LE NORD AND PICARDY
Pages 182–195

CHAMPAGNE
Pages 196–207

ALSACE AND LORRAINE
Pages 208–223

 Reims

NORTHEAST FRANCE

Strasbourg

Troyes

Dijon

CENTRAL FRANCE AND THE ALPS

Lyon

Grenoble

BURGUNDY AND FRANCHE-COMTÉ
Pages 316–341

THE MASSIF CENTRAL
Pages 342–361

THE RHÔNE VALLEY AND FRENCH ALPS
Pages 362–381

THE SOUTH OF FRANCE

LANGUEDOC-ROUSSILLON
Pages 466–487

PROVENCE AND THE CÔTE D'AZUR
488–521

Ajaccio

CORSICA
Pages 522–533

EYEWITNESS TRAVEL GUIDES

FRANCE

EYEWITNESS TRAVEL GUIDES

FRANCE

DK PUBLISHING

LONDON • NEW YORK • MUNICH
MELBOURNE • DELHI

PROJECT EDITOR Rosemary Bailey
ART EDITOR Janis Utton
EDITORS Tanya Colbourne, Fiona Morgan,
Anna Streiffert, Celia Woolfrey
US EDITORS Laaren Brown, Mary Ann Lynch, Mary Sutherland
DESIGNERS Joy FitzSimmons, Erika Lang, Clare Sullivan

MAIN CONTRIBUTORS
John Ardagh, Rosemary Bailey, Judith Fayard, Lisa Gerard-Sharp,
Colin Jones, Alister Kershaw, Alec Lobrano, Anthony Roberts,
Alan Tillier, Nigel Tisdall

PHOTOGRAPHERS
Max Alexander, Neil Lukas, John Parker, Kim Sayer

ILLUSTRATORS
Stephen Conlin, John Lawrence, Maltings Partnership,
John Woodcock

Reproduced by Colourscan (Singapore)
Printed and bound by South China Printing Co. Ltd., China

First American Edition, 1994
10 9

Published in the United States by
DK Publishing, Inc., 375 Hudson Street,
New York, New York 10014

**Reprinted with revisions 1996, 1997, 1998, 1999,
2000, 2001, 2002, 2003**

Copyright © 1994, 2003 Dorling Kindersley Limited, London

A CATALOGING-IN-PUBLICATION RECORD IS AVAILABLE
FROM THE LIBRARY OF CONGRESS

ISBN 0-7894-9387-X

THROUGHOUT THIS BOOK, FLOORS ARE REFERRED TO IN ACCORDANCE WITH
EUROPEAN USAGE, I.E., THE "FIRST FLOOR" IS ONE FLIGHT UP.

See our complete product line at
www.dk.com

**The information in this
Dorling Kindersley Travel Guide is checked annually**.
Every effort has been made to ensure that this book is as up-to-date
as possible at the time of going to press. Some details, however,
such as telephone numbers, opening hours, prices, gallery hanging
arrangements and travel information are liable to change. The
publishers cannot accept responsibility for any consequences arising
from the use of this book, nor for any material on third party
websites, and cannot guarantee that any website address in this
book will be a suitable source of travel information. We value the
views and suggestions of our readers very highly. Please write to:
Publisher, DK Eyewitness Travel Guides,
Dorling Kindersley, 80 Strand, London WC2R 0RL, Great Britain.

CONTENTS

HOW TO USE THIS GUIDE 6

Bust of Charlemagne

INTRODUCING FRANCE

PUTTING FRANCE ON THE MAP *10*

A PORTRAIT OF FRANCE *14*

FRANCE THROUGH THE YEAR *32*

THE HISTORY OF FRANCE *38*

PARIS AND ILE DE FRANCE

INTRODUCING PARIS AND ILE DE FRANCE *68*

A RIVER VIEW OF PARIS *70*

ILE DE LA CITÉ, MARAIS AND BEAUBOURG *76*

TUILERIES AND OPÉRA *90*

CHAMPS-ELYSÉES AND INVALIDES *100*

THE LEFT BANK *112*

The fishing village of St-Jean-de-Luz in the Pyrenees

Grape harvest in Alsace

Palais des Papes, Avignon

HOW TO USE THIS GUIDE

THIS GUIDE helps you get the most from your visit to France. It provides expert recommendations and detailed practical information. *Introducing France* maps the country and sets it in its historical and cultural context. The 15 regional chapters, plus *Paris and Ile de France,* describe important sights, with maps, pictures and illustrations. Throughout, features cover topics from food and wine to culture and beaches. Restaurant and hotel recommendations can be found in *Travelers' Needs*. The *Survival Guide* has tips on everything from the French telephone system to transportation.

PARIS AND ILE DE FRANCE

The center of Paris has been divided into five sightseeing areas. Each has its own chapter, which opens with a list of the sights described. A separate section covers Ile de France. All sights are numbered and plotted on an area map. The detailed information for each sight follows the map's numerical order, making sights easy to locate within the chapter.

Sights at a Glance lists the chapter's sights by category: Churches; Museums and Galleries; Historic Buildings; Squares and Gardens.

All pages relating to Paris and Ile de France have green thumb tabs.

A locator map shows where you are in relation to other areas of the city center.

1 Area Map
For easy reference, the sights are numbered and located on a map. Sights in the city center are also shown on the Paris Street Finder *on pages 146–59.*

2 Street-by-Street Map
This gives a bird's-eye view of the key areas in each chapter.

A suggested route for a walk is shown in red.

Stars indicate the sights that no visitor should miss.

3 Detailed information
The sights in Paris and Ile de France are described individually. Addresses, telephone numbers, opening hours and information on admission charges and wheelchair access are also provided for each entry.

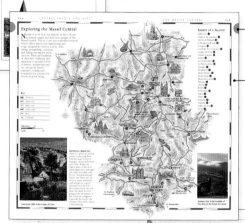

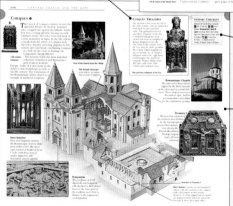

1 Introduction
The landscape, history and character of each region are described here, showing how the area has developed over the centuries and what it offers to the visitor today.

FRANCE AREA BY AREA

Apart from Paris and Ile de France, France has been divided into 15 regions, each of which has a separate chapter. The most interesting towns and places to visit have been numbered on a *Pictorial Map*.

Each area of France can be quickly identified by its color coding, shown on the inside front cover.

2 Pictorial Map
This shows the road network and gives an illustrated overview of the whole region. All interesting places to visit are numbered, and there are also useful tips on getting around the region by car and train.

3 Detailed information
All the important towns and other places to visit are described individually. They are listed in order, following the numbering on the Pictorial Map. Within each town or city, there is detailed information on important buildings and other sights.

Story boxes highlight noteworthy features of the top sights.

For all the top sights, a Visitor's Checklist provides the practical information you will need to plan your visit.

4 France's top sights
These are given two or more full pages. Historic buildings are dissected to reveal their interiors. The most interesting towns or city centers are shown in a bird's-eye view, with sights pointed out and described.

INTRODUCING
FRANCE

Putting France on the Map

FRANCE, ONE OF THE LARGEST countries in Europe, has airline connections with most cities in the world. Paris is the major transportation hub with two international airports; others include Bordeaux, Lille, Lyon, Nice and Toulouse. There are good, high-speed rail links with the rest of Europe, and a network of efficient highways. A number of ferry routes cross the Mediterranean to Corsica and beyond. Cross-Channel ferries serve several ports, with the Channel Tunnel providing an alternative link by rail.

France, known as the "Hexagon" due to its six-sided shape, is bordered by six countries: Spain across the Pyrenees to the south; Italy and Switzerland beyond the Alps; Luxembourg and Belgium to the north; and Germany on the other side of the Rhine. The United Kingdom lies across the English Channel (La Manche).

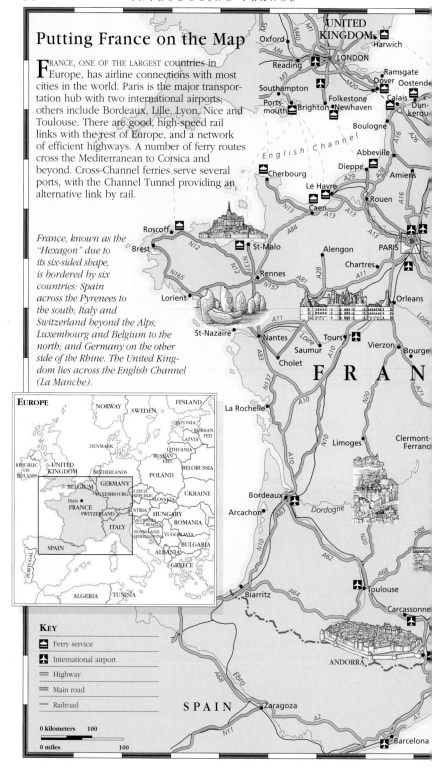

KEY

- 🚢 Ferry service
- ✈ International airport
- ▬ Highway
- ▬ Main road
- — Railroad

0 kilometers   100

0 miles   100

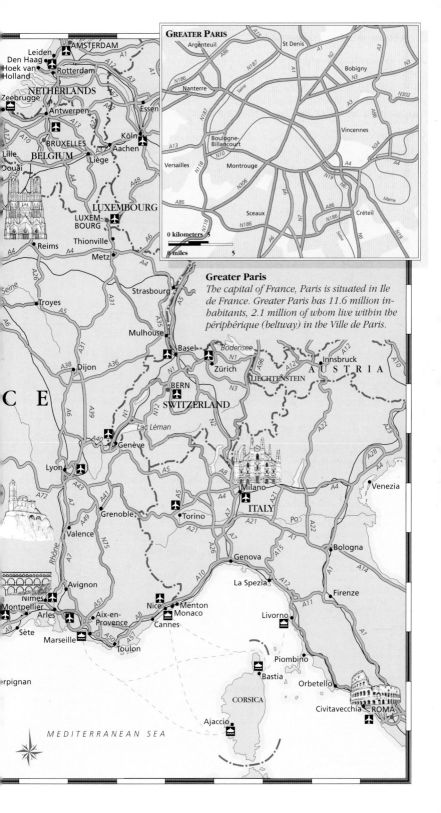

GREATER PARIS

Argenteuil · St Denis · Bobigny · Nanterre · Seine · Vincennes · Boulogne-Billancourt · Versailles · Montrouge · Sceaux · Créteil · Marne

N186 · N187 · A15 · A86 · N2 · N3 · A1 · A3 · N302 · N94 · A4 · A13 · N10 · N118 · N206 · A6 · N19 · N6 · A86 · N7 · N186 · N19 · Seine

0 kilometers 5
0 miles 5

Greater Paris

The capital of France, Paris is situated in Ile de France. Greater Paris has 11.6 million inhabitants, 2.1 million of whom live within the périphérique (beltway) in the Ville de Paris.

AMSTERDAM · Leiden · Den Haag · Hoek van Holland · Rotterdam · NETHERLANDS · Zeebrugge · Antwerpen · Essen · BRUXELLES · Köln · BELGIUM · Aachen · Lille · Liège · Douai · Reims · LUXEMBOURG · LUXEM-BOURG · Thionville · Metz · Troyes · Strasbourg · Seine · Mulhouse · Basel · Bodensee · Innsbruck · Dijon · Zürich · LIECHTENSTEIN · AUSTRIA · BERN · SWITZERLAND · Lac Léman · Genève · Lyon · Milano · ITALY · Venezia · Grenoble · Torino · Valence · Po · Bologna · Rhône · Genova · Avignon · La Spezia · Firenze · Nîmes · Nice · Menton · Livorno · Montpellier · Arles · Aix-en-Provence · Monaco · Sète · Cannes · Marseille · Toulon · Piombino · Bastia · rpignan · CORSICA · Orbetello · Civitavecchia · ROMA · Ajaccio · MEDITERRANEAN SEA

FRANCE

A1 · A12 · A3 · A57 · A67 · A2 · A13 · A31 · A4 · A48 · A4 · A26 · A5 · A6 · A31 · A5 · A35 · A4 · A38 · A36 · A39 · N1 · A12 · A86 · A12 · A10 · N3 · A22 · A23 · N1 · N2 · A28 · A72 · A43 · A41 · A5 · A8 · A4 · A21 · A4 · A26 · A7 · A21 · A49 · N75 · A15 · A1 · A14 · A51 · A10 · A12 · A11 · A8 · A50 · A57 · A9 · A1

Regional France

FRANCE HAS A POPULATION of around 60 million, and receives over 75 million visitors a year. It covers an area of 543,965 sq km (210,025 sq miles). Paris is the largest city, followed by Lyon, Marseille and the Lille-Lens-Valenciennes urban area. The Loire, Seine, Garonne and Rhône are the longest of France's many rivers. This book divides the country into 15 regions, plus a separate section for Paris and Ile de France, although officially France comprises 22 *régions*.

GETTING AROUND

In spite of its size, France is relatively easy to travel around. There is a well-organized rail network, and traveling times are considerably shortened between towns with a high-speed TGV link *(see p635)*. Most highways have expensive tolls but are fast and efficient for longer distances. City by-passes are usually free and some longer sections of highway may also be free. Smaller roads are usually a more interesting way to discover the country's varied landscape *(pp638–40)*, and they are almost invariably well maintained and marked.

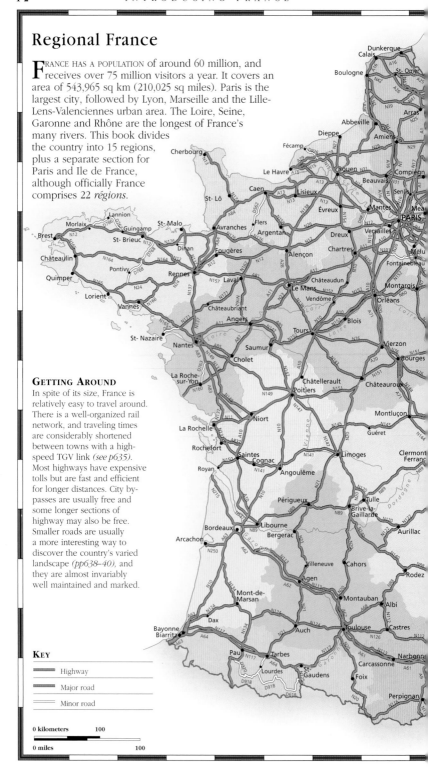

KEY

▰▰▰	Highway
▰▰▰	Major road
══	Minor road

0 kilometers   100

0 miles   100

Eyewitness France Regions

Each of the chapters in this guide has a color code. The chapters are grouped into five sections – Northeast France, Western France, Central France and the Alps, Southwest France and the South of France – plus Paris and Ile de France.

KEY TO COLOR-CODING

Paris and Ile de France

Northeast France

Le Nord and Picardy

Champagne

Alsace and Lorraine

Western France

Normandy

Brittany

The Loire Valley

Central France and the Alps

Burgundy and Franche-Comté

Massif Central

The Rhône Valley and French Alps

Southwest France

Poitou and Aquitaine

Périgord, Quercy and Gascony

The Pyrenees

The South of France

Languedoc-Roussillon

Provence and the Côte d'Azur

Corsica

CORSICA

Corsica

Situated 193 km (120 miles) from the Côte d'Azur, Corsica can be reached by ferry or air. Covering an area of 8,680 sq km (3,350 sq miles), it is the fourth largest island in the Mediterranean.

A PORTRAIT OF FRANCE

THE FRENCH ARE *convinced that their way of life is best, and that their country is the most civilized on earth. Many millions of visitors agree with them. The food and wine are justly celebrated. French culture, literature, art, movies, and architecture can be both profound and provocative. Whether cerebral, sensual or sportif, France is a country where anyone might feel at home.*

France's landscape ranges from high mountain plateaux to lush farmland, traditional villages to chic boulevards. Its regional identities are equally diverse. The country belongs to both northern and southern Europe, and encompasses Brittany with its Celtic maritime heritage, the Mediterranean sunbelt, Germanic Alsace-Lorraine, and the hardy mountain regions of the Auvergne and the Pyrenees. Paris remains the linchpin, with its famously brusque citizens and intense tempo. Other cities range from the huge industrial conglomeration of Lille in the north, to Marseille, the biggest port on the Mediterranean. The differences between north and south, country and

Marianne, symbol of France

city are well-entrenched, indeed cherished, despite the determination of the forward-thinking French to link their country by TGV (high-speed train) and the home databank service, Minitel. High-tech advances like these have provoked an equal and opposite reaction: as life in France becomes more city-based and industrialized, so the desire grows to safeguard the old, traditional ways and to value rural life.

The idea of life in the country – *douceur de vivre* (the Good Life), long tables set in the sun for the wine and anecdotes to flow – is as seductive as ever for residents and visitors alike. Nevertheless, the rural way of life has been changing. Whereas in 1945 one

Château de Saumur, one of the Loire's most romantic and complete castles

◁ Café life in St-Tropez, one of the country's many pleasures

person in three worked in farming, today it is only one in 16. France's main exports used to be luxury goods like perfumes and Cognac; today, such exports have been overtaken by cars, telecommunications equipment, nuclear power stations, and fighter aircraft.

The popular *moto* (scooter)

People remain firmly committed to their roots, however, and often retain a place in the country where they go back for vacations or retirement. On average, there are more French people who have second homes than any other nationality; and in many areas such as Provence, the dying villages have found a new life as chic summer residences for Parisians and foreigners. Many artists and artisans

Chanel chic

from the towns now live and work in the country; and entrepreneurs have set up factory workshops there, more feasible in the age of the fax, the computer and the Internet.

Social changes have come about since the steep decline in the influence of the Catholic Church. Today only 14 percent of people attend mass regularly. Nearly half of all couples live together before marriage, and many never marry at all. Abortion is now legal.

Feminism in France has quite a different look than in Anglo-Saxon countries. It seems that in France, even feminists are unwilling to condemn frivolous feminity and sex-appeal. As EU citizens, women in France have full legal equality with men, but French attitudes remain traditional. A flirtatious gallantry is the norm between the sexes, even in public life. The election of Edith Cresson in 1991 as France's first woman prime minister may have appeared a milestone, but her crushing unpopularity in that role, followed by the 1999 corruption case against her as an EU Commissioner (leading to the resignation of the entire Commission), arguably held back the cause of women's equality in French politics.

SOCIAL CUSTOMS AND POLITICS

French social life, except between close friends, has always been marked by formality – handshaking, the use of titles (*"Monsieur le President"*), the infrequent use of first names, the preference for the formal *vous* rather than the intimate *tu*. However, this is changing among the younger generation, who

The May 1968 uprising, a catalyst for profound change in France

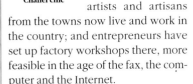

Farming in Alsace-Lorraine

now call you by your first name, and use *tu* even in an office context. Standards of dress have become much more informal too, though the French are still very concerned to dress well, and they judge others by their clothes: they prefer an elegantly casual Cardin pullover to an ill-fitting formal suit.

Formality lingers on, however, and France remains very legalistic – whether you are buying a house, exporting an antique or getting divorced. But the French also display a charming insouciance about their famous red tape. Rules and laws are there to be ingeniously evaded, twisted or made more human. This sport of avoiding cumbersome bureaucracy has a name of its own, *le système D*, to be accompanied with a shrug and a smile. For example, since 1992 the law insists on no smoking areas in public places, even in the most nicotine-stained of tiny bars – but no one really minds if it is not always applied too literally.

The old sharp Left/Right ideological divide which used to dominate French politics, had recently given way to a more center-focused consensus fos-

Charles de Gaulle

tered by the influential François Mitterrand, President from 1981 to 1995. It reappeared however in a dramatic manner in May 2002, with the re-election of the Conservative Jacques Chirac as President, after an uncomfortable five-year 'cohabitation' with the Socialist Lionel Jospin as Prime Minister, followed a month later by a massive swing to the right in the general elections. The real power though remains largely in the hands of the upper bourgeoisie through both state and business appointments, notwithstanding the occasional flash of Republican spirit in the form of strikes and mass demonstrations, which often result in government retraction. Unemployment and a sense of insecurity continue to fuel support of the far right and growing racism against Arabs and black immigrants, many of whom are from former French colonies.

CULTURE AND THE ARTS

Culture is taken seriously in France, and writers, intellectuals, artists and fashion designers are held in high social esteem. As a result, the state finances a

Designer Thierry Mugler at the Paris collections

large network of provincial arts centers, and has traditionally given subsidies which have allowed experimentation in art and design. The French remain justly proud of their own serious cinematic tradition, and are determined to defend it against pressures from Hollywood. Other activities – from the music industry to the French language itself – are subject to the same protectionist attitudes.

Avant-garde art and literature and modern architecture all enjoy strong patronage in France. Some of the more exciting architectural projects range from the striking modern buildings in Paris – the Louvre pyramid and La Grande Arche at La

Défense – to the post-modern housing developments of Nîmes, Montpellier and Marseille in the south.

MODERN LIFE

Whilst one half of the French were heralding in the new millennium in true Gallic style, the other half were plunged into darkness caused by the worst storms to hit Europe since records began. This is an extreme illustration of French ambivalence toward modernism. France's agro-business is one of the most modern in the world, but the peasant farmer is deeply revered. France hankers after a leading role in the world, yet the country effectively closes down for the whole of August, when the French take to the roads and coastal resorts ... of France! However, two recent changes have somewhat forced the pace: the Internet, which France has embraced keenly, despite the obvious threat to its previously revolutionary communications network, Minitel; and the Euro, which, in one fell swoop, has swept away Europe's oldest decimalized currency, the Franc.

Traditional Breton costumes, worn for festivals and *pardons*

A view through the base of La Grande Arche, part of the huge business complex on the edge of Paris

The traditional game of *boules* or *pétanque*, still extremely popular – especially in the south

The French are enthusiastic, discerning consumers. Even small towns have excellent, stylish clothes shops. Street markets bring in the best of local produce. In addition, France has Europe's largest hypermarkets, which have been steadily ousting the local grocery or corner shop. These are remarkably French in what they sell: a long delicatessen counter may have a wonderful display of 100 or so French cheeses and *charcuterie*, while the huge range of fresh vegetables and fruit is a tribute to their role in French cuisine.

Southern produce: melons, peaches, and apricots

However, under modern pressures, eating habits have been polarizing in a curious way. The French used to eat well every day as a matter of course. Today they are in a hurry, and for most meals of the week they will eat simply – either a quick fried steak or pasta dish at home, or a snack in town (hence the wave of fast-food places that have sprung up, in defiance of French tradition). But meals still remain an important part of French culture – not just for the food and wines themselves, but also for the pleasure of lengthy, unhurried meals and good conversation around a table, among family or friends. They will reserve their gastronomy for the once-or-twice-a-week special occasion, or the big family Sunday lunch which remains an important French ritual. It is at these times that the French zest for life really comes into its own.

Remote farm – a nostalgic reminder of rural life

The Classic French Menu

THE TRADITIONAL French meal consists of at least three courses. *Les entrées* or *hors d'oeuvre* (appetizers) include soups, egg dishes, salads or *charcuterie*, such as sliced sausage or ham. For *les plats* (main courses), fish or meat is served often with sauce, and accompanied by potatoes, rice or pasta, and vegetables. Cheese comes before dessert, which can include sorbets, fruit tarts or *pâtisserie*. A fixed-price menu is the cheapest option. For more information on French restaurants, see pp576–9.

Soupe à l'oignon *is a favorite in bistros. Croutons, grated cheese and sometimes egg yolk are added to the onion soup.*

Fish soup

Endive salad with diced fried bacon

Goat's cheese melted on toast with salad

Oeufs en Cocotte *are prepared by baking eggs, cream and butter in a china ramekin. They may be sprinkled with fresh herbs and garnished with mushrooms.*

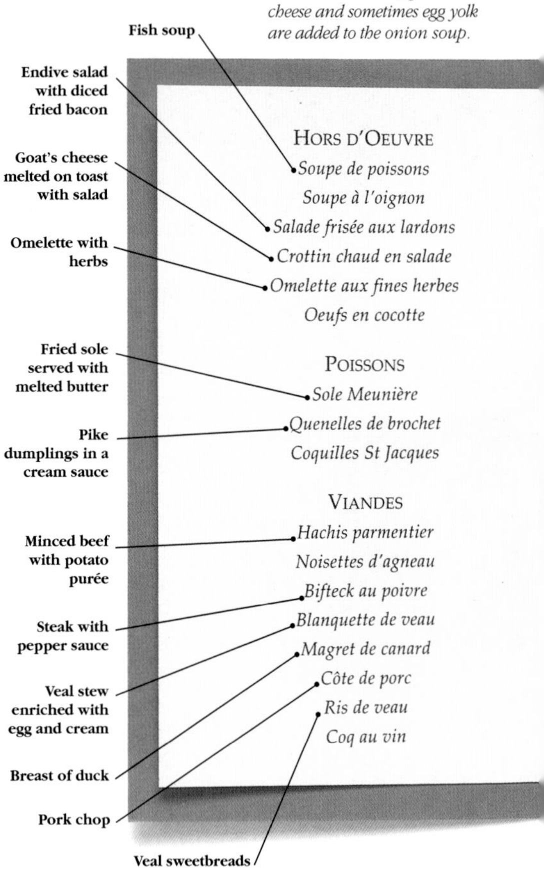

Omelette with herbs

Fried sole served with melted butter

Pike dumplings in a cream sauce

Coquilles Saint-Jacques *are plump sea scallops. They are cooked simply in a little butter. Their orange tails, containing edible roe, are delicious.*

Minced beef with potato purée

Steak with pepper sauce

Veal stew enriched with egg and cream

Breast of duck

Pork chop

Veal sweetbreads

HORS D'OEUVRE

Soupe de poissons
Soupe à l'oignon
Salade frisée aux lardons
Crottin chaud en salade
Omelette aux fines herbes
Oeufs en cocotte

POISSONS

Sole Meunière
Quenelles de brochet
Coquilles St Jacques

VIANDES

Hachis parmentier
Noisettes d'agneau
Bifteck au poivre
Blanquette de veau
Magret de canard
Côte de porc
Ris de veau
Coq au vin

Noisettes d'Agneau *are small, tender lamb cutlets, sautéed in butter and served rare with mushrooms and herb-and-garlic butter.*

Coq au vin *is one of the best-known French dishes, made of chicken braised in a sauce of red wine, herbs, garlic, pearl onions and button mushrooms.*

BREAKFAST

The French rarely eat cereal, eggs or meat for breakfast, so assorted breads spread with butter and jams are the morning choice. These include *croissants*: flaky, buttery crescent-shaped pastries; a piece of *baguette* (the classic long thin loaf), which is split in half and spread with butter and jam to create a *tartine*; *pain au chocolat*: a buttery square roll with a melted tablet of chocolate inside; and *brioche*, an airy muffin-shaped, egg-enriched yeast bread. This is washed down with coffee or tea and, in some cafés, a glass of red wine, which is said to be good for digestion. The most common form of coffee at breakfast is *café au lait*, espresso coffee served with warm milk.

Croissants

Brioches

Pains au chocolat

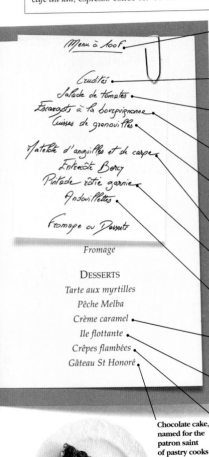

Menu à 100 f.

Crudités

Salade de tomates

Escargots à la bourguignonne

Cuisses de grenouilles

Matelote d'anguilles et de carpe

Entrecôte Bercy

Pintade rôtie garnie

Andouillettes

Fromage ou Dessert

Fromage

DESSERTS

Tarte aux myrtilles

Pêche Melba

Crème caramel

Ile flottante

Crêpes flambées

Gâteau St Honoré

Fixed-price menu of the day

Raw vegetables

Sliced tomatoes in vinaigrette dressing

Snails in garlic butter

Frogs' legs in garlic butter

A stew of eel and carp

Roast guinea fowl

Small tripe sausages

Egg custard with a caramel sauce

Meringues floating in a creamy custard sauce

Chocolate cake, named for the patron saint of pastry cooks

Sugared crêpes flamed in a liqueur

Entrecôte Bercy *is rib steak served with a white wine sauce, named after Quai de Bercy in Paris where wine was unloaded.*

The cheese board *may include goat's, cow's and sheep's milk cheeses, to be eaten with bread or a knife and fork.*

Pêche Melba *is peaches, ice cream and raspberry sauce, created by famed chef Escoffier for the singer Dame Nellie Melba.*

Tarte aux Myrtilles *is blueberry tart. Like most French fruit tarts, it consists of a shallow shortbread crust filled with fruit.*

The Wine of France

WINEMAKING IN FRANCE dates back to pre-Roman times, although it was the Romans who disseminated the culture of the vine and the practice of winemaking throughout the country. The range, quality and reputation of the fine wines of Bordeaux, Burgundy, the Rhône, and Champagne in particular have made them rôle models the world over. France's everyday wines can be highly enjoyable too, and there are also good wines now emerging from the southern regions.

Picker's hod

Traditional vineyard cultivation

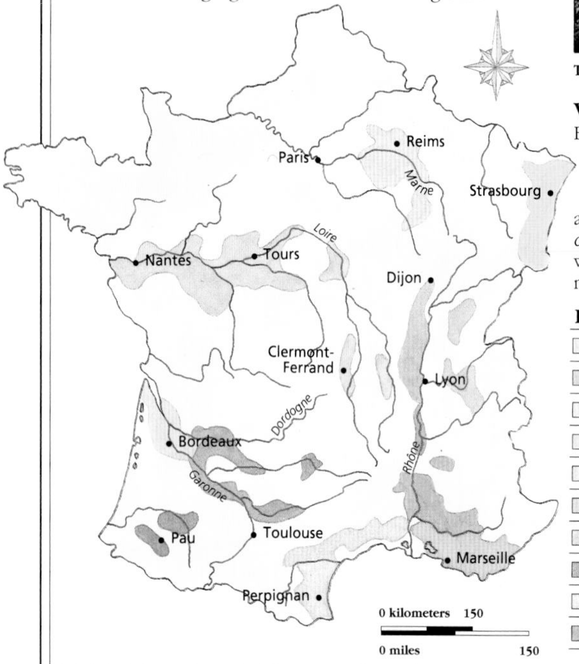

WINE REGIONS

Each of the 10 principal wine-producing regions has its own identity, based on grape varieties, climate and *terroir*. *Appellation contrôlée* laws guarantee a wine's origins and production methods.

KEY

- [ ] Bordeaux
- [ ] Burgundy
- [ ] Champagne
- [ ] Alsace
- [ ] Loire
- [ ] Provence
- [ ] Jura and Savoie
- [ ] The Southwest
- [ ] Languedoc-Roussillon
- [ ] Rhône

Map labels: Paris, Reims, Strasbourg, Nantes, Tours, Dijon, Clermont-Ferrand, Lyon, Bordeaux, Pau, Toulouse, Marseille, Perpignan; rivers Marne, Loire, Dordogne, Garonne, Rhône.

0 kilometers 150
0 miles 150

HOW TO READ A WINE LABEL

Even the simplest label will identify the wine and provide a key to its quality. It will bear the name of the wine and its producer, its vintage if there is one, and whether it comes from a strictly defined area (*appellation contrôlée* or VDQS) or is a more general *vin de pays* or *vin de table*. It may also have a regional grading, as with the *crus classés* in Bordeaux. The shape and color of the bottle is also a guide to the kind of wine it contains. Green glass is often used since this helps to protect the wine from light.

The property or producer

Château-bottled, rather than a blend from a merchant or grower's cooperative

MIS EN BOUTEILLE AU CHÂTEAU

CHÂTEAU MARGAUX
GRAND VIN

Pictures may be realistic or fanciful

PREMIER GRAND CRU CLASSÉ
1985
MARGAUX
APPELLATION MARGAUX CONTRÔLÉE
S.C.A. CHATEAU MARGAUX PROPRIETAIRE A MARGAUX - FRANCE

Capacity of the bottle

The vintage, from the French word *vendange*, or harvest

The wine's *appellation contrôlée*

How Wine is Made

Wine is the product of the juice of freshly picked grapes, after natural or cultured yeasts have converted the grape sugars into alcohol during the fermentation process. The yeasts, or lees, are normally filtered out before bottling.

WHITE WINE   RED WINE

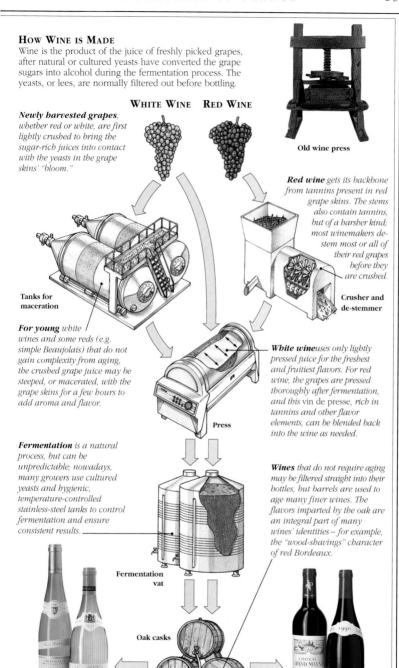

Old wine press

Newly harvested grapes, whether red or white, are first lightly crushed to bring the sugar-rich juices into contact with the yeasts in the grape skins' "bloom."

Red wine gets its backbone from tannins present in red grape skins. The stems also contain tannins, but of a harsher kind; most winemakers de-stem most or all of their red grapes before they are crushed.

Tanks for maceration

Crusher and de-stemmer

For young white wines and some reds (e.g. simple Beaujolais) that do not gain complexity from aging, the crushed grape juice may be steeped, or macerated, with the grape skins for a few hours to add aroma and flavor.

White wine uses only lightly pressed juice for the freshest and fruitiest flavors. For red wine, the grapes are pressed thoroughly after fermentation, and this vin de presse, rich in tannins and other flavor elements, can be blended back into the wine as needed.

Press

Fermentation is a natural process, but can be unpredictable; nowadays, many growers use cultured yeasts and hygienic, temperature-controlled stainless-steel tanks to control fermentation and ensure consistent results.

Wines that do not require aging may be filtered straight into their bottles, but barrels are used to age many finer wines. The flavors imparted by the oak are an integral part of many wines' identities – for example, the "wood-shavings" character of red Bordeaux.

Fermentation vat

Oak casks

Different shades of glass identify the wine regions

Bottle shapes typical of red Bordeaux (left) and Burgundy

Artists in France

Aʀᴛɪsᴛs ʜᴀᴠᴇ always been inspired by France, especially since landscape became a legitimate subject for art in the 19th century. Art and tourism have been closely linked for more than a century. The establishment of artists' colonies in Brittany, the forest of Fontainebleau and the south of France did much to make these areas attractive to visitors. Today, one of the pleasures of touring the countryside is seeing the landscapes made famous in paintings.

Follower of *the French Classical tradition of landscape painting, Jean-Baptiste-Camille Corot recorded* The Belfry of Douai *(1871).*

Le Nord a Picardy

Gustave Courbet, *socialist and leader of the Realist School of painting, captured this famous coastal town in* The Cliffs at Etretat after a Storm *(1869).*

Normandy

Paris and Ile Franc

Brittany

Loire Valley

Emile Bernard *was fascinated by the wild, almost primitive character of the Breton landscape and the individuality of its inhabitants. He was one of the community of artists based in Pont Aven. His* La Ronde Bretonne *(1892) portrays local Celtic customs.*

Poitou and Aquitaine

Neo-Impressionist *artist and exponent of Pointillism, Paul Signac indulged his love of maritime subjects on the coasts of France.* Entrance to the Port at La Rochelle *(1921) shows his use of myriad dots of color to represent nature.*

Périgord, Quercy and Gascony

Pyrenees

Langued Roussillo

Théodore Rousseau, *the leading light of the Barbizon School (see p171) of landscape painters, visited the Auvergne in 1830. It was here that he began to paint "en plein air" (in the open air). The results are seen in this sensitively observed scene,* Sunset, Auvergne *(c.1830).*

A few months before his tragic death in July 1890, Vincent Van Gogh painted the Church at Auvers. *He noted that the building "appears to have a violet-hued blue color; pure cobalt".*

In his **Eiffel Tower** *(1926) Robert Delaunay investigated the abstract qualities of color. His wife, artist Sonia Delaunay, said, "The Eiffel Tower and the Universe were one and the same to him."*

Scenes from everyday life were realistically rendered by Gustave Courbet, as here in Young Ladies of the Village Giving Alms to a Cow Girl in a Valley near Ornans *(1851–2).*

Maurice Utrillo *painted this village scene,* The Church of Saint Bernard in Summer *(1924), while staying at his mother's home. The somber tone and emptiness reflect his unhappy life.*

Alsace and Lorraine

Champagne

Burgundy and Franche-Comté

The Massif Central

The Rhône Valley and French Alps

Provence and the Côte d'Azur

The French Riviera attracted many artists (see pp462–3). Raoul Dufy particularly appreciated its pleasures, seen in this typical scene of blue skies and palm trees, La Jetée Promenade à Nice (1928).

Landscape at Collioure (1905) depicts the vivid colors of this little Catalan fishing village. It was here that Henri Matisse founded the art movement of the Fauves, or "Wild Beasts," who used exceptionally bright, expressive colors.

0 kilometers 100

0 miles 100

Writers in France

Writers and intellectuals traditionally enjoy great prestige in France. One of the most august of French institutions is the Academie Française, whose 40 members, most of them writers, have pronounced on national events and have, on occasion, held public office.

The work of many French novelists is deeply rooted in their native area, ranging from the Normandy of Gustave Flaubert to Jean Giono's Provence. In addition to their literary merit, these novels provide a unique guide to France's regional identities.

Monument to Baudelaire

Colette's house in Burgundy

The Novel

The farmland of the Beauce, where Zola based his novel, *La Terre*

Marcel Proust, author of *Remembrance of Things Past*

The first great French writer was Rabelais in the 16th century, a boisterous, life-affirming satirist *(see p285)*. Many writers in the Age of Enlightenment that followed emphasized the classic tradition of reason, clarity and objectivity in their work. The 19th century was the golden age of the French humanist novel, producing Balzac, with his vast fresco of contemporary society; Stendhal, a fierce critic of the frailties of ambition in *Scarlet and Black*; and Victor Hugo, known for epics such as *Les Misérables*. George Sand broke ground with her novels such as *The Devil's Pool*, which depicted peasant life, albeit in an idealized way. In the same century, Flaubert produced *Madame Bovary*, a study of provincialism and misplaced romanticism. In contrast, Emil Zola wrote *Germinal*, *La Terre* and other studies of lower-class life.

Marcel Proust combined a poetic evocation of his boyhood with a portrait of high society in his long novel *Remembrance of Things Past*.

Others have also written poetically about their childhood, including Alain-Fournier in *Le Grand Meaulnes* and Colette in *My Mother's House*.

A new kind of novel emerged after World War I. Jean Giono's *Joy of Man's Desiring* and François Mauriac's masterly *Thérèse Desqueyroux* explored the impact of landscape upon human character. Mauriac, and also George Bernanos in his *Diary of a Country Priest*, used lone spiritual struggle as a theme. The free-thinker André Gide was another leading writer of the interwar years with his *Strait is the Gate* and the autobiographical *If it Die*.

In the 1960s Alain Robbe-Grillet and others experimented with the Nouveau Roman which subordinated character and plot to detailed physical description. Critics held it in part responsible for the recent decline of the novel. Despite this decline, new, avant-garde works continue to see the light of day.

Hugo's novel *Les Misérables*, made into a musical in the 1980s

THEATER

THE THREE classic playwrights of French literature, Racine, Molière and Corneille, lived in the 17th century. Molière's comedies satirized the vanities and foibles of human nature. Corneille and Racine wrote noble verse tragedies. They were followed in the 18th century by Marivaux, writer of romantic comedies, and Beaumarchais, whose *Barber of Seville* and *Marriage of Figaro* later became operas.

Molière, the 17th-century dramatist

Victor Hugo's dramas were the most vigorous product of the 19th century. The exceptional dramatists of the 20th century range from Jean Anouilh, author of urbane philosophical comedies, to Jean Genet, ex-convict critic of the establishment. In the 1960s, Eugene Ionesco from Romania and Samuel Beckett from Ireland were among the pioneers of a new genre, the "theater of the absurd." Since then, no major playwrights have emerged, but experimental work flourishes in state-subsidized theater companies.

POETRY

THE GREATEST of early French poets was Ronsard, who wrote sonnets about nature and love in the 16th century. Lamartine, a major poet of the early 19th century, also took nature as one of his themes (his poem *Le Lac* laments a lost love). Later the same century, Baudelaire (*Les Fleurs du mal*) and Rimbaud (*Le Bateau Ivre*) were considered provocative in their day. Nobel prizewinner in 1904, Frédéric Mistral wrote in his native Provençal tongue. The greatest poet of the 20th century is considered to be Paul Valéry, whose work is profoundly philosophical.

PHILOSOPHY

FRANCE has produced a large number of leading philosophers in the European humanist tradition. One of

Novels by Albert Camus, who won the Nobel Prize in 1957

Sartre and de Beauvoir in La Coupole restaurant in Paris, 1969

the first was Montaigne in the 16th century, an inspired moralist who established the essay as an art form. Then came Descartes, the master of logic, and the philosopher Pascal. The 18th century produced two great figures – Voltaire, the supreme liberal, and Rousseau, who preached the harmonizing influence of living close to nature.

In the 20th century Sartre, de Beauvoir and Camus used the novel as a philosophical vehicle. Sartre led the existentialist movement in Paris in the early 1940s with his novel *Nausea* and his treatise *Being and Nothingness.* Camus' novel *The Outsider,* was equally influential.

Throughout the '70s and '80s the radical ideas of the structuralists seized Paris (Barthes, Foucault etc). Post-structuralism relayed this rationalist approach into the '90s with Derrida, Kristeva, Deleuze and Lyotard.

FOREIGN WRITERS

Many foreign writers have visited and been inspired by France, from Petrarch in 14th-century Avignon to Goethe in Alsace in 1770–71. The Riviera attracted many English writers, including Somerset Maugham, Katharine Mansfield and Graham Greene. In 1919 the American Sylvia Beach opened the first Shakespeare and Company bookstore in Paris, which became a cultural center for expatriate writers. In 1922 she was the first to publish James Joyce's masterwork, *Ulysses.*

Hemingway with Sylvia Beach and friends, Paris 1923

Romanesque and Gothic Architecture in France

FRANCE IS RICH in medieval architecture, ranging from small Romanesque churches to great Gothic cathedrals. As the country emerged from the Dark Ages in the 11th century, there was a surge in Romanesque building, based on the Roman model of thick walls, round arches and heavy vaults. French architects improved this basic structure, leading to the flowering of Gothic in the 13th century. Pointed arches and flying buttresses were the key features that allowed for much taller buildings with larger windows.

LOCATOR MAP

① *Romanesque abbeys & churches*

⑬ *Gothic cathedrals*

ROMANESQUE FEATURES

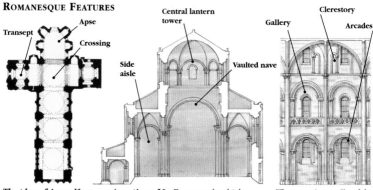

Transept — Apse — Crossing

Central lantern tower — Side aisle — Vaulted nave

Clerestory — Gallery — Arcades

The plan of Angoulême shows the cross shape and the rounded eastern apse typical of Romanesque architecture.

A section of Le Puy reveals a high barrel-vaulted nave with round arches and low side aisles. Light could enter through windows in the side aisles and the central lantern tower.

The massive walls of the nave bays of St-Etienne support a three-story structure of arcades, a gallery and clerestory.

GOTHIC FEATURES

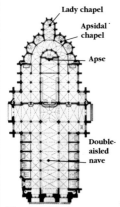

Lady chapel — Apsidal chapel — Apse — Double-aisled nave

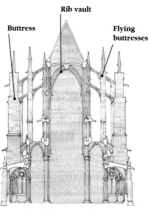

Rib vault — Buttress — Flying buttresses

Triforium — Pointed arch — Tracery

The plan of Amiens shows the nave and apse flanked by a continuous row of chapels.

A section of Beauvais shows how the nave could be raised to staggering heights thanks to exterior support from flying buttresses.

Pointed arches withstood greater stress, permitting larger windows as in the nave at Reims.

WHERE TO FIND ROMANESQUE ARCHITECTURE

① St-Etienne, Caen *p244*
② Mont-St-Michel, Normandy *p248*
③ St-Pierre, Angoulême *p409*
④ Notre-Dame, Le Puy *p355*
⑤ St-Pierre, Moissac *pp432–3*
⑥ St-Sernin, Toulouse *pp436–7*
⑦ Ste-Foy, Conques *pp356–7*
⑧ Sacré-Coeur, Paray-le-Monial *p335*
⑨ St-Philibert, Tournus *p334*
⑩ St-Etienne, Nevers *p328*
⑪ Ste-Madeleine, Vézelay *pp326–7*
⑫ Marmoutier, Saverne *p223*

WHERE TO FIND GOTHIC ARCHITECTURE

⑬ Notre-Dame, Strasbourg *p221*
⑭ Notre-Dame, Reims *pp202–3*
⑮ Notre-Dame, Laon *p195*
⑯ Notre-Dame, Amiens *pp192–3*
⑰ St-Pierre, Beauvais *p190*
⑱ St-Denis, Ile-de-France *p162*
⑲ Sainte-Chapelle, Paris *pp80–81*
⑳ Notre-Dame, Paris *p82–3*
㉑ Notre-Dame, Chartres *pp298–301*
㉒ St-Etienne, Bourges *p303*

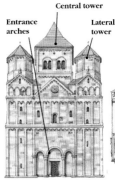

Central tower
Entrance arches
Lateral tower

The west façade of Marmoutier Abbey, *with its towers, narrow windows and small portal, has a fortified appearance.*

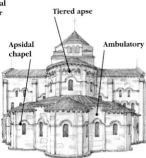

Tiered apse
Apsidal chapel
Ambulatory

The east end of Nevers *has a rounded apse surrounded by a semicircular ambulatory and radiating chapels. The chapels were added to provide space for altars.*

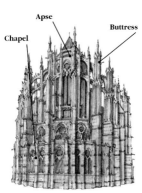

Stepped tower
Sculpted portal
Rose
Apse
Buttress
Chapel

The west façade of Laon *has decorative, sculpted portals and a rose window characteristic of Gothic style.*

The east end of Beauvais, *with its delicate buttresses topped by pinnacles, is the culmination of High Gothic.*

TERMS USED IN THIS GUIDE

Basilica: Early church with two aisles and nave lit from above by clerestory windows.

Clerestory: A row of windows illuminating the nave from above the aisle roof.

Rose: Circular window, often stained glass.

Buttress: Mass of masonry built to support a wall.

Flying buttress: An arched support transmitting thrust of the weight downward.

Portal: Monumental entrance to a building, often decorated.

Tympanum: Decorated space, often carved, over a door or window lintel.

Vault: Arched stone ceiling.

Transept: Two wings of a cruciform church at right angles to the nave.

Crossing: Center of cruciform where transept crosses nave.

Lantern: Turret with windows to illuminate interior, often with cupola (domed ceiling).

Triforium: Middle story between arcades and clerestory.

Apse: Termination of the church, often rounded.

Ambulatory: Aisle running around east end, passing behind the sanctuary.

Arcade: Set of arches and supporting columns.

Rib vault: Vault supported by projecting ribs of stone.

Gargoyle: Carved grotesque figure, often a water spout.

Tracery: Ornamental carved stone pattern within Gothic window.

Flamboyant Gothic: Carved stone tracery resembling flames.

Capital: Top of a column, usually carved.

Rural Architecture

FRENCH FARMHOUSES ARE ENTIRELY products of the soil, built of stone, clay or wood, depending on what materials are found locally. As the topography changes so does the architecture, from the steeply sloped roofs covered in flat tiles in the north to the broad canal-tiled roofs of the south.

Despite this rich regional diversity, French farmhouses fall into three basic categories: the *maison bloc*, where house and outbuildings share the same roof; the high house, with living quarters upstairs and livestock or wine cellar below; and courtyard farmsteads, their buildings set around a central court.

Shuttered window in Alsace

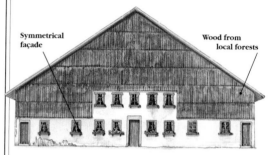

Symmetrical façade

Wood from local forests

The chalet is typical of the Jura, Alps and Vosges mountains. The maison bloc housed both family and livestock throughout the winter. Gaps between the gable planks allowed air to circulate around crops stored in the loft, and an earth ramp behind gave wagons access. Many lofts also had a threshing floor.

Normandy wood structure

Flat-tiled roof

Half-timbered houses are typical of Normandy, Alsace, Champagne, Picardy, the Landes and Basque country. The filling between the timbers was wattle and daub or in some cases brick, but it is the arrangement of the smaller posts, different in each region, that best expresses the local style.

Raised stone foundations

Dovecote with flat tiles

Steps to front door

Animals or wine housed here

The high house is most prominent in the southeast, and is normally built of stone with an exterior stone staircase and upstairs porch. Wine growers' barrels could be stored on the ground floor without hoisting, or livestock stabled there. High houses in the Lot Valley often boast a dovecote.

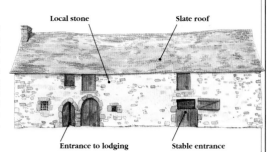

The long house is the oldest form of maison bloc, *with family and livestock at opposite ends of the building – originally one room. In this Breton version, separate doorways lead to house and stable. A dividing wall became common only in the 19th century.*

Local stone

Slate roof

Entrance to lodging

Stable entrance

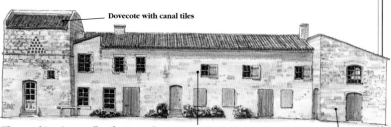

Dovecote with canal tiles

*The word "*mas" *generally refers to any Provençal farmhouse. In the Camargue and the Crau, it is a farmstead for large-scale sheep farming built in an "agglomerated" style: the outbuildings, although attached to one another, are of different heights. Often, a dovecote is included.*

Ocher and beige colors of the south

Rendered façade

Pebble and brick wall

Half-timber and brick

Compressed cob: *pisé*

Sun-dried adobe bricks

Pebbles in lime mortar

Brick, flint and chalk

WALLS

Limestone, granite, sandstone and pebbles were all used for building walls. But if no stone was available, clay was dug for infilling half-timbered houses, as wattle and daub. The alternative was to use a cob mixture *(pisé)*, pressed into blocks in a process called *banchange*. Adobe (sun-dried brick) was also used, but fired brick was fairly rare as it was expensive to bake. Still, brick was sometimes used as trim or combined with chalk or pebbles in a "composite" walling. Walls were generally rendered with mortar.

Flat terra-cotta tiles in colors of local sand

Pantiles, used in Flanders and Picardy

Canal clay tiles typical of the south

ROOFING

Two roof styles distinguish the north and south. Northern roofs are steeply pitched, so that any rainwater runs off easily. In the south, roofs are covered with canal clay tiles, and more gently sloped to prevent the tiles from sliding off.

FRANCE THROUGH THE YEAR

THE FRENCH, with their farming roots, are deeply aware of the changing seasons, and the mild climate means they can celebrate outdoors most of the year. History and tradition are honored with *fêtes*, such as Bastille Day (July 14). For culture lovers, thousands of arts festivals are held in various locations, from the huge Avignon Theater Festival down to small village events. Large national sports events, such as the Tour de France bicycle race, are featured annual events. There are also festivals throughout the year, featuring every kind of food and wine. In high season in the summer, the cities empty and locals and tourists flock to the beaches and countryside.

Formula One racing at the Monaco Grand Prix

SPRING

FRANCE'S OUTDOOR life resumes in spring, terrace cafés filling up in the sunshine. Easter is a time of Catholic processions and concerts of sacred music. The Cannes Film Festival in May is the best known of the season's many conventions and trade fairs.

MARCH

Tinta' Mars *(two weeks)*, Langres. Cabaret and musical evenings at various venues.
Grenoble Jazz Festival *(two weeks Mar)*. Jazz concerts.
Musical Flower Show *(end Mar–May)*, Epinal. Classical concerts.

Rugby ball

APRIL

Six Nations Rugby Tournament, Stade de France, Paris.

La Bravade procession honoring Saint Torpes in St-Tropez

Lourdes Pilgrimage *(Palm Sun to Oct, see p449)*. **Good Friday penitential processions** Sartène *(see p533)*, & Perpignan *(see p474)*.
Passion Plays *(Easter)*, reenactments of the Crucifixion throughout France. **Festival de Pâques** *(Easter week)*, Chamber music festival, Deauville *(see p245)*.
Bourges Spring Festival *(see p303)*, modern music.
Europa Jazz Festival *(last two wks)*, Le Mans. Young jazz musicians from all over the world perform.
Foire de Paris *(end Apr–first wk May)*, Paris Expo, Port de Versailles, Paris. Food, wine, homes & tourism show.
Joan of Arc Festival *(end Apr–early May)*, Orléans *(see p302)*.
Paris International Marathon, from Place de la Concorde to Avenue Foch. **Festival d'Amiens** *(late Mar/early Apr)*. Jazz festival at various venues.

MAY

Spring asparagus

Asparagus harvest, notably in the Loire.
International Grand Prix de Monaco *(Ascension weekend, see p520)*.
La Bravade *(May 16–18)*, St-Tropez *(see p506)*.

Cannes Film Festival *(second and third week).*
Gypsy Pilgrimage *(May 24–26),* Stes-Maries-de-la-Mer *(see p500).*
Fête de la Transhumance *(end May).* Herds are taken up to summer pastures.
Le Printemps des Arts *(May–Jun),* St –Tropez *(see p506).*
Nîmes Feria *(Pentecost),* bullfights and street music festival *(see p486).*
Grandes Eaux Musicales *(Apr–Oct: Sun; Jul–Sep: Sat–Sun),* Versailles. Classical music in the grounds of the château.

Traditional movement of animals to summer pastures

Puy-du-Fou Pageant *(Jun–Aug),* Audio–guides, fireworks and horse-riding stunts evoke local French life through the ages *(see p280).*

Football Cup Final *(second week),* Stade de France, Paris.
Le Printemps des Arts *(mid May–Jun),* Nantes area. Baroque dance and music.

SUMMER

THE FRENCH vacation season begins in mid-July, with the return to work and school *(la rentrée)* in early September. Beaches, marinas and campsites are all full to bursting. Every village has its *fête* and there are countless festivals and sports events.

JUNE

French Tennis Open *(last wk May – first wk Jun),* Stade Roland Garros, Paris.
Strasbourg International Music Festival *(until Jul).*
International Sailing Week *(early Jun),* La Rochelle.

The rose season in full bloom

Le Mans 24-Hour Automobile Race *(second or third w/e, see p281).*
Rose Show, Jardins de Bagatelle, Bois de Boulogne, Paris.
Fête de la Musique *(21 Jun),* Music events all over France.
Fête de St-Jean *(Jun 24),* music, bonfires and fireworks all over France.
Tarasque Festival *(last w/e),* Tarascon *(see p497).*

JULY

Festival d'Art Lyrique *(Jun–Jul),* Aix-en-Provence *(see p501).*
Avignon Theater Festival *(all month, see p493).*
Eté Girondin *(Jul–Aug).* Jazz concerts throughout

Cyclists in the final stage of the Tour de France cycle race

Bullfighting in Mont-de-Marsan

Aquitaine *(see p411).*
Tombées de la Nuit *(first week),* Rennes. Arts festival.
Troménie *(2nd Sun Jul),* Locronan. Procession of penitents *(see p263).*
Comminges Music Festival *(Jul–end Aug, see p452).*
Nice Jazz Festival *(late-Jul)*
Mont-de-Marsan Feria *(third w/e).* Bullfights and music *(see p415).*
International Jazz Festival *(second half),* Antibes and Juan-les-Pins *(see p511).*
Jazz Vienne *(first two weeks),* Vienne *(see p372).*
Fête de St-Louis *(around Aug 25),* Sète *(see p482).*
Tour de France cycle race *(1st three weeks).* The grand finale takes place on the Champs-Elysées, Paris.
Sardana Dance Festival *(third w/e),* Céret *(see p472).*

Vacationers on a crowded beach in Cannes on the Côte d'Azur

AUGUST

Pablo Casals Festival *(end Jul–mid-Aug)*, Prades (*see p470*).
Les Rendezvous de l'Erdre *(last w/e)*, Nantes. Jazz and river-boats (*see p280*).
Mimos *(1st week)*, Périgueux. International mime festival.
Fête du Jasmin *(first*

w/e), Grasse (*see p.507*) .
Floats, music, dancing in the town.
Foire aux Sorciers *(first Sun)*, Bué (nr Bourges). Costumed witch and wizard fest-ival and folk groups.
Parade of Lavender Floats *(first or second w/e)*, Digne (*see p507*).
Fête de la Véraison

Avignon Theater Festival performer

(first or second w/e), medieval celebrat-ion of fruit harvest, Châteauneuf-du-Pape (*see p492*).
Interceltic Festival *(second week)*, Celtic arts and music, Lorient.
Feria – Bullfight *(mid-Aug)*, Dax (*see p415*).
St-Jean-Pied-de-Port-Basque Fête *(mid-Aug, see p444)*.
Deauville American film Festival *(last week, see p245)*.

AUTUMN

IN WINE REGIONS, the grape harvest is the occasion for much gregarious jollity, and every wine village celebrates with a wine festival. When the new wine is ready in November there are more festivities. The hunting season begins – hunters are out everywhere. In the south-west, small migrating birds are trapped in nets, often to the fury of ecologists.

Ceremony for the Induction of new Chevaliers at the Hospice de Beaune

SEPTEMBER

Picardy Cathedral Festival *(mid-Sep)*, classical concerts in the region's cathedrals.
"Musicades" *(first two weeks)*, Lyon. Classical concerts.
Le Puy "Roi de l'Oiseau," *(third week)*, Renaissance-style festival (*see p355*).
Grape harvest, wine regions throughout France.
Journées du Patrimoine, *(3rd w/e)*, Over 14,000 histor-ical buildings can be visited, many not normally open.

OCTOBER

Dinard British film Festival *(first week, see p271)*.
Prix de l'Arc de Triomphe *(first Sun)*, Horse racing at Longchamp, Paris.
Espelette Red Pepper Festival *(last w/e, see p443)*, Basque region.
Abbaye de Fontevraud Season of Music *(autumn to spring, see p284)*.

Classical cello

NOVEMBER

Dijon International Food and Wine Festival *(first two weeks)*. Traditional gastronomic fair.
Apple Festival *(mid-Nov)*, Le Havre.
Wine Auctions and Les Trois Glorieuses *(third w/e)*, Beaune (*see p336*).
Truffle season *(until Mar)*, Périgord, Quercy and Provence.

WINTER

Christmas wreath

AT CHRISTMAS, traditional nativity plays are held in churches and there are fairs and markets throughout France. In the Alps and the Pyrenees, and even the Vosges and Massif Central, the ski slopes are crowded. In Flanders and Nice, carnivals take place before Lent.

DECEMBER

Critérium International de la Première Niege *(early Dec)*, Val d'Isère. First competition of the season.

JANUARY

Monte-Carlo Rally *(usually mid-Jan, see p520).*
Limoux Carnival *(until Mar).* Street festival held since the Middle Ages.
Fashion shows. Summer

Downhill skier on the slopes in the French Alps

The Taj Mahal re-created at the Lemon Festival in Menton

collections, Paris.
Festival du Cirque *(end)*, Monaco. International event.
Festival de la Bande Dessinée *(last w/e).* International strip cartoon festival, Angoulême.

FEBRUARY

Lemon Festival *(mid-Feb–Mar)*, Menton *(see p519).*
Nice Carnival and the Battle of Flowers *(late Feb–early Mar, see p516).*
Paris Carnaval *(date varies, check)*, Quartier St-Fargeau.
Fête de Mimosa *(3rd Sun)*, Bornes-les-Mimosas.

Celebrating the Nice Carnival and the Battle of Flowers

Bastille Day parade past the Arc de Triomphe

PUBLIC HOLIDAYS

New Year's Day (Jan 1)
Easter Sunday and Monday
Ascension Day (sixth Thursday after Easter)
Whit Monday (second Monday after Ascension)
Labor Day (May 1)
VE Day (May 8)
Bastille Day (Jul 14)
Assumption Day (Aug 15)
All Saints' Day (Nov 1)
Remembrance Day (Nov 11)
Christmas Day (Dec 25)

The Climate of France

S ET ON EUROPE's western edge, France has a varied, temperate climate. An Atlantic influence prevails in the northwest, with westerly sea winds bringing humidity and warm winters. The east experiences Continental temperature extremes, with frosty, clear winters and often stormy summers. The south enjoys a Mediterranean climate, with hot, dry summers and mild winters punctuated by violent winds.

PARIS AND ILE DE FRANCE

°F			
		75	
58	59	61	
44		49	44
			36
6 hrs	8 hrs	4.5 hrs	2 hrs
2 in	2.25 in	2.25 in	2.25 in
month	Apr	Jul	Oct	Jan

- Average monthly maximum temperature
- Average monthly minimum temperature
- Average daily hours of sunshine
- Average monthly rainfall

NORMANDY

°F			
	71		
55	55	61	
41		46	46
			36
5.5 hrs	7 hrs	4 hrs	2 hrs
1.75 in	2 in	2.75 in	2.5 in
month	Apr	Jul	Oct	Jan

BRITTANY

°F			
	75		
58	55	63	
42		47	46
			36
6 hrs	8 hrs	4.5 hrs	2 hrs
1.75 in	1.5 in	2.5 in	2.5 in
month	Apr	Jul	Oct	Jan

LOIRE VALLEY

°F			
	76		
59	57	64	
43		48	47
			37
6 hrs	8.5 hrs	4.5 hrs	2.5 hrs
2 in	1.75 in	3 in	3.5 in
month	Apr	Jul	Oct	Jan

POITOU AND AQUITAINE

°F			
	79		
62	58	66	
44		48	49
			37
6.5 hrs	9 hrs	5.5 hrs	2.5 hrs
2.75 in	1.75 in	3.5 in	4 in
month	Apr	Jul	Oct	Jan

PYRENEES

°F			
	77		
59	56	66	
41		46	50
			33
5 hrs	7.5 hrs	5.5 hrs	3.5 hrs
3.75 in	2.5 in	3 in	3.75 in
month	Apr	Jul	Oct	Jan

PÉRIGORD, QUERCY AND GASCONY

°F			
	81		
62	58	66	
43		48	47
			36
6 hrs	9 hrs	4.5 hrs	2.5 hrs
2.25 in	2 in	2.25 in	2.5 in
month	Apr	Jul	Oct	Jan

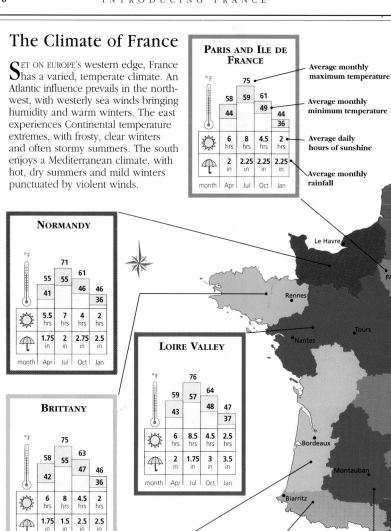
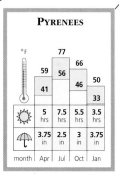
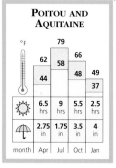

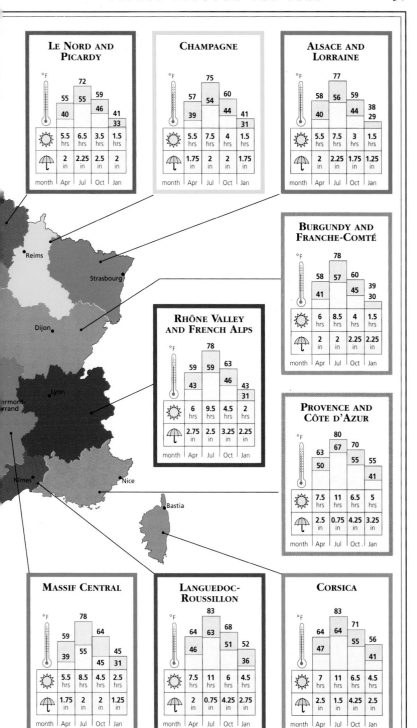

THE HISTORY OF FRANCE

THE ONLY European country to face both the North Sea and the Mediterranean, France has been subject to a particularly rich variety of cultural influences. Though famous for the rootedness of its peasant population, it has also been a European melting pot, from before the arrival of the Celtic Gauls in the centuries before Christ, through to the Mediterranean immigrations of the 20th century.

Roman conquest by Julius Caesar had an enduring impact, but from the 4th and 5th centuries AD, waves of Barbarian invaders destroyed much of the Roman legacy. The Germanic Franks provided political leadership in the following centuries, but when their line died out in the late 10th century, France was socially and politically fragmented.

Fleur-de-lys, the royal emblem

THE FORMATION OF FRANCE

The Capetian dynasty gradually pieced France together over the Middle Ages, a period of great economic prosperity and cultural vitality. The Black Death and the Hundred Years' War brought setbacks, and the dynasty's power was seriously threatened by the rival Burgundian dukes. France recovered, however, and flourished during the Renaissance, followed by the grandeur of Louis XIV's reign. During the Enlightenment, in the 18th century, French culture and institutions were the envy of Europe.

The Revolution of 1789 ended the absolute monarchy and introduced major social and institutional reforms, many of which were endorsed and consolidated by Napoleon. Yet the Revolution also inaugurated the instability that has remained a hallmark of French politics: since 1789, France has known five republics, two empires and three brands of royal power, plus the Vichy government during World War II.

Modernization in the 19th and 20th centuries proved a slow process. Railroads, the military service and radical educational reforms were crucial in forming a sense of French identity among the citizens.

Rivalry with Germany dominated French politics for most of the late 19th and early 20th centuries. The population losses in World War I were traumatic for France, and so was its occupation by Germany from 1940–44. Yet since 1945, the two countries have proved the backbone of the developing European Union.

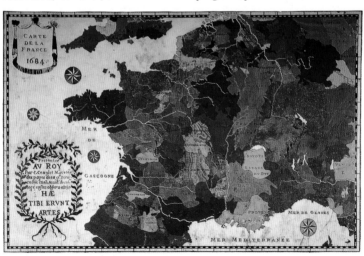

Inlaid marble tabletop showing the map of France in 1684

◁ *La République*, painted by Charles Landelle in 1848

Prehistoric France

THE EARLIEST TRACES of human life in France date back to around 2 million BC. From around 40,000 BC, *Homo sapiens* lived an itinerant existence as hunters and gatherers. Around 6000 BC, following the end of the Ice Age, a major shift in lifestyle occurred, as people settled down to herd animals and cultivate crops. The advent of metalworking allowed more effective tools and weapons to be developed. The Iron Age is associated particularly with the Celts, who arrived from the east during the first millennium BC. A more complex social hierarchy developed, consisting of warriors, farmers, artisans and druids (Celtic priests).

Bronze Age vase, Brittany

FRANCE IN 8000 BC

☐ *Former coastline*

☐ *Present-day land mass*

Carnac Stone Alignments *(4500–4000 BC)*
The purpose of the extensive networks of megaliths around Carnac (see p268) remains obscure. They possibly served in pagan rituals or as an astronomical calendar.

These carvings of horses' heads were found in the Pyrenees and date from around 9000 BC.

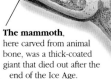

The mammoth, here carved from animal bone, was a thick-coated giant that died out after the end of the Ice Age.

Cro-Magnon Man
This skull, dating to c.25,000 BC, was discovered at Cro-Magnon in the Dordogne in 1868. In comparison with most of his predecessors, Cro-Magnon Man was tall, robust and had a large head. He differed only marginally from us.

PREHISTORIC ART
The rich deposits of cave art in France have only been recognized as authentic for just over a century. They include wall paintings and sketches as well as various engraved objects. Venus figurines, carved with flint tools, probably had ritual and religious rather than erotic purposes.

TIMELINE

Painting of bulls in Lascaux

2,000,000 BC Early hominid societies

30,000 Cro-Magnon Man

2,000,000 BC	30,000	25,000	20,000

400,000 Discovery of fire by *Homo erectus*

28,000 The first Venus sculptures, possibly representing fertility goddesses

Primitive stone tool

Doorway, Roquepertuse
Religion was an important part of Celtic life. The Celts made a cult of severed heads – presumably of their enemies – as seen in this sanctuary doorway dating from the 3rd century BC.

WHERE TO SEE PREHISTORIC FRANCE

The Lascaux cave paintings in Périgord *(see p424)* are among the best in the world. Other cave decoration is found around Les Eyzies *(pp424–5)*, at the Vallée des Merveilles near Tendes in the Alpes-Maritimes *(p519)* and in the Grotte du Pech Merle in the Lot Valley *(p428)*. The intriguing menhirs at Filitosa in Corsica *(pp532–3)* are about 4,000 years old.

***The Lascaux** cave paintings, dating from 16,000–14,000 BC, include images of bulls and mammoths.*

The prehistoric hunter's quarry is here represented by a flock of chamois (goatlike antelopes) carved on bone.

This carved bone, found in Laugerie Basse in the Dordogne, shows a bison chased by a man with a spear.

Copper Ax *(c.2000 BC)*
Copper tools preceded the arrival of the stronger and more malleable bronze alloy. Iron was to prove the toughest and most useful metal of all.

Bronze Armor
Bronze and Iron Age people were highly warlike. The Celtic Gauls were feared even by Romans. Their protective armor, such as this breastplate dating from 750–475 BC, was light but reasonably effective.

This highly stylized female figure, a Venus figurine found in southwest France, was carved from mammoth tusk in around 20,000 BC.

15,000 Hunters live on wandering herds of mammoth, rhinoceros and reindeer. Art includes the Lascaux caves and Val Camonica/Mont Bego engravings

7000–4500 Neolithic revolution: farming, megaliths and menhir stone sculptures

600 Greek colony at Marseille. Mediterranean luxury goods exchanged for tin, copper, iron and slaves. Early urban development

15,000	10,000	5,000

10,000 End of Ice Age. More regions become inhabitable

10,000–6000 Mammoth herds disappear and hunters must rely on animals of the forest, including wild boar and aurochs

1200–700 Arrival of the Celts during the Bronze and Iron Ages

500 Celtic nobles bury their dead with riches such as the Vix treasure *(see p324)*

Celtic helmet

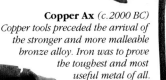

Roman Gaul

Roman mosaic from Vienne

THE ROMANS HAD ANNEXED the southern fringe of France by 125–121 BC. Julius Caesar brought the rest of Gaul under Roman control in the Gallic Wars (58–51 BC). The province of Gaul prospered: it developed good communications, a network of cities crammed with public buildings and leisure facilities such as baths and amphitheaters, while in the countryside large villas were established. By the 3rd century AD, however, barbarian raids from Germany were causing increasing havoc. From the 5th century barbarians began to settle throughout Gaul.

FRANCE IN 58 BC

☐ *Roman Gaul*

Emperor Augustus, who was considered a living God, was worshiped at this altar.

Roman Dolce Vita
The Romans brought material comfort and luxury, and wine production became widespread. This 19th-century painting by Couture conveys a contemporary view of Roman decadence.

Vercingetorix
The Celtic chieftain Vercingetorix was Julius Caesar's greatest military opponent. This bronze statue is at Alise-Sainte-Reine (see p324), the Gauls' final stand in 51 BC.

LA TURBIE
This impressive monument near Monaco was erected in 6 BC by the Roman Senate. It celebrates Augustus's victory over the Alpine tribes in 14–13 BC. Badly pillaged for its stone, restoration only began in the 1920's.

TIMELINE

Augustus

125–121 BC Roman colonization of Southern Gaul

31 BC Frontiers of the Three Gauls (*Gallia Celtica, Gallia Aquitania* and *Gallia Belgica*) established by Augustus

200 BC	100	0	AD 100

Julius Caesar

58–51 BC Julius Caesar's Gallic Wars result in establishment of Roman Gaul

16 BC Maison Carrée built in Nîmes (*see pp486–7*)

52–51 BC Vercingetorix revolt

AD 43 Lugdunum (Lyon) established as capital of the Three Gauls

Dancing Girl
*Celtic art continued,
uninfluenced by Roman naturalistic ideals. This bronze statuette
of a young woman dates from
the 1st–2nd century AD.*

A statue of Augustus
was placed at the
top of the original
monument.

Enameled Brooch
*This decorative Gallo-
Roman brooch dates
from the second half
of the 1st century BC.*

WHERE TO SEE GALLO-ROMAN FRANCE

Gallo-Roman remains are to be found
all over France, many of them in
Provence. In addition to La Turbie *(see
p519)*, there is the Roman amphitheater
in Arles *(p475)* and the theater and
triumphal arch in Orange *(p492)*.
Elsewhere, there are ruins at Autun in
Burgundy *(p329)*, the Temple d'Auguste
et Livie in Vienne *(p372)*, Les Arènes
at Nîmes *(pp486–7)* and fragments of
Vesunna in Périgueux *(p424)*.

Les Arènes in Nîmes, *built at the end of
the 1st century AD, is still in use today.*

The Claudian Tables
*In AD 48, Emperor
Claudius persuaded the
Senate to allow Gauls full
Roman citizenship. The
grateful Gauls recorded
the event on stone tables,
found at Lyon.*

The 44 tribes subjugated
by Augustus are listed on
an inscription, with a dedi-
cation to the emperor.

**Emperor
Augustus**
*Augustus, the first
Roman Emperor (27 BC–AD
14), upheld the Pax Romana, a
peace agreement that allowed
the Gauls to concentrate on
culture rather than war.*

AD 177 First execution
of Christian martyrs,
Lyon. Sainte Blandine is
thrown to the lions, who
refuse to harm her

Sainte Blandine

360 Julian, prefect of Gaul,
proclaimed Roman Emperor.
Lutetia changes name to Paris

200	300	400

275 First Barbarian raids

313 Christianity officially recognized as
religion under the rule of Constantine,
the first Christian emperor

406 Barbarian invasion
from the east. Settlement
of the Franks and
Germanic tribes

476 Overthrow of
the last Roman
emperor leads to
end of the western
Roman Empire

The Monastic Realm

THE COLLAPSE of the Roman Empire led to a period of instability and invasions. Both the Frankish Merovingian dynasty (486–751) and the Carolingians (751–987) were unable to bring more than spasmodic periods of political calm. Throughout this turbulent period, the Church provided an element of continuity. As centers for Christian scholars and artists, the monasteries helped to restore the values of the ancient world. They also developed farming and viticulture; and some became extremely powerful, dominating the country economically as well as spiritually.

9th-century gold chalice

FRANCE IN 751

☐ *Carolingian Empire*

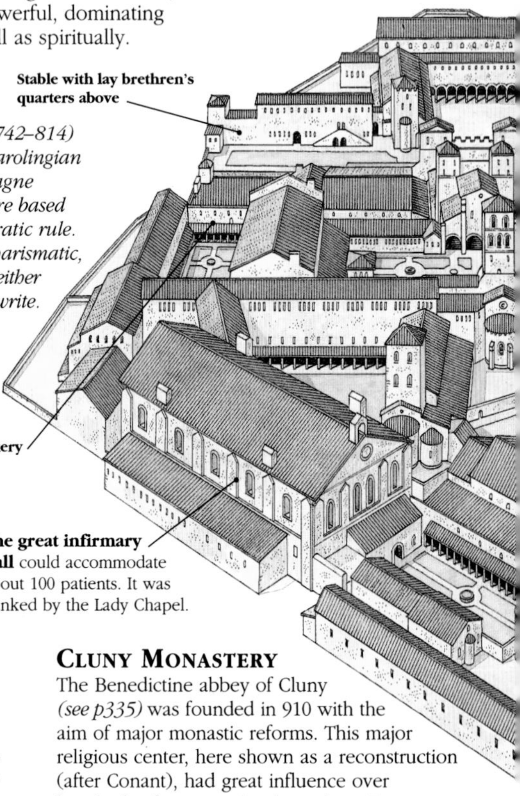

Stable with lay brethren's quarters above

Charlemagne *(742–814)*
The greatest of Carolingian rulers, Charlemagne created an empire based on strictly autocratic rule. Powerful and charismatic, he could neither read nor write.

Bakery

The great infirmary hall could accommodate about 100 patients. It was flanked by the Lady Chapel.

CLUNY MONASTERY

The Benedictine abbey of Cluny *(see p335)* was founded in 910 with the aim of major monastic reforms. This major religious center, here shown as a reconstruction (after Conant), had great influence over hundreds of monasteries throughout Europe.

Saint Benedict
Saint Benedict established the Benedictine rule: monks were to divide their time between work and prayer.

TIMELINE

481 Clovis the Frank becomes first Merovingian king	**c.590** Saint Colombanus introduces Irish monasticism to France	**732** Battle of Poitiers: Charles Martel repulses Arab invasion
507 Paris made capital of the Frankish kingdom		
500	**600**	**700**
496 Conversion of Clovis, king of the Franks, to Christianity	**628–37** Dagobert I, the last effective ruler of the Merovingian dynasty, brings temporary unity to the Frankish kingdom	**751** Pepin becomes first king of the Carolingian dynasty

Dagobert I

Baptism of Clovis
The Frankish chieftain Clovis was the first barbarian ruler to convert to Christianity. He was baptized in Reims in 496.

The abbey church, begun in 1088, was the largest church in Europe before St. Peter's was built in Rome in the 16th century.

Cemetery chapel

WHERE TO SEE MONASTIC FRANCE

The monastic realm has survived in austere Cistercian abbeys in Burgundy, such as Fontenay *(see pp322–3)*. Little remains of Cluny, but some of the superb capitals can still be admired *(p335)*. The best way to experience monastic France might be to retrace the steps of medieval pilgrims and visit the monastic centers on the route to Santiago de Compostela *(pp390–91)*, such as Vézelay *(pp326–7)*, Le Puy *(pp354–5)*, Conques *(pp358–9)*, Moissac *(pp432–3)* and St-Sernin in Toulouse *(pp436–7)*.

Cluny capitals

Monastic Arts
In scriptoriums, talented artists dedicated their time to the meticulous art of illuminating and copying manuscripts for the libraries.

Monastic Labor
Monks of the Cistercian rule were renowned for their commitment to manual labor such as cultivating the land and producing wine and liqueurs.

Carolingian soldiers

987 Hugh Capet, first Capetian ruler

1096 First Crusade

1066 Conquest of England by the Normans

800	900	1000

843 Treaty of Verdun: division of the Carolingian Empire into three parts including West Francia

800 Coronation of Charlemagne as Holy Roman Emperor

910 Foundation of the Benedictine monastery of Cluny

1077 Bayeux tapestry

William the Conqueror steering his ship on the Bayeux tapestry

Gothic France

THE GOTHIC STYLE, epitomized by soaring cathedrals *(see pp28–9)*, emerged in the 12th century at a time of growing prosperity and scholarship, crusades and an increasingly dominant monarchy. The rival French and Burgundian courts *(see p333)* became models of fashion and etiquette for all of Europe. *Chansons des gestes* (epic poems) performed by troubadours celebrated the code of chivalry.

FRANCE IN 1270

☐ *Royal territory*
▨ *Other fiefs*

Medieval knights in combat

Ciborium of Alpais

Alpais, a renowned 12th-century goldsmith in Limoges, made this superb ciborium, used to hold wafers for the Holy Communion.

Winch to lift stone sections

Courtly Love

According to the code of chivalry, knights dedicated their service to an ideal but unapproachable lady. Courtesy and romance were introduced in art and music.

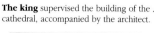
The king supervised the building of the cathedral, accompanied by the architect.

Draper's Window

The textile trade benefited from the era of urban prosperity. This stained-glass window in a church in Semur-en-Auxois (see p325) shows wool washers at work.

TIMELINE

c.1100 First edition of the epic poem *Chanson de Roland*

1117 Secret marriage of the scholar Abelard and his student Héloise. Her uncle, canon Filibert, does not approve and forces him to become a monk while she retires as a nun

1154 Angevin Empire created by Anglo-Norman dynasty starting with Henry Plantagenet, a Count of Anjou and King of England (as Henry II)

1100	1125	1150	1175

1115 Saint Bernard founds the Cistercian Abbey at Clairvaux

1120 Rebuilding of the Abbey of St-Denis; birth of the Gothic style

King Philip Augustus, who adopted the fleur-de-lys emblem

1180–1223 Reign of Philip Augustus

The Crusades
In an attempt to win back the Holy Land from the Turks, Philip Augustus set out on the Third Crusade (1189) alongside England's Richard the Lion-Heart and Holy Roman Emperor Frederick Barbarossa.

Lacelike sculpture adorned the façades of the Gothic cathedrals.

Stonemasons cut stones on site.

ELEANOR OF AQUITAINE

Strong-willed and vivacious Eleanor, duchess of independent Aquitaine, contributed to the conflict between France and England. In 1137 she married the pious Louis VII of France. Returning from a crusade, Louis found that their marriage had broken down. After the annulment in 1152, Eleanor married Henry of Anjou, taking her duchy with her. Two years later Henry successfully claimed the throne of England. Aquitaine came under English rule, and thus the Angevin Empire began.

***Eleanor of Aquitaine** and Henry II are buried in Fontevraud (p284).*

Holy Relic
Throughout the Middle Ages most churches could boast at least one saint's relic. The cult of relics brought pilgrims and more riches.

St. Bernard *(1090–1153) Key figure of the Cistercian rule and counselor to the pope, St. Bernard preached rigorous simplicity of life.*

THE BUILDING OF A CATHEDRAL
In affluent, mercantile towns, skilled masons constructed towering Gothic cathedrals of revolutionary design, such as Chartres *(see pp298–301)* and Amiens *(pp192–3)*. With their improbable height and lightness, they were a testimony to both faith and prosperity.

Louis IX on his death bed

1226 Louis IX crowned king

1270 Death of Louis IX at Tunis in the Eighth Crusade

1305 Papacy established in Avignon

1200	1225	1250	1275	1300

1214 Battle of Bouvines. Philip Augustus begins to drive the English out of France

1259 Normandy, Maine, Anjou and Poitou acquired from England

1285 Philip the Fair crowned

1297 Louis IX is canonized, becoming Saint Louis

The Hundred Years' War

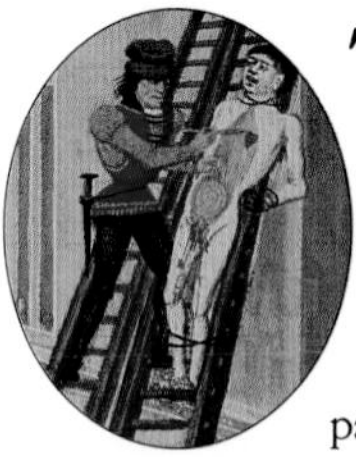

THE HUNDRED YEARS' WAR (1337–1453), pitting England against France for control of French land, had devastating effects. The damage of warfare was amplified by frequent famines and the ravages of bubonic plague in the wake of the Black Death in 1348. France came close to being permanently partitioned by the king of England and the duke of Burgundy. In 1429–30 the young Joan of Arc helped rally France's fortunes, and within a generation the English had been driven out of France.

Public execution, in Froissart's 14th-century chronicle

FRANCE IN 1429

☐ France

▨ Anglo-Burgundy

Angels with trumpets announce the Last Judgment.

Men of War
One of the reasons men enlisted as soldiers was hope for plunder. Both the French and English armies lived off the land, at the expense of the peasantry.

The elect, springing resurrected from their graves, are ushered into heaven.

The Black Death
The plague of 1348–52 caused 4–5 million deaths, about 25 percent of the French population. For want of medicines people had to put their faith in prayers and holy processions.

TIMELINE

1346 Battle of Crécy: French defeated by English

1328 Philip VI, first Valois monarch

1356 French defeat at Battle of Poitiers

14th-century flame-throw

1325	1350	1375

1337 Start of the Hundred Years' War

1348–52 The Black Death

1358 Bourgeois uprising in Paris led by Etienne Marcel. The Jacquerie peasant uprising in Northern France

Plague victims

Medieval Medicine
The state of the heavens was widely held to influence earthly conditions, such as health, and a diagnosis based on the zodiac was considered reliable. The standby cure for all sorts of ailments was bloodletting.

English Longbow
The king's troops fought against England, but the individual French duchies supported whichever side seemed more favorable. In the confused battles, English bowmen excelled. Their longbows caused chaos among the hordes of mounted French cavalry.

Christ as Supreme Judge is flanked by angels bearing the instruments of the Passion.

Archangel Michael, resplendent with peacock wings, holds the judgment scales. The weight of sinners outbalances the elect.

John the Baptist is accompanied by the 12 apostles and the Virgin Mary, dressed in blue.

The damned, with hideously twisted faces, fall into Hell.

THE LAST JUDGMENT
With war, plague and famine as constant visitors, many people feared that the end of the world was nigh. Religious paintings, such as the great 15th-century altar screen by Rogier van der Weyden in the Hôtel-Dieu in Beaune *(see pp336–7)*, reflected the moral fervor of the time.

Attack on Heresy
The general anxiety spilled over into anti-Semitic pogroms and attacks on alleged heretics, who were burned at the stake.

1415 Battle of Agincourt. French defeat by Henry V of England

1429 Intervention of Joan of Arc: Charles VII crowned king

1453 End of the Hundred Years' War. Only Calais remains in English hands

1400   **1425**   **1450**

1411 *Les Très Riches Heures du Duc du Berry* prayer book, by Paul and Jean de Limbourg *(see p194)*

1431 Joan of Arc burned at stake as witch by the English

1419 Charles VI of France makes Henry V of England his heir

Joan of Arc

Renaissance France

AS A RESULT OF the French invasion of Italy in 1494, the ideals and aesthetic of the Italian Renaissance spread to France, reaching their height during the reign of François I. Known as a true Renaissance prince, he was skilled in letters and art as well as sports and war. He invited Italian artists, such as Leonardo and Cellini, to his court and enjoyed Rabelais' bawdy stories. Another highly influential Italian was Catherine de' Medici (1519–89). Widow of Henri II, she virtually ruled France through her sons, François II, Charles IX and Henri III. She was also one of the major **Masked** players in the Wars of Religion (1562–93) **lute-player** between Catholics and Protestants, which divided the nobility and tore the country to pieces.

FRANCE IN 1527

☐ *Royal territory*

■ *Other fiefs*

The corner towers are a Gothic feature transformed by Italian lightness of touch into pure decoration.

Galerie François I, Fontainebleau
*The artists of the School of Fontaine-
bleau blended late Italian Renaissance
style with French elements.*

**Power Behind
the Throne**
*Catherine de'
Medici domi-
nated French
politics from
1559–89.*

AZAY-LE-RIDEAU
One of the loveliest of the Loire châteaux, Azay was begun in 1518 *(see p286).* Italian influences are visible, and it is clear that this is a dwelling meant for pleasure rather than defense.

TIMELINE

1470 First printing presses established in France

*Prototype tank by
Leonardo da Vinci*

1519 Leonardo da Vinci dies in the arms of François I at the French court in Amboise

1536 Calvin's *Institutes
of the Christian Religion*
leads to a new form of
Protestantism

1470	1480	1490	1500	1510	1520	1530

1477 Final defeat of the Dukes of Burgundy, who sought to establish a middle kingdom between France and Germany

1494–1559 France and Austria fight over Italian territories in the Italian Wars

1515 Reign of François I begins

*Golden coin
showing the
fleur-de-lys
and the
salamander
of François I*

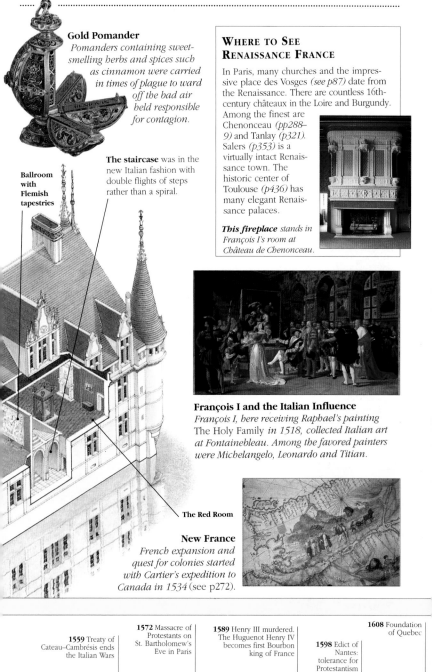

Gold Pomander
Pomanders containing sweet-smelling herbs and spices such as cinnamon were carried in times of plague to ward off the bad air held responsible for contagion.

The staircase was in the new Italian fashion with double flights of steps rather than a spiral.

Ballroom with Flemish tapestries

WHERE TO SEE RENAISSANCE FRANCE

In Paris, many churches and the impressive place des Vosges *(see p87)* date from the Renaissance. There are countless 16th-century châteaux in the Loire and Burgundy. Among the finest are Chenonceau *(pp288–9)* and Tanlay *(p321)*. Salers *(p353)* is a virtually intact Renaissance town. The historic center of Toulouse *(p436)* has many elegant Renaissance palaces.

This fireplace *stands in François I's room at Château de Chenonceau.*

François I and the Italian Influence
François I, here receiving Raphael's painting The Holy Family *in 1518, collected Italian art at Fontainebleau. Among the favored painters were Michelangelo, Leonardo and Titian.*

The Red Room

New France
French expansion and quest for colonies started with Cartier's expedition to Canada in 1534 (see p272).

1540	1550	1560	1570	1580	1590	1600

1559 Treaty of Cateau–Cambrésis ends the Italian Wars

1572 Massacre of Protestants on St. Bartholomew's Eve in Paris

1589 Henry III murdered. The Huguenot Henry IV becomes first Bourbon king of France

1598 Edict of Nantes: tolerance for Protestantism

1608 Foundation of Quebec

1539 Edict of Villers otterets makes French the official language of state

1562 Wars of Religion between Catholics and Protestants start

St. Bartholomew's Eve Massacre

1593 Henry IV converts to Catholicism and ends the Wars of Religion

The Grand Siècle

THE END OF THE RELIGIOUS WARS heralded a period of exceptional French influence and power. The cardinal ministers Richelieu and Mazarin paved the way for Louis XIV's absolute monarchy. Political development was matched by artistic styles of unprecedented brilliance: enormous Baroque edifices, the drama of Molière and the music of Lully.

Emblem of the Sun King

Versailles *(see pp164–7)*, built under the supervision of Louis' capable finance minister Colbert, was the glory of Europe, but its cost and Louis XIV's endless wars proved expensive for the French state and led to widespread misery by the end of his reign.

FRANCE IN 1661

☐ *Royal territory*

▨ *Avignon (papal enclave)*

Molière *(1622–73)*
Actor-playwright Molière performed many plays for Louis XIV and his court, though some of his satires were banned. After his death, his company became the basis of the French state theater, the Comédie Française.

Madame (married to Monsieur) as Flora

Monsieur, the king's brother

Madame de Maintenon
In 1684, following the death of his first wife, Marie-Thérèse, Louis secretly married his mistress Mme. de Maintenon, then aged 49.

THE SUN KING AND HIS FAMILY
Claiming to be monarch by divine right, Louis XIV commanded court painter Jean Nocret to devise this allegorical scene in 1665. Surrounded by his family, the king appears as the sun god Apollo.

TIMELINE

1610–17 Marie de' Medici acts as Regent for Louis XIII		*Cardinal Richelieu* **1624** Cardinal Richelieu becomes principal minister	**1634** Foundation of the literary society Académie Française	**1642–3** Death of Louis XIII and Cardinal Richelieu. Accession of Louis XIV with Mazarin as principal minister
1610	**1620**	**1630**	**1640**	**1650**
	1617 Louis XIII accedes at the age of 17	**1631** Foundation of *La Gazette*, France's first newspaper	**1637** Descartes' *Discourse on Method* **1635** Richelieu actively involves France in the Thirty Years' War	**1648–52** The Fronde: French civil wars

Louis XIV's Book of Hours
After a lively and libertine youth, Louis became increasingly religious. His Book of Hours *(1688–93) is in Musée Condé (see p195).*

Royal Wedding
Louis XIII and Anne of Austria were married in 1615. After his death, Anne became regent for the young Louis XIV with Cardinal Mazarin as minister.

Baroque Figurine
The royal glory was reflected in the arts. This objet d'art *features a Christ in jasper on a pedestal decorated with gilded cherubs and rich enameling.*

Louis XIV as Apollo

Anne of Austria as Cybele

WHERE TO SEE ARCHITECTURE OF THE GRAND SIÈCLE

Paris boasts many imposing Grand Siècle buildings, such as the Hôtel des Invalides (*see p110*), the Dôme church (*p111*) and the Palais du Luxembourg (*pp122–3*), but the Château de Versailles (*pp164–7*) is the ultimate example of the flamboyance of the period. Reminders of this glory include the sumptuous Palais Lascaris in Nice (*p518*) and the Corderie Royale in Rochefort (*p407*). At the same time, military architect Vauban constructed mighty citadels, such as Neuf-Brisach (*see p216*).

***Versailles's** interior is a typical example of the gilded Baroque style.*

The dauphin (the king's son)

Grande Mademoiselle, the king's cousin, as Diana

Queen Marie-Thérèse as Juno

Playwright Jean Racine (1639–99)

1661 Death of Mazarin: Louis XIV becomes his own principal minister

1662 Colbert, finance minister, reforms finances and the economy

1680 Creation of the theater Comédie Française

1682 Royal court moves to Versailles

1685 Revocation of the Edict of Nantes of 1598: Protestantism banned

1686 Opening of the Café Procope (first coffeehouse in Paris)

1689 Major wars of Louis XIV begin

1709 Last great famine in French history

1660	1670	1680	1690	1700

17th-century cannon

Enlightenment and Revolution

I**N THE** 18TH CENTURY, Enlightenment philosophers such as Voltaire and Rousseau redefined man's place within a framework of natural principles, thus challenging the old aristocratic order. Their essays were read across Europe and even in the American colonies. But although France exported worldly items as well as ideas, the state's increasing debts brought social turmoil, triggering the 1789 Revolution. Under the motto "Liberty, Equality, Fraternity," the new Republic and its reforms had a far-reaching impact on the rest of Europe.

Plate of Louis XVI's execution

FRANCE IN 1789

☐ *Royal France*

▨ *Avignon (papal enclave)*

Voltaire *(1694–1778)*
Voltaire, master of satire, wrote numerous essays and the novel Candide. *His fierce critiques sometimes forced him into exile abroad.*

National Assembly

Jacobin Club

The Guillotine
This infamous invention was introduced in 1792 as a humane alternative to other forms of capital punishment, which had usually involved torture.

Place de la Révolution
(see p94) is where Louis XVI's execution took place in 1793.

The Tuileries

Café Le Procope was the haunt of Voltaire and Rousseau.

Palais Royal
The private residence of the Duke of Orléans, the Palais Royal (see p95) became a center of revolutionary agitation from 1789. It was also the site of several printing presses.

TIMELINE

1715 Death of Louis XIV, accession of Louis XV

1743–64 Mme. de Pompadour, Louis XV's favorite, uses her influence to support artists and philosophers during her time at court

1715	1725	1735	1745	1755

1720 Last outbreak of plague in France: population of Marseilles decimated

Physician's protective costume worn during the plague

1751 Publication of the first volume of Diderot's *Encyclopedia*

1756–63 Seven Years' War: France loses Canada and other colonial possessions

Revolutionary Symbols
The motifs of the Revolution, such as the blue, white and red of the tricolor, even appeared on wallpaper in the 1790s.

WHERE TO SEE 18TH-CENTURY FRANCE

The Palais de l'Elysée, built in 1718 *(see p104)*, is an outstanding example of 18th-century Parisian architecture. Examples across France include the curious Saline Royale in Arc-et-Senans *(p340)*, the Grand Théâtre in Bordeaux *(p412)*, the elegant mansions in Condom *(p430)* and the merchants' houses in Ciboure *(p443)*. The Château de Laàs in Sauveterre de Béarn is a feast of 18th-century art and furniture *(p448)*.

The Grand Théâtre *in Bordeaux is an excellent example of elegant 18th-century architecture.*

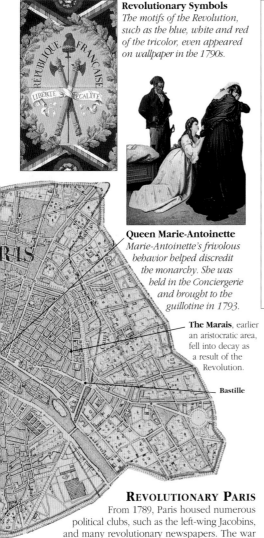

Queen Marie-Antoinette
Marie-Antoinette's frivolous behavior helped discredit the monarchy. She was held in the Conciergerie and brought to the guillotine in 1793.

The Marais, earlier an aristocratic area, fell into decay as a result of the Revolution.

Bastille

REVOLUTIONARY PARIS

From 1789, Paris housed numerous political clubs, such as the left-wing Jacobins, and many revolutionary newspapers. The war tune "La Marseillaise," introduced by volunteers from the south, was soon heard everywhere.

Revolutionary Calendar
A new calendar was introduced, the months named after seasonal events. This engraving shows Messidor, the month of harvest.

1768 Annexation of Corsica

1789 Storming of the Bastille, and establishment of constitutional monarchy: abolition of feudalism

1783 First balloon ascent, by the Montgolfier brothers

Model of the Bastille

1765	1775	1785	1795

1774 Accession of Louis XVI

Electors' card for the Convention of 1792

1794 Overthrow of Robespierre and end of the Terror

1762 Rousseau's *Emile* and the *Social Contract*

1778–83 France aids the 13 colonies in the American Revolution

1792 Overthrow of Louis XVI: establishment of First Republic

Napoleonic France

TWO GENERATIONS of Napoleons dominated France from 1800 to 1870. Napoleon Bonaparte took the title of Emperor Napoleon I. He extended his empire throughout most of western Europe, placing his brothers and sisters on the thrones of conquered countries. Defeated in 1814 and replaced by the restored Bourbon dynasty, followed by the 1830 Revolution and the so-called July Monarchy, the Napoleonic clan made a comeback after 1848. Napoleon I's nephew, Louis Napoleon, became President of the Second Republic, then made himself emperor as Napoleon III. During his reign, Paris was modernized and the industrial transformation of France began.

Légion d'Honneur

EUROPE IN 1812

☐ *Napoleonic rule*

☐ *Dependent states*

Musée du Louvre
The museum had opened in 1792, but it flourished during Napoleon's reign. He took a personal interest in both acquisitions and organization.

The laurel crown of the Roman emperors

Napoleon, as First Consul, is crowned by Chronos, the God of Time.

The revolutionary tricolor flag was kept throughout the empire.

Imperial Insignia
Napoleon I created a new titled aristocracy, who were allowed coats of arms. Only his, however, was permitted a crown. The eagle symbol was adopted in 1800, an evocation of Imperial Rome.

Légion d'Honneur medal

TIMELINE

Josephine's bed at Malmaison

1800 Establishment of the Bank of France

1804 Napoleon crowned as Emperor. Napoleonic Civil Code established

1809 Josephine and Napoleon divorce. She retains Château Malmaison *(see p163)*

1814 Defeat of Napoleon by the Allies (England, Russia, Austria and Prussia). Napoleon exiled to Elba

1800	1810	1820

1801–3 Treaty of Amiens brings temporary peace to Europe

1802 Establishment of the Légion d'Honneur

1803 Resumption of wars to create the Napoleonic Empire

1806 Arc de Triomphe commissioned

1815 The "Hundred Days": Napoleon returns from Elba, is defeated at Waterloo and exiled to St. Helena

THE HISTORY OF FRANCE

July Revolution
Three days of street fighting in July 1830 ended unpopular Bourbon rule.

The Napoleons
This imaginary group portrait depicts Napoleon I (seated), his son "Napoleon II" – who never ruled (right) – Napoleon's nephew Louis Napoleon (Napoleon III) and the latter's young son.

The Civil Code, created by Napoleon, is here shown as a tablet.

Napoleon on Campaign
A dashing general in the late 1790s, Napoleon remained a remarkable military commander throughout his reign.

EMPIRE FASHION

Greek and Roman ideals were evident in architecture, furniture, design and fashion. Women wore light, Classical tunics, the most daring with one shoulder or more bare. David and Gérard were the fashionable portraitists, while Delacroix and Géricault created many Romantic masterpieces.

Madame Récamier held a popular salon and was renowned for her beauty and wit. David painted her in 1800.

NAPOLEONIC GLORY

Though professing himself a true revolutionary, Napoleon developed a taste for imperial pomp. However, he also achieved some long-lasting reforms such as the Civil Code, the new school system and the Bank of France.

1832 Cholera epidemics begin

1838 Daguerre experiments with photography

1848 Revolution of 1848: end of July Monarchy and establishment of the Second Republic

1851 Coup d'état by Louis Napoleon

1852 Louis Napoleon crowned as Emperor Napoleon III

1830	1840	1850	1860

1830 Revolution of 1830: Bourbon Charles X replaced by the July Monarchy of King Louis-Philippe

1840 Large-scale railroad building

1853 Modernization of Paris by Haussmann

1857 Baudelaire (*Les Fleurs du Mal*) and Flaubert (*Mme. Bovary*) prosecuted for public immorality

1859–60 Annexation of Nice and Savoy

Train on the Paris – St-Germain line

The Belle Epoque

Art Nouveau vase by Lalique

THE DECADES before World War I became the *Belle Epoque* for the French, remembered as a golden era forever past. Nevertheless, this was a politically turbulent time, with working-class militancy, organized socialist move-ments and the Dreyfus Affair polarizing the country between Left and anti-semitic Right. New inventions such as electricity and vaccination against disease made life easier at all social levels. The cultural scene thrived and took new forms with Impressionism and Art Nouveau, the realist novels of Gustave Flaubert and Emile Zola, cabaret and cancan and, in 1895, the birth of the movie theater.

FRANCE IN 1871

☐ *Under Third Republic*

☐ *Alsace and Lorraine*

Universal Exhibition
The 1889 Paris exhi-bition was attended by 3.2 million people. Engineer Eiffel's breathtaking iron structure dominated the exhibition and caused great controversy at the time.

Statue of Apollo by Aimé Millet

Stage

Copper-green roofed cupola

Backstage area

Peugeot Car *(1899)*
The car and bicycle brought new free-dom, becoming a part of people's leisure time. Peugeot, Renault and Citroën were all founded before World War I.

The auditorium decorated in gold and purple seated over 2,000 guests.

TIMELINE

Woman on the barricades in 1871

1869 Opening of the Suez Canal, built by Ferdinand de Lesseps

1871 The Paris Commune leads to the Third Republic

1880s Scramble for colonies in Africa and Asia begins

1889 Universal Exhibition in Paris; Eiffel Tower built

1865	1870	1875	1880	1885	1890

1870–71 Franco-Prussian War: defeat and overthrow of Napoleon III; France cedes Alsace and Lorraine to Germany

1874 Impressionist movement begins

1881–6 Reforms in education by Jules Ferry

1885 Pasteur produces vaccine for rabies, the first tested on a human

1890 Peugeot constructs one of the earliest automobiles

Poster Art
The poster was revolutionized by Art Nouveau, with designs by Alphonse Mucha particularly popular. This one from 1897 is for beer, the beverage of the lost Alsace and Lorraine, which became a "patriotic" drink.

Staircase at the Opera
The grand staircase had colored marble columns and a frescoed ceiling. As this painting by Beroud from 1887 shows, it soon became a showcase for high society.

WHERE TO SEE THE BELLE EPOQUE

Belle Epoque buildings include the Negresco Hotel, Nice *(see p516)*, the Grand Casino in Monte-Carlo *(p520)* and the Palais Hotel in Biarritz *(p442)*. The Musée d'Orsay in Paris *(pp116–17)* exhibits Art Nouveau objects and furniture.

***Guimard's** Metro entrance is a typical example of the elegant, swirling lines of Art Nouveau.*

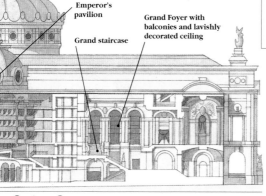

Emperor's pavilion

Grand Foyer with balconies and lavishly decorated ceiling

Grand staircase

OPÉRA GARNIER
Founded by Napoleon III in 1862, the new opera was opened to great public acclaim in 1875 and became a focus of Belle Epoque social life. Designed by Charles Garnier, its extravagant exterior was matched by its sumptuous interior decor.

The Divine Sarah
Actress Sarah Bernhardt (1844–1923) worked in all theatrical genres, dominating the Paris stage.

1895 First movie shown by the Lumière brothers

Caricature of Zola

1894–1906 The alleged treason of Dreyfus sparks the Dreyfus Affair, involving the author Zola among others

1909 Blériot flies the Channel

1918 Armistice ends the war

1917 Mutinies in the army suppressed by Pétain

1916 Battle of Verdun

1895	1900	1905	1910	1915

1905 Official separation of church and state

1913 Publication of Proust's first volume of *Remembrance of Things Past*

1898 Marie and Pierre Curie discover radium

1914 World War I breaks out

French recruit, 1916

1919 Treaty of Versailles

Avant-Garde France

DESPITE THE DEVASTATION wrought by two world wars, France retained its international renown as a center for the avant garde. Paris in particular was a magnet for experimental writers, artists and musicians. The cafés were full of American authors and jazz musicians, French surrealists and filmmakers. The French Riviera also attracted colonies of artists and writers, from Matisse and Picasso to Hemingway and F. Scott Fitzgerald, along with the wealthy industrialists and aristocrats arriving in automobiles or the famous Train Bleu. And from 1936, paid vacations meant that the working classes could also enjoy the new fashion for sunbathing.

FRANCE IN 1919

☐ *French territory*

African Gods of Creation

Art Deco 1925
The International Exhibition in Paris in 1925 launched the Art Deco style: geometrical shapes and utilitarian designs, adapted for mass production.

PARIS-1925

MINISTÈRE DU COMMERCE ET DE L'INDUSTRIE

EXPOSITION INTERNATIONALE DES ARTS DÉCORATIFS ET INDUSTRIELS MODERNES AVRIL-OCTOBRE

Dancers in heavy cardboard costumes

The Jazz Age
Paris welcomed American jazz musicians, such as Sidney Bechet in 1925 and Dizzy Gillespie (left), co-founder of Bebop, in the 1940s.

Citroën Goddess *(1956)*
This elegant model became an icon of the new French consumerism evident in the 1950s and '60s.

The costumes
and scenery by the Cubist Léger were striking and made to look partly mechanical.

TIMELINE

1920 French Communist Party founded. Publication of Tristan Tzara's *Dadaist Manifesto*

1928 Premiere of *Un Chien Andalou* by Luis Buñuel and Salvador Dalí

Air France airplane, 1937

1933 Air France begins operation

1937 Premiere of *La Grande Illusion* by Jean Renoir

1920

1930

1924 Olympic Games in Paris. André Breton publishes the *Surrealist Manifesto*

Detail of poster for the 1924 Olympics

1936–38 The "Popular Front": radical social program introduced, including paid vacations

1929–39 The Depression

1938 Munich Conference: height of appeasement

Coco Chanel *(1883–1971)*
Chanel, here photographed by Man Ray, revolutionized fashion in the 1920s with her elegant but comfortable clothes.

Par Avion
France pioneered the use of airmail, starting in 1927.

First Man and Woman

WORLD WAR II

Following the collapse of the Third Republic in 1940, Paris and the north and west parts of France were occupied by the Germans until the Liberation in 1944. Southeast France formed the collaborationist Vichy state, led by Marshal Pétain and Pierre Laval. Meanwhile, the Free French movement was led by Charles de Gaulle, with Jean Moulin coordinating the operations of the many different Resistance factions.

German soldiers *liked to pose in front of the Eiffel Tower during the occupation of Paris.*

LA CRÉATION DU MONDE *(1923)*
Artistic experimentation thrived in the early 20th century. *La Création du Monde* by Les Ballets Suédois had costumes by Léger and music by Milhaud. Diaghilev's Ballets Russes also competed for avant-garde artists such as Picabia, Cocteau, Satie and Sonia Delaunay.

The African theme was based on text by Blaise Cendrars.

Josephine Baker *(1906–75)*
The music hall flourished in the 1920s with Mistinguett and Josephine Baker as its undisputed queens.

1940 German offensive: the Fall of France. Vichy government led by Pétain

1942 The whole of France controlled by Germany

1949 Establishment of NATO. Founding of the Council of Europe

1958 5th Republic begins under President de Gaulle

1956 Late in her career, Edith Piaf crowns her success at Carnegie Hall, New York

1940

1950

1944 D-Day: Allied landings in Normandy (June). Liberation of Paris (August)

1939 Declaration of World War II

1946 Sartre establishes *Les Temps Modernes*. First Cannes Film Festival

1945 End of the war. Votes for women

1954 France withdraws from Indo-China after Battle of Dien Bien Phu. Start of Algerian insurrection

Modern France

AFTER THE 1950s, the traditional foundations of French society changed: the number of peasant farmers plummeted, old industries decayed, jobs in the service sector and high-technology industries grew dramatically, and the French came to enjoy the benefits of mass culture and widespread consumerism. High prestige projects, such as Concorde, TGV, La Défense and the Pompidou Center, brought international acclaim. Efforts for European integration and the inauguration of the Channel Tunnel aim toward closer relations with France's neighbors.

Lemon squeezer by Philippe Starck

FRANCE TODAY

☐ *France*

◼ *European Union*

Pompidou Center *(1977)*
The Pompidou Center's controversial building changed the aspect of the historic quarter of Beaubourg. A major arts center, it has re-vitalized the formerly rundown area (see pp88–9).

New Wave Film
Directors like Godard and Truffaut launched a refreshing, personal style of films, such as Jules et Jim *(1961).*

La Grande Arche was opened in 1989 to commemorate the bicentenary of the Revolution.

Shopping center

LA DÉFENSE
The huge modernist business center at La Défense *(see p126),* on the edge of Paris, was developed in the 1960s and has become a prime site for the headquarters of major multinational companies.

TIMELINE

1960 First French atomic bomb. Decolonization of black Africa	**1963** First French nuclear power station	**1968** May demonstrations	**1973** Extension of the Common Market (EU) from six to nine states
		1969 Pompidou replaces de Gaulle as president	
	1966 France leaves NATO		**1974** Giscard d'Estaing elected president

1960   **1970**

1962 Evian agreements lead to Algerian independence	**1965** First French satellite	**1970** Charles de Gaulle dies	**1976** First commercial flight for Concorde airplane
	1967 Common Agricultural Policy, subsidizing Europe's farmers		

1977 Jacques Chirac first mayor of Paris since 1871. Opening of the Pompidou Center

EU Flag
France has been one of the leading forces in the European Union ever since the move toward closer European collaboration began in the 1950s.

TGV
The TGV (Train à Grande Vitesse) is one of the world's fastest trains (see pp634–5). It typifies the French government's commitment to high technology and improved communications.

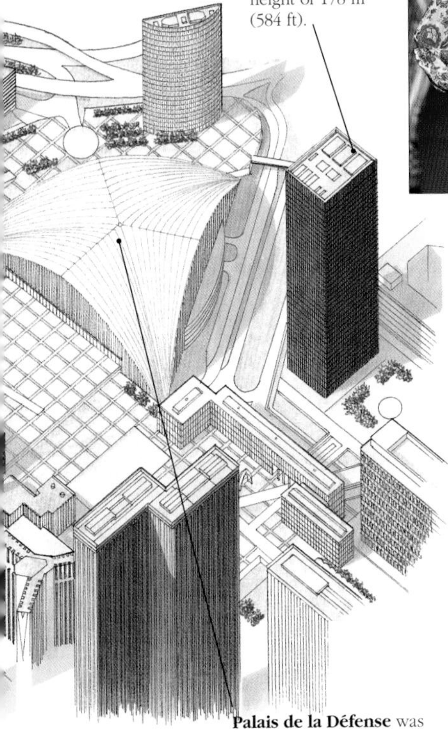

The Fiat Tower is one of Europe's tallest towers, at a height of 178 m (584 ft).

Fashion by Lacroix
Despite less demand for haute couture, Paris is still a major fashion center. The designs shown on the catwalk, here by Christian Lacroix, remain proof of the world-renowned skills of French designers.

MAY 1968

The events of May 1968 began as a political revolt by left-wing students against the Establishment and had a profound influence on French society. Around 9 million workers, and leading intellectuals like Jean-Paul Sartre, joined the rebellion, demanding better pay, better study conditions and the overhaul of traditional values and institutions.

***Student riots** starting in Nanterre, just outside Paris, sparked widespread rioting and industrial unrest in France.*

Palais de la Défense was built first and houses the center for industry.

1980 Giverny, Monet's garden, opens to the public (see p256)

1989 Bicentennial celebration of the French Revolution

1991 Edith Cresson is first woman prime minister

2002 National Front defeats Socialists in 1st round of Presidential campaign. France rallies to re-elect Jacques Chirac to save the day.

1980

1990

2000

1981 Mitterrand becomes president and heads Socialist governments 1981–6

François Mitterrand

1987 Mitterrand and Thatcher sign agreement for Channel Tunnel. Trial in Lyons of ex-SS Officer Klaus Barbie

1994 Channel Tunnel opens

1996 France mourns Mitterrand, who dies after a long illness

2002 Euro replaces Franc as legal tender

Kings and Emperors of France

Following the breakup of the Roman Empire, the Frankish king Clovis consolidated the Merovingian dynasty. It was followed by the Carolingians, and, from the 10th century, by Capetian rulers. The Capetians established royal power, which passed to the Valois branch in the 14th century, and then to the Bourbons in the late 16th century, following the Wars of Religion. The Revolution of 1789 seemed to end the Bourbon dynasty, but it made a brief comeback in 1814–30. The 19th century was dominated by the Bonapartes, Napoleon I and Napoleon III. Since the overthrow of Napoleon III in 1870, France has been a republic.

768–814 Charlemagne

743–751 Childéric III
716–721 Chilpéric II
695–711 Childebert II
566–584 Chilpéric I
674–691 Thierri III
558–562 Clothaire I
447–458 Merovich
655–668 Clothaire III
458–482 Childéric I
628–637 Dagobert I

954–986 Lothaire
898–929 Charles III, the Simple
884–888 Charles II, the Fat
879–882 Louis III
840–877 Charles I, the Bald

1137–80 Louis VII
987–996 Hugh Capet
1031–60 Henri I
1060–1108 Philippe I

400	500	600	700	800	900	1000	11
MEROVINGIAN DYNASTY				**CAROLINGIAN DYNASTY**		**CAPETIAN DYNASTY**	
400	500	600	700	800	900	1000	11

751–768 Pépin the Short
721–737 Thierri IV
711–716 Dagobert III
691–695 Clovis III
668–674 Childéric II
637–655 Clovis II
584–628 Clothaire II
562–566 Caribert
511–558 Childebert I

996–1031 Robert II, the Pious
986–987 Louis V
936–954 Louis IV, the Foreigner
888–898 Odo, Count of Paris
882–884 Carloman
877–879 Louis II, the Stammerer
814–840 Louis I, the Pious

482–511 Clovis I

1108–37 Louis VI, the Fat

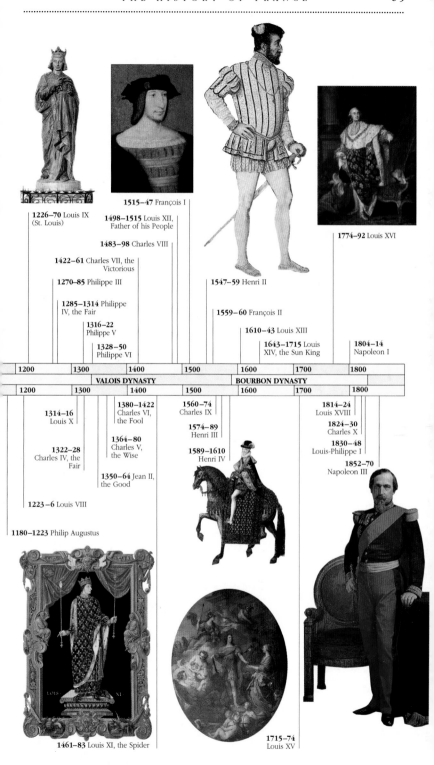

1226–70 Louis IX
(St. Louis)

1498–1515 Louis XII,
Father of his People

1515–47 François I

1483–98 Charles VIII

1774–92 Louis XVI

1422–61 Charles VII, the
Victorious

1270–85 Philippe III

1547–59 Henri II

1285–1314 Philippe
IV, the Fair

1559–60 François II

1316–22
Philippe V

1610–43 Louis XIII

1328–50
Philippe VI

1643–1715 Louis
XIV, the Sun King

1804–14
Napoleon I

1200	1300	1400	1500	1600	1700	1800	

VALOIS DYNASTY   **BOURBON DYNASTY**

1200	1300	1400	1500	1600	1700	1800	

1314–16
Louis X

1380–1422
Charles VI,
the Fool

1560–74
Charles IX

1814–24
Louis XVIII

1574–89
Henri III

1824–30
Charles X

1322–28
Charles IV, the
Fair

1364–80
Charles V,
the Wise

1589–1610
Henri IV

1830–48
Louis-Philippe I

1852–70
Napoleon III

1350–64 Jean II,
the Good

1223–6 Louis VIII

1180–1223 Philip Augustus

1461–83 Louis XI, the Spider

1715–74
Louis XV

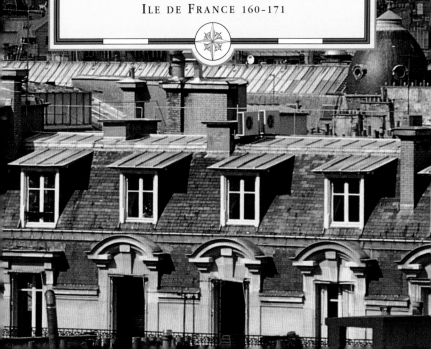

PARIS AND
ILE DE FRANCE

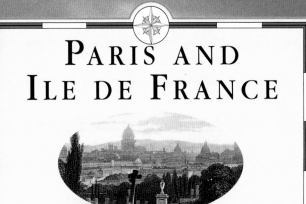

Introducing Paris and Ile de France

THE FRENCH CAPITAL is rich in museums, art galleries and monuments. The Louvre, Eiffel Tower and Pompidou Center are among the most popular sights. Surrounding Paris, the Ile de France takes in 12,000 sq km (4,600 sq miles) of busy suburbs and commuter towns punctuated by châteaux, the most celebrated being Versailles. Farther out, suburbia gives way to farmland, forests and the magnificent palace of Fontainebleau.

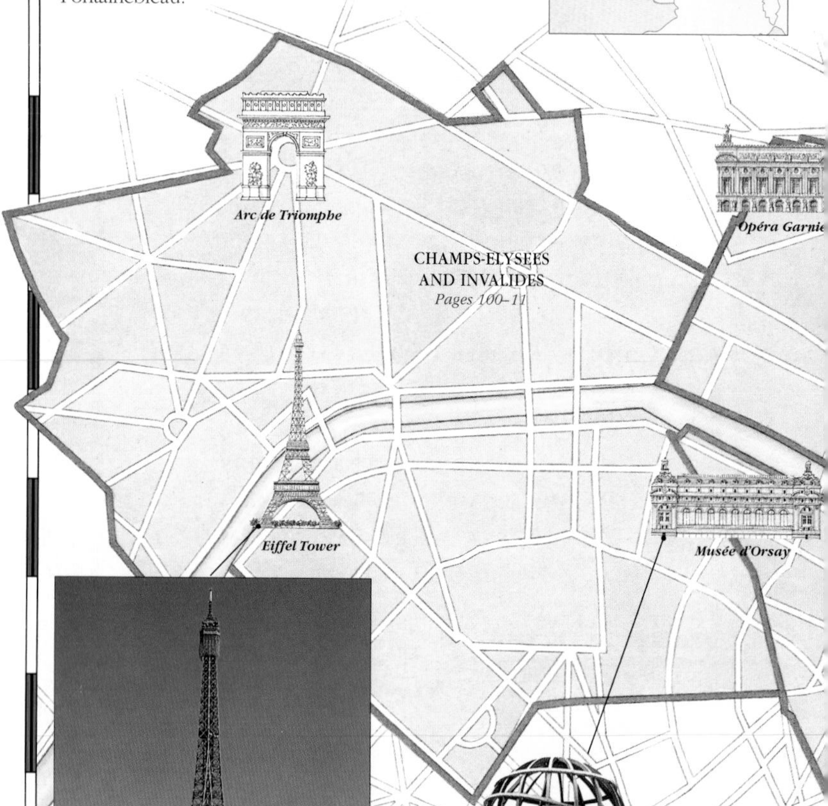

Arc de Triomphe

Opéra Garnie

CHAMPS-ELYSEES AND INVALIDES
Pages 100–11

Eiffel Tower

Musée d'Orsay

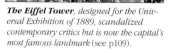

The Eiffel Tower, *designed for the Universal Exhibition of 1889, scandalized contemporary critics but is now the capital's most famous landmark (see p109).*

The Musée d'Orsay, *opened in 1986, was created from a late 19th-century railroad station (see pp116–17). Its magnificent collection of 19th- and early 20th-century art, (notably Impressionist art), includes Jean-Baptiste Carpeaux's* Four Quarters of the World *(1867–72).*

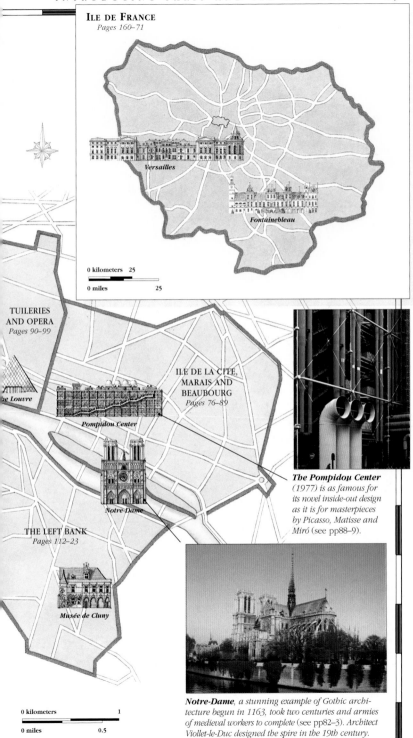

ILE DE FRANCE
Pages 160–71

Versailles

Fontainebleau

0 kilometers   25

0 miles   25

**TUILERIES
AND OPERA**
Pages 90–99

le Louvre

**ILE DE LA CITÉ,
MARAIS AND
BEAUBOURG**
Pages 76–89

Pompidou Center

Notre-Dame

THE LEFT BANK
Pages 112–23

Musée de Cluny

0 kilometers   1

0 miles   0.5

The Pompidou Center
*(1977) is as famous for
its novel inside-out design
as it is for masterpieces
by Picasso, Matisse and
Miró* (see pp88–9).

Notre-Dame, *a stunning example of Gothic architecture begun in 1163, took two centuries and armies
of medieval workers to complete* (see pp82–3). *Architect
Viollet-le-Duc designed the spire in the 19th century.*

A RIVER VIEW OF PARIS

Sculpture on the Pont Alexandre III

THE REMARK-ABLE French music-hall star Mistinguett described the Seine as a "pretty blonde with laughing eyes." The river most certainly has a beguiling quality, but the relationship that exists between it and the city of Paris is far more than one of flirtation.

No other European city defines itself by its river in the same way as Paris. The Seine is the essential point of reference to the city: distances are measured from it, street numbers determined by it, and it divides the capital into two distinct areas, the Right Bank on the north side of the river and the Left Bank on the south side. These are as well-defined as any of the official boundaries. The city is also divided historically: the east is linked to the city's ancient roots, and the west to the 19th–20th centuries.

Practically every building of note in Paris is either along the riverbank or within a stone's throw of it. The quays are lined by fine bourgeois apartments, magnificent town houses, world-renowned museums and striking monuments.

Above all, the river is very much alive. For centuries, fleets of small boats used it, but motorized land traffic stifled this once-bustling scene. Today, the river is busy with commercial barges and massive *bateaux-mouches* – pleasure boats carrying sightseers up and down the river.

The Latin Quarter Quayside is on the left bank of the Seine. Associated with institutes of learning since the Middle Ages, it acquired its name from the early Latin-speaking students.

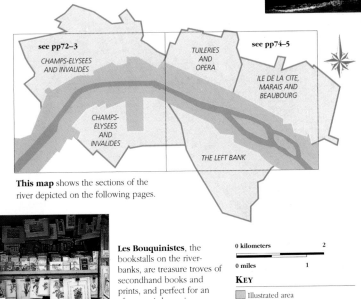

see pp72–3

CHAMPS-ELYSEES AND INVALIDES

CHAMPS-ELYSEES AND INVALIDES

TUILERIES AND OPERA

see pp74–5

ILE DE LA CITE, MARAIS AND BEAUBOURG

THE LEFT BANK

This map shows the sections of the river depicted on the following pages.

Les Bouquinistes, the bookstalls on the river-banks, are treasure troves of secondhand books and prints, and perfect for an afternoon's browsing.

0 kilometers		2
0 miles	1	

KEY

Illustrated area

◁ **Pont Alexandre III, encrusted with exuberant statuary**

From Pont de Grenelle to Pont de la Concorde

THE GRAND monuments along this stretch of the river are remnants of the Napoleonic era and the Industrial Revolution. The elegance of the Eiffel Tower, the Petit Palais and the Grand Palais is matched by more recent buildings, such as the Palais de Chaillot and the skyscrapers on the Left Bank.

Palais de Chaillot
Built for the 1937 Exhibition, the colonnaded wings house several museums, a theater and a movie theater (p106).

The Palais de Tokyo
Bourdelle's statues adorn the facades (p106).

The Pont Bir-Hakeim has a dynamic statue by Wederkinch rising at its north end.

Maison de Radio France
is an imposing circular building, designed in 1960, which houses studios as well as a radio museum.

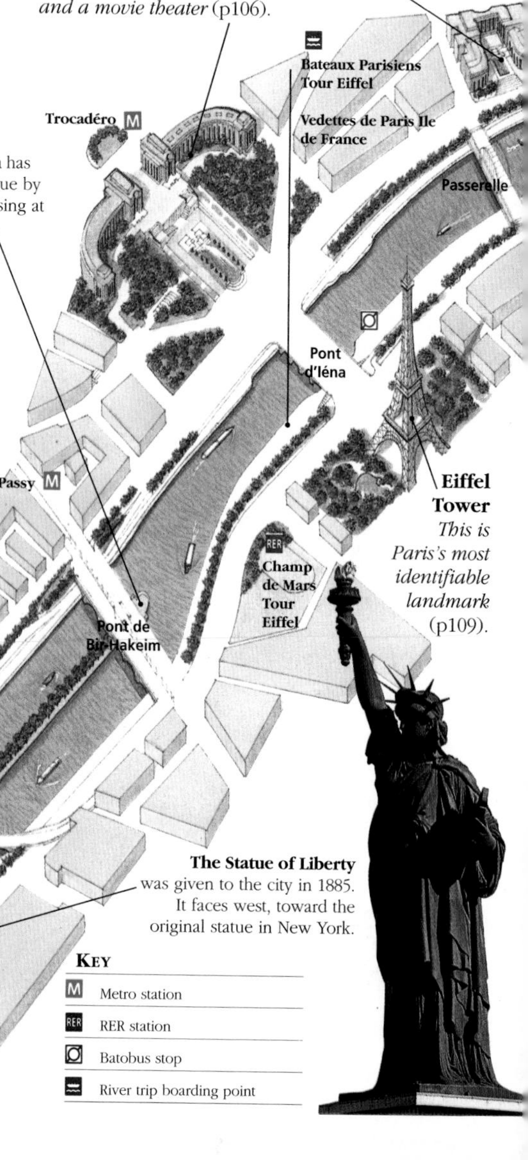

Trocadéro Ⓜ

Bateaux Parisiens Tour Eiffel

Vedettes de Paris Ile de France

Passerelle

Pont d'Iéna

Passy Ⓜ

Champ de Mars Tour Eiffel

Pont de Bir-Hakeim

Eiffel Tower
This is Paris's most identifiable landmark (p109).

Prés. Kennedy Radio France

The Statue of Liberty
was given to the city in 1885. It faces west, toward the original statue in New York.

Pont de Grenelle

KEY

Ⓜ	Metro station
RER	RER station
◻	Batobus stop
▬	River trip boarding point

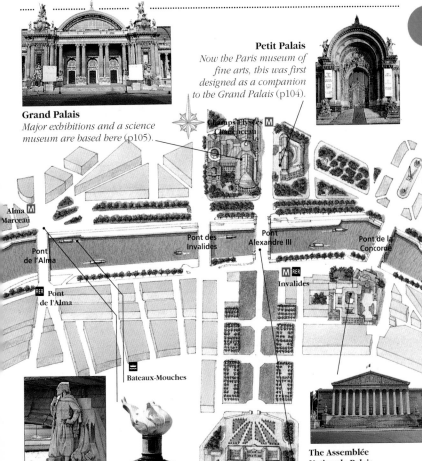

Grand Palais
Major exhibitions and a science museum are based here (p105).

Petit Palais
Now the Paris museum of fine arts, this was first designed as a companion to the Grand Palais (p104).

The Zouave, a statue on the central pier, is a useful gauge for checking flood levels.

The Liberty Flame is a memorial to the fighters of the French Resistance during World War II.

The Assemblée Nationale Palais-Bourbon was originally built for Louis XIV's daughter. It has accommodated the lower house of the French Parliament since 1830.

Dôme Church
The majestic gilded dome (p111) is here seen from Pont Alexandre III. Napoleon's tomb is installed in the crypt.

Pont Alexandre III
Flamboyant statuary decorates Paris's most ornate bridge (p105).

From Pont de la Concorde to Pont de Sully

The HISTORIC heart of Paris lies on the banks and islands of the east river. At its center is the Ile de la Cité, a natural stepping stone across the Seine and the cultural core of medieval Paris. Today it is still vital to Parisian life.

Jardin des Tuileries
These are laid out in the formal style (pp94–5).

Musée du Louvre
Before becoming the world's greatest museum and home to the Mona Lisa, this was Europe's largest royal palace (pp96–9).

Pont de la Concorde

Assemblée Nationale

Passerelle Solférino

Quai d'Orsay

Pont Royal

Pont du Carrousel

Passerelle des Arts

Musée de l'Orangerie
An important collection of 19th-century paintings is on display here (p94).

Musée d'Orsay
This converted train station houses Paris's outstanding collection of Impressionist art (pp116–17).

Bateaux Vedettes du Pont Neuf

BATOBUS
PARIS

The Batobus shuttle service departs Apr–Nov: 10am–7pm (9pm Jun–Sep) daily, every 20 min. Board at:
Eiffel Tower. Map 6 D3. **M** Bir Hakeim. **Champs-Elysées. Map** 7 A1. **M** Champs-Elysées-Clemenceau. **Musée d'Orsay. Map** 8 D2. **M** Assemblée Nationale. **Louvre. Map** 8 D2. **M** Palais Royal-Musée du Louvre. **Hôtel de Ville. Map** 9 B4. **M** Hôtel de Ville. **Notre-Dame. Map** 9 B4. **M** Saint-Michel. **Saint-Germain des Prés. Map** 8 E3. **M** Saint-Germain des Prés.

Passerelle des Arts
This steel reconstruction of Paris's first cast-iron bridge (1804) was inaugurated in 1984.

Hôtel des Monnaies, the Mint, was built in 1778, and has an extensive coin and medallion collection in its old milling halls.

How to Take a Seine Cruise

Bateaux Vedettes Pont Neuf Seine Cruise

The boarding point is: **Square du Vert-Galant** (Pont Neuf).
Map 8 F3.
01 46 33 98 38.
M Pont Neuf.
RER Châtelet.
24, 27, 58, 67, 70, 72, 74, 75.
Departures Apr–Oct: 10:30am, 11:15am, noon, 1:30pm–6:30pm, 9–10:30pm (every 30 min) daily; Nov–Mar: 10:30am, 11:15am, noon, 2–5pm (6:30pm w/e), Mon–Fri (every 45 min).
Duration 1 hr.

Bateaux Mouches Seine Cruise

The boarding point is: **Pont de l'Alma. Map** 6 F1.
01 42 25 96 10.
M Alma-Marceau.
RER Pont de l'Alma. 28, 42, 63, 72, 80, 92.
Departures Mar–Sep: 10am–11:30pm daily (every 30 min); Oct–Feb: 11am–10pm (every 45 min; extra departures w/e & public hols).
Duration 1 hr 15 min.
Lunch cruise Mar–Nov: 1pm Tue–Sun (w/e in winter). **Dinner cruise** 8:30pm daily. Jacket and tie. Bateaux Mouches are the largest cruise boats.

Vedettes de Paris Ile de France Seine Cruise

The boarding point is: **Pont d'Iéna. Map** 6 D2.
01 47 05 71 29.
M Bir Hakeim.
RER Champ-de-Mars–Tour Eiffel. 30, 32, 42, 63, 72, 82, 87.
Departures May–Oct: 10am–11pm daily (every 30 min); Nov–Apr: 11am–9pm Mon–Fri (every hour); 11am–8pm Sat, Sun (every 30 min).
Duration 1 hr.
Vedettes are small boats which allow passengers to view the surroundings through glass walls.

Bateaux Parisiens Tour Eiffel Seine Cruise

The boarding point is: **Pont d'Iéna. Map** 6 D2.
01 44 11 33 44.
M Trocadéro, Bir Hakeim.
RER Champ-de-Mars–Tour Eiffel. 30, 32, 42, 72, 82, 87. **Departures** Apr–Oct: 10am–11pm daily (every 30 min); Nov–Mar: 10am–9pm (10pm Fri–Sat) daily (every hour). **Lunch cruise** 12:30pm daily.
Dinner cruise 8pm daily.
Duration 3 hr. Jacket and tie. Bateaux Parisiens are a more luxurious version of Bateaux Mouches.

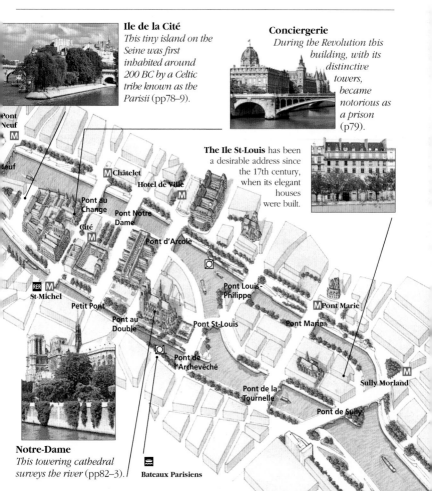

Ile de la Cité
This tiny island on the Seine was first inhabited around 200 BC by a Celtic tribe known as the Parisii (pp78–9).

Conciergerie
During the Revolution this building, with its distinctive towers, became notorious as a prison (p79).

The Ile St-Louis has been a desirable address since the 17th century, when its elegant houses were built.

Pont Neuf
M
euf
M Châtelet
Hotel de Ville
M
Pont au Change
Pont Notre Dame
Cité
M
Pont d'Arcole
RER M
St-Michel
Petit Pont
Pont au Double
Pont St-Louis
Pont Louis-Philippe
M Pont Marie
Pont Marie
Pont de l'Archevêché
Pont de la Tournelle
Sully Morland
M
Pont de Sully

Notre-Dame
This towering cathedral surveys the river (pp82–3).

Bateaux Parisiens

ILE DE LA CITÉ, MARAIS AND BEAUBOURG

THE RIGHT BANK is dominated by the modernistic Forum des Halles and Pompidou Center in the Beaubourg. These are Paris's most thriving public areas, with millions of tourists, shoppers and students flowing between them. Young people flock to Les Halles, shopping for the latest street fashions beneath the concrete and glass bubbles of the underground arcades. All roads from Les Halles appear to lead to the Pompidou Center, an avant-garde assembly of pipes, ducts and cables housing the Musée National d'Art Moderne. The smaller streets around the center are full of art galleries housed in crooked, gabled buildings.

The motto of the city of Paris

The neighboring Marais was abandoned by its royal residents during the 1789 Revolution, and it descended into architectural wasteland before being rescued in the 1960s. It has since become a very fashionable address, though small cafés, bakeries and artisans still survive in its streets.

Notre-Dame cathedral, the Palais de Justice and Sainte-Chapelle continue to draw tourists to the Ile de la Cité, despite extensive redevelopment of the island in the last century. At the eastern end, a bridge connects with the Ile St-Louis, a former swampy pastureland transformed into a residential area with lovely, tree-lined quays.

SIGHTS AT A GLANCE

Islands & Squares
Ile St-Louis **7**
Forum des Halles **13**
Place des Vosges **19**
Place de la Bastille **21**

Churches
Sainte-Chapelle **4**
Notre-Dame pp82–3 **6**
St-Gervais–St-Protais **9**
St-Eustache **12**

Historic Buildings
Conciergerie **2**
Palais de Justice **3**
Hôtel de Ville **10**
Tour St-Jacques **11**

Museums and Galleries
Crypte Archéologique **5**
Hôtel de Sens **8**
Pompidou Centre pp88–9 **14**
Musée d'Art et d'Histoire du Judaisme **15**
Hôtel de Soubise **16**
Musée Picasso **17**
Musée Carnavalet **18**
Maison de Victor Hugo **20**

Bridges
Pont Neuf **1**

GETTING THERE
Metro stations include Châtelet, Hôtel-de- Ville and Cité. Buses 47 and 29 serve Beaubourg and the Marais respectively. Several bus routes cross Ile de la Cité and Ile St-Louis.

KEY

	Street-by-Street map *pp78–9*
	Street-by-Street map *pp84–5*
M	Metro station
	Batobus boarding point
P	Parking
RER	RER station

◁ **View of the Conciergerie and the Pont au Change**

Street-by-Street: Ile de la Cité

THE ORIGINS OF PARIS are on the Ile de la Cité, the boat-shaped island on the Seine first inhabited by Celtic tribes in the 3rd century BC. One tribe, the Parisii, eventually gave its name to the city. The island offered a convenient river crossing on the route between northern and southern Gaul and was easily defended. In later centuries, the settlement was expanded by the Romans, the Franks and the Capetian kings to form the nucleus of today's city.

Remains of the first buildings can still be seen today in the archaeological crypt of the great medieval cathedral of Notre-Dame. At the other end of the island is Sainte-Chapelle, another Gothic masterpiece.

★ Conciergerie
This sinister-looking building was the country's main prison during the Revolution ❷

The Marché aux Fleurs et Oiseaux in place Louis-Lépine is one of the largest flower markets in Paris, with birds for sale on Sundays.

Metro Cité

To Pont Neuf

★ Sainte-Chapelle
A jewel of Gothic architecture, Sainte-Chapelle is famous for its magnificent stained-glass windows ❹

Palais de Justice
With a history spanning over 16 centuries, the old palace is today a massive complex of law courts ❸

Point Zéro marks the spot from which all road distances are measured in France.

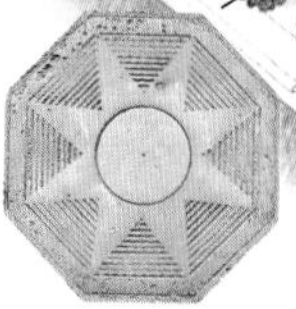

STAR SIGHTS

★ Notre-Dame

★ Sainte-Chapelle

★ Conciergerie

KEY

‒ ‒ ‒ Suggested route

Crypte Archéologique
Deep under the square lie remnants of houses dating back 2,000 years ❺

To Latin Quarter

Hôtel Dieu, a large hospital serving central Paris, was founded in AD 651 by St. Landry, Bishop of Paris.

TUILERIES AND OPERA

ILE DE LA CITE, MARAIS AND BEAUBOURG

THE LEFT BANK

Seine

LOCATOR MAP
See Street Finder maps 8, 9

★ **Notre-Dame**
This cathedral is a superb example of French medieval architecture ❻

Musée Notre-Dame, founded in 1951, contains exhibits and documents commemorating the great events in Notre-Dame's history.

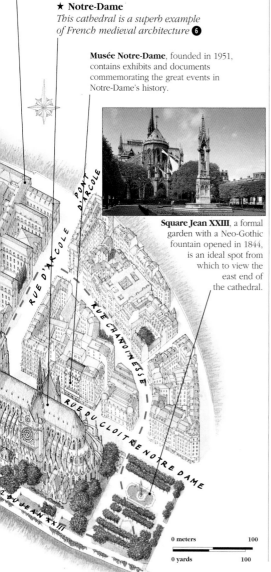

Square Jean XXIII, a formal garden with a Neo-Gothic fountain opened in 1844, is an ideal spot from which to view the east end of the cathedral.

RUE D'ARCOLE

PONT D'ARCOLE

RUE CHANOINESSE

RUE DU CLOITRE NOTRE DAME

SQU JEAN XXIII

| 0 meters | 100 |
| 0 yards | 100 |

Pont Neuf, the city's oldest bridge

Pont Neuf ❶

75001. **Map** 8 F3. Ⓜ Pont Neuf, Cité.

DESPITE ITS NAME (New Bridge), this bridge is the oldest in Paris and has been immortalized by major literary and artistic figures. The first stone was laid by Henri III in 1578, but it was Henri IV (whose statue stands at the center) who inaugurated it and gave it its name in 1607.

Conciergerie ❷

1 quai de l'Horloge 75001. **Map** 9 A3. 🏛 01 53 73 78 50. Ⓜ Cité. ◗ Apr–Sep: 9:30am–6:30pm daily; Oct–Mar: 10am–5pm daily (last adm: 30 mins before closing). ● Jan 1, May 1, Nov 1 & 11, Dec 25. 🗷 🖸 🗷 11am, 3pm daily. 🚻

FORMING PART of the huge Palais de Justice, the historic Conciergerie served as a prison from 1391–1914. Henry IV's assassin, François Ravaillac, was imprisoned and tortured here in 1610.

During the Revolution, the building was packed with over 4,000 prisoners. Its most celebrated inmate was Marie-Antoinette, who was held in a tiny cell until her execution in 1793. Others included Charlotte Corday, who stabbed Revolutionary leader Marat while he bathed.

The Conciergerie has a superb four-aisled Gothic hall, where guards of the royal household once lived. Renovated during the 19th century, the building retains its 11th-century torture chamber and the 14th-century clock tower.

A sculptured relief on the Palais de Justice

Palais de Justice ❸

4 boulevard du Palais (entrance by
the Cour de Mai) 75001. **Map** 9 A3.
🕿 01 44 32 50 00. **M** Cité.
◷ 8:30am–6:30pm Mon–Fri.
⬤ public holidays & Aug recess.

THIS HUGE BLOCK of build-
ings making up the law
courts of Paris stretches the
entire width of the Ile de la
Cité. It is a splendid sight
with its Gothic towers lining
the quays. The site has been

occupied since Roman times
when it was the governors'
residence. It was the seat of
royal power until Charles V
moved the court to the Marais
following a bloody revolt
in 1358. In April 1793, the
notorious Revolutionary
Tribunal began dispensing
justice from the Première
Chambre Civile, or first
civil chamber. Today, the
site embodies Napoleon's
great legacy – the French
judicial system.

Crypte Archéologique ❺

Place du Parvis Notre-Dame 75004.
Map 9 A4. 🕿 01 43 29 83 51. **M** Cité.
◷ Tue–Sun 10am–6pm. ⬤ Jan 1,
May 1, Nov 1 & 11, Dec 25. 🖾 🖾 🖾
W www.paris-france.org/musees

SITUATED BENEATH the *parvis*
(main square) of Notre-Dame
and stretching 120 m (393 ft)
underground, the crypt was
opened in 1980.
   There are Gallo-Roman
streets and houses with an
underground heating system,
sections of Lutetia's 3rd-cen-
tury BC wall, and remains of
the cathedral. Models explain
the development of Paris from
a settlement of the Parisii, the
Celtic tribe who inhabited the
island 200 years ago, giving
their name to the present city.

Notre-Dame ❻

See pp82–3.

Sainte-Chapelle ❹

4 boulevard du Palais 75001.
Map 9 A3. 🕿 01 53 73 78 50.
M Cité. ◷ Apr–Sep: 9:30am–
6:30pm daily; Oct–Mar: 10am–5pm
daily. ⬤ Jan 1, May 1, Nov 1 & 11,
Dec 25. 🖾 🖾 🖾 🖾

ETHEREAL AND MAGICAL,
Sainte-Chapelle has
been hailed as one of
the greatest architectural
masterpieces of the
Western world. In the
Middle Ages the devout
likened this church to
"a gateway to heaven."
No visitor can fail to
be transported by the
blaze of light created
by the 15 magnificent
stained-glass windows,
separated by pencil-like
columns soaring 15 m
(50 ft) to the star-studded
roof. The windows
portray more than 1,000
biblical scenes in a
kaleidoscope of red,
gold, green and blue.
Starting from the left
near the entrance and
proceeding clockwise,
you can trace the

scriptures from Genesis
through to the Crucifixion
and the Apocalypse.
   The chapel was completed
in 1248 by Louis IX to house
what was believed to be
Christ's Crown of Thorns and
fragments of the True Cross

(now in the treasury at Notre-
Dame). The king, who was
canonized for his good works,
purchased these relics from the
Emperor of Constantinople,
paying three times more for
them than for the entire construction of Sainte-Chapelle.
   The building actually
consists of two separate
chapels. The somber
lower chapel was used
by servants and lower
court officials, while the
exquisite upper chapel,
reached by means of a
narrow spiral staircase,
was reserved for the roy-
al family and its cour-
tiers. A discreetly placed
window enabled the
king to take part in the
celebrations unobserved.
   During the Revolution
the building was badly
damaged and became a
warehouse for storing
flour. It was renovated a
century later by architect
Viollet-le-Duc.
   Today, evening con-
certs of classical music
are held regularly in the
chapel, taking advantage
of its superb acoustics.

The magnificent interior of Sainte-Chapelle

Ile St-Louis **⑦**

75004. **Map** 9 B–C4–5. **M** *Pont Marie. Sully Morland.* **St-Louis-en-l'Ile** **☎** *01 46 34 11 60.* **◑** *9am–noon, 3–6pm Tue–Sun.* **●** *public hols.* **Concerts**

ACROSS PONT ST-LOUIS from Ile de la Cîté, smaller Ile St-Louis is a little haven of quiet streets and riverside quays. There are luxurious restaurants and stores, including the famous ice-cream maker Berthillon. Almost everything on the Ile was built in classical style in the 17th-century. The church of **St-Louis-en-l'Ile**, with its marble and gilt Baroque interior, was completed in 1726 from plans by royal architect Louis de Vau, an island resident. Note the 1741 iron clock at the church entrance, the pierced iron spire, and a plaque given in 1926 by St-Louis, Missouri, in the USA. The church is also twinned with Carthage cathedral in Tunisia, where St-Louis is buried.

The interior of St-Louis-en-l'Ile

Hôtel de Sens **⑧**

1 rue du Figuier 75004. **Map** 9 C4. **☎** *01 42 78 14 60.* **M** *Pont-Marie.* **◑** *1:30–8:30pm Tue–Fri; 10am–8:30pm Sat.* **●** *public hols.* **◪**

ONE OF ONLY a handful of medieval buildings still standing in Paris, the Hôtel de Sens is home to the Forney arts library. During the period of the Catholic League in the 16th century, it was turned into a fortified mansion and occupied by the Bourbons, the Guises and Cardinal de Pellevé.

St-Gervais– St-Protais **⑨**

Pl St-Gervais 75004. **Map** 9 B3. **☎** *01 48 87 32 02.* **M** *Hôtel de Ville.* **◑** *6am–9pm daily.* **Organ concerts**

NAMED AFTER Gervase and Protase, two Roman soldiers martyred by the Emperor Nero, the origins of this magnificent church go back to the 6th century. It boasts the earliest Classical façade in Paris, dating from 1621 and with a triple-tiered arrangement of Doric, Ionic and Corinthian columns.

Behind the façade lies a late Gothic church renowned for its association with religious music. It was for this church's organ that François Couperin (1668–1733) composed his two masses.

UPPER CHAPEL WINDOWS

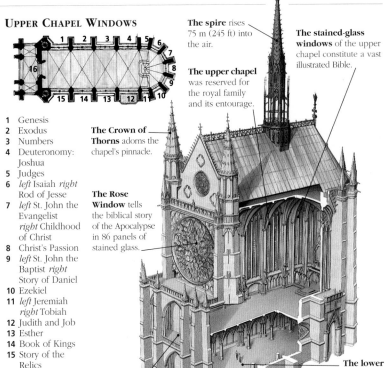

1 Genesis
2 Exodus
3 Numbers
4 Deuteronomy: Joshua
5 Judges
6 *left* Isaiah *right* Rod of Jesse
7 *left* St. John the Evangelist *right* Childhood of Christ
8 Christ's Passion
9 *left* St. John the Baptist *right* Story of Daniel
10 Ezekiel
11 *left* Jeremiah *right* Tobiah
12 Judith and Job
13 Esther
14 Book of Kings
15 Story of the Relics
16 Rose Window: The Apocalypse

The Crown of Thorns adorns the chapel's pinnacle.

The Rose Window tells the biblical story of the Apocalypse in 86 panels of stained glass.

The spire rises 75 m (245 ft) into the air.

The upper chapel was reserved for the royal family and its entourage.

The stained-glass windows of the upper chapel constitute a vast illustrated Bible.

Main portals

The lower chapel was used by servants and commoners.

Notre-Dame ❻

No OTHER BUILDING epitomizes the history of Paris more than Notre-Dame. Built on the site of a Roman temple, the cathedral was commissioned by Bishop de Sully in 1159. The first stone was laid in 1163, marking the start of two centuries of toil by armies of Gothic architects and medieval craftsmen. It has been witness to great events of French history ever since, including the coronations of Henry VI in 1422 and Napoleon Bonaparte in 1804. During the Revolution, the building was desecrated and rechristened the Temple of Reason. Extensive renovations (including the addition of the spire and gargoyles) were carried out in the 19th century by architect Viollet-le-Duc.

★ **West Façade**
The beautifully proportioned west façade is a masterpiece of French Gothic architecture.

387 steps lead to the top of the south tower, where the famous Emmanuel bell is housed.

★ **Galerie des Chimères**
The cathedral's legendary gargoyles (chimères) *gaze menacingly from the cathedral's ledge.*

★ **West Rose Window**
This window depicts the Virgin in a medallion of rich reds and blues.

The Kings' Gallery features 28 stone images of the kings of Judah.

Portal of the Virgin
The Virgin surrounded by saints and kings is a fine composition of 13th-century statues.

STAR FEATURES

★ **West Façade and Portals**

★ **Flying Buttresses**

★ **Rose Windows**

★ **Galerie des Chimères**

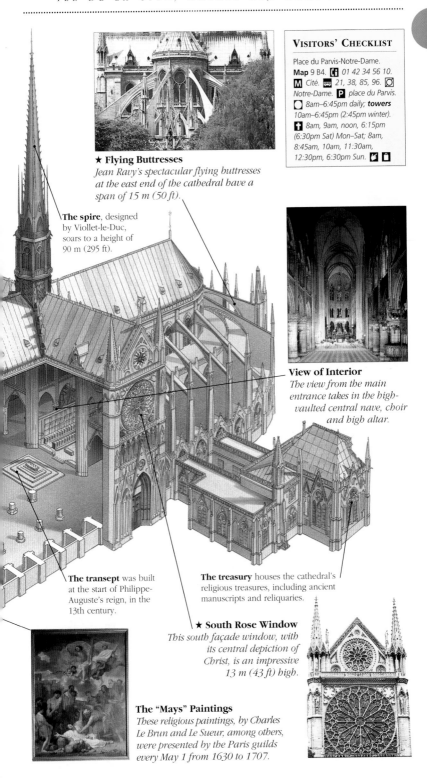

★ Flying Buttresses
Jean Ravy's spectacular flying buttresses at the east end of the cathedral have a span of 15 m (50 ft).

The spire, designed by Viollet-le-Duc, soars to a height of 90 m (295 ft).

VISITORS' CHECKLIST

Place du Parvis-Notre-Dame.
Map 9 B4. **☎** *01 42 34 56 10.*
Ⓜ *Cité.* **🚌** *21, 38, 85, 96.* **Ⓟ**
Notre-Dame. **Ⓟ** *place du Parvis.*
⛪ *8am–6:45pm daily;* **towers**
10am–6:45pm (2:45pm winter).
✝ *8am, 9am, noon, 6:15pm
(6:30pm Sat) Mon–Sat; 8am,
8:45am, 10am, 11:30am,
12:30pm, 6:30pm Sun.* **📷 ♿**

View of Interior
The view from the main entrance takes in the high-vaulted central nave, choir and high altar.

The transept was built at the start of Philippe-Auguste's reign, in the 13th century.

The treasury houses the cathedral's religious treasures, including ancient manuscripts and reliquaries.

★ South Rose Window
This south façade window, with its central depiction of Christ, is an impressive 13 m (43 ft) high.

The "Mays" Paintings
These religious paintings, by Charles Le Brun and Le Sueur, among others, were presented by the Paris guilds every May 1 from 1630 to 1707.

Street-by-Street: The Marais

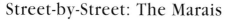

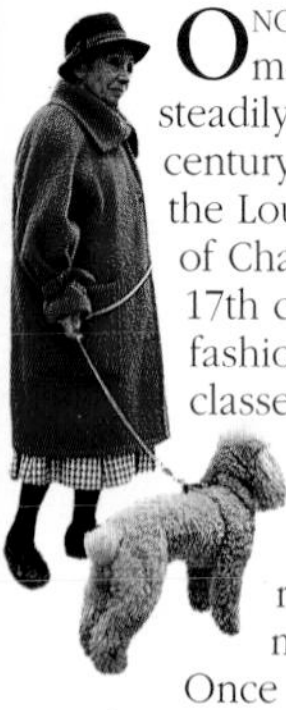

ONCE AN AREA of marshland (*marais* means swamp), the Marais grew steadily in importance from the 14th century, by virtue of its proximity to the Louvre, the preferred residence of Charles V. Its heyday was in the 17th century, when it became a fashionable area for the monied classes, many of whose grand mansions, (*hôtels*) have now been restored as museums.

Once again fashionable, chic designer boutiques alternate with small restaurants and stores.

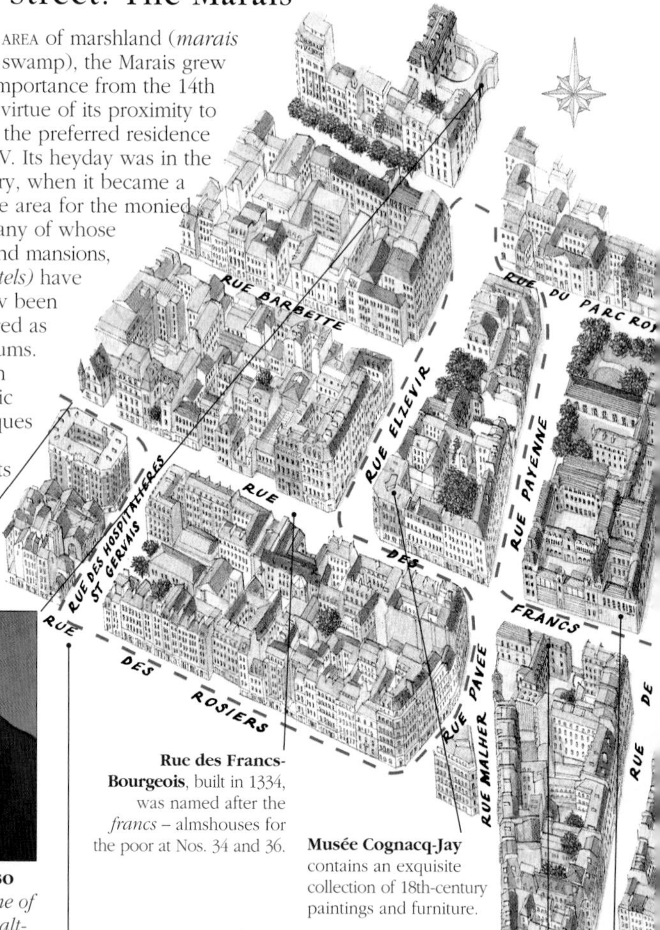

To the Pompidou Center

RUE BARBETTE

RUE DU PARC ROY

RUE ELZEVIR

RUE PAYENNE

RUE DES HOSPITALIERES ST GERVAIS

RUE DES ROSIERS

RUE

DES

FRANCS

RUE MALHER PAVEE

RUE MALHER

RUE

★ **Musée Picasso**
The palatial home of a 17th-century salt-tax collector is the setting for the most extensive collection of Picassos in the world **17**

Rue des Francs-Bourgeois, built in 1334, was named after the *francs* – almshouses for the poor at Nos. 34 and 36.

Musée Cognacq-Jay contains an exquisite collection of 18th-century paintings and furniture.

Hôtel de Lamoignon was built in 1584 and houses Paris's historical library.

Rue des Rosiers, heart of the city's oldest Jewish quarter, is lined with 18th-century houses, shops and restaurants serving hot pastrami and borscht.

KEY

– – – Suggested route

| 0 meters | 100 |
| 0 yards | 100 |

★ **Musée Carnavalet**
Occupying two large mansions, this museum covers the history of Paris from Prehistoric and Gallo-Roman times **18**

★ **Place des Vosges**
This enchanting square is an oasis of peace and tranquility ⑲

LOCATOR MAP
See Street Finder maps 9, 10

Maison de Victor Hugo
Author of Les Misérables, *Victor Hugo lived at No. 6 place des Vosges, now a museum of his life and work* ⑳

To Metro Sully Morland

STAR SIGHTS

★ **Musée Picasso**

★ **Musée Carnavalet**

★ **Place des Vosges**

Hôtel de Sully, with its orangerie and courtyard, is an elegant Renaissance mansion.

Hôtel de Ville ⑩

4 place de l'Hôtel de Ville 75004.
Map 9 B3. ☎ *01 42 76 50 49.*
Ⓜ *Hôtel-de-Ville.* ⌚ *to groups: call to arrange.* ● *public hols, and for official functions (call to check).*
♿ Ⓦ *www.paris-france.org*

HOME OF THE city council, the Hôtel de Ville is a 19th-century reconstruction of the 17th-century town hall burned down by insurgents of the Paris Commune in 1871. It is a highly ornate example of Third Republic architecture, with elaborate stonework, turrets and statues overlooking a pedestrianized square.

The 16th-century Tour St-Jacques

Tour St-Jacques ⑪

Square de la Tour St-Jacques 75004.
Map 9 A3. Ⓜ *Châtelet.* **Not open** *to the public.*

THIS IMPOSING late Gothic tower, dating from 1523, is all that remains of a medieval church used as a rendezvous by pilgrims setting out for Compostela in Spain. The building was destroyed by revolutionaries in 1797.

Earlier, Blaise Pascal, the 17th-century philosopher, mathematician, physicist and writer, used the tower for barometric experiments. His statue stands at the base of the tower, which is now used as a meteorological station.

St-Eustache ⑫

Place du Jour 75001. **Map** 9 A1.
📞 01 40 26 47 99. Ⓜ *Les Halles.*
🚇 *Châtelet-Les-Halles.* ⏱ *9am–8pm daily (7pm winter).* **Concerts**

Wᴵᵀᴴ ɪᴛꜱ ɢᴏᴛʜɪᴄ ᴘʟᴀɴ and Renaissance decoration, St-Eustache is one of Paris's most beautiful churches. Its massive interior is modeled on Notre-Dame, with five naves and side and radial chapels. The 105 years (1532–1637) it took to complete the church saw the flowering of the Renaissance style, which is evident in the magnificent arches, pillars and columns.

St-Eustache has been the setting for many ceremonial events, including the baptisms of Cardinal Richelieu and Madame de Pompadour, and the funerals of fabulist La Fontaine, Colbert (prime minister of Louis XIV), 17th-century dramatist Molière, composer Rameau and revolutionary orator Mirabeau. It was here that Berlioz first performed his *Te Deum* in 1855 and Liszt his *Messe Solenelle* in 1866. Today, talented choir groups perform here regularly and organ recitals are held on Sundays at 5:30pm.

Forum des Halles ⑬

75001. **Map** 13 A2. Ⓜ *Les Halles.*
🚇 *Châtelet-Les-Halles.*

Tʜᴇ ᴘʀᴇꜱᴇɴᴛ Forum des Halles, which is simply known as Les Halles, was built in 1979, amid much controversy, on the site of the famous old fruit and vegetable market. The present complex occupies 7 ha (750,000 sq ft), partly above and partly below ground. The underground levels 2 and 3 are occupied by a varied array of shops, from smart boutiques to megastores. Above ground there are well-tended gardens, pergolas and mini-pavilions. Also outside are the palm-shaped buildings of metal and glass which house the Pavillon des Arts and the Maison de la Poésie, which are cultural centers for contemporary art and poetry respectively.

St-Eustache and sculptured head,
l'Ecoute, **by Henri de Miller**

Pompidou Centre ⑭

See pp88–9.

Musée d'Art et d'Histoire du Judaïsme ⑮

Hôtel de St-Aignan, 71 rue du Temple 75003. **Map** 13 B2. 📞 01 53 01 86 53. Ⓜ *Rambuteau.* ⏱ *11am–6pm Mon–Fri, 10am–6pm Sun.* ● *Jewish hols* 📷 🕙 🚹 🛒 🛈

Tʜɪꜱ museum in a Marais mansion, the elegant Hôtel de St-Aignan, brings together collections formerly scattered around the city, and commemorates the culture of French Jewry from medieval times to the present. Visitors learn that there has been a sizeable Jewish community in France since Roman times, and some of the world's greatest Jewish scholars – Rashi, Rabenu Tam, the Tosafists – were French. Much exquisite craftsmanship is displayed, with elaborate silverware, Torah covers, fabrics, and items of fine Judaica and religious objects for use both in the synagogue and in the home. There are also photographs, paintings and cartoons and historical documents, including some on the antisemitic Dreyfus Affair a century ago.

Hôtel de Soubise ⑯

60 rue des Francs-Bourgeois 75003.
Map 9 C2. 📞 01 40 27 62 18.
Ⓜ *Rambuteau.* ⏱ *10am–5:45pm Wed–Mon, 2–5:45pm Sat–Sun.*
● *public hols.* 📷

Tʜɪꜱ ɪᴍᴘᴏꜱɪɴɢ ᴍᴀɴꜱɪᴏɴ, built from 1705 to 1709 for the Princesse de Rohan, is one of two main buildings housing the national archives (the other one being the Hôtel de Rohan). It boasts a majestic courtyard and 18th-century interior decoration by some of the best-known artists of the time.

Natoire's *rocaille* work in the Princess's bedchamber, can be admired in the museum now housed here. Other exhibits include Napoleon's will, in which he asks for his remains to be returned to France.

Musée Picasso ⑰

Hôtel Salé, 5 rue de Thorigny, 75003
Map 10 D2. 📞 01 42 71 25 21.
Ⓜ *St-Sébastien Froissart.* ⏱ *Oct–Apr: 9:30am–5:30pm Wed–Mon; May–Sep: 9:30am–6pm Wed–Mon.*
● *Jan 1, Dec 25.* 📷 📷 🕙 🚹 🛒 🛈
🛈 🖥 *www.musee-picasso.fr*

Uᴘᴏɴ ᴛʜᴇ ᴅᴇᴀᴛʜ ᴏꜰ the Spanish-born artist Pablo Picasso (1881–1973), who lived most of his life in France, the French State inherited one-quarter of his works in lieu of death taxes. In 1986, it used them to create the Musée Picasso in the beautifully

Woman Reading (1932) by
Pablo Picasso

restored Hôtel Salé, one of the loveliest buildings in the Marais. It was built in 1656 for Aubert de Fontenay, collector of the dreaded salt tax (*salé* means "salty").

Comprising over 200 paintings, 158 sculptures, 88 ceramic works and some 3,000 sketches and engravings, this unique collection shows the enormous range and variety of Picasso's work, including examples from his Blue, Pink and Cubist periods.

Highlights to watch for are his Blue period *Self-portrait*, painted at age 20; studies for his masterpiece *Les Demoiselles d'Avignon; Still Life with Caned Chair*, which introduced collage to Cubism; the Neo-Classical *Pipes of Pan;* and *The Crucifixion*.

Also exhibited are works from Picasso's private art collection, including paintings by Rousseau, Renoir, Cézanne, Braque, Balthus, Miró and Matisse.

A magnificent 17th-century ceiling painting by Charles Le Brun

Musée Carnavalet ⑱

23 rue de Sevigné 75003. **Map** 10 D3.
☎ *01 44 59 58 58.* Ⓜ *St-Paul.*
◯ *10am–6pm Tue–Sun.* ● *public hols.* 🚫 🖾 🎟 *ring for times.* ❑
🆆 *www.paris-france.org*

D EVOTED TO the history of Paris since Prehistoric times, this vast museum is in two adjoining mansions. They include entire decorated rooms with gilded paneling, furniture and *objets d'art*; many works of art, such as paintings and sculptures of prominent personalities; and engravings

showing Paris being built.

The main building is the Hôtel Carnavalet, built as a town house in 1548 by Nicolas Dupuis. The literary hostess Madame de Sévigné lived here between 1677 and 1696, entertaining the intelligentsia of the day and writing her celebrated *Lettres*. Many of her possessions are in the first-floor exhibit covering the Louis XIV era.

The 17th-century Hôtel le Peletier, opened in 1989, features superb reconstructions of early 20th-century interiors, and artifacts from the Revolution and Napoleonic era. The Orangery houses a new department devoted to Prehistory and Gallo-Roman Paris. The collection includes pirogues discovered in 1992, during an archaeological dig in the Parc de Bercy, which unearthed a neolithic village.

Place des Vosges ⑲

75003, 75004. **Map** 10 D3.
Ⓜ *Bastille, St-Paul.*

T HIS PERFECTLY symmetrical square, laid out in 1605 by Henri IV, is considered among the most beautiful in the world by Parisians and visitors alike. Thirty-six houses, nine on each side, are built over arcades that today accommodate antiques shops and fashionable cafés. The square has been the scene of many historical events over the centuries, including a three-day tournament in celebration of the marriage of Louis XIII to Anne of Austria in 1615.

Maison de Victor Hugo ⑳

6 place des Vosges 75004. **Map** 10 D4.
☎ *01 42 72 10 16.* Ⓜ *Bastille.*
◯ *10am–6pm Tue–Sun.* ● *public hols.* 🚫 🎟 *Library.*

T HE FRENCH POET, dramatist and novelist lived on the second floor of the former Hôtel Rohan-Guéménée, the

largest house on the square, from 1832 to 1848. It was here that he wrote most of *Les Misérables* and completed other famous works. On display are reconstructions of some of the rooms in which he lived, complete with his desk, the furniture he made, his pen-and-ink drawings and mementos from the crucially important periods of his life, from his childhood to his exile between 1852 and 1870.

Marble bust of Victor Hugo by Auguste Rodin

Place de la Bastille ㉑

75004. **Map** 10 E4. Ⓜ *Bastille.*

N OTHING REMAINS of the infamous prison stormed by the revolutionary mob on July 14, 1789, the event that sparked the French Revolution.

The 52-m (170-ft) Colonne de Juillet stands in the middle of the traffic-clogged square to honor the victims of the July Revolution of 1830. On the south side of the square (at 120 rue de Lyon) is the 2,700-seat Opéra Bastille, completed in 1989, the bicentennial of the French Revolution.

The "genius of liberty" statue on top of the Colonne de Juillet

Pompidou Centre ⓮

THE POMPIDOU IS LIKE a building turned inside out: escalators, elevators, air and water ducts, and even the massive steel struts that make up the building's skeleton are all on the outside. This allowed architects Richard Rogers, Renzo Piano, and Gianfranco Franchini, to create a flexible exhibition space. Artists featured in the museum include Matisse, Picasso, Miró, and Pollock, representing such schools as Fauvism, Cubism, and Surrealism. Outside in the Piazza, large crowds gather to watch the street performers. The Pompidou has been completely renovated for the new Millennium.

KEY

☐ Exhibition space

☐ Nonexhibition space

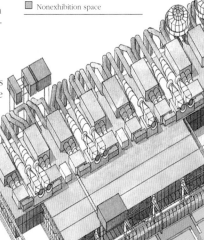

This riotous jumble of glass and steel, known as Beaubourg, is Paris's top tourist attraction, built in 1977 and drawing over seven million visitors a year.

Mobile on Two Planes (1955)
20th-century American artist Alexander Calder introduced the mobile as an art form.

To the Atelier Brancusi

GALLERY GUIDE

The permanent collections are on the fifth and fourth levels: works from 1905–60 are on the former, contemporary art on the latter. The first and sixth levels are for temporary exhibitions; the first, second and third house a library. The lower levels make up "The Forum," the focal public area, with a performance center, movie theater, and children's workshop.

Sorrow of the King (1952)
This collage was created by Matisse using gouache-painted paper cutouts.

Basin and Sculpture Terrace

Portrait of the Journalist Sylvia von Harden *(1926)*
The surgical precision of Otto Dix's style makes this a harsh caricature.

Le Duo *(1937)*
Georges Braque, like Picasso, developed the Cubist technique of representing different views of a subject in a single picture.

With the Black Arc
(1912) The transition to Abstraction, one of the major art forms of the 20th century, can be seen in the works of Wassily Kandinsky.

VISITORS' CHECKLIST

Centre d'Art et de Culture Georges Pompidou, Pl G Pompidou, 75004. **Map** 9 B2. 01 44 78 12 33.
Rambuteau, Châtelet, Hôtel de Ville. 21, 29, 38, 47, 58, 69, 70, 72, 74, 75, 76, 81, 85, 96.
RER Châtelet-Les-Halles. P Centre G Pompidou. MNAM & temp exhibs: 11am–9pm Wed–Mon; (11pm Thu); Atelier Brancusi: 2–6pm Wed–Sun; Library: noon–10pm Mon–Fri, 11am–10pm w/e.
www.centrepompidou.fr

Stravinsky Fountain
This fountain, which was inaugurated in 1983, is in the Place Igor Stravinsky near the Pompidou Centre. It was designed by sculptors Jean Tinguely and Niki de Saint Phalle, both of whom are represented in the Pompidou Centre.

BRANCUSI WORKSHOP

The Atelier Brancusi, on the rue Rambuteau side of the piazza, is a reconstruction of the workshop of the Romanian-born artist Constantin Brancusi (1876–1957), who lived and worked in Paris. He bequeathed his entire collection of works to the French state on condition that his workshop be rebuilt as it was. The collection includes over 200 sculptures and plinths, 1600 photographs, exhibited in rotation, and the tools Brancusi used in his work. Also featured are some of his more personal items such as documents, pieces of furniture, and his book collection.

Interior of the Brancusi workshop, designed by Renzo Piano

TUILERIES AND OPÉRA

THE 19TH-CENTURY grandeur of Baron Haussmann's *grands boulevards* offsets the bustle of bankers, theater-goers, sightseers and shoppers who frequent the area around the Opéra. A profusion of shops and department stores, ranging from the exclusively expensive to the popular, draws the crowds. Much of the area's older character is found in the early 19th-century shopping arcades, with elaborate steel and glass roofs. They are known as *galeries,* or *passages,* and were restored to their former glory in the 1970s. Galerie Vivienne, the most impressive, has an elaborate, patterned mosaic floor. The passage des Panoramas, passage Verdeau and the tiny passage des Princes are more old-style Parisian. These streets abound with food shops of all kinds,

Lamppost of vestal virgin outside the Opéra

noted for their mouthwatering displays of expensive jams, spices, pâtés, mustards and sauces.

The Tuileries area lies between the Opéra and the river, bounded by the vast place de la Concorde in the west and the Louvre to the east. The Louvre palace combines one of the world's greatest art collections with I.M. Pei's avant-garde glass pyramid. Elegant squares and formal gardens give the area its special character. Monuments to monarchy and the arts coexist with modern luxury at its most ostentatious. Place Vendôme, home to exquisite jewelry shops and the luxurious Ritz Hotel, is a heady mix of the wealthy and the chic. Parallel to the Jardin des Tuileries are two of Paris's foremost shopping streets, the rue de Rivoli and rue St-Honoré, full of expensive boutiques, bookshops and five-star hotels.

SIGHTS AT A GLANCE

Museums and Galleries
Galerie Nationale du Jeu de Paume **6**
Musée des Arts Décoratifs **11**
Musée Grévin **3**
Musée du Louvre pp96–9 **14**
Musée de l'Orangerie **8**

Squares, Parks and Gardens
Jardin des Tuileries **9**
Place de la Concorde **7**
Place Vendôme **5**

Monuments
Arc de Triomphe du Carrousel **12**

Historic Buildings
Opéra de Paris Garnier **2**
Palais Royal **13**

Churches
La Madeleine **1**
St-Roch **10**

Shops
Les Passages **4**

GETTING THERE
This area is well served by the metro system, with stations at Tuileries, Pyramides, Palais Royal, Madeleine and Opéra, among others. Bus routes 24 and 72 pass along quai des Tuileries and quai du Louvre, while routes 21, 27 and 29 serve avenue de l'Opéra.

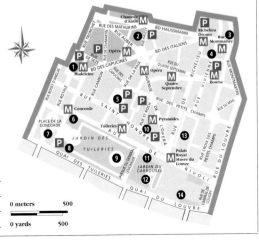

KEY
	Street-by-Street map *pp92–3*
M	Metro station
P	Parking

0 meters 500
0 yards 500

◁ **View of the place de la Concorde and the Obelisk**

Street-by-Street: Opéra Quarter

IT HAS BEEN SAID that the whole world will pass you by if you sit for long enough at the Café de la Paix (opposite the Opéra Garnier). During the day, the area is a center of commerce, tourism and shopping, with mammoth department stores lining the *grands boulevards*. In the evening, the clubs and theaters attract a totally different crowd, and the cafés along boulevard des Capucines throb with life.

Statue by Gurnery on the Opéra

★ Opéra Garnier
Dating from 1875, the grandiose opera house has come to symbolize the opulence of the Second Empire ❷

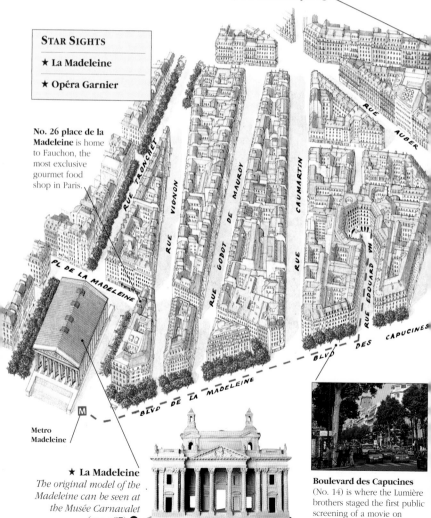

STAR SIGHTS

★ **La Madeleine**

★ **Opéra Garnier**

No. 26 place de la Madeleine is home to Fauchon, the most exclusive gourmet food shop in Paris.

RUE TRONCHET
RUE VIGNON
RUE GODOT DE MAUROY
RUE CAUMARTIN
RUE AUBER
RUE EDOUARD VII
PL DE LA MADELEINE

Metro Madeleine

Ⓜ

BLVD DE LA MADELEINE

BLVD DES CAPUCINES

★ La Madeleine
The original model of the Madeleine can be seen at the Musée Carnavalet (see p87) ❶

Boulevard des Capucines
(No. 14) is where the Lumière brothers staged the first public screening of a movie on December 28, 1895.

LOCATOR MAP
*See Street Finder
maps 4, 7, 8*

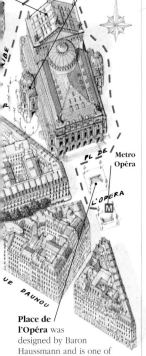

PL DIAGHILEV

Musée de l'Opéra contains the scores of every ballet and opera performed at the Opéra, and memorabilia ranging from Nijinsky's dancing shoes to Pavlova's tiara.

Metro Opéra

L'OPÉRA

PL DE

VE DAUNOU

Place de l'Opéra was designed by Baron Haussmann and is one of Paris's busiest intersections.

KEY

— — — Suggested route

0 meters	100
0 yards	100

Marochetti's *Mary Magdalene Ascending to Heaven* in La Madeleine

La Madeleine ❶

Place de la Madeleine 75008.
Map 3 C5. ☎ 01 44 51 69 00.
Ⓜ *Madeleine.* ⏰ 8:30am–7pm daily (9am Sat). 🔲 🅿 **Concerts**.

MODELED AFTER a Greek temple, La Madeleine was begun in 1764 but not consecrated until 1845. Before that, there were proposals to turn it into a stock exchange, a bank, a theater, a railroad station, or yet another monument to Napoleon.

A colonnade of Corinthian columns encircles the building and supports a sculptured frieze. The inside is crowned by three ceiling domes and lavishly decorated with fine sculptures, rose marble and gilt.

Opéra de Paris Garnier ❷

Place de l'Opéra 75009. **Map** 4 DF.
01 40 01 22 63. Ⓜ *Opéra.* ⏰ 10am–5pm daily. ● *public hols.* 🔲 🗹

SOMETIMES COMPARED to a giant wedding cake, this extravagant building was designed by Charles Garnier for Napoleon III in 1862. The Prussian War and the 1871 uprising delayed the opening of the building till 1875.

The interior of the Opéra is famous for its Grand Staircase made of white Carrara marble, topped by a huge chandelier, as well as for its auditorium bedecked in red velvet and gold, with a false ceiling painted by Chagall in 1964.

Restored to its full glory, it is primarily used for dance (it is home to the Ballet de l'Opéra de Paris), but shares operatic productions with the Bastille.

Musée Grévin ❸

10 boulevard Montmartre 75009.
Map 4 F4. ☎ 01 47 70 85 05. Ⓜ *rue Montmartre.* ⏰ 10am–6pm daily. 🔲 🅿 Ⓦ www.musee-grevin.com

FOUNDED IN 1882, this museum is now a Paris landmark, on a par with Madame Tussauds in London. It shows important historical scenes such as Louis XIV at Versailles and the arrest of Louis XVI. Figures from the arts, politics, film and sports are also on display. On the first floor, there is a holography museum devoted to optical tricks. The museum also houses a 320-seat theater.

Sign outside the Musée Grévin

Les Passages ❹

75002. **Map** 4 F5. Ⓜ *Bourse.*

THE EARLY 19th-century glass-roofed shopping arcades (known as *galeries* or *passages*) are concentrated between boulevard Montmartre and rue St-Marc. They house an eclectic mixture of small shops selling everything from designer jewelry to rare books and art supplies. One of the most charming is the Galerie Vivienne (off the rue Vivienne or the rue des Petits Champs), with its mosaic floor and excellent tearoom.

Place Vendôme ❺

75001. **Map** 8 D1. **M** *Tuileries.*

Perhaps the best example of 18th-century elegance in the city, the architect Jules Hardouin-Mansart's royal square was begun in 1698. The original plan was to house academies and embassies behind its arcaded façades, but instead bankers moved in and created sumptuous mansions for themselves. The square's most famous residents include Frédéric Chopin, who died here in 1849 at No. 12, and César Ritz, who established his famous hotel at No. 15 in 1898.

Monet's *Waterlilies (Nymphéas)* on display in the Musée de l'Orangerie

Galerie Nationale du Jeu de Paume ❻

Jardin des Tuileries, place de la Concorde 75008. **C** 01 47 03 12 50. **F** 01 47 03 12 52. **M** *Concorde.* ◯ *noon–9:30pm Tue, noon–7pm Wed–Fri, 10am–7pm Sat & Sun.* ● *Jan 1, May 1 & Dec 25.* 🖥 🔊 🗞 🖒 📷 🖸

The jeu de paume – literally "game of the palm" – was built as two royal tennis courts by Napoleon III in 1851. When the game's popularity waned, the courts were converted into a gallery devoted to French Impressionist art. In 1986, the collection was moved to the Musée d'Orsay across the river *(see pp116–17)*. The Jeu de Paume now exhibits contemporary art.

Place de la Concorde ❼

75008. **Map** 7 C1. **M** *Concorde.*

One of Europe's most magnificent and historic squares, covering over 20 acres, the place de la Concorde was a swamp until

The 3,200-year-old obelisk from Luxor

the mid-18th century. It became the place Louis XV in 1775, when royal architect Jacques-Ange Gabriel was asked by the king to design a suitable setting for an equestrian statue of himself.

The monument, which lasted here less than 20 years, was replaced by the guillotine (the Black Widow, as it came to be known), and the square was renamed place de la Révolution. On January 21, 1793, Louis XVI was beheaded, followed by over 1,300 other victims including Marie Antoinette, Madame du Barry, Charlotte Corday (Marat's assassin) and revolutionary leaders Danton and Robespierre.

The blood-soaked square was optimistically renamed place de la Concorde after the Reign of Terror finally came to an end in 1794. A few decades later, the 3,200-year-old obelisk was presented to King Louis-Philippe as a gift from the viceroy of Egypt (who also donated Cleopatra's Needle in London).

Flanking the rue Royale on the north side of the square are two of Gabriel's Neo-Classical mansions – the Hôtel de la Marine and the exclusive Hôtel Crillon.

Musée de l'Orangerie ❽

Jardin des Tuileries, place de la Concorde 75008. **Map** 7 C1. **C** 01 42 97 48 16. **M** *Concorde.* ● *for renovation until early 2004.* 🖼 📷 🖒 🗞 *by appt.* 🖸

Paintings from Claude Monet's crowning work, representing part of his water-lily series, fill the two oval ground floor rooms. Known as the *Nymphéas*, most of the canvases were painted between 1899 and 1921 in his garden at Giverny, near Paris.

This superb work is complemented by the Walter-Guillaume collection, including 27 canvases by Renoir, notably *Young Girls at the Piano;* dramatic works by Soutine; and 14 Cézannes, including *The Red Rock.* Picasso is represented by early works, including *The Female Bathers,* and Rousseau by 9 paintings, notably *The Wedding* and *Old Junier's Cart.* Other outstanding works are by Sisley, Derain, Modigliani and Utrillo.

Jardin des Tuileries ❾

75001. **Map** 8 D1. **M** *Tuileries, Concorde.* ◯ *7:30am–7:30pm daily.*

These neo-classical gardens once belonged to the Palais des Tuileries, which the Communards razed to the ground in 1871. They were laid out in the 17th century by André Le Nôtre, who created the broad central avenue and topiary arranged in geometric designs. Recent restoration has created a new garden with lime and chestnut trees, and striking modern sculptures throughout.

St-Roch ⑩

296 rue St-Honoré 75001. **Map** 8 E1.
☎ 01 42 44 13 20. Ⓜ Tuileries.
◯ 9am–6pm daily. ● non-religious public hols. ◉ Concerts

THIS HUGE CHURCH was designed by Jacques Lemercier, architect of the Louvre, and its foundation stone was laid by Louis XIV in 1653. It is a treasure house of religious art, much of it from now-vanished churches and monasteries, and contains the tombs of the playwright Pierre Corneille, the royal gardener André Le Nôtre and the philosopher Denis Diderot.

Vien's *St. Denis Preaching to the Gauls* (1767) in St-Roch

Musée des Arts Décoratifs ⑪

Palais du Louvre, 107 rue de Rivoli 75001. **Map** 8 E2. ☎ 01 44 55 57 50. Ⓜ Palais Royal, Tuileries. ◯ 11am–6pm Tue, Thu, Fri; 11am–9pm Wed; 10am–6pm Sat & Sun. **Library** ●
until 2004. 📷 Ⓦ www.ucad.fr

OCCUPYING THE northwest wing of the Palais du Louvre (along with the Musée de la Publicité and the Musée de la Mode et du Textile) this museum offers an eclectic mix of decorative art and domestic design from the Middle Ages to the present day. The Art Nouveau and Art Deco rooms, include a reconstruction of the home of couturier Jeanne Lanvin. Other floors show Louis XIV, XV and XVI styles of decoration and furniture. Contemporary designers such as Jean-Michel Wilmotte, Philippe Starck and Andrée Putmann are also represented.

Arc de Triomphe du Carrousel ⑫

Place du Carrousel 75001. **Map** 8 E2. Ⓜ Palais Royal.

THIS ROSE-MARBLE ARCH was built by Napoleon to celebrate various military triumphs, notably the Battle of Austerlitz in 1805. The crowning statues, added in 1828, are copies of the famous Horses of St. Mark's that Napoleon stole from Venice, which he was subsequently forced to return after his defeat at Waterloo in 1815.

The Buren Columns in the main courtyard of the Palais Royal

Palais Royal ⑬

Place du Palais Royal 75001. **Map** 8 E1. Ⓜ Palais Royal. **Buildings** ● to the public.

THIS FORMER royal palace has had a turbulent history. It was built by Cardinal Richelieu in the early 17th century, passing to the Crown on his death and becoming the childhood home of Louis XIV. Under the 18th-century royal dukes of Orléans, it became the epicenter of brilliant gatherings, interspersed with periods of gambling and de-bauchery. It was from here that the clarion call to revolution roused the mobs to storm the Bastille on July 14, 1789.

The southern section of the building now houses the Councils of State and the Ministry of Culture. Just west of the palace at 2 rue de Richelieu is the Comédie Française, established by Louis XIV in 1680. Luxury shops occupy the rear section of the palace, where artists such as Colette and Cocteau once lived.

The Arc de Triomphe du Carrousel crowned by Victory riding a chariot

Musée du Louvre ⓮

T HE MUSÉE DU LOUVRE, containing one of the most important art collections in the world, has a history dating from medieval times. Built as a fortress in 1190 by King Philippe-Auguste to protect Paris against Viking raids, it lost its keep in the reign of François I, who replaced it with a Renaissance-style building. Thereafter, four centuries of kings and emperors improved and enlarged it. The latest addition is the collection of arts from Africa, Asia, Oceania and the Americas, in the Pavillion des Sessions until 2004.

The Louvre's east façade, facing St-Germain l'Auxerrois

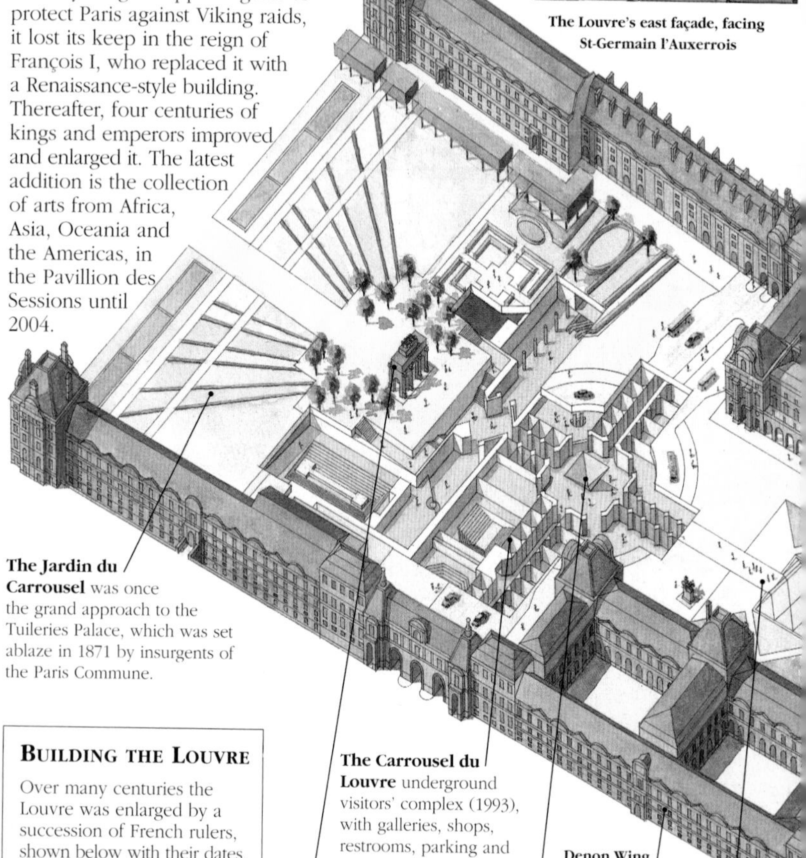

The Jardin du Carrousel was once the grand approach to the Tuileries Palace, which was set ablaze in 1871 by insurgents of the Paris Commune.

BUILDING THE LOUVRE

Over many centuries the Louvre was enlarged by a succession of French rulers, shown below with their dates.

MAJOR ALTERATIONS

☐	Reign of François I (1515–47)
☐	Catherine de' Medici (about 1560)
■	Reign of Henri IV (1589–1610)
■	Reign of Louis XIII (1610–43)
☐	Reign of Louis XIV (1643–1715)
■	Reign of Napoleon I (1804–15)
☐	Reign of Napoleon III (1852–70)
■	I.M. Pei (1989) (architect)

The Carrousel du Louvre underground visitors' complex (1993), with galleries, shops, restrooms, parking and an information desk, lies beneath the Arc de Triomphe du Carrousel.

★ Arc de Triomphe du Carrousel
This triumphal arch was built to celebrate Napoleon's military victories in 1805.

Denon Wing

Pyramid entrance

The inverted glass pyramid brings light to the subterranean complex, echoing the museum's new main entrance in the Cour Napoléon.

STAR FEATURES

★ **Perrault Colonnade**

★ **Medieval Moats**

★ **Arc de Triomphe du Carrousel**

THE GLASS PYRAMID

Plans for the modernization and expansion of the Louvre were first conceived in 1981. They included the transfer of the Ministry of Finance from the Richelieu wing of the Louvre to new offices elsewhere, as well as a new main entrance designed by architect I.M. Pei in 1989. Made of metal and glass, the pyramid enables the visitor to see the buildings around the palace, while allowing light down into the underground visitors' reception area.

VISITORS' CHECKLIST

Map 12 E2. 01 40 20 53 17. 01 40 20 51 51. M Palais Royal, Musée du Louvre. 21, 27, 39, 48, 68, 69, 72, 95. Châtelet-Les-Halles. Louvre. P Carrousel du Louvre (entrance via avenue du General Lemmonier); Pl du Louvre, Rue St-Honoré. 9am–6pm Wed–Mon (open till 9:45pm Mon & Wed), History of the Louvre rooms only open Mon & Fri, same hrs as above. some public hols. (reduced price after 3pm & all day Sun; free 1st Sun of each month and for under 18). partial 01 40 20 53 17. call 01 40 20 52 63. Lectures, movies, concerts 01 40 20 54 55. W www.louvre.fr

Cour Marly is the glass-roofed courtyard that now houses the *Marly Horses (see p99)*.

Richelieu Wing

Cour Puget

Hall Napoléon is situated under the pyramid.

Cour Khorsabad

Sully Wing

Cour Carrée

Cour Napoléon

★ **Perrault's Colonnade**
The east façade, with its majestic rows of columns, was built by Claude Perrault, who worked on the Louvre with Louis Le Vau in the mid-17th century.

The Salle des Caryatides
is named after the four monumental statues created by Jean Goujon in 1550 to support the upper gallery. Built for Henri II, it is the oldest room in the palace.

The Louvre of Charles V
In about 1360, Charles V transformed Philippe-Auguste's old fortress, with its distinctive tower and keep, into a royal residence.

★ **Medieval Moats**
The base of the twin towers and the drawbridge support of Philippe-Auguste's fortress can be seen in the excavated area.

Exploring the Louvre's Collection

DUE TO THE VAST SIZE of the Louvre's collection, it is useful to set a few viewing priorities before starting. The collection of European paintings (1400–1848) is comprehensive, with over half the works by French artists. The extensively renovated departments of Oriental, Egyptian, Etruscan, and Roman antiquities feature numerous new acquisitions and rare treasures. The varied display of *objets d'art* includes furniture and jewelry.

Paintings after this date are housed in the Musée d'Orsay *(see pp116–17)*. Outstanding is Enguerrand Quarton's *Villeneuve-les-Avignon Pietà* (1455). The great 18th-century painter of melancholy, J.A. Watteau, is represented, as is J.H. Fragonard, master of the Rococo, whose delightfully frivolous subjects are evident in *The Bathers* from 1770.

The Raft of the Medusa (1819) by Théodore Géricault

EUROPEAN PAINTING: 1200 TO 1848

PAINTING FROM northern Europe (Flemish, Dutch, German and English) is well covered. One of the earliest Flemish works is Jan van Eyck's *Madonna of the Chancellor Rolin* (about 1435), which shows the Chancellor of Burgundy kneeling in prayer before the Virgin and Child. Hieronymus Bosch's *Ship of Fools* (1500) is a satirical account of the futility of human existence.

Mona Lisa (about 1504) by Leonardo da Vinci

In the Dutch collection, Rembrandt's *Self-portrait*, his *Disciples at Emmaus* (1648) and *Bathsheba* (1654) are examples of the artist's genius.

The three major German painters of the 15th and 16th centuries are represented by important works. There is a youthful *Self-portrait* (1493) by Albrecht Dürer, a *Venus* (1529) by Lucas Cranach and a portrait of the great humanist scholar Erasmus by Hans Holbein.

The museum's collection of Italian paintings is large, covering the period from 1200 to 1800. The father figures of the early Renaissance, Cimabue and Giotto, are here, as is Fra Angelico, with his *Coronation of the Virgin* (1435), and Pisanello, with his delightful *Portrait of Ginevra d'Este* (about 1435). Several paintings by Leonardo da Vinci are on display, for instance the *Virgin with the Infant Jesus and St. Anne* which is as enchanting as his *Mona Lisa*.

The Louvre's fine collection of French painting ranges from the 14th century to 1848.

EUROPEAN SCULPTURE: 1100 TO 1848

EARLY FLEMISH and German sculpture in the collection includes such masterpieces as Tilman Riemenschneider's *Virgin of the Annunciation*, from the end of the 15th century, and a life-size nude figure of the penitent Mary Magdalen by Gregor Erhart (early 16th century). An important work of Flemish sculpture is Adrian de Vries's long-limbed *Mercury and Psyche* from 1593, which was originally made for the court of Rudolph II in Prague.

The French section opens with early Romanesque works, such as the figure of Christ by a 12th-century Burgundian sculptor, and a head of St. Peter. With its eight black-hooded mourners, the late 15th-century tomb of Philippe Pot (a high-ranking official in Burgundy) is one of the more unusual pieces. Diane de Poitiers, Henri II's mistress, had a large figure of her namesake Diana, goddess of the hunt, installed in the courtyard of her castle west of Paris. It is now in the Louvre.

The tomb of Philippe Pot (late 15th century) by Antoine le Moiturier

**The celebrated *Marly Horses*
(1745) by Guillaume Coustou**

The works of French sculptor
Pierre Puget (1620–94) have
been assembled in the Cour
Puget. They include a figure of
Milo of Crotona, the Greek ath-
lete who got his hands caught
in the cleft of a tree stump and
was eaten by a lion. The wild
horses of Marly now stand in
the Cour Marly, surrounded by
other masterpieces of French
sculpture, including Jean-
Antoine Houdon's early 19th-
century busts of famous men
such as Diderot and Voltaire.

The collection of Italian
sculpture includes such splendid exhibits as Michelangelo's
Slaves and Benvenuto Cellini's
Fontainebleau *Nymph*.

ORIENTAL, EGYPTIAN, GREEK, ETRUSCAN AND ROMAN ANTIQUITIES

A SUBSTANTIAL overhaul of the
Louvre has boosted its
collection of antiquities, which
range from the Neolithic period to the fall of the Roman
Empire. Among the new ex-
hibits are Greek and Roman
glassware dating from the 6th
century BC. Important works
of Mesopotamian art include
one of the world's oldest legal
documents, a basalt block
bearing the code of the
Babylonian King Hammurabi,
dating from about 1700 BC.

The warlike Assyrians are
represented by delicate carvings and a spectacular reconstruction of part of Sargon II's
(722–705 BC) palace with its

winged bulls. A fine example
of Persian art is the enameled
brickwork depicting the king
of Persia's personal guard of
archers (5th century BC).

Most Egyptian art was
made for the dead, who
were provided with the
things they needed for the
afterlife. Examples include
the lifelike funeral
portraits, such as the
Squatting Scribe, and
several sculptures of
married couples.

The departments of
Greek, Roman and
Etruscan antiquities
contain a vast array of
fragments, among them
some exceptional
pieces. There is a
geometric head from
the Cyclades (2700
BC) and an elegant
swan-necked bowl
hammered out of a
gold sheet (2500 BC).
The two most famous
Greek marble statues,
the *Winged Victory of
Samothrace* and the
Venus de Milo,
both belong to the
Hellenistic
period (late 3rd to
2nd century BC),
when more
natural-looking
human forms were produced.

**Venus de Milo
(Greece, late 3rd–early
2nd century BC)**

The undisputed star of the
Etruscan collection is the
terracotta sarcophagus of a
married couple who look as
though they are attending an
eternal banquet, while the
highlight of the Roman section
is a 2nd-century
bronze head of
the Emperor
Hadrian.

***Squatting Scribe* (about 2500 BC), a lifelike
Egyptian funeral sculpture**

OBJETS D'ART

T HE CATCH-ALL term *objets
d'art* (art objects) covers a
vast range of items: jewelry,
furniture, clocks, watches,
sundials, tapestries, miniatures,
silver and glassware, cutlery,
Byzantine and Parisian carved
ivory, Limoges enamels,
porcelain, French and
Italian stoneware, rugs,
snuffboxes, scientific
instruments and
armor. The Louvre
has well over 8,000
pieces, from many
ages and regions.

Many of these
precious objects came
from the Abbey of
St-Denis, where the
kings of France were
crowned. The treasures
include a serpentine
stone plate from the 1st
century AD with a 9th-
century border of gold
and precious stones; a
porphyry vase that
Suger, Abbot of St-
Denis, had mounted in
gold in the shape of an
eagle; and the golden
scepter made for
King Charles V in
about 1380.

The French crown
jewels include the coronation
crowns of Louis XV and
Napoleon, scepters, swords
and other accessories of the
coronation ceremonies. On
display also is the Regent, one
of the purest diamonds in the
world, which Louis XV wore
at his coronation in 1722.

One whole room is taken
up with a series of tapestries
called the *Hunts of Maximilian,*
originally executed for
Emperor Charles V in 1530.
The large collection of French
furniture ranges from the 16th
to the 19th centuries and is
assembled by period, or in
rooms devoted to donations
by distinguished collectors.
On display are pieces
by such exceptionally
prominent furniture-
makers as André-
Charles Boulle, cabinet-
maker to Louis XIV,
who worked in the
Louvre in the late 17th
to mid-18th centuries.

Gilded bronze statues by a number of sculptors, decorating the central square of the Palais de Chaillot

CHAMPS-ELYSÉES AND INVALIDES

THE RIVER SEINE bisects this area, much of which is built on a monumental scale, from the imposing 18th-century buildings of Les Invalides to the Art Nouveau avenues surrounding the Eiffel Tower. Two of Paris's grandest avenues dominate the neighborhood to the north of the Seine: the Champs-Elysées has many chic hotels and shops but today is more downscale;

Ornate lamppost on Pont Alexandre III

while the more chic rue du Faubourg St-Honoré boasts the heavily guarded Palais de l'Elysée. The village of Chaillot was absorbed into the city in the 19th century, and many of its opulent Second Empire mansions are now embassies or company headquarters. Streets around the place du Trocadéro and the Palais de Chaillot are packed full of museums and elegant cafés.

SIGHTS AT A GLANCE

Historic Buildings and Streets
Avenue des Champs-Elysées ❷
Palais de l'Elysée ❸
No. 29 Avenue Rapp ⓰
Champ-de-Mars ⓱
Ecole Militaire ⓲
Hôtel des Invalides ⓴
Les Egouts ⓮

Museums and Galleries
Petit Palais ❹
Grand Palais ❺
Musée d'Art Moderne de la Ville de Paris ❼
Musée de la Mode et du Costume Palais Galliera ❽
Musée National des Arts Asiatiques Guimet ❾
Musée National d'Ennery ❿
Musée Dapper ⓫
Palais de Chaillot ⓭
Musée de l'Armée ㉑
Musée Rodin ㉔
Musée Maillol ㉖

Churches
St-Louis-des-Invalides ㉒
Dôme Church ㉓
Sainte-Clotilde ㉕

Monuments and Fountains
Arc de Triomphe ❶
Eiffel Tower p109 ⓯

Modern Architecture
UNESCO ⓳

Gardens
Jardins du Trocadéro ⓬

Bridges
Pont Alexandre III ❻

GETTING THERE
Metro stations in this area include Etoile, Trocadéro and Champs-Elysées. Bus routes 42 and 73 serve the Champs-Elysées; routes 87 and 69 serve avenue de Suffren and rue St-Dominique respectively.

KEY

▢	Street-by-Street map *pp102–3*
Ⓜ	Metro station
RER	RER station
▢	Batobus boarding point
P	Parking

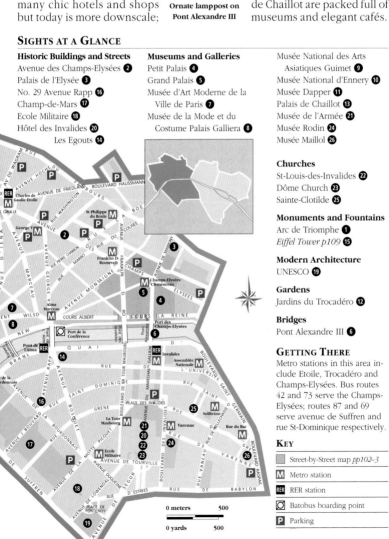

0 meters 500

0 yards 500

Street-by-Street: Champs-Elysées

T HE FORMAL GARDENS that line the Champs-Elysées from the place de la Concorde to the Rond-Point have changed little since they were laid out by the architect Jacques Hittorff in 1838. The gardens were used as the setting for the World's Fair of 1855, which included the Palais de l'Industrie, Paris's response to London's Crystal Palace. The Palais was later replaced by the Grand Palais and the Petit Palais, which was created as a showpiece of the Third Republic for the Universal Exhibition of 1900. They sit on either side of an impressive vista that stretches from the place Clémenceau across the elegant curve of the Pont Alexandre III, with its four strong anchoring columns, to the Invalides.

Théâtre du Rond Point, an original Champs-Elysées building, is home to the Marcel-Maréchal Company.

Metro Franklin D. Roosevelt

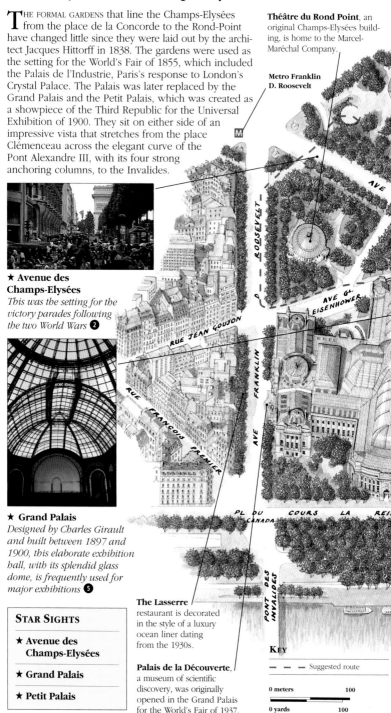

★ **Avenue des Champs-Elysées**
This was the setting for the victory parades following the two World Wars ❷

★ **Grand Palais**
Designed by Charles Girault and built between 1897 and 1900, this elaborate exhibition hall, with its splendid glass dome, is frequently used for major exhibitions ❺

The Lasserre restaurant is decorated in the style of a luxury ocean liner dating from the 1930s.

Palais de la Découverte, a museum of scientific discovery, was originally opened in the Grand Palais for the World's Fair of 1937.

STAR SIGHTS

★ Avenue des Champs-Elysées

★ Grand Palais

★ Petit Palais

KEY

– – – Suggested route

| 0 meters | | 100 |
| 0 yards | | 100 |

The Jardins des Champs-Elysées, with their fountains, flower beds and pleasure pavilions, have been a popular spot since the 19th century.

CHAMPS-
ELYSEES
AND
INVALIDES

Seine

LOCATOR MAP
*See Street Finder maps
2, 3, 6, 7*

Metro
Champs-
Elysées-
Clémenceau

To place
de la
Concorde

★ Petit Palais
The art collections of the city of Paris are housed here. They contain artifacts ranging from antique sculptures to landscape paintings by the Barbizon School ④

To the Invalides

Pont Alexandre III
This highly ornate, single-span structure symbolizes the optimism of the Belle Epoque at the turn of the century ⑥

The east façade of the Arc de Triomphe

Arc de Triomphe ①

Place Charles de Gaulle, 75008.
Map 2 D4. **M** *Charles de Gaulle-Etoile.* **C** *01 55 37 73 77.* ○ *Apr–Sep: 9:30am–11pm daily; Oct–Mar: 10am–10:30pm daily.* ● *public hols.* ○ 🖼 🚻

AFTER HIS greatest victory, the Battle of Austerlitz in 1805, Napoleon promised his men they would "go home beneath triumphal arches." The first stone of what was to become the world's most famous triumphal arch was laid the following year. But disruptions to architect Jean Chalgrin's plans, combined with the demise of Napoleonic power delayed its completion until 1836. Standing 50 m (164 ft) high, the Arc is encrusted with flamboyant reliefs, shields, and sculptures. The viewing platform offers fascinating views of the city.

On November 11, 1920, the body of the Unknown Soldier was placed beneath the arch to commemorate the dead of World War I, and the eternal flame is lit every evening.

High relief by J.P. Corot, celebrating the Triumph of Napoleon

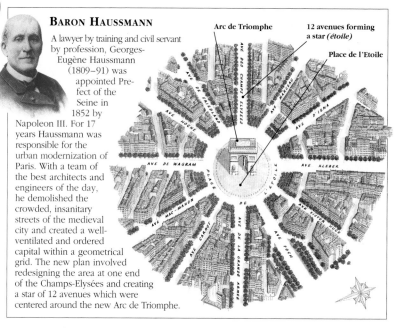

BARON HAUSSMANN

A lawyer by training and civil servant by profession, Georges-Eugène Haussmann (1809–91) was appointed Prefect of the Seine in 1852 by Napoleon III. For 17 years Haussmann was responsible for the urban modernization of Paris. With a team of the best architects and engineers of the day, he demolished the crowded, insanitary streets of the medieval city and created a well-ventilated and ordered capital within a geometrical grid. The new plan involved redesigning the area at one end of the Champs-Elysées and creating a star of 12 avenues which were centered around the new Arc de Triomphe.

Arc de Triomphe

12 avenues forming a star (*étoile*)

Place de l'Etoile

Avenue des Champs-Elysées ❷

75008. **Map** 3 A5. **M** *Charles de Gaulle-Etoile, George V, Franklin D. Roosevelt, Champs-Elysées-Clemenceau, Concorde.*

THE MAJESTIC avenue "of the Elysian Fields" (the name refers to a mythical Greek heaven for heroes), first laid out in the 1660s by the landscape designer André Le Nôtre, forms a 3km straight line from the huge Place de la Concorde to the Arc de Triomphe. The 19th-century saw it transformed from horseride into elegant boulevard. Today it's a crowded tourist trap with notorious traffic, but the Champs-Elysées keeps its style, its memories – and a special place in the French heart. National parades are held here, and the finish of the annual Tour de France cycle race is always in the Champs-Elysées, and above all, it is where Parisians instinctively go at times of great national celebration.

Palais de l'Elysée ❸

55 rue du Faubourg-St-Honoré 75008. **Map** 3 B5. **M** *St-Philippe-du-Roule.* ● *to the public.*

AMID SPLENDID gardens, the Elysée Palace was built in 1718 and has been the official residence of the President of the Republic since 1873. Several occupants left their mark. Louis XV's mistress, Madame de Pompadour, had the whole site enlarged. After the Revolution, it became a dance hall. In the 19th-century, it was home to Napoleon's

Elysée guard

sister Caroline Murat, and his wife Empress Josephine. The President's Apartments are today on the first floor.

Petit Palais ❹

Av Winston Churchill 75008. **Map** 7 B1. **C** *01 42 65 12 73.* **M** *Champs-Elysées-Clemenceau.* ● *for renovation until 2004.* ▨ ▸ *for exhibitions.* ▢ ▸

BUILT FOR the Universal Exhibition in 1900, to stage a major display of French art, this jewel of a building now houses the Musée des Beaux-Arts de la Ville de Paris. The architect, Charles Girault, arranged the palace around a semicircular

GRAND PALAIS

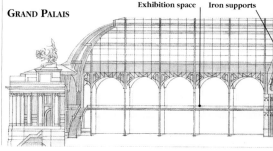

Exhibition space   Iron supports

Pont Alexandre III, built between 1896–1900 for the Universal Exhibition

courtyard and garden, similar in style to the Grand Palais. The exhibits, which were donated by private collectors, are divided into sections. These include the Dutuit Collection of medieval and Renaissance *objets d'art*, paintings and drawings; the Tuck Collection of 18th-century furniture and *objets d'art*; and the City of Paris collection, with work by such artists as Ingres, Delacroix and Courbet, and the landscape painters of the Barbizon School.

Grand Palais ➎

Porte A, Ave Eisenhower 75008. **Map** 7 A1. 🄲 01 44 13 17 30. Ⓜ *Champs-Elysées-Clemenceau.* ⭘ *for temporary exhibitions (phone to check).* 🈳 ⬧ 🅰 🅲 🄰 🄰 🄰
Palais de la Découverte: Ave Franklin D Roosevelt 75008 🄲 01 56 43 20 21. Ⓜ *Franklin D Roosevelt.* ⭘ *9:30am–6pm Tues–Sat, 10am–7pm Sun.* 🈳 🄰 🄰 Ⓦ *www.palais-decouverte.fr*

Ⓑuilt at the same time as the Petit Palais opposite, this glass-roofed palace has a fine Classical façade adorned with a riot of statuary and Art Nouveau ironwork. Bronze flying horses and chariots stand at the four corners. The Great Hall and glass cupola can be admired from inside during exhibitions and trade shows. On the west side of the building, and with its own separate entrance, the **Palais de la Découverte** is an imaginative, very popular child-orientated science museum.

Pont Alexandre III ➏

75008. **Map** 7 A1. Ⓜ *Champs-Elysées-Clemenceau.*

Ⓣhis is Paris's prettiest bridge, with exuberant Art Nouveau decoration of gilt and bronze lamps, cupids and cherubs, nymphs and winged horses at either end. It was built between 1896 and 1900 to commemorate the 1892 French-Russian alliance, and in time for the Universal Exhibition in 1900. Pont Alexandre III was named after Tsar Alexander III (father of Nicholas II), who laid the foundation stone in October 1896.

The style of the bridge re-flects that of the Grand Palais, to which it leads on the Right Bank. The construction of the bridge is a marvel of 19th-century engineering. It consists of a 6-meter-high (18 ft) single-span steel arch across the Seine. The design was subject to strict controls that prevented the bridge from obscuring the view of the Champs-Elysées or the Invalides, so today you can still enjoy the magnificent views from here.

Entrance to the Petit Palais

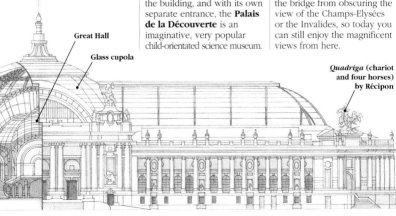

Great Hall

Glass cupola

Quadriga (chariot and four horses) by Récipon

Musée d'Art Moderne de la Ville de Paris ❼

Palais de Tokyo, 11 av du Président-Wilson 75116. **Map** 6 E1. ⬛ *01 53 67 40 00.* Ⓜ *Iéna.* ◯ *10am–5:30pm Tue–Sun.* ⬛ *Jan 1.* 🎫 ♿ 📷 ▯ 📷 ⬤ ⬛ *www.palaisdetokyo.com*

THIS MUSEUM covers trends in 20th-century art and is located in the east wing of the Palais de Tokyo. The Fauves and Cubists are well represented here. Highlights include Raoul Dufy's gigantic mural *The Spirit of Electricity*, (created for the 1937 World's Fair), and Matisse's *The Dance* (1932). Also exhibited here is a collection of Art Deco furniture from the period 1920–37.

Musée de la Mode et du Costume Palais Galliera ❽

10 av Pierre 1er de Serbie 75116. **Map** 6 D1. ⬛ *01 56 52 86 00.* Ⓜ *Iéna, Alma–Marceau.* ◯ *10am–6pm Tue–Sun, but check as only open for exhibitions.* ⬤ *public hols.* 🎫 ⬛ *www.paris-france.org/musees*

DEVOTED TO the evolution of fashion, this museum is housed in the Renaissance-style palace built for the Duchesse Maria de Ferrari Galliera in 1892. The collection includes more than 100,000 outfits and fashion accessories, from the 18th century to the present day. Donations have been made by such fashionable women as Baronne Hélène de Rothschild and Princess Grace of Monaco. Eminent couturiers such as Balmain and Balenciaga have donated their designs to the museum.

Because they are often extremely fragile, the fashion exhibits are displayed in rotation, usually in two major exhibitions each year. These shows can highlight a particular couturier's career or explore a single theme.

Trocadéro fountains in front of the Palais de Chaillot

Musée Dapper ⓫

35 bis rue Paul-Valéry 75016. ⬛ *01 45 00 01 50.* Ⓜ *Victor-Hugo.* ◯ *11am–7pm Wed–Sun.* 🎫 *(free Wed).*

NOT JUST a museum, but a world-class ethnographic research center, this is France's premier showcase of African art and culture. Located in an attractive building with an "African" garden, it is a treasure house of color and powerful, evocative work from the black nations. The focus is on pre-colonial folk arts, with sculpture, carvings and tribal work, but there is later art too. The highlight is tribal masks, with a dazzling, extraordinary array of richly carved religious, ritual and funerary masks, as well as theatrical ones used for comic, magical or symbolic performances.

Jardins du Trocadéro ⓬

75016. **Map** 6 D2. Ⓜ *Trocadéro.*

THESE BEAUTIFUL gardens cover 10ha (25 acres). Their centerpiece is a long, rectangular ornamental pool, bordered by stone and bronze-gilt statues, which looks spectacular at night when the fountains are illuminated. The statues include *Woman* by Georges Braque and *Horse* by Georges Lucien Guyot. On either side of the pool, the slopes of the Chaillot hill lead gently down to the Seine and the Pont d'Iéna. There is a freshwater aquarium in the northeast corner of the gardens, which are richly laid out with trees, walkways, small streams and bridges.

Palais de Chaillot ⓭

Place du Trocadéro 75016. **Map** 5 C2. Ⓜ *Trocadéro.* ◯ *9:45am–5:15pm Wed–Mon.* ⬤ *public hols.* **Cinémathèque Française** 📷 *01 56 26 01 01.* **Museums** ◯ *Wed–Mon.*

THE PALAIS, with its huge, curved colonnaded wings, each culminating in a vast pavilion, currently has two museums, a theater and a cinema with major changes underway for 2003. Designed in Neo-Classical style for the 1937 Paris Exhibition by Azéma, Louis-Auguste Boileau and Jacques Carlu, it is adorned with sculptures and bas-reliefs. On the walls of the pavilions are gold inscriptions which were written by the poet and essayist Paul Valéry. The square (*parvis*), between the two pavilions has bronze

Musée National des Arts Asiatiques Guimet ❾

6 place d'Iéna 75016. **Map** 6 D1. ☎ 01 56 52 53 00. Ⓜ Iéna. ◯ 10am–6pm Wed–Mon. 🈺 🄍 ♿ 🛍 Panthéon Bouddhique, 19 Av d'Iéna. ☎ 01 40 73 88 00. ⓦ www.museeguimet.fr

ONE OF THE WORLD'S leading museums of Asian art, the Guimet has the finest collection of Cambodian (Khmer) art in the West. It was originally set up in Lyon in 1879 by the industrialist and Orientalist Emile Guimet and moved to Paris in 1884. It includes an Asian research center.

Buddha head from Musée Guimet

Musée National d'Ennery ❿

59 avenue Foch 75016. **Map** 1 B5. ☎ 01 45 53 57 96. Ⓜ Porte Dauphine. ◯ for refurbishment until further notice.

THIS MANSION, which dates from the Second Empire period, contains two highly personal museums of precious *objets d'art*. Adolphe d'Ennery, the 19th-century dramatist and collector of Far Eastern art, assembled this array of Chinese and Japanese figures, ceramic boxes, ornaments and furniture, dating from the 17th to the 19th century.

PALAIS DE CHAILLOT

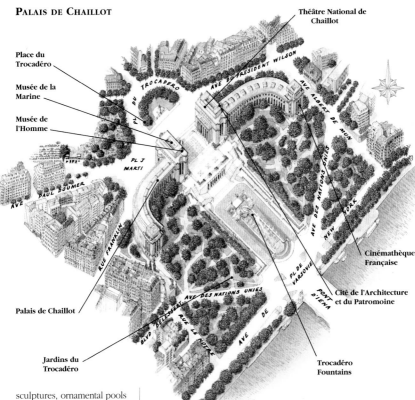

Théâtre National de Chaillot

Place du Trocadéro

Musée de la Marine

Musée de l'Homme

PL J MARTI

PL DU TROCADÉRO

AVE DU PRÉSIDENT WILSON

AVE ALBERT DE MUN

AVE PAUL DOUMER

RUE FRANKLIN

AVE DES NATIONS UNIES

NEW YORK

Cinémathèque Française

Cité de l'Architecture et du Patromoine

PL DE VARSOVIE

PONT D'IÉNA

AVE DES NATIONS UNIES

BLVD DELESSERT

RUE LE NOTRE

AVE DE

Palais de Chaillot

Jardins du Trocadéro

Trocadéro Fountains

sculptures, ornamental pools and fountains. Steps lead down from the terrace to the Théâtre National de Chaillot.

The basement of the palace institute, the **Cinémathèque Française**, founded by Henri Langlois in 1936, screens a schedule of film classics.

The **Musée de l'Homme** in the west wing traces human evolution through a series of anthropological, archaeological and ethnological displays. Highlights include an Incan mummy and a rich African section, with frescoes from the Sahara, magical figures and musical instruments. Next door is the **Musée de la Marine**, devoted to French naval history.

Les Egouts ⑭

In front of 93 quai d'Orsay 75007.
Map 6 F2. ☎ 01 53 68 27 81 (in English). Ⓜ Alma Marceau. ⭕ 11am–4pm (5pm in summer) Sat–Wed. ⭕ last 3 wks Jan. ♿ ✔ ⬛

O NE OF BARON HAUSSMANN'S finest achievements, the majority of Paris's sewers (égouts) date from the Second Empire. If laid end to end the 2,100 km (1,300 miles) of sewers would stretch from Paris to Istanbul. They are a popular tourist attraction. All tours have been limited to a small area around the quai d'Orsay entrance and are now on foot. A sewer museum has been established here where visitors can discover the mysteries of underground Paris. There are also displays showing how the machinery used in the sewers has changed over the years.

Eiffel Tower ⑮

See p109.

No. 29 Avenue Rapp ⑯

75005. **Map** 6 E2. Ⓜ Pont-de-l'Alma.

A PRIME EXAMPLE of Art Nouveau architecture, No. 29 avenue Rapp won its designer, Jules Lavirotte, first prize at the Concours des

Original Art Nouveau doorway at No. 29 avenue Rapp

Façades de la Ville de Paris in 1901. Its ceramics and brickwork are decorated with animal and flower motifs intermingling with female figures. These are super-imposed on a multicolored sandstone base to produce a façade that is deliberately erotic and was certainly subversive in its day. Also worth visiting nearby is Lavirotte's building, complete with watchtower, which can be found in the square Rapp.

Champ-de-Mars ⑰

75007. **Map** 6 E3. Ⓜ Ecole-Militaire. ⒭ Champ-de-Mars–Tour-Eiffel.

T HE VAST GARDENS stretching from the Eiffel Tower to the Ecole Militaire (Military School) were originally a parade ground for young officer cadets. The area has since been used for horse racing, hot-air ballooning and mass ceremonies to celebrate the anniversary of the Revolution on July 14. The first ceremony was held in 1790, in the presence of a glum, captive, Louis XVI.
    Mammoth exhibitions were held here in the late 19th century, among them the 1889 World's Fair, for which the Eiffel Tower was erected.

A Paris balloon ascent

Ecole Militaire ⑱

1 place Joffre 75007. **Map** 6 F4. Ⓜ Ecole-Militaire. **Visits** by special permission only – contact the Commandant in writing.

T HE ROYAL MILITARY academy of Louis XV was founded in 1751 to educate 500 sons of impoverished officers. Louis XV and Madame de Pompadour commissioned architect Jacques-Ange Gabriel to design a building that would rival Louis XVI's Hôtel des Invalides. Financing the building became a problem, so a lottery was authorized and a tax was raised on playing cards.

ETABLISSEMENT DE L'ECOLE MILITAIRE.

A 1751 engraving showing the planning of the Ecole Militaire

One of the main features is the central pavilion – a magnificent example of the French Classical style, with ten Corinthian columns and a quadrangular dome. Four figures adorn the entablature frieze, symbolizing France, Victory, Force and Peace. An early cadet at the academy was Napoleon, whose graduation report stated that "he could go far if the circum-stances are right."

UNESCO ⑲

7 place de Fontenoy 75007. **Map** 6 F5. ☎ 01 45 68 10 60 (in English). Ⓜ Ségur, Cambronne. ⭕ 9:30am–12:30pm, 2:30–5pm Mon–Fri. ⭕ public hols & during conference sessions. ♿ ✔ 🍴 ⬛

T HIS IS the headquarters of the United Nations Educational, Scientific and Cultural Organization (UNESCO). The aim of the organization is to contribute to international peace and security through education, science and culture.
    UNESCO is a treasure trove of modern art, including an enormous mural by Picasso, ceramics by Joan Miró and sculptures by Henry Moore, and the calm Japanese garden by Nogushi. Exhibitions and movies are also held here.

Eiffel Tower ⑮

BUILT FOR the Universal Exhibition of 1889, and to commemorate the centennial of the Revolution, the 324-m (1,063-ft) Eiffel Tower (Tour Eiffel) was meant to be a temporary addition to Paris's skyline. Designed by Gustave Eiffel, it was fiercely decried by 19th-century aesthetes. It stood as the world's tallest building until 1931, when New York's Empire State Building was completed.

Eiffel Tower seen from the Trocadéro

VISITORS' CHECKLIST

Champ-de-Mars–Tour Eiffel 75007. **Map** 6 D3. **C** 01 44 11 23 11. **M** Bir Hakeim. 🚌 42, 69, 82, 87, to Champ-de-Mars. **RER** Champ-de-Mars. **O** Tour Eiffel. **O** Sep–Jun: 9:30am–11pm; Jul & Aug: 9am–mid-night. 🎫 📷 **11** 🍴 📷 **w** www.tour-eiffel.fr

DARING FEATS

The tower has always inspired crazy stunts. In 1912, Reichelt, a Parisian tailor, attempted to fly from the parapet with only a cape for wings. He plunged to his death in front of a large crowd.

Stuntman Reichelt

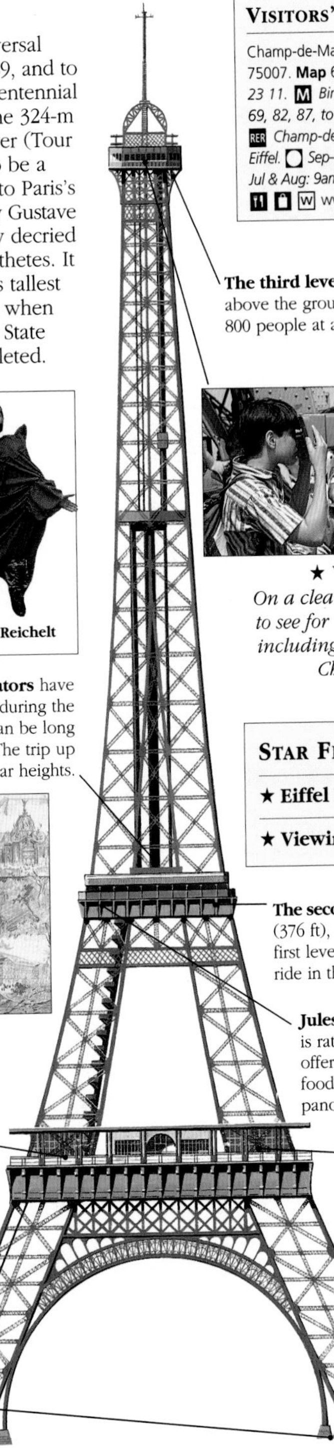

The third level, 276 m (905 ft) above the ground, can hold 800 people at a time.

★ Viewing Gallery
On a clear day it is possible to see for 72 km (45 miles), including a distant view of Chartres Cathedral.

The double-decker elevators have a limited capacity, and during the tourist season there can be long waits for the elevators. The trip up is not for those who fear heights.

STAR FEATURES

★ Eiffel Bust

★ Viewing Gallery

Cinémax
This small audiovisual museum shows historical film footage of the tower.

The second level is at 115 m (376 ft), 359 steps above the first level, or a few minutes ride in the elevator.

Jules Verne restaurant is rated highly in Paris, offering not only superb food, but a breathtaking panoramic view.

★ Eiffel Bust
The achievement of Eiffel (1832–1923) was honored by Antoine Bourdelle, who placed this bust under the tower in 1929.

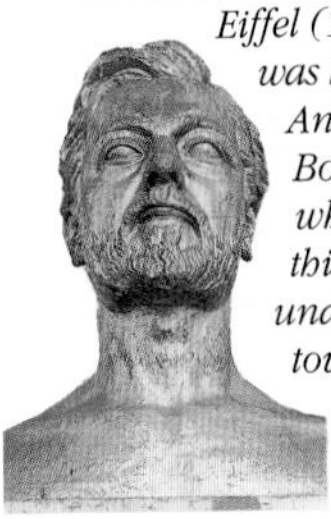

The first level, is 57 m (187 ft) high. Take the elevator or walk up 360 steps. There's a post office here.

LES INVALIDES

Musée de l'Armée   Hôtel des Invalides   Cour d'Honneur

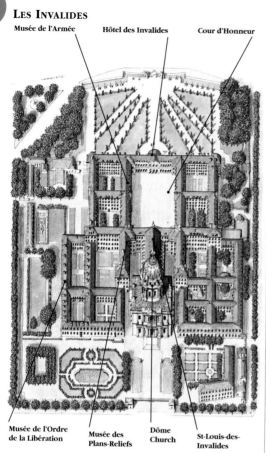

Musée de l'Ordre
de la Libération   Musée des
Plans-Reliefs   Dôme
Church   St-Louis-des-
Invalides

Hôtel des Invalides ⑳

75007. **Map** 7 A3. 🄲 *01 44 42 37 70.*
Ⓜ *Latour-Maubourg, Invalides,
Varenne.* ⏰ *10am–6pm (5pm winter)
daily.* ⬤ *Jan 1, May 1, Nov 1, Dec 25.*

THIS IMPOSING building, from
which the area takes its
name, was commissioned by
Louis XIV in 1670 for his
wounded and homeless
veterans, many of whom had
become beggars. Designed
by Libéral Bruand, it was
completed in 1676 by Jules
Hardouin-Mansart. He later
incorporated the Dôme Church,
with its glittering golden roof,
which was built as Louis XIV's
private chapel. Nearly 6,000
soldiers once lived here. Today
there are fewer than 100.
The harmonious Classical

façade is one of the most
impressive sights in Paris, a
masterpiece of French 17th-
century architecture. The entire
ensemble is vast, brimming
with architectural and historical
splendor, with its tree-lined
esplanade stretching to the
Seine. The building houses
the Musée de l'Armée and
the Musée de l'Ordre de la
Libération. This was set up
to honor feats of heroism
during World War II under
the leadership of Charles de
Gaulle. The story is told using

documents, photographs and
mementos. The Musée des
Plans-Reliefs in the right wing
houses a large collection of
detailed military models of
French forts and fortified
towns considered top secret
until the 1950s. Bruand's Cour
d'Honneur is still used for
military parades.

Musée de l'Armée ㉑

Hôtel des Invalides 75007. **Map** 7 A3.
🄲 *01 44 42 37 72.* Ⓜ *Varenne,
Latour-Maubourg, Invalides.* ⏰ *10am–
6pm (5pm winter) daily.* ⬤ *some
public hols.* 🎨 📷 ♿ 🎁 🛒 📖 ⓘ

THIS IS ONE of the most
comprehensive museums
of military history in the world.
It is housed in two galleries,
situated on either side of the
magnificent courtyard of the
Hôtel des Invalides and in the
newly-opened "Priests' Wing"
with the World War II galleries.
Among the vast collection
is an exhibit recalling the
victories and defeats of France
through history, dedicated
mainly to the Napoleonic
era. Uniforms, weapons and
models are on display, as well
as the emperor's death mask
and stuffed horse, Vizier. Other
exhibits include François I's
ivory hunting horns, Oriental
arms from China, Japan and
Turkey, and a model of the
1944 Normandy landing.

St-Louis-des-Invalides ㉑

Hôtel des Invalides 75007. **Map** 7 A3.
Ⓜ *Varenne, Latour-Maubourg,
Invalides.* 🄲 *01 44 42 37 65.*
⏰ *10am–6pm (5pm winter) daily.*

ALSO KNOWN AS the "soldiers'
church," this is the chapel
of the Hôtel des Invalides. It
was built from 1679 to 1708

The façade of the Musée de l'Armée

**Altar of St-Louis-des-Invalides
with banners seized in battle**

by Jules Hardouin-Mansart,
according to Bruand's design.
The stark, Classical interior is
well-proportioned, designed
in the shape of a Greek cross.

There is a fine 17th-century
organ, built by Alexandre
Thierry, on which the first
performance of Berlioz's
Requiem was given on
December 5 1837. More than
200 musicians and choristers
participated in the concert.

Dôme Church ㉓

Hôtel des Invalides, 129 rue de
Grenelle 75007. **Map** 7 A3. 01 44
42 37 72. Latour-Maubourg,
Varenne, Invalides. 28, 49, 63, 69,
82, 83, 87, 92 to Les Invalides. RER
Invalides. Tour Eiffel. Oct–Mar:
10am–5pm; Apr–Sep: 10am–6pm
daily. Jan 1, May 1, Jun 17, Nov 1,
Dec 25. restr.

JULES HARDOUIN-MANSART was
asked in 1676 by the Sun
King, Louis XIV, to build the
Dôme Church to complement
the existing buildings of the
Invalides military refuge,
designed by Libéral Bruand,
and to reflect the splendor of
his reign. The Dôme was to be
reserved for the exclusive use
of the Sun King and as the
location of royal tombs.

The resulting masterpiece
is one of the greatest examples
of 17th-century French
architecture, the period
known as the *grand siècle*.
After Louis XIV's death, plans
to bury the royal family in the

church were abandoned; it
became a monument to
Bourbon glory.

The main attraction has to be
the tomb of Napoleon; 20
years after his death on the
island of St. Helena, his body
was returned to France on
the authority of Louis-Philippe.
His remains were installed in
the crypt, encased in six
coffins within an enormous
red porphyry sarcophagus,
resting on a pedestal of green
granite. His son and brothers,
Jerôme and Joseph, are also
entombed in the crypt.

Marshal Foch, commander of
the Allied troops during World
War I, is buried here. There is
also a memorial to Sébastien
le Prestre de Vauban, Louis
XIV's military architect.

**Dôme Church with cupola, first
gilded in 1715**

Musée Rodin ㉔

77 rue de Varenne 75007. **Map** 7 B3.
01 47 05 01 34. Varenne.
9:30am–5:45pm (4:45pm winter) Tue
–Sun; gdn 1 hr later. Jan 1, May
1, Dec 25. restricted.

AUGUSTE RODIN (1840–1917),
widely regarded as
one of the greatest French
sculptors, lived and
worked in the Hôtel
Biron, an elegant 18th-
century mansion, from
1908 until his death.
In return for a state-
owned flat and studio,
Rodin left his work to
the nation, and it is
now exhibited
here. Some of his
most celebrated

sculptures are on display in
the garden: *The Burghers of
Calais, The Thinker, The Gates
of Hell (see p116)* and *Balzac*.

The indoor exhibits are
arranged in chronological
order, spanning Rodin's
entire career. Highlights of
the collection include *The
Kiss* and *Eve*.

Sainte-Clotilde ㉕

12 rue Martignac 75007. **Map** 7 B3.
01 44 18 62 60. Solférino,
Varenne, Invalides. 9am–7pm
daily. non-relig pub hols. **Concerts**

DESIGNED BY the German-
born architect Franz
Christian Gau and built in
1846–56, this Neo-Gothic
church was inspired by the
mid-19th-century enthusiasm
for the Middle Ages, made
fashionable by such writers as
Victor Hugo.

The interior decoration
includes wall paintings by
James Pradier and stained-
glass windows with scenes
relating to the patron saint of
the church. The composer
César Franck was organist
here from 1858 to 1890.

Musée Maillol ㉖

61 rue de Grenelle 75007. **Map** 7 C4.
01 42 22 59 58. rue du Bac,
Sèvres-Babylone. 11am–6pm
Wed–Mon. publ. hols.

IT WAS Dina Vierny, former
model and muse to Aristide
Maillol, who created this museum, once lived in by novelist
Alfred de Musset. Maillol's
work is here in all its forms:
drawings, engravings, paintings,
sculpture and
decorative
objects. Also
displayed is
Dina Vierny's
private collec-
tion, which
includes naïve
art and works by
Matisse, Dufy,
Picasso and Rodin.
Allegorical figures of
the city of Paris and
the four seasons adorn
Bouchardon's fountain
in front of the house.

**Rodin's *The Thinker*
in museum garden**

THE LEFT BANK

THE LEFT BANK has long been associated with poets, philosophers, artists and radical thinkers of all kinds. It still has its share of bohemian street life and pavement cafés, but the smart set has moved in, patronizing Yves St-Laurent and the exclusive interior design shops in rue Jacob.

The Latin Quarter is the ancient area lying between the Seine and Luxembourg Gardens, and is today filled with bookstores, art galleries and cafés. The boulevard St-Michel, bordering the Latin quarter and St-Germain-des-Prés, has slowly given way to commerce, and is full of

Clock in the Musée d'Orsay

fast-food places and cheap shops. The surrounding maze of narrow, cobbled streets has retained its character, with ethnic shops and avant-garde theaters dominated by the façade of the Sorbonne, France's first university, built in 1253.

Many Parisians dream of living near the Luxembourg Gardens, a quiet area with charming old streets, gateways and elaborate gardens full of paths, lawns and tree-lined avenues. Students come here to chat, and on warm days, old men still meet underneath the chestnut trees to play chess or the traditional French game of *boules*.

SIGHTS AT A GLANCE

Churches
Panthéon ❸
St-Etienne-du-Mont ❷
St-Germain-des-Prés ❺
St-Julien-le-Pauvre ❿
St-Séverin ❾

St-Sulpice ⓯
Val-de-Grâce ⓱

Museums and Galleries
Musée de Cluny ❽
Musée Eugène Delacroix ❻
Musée d'Orsay pp116–17 ❶

Fountains
Fontaine de l'Observatoire ⓰

Historic Buildings and Streets
Boulevard St-Germain ❷
Ecole Nationale Supérieure des Beaux Arts ❹
Palais du Luxembourg ⓮
Quai Voltaire ❸
Rue de l'Odéon ❼
La Sorbonne ⓫

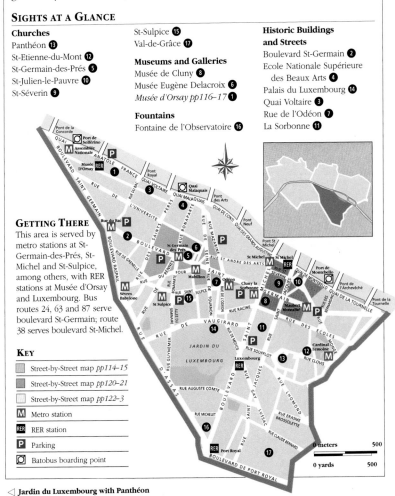

GETTING THERE
This area is served by metro stations at St-Germain-des-Prés, St-Michel and St-Sulpice, among others, with RER stations at Musée d'Orsay and Luxembourg. Bus routes 24, 63 and 87 serve boulevard St-Germain; route 38 serves boulevard St-Michel.

KEY

	Street-by-Street map *pp114–15*
	Street-by-Street map *pp120–21*
	Street-by-Street map *pp122–3*
M	Metro station
RER	RER station
P	Parking
	Batobus boarding point

◁ **Jardin du Luxembourg with Panthéon**

Street-by-Street: St-Germain-des-Prés

Organ grinder in St-Germain

AFTER WORLD WAR II, St-Germain des-Prés became synonymous with intellectual life centered on bars and cafés. Philosophers, writers, actors and musicians mingled in the cellar nightspots and brasseries, where existentialist philosophy co-existed with American jazz.

The area is now more upscale than in the heyday of Jean-Paul Sartre and Simone de Beauvoir, the enigmatic singer Juliette Greco and the New Wave filmmakers. However, the writers are still around, enjoying the pleasures of sitting in Les Deux Magots, Café de Flore and other haunts. The 17th-century buildings have survived, but signs of change are evident in the affluent shops dealing in antiques, books and fashion.

Les Deux Magots became a focus of bohemian and literary activity in the 1920s.

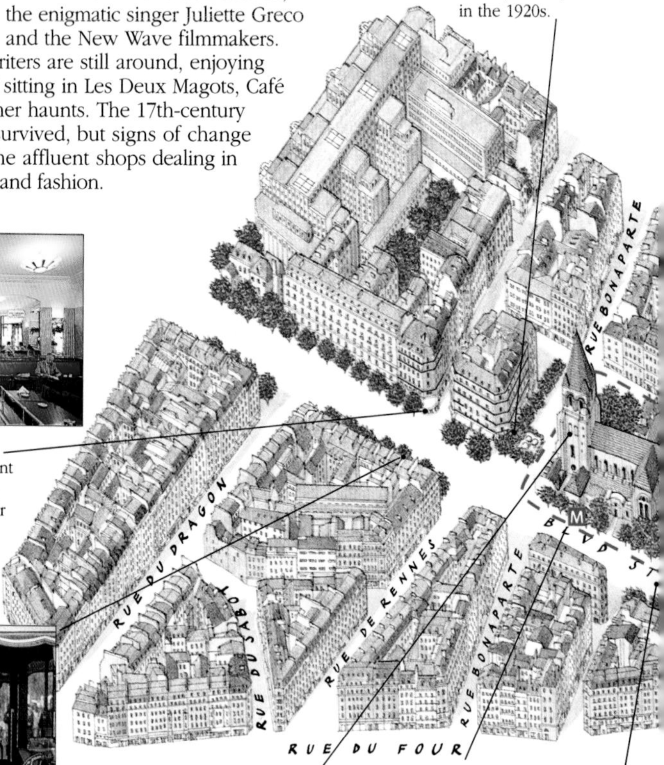

Café de Flore, the former favorite haunt of Jean-Paul Sartre, Simone de Beauvoir and other French intellectuals, still has a classic Art Deco interior.

RUE BONAPARTE

RUE DU DRAGON

RUE DU SABOT

RUE DE RENNES

RUE BONAPARTE

BD ST

M

RUE DU FOUR

Metro St-Germain-des-Prés

Brasserie Lipp, decorated with colorful ceramics, is a renowned brasserie frequented by politicians.

★ **St-Germain-des-Prés**
The philosopher René Descartes is among the notables buried here in Paris's oldest church **5**

★ **Boulevard St-Germain**
Café terraces, boutiques, movies, restaurants and bookstores characterize the central section of the Left Bank's main street **2**

STAR SIGHTS

★ St-Germain-des-Prés

★ Boulevard St-Germain

★ Musée Delacroix

KEY

━ ━ ━ Suggested route

LOCATOR MAP
See Street Finder maps 7, 8

★ Musée Delacroix
The home of the Romantic painter Eugène Delacroix (1798–1863) is now a museum devoted to his art **6**

Palais Abbatial was the residence of abbots from 1586 till the 1789 Revolution.

Rue de Buci was for centuries an important street and the site of some Real Tennis courts. It now holds a lively market.

Metro Mabillon

0 meters　　　　100

0 yards　　　　100

Musée d'Orsay ❶

See pp116–17.

Boulevard St-Germain ❷

75006, 75007. **Map** 8 D4.
Ⓜ Solférino, Rue du Bac, St-Germain-des-Prés, Mabillon, Odéon.

THE LEFT BANK'S most celebrated thoroughfare curves across three districts from the Ile St-Louis to the Pont de la Concorde. The architecture is homogeneous because the boulevard was another of Baron Hauss-mann's bold strokes of 19th-century urban planning, but it encompasses a wide range of different lifestyles, from bohemian to bourgeois.

Starting from the east, it passes Musée de Cluny and the Sorbonne. It is most lively from boulevard St-Michel to St-Germain-des-Prés, with its café culture.

Quai Voltaire ❸

75006, 75007. **Map** 8 D3.
Ⓜ Rue du Bac.

THE QUAI VOLTAIRE is now home to some of the most important antiques dealers in Paris. Many famous people have lived in the attractive 18th-century houses, among them Voltaire at No. 27 and Richard Wagner, Jean Sibelius and Oscar Wilde at No. 19.

Plaque marking the house in quai Voltaire where Voltaire died in 1778

Musée d'Orsay ❶

IN 1986, 47 YEARS AFTER it had closed as a mainline railroad station, Victor Laloux's superb turn-of-the-century building reopened as the Musée d'Orsay. Originally built as the Orléans railroad terminus in the heart of Paris, it narrowly avoided demolition in the 1970s. During its conversion to a museum, much of the original architecture was retained. The new museum presents the rich diversity of visual arts from 1848 to 1914 and explains the social, political and technological context in which they were created. Most of the exhibits are paintings and sculptures, but there are also displays of furniture, the decorative arts and the newspaper and motion picture industries.

Young Dancer of Fourteen (1881) by Edgar Dégas

The Gates of Hell *(1880–1917)*
Rodin included figures that he had already created, such as The Thinker *and* The Kiss, *in this famous gateway.*

Dancing at the Moulin de la Galette *(1876)*
To capture the light filtering through the trees, Renoir painted this colorful picture outdoors.

The Dance *(1867–8)*
Carpeaux's dynamic sculpture caused a scandal when it was first unveiled in 1869.

KEY TO FLOORPLAN

☐ Architecture & Decorative Arts	☐ Naturalism and Symbolism
☐ Sculpture	☐ Art Nouveau
☐ Painting before 1870	☐ Temporary exhibitions
☐ Impressionism	☐ Nonexhibition space
☐ Neo-Impressionism	

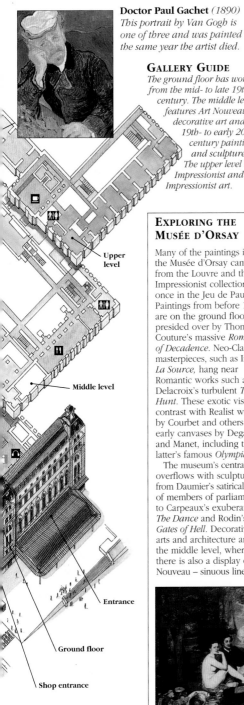

Doctor Paul Gachet *(1890)*
*This portrait by Van Gogh is
one of three and was painted
the same year the artist died.*

GALLERY GUIDE

*The ground floor has works
from the mid- to late 19th
century. The middle level
features Art Nouveau
decorative art and late
19th- to early 20th-
century paintings
and sculptures.
The upper level has
Impressionist and Neo-
Impressionist art.*

Upper level

Middle level

Entrance

Ground floor

Shop entrance

VISITORS' CHECKLIST

1 rue de Bellechasse, 75007.
Map 8 D2. 📞 *01 40 49 48 14.*
Ⓜ️ Solférino. 🚌 *24, 68, 69, 84
to Quai A. France; 73 to Rue de
la Légion d'Honneur; 63, 83, 84,
94 to Bd St-Germain.*
RER & ⏣ *Musée d'Orsay.*
🅿️ *Quai A.France.* ⏰ *Jun–Sep:
9am– 6pm Tue –Sun (9:45pm
Thu); Oct– May: 10am–6pm Tue–
Sat (9:45pm Thu), 9am–6pm
Sun.* ● *Jan 1, May 1, Dec 25.*
📷 🅞 ♿ 🎁 🍴 🎭 **Concerts**
🆆 *www.musee-orsay.fr*

EXPLORING THE MUSÉE D'ORSAY

Many of the paintings in
the Musée d'Orsay came
from the Louvre and the
Impressionist collection
once in the Jeu de Paume.
Paintings from before 1870
are on the ground floor,
presided over by Thomas
Couture's massive *Romans
of Decadence*. Neo-Classical
masterpieces, such as Ingres'
La Source, hang near
Romantic works such as
Delacroix's turbulent *Tiger
Hunt*. These exotic visions
contrast with Realist works
by Courbet and others and
early canvases by Degas
and Manet, including the
latter's famous *Olympia*.
    The museum's central aisle
overflows with sculpture,
from Daumier's satirical busts
of members of parliament
to Carpeaux's exuberant
The Dance and Rodin's *The
Gates of Hell*. Decorative
arts and architecture are on
the middle level, where
there is also a display of Art
Nouveau – sinuous lines

Blue Waterlilies *(1919)*
by Claude Monet

characterize Lalique's
jewelry and glassware and
the designs of Hector
Guimard, who produced
the characteristic curved
entrances of the Paris metro.
    Among the many high-
lights of the Impressionist
rooms on the upper level
are Monet's *Rouen Cathedral*
series (*see p257*) and Renoir's
joyful *Moulin de la Galette*.
The Post-Impressionist
collection includes the *Eglise
d'Auvers* by Van Gogh;
works by Cézanne; Seurat's
pointillist compositions such
as *Le Cirque*; Gauguin's
highly-colored Symbolist
works; Toulouse-Lautrec's
depictions
of Parisian
women and
nightlife; and
Rousseau's
charmingly
naive dream
world. Among
the highlights
of the post-
1900 display
is Matisse's
*Luxe, Calme
et Volupté*.

Le Déjeuner sur l'Herbe (1863) by Edouard Manet

The façade of the Ecole Nationale Supérieure des Beaux Arts

Ecole Nationale Supérieure des Beaux Arts ❹

14 rue Bonaparte 75006. **Map** 8 E3.
[C] 01 47 03 50 00. [M] St-Germain-des-Prés. ⬤ groups only (01 47 03 52 15 to book). 📷 ♿ **Library**

Tᴴᴇ ᴍᴀɪɴ ꜰʀᴇɴᴄʜ school of fine arts has an enviable position at the corner of the rue Bonaparte and the riverside quai Malaquais. It is housed in several buildings, the most imposing being the 19th-century Palais des Etudes. A host of budding French and foreign painters and architects have crossed the large courtyard, which contains a 17th-century chapel, to study in the ateliers of the school. Young American architects, in particular, have come here to study over the past century.

St-Germain-des-Prés ❺

3 place St-Germain-des-Prés 75006. **Map** 8 E4. [C] 01 43 25 41 71. [M] St-Germain-des-Prés. ⬤ 8am–7pm daily. **Concerts**

Tʜɪꜱ ɪꜱ ᴛʜᴇ ᴏʟᴅᴇꜱᴛ ᴄʜᴜʀᴄʜ in Paris, originating in 542 as a basilica to house holy relics. It became an immensely powerful Benedictine abbey, rebuilt in the 11th century, but most of it was destroyed by fire in 1794. Major restoration took place in the 19th century. One of the three original towers survives, housing one of the oldest belfries in France. The interior of the church is an interesting mix of architectural styles, with 6th-century marble columns, Gothic vaulting and Romanesque arches. Famous tombs include that of 17th-century philosopher René Descartes.

Musée Eugène Delacroix ❻

6 rue de Fürstenberg 75006. **Map** 8 E4. [C] 01 44 41 86 50. [M] St-Germain-des-Prés. ⬤ 9:30am–5pm Wed–Mon. 📷 ♿ [W] www.musee-delacroix.fr

Tʜᴇ ʟᴇᴀᴅɪɴɢ nonconformist Romantic painter Eugène Delacroix lived and worked here from 1857 till his death in 1863. Here, he painted *The Entombment of Christ* and *The Way to Calvary* (which now hang in the museum). He also created superb murals for the Chapel of the Holy Angels in the nearby St-Sulpice church.

The apartment and garden studio has a portrait of Georges Sand, Delacroix self-portraits and sketches. There are also temporary exhibitions.

Jacob Wrestling with the Angel by Delacroix, in St-Sulpice *(see p123)*

Rue de l'Odéon ❼

75006. **Map** 8 F5. [M] Odéon.

Oᴘᴇɴᴇᴅ ɪɴ 1779 to improve access to the Odéon theater, this was the first street in Paris to have pavements with gutters, and it still has many 18th-century houses.

Sylvia Beach's bookstore, the original Shakespeare & Company, stood at No. 12 from 1921 to 1940. It was a magnet for writers like James Joyce, Ezra Pound and Hemingway.

Musée National du Moyen Age ❽

6 pl Paul-Painlevé. **Map** 9 A5. [C] 01 53 73 78 00. [M] St-Michel, Odéon, Cluny. [RER] St-Michel. ⬤ 9:15am– 5:45pm Wed–Mon. 📷 ♿ **Concerts** [W] www.musee-moyenage.fr

Tʜᴇ ᴍᴜꜱᴇᴜᴍ is a unique combination of Gallo-Roman ruins, incorporated

Stone heads of the Kings of Judah carved around 1220

St-Séverin ❾

1 rue-des-Prêtres-St-Séverin 75005. **Map** 9 A4. [C] 01 42 34 93 50. [M] St-Michel. ⬤ 11am–7:30pm Mon–Fri, 11am–7:40pm Sat, 9am–8:30pm Sun.

Sᴛ-ꜱᴇᴠᴇʀɪɴ, one of the most beautiful churches in Paris, is named after a 6th-century hermit. It is a perfect example of the Flamboyant Gothic style. Construction finished in the early 16th century and included a remarkable double aisle encircling the chancel. In the garden stands the church's medieval gable-roofed charnel house.

Gargoyles adorning the gables of the Flamboyant Gothic St-Séverin

The School woodcarving (English, early 16th century)

LADY WITH THE UNICORN TAPESTRIES

These six outstanding tapestries are fine examples of the *millefleurs* style. Developed in the 15th and early 16th centuries, the style is noted for its graceful depiction of animals and people and its fresh and harmonious colors.

The poetic elegance of a unicorn on the sixth tapestry

into a medieval mansion (in newly-created medieval gardens), and one of the world's finest collections of medieval art and crafts. Its name comes from Pierre de Chalus, Abbot of Cluny, who bought the ruins in 1330. The present building dates from 1485–98.

Among the star exhibits are the tapestries, remarkable for their quality, age and state of preservation. The highlight of the sculpture section is the Gallery of the Kings, while one of Cluny's most precious items, the Golden Rose of Basel from 1330, is found in the collection of jewelry and metalwork. Other parts of the collection include stained glass, woodcarvings, Books of Hours and enamelwork.

St-Julien-le-Pauvre ❿

1 rue St-Julien-le-Pauvre 75005. **Map 9 A4.** ☎ 01 43 29 09 09. Ⓜ *St-Michel.* Ⓡ *St-Michel.* ⏱ *9am–1pm, 3pm–6:30pm daily.* **Concerts**

THE CHURCH is one of the oldest in Paris, dating from between 1165 and 1220. The university held its official meetings in the church until 1524, when a student protest created so much damage that university meetings were barred from the church by parliament. It has belonged to the Melchite sect of the Greek Orthodox Church since 1889 and is now the setting for classical and religious concerts.

La Sorbonne ⓫

47 rue des Ecoles 75005. **Map 9 A5.** ☎ 01 40 46 22 11. Ⓜ *Cluny-La Sorbonne, Maubert-Mutualité.* 🎟 *only by appt. Write to Service des Visites.*

THE SORBONNE, seat of the University of Paris until 1969, was established in 1253 by Robert de Sorbon, confessor to Louis IX, for 16 poor scholars to study theology. From these modest origins,

the college became the center of scholastic theology. In 1469, three printing machines were brought from Mainz, and the first printing house in France was founded. The college's opposition to liberal 18th-century philosophical ideas led to its suppression during the Revolution. It was re-established by Napoleon in 1806, and the 17th-century buildings replaced. In 1969, the Sorbonne split into 13 separate universities, but the building still holds some lectures.

St-Etienne-du-Mont ⓬

Place Ste-Geneviève 75005. **Map 13 A1.** ☎ 01 43 54 11 79. Ⓜ *Cardinal Lemoine.* ⏱ *8am–7:30pm Mon–Fri, 8am–noon, 2–7:30pm Sat; 9am–noon, 2:30–7:30pm Sun.* ● *Mon in Jul–Aug.* 📷 🚻

THIS REMARKABLE church houses the shrine of Saint Geneviève, patron saint of Paris, and the remains of the great literary figures Racine and Pascal. Some parts are Gothic while others date from the Renaissance, including the rood screen.

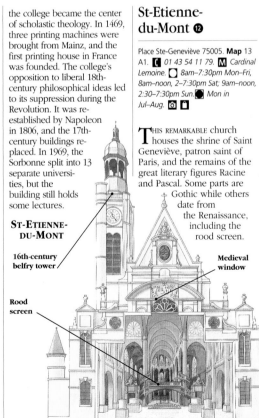

ST-ETIENNE-DU-MONT

16th-century belfry tower

Rood screen

Medieval window

Street-by-Street: Latin Quarter

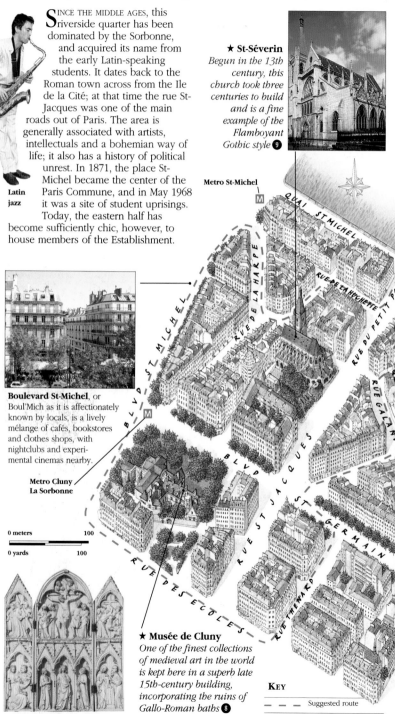

SINCE THE MIDDLE AGES, this riverside quarter has been dominated by the Sorbonne, and acquired its name from the early Latin-speaking students. It dates back to the Roman town across from the Ile de la Cité; at that time the rue St-Jacques was one of the main roads out of Paris. The area is generally associated with artists, intellectuals and a bohemian way of life; it also has a history of political unrest. In 1871, the place St-Michel became the center of the Paris Commune, and in May 1968 it was a site of student uprisings. Today, the eastern half has become sufficiently chic, however, to house members of the Establishment.

Latin jazz

★ **St-Séverin**
Begun in the 13th century, this church took three centuries to build and is a fine example of the Flamboyant Gothic style ❾

Metro St-Michel

Boulevard St-Michel, or Boul'Mich as it is affectionately known by locals, is a lively mélange of cafés, bookstores and clothes shops, with nightclubs and experimental cinemas nearby.

Metro Cluny La Sorbonne

0 meters   100

0 yards   100

QUAI ST MICHEL
RUE DE LA HARPE
RUE DE LA HUCHETTE
RUE DU PETIT PO
RUE GALANDE
BLVD ST MICHEL
BLVD ST GERMAIN
RUE ST JACQUES
RUE DES ECOLES
RUE THENARD

★ **Musée de Cluny**
One of the finest collections of medieval art in the world is kept here in a superb late 15th-century building, incorporating the ruins of Gallo-Roman baths ❽

KEY

--- ---   Suggested route

LOCATOR MAP
See Street Finder maps 8, 9, 12, 13

★ St-Julien-le-Pauvre
Rebuilt in the 17th century, this church was used to store animal feed in the Revolution 🔟

**Metro
Maubert
Mutualité**

STAR SIGHTS

★ **Musée de Cluny**

★ **St-Séverin**

★ **St-Julien-le-Pauvre**

Panthéon ⑬

Pl du Panthéon 75005. **Map** 13 A1.
☎ 01 44 32 18 00. Ⓜ Maubert-Mutualité, Cardinal-Lemoine. RER Luxembourg ☐ Oct–Mar: 10am–6pm; Apr–Sep: 10am–6:30pm; daily. ● Jan 1, May 1, Nov 11, Dec 25. 📷 ⓩ

WHEN LOUIS XV recovered from a desperate illness in 1744, he was so grateful to be alive that he conceived a magnificent church to honor Saint Geneviève, the patron saint of Paris. The French architect Jacques-Germain Soufflot, planned the church in Neo-Classical style. Work began in 1764 and was completed in 1790 under the control of Guillaume Rondelet, ten years after Soufflot's death. But with the Revolution underway, the church was soon turned into a pantheon – a monument housing the tombs of France's great heroes. Napoleon returned it to the Church in 1806, but it was secularized and then desecularized once more before finally being made a civic building in 1885.

The façade, inspired by the Rome Pantheon, has a pediment relief by David d'Angers, depicting the mother country granting laurels to her great men. Those resting here include Voltaire, Rousseau, and Zola, and the ashes of Pierre and Marie Curie, Alexandre Dumas and André Malraux.

Iron-Framed Dome
The fresco in the dome's stone cupola represents the Glorification of Sainte Geneviève, commissioned by Napoleon in 1811.

The dome lantern

The dome galleries

The Panthéon Interior
The interior has four aisles arranged in the shape of a Greek cross, from the center of which the great dome rises.

Entrance

Crypt
Under the building, the vast crypt divides into galleries flanked by Doric columns. Many French notables rest here, including Voltaire and Emile Zola.

Street-by-Street: Luxembourg Quarter

Situated only a few steps from the bustle of St-Germain-des-Prés, this graceful and historic area offers a peaceful haven in the heart of a modern city. The Jardin du Luxembourg and Palais du Luxembourg dominate the surroundings. The gardens became fully open to the public in the 19th century under the ownership of the Comte de Provence (later to become Louis XVIII), when, for a small fee, visitors could come in and feast on fruit from the orchard. Today, the gardens, palace and old houses on the streets to the north remain unspoiled and attract many visitors.

To St-Germain-des-Prés

STAR SIGHTS

★ St-Sulpice

★ Palais du Luxembourg

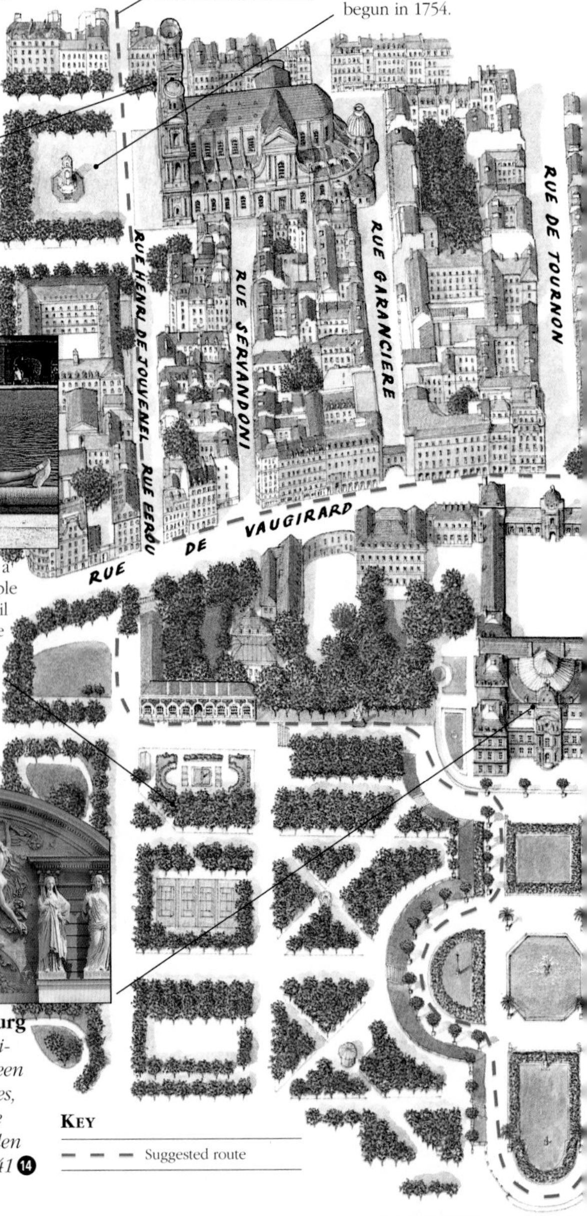

Place St-Sulpice, ringed by flowering chestnut trees, was begun in 1754.

★ St-Sulpice
This huge Classical church, by six different architects, took over a century to build ⓯

Jardin du Luxembourg is a popular garden where people come to relax, sunbathe, sail boats in the pond or admire the many beautiful statues erected in the 19th century.

RUE HENRI DE JOUVENEL   RUE FÉROU
RUE SERVANDONI
RUE GARANCIÈRE
RUE DE TOURNON
RUE DE VAUGIRARD

0 meters   100
0 yards   100

★ Palais du Luxembourg
First built as a royal residence, the palace has been used for various purposes, from prison to Luftwaffe headquarters. This garden façade was added in 1841 ⓮

KEY

- - - Suggested route

LOCATOR MAP
See Street Finder maps 8, 12, 13

Fontaine de Médicis is a 17th-century fountain in the style of an Italian grotto. It is thought to have been designed by Salomon de Brosse.

Saint Geneviève, patron saint of Paris, whose prayers saved Paris from the Huns in AD 451, is honored by this statue by Michel-Louis Victor in 1845.

Palais du Luxembourg ⑭

15 rue de Vaugirard 75006. **Map** 8 E5. 🛈 *01 42 34 20 60.* Ⓜ *Odéon.* 🚇 *Luxembourg.* ⬛ *groups only by appt: Mon, Fri, Sat. Apply 3 months in advance.* 🛈 *01 42 34 20 60.* ⊘

Nᴏᴡ ᴛʜᴇ ʜᴏᴍᴇ of the French Senate, this palace was built to remind Marie de' Médici, widow of Henri IV, of her native Florence. By the time it was finished (1631), she had been banished from Paris, but it remained a royal palace until the Revolution. Since then the palace has been used as a prison, and in World War II it served as headquarters for the German Luftwaffe, with numerous air-raid shelters built underneath its famous gardens.

It was designed by Salomon de Brosse in the style of the Pitti Palace in Florence.

St-Sulpice ⑮

Place St-Sulpice 75006. **Map** 8 E5. 🛈 *01 46 33 21 78.* Ⓜ *St-Sulpice.* ◯ *8am–7pm daily.* 🎵 **Concerts**

Tʜɪs ʜᴜɢᴇ and imposing church was started in 1646 and took more than a century to finish. The result is a simple façade with two tiers of elegant columns and two mismatched towers at the ends. Large arched windows fill the vast interior with light.

In the side chapel to the right are murals by Eugène Delacroix, including *Jacob Wrestling with the Angel (see p118)* and *Heliodorus Driven from the Temple.*

The Classical two-story west front of St-Sulpice with its two towers

Carpeaux's fountain sculpture

Fontaine de l'Observatoire ⑯

Place Ernest Denis, avenue de l'Observatoire 7500. **Map** 12 E2. 🚇 *Port Royal.*

Sɪᴛᴜᴀᴛᴇᴅ ᴀᴛ ᴛʜᴇ southern tip of the Jardin du Luxembourg, this is one of the finest fountains in Paris. The central sculpture, by Jean-Baptiste Carpeaux, was erected in 1873. Made of bronze, it has four women holding aloft a globe representing four continents – the fifth, Oceania, was left out for reasons of symmetry. There are some subsidiary figures, including dolphins, horses and a turtle.

Val-de-Grâce ⑰

Pl Alphonse-Laveran 75005. **Map** 12 F2. 🛈 *01 40 51 51 92.* Ⓜ *Gobelins.* 🚇 *Port Royal.* ◯ *noon–6pm Tue, Wed, Sat, Sun.* ⬛ *Aug.* 🎫 📷 ♿

Tʜɪs ɪs ᴏɴᴇ of the most beautiful churches in France, built for Anne of Austria (wife of Louis XIII) in gratitude for the birth of her son. Young Louis XIV himself laid the first stone in 1645.

The church is noted for its lead-and-gilt dome. In the cupola is Pierre Mignard's enormous fresco, with over 200 triple-life-size figures. The six huge, twisted marble columns that frame the altar are similar to those made by Bernini for St. Peter's in Rome.

FARTHER AFIELD

ANY OF PARIS'S famous sights are slightly out of the city center. Montmartre, long a mecca for artists and writers, still retains much of its bohemian atmosphere, and Montparnasse is full of bustling cafés and theater crowds. The famous Cimetière du Père Lachaise numbers Chopin, Oscar Wilde and Jim Morrison among its dead, and, along with the parks and gardens, provides a tranquil escape from sightseeing. Modern architecture can be seen at Fondation Le Corbusier and La Défense, and there is a huge selection of museums to visit. To the northeast, the science museum at La Villette provides an educational family outing.

SIGHTS AT A GLANCE

Museums and Galleries
Musée Marmottan **5**
Musée Gustave Moreau **8**
Musée du Cristal de Baccarat **9**
Musée National des Arts
  d'Afrique et d'Océanie **20**
Museum National d'Histoire
  Naturelle **24**

Churches and Mosques
St-Alexandre-Nevsky **6**
Sacré-Coeur **11**
Mosquée de Paris/Institut
  musulman **27**

Parks and Gardens
Bois de Boulogne **2**
Parc Monceau **7**
Parc des Buttes-Chaumont **17**
Parc Montsouris **23**
Jardin des Plantes **25**
Parc André Citroën **28**

Cemeteries
Cimetière de Montmartre **13**
Cimetière du Père Lachaise **18**
Cimetière du Montparnasse **30**

Historic Districts
Montmartre pp128–9 **10**
Canal St-Martin **16**
Montparnasse **29**

Historic Buildings and
Streets
Rue La Fontaine **4**
Moulin Rouge **12**
Château de Vincennes **21**
Catacombes **31**

KEY
    Main sightseeing area
    Major roads

Modern Architecture
La Défense **1**
Fondation Le Corbusier **3**
Bercy **19**
Bibliothèque Nationale
  de France **22**
Institut du Monde
  Arabe **26**

Markets
Marché aux Puces
  de St-Ouen **14**

Theme Parks
*Cité des Sciences et
  de l'Industrie pp132–3* **15**

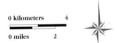

0 kilometers   4

0 miles   2

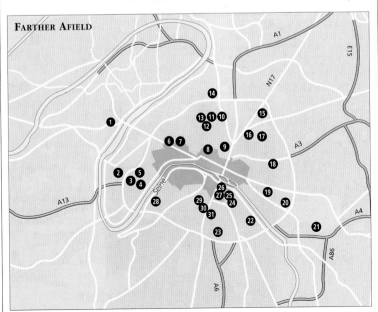

FARTHER AFIELD

◁ **The narrow rue St-Rustique winding up the hill to Sacré-Coeur**

West of the City

La Défense ❶

La Grande Arche. 📞 *01 49 07 27 57.*
RER *La Défense.* ○ *10am–10pm daily
(7pm Oct–Mar).* ♿ 🍴 📷 *See
The History of France pp62–3.*
W *www.grandearche.com*

Tʜɪꜱ ꜱᴋʏꜱᴄʀᴀᴘᴇʀ business
city on the western edge
of Paris is the largest office
development in Europe. La
Grande Arche is an enormous
hollow cube large enough to
contain Notre-Dame cathedral.
Designed by Danish architect
Otto von Spreckelsen in the
late 1980s, the arch houses a
gallery and a conference
center, and has superb views.

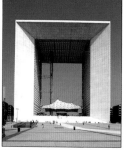

La Grande Arche in La Défense

Bois de Boulogne ❷

75016. **M** *Porte Maillot, Porte
Dauphine, Porte d'Auteuil, Sablons.*
○ *24 hrs daily.* 📷 *to specialized
gardens and museum.* ♿

Lᴏᴄᴀᴛᴇᴅ ʙᴇᴛᴡᴇᴇɴ the
western edges of
Paris and the Seine
River, this 865-ha
(2,137-acre) park offers
a vast belt of greenery
for strolling, cycling,
riding, boating, pic-
nicking or spending a
day at the races. The
Bois de Boulogne was
once part of the im-
mense Forêt du Rouvre.
In the mid-19th century
Napoleon III had the
Bois designed and
landscaped by Baron
Haussmann along the
lines of Hyde Park in
London. Several self-
contained parks within

the forest include the Pré
Catelan and the Bagatelle gardens, with architectural follies
and an 18th-century villa
famous for its rose garden.
The villa was built in just 64
days as the result of a bet
between the Comte d'Artois
and Marie Antoinette.
   By day the Bois is busy with
families, joggers and walkers,
but after dark it is notoriously
seedy – and best avoided.

Fondation Le Corbusier ❸

8 square du Docteur-Blanche 75016.
📞 *01 42 88 41 53.* **M** *Jasmin.*
○ *10am–12:30pm, 1:30–6pm (5pm
Fri) Mon–Fri.* ● *pub hols, Aug, Dec
24–Jan 2.* 📷 *Films, videos*
W *www.fondationlecorbusier.asso.fr*

Iɴ ᴀ ǫᴜɪᴇᴛ ᴄᴏʀɴᴇʀ of Auteuil
stand the villas La Roche
and Jeanneret, the first two
Parisian houses built by the
brilliant and influential 20th-
century architect Charles-
Edouard Jeanneret, better
known as Le Corbusier. Built
at the start of the 1920s, they
demonstrate his revolutionary
use of white concrete in Cubist
forms. Rooms flow into each
other, allowing maximum light
and volume, and the houses
stand on stilts with windows
along their entire length.
   Villa La Roche was owned by
the art patron Raoul La Roche.
Today, the villas are documentation centers, with lectures on
Le Corbusier and his work.

**An Art Nouveau window in the
rue la Fontaine**

Rue la Fontaine ❹

75016. **Map** 5 A4. **M** *Michel-Ange
Auteuil, Jasmin.* **RER** *Radio-France.*

Tʜᴇ ʀᴜᴇ ʟᴀ ꜰᴏɴᴛᴀɪɴᴇ and
surrounding streets act
as a showcase for some of
the most exciting early 20th-
century, low-cost architecture,
featuring sinuous decorative
detail. At No. 14 stands the
Castel Béranger, which firmly
established the reputation of
architect Hector Guimard. He
went on to design the city's
Art Nouveau metro entrances.

Musée Marmottan ❺

2 rue Louis Boilly 75016. 📞 *01 44 96
50 33.* **M** *Muette.* ○ *10am–6pm
Tue–Sun.* ● *Jan 1, Dec 25, May 1.*
📷 ♿ 📷 W *www.marmottan.com*

Tʜᴇ ᴍᴜꜱᴇᴜᴍ ᴡᴀꜱ
created in the 19th-
century mansion of the
famous art historian
Paul Marmottan in
1932. He bequeathed
his house, plus his
Renaissance, Consular
and First Empire paint-
ings and furniture, to
the Institut de France.
   In 1971 the museum
acquired one of the
world's most important
collections of work by
Impressionist painter
Claude Monet, at the
bequest of his son,
Michel. Some of Monet's
most famous paintings
are here, including
Impression – Sunrise

A landscaped island in the Bois de Boulogne

(from which came the term "Impressionist"), a painting of Rouen Cathedral *(see p257)* and several from the *Water-lilies* series *(see p94)*. Also on show is the body of work painted at Giverny during the last years of Monet's life. This includes paintings such as *The Japanese Bridge* and *The Weeping Willow*. The wild, expressive brushstrokes and iridescent colors make these some of the museum's most powerful works.

Part of Monet's personal art collection was passed on to the museum, including work by fellow Impressionists Camille Pissarro, Pierre-Auguste Renoir and Alfred Sisley. The museum also displays medieval illuminated manuscripts and 16th-century Burgundian tapestries.

Colonnade beside the *naumachia* basin in Parc Monceau

North of the City

St-Alexandre-Nevsky Cathedral

St-Alexandre-Nevsky ❻

12 rue Daru 75008. **Map** 2 F3. 🇨 *01 42 27 37 34.* 🄼 *Courcelles, Ternes.* ◯ *3–5pm Tue, Fri, Sun.* ☑ 🕇 *6pm Sat, 10:30am Sun*

Tʜɪs ɪᴍᴘᴏsɪɴɢ Russian Orthodox cathedral, with its five golden-copper domes, signals the presence of a large Russian community in Paris. Designed by members of the St. Petersburg Fine Arts Academy and financed jointly by Tsar Alexander II and the local Russian community, it was completed in 1861. A wall of icons divides the interior.

The Greek-cross plan and the rich interior mosaics and frescoes are Neo-Byzantine in style, while the exterior and gilt domes are traditional Russian Orthodox in design.

Parc Monceau ❼

Bd de Courcelles 75017. **Map** 3 A3. 🇨 *01 42 27 08 64.* 🄼 *Monceau.* ◯ *7am–9pm daily (10pm summer).*

Tʜɪs ɢʀᴇᴇɴ ʜᴀᴠᴇɴ dates back to 1778, when the Duc de Chartres commissioned the painter-writer and amateur landscape designer Louis Carmontelle to create a magnificent garden. The result was an exotic landscape full of architectural follies in the English and German style.

Over the years the land changed hands and in 1852 was acquired by the state and made into a chic public park. A few of the original features still remain. Among them is the *naumachia* basin – an ornamental version of a Roman pool used for simulating naval battles.

Musée Gustave Moreau ❽

14 rue de la Rochefoucauld 75009. **Map** 4 E3. 🇨 *01 48 74 38 50.* 🄼 *Trinité.* ◯ *10am–12:45pm, 2–5:15pm Wed–Mon.* ⬤ *some public hols.* ☑ 📷 🕇

Tʜᴇ sʏᴍʙᴏʟɪsᴛ painter Gustave Moreau (1826–98), known for his symbolic works depicting biblical and

mythological fantasies, lived and worked in this handsome town house at the end of the 19th century. *Jupiter and Semele,* one of the artist's outstanding works, is displayed here, along with other major paintings and some of the 7,000 drawings and 1,000 oils and watercolors that Moreau bequeathed to the state.

Musée du Cristal de Baccarat ❾

30 bis rue de Paradis 75010. 🇨 *01 47 70 64 30.* 🄼 *Château d'Eau, Poissonnières.* ◯ *10am– 6pm Mon–Sat.* ⬤ *public hols.* ☑ 🕇 ☑ *by appt.* 🅆 *www.baccarat.fr*

Tʜᴇ ʀᴜᴇ ᴅᴇ ᴘᴀʀᴀᴅɪs has a number of glass and ceramics retailers, including the Baccarat company, founded in 1764 in Lorraine. The Musée du Cristal is beside the Baccarat showroom and displays over 1,200 articles made by the company. These include services created for the royal and imperial courts of Europe and many of the best pieces produced in the workshops.

Also on display are some of the techniques for shaping the crystal ware. These are as intricate as the finished work itself.

Le Vase d'Abyssinie, made of Baccarat crystal and bronze

Montmartre ⑩

THE STEEP *butte* (hill) of Montmartre has been associated with artists for 200 years. Théodore Géricault and Camille Corot came here at the start of the 19th century, and in the 20th century Maurice Utrillo immortalized the streets in his works. Today, street artists thrive predominantly on the tourist trade, but much of the area still preserves its villagey, sometimes seedy, prewar atmosphere. The name of the area is ascribed to martyrs tortured and killed in the area around AD 250, hence *mons martyrium*.

Streetside painter

Montmartre Vineyard
This is the last Parisian vineyard. The harvest is celebrated on the first Saturday in October.

Metro Lamarck Caulaincourt

Au Lapin Agile
"The Agile Rabbit," once a literary haunt, is now a nightclub.

A la Mère Catherine
This was a favorite restaurant of Russian cossacks. They would shout "Bistro!" (meaning "quick") – which gave the bistro its name.

Espace Montmartre Salvador Dalí
Some 330 works by the Surrealist painter and sculptor are on display here.

Place du Tertre
The tourist center of Montmartre is full of portraitists. Artists first exhibited in the square in the 19th century.

KEY

 Suggested route

0 meters		100
0 yards		100

Musée de Montmartre
Changing, Montmarte-related exhibitions usually include works by artists who lived here, such as this Portrait of a Woman *(1918) by Amedeo Modigliani.*

LOCATOR MAP
See Street Finder maps 3, 4

MONTMARTRE

TUILERIES
AND
OPERA

BEAUBOURG

Sacré-Coeur
This Neo-Romanesque church, started in the 1870s and completed in 1914, contains many treasures, such as this figure of the Virgin Mary and Child *(1896) by P. Brunet* ⓫

RUE DU MONT CENIS

RUE DU CHEVALIER

RUE DU CARDINAL GUIBERT

RUE LAMARCK

RUE PAUL ALBERT

PL DU PARVIS
DU SACRE
COEUR

RUE AZAIS

RUE ST ELEUTHERE

RUE DU CARDINAL DUBOIS

GABRIELLE

RUE CHAPPE

RUE CH NODIER

SQ RE
WILLETTE

PL ST-PIERRE

RUE TARDIEU

RUE DE LA
STEINKERQUE

To metro Anvers

St-Pierre de Montmartre
This is an early Parisian church with origins dating back to the 6th century.

The funiculaire, or cable car, at the end of the rue Foyatier takes you to the foot of the basilica of the Sacré-Coeur. Metro tickets are valid for it.

Square Willette lies below the forecourt of the Sacré-Coeur. It is laid out on the side of the hill in a series of descending terraces with lawns, shrubs, trees and flower beds.

Musée d'Art Naïf Max Fourny
Almost 600 examples of naive art are housed here, including The Wall *(1944) by F. Tremblot.*

Sacré-Coeur ⓫

35 rue de Chevalier 75018. **Map** 4 F1.
☎ 01 53 41 89 00. Ⓜ *Abbesses (then
funiculaire to steps of Sacré- Coeur),
Anvers, Barbès-Rochechouart, Château-
Rouge, Lamarck-Caulaincourt.* 🚌 *30,
54, 80, 85.* **Basilica** ◯ *6:15am–10:30
pm daily.* **Dome & crypt** ◯ *10am–
7pm daily (6pm winter).* 🎫 👢 *restr.*
✝ *11:30am, 6:30pm, 9pm Mon–Thu;
11:30am, 3pm, 6:30pm Fri; 11:30am,
9pm Sat; 11am, 4pm, 9pm Sun.*

T HE SACRE-COEUR basilica,
dedicated to the Sacred
Heart of Christ, was built as a
result of a private religious
vow made at the outbreak of
the Franco-Prussian war.
Two businessmen, Alexandre
Legentil and Rohault de
Fleury, promised to finance
the basilica should France be
spared from assault. Despite
the war and the Siege of
Paris, invasion was averted
and work began in 1875 to
Paul Abadie's designs. Never
considered particularly graceful, the basilica is nonetheless
vast and impressive, and one
of France's most important
Roman Catholic buildings.

**The stained glass
gallery** affords a view
of the whole interior.

**The Great Mosaic
of Christ** (1912–22)
by Luc Olivier
Merson,
dominates the
chancel vault.

The ovoid dome is
the second-highest
point in Paris, after
the Eiffel Tower.

Bronze doors
in the portico
show the Last
Supper and
other biblical
scenes.

The crypt vaults house a
chapel containing Alexandre
Legentil's heart in a stone urn.

Moulin Rouge ⓬

82 bd de Clichy 75018. **Map** 4 E1.
☎ 01 53 09 82 82. Ⓜ *Blanche.*
◯ *7pm–1am daily.* 🎫 *See p141.*
🌐 *www.moulinrouge.fr*

B UILT IN 1885, the Moulin
Rouge was turned into
a dance hall as early as 1900.
Henri de Toulouse-Lautrec
immortalized the wild and
colorful cancan shows here
in his posters and drawings of
famous dancers such as Jane
Avril. The high-kicking routines
continue today in glittering,
Las Vegas-style revues.

Cimetière de
Montmartre ⓭

20 avenue Rachel 75018. **Map** 4 D1.
☎ 01 53 42 36 30. Ⓜ *Place de
Clichy.* ◯ *8am–5.30pm Mon–Sat,
9am–5.30pm Sun (6pm summer).* 👢

T HIS HAS been the resting
place for many luminaries
of the creative arts since the
beginning of the 19th century.

The composers Hector Berlioz
and Jacques Offenbach (who
wrote the famous cancan
tune), Russian dancer Waslaw
Nijinsky, and film director
François Truffaut are just
a few of the famous people
who have been buried here
over the years.
    There is also a Montmartre
cemetery near square Roland-
Dorgelès, known as the St-
Vincent cemetery. This is
where the French painter
Maurice Utrillo is buried.

**African stall in the Marché aux
Puces de St-Ouen**

Marché aux Puces
de St-Ouen ⓮

Rue des Rosiers, St-Ouen 75018.
Ⓜ *Porte-de-Clignancourt.*
◯ *9am–6pm Sat–Mon. See* **Shops
and Markets** *p138.*

T HIS IS THE OLDEST and largest of the Paris flea markets, covering 6 ha (15 acres)
near the Porte de Clignancourt.
In the 19th century, rag merchants and tramps would
gather outside the fortifications that marked the city
limits and offer their wares
for sale. Today the area is
divided into separate markets
and is well-known for its
heavy Second Empire furniture and ornaments. Although
there are few bargains to be
had, this does not deter the
huge weekend crowds.

Cité des Sciences et
de l'Industrie ⓯

See pp132–3.

Canal St-Martin **16**

M *Jaurès, J Bonsergent, Goncourt.*

A WALK ALONG THE QUAYS on either side of the Canal St-Martin gives a glimpse of how this thriving, industrial, working-class area of the city looked at the end of the 19th century. The 5-km (3-mile) canal, opened in 1825, provided a shortcut for river traffic between loops of the Seine. A smattering of brick-and-iron factories and warehouses survive from this time along the Quai de Jemmapes. Here, too, you will find the legendary Hôtel du Nord, which featured in Marcel Carné's 1930s film of the same name. The canal itself is quietly busy with barges and anglers; around it the tree-lined quays, iron footbridges and public gardens are ideal for a leisurely stroll.

Parc des Buttes-Chaumont **17**

Rue Manin 75019 (access from Rue Armand Carrel). **[** 01 53 35 89 35. M *Botzaris, Buttes-Chaumont.* **○** 7am–9pm (11pm summer) daily.

F OR MANY THIS is the most pleasant and unexpected park in Paris. Urban planner Baron Haussmann converted the hilly site from a garbage dump and quarry with gallows at the foot, to English-style gardens in the 1860s. His part- ner on the project was landscape architect Adolphe Alphand, who became chief organizer of a vast 1860s program to provide the pavement-lined Parisian avenues with benches, streetlights, newspaper kiosks and urinals.

Others involved in the creation of this highly praised park were the engineer Darcel and the landscape gardener Barillet-Deschamps. They created a lake, made an island with real and artificial rocks, gave it a Roman-style temple and added a waterfall, streams, and footbridges leading to the island. Today,

Boats moored at Port de l'Arsenal

in summer, visitors will also find boating facilities, donkey rides and sun worshipers on the beautifully kept lawns.

East of the City

Cimetière du Père Lachaise **18**

16 rue du Repos, 75020. **[** 01 55 25 82 10. M *Père Lachaise, A Dumas.* **○** 8am–6pm daily (8:30am Sat, 9am Sun).

P ARIS'S most prestigious cemetery is set on a wooded hill overlooking the city. The land was once owned by Père de la Chaise, Louis XIV's confessor, but it was bought by order of Napoleon in 1803 to create a completely new cemetery. This became so popular with the Parisian bourgeoisie that the boundaries were extended six times during the 19th century. Here are buried celebrities such as writer Honoré de Balzac and the composer Frédéric Chopin, and more recently, singer Jim Morrison and actors Simone Signoret and Yves Montand.

Bercy **19**

75012. M *Bercy, Cour St-Emilion.* ⬛ *Port de Bercy (01 43 43 40 30).* W www.marinadebercy.fr

T HIS FORMER wine-trading quarter just east of the city center, with its once-grim riverside warehouses and pavilions and slum housing, has been transformed into an ultra-modern district beside the Seine. A new automatic metro line (Line 14) links it to the heart of the city.

Centerpiece of this new district is the Palais d'Omnisports de Paris-Bercy (POPB), now the city center's principal venue for major concerts, as well as its premier sports stadium. The vast pyramidal structure, its steep sides clad with real lawns, has become a contemporary landmark for the eastern part of central Paris.

Other architecturally adventurous administrative and commercial buildings dominate the skyline, notably Chemetov's Ministry of Finance building, and Frank Gehry's American Center (due to reopen in 2003 as the Museum of Cinema and Cinemathèque Française).

At the foot of these structures, the imaginative 70-ha (173-acre) Parc de Bercy provides a welcome green space. Former wine stores and cellars along Cours St Emilion have been restored as restaurants, bars, and shops. Some of the warehouses have been restructured as the Pavillons de Bercy, one of which contains the Musée des Arts Forains (Fairground Museum). Rivertrips can be taken from the Marina de Bercy.

Bercy's striking American Center, designed by Frank Gehry

Cité des Sciences et de l'Industrie ⓯

THIS HUGELY popular science and technology museum occupies the largest of the old Villette slaughterhouses, which now form part of a massive urban park. Architect Adrien Fainsilber has created an imaginative interplay of light, vegetation, and water in the high-tech, five-story building, which soars 40 m (133 ft) high, stretching over 7 acres. At the museum's heart is the Explora exhibit, a fascinating guide to the worlds of science and technology. Visitors can play computerized games on space, the earth and ocean, computers, and sound. On other levels there are theaters, a science newsroom, a library, and shops.

Modern folly in the Parc de la Villette

Planetarium
In this 260-seat auditorium, special effects projectors and the latest sound systems create exciting images of the stars and planets.

Starball
The Planetarium's 10,000 lenses reproduce images of the sky as it is viewed by astronauts beyond the earth's atmosphere.

★ **Ariane**
Rocket displays explain how astronauts are sent into space and include an example of the European rocket Ariane.

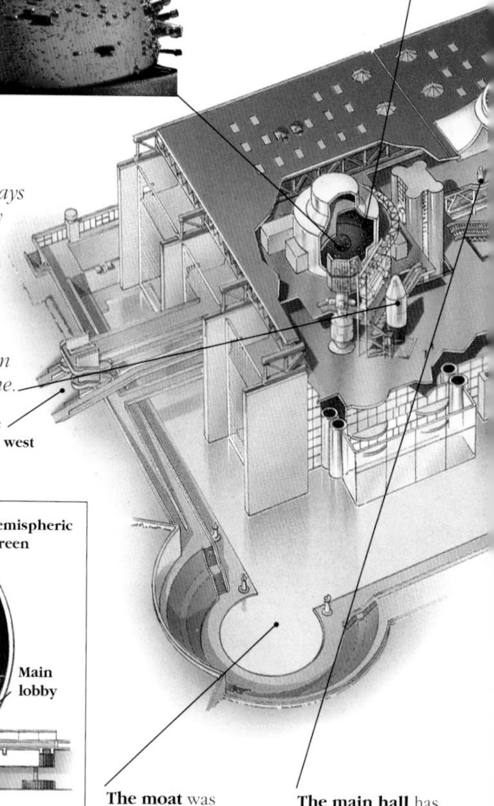

Entrance from the west

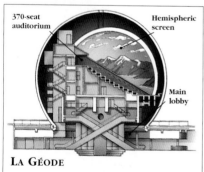

370-seat auditorium

Hemispheric screen

Main lobby

LA GÉODE

This giant entertainment sphere houses a huge hemispheric movie screen, 1,000 sq m (11,000 sq ft), showing IMAX films on nature, travel, and space.

The moat was designed by Fainsilber so that natural light could penetrate into the lower levels of the building.

The main hall has a vast, cathedral-like atmosphere, with its soaring network of shafts, bridges, escalators and balconies.

STAR EXHIBITS

★ Children's City

★ Ariane

★ La Géode

Cupolas
*The two glazed domes,
17 m (56 ft) in diameter,
filter the flow of natural
light into the main hall.*

VISITORS' CHECKLIST

30 av Corentin-Cariou 75019.
📞 01 40 05 80 00. Ⓜ *Porte de
la Villette.* 🚌 *75, 150, 152, PC
to Pte de la Villette.* ⏱ *10am–
6pm Tue–Sat (Sun 7pm).* ♿ ♿
🚻 ◻ ⛰ ◻ ◻ *Concerts.
Films, videos. Library.*
🅦 www.cite-sciences.fr

The greenhouses are
square hothouses, 32 m
(105 ft) high and wide,
linking the park to the
building.

Mirage Aircraft
*A full-size model of the
French-built jet fighter is one
of the exhibits illustrating
advances in technology.*

To La Géode

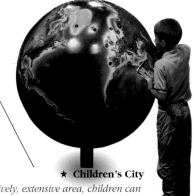

Walkways
*The walkways cross the
encircling moat to link the
various floors of the museum
to the Géode and the park.*

★ **Children's City**
*In this lively, extensive area, children can
experiment and play with machines that
show how scientific principles work.*

Bibliothèque Nationale de France

Musée National des Arts d'Afrique et d'Océanie ⑳

293 ave Daumesnil 75012. **℄** *01 44 74 84 80.* **Ⓜ** *Porte Dorée.* **◯** *10am–5:30 pm Wed–Mon,* **●** *May 1.* 📷 **⅋** *restr.* 🔲 **ⓦ** *www.musee-afriqueoceanie.fr*

THIS MUSEUM IS housed in an Art Deco building designed by architects Albert Laprade and Léon Jaussely for the city's grand colonial exhibition in 1931. Inside is a remarkable collection of African and Australasian art, including antelope masks from Mali, Moroccan jewelry, Aborigine bark paintings, and African wood and copper figures on the themes of life and death.

Château de Vincennes ㉑

Avenue de Paris 94300 Vincennes. **℄** *01 48 08 31 20.* **Ⓜ** *Château de Vincennes.* **RER** *Vincennes.* **◯** *10am–5pm daily (last adm 4:15pm); May–Sep until 6pm.* **Chapel** 📷 *only.*

THE CHÂTEAU de Vincennes was the permanent royal residence until the 17th century, before the court moved to Versailles. The royal chambers and beautiful Gothic chapel are all worth seeing; so is the large, impressive museum in the medieval keep.

Beyond the château moat lies the Bois de Vincennes. Once a royal hunting ground, it is now a landscaped forest with ornamental lakes and cascades, a racecourse, a zoo, and a good playground.

Bibliothèque Nationale de France ㉒

Quai François-Mauriac 75013. 📠 *01 53 79 59 59.* **Ⓜ** *Bibliothèque François Mitterrand.* **◯** *10am–8pm Tue–Sun, (noon Sun).* **●** *public hols, 2 wks mid-Sep.* 📷 **⅋** 🍴 🔲 **ⓦ** *www.bnf.fr*

THESE FOUR great book-shaped towers house ten million volumes. The reference and research libraries, in the central podium, offer over 400,000 titles. Other resources include digitized illustrations, sound archives, and CD-ROMs.

South of the City

Parc Montsouris ㉓

Bd Jourdan 75014. 📞 *01 45 88 28 60.* **Ⓜ** *Porte d'Orléans.* **RER** *Cité Universitaire.* **◯** *7:30am–7pm (5:30pm winter) daily.*

THIS ENGLISH-STYLE park, the second largest in Paris, was laid out by the landscape architect Adolphe Alphand from 1865–1878. With its restaurant, lawns, and lake – home to a variety of birds – it is popular with students and children.

Skull of the reptile dimetrodon

Muséum National d'Histoire Naturelle ㉔

2 rue Buffon 75005. **Map** *14 D1.* 📞 *01 40 79 30 00.* **Ⓜ** *Jussieu, Austerlitz.* **◯** *10am–5pm Wed–Mon (10pm Thu).* **●** *May 1.* 📷 **⅋** *restr.* 🔲 🔲 📷 **Library** **ⓦ** *www.mnhn.fr*

THE HIGHLIGHT OF the museum is the Grande Galerie de l'Evolution. There are also four other departments: palaeontology, featuring skeletons, casts of various animals and an exhibition showing the evolution of the vertebrate skeleton; palaeobotany, devoted to plant fossils; mineralogy, including gemstones; and entomology, with some of the oldest fossilized insects on earth. The bookstore is in the house that was occupied by the naturalist Buffon, from 1772 until his death in 1788.

Jardin des Plantes ㉕

57 rue Cuvier 75005. **Map** *13 C1.* **Ⓜ** *Jussieu, Austerlitz.* **◯** *9am–6pm (5pm winter) daily.*

THE BOTANICAL gardens were established in 1626 when Jean Hérouard and Guy de la Brosse, Louis XIII's physicians, obtained permission to found a royal medicinal herb garden. A school of botany, natural history, and pharmacy followed, and the garden opened to the public in 1640. One of the city's great parks, it contains a natural history museum, botanical school, and zoo.

The park has an alpine garden with plants from Corsica, Morocco, the Alps, and the Himalayas, and an unrivaled display of herbaceous and wild plants, as well as beautiful vistas and walkways flanked by ancient statues. The Cedar of Lebanon here, originally from Britain's Kew Gardens, was the first to be planted in France.

Rue Mouffetard, one of several markets near Jardin des Plantes

Institut du Monde Arabe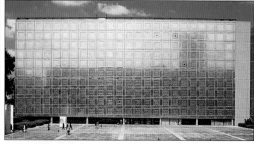

1 rue des Fossés St-Bernard 75005.
Map 9 C5. **C** *01 40 51 38 38.*
M *Jussieu, Cardinal-Lemoine.*
Museum & temp exhibs ◯ *10am–6pm Tue–Sun.* **Library** ◯ *1–8pm Tue–Sat.*

T HIS MAGNIFICENT modern building was designed by French architect Jean Nouvel, and cleverly combines high-tech details with the spirit of traditional Arab architecture.

From the fourth to seventh floors there is a comprehensive display of Islamic works of art from the 9th to the 19th centuries including glassware, ceramics, and sculpture. The museum's highlight is the fine collection of *astrolabes*, the much-prized tool used by the ancient Arabic astronomers.

Mosquée de Paris/Institut Musulman

Place du Puits de l'Ermite 75005.
C *01 45 35 97 33.* **M** *Place Monge.*
◯ *9am–noon, 2–6pm Sat–Thu.* ●
Muslim hols. **Library**

B UILT IN THE 1920s in the Hispano-Moorish style, these buildings are the spiritual center for Paris's Muslim community and the home of the Grand Imam. Once used solely by scholars, the mosque has expanded over the years and now houses the best Turkish baths in the city, a restaurant, and beautiful *salon de thé*.

Parc André Citroën

Rue Balard 75015. **C** *01 40 71 74 03.* **M** *Javel, Balard.* ◯ *7:30am–dusk Mon–Fri (9am w/e, public hols).*

D ESIGNED BY both landscapers and architects, this park is a fascinating blend of styles, ranging from wildflower meadow in the north to sophisticated monochrome mineral and sculpture gardens in the southern section. Modern water sculptures dot the park.

Institut du Monde Arabe, covered with photosensitive light screens

Tour Montparnasse

Montparnasse

75014 & 75015. **Map** 11 & 12.
M *Vavin, Raspail, Edgar Quinet.*

T HE NAME Montparnasse was first used ironically in the 17th century, when art students performed their work on a "mount" of rubble left over from quarrying.
In ancient Greece, Mount Parnassus was dedicated to poetry, music, and beauty. By the 19th century, crowds were drawn to the local cabarets and bars by duty-free prices. The mixture of art and high living was particularly potent in the 1920s and 1930s when Hemingway, Picasso, Cocteau, Giacometti, Matisse, and Modigliani were "Montparnos," as the residents were called. This epoch ended with World War II. The modern *quartier* is dominated by the much-hated Tour Montparnasse, visible from all over Paris, and vast office developments.

Cimetière du Montparnasse

3 bd Edgar Quinet 75014. **Map** 12 D3.
C *01 44 10 86 50.* **M** *Edgar Quinet.*
◯ *8am–6pm Mon–Fri, 8:30am–6pm Sat, 9am–6pm Sun (5:30pm in winter).*

M ONTPARNASSE cemetery opened in 1824 and fast became a chic burial place. Among those buried here are Serge Gainsbourg, Charles Baudelaire, Left-Bank personalities Jean-Paul Sartre and Simone de Beauvoir, and Guy de Maupassant.

Catacombes

1 place Denfert-Rochereau 75014.
Map 12 E3. **C** *01 43 22 47 63.*
M *Denfert-Rochereau.* ◯ *11am–4pm Tue, 9am–4pm Wed–Sun.*
● *public hols.*

A LONG SERIES of quarry tunnels built in Roman times, the catacombs are now lined with ancient bones and skulls. Thousands of rotting corpses were transported here in the 1780s to absorb the excess from the unsanitary Les Halles cemetery.

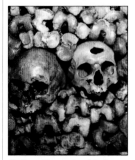

Skulls and bones stored in the catacombs

SHOPS AND MARKETS

FOR MANY PEOPLE, Paris epitomizes luxury and good living. Exquisitely dressed men and women sip wine by the banks of the Seine against the backdrop of splendid French architecture, or shop at small specialized stores. The least expensive way of joining the chic set is to create French style with accessories or costume jewelry. Alternatively, try shopping in the January or July sales. If your budget allows, take the opportunity to buy world-famous Parisian fashions, or feast on the wonderful gourmet delicacies, displayed with consummate artistry. Parisian shopping streets and markets are the ideal place to indulge in the French custom of strolling for the express purpose of seeing and being seen. For up-to-the-minute high fashion, the rue du Faubourg-St-Honoré is hard·to beat, with its exquisite couture window displays. Browsing around the bookstands along the Seine is another favorite French pastime. A brief survey of some of the best and most famous places to shop follows.

Shopping in avenue Montaigne

OPENING HOURS

SHOPS GENERALLY OPEN from 9:30am to 7pm, Monday to Saturday. Markets and local shops close on Mondays and some places also close for the month of August.

PAYMENT AND VAT

CASH IS READILY available from the ATMs in most banks, which accept credit/bank debit cards. For further information, see pages 620–21. Prices will normally include sales tax (TVA), which varies from 5.5% to 19.6%. Non-EU residents are entitled to a refund, provided you spend a minimum of 175¤ in one shop on one day, and are staying in France for under six months. Fill in a form (*bordereau de détaxe* or *bordereau de vente*) and present it to customs upon departure.

WOMEN'S FASHIONS

PARIS IS THE HOME of haute couture. Original haute couture garments, as opposed to imitations and adaptations, are unique creations designed by the 23 couture houses listed with the Fédération Française de la Couture. The rules governing the classification "haute couture" are fairly strict, and many of the world's top designers, such as Claude Montana and Karl Lagerfeld, are not included on this prestigious list. Astronomical prices put haute couture beyond the reach of most pockets, yet it still remains the lifeblood and focus of the French fashion industry. Most couture houses are on or near rue du Faubourg-St-Honoré and avenue Montaigne, including **Chanel**, **Christian Lacroix**, **Guy Laroche**, **Nina Ricci**, **Yves Saint Laurent** and **Christian Dior**.

Hermès has classic country chic, and no one can resist **MaxMara**'s Italian elegance or a **Giorgio Armani** suit. **Karl Lagerfeld** designs for Chanel and has created his own sleek line. One of the best collections of designer labels is found at **Victoire**, in the Place des Victoires, not far from **Kenzo**. **Comme des Garçons** with its avant-garde, quirky clothes for both sexes is just nearby.

The Chanel logo, recognized worldwide

THE CENTER OF PARIS COUTURE

The couture houses are concentrated on the Right Bank, around rue du Faubourg-St-Honoré and avenue Montaigne.

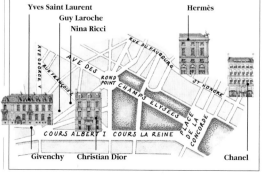

Yves Saint Laurent
Guy Laroche
Nina Ricci
Hermès
Givenchy
Christian Dior
Chanel

For accessories to complete the look, **Cartier** and **Christian Lacroix** are hard to beat.

Farther east on the Rue de Jour, **Diapositive**'s body-hugging clothes are popular, while **Agnès B**'s clothes combine the vary latest chic with comfort. The Marais is full of new designers, many in the Rue des Rosiers and the Rue des Francs-Bourgeois. Daring designer **Azzedine Alaïa**'s shop is just around the corner. The Bastille area also has many trendy boutiques and some more established names such as **Jean-Paul Gaultier** in the Rue du Faubourg St-Antoine.

La Samaritaine department store in Beaubourg and Les Halles

Kenzo designerwear in the place des Victoires

MEN'S CLOTHES

Men don't have the luxury of haute couture dressing; their choice is limited to ready-to-wear, but most of the big name womenswear designers also produce a line for men, although they tend to be rather expensive. A good example is **Gianni Versace**, with his classic Italian clothes for men.

On the Right Bank, the household name designers include the stylish **Giorgio Armani**, **Pierre Cardin**, **Yves Saint Laurent** and **Lanvin**, who is particularly popular for his beautifully made leather accessories. Across the Seine, **Francesco Smalto**'s elegant creations are bought by the likes of Jean-Paul Belmondo, and for those who are not afraid to make a bold fashion statement, there is **Yohji Yamamoto**.

DEPARTMENT STORES

If time is short and you want to make all your purchases under one roof, try the *grands magasins* (department stores), all of which have restaurants as well. Most still operate a ticket system for selling goods. The assistant writes a ticket for goods from a single boutique, which you take to a cashier to be validated. You then return to the assistant to pick up your purchase. This can be time-consuming, so shop early in the day and avoid Saturdays. Be assertive, as the French don't pay attention to lines!

Au Printemps is huge, with separate buildings for menswear, household goods and women's and children's clothes. Fashion shows are held on Tuesdays at 10am (also on Fridays in summer). The beauty department, with a vast perfume selection, is definitely worth a visit.

Cartier, one of the world's most exclusive stores

Le Bon Marché, on the Left Bank, was the first department store in Paris and is the most chic, with a good food hall. **Galeries Lafayette** has a wide range of clothes at all price levels. Fashion shows are held at 11am on Wednesdays and also on Fridays in summer. **La Samaritaine** is one of the oldest shops in Paris, and full of bargains. It includes a sportswear shop and has good sales on household goods and furnishings. The store has a panoramic view of the Seine from its restaurant Le Toupary.

ART AND ANTIQUES

You can buy art and antiques from shops and galleries of established reputations, or from flea markets and avant-garde galleries.

To avoid paying duty, you will need a certificate of authenticity when exporting *objets d'art* over 20 years old and any goods over a century old worth more than 150,000₀. Seek professional advice and declare the item at customs if in doubt.

Many of the prestigious antique shops and galleries are near the rue St-Honoré, including **Le Louvre des Antiquaires**, which comprises 250 different shops. On the Left Bank is the Carré Rive Gauche, an organization of 30 antiques dealers. Here, **Didier Aaron** is an international expert on the 17th and 18th centuries. Two galleries worth a visit are **Artcurial**, for books and prints, and **Lavignes-Bastille**.

CHILDREN

THE CITY has many appealing toy shops, including one of the world's most famous, **Au Nain Bleu**, situated in rue St-Honoré. Unfortunately, the toys tend to be rather expensive, so a visit to the store is best kept as a special treat.

There is no shortage of children's fashion in Paris, in all styles and price ranges. A good place to start is the rue du Jour in Beaubourg and Les Halles, which has a number of children's boutiques. Many designers of adult clothes also have boutiques for children, including **Kenzo**, **Baby Dior** and **Agnès B**. Prices can be extremely high, though. Ready-to-wear chains such as **Bonpoint** sell chic, expensive, but well-made clothes, and the shops are also conveniently located. Perhaps not surprisingly, the best-selling children's garments at **Tartine et Chocolat** on rue du Faubourg-St-Honoré are overalls.

For little feet, **Froment-Leroyer** offers the best all-around classics.

Characters from the Tintin series, Au Nain Bleu toy shop

BOOKS, NEWSPAPERS AND MAGAZINES

BRITISH AND OTHER European papers can be bought on the day of publication at large newsagents or kiosks. Some are European or international editions, such as the *Financial Times Europe*, *The Guardian Europe* and the *Guardian International*, *The Weekly Telegraph*, *The Economist*, *USA Today*, and *The International Herald Tribune*. For what's on, see the French weekly

Bookstall at Vanves market

listing magazines *Pariscope* and *L'Officiel des Spectacles*.

Some large department stores have a book department, and there are many English-language bookstores such as **WH Smith**, **Brentano**, and **Village Voice.** **Gibert Joseph** is a French-language bookstore selling general and educational books, while **La Hune** specializes in art, design, cinema, fashion, and photography. **Tea and Tattered Pages** is a British secondhand bookstore.

Elegantly packaged produce from Fauchon

FOOD AND WINE

PARIS'S GASTRONOMIC treats include *foie gras, charcuterie*, cheese and wine. Some streets positively overflow with food shops – try rue Montorgueil or rue Rambuteau, which has a marvelous row of fishmongers, delicatessens and shops selling prepared food. Charcuteries such as **Fauchon**, in place Madeleine, and the basement of **Le Bon Marché** department store sell cheese, snails, truffles, caviar and regional produce.

L'établissement Poilâne sells perhaps the only bread in Paris known by the name of its baker. Be prepared for big crowds on weekends and around 4pm when a fresh batch comes out of the oven.

Chocolate is another French obsession. **Christian Constant**'s low-sugar creations, well-known to connoisseurs, are made from pure cocoa. **Barthélemy** in the rue de Grenelle has exceptional

Roquefort. **Caves Taillevent**, an enormous wine cellar with some of France's most expensive wine, is worth a tour.

MARKETS

THE FRENCH still shop daily, hence food markets are always packed. Most fruit and vegetable markets are open from around 8am to 1pm and from 4pm to 7pm Tuesday to Saturday, and 9am to 1pm Sunday. Watch out for rotten produce – buy products loose, not in boxes. A little language is useful for specifying *pas trop mûr* (not too ripe), or *pour manger ce soir* (to be eaten tonight). The newly renovated **Marché St-Germain** is a good bet for Italian, Mexican, Greek, Asian and organic produce. The **Rue Lepic** fruit and vegetable market, close to Montmartre, is at its most lively on weekends. The **Rue Poncelet** food market is worth a trip for its variety of bakeries, pâtisseries and charcuteries. **Rue de Seine** and **Rue de Buci** have florists and two excellent pâtisseries.

Paris's biggest and best-known flea market is the **Marché aux Puces de St-Ouen**. Divided into separate markets, it specializes in furniture, antiques, old jewelry and secondhand clothes. The smaller **Marché de la Porte de Vanves** has good-quality bric-a-brac – get there early for the best choice.

Lionel Poilâne's bread bearing his trademark – a square

DIRECTORY

WOMEN'S FASHION

Agnès B
6 rue de Jour 75001.
Map 9 A1.
01 45 08 56 56.

Azzedine Alaïa
7 rue de Moussy 75004.
Map 9 C3.
01 40 27 85 58.

Cartier
13 rue de la Paix 75002.
Map 4 D5.
01 42 61 58 56.

Chanel
42 av Montaigne 75008.
Map 3 A5.
01 47 23 74 12.

Christian Dior
30 av Montaigne 75008.
Map 6 F1.
01 40 73 54 44.

Christian Lacroix
73 rue du Faubourg-St-Honoré 75008. **Map** 3 B5.
01 42 68 79 00.

Comme des Garçons
54 rue du Faubourg St-Honoré 75008. **Map** 3 B5.
01 53 30 27 27.

Diapositive
12 Rue du Jour
75001.
Map 9 A1.
01 42 21 34 41.

Giorgio Armani
6 pl Vendôme 75001.
Map 4 D5.
01 42 61 55 09.

Guy Laroche
30 rue du Faubourg-St-Honoré 75008.
Map 3 C5.
01 40 06 01 70.

Jean-Paul Gaultier
6 rue Vivienne 75002.
Map 8 F1.
01 42 86 05 05.

Hermès
24 rue du Faubourg-St-Honoré 75008.
Map 3 C5.
01 40 17 47 17.

Kenzo
3 pl des Victoires 75001.
Map 8 F1.
01 40 39 72 03.

MaxMara
37 rue du Four 75006.
Map 8 D4.
01 43 29 91 10.

Nina Ricci
39 av Montaigne 75008.
Map 6 F1.
01 40 88 64 96.

Victoire
12 Place de Victoires
75002. **Map** 8 F1.
01 42 61 09 02.

Yves Saint Laurent
38 rue du Faubourg-St-Honoré 75008. **Map** 3 C5.
01 42 65 74 59.

MEN'S CLOTHES

Francesco Smalto
44 rue François 1er
75008. **Map** 2 F5.
01 47 20 70 63.

Gianni Versace
62 rue du Faubourg-St-Honoré 75008. **Map** 3 C5.
01 47 42 88 02.

Lanvin
32 rue Marbeuf 75008.
Map 4 F5.
01 53 75 02 20.

Pierre Cardin
59 rue du Faubourg-St-Honoré 75008. **Map** 3 C5.
01 42 66 64 74.

Yohji Yamamoto
69 rue des Saints-Pères
75006. **Map** 8 D4.
01 42 48 22 56.

DEPARTMENT STORES

Le Bon Marché
24 rue de Sèvres 75007.
Map 7 C5.
01 44 39 80 00.

Au Printemps
64 bd Haussman 75009.
Map 4 D4.
01 42 82 50 00.

Galeries Lafayette
40 bd Haussmann 75009.
Map 4 E4.
01 42 82 34 56.

La Samaritaine
19 rue de la Monnaie
75001. **Map** 8 F2.
01 40 41 20 20.

ART AND ANTIQUES

Artcurial
9 av Matignon 75008.
Map 3 A5.
01 42 99 16 16.

Le Louvre des Antiquaires
2 pl du Palais-Royal
75001. **Map** 8 F2.
01 42 97 27 00.

Didier Aaron
118 rue du Faubourg-St-Honoré 75008. **Map** 3 C5.
01 47 42 47 34.

Lavignes-Bastille
27 rue de Charonne
75011. **Map** 10 F4.
01 47 00 88 18.

CHILDREN

Au Nain Bleu
408 rue St-Honoré 75008.
Map 3 C5.
01 42 60 39 01.

Baby Dior
28 av Montaigne 75008.
Map 6 F1.
01 49 52 04 50.

Bonpoint
15 rue Royale 75008.
Map 3 C5.
01 47 42 52 63.

Froment-Leroyer
7 rue Vavin 75006.
Map 12 E1.
01 43 54 33 15.

Tartine et Chocolat
105 rue du Faubourg-St-Honoré 75008. **Map** 3 B5.
01 45 62 44 04.

BOOKS

Brentano
37 av de l'Opera 75002.
Map 4 E5.
01 42 61 52 50.

Gibert Joseph
26 bd St-Michel 75006.
Map 8 F5.
01 44 41 88 88.

La Hune
170 bd St-Germain
75006. **Map** 8 D4.
01 45 48 35 85.

Tea and Tattered Pages
24 rue Mayet 75006.
Map 11 B1.
01 40 65 94 35.

Village Voice
6 rue Princesse 75006.
Map 8 E1.
01 46 33 36 47.

WH Smith
248 rue de Rivoli 75001.
Map 7 C1.
01 44 77 88 99.

FOOD AND WINE

Barthélemy
51 rue de Grenelle 75007.
Map 8 D4.
01 45 48 56 75.

Caves Taillevent
199 rue du Faubourg-St-Honoré 75008. **Map** 2 F3.
01 45 61 14 09.

Christian Constant
37 rue d'Assas 75006.
Map 12 E1.
01 53 63 15 15.

L'établissement Poilâne
8 rue du Cherche-Midi
75006. **Map** 8 D4.
01 45 48 42 59.

Fauchon
26 pl de la Madeleine
75008. **Map** 3 C5.
01 47 42 60 11.

MARKETS

Marché St-Germain
Rue Mabillon and rue
Lobineau 75005.
Map 8 E4.

Rue Lepic
75018. **Map** 4 F1.

Rue Poncelet
75017. **Map** 2 E3.

Marché de la Porte de Vanves
Av Georges-Lafenestre &
av Marc-Sangnier 75014.

Marché aux Puces de St-Ouen
Rue des Rosiers, St-Ouen
75018.

Rue de Seine and Rue de Buci
75006. **Map** 8 E4.

ENTERTAINMENT IN PARIS

WHETHER YOUR preference is for classical drama, avant-garde theater, ballet, opera or jazz, movies or dancing the night away, Paris has it all. There is plenty of free entertainment, too, from the street performers outside the Pompidou Center to musicians found all over the city and in the metros.

Parisians themselves like nothing better than strolling along the boulevards or sitting at a sidewalk café nursing a drink as they watch the world go by. If, however, you're looking for the ultimate "Oh la-la!" experience, you can take in any of the celebrated nightclubs.

For fans of spectator sports there is tennis, the Tour de France or horse racing. Fitness centers and gyms cater to the more active. And for those disposed to more leisurely pursuits, there is always a game of lawn bowling (boules) to be played in the park.

The glass façade of the Bastille Opéra

BOOKING TICKETS

DEPENDING on the event, tickets can often be bought at the door, but for popular events it is wiser to purchase tickets in advance at the **FNAC** chain or **Virgin Megastore**. Theater box offices open daily from about 11am–7pm. Most accept credit card bookings by telephone. The **Kiosque Théâtre** sells leftover tickets for up to half the price the day of performance.

THEATER

FROM THE GRANDEUR of the **Comédie Française** to slapstick farce and avant-garde drama, theater is flourishing in Paris. Founded in 1680 by royal decree, the Comédie Française is the bastion of French theater, aiming to keep classical drama in the public eye and to perform works by the best modern playwrights. Formerly the second theater of the Comédie Française, the **Odéon Théâtre de l'Europe** now specializes in plays from other countries, performed in their original language. In an underground auditorium in the Art Deco Palais de Chaillot, the **Théâtre National de Chaillot** stages lively productions of European classics. The **Théâtre National de la Colline** specializes in contemporary dramas.

Among the most important of the serious independents is the **Comédie des Champs-Elysées**, while for over 100 years, the **Palais Royal** has been the temple of risqué farce. The café theaters such as **Café d'Edgar** and **Au Bec Fin** are good places for seeing new talent.

In the summer, street theater thrives in tourist areas such as the Pompidou Center, Les Halles and St-Germain-des-Prés. Outdoor performances of Shakespeare and classic French plays are given at the Shakespeare Garden in the Bois de Boulogne.

CLASSICAL MUSIC

THE MUSIC SCENE in Paris has never been so busy. There are many first-class venues with an excellent range of opera, classical and contemporary music productions.

Opened in 1989, the ultramodern 2,700-seat **Opéra de Paris Bastille** stages classic and modern operas. The beautifully renovated **Opéra Garnier** now also puts on operatic productions.

The **Salle Pleyel** is Paris's principal concert hall, with 2,300 seats. Both the **Théâtre des Champs-Elysées** and the **Théâtre du Châtelet** are recommended for their varied, high-quality programs. Venues for chamber music include the **Salle Gaveau**, the **Théâtre de la Ville** and the charming

LISTINGS MAGAZINES

Pariscope, Zurban and *L'Officiel des Spectacles* are the best listings magazines in Paris. Published every Wednesday, you can pick them up at any news-stand. *Le Figaro* also has a good listings section on Wednesdays. *The City* is published quarterly in English, and is available at newsstands or W.H. Smith *(see p139)*.

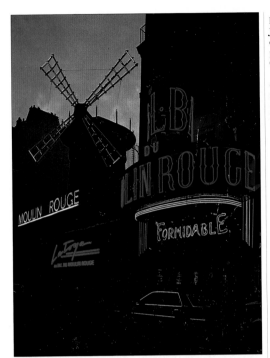

The famous silhouette of the Moulin Rouge nightclub

rococo **Théâtre du Musée Grévin** *(see p93)*. Paris's newest venue is the **Cité de la Musique** in the Parc de la Villette. It is home to the renowned contemporary music group, the Ensemble InterContemporain, directed by Jonathan Nott.

DANCE

THE FRENCH are very vocal in their appreciation or dislike of dance, and those who fail to please are subjected to boos, hisses and mass walkouts in mid-performance.

The opulent **Opéra Garnier** has performance space for 450 artists and is home to the Ballet de l'Opéra de Paris, which has earned a reputation as one of the best classical ballet companies in the world. Government support has helped the **Théâtre de la Ville** to become Paris's most important venue for modern dance, with subsidies keeping ticket costs relatively low.

The **Maison des Arts de Créteil** stages famous overseas companies, as well as its own much-praised productions.

CLUBS AND CABARET

MUSIC IN PARIS CLUBS tends to follow the trends set in the US and Britain. Only a few clubs, such as **Balajo**, once frequented by Edith Piaf, and the ultra-hip **Folies Pigalle**, a former strip joint, are genuinely up-to-the-minute with their music.

La Locomotive attracts a mixed crowd to its three-level mainstream house nights. **Les Bains** is the old standby nightspot attracting fashion and show business people.

For a more Latin touch, try **La Java**. The dance floor of this club, where Edith Piaf once performed, now sways to Cuban and Brazilian sounds.

When it comes to picking a cabaret, the rule of thumb is simple: the better known places are best. The **Folies-Bergères** is the oldest music hall in Paris and probably the most famous in the world. It is closely rivaled by the **Lido** and the **Moulin Rouge**, birthplace of the cancan. **Paradis Latin** is the most "French" cabaret in the city. It presents variety acts whose sketches are enlivened by remarkable special effects and scenery.

ROCK, JAZZ AND WORLD MUSIC

THE TOP international acts are usually to be found at the enormous arenas such as **Palais Omnisports Paris-Bercy** or the **Zénith**. For a more intimate atmosphere, the legendary **Olympia** has assigned seating and good acoustics. To hear indigenous rock groups like Les Negresses Vertes and Mano Negra, go to **La Cigale** or **Elysée-Montmartre** in the Pigalle area.

Jazz-crazy Paris has innumerable packed clubs where the best talent in the world can be heard on any evening. All the great jazz musicians have performed at **New Morning**, which also hosts African, Brazilian and other sounds. For Dixieland, go to **Le Petit Journal St-Michel**.

World music and jazz lovers alike can see leading acts and dance until dawn at the excellent **Chapelle des Lombards**.

La Locomotive, a huge disco on three levels

FILM

PARIS IS THE WORLD'S capital of film appreciation. It was the cradle of the cinematograph nearly 100 years ago. Then in the late 1950s and early 1960s, the city nurtured that very Parisian vanguard movement, the New Wave, when film directors such as François Truffaut and Jean-Luc Godard revolutionized the way films were made and perceived.

There are now more than 300 screens within the city limits, distributed among 100 theaters. Most are concentrated in movie belts, which enjoy the added appeal of nearby restaurants and shops. The Champs-Elysées has the densest movie theater strip in town, where you can see the latest Hollywood smash or French *auteur* triumph, as well as classic reissues.

In the vicinity of the Opéra de Paris Garnier, the movie theaters in the Grands Boulevards include two notable landmarks: the 2,800-seat **Le Grand Rex**, with its Baroque decor, and the **Max Linder Panorama**, which was completely refurbished in the 1980s. The place de Clichy is the last Parisian stronghold of Pathé, while the newest hub of Right Bank movies is in the Forum des Halles shopping mall. The largest screen in France, except for a special screen at **La Géode**, is the **Gaumont** flagship in the place d'Italie district.

On the Left Bank, Odéon-St-Germain-des-Prés has taken over from the Latin Quarter as the city's heartland for art and repertory film theaters.

The dome of the 2,800-seat Le Grand Rex movie theater

SPORT

PARIS IS HOST to some of the foremost sporting events in the world. City-wide frenzy sweeps Paris when the Tour de France bicycle race finishes there in July. From late May to mid-June, Parisians live and breathe tennis during the **Roland Garros** national tennis championship. The Prix de l'Arc de Triomphe, held at the **Hippodrome de Longchamp** on the first Sunday in October, provides the opportunity to see the rich in all their finery as well as first-class flat horse-racing.

The **Palais Omnisports Paris-Bercy** is the venue for a vast range of events, including the Paris tennis open, and rock concerts, as is the new **Stade de France** at St-Denis. **Parc des Princes** is home to Paris's top soccer team, Paris St-Germain.

THE CELEBRATED CAFÉS OF PARIS

One of the most enduring images of Paris is the Left Bank café scene, where great artists, writers and eminent intellectuals consorted. Before World War I, hordes of Russian revolutionaries, including Lenin and Trotsky, whiled away their days in the Rotonde and the Dôme in Montparnasse. In the 1920s, Surrealists dominated café life. Later came the American writers led by Ernest Hemingway and F. Scott Fitzgerald, whose haunts included La Coupole. After World War II, Jean-Paul Sartre and other Existentialists shifted the cultural scene northward to St-Germain.

Newspaper reading remains a typical café pastime

DIRECTORY

BOOKING TICKETS

FNAC
26 av des Ternes 75017.
Map 2 D3.
📞 01 44 09 18 00.
Forum Les Halles, 1 rue
Pierre Lescot 75001.
Map 9 A2.
📞 01 40 41 40 00.

Virgin Megastore
52–60 av des Champs-
Elysées 75008. **Map** 2 F5.
📞 01 49 53 50 00.

Kiosque Théâtre
15 pl de la Madeleine
75008. **Map** 3 C5.

THEATER

Au Bec Fin
6 rue Thérèse 75001.
Map 8 E1.
📞 01 42 96 29 35.

**Comédie des
Champs-Elysées**
15 av Montaigne 75008.
Map 6 F1.
📞 01 53 23 99 19.

Comédie Française
2 rue de Richelieu 75001.
Map 8 E1.
📞 01 44 58 15 15.

**Odéon Théâtre de
l'Europe**
Pl de l'Odéon 75006.
Map 8 F5.
📞 01 44 41 36 36.

Palais Royal
38 rue Montpensier
75001. **Map** 8 E1.
📞 01 42 97 59 85.

Café d'Edgar
58 bd Edgar-Quinet
75014.
Map 12 D2.
📞 01 42 79 97 97.

**Théâtre National
de Chaillot**
Pl du Trocadéro
75016.
Map 5 C2.
📞 01 53 65 30 00.

**Théâtre National
de la Colline**
15 rue Malte-Brun 75020.
📞 01 44 62 52 52.

CLASSICAL MUSIC

Cité de la Musique
221 av Jean-Jaurès 75019.
📞 01 44 84 44 84.
🌐 www.cite-musique.fr

**Opéra de Paris
Bastille**
120 rue de Lyon 75012.
Map 10 E4.
📞 08 36 69 78 68.

**Opéra de Paris
Garnier**
Pl de l'Opera 75009.
Map 4 E5.
📞 08 36 69 78 68.

Salle Gaveau
45 rue la Boétie 75008.
Map 3 B4.
📞 01 45 62 69 71.

Salle Pleyel
252 rue du Faubourg St-
Honoré 75008. **Map** 2 E3.
📞 01 45 61 53 00.

**Théâtre des
Champs-Elysées**
15 av Montaigne 75008.
Map 6 F1.
📞 01 49 52 50 50.

Théâtre du Châtelet
Pl du Châtelet 75001.
Map 9 A3.
📞 01 40 28 28 40.

Théâtre de la Ville
2 pl du Châtelet 75004.
Map 9 A3.
📞 01 42 74 22 77.

Théâtre du Grévin
10 blvd Montmartre
75009.
Map 4 F4.
📞 01 47 70 85 05.

DANCE

**Maison des Arts de
Créteil**
Pl Salvador Allende 94000
Créteil. 📞 01 45 13 19 19.

Opéra Garnier
(See Classical Music.)

Théâtre de la Ville
(See Classical Music.)

CLUBS AND
CABARET

Les Bains
7 rue du Bourg-L'Abbé
75003. **Map** 9 B1.
📞 01 48 87 01 80.

Balajo
9 rue de Lappe 75011.
Map 10 E4.
📞 01 47 00 07 87.

Folies-Bergères
32 rue Richer 75009.
📞 01 44 79 98 98.

Folies Pigalle
11 pl Pigalle 75009.
Map 4 E2.
📞 01 48 78 55 25.

La Java
105 rue du Faubourg-du-
Temple 75010.
📞 01 42 02 20 52.

La Locomotive
90 bd de Clichy 75018.
Map 4 D1.
📞 08 36 69 69 28.

Lido
116 bis av des Champs-
Elysées 75008. **Map** 2 E4.
📞 01 40 76 56 10.

Moulin Rouge
82 bd de Clichy 75018.
Map 4 E1.
📞 01 53 09 82 82.

Paradis Latin
28 rue du Cardinal-Lemoine
75005. **Map** 9 B5.
📞 01 43 25 28 28.

ROCK, JAZZ AND
WORLD MUSIC

**Chapelle des
Lombards**
19 rue de Lappe 75011.
Map 10 F4.
📞 01 43 57 24 24.

La Cigale
120 bd Rochechouart
75018. **Map** 4 F2.
📞 01 49 25 89 99.

Elysée-Montmartre
72 bd Rochechouart
75018. **Map** 4 F2.
📞 01 44 92 45 45.

New Morning
7–9 rue des Petites-Ecuries
75010.
📞 01 45 23 51 41.

Olympia
28 bd des Capucines
75009. **Map** 4 D5.
📞 01 55 27 10 00.

**Palais Omnisports
Paris-Bercy**
8 bd de Bercy 75012. **Map**
14 F2. 📞 08 03 03 00 31.
🌐 www.ticketnet.fr

**Le Petit Journal St-
Michel**
71 bd St-Michel
75005.**Map** 12 F1.
📞 01 43 26 28 59.

Zénith
211 av de Jean-Jaurès
75019.
📞 01 42 08 60 00.

FILM

Gaumont Gobelins
58 & 73 av des Gobelins
75013. **Map** 13 B4.
📞 08 36 68 75 55.
📞 01 40 30 730 31 (reserv).

La Géode
26 av Corentin-Cariou
75019. 📞 08 92 68 45 40.

Le Grand Rex
1 bd Poissonnière 75002.
📞 08 36 68 70 23.

**Max Linder
Panorama**
24 bd Poissonnière 75009.
📞 08 92 68 50 52.

SPORT

**Hippodrome de
Longchamp**
Bois de Boulogne 75016.
📞 01 44 30 75 00.

**Palais Omnisports
Paris-Bercy**
(See Rock section.)

Stade de France
93210 La Plaine St-Denis.
📞 01 55 93 00 00.

Parc des Princes
24 rue du Commandant-
Guilbaud 75016.
📞 01 47 43 71 71.

**Stade Roland
Garros**
2 av Gordon-Bennett
75016. 📞 01 47 43 48 00.

PARIS STREET FINDER

THE MAP REFERENCES given for sights, shops and entertainment venues described in the Paris section of the guide refer to the maps on the following pages. Map references are also given for Paris hotels *(see pp540–44)*, and restaurants *(pp580–84),* and for useful addresses in the *Travelers' Needs* and *Survival Guide* sections at the back of the book. The maps include not only the main sightseeing areas but also the most important districts for hotels, restaurants, shopping and entertainment venues. The key map below shows the area of Paris covered by the *Street Finder*, with the arrondissement numbers for the various districts. The symbols used for sights and other features on the *Street Finder* maps are listed opposite.

Paris is divided into 20 arrondissements, outlined in orange and numbered on this map.

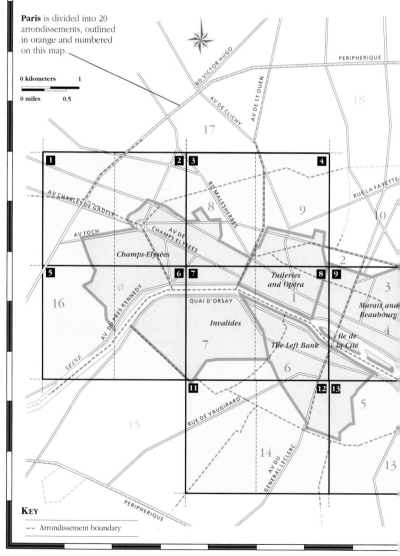

0 kilometers   1

0 miles   0.5

KEY

-- Arrondissement boundary

HOW THE MAP REFERENCES WORK

The first figure tells you which *Street Finder* map to turn to.

Map 9 B3.

Hôtel de Ville ⑩

4 place de l'Hôtel-de-Ville 75004.
Map 9 B3. (42 76 50 49.
M *Hôtel-de-Ville.* ◯ 10:30am Mon
for tours in French, leaving from the
info office at 29 rue de Rivoli.
● public hols, official functions. &

The letter and number give
the grid reference. Letters go
across the map's top and
bottom; numbers on its sides.

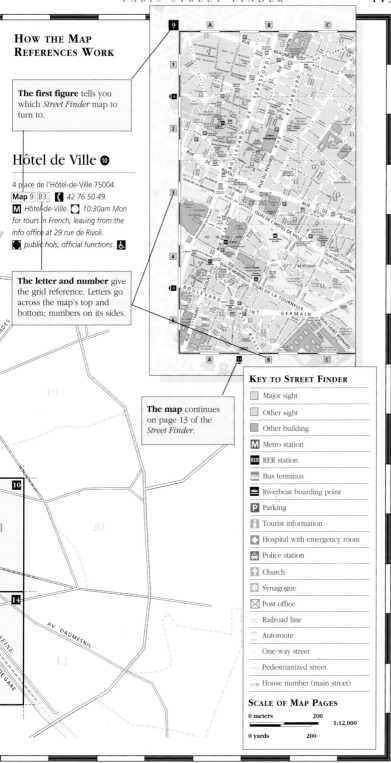

The map continues
on page 13 of the
Street Finder.

KEY TO STREET FINDER

▨	Major sight
▨	Other sight
▨	Other building
M	Metro station
RER	RER station
▦	Bus terminus
▦	Riverboat boarding point
P	Parking
▮	Tourist information
✚	Hospital with emergency room
▣	Police station
✝	Church
✡	Synagogue
⊠	Post office
══	Railroad line
---	Autoroute
—	One-way street
---	Pedestrianized street
⊲130	House number (main street)

SCALE OF MAP PAGES

0 meters	200	
		1:12,000
0 yards	200	

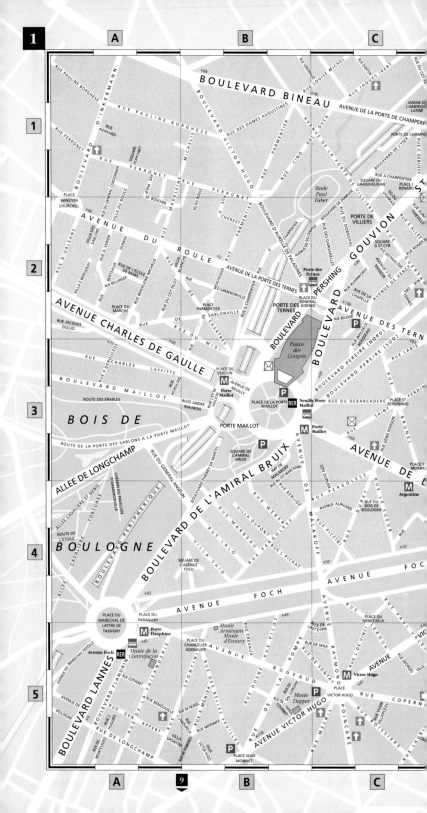

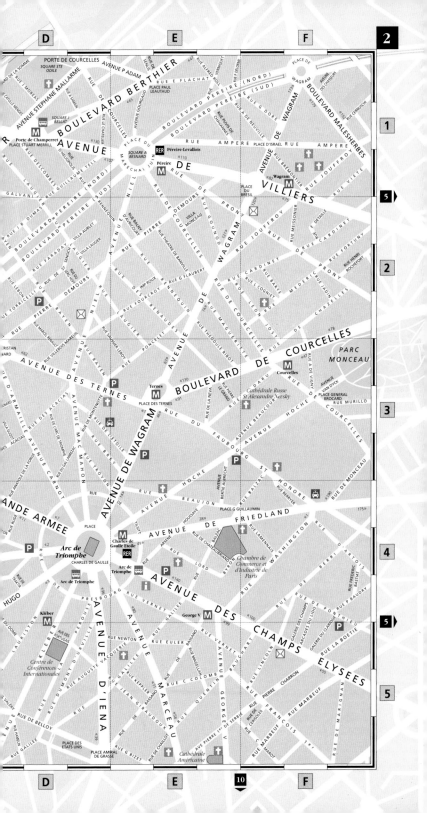

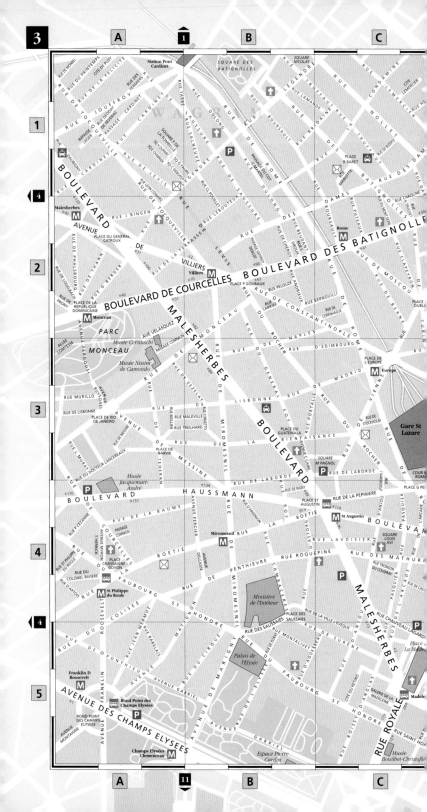

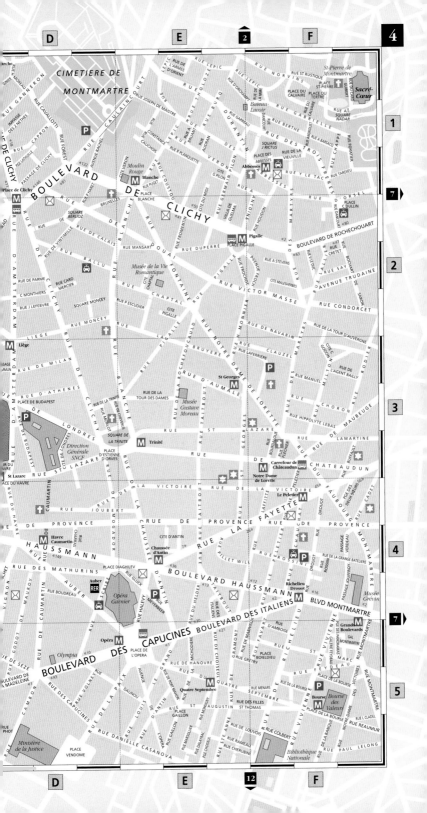

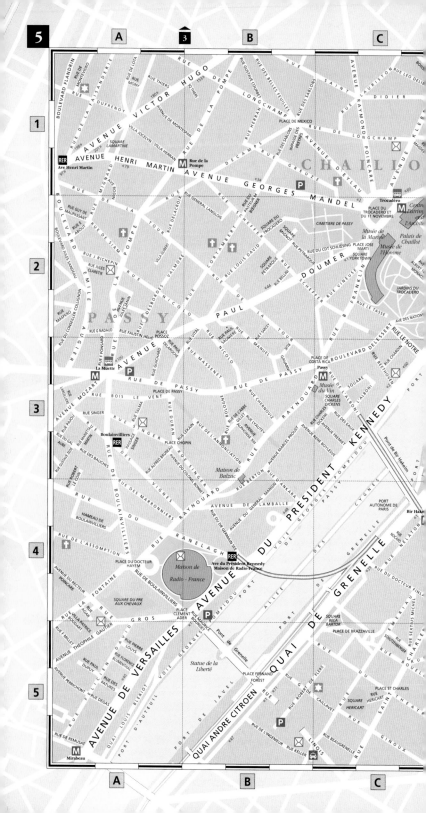

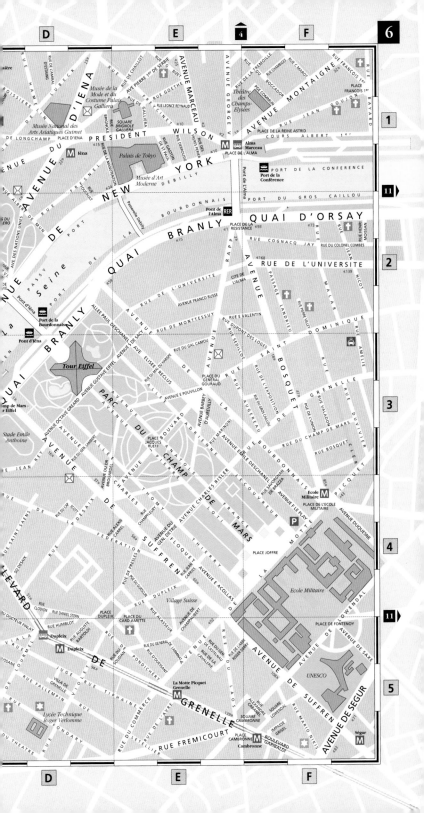

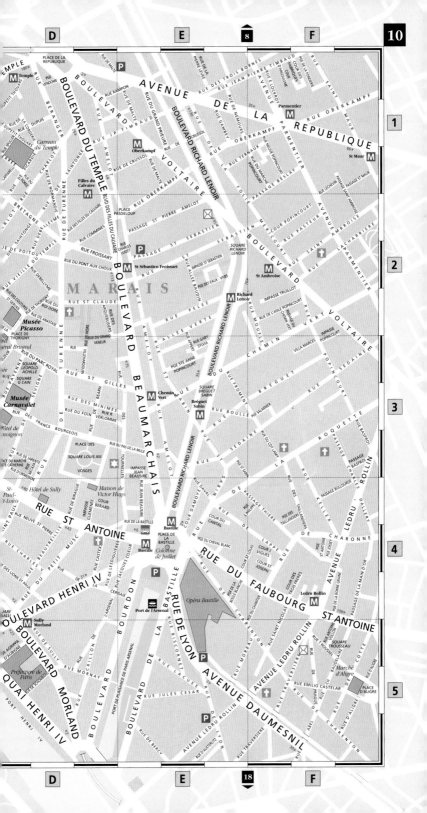

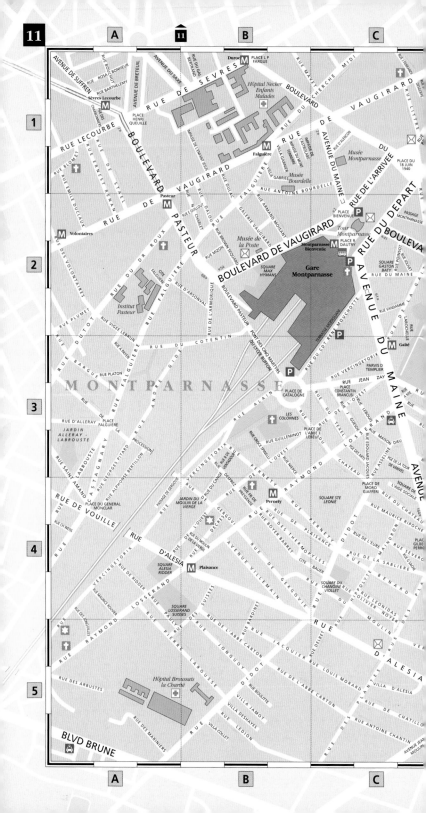

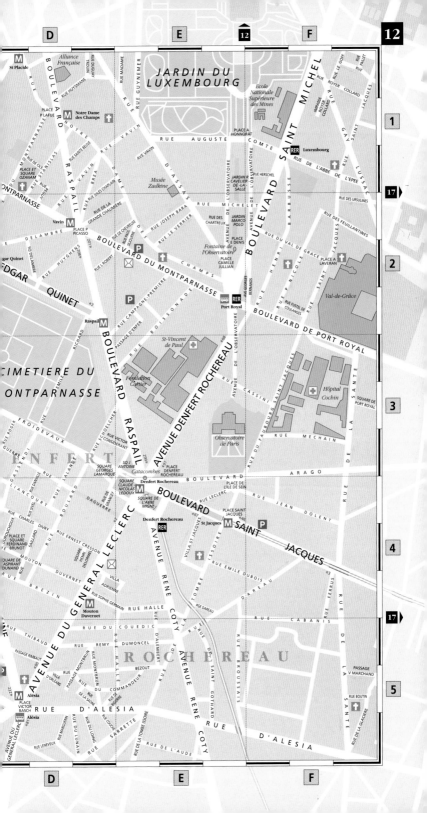

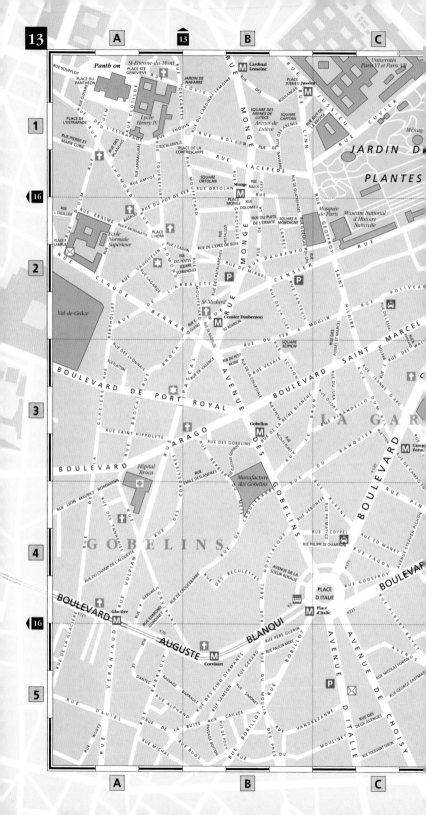

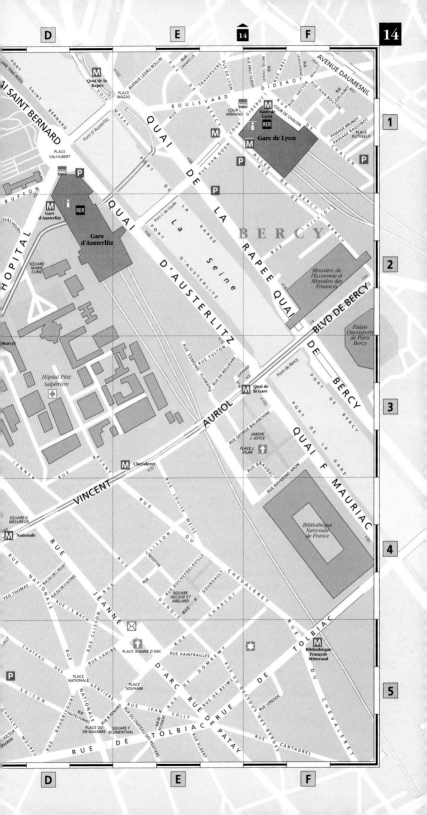

ILE DE FRANCE

SET AT THE HEART OF FRANCE, with Paris as its hub, Ile de France extends well beyond the densely populated suburbs of the city. Its rich countryside incorporates a historic royal region of monumental splendor central to *"la gloire de la France."*

The region became a favorite with French royalty after François I transformed Fontainebleau into a Renaissance palace in 1528. Louis XIV kept the Ile de France as the political axis of the country when he started building Versailles in 1661. This Classical château, created by the combined genius of Le Nôtre, Le Vau, Le Brun and Jules Hardouin-Mansart, is France's most visited sight. It stands as a monument to the power of the Sun King and is still used for state occasions. Rambouillet, closely linked with Louis XVI, is now the summer residence of the French president, while Malmaison was the favorite home of Empress Josephine. To the north, the Château d'Ecouen offers a showcase of Renaissance life, and to the south, Vaux-le-Vicomte boasts some of the loveliest formal gardens in France.

Nourished by the Seine and Marne rivers, the Ile de France is a patchwork of chalky plains, wheatfields and forests. The serene, poplar-lined avenues and rustic charm of the region have been an inspiration to painters such as Corot, Rousseau, Pissarro and Cézanne.

SIGHTS AT A GLANCE

Châteaux and Museums
Château de Dampierre **8**
Château de Fontainebleau **13**
Château de Malmaison **5**
Château de Rambouillet **9**
Château de Sceaux **7**
Château Vaux-le-Vicomte **11**
Château de Versailles **6**
Musée National de la Renaissance **2**

Towns
Provins **12**
St-Germain-en-Laye **4**

Abbeys and Churches
Abbaye de Royaumont **1**
Basilique St-Denis **3**

Theme Parks
Disneyland Paris **10**

KEY

☐	Greater Paris
☐	Central Paris
✈	International airport
▬	Highway
▬	Major road
▬	Minor road

0 kilometers 20
0 miles 10

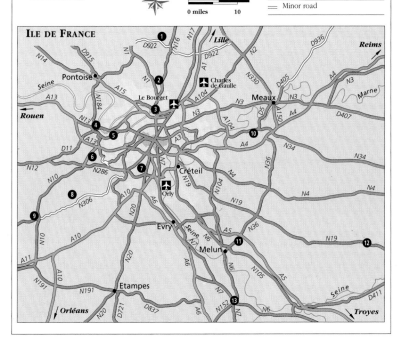

◁ **Magnificent formal gardens at the Château Vaux-le-Vicomte**

The vaulted Gothic refectory of Abbaye de Royaumont

Abbaye de Royaumont ❶

Fondation Royaumont, Asnières-sur-Oise, Val-d'Oise. 📞 01 30 35 59 00. ⬜ daily. 🕮 ♿ 📷 call 01 30 35 59 91. 🎵 **Concerts.**

SET AMONG WOODS "near water and far from man-kind," 30 km (20 miles) north of Paris, Royaumont is the finest Cistercian abbey in the Ile de France. Chosen for its remoteness, the abbey's stark stonework and simplicity of line reflect the austere teachings of St. Bernard. However, unlike his Burgundian abbeys, Royaumont was founded in 1228 by Louis IX and his mother, Blanche de Castile. "St. Louis" showered the abbey with riches and chose it as a royal burial site.

The abbey retained its royal links until the Revolution, when much of it was destroyed. It was then a cotton mill and orphanage until its revival as a cultural center. The original pillars still remain, along with a gravity-defying corner tower and the largest Cistercian cloisters in France, which enclose a charming Classical garden. The monastic quarters border one side of the cloisters.

The Château de Royaumont, erected as the abbot's palace on the eve of the Revolution, is set apart and resembles an Italianate villa. A stroll around the grounds will reveal the monks' workshops, woods, ponds and Cistercian canals.

In summer, concerts are held in the abbey at weekends (01 34 68 05 55 for details).

Musée National de la Renaissance ❷

Chateau d'Ecouen, Val-d'Oise. 📞 01 34 38 38 50. ⬜ Wed–Mon. ● Jan 1, May 1, Dec 25. 🕮 ♿ 📷 🍴

THIS IMPOSING moated château is curiously adrift, halfway between St-Denis and Royaumont. Now a Renaissance museum, Ecouen's magnificent quadrilateral exterior provides an authentic setting for an impressive collection of paintings, tapestries, coffers, carved doors and staircases salvaged from other 16th-century châteaux.

Ecouen was built in 1538 for Anne de Montmorency, advisor to François I and commander in chief of his armies. As the second most powerful person in the kingdom, he employed Ecole de Fontainebleau artists and craftsmen to adorn his palace. Their influence is apparent in the ravishing painted fireplaces, depicting biblical and Classical themes in mysterious landscapes. The most striking room is the chapel, containing a minstrels' gallery and vaulted ceilings painted with the Montmorency coat of arms.

Upstairs, a long gallery contains one of the finest series of 16th-century tapestries in France. Equally compelling are the princely apartments, the Renaissance tiled floors, the library of illuminated manuscripts, a collection of vivid ceramics from Lyon, Nevers, Venice and Faenza and Iznik, and a display of early mathematical instruments and watches.

Since the ground floor is open in the morning and the second floor in the afternoon, lunching at Ecouen is advised.

Basilique St-Denis ❸

1 pl de la Légion d'Honneur, St-Denis. Seine-St-Denis. 📞 01 48 09 83 54. ⬜ daily. ● Jan 1, May 1, Dec 25. 🕮 ♿

ACCORDING TO LEGEND, the decapitated St. Denis struggled here, clutching his head, and an abbey was erected to commemorate the martyred bishop. Following the burial of Dagobert I in the basilica in 638, a royal link with St-Denis began, which was to span 12 centuries. Most French kings were entombed in St-Denis, and all the queens of France were crowned here. The elegant, early Gothic basilica rests on Carolingian and Romanesque crypts.

Statue of Louis XVI at St-Denis

Of the medieval effigies, the most impressive are of Charles V (1364) and a 12th-century likeness in enameled copper of Blanche de France with her dog.

The masklike serenity of these effigies is in sharp

The west wing of Musée National de la Renaissance

The Renaissance tomb of Louis XII and Anne de Bretagne in St-Denis

contrast to the graphically realistic Renaissance portrayal of agony present in the grotesque mausoleum of Louis XII and Anne de Bretagne. Both are represented as naked figures in the tabernacle, their faces eerily captured at the moment of death. Above the mausoleum, effigies of the finely dressed royal couple contemplate their own nakedness. As a reflection of humanity in the face of death, the basilica's tombs have few rivals.

St-Germain-en-Laye ❹

Yvelines. 🚆 41,000. 🚉 🚌 ℹ️
Musée Claude Debussy, 38 rue au Pain. 📞 01 34 51 05 12.
📅 *Tue, Fri–Sun.*

Dominating the place Général de Gaulle in this chic suburb is the legendary Château de St-Germain, birthplace of Louis XIV.

Louis VI built the original stronghold in 1122 but only the keep and St-Louis chapel remain. Under François I and Henri II, the medieval upper tiers were demolished, leaving a moated pentagon. Henri IV built the pavilion and terraces that run down to the Seine, and Louis XIV had Le Nôtre landscape the gardens before leaving for Versailles in 1682.

Today the château houses the **Musée des Antiquités Nationales**, which exhibits archaeological finds from prehistory to the Middle Ages. Created by Napoleon III, the collection includes a 22,000-year-old carved female, a megalithic tomb, a bronze helmet from the 3rd century BC and Celtic jewelry. The finest treasure is the Gallo-Roman mosaic pavement.

🏛 Musée des Antiquités Nationales

Château de St-Germain-en-Laye.
📞 01 39 10 13 00.
📅 *Wed–Mon.* 🚫 ✔️ 👁 ℹ️

Château de Malmaison ❺

Rueil-Malmaison, Hauts-de-Seine.
📞 01 41 29 05 55. 📅 10am Wed–Mon; closing times vary according to season; call for details. 🚫 Jan 1, Dec 25.
📷 ♿ restr. 🌐 www.napoleon.org

Situated 15 km (9 miles) west of Paris, Richelieu's 17th-century estate is now best known for its Napoleonic associations. Bought by Josephine as a retreat from the formality of the Emperor's residences at the Tuileries and Fontainebleau, it still has charming rural grounds. While Josephine loved this country manor, Napoleon scorned the front entrance as fit only for servants. Instead, he had a curious drawbridge built at the back of the château.

The finest rooms are the frescoed and vaulted library, the canopied campaign room, and the sunny Salon de Musique, hung with paintings from Josephine's private collection. Contrast Napoleon's restrained yellow canopied bedroom with the bedchamber in which Josephine died. Many of the rooms overlook the romantic "English" gardens and the famous rose garden which was cultivated by Josephine after her divorce.

Memorabilia abound, from Imperial eagles to David's moody portrait of Napoleon, or Gérard's painting of the languid Josephine reclining on a chaise longue.

Château Bois Préau, set in the wooded grounds, houses a museum dedicated to Napoleon's exile and death.

Empress Josephine's bed at Château de Malmaison

Château de Versailles ⑥

THE PRESENT PALACE, started by Louis XIV in 1668, grew around Louis XIII's original hunting lodge. Architect Louis Le Vau built the first section, which expanded into an enlarged courtyard. From 1678, Jules Hardouin-Mansart added north and south wings and the Hall of Mirrors. He also designed the chapel, completed in 1710. The Opera House (L'Opéra) was added by Louis XV in 1770. André Le Nôtre enlarged the gardens and broke the monotony of the symmetrical layout with expanses of water and creative use of uneven ground. Opposite the château is the Musée des Carrosses, housing a collection of royal carriages.

Garden statue of a flautist

★ **Formal Gardens**
Geometric paths and shrubs are features of the gardens.

The Orangery was built beneath the Parterre du Midi to house exotic plants in winter.

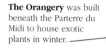

Fountain of Latona
Four marble basins rise to Balthazar Marsy's statue of the goddess Latona.

Water Parterre

★ **Château**
Under Louis XIV, Versailles became the center of political power in France.

Dragon Fountain
The fountain's centerpiece is a winged monster.

The King's garden features a mirror pool in the 19th-century garden created by Louis XVIII.

Colonnade
Mansart designed this circle of marble arches in 1685.

VISITORS' CHECKLIST

Versailles, Yvelines. ☎ 01 30 83 77 88. 🚌 171 from Paris. **RER** *Versailles Rive Gauche.* 🚉 *Versailles Chantiers, Versailles Rive Droite.* **Château** ⏰ *9am–6:30 pm (5:30pm winter) Tue–Sun.* 🎫
Grand Trianon & Petit Trianon
⏰ *noon–6:30pm (5:30pm winter) daily (last adm: 30 mins before closing).* 🎫 ♿ 🎫 🏛
🎫 🏛 **Musée des Carrosses** ⏰
12:30–6:30pm (5:30pm winter) Sat & Sun. 🎫 🎆 *Les Fêtes de Nuit (Aug–Sep); Les Grandes Eaux Musicales (Apr–Oct).*
W *www.chateauversailles.fr*

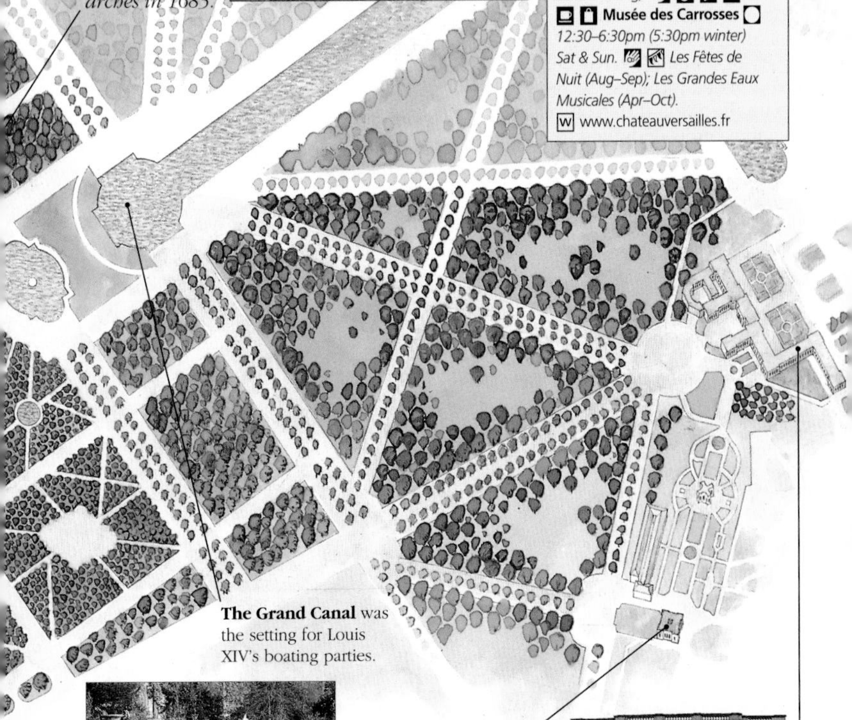

The Grand Canal was the setting for Louis XIV's boating parties.

Petit Trianon
Built in 1762 as a retreat for Louis XV, this small château became a favorite with Marie Antoinette.

Fountain of Neptune
Groups of sculptures spray spectacular jets of water in Le Nôtre's 17th-century garden.

★ **Grand Trianon**
Louis XIV built this small palace of stone and pink marble in 1687 to escape the rigors of court life, and to enjoy the company of Madame de Maintenon.

STAR FEATURES

★ **Château**

★ **Formal Gardens**

★ **Grand Trianon**

Inside the Château de Versailles

THE SUMPTUOUS main apartments are on the first floor of this vast château complex. Around the Marble Courtyard are the private apartments of the king and queen. On the garden side are the state apartments where official court life took place. These were richly decorated by Charles Le Brun with colored marble, stone and wood carvings, murals, velvet, silver and gilded furniture. Beginning with the Salon d'Hercule, each state room is dedicated to an Olympian deity. The climax is the Hall of Mirrors, where 17 great mirrors face tall arched windows.

KEY TO FLOORPLAN

- South wing
- Coronation room
- Madame de Maintenon's apartments
- Queen's apartments and private suite
- State apartments
- King's apartments and private suite
- North wing
- Non-exhibition space

★ Queen's Bedroom
In this room the queens of France gave birth to the royal children in public view.

The Marble Courtyard is overlooked by a gilded balcony.

Entrance

The Salon du Sacre is **Entrance** adorned with huge paintings of Napoleon by Jacques-Louis David.

★ Salon de Vénus
A statue of Louis XIV stands amid the rich marble decor of this room.

Stairs to ground floor reception area

★ Chapelle Royale
The chapel's first floor was reserved for the royal family and the ground floor for the court. The beautiful interior is decorated with Corinthian columns and white marble, gilding and Baroque murals.

STAR FEATURES
★ Chapelle Royale
★ Salon de Vénus
★ Hall of Mirrors
★ Queen's Bedroom

★ Hall of Mirrors
Great state occasions were held in this room stretching 70 m (233 ft) along the west façade. Here, in 1919, the Treaty of Versailles was ratified, ending World War I.

Oeil-de-Boeuf

The King's Bedroom is where Louis XIV died in 1715.

The Cabinet du Conseil was used by the king to receive his ministers and family.

Salon de la Guerre
The room's theme of war is reinforced by Antoine Coysevox's stuccoed relief of Louis XIV riding to victory.

Louis XVI's library features Neo-Classical paneling and the king's terrestrial globe.

Salon d'Apollon
Designed by Le Brun and dedicated to the god Apollo, this was Louis XIV's throne room. A copy of Hyacinthe Rigaud's famous portrait of the king (1701) hangs here.

Salon d'Hercule

TIMELINE

Louis XV

1667 Grand Canal begun		**1793** Louis XVI and Marie Antoinette executed	**1833** Louis-Philippe turns the château into a museum	
1668 Construction of new château by Le Vau	**1722** 12-year-old Louis XV occupies Versailles			

1650	1700	1750	1800	1850

1671 Interior decoration by Le Brun begun	**1715** Death of Louis XIV. Versailles abandoned by court	**1789** King and queen forced to leave Versailles for Paris	
			1919 Treaty of Versailles signed on June 28
1661 Louis XIV enlarges château	**1682** Louis XIV and Marie-Thérèse move to Versailles	**1774** Louis XVI and Marie Antoinette live at Versailles	

Château de Sceaux ❼

Sceaux, Hauts-de-Seine. ☎ 01 46 61 06 71. ◯ Wed–Mon. ● public hols. ▨ ♿ 📷 groups.

Tʜᴇ ᴘᴀʀᴄ ᴅᴇ sᴄᴇᴀᴜx, bounded by elegant villas, is an appealing mixture of formal gardens, woods and water, featuring Classical gardens designed by Le Nôtre. The gardens use water to great effect, with tiered waterfalls and fountains presenting a moving staircase that cascades into an octagonal basin. This feeds into the Grand Canal and offers a poplar-lined view to the Pavillon de Hanovre. This elegant pavilion is one of several that adorn the park, which also contains Mansart's Classical Orangerie. Today this is the setting for exhibitions and, in summer, classical music concerts.

Built for Colbert in 1670, the original château was demolished and rebuilt in Louis XIII style in 1856. The stylish fake contains the Musée de l'Ile de France, which celebrates the landscapes, châteaux and history of the region through paintings, furniture, sculpture and ceramics.

Château de Dampierre ❽

Dampierre-en-Yvelines, Yvelines. ☎ 01 30 52 53 24. ◯ Apr–mid-Oct: daily pm. ▨ ♿ restricted. 📷

Aғᴛᴇʀ ᴠᴇʀsᴀɪʟʟᴇs and Rambouillet, Dampierre is the most celebrated château southwest of Paris. Built in 1675 for the Duc de Chevreuse, the exterior of the château is a harmonious composition of rose-colored brick and cool stone, designed by Hardouin-Mansart.

By contrast, the interior sumptuously evokes Versailles, particularly in the royal apartments and the Louis XIV dining room. The grandest room is the frescoed Salle des Fêtes, remodeled in the 19th century in triumphal Roman style. The rooms overlook gardens landscaped around a canal by Le Nôtre.

Château de Rambouillet

Château de Rambouillet ❾

Rambouillet, Yvelines. ☎ 01 34 83 00 25. ◯ Wed–Mon. ● Jan 1, May 1, Nov 1 & 11, Dec 25, and when president in residence. ▨ 📷

Tʜᴇ ᴄʜᴀ̂ᴛᴇᴀᴜ borders the deep Forêt de Rambouillet, once the favorite royal hunting ground. This ivy-covered red-brick château, flanked by five stone towers, is curious rather than beautiful. Adopted as a feudal castle, country estate, royal palace and Imperial residence, it reflects a composite of French royal history. Since 1897, it has been the president's official summer residence.

Inside, oak-paneled rooms are adorned with Empire-style furnishings and Aubusson tapestries. The main façade overlooks Classical parterres. Nearby is the Queen's Dairy, given by Louis XVI to Marie Antoinette so that she could play milkmaid.

Environs
About 28 km (17 miles) north on the D11 is the **Château de Thoiry,** which has a large zoo of around 800 animals in its grounds and an innovative play area for children.

Disneyland Paris ❿

Marne-la-Vallée, Seine-et-Marne. ☎ 01 64 74 30 00. ◯ daily. 🚆 Marne-la-Valée-Chessy. 🚄 TGV from Lille or Lyon. ✈ from both airports. ▨ ♿ ⓦ www.disneyland.paris.com

Dɪsɴᴇʏʟᴀɴᴅ ᴘᴀʀɪs as a whole covers 200 ha (500 acres), with two theme parks; six hotels; facilities for shopping, dining and leisure; convention centers and a campsite. But of most inter-est to children of all ages are the Parks – the first with its five themed Lands, offering a wealth of magical experiences and dominated by **Minnie Mouse**
Sleeping Beauty's Castle, and the new Walt Disney Studios, paying homage to the movies.

Château Vaux-le-Vicomte ⓫

Maincy, Seine-et-Marne. ☎ 01 64 14 41 90. ◯ late-Mar–Nov 11: daily. ▨ 🍴

Sᴇᴛ ɴᴏʀᴛʜ ᴏғ ᴍᴇʟᴜɴ, not far from Fontainebleau, the château enjoys a peaceful rural location. Nicolas Fouquet, a

ANDRÉ LE NÔTRE

As the greatest French landscape gardener, Le Nôtre (1613–1700) created masterpieces in château gardens all over France. His Classical vision shaped many in the Ile de France, such as those at Dampierre, Sceaux and Vaux-le-Vicomte. At Vaux he perfected the concept of the *jardin à la française*: avenues framed by statues and box hedges; water gardens with fountains and ornate pools; graceful terraces and geometrical parterres "embroidered" with motifs. His genius lay in architectural orchestration and a sense of symmetry, typified by the sweeping vistas of Versailles, his greatest triumph.

powerful court financier to Louis XIV, challenged the architect Le Vau and the decorator Le Brun to create the most sumptuous palace of the day. The result, one of the greatest 17th-century French châteaux, surpassed Fouquet's dreams. However, it also led to his downfall. Louis and his ministers were so enraged – because its luxury cast the royal palaces into the shade – that they arrested Fouquet and confiscated all his estates.

As befits Fouquet's grand tastes, the interior is a gilded banquet of frescoes, stucco, caryatids and giant busts. The Salon des Muses boasts Le Brun's magnificent frescoed

ceiling of dancing nymphs and poetic sphinxes. La Grande Chambre Carrée is decorated in Louis XIII style with paneled walls and an impressive triumphal frieze, evoking Rome. Unlike Versailles or even Fontainebleau, its many rooms feel touchingly intimate and the scale is not overwhelming.

Yet Vaux-le-Vicomte's continuing fame is due to André Le Nôtre's stunning gardens, the finest in the Ile de France. The landscape designer's early training as a painter is evident in the magnificent succession of terraces, ornamental lakes and fountains, which descend to a formal canal.

Provins ⑫

Seine-et-Marne. 🚶 *12,000*. 🚊 🚌
🛈 *Chemin de Villecran (01 64 60 26 26)*. 🚍 *Sat*.

AS A ROMAN OUTPOST, Provins commanded the border of Ile de France and Champagne. Today, it offers a coherent vision of the medieval world. Ville Haute, the upper town, is clustered within high 12th-century ramparts, complete with crenelations and defensive ditches. The ramparts to the west are the best preserved. Here, between the fortified gateways of Porte de Jouy and Porte St-Jean, the fortifications are dotted with square, round and rectangular towers.

The town is dominated by Tour César, a keep with four corner turrets and a pyramid-shaped roof. The moat and fortifications were added by the English during the Hundred Years' War. A guard-room leads to a gallery and views over the place du Chatel, a dusty square of medieval gabled houses, and the Grange aux Dîmes to the endless wheatfields beyond.

Provins is proud of its crimson roses. Every June, a floral celebration is held in the riverside rose garden, marked by a medieval festival.

Château Vaux-le-Vicomte seen across the gardens designed by Le Nôtre

Château de Fontainebleau ⓫

Ceiling detail from the Salle de Bal

FONTAINEBLEAU is not the product of a single vision, but a bewildering cluster of styles from different periods. Louis VII built an abbey here that was consecrated by Thomas à Beckett in 1169. A medieval tower survives, but the present château harks back to François I. Originally drawn by the local hunting, the Renaissance king created a decorative château modeled on Florentine and Roman styles.

Fontainebleau's abiding charm comes from its relative informality and spectacular forest setting. While impossible to cover in a day, the *grands appartements* provide a sumptuous introduction to this royal palace.

Ground floor

Jardin de Diane
Now more romantic than Classical, the garden features a bronze fountain of Diana as huntress.

★ Escalier du Fer-à-Cheval
This imposing horseshoe-shaped staircase by Jean Androuet du Cerceau, built in 1634, lies at the end of Cour du Cheval Blanc. Its ingenious design allowed carriages to pass beneath the two arches.

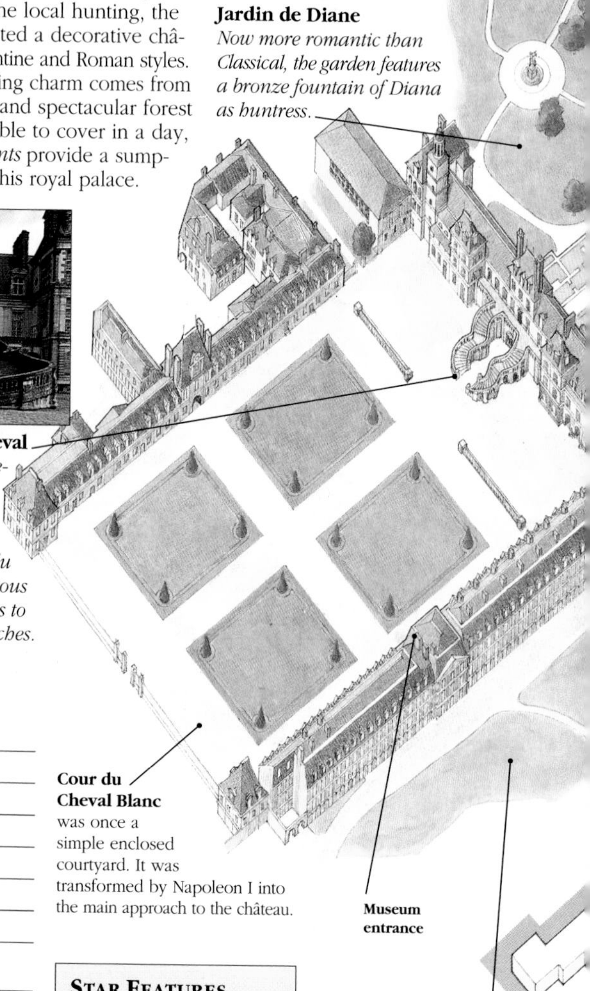

KEY TO FLOOR PLAN

- ☐ Petits Appartements
- ☐ Galerie des Cerfs
- ■ Musée Chinois
- ☐ Musée Napoléon
- ☐ Grands Appartements
- ☐ Salle Renaissance
- ☐ Appartements de Madame de Maintenon
- ☐ Grands Appartements des Souverains
- ☐ Escalier de la Reine/ Appartements des Chasses
- ☐ Chapelle de la Trinité
- ☐ Appartement Intérieur de l'Empereur

Cour du Cheval Blanc
was once a simple enclosed courtyard. It was transformed by Napoleon I into the main approach to the château.

Museum entrance

The Jardin Anglais is a romantic "English" garden, planted with cypress and plantain trees. It was re-designed in the 19th century.

STAR FEATURES

- **★ Escalier du Fer-à-Cheval**
- **★ Salle de Bal**
- **★ Galerie François I**

Porte Dorée
Originally a feudal gate-house, this was transformed into the entrance pavilion to the forest by Gilles Le Breton for François I.

Cour Oval

First floor

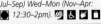

VISITORS' CHECKLIST

Seine-et-Marne. ☎ 01 60 71 50 60. ◯ 9:30am–5pm (6pm Jul–Sep) Wed–Mon (Nov–Apr: ◯ 12:30–2pm). 🎦 ♿ 🅿 🛍

★ Salle de Bal
The Renaissance ballroom, de-signed by Primaticcio (1552), was finished under Henri II. His emblems adorn the walnut cof-fered ceiling, forming a pattern reflected in the parquet floor.

The Appartements de Napoleon I house his grandiose throne in the Emperor's Salle du Trône, formerly the Chambre du Roi.

Cour de la Fontaine

★ Galerie François I
This gilded gallery is a tribute to the Italian artists in the Ecole de Fontainebleau. Rosso Fiorentino's allegorical frescoes pay homage to the king's wish to create "a second Rome."

Chapelle de la Sainte Trinité was designed by Henri II in 1550. The chapel acquired its vaulted and frescoed ceiling under Henri IV and was completed by Louis XIII.

THE BARBIZON SCHOOL

Artists have been drawn to the glades of Fontainebleau since the 1840s, when a group of landscape painters, determined to paint only from nature, formed around Théodore Rousseau and Millet. They settled in the hamlet of Barbizon where, today, Rousseau's workshop is a museum dedicated to the Ecole de Barbizon.

Spring at Barbizon, painted by Jean-François Millet (1814–75)

NORTHEAST
FRANCE

Introducing Northeast France

THE ROLLING PLAINS of Northern France run from the English Channel to the wooded Ardennes hills and the Vosges mountains of Alsace. Apart from sombre battle memorials, the area has France's finest gothic cathedrals – and a long tradition of brewing good quality beers. There is fine wine too, in Champagne and Alsace. The old heavy industry has gone, while Lille's growth as a transport hub has brought new prosperity. This map shows some of the most interesting sights.

Amiens Cathedral *is renowned for its fine wood carvings and its nave, the highest in France (see pp192–3).*

Amiens Cathedral

LE NORD AND PICARDY
(See pp182–95)

Beauvais Cathedral

Château de Compiègne

Reims Cathedral

Troyes Cathedral

The pride of Beauvais *is its Gothic cathedral and astronomical clock (see p190), which escaped heavy bombing during World War II.*

Half-timbered houses *and Renaissance mansions line the streets and alleys of Troyes' Old Town (see p206), rebuilt after the great fire in 1524. Its cathedral has remarkable stained-glass windows.*

The legacy of World War I *is strong in this area of former battlefields. The Douaumont Memorial outside Verdun (see pp180–81), with its 15,000 graves, is only one of many memorials and cemeteries here.*

Haut-Koenigsbourg, *a castle rebuilt in Neo-Gothic style by Kaiser Wilhelm II when Alsace-Lorraine was under German rule, is one of Alsace's most popular attractions (see p218).*

Strasbourg, *seat of the European Council, has a fine Gothic cathedral (see pp220–21) surrounded by delightful historic buildings.*

Douaumont Memorial

Porte Chaussée, Verdun

Place Stanislas, Nancy

Strasbourg Cathedral

CHAMPAGNE
(See pp196–207)

ALSACE AND LORRAINE
(See pp208–23)

Haut-Koenigsbourg

| 0 kilometers | 50 |
| 0 miles | 50 |

Regional Food: Northeast France

Visitors to Boulogne, Le Touquet and Calais know the northeast best for its sea catch. Besides heaped platters of *fruits de mer*, a plate of steamed mussels and french fries is one of the pleasures of this coast. A giant waffle dusted with sugar completes the meal.

Moutarde de Meaux

Hops, used to make the local beer, grow inland, along with fields of chicory. Both hops and chicory are served as vegetables. Alsace and Lorraine share in the tradition of beer-making – beer is commonly used in cooking in Lorraine, while Riesling wine is more popular in Alsace. Alsatian cooking centers around *charcuterie* (cooked meats), culminating in the classic *choucroute garnie* (sauerkraut with pork and sausages).

Rich cakes and tarts are also popular, especially the *kougelhopf*, a ring-shaped cake studded with raisins, currants and almonds, and sometimes soaked in Kirsch.

Potato salad with sausage *reveals the German influence in robust Alsatian fare. This dish is usually served warm.*

Brioche *is a buttery, egg-enriched bread. In Alsace, various brioches are associated with festivals – neujohweka are eaten on New Year's Day, and on St. Nicholas Day (Dec 6) bakers make small brioche figures called* bonshommes.

Herrings, *found along the northeast coast of France, are popular grilled or cured, and served with potatoes.*

Bacon   **Frankfurter**

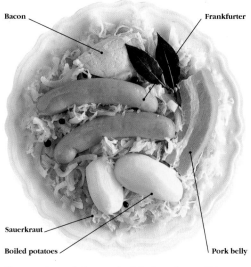

Sauerkraut

Boiled potatoes   **Pork belly**

Pâté en croûte *is cooked in a pastry case. The pastry keeps the pâté moist and faintly pink while it is baked in the oven.*

Choucroute garnie *is an earthy dish of sauerkraut with bacon, cured pork loin or knuckle, and fresh and smoked sausages – among them* boudin noir *(black pudding),* saucisse de Strasbourg *(a plump frankfurter) and* boudin blanc *(white pork sausage). It should be accompanied by boiled potatoes and strong* moutarde de Meaux, *along with a glass of chilled Alsatian Riesling wine.*

Pea soup, *also known as* Potage St-Germain, *is made with fresh peas, which abound in the market gardens of Amiens.*

Truite Ardennaise, *pan-fried trout with smoked ham and cream, is an old-time classic from the Ardennes region.*

Zewelwai *or* **onion quiche** *is a tart made with a filling of onions, eggs and cream, typical of Lorraine.*

Porc aux deux pommes *is the quintessential Alsatian dish, consisting of pork served with potatoes and apples.*

Ardennes ham, *cured in the traditional local method, takes its name from the area. It is then salted and cold-smoked.*

Carbonnade *is a beef stew braised in beer; the name derives from "carbon," when the meat was grilled over coals.*

Tarte Alsacienne *is a fruit- and custard-filled tart, often made with yeasted dough instead of shortbread pastry.*

Madeleines *are little sponge cakes immortalized by Proust in* Remembrance of Things Past.

Rum babas *are rum and sugar syrup-soaked yeast pastries baked in individual molds.*

Macaroons *are almond meringue biscuits, a specialty of Nancy, capital of Lorraine.*

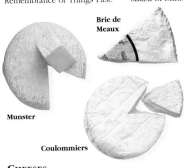

Brie de
Meaux

Munster

Coulommiers

DRINKS

Beer is often drunk with meals in the northeast. Traditional methods of beer-making are still followed by big breweries such as Krönenbourg, as well as many smaller breweries.

CHEESES

In addition to the familiar Brie de Meaux and tangy Munster of Alsace, the northeast has many lesser known but equally flavorful cheeses such as the pungent Maroilles, Vieux Lille, Boulette d'Avesnes, Dauphin, Rollot and Coulommiers.

Savenne

Krönenbourg

Bière de Garde

France's Wine Regions: Champagne

Giant carved barrel, Épernay

SINCE ITS FABLED "INVENTION" by the monk Dom Pérignon in the 17th century, no other wine has rivaled champagne as the symbol of luxury and celebration. Only wines made in this region by the *Méthode Champenoise* can be called champagne *(see p200)*. Most champagne is non-vintage: the skill of the blenders using reserves of older wines, creates consistency and excellence year after year. The "big names" *(grandes marques)* command the prestige and prices, but many small growers and cooperatives also produce excellent-value wines well worth seeking out.

LOCATOR MAP

▨ *Champagne wine region*

Grapes going for pressing, Montagne de Reims

WINE REGIONS

Champagne is a compact wine region, largely in the French *département* of the Marne. Certain areas within it are particularly identified with certain styles of wine. The Aube is famous not only for champagne but also for pricey and eccentric still wine, Rosé des Riceys.

KEY FACTS ABOUT CHAMPAGNE

Location and Climate

The cool, marginal climate creates the quality that other sparkling wines strive for, but seldom achieve. Chalky soils and east- and north-facing aspects help produce the relatively high acidity champagne needs.

Grape Varieties

Three varieties are grown, red **Pinot Noir** and **Pinot Meunier**, and white **Chardonnay**. Most champagne is a blend of all three, though Blanc de Blancs is 100 per cent Chardonnay and Blanc de Noirs, although white, is made only from red grapes.

Good Producers

Grandes Marques: Bollinger, Gosset, Krug, Möet et Chandon, Joseph Perrier, Louis Roederer, Pol Roger, Billecart-Salmon, Veuve Clicquot, Taittinger, Ruinart, Laurent Perrier, Salon.
Négociants, cooperatives & growers: Boizel, M.Arnould, Cattier, Bricout, Drappier, Ployez-Jacquemart, H. Blin, Gimmonet, Andre Jacquart, Chartogne-Taillet, Vilmart, Alfred Gratien, Emile Hamm, B. Paillard, P. Gerbais.

Good Vintages

1998, 1996, 1990, 1989, 1988, 1985.

BOLLINGER
Spécial Cuvée
BRUT
Champagne   *Aÿ France*

From a name famous even to nonwine lovers, this is in the classic brut *(dry)* style; only brut non dosage *or* brut sauvage *is drier.*

KEY

▨ Champagne *appellation* area

▨ Vallée de la Marne district

▨ Montagne de Reims district

▨ Côte de Sézanne district

▨ Côte des Blancs district

▨ Aube district

0 kilometers   15

0 miles   15

Soissons

Château Thierry

La Ferté-sous-Jouarre

Petit Morin

Grand Morin

Nogent-sur-Seine

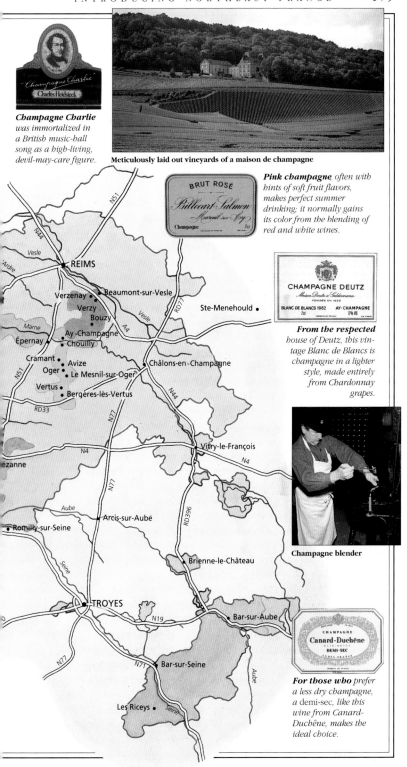

Champagne Charlie *was immortalized in a British music-hall song as a high-living, devil-may-care figure.*

Meticulously laid out vineyards of a maison de champagne

Pink champagne *often with hints of soft fruit flavors, makes perfect summer drinking; it normally gains its color from the blending of red and white wines.*

From the respected *house of Deutz, this vintage Blanc de Blancs is champagne in a lighter style, made entirely from Chardonnay grapes.*

Champagne blender

For those who *prefer a less dry champagne, a demi-sec, like this wine from Canard-Duchêne, makes the ideal choice.*

The Battle of the Somme

THE MANY CEMETERIES that cover the Somme region serve as poignant reminders of the mass slaughter that took place on the Western Front in World War I (which ended with the Armistice on November 11, 1918). Between July 1 and November 21, 1916, the Allied forces lost more than 600,000 men and the Germans at least 465,000. The Battle of the Somme, a series of campaigns conducted by British and French armies against fortified positions held by the Germans, relieved the hard-pressed French at Verdun; but hopes of a breakthrough never materialized, and the Allies only managed to advance 16 km (10 miles).

British World War I soldier

LOCATOR MAP

☐ *Somme battlefield*

Beaumont Hamel Memorial Park, a tribute to the Royal Newfoundland Regiment, features a huge bronze caribou.

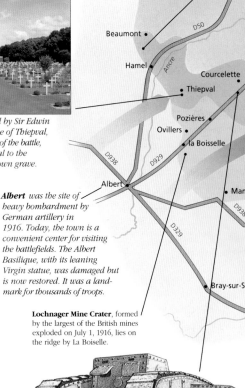

Thiepval Memorial *was designed by Sir Edwin Lutyens. It dominates the landscape of Thiepval, one of the most hard-fought areas of the battle, appropriately chosen as a memorial to the 73,367 British soldiers with no known grave.*

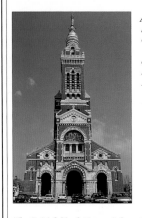

Albert *was the site of heavy bombardment by German artillery in 1916. Today, the town is a convenient center for visiting the battlefields. The Albert Basilique, with its leaning Virgin statue, was damaged but is now restored. It was a landmark for thousands of troops.*

Lochnager Mine Crater, formed by the largest of the British mines exploded on July 1, 1916, lies on the ridge by La Boiselle.

The British Tank Memorial, *on the main road from Albert to Bapaume, commemorates the first use of tanks in warfare on September 15, 1916. The attack was a limited success; World War I tanks were too slow and unreliable to transform warfare and it continued to be fought mainly by heavy artillery and machine guns.*

Propaganda in World War I *was employed by both sides to maintain support at home. This French postcard has an especially popular image. It shows a dying soldier kissing the flag, under the tender gaze of a ministering nurse, affirming his faith in the cause as he breathes his last breath.*

Delville Wood *South African Memorial and Museum show the importance of Common-wealth forces in the Somme.*

VISITORS' CHECKLIST

D929, D938 from Albert. **i** *9 rue Gambetta, Albert.* **C** *03 22 75 16 42.* **W** *www.ville-albert.fr* **Albert Basilique, Beaumont Hamel Memorial Park, Delville Wood, La Boiselle, Thiepval & Pozières memorials** ☐ *daily.* **Ulster Tower** ☐ *Feb–Mar: Tue–Sun; Apr–Nov: daily.* **South African Memorial Museum**, *Delville Wood, Long-ueval.* **C** *03 22 85 02 17.* ☐ *Feb–Nov: Tue–Sun.* ● *public hols.* **Historial de Péronne** **C** *03 22 83 14 18.* ☐ *May–Sep: daily; Oct–Apr: Tue–Sun.* ● *mid-Dec–mid-Jan.*

Poppies *were one of the few plants to grow on the battlefield. Ghengis Khan brought the first white poppy from China and, according to legend, it turned red after battle. Today poppies are a symbol of remembrance.*

KEY

▨	Allied forces
▨	German forces
☐	Front Line before July 1, 1916
▨	Front Line progress July–September 1916
▨	Front Line progress September–November 1916

```
0 kilometers          5
0 miles               5
```

Map labels: Bapaume, D929, A1, N17, A2, Flers, Morval, Ginchy, Maricourt, Maurepas, Canal du Nord, D917, N17, Canal de la Somme, A1, D1, Péronne

The Front Line trenches *stretched from the North Sea to the Swiss frontier; only by keeping underground could men survive the terrible conditions. Trenches remain in a few areas, including the Beaumont Hamel Park.*

LE NORD
AND PICARDY

PAS DE CALAIS · NORD · SOMME · OISE · AISNE

BENEATH THE MODERN SKIN *of France's northernmost region, the sights and monuments bear witness to the triumphs and turbulence of its past: soaring Gothic cathedrals, stately châteaux along the Oise River and the battlefields and memorials of World War I.*

The Channel ports of Dunkerque, Calais and Boulogne and the refined resort of Le Touquet are the focal points along a busy coastline that stretches from the Somme estuary to the Belgian frontier. Boulogne has a genuine maritime flavor, and the white cliffs running from here to Calais provide the most dramatic scenery along the Côte d'Opale.

Flemish culture holds sway along the border with Belgium: an unfamiliar France of windmills and canals where the local taste is for beer, savory stews and festivals with gallivanting giants. Lille is the dominant city here, a sprawling modern metropolis with a lively historic heart and an excellent art museum. To the southwest, the grace of Flemish architecture is handsomely displayed in the central squares of Arras, the capital of Artois.

From here to the Somme Valley, the legacy of World War I, with its memorial cemeteries and poppy-strewn battlefields, makes for compelling viewing.

Cathedrals are the main appeal of Picardy. In Amiens, its capital, Cathédrale Notre-Dame is a pinnacle of the Gothic style – its magnificence echoed by the dizzying achievements at Beauvais farther south. Splendid cathedrals in Noyon, Senlis and the delightful hilltop town of Laon chart the evolution of the Gothic. Closer to Paris, two châteaux command attention. Chantilly, the epicenter of French equestrianism, boasts gardens by Le Nôtre and a 19th-century château housing copious art treasures. Compiègne, bordered by a large and inviting forest, plays host to a lavish royal palace favored by French rulers from Louis XV to Napoleon III.

Memorial cemetery in Vallée de la Somme, an area still haunted by the memory of World War I

◁ **Catamarans on the busy beach of Le Touquet Paris-Plage**

Exploring Le Nord and Picardy

As the gateway to England and Belgium, this northern corner of France is buzzing with businesses and industries, with the large, Euro-oriented city of Lille offering great culture as well as a new hi-tech district. Yet peace and quiet is never far away. The coast between the historic port of Boulogne-sur-Mer and the Vallée de la Somme has a rich birdlife and is perfect for a relaxing seaside visit. Inland, the many Gothic cathedrals such as Amiens and Beauvais make an impressive tour, and the World War I battlefields and memorials provide an important insight into 20th-century history. Farther south, the grand châteaux at Compiègne and Chantilly – which has the fascinating Musée Condé – are easily visited en route to or from Paris.

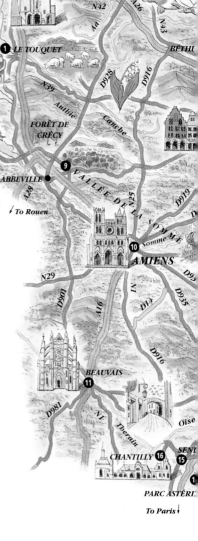

KEY

▨	Highway
▨	Major road
▨	Minor road
▨	Scenic route
≈	River
☆	Viewing point

0 kilometers — 25

0 miles — 25

**Lively outdoor café in the historic Grand'
Place in the heart of Arras**

SIGHTS AT A GLANCE

The meandering waters in the Vallée de la Somme

GETTING AROUND

The main entry point into the region is Calais (and the Channel Tunnel terminal 3km south). From here, autoroutes A16 and A26/A1, several major N roads, and mainline rail services, run directly to Paris. In addition, TGVs serve Calais-Frethun, Lille and Paris. There is a dense road network throughout the region. With their many local buses and train connections, Lille and Amiens make good bases. The A26 (or *Autoroute des Anglais*) crosses the whole region from Calais to Troyes, via Arras and Laon, giving easy access to eastern Picardy. It's also a useful route if you're heading south and want to avoid Paris.

Poppies, the symbol of World War I battlefields, in Vallée de la Somme

Le Touquet beach at low tide

Le Touquet ❶

Pas de Calais. 🏠 6,000. 🚇 🚉
🛈 *Palais de l'Europe (03 21 06 72 00).*
🛒 *Thu & Sat (Jun–mid-Sep: also Mon).*

PROPERLY KNOWN as Le Touquet Paris-Plage, this resort was created in the 19th century and became fashionable with the rich and famous between the two World Wars.

A vast pine forest, planted in 1855, spreads around the town, sheltering stately villas. To the west, a grid of stylish hotels, vacation residences and sophisticated shops and restaurants borders a long, sandy beach. A racecourse and a casino help retain Le Touquet's affluent atmosphere, complemented by seaside amusements and sports facilities, including horseback-riding, golf and land yachting.

Farther inland, the hilltop town of **Montreuil** has lime-washed 17th-century houses, abundant restaurants and a tree-shaded rampart walk.

Boulogne-sur-Mer ❷

Pas de Calais. 🏠 44,000. 🚇 🚉 🚌
🛈 *24 quai Gambetta (03 21 10 88 10).*
🛒 *Wed & Sat.*

AN IMPORTANT fishing port and busy marina, Boulogne rewards its visitors well. Its historical attractions come neatly boxed in a walled Haute Ville, with the Porte des Dunes opening onto a 17th–19th-century ensemble of Palais de Justice, Biblio-

thèque and Hôtel de Ville in **place de la Résistance**.

The 19th-century **Basilique Notre-Dame** is capped by a huge dome visible for miles around. Inside, a bejeweled wooden statue represents Boulogne's patroness, Notre-Dame de Boulogne. She is wearing a *soleil*, a radiant headdress also worn by the women of the town during the *Grande Procession* held annually in her honor. Nearby, the powerful moated 13th-century **Château**, built for the counts of Boulogne, is now a well-organized historical museum.

In the center of town, shops, hotels and fish restaurants line the quai Gambetta on the east bank of the Liane River. To the north lie Boulogne's beach and **Nausicaa**, a vast, spectacular and innovative aquarium and sea center.

North of the town, the **Colonne de la Grande Armée** was erected in 1841 as a monument to Napoleon I's planned invasion of England in 1803–5. From the top there is a panoramic view along the coast toward Calais. This is the most scenic stretch of the Côte d'Opale (Opal Coast),

with the windblown headlands of **Cap Gris-Nez** and **Cap Blanc-Nez** offering extensive views across the Channel.

♣ **Château**
Rue de Bernet. 🛈 *03 21 10 02 20.*
🕐 *Wed–Mon.* ● *Jan 1, May 1, Dec 25.*
🗡 **Nausicaa**
Bd Sainte-Beuve. 🛈 *03 21 30 99 99.*
🕐 *daily.* ● *3 weeks in Jan, Dec 25.*
🅿 🛒

Calais ❸

Pas de Calais. 🏠 80,000. 🚇 🚉 🚌
🛈 *12 bd Clémenceau (03 21 96 62 40).* 🛒 *Wed, Thu & Sat.*

CALAIS IS A BUSY cross-Channel port with a sandy beach to the west. Clumsily rebuilt after World War II, it seems to have little to offer at first sight. For the brave-hearted, the huge shopping complex beside the Eurotunnel terminal suffices.

The **Musée des Beaux Arts et de la Dentelle**, however, has works by the Dutch and Flemish Schools, and recalls the town's lace-making industry. Also on display are studies for Auguste Rodin's famous statue

The windswept Cap Blanc-Nez on the Côte d'Opale

The Burghers of Calais **by Auguste Rodin (1895)**

The Burghers of Calais (1895). Freshly renovated, the statue stands outside the Flemish Renaissance-style Hôtel de Ville in the southern part of town. It celebrates an event during Edward III's siege of Calais in 1347, when six burghers offered their lives to save the town.

Musée de la Guerre, housed in a battle-scarred German blockhouse, offers a detailed account of local events during World War II.

Musée des Beaux Arts et de la Dentelle
25 rue Richelieu. [*03 21 46 48 40.*] ☐ *Wed–Mon (Sun pm).* ● *public hols.* ⚅ ⚄

Musée de la Guerre
Parc Saint Pierre. [*03 21 34 21 57.*] ☐ *May–Sep: daily; mid-Feb–Apr & Oct–mid-Nov: Wed–Mon.* ⚅ ⚄

Dunkerque ➍

Nord. 🔼 *70,000.* 🚊 🚌 ⛴
🛈 *rue Amiral Ronarc'h (03 28 66 79 21).* ☐ *Wed, Sat.*

THOUGH A MAJOR industrial port, Dunkerque has much Flemish character. Start a tour (on foot or by boat) from Place du Minck, with its fresh fish stalls. Nearby **Musée Portuaire**, celebrates the town's maritime history. In the old center, a statue commemorates local hero Jean Bart, a 17th–century corsair, who lies in **Eglise St-Eloi**. Its belfry (1440) offers fine views.

Musée des Beaux Arts has an exhibition of the dramatic evacuation of 350,000 British

and French troops in 1940, and works by artists Vasarely and César. The **Musée d'Art Contemporain** features ceramics and glassware.

Musée Portuaire
9 quai de la Citadelle. [*03 28 63 33 39.*] ☐ *Wed–Mon.* ● *Jan 1, May 1, Dec 25.* ⚅ ⚄

The port at Dunkerque

Musée des Beaux Arts
Place du Général de Gaulle. [*03 28 59 21 65.*] ☐ *Wed–Mon.* ● *Jan 1, Nov 1, Dec 25.* ⚅ ⚄ *gr. fl. only.*

Musée d'Art Contemporain
Avenue des Bains. [*03 28 59 21 65.*] ● *for renovations until Spring 2003.* ⚅ ⚄

St-Omer ➎

Pas de Calais. 🔼 *15,000.* 🚊 🚌 🛈 *4 rue Lion d'Or (03 21 98 70 00).* ☐ *Sat.*

REFINED, old-fashioned St-Omer seems untouched by the war. Pilasters adorn the 17th- and 18th-century houses lining the cobbled streets, one of which **Hôtel Sandelin**, is now a museum of fine and decorative arts. The cathedral has original 13th-century tiles and a huge Classical organ. The **Bibliothèque Municipale** contains rare manuscripts from the Abbaye St-Bertin, a ruined 15th-century abbey east of town.

5km (3 miles) from St-Omer, **La Coupole** is a well-arranged, informative WW2 museum inside a converted bunker.

Hôtel Sandelin
14 rue Carnot. [*03 21 38 00 94.*] ☐ *Wed–Sun.* ● *for renovation until sometime in 2003.* ⚅ ⚄ *gr. fl.*

Bibliothèque Municipale
40 rue Gambetta. [*03 21 38 35 08.*] ☐ *Tue–Sat.* ● *public hols.*

La Coupole
[*03 21 93 07 07.*] ☐ *daily.* ● *2 weeks in Jan.*

CHANNEL CROSSINGS

Calais is only 36 km (22 miles) southeast of the English coast, and crossing the waters of the Channel – which the French know as La Manche (the Sleeve) – has inspired many intrepid exploits. The first crossing by balloon was in 1785 by Jean Pierre Blanchard; Captain M. Webb made the first swim in 1875; and Louis Blériot's pioneering flight followed in 1909. Plans for an undersea tunnel, first laid as early as 1751, were finally achieved in 1994 with the opening of a rail link between Fréthun and Folkestone.

Children watching Louis Blériot taking off, 1909

Flandre Maritime ⑥

Nord. 🚊 *Lille*. 🚉 *Bergues*. 🚌 *Dunkerque*. 🛈 *Bergues, pl de la République (03 28 68 71 06)*.

SOUTH OF DUNKERQUE lies a flat, agricultural plain with narrow waterways and expansive skies – an archetypal Flemish landscape with canals, cyclists and ancient windmills. The **Noordmeulen**, built just north of Hondschoote in 1127, is thought to be the oldest windmill in Europe.

From Hondschoote the D3 follows the Canal de la Basse Colme west to Bergues, a fortified wool town with fine 16th–17th-century Flemish works in its **Musée Municipal**. Farther south, the hilltop town of **Cassel** has a cobbled Grande Place with 16th–18th-century buildings, and views across Flanders and Belgium from its Jardin Public.

🏛 Musée Municipal

1 rue du Mont de Piété, Bergues. 📞 *03 28 68 13 30.* ⏰ *Wed–Mon.* ⬛ *25 Dec–Jan.* ▨

Lille ⑦

Nord. 🚶 *214,000.* 🚉 🚌 🛈 *Palais Rihour (03 20 21 94 21).* 🛒 *daily.* 🌐 *www.lilletourism.com*

TRANSFORMED IN recent years, not least by the advent of Eurostar, Lille has excellent stores and markets and a

Flower stands in the arcades of the Vieille Bourse in Lille

Musicians in place du Général de Gaulle, in the heart of Vieux Lille

powerful sense of its historic Flemish identity – the Flemish name, Rijssel, is still used and some of the area's one million residents speak a Franco-Flemish patois. With heavy industry declining, the city has turned to high-tech. A modern commercial quarter, including the Euralille shopping complex, adjoins Lille Europe station, the TGV/ Eurostar/Thalys rail interchange. The city's 'metro', VAL, is a driverless automatic train.

The city's charm lies in its historic center, Vieux Lille – a vibrant concentration of cobbled squares and narrow streets that are packed with stylish stores, cafés and restaurants. Place du Général de Gaulle forms its hub, with impressive façades including the 17th-century **Vieille Bourse** (Old Exchange). Adjacent stand the imposing **Nouvelle Bourse** and the **Opéra**, both built in the early years of the 20th-century. The

huge, moated five-point brick Citadel is also worth a look.

⚕ Hospice Comtesse

32 rue de la Monnaie. 📞 *03 28 36 84 00.* ⏰ *Wed–Sun, Mon pm.* ▨ A hospital was founded here in 1237. Today its 15th- and 17th-century buildings house exhibitions. The Sick Room (1470) has a splendid barrel-vaulted ceiling, the Community Wing a fine Delft-tiled kitchen. There's also a collection of ancient musical instruments.

🏛 Musée des Beaux Arts

Pl de la République. 📞 *03 20 06 78 00.* ⏰ *Wed–Sun, Mon pm.* ▨ 🚻 ♿ One of the best art collections outside Paris, the museum is strong on Flemish works, including Rubens and Van Dyck. Other highlights are *Paradise and Hell* by Dirk Bouts, Van Goyen's *The Skaters*, Goya's *The Letter*, Delacroix's *Médée* as well as works by Courbet and Impressionist paintings.

Arras ❽

Pas de Calais. 👥 42,000. 🚉 🚌
ℹ️ Hôtel de Ville, place des Héros
(03 21 51 26 95). 🛒 Wed, Sat.

THE CENTER of Arras, capital of the Artois region, is graced by two picturesque cobbled squares enclosed by 155 houses with 17th-century Flemish-style façades. A triumph of postwar reconstruction, each residence in the **Grand' Place** and the smaller Place des Héros has a slightly varying design, with some original shop signs still visible.

A monumental **Hôtel de Ville** rebuilt in the Flamboyant Gothic style stands at the west end of place des Héros – in the foyer are two giants, Colas Dédé and Jacqueline, who swagger around the town during local festivals. From the basement you can take an elevator up to the belfry, which offers superb views, or take a guided tour into the labyrinth of underground passages below Arras. These were cut in the limestone as early as the 10th century. They have often served as shelter, and during World War I as a subterranean army camp.

The huge Abbaye St-Vaast includes an 18th–19th-century Neo-Classical cathedral and the **Musée des Beaux-Arts**. The museum contains some fine medieval sculpture including a pair of beautifully carved 13th-century angels. Among other exhibits are a local *arras* (hanging tapestry), and 19th-century works by the School of Arras, a group of realist landscape painters influenced by Corot.

🏛️ Hôtel de Ville
Pl des Héros. 📞 03 21 51 26 95.
🕐 daily. 🎫 oblig for les boves.
🏛️ Musée des Beaux Arts
22 rue Paul Doumer. 📞 03 21 71 26 43. 🕐 Wed–Mon. 🅿️ public hols. 🎫

Vallée de la Somme ❾

Somme. 🚗 🚉 🚌 Amiens.
ℹ️ Péronne (03 22 84 42 38).

THE NAME OF THE Somme remains synonymous with the slaughter and horror of trench warfare during World War I (see pp180-81). Yet the Somme valley also means pretty countryside, a vast estuary wetland, and abundant wildlife. The river winds across Picardy. Small lakes and woods alongside provide enjoyable camping, walking and fishing.

The battlefields lie along the river and its tributaries north and northeast of Amiens, and extend north to Arras. Neat World War I Commonwealth cemeteries, immaculately maintained, cover the area. The **Historial de la Grande Guerre** at Péronne gives a thoughtful introduction.

Roadside shrine, Somme Valley

Boating on the Somme

Parc Mémorial Beaumont-Hamel, near Albert, is a real battlefield being allowed to disappear in its own time. Travel to Vimy Ridge Canadian Memorial, near Arras, to see a bloodbath battle site preserved as it was, and to Notre-Dame de Lorette, the landmark French National Cemetery.

West of Amiens, **Samara** – Amiens' Gallo-Roman name – is France's largest archaeological park, with reconstructions of prehistoric dwellings, and exhibitions explaining early crafts like flint-cutting and corn-grinding. Further downstream, Eglise St-Vulfran at Abbeyville is noted for its Flamboyant Gothic west front with beautifully carved 16th-century door panels.

St-Valéry-sur-Somme is a charming harbor resort with a historic upper town and a tree-lined promenade looking across the estuary. William departed for England from here in 1066. Birdwatchers should visit the Maison de l'Oiseau on the D3 nearby, or the Parc Ornithologique de Marquenterre on the far shore near delightful Le Crotoy. In summer, a little train links the two sides, passing through dunes and marshlands.

🏛️ Historial de la Grande Guerre
Château de Péronne. 📞 03 22 83 14 18. 🕐 Nov–Mar: Tue–Sun; Apr–Oct: daily. 🅿️ mid-Dec–mid-Jan.
🎫 ♿
🏛️ Samara
La Chaussée-Tirancourt. 📞 03 22 51 82 83. 🕐 mid-Mar–mid-Nov: daily. 🎫 ♿

16th-century carvings on Eglise St-Vulfran in Abbeville, Somme Valley

Amiens ⑩

Somme. 🏛 *130,000*. 🚌 🚃 ⊞ *6 bis rue Duseval (03 22 71 60 50)*. 🚢 *Thu & Sat*. ⓦ *www.amiens.com*

THERE IS MORE to Amiens, the capital of Picardy, than its **Cathédrale Notre-Dame** *(see pp192–3)*. The picturesque quarter of St-Leu is a pedestrianized area of low houses and flower-lined canals with waterside restaurants, bars and artisans' shops. Farther east are **Les Hortillonnages**, a colorful patchwork of marshland market gardens, once tended by farmers using punts which now ferry visitors around the protected natural site.

The **Musée de Picardie** has fine medieval and 19th-century sculpture and 16th–20th-century paintings, including a remarkable set of 16th-century group portraits, commissioned annually as offerings to the cathedral. To the south is the Cirque d'Hiver which author Jules Verne (1828– 1905) inaugurated in 1889. **Maison à la Tour**, his home, is open to visitors. Regional furniture and *objets d'art* can be seen at the **Musée d'Art Local et d'Histoire Régionale**.

🏛 **Musée de Picardie**
48 rue de la République. 📞 *03 22 97 14 00*. ◯ *Tue–Sun*. ◯ *Jan 1, May 1, Nov 1 & 11, Dec 25*. 🎫 ♿
🏛 **Musée d'Art Local et d'Histoire Régionale**
36 rue V Hugo. 📞 *03 22 97 14 00*. ◯ *Easter–Sep: Thu–Sun pms; Oct–Easter: Sun pm*. ◯ *undergoing renovation so phone to check*. 🎫 ♿

The clock depicts Christ surrounded by the 12 apostles.

Solstice indicator

Mechanical figures perform scenes from the Last Judgment.

Clock showing age of the world

Astronomical clock in Beauvais cathedral

Beauvais ⑪

Oise. 🏛 *56,000*. 🚌 🚃 🚃
ℹ *1 rue Beauregard (03 44 15 30 30)*.
🚢 *Wed & Sat*.

HEAVILY BOMBED in World War II, Beauvais is now a modern town with one outstanding jewel. Though never completed, **Cathédrale St-Pierre** is a poignant, neck-cricking finale to the vaulting ambition that created the great Gothic cathedrals. In 1227 work began on a building designed to soar above all predecessors, but the roof of the chancel caved in twice from lack of support before its completion in the early 14th century. Delayed by wars and inadequate funds, the transept was not completed until 1550. In 1573 its crossing collapsed after a tower and spire were added. What remains today is nevertheless a masterpiece, rising 48 m (157 ft) high. In the transept much of the original 16th-century stained glass survives, while near the north door is a 90,000-part astronomical clock assembled in the 1860s. What would have been the nave is still occupied by the remnants of a 10th-century church known as the Basse-Oeuvre.

The former Bishop's Palace is now home to the **Musée Départemental de l'Oise**. The collection includes archaeological finds, medieval sculpture, tapestries and local ceramics. Beauvais has a long tradition of tapestry manufacturing, and examples from

VIOLLET-LE-DUC

The renowned architectural theorist Viollet-le-Duc (1814–79) was the first to fully appreciate Gothic architecture. His 1854 dictionary of architecture celebrated medieval building techniques, showing that the arches and tracery of Gothic cathedrals were solutions to architectural problems, not mere decoration. His restoration work included Château de Pierrefonds, Notre-Dame in Paris *(see pp82–3)* and Carcassonne *(see pp478–9)*.

Medieval architects, as drawn by Viollet-le-Duc

the French national collection are shown in the **Galerie Nationale de la Tapisserie**.

🏛 **Musée Départemental de l'Oise**
Ancien Palais Episcopal, 1 rue du Musée. **[** 03 44 11 43 83.
⬜ Wed–Mon. ⬤ public hols. ⬛
🏛 **Galerie Nationale de la Tapisserie**
22 Rue St-Pierre. **[** 03 44 15 39 10.
⬜ Tue–Sun. ⬛

Noyon ⑫

Oise. 🗺 15,000. 🚉 🛈 place de l'Hôtel de Ville (03 44 44 21 88). ⬤ Wed & Sat, first Tue of each month.

N OYON has long been a religious center. The **Cathédrale de Notre-Dame**, dating from 1150, is the fifth to be built on this site and was completed by 1290. It provides a harmonious example of the transition from Romanesque to Gothic style. A local history museum, the **Musée du Noyonnais**, occupies part of the former Bishop's Palace, and at the cathedral's east end is a rare half-timbered chapter library built in 1506.

Jean Calvin, the Protestant theologian and one of the leaders of the Reformation, was born here in 1509 and is commemorated in the small **Musée Jean Calvin**.

🏛 **Musée du Noyonnais**
Ancien Palais Episcopal, 7 rue de l'Evêché. **[** 03 44 09 43 41.
⬜ Wed–Mon. ⬤ Jan 1, Nov 11, Dec 25. ⬛

The rib-vaulted nave of Cathédrale de Notre-Dame, Noyon

Path through Forêt de Compiègne

Compiègne ⑬

Oise. 🗺 50,000. 🚉 🚌 🛈 place de l'Hôtel de Ville (03 44 40 01 00). ⬤ Wed & Sat.

C OMPIÈGNE is where Joan of Arc was captured by the Burgundians in 1430. A 16th-century Hôtel de Ville with a towering belfry rules over the center, but the town is most famous for its royal **château**.

Designed as a summer residence for Louis XV by Jacques Ange Gabriel, the château was completed by Louis XVI, restored by Napoleon and later became a favorite residence of Napoleon III and Empress Eugénie. Guided tours of the imperial apartments progress through stately and private chambers, such as the sumptuous bedrooms of Napoleon I and Marie-Louise.

Within the château, the Musée du Second Empire and Musée de l'Impératrice display furniture, portraits and memorabilia, while the Musée de la Voiture is an entertaining assembly of historic carriages, bicycles and early automobiles.

South and east of the town, the old hunting grounds of **Forêt de Compiègne** spread as far as Pierrefonds, with ample space for walks and picnics beneath its oaks and beeches. East of the D130, Les Beaux Monts provide majestic views back to the château.

The Clairière de l'Armistice, north of the N31, marks the spot where the armistice of World War I was signed on November 11, 1918. The small **Musée Wagon de l'Armistice**

contains a replica of the train car where the ceremony took place, which was used again in World War II by Hitler as a humiliating venue for the signing of the French surrender on June 22, 1940.

♠ **Château de Compiègne**
Place du Général de Gaulle.
[03 44 38 47 00. ⬜ Wed–Mon.
⬤ Jan 1, May 1, Nov 1, Dec 25. ⬛ &
🏛 **Musée Wagon de l'Armistice**
Clairière de l'Armistice (direc. Soissons).
[03 44 85 14 18. ⬜ Wed–Mon.
⬤ Jan: Mon ams, Jan 1, Dec 25. ⬛

Château de Pierrefonds

Château de Pierrefonds ⑭

Oise. **[** 03 44 42 72 72.
⬜ daily. ⬤ Jan 1, May 1, Nov 11, Dec 25. ⬛ 🎵 **Concerts**

T HE IMMENSE Château de Pierrefonds dominates the small village below. A mighty castle was constructed here by Louis d'Orléans in the 14th century, but by 1813 it had become a picturesque ruin, which Napoleon I purchased for less than 3,000 francs.

In 1857, Napoleon III commissioned the architect Viollet-le-Duc to restore it, and in 1884 Pierrefonds was reborn as an imperial residence. The exterior, with its moat, drawbridge, towers and double sentry walks, is a diligent reconstruction of medieval military architecture. The interior, by contrast, is enlivened by the romantic fancies of Viollet-le-Duc and his patron. There are guided tours and a historical exhibition.

Amiens Cathedral

WORK ON THE LARGEST cathedral in France started around 1220, financed by profits from the cultivation of woad, a plant valued for its blue dye. It was built to house the head of St. John the Baptist, brought back from the Crusades in 1206 and a magnet for pilgrims, which is still displayed here. Within 50 years Notre-Dame was complete, a masterpiece of engineering – Gothic architecture carried to a bold extreme. Restored in the 1850s by Viollet-le-Duc *(see p190)*, and having miraculously survived two world wars, the cathedral is famous for its rich array of statues and reliefs, which inspired John Ruskin's *The Bible of Amiens* in 1884.

★ West Front
The King's Gallery, a row of 22 colossal statues representing the kings of France, spans the west front. The statues are also thought to symbolize the kings of Judah.

St. Firmin Portal is decorated with figures and scenes from the life of St. Firmin, the martyr who brought Christianity to Picardy and became the first bishop of Amiens.

The calendar shows signs from the zodiac, with the corresponding monthly labors below. It depicts everyday life in the 13th century.

Weeping Angel
Sculpted by Nicolas Blasset in 1628, this sentimental statue in the ambulatory became a popular image during World War I.

STAR FEATURES
★ West Front
★ Nave
★ Choir Stalls
★ Choir Screens

Central Portal
Scenes from the Last Judgment adorn the tympanum, with the Beau Dieu, *a statue of Christ, between the doors.*

Towers
Two towers of unequal height frame the west front. The south tower was completed in 1366, the north in 1402. The spire was replaced twice, in 1627 and 1887.

The Flamboyant tracery of the rose window was created in the 16th century.

VISITORS' CHECKLIST

Cathédrale Notre-Dame, place Notre-Dame. ☎ 03 22 80 03 41. ◯ 8:30am–6:45pm (closes 5pm & noon–2pm winter). ◖ Jan1, last Sun Sep. ✝ 9am daily (Wed 12:10pm), Sun 9am, 10:15am, 11:30am, 6pm. ▣ ✦

A double row comprising 22 elegant flying buttresses supports the construction.

★ **Nave**
Soaring 42 m (138 ft) high, with support from 126 slender pillars, the brightly illuminated interior of Notre-Dame is a hymn to the vertical.

★ **Choir Stalls**
The 110 oak choir stalls (1508–19) are delicately carved with over 4,000 biblical, mythical and real life figures.

★ **Choir Screens**
Vivid scenes from the lives of St. Firmin and St. John, carved in the 15th–16th centuries, adorn the ambulatory.

The flooring was laid down in 1288 and reassembled in the late 19th century. The faithful followed its labyrinthine shape on their knees.

Senlis ⑮

Oise. 🏠 16,000. 🚌 ℹ️ *place du Parvis Notre-Dame (03 44 53 06 40).* 🛒 *Tue & Fri.*

Senlis, 10 km (6 miles) east of Chantilly, is worth visiting for its Gothic cathedral and the well-preserved historic streets in the old town that surround it. **Cathédrale Notre-Dame** was constructed during the second half of the 12th century, and the sculpted central doorway of its west front, depicting the Assumption of the Virgin, influenced later cathedrals such as Amiens (*see pp192–3*). The spire of the south tower dates from the 13th century, while the Flamboyant south transept, built in the mid-16th century, makes an ornate contrast with the austerity of earlier years. Opposite the west front, a gateway leads to the ruins of the Château Royal and its gardens. Here the **Musée de la Vénerie**, housed in a former priory, celebrates hunting through paintings, old weapons and trophies.

The **Musée d'Art** recalls the town's Gallo-Roman past and also has an excellent collection of early Gothic sculpture.

🏛 **Musée de la Vénerie**
Château Royal, place du Parvis Notre-Dame. 📞 *03 44 32 00 83.* ⬜ *Wed pm–Mon.* ● *Jan 1, May 1, Dec 25.* 📷 📹 *obligatory.*

🏛 **Musée d'Art et d'Archéologie**
Ancien Evêché, 2 place Notre-Dame. 📞 *03 44 32 00 81.* ⬜ *Wed pm–Mon.* ● *Jan 1, May 1, Dec 25.* 📷

Les Très Riches Heures du Duc de Berry, on display in Chantilly

Chantilly ⑯

Oise. 🏠 11,000. 🚇 🚌 ℹ️ *60 avenue du Maréchal Joffre (03 44 67 37 37).* 🛒 *Wed & Sat.*

The horse-racing capital of France, Chantilly offers a classy combination of château, park and forest that has long made it a popular excursion.

With origins from Gallo-Roman times, the château of today started to take shape in 1528, when the famous Anne de Montmorency, constable of France, had the old fortress replaced and added the Petit Château. During the time of the Great Prince of Condé (1621–86), renovation work continued and Le Nôtre created a park and fountains that made even Louis XIV jealous.

Destroyed in the Revolution, the Grand Château was again

CHANTILLY HORSE RACING

Chantilly is the capital of thoroughbred racing in France, a shrine to the long-standing love affair between the French upper classes and the world of horses. It was the firm belief of Prince Louis-Henri de Bourbon, creator of Chantilly's monumental Grandes Ecuries, that he would one day be reincarnated as a horse. Horse racing was introduced from England around 1830 and soon became very popular. The first official race meeting was held here in 1834, and today around 3,000 horses are trained in the surrounding forests and countryside. Every June, Chantilly becomes the focus of the social and flat racing season when top riders and their thoroughbreds compete for its two historic trophies, the Prix du Jockey-Club and Prix de Diane-Hermès.

Prix Equipage de Hermès, one of many prestigious races at Chantilly

rebuilt and its receptions and hunting parties became crowded by the fashionable high society of the 1820s–30s. It was finally replaced by a Renaissance-style château in the late 19th century.

Today the Grand Château and the Petit Château form the **Musée Condé**, displaying art treasures collected by its last private owner, the Duke of Aumale. These include work by Raphael, Botticelli, Poussin and Ingres, and an entertaining gallery of 16th-century portraits by the Clouet brothers. Among the most precious items is the famous 15th-century illuminated manuscript *Les Très Riches Heures du Duc de Berry*; reproductions are on display. You can also tour the stately apartments, with decorative conceits ranging from frolicking monkeys to triumphant battles.

Both châteaux are somewhat upstaged by the magnificent stables (Grandes Ecuries), an equestrian palace designed by Jean Aubert in 1719 that could accommodate 240 horses and 500 dogs. Adjacent to the hippodrome, it is occupied by the **Musée Vivant du Cheval**, presenting various breeds of horses and ponies as well as riding displays.

🏛 **Musée Condé**
Château de Chantilly. 【 03 44 62 62 62. ◯ *Wed–Mon.* 🌃 ⅃

🐎 **Musée Vivant du Cheval**
Grandes Ecuries du Prince de Condé, Chantilly. 【 03 44 57 40 40. ◯ *Wed–Mon (winter pms only).* 🌃 ⅃

Parc Astérix ⑰

Plailly. 🎫 08 36 68 30 10. ◯ *Apr– Aug: daily, Sep–early Oct: Wed & w/e.* 🌐 *Some Mon & Fri in May–June (check).* 🌃 ⅃ 🌐 www.parcasreix.fr

NEAR CHARLES DE Gaulle Airport a small fortified Gaulish village has its own customs controls, currency and radio station (Menhir FM).

One of the most popular theme parks in France, it is dedicated to Asterix the Gaul and all the other characters in Goscinny and Uderzo's famous cartoon strip: Getafix, Obelix, Cacofonix et al. The Romans are driven crazy as they try to subdue these larger than life Gauls, who dodge patrolling Roman centurions. Hilarious battles take place.

The Parc is as much about French history as about the cartoons. Via Antiqua and the Roman City are lighthearted but genuinely educational. Rue de Paris shows Paris through the centuries, including the construction of Notre-Dame cathedral. There are non-historical attractions too, like a dophinarium and Zeus' Thunder highspeed rollercoaster. Check out the latest rides – there's usually something new every year.

Asterix with friends, Parc Astérix

Laon ⑱

Aisne. 🏙 *36,000.* 🚉 🚌 *pl du Parvis de la Cathédrale (03 23 20 28 62).* 🛒 *Wed–Thu & Sat.*

THE CAPITAL of the Aisne *département*, Laon occupies a dramatic site on top of a long, narrow ridge surrounded by wide plains.

The pedestrianized rue Châtelaine, a main shopping street in Laon

Rose window in the 13th-century Cathédrale de Notre-Dame, Laon

The old town, on top of the mount, is best approached by Poma, an automated cable car that swings up from the railroad station to the place du Général Leclerc.

The pedestrianized rue Châtelaine leads to Laon's splendid **Cathédrale de Notre-Dame**. Completed in 1235, the cathedral lost two of its original seven towers in the Revolution but remains an impressive monument to the early Gothic style.

Notable details include the deep porches of the west façade, the four-story nave, and the carved Renaissance screens enclosing its side chapels. The immense 13th-century rose window in the apse beautifully represents the Glorification of the Church. Protruding from the cathedral's western towers are statues paying tribute to the oxen used to haul stone for its construction.

The rest of medieval Laon rewards casual strolling: a promenade rings the 16th-century **Citadelle** farther east, while to the south you can follow the ramparts past the Porte d'Ardon and Porte des Chenizelles to **Eglise St-Martin**, with good views back over the rooftops to the cathedral from rue Thibesard.

South of Laon is Chemin des Dames, named after Louis XV's daughters, who used to take this route. It is more often remembered as a World War I battlefield, now lined with cemeteries and memorials.

CHAMPAGNE

······························

MARNE · ARDENNES · AUBE · HAUTE-MARNE

C HAMPAGNE IS A NAME *of great resonance, conjuring up images of celebration and the world-famous cathedral in Reims. Yet beyond the glamour lies an unspoiled rural area of strikingly contrasting landscapes: the rolling plains of Champagne, giving way to lakes and water meadows to the south, and the dense forests and hills of the Ardennes in the north.*

The so-called "sacred triangle of Champagne," linking Épernay, Reims and Châlons-en-Champagne, is like a magnet for wine lovers. Here, the experience of drinking fine champagne is enhanced by gourmet meals of stuffed trout, Ardennes ham and the famous sausages called *andouillettes*.

The well-marked *route touristique du champagne* wends its way through vineyards toward endless cereal plains stretching southward to the "lake district," an area of oak forests, water meadows and streams.

On the border between France and Belgium lies the Ardennes, named after the Celtic word for deep forest. This wild border land of dramatic valleys, deciduous forests and hills is cut by the meanderings of the Meuse River. Border fortifications include the vast citadel of Sedan and the star-shaped bastion of Rocroi, as well as the Maginot Line outposts built before World War II.

The Ardennes may offer appealing countryside but Champagne is culturally superior, with impressive towns and their painstakingly restored historic centers. It has some striking churches, from the Gothic majesty of Reims Cathedral to the rustic charm of its typical wooden *champenois* churches. These feature vivid stained-glass windows by the famous School of Troyes, whose subtle craftsmanship seems to typify the appeal of this quiet region.

Timber-framed *champenois* church at Lac du Der-Chantecoq

◁ **Cathédrale St-Etienne in Châlons-en-Champagne**

Exploring Champagne

CHAMPAGNE draws wine lovers to the sacred triangle between Reims, Epernay and Châlons-en-Champagne, but the region also attracts culture lovers to its great churches, notably Reims Cathedral. Reims abounds in gastronomic restaurants but Troyes, the former capital of Champagne, makes the most delightful base. Much of Champagne is flat or gently undulating, and the wild and wooded Ardennes to the north attracts walkers and nature lovers. North of Reims, the Ardennes Canal can be explored by barge or pleasure boat from Rethel; to the south, water sports are popular on the lakes east of Troyes.

Fishing by a canal in Montier-en-Der near Lac du Der-Chantecoq

GETTING AROUND

The region's main autoroute is the A26, which reaches Reims in under 3 hours from Calais, and also provides easy access to most of the region all the way down to Troyes and Langres (via the A5). The A4 highway also links reims to Paris and Alsace. Paris-Reims by train takes 90 minutes. Rail transport within the region is reasonably good, and so are the roads. To explore the wine-growing region, follow the signposted roads marked "Route de Champagne."

Windmill at Verzenay, Parc Naturel de la Montagne de Reims

To Brus
RO
N43

To St-Quentin
Amiens

RETHEL

Aisne

A26
N44
N31

REIMS ①

A4

PARC NATUREL
RÉGIONAL DE LA
MONTAGNE DE REIMS

ÉPERNAY ②

CHÂLONS-
EN-CHAMPAGNE

RD33

RD273

RD51

N4

N4

Aube

To Provins

D441

D951

Seine

⑩

TROYES

N7

D444

N51
VALLÉE DE LA MEUSE
3
5
6
SEDAN
Canal des Ardennes
Meuse
D977
To Luxembourg
D947
7
ARGONNE
Aisne
STE-MENEHOULD
To Metz
RD394
RD395
VITRY-LE-FRANÇOIS
N35
ST-DIZIER
Lac du Der-Chantecoq
Marne
D60
D400
N67
N74
D27
BAR-SUR-AUBE
D74
Meuse
11
CHAUMONT
D65
A5
A31
Marne
Aube
12
LANGRES
D428
To Dijon

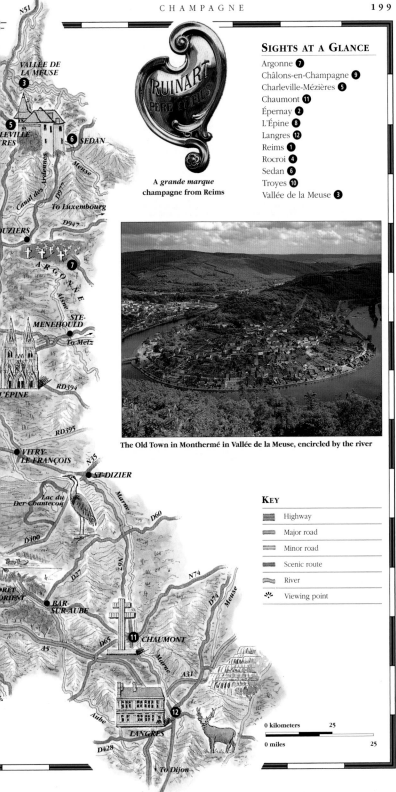

A *grande marque* champagne from Reims

Sights at a Glance

Argonne 7
Châlons-en-Champagne 9
Charleville-Mézières 5
Chaumont 11
Épernay 2
L'Épine 8
Langres 12
Reims 1
Rocroi 4
Sedan 6
Troyes 10
Vallée de la Meuse 3

The Old Town in Monthermé in Vallée de la Meuse, encircled by the river

Key

- Highway
- Major road
- Minor road
- Scenic route
- River
- Viewing point

0 kilometers 25

0 miles 25

Gilded reliquary (1896), with body of St. Remi, in Basilique St-Remi, Reims

Reims ❶

Marne. 🏛 *185,000*. ✈ 🏢 🚌 🚊 ❶ *2 rue Guillaume de Machault (03 26 77 45 25)*. 🛏 *daily*. 🌐 *www.tourisme.fr*

PRONOUNCED like the French word "prince" without the "p", Reims is home to some of the best-known *grandes marques* in Champagne, mostly grouped around the Basilique St-Rémi. But the city has another, much earlier, claim to fame: since the 11th cent-ury, all the kings of France have come to this "city of coronations" to be crowned in its remarkable Gothic **Cathédrale Notre-Dame** *(see pp202–3)*.

Although World War II bombing destroyed much of Reims' architectural coherence, there are some remarkable monuments here. The **Crypto-portique**, part of the forum, and Porte Mars, a triumphal Augustan arch, recall the city's Roman past. In 1945, the German surrender was taken in the **Musée de la Reddition** in Eisenhower's French headquarters during World War II. **Musée des Beaux Arts** houses a fine collection of 15th- and 16th-century canvases depicting biblical scenes; portraits by the Cranachs; *The Death of Marat* by David, and more than 20 landscapes by Corot. Also featured are the Barbizon School, Impressionists and modern masters.

In 1996 Reims celebrated the 1,500-year anniversary of the baptism of Clovis, first King of the Franks, in its cathedral.

🚇 Ancien Collège des Jésuites & Planetarium

1 place Museux. 📞 *03 26 85 51 50.* **College** 🕐 *daily.* 🌙 *ams: Tue, Sat–Sun; publ hols.* **Planetarium** 🕐 *w/e & sch hols:* 2:45pm, 3:45pm, 4:45pm. 📷
Founded in 1606, this college was a hospice until 1976.

Nowadays its 300-year-old vines, Romanesque wine cellars and Baroque interior play their part as atmospheric film sets, notably for the film of Zola's *Germinal* (1992) and *Queen Margot* (1993). Highlights include the refectory's ceiling and the kitchen, the only room where fireplaces were allowed in an austere Jesuit establishment. A double spiral staircase leads to a Baroque library with yet another magnificent ceiling. Housed in the same building since 1979 is the **Planetarium** with views of the sky from everywhere in the world.

⛪ Basilique St-Rémi

Place de Lenoncourt. **Open** *daily.* ♿
Now marooned in a modern quarter, this Benedictine abbey church, the oldest church in Reims, began as a Carolingian

Porte Mars, a reminder of Reims in Roman times

MÉTHODE CHAMPENOISE

To produce its characteristic bubbles, champagne has to undergo a process of double fermentation.
• **First fermentation:** The base wine, made from rather acidic grapes, is fermented at 68°–72°F in either stainless steel tanks or, traditionally, in oak barrels. It is then siphoned off from the sediment and kept at colder temperatures to clear completely, before being drawn off and blended with wines from other areas and years (except in the case of vintage champagne). The wine is bottled and the *liqueur de tirage* (sugar, wine and yeast) is added.
• **Second fermentation:** The bottles are stored for a year or more in cool, chalky cellars. The yeast converts the sugar to alcohol and carbon dioxide, which produces the sparkle, and the yeast cells die leaving a deposit. To remove this, the inverted bottles are turned and tapped *(remuage)* daily to shift the deposits into the neck of the bottle. Finally, the deposits are expelled by the process known as *dégorgement*, and a bit of sugar *(liqueur d'expédition)* is added to adjust the sweetness before the final cork is inserted.

Champagne Mumm of Reims

basilica dedicated to Saint Rémi (440–533). Inside, an Early Gothic choir and radiating chapels can be seen, as well as sculpted Romanesque capitals in the north transept.

🏛 Musée St-Rémi

53 rue Simon. 📞 *03 26 85 23 36.* ⭘ *daily, pm only.* ⬤ *Jan 1, May 1, Jul 14, Nov 1 & 11, Dec 25.* 📷

Set in the former abbey, the adjoining museum encloses the original Gothic chapter house within its cloistered 17th-century shell. On display in the museum are archaeological artifacts, 15th-century tapestries depicting the life of Saint Rémi, and a varied collection of weapons dating from the 16th–19th centuries.

Epernay ❷

Marne. 👥 *28,000.* 🚉 ℹ️ *7 av de Champagne (03 26 53 33 00).* 🛒 *Wed, Sat & Sun.*

THE SOLE REASON for visiting Épernay is to burrow into the chalky *caves* and taste the champagne. This rather undistinguished town dominates the champagne industry, and has the highest per capita income in France. As proof, the avenue de Champagne quarter abounds in mock-

Dégorgement *is the final removal of the yeast deposits from the bottle. The neck of the bottle is plunged in freezing brine and the frozen block of sediment is then removed.*

Statue of Dom Perignon at Moët

Renaissance mansions. **Moët & Chandon**, dating back to 1743, is the largest and slickest *maison*, the star of the Moët-Hennessy stable.

The group also owns other champagnes houses, such as Mercier, Krug, Pommery, Veuve Cliquot, and Canard Duchêne. When the recession took the fizz out of Champagne in 1993, Moët made a number of people redundant and provoked the first ever

strike in the industry. The cellars of Moët & Chandon or **Mercier** – both are in avenue de Champagne. Mercier has the distinction of displaying a giant cask created for the 1889 Paris Exhibition, and takes visitors trundling through the *caves* in an electric train.

De Castellane, in avenue de Verdun, offers a more personalized tour, complete with a chance to taste their champagne.

🍾 Moët & Chandon

18 avenue de Champagne. 📞 *03 26 51 20 20.* ⭘ *Apr–mid-Nov: daily, mid-Nov–Mar: Mon–Fri.* 📷 🎫 *only.*

🍾 Mercier

70 avenue de Champagne. 📞 *03 26 51 22 22.* ⭘ *mid-Mar–Nov: daily; Dec–mid-Mar: Thu–Mon.* 📷 ♿ *oblig.*

🍾 De Castellane

57 rue de Verdun. 📞 *03 26 51 19 11.* ⭘ *Mar–late-Dec: daily.* 📷 ♿ *restr.* 🎫 *oblig.*

Seductive marketing *of champagne since the last century has ensured its continuing success.*

The bubbles in champagne *are produced during the second fermentation. Champagnes, especially vintage ones, improve with ageing.*

Reims Cathedral

THE MAGNIFICENT GOTHIC Cathédrale Notre-Dame at
Reims is noted for its harmony and monumentality.
A cathedral has stood on this site since 401 but the
present building was begun in 1211. Reims has been
the backdrop for coronations from medieval times till
1825, when Charles X was crowned. The coronation of
Charles VII here in 1429 was attended by Joan of Arc.

During the Revolution, the rood screen and windows
were destroyed but the stonework survived. World War I
damage was finally fully restored in 1996, to coincide
with the 1,500th anniversary of the baptism of Clovis,
King of the Franks, at Reims, which was considered the
first coronation of a French king.

★ Great Rose Window
*Best seen at sunset, the
13th-century window
shows the Virgin sur-
rounded by the apostles
and angel musicians. It is
set within a larger window,
a feature common in
13th-century architecture.*

The Nave
*Compared with the nave at
Chartres (see pp298–301),
Reims is taller. Its elegant
capitals are decorated with
naturalistic floral motifs
such as ivy and berries.*

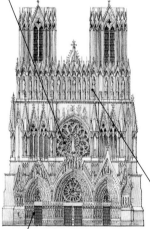

WEST FAÇADE

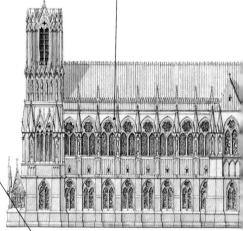

SOUTH FAÇADE

★ Smiling Angel
*Rich in statuary,
Reims is often called
"the cathedral of
angels." Situated
above the left (north)
portal, this enigmatic
angel with unfurled
wings is the most cele-
brated of the many
that grace the building.*

★ Gallery of the Kings
*The harmonious west façade, decorated
with over 2,300 statues, is the most notable
feature at Reims. Fifty-six stone effigies of
French kings form the Gallery of the Kings.*

Palais Du Tau

The archbishop's palace adjoining the cathedral is named after its T-shaped design, based on early episcopal crosses. (Tau is Greek for T.) The palace, built in 1690 by Mansart and Robert de Cotte, encloses a Gothic chapel and the 15th-century Salle du Tau, rooms associated with French coronations. On the eve of a coronation, the future king spent the night in the palace. After being crowned in the cathedral, he held a magnificent banquet in the palace. The Salle du Tau, or banquet hall, is the finest room in the palace, with a magnificent barrel-vaulted ceiling and walls hung with 15th-century Arras tapestries. The palace now houses a museum of statuary and tapestries from the cathedral, including a 15th-century tapestry of the baptism of Clovis, the first Christian king.

Salle du Tau – the banquet hall

Visitors' Checklist

Cathédrale Notre-Dame, place du Cardinal Luçon. 03 26 47 55 34. 7:30am–7:30pm daily. 8am & 7pm Mon–Fri; 8am Sat; 9am & 10:15am Sun. by appt only.
Palais du Tau 03 26 47 81 79. Tue–Sun. Jan 1, May 1, Nov 1 & 11, Dec 25.

Apse Gallery
The restored claire-voie (open work) gallery on the apse is crowned by statues of mythological beasts.

The radiating chapels of the apse are supported by flying buttresses and adorned with octagonal pinnacles.

South transept

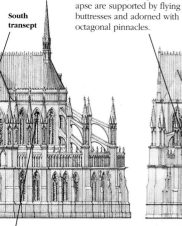

APSE

SIDE SECTION

The clerestory windows pioneered Gothic tracery by dividing the lights with slender bars of stone, creating a decorative, intersecting pattern.

Pinnacles on the flying buttresses shelter guardian angels, symbolic protectors of the cathedral.

Star Features

★ **Gallery of the Kings**

★ **Smiling Angel**

★ **Great Rose Window**

Chagall Window
The windows in the axial chapel were designed by the 20th-century artist Marc Chagall and made by local craftsmen. This one depicts the Crucifixion and the Sacrifice of Isaac.

The *sentier touristique*, a walk along the ramparts of Rocroi

Vallée de la Meuse ❸

Ardennes. 🚂 *Revin.* 🛈 *Revin (03 24 40 19 59).*

THE MEUSE meanders through the Ardennes among spectacular scenery of wild gorges, woods and warped rock formations of granite or schist.

Dramatically situated on a double meander of the Meuse, **Revin** is an unremarkable town in an exceptional site, with the Vieille Ville enfolded in the north bend. From the quay, you can see wooded **Mont Malgré Tout** and a route dotted with observation points and steep trails. Just south is **Dames de la Meuse**, a rocky outcrop over the river gorge.

Monthermé lies on two banks, with the Vieille Ville clustered on the charming left bank. The rocky gorges around **Roche à Sept Heures** on the far bank entice climbers and ramblers. Farther on is **Rocher des Quatre Fils d'Aymon**, a ridge whose jagged crest suggests the silhouette of four legendary local horsemen.

Rocroi ❹

Ardennes. 🚶 *2,600.* 🚂 🚂 *Revin.* 🛈 *14 place d'Armes (03 24 54 20 06).* 🍽 *Tue & 1st Mon of month.*

SET ON the Ardennes plateau, the star-shaped citadel of Rocroi was originally built under Henri II in 1555, and later made impregnable by Vauban in 1675 *(see p216)*.

The main attraction is the walk along the ramparts from the Porte de France, the southern gateway. The nature preserve at Rièzes is home to orchids and carnivorous plants.

Charleville-Mézières ❺

Ardennes. 🚶 *57,000.* 🚂 🚍 🛈 *4 place Ducale (03 24 55 69 90).* 🍽 *Tue, Thu & Sat.*

KNOWN AS the gateway to the Ardennes, this riverside ford was originally two towns. The somber medieval citadel of Mézières merged with the neat Classical town of Charleville in 1966. Mézières has irregular slate-covered houses curving around a bend in the Meuse. Battered fortifications and gateways are visible from avenue de St-Julien. Tucked into the ramparts is the much-remodeled Gothic **Notre-Dame de l'Espérance**.

The centerpiece of Charleville is **place Ducale**, a model of Louis XIII urban planning, echoing place des Vosges in Paris *(see p87)*. The poet Arthur Rimbaud was born nearby in 1854. His modest birthplace at No. 12 rue Bérégovoy is still there, along with his childhood home on the Meuse at 7 quai Arthur Rimbaud.

Just along the quayside is the Vieux Moulin, the town house whose view inspired *Le Bateau Ivre*, Rimbaud's greatest poem. Inside is the small **Musée Rimbaud**, with manuscripts and photographs by the poet.

🏛 **Musée Rimbaud**
Quai Arthur Rimbaud. 📞 *03 24 32 44 65.* **Open** *Tue–Sun.* **Closed** *Jan 1, May 1, Dec 25.* 🖼

Sedan ❻

Ardennes. 🚶 *22,000.* 🚂 🚍 🛈 *Château Fort, place du Château (03 24 27 73 73).* 🍽 *Wed & Sat.*

JUST TO THE EAST of Charleville is the **Château de Sedan**, the largest fortified castle in the whole of Europe. There has been a bastion on these slopes since the 11th century, but each Ardennes conflict has meant a new tier of defenses for Sedan.

In 1870, during the Franco-Prussian War, with 700 Prussian cannons turned on Sedan, Napoleon III surrendered, and 83,000 French prisoners were deported to Prussia. In May 1940, after capturing Sedan, German forces reached the French coast a week later.

The seven-story bastion contains sections dating from medieval times to the 16th

The 19th-century poet Rimbaud, whose birthplace was Charleville

century. Highlights of any visit are the ramparts, the 16th-century fortifications and the magnificent 15th-century eaves in one tower. The **Musée du Château**, that is located in the south wing has a section devoted to military campaigns.

The bastion is surrounded by 17th-century slate-roofed houses which hug the banks of the Meuse. These reflect the city's earlier prosperity as a Huguenot stronghold.

🏛 **Musée du Château**

1 place du Château. 📞 03 24 27 73 73. 🕐 mid-Mar–mid-Sep: daily; mid-Sep–mid-Mar: w/e & Tue–Fri pms. 🏷

Environs

Farther south is **Fort de Vitry-la-Ferté**, one of the few forts on the Maginot line to have come into direct and devastating combat with the enemy in 1940.

Courtyard inside the heavily fortified Château de Sedan

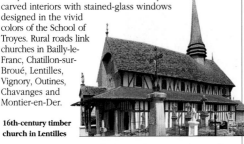

Gargoyle on Basilique de Notre-Dame de l'Epine

Argonne ❼

Ardennes & Meuse. 🚉 Châlons. 🚌 Ste-Menehould. 🛈 Ste-Menehould (03 26 60 85 83).

EAST OF REIMS, the Argonne is a compact region of picturesque valleys and forests, dotted with priories, trenches and war cemeteries.

As a wooded border between the rival bishoprics of Champagne and Lorraine, the Argonne was home to abbeys and priories. Now ruined, the Benedictine abbey of **Beaulieu-en-Argonne** boasts a 13th-century wine press and has forest views. Just north is **Les Islettes**, known for its faïence pottery and tiles. The hilly terrain here was a battleground during the Franco-Prussian War and lay on the Western front in World War I. The disputed territory of **Butte de Vauquois**, north of Les Islettes, bears a war memorial.

L'Epine ❽

Marne. 🏠 650. 🚉 Châlons. 🛈 Mairie (03 26 66 96 99).

L'EPINE IS WORTH visiting if only for a glimpse of the **Basilique de Notre-Dame de l'Epine**, surrounded by wheatfields. Designed on the scale of a cathedral, this 15th-century Flamboyant Gothic church has been a pilgrimage site, since medieval times. Even French kings have come here to venerate a "miraculous" statue of the Virgin.

On the façade, three gabled portals are offset by floating tracery, a gauzy effect reminiscent of Reims cathedral. All around are gruesome gargoyles symbolizing evil spirits and deadly sins, chased out by the holy presence within. Unfortunately, the most risqué sculptures were destroyed, judged obscene by 19th-century puritans. The subdued Gothic interior contains a 15th-century rood screen and the venerated statue of the Virgin.

CHAMPAGNE TIMBER CHURCHES

Skirting Lac du Der-Chantecoq lies a region of woodland, water meadows and characteristic Romanesque and Renaissance timber-framed churches with curious pointed gables and *caquetoirs*, rickety wooden porches. Many have intimate and often beautifully carved interiors with stained-glass windows designed in the vivid colors of the School of Troyes. Rural roads link churches in Bailly-le-Franc, Chatillon-sur-Broué, Lentilles, Vignory, Outines, Chavanges and Montier-en-Der.

16th-century timber church in Lentilles

Châlons-en-Champagne ❾

Marne. 🏛 48,000. 🚊 🚌
🛈 3 quai des Arts (03 26 65 17 89).
🛒 Wed, Fri, Sat & Sun.

ENCIRCLED BY the Marne River and minor canals, Châlons' sleepy bourgeois charm is made up of half-timbered houses and gardens mirrored in canals. Nearby are vineyards producing Blanc de Blancs.

From quai de Notre-Dame there are views of old bridges and the Romanesque towers of **Notre-Dame-en-Vaux**, a masterpiece of Romanesque-Gothic. Behind the church is a well-restored medieval quarter and the **Musée du Cloître de Notre-Dame-en-Vaux**, containing the original Romanesque cloisters.

Cathédrale St-Etienne, by the canal, is a Gothic affair with a Baroque portal, Romanesque crypt and vivid medieval windows. Beyond is **Le Petit Jard**, riverside gardens overlooking the Château du Marché, a turreted toll-gate built by Henri IV. The neighboring place de la République has lively bars and restaurants.

🏛 **Musée du Cloître de Notre-Dame-en-Vaux**
Rue Nicolas Durand. 【 03 26 64 03 87. ◯ Wed–Mon. ◯ Jan 1, May 1, Nov 1 & 11, Dec 25. 🌐 ✓

Troyes ❿

Aube. 🏛 60,000. 🚊 🚌 🛈 16 bd Carnot (03 25 82 62 70). 🛒 daily.

TROYES IS A DELIGHT, a city of magnificent Gothic churches and charming 16th-century courtyards, in a historic center shaped like a champagne cork. The city is famous for its heritage of stained glass and sausages (*andouillettes*), its knitwear industry and factory outlets.

The battered Flamboyant Gothic west front of the **Cathédrale St-Pierre-et-St-Paul** opens onto a splendid vaulted interior. The nave is bathed in mauvish-red rays from the 16th-century rose

Statuary in Troyes' Cathédrale St-Pierre-et-St-Paul

window, complemented by the discreet turquoise of the Tree of Jesse window and the intense blue of the medieval windows of the apse.

Nearby, **Eglise St-Nizier** glitters in the faded quarter behind the cathedral, with its shimmering tiled Burgundian roof. Inside, it is lit by windows in a range of warm mauves and soothing blues.

The harmonious Gothic **Basilique St-Urbain** boasts grand flying buttresses and particularly fine windows which have recently been restored. **Eglise Ste-Madeleine** is noted for its elaborate 16th-century rood screen resembling lacy

Rue Larivey, a typical street with half-timbered houses, in Troyes

foliage, grapes and figs. Beyond is a wall of windows in browns, reds and blues. The ruelle des Chats, which is a quaint covered passageway, connects rue Charbonnet and rue Champeaux.

Set in one of the best-preserved quarters, **Eglise St-Pantaléon** faces a Renaissance mansion. A Gothic and Renaissance interior houses an imposing collection of 16th-century statuary and severe *grisaille* windows.

🏛 **Musée d'Art Moderne**
Palais Episcopal, place St-Pierre.
【 03 25 76 26 80. ◯ Tue–Sun.
◯ public hols. 🌐 ♿
Beside the cathedral, the former episcopal palace is now a museum of modern art, with a sculpture by Rodin and an especially fine collection of Fauvist paintings, as well as other modern art.

🏛 **Hôtel du Petit Louvre**
Rue de la Montée St-Pierre.
Courtyard only ◯ daily.
Set off quai Dampierre, this newly restored *hôtel particulier* boasts a fish-scale roof, medieval tower, Renaissance courtyard, staircase and well. The highlight is a façade adorned with quizzical multi-colored faces.

Environs

The city's green playground, **Lac et Forêt d'Orient**, is 25 km (15 miles) east of Troyes. The forest is dotted with marshes, nature reserves and smaller lakes. Lac d'Orient, a large artificial lake, is popular for sailing, and there's water-skiing on Lac Amance and fishing at Lac du Temple.

Chaumont ⓫

Haute-Marne. 🏠 29,000. 🚉
🛈 place du Général de Gaulle (03 25 03 80 80). 🗓 Wed & Sat.

As the former residence of the Counts of Champagne, this feudal town enjoyed great prestige in the 13th century. On the far side of a ravine, the old town is on a rocky spur, with the Palais de Justice and the medieval castle keep dominating.

The keep, is a reminder that this quiet administrative center had a formidable past. This impression is confirmed by the Renaissance town houses which are bulging with *tourelles d'escaliers*, turreted staircases.

Basilique St-Jean-Baptiste, a gray stone Champenois church, is the most remarkable monument in Chaumont. The interior is enlivened by a spider's web of vaulting, a striking turreted staircase and Renaissance galleries. Near the entrance is a tiny chapel containing an unsettling *Mise au Tombeau* (1471), an intense multicolored stone group of 10 mourners gathered around Christ laid out on a shroud in his tomb. In the left transept is a bizarre but beguiling *Tree of Jesse*. On this ill-lit Renaissance stone relief, a family tree sprouts from the sleeping Jesus, who slumbers unawares – much like Chaumont itself.

Environs

Twenty-three kilometers (14 miles) northwest of Chaumont, **Colombey-les-Deux-Eglises** will forever be associated with General Charles de Gaulle (1890–1970). The de Gaulles bought their home, **La Boisserie**, in 1933,

Cathédrale St-Mammès in Langres

but had to abandon it during the war, when it was badly damaged. After its restoration, de Gaulle would return to La Boisserie from Paris on weekends to write his memoirs and plan comebacks. He eventually died here on November 9, 1970. The house is now a museum, with memorabilia from his life.

In the village churchyard, the General and President of France (1958-69) lies in a simple tomb. However, a giant granite cross of Lorraine, erected in 1972, dominates the skyline – a grandiose memorial more in keeping with de Gaulle's notion of *la gloire*.

🏛 **La Boisserie**
Colombey-les-Deux-Eglises. 📞 03 25 01 52 52. 🕐 Feb–Nov: Wed–Mon. 🖼 ♿

Langres ⓬

Haute-Marne. 🏠 10,000. 🚉 🚌
🛈 square Olivier Lahalle (03 25 87 67 67). 🗓 Fri.

Set on a rocky spur, Langres lies beyond Chaumont, in the backwaters of southern Champagne. This ancient bishopric was one of the gateways to Burgundy and the birthplace of the encyclopedist, Denis Diderot (1713–84). Langres promotes itself as a land of springs, claiming that its proximity to the sources of the Seine and Marne grant it mystical powers.

Virtually the whole town is enclosed by medieval ramparts, Langres' undoubted attraction. A succession of towers and parapets provides glimpses of romantic town gates, sculpted Renaissance mansions and dim alleys. From the ramparts stretch panoramic views of the Marne Valley, the Langres plateau, the Vosges, and, on a clear day, even Mont Blanc.

Near Porte Henri IV is the much-remodeled **Cathédrale St-Mammès**. The gloomy vaulted interior, in Burgundian Romanesque style, is redeemed by the sculpted capitals in the apse, reputedly taken from a temple of Jupiter. The town's Musée d'Art et d'Histoire has some interesting collections.

Langres' lively summer season includes historical re-enactments, theater and fireworks.

Memorial to General de Gaulle at Colombey-les-Deux-Eglises

ALSACE AND LORRAINE

MEURTHE-ET-MOSELLE · MEUSE · MOSELLE · BAS-RHIN
HAUT-RHIN · VOSGES

S BORDER REGIONS, *Alsace and Lorraine have been fought over for centuries by France and Germany, their beleaguered past recalled by many military strongholds and cemeteries. But today, peace pervades the region, with its pastel-painted villages, fortified towns and sleepy vineyards.*

At the northeast frontier of France, bordered by the Rhine, Alsace forms a fertile watershed between the mountains of the Vosges and the Black Forest in Germany. Lorraine, with its gentle rolling landscape on the other side of the mountains, is the poorer cousin but is more overtly French in character.

EMBATTLED TERRITORY

Caught in the wars between France and Germany, Alsace and Lorraine have changed nationality four times since 1871. Centuries of strife have made border citadels of Metz, Toul and Verdun in Lorraine, while Alsace abounds with castles, from the pastiche folly of Haut-Koenigsbourg to Saverne's ruined fortress, built to guard a strategic pass in the Vosges. However, the area has a strong identity of its own, taking pride in local costumes, traditions and dialects. In Alsace, Route du Vin vineyards nudge pretty villages in the Vosges foothills. Strasbourg, the capital, is a cosmopolitan city with a 16th-century center, while Nancy, Lorraine's historic capital, represents elegant 18th-century architecture and town planning.

Much of the attraction of this region lies in its cuisine. Lorraine offers beer and quiche lorraine. In Alsace, cozy *winstubs*, or wine cellars, serve sauerkraut and flowery white wines, such as Riesling and Gewürztraminer.

Villagers enjoying the view from their window in Hunspach, north of Strasbourg in the northern Vosges

◁ Half-timbered houses with flower-clad balconies along the Route du Vin in Alsace

Exploring Alsace and Lorraine

Visitors seeking art and architecture will be amply
rewarded by the charming medieval towns and excellent
city museums of the region. Undiscovered Lorraine is the
place to clamber over military citadels, walk in unspoiled
countryside and unwind at
relaxing spas. By contrast, Alsace
offers magnificent forests and
rugged mountain drives in the
Vosges; quaint villages; and rich
wines. The Route du Vin *(see
pp222–3)* is one of the region's
many scenic routes. It is
particularly popular during the
wine harvest festivities but is
worth visiting in any season.

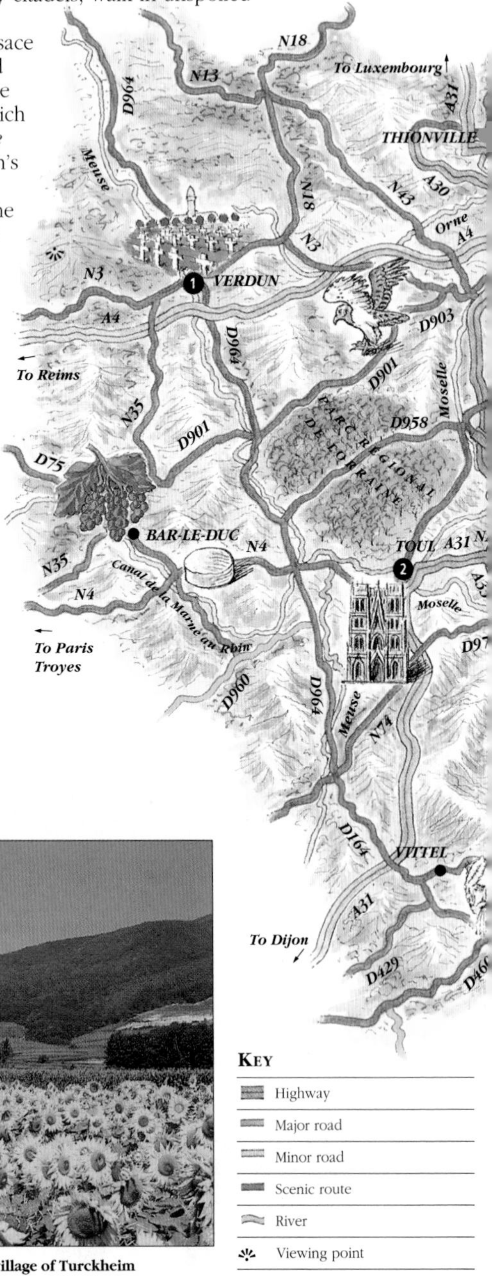

Sights at a Glance

Betschdorf **18**
Château du Haut-
  Koenigsbourg **13**
Colmar **10**
Eguisheim **9**
Gérardmer **5**
Guebwiller **7**
Metz **3**
Mulhouse **6**
Nancy **4**
Neuf-Brisach **8**
Obernai **15**
Ribeauvillé **12**
Riquewihr **11**
Saverne **17**
Sélestat **14**
Strasbourg **16**
Toul **2**
Verdun **1**

Key

▦ Highway
▦ Major road
▦ Minor road
▦ Scenic route
〰 River
☀ Viewing point

Field of sunflowers just outside the village of Turckheim

The picturesque village of Riquewihr on the Route du Vin

GETTING AROUND

There are good road and rail links between Strasbourg, Colmar and Nancy, and on to Switzerland and Germany. The main roads to and through the regions are the N3, N4, A31 and A35, the A4 to Paris, and the N59 and the tunnel under the Vosges. The spectacular journey over the Vosges and along the Route du Vin is best made by car or on organized trips from Colmar or Strasbourg.

To Karlsrube
Mannheim

To Besançon

To Basel
Bern
Zurich

0 kilometers   20

0 miles   10

The Ossuaire de Douaumont, a sentinel for the regiments of crosses on the battlefields of Verdun

Verdun ❶

Meuse. 🏠 23,000. 🚉 🚌 🚏 place de la Nation (03 29 86 14 18). 🕭 Fri.

VERDUN WILL be forever remembered for the horrors of the 1916–1917 Battle of Verdun, when about a million men died in almost a whole year of continuous bloodshed that is considered the worst single battle of the Great War. The Germans intended to strike a blow at French morale by destroying the forts of Douaumont and Vaux (which had been built to prevent a repeat of the humiliating French defeat of the Franco-Prussian war of 1870) and capturing Verdun, France's northeastern stronghold. The French fought simply to prevent the town being taken. The stalemate and the killing continued here right up to the end of the war, and not until 1918 did the Germans draw back from their positions just 5km from the town.

Several poignant museums, memorials, battle sites and cemeteries can be visited in the hills just outside Verdun on the north side. In this devastated region, nine villages were obliterated without trace. The **Musée-Memorial de Fleury** tells their story. Nearby, the **Ossuaire de Douaumont** contains the unidentified bones of over 130,000 French and German dead. One of the most striking monuments to the Battle of Verdun is Rodin's memorial in Verdun itself. It depicts the winged figure of Victory unable to soar triumphant because she has

become caught in the remains of a dead soldier.

The town of Verdun was heavily fortified over the centuries. The crenelated **Porte Chaussée**, a medieval river gateway, still guards the eastern entrance to the town and is the most impressive of the remaining fortifications.

Although battered by war damage, the **Citadelle de Verdun** retains its 12th-century tower, the only relic from the original abbey that Vauban incorporated into his new military design. Now a war museum, the **Musée de la Citadelle Militaire**, it recreates through an audio-visual display Verdun's role in WWI. The citadel casemates come to life as grim trenches, and the presentation ends by showing how the "Unknown Soldier" was chosen for the symbolic tomb under the Arc de Triomphe in Paris *(see p103)*.

The town center is dominated by the cathedral, where Romanesque elements were rediscovered after the 1916 bombardments.

The 16th-century cloisters of Eglise St-Gengoult in Toul

🏛 **Musée de la Citadelle Militaire**
La Citadelle. 📞 03 29 86 14 18.
🕐 daily. 🌑 Jan. 🎟 ♿

Toul ❷

Meurthe-et-Moselle. 🏠 18,000.
🚉 🚌 🚏 parvis de la Cathédrale (03 83 64 11 69). 🕭 Wed & Fri.

LYING WITHIN dark forests west of Nancy, the octagonal fortress city of Toul is encircled by the Moselle and the Canal de la Marne. Along with Verdun and Metz, Toul was one of the 4th-century bishoprics. In the early 18th century, Vauban built the citadel, from which the ring of defensive waterways, the octagonal city ramparts and the **Porte de Metz** remain.

The **Cathédrale St-Etienne**, begun in the 13th century, took over 300 years to build. It suffered damage in World War II, but the purity of the Champenois style has survived, notably in the arched, high-galleried interior. The imposing Flamboyant Gothic façade is flanked by octagonal towers. Other highlights are the two Renaissance chapels close to the transepts and the vast Champenois cloisters, decorated with sculpted foliage and stone gargoyles. Rue du Général-Gengoult, behind the Gothic **Eglise St-Gengoult** (with its stained-glass windows depicting the life of the saint), contains a clutch of sculpted Renaissance houses.

Just north of the city are vineyards producing the local "grey" Côtes de Toul wines.

Environs

Accessible from either Metz or Toul, the vast **Parc Régional de Lorraine** takes in red-tiled cottages, vineyards, forests, cropland, *chaumes* (high pastureland), marshes and lakes. Inns in the area are especially noted for their quiche lorraine and *potée lorraine*, a bacon casserole.

Jupiter Slaying a Monster on the Column of Merten in La Cour d'Or

Metz ❸

Moselle. 👥 124,000. ✈ 🚆 🚌
ℹ *place d'Armes (03 87 55 53 76).*
📅 *Sat.* 🌐 *www.tourisme.mairie-metz.fr*

A N AUSTERE yet appealing city, Metz sits at the confluence of the Moselle and the Seille. Twenty bridges crisscross the rivers and canals, and there are pleasant walks along the banks. This Gallo-Roman city, now the capital of Lorraine, has always been a pawn in the game of border chess – annexed by Germany in 1870, regained by France in 1918.

Set on a hill above the Moselle, the **Cathédrale St-Etienne** overlooks the historic center. The Gothic exterior flaunts impressive flying buttresses and long-necked gargoyles. Inside, stained-glass windows, from Gothic to modern, including some by Chagall, present walls of shimmering light.

To the northwest of the cathedral, a narrow wooden bridge leads across to the island of Petit Saulcy, where the oldest French theater is still in use. Located on the other side of the cathedral, the

Porte des Allemands, spanning a river, more resembles a medieval castle because of its bridge, defensive towers and 13th-century gate with pepper mill-shaped towers.

In the Vieille Ville, place St-Louis is a delightful square bordered by lofty, arcaded 14th-century mansions. **Eglise St-Pierre-aux-Nonnains** claims to be one of the oldest churches in France. The external walls and the ruined façade date from Roman times, while much of the rest belongs to the 7th-century convent that occupied the site. Nearby is the frescoed 13th-century **Chapelle des Templiers**, built by the Knights Templar.

🏛 **Musée de la Cour d'Or**

2 rue du Haut-Poirier. 📞 *03 87 68 25 00.* 🕐 *Wed–Mon.* ⬤ *publ. hols.* 📷
Also known as the Musée d'Art et d'Histoire, this fascinating collection is set in the Petits-Carmes, a deconsecrated 17th-century monastery incorporating Gallo-Roman thermal baths and a medieval tithe barn. On display are Merovingian stone carvings, Gothic painted ceilings, and German, Flemish and French paintings.

WHITE STORKS

Until recently, the white stork, traditionally a symbol of good fortune, was a frequent sight in northeast France. White storks spend the winter in Africa, but migrate north to breed. However, the gradual draining of marshy ground and pesticides and electric cables have threatened their survival here. A program to reintroduce them to the area has set up breeding centers, as at Molsheim and Turckheim, which means these striking birds can once again be seen in Alsace-Lorraine.

The 13th-century Chapelle des Templiers, with restored frescoes, in Metz

Place Stanislas in Nancy, with statue of Stanislas Leczinski, Duke of Lorraine and father-in-law of Louis XV

Nancy ❹

Meurthe-et-Moselle. 🏛 102,000.
✈ 🚂 🚌 ❚ 14 place Stanislas
(03 83 35 22 41). 🗓 Tue–Sat.
🌐 www.ot-nancy.fr

L ORRAINE'S HISTORIC capital
backs onto the Canal du
Marne and the Meurthe River.
In the 18th century, Stanislas
Leczinski, Duke of Lorraine
(see p292), transformed the
city, making it a model of
18th-century town planning.

The second golden age was
at the turn of this century,
when glassmaker Emile Gallé
founded the Ecole de Nancy,
a forerunner of the Art
Nouveau movement in France.

Nancy's principal and most
renowned landmark is **place
Stanislas**. Laid out in the
1750s, this elegantly proportioned square is enclosed by
highly ornate gilded wrought-
iron gates and railings, a hallmark of the city. Lining the
square are fine *hôtels
particuliers* (town houses),
and stylish restaurants.

An Arc de Triomphe leads
to place de la Carrière, a
gracious, tree-lined square. At
the far end, flanked by semicircular arcades, is the Gothic
Palais du Gouvernement.
Next door in the Parc de la

Pépinière is Rodin's statue of
Claude Lorrain, the landscape
painter, born near Nancy.

The Grande Rue provides a
glimpse of medieval Nancy.
Of the original fortifications
only the Porte de la Craffe
remains, which was used as a
prison after the Revolution.

♟ Eglise et Couvent des
Cordeliers et Musée
Régional des Arts et
Traditions Populaires

64 & 66 Grande Rue. ❚ 03 83 32 18
74. 🗓 Wed–Mon. ● Jan 1, Easter
Sun, May 1, Jul 14, Nov 1, Dec 25. 🖼
The Dukes of Lorraine are
buried in the crypt, and the
adjoining converted monastery
contains the Musée Régional
des Arts et Traditions Populaires, covering folklore,
furniture, costumes and crafts.

🏛 Musée des Beaux Arts

3 place Stanislas. ❚ 03 83 85 30 72.
🗓 Wed–Mon. ● some public hols.
🖼 ♿ 🖼
Recent renovation and a modern extension have enabled
40 percent more of the museum's remarkable collection of
14th-to 20th-century European
art to be seen, including
works by Delacroix, Manet,
Monet, Morisot, Utrillo, Dufy
and Modigliani. The Daum
glassware is stunning.

🏛 Musée Historique
Lorraine

Palais Ducal, 64 Grande Rue. ❚ 03 83
32 18 74. 🗓 Wed–Mon. ● Jan 1,
May 1, Jul 14, Nov 1, Dec 25. 🖼
The museum of the history of
Lorraine has a rich collection
of archaeological finds, sculptures and paintings, including
two by Georges de la Tour.

🏛 Musée de l'Ecole de
Nancy

36–38 rue de Sergent Blandan.
❚ 03 83 40 14 86. 🗓 Wed–Sun.
● Jan 1, May 1, Jul 14, Nov 1,
Dec 25. 🖼 🖼
Exhibits in reconstructed Art
Nouveau settings include
furniture, fabrics and jewelry,
as well as the fanciful glassware of Emile Gallé, founder
of the Ecole de Nancy.

Arc de Triomphe in place Stanislas,
leading to place de la Carrière

Vosges landscape seen from the Route des Crêtes

THE ROUTE DES CRÊTES

This strategic mountain road (83 km/50 miles
long) connects the Vosges Valley from Col du
Bonhomme to Cernay, east of Thann, often
through woodland. Hugging the western side
of the Vosges, the Route des Crêtes was
created during World War I to prevent the
Germans from observing French troop
movements. When not shrouded in mist, there
are breathtaking views over Lorraine from its
many "crests" (*crêtes*).

Gérardmer ⑤

Vosges. 🏔 *10,000.* 🚉 🚤 ℹ️ *place des Déportés (03 29 27 27 27).* 🏪 *Thu & Sat.*

NESTLING ON the Lorraine side of the Vosges, on the shore of a magnificent lake stretching out before it, Gérardmer is a setting rather than a city. In November 1944, just before its liberation, Gérardmer was razed by the Nazi scorched-earth policy, but has since been reconstructed. Saw mills and wood-carving remain local trades, though tourism is fast replacing the textile industry.

Gérardmer is now a popular vacation resort. In winter, the steep slopes of the Vosges Cristallines around the town turn it into a ski resort, while the lake is used for water sports in summer. The town's attractions also include lakeside walks and boat trips, as well as Géromée cheese, similar to the more famous Munster, from just over the Alsatian border. Gérardmer also boasts the oldest tourist information office in the country, dating from 1875.

Yet, ultimately, it is the scenic drives and mountain hikes in the Vosges that attract adventurous visitors. Most leave the lakeside bowl to head for the Alsatian border via the magnificent **Route des Crêtes**, which can be joined at the mountain pass of Col de la Schlucht.

Re-creating village crafts in Ecomusée d'Alsace in Ungersheim

Mulhouse ⑥

Haut Rhin. 🏔 *109,000.* ✈️ 🚉 🚌 ℹ️ *9 av du Maréchal Foch (03 89 35 48 48).* 🏪 *Tue, Thu & Sat.*

CLOSE TO the Swiss border, Mulhouse is primarily an industrial city, badly damaged in World War II. However, there are numerous technical museums and shopping galleries, as well as Alsatian taverns and Swiss wine bars. Most visitors use the city as a base for exploring the rolling hills of the Sundgau on the Swiss border.

Of the museums, **Musée de l'Impression sur Etoffes**, at 14 rue Jean-Jaques Henner, is devoted to textiles and fabric painting, while **Musée Français du Chemin de Fer**, at 2 rue Alfred Glehn, has a collection of steam and electric locomotives. **Musée National de l'Automobile**, at 192 avenue de Colmar, boasts over 100 Bugattis, plus several Mercedes and Ferraris and Charlie Chaplin's Rolls Royce. The place de la République, the liveliest part of town, has a **Musée Historique**, in the Renaissance former town hall.

Alsatian black pig in Ecomusée d'Alsace in Ungersheim

Environs

At Ungersheim, north of Mulhouse, the **Ecomusée d'Alsace** consists of rural settings transplanted here to preserve and display the region's heritage. The 12th-century fortified house from Mulhouse is a dramatic building, complete with Gothic garden. Farms are run along traditional lines, with livestock such as the Alsatian black pig. Rural crafts can be seen in their original settings.

🏛 **Ecomusée d'Alsace**
Chemin du Grosswald. 📞 *03 89 74 44 74.* ☐ *daily.* 🎦 ♿ 🎫

The lake at Gérardmer, offering sports and leisure activities

Guebwiller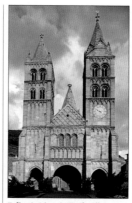

Haut Rhin. 🚶 11,000. 🚆 ℹ️ 73 rue de la République (03 89 76 10 63). 🛒 Tue & Fri.

SURROUNDED BY vineyards and flower-filled valleys, Guebwiller is known as "the gateway to the valley of flowers." However, as an industrial town producing textiles and machine tools, it feels cut off from its rural setting. The houses are dignified, but the *caves* and churches make it worth a visit.

Set on a pretty square, **Eglise Notre-Dame** combines Baroque theatricality with Neo-Classical elegance, while **Eglise des Dominicains** boasts Gothic frescoes and a fine rood screen. **Eglise St-Léger**, the richly ornamented Romanesque church, is the most rewarding, especially the façade, triple porch and portal.

Eglise St-Léger in Guebwiller

Environs

The scenic Lauch Valley, northwest of Guebwiller, is known as "Le Florival" because of its flowers and foliage. **Lautenbach** is used as a starting point for hikes through this recognized *zone de tranquillité*. The village has a pink Romanesque church, whose portal depicts human passion and the battle between Good and Evil. The square leads to the river, a small dam, a *lavoir* (public washing place) and houses overhanging the water.

Neuf-Brisach

Haut Rhin. 🚶 2,100. 🚆 ℹ️ Palais du Gouverneur, 6 place d'Armes (03 89 72 56 66). 🛒 1st & 3rd Mon of each month.

SITUATED NEAR the German border, this octagonal citadel is the military strategist Vauban's masterpiece. Built between 1698 and 1707, the citadel forms a typical star-shaped pattern, with symmetrical towers enclosing 48 equal squares. In the center, from where straight streets radiate for ease of defense, is

THE CITADEL OF NEUF-BRISACH

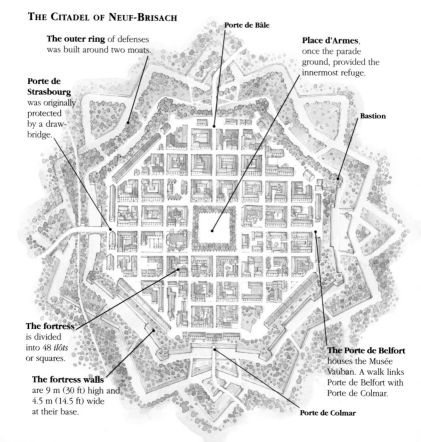

The outer ring of defenses was built around two moats.

Porte de Bâle

Place d'Armes, once the parade ground, provided the innermost refuge.

Porte de Strasbourg was originally protected by a drawbridge.

Bastion

The fortress is divided into 48 *îlôts* or squares.

The fortress walls are 9 m (30 ft) high and 4.5 m (14.5 ft) wide at their base.

The Porte de Belfort houses the Musée Vauban. A walk links Porte de Belfort with Porte de Colmar.

Porte de Colmar

The celebrated Issenheim altarpiece by Matthias Grünewald in Colmar

the place d'Armes and the Eglise St-Louis, which was added in 1731–6. It was Vauban's usual homage to his patron, Louis XIV, implying that the church was dedicated to the Sun King, rather than the saint.

The Porte de Belfort houses the **Musée Vauban**, which includes a model of the town, showing the outlying defenses, now concealed by woodland. They represent Vauban's barrier to the fortress and it is to his credit that the citadel was never taken.

🏛 **Musée Vauban**
Place Porte de Belfort. 📞 03 89 72 56 66. ◯ Apr–Oct: Wed–Mon; Nov–Mar: groups only by appt. 🈲 ♿

Eguisheim ❾

Haut Rhin. 🏘 1,500. 🚆 🚌 🛈 22a Grand'Rue (03 89 23 40 33).

EGUISHEIM is a most exquisite small town, laid out within three concentric rings of ramparts. Curled up within these 13th-century walls, the ensemble of austere fortifications and domestic elegance makes for a surprisingly harmonious whole.

In the center of town is the octagonal feudal **castle** of the Counts of Eguisheim. A Renaissance fountain in front has the statue of Bruno Eguisheim, born here in 1002. He became Pope Léon IX and was later canonized.

The Grand'Rue is lined with half-timbered houses, many showing their construction

date. Close to the castle is the **Marbacherhof**, a monastic tithe barn and cornhall. On a neighboring square, the modern parish church retains the original Romanesque sculpted tympanum.

The rest of the town has its share of Hansel-and-Gretel atmosphere, while inviting courtyards offer tastings of *grands crus*. From rue de Hautvilliers, outside the ramparts, a marked path leads through scenic vineyards.

Colmar ❿

Haut Rhin. 🏘 65,000. 🚆 🚌 🛈 4 rue d'Unterlinden (03 89 20 68 92). 🈲 Mon, Wed, Thu & Sat.

COLMAR IS THE BEST-preserved city in Alsace. As a trading post and river port, Colmar had its heyday in the 16th century, when wine merchants shipped their wine along the waterways running through the picturesque canal quarter,

now known as **Petite Venise**. "Little Venice" is best seen on a leisurely boat trip that takes you from the tanners' quarter to the rue des Tanneurs. The adjoining place de l'Alsacienne Douane is dominated by the **Koïfhüs**, a galleried customs house with a Burgundian tiled roof, overlooking half-timbered pastel houses that sport sculpted pillars.

Nearby, the place de la Cathédrale quarter is full of 16th-century houses with picturesque hanging signs. **Eglise St-Martin**, essentially Gothic, has a noted south portal. Just to the west, the place des Dominicains, with cafés, is dwarfed by the Gothic **Eglise Dominicains**. Inside is *La Vierge au Buisson de Rose*s (1473), the glittering red and gold "Virgin of the Rose-bush" by Martin Schongauer, a renowned Alsatian painter and native of Colmar.

Place d'Unterlinden, the adjoining square, has the **Musée d'Unterlinden**. Set in a Dominican monastery, it displays early Rhenish paintings. The highlight is the Issenheim altarpiece. A master-piece of emotional intensity, it is part of an early 16th-century Alsatian panel painting by Matthias Grünewald.

In the historic center, the quaint rue des Têtes has the former wine exchange, a Renaissance town house known as the Maison des Têtes because of the grimacing heads on the gabled façade. And in rue Mercière, **Maison Pfister**, with its slender stair turret and galleried flower-decked façade, has come to typify the city.

Along the quai de la Poissonerie in the Petite Venise area of Colmar

Riquewihr **⓫**

Haut Rhin. 👥 *1,100.* 🚂
ℹ️ *2 rue de 1ère Armèe (03 89 49 08 40).* 🏛️ *Fri.*

VINEYARDS RUN right up to the ramparts of Riquewihr, the prettiest village on the Route du Vin (*see pp222–3*). Deeply pragmatic, Riquewihr winemakers plant roses at the end of each row of vines – both for their pretty effect and as early detectors of parasites. The village belonged to the Counts of Wurtemberg until the Revolution and has grown rich on wine, from Tokay and Pinot Gris to Gewürztraminer and Riesling. Virtually an outdoor museum, Riquewihr abounds in cobbled alleys, geranium-clad balconies, galleried courtyards, romantic double ramparts and watchtowers.

From the Hôtel de Ville, the **rue du Général de Gaulle** climbs gently past medieval and Renaissance houses, half-timbered, stone-clad or corbelled. Oriel windows vie with sculpted portals and medieval sign boards. On the right lies the idyllic **place des**

Trois Eglises. A passageway leads through the ramparts to the vineyards, stacked up on the hill. Farther up lies the **Dolder**, a 13th-century belfry, followed by the **Tour des Voleurs** (both are museums, the latter with a grueling medieval torture chamber), marking the second tier of ramparts. Beyond the gateway is the **Cour des Bergers**, gardens laid out around the 16th-century ramparts. Visitors outnumber the local population several times over, in summer or during the wine festival.

The pretty – and popular – village of Riquewihr, set among vineyards

Ribeauvillé **⓬**

Haut Rhin. 👥 *4,800.* 🚂 🚌
ℹ️ *1 Grand'Rue (03 89 73 62 22).* 🏛️ *Sat.*

OVERLOOKED by three ruined castles, Ribeauvillé is stiflingly prettified, as may be expected from a popular town on the Route du Vin. This status is partly due to healthy sales of the celebrated *grands crus* of Alsace, especially Riesling. There are ample opportunities for tastings, particularly near the park, in the lower part of town (*see pp222–3*).

On the Grand'Rue (No. 14) is the **Pfifferhüs**, the minstrels' house, now a regional restaurant. As local cooks declare, Ribeauvillé is the capital of the *kougelhopf*, the light, almond-flavored Alsatian cake.

Tortuous alleys wind past steep-roofed artisans' and wine-growers' houses in the upper part of the town. Beyond are Renaissance fountains, painted façades and **St Grégoire-le-Grand**, the Gothic parish church. A marked path, which begins in this part of town, leads into the vineyards.

Château du Haut-Koenigsbourg **⓭**

Orschwiller. 📞 *03 88 82 50 60.*
⭕ *daily.* ⬤ *Jan 1, May 1, Dec 25.*
📷 🚗 ♿ 🏠 🍴

LOOMING ABOVE the lovely village of St-Hippolyte, this castle is the most popular attraction in Alsace. In 1114, the Swabian Emperor, Frederick of Hohenstaufen, built the first Teutonic castle here, which was destroyed in 1462. Rebuilt and added to under the Habsburgs, it burned down in 1633. At the end of the 19th century, Kaiser Wilhelm II commissioned Berlin architect Bodo Ebhardt to restore the castle. The result of his painstaking work was a precise reconstruction of the original building.

Despite a drawbridge, fierce keep and rings of fortifications, this warm sandstone hybrid is too sophisticated for a feudal

château. The Cour d'Honneur is a breathtaking re-creation, with a pointed corner turret and creaky arcaded galleries. Within the castle are suitably gloomy "Gothic" chambers and airy "Renaissance" rooms. La Grande Salle is the most elaborate, with a Neo-Gothic gallery and ornate paneling. From the battlements,

almost 750 m (2,500 ft) above the Alsace plain, stretches a glorious Rhineland panorama, bordered by the Black Forest and the Alps. On the other side are sweeping views, from the high Vosges to villages and vineyards below.

Upper garden

West bastion

West wing

Outer walls

Chapelle St-Sébastien outside Dambach-la-Ville, along the Route du Vin

Sélestat 🄤

Bas Rhin. 🚶 16,000. 🚉 🚌
🛈 Commanderie Saint Jean, boulevard du Général Leclerc (03 88 58 87 20). 🚇 Tue.

D URING THE RENAISSANCE, Sélestat was the intellectual center of Alsace, with a tradition of humanism fostered by Beatus Rhenanus, a friend of Erasmus. The famous **Bibliothèque Humaniste** has a magnificent collection of leather-bound editions of some of the earliest printed books and unique illuminated manuscripts. Nearby are the Cour des Prélats, a turreted ivy-covered mansion, and the Tour de l'Horloge, a medieval clock tower. **Eglise Ste-Foy** is 12th-century, with an octagonal belltower. Opposite is **Eglise St-Georges**, glittering with green and red "Burgundian tiles."

🏛 **Bibliothèque Humaniste**
1 rue de la Bibliothèque.
📞 03 88 58 07 20.
⏰ Mon, Wed–Sat am; (Jul–Aug: Wed–Mon exc. Sun am). ⬤ public hols. 📷

Environs
Medieval **Dambach-la-Ville**, another pretty town, is linked to Andlau and red-tiled Itterswiller by a delightful rural road through vineyards.

Ebersmunster, a picturesque hamlet, has an onion-domed abbey church, whose Baroque interior is a sumptuous display of gilded stucco.

Obernai 🄯

Bas Rhin. 🚶 10,000. 🚉 🚌
🛈 place du Beffroi (03 88 95 64 13).
🚇 Thu.

A T THE NORTH END of the Route du Vin, Obernai retains a flavor of authentic Alsace: residents speak Alsatian, at festivities women wear traditional costume, and church services are well attended in the cavernous Neo-Gothic **Eglise St-Pierre-et-St-Paul**. The place du Marché is well preserved, and features the gabled **Halle aux Blés**, a 16th-century corn hall (now a restaurant) above a former butcher's shop, with a façade adorned with cows' and dragons' heads. Place de la Chapelle, the adjoining square, has a Renaissance fountain and the 16th-century **Hôtel de Ville** and the **Kapellturm**, the galleried Gothic belfry. Side streets have Renaissance and medieval timber-framed houses. A stroll past the cafés on rue du Marché ends in a pleasant park by the ramparts.

Young *Alsaciens* in traditional costume

Environs
Odile, Alsace's seventh-century patron saint, was born in Obernai but she is venerated on **Mont Sainte-Odile** to the west, where she is buried in the Chapelle Ste-Odile.

Molsheim, a former bishopric and fortified market town 10 km (6 miles) north, is noted for its attractive marketplace with fountain. The star attraction is the Metzig, a Renaissance-style butchers' guildhall, now the town hall.

North wing, with kitchens

South wing, with chapel

Entrance ramp to upper castle

Hostelry

Outer walls

Guardroom

Entrance

Well tower

Drawbridge within the walls of Château du Haut-Koenigsbourg

Strasbourg ⑯

HALFWAY BETWEEN PARIS and Prague, Strasbourg is often known, not surprisingly, as "the crossroads of Europe." The city wears its European cosmopolitanism with ease – after all, its famous cathedral has catered to both Catholic and Protestant congregations – and, as one of the capitals of the European Union has sensibly located the futuristic European Parliament building some way off the historic center. One way to see this, along with more traditional city sights, is to take a boat trip along the waterways encircling the Old Town. On the way you will pass the Ponts-Couverts, covered bridges linked by medieval watchtowers that provide an observation point for the four Ill canals, and the scenic Petite France, once the tanners' district, dotted with mills and crisscrossed by bridges.

Cathedral statue

Barge on the canal

The central portal of the west façade of the cathedral

⛪ Cathédrale Notre-Dame

A masterpiece of stone lacework, the sandstone cathedral "rises like a most sublime, widearching tree of God," as Goethe marveled. Though construction began in the late 11th century (the choir is Romanesque, the nave is Gothic), it ended only in 1439, with the completion of the west façade begun in 1277. The three portals are ornamented with statues. But the crowning glory is the rose window. The south portal leads to the Gothic Pillar of Angels (*circa* 1230), set beside the Astronomical Clock: mechanical figures appear accompanied by chimes at 12:31pm. There are wonderful views over the city from the viewing platform, and on some summer evenings there are organ concerts.

In place de la Cathédrale, Maison Kammerzell, now a popular restaurant, was once a rich merchant's mansion, its highly elaborate, carved facade dating from mid-15th–late-16th centuries.

🏛 Palais Rohan

2 pl du Château. 📞 03 88 52 50 00.
🕐 Wed–Mon. ⬤ Jan 1, Good Fri,
May 1, Nov 1 & 11, Dec 25.
📷 ♿

Designed by the king's architect, Robert de Cotte, in 1730, this grand Classical palace was intended for the Prince-Bishops of Strasbourg. It houses three museums: the Musée des Beaux Arts; the Musée Archéologique; and the Musée des Arts Décoratifs, which contains the sumptuous State Apartments and one of the finest collections of ceramics in France.

The Musée d'Art Moderne et Contemporain on Strasbourg's waterfront

VISITORS' CHECKLIST

Bas Rhin. 250,000. 12 km
(7.5 miles) SW Strasbourg. pl
de la Gare (08 36 35 35 35).
pl des Halles (03 88 77 70 09).
17 pl de la Cathédrale (03 88
52 28 22). Mon, Wed–Sat.
International Music Festival
(Jun); Musica, contemporary
music festival (mid-Sep–early-Oct);
Jazz Festival (Nov).

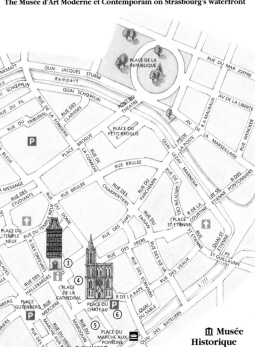

buildings, the museum has
exhibits on local traditions
and popular arts and crafts.

🏛 Musée de l'Oeuvre Notre-Dame

3 place du Château. 03 88
52 50 00. Wed–Mon.
Jan 1, Good Fri, May 1,
Nov 1, Dec 25. ground fl.
The cathedral's impressive
museum contains much of
its original sculpture,
as well as magnifi-
cent 11th-century
stained glass. This
sombre gabled
house also displays
a collection of
Medieval and Renais-
sance Alsatian art.

🏛 Musée d'Art Moderne et Contemporain

1 pl Jean Hans-Arp. 03 88 23 31 31.
Tue–Sun. Jan 1, Good Fri,
May 1, Nov 1 & 11, Dec 25.
Concerts, cinema.
Adrien Fainsilber's cultural
flagship for the 21st century
is a marvel of glass and light
(particularly at night when it
appears to float on the river).
Its superb collections run from
1860–1950 and from 1950 onward. The Art Café is welcome respite for art-weary feet.

🏛 Musée Historique

3 place de la Grande
Boucherie. 03 88 52 50
00. for renovation until
2004.
The museum occupies the
cavernous 16th-century city
abattoir and focuses on Strasbourg's political, economic
and military history.

🏛 Musée Alsacien

23 quai St-Nicolas. 03 88 52 50 00.
Wed–Mon. Jan 1, Good Fri,
May 1, Nov 1, Dec 25.
Housed in a series of inter-
connecting Renaissance

KEY

🚢	River boat service
🅿	Parking
ℹ	Tourist information
✚	Church

STRASBOURG CITY CENTER

Ponts-Couverts ①
Petite France ②
Maison Kammerzell ③
Cathédrale Notre-Dame ④
Musée de l'Oeuvre
 Notre-Dame ⑤
Palais Rohan ⑥
Musée Alsacien ⑦

0 meters   250

0 yards   250

**Ponts-Couverts with medieval
watchtowers over the canals**

The Alsace Route du Vin

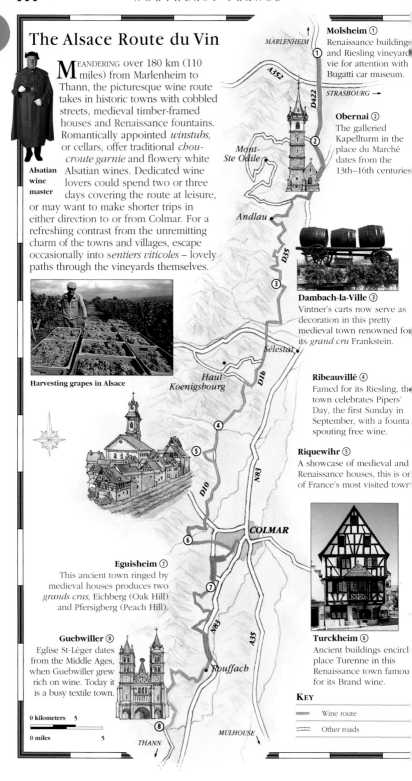

MEANDERING over 180 km (110 miles) from Marlenheim to Thann, the picturesque wine route takes in historic towns with cobbled streets, medieval timber-framed houses and Renaissance fountains. Romantically appointed *winstubs*, or cellars, offer traditional *choucroute garnie* and flowery white Alsatian wines. Dedicated wine lovers could spend two or three days covering the route at leisure, or may want to make shorter trips in either direction to or from Colmar. For a refreshing contrast from the unremitting charm of the towns and villages, escape occasionally into *sentiers viticoles* – lovely paths through the vineyards themselves.

Alsatian wine master

Harvesting grapes in Alsace

Molsheim ①
Renaissance buildings and Riesling vineyards vie for attention with Bugatti car museum.

Obernai ②
The galleried Kapellturm in the place du Marché dates from the 13th–16th centuries.

Dambach-la-Ville ③
Vintner's carts now serve as decoration in this pretty medieval town renowned for its *grand cru* Frankstein.

Ribeauvillé ④
Famed for its Riesling, the town celebrates Pipers' Day, the first Sunday in September, with a fountain spouting free wine.

Riquewihr ⑤
A showcase of medieval and Renaissance houses, this is one of France's most visited towns.

Eguisheim ⑦
This ancient town ringed by medieval houses produces two *grands crus*, Eichberg (Oak Hill) and Pfersigberg (Peach Hill).

Guebwiller ⑧
Eglise St-Léger dates from the Middle Ages, when Guebwiller grew rich on wine. Today it is a busy textile town.

Turckheim ⑥
Ancient buildings encircle place Turenne in this Renaissance town famous for its Brand wine.

KEY

▬▬	Wine route
═══	Other roads

0 kilometers   5
0 miles   5

LSACE WINE

ace wines are usually
matic, dry and full-bodied.
are white except Pinot Noir,
d for light reds.

ate-harvested Alsatian classic

KEY FACTS

Location and climate
Protected by the
Vosges, Alsace has
a semi-continental, fairly
dry, warm climate.

Grape varieties
Alsace wines are
known simply by
their grape variety.
Gewürztraminer, with its
exotic rose-petal character,
is most typically Alsatian,
although the *Riesling* is
arguably the finest. *Muscat*
is another aromatic variety.
spicy but less assertive than
Gewürztraminer, *Pinot
Gris* and the crisper, dry
Pinot Blanc go well with
food. *Pinot Noir* is the
only red variety.

Lusciously rich, sweet,
ate-harvested wines are an
Alsace specialty.

Best producers
Albert Boxler,
Marcel Deiss,
Rolly Gassmann,
Bayer, Mayer-
Fonne, Kuentz-Bas,
Domaine Weinbach, Dopff
& Irion, Olivier Zind-
Humbrecht, Charles Schléret,
Domaines Schlumberger,
Domaine Ostertag,
Domaine Trimbach, Hugel
& Fils, Cave de Turckheim.

Good vintages
1998, 1996, 1995,
1990, 1989, 1988.

The 12th-century chapel of the Château du Haut-Barr, near Saverne

Saverne ⑰

Bas Rhin. 🕭 10,300. 🚊 🚌
🛈 37 Grand Rue (03 88 91 80 47).
🔄 Tue & Thu.

FRAMED BY HILLS, and situated
on the Zorn River and the
Marne-Rhine Canal, Saverne is
a pretty sight. The town was a
fief of the prince-bishops of
Strasbourg, and its sandstone
Château des Rohan was a
favorite summer residence.
Today, it houses the
**Musée de la Ville
de Saverne**, whose
collection traces
Saverne's past. On
the far side of the
château, the Grand'Rue
is studded with res-
taurants and timber-
framed Renaissance
houses.

🏛 Musée de la Ville de Saverne

Château des Rohan. 📞 03 88 91 06
28. ⭕ Mar–Nov: Wed–Mon pms
(mid-Jun–mid-Sep: all day); Dec–Jan:
Sun pm. 🎦 ♿ restricted.

Environs

To the southwest, perched on
a rocky spur, the ruined
Château du Haut-Barr – the
"Eye of Alsace" – once commanded the vital pass of Col
de Saverne. In **Marmoutier**,
6 km (3.5 miles) further south,
is a renowned abbey church
with a Romanesque-Lombard
façade and octagonal towers.

Betschdorf ⑱

Bas Rhin. 🕭 3,600. 🛈 La Mairie
(03 88 54 48 00).

THE VIBRANT village of
Betschdorf borders the
Forêt de Haguenau, 45 km
(27 miles) north of Strasbourg.
Many residents occupy timber-
framed houses dating from
the 18th century, when
pottery made the village prosperous. Generations of
potters have passed
down the knowledge
of the characteristic
blue-gray glaze to
their sons, while the
women have been
entrusted with deco-
rating it in cobalt
blue. A pottery
museum, with a work-
shop attached, dis-
plays rural
ceramics. Also worth visiting
are the frescoed Gothic Nieder-
betschdorf church and the
Lutheran Kuhlendorf church,
the only timber-framed church
in Alsace. Nearby is the Wacht,
the former nightwatchmen's
quarters. Betschdorf is a good
place to try *tartes flambées* –
hot, crispy bases topped with
cheese or fruit.

Betschdorf pottery

Environs

Another pottery village,
Soufflenheim, lies 10 km
(6 miles) southeast. Its earth-
colored pottery is usually
painted with bold flowers.

WESTERN
FRANCE

Introducing Western France

THE WESTERN REGIONS of France have played very
different historical roles, from the royal heartland
of the Loire Valley to separatist Celtic Brittany. These
are mainly rich farming regions, with fishing important
along the coasts. Heavy industry and oil refineries are
concentrated around Rouen and Le Havre. Visitors
come for the wonderful beaches, quiet rural byways
and the sumptuous Loire châteaux. This map shows
some of the region's most celebrated sights.

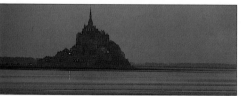

The evocative silhouette of Mont-St-Michel *has welcomed
pilgrims since the 11th century. Today nearly one million visitors
a year walk across the causeway to the island abbey (see pp246–51).*

Guimiliau Parish Close

Mont-St-Michel

BRITTANY
(See pp258–75)

Carnac Megaliths

The megaliths of Carnac *are evidence of early settlers
in Brittany. These ancient granite blocks, arranged in
intriguing patterns, date to 4000 BC and are thought to
have had a religious or astronomical significance (see p269).*

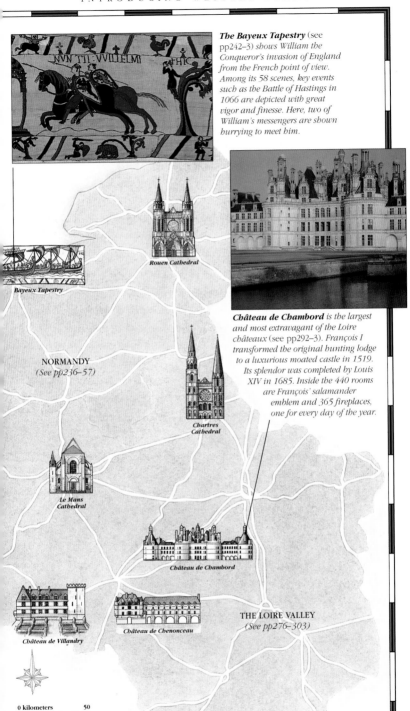

The Bayeux Tapestry (see pp242–3) shows William the Conqueror's invasion of England from the French point of view. Among its 58 scenes, key events such as the Battle of Hastings in 1066 are depicted with great vigor and finesse. Here, two of William's messengers are shown hurrying to meet him.

Château de Chambord is the largest and most extravagant of the Loire châteaux (see pp292–3). François I transformed the original hunting lodge to a luxurious moated castle in 1519. Its splendor was completed by Louis XIV in 1685. Inside the 440 rooms are François' salamander emblem and 365 fireplaces, one for every day of the year.

Bayeux Tapestry

Rouen Cathedral

NORMANDY
(See pp236–57)

Chartres
Cathedral

Le Mans
Cathedral

Château de Chambord

Château de Villandry

Château de Chenonceau

THE LOIRE VALLEY
(See pp276–303)

0 kilometers 50

0 miles 50

Regional Food: Western France

W ITH 480 KM (300 MILES) of coastline, Normandy cooking naturally draws on an abundance of fish and shellfish. Lambs graze on the salt marshes, giving the meat its slightly salty, distinctive flavor. Inland, dairy cattle produce rich milk for cream, cheese and butter. Calvados, the famous apple brandy, is derived from the apples that thrive here.

Camembert cheese

Seafood, salt-marsh lamb, cider, and cider *eau-de-vie* all cross the border into Breton cuisine, but particular to Brittany is fresh curd cheese or buttermilk with buckwheat *galettes* – foods once regarded as humble but that have now become much sought-after ingredients of chic regional cuisine.

In the Loire Valley, the river is a source of tasty fresh-water fish, and plump mushrooms are cultivated in caves along the riverbanks. The rich alluvial soils produce luscious vegetables, fruit, cheese and wine.

Moules marinières *are mussels cooked in white wine, with onions, shallots, parsley and butter.*

Oysters *can be eaten raw straight from the shell or grilled quickly and served with a sauce.*

Pure sea salt crystals, seen glistening on the Guérande Peninsula of southeast Brittany, are raked in pans by farmers in the traditional way. This fine natural salt retains all its minerals and the unmistakable scent of the sea.

Shrimps

Clams

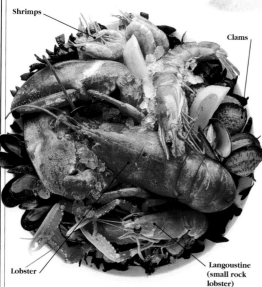

Lobster

Langoustine (small rock lobster)

Fruits de mer is a selection of local seafood which includes oysters, clams, mussels, crabs, langoustines, whelks (a type of snail), shrimps and winkles, often served on a great bed of ice and seaweed. Necessary accompaniments include lemons, shallot-and-vinegar sauce, chilled Muscadet, fresh rye bread and butter.

Rillettes *are chunks of pork or goose meat, cooked slowly in lard, then shredded and potted.*

Artichokes *can be cooked in water or wine with herbs, stuffed, or served with herb or lemon-flavored butter.*

Gigot d'agneau à la Bretonne *is roast lamb served with haricot beans simmered with tomatoes, garlic and onions.*

***Salmon with* beurre blanc,** *a sauce of butter, wine and shallots, is a popular dish in both Brittany and the Loire.*

Tripe à la mode de Caen *is a Normandy dish of steamed tripe and vegetables cooked together very slowly in cider.*

Tarte tatin *is a caramelized upside-down apple tart, originally created at the Hôtel Tatin in the Loire Valley.*

Crêpes Suzettes, *one of Brittany's most famous dishes, is flavored with oranges and Grand Marnier liqueur.*

***Galette biscuits* from Brittany** *are quite noticeably flavored with the slightly salty butter used in the regional cuisine.*

CHEESES
Some of France's finest cheeses come from Normandy – Camembert, pungent Livarot and creamy Pont-l'Evêque. Crottin de Chavignol from the Loire is one of the most popular *chèvres* (goat's cheeses).

Pont l'Evêque

Crottins de Chavignol

Livarot

Camembert

DRINKS
In Normandy and most of Brittany, still or sparkling cider is the local drink, an excellent accompaniment to savory and sweet *galettes* and *crêpes*. Much stronger is the apple brandy known as Calvados (*lambig* in Brittany). The herbal liqueur Benedictine was first concocted by a monk at Fécamp in 1510.

Benedictine

Calvados

Cider

France's Wine Regions: the Loire

W ITH A FEW EXCEPTIONS, the Loire is a region of good rather than great wines. The fertile agricultural soils of the meandering flatlands of the "Garden of France" are fine for fruit and vegetables, less so for the production of great wines. The cool, northern, Atlantic-influenced climate nonetheless produces refreshing reds and summer rosés, both dry and lusciously sweet white wines and attractively bracing sparkling wines. Dry white wines are very much in the majority here, and are usually intended for early consumption, so vintages in the Loire tend to matter less than in the classic red wine regions.

Cabernet Franc, red grape of the Loire

LOCATOR MAP
☐ *Loire wine region*

The sweet wine of Quarts de Chaume, within the Coteaux du Layon appellation, is little-known outside France.

Muscadet with the words sur lie *on the label has been aged on its "lees" (see p23), giving the wine more flavor and interest.*

WINE REGIONS

The Loire, flowing for some 1,000 km (620 miles), links the major wine areas of the Loire Valley. From its source in the Ardèche, it flows north through the center of France to the Sancerre and Pouilly Fumé vineyards, then west through Touraine and Anjou, finally reaching the coastal flats of the Pays Nantais, home of Muscadet.

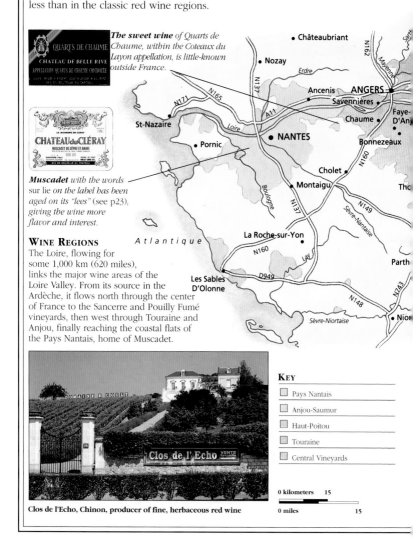

KEY
☐ Pays Nantais
☐ Anjou-Saumur
☐ Haut-Poitou
☐ Touraine
☐ Central Vineyards

0 kilometers   15

0 miles   15

Clos de l'Echo, Chinon, producer of fine, herbaceous red wine

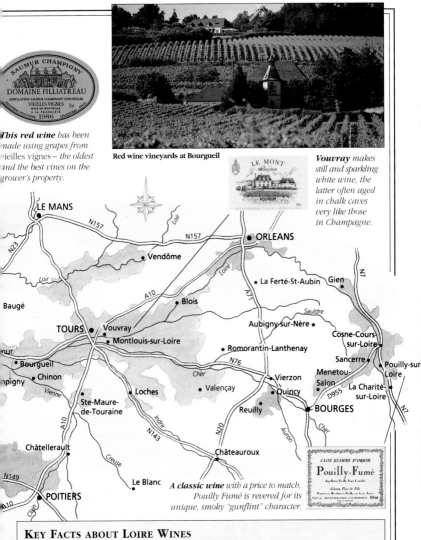

This red wine has been made using grapes from vieilles vignes – the oldest and the best vines on the grower's property.

Red wine vineyards at Bourgueil

Vouvray *makes still and sparkling white wine, the latter often aged in chalk caves very like those in Champagne.*

LE MANS

N157

N23

Vendôme

ORLEANS

N157

Baugé

A10

La Ferté-St-Aubin   Gien

N7

Blois

TOURS   Vouvray

Montlouis-sur-Loire

Aubigny-sur-Nère

Cosne-Cours-sur-Loire

Romorantin-Lanthenay

N76

Sancerre   Pouilly-sur-Loire

Bourgueil

Chinon

Cher

Vierzon

Menetou-Salon

pigny

Vienne

Loches

Valençay

Quincy   La Charité-sur-Loire

D955

Ste-Maure-de-Touraine

Indre

Reuilly   **BOURGES**

N143

N20

Auron

Cher

Châtellerault

Creuse

Châteauroux

N7

N149

Le Blanc   *A classic wine with a price to match, Pouilly Fumé is revered for its unique, smoky "gunflint" character.*

POITIERS

A10

KEY FACTS ABOUT LOIRE WINES

Location and Climate
Fertile agricultural soils support fruit, vegetables and cereals as well as grapes. The climate is cool, influenced by the nearby Atlantic, giving the wines a refreshing acidity.

Grape Varieties
The ***Muscadet*** makes simple, dry white wines. The ***Sauvignon*** makes gooseberryish, flinty dry whites; it is at its finest in Sancerre and Pouilly Fumé, but is also good in Touraine. The ***Chenin Blanc*** makes dry and medium Anjou, Savennières, Vouvray, Montlouis and Saumur, sparkling Vouvray and Saumur, and the famous sweet whites, Bonnezeaux,

Vouvray and Quarts de Chaume. Summery reds are made from the ***Gamay*** and the grassy, herbaceous ***Cabernet Franc***.

Good Producers
Muscadet: Sauvion, Guy Bossard, Luneau-Papin. *Anjou, Savennières, Vouvray*: Richou, Ogereau, Nicolas Joly, Huet, Domaine des Aubuissières, Bourillon-Dorléans. *Touraine* (white): Château de Chenonceaux. *Saumur-Champigny* (red): Filliatreau, Château du Hureau. *Chinon, Bourgueil* (red): Couly-Dutheil, Yves Loiseau. *Sancerre, Pouilly Fumé, Ménétou-Salon*: Francis Cotat, Dagueneau, Reverdy, Vacheron, Mellot, Vincent Pinard.

From Defense to Decoration

THE GREAT CHATEAUX of the Loire Valley gradually evolved from purely defensive structures to decorative palaces. With the introduction of firearms, castles lost their defensive function and comfort and taste predominated. Defensive elements like towers, battlements, moats and gatehouses were retained largely as symbols of rank and ancestry. Renaissance additions, like galleries and dormer windows, added elegance.

Salamander emblem of François 1

Slate and stone walls

Fortifications with towers removed

Circular tower, formerly defensive

Corbeled walkways, once useful in battle

Angers (see p281), *a fortress built from 1230–40 by Louis IX, stands on a rocky hill in the town center. In 1585, Henri III removed the towers from 17 fortifications that were formerly 30 m (98 ft) high.*

Chaumont (see p296) *was rebuilt in 1445–1510 in Renaissance style by the Amboise family. Although it has a defensive appearance, with circular towers, corbeled walkways and a gatehouse, these features are mainly decorative. It was restored after c.1833.*

Decorated turret

Azay-le-Rideau (see p286), *regarded as one of the most elegant and well-designed Renaissance châteaux , was built by finance minister Gilles Berthelot (1518–1527) and his wife Philippa Lesbahy. It is a mixture of traditional turrets with Renaissance pilasters and pinnacles. Most dramatic is the interior staircase with its three stories of twin bays and an intricately decorated pediment.*

Renaissance carved windows

Pilasters (columns)

Cylindrical tower

Dormer windows

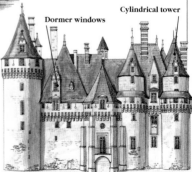

Ussé (see p285) *was built in 1462 by Jean de Bueil as a fortress with parapets containing openings for missiles, battlements and gunloops. The Espinay family, chamberlains to both Louis XI and Charles VIII, bought the château and changed the walls overlooking the main court-yard to Renaissance style with dormer windows and pilasters. In the 17th century the north wing was demolished to create palatial terraces.*

Breton Traditions

BRITTANY WAS CHRISTENED Breiz Izel (Little Britain) by the migrants who fled here from Cornwall and Wales in the 5th and 6th centuries AD and imposed their customs, language and religion on the local Gauls. Brittany resisted Charlemagne, the Vikings, the Normans, English alliances and even French rule until 1532. Today, Breton is taught in some schools, and a busy calendar keeps Brittany in touch with its past and with other Celtic regions.

Bigouden lace headdresses

Breton music has strong Celtic links. Instruments like the biniou, similar to the bagpipes, and the oboelike bombarde are often heard at local festivals.

A **pardon** *is an annual religious festival honoring a local saint. The name derives from the granting of indulgences to pardon the sins of the past year. Some pardons, like those at Ste-Anne d'Auray and Ste-Anne-la-Palud, still attract thousands of pilgrims who carry banners and holy relics through the streets. Most pardons take place between April and September.*

Lace *coiffe*   Felt hat   Linen *coiffe*   **Small headdress**

Wooden clogs

Embroidered apron

Baggy Breton trousers

Breton costumes, *still seen at pardons and weddings, varied as each area had distinctive headdresses or coiffes. Artists like Gauguin often painted the costumes. There are good museum collections in Quimper (see p264) and Pont l'Abbé in Pays Bigouden (see p263).*

Brittany's Coastal Wildlife

WITH ITS GRANITE CLIFFS, sweeping bays, rias and deep estuaries, the Brittany coastline contains a wealth of different wildlife habitats. Parts of the coast have a tidal range of more than 50 m (150 ft), the highest in France, and this great variation in sea level divides marine life into several distinct zones. Most of the

Starfish   region's famous shellfish, including mussels, clams and oysters, live on the lower shore, either on rocks or in muddy sand where they are submerged for most of the day. Higher zones are the preserve of limpets and barnacles and several kinds of seaweed that can survive out of the water for long periods. Above the sea, towering cliffs offer a nursery for seabirds and a foothold for many kinds of wildflowers.

Cliffs at the Pointe du Raz, Brittany

The Ile de Bréhat at low tide

FEATURES OF THE COAST

This scene shows some of the wildlife habitats found on the Brittany coastline. When exploring the shore, make a note of the tide times, particularly if you plan to walk along the foot of the cliffs.

Salt-marsh flowers are a their best in late summer

Dunes, where marram grass grows, stabilize the sand.

Mud and sand are inhabited by clams and cockles that filter food from the water.

Rock stacks provide secure nurseries for nesting seabirds.

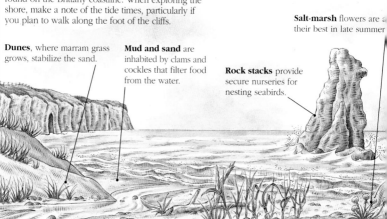

OYSTER BEDS

Like most marine mollusks, oysters begin their lives as tiny floating larvae. The first step in *ostréiculture*, or oyster cultivation, consists of providing the larvae with somewhere to settle, which is usually a stack of submerged tiles. The developing oysters are later transferred to beds and left to mature before being collected for the market.

Oyster beds at Cancale

Clifftop turf often contains a narrow band of wildflowers sandwiched between fields and the sea.

Tidepools are flooded twice daily by the tide. They are inhabited by fish, mollusks, sea anemones and sponges.

COASTAL WILDLIFE

The structure of this shore determines the wildlife that lives on it. In a world beset by wind and waves, rocks provide solid anchorage for plants and a secure habitat for many small animals. Muddy sand is rich in nutrients, and has a greater abundance of life – although most of this is concealed beneath the surface.

Cliffs

The rock dove *is a cliff-dwelling ancestor of the well-known city pigeon.*

Thrift *is a common spring flower, found on exposed ledges near the sea.*

Rocks and Tidepools

Seaweed *of many different varieties is exposed each day by the falling tide.*

The limpet, *a slow-moving creature, scrapes tiny plants from the rock surface.*

The goby, *with its sharp eyesight, dashes for cover at the first sign of movement above.*

Crabs *live at many different water depths. Some species are extremely good swimmers.*

Mud and Sand

Cockles *live in large numbers just beneath the surface of muddy sand.*

The curlew *has a forceps-like curved beak for extracting shell-fish from mud and sand.*

NORMANDY

EURE · SEINE-MARITIME · MANCHE · CALVADOS · ORNE

THE QUINTESSENTIAL IMAGE *of Normandy is of a lush, pastoral region of apple orchards and contented cows, cider and pungent cheeses – but this area also embraces the windswept beaches of the Cotentin and the wooded banks of the Seine Valley. Famous attractions include the great abbey churches of Caen, the mighty island of Mont-St-Michel and Monet's garden at Giverny.*

Normandy gets its name from the Viking Norsemen who sailed up the Seine River in the 9th century. Pillagers turned settlers, they made their capital at Rouen – today a cultured cathedral city seated in the eastern part of the region. Here the Seine meanders seaward past the ancient abbeys at Jumièges and St-Wandrille to a coast that became an outdoor studio for Impressionist painters during the mid- and late 19th century.

North of Rouen are the chalky cliffs of the Côte d'Albâtre. The mood softens at the port of Honfleur and the elegant resorts of the Côte Fleurie to the west. Inland lies the Pays d'Auge, with its half-timbered manor houses and patch-eyed cows. The western half of Normandy is predominantly rural, a *bocage* countryside of small, high-hedged fields with windbreaks composed of beech trees.

The modern city of Caen is worth visiting for its two great 11th-century abbey churches built by William the Conqueror and his queen, Matilda. Nearby in Bayeux, the story of William's invasion of England is told in detail by the town's famous tapestry. Memories of another invasion, the D-Day Landings of 1944, still linger along the Côte de Nacre and the Cotentin Peninsula. Thousands of Allied troops poured ashore onto these magnificent beaches in the closing stages of World War II. The Cotentin Peninsula is capped by the port of Cherbourg, still a strategic naval base. At its western foot stands one of France's greatest attractions: the monastery island of Mont-St-Michel.

Half-timbered manor house in the village of Beuvron-en-Auge, near Lisieux

◁ Rich pastures and brown and white Norman cattle, the traditional wealth of the province

Exploring Normandy

Normandy's rich historical sights and diverse land-scape make it ideal for touring by car or bicycle. Rewarding coastal drives and good beaches can be found along the windswept Côte d'Albâtre and the Cotentin Peninsula. Farther south is one of France's most celebrated sights, Mont-St-Michel. Inland, follow the meandering lovely Seine Valley, passing cider orchards and half-timbered houses along the way, to visit historic Rouen and Monet's garden at Giverny.

Apple trees in blossom in the Pays d'Auge

The Côte d'Albâtre coastline

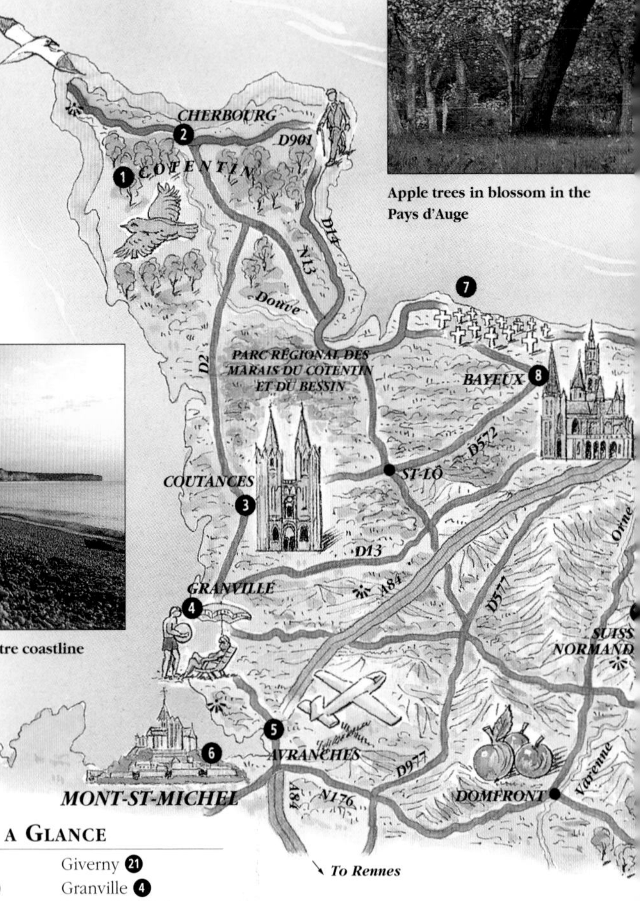

Sights at a Glance

Avranches ⑤	Giverny ㉑
Basse-Seine ⑱	Granville ④
Bayeux ⑧	Haute-Seine ⑳
Caen ⑨	Honfleur ⑭
Cherbourg ②	Le Havre ⑮
Côte d'Albâtre ⑯	Mont-St-Michel ⑥
Côte Fleurie ⑫	Parc Régional de
Côte de Nacre ⑦	Normandie-Maine ⑪
Cotentin ①	Pays d'Auge ⑬
Coutances ③	Rouen ⑲
Dieppe ⑰	Suisse Normande ⑩
Évreux ㉒	

To Rennes

Key

▬▬	Highway
▬▬	Major road
▬▬	Minor road
▬▬	Scenic route
〜	River
☀	Viewing point

GETTING AROUND

Access to and through the region from Calais is quick and direct on the A28–A29, which links up with the A13 highway to Paris, and runs west to Caen, and beyond on the A84. There are also main road and rail links to the cross-Channel ports of Dieppe, Le Havre, Caen (Ouistreham) and Cherbourg. Travel by public transportation beyond these arteries is limited. The region is threaded with minor roads, particularly delightful in the Pays d'Auge and Cotentin Peninsula. The main airports are Rouen, Le Havre and Caen.

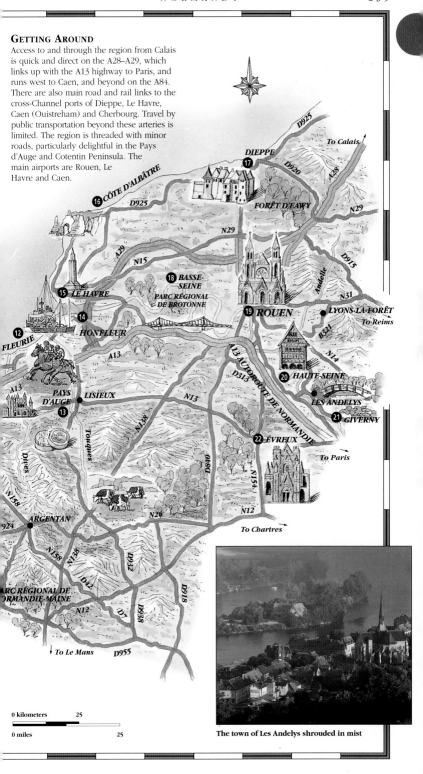

D925

To Calais

DIEPPE
17

CÔTE D'ALBÂTRE
16

D925

D920

A28

FORÊT D'EAWY

N29

N29

N15

A29

D915

BASSE-
SEINE
18

PARC RÉGIONAL
DE BROTONNE

Andelle

N31

LE HAVRE
15

14

ROUEN
19

LYONS-LA-FORÊT

To Reims

HONFLEUR

FLEURIE
12

A13

B321

N14

HAUTE-SEINE
20

A13 AUTOROUTE DE NORMANDIE

D313

LES ANDELYS

PAYS
D'AUGE
13

LISIEUX

N13

GIVERNY
21

Touques

N138

D840

ÉVREUX
22

To Paris

Dives

N154

N158

ARGENTAN

N26

N12

To Chartres

924

N158

N138

D932

D918

PARC RÉGIONAL DE
NORMANDIE-MAINE

D41

N12

D7

D938

To Le Mans

D955

0 kilometers   25

0 miles   25

The town of Les Andelys shrouded in mist

Rugged cliffs on the Cotentin Peninsula

Cotentin ●

Manche. 🚉 🚍 🏛 🚢 *Cherbourg.*
ℹ *Cherbourg (02 33 93 52 02).*

THRUSTING INTO the English Channel, the Cotentin Peninsula has a landscape similar to Brittany's. Its long sandy beaches are relatively undeveloped, with wild and windblown headlands around Cap de la Hague and Nez de Jobourg. The latter is a worthwhile goal for bird-watchers – gannets and shearwaters fly by in large numbers. Along the east coast stretch the expansive sands of Utah Beach, where American troops landed as part of the Allied invasion on June 6, 1944. Inland, Ste-Mère-Eglise commemorates these events with its poignant **Musée Airborne** (Airborne Troops Museum). Just outside Ste-Mère-Eglise, the **Ferme Musée du Cotentin** has farm animals and activities which give an insight into rural life in the early 1900s, while farther north in the market town of Valognes, the **Musée Régional du Cidre et du Calvados** celebrates the thriving local talent for making cider and Calvados.

Two fishing ports command the peninsula's northeast corner: Barfleur and St-Vaast-la-Hougue, the latter famous for oysters and a base for boat trips to the Ile de Tatihou. The Val de Saire is ideal for a scenic drive, with the viewpoint a la Pernelle the best place to survey the coast. On the west side of the Peninsula,

warmed by the Gulf Stream, the resort of Barneville-Carteret offers sandy beaches and summer boat trips to the Channel Islands. The low-lying marshy landscape east of Carentan forms the heart of the Parc Régional des Marais du Cotentin et du Bessin.

🏛 **Musée Airborne**
14 rue Eisenhower, Ste-Mère-Eglise.
📞 *02 33 41 41 35.* ◯ *Feb–Nov: daily.* ● *Dec–Jan.* 🔲 🔖
🖥 www.airborne.museum.org
🏛 **Ferme Musée du Cotentin**
Rte de Beauvais, Ste-Mère-Eglise. 📞 *02 33 41 30 25.* ◯ *Jun–Sep: daily; Feb sch hols–May & Oct sch hols: daily pms.* 🔲
🏛 **Musée Régional du Cidre et du Calvados**
Rue du Petit-Versailles, Valognes.
📞 *02 33 40 22 73.* ◯ *Apr–Sep: Wed–Mon (Jul & Aug: daily).* ● *Sun am.* 🔲

Cherbourg ●

Manche. 🚹 *44,000.* 🚉 🚍 🏛 🚢 ℹ *2 quai Alexandre III (02 33 93 52 02).* 🅿 *Tue, Thu & Sat.*
🖥 www.ot-cherbourg-cotentin.fr

CHERBOURG has been a strategic port and naval base since the mid-19th century. The French Navy still uses its harbors, along with transatlantic ships and cross-Channel ferries from England and Ireland. For a good view of the port, drive to the hilltop **Fort du Roule**, which houses the **Musée de la Libération**, recalling the D-Day invasion and the subsequent liberation of Cherbourg. Most activity is centered around the flower-

filled market square, place Général de Gaulle, and along shopping streets such as rue Tour-Carrée and rue de la Paix. The town's collection of fine art in the spacious **Musée Thomas-Henry**, includes 17th-century Flemish works, and portraits by Jean François Millet, born in Gréville-Hague nearby. **Parc Emmanuel Liais** has lovely small botanical gardens and a densely packed **Musée d'Histoire Naturelle**.

Opened in 2002 is the **Cité de la Mer**, with its cylindrical deep-sea aquarium, the world's largest visitable submarine and many other wonders.

🏛 **Musée de la Libération**
Fort du Roule. 📞 *02 33 20 14 12.* ◯ *May–Sep: Mon pm–Sat & Sun pm; Oct–Apr: Wed–Sun pms.* ● *pub hols.* 🔲 🔖
🏛 **Musée Thomas-Henry**
Rue Vastel. 📞 *02 33 23 02 23.* ◯ *Tue–Sun.* ● *public hols.* 🔲 🔖
🏛 **La Cité de la Mer**
Gare Maritime Transatlantique. 📞 *02 33 20 26 26.* ◯ *daily.* ● *Dec 25, Jan 1, 3 wks Jan* 🔲 🍴 🔲 🔲 🖥 www.citedelamer.com

Cherbourg town center

Coutances ●

Manche. 🚹 *10,000.* 🚍 🏛 ℹ *place Georges Leclerc (02 33 19 08 10).* 🅿 *Thu.*

FROM ROMAN TIMES until the Revolution, the hilltop town of Coutances was the capital of the Cotentin. The slender **Cathédrale Notre-Dame**, a fine example of Norman Gothic architecture, with a soaring 66m (217 ft.) lantern tower. Founded in the 1040s by Bishop Geoffroi de Montbray, it was financed by the local de Hautville family using monies gained in Sicily where they had founded a kingdom a few years earlier. The town was badly damaged during World War II, but the cathedral, the churches of St Nicholas and St Peter, and the beautiful public gardens with their rare plants, all survived.

The back of Coutances cathedral with its squat lantern tower

Granville ❹

Manche. 🏔 *13,000.* 🚉 🚌 ⛴
🛈 *4 cours Jonville (02 33 91 30 03).*
🛒 *Wed, Sat.*

Ramparts enclose the upper town of Granville, which sits on a rocky spur overlooking the Baie du Mont-St-Michel. The walled town developed from fortifications built by the English in 1439 as part of their assault on Mont-St-Michel. The **Musée de Vieux Granville**, in the town gatehouse, recounts Granville's long-established seafaring tradition. The chapel walls of the **Eglise de Notre-Dame** are lined with tributes from local fishermen to their patroness

Notre-Dame du Cap Lihou. The lower town is an old-fashioned seaside resort with a casino, promenades and public gardens. From the port, there are boat trips to the Iles Chausey, a scattering of low-lying granite islands.
   Le Musée Christian Dior is housed in Les Rhumbs, the fashion designer's childhood home, surrounded by a beautiful cliff garden.

🏛 **Musée de Vieux Granville**
2 rue Lecarpentier. 📞 *02 33 50 44
10.* ⊙ *Apr–Sep: Wed–Mon;
Oct–Mar: Wed, Sat & Sun pms.*
● *Nov 1, Dec 22–Jan.* 🎟
🏛 **Musée Christian Dior**
Jardin Public Christian Dior. 📞 *02
33 61 48 21.* ⊙ *Jun–Sep: Tue–Sun.*

D-Day Landings

In the early hours of June 6, 1944, Allied forces began landing on the shores of Normandy, the first step in a long-planned invasion of German-occupied France, known as Operation Overlord. Parachutists were dropped near Ste-Mère-Eglise and Pegasus Bridge, and seaborne assaults were made along a string of code-named beaches. US troops landed on Utah and Omaha in the west, while British and Canadian troops, which included a contingent of Free French commandos, landed at Gold, Juno and Sword. Fifty years later, the beaches are still referred to by their code names.

American troops coming ashore during the Allied invasion of France

Pegasus Bridge, where the first French house was liberated, is a natural starting point for a tour around the sights and memorials. Farther west, evocative ruins of the artificial harbor towed across from England survive at Arromanches-les-Bains. There

are British, German and American war cemeteries at La Cambe, Ranville and St-Laurent-sur-Mer. War museums at Bayeux, Caen, St-Mère-Eglise and Cherbourg provide background on D-Day and the ensuing Battle for Normandy.

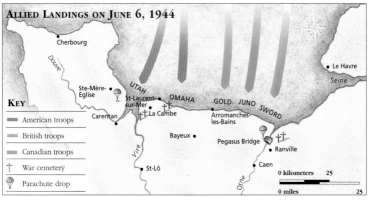

ALLIED LANDINGS ON JUNE 6, 1944

Cherbourg

Le Havre

Douve

Seine

Ste-Mère-Eglise

UTAH

St-Laurent-sur-Mer   OMAHA   GOLD   JUNO   SWORD

KEY

Carentan

La Cambe

Arromanches-les-Bains

▬ American troops

▬ British troops

Bayeux

▬ Canadian troops

Vire

Pegasus Bridge

✝ War cemetery

Ranville

🪂 Parachute drop

Caen

St-Lô

Orne

0 kilometers   25

0 miles   25

By the end of D-Day, over 135,000 men had been brought ashore, with losses totaling around 10,000

Avranches ❺

Manche. 🏛 8,500. 🚊 🚌 ℹ️ 2 rue Général de Gaulle (02 33 58 00 22). 🅿️ Sat. 🌐 www.ville-avranches.fr

AVRANCHES has been a religious center since the 6th century and is the final stopping point for visitors to the abbey on Mont-St-Michel. The origins of the abbey lie in a vision experienced by Aubert, the Bishop of Avranches. One night in 708 the Archangel Michael instructed him to build a church on the nearby island. Aubert's skull, with the finger-hole made by the angel, can be seen in the treasury of **St-Gervais** church in Avranches. The best views of Mont-St-Michel are from the **Jardin des Plantes**.

After the Revolution, 203 illuminated manuscripts were rescued from Mont-St-Michel's abbey. These, and some 14,000 others from surrounding abbeys are held in the **Musée Hôtel de Ville**. Nearby, the **Musée Municipal** illustrates life in the Cotentin over the past centuries, with a model of Avranches cathedral, which was torn down in 1794. Just outside the town, in Le Val St-Père, is the **Musée de la Seconde Guerre Mondiale**.

🏛 **Musée Hôtel de Ville**
Place Littré. 📞 02 33 89 29 40.
🕐 Jun–Sep: daily. 📷 ♿
🏛 **Musée Municipal**
Place Jean de Saint-Avit. 📞 02 33 58 25 15. 🕐 Jun–Sep: daily. 📷

Remains of Mulberry Harbor from World War II off the Côte de Nacre

Mont-St-Michel ❻

See pp246–9.

Côte de Nacre ❼

Calvados. ✈ Caen. 🚊 🚌 Caen, Bayeux. ⛴ Caen-Ouistreham. ℹ️ Caen (02 31 27 14 14).

THE STRETCH of coast between the mouths of the Orne and Vire rivers was dubbed the Côte de Nacre (Mother of Pearl Coast) in the 19th century. More recently it has become known as the site of the D-Day Landings, when Allied troops poured ashore at the start of Operation Overlord *(see p241)*. The associated cemeteries, memorials and museums, and the remnants of the Mulberry Harbor at Arromanches-les-Bains, provide focal points for a visit. However, the coastline is equally popular as a summer vacation destination, offering long, sandy beaches with seaside resorts such as Courseulles-sur-Mer and Luc-sur-Mer. Both are less expensive and more relaxed than the resorts of the Côte Fleurie farther east.

Bayeux ❽

Calvados. 🏛 15,000. 🚊 🚌 ℹ️ Pont-St-Jean (02 31 51 28 28). 🅿️ Sat, Wed. 🌐 www.bayeux-tourism.com

BAYEUX was the first town to be liberated by the Allies in 1944 and fortunate to escape war damage. Today, an attractive nucleus of 15th–19th-century buildings remains around its central high streets,

BAYEUX TAPESTRY

A lively picture story justifying William the Conqueror's invasion of England, this 70-m-long (230-ft) embroidered hanging was probably commissioned by Bishop Odo of Bayeux. Offering insights into 11th-century life, and an action-packed account of the defeat of Harold, King of England, at the Battle of Hastings, the tapestry is valued as a work of art and as an entertaining historical document.

Harold's retinue sets off for France to inform William that Harold will succeed to the English throne.

Trees with interlacing branches are sometimes used to divide the tapestry's 58 scenes.

rue St-Martin and rue St-Jean. The latter, pedestrianized in summer, is lined with shops and cafés. Above the town rise the spires and domed lantern tower of the Gothic **Cathédrale Notre-Dame**. Beneath its harmoniously proportioned interior is an 11th-century crypt decorated with restored 15th-century frescoes of angels playing musical instruments. The original Romanesque church that stood here was consecrated in 1077, and it is likely that Bayeux's famous tapestry was commissioned for this occasion by one of its key characters, Bishop Odo.

The tapestry is displayed in a renovated seminary, **Centre Guillaume-le-Conquérant**, which gives a detailed audio-visual explanation of events leading up to the Norman conquest. On the southwest side of the highway circling the town, the **Musée Mémorial de la Bataille de Normandie** traces the events of the Battle of Normandy and includes an excellent film compilation made from World War II newsreels.

🏛 **Centre Guillaume-le-Conquérant**
Rue de Nesmond. ☎ 02 31 51 25 50. ◯ daily. ● Jan 1–2, Dec 25–26. 🏷 ᕔ
🏛 **Musée Mémorial de la Bataille de Normandie**
Boulevard Fabian-Ware. ☎ 02 31 92 93 41. ◯ daily. ● Jan 1, Dec 25–26, last 2 wks Jan. 🏷 ᕔ

The Abbaye aux Hommes in Caen

Caen ❾

Calvados. 🏘 200,000. ✈ 🚆 🚌
🚌 ℹ place St-Pierre (02 31 27 14 14).
� Fri & Sun. ⓦ www.ville-caen.fr

IN THE MID-11TH century Caen became the favorite residence of William the Conqueror and Queen Matilda, and despite the destruction of three-quarters of the city during World War II, much remains of their creation. The monarchs built two great abbeys and a castle on the north bank of the Orne River, bequeathing Caen a core of historic interest worth looking for beyond its industrial estates and postwar housing.

Much-loved by the citizens of Caen, the **Eglise St-Pierre** was built on the south side of the castle in the 13th–14th centuries, with an impressively ornate Renaissance east end added in the early 16th century. The frequently copied 14th-century bell tower was destroyed in 1944 but has now been restored. To the east, rue du Vaugeux is the central street in Caen's small Vieux Quartier (Old Quarter). Now pedestrianized, the street still has some lovely half-timbered buildings. A walk west along rue St-Pierre or boulevard du Maréchal Leclerc leads to the city's main shopping district.

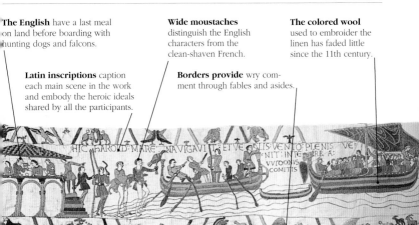

The English have a last meal on land before boarding with hunting dogs and falcons.

Wide moustaches distinguish the English characters from the clean-shaven French.

The colored wool used to embroider the linen has faded little since the 11th century.

Latin inscriptions caption each main scene in the work and embody the heroic ideals shared by all the participants.

Borders provide wry comment through fables and asides.

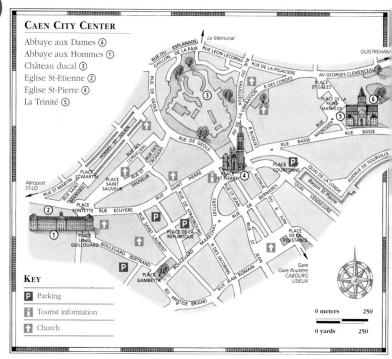

CAEN CITY CENTER

Abbaye aux Dames ⑥
Abbaye aux Hommes ①
Château ducal ③
Eglise St-Etienne ②
Eglise St-Pierre ④
La Trinité ⑤

KEY

🅿 Parking

ℹ Tourist information

✝ Church

0 meters   250
0 yards   250

🏛 Abbaye aux Hommes

Esplanade Jean-Marie Louvel. 📞 *02 31 30 42 81.* ⏰ *daily.* ● *Jan 1, May 1, Dec 25.* 🎫 ♿ *rest.* 🎫 *oblig.*
Work began on William's Abbey for Men in 1063 and was almost complete by his death 20 years later. The abbey church, **Eglise St-Etienne**, is a Norman Romanesque masterpiece, with a severe, unadorned west front crowned with 13th-century spires. The sparingly decorated nave was roofed in the early 12th century with stone vaulting that anticipates the Gothic style.

🏛 Abbaye aux Dames

Place de la Reine Mathilde. 📞 *02 31 06 98 98.* ⏰ *daily.* ● *Jan 1, May 1, Dec 25.* 🎫 *oblig.* ♿
Like William's Abbaye aux Hommes, Matilda's Abbey for Women also has a Norman Romanesque church, **La Trinité**, flanked by 18th-century buildings. Begun in 1060, it was consecrated six years later. Queen Matilda lies buried in the choir under a slab of black marble, and her beautifully restored abbey, with its creamy Caen stone, makes a serene, dignified mausoleum.

🏛 Château ducal

Esplanade du Château. **Musée des Beaux Arts** 📞 *02 31 30 47 70.* **Musée de Normandie** 📞 *02 31 30 47 50.* **Museums** ⏰ *Wed–Mon.* ● *Jan 1, Easter, May 1, Ascension, Nov 1, Dec 25.* ♿
The ruins of Caen's castle, one of the largest fortified enclosures in Europe, offer spacious lawns, museums and rampart views. An extensive fine art collection, strong on 17th-century French and Italian painting, is on exhibit in the **Musée des Beaux Arts**. The **Musée de Normandie** recalls traditional life in the region with utensils and displays on farming and lace.

🏛 Mémorial de Caen

Esplanade Dwight-Eisenhower. 📞 *02 31 06 06 44.* ⏰ *mid-Jan–Dec:* *daily.* ● *Dec 25.* 🎫 ♿ 🌐 *www.memorial-caen.fr*
In the northwest of Caen, close to the N13 highway (exit 7), Mémorial is a museum dedicated to peace, placing the events of D-Day into the context of World War II using a host of interactive and audiovisual techniques, including stunning compilations of archival and fictional film.
A recent extension gives a wider perspective on cultural, religious, border and ecological conflicts in the second half of the 20th-century.

Lush Orne Valley in the Suisse Normande

Suisse Normande ⑩

Calvados & Orne. ✈ Caen. 🚌 🚋 Caen, Argentan. 🛈 Thury Harcourt Clécy (02 31 79 70 45).

THOUGH HARDLY LIKE the mountains of Switzerland, the cliffs and valleys carved out by the Orne River as it winds north to Caen have become a popular site for walking, climbing, camping and river sports. The area is also ideal for a lazy, rural drive. Its highest and most impressive point is the Oëtre Rock, off the D329, where you can look down over the dramatic gorges created by the Rouvre River.

Parc Régional de Normandie-Maine ⑪

Orne & Manche. ✈ Alençon. 🚋 🚌 Argentan. 🛈 Carrouges (02 33 27 40 62).

THE SOUTHERN FRINGES of central Normandy have been incorporated into France's largest regional park. Among the farmland and forests of oak and beech are several small towns. **Domfront** rests on a spur overlooking the Varenne River. The lakeside spa town **Bagnoles-de-l'Orne** offers a casino and sports facilities, while farther east, **Sées** has an attractive Gothic cathedral. The **Maison du Parc** at Carrouges provides information on

Poster of Deauville, about 1930

walks, riding, cycling, climbing and canoeing in the park.

🏠 Maison du Parc
Carrouges. 📞 02 33 81 75 75. 🕐 Mon–Fri. ⬤ public hols.

Environs
Just north of the park, outside Mortrée, is the **Chateau d'O**, a moated Renaissance château with fine 17th-century frescoes. The **Haras du Pin** nearby is France's national stud, called "a horses' Versailles" for its grandeur and 17th-century architecture. Horse shows, dressage events and tours take place throughout the year.

Côte Fleurie ⑫

Calvados ✈ 🚋 🚌 Deauville. 🛈 Deauville (02 31 14 40 00).

THE COTE FLEURIE (Flowery Coast) between Villerville and Cabourg has been planted with chic resorts that burst

into bloom every summer. **Trouville** was once a humble fishing village, but in the mid-19th century caught the attention of writers Gustave Flaubert and Alexandre Dumas. By the 1870s, Trouville had acquired grand hotels, a railroad station and pseudo-Swiss villas along the beachfront. It has, however, long been outclassed by its neighbor, **Deauville**, created by the Duc de Morny in the 1860s. This resort boasts a casino, racetracks, marinas and the famous beachside catwalk, Les Planches.

For something quieter, head west to smaller resorts such as Villers-sur-Mer or Houlgate. **Cabourg** farther west is dominated by the turn-of-the-century Grand Hôtel (see p551), where novelist Marcel Proust spent many summers. Proust used the resort as a model for the fictional Balbec in his novel Remembrance of Things Past.

Pays d'Auge ⑬

Calvados. ✈ Deauville. 🚋 🚌 Lisieux. 🛈 Lisieux (02 31 48 18 10).

INLAND from the Côte Fleurie, the Pays d'Auge is classic Normandy countryside, lushly woven with fields, wooded valleys, cider orchards, dairy farms and manor houses. Its capital is **Lisieux**, a cathedral town devoted to St. Thérèse of Lisieux, canonized in 1925, who attracts hundreds of thousands of pilgrims each year. Lisieux is an obvious base for exploring the region, but nearby market towns, such as St-Pierre-sur-Dives and Orbec, are smaller and more attractive.

The best way to enjoy the Pays d'Auge is to sightsee around on its minor roads. Two marked tourist routes are devoted to cider and cheese, while picturesque half-timbered manor houses, farmhouses, and châteaux testify to the wealth of this fertile land. The manor of **St-Germain-de-Livet**, can be visited, as can **Crèvecoeur-en-Auge**, with its unexpected Schlumberger oil museum, and the half-timbered village of **Beuvron-en-Auge** is charming.

APPLES AND CIDER

Apple orchards are a familiar feature of the Normandy countryside, and their fruit a fundamental ingredient in the region's gastronomic repertoire. No self-respecting pâtisserie would be without its *tarte normande* (apple tart), and every country lane seems to sport an *Ici Vente Cidre* (cider sold here) sign. Much of the harvest forms the raw material for cider and Calvados, an apple brandy aged in oak barrels for at least two years. Another local brew is made from pears, and known as *poiré* (perry).

Crops range from sour cider apples to sweet edible varieties

Mont-St-Michel ⑥

The 10th century abbey

The 11th-century abbey

The mid-18th century abbey

SHROUDED BY MIST, encircled by sea, soaring proudly above glistening sands – the silhouette of Mont-St-Michel is one of the most enchanting sights in France. Now linked to the mainland by a causeway, the island of Mont-Tombe (Tomb on the Hill) stands at the mouth of the Couesnon River, crowned by a fortified abbey that almost doubles its height. Lying strategically on the frontier between Normandy and Brittany, **St. Michael** Mont-St-Michel grew from a humble 8th-century oratory to become a Benedictine monastery that had its greatest influence in the 12th and 13th centuries. Pilgrims known as *miquelots* journeyed from afar to honor the cult of St. Michael, and the monastery was a renowned center of medieval learning. After the Revolution, the abbey became a prison. It is now a national monument that draws one million visitors a year.

St-Aubert's Chapel
A small 15th-century chapel built on an outcrop of rock is dedicated to Aubert, the founder of Mont-St-Michel.

Gabriel Tower

★ **Ramparts**
English attacks during the Hundred Years' War led to the construction of fortified walls with imposing towers.

Entrance

TIMELINE

700	1000	1300	1600	1900
966 Benedictine abbey founded by Duke Richard I	**1211–28** Construction of La Merveille	**1434** Last assault by English forces. Ramparts surround the town	**1789** French Revolution: abbey becomes a political prison	**1874** Abbey declared a national monument
				1922 Services again held in abbey church
1017 Work on abbey church starts		**1516** Abbey falls into decline	**1877–9** Causeway built	**1895–7** Belfry, spire and statue of St. Michael added
708 St. Aubert builds an oratory on Mont-Tombe	**1067–70** Mont-St-Michel depicted in Bayeux Tapestry *Bayeux Tapestry detail*			**1969** Benedictine monks return

Tides of Mont-St-Michel
Extremely strong tides in the Baie du Mont-St-Michel act as a natural defense. They rise and fall with the lunar calendar and can reach speeds of 10 km/h (6 mph) in spring.

★ Abbey
Protected by high walls, the abbey and its church occupy an impregnable position on the island.

Gautier's Leap
At the top of the Inner Staircase, this terrace is named after a prisoner who leaped to his death.

Eglise St-Pierre

Liberty Tower

The Arcade Tower provided lodgings for the abbot's soldiers.

King's Tower

STAR FEATURES

★ Abbey

★ Ramparts

★ Grande Rue

★ Grande Rue
Now crowded with restaurants, the pilgrims' route, followed since the 12th century, climbs up past Eglise St-Pierre to the abbey gates.

The Abbey of Mont-St-Michel

THE PRESENT BUILDINGS bear witness to the time when the abbey served both as a Benedictine monastery and, for 73 years after the Revolution, as a political prison. In 1017 work began on a Romanesque church at the island's highest point, building over its 10th-century predecessor, now the Chapel of Our Lady Underground. A monastery built on three levels, La Merveille (The Miracle) was added to the church's north side in the early 13th century.

Cross in the choir

★ Church
Four bays of the Romanesque nave survive. Three were torn down in 1776, creating the West Terrace.

★ La Merveille
The Miracle is a Gothic masterpiece – a three-story monastic complex built in only 16 years.

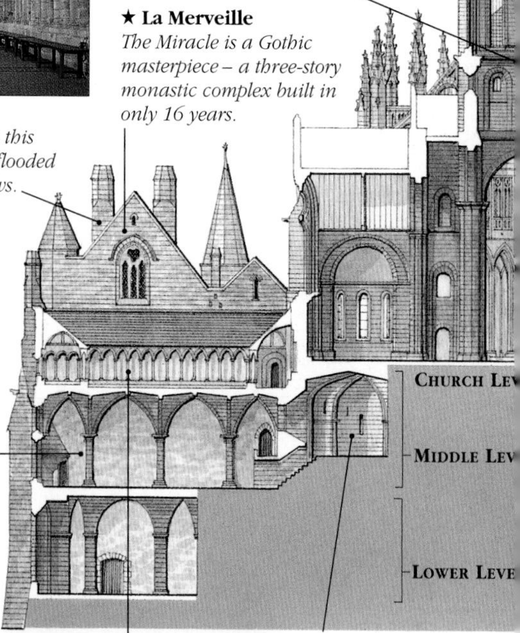

Refectory
The monks had their meals in this long, narrow room, which is flooded with light through tall windows.

Knights' Room
The rib vaults and finely decorated capitals are typically Gothic.

CHURCH LEVEL

MIDDLE LEVEL

LOWER LEVEL

Crypt of the Thirty Candles is one of two 11th-century crypts built to support the transepts of the main church.

★ Cloisters
The cloisters with their elegant columns in staggered rows are a beautiful example of early 13th-century Anglo-Norman style.

VISITING THE ABBEY

The three levels of the abbey reflect the monastic hierarchy. The monks lived at the highest level, in an enclosed world of church, cloister and refectory. The abbot entertained his noble guests on the middle level. Soldiers and pilgrims further down on the social scale were received at the lowest level. Guided tours begin at the West Terrace at the church level and end in the almonry, where alms were dispensed to the poor. The almonry is now a bookstore and souvenir hall.

CHURCH LEVEL

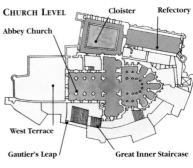

Abbey Church
Cloister
Refectory
West Terrace
Gautier's Leap
Great Inner Staircase

MIDDLE LEVEL

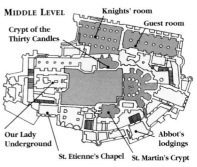

Crypt of the Thirty Candles
Knights' room
Guest room
Our Lady Underground
St. Etienne's Chapel
St. Martin's Crypt
Abbot's lodgings

LOWER LEVEL

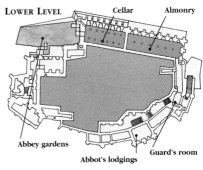

Cellar
Almonry
Abbey gardens
Abbot's lodgings
Guard's room

Church Interior
A Flamboyant Gothic choir was built in 1446–1521, held up by crypts with massive supporting pillars.

St. Martin's Crypt is an 11th-century barrel-vaulted chapel that preserves the austere forms of the original Romanesque abbey.

The abbot's lodgings were close to the abbey entrance, and he received prestigious visitors in the guest room. Poorer pilgrims were received in the almonry.

Benedictine Monks
Today a small monastic community lives in the abbey, continuing the religious traditions introduced by the Benedictines in 966.

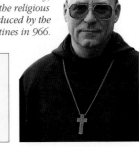

STAR FEATURES
★ Church
★ La Merveille
★ Cloisters

Mont-St-Michel by night ▷

Honfleur ⑭

Calvados. 🏠 8,400. 🚉 Deauville.
🛈 quai Lepaulmier (02 31 89 23 30).
🚌 Sat. [W] www.ot-honfleur.fr

A MAJOR DEFENSIVE PORT in the 15th century, Honfleur has blossomed into one of Normandy's most appealing harbors. At its heart is the 17th-century Vieux Bassin (Old Dock), with its pictures-que tall houses (6–7 stories).

Honfleur became a center of artistic activity in the 19th century. Eugène Boudin, the seascape painter, was born here in 1824, as was the composer Erik Satie in 1886. Courbet, Sisley, Pissarro, Renoir and Cézanne all visited Honfleur, often meeting at the Ferme St-Siméon, which is now a luxury hotel. Painters still work from Honfleur's quayside and exhibitions are held in the **Greniers à Sel**, two salt warehouses built in 1670. These lie to the east of the Vieux Bassin in an area known as l'Enclos, which made up the fortified heart of the town in the 13th century.

The **Musée de la Marine** displays mementos of Hon-fleur's nautical past, with a warren of Norman interiors next door in the former prison. Place Ste-Catherine has an unusual 15th-Century church built by ship's carpenters. The **Musée Eugène Boudin** documents the artistic appeal of Honfleur and the Seine estuary, with works ranging from Eugène Boudin to Raoul Dufy. **Les Maisons Satie** use extracts from Satie's music to guide you round imaginative reconstructions of the rooms.

🏛 Greniers à Sel
Rue de la Ville/quai de la Tour.
📞 02 31 89 02 30. ⭘ for guided tours & exhibitions. ☑ obligatory, except during summer exhibs. 🦽 ♿

🏛 Musée de la Marine
Quai St Etienne. 📞 02 31 89 14 12.
⭘ Apr–Jun & Sep: Tue–Sun; Jul & Aug: daily; mid-Nov–mid-Feb: daily (Mon–Fri pms only). ⬤ May 1. 🦽 ♿

🏛 Musée Eugène Boudin
Place Erik Satie, rue de l'Homme de Bois. 📞 02 31 89 54 00.
⭘ mid-Mar–Sep: Wed–Mon; Oct–Dec & mid-Feb–mid-Mar: Wed–Mon pm, Sat, Sun. 🦽 ♿

🏛 Les Maison Satie
67 Blvd Charles V. 📞 02 31 89 11 11.
⭘ Wed–Mon. ⬤ Jan–mid-Feb. 🦽

Quai St-Etienne in Honfleur

Le Havre ⑮

Seine-Maritime. 🏠 197,000. ✈ 🚉
🚌 ⛴ 🛈 186 bd Clemenceau (02 32 74 04 04). 🚌 Mon–Sat.
[W] www.lehavretourisme.com

STRATEGICALLY positioned on the Seine estuary, Le Havre (The Harbor) was created in 1517 by François I after the nearby port of Harfleur silted up. During World War II it was virtually obliterated by Allied bombing, but despite the vast oil refineries and industrial zone which stands beside the port, it still has appeal. It is an important yachting center, and its beach has two blue flags (very clean!)

Much of the city center was rebuilt in the 1950s–1960s by August Perret, whose towering **Eglise St-Joseph**, pierces the skyline. The **Musée Malraux**, built entirely of glass and metal, right on the seafront has an exhilarating collection of works amongst others, local artist Raoul Dufy.

🏛 Musée Malraux
2 bd Clemenceau. 📞 02 35 19 62 62. ⭘ Wed–Mon. ⬤ public hols.

Côte d'Albâtre ⑯

Seine-Maritime. 🚉 🚌 ⛴
🛈 Dieppe (02 32 14 40 60).

THE ALABASTER COAST gets its name from the chalky cliffs and milky waters that characterize the Normandy coastline between Le Havre and Le Tréport. It is best known for the **Falaise d'Aval** west of Etretat, eroded into an arch. The author Guy de Mau-passant, born near Dieppe in 1850, compared these cliffs to an elephant dipping its trunk into the sea. From Etretat, a chain of coastal roads runs east across a switchback of breezy headlands and wooded valleys to Dieppe.

Fécamp is the only major town along this route. Its Benedictine abbey was once an important pilgrimage center after a tree trunk containing drops of Christ's Blood was washed ashore here during the 7th century. This is enshrined in a reliquary at the entrance to the Lady Chapel of the abbey church, La Trinité.

The vast **Palais Bénédictine** is a neo-Gothic-and-Renaissance homage to the ego of Alexander Le Grand, a local wine and spirits merchant who rediscovered the monks' recipe for Bénédictine, the famous herbal liqueur. Build-ing of the palace began in 1882 and today, incorporates

Woman with Parasol (1880) by Boudin in the Musée Eugène Boudin

The cliffs at Falaise d'Aval, famously likened to an elephant dipping its trunk into the sea

a distillery and an eccentric museum packed with curios and art treasures. The adjacent halls provide an aromatic account of the 27 herbs and spices that make up the elixir, and include tastings.

🏛 Palais Bénédictine
110 rue Alexandre Le Grand, Fécamp. 📞 02 35 10 26 10. ⏰ daily. ⬤ Jan. 📷 🚻

View of Dieppe from the château and museum above the town

Dieppe ⑰

Seine-Maritime. 🚶 36,000. 🚇 🚌 🚢 🅸 pont Jehan Ango (02 32 14 40 60). 🛒 Tue, Thu & esp. Sat. 🌐 www.dieppetourisme.com

DIEPPE exploits a break in the chalky cliffs bordering the Pays de Caux, and has won historical prestige as a Channel fort, port and resort. Prosperity came during the 16th and 17th centuries, when local privateer Jehan Ango raided the Portuguese and English fleets, and a trading post called Petit Dieppe was founded on the West African coast. At that time, Dieppe's population was already 30,000, and included a 300-strong

community of craftsmen carving imported ivory. This maritime past is celebrated in the **Musée du Château**, the 15th-century castle crowning the headland to the west of the seafront. Here you can see historical maps and model ships, a collection of Dieppe ivories (the most important in Europe), and paintings that evoke the town's development as a fashionable seaside resort during the 19th century. Dieppe had the beach closest to Paris, and it quickly responded to the developing passion for promenading, seawater cures and bathing.

Today, Dieppe's broad seafront includes lawns, seaside amusements and parking lots, and its liveliest streets surround the battle-scarred **Eglise St-Jacques** to the south. If the weather is poor, visit the **Cité de la Mer**, an exhibition center featuring models on maritime themes, and fun for kids.

🏛 Musée du Château
📞 02 35 84 19 76. ⏰ Jun–Sep: daily; Oct–May: Wed–Mon. ⬤ Jan 1, May 1, Nov 1, Dec 25. 📷
🏛 Cité de la Mer
37 Rue de l'Asile Thomas. 📞 02 35 06 93 20. ⏰ daily. 📷 ♿

Basse-Seine ⑱

Seine-Maritime & Eure. ✈ Le Havre, Rouen. 🚇 🚌 🚢 Yvetot. ✈ Le Havre. 🅸 Caudebec-en-Caux (02 32 70 46 32), Yvetot (02 35 95 08 40).

MEANDERING seaward from Rouen to Le Havre, the Seine River is crossed by three spectacular road bridges: the Pont de Brotonne, the Pont

de Tancarville and the Pont de Normandie (completed in 1995, it links Le Havre and Honfleur). The grace and daring of these modern bridges echoes the soaring aspirations of the abbeys, founded on the river's banks in the 7th and 8th centuries. The abbeys now provide good stepping stones for a tour of the Lower Seine Valley.

West of Rouen is the harmonious Eglise de St-Georges at **St-Martin-de-Boscherville** which, until the Revolution, was the church of a small walled abbey. Its 12th-century chapter house has remarkable biblical statues and carved capitals. From here the D67 highway runs south to the riverside village of La Bouille.

As you head northwest, an hourly car ferry at Mesnil-sous-Jumièges takes you over to the colossal ruins of the **Abbaye de Jumièges**. The abbey was founded in 654 and once housed 900 monks and 1,500 servants. The main abbey church dates from the 11th century; its consecration in 1067 was a major event, with William the Conqueror in attendance.

The D913 highway passes through oak and beech woods in the Parc Régional de Brotonne to the 7th-century **Abbaye de St-Wandrille**. The Musée de la Marine de Seine at **Caudebec-en-Caux** gives an engrossing account of life on this great river over the past 120 years.

Monk from Abbaye de St-Wandrille

Rouen ⑲

FOUNDED AT THE LOWEST POINT where the Seine could be bridged, Rouen has prospered through maritime trade and industrialization to become a rich and cultured city. Despite the severe damage of World War II, the city boasts a wealth of historic sights on its right bank, all within walking distance of the central Cathédrale Notre-Dame, frequently painted by Monet. In turn a Celtic trading post, Roman garrison and Viking colony, Rouen became the capital of the Norman Duchy in 911. It was captured by Henry V in 1419 after a siege during the Hundred Years' War. In 1431, Joan of Arc was burned at the stake here in place du Vieux-Marché.

Rouen, a thriving port on the Seine River

Exploring Rouen

From the cathedral, the rue du Gros Horloge runs west under the city's Great Clock, to the place du Vieux Marché and its post-war Eglise Ste-Jeanne-d'Arc. Rue aux Juifs leads past the 15th-century Gothic **Palais de Justice**, once Normandy's parliament, to the chic shops and cafés around rue des Carmes. Farther east, between the St-Maclou and St-Ouen churches, are half-timbered houses in the rue Damiette and rue Eau de Robec. North, in place Général de Gaulle, is the 18th-century **Hôtel de Ville**.

🏛 Cathédrale Notre-Dame

This Gothic masterpiece is dominated by the famous west façade *(see p257)*, painted

Cathédrale Notre-Dame, Rouen

by Monet, which is framed by two un-equal towers – the northern Tour St-Romain, and the later Tour du Beurre, supposedly paid for by a tax on butter consumption in Lent. Above the central lantern tower rises an Neo-Gothic spire, made from cast iron and erected in 1876. Recently restored, both the 14th-century northern Portail des Libraires and the 14th-century southern Portail de la Calende are worth seeing for their precise sculpting and delicate tracery. Many of the cathedral's riches can be seen by guided tour only, including the tomb of Richard the Lionheart, whose heart was buried here, and the rare 11th-century semi-circular hall crypt, rediscovered in 1934. The choir/chancel was badly hit by the 1999 storm.

KEY

🅿	Parking
ℹ	Tourist information
✝	Church

0 meters   250

0 yards   250

🔒 Eglise St-Maclou

This Flamboyant Gothic church has an elaborately decorated west façade with a five-bay porch and carved wooden doors depicting biblical scenes. Behind the church, its *aître*, or ossuary, is a rare surviving example of a medieval cemetery for the burial of plague victims. The timbers of its buildings, set around the quadrangle, are carved with a macabre array of grinning skulls, crossed bones, coffins, hourglasses, buckets, beds and grave-diggers' implements.

Pitcher, Musée de la Céramique

🔒 Eglise St-Ouen

Once part of a formidable Benedictine abbey, St-Ouen is a solid Gothic church with a lofty, unadorned interior made all the more beautiful by its restored 14th-century stained glass. Behind the church, there is a pleasant park which is an ideal spot for picnics.

🏛 Musée des Beaux Arts

Square Verdrel. ☎ 02 35 71 28 40. ⬤ Wed–Mon. ⬤ public hols except Easter & Pentecost. 🈁 🛗
The city's collection includes masterpieces by Caravaggio and Velázquez, and paintings by Normandy-born artists Théodore Géricault, Eugène Boudin and Raoul Dufy. Also on display is Monet's work entitled *Rouen Cathedral, The Portal, Gray Weather*.

VISITORS' CHECKLIST

Seine Maritime. 🏚 102,000. ✈ 11 km (7 miles) SE Rouen. 🚉 gare rive droite, place Bernard Tissot (08 92 35 35 35). 🚌 25 rue des Charrettes (0825 076 027). 🛈 25 place de la Cathédrale (02 32 08 32 40). 🛒 Tue–Sun. 🎭 Feast of Joan of Arc (late May).

🏛 Musée de la Céramique

Hôtel d'Hocqueville, 1 rue Faucon. ☎ 02 35 07 31 74. ⬤ Wed–Mon. ⬤ public hols. 🈁
Exhibits of 1,000 pieces of Rouen faïence – colorful glazed earthenware – together with other pieces of French and foreign china are displayed in a 17th-century town house. The works trace the history of Rouen faïence to its zenith in the 18th century.

🏛 Musée Le Secq des Tournelles

Rue Jacques-Villon. ☎ 02 35 88 42 92. ⬤ Wed–Mon. ⬤ public hols. 🈁 ♿ ground floor only.
Located in a 15th-century church, this wrought ironwork museum exhibits antique iron-mongery ranging from keys to corkscrews, Gallo-Roman spoons to mighty tavern signs.

🏛 Musée Flaubert

51 rue de Lecat. ☎ 02 35 15 59 95. ⬤ Tue–Sat. ⬤ public hols. 🈁
Flaubert's father was a surgeon at Rouen Hospital, and his family home combines memorabilia with an awesome – and occasionally gruesome – display of 17th–19th-century medical equipment and a medicinal herb garden.

SIGHTS AT A GLANCE

GUSTAVE FLAUBERT

The novelist Gustave Flaubert (1821–80) was born and raised in Rouen, and the city provides the backdrop for some memorable scenes in his masterpiece *Madame Bovary*. Published in 1857, this realistic study of a country doctor's wife driven to despair by her love affairs provoked a scandal that made Flaubert's name. His famous stuffed green parrot, which can be seen in the Musée Flaubert, was always perched on his writing desk.

Flaubert's stuffed parrot

Château Gaillard and the village of Les Andelys, in a loop of the Seine River

Haute-Seine ❷⓪

Eure. 🚆 Rouen. 🚌 Vernon, Val de Renvil. 🚌 Gisors, Les Andelys. 🛈 Les Andelys (02 32 54 41 93).

Southeast of rouen, the Seine River follows a convoluted course, with most points of interest on its north bank. At the center of the Forêt de Lyons, once the hunting ground for the Dukes of Normandy, is the country town of **Lyons-la-Forêt**, with half-timbered houses and an 18th-century covered market.

To the south, the D313 follows the gracefully curving Seine to the town of **Les Andelys**. Above it tower the ruins of Château Gaillard, which Richard the Lion-Heart, as king of England and duke of Normandy, built in 1197 to defend Rouen from the French. They eventually took the castle in 1204 by forcing a way in through the latrines.

Giverny ❷①

Eure. 👥 600. 🛈 36 rue Carnot, Vernon (02 32 51 39 60).

In 1883 the Impressionist painter Claude Monet rented a house in the small village of Giverny, and worked there until his death

at the age of 86. The house, known as the **Fondation Claude Monet**, and its magnificent gardens are open to the public. The house is decorated in the original color schemes that Monet admired; the gardens are famous as the subject of some of the artist's best-loved studies. Only copies are on display in the small gallery, but there are outstanding original 19th- and 20th-century artworks in the **Musée d'Art Américain Giverny** nearby.

🏛 **Fondation Claude Monet**
Giverny, Gasny. 📞 02 32 51 28 21. 🕐 Apr–Oct: Tue–Sun. 📷
🏛 **Musée d'Art Américain Giverny**
99 rue Claude Monet, Giverny. 📞 02 32 51 94 65. 🕐 Apr–Oct: Tue–Sun; Nov: Thu–Sun. 📷 ♿

Monet's garden at Giverny, restored to its original profuse glory

Évreux ❷❷

Eure. 👥 55,000. 🚆 🚌 🛈 1 ter place du Général de Gaulle (02 32 24 04 43). 🛒 Wed & Sat.

Though considerably damaged in the war, Évreux is a pleasant cathedral town set in wide, agricultural plains. At its heart, the **Cathédrale Notre-Dame** is renowned for its 14th–15th-century stained glass. The building is predominantly Gothic, though Romanesque arches survive in the nave and Renaissance screens adorn its chapels. Next door, the former Bishop's Palace houses the **Musée Municipal**, with exhibits ranging from two Roman bronze statues of Jupiter and Apollo to fine 18th-century furniture and decorative art.

Monet's Cathedral Series

IN THE 1890s, Claude Monet made almost 30 paintings of Rouen's cathedral, several of which are now in the Musée d'Orsay in Paris *(see pp116–17)*. He studied the effects of changing light on its façades, and described both the surface detail and huge bulk, putting color before contour. The archetypal Impressionist, Monet said he conceived this series when he watched the effects of light on a country church, "as the sun's rays slowly dissolved the mists . . . that wrapped the golden stone in an ideally vaporous envelope."

HARMONY IN BLUE AND GOLD *(1894)*
Monet selected a close vantage point for the series and especially liked this southwest view. The sun would cast afternoon shadows across the carved west front, accentuating the cavernous portals and the large rose window.

Monet's sketch, one of many of Rouen, parallels the shimmering effect of the paintings.

Harmony in Brown (1894) is the only finished version of a frontal view of the west façade. Analysis has shown that it was begun as a southwest view, like the others.

Harmony in Blue (1894), compared with Harmony in Blue and Gold, shows the stone of the west façade farther softened by the diffuse light of a misty morning.

The Portal, Gray Weather (1894) was one of several canvases in the gray color group that showed the cathedral façade in the soft light of an overcast day.

BRITTANY

FINISTÈRE · CÔTES D'ARMOR · MORBIHAN · ILLE-ET-VILAINE

JUTTING DEFIANTLY INTO THE ATLANTIC, *France's northwest corner has long been culturally and geographically distinct from the rest of the country. Known to the Celts as Armorica, the land of the sea, Brittany's past swirls with the legends of drowned cities and Arthurian forests. Prehistoric megaliths arise mysteriously from land and sea, and the medieval is never far from the modern.*

A long, jagged coastline is the region's great attraction. Magnificent beaches line its northern shore, swept clean by huge tides and interspersed with well-established seaside resorts, seasoned fishing ports and abundant oyster beds. The south coast is gentler, with wooded river valleys and a milder climate, while the west, being exposed to the Atlantic winds, has a drama that justifies its name: Finistère – "the End of the Earth."

Inland lies the Argoat – once the Land of the Forest, now a patchwork of undulating fields, woods and rolling moorland. Parc Régional d'Armorique occupies much of central Finistère, and it is in western Brittany that Breton culture remains most evident. In Quimper, and in the Pays Bigouden, crêpes and cider, traditional costumes and Celtic music are still a genuine part of the Breton lifestyle. Eastern Brittany has a more conventional appeal. Vannes, Dinan and Rennes, the Breton capital, have well-preserved medieval quarters where half-timbered buildings shelter inviting markets, shops, crêperies and restaurants. The walled port of St-Malo on the Côte d'Emeraude recalls the region's maritime prowess, while the remarkably intact castles at Fougères and Vitré are a reminder of the mighty border-fortresses that protected Brittany's eastern frontier before its final union with France in 1532.

Women dressed in traditional costume and *coiffe,* the typical Breton lace headdress

◁ **Characteristic pink granite cliffs on the Côte de Granit Rose, northern Brittany**

Exploring Brittany

IDEAL FOR A SEASIDE HOLIDAY, Brittany offers enjoyable drives along the headlands and beaches of the northern Côte d'Emeraude and Côte de Granit Rose, while the south coast boasts wooded valleys and the prehistoric sites of Carnac and the Golfe du Morbihan. The parish closes (see pp266–7) provide an intriguing insight into Breton culture, as does the cathedral town of Quimper. Be sure to visit the regional capital, Rennes, and the great castle at Fougères, and in summer take a boat trip to one of Brittany's islands.

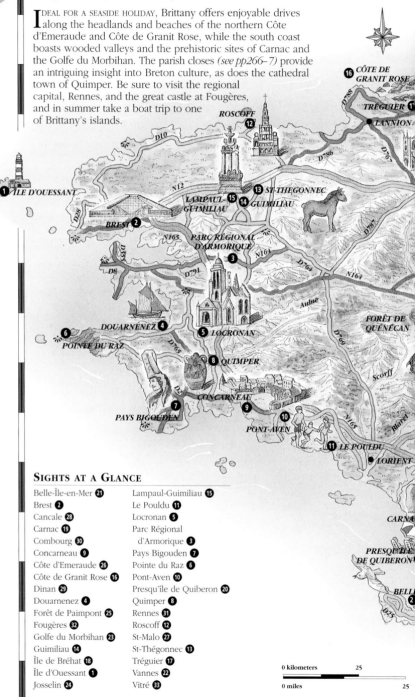

SIGHTS AT A GLANCE

0 kilometers   25

0 miles   25

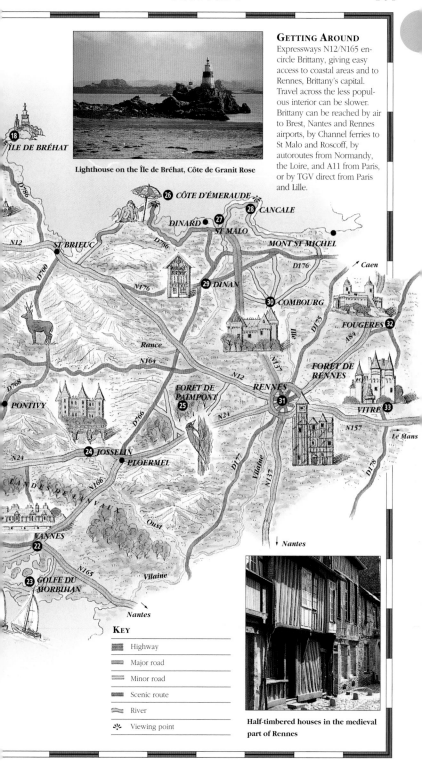

Lighthouse on the Île de Bréhat, Côte de Granit Rose

GETTING AROUND

Expressways N12/N165 encircle Brittany, giving easy access to coastal areas and to Rennes, Brittany's capital. Travel across the less populous interior can be slower. Brittany can be reached by air to Brest, Nantes and Rennes airports, by Channel ferries to St Malo and Roscoff, by autoroutes from Normandy, the Loire, and A11 from Paris, or by TGV direct from Paris and Lille.

ÎLE DE BRÉHAT

18

N12

ST BRIEUC

D700

D780

D786

26 CÔTE D'ÉMERAUDE

DINARD

27 ST MALO

28 CANCALE

MONT ST MICHEL

D176

Caen

N176

29 DINAN

30 COMBOURG

D75

FOUGÈRES 32

A84

Rance

N164

FORÊT DE RENNES

N12

D768

PONTIVY

D766

FORÊT DE PAIMPONT

25

N24

RENNES

31

VITRÉ 33

N157

Le Mans

24 JOSSELIN

PLOERMEL

D177

Vilaine

N137

D178

N24

N166

LANDES DE LANVAUX

Oust

VANNES

22

N165

Vilaine

Nantes

23 GOLFE DU MORBIHAN

Nantes

N12

Nantes

KEY

- Highway
- Major road
- Minor road
- Scenic route
- River
- Viewing point

Half-timbered houses in the medieval part of Rennes

Île d'Ouessant **1**

Finistère. ✈ Ouessant (via Brest).
▣ Brest, then boat. ▣ Le Conquet,
then boat. **ℹ** place de l'Eglise,
Lampaul (02 98 48 85 83).

A WELL-KNOWN Breton proverb
declares "He who sees
Ouessant sees his own blood."
Also known as Ushant, the
island is notorious among
sailors for its fierce storms and
strong currents. However, this
westerly point of France has a
pleasant climate in summer
and, though often bleak and
stormy, can be surprisingly
mild in winter. Part of the Parc
Naturel Régional d'Armorique,
the windswept island is a
popular stopover for migrating
birds. These, along with a
small seal population, may be
observed from the Pern and
Pen-ar-Roc'h headlands.

Two museums shed light on
the islands defiant history,
dogged by shipwreck and
tragedy. At Niou Uhella, the
EcoMusée d'Ouessant has
furniture made from driftwood
and wrecks, often painted blue
and white in honor of the
Virgin Mary. Nearby, at Phare
du Créac'h, the **Musée des
Phares et Balises** explains
the history of Brittany's many
lighthouses and their keepers.

🏛 **EcoMusée d'Ouessant**
Niou Uhella. **☎** 02 98 48 86 37.
◯ Apr–Sep & sch hols: daily; Oct–Mar:
Tue–Sun (pm only). 🎫 ♿ restricted.
🏛 **Musée des Phares et
Balises**
Phare du Créac'h. **☎** 02 98 48 80 70.
◯ Apr–Sep & sch hols: daily;
Oct–Mar: Tue–Sun (pm only). 🎫 ♿

Brest **2**

Finistère. 🏘 153,000. ⛴ ▣ ▣ ⛴
to islands only. **ℹ** place de la Liberté
(02 98 44 24 96). ⛴ daily.

A NATURAL HARBOR protected
by the Presqu'île de
Crozon, Brest is France's premiere Atlantic naval port, with a
rich maritime history. Heavily
bombed during World War II,
it is now a modern commercial
city where cargo vessels, yachts
and fishing boats ply the
waters. The Cours Dajot
promenade has good views

Windswept moorlands near Ménez-Meur, Parc Régional d'Armorique

of the Rade de Brest. The
Château houses a naval
museum with historic maps,
maritime paintings, model
ships, carved wooden figureheads and nautical instruments.
Across the Penfeld River –
reached by Europe's largest
lifting bridge, the Pont de
Recouvrance – is the 14th-
century **Tour Tanguy**. By the
Port de Plaisance, **Océanopolis**
is an entertaining, educational
"sea center", with three vast
pavilions (polar, temperate
and tropical) simulating these
varied underwater ecosystems.

⚓ **Château de Brest**
☎ 02 98 22 12 39. ◯ Apr–mid-Sep:
daily; mid-Sep–mid-Dec & Feb–Mar:
Wed pm–Mon. 🎫
🏰 **Tour Tanguy**
Sq Pierre Peron. **☎** 02 98 00 88 60.
◯ Jun–Sep: daily; Oct–May: Wed–Thu,
Sat–Sun pms. ● Jan 1, May 1, Dec 25.
🐠 **Océanopolis**
Port de Plaisance du Moulin Blanc.
☎ 02 98 34 40 40. ◯ Apr–Aug &
sch hols: daily; Sep–Mar: Tue–Sun. ●
Jan 1, 2 wks in Jan, Dec 25. 🎫 ♿
🌐 www.oceanopolis.com

**Traditional boatbuilding at Le
Port-Musée, Douarnenez**

Parc Naturel
Régional
d'Armorique **3**

Finistère. 🛫 Brest. ▣ Chateaulin,
Landernau. ▣ Le Faou, Huelgoat,
Carhaix. **ℹ** Le Faou (02 98 81 90 08).

T HE ARMORICAN Regional
Nature Park stretches west
from the moorlands of the
Monts d'Arrée to the Presqu'île
de Crozon and Ile d'Ouessant.
Within this protected area lies
a mixture of farmland, heaths,
remains of ancient oak forest
and wild, open spaces. The
park and its scenic coastline
are ideal for walking, riding
and touring by bicycle or car.

Huelgoat is a good starting
point for inland walks, while
Ménez-Hom (300 m/1,082 ft)
at the beginning of the Crozon
Peninsula, has excellent views.

The main information center
for the park is at **Le Faou**.
Nearby at **Ménez-Meur**, is a
wooded estate with wild and
farm animals, and a Breton
horse museum. Scattered
around the park are 16 small,
specialist museums, some
paying tribute to country
traditions like hunting, fishing
and tanning. The **Musée de
l'Ecole Rurale** at Trégarven
recreates a 20th-century rural
school, while other museums
cover subjects as diverse as
medieval monastic life, rag-
pickers and the lifestyle of a
Breton country priest.
Contemporary crafts and art
can be seen at the **Maison
des Artisans** in Brasparts.

Douarnenez ❹

Finistère. ⋒ 16,700. ⚏
🛈 2 rue Docteur Mevel (02 98 92 13 35). ⚏ Mon–Fri.

AT THE START of this century, Douarnenez used to be France's leading sardine port; today, it is still devoted to fishing, but is also a tourist resort, with beaches on both sides of the Pouldavid estuary.

Nearby lies the tiny **Île Tristan**, linked with the tragic love story of Tristan and Iseult. In the 16th century, it was the stronghold of a notorious brigand, La Fontenelle.

The picturesque **Port du Rosmeur** offers cafés, fish restaurants and boat trips around the bay, with a lively early morning *criée* (fish auction) held in the nearby Nouveau Port. The Port-Rhu has been turned into a floating museum, **Le Port-Rhu Musée**, with over 100 boats and several shipyards. Some of the larger vessels can be visited in tourist season.

🏛 Le Port-Rhu Musée
Place de l'Enfer. ⚏ 02 98 92 65 20.
⚏ mid-Jun–mid-Sep: daily; mid-Sep–Nov 3 & Apr–mid-Jun: Tue–Sun. ⚏ &

Locronan's 15th-century Eglise St-Ronan, seen from the churchyard

Locronan ❺

Finistère. ⋒ 800. 🛈 place de la Mairie (02 98 91 70 14).

DURING THE 15th–17th centuries, Locronan grew wealthy from the manufacture of sailcloth. After Louis XIV ended the Breton monopoly on this trade, the town declined – leaving an elegant ensemble of Renaissance buildings that today attract huge numbers of visitors. In the town's central cobbled square stands a late 15th-century church dedicated to the Irish missionary St. Ronan. Down Rue Moal is the delightful **Chapelle Notre-Dame-de-Bonne-Nouvelle**, with a calvary and a fountain.

Every July, Locronan is the scene of a *Troménie*, a hilltop pilgrimage held in honor of St. Ronan. The more elaborate *Grande Troménie* takes place every six years.

Pointe du Raz ❻

Finistère. ✈ Quimper. ⛟ Quimper, then bus. 🛈 Audierne (02 98 70 12 20). Maison du Site (02 98 70 67 18).

THE DRAMATIC Pointe du Raz, almost 80 m (262 ft) high, is a narrow headland jutting into the Atlantic at the tip of Cap Sizun. The views of jagged rocks and pounding seas are breathtaking. Farther west lies the flat, treeless Ile de Sein and beyond that the lighthouse of Ar Men. Despite being only an average 1.5 m (5 ft) above sea level, Ile de Sein is home to some 260 resolute inhabitants, and can be reached by boat from Audierne in an hour.

The awe-inspiring cliffs of Pointe du Raz

Pays Bigouden ❼

Finistère. ⛟ Pont l'Abbé. 🛈 Pont l'Abbé (02 98 82 30 30).

BRITTANY'S SOUTHWEST tip is known as the Pays Bigouden, a windy peninsula with proud and ancient traditions. The region is famous for the women's tall *coiffes* still worn at festivals and *pardons* (see p233), which can also be seen at the **Musée Bigouden**.

Along the Baie d'Audierne is a brooding landscape of weather-beaten hamlets and isolated chapels – the 15th-century calvary at **Notre-Dame-de-Tronoën** is the oldest in Brittany. There are invigorating sea views from **Pointe de la Torche** (a good surfing spot) and from the **Eckmühl lighthouse**.

🏛 Musée Bigouden
Le Château, Pont l'Abbé. ⚏ 02 98 66 09 09. ⚏ Easter hols–May: Mon–Sat; Jun–Sep: daily. ● May 1. ⚏

Quimper **8**

Finistère. 🚶 *63,000.* 🚢 🚌 🚂 ⛴
ℹ *place de la Résistance (02 98 53 04 05).* 🎪 *Wed, Sat.*

THE ANCIENT capital of Cornouaille, Quimper has a distinctly Breton character. Here you can find Breton language books and music for sale, buy a traditional costume or enjoy some of the best crêpes and cider in Brittany. Quimper gets its name from *kemper*, a Breton word meaning the confluence of two rivers, and the Steir and Odet still flow through this relaxed cathedral city.

West of the cathedral lies a pedestrianized area known as **Vieux Quimper**, full of shops, crêperies and half-timbered houses. Rue Kéréon is the main thoroughfare, with the place au Beurre and the picturesque *hôtel particuliers* (mansions) of rue des Gentilshommes to the north.

Quimper has been producing faïence, elegant hand-painted pottery, since 1690. The design often features decorative flowers and animals framed by blue and yellow borders. Originally made for daily use, but now mainly decorative, faïence is today exported to collectors all over the world. In the southwest of the city lies the oldest factory, **Faïenceries HB-Henriot**, which is open to visitors from March to October.

🔒 **Cathédrale St-Corentin**

Quimper's cathedral is dedicated to the city's founder-bishop, St. Corentin. Begun in 1240 – its colorfully painted interior now restored – it is the earliest Gothic building in Lower Brittany, and was bizarrely constructed its choir at a slight angle to the nave, perhaps to fit in with some since-disappeared buildings. The two spires of the west façade were added in 1856. Between them is a statue of King Gradlon, the

The Martyrdom of St. Triphine (1910) by Sérusier, Pont-Aven School

mythical founder of the drowned city of Ys. After this deluge, he chose Quimper as his new capital and St. Corentin as his spiritual guide.

🏛 **Musée des Beaux-Arts**

40 place St-Corentin. 📞 *02 98 95 45 20.* ⏱ *Jul–Aug: daily; Sep–Jun: Wed–Mon.* ● *most public hols; Nov–Mar: Sun am.* 💰 ♿

Quimper's art museum, is one of the best in the region. The collection is strong in late 19th- and early 20th-century artists, whose work – such as Jean-Eugène Buland's *Visite à Ste-Marie de Bénodet* – offers a valuable insight into the way visiting painters perpetuated a romantic view of Brittany. Also on exhibit are works by members of the Pont-Aven School and local artists J.J. Lemordant and Max Jacob.

Typical faïence plate from Quimper

🏛 **Musée Departemental Breton**

1 rue de Roi-Gradlon. 📞 *02 98 95 21 60.* ⏱ *Jun–Sep: daily; Oct–May: Tue–Sat, Sun pm.* ● *public hols.* 💰 ♿

The 16th-century Bishop's Palace has interesting collections of Breton costumes, furniture and faïence, including elaborate Cornouaille, *coiffes,* ornately carved box-beds and wardrobes, and turn-of-the-century tourist posters for Brittany.

Concarneau **9**

Finistère. 🚶 *20,000.* 🚌 ⛴ *only for islands* ℹ *quai d'Aiguillon (02 98 97 01 44).* 🎪 *Mon & Fri.*

AN IMPORTANT fishing port, Concarneau's principal attraction is its 14th-century **Ville Close** (walled town), built on an island in the harbor and completely encircled by massive lichen-covered granite ramparts. Access is by bridge from the place Jean Jaurès. Parts of the ramparts can be toured, and the narrow streets are full of shops and restaurants. The **Musée de la Pêche**, housed in the port's ancient barracks, explains the local techniques and history of sea-fishing.

🏛 **Musée de la Pêche**

Rue Vauban. 📞 *02 98 97 10 20.* ⏱ *daily.* ● *Jan.* 💰 ♿

Fishing boats in Concarneau's busy harbor

Pont-Aven ⑩

Finistère. 🏠 *3,000.* 🚌 🛈 *place de l'Hôtel de Ville (02 98 06 04 70).* 🛒 *Tue (daily in summer).*

O NCE A MARKET town of "14 mills and 15 houses," Pont-Aven's picturesque location in the wooded Aven estuary made it attractive to many late 19th-century artists.

In 1888, Paul Gauguin, along with like-minded painters Emile Bernard and Paul Sérusier, developed a crude, colorful style of painting known as Synthetism. Drawing inspiration from the Breton landscape and its people, the Ecole de Pont-Aven (Pont-Aven School) worked here and in nearby Le Pouldu until 1896.

Today, the town remains devoted to art and has some 50 private galleries, along with the informative **Musée de Pont-Aven**, which documents the achievements of the Pont-Aven School. The surrounding woods proved inspirational to many visiting artists, and offer pleasant walks in their footsteps – one leads through the Bois d'Amour to the **Chapelle de Trémalo**, where the wooden Christ in Gauguin's *Le Christ Jaune* still hangs.

🏛 Musée de Pont-Aven
Pl de l'Hôtel de Ville. 📞 *02 98 06 14 43.* ⭕ *daily.* ⬤ *Jan; between exhibitions.* 📷 ♿

Notre-Dame-de-Kroaz-Baz, Roscoff

Le Pouldu ⑪

Finistère. 🏠 *4,000.* 🚌 🛈 *boulevard Charles Filiger (02 98 39 93 42).*

A QUIET PORT at the mouth of the River Laïta, Le Pouldu has a small beach and good walks. Its main attraction is **Maison de Marie Henry**, a reconstruction of the inn where Paul Gauguin and other artists stayed between 1889 and 1893. They covered every inch of the dining room, including the windowpanes, with self-portraits, caricatures and still-lifes. These were discovered in 1924 beneath layers of wallpaper.

🏛 Maison de Marie Henry
Rue des Grandes Sables. 📞 *02 98 39 98 51.* ⭕ *Apr–May: Sat–Sun &, public hols pms; Jun–Sep: Wed pm–Mon pm; July–Aug: daily.* 📷

Roscoff ⑫

Finistère. 🏠 *3,700.* 🚌 🚌 ⛴ 🛈 *46 rue Gambetta (02 98 61 12 13).* 🛒 *Wed.*

O NCE A PIRATES' haunt, Roscoff is now a thriving Channel port and seaside resort. Signs of its wealthy seafaring past can be found in the old port, particularly along rue Amiral Réveillère and in place Lacaze-Duthiers. Here, the granite façades of the 16th- and 17th-century shipowners' mansions, and the weatherbeaten caravels and cannon decorating the 16th-century **Eglise Notre-Dame-de-Kroaz-Baz**, testify to the days when the pirates of Roscoff were as notorious as those of St-Malo *(see p272).*

The famous French onion sellers (Johnnies) first crossed the Channel in 1828, selling their plaited onions door to door as far as Scotland. The **Maison des Johnnies** tells their colorful history. The **Charles Perez Aquarium** is devoted to the weird and wonderful creatures that swim in the Channel, while Thalado is a seaweed exhibition center. From the harbor, you can take a short boat trip to the peaceful **Ile de Batz**. Near the Pointe de Bloscon there are colorful tropical gardens.

🐟 Charles Perez Aquarium
Place Georges Teissier. 📞 *02 98 29 23 25.* ⭕ *Apr–early Nov: daily;* 📷 ♿ *restr.*

PAUL GAUGUIN IN BRITTANY

Carving, Chapelle de Trémalo

Paul Gauguin's (1848–1903) story reads like a romantic novel. At the age of 35, he left his career as a stockbroker to become a fulltime painter. From 1886 to 1894, he lived and worked in Brittany, at Pont-Aven and Le Pouldu, where he painted the landscape and its people. He chose to concentrate on the intense, almost "primitive" quality of the Breton Catholic faith, attempting to convey it in his work. This is evident in *Le Christ Jaune* (Yellow Christ), inspired by a woodcarving in the Trémalo chapel. In Gauguin's painting, the Crucifixion is a reality in the midst of the contemporary Breton landscape, rather than a remote or symbolic event. This theme recurs in many of his paintings from the period, including *Jacob Wrestling with the Angel* (1888).

Le Christ Jaune (1889) by Paul Gauguin

St-Thégonnec ⓭

Finistère. 🚌 🅿 *daily.* ♿

Tʜɪs ɪs ᴏɴᴇ ᴏꜰ ᴛʜᴇ most complete parish closes in Brittany. Passing through its triumphal archway, the ossuary is to the left. The calvary, directly ahead, was built in 1610 and perfectly illustrates the extraordinary skills Breton sculptors developed as they worked with the local granite. Among the many animated figures surrounding the central cross, a small niche contains a statue of St. Thégonnec with a cart pulled by wolves.

Guimiliau ⓮

Finistère. 🅿 *daily.* ♿

Aʟᴍᴏsᴛ 200 figures adorn Guimiliau's intensely decorated calvary (1581–88), many wearing 16th-century dress. Among them you can contemplate the legendary torment of Katell Gollet, a servant girl tortured by demons for stealing a consecrated wafer to please her lover. The church is dedicated to St. Miliau and has a richly decorated south porch. The baptistry's elaborately-carved oak canopy dates from 1675.

Font canopy from 1675, Guimiliau

Lampaul-Guimiliau ⓯

Finistère. 🅿 *daily.* ♿

Eɴᴛᴇʀɪɴɢ ᴛʜʀᴏᴜɢʜ the monu-mental gate, the chapel and ossuary lie to the left, while the calvary is to the right. Here, however, it is the church that demands most attention. The interior is zealously painted and carved, including some naïve scenes from the Passion depicted along the 16th-century rood beam dividing the nave and choir.

Parish Closes

Rᴇꜰʟᴇᴄᴛɪɴɢ ᴛʜᴇ ʀᴇʟɪɢɪᴏᴜs ꜰᴇʀᴠᴏʀ of the Bretons, the Enclos Paroissiaux (parish closes) were built during the 15th–18th centuries. At that time, Brittany had few urban centers but many wealthy rural settlements, which profited from maritime trading and the manufacture of cloth. Grand religious monuments, some taking over 200 years to complete, were built by small villages inspired by spiritual zeal and the more earthly desire to rival their neighbors. Some of the finest parish closes lie in the Elorn valley, linked by a well-marked Circuit des Enclos Paroissiaux.

***The enclosure**, surrounded by a stone wall, is the hallowed area. By following the wall, visitors are drawn toward the triumphal arch, shown here in Pleyben.*

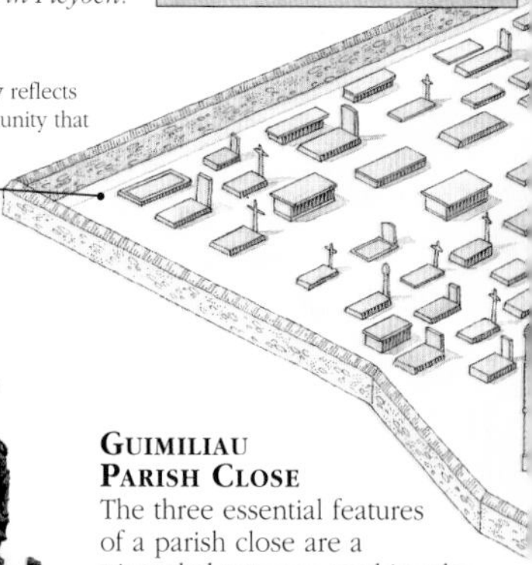

The small cemetery reflects the size of the community that built these great churches.

Gᴜɪᴍɪʟɪᴀᴜ Pᴀʀɪsʜ Cʟᴏsᴇ
The three essential features of a parish close are a triumphal gateway marking the entry into the hallowed enclosure, a calvary depicting scenes from the Passion and Crucifixion, and an ossuary beside the church porch.

***The calvary** is unique to Brittany, and may have been inspired by the crosses set on top of menhirs (see p269) by the early Christians. They provide a unique Bible lesson, often with the characters in 17th-century costumes, as in this example from St-Thégonnec.*

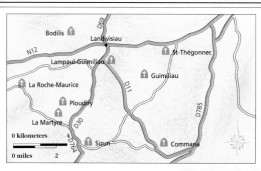

Brittany's parish closes are mostly in the Elorn Valley. As well as St-Thégonnec, Lampaul-Guimiliau and Guimiliau, other parish closes to visit include Bodilis, La Martyre, La Roche-Maurice, Ploudiry, Sizun and Commana. Farther afield lie Plougastel-Daoulas and Pleyben, while Guébenno is in the Morbihan region.
🛈 14 av Maréchal Foch, Landivisiau (02 98 68 33 33).

Church interiors are usually adorned with depictions of local saints and scenes from their lives, along with ornately carved beams and furniture. This is the altarpiece in Guimiliau.

In the ossuary, bones exhumed from the cemetery were stored. Built close to the church entrance, the ossuary was considered a bridge between the living and the dead.

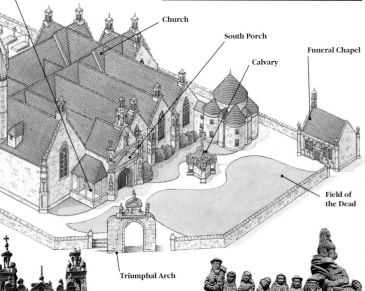

Church

South Porch

Calvary

Funeral Chapel

Field of the Dead

Triumphal Arch

The triumphal arch at St-Thégonnec, a monumental entrance, heralds the worshipper's arrival on sacred ground, like the righteous entering heaven.

Carvings in stone were created as biblical cartoons to instruct and inspire visitors. Their clear message is now often obscured by weather and lichen, but this one in St-Thégonnec is well preserved.

The chapel of Notre-Dame, perched on the cliffs above the beach of Port-Blanc, Côte de Granit Rose

Côte de Granit Rose ⑯

Côtes d'Armor. ✗ 🚉 🚌 Lannion. 🛈 Lannion (02 96 46 41 00).

THE COAST between Paimpol and Trébeurden is known as the Côte de Granit Rose due to its reddish-pink cliffs. These are best seen between Trégastel and Trébeurden, but the pink granite is also used in the nearby towns. The stretch of coast between Trébeurden and Perros-Guirec is one of Brittany's most popular family vacation areas.

Farther east are quieter beaches and coves, at **Trévou-Tréguignec** and **Port-Blanc**. Beyond Tréguier, **Paimpol** is a working fishing port that once sent huge cod and whaling fleets to fish off Iceland and Newfoundland.

Tréguier ⑰

Côtes d'Armor. 👥 2,900. 🛈 Les Quais (02 96 92 30 19). 🖭 Wed.

OVERLOOKING THE estuary of the Jaundy and Guindy rivers, Tréguier stands apart from the seaside resorts of the Côte de Granit Rose. It is a typically Breton market town, with one main attraction, the 14th–15th century **Cathédrale St-Tugdual**. It has three towers, one Romanesque, one Gothic, and one 18th-century. The last, financed by Louis XVI with winnings from the Paris Lottery, has holes pierced in the shapes of playing card suits.

Environs
Chapelle St-Gonery in Plougrescant has a leaning lead spire and a 15th-century painted wooden ceiling.

Île de Bréhat ⑱

Côtes d'Armor. 🚉 🚌 Paimpol, then bus to Pointe de l'Arcouest (Mon–Sat in winter; daily in summer), then boat. 🛈 Paimpol (02 96 20 83 16).

A 15-MINUTE CROSSING from the Pointe de l'Arcouest, the Île de Bréhat is actually two islands, joined by a small bridge, which together are only 3.5 km (2.2 miles) long. With motorized traffic banned, and a climate mild enough for oleander, mimosa and a variety of fruit trees to flourish, it has a relaxing, pastoral atmosphere. Bicycle rentals and boat tours of the island are available in the main town, **Port-Clos**, and you can walk to the island's highest point, the **Chapelle St-Michel**.

Chapelle St-Michel, a landmark on Ile de Bréhat

Carnac ⑲

Morbihan. 👥 4,400. 🚉 🛈 74 avenue des Druides (02 97 52 13 52). 🖳 www.carnac.fr

CARNAC IS ONE of the world's great prehistoric sites, with almost 3,000 menhirs in parallel rows, and an excellent **Musée de Préhistoire**.

The 17th-century **Eglise St-Cornély** is dedicated to St. Cornelius, patron saint of horned animals, scenes from whose life are painted on its wooden ceiling. The town is a popular seaside resort.

♦ **Accueil de Kermario** (site) 📞 02 97 52 89 99. ⏰ daily. 🔲 summer only. 🎟 obligatory Apr–Sep.
🏛 **Musée de Préhistoire** 10 pl de la Chapelle. 📞 02 97 52 22 04. ⏰ Jun–Sep daily; Oct–May: Wed–Mon. ● Jan 1, May 1, Dec 25. 🎟 🔲

Presqu'île de Quiberon ⑳

Morbihan. ✗ Quiberon (via Lorient). 🚉 Jul–Aug. 🚉 ⛴ Quiberon. 🛈 Quiberon (02 97 50 07 84).

ONCE AN ISLAND, the slender Quiberon peninsula has a bleak and windy west coast with sea-punished cliffs, known as the Côte Sauvage. The east is more benign, with sheltered beaches. At the southern tip of the peninsula is the fishing port and resort of **Quiberon**, departure point for the car ferry to Belle-Ile. In 1795, 10,000 Royalist troops were massacred here in an ill-fated attempt to reverse the French Revolution.

Brittany's Prehistoric Monuments

A T CARNAC, thousands of ancient granite rocks were arranged in mysterious lines and patterns by Megalithic tribes as early as 4000 BC. Their original purpose remains obscure: the significance was probably religious, but the precise patterns also suggest an early astronomical calendar. Celts, Romans and Christians have since adapted them to their own beliefs.

The Gavrinis Tumulus, Golfe du Morbihan

MEGALITHS

There are many different formations of megaliths, all with a particular purpose. Words from the Breton language, such as *men* (stone), *dole* (table) and *bir* (long), are still used to describe them.

Menhirs, *the most common megaliths, are upright stones, standing alone or arranged in lines. Those in circles are known as cromlechs.*

Dolmen, *two upright stones roofed by a third, were used as a burial chamber, such as the Merchant's Table at Locmariaquer.*

Allée couverte, *upright stones placed in a row and roofed to form a covered alley, can be seen at Carnac.*

A tumulus *is a dolmen covered with stones and soil to form a burial mound.*

KEY

	Megalithic sites
	Alignments

0 kilometers 10

0 miles 5

Brittany's major megalithic sites

Alignment at Carnac

Menhirs of all shapes in a field near Carnac

Belle-Île-en-Mer ㉑

Morbihan. ✕ *Quiberon (via Lorient).*
⛴ *from Quiberon.* ℹ *Le Palais*
(02 97 31 81 93). 🆆 www.belle-ile.com

BRITTANY'S largest island lies
14 km (9 miles) south of
Quiberon and can be reached
in 45 minutes by car ferry
from Quiberon. Its coast
offers both rugged cliffs and
good beaches, while inland
lie exposed highlands inter-
sected by sheltered valleys.
In the main town, Le Palais,
stands the **Citadelle Vauban**,
a 16th-century star-shaped
fortress, and there are fine
walks and views along the
southern Côte Sauvage.

Cloisters of St-Pierre in Vannes

Vannes ㉒

Morbihan. 🏛 *54,000.* 🚆 🚌 ⛴ ℹ *1 rue*
Thiers (02 97 47 24 34). 🛒 *Wed & Sat.*
🆆 www.pays-de-vannes.com

STANDING AT THE HEAD of the
Golfe du Morbihan, Vannes
was the capital of the Veneti,
a seafaring Armorican tribe
defeated by Caesar in 56 BC.
In the 9th century, Nominoë,
the first Duke of Brittany,
made it his power base. The
city remained influential up
until the signing of the union
with France in 1532, when
Rennes became the Breton
capital. Today, it is a busy
commercial city with a well-
preserved medieval quarter,
and a good base for exploring
the Golfe du Morbihan.
   The impressive eastern
walls of old Vannes can be
viewed from the promenade
de la Garenne. Two of the
city's old gates survive at
either end: Porte-Prison in the

Breton seafarer, off Belle-Île's coast

north, and the southern Porte-
Poterne with a row of 17th-
century wash houses close by.
   Walking up from Porte St-
Vincent, you find the city's
old market squares, still in
use today. The **place des
Lices** was once the scene of
medieval tournaments, and
the streets around the rue de
la Monnaie are full of well-
preserved 16th-century houses.
   Begun in the 13th century,
Cathédrale St-Pierre has since
been drastically remodeled
and restored. The Chapel of
the Holy Sacrament houses
the revered tomb of Vincent
Ferrier, a Spanish saint who
died in Vannes in 1419.
   Opposite the west front of
the cathedral, the old covered
market **La Cohue** (meaning
throng or hubbub) was once
the city's central meeting place.
Parts of the building date from
the 13th century, and a small
museum inside displays art
and artifacts relevant to the
history of the area.
   Housed in the 15th-century
Château Gaillard, the **Musée
d'Archéologie du Morbihan**

is a rich assembly of finds
from Morbihan's many
prehistoric sites, including
jewelry, pottery and
weapons. There is also a
gallery of medieval and
Renaissance *objets d'art*.

🏛 **Musée d'Archéologie du
Morbihan**
Château Gaillard, 2 rue Noé. 📞 *02*
97 47 35 86. ⏰ *daily (Oct– mid-Jun:*
pms only) ● *public hols.* 📷

Environs
To the south of the city, the
Parc du Golfe is a park with
many amusements, a but-
terfly conservatory, an
automatum museum and
an aquarium with over 400
species of fish. Northeast of
Vannes, off the N166, lie the
romantic ruins of the 15th-
century **Tours d'Elven**.

Golfe du Morbihan ㉓

Morbihan. ✕ *Lorient.* 🚆 🚌 ⛴
Vannes. ℹ *Vannes (02 97 47 24 34).*

MORBIHAN MEANS "little sea"
in Breton, an apt de-
scription for this landlocked
expanse of tidal water.
Connected to the Atlantic by
only a small channel between
the Locmariaquer and Rhuys
peninsulas, the gulf is dotted
with islands. Around 40 are
inhabited, with the **Ile d'Arz**
and the **Ile aux Moines** the
largest. These are served by
regular ferries from Conleau
and Port-Blanc, respectively.
   Around the gulf several
small harbor towns thrive on
fishing, oyster cultivation and
tourism. There is a wealth of

The picturesque fishing port of Le Bono in Golfe du Morbihan

Young vacationers on the beach at Dinard, a classic seaside resort on the Emerald Coast

megalithic sites, notably the island of **Gavrinis** where a tumulus has been excavated to reveal extraordinary stone carvings *(see p269)*. There are boat trips to Gavrinis from Larmor-Baden and around the gulf from Locmariaquer, Auray, Vannes and Port-Navalo.

The medieval Château de Josselin on the banks of the River Oust

Josselin 24

Morbihan. 🏠 *2,600*. 🚌 ℹ *place de la Congrégation (02 97 22 36 43).* 🛒 *Sat.*

OVERLOOKING the River Oust, Josselin is dominated by a medieval **Château** owned by the de Rohan family since the end of the 15th century. Only four of its nine towers survive. The elaborate inner granite façade incorporates the letter "A" – a tribute to the much-loved Duchess Anne of Brittany (1477–1514), who presided over Brittany's "Golden Age." Tours are given of the 19th-century interior, and in the former stables is the Musée des Poupées, with 600 dolls. In the town, **Basilique Notre-Dame-du-Roncier** contains

the mausoleum of the castle's most famous owner and constable of France, Olivier de Clisson (1336–1407). West of Josselin at Kerguéhennec, the grounds of an 18th-century château have become a modern sculpture park.

🏰 **Château de Josselin**
📞 *02 97 22 36 45.* ⏰ *Apr – May, Oct & sch hols: Sat–Sun & public hols; pms only; Jun –Sep: daily (Jun–mid-Jul & Sep: pms only).* 🎫 ♿

Forêt de Paimpont 25

Ille-et-Vilaine. 🚌 *Rennes.* 🚉 *Monfort-sur-Meu.* 🚌 *Rennes.* ℹ *Plélan (02 99 06 86 07).*

ALSO KNOWN AS the Forêt de Brocéliande, this forest is a last remnant of the dense primeval woods that once covered much of Armorica. It has long been associated with the legends of King Arthur, and visitors still come to search for the magical

Legendary sorcerer Merlin and Viviane, the Lady of the Lake

spring where the sorcerer Merlin first met Viviane, the Lady of the Lake. The small village of **Paimpont** provides a good base for exploring both the forest and its myths.

Côte d'Emeraude 26

Ille et Vilaine & Côtes d'Armor. 🛬 🛫 *Dinard–St-Malo.* 🚉 🚌 ⛴ ℹ *Dinard (02 99 46 94 12).*

BETWEEN Le Val-André and the Pointe du Grouin near Cancale, sandy beaches, rocky headlands and classic seaside resorts stretch along Brittany's northern shore. Known as the Emerald Coast, its self-proclaimed Queen is the aristocratic resort of **Dinard**, "discovered" in the 1850s and still playing host to the international rich.

To its west, the summer holiday mood is sustained by such resorts as St-Jacut-de-la-Mer, St-Cast-le-Guildo, Sables d'Or-les-Pins and Erquy, all with tempting beaches. In the Baie de la Frênaye, the medi-eval **Fort La Latte** provides good views from its ancient watchtower, while the light-house that dominates **Cap Fréhel** nearby offers even more extensive panoramas.

East of Dinard, the D186 runs across the **Barrage de la Rance** to St-Malo. Built in 1966, it was the world's first dam to generate electricity using tidal power. Beyond St-Malo, coves and beaches surround La Guimorais, while around the Pointe du Grouin the seas are truly emerald.

SEAFARERS OF ST-MALO

St-Malo owes its wealth and reputation to the exploits of its mariners. In 1534 Jacques Cartier, born in nearby Rothéneuf, discovered the mouth of the St. Lawrence River in Canada and claimed the territory for France. It was Breton sailors who voyaged to South America in 1698 to colonize the Iles Malouines, known today as Las Malvinas, or the Falklands. By the 17th century, St-Malo was the largest port in France and famous for its corsairs – privateers licensed by the king to prey on foreign ships. The most illustrious were the swashbuckling René Duguay-Trouin (1673–1736), who captured Rio de Janeiro from the Portuguese in 1711, and the intrepid Robert Surcouf (1773–1827), whose ships hounded vessels of the British East India Company. The riches won by trade and piracy enabled St-Malo's ship-owners to build great mansions known as *malouinières*.

Explorer Jacques Cartier (1491–1557)

St-Malo ㉗

Ille-et-Vilaine. 53,000. esplanade St-Vincent (02 99 56 64 48). Mon–Sat.

ONCE A FORTIFIED island, St-Malo stands in a commanding position at the mouth of the River Rance.
The city is named after Maclou, a Welsh monk who came here in the 6th century to spread the Christian message. During the 16th–19th centuries, the port won prosperity and power through the exploits of its seafarers. St-Malo was heavily bombed in 1944 but has since been scrupulously restored and is now a major port and ferry terminal as well as a resort.

Intra-muros, the old walled city, is encircled by ramparts that provide fine views of St-Malo and its offshore islands. Take the steps up by the **Porte St-Vincent** and walk clockwise, passing the mighty 15th-century **Grande Porte**.

Within the city is a web of narrow, cobbled streets with tall 18th-century buildings housing souvenir shops, sea-food restaurants and crêperies. Rue Porcon-de-la-Barbinais leads to **Cathédrale St-Vincent**, whose somber 12th-century nave contrasts with the brilliant modern stained glass of the chancel. On cour La Houssaye, the 15th-century Maison de la Duchesse Anne has been carefully restored.

St-Malo seen at low tide through the gate of Fort National

♣ Château de St-Malo

02 99 40 71 57. Apr–Sep: daily; Oct–Mar: Tue–Sun. Jan 1, Nov 1 & 11, Dec 25.
St-Malo's castle dates from the 14th–15th centuries. The great keep, built in 1424, contains a museum of the city's history, including the adventures of its state-sponsored corsairs. From its watch towers, there is an impressive view. Nearby, in the place Vauban, a tropical freshwater aquarium has been built into the ramparts, while on the edge of town, the Grand Aquarium has a ring-shaped shark tank and deep-sea simulated submarine rides.

⚓ Fort National

Jun–Sep: daily at low tide.
Constructed in 1689 by Louis XIV's famous military architect, Vauban, this fort can be reached on foot at low tide and offers good views of St-Malo and its ramparts. At low tide you can also walk out to **Petit Bé Fort** (open Easter–mid -Nov) and **Grand Bé**, where St-Malo-born writer François-René de Chateaubriand is buried. From the top there are great views along the whole of Côte d'Emeraude (*see p271*).

⚓ Tour Solidor

St-Servan. 02 99 40 71 58. Apr–Sep: daily; Oct–Mar: Tue–Sun. Jan 1, May 1, Nov 1 & 11, Dec 25.
To the west of St-Malo in St-Servan, the three-towered Tour Solidor was built in 1382. Formerly a toll house it was also a prison under the Revolution, and it now houses an intriguing museum devoted to the ships and sailors that rounded Cape Horn, displaying ship models, logs and various instruments of a nautical flavor.

Environs

When the tide is out, good beaches are revealed around St-Malo and in the neighboring suburbs of St-Servan and Paramé. A passenger ferry runs to Dinard in the summer (*see p271*) and the Channel Islands, and there are boat trips up the Rance to Dinan, and to the Iles Chausey, Ile de Cézembre and Cap Fréhel.

At Rothéneuf, you can visit the **Manoir Limoëlou**, home of the navigator Jacques Cartier. Nearby, on the coast, Les Rochers Sculptés is a

22f/Dz

Cancale oysters, prized for their taste since Roman times

beguiling array of granite faces and figures carved into the cliffs by a local priest, Abbé Fouré, at the end of the 19th century.

🏠 Manoir Limoëlou
Rue D Macdonald-Stuart, Limoëlou-Rothéneuf. 📞 02 99 40 97 73. ⭘ Jul–Aug: daily; Sep–Jun: Mon–Sat. 📷 ♿

Cancale 28

Ille-et-Vilaine. 🏠 5,000. 🚌
🛈 44 rue du Port (02 99 89 63 72).
🐟 Sun. 🌐 www.ville-cancale.fr

A SMALL PORT with views across the Baie du Mont-St-Michel, Cancale is entirely devoted to the cultivation and consumption of oysters. Prized by the Romans, the acclaimed flavor of Cancale's oysters is said to derive from the strong tides that wash over them daily. You can survey the beds from a *sentier des douaniers* (coastguards' footpath, the GR34) running along the cliffs.

There are plenty of opportunities for sampling the local specialty provided by a multitude of bars and restaurants along the busy quays of the Port de la Houle, where the fishing boats arrive at high tide. Devotees should pay a visit to the **Musée de l'Huître et du Coquillage**.

🏛 Musée de l'Huître et du Coquillage – La Ferme Marine
Aurore. 📞 02 99 89 69 99. ⭘ mid-Jun–mid-Sep: daily; mid-Feb–mid-Jun & mid-Sep–Oct: Mon–Fri. 📷

Dinan 29

Côtes d'Armor. 🏠 10,000. 🚌 🚆
🛈 9 rue du Château (02 96 87 69 76).
🐟 Thu. 🌐 www.dinan-tourisme.com

S ET ON A HILL overlooking the wooded Rance valley, Dinan is a modern market town with a medieval heart. Surrounded by ramparts, the well-kept, half-timbered houses and cobbled streets of its Vieille Ville have an impressive, unforced unity best appreciated by climbing to the top of its 15th-century **Tour d'Horloge**, in rue de l'Horloge. Nearby, **Basilique St-Sauveur** contains the heart of Dinan's most famous son, the 14th-century warrior Bertrand du Guesclin.

Behind the church, Les Jardins Anglais offer good views of the River Rance and the viaduct spanning it. A short distance farther north, the steep, geranium-decorated rue du Jerzual winds down through the 14th-century town gate to the port. Once a busy harbor from which cloth was shipped, it is now a quiet backwater where you can take a pleasure cruise, or walk along a towpath to the restored 17th-century **Abbaye St-Magloire** at Léhon.

The **Musée-Château** houses a small museum of local history. Next to it is the 15th-century **Tour de Coëtquen**. From here, there are pleasant walks beside the ramparts along the promenade des Petits Fossés and the promenade des Grands Fossés.

♜ Musée-Château
Château de la Duchesse Anne, rue du Château. 📞 02 96 39 45 20.
⭘ Jun–Sep: daily; Oct–May: Wed–Mon (mid-Nov–Dec: pms only).
⭘ Dec 25. 📷

Author and diplomat François-René de Chateaubriand (1768–1848)

Combourg 30

Ille-et-Vilaine. 🏠 5,000. 🚌 🚆
🛈 place Albert Parent (02 99 73 13 93). 🐟 Mon. 🌐 www.combourg.net

A SMALL, SLEEPY town beside a lake, Combourg is completely overshadowed by the great, haunting **Château de Combourg**. The buildings seen today date from the 14th and 15th centuries. In 1761, the château was bought by the Comte de Chateaubriand, and the melancholic childhood spent there by his son, the author and diplomat François-René de Chateaubriand (1768–1848), is candidly described in his entertaining chronicle, *Mémoires d'Outre-Tombe*.

Empty after the Revolution, the château was restored in the late 19th century and is now open for guided tours. In one room are papers and furniture relating to the life of François-René de Chateaubriand.

♜ Château de Combourg
23 rue des Princes. 📞 02 99 73 22 95.
⭘ Apr–Jun & Oct: Sun–Fri; Jul–Aug: daily. 📷

View over Dinan and the Gothic bridge crossing the River Rance

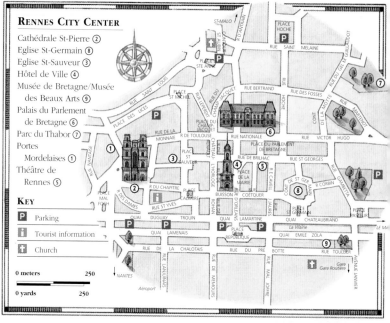

RENNES CITY CENTER

Cathédrale St-Pierre ②
Eglise St-Germain ⑧
Eglise St-Sauveur ③
Hôtel de Ville ④
Musée de Bretagne/Musée
　des Beaux Arts ⑨
Palais du Parlement
　de Bretagne ⑥
Parc du Thabor ⑦
Portes
　Mordelaises ①
Théâtre de
　Rennes ⑤

KEY

P Parking

i Tourist information

✝ Church

0 meters 　　　250
0 yards 　　　　250

Rennes ③

Ille-et-Vilaine. 🏠 *204,000.* ✈ 🚆
🚌 **i** *rue St-Yves (02 99 67 11 11).*
🗓 *Tue–Sat.* **W** *www.ville-rennes.fr*

FOUNDED BY the Gauls and
colonized by the Romans,
Rennes is strategically located
where the Vilaine and Ille
rivers meet. After Brittany's
union with France in 1532, the
town became regional capital.
In 1720, a fire lasting for six
days devastated the city. Today,
a small part of the medieval
city survives, together with
the neat grid of 18th-century

**The lively market at place des
Lices in the heart of Rennes**

buildings that arose from the
ashes. Around this historic
core are the tower blocks and
hi-tech factories of modern
Rennes – a confident provincial
capital with two universities
and a thriving cultural life.
　Wandering through the
streets that radiate from the
place des Lices and the place
Ste-Anne, it is easy to imagine
what Rennes was like before
the Great Fire. Now mostly
pedestrianized, this area has
become the city's youthful
heart, with plenty of bars,
crêperies and designer shops.
At the western end of rue de
la Monnaie stands the 15th-
century **Portes Mordelaises**,
once part of the city's ramparts.
　Close by, **Cathédrale St-
Pierre** was completed in 1844,
the third on this site. Note the
carved 16th-century Flemish
altarpiece. Nearby is the 18th-
century **Eglise St-Sauveur**.
Just south of the attractive rue
St-George, **Eglise St-Germain**
has a typically Breton belfry
and wooden vaulting. In the
place de la Mairie stands the
early 18th-century **Hôtel de
Ville** and the Neo-Classical
Théâtre de Rennes. The
Parc du Thabor, once part
of a Benedictine monastery,
is ideal for walks and picnics.

**Half-timbered houses lining the
narrow streets of old Rennes**

🏛 Palais du Parlement
de Bretagne

Place du Parlement. 🚪 *guided tours
organised by Tourist Office: book 2
wks ahead (02 99 67 11 11).*
Rennes' Law Courts, built in
1618–55 and designed by
Salomon de Brosse, were the
seat of the region's governing
body until the Revolution. Sev-
erely damaged by fire during
riots over fish prices in 1994,
the major restoration work is
all but complete, including the
unique coffered ceiling and
gilded woodwork of the
Grande Chambre. Only the
Salle des Pas Perdus, with its
vaulted ceilings, remain closed.

🏛 Musée de Bretagne, Musée des Beaux Arts

20 quai Emile Zola. 📞 *02 99 28 55 84 (Musée de Bretagne).* 📞 *02 99 28 55 85 (Musée des Beaux Arts).* ⬤ *Wed–Mon.* ⬤ *public hols.* 📷 ♿

The permanent collection of the Musée de Bretagne includes examples of traditional Breton furniture and costume, and displays on Brittany's prehistoric megaliths, the growth of Rennes, rural crafts and the fishing industry. However, these are not on show until 2004, when the museum will reopen in new premises.

In the same building, the Musée des Beaux Arts has a wide-ranging collection of art from the 14th century to the present, including a room of art on Breton themes. There are paintings by Gauguin, Bernard and other members of the Pont-Aven School *(see p265)*, and three works by Picasso, including the lively *Baigneuse* painted at Dinard in 1928.

Environs

Just south of Rennes, the **Ecomusée du Pays de Rennes** traces the history of a local farm since the 17th century.

Some 16 km (10 miles) to the southeast of Rennes is **Châteaugiron**, a charming medieval village, with an imposing castle and houses preserving their wooden eaves.

🏛 Ecomusée du Pays de Rennes
Ferme de la Bintinais, Rte de Châtillon-sur-Seiche. 📞 *02 99 51 38 15.* ⬤ *Feb–mid-Jan: Tue–Sun.* ⬤ *w/e ams, public hols.* 📷 ♿

♣ Château de Châteaugiron
📞 *02 99 37 89 02.* ⬤ *mid-Jun–mid-Sep: daily; by appt rest of year.* 📷

Fougères 32

Ille-et-Vilaine. 👥 *23,000.* 🚉 🅸 *2 rue Nationale (02 99 94 12 20).* 🚌 *Sat.* Ⓦ *www.ot-fougeres.fr*

A FORTRESS TOWN close to the Breton border, Fougères rests on a hill overlooking the Nançon river. In the valley below, and still linked to the Haute Ville by a curtain of ancient ramparts, stands the mighty 11th–15th century

The mighty fortifications of Château de Fougères

Château de Fougères. To get a good overview of the château, go to the gardens of place aux Arbres behind the 16th-century **Eglise St-Léonard.** From here you can descend to the river and the medieval houses around place du Marchix. The Flamboyant Gothic **Eglise St-Sulpice**, with its 18th-century wood-panelled interior and granite retables, is well worth visiting.

A walk around the castle's massive outer fortifications reveals the ambitious scale of its construction, with 13 towers and walls over 3 m (10 ft) thick. You can still climb the castle's ramparts and towers to get a feel of what it was like to live and fight within its staggered defences. Much of the action in Balzac's novel *Les Chouans* (1829) takes place in and around Fougères and its castle.

♣ Château de Fougères
Place Pierre-Simon. 📞 *02 99 99 79 59.* ⬤ *Feb–Dec: daily.* 📷

Overhanging timber-frame houses on rue Beaudrairie, Vitré

Vitré 33

Ille-et-Vilaine. 👥 *16,000.* 🚉 🅿 🅸 *place Général de Gaulle (02 99 75 04 46).* 🚌 *Mon & Sat.*

THE FORTIFIED TOWN of Vitré is set high on a hill overlooking the Vilaine Valley. Its medieval **Château** is complete with pencil-point turrets and picturesque 15th–16th century buildings in attendance. The castle was rebuilt in the 14th–15th centuries and follows a triangular plan, with some of its ramparts walkable. There is a museum of local treasures in the Tour St-Laurent.

To the east, rue Beaudrairie and rue d'Embas have overhanging timber-frame houses with remarkable patterning.

The 15th–16th century **Cathédrale Notre-Dame**, built in Flamboyant Gothic style, has an elaborate south façade with an exterior stone pulpit. Farther along rue Notre-Dame, the promenade du Val skirts around the town's ramparts.

To the southeast of Vitré on the D88, the **Château des Rochers-Sévigné** was once the home of Mme. de Sévigné (1626–96), famous letter-writer and chronicler of life at the court of Louis XIV. The park, chapel and some of her rooms are open to the public.

♣ Château de Vitré
📞 *02 99 75 04 54.* ⬤ *Apr–Sep: daily; Oct–Mar: Wed–Mon (Sat–Mon pms only).* ⬤ *Jan 1, Easter, Nov 1, Dec 25.* 📷

♣ Château des Rochers-Sévigné
📞 *02 99 96 76 51.* ⬤ ⬤ *same as above.* 📷 ♿ *restricted.*

THE LOIRE VALLEY

INDRE · INDRE-ET-LOIRE · LOIR-ET-CHER · LOIRET · EURE-ET-LOIR
CHER · VENDÉE · MAINE-ET-LOIRE · LOIRE-ATLANTIQUE · SARTHE

RENOWNED FOR ITS SUMPTUOUS CHATEAUX, *the glorious valley of the Loire, now classified a UNESCO World Heritage Site, is rich both in history and architecture. Like the Loire River, this vast region runs through the heart of French life. Its sophisticated cities, luxuriant landscape and magnificent food and wine add up to a bourgeois paradise.*

The lush Loire Valley is supremely regal. Orléans was France's intellectual capital in the 13th century, attracting artists, poets and troubadours to the royal court. But the medieval court never stayed in one place for long, which led to the building of magnificent châteaux all along the Loire. Chambord and Chenonceau, the two greatest Renaissance châteaux, remain prestigious symbols of royal rule, resplendent amid vast hunting forests and waterways.

Due to its central location, culture and fine cuisine, Tours is the natural visitors' capital. Angers is a close second, but more authentic are the historic towns of Saumur, Amboise, Blois and Beaugency, strung out like jewels along the river. This is the classic Loire Valley, a château trail that embraces the Renaissance gardens of Villandry and the fairy-tale turrets of Ussé.

Venture northward and the cathedral cities of Le Mans and Chartres reign supreme, their medieval centers bordered by Gallo-Roman walls. Nantes in the west is a breezy, forward-looking port and gateway to the Atlantic.

Southward, the windswept Vendée is edged by a wild, sandy coastline that is perfect for windsurfers and nature lovers alike. Inland, the Loire's more peaceful tributaries and the watery Sologne beg to be explored. Also ripe for discovery are troglodyte caves, sleepy hamlets and small Romanesque churches decorated with frescoes. Inviting inns offer game, fish and abundant fresh vegetables to be lingered over with a light white Vouvray wine or a full-bodied Bourgueil. Overindulgence is no sin in this rich region.

The Loire River at Montsoreau, southeast of Saumur

◁ The fairytale Château de Saumur towering above the town and the Loire River

Exploring the Loire Valley

THE LUSH RIVER PLAIN, studded with France's greatest châteaux, is the main attraction. Numerous river cruises are available, while the sandy Atlantic coast offers beach resorts. Peaceful country vacations can be had in the Vendée, and in the Loir and Indre valleys. Wine tours focus on Bourgueil, Chinon, Saumur, and Vouvray vintages. The most charming bases are Amboise, Blois, Beaugency and Saumur, but culture-lovers are well-provided for throughout the region.

Countryside around Vouvray

To Caen

N12

To Rennes
Brest

N157   LAVAL

To Rennes
St-Malo

CHÂTEAUBRIANT

Erdre

ANGERS

NANTES

CLISSON

CHOLET

ÎLE DE NOIRMOUTIER

SAUMUR

LANGEA

USSÉ

ABBAYE
DE FONTEVRA

MONTREUIL-BELLAY

ÎLE D'YEU

LA ROCHE-SUR-YON

VENDÉE

LES SABLES D'OLONNE

To Poi

KEY

▬▬	Highway
▬▬	Major road
▬▬	Minor road
▬▬	Scenic route
〜	River
✹	Viewing point

0 kilometers   25

0 miles   25

**The 16th-century Château de
Villandry and its famous gardens**

SIGHTS AT A GLANCE

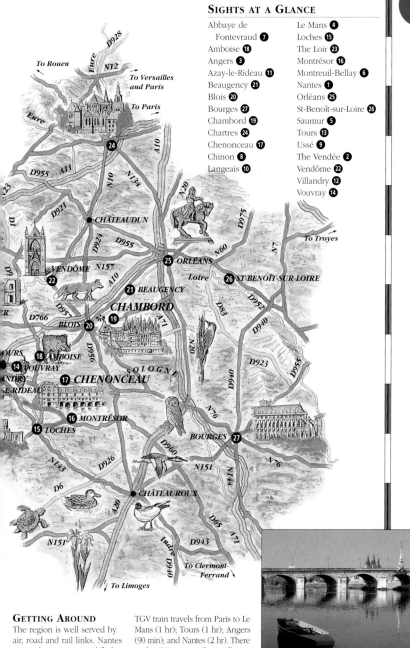

GETTING AROUND

The region is well served by air, road and rail links. Nantes airport has international flights, while Tours airport serves Paris. Chartres, Le Mans, Angers and Nantes are reached from Paris by the A11, and the A10 links Orléans, Blois and Tours. The TGV train travels from Paris to Le Mans (1 hr); Tours (1 hr); Angers (90 min); and Nantes (2 hr). There is also TGV access from Lille (easy Eurostar interchange). The smaller châteaux can be difficult to reach by public transportation, but there are often tours from the major tourist centers.

A bridge over the river Loire pictured at dawn

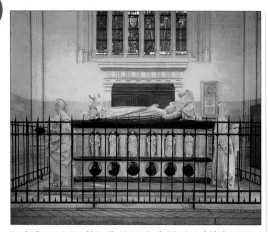

Tomb of François II and his wife, Marguerite de Foix, in Cathédrale St-Pierre

Nantes ❶

Loire-Atlantique. 🏙 270,000.
✈ 🚉 🚌 🛈 *place du Commerce
(02 40 20 60 00).* 🅿 *Tue–Sun.*

FOR CENTURIES, Nantes disputed with Rennes over the title of capital of Brittany. Yet links with the Plantagenets and Henri IV also bound it to the "royal" Loire River. Since the 1790s it has officially ceased to be part of Brittany; though still Breton at heart, it is today capital of the Pays de la Loire.

Visually, Nantes is a city of variety, with high-tech towers overlooking the port, canals and Art Nouveau squares. Chic bars and restaurants cram the medieval nucleus, bounded by place St-Croix and the château.

The **Cathédrale St-Pierre et St-Paul**, started in 1434 but not completed until 1893, is notable for its sculpted Gothic portals and Renaissance tomb of François II, the last duke of Brittany.

More impressive is the **Château des Ducs de Bretagne**, where Anne of Brittany was born in 1477 and where the Edict of Nantes was signed by Henri IV in 1598, granting Protestants religious freedom. The château is at present undergoing major restoration work and will reopen definitively in 2006. It will house a new museum charting the history of Nantes, including the city's colonial links and slave-trading activities in the 18th and 19th centuries.

♣ Château des Ducs de Bretagne
Place Marc Elder. 📞 *02 40 41 56 56.*
🅾 *Wed–Mon during temp exhibits; main re-opening due 2006.* 🎫

Environs
From Nantes, boats cruise the Erdre and Sèvre Nantaise rivers, passing a succession of minor châteaux, Muscadet vineyards and gentle rolling countryside. Some 30 km (20 miles) southeast of Nantes is **Clisson**, a town razed to the ground during the Vendée Uprising of 1793, and later rebuilt along Italian lines, acquiring Neo-Classical villas, brick bell towers and red-tiled roofs. On a rocky spur overlooking the Sèvre Nantaise River is the ruined 13th-century **Château de Clisson**, under restoration.

♣ Château de Clisson
📞 *02 40 54 02 22.* 🅾 *Apr–Sep: Wed–Mon; Oct–Mar: Wed–Sun* 🎫 🎦

The Vendée ❷

Vendée and Maine-et-Loire.
✈ *Nantes.* 🚉 🚌 *La Roche-sur-Yon.*
🛈 *La Roche-sur-Yon (02 51 36 00 85).*

THE COUNTER-REVOLUTIONARY movement that swept western France between 1793 and 1799 began as a series of uprisings in the Vendée, still an evocative name to the French. As a bastion of the *Ancien Régime*, the region rebelled against urban Republican values. But a violent massacre in 1793 left 80,000 royalists dead in one day as they tried to cross the Loire at St-Florent-le-Vieil. The Vendée farmers were staunch royalists, and, although they ultimately lost, the region remains colored by conservatism and religious fervor to this day.

This local history is dramatically retraced at **Le Puy du Fou** in Les Epesses, south of Cholet, with its spectacular summer evening live show, "Cinéscenie." More sober accounts are given at La Chabotterie Museum near St-Sulpice-de-Verdon, and the Musée du Textile in Cholet, whose flax and hemp textiles, provided the royalist heroes with their kerchiefs: originally white, then blood-red.

Today, the tranquil Vendée offers "green" tourism inland, in the *bocage vendéen*, a wooded backwater with bridle paths and nature trails. The Atlantic coast between the Loire and La Rochelle has long sandy beaches, yet the only sizeable resort here is **Les Sables d'Olonne**, with boat trips to the salt marshes, out to sea or to the nearby **Ile**

The harbor at Ile de Noirmoutier in the Vendée

d'Yeu. To the north, the marshy **Ile de Noirmoutier** is connected to the mainland at low tide via the Gois causeway.

Inland lies **Marais Poitevin** *(see p398)*, its marshes home to bird sanctuaries and fine churches (Maillezais, Vix, Maillé) in hamlets bordered by canals. It is France's largest complex of man-made waterways, largely reclaimed for farming in the west, whilst further east is a nature lover's paradise. Coulon is the main center for hiring punts.

The Apocalypse Tapestry in Angers

Angers ❸

Maine-et-Loire. 🏠 156,000. 🚊 🚌
🛈 pl Kennedy (02 41 23 50 00).
🛒 Tue–Sun.

ANGERS SEES ITSELF as the quintessential Loire city. It is the historic capital of Anjou, home of the Plantagenets and gateway to the Loire Valley.

Angers has a formidable 13th-century **Château** *(see p232)*. Inside is the longest (103m) and one of the finest medieval tapestries in the world. It tells the story of the Apocalypse, depicting battles between hydras and angels.

A short walk from the castle is the **Cathédrale St-Maurice**, noted for its Romanesque façade and 13th-century stained-glass windows. Close by, in place St-Croix, is the timber-framed **Maison d'Adam**, with carvings of the tree of life. The nearby **Musée David d'Angers**, housed in the glass-covered ruins of a 13th-century church, is a tribute to the eponymous 19th-century sculptor born in Angers. Across the Maine River, the Hôpital St-Jean, a hospital for the poor from 1174 to 1854, is today the home of the **Musée Jean Lurçat**. Its prize exhibit is the dramatic *Chant du Monde* tapestry created by Lurçat in 1957.

⚜ Château d'Angers

📞 02 41 87 43 47. ⏱ daily. ⬤ Jan 1, May 1, Nov 1 & 11, Dec 25. 🔲 🎫 📷 ♿

🏛 Musée David d'Angers

33 rue Toussaint. 📞 02 41 87 21 03.
⏱ mid-June–mid-Sep: daily; mid-Sep–mid-Jun: Tue–Sun. ⬤ most public hols. 🔲

🏛 Musée Jean Lurçat

4 boulevard Arago. 📞 02 41 24 18 45.
⏱ mid-Jun–mid-Sep: daily; mid-Sep–mid-Jun: Tue–Sun. ⬤ most public hols. 🔲 ♿

Environs

Within a 20-km (13-mile) radius of Angers lie the Classical **Château de Serrant** and the moated **Château du Plessis-Bourré**, a decorative pleasure dome encased in a feudal shell. Follow the Loire east along the sandbanks and dikes, enjoying the rustic fish restaurants and maybe a game of local *boule de fort* en route.

⚜ Château de Serrant

St-Georges-sur-Loire. 📞 02 41 39 13 01. ⏱ Jul–Aug: daily; Apr–Jun & Sep –mid-Nov: Wed–Sun; ⬤ mid-Nov–Mar 🔲 🎫 oblig.

⚜ Château du Plessis-Bourré

Ecuillé. 📞 02 41 32 06 72. ⏱ Jul–Aug: daily; Apr–Jun & Sep: Thu pm–Tue (Feb, Mar, Oct, Nov): Thu–Tue pms only). 🔲 🎫 oblig.

Le Mans ❹

Sarthe. 🏠 150,000. ✈ 🚊 🚌
🛈 rue de l'Etoile (02 43 28 17 22).
🛒 Tue–Sun.

EVER SINCE Monsieur Bollée became the first designer to place an engine under a car hood, Le Mans has been synonymous with the motor trade. Bollée's son created an embryonic Grand Prix; ever since, the event *(see p33)* and associated **Musée de l'Automobile**

Stained-glass Ascension window in the Cathédrale St-Julien, Le Mans

have remained star attractions. Vieux Mans, the ancient fortified center, is surrounded by the greatest Gallo-Roman walls in France, best seen from the quai Louis Blanc. Once insalubrious and abandoned, the area has been extensively restored, and is now used for filming epics such as *Cyrano de Bergerac*, set amongst its Renaissance mansions, half-timbered houses, arcaded alleys and tiny courtyards. The crowning point is the Gothic **Cathédrale St-Julien**, borne aloft on flying buttresses, with its Romanesque portal rivaling that of Chartres. Inside, the Angevin nave opens into a Gothic choir, complemented by sculpted capitals and a 12th-century Ascension window.

🏛 Musée de l'Automobile

Circuit des 24 Heures du Mans.
📞 02 43 72 72 24. ⏱ Feb–Dec daily; Jan: w/e. 🔲 ♿

Le Mans racetrack: a 1933 print from the French magazine *Illustration*

Saumur ❺

Maine-et-Loire. 🚶 *32,000.* 🚉 🚌 ℹ️ *pl de la Bilange (02 41 40 20 60).* 🛒 *Thu, Sat.*

Saumur is celebrated for its fairy-tale château, cavalry school, mushrooms and sparkling wines. Its stone mansions recall the city's 17th-century heyday, when it was a bastion of Protestantism and vied with Angers as the intellectual capital of Anjou.

Towering high above both town and river is the turreted **Château de Saumur**. The present structure was started in the 14th century by Louis I of Anjou and remodeled a century later by his grandson, King René. Collections include outstanding medieval sculpture, ceramics, and equestrian exhibits.

The Military Cavalry School, established in Saumur in 1814, led to the creation of the **Musée des Blindés**, which exhibits 150 different armored vehicles, and of the prestigious Cadre Noir horse-riding formation.

The Château de Saumur and spire of St-Pierre seen from the Loire

Morning training sessions and stable visits, along with occasional evening performances, can be seen at the **Ecole National d'Equitation**. The nearby subterranean **Parc Pierre et Lumière** (sculptures in the tufa cave walls of prominent local tourist sites), is well worth a visit; as is Europe's largest dolmen, with its collection of prehistoric implements in Bagneux.

Before you leave the area, be sure to sample the local *méthode champenoise* sparkling wine – the best in France outside Champagne – in one of the many wine cellars or at the Maison des Vins in town.

King René's coat of arms

♣ **Château de Saumur**
🕐 *02 41 40 24 40.* 🕐 *Apr–Sep: daily; Oct–Mar: Wed–Mon.* ⬤ *Jan 1, Dec 25.* 📷 ✔

Ecole Nationale d'Equitation
St-Hilaire-St-Florent. 🕐 *02 41 53 50 60.* 🕐 *Apr–Sep: Tue–Sat. For performances call for details.*
⬤ *public hols.* 📷 ♿ ✔ *oblig.* 🖥️

Environs
The lovely **Eglise Notre-Dame** at Cunault, an 11th-century Romanesque priory church has a fine west door and carved capitals, while an amazing subterranean fort and myriad caves and tunnels can be seen at **Château de Brézé**.

Montreuil-Bellay ❻

Maine-et-Loire. 🚶 *4,300.* 🚉 🚌 ℹ️ *pl du Concorde (02 41 52 32 39).* 🛒 *Tue (& Sun, mid-Jun–Sep).*

Set on the Thouet River 17 km (11 miles) south of Saumur, Montreuil-Bellay is one of the region's most gracious small towns. It makes an ideal base for touring Anjou. The towering roofline of the Gothic collegiate church overlooks walled mansions and surrounding vineyards (wine-tasting recommended). The **Chapelle St-Jean**, was an ancient hospice and pilgrimage center.

The imposing **Château de Montreuil-Bellay**, established in 1025, is a veritable fortress with its 13 interlocking towers, barbican and ramparts. A gracious 15th-century house lies beyond the fortified gateway, complete with vaulted medieval kitchen, ancient wine cellars and an oratory decorated with 15th-century frescoes.

♣ **Château de Montreuil-Bellay**
🕐 *02 41 52 33 06.* 🕐 *Apr–Oct: Wed–Mon.* 📷 ✔ *oblig.*

TROGLODYTE DWELLINGS

Some of the best troglodyte settlements in France have been carved out of the soft limestone (tufa) of the Loire Valley, especially around Saumur, Vouvray and along the Loir River. The caves, cut out of cliff-faces or dug underground, have been a source of cheap, secure accommodation for centuries. Today they are popular as *résidences secondaires*, or used for wine storage and mushroom growing. Some are now restaurants or hotels, and old quarries at Doué-la-Fontaine accommodate a zoo and a 15th-century amphitheater. At Rochemenier, near Saumur, is a well-preserved troglodyte village museum. A central pit is surrounded by a warren of caves, barns, wine cellars, dwellings and even a simple underground chapel.

Heralded by chimneys, the underground hamlet of nearby La Fosse was inhabited by one family that has made their eccentric home into a living museum open to visitors.

A typical troglodyte dwelling

Court Life in the Renaissance

FRANÇOIS I'S REIGN, from 1515 to 1547, witnessed the pinnacle of the French Renaissance, characterized by an intense period of château-building and an interest in humanism and the arts. The itinerant court traveled between the pleasure palaces of Amboise, Blois and Chambord in the Loire. Days were devoted to hunting, falconry, *fêtes champêtres* (country festivals) or *jeu de paume*, a forerunner of tennis. Nights were given over to feasting, balls, poetry and romantic rendezvous.

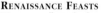

Lute and mandolin music were much in vogue, as were Italian recitals and masquerades. Musicians played at the twice-weekly balls, where the pavane and galliard were danced.

The antics of François I's fools, Triboulet and Caillette, amused the court. Yet they were often mistreated: courtiers regularly nailed Caillette's ears to a post for fun, daring him to remain silent.

RENAISSANCE FEASTS

Dinner usually took place before 7pm to the accompaniment of Italian music. Humanist texts were read aloud and the king's fools amused the courtiers.

Courtiers used their own knives at dinner. Forks were still rare, although their use was spreading from Italy.

A typical royal dinner comprised smoked eel, salted ham, veal pâté, egg and saffron soups, roast game and boiled meats, as well as fish dishes in lemon or gooseberry sauce.

The cost of lavish damask, satin and silk costumes often sent courtiers into debt.

Diane de Poitiers (1499–1566) became the mistress of the future Henri II when he was 12 years old. Two years later he married Catherine de' Medici, but Diane remained his favorite until his death.

Artists symbolized love in different ways during the Renaissance. Winged hearts charmingly perform the function here.

The Grand Moûtier cloisters

Abbaye de Fontevraud **❼**

Maine-et-Loire. 🚌 *from Saumur.*
📞 *02 41 51 71 41.* ⬭ *daily.* ⬤ *Jan 1, Nov 1 & 11, Dec 25.* 🅰 🅱

The Plantagenets

The legendary counts of Anjou were named after the *genêt*, the sprig of broom Geoffrey Plantagenet wore in his cap. He married Matilda, daughter of England's Henry I. In 1154, when their son Henry – who had married Eleanor of Aquitaine *(see p47)* – acceded to the English throne, the Plantagenet dynasty of English kings was founded, fusing French and English destinies for 300 years.

Effigies of Henry II, Plantagenet king of England, and Eleanor of Aquitaine

THE ABBAYE DE FONTEVRAUD is the largest and most intact medieval abbey in Europe. It was founded in the early 12th century by Robert d'Arbrissel, a visionary itinerant preacher who set up a Benedictine community of monks, nuns, nobles, lepers, vagabonds and re-pentant prostitutes.

The radical founder entrusted the running of the abbey to an abbess, usually from a noble family, and the abbey became a favorite sanctuary for the female aristocracy, in-cluding Eleanor of Aquitaine.

From 1804 to 1963 the abbey was used as a prison; since then the buildings have been undergoing painstaking restoration by the French State. Wandering around the ab-bey buildings, orangery and gardens gives a fas-cinating insight into monastic life. The focal point was the Romanesque

abbey church, consecrated in 1119. It boasts beautifully carved capitals and an immense single nave with four domes, one of the finest examples of a cupola nave in France. Inside are the painted effigies of the Plantagenets dating from the early 13th century: Henry II of England, his redoubtable wife Queen Eleanor of Aquitaine, their crusading, non-English-speaking son Richard the Lion-Heart and Isabelle d'Angoulême, widow of his infamous brother, King John of England.

The abbey's nuns lived around the Renaissance **Grand Moûtier cloisters**, forming one of the largest nunneries in France, and the leper colony was housed in the **St-Lazare priory**, now the atmospheric abbey hotel *(see p555)*. Little remains of the monastic quarters, but the **St-Benoît chapel and cloisters** survive. Most impressive is the octagonal kitchen with its fireplaces and chimneys in the **Tour Evraud** which is a rare example of secular Romanesque architecture.

The abbey, now an import-ant arts center, regularly hosts concerts and exhibitions.

TOUR EVRAUD

Pepperpot chimneys top the towers of the kitchen, restored in the 20th century.

Fireplace alcoves that look like side chapels housed the ovens.

Chinon **❽**

Indre-et-Loire. 🔼 *9,000.* 🚌 🚉 **i** *1 place d'Hofheim (02 47 93 17 85).* 🔽 *Thu, Sat & Sun.*

THE CHATEAU DE CHINON is an important shrine in Joan of Arc country and, as such, wheedles money from all passing pilgrims. It was here in 1429 that the saint first recognized the disguised dauphin (later Charles VII)

and persuaded him to give her an army in order to drive the English out of France. Before that, Chinon was the Plantagenet kings' favorite castle. Although the **château** is now mostly in ruins, the ramparts are an impressive sight from the opposite bank of the Vienne River. The town's bijou

Stallholder at Chinon's market

center is like a medieval movie set. **Rue Voltaire**, lined with 15th- and 16th-century houses and once enclosed by the castle walls, repre-sents a cross-section of Chinonais history. At No. 12 is the **Musée Animé du Vin**, where animated figures tell the story of wine-making. **No. 44** is a stone mansion where,

Vineyard in the Chinon wine region

in 1199, Richard the Lion-Heart is said to have died. The grandest mansion is the **Palais du Gouvernement**, with its double staircase and loggia. More charming is the **Maison Rouge** in the Grand Carroi, studded with a red-brick herringbone pattern.

The 15th-century **Hostellerie Gargantua**, where Rabelais's lawyer father once practiced, is now an agreeable inn *(see p555)*. The great Renaissance writer lived nearby, in the Rue de la Lamproie.

The 1900s market is not to be missed (3rd Sat Aug): the stallholders wear period costume and folk dancing and music fill the streets.

🏛 Musée Animé du Vin
12 rue Voltaire. **⟦** *02 47 93 25 63.*
◯ *Easter–Sep: daily.* 📷 ☑

Environs
5 km (3 miles) southwest of Chinon is **La Devinière**, birthplace of François Rabelais, the 16th-century writer, priest, doctor and humanist scholar.

🏛 La Devinière
Seuilly. **⟦** *02 47 95 91 18.* ◯ *daily.*
● *Jan 1, Dec 25.* 📷 ☑

Château d'Ussé ❾

Indre-et-Loire. 🚆 *Langeais, then taxi.* **⟦** *02 47 95 54 05.* ◯ *mid-Feb–mid-Nov: daily.* 📷 ☑ *oblig.*

THE FAIRY-TALE Château d'Ussé enjoys a bucolic setting overlooking watery meadows and the Indre River. Its romantic white turrets, pointed towers and chimneys inspired Charles Perrault's *Sleeping Beauty*.

Constructed in the 15th century, the castle was gradually transformed into an aristocratic château, which is still privately owned *(see p232)*. However, the sunless and musty interior is rather disappointing and the *Sleeping Beauty* tableaux are clumsily presented.

The château's delightful Renaissance chapel, framed by the oak forest of Chinon, has lost its Aubusson tapestries, but retains a lovely della Robbia terra-cotta *Virgin*.

Château de Langeais ❿

Indre-et-Loire. 🚆 *Langeais.*
⟦ *02 47 96 72 60.* ◯ *daily.*
● *Dec 25.* 📷 ☑

COMPARED with neighboring towns, Langeais is distinctly untouristy and has a welcoming, unpretentious feel. Its château is fiercely feudal, built strictly for defense with a drawbridge, portcullis and no concessions to the Renaissance. It was constructed by Louis XI in just four years, from 1465–9, with hardly an alteration since then. The ruins of an impressive keep, built by Foulques Nerra in AD 994, stand in the small château courtyard.

A *son et lumière* in the Salle de la Chapelle represents the marriage of Charles VIII and his child-bride Anne of Brittany in 1491. Many of the well-furnished rooms have intricate designs on the tiled floors, and all are hung with fine 15th- and 16th-century Flemish and Aubusson tapestries.

FRANÇOIS RABELAIS

Rabelais, born in 1494, was a priest, doctor, diplomat and humanist scholar noted for his wisdom and tolerance. He is best remembered for his many ribald satires (written as "medicine" for his patients), such as *Pantagruel* and *Gargantua*, set around his native Chinon.

Infant Pantagruel, depicted by Doré in 1854, was fed on the milk of 17,913 cows

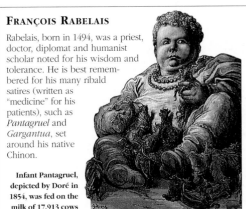

Château d'Azay-le-Rideau ⓫

Indre-et-Loire. 🚆 🚍 *Azay-le-Rideau.*
🔴 *02 47 45 42 04.* ⭕ *Apr–Sep daily;*
Oct–Mar Wed–Mon. ⚫ *Jan 1, May 1,*
Nov 1 & 11, Dec 25. 🖼️ ✅

Bᴀʟᴢᴀᴄ ᴄᴀʟʟᴇᴅ Azay-le-Rideau "a multifaceted diamond set in the Indre." It is the most beguiling and feminine of Loire châteaux, created in the early 16th century by Philippa Lesbahy, wife of François I's corrupt finance minister. Although Azay is superficially Gothic *(see pp50–51, 232)*, it clearly shows the transition to the Renaissance: the turrets are purely decorative and the moats are picturesque pools. Azay was a pleasure palace, lived in during fine weather and deserted in winter.

The interior is equally delightful – an airy, creaking mansion smelling faintly of cedarwood and full of lovingly re-created domestic detail. The first floor is furnished in the Renaissance style, with a fine example of a portable Spanish cabinet and exquisite tapestries. The ground floor has 19th-century furniture, dating from the period of the château's restoration. The four-story grand staircase is unusual for its time, being straight as opposed to spiral.

Wine-tasting opportunities in the village are a welcome reminder that vineyards are all around. Unlike most Loire villages, Azay is lively at night, thanks to the château's poetic *son et lumière.*

The Château de Villandry's *jardin d'ornement*

Château de Villandry ⓬

Indre-et-Loire. 🚆 *Tours, then taxi.* 🔴
02 47 50 02 09. ⭕ **Château:**
Feb–mid-Nov and Christmas hols:
daily. **Gardens:** *daily.* 🖼️ ✅
🏨 *Mar–Oct*

Vɪʟʟᴀɴᴅʀʏ was the last great Renaissance château built in the Loire Valley, a perfect example of 16th-century architecture. Its spectacular gardens were restored to their Renaissance splendor earlier this century by Dr. Joachim Carvallo, whose grandson continues his work unstintingly.

The result is a patchwork of sculpted shrubs and flowers on three levels: the kitchen garden *(jardin potager)*, the ornamental garden *(jardin d'ornement)* and, on the highest level, the water garden *(jardin d'eau)*. There are signs to explain the history and meaning behind each plant: the zucchini, for instance, symbolized fertility; the cabbage, sexual and spiritual corruption. Plants were also prized for their medicinal properties: cabbage helped to cure hangovers, while pimento aided digestion.

The delicate roots of the 52 kms (32 miles) of box hedge that outline and highlight each section mean that the whole 10 acres of gardens must be hand-weeded.

A *chocolatier* in Tours

Tours ⓭

Indre-et-Loire. 👥 *130,000.* ✈️ 🚆 🚍
ℹ️ *78 rue Bernard Palissy*
(02 47 70 37 37). 🛒 *Tue–Sun.*

Tᴏᴜʀs ɪs ᴛʜᴇ ᴍᴏsᴛ appealing of the major Loire cities, thanks to bourgeois prosperity, an intelligent restoration program and a lively university population. It is built on the site of a Roman town, and became an important center of Christianity in the 4th century under St. Martin, bishop of Tours. In 1461, Louis XI made the city the French capital, and it prospered on arms and fabrics. However, during Henri IV's reign the city lost favor with the monarchy, and the capital left Tours for Paris.

Bombarded by the Prussians in 1870, and bombed in World War II, Tours suffered extensive damage. By 1960, the middle classes had abandoned the historic center and

Château d'Azay-le-Rideau reflected in the river Indre

it became a slum, full of crumbling medieval masonry. Regeneration of the city has succeeded due to the popular policies of Jean Royer, mayor of Tours from 1958 to 1996.

The pedestrianized **place Plumereau** is Tours's most atmospheric quarter, set in the medieval heart of the city and full of cafés, boutiques and galleries. Streets such as rue Briçonnet reveal half-timbered façades, hidden courtyards and crooked towers. A gateway leads to place St-Pierre-le-Puellier, a square with sunken Gallo-Roman remains and a Romanesque church converted into a café. A few streets away in place de Châteauneuf lies the Romanesque **Tour Charlemagne**, all that remains of St. Martin's first church. West of here is the highly yuppified artisans' quarter, centered on the rue du Petit St-Martin.

The **Cathédrale St-Gatien**, in the eastern sector of the city, was begun in the early 13th century and completed in the 16th. Its Flamboyant Gothic façade is blackened and crumbling but still truly impressive, as are the medieval stained-glass windows.

The **Musée des Beaux Arts**, set in the former arch-

Cathédrale St-Gatien in Tours

bishop's palace nearby, over-looks Classical gardens and a giant cedar of Lebanon. Its star exhibits are *Christ in the Garden of Olives* and *The Resurrection* by Mantegna, and a room devoted to the modern artist Olivier Debré.

Further west is the **Eglise St-Julien**, whose Gothic monastic cells and chapter-house contain a small wine museum. The **Musée du Compagnonnage** next door displays works by master craftsmen of the guilds.

Across the Rue Nationale lies

the town's finest Renaissance building, the **Hôtel Goüin**. A former silk merchant's house, it is now the Touraine history museum, and contains fine Renaissance statuary.

Musée des Beaux Arts
18 place François Sicard. 02 47 05 68 73. Wed–Mon. some public hols.

Hôtel Goüin
25 rue du Commerce. 02 47 66 22 32. daily. Jan 1, Dec 25.

Environs
Just outside Céré la Ronde, on the D764 from Montrichard to Loches, lies the 15th-century **Château de Montpoupon** and its excellent Musée de la Chasse (open daily in summer; weekends only in winter).

Backgammon players in Tours' place Plumereau

TOURS TOWN CENTER

Cathédrale St-Gatien ⑤
Château Royal ④
Eglise St-Julien ③
Hôtel Goüin ②
Musée des Beaux Arts ⑥
Tour Charlemagne ①

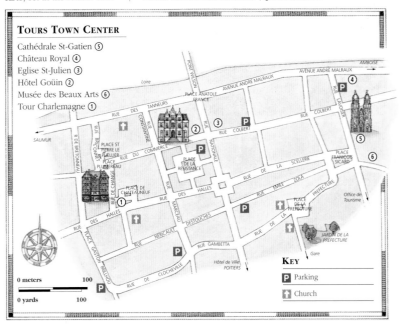

KEY

P Parking

✝ Church

0 meters 100
0 yards 100

Château de Chenonceau ⑰

A ROMANTIC PLEASURE PALACE, Chenonceau was created from the Renaissance onward by a series of aristocratic women. A magnificent avenue bordered by plane trees leads to symmetrical gardens and the serene vision that Flaubert praised as "floating on air and water." The château stretches across the Cher River with a 60-m (197-ft) gallery built over a series of arches, its elegant beauty reflected in the languid waters. The grandeur continues inside with splendidly furnished rooms, airy bedchambers and fine paintings and tapestries.

Turreted Pavilion
This was built between 1513 and 1521 by Catherine Briçonnet and her husband, Thomas Bohier, over the foundations of an old water mill.

Chapelle
The chapel has a vaulted ceiling and pilasters sculpted with acanthus leaves and cockleshells. The stained glass, destroyed by a bomb in 1944, was replaced in 1953.

Catherine de' Medici's Garden
Lavish court receptions and transvestite balls were held under Catherine's auspices.

TIMELINE

Catherine de' Medici

1533 Marriage of Catherine de' Medici (1519–89) to Henri II (1519–59). Chenonceau becomes a Loire royal palace

1559 Upon Henri's death, Catherine forces the disgraced Diane to accept the Château de Chaumont in exchange for Chenonceau

1789 Chenonceau is spared in the French Revolution thanks to Madame Dupin

1500	1600	1700	1800

1575 Louise de Lorraine (1554–1601) marries Henri III, Catherine's third and favorite son

1547 Henri II offers Chenonceau to Diane de Poitiers, his lifelong mistress

1512 Thomas Bohier acquires medieval Chenonceau. His wife, Catherine Briçonnet, rebuilds it in Renaissance style

1863 Madame Pelo restores the châtea its original

1730–99 Madame Dupin, a "farmer-general's" wife, makes Chenonceau a salon for writers and philosophers

The Creation of Chenonceau

THE WOMEN RESPONSIBLE for Chenonceau each left their mark. Catherine Briçonnet, wife of the first owner, built the turreted pavilion and one of the first straight staircases in France; Henri II's mistress, Diane de Poitiers, added the formal gardens and arched bridge over the river; Catherine de' Medici transformed the bridge into an Italian-style gallery (having evicted Diane following her husband's death in 1559); Louise de Lorraine, bereaved wife of Henri III, inherited the château in 1590 and painted the ceiling of her bedchamber black and white (the colors of royal mourning); Madame Dupin, a cultured 18th-century châtelaine, saved the château from destruction in the Revolution; and Madame Pelouze undertook a complete restoration in 1863.

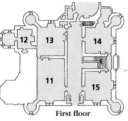

Ground floor   **First floor**

CHÂTEAU GUIDE

The main living area was in the square-shaped turreted pavilion in the middle of the Cher River. Four principal rooms open off the Vestibule on the ground floor: the Salle des Gardes and the Chambre de Diane de Poitiers, both hung with 16th-century Flemish tapestries; the Chambre de François I, with a Van Loo painting; and the Salon Louis XIV. On the first floor, reached via the Italianate staircase are other sumptuous apartments including the Chambre de Catherine de' Medici and the Chambre de Vendôme.

1   Vestibule
2   Salle des Gardes
3   Chapelle
4   Terrasse
5   Librairie de Catherine de' Medici
6   Cabinet Vert
7   Chambre de Diane de Poitiers
8   Grande Galerie
9   Chambre de François I
10 Salon Louis XIV
11 Chambre des Cinq Reines
12 Cabinet des Estampes
13 Chambre de Catherine de' Medici
14 Chambre de Vendôme
15 Chambre de Gabrielle d'Estrées

Grande Galerie
The elegant gallery crowning the bridge is Florentine in style, created by Catherine de' Medici from 1570–76.

1913 The château is bought by the Menier family, the *chocolatiers* who still own it today

1941 Chenonceau chapel is damaged in a bombing raid

Diane de Poitiers

Chambre de Catherine de' Medici

Vouvray ⓮

Indre-et-Loire. 🏠 *3,000.*
ℹ️ *(02 47 52 68 73/70 88
summer/winter).* 🛒 *Tue & Fri.*

JUST EAST OF TOURS is the village of Vouvray, home of the delicious white wine that Renaissance author Rabelais likened to taffeta.

Nothing has changed in the quality of Vouvray's wines. The star vineyard is **Huet** where, since 1990, grapes have been grown according to bio-dynamic methods: manual weeding, natural fertilizers, and no chemicals. In the preface to his novel *Quentin Durward*, Sir Walter Scott sang the praises of its dry white wines which are still to this day matured in chestnut barrels. Gaston Huet also hit the headlines in 1990 with his protests against the building of tracks for the TGV train over Vouvray vineyards. A French compromise was eventually reached, and tunnels were built under the hilly vineyards.

The **Château de Montcontour**, where monks first planted vines in the 4th century, has its own wine-making museum in the impressive 10th-century cellars hewn out of the tufa rock.

The medieval town of Loches

🌸 **Huet**
11–13 rue de la Croix-Buisée.
📞 *02 47 52 78 87.* 🕐 *Mon–Sat for wine tastings; cellar visits by reservation only.* ⚫ *public hols.*

⚜️ **Château de Moncontour**
Route de Rochecorbon. 📞 *02 47 52 60 77.* 🕐 *Apr–Nov: daily.* 🎟️ 🅿️
Visits can be followed by wine tastings.

Loches ⓯

Indre-et-Loire. 🏠 *7,000.* 🚆 🚌
ℹ️ *place de la Marne (02 47 91 82 82).*
🛒 *Wed & Sat.*

THIS UNSPOILED medieval town is slightly removed from the château trail in the Indre Valley. It is a backwater of late Gothic gateways and sculpted façades. Its keep (*donjon*) dominates the scene and boasts the deepest dungeons in the Loire. The Logis Royal is associated with Charles VII and his beautiful mistress Agnès Sorel. It is also where Joan of Arc, after her historic victory in Orléans, pleaded with Charles to go to Reims and be crowned. Anne of Brittany's chapel is decorated with ermines (her emblem) and contains a poignant alabaster effigy of Agnès Sorel.

⚜️ **Logis Royal de Loches**
📞 *02 47 59 01 32.* 🕐 *daily.* 🎟️ 🅿️

THE HEROINE OF FRANCE

Joan of Arc is the quintessential French national heroine, a virginal warrior, a woman martyr, a French figurehead. Her divinely led campaign to "drive the English out of France" during the Hundred Years' War has inspired plays, poetry and films from Voltaire to Cecil B. de Mille. Responding to heavenly voices, she appeared on the scene as champion of the dauphin, the uncrowned Charles VII. He faced an Anglo-Burgundian alliance that held most of northern France, and had escaped to the royal châteaux on the Loire.

Joan convinced him of the importance of her mission, mustered the French troops and in May 1429 led them to victory over the English at Orléans. She then urged the dithering Charles to go to Reims to be crowned. However, in 1430 she was captured and handed over to the English. Accused of witchcraft, she was burned at the stake in Rouen in 1431 at the age of 19. Her legendary bravery and tragic martyrdom led to her canonization in 1920.

Earliest known drawing of Joan of Arc (1429)

Portrait of Joan of Arc *in the Maison Jeanne d'Arc in Orléans (see p302). She saved the city from the English on May 8, 1429, a date the Orléannais still celebrate annually.*

Montrésor 🔟

Indre-et-Loire. 🚹 395. 🛈 *Grande Rue (02 47 92 70 71).*

Classed as one of "the most beautiful villages in France," Montrésor does not disappoint. It is set on the Indrois River, in the loveliest valley in Touraine. Once a fief of the Tours' cathedral, the village became a Polish enclave in the 1840s. In 1849 a Polish nobleman, Count Branicki, bought the 15th-century **Château**, built on the site of one of Foulques

Farm building and poppy fields near the village of Montrésor

Nerra's 11th-century fortifications. It has remained in the family ever since, its interior virtually unchanged.

♣ **Château de Montrésor**
📞 02 47 92 60 04. ◻ Apr–Oct: daily. 🈲 🎫 oblig. ♿ restricted.

Château de Chenonceau 🔟

See pp288–9.

Amboise 🔟

Indre-et-Loire. 🚹 12,000. 🚆 🚌 🛈 Quai du Général de Gaulle (02 47 57 01 37). 🛒 Fri & Sun.

Few buildings are more historically important than the **Château d'Amboise**. Louis XI lived here; Charles VIII was born and died here; François I was brought up here, as were Catherine de' Medici's 10 children. The château was also the setting for the 1560 Amboise Conspiracy an ill-fated Huguenot plot against François II. Visitors are shown the metal lacework balcony which served as a gibbet for 12 of the 1,200 conspirators who were put to death.

The **Tour des Minimes**, the château's original entrance, is

Amboise seen from the Loire

famous for its huge spiral ramp up which horsemen could ride to deliver provisions.

Perched on the ramparts is the Gothic **Chapelle St-Hubert**, believed to be Leonardo da Vinci's burial place. Under the patronage of François I, the artist spent the last years of his life in the nearby manor house of **Clos-Lucé**, whose cellars exhibit models of Leonardo's inventions constructed from his mechanical sketches.

♣ **Château d'Amboise**
📞 02 47 57 00 98. ◻ daily. ● Jan 1, Dec 25. 🈲 🎫
🏛 **Clos-Lucé**
2 rue de Clos-Lucé. 📞 02 47 57 62 88. ◻ daily. ● Jan 1, Dec 25. 🈲 ♿ restr.

A romantic heroine, Joan of Arc was a popular subject for artists. This painting of her is by François Léon Benouville (1821–59).

Burned at the stake – *a scene from* St. Joan, *Otto Preminger's 1957 epic film, which starred Jean Seberg.*

Château de Chambord ⓳

Henry James once said, "Chambord is truly royal – royal in its great scale, its grand air, and its indifference to common considerations." The Loire's largest residence, brainchild of the extravagant François I, began as a hunting lodge in the Forêt de Boulogne. In 1519 this was razed and the creation of present-day Chambord began, to a design probably initiated by Leonardo da Vinci. By 1537 the towers, keep and terraces had been completed by 1,800 men and three master masons. At one point, François suggested diverting the Loire to flow in front of his château, but he settled for redirecting the nearer Cosson instead. His son Henry II continued his work, and Louis XIV completed the 440-roomed edifice in 1685.

The Château de Chambord with the Cosson River, a tributary of the Loire, in the foreground

The Salamander
François I chose the salamander as his enigmatic emblem. It appears over 800 times throughout the château.

The chapel was begun by François I shortly before his death in 1547. Henri II added the second story and Louis XIV the roof.

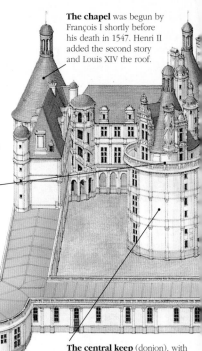

★ **Roof Terraces**
This skyline of delicate cupolas has been likened to a miniature Oriental town. The roof terraces include a forest of elongated chimneys, miniature spires, shell-shaped domes and richly sculpted gables.

The central keep (donjon), with its four circular towers, forms the nucleus of the château.

STAR FEATURES

★ **Roof Terraces**

★ **Vaulted Guardrooms**

★ **Grand Staircase**

TIMELINE

1519–47 The Count of Blois' hunting lodge demolished by François I and the château created

1547–59 Henri II adds the west wing and second story of the chapel

1725–33 Inhabited by Stanislas Leczinski, exiled king of Poland who was made duke of Lorraine

1748 The Maréchal de Saxe acquires Chambord. On his death two years later, the château yet again falls into decline

1500	1600	1700	1800	1900

1547 Death of François I

1669–85 Louis XIV completes the building, then abandons it

1670 Molière's *Le Bourgeois Gentilhomme* staged at Chambord

1840 Chambord declared a *Monument Historique*

1970s Chambord is restored and refurnished, and the moats re-dug

★ **Vaulted Guardrooms**
Arranged in the form of a Greek cross around the Grand Staircase, the vaulted guardrooms were once the setting for royal balls and plays. Their ceilings are decorated with François I's initials and salamander motif.

VISITORS' CHECKLIST

🚃 *Blois, then taxi or bus.* 📞 *02 54 50 40 00.* 🕐 *9am–6:15pm daily (Jul–Aug: 6:45pm; Nov–Mar: 5:15pm).* ⬤ *Jan 1, May 1, Dec 25. Musée de la Chasse in château. Son et Lumière: Apr–Sep.* 🖼️ 🍴 W *www.chambord.org*

The lantern tower is 32 m (105 ft) high. Surmounting the terrace, it is supported by arched buttresses and crowned by a fleur-de-lys.

François I's Bedchamber is where the king, hurt by a failed romance, scratched a message on a pane of glass: "*Souvent femme varie, bien fol est qui s'y fie.*" (Every woman is fickle, he who trusts one is a fool.)

Cabinet de François I
The king's barrel-vaulted study (cabinet) in the outer north tower was turned into an oratory in the 18th century by Queen Catherine Opalinska, wife of Stanislas Leczinski (Louis XV's father-in-law).

★ **Grand Staircase**
This innovative double-helix staircase was supposedly designed by Leonardo da Vinci. It ensures that the person going up and the person going down cannot meet.

Louis XIV's Bedchamber
Louis XIV's bedchamber lies within the Sun King's state apartments, the grandest quarters in the château.

Blois's Cathédrale St-Louis and Hôtel de Ville seen from across the Loire

Blois ⑳

Loir-et-Cher. 🏠 59,000. 🚍 🚉
ℹ *Voûte du Château (02 54 90 41
41).*🚌 *Tue, Thu, & Sat (Jul & Aug:
Thu pm, in period dress).*

ONCE A FIEF of the counts of
Blois, the town rose to
prominence as a royal domain
in the 15th century, retaining
its historic façades and refined
atmosphere to this day. Architectural interest abounds in
Vieux Blois, the hilly, partially
pedestrianized quarter enclosed
by the château, cathedral and
river. Four well-signposted
walking tours act as a gentle
introduction to the noble
mansions and romantic
courtyards that grace the
Loire's most beguiling town.

Set back from the north
bank of the river, the **Château
de Blois** was the principal
royal residence until Henri IV
moved the court to Paris in
1598 – Louis XIV's creation
of Versailles *(see pp164–7)*
was to mark the final eclipse
of Blois. The château's four
contrasting wings make a har-

monious whole. The Salle des
Etats Generaux, the only part
of the building surviving from
the 13th century, housed the
council and court, and is the
largest and best-preserved
Gothic hall in the France. The
adjoining late 15th-century
Louis XII wing infuses Gothic
design with Renaissance spirit,
sealed with the king's porcupine symbol and motto.

The 16th-century François I
wing is a masterpiece of the
French Renaissance, containing
a monumental spiral staircase
in an octagonal tower. By
contrast, the 17th-century
Gaston d'Orléans wing is a
model of Classical sobriety.

Blois is authentically furnished and hung with
paintings portraying its
troubled past. These include a
graphic portrayal of
the murder of the
Duc de Guise in
1588. Suspected of
head- ing a Catholic
plot against Henri
III, he was
stabbed to death
by guards in the

King Louis XII's porcupine symbol

king's chamber. The most
intriguing room is Catherine
de' Medici's study where, of
the 237 carved wooden wall
panels, 4 are secret cabinets
said to have stored her poisons.

François I Staircase
*Built between 1515 and
1524, this octagonal
staircase is a master-
piece of the
early French
Renaissance.*

The gallery
provided an
ideal setting
for viewing
jousts and re-
ceptions held
in the inner
courtyard.

**François I's
salamander
motif** adorns
the openwork
balustrades.

The staircase
within the
tower slopes
appreciably
more steeply
than the
balustrades.

Louis XII wing of the Château de Blois

Dominating the eastern sector of the city, the **Cathédrale St-Louis** is a 17th-century reconstruction of a Gothic church that was almost completely destroyed by a hurricane in 1678. Behind the cathedral the former bishop's palace, built in 1700, is the **Hôtel de Ville** (town hall). The surrounding terraced gardens have lovely views over the city and river. Opposite the cathedral is the **Maison des Acrobates**, carved with characters from medieval farces including acrobats and jugglers.

Place Louis-XII, the marketplace, is overlooked by splendid 17th-century façades, balconies and half-timbered houses.

Rue Pierre de Blois, a quaint alley straddled by a Gothic passageway, winds downhill to the medieval Jewish ghetto. The Rue des Juifs boasts several distinguished *hôtels particuliers* (mansions), including the galleried **Hôtel de Condé**, with its Renaissance archway and courtyard, and the **Hôtel Jassaud**, with magnificent 16th-century bas-reliefs above the main doorway. On the rue du Puits-Châtel, also rich in Renaissance mansions, is the galleried **Hôtel Sardini**, once owned by wealthy Renaissance bankers.

Place Vauvert is the most charming square in Vieux Blois, with a fine example of a half-timbered house.

⛪ **Château de Blois**
📞 02 54 90 33 33. ⭘ *daily (call to check).* ⬤ *Jan 1, Dec 25* 🖼 🎫

Covered Gothic passageway in rue Pierre de Blois

The nave of the abbey church of Notre-Dame in Beaugency

Beaugency ㉑

Loiret. 👥 *7,300.* 🚂 🚌 🛈 *3 pl de Docteur-Hyvernaud (02 38 44 54 42).* 🛒 *Sat.*

Beaugency has long been the eastern gateway to the Loire. This compact medieval town makes a peaceful base for exploring the Orléanais region. Exceptionally for the Loire, it is possible to walk along the riverbanks and stone *levées*. At quai de l'Abbaye there is a good view of the 11th-century bridge, which, until modern times, was the only crossing point between Blois and Orléans. An obvious target for enemy attack, it was captured four times by the English during the Hundred Years' War before being retaken by Joan of Arc in 1429.

The center of town is dominated by a ruined 11th-century watchtower. It stands on **place St-Firmin**, along with a 16th-century bell tower (the church was destroyed in the Revolution) and a statue of Joan of Arc.

Period houses line the square. Further down is the **Château Dunois**, built on the site of the feudal castle by one of Joan of Arc's *compagnon d'armes*. Its regional museum features an array of costumes, furniture, and antique toys. Facing the Château Dunois is **Notre-Dame**, a Romanesque abbey church that witnessed the annulment of the marriage between Eleanor of Aquitaine and Louis VII in 1152, leaving Eleanor free to marry the future Henry II of England.

Nearby is the medieval clock tower in Rue du Change and the Renaissance **Hôtel de Ville**, with its façade adorned with the town's arms. Equally charming is the nearby ancient mill district, around the Rue du Pont and the Rue du Rü, with its streams and riot of flowers.

⛪ **Château Dunois (Musée Daniel Vannier)**
Place Dunois. 📞 02 38 44 55 23. ⭘ *Wed–Mon (call first).* ⬤ *Jan 1, May 1, Dec 25.* 🖼 🎫 *oblig.*

Châteaux Tour of the Sologne

The mysterious Sologne is a secretive landscape of woods and marshes edged by vineyards. Wine-lovers can indulge in tastings of Loire Valley wines, accompanied, in season, by a dinner of succulent wild game from the region's forests, popular hunting grounds for centuries. The Sologne is a hunter's paradise and devotees of the sport can see today's hounds, as well as hunting trophies of the past.

This ambling rural route takes in some of the Loire's most varied châteaux. The five on this tour – for which a couple of days is required – represent a delightful encapsulation of regional architecture. All styles are here, from feudal might to Renaissance grace and Classical elegance. Several are inhabited but can still be visited.

Château de Beauregard ②
Beauregard was built around 1520 as a hunting lodge for François I. It contains a gallery with 327 portraits of royalty.

Château de Chaumont ①
Chaumont is a feudal castle with Renaissance embellishments and lofty views over the Loire River (*see p232*).

N152   D751
← AMBOISE
D764
Pontlevoy

```
0 kilometers        5
0 miles             5
```

KEY

▬▬ Tour route

══ Other roads

Vendôme ㉒

Loir-et-Cher. 🏛 18,500. 🚉 🚌
ℹ *Hôtel du Saillant (02 54 77 05 07).* 🛒 *Fri & Sun.*

Once an important stop for pilgrims en route to Compostela in Spain, Vendôme is still popular with modern pilgrims, thanks to the TGV rail service. Though a desirable address with Parisian commuters, the town still manages to retain its provincial charm. Vendôme's old stone buildings are encircled by the Loir River, its lush gardens and chic restaurants reflected in the water.

The town's greatest monument is the abbey church of **La Trinité**, founded in 1034. Its Romanesque bell tower (all that remains of the original structure) is overshadowed by the church portal, a masterpiece of Flamboyant Gothic tracery. The interior is embellished with Romanesque capitals and 15th-century choir stalls.

Commanding a rocky spur high above the Loir is the ruined **château**, built by the counts of Vendôme in the 13th–14th centuries. Down below, rowboats may be rented for gently exploring the meandering backwaters of the Loir, past a medieval *lavoir*, elegant buildings, and a plane tree planted in 1759.

Vendôme's native son Rochambeau, hero of the American Revolution

The Loir ㉓

Loir-et-Cher. 🚉 Tours. 🚌 Vendôme
🚌 Montoire-sur-le-Loir. ℹ *Montoire-sur-Loir (02 54 85 23 30).*

Compared with the royal Loire River, the tranquil Loir to the north has a more rural charm. The stretch between Vendôme and Trôo is the most rewarding, offering troglodyte caves (*see p282*), walking trails, wine tasting, fishing and boat trips.

Les Roches-l'Evêque is a fortified village with cave dwellings visible in the cliffs. Just downstream is **Lavardin**, with its Romanesque church, half-timbered houses, Gothic bridge and ruined château ringed by ramparts. In **Montoire-sur-le-Loir**, the Chapelle St-Gilles, a former leper colony, has Romanesque frescoes. **Trôo**, the next major village, is known for its Romanesque Eglise de St-Martin and a labyrinth of troglodyte dwellings.

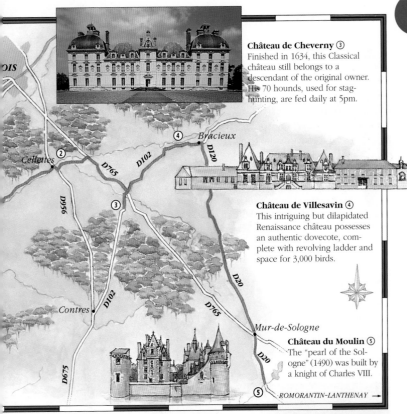

Château de Cheverny ③
Finished in 1634, this Classical château still belongs to a descendant of the original owner. His 70 hounds, used for stag-hunting, are fed daily at 5pm.

Bracieux

Cellettes ②

Château de Villesavin ④
This intriguing but dilapidated Renaissance château possesses an authentic dovecote, complete with revolving ladder and space for 3,000 birds.

Contres

Mur-de-Sologne

Château du Moulin ⑤
The "pearl of the Sologne" (1490) was built by a knight of Charles VIII.

ROMORANTIN-LANTHENAY →

St-Jacques-des-Guérets, facing the village of Trôo, has a frescoed Romanesque chapel, as does **Poncé-sur-le-Loir**, farther downstream. On the slopes are vineyards producing Jasnières and Côteaux du Vendômois. Wine tastings enliven sleepy **Poncé** and **La Chartre-sur-le-Loir**. The cliffs on the opposite bank are studded with caves, commonly used as wine cellars.

Northward, the **Forêt de Bercé** abounds with paths and streams, while to the west the small town of **Le Lude** sits on the south bank of the Loir, dominated by its romantic 15th-century château with formal gardens and fountains.

Some 20 km (12 miles) west of Le Lude lies the town of **La Flèche**, whose main attraction is the Prytanée Nationale Militaire, originally a Jesuit college founded by Henri IV in 1603. Philosopher René Descartes was one of the college's earliest and most illustrious pupils.

Chartres ㉔

Eure-et-Loir. 👥 42,000. 🚉 🚌
🛈 pl de la Cathédrale (02 37 18 26 26). 🛒 Sat.

CHARTRES MAY have the greatest Gothic cathedral in Europe (*see pp298–301*), but the town's churches should not be ignored. The Benedictine abbey church of **St-Pierre** has lovely medieval stained-glass windows, while **St-Aignan**, with its painted interior, abuts 9th-century ramparts. By the river is the Romanesque **Eglise de St-André**, a deconsecrated church used for art exhibitions and concerts. The **Musée des Beaux Arts**, in the former episcopal palace, offers a fine collection of 17th- and 18th-century furniture, Renaissance enamels and paintings by Vlaminck.

As one of the first urban conservation sites in France, Chartres is a success story. Quirky half-timbered houses

One of the many washhouses along the Eure River

abound along cobbled streets such as the rue des Ecuyers. Steep staircases known as *tertres* lead down to the Eure River, providing views of mills, humpback stone bridges, washhouses and the cathedral.

In the Grenier de Loens, next to the cathedral, is the Centre International du Vitraux. The building's 13th-century vaulted storerooms are also used for temporary exhibitions.

🏛 Musée des Beaux Arts
29 cloître Notre-Dame. 📞 02 37 36 41 39. ◯ Wed–Mon. ● Sun am, and some public hols. 📷 📹

Chartres Cathedral

ACCORDING TO ART HISTORIAN Emile Male, "Chartres is the mind of the Middle Ages manifest." Begun in 1020, the Romanesque cathedral was destroyed by fire in 1194. Only the north and south towers, south steeple, west portal and crypt remained; the sacred *Veil of the Virgin* relic was the sole treasure to survive. Peasant and lord alike helped to rebuild the church in just 25 years. Few alterations were made after 1250 and, fortunately, Chartres was unscathed by the Wars of Religion and the French Revolution. The result is a Gothic cathedral with a true "Bible in stone" reputation.

Part of the Vendôme Window

Elongated Statues
These statues on the Royal Portal represent Old Testament figures.

The taller of the two spires dates from the start of the 16th century. Flamboyant Gothic in style, it contrasts sharply with the solemnity of its Romanesque counterpart.

STAR FEATURES

★ **Stained-Glass Windows**

★ **South Porch**

★ **Royal Portal**

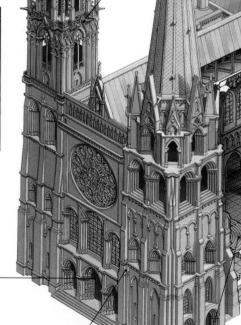

Gothic Nave
As wide as the Romanesque crypt below it, the nave reaches a lofty height of 37 m (121 ft).

★ Royal Portal
The central tympanum of the Royal Portal (1145–55) shows Christ in Majesty.

The lower half of the west front is a survivor of the original Romanesque church, the portal dating from the mid-12th century.

Labyrinth

THE LABYRINTH

The 13th-century labyrinth, inlaid in the nave floor, was a feature of most medieval cathedrals. As a penance, pilgrims used to follow the tortuous route on their knees, echoing the Way of the Cross. The journey of 262 m (851 ft), around 11 bands of broken concentric circles, took at least one hour to complete.

VISITORS' CHECKLIST

Pl de la Cathédrale. 02 37 21 75 02. 7:30am–7:15pm Mon–Sat; 8am Sun & publ hols. 9am Tue & Fri; 11:45am & 6:15pm Mon–Sat (6pm Sat); 9:15am (in Latin), 11am, 6pm Sun. W www.cathedrale-chartres.com

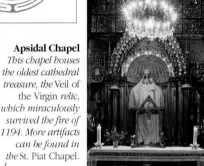

Apsidal Chapel
This chapel houses the oldest cathedral treasure, the Veil of the Virgin relic, which miraculously survived the fire of 1194. More artifacts can be found in the St. Piat Chapel.

Vaulted Ceiling
A network of ribs supports the vaulted ceiling.

★ Stained-Glass Windows
The windows cover a surface area of over 2,600 sq m (28,000 sq ft).

★ South Porch
Sculpture on the South Porch (1197–1209) reflects New Testament teaching.

The Crypt
This is the largest crypt in France, most of it dating from the early 11th century. It comprises two parallel galleries, a series of chapels and the 9th-century St. Lubin's vault.

The Stained Glass of Chartres

DONATED BY royalty, aristocracy and the merchant brotherhoods between 1210 and 1240, this glorious collection of stained glass is world-renowned. Over 150 windows illustrate biblical stories and daily life in the 13th century. During both World Wars the windows were dismantled piece by piece and removed for safety. There is an on-going program, begun in the 1970s, to restore the windows in the cathedral.

Stained glass above the apse

Redemption Window
Six scenes illustrate Christ's Passion *and death on the* Cross (c.1210).

★ Tree of Jesse
This 12th-century stained glass shows Christ's genealogy. The tree rises up from Jesse, father of David, at the bottom, to Christ enthroned at the top.

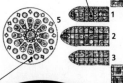

★ West Rose Window
This window (1215), with Christ seated in the center, shows the Last Judgment.

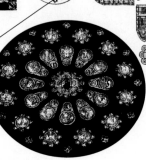

KEY

1 Tree of Jesse	**12** Noah	**22** St. Anthony and St. Paul	**33** St. Theodore and St. Vincent
2 Incarnation	**13** St. John the Evangelist	**23** Blue Virgin	**34** St. Stephen
3 Passion and Resurrection	**14** Mary Magdalene	**24** Life of the Virgin	**35** St. Cheron
4 North Rose Window	**15** Good Samaritan and Adam and Eve	**25** Zodiac Window	**36** St. Thomas
5 West Rose Window	**16** Assumption	**26** St. Martin	**37** Peace Window
6 South Rose Window	**17** Vendôme Chapel Windows	**27** St. Thomas à Becket	**38** Modern Window
7 Redemption Window	**18** Miracles of Mary	**28** St. Margaret and St. Catherine	**39** Prodigal Son
8 St. Nicholas	**19** St. Apollinaris	**29** St. Nicholas	**40** Ezekiel and David
9 Joseph	**20** Modern Window	**30** St. Remy	**41** Aaron
10 St. Eustache	**21** St. Fulbert	**31** St. James the Greater	**42** Virgin and Child
11 St. Lubin		**32** Charlemagne	**43** Isaiah and Moses
			44 Daniel and Jeremiah

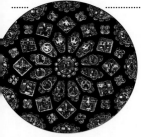

North Rose Window
This depicts the Glorification of the Virgin, *surrounded by the kings of Judah and the prophets (c.1230).*

4

GUIDE TO READING THE WINDOWS

Each window is divided into panels, which are usually read from left to right, bottom to top (earth to heaven). The number of figures or abstract shapes used is thought to be symbolic: three stands for the Church, while the number four symbolizes the material world or the four elements.

Mary and Child in the sacred mandorla (c.1150)

Two angels doing homage before the celestial throne

Christ's triumphal entry into Jerusalem on Palm Sunday

Upper panels of the Incarnation Window

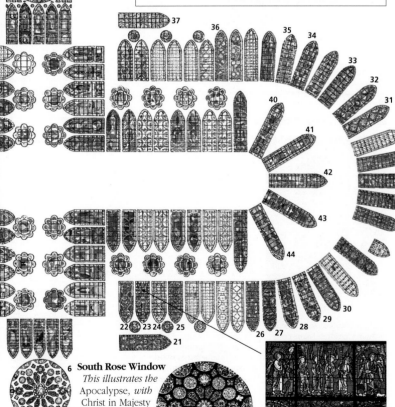

37
36
35
34
33
32
31
40
41
42
43
44
30
29
28
27
26
25 24 23 22
21

6 **South Rose Window**
This illustrates the Apocalypse, *with* Christ in Majesty *(c.1225).*

★ **Blue Virgin Window**
The window's bottom panel depicts the conversion of water into wine by Christ at The Marriage at Cana.

STAR WINDOWS

★ **West Rose Window**

★ **Tree of Jesse**

★ **Blue Virgin Window**

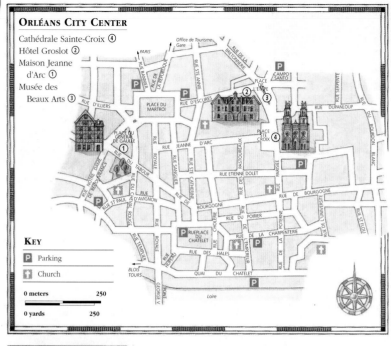

ORLÉANS CITY CENTER

Cathédrale Sainte-Croix ④
Hôtel Groslot ②
Maison Jeanne
    d'Arc ①
Musée des
    Beaux Arts ③

KEY

P Parking

† Church

0 meters   250
0 yards   250

Orléans' Cathédrale Sainte-Croix

Orléans ㉕

Loiret. 👥 113,000. ✈ 🚆 🚌
ℹ 6 rue Albert 1er (02 38 24 05 05).
🗓 Tue–Sun.

O RLEANS' dazzling new
    bridge symbolizes the
city's increasing importance at
the geographic heart of both
France and Europe.

As a tourist, however, one is
struck by the city's continued
attachment to its past, most
particularly to Joan of Arc. It
was from here that the Maid

of Orléans saved France from
the English in 1429 *(see p290)*.
Since her martyrdom at
Rouen in 1431, Joan remains
a presence in Orléans. Every
April 29 and May 1, 7–8 her
liberation of the city is re-
enacted in a pageant and a
blessing in the cathedral.

Orléans' historic center was
badly damaged in World War
II, but much has been reconstructed, and a faded grandeur
lingers in Vieil Orléans, the
quarter bounded by the cathedral, the river Loire and the
Place du Martroi. The latter,
a Classical but rather windswept
square, has an equestrian statue
of the city's heroine. Nearby,
the half-timbered **Maison
Jeanne d'Arc** was rebuilt
from period dwellings in 1961
on the site where Joan lodged
in 1429. Inside are audio-
visual re-creations of her life.

From Place du Martroi, the
Rue d'Escures leads past
Renaissance mansions to the
cathedral. **Hôtel Groslot** is the
grandest, a 16th-century red-
brick mansion where kings
Charles IX, Henri III and Henri
IV all stayed. The 17-year-old
François II died here in 1560
after attending a meeting of

the Etats Généraux with his
child-bride, Mary, later Queen
of Scots. The building served
as Orléans' town hall from
1790 to 1982, and the sumptuously decorated interior,
with its Joan memorabilia, is
still used for marriages and
official ceremonies.

Virtually opposite the Hôtel
Groslot and alongside the new
town hall is the **Musée des
Beaux Arts**, displaying European works of art from the
16th to the 20th centuries.

The **Cathédrale Sainte-
Croix** nearby is an imposing
edifice that was begun in the
late 13th century, destroyed by
the Huguenots (Protestants) in
1568, and then rebuilt in supposedly Gothic style between
the 17th and 19th centuries.

🏛 **Hôtel Groslot**
Place de l'Etape. 📞 02 38 79 22 30.
◯ daily. ● sporadically.

🏛 **Musée des Beaux Arts**
Place Ste-Croix. 📞 02 38 79 21 55.
◯ Tue–Sat & Sun pm. ● Jan 1, May
1, Nov 1, Dec 25. 🎫 &

🏛 **Maison Jeanne d'Arc**
3 place du Général de Gaulle. 📞 02 38
52 99 89. ◯ Tue–Sun. ● Jan 1, May
1 & 8, Nov 1, Dec 25; Nov–Apr: ams.
🎫 🎫

Joan of Arc stained-glass window in Orléans' Cathédrale Sainte-Croix

St-Benoît-sur-Loire ㉖

Loiret. 👥 1,876. 🚉 ℹ️ *44 rue Orléannais (02 38 35 79 00).*

SITUATED ALONG the river Loire between Orléans and Gien, St-Benoît-sur-Loire boasts one of the finest Romanesque abbey churches in France, constructed between 1067 and 1108. It is all that survives of an important monastery founded in AD 650 and named after St. Benedict, patron saint of Europe. His relics were transported from Italy at the end of the 7th century.

The church's belfry porch is graced with carved capitals depicting biblical scenes. The nave is tall and light, and the choir floor is an amazing patchwork of Italian marble. Daily services with Gregorian chant are open to the public.

Bourges ㉗

Cher. 👥 76,000. ✈️ 🚉 🚌
ℹ️ *21 rue Victor Hugo (02 48 23 02 60).* 🎭 *Tue–Sun.*

THIS GALLO-ROMAN city retains its original walls but is best known as the city of Jacques Coeur, financier and foreign minister to Charles VII. The greatest merchant of the Middle Ages and a self-made man *par excellence*, it was in his capacity as an arms dealer that he established a tradition maintained for four centuries, as Napoléon III had cannons manufactured here in 1862.

Built over part of the walls, the **Palais Jacques Coeur** is a Gothic gem and a lasting memorial to its first master. It was finished in 1453, and incorporates Coeur's two emblems, scallop shells and hearts, as well as his punning family motto: *"A vaillan coeur, rien impossible"* – to the valiant heart, nothing is impossible. The obligatory tour reveals a barrel-vaulted gallery, a painted chapel and a chamber that housed Turkish baths.

Bourges also flourishes as a university town and cultural mecca, renowned for its spring festival of music.

Rue Bourbonnoux leads to **St-Etienne**, the widest Gothic cathedral in France and the one most similar to Paris's Notre-Dame. The west façade has five sculpted portals, the central one depicting an

Stained-glass window in the Cathédrale St-Etienne

enthralling *Last Judgment*. In the choir are vivid 13th-century stained-glass windows presented by the guilds. The crypt holds the marble tomb of the 14th-century Duc de Berry, best known for commissioning the illuminated manuscript the *Très Riches Heures (see pp194–5).* From the top of the north tower stretch views of the beautifully restored medieval quarter and the marshes beyond. Beside the cathedral is a magnificent tithe barn and the remains of the Gallo-Roman ramparts.

The **Jardin des Prés Fichaux**, set along the river Yèvre, contains pools, parterres and an open-air theater. On the northern edge of town lie the **Marais de Bourges**, where market gardeners transport their produce by flat-bottomed boat.

Statue of Jacques Coeur

⚜️ **Palais Jacques Coeur**
Rue Jacques Coeur. 📞 *02 48 24 06 87.*
🕐 *daily.* ⬤ *Jan 1, May 1, Nov 1 & 11, Dec 25.* 🚫 🎫

Environs
About 35 km (22 miles) south of Bourges in the Berry region is the **Abbaye de Noirlac**. Founded in 1136, it is one of the best-preserved Cistercian abbeys in France.

Statue in the Jardin des Prés Fichaux

CENTRAL FRANCE
AND THE ALPS

Introducing Central France and the Alps

THE GEOLOGICAL CONTRASTS of this region reflect its enormous variety, from the industrial and gastronomic metropolis of Lyon to the largely agricultural landscape of Burgundy. The mountains of the Massif Central and the Alps attract visitors for winter sports, superb walking and other outdoor activities. The major sights of this richly rewarding area, both natural and architectural, are shown here.

Basilique Ste-Madeleine, the famous pilgrimage church crowning the hilltop village of Vézelay, is a masterpiece of Burgundian Romanesque. It is renowned for its vividly decorated tympanum and capitals (see pp326–7).

The Abbaye de Ste-Foy in the village of Conques (see pp356–7) is one of the great pilgrimage churches of France, with a fabulous treasury of medieval and Renaissance gold reliquaries.

THE MASSIF CENTRAL
(See pp342–61)

Abbaye de Ste-Foy, Conques

The Gorges du Tarn have some of France's most spectacular natural scenery. The road which follows the plunging course of the Tarn River gives dramatic viewing points along the canyon and across the limestone Causses (see pp360–61).

The Abbaye de Fontenay, *founded by Saint Bernard in the early 12th century, is the oldest Cistercian monastery in France (see pp322–3). This well-preserved Romanesque abbey is a perfect testimony to the severe ideal of the Cistercian life.*

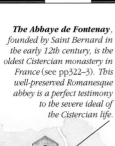

eleine, elay

Abbaye de Fontenay

Palais des Ducs, Dijon

Théâtre Romain, Autun

BURGUNDY AND FRANCHE-COMTE
(See pp316–41)

Brou Abbey Church,
Bourg-en-Bresse

Mont Blanc

Temple d'Auguste
et Livie, Vienne

THE RHONE VALLEY AND FRENCH ALPS
(See pp362–81)

Palais Idéal du Facteur
Cheval, Hauterives

Le Puy

Gorges du Tarn

0 kilometers	50
0 miles	50

Regional Food: Central France

Renowned FOR ITS gastronomic tradition, Lyon is the place to savor Lyonnais and Burgundian food at its best – its old streets are packed with high quality yet modestly priced small restaurants, called *bouchons* or *mères*. This eminent culinary flair is complemented by the wealth of fine local produce: the famed chicken from Bresse; prime lean beef from Charolais; ham from the Morvan hills; wild fowl and frogs from the marshes of the Dombes; fish from the Saône and the Rhône; and snails known as the "oysters of Burgundy." Franche-Comté and the Jura contribute to the regional repertoire with smoked sausages, farmhouse cheeses, walnut oil, and fish from glacier-fed lakes. In the Auvergne, regional fare features salted hams, pork, cheeses, potatoes, cabbage and lentils.

Oeufs en meurette *is a famous Burgundian dish of eggs poached in a red wine sauce with onions, mushrooms and bacon.*

Pain d'epices

Dijon mustard owes *its distinctive flavor to the combination of high quality mustard seeds, local wine, and* verjus *(the juice of unripe grapes). A staple condiment in French households, the smooth and coarse-grained varieties are also used in cooking.*

Coarse-grained Dijon mustard

Smooth Dijon mustard

Rosette de Lyon *is the most famous of Lyon sausages. It is made of meat from leg of pork and served in thin slices.*

Bacon

Mushrooms

Escargots à la Bourguignonne *are snails served with parsley and garlic butter. Small tongs are used to pluck the snails out of the shells.*

Beef

Wine sauce

Boeuf bourguignon, *the famous classic stew, is more refined than many other French stews. Burgundians prefer to use cuts of beef from Charolais cattle. The marinated meat is cooked slowly in Burgundy or Beaujolais wine until tender. Cubes of lardons, baby onions and mushrooms are then added.*

Falette *(stuffed mutton breast) is a specialty from the Auvergne. It can be served hot with braised cabbage or haricot beans.*

Minute steak Dijonnaise *is steak served in a cream and mustard sauce. Veal, rabbit and pork are also served in this way.*

Bresse chicken, *the appellation contrôlée chicken, is delicious served with a creamy sauce and wild morels.*

Andouillettes à la Lyonnaise *are tripe sausages stuffed with veal. Served with fried onions, they are typically Lyonnaise.*

Salt pork with lentils, *a specialty of the Auvergne, is salt-cured pork poached in wine with tiny green Puy lentils.*

Walnut and pear pie *is a double-crusted pie made with ground walnut pastry and filled with sliced pears.*

Cherry flan or clafoutis *is made with dark cherries covered in a batterlike dough and laced with kirsch, a cherry liqueur.*

CHEESES

Central France produces the richest selection of cheeses in France. These range from soft, tangy, brandy-soaked Epoisses from Burgundy and the Swiss-type cheeses of the Alps, used in fondue, to cheddarlike Cantal and blue-veined cheeses such as Roquefort.

Burgundy cheeses

Epoisses

Pipo Crem'

Bleu de Bresse

Alpine cheeses

Tomme au raisin

Raclette

Emmenthal Français

Vacherin

Massif Central cheeses

St-Nectaire

Roquefort

Fourme d'Ambert

Cantal

France's Wine Regions: Burgundy

Grape-picker's basket

Burgundy and its fine wines have inspired awe for centuries. The fame of the region's wines spread throughout Europe in the 14th century, under the Valois Dukes of Burgundy. After the French Revolution, Napoleonic laws of equal inheritance split vineyards into tiny fractions, resulting in a bewildering number of *appellations*. Even today, the classification system remains dauntingly complex. But despite its impenetrable image, this is must-see territory for the "serious" wine lover, with its rich vinous history and tradition and dazzling *grands crus*.

LOCATOR MAP

◻ *Burgundy wine region*

Clos de Vougeot on the Côte de Nuits

WINE REGIONS

Between Chablis in the north and the Côte Chalonnaise and Mâconnais in the south is the Côte d'Or, incorporating Côte de Nuits and Côte de Beaune. The Beaujolais region *(see pp366–7)* lies below Mâcon.

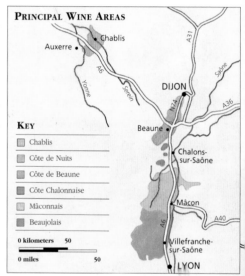

PRINCIPAL WINE AREAS

Chablis
Auxerre ●

DIJON

KEY

◻ Chablis
◻ Côte de Nuits
◻ Côte de Beaune
◻ Côte Chalonnaise
◻ Mâconnais
◻ Beaujolais

Beaune ●

Chalons-sur-Saône

Mâcon

0 kilometers   50

0 miles   50

Villefranche-sur-Saône

LYON

KEY FACTS ABOUT BURGUNDY

Location and Climate
The continental climate (bleak winters and hot summers) can be very variable, making vintages a crucial quality factor. The best vineyards have chalky soil and face south or east.

Grape Varieties
Burgundy is at least relatively simple in its grape varieties. Red Burgundy is made from **Pinot Noir**, with its sweet flavors of raspberries, cherries and strawberries, while the **Gamay** makes red Mâcon and Beaujolais. **Chardonnay** is the principal white variety for Chablis and white Burgundy, though small amounts of **Aligoté** and **Pinot Blanc** are grown and the **Sauvignon** is a specialty of St. Bris.

Good Producers
White Burgundy: Jean-Marie Raveneau, René Dauvissat, La Chablisienne, Comtes Lafon, Guy Roulot, Etienne Sauzet, Pierre Morey, Louis Carillon, Jean-Marc Boillot, André Ramonet, Hubert Lamy, Jean-Marie Guffens-Heynen, Olivier Merlin, Louis Latour, Louis Jadot, Olivier Leflaive.
Red Burgundy: Denis Bachelet, Daniel Rion, Domaine Dujac, Armand Rousseau, Joseph Roty, De Montille, Domaine de la Pousse d'Or, Domaine de l'Arlot, Jean-Jacques Confuron, Robert Chevillon, Georges Roumier, Leroy, Drouhin.

Good Vintages
(Reds) 1996, 1993, 1990, 1988.
(Whites) 1996, 1995, 1992, 1989.

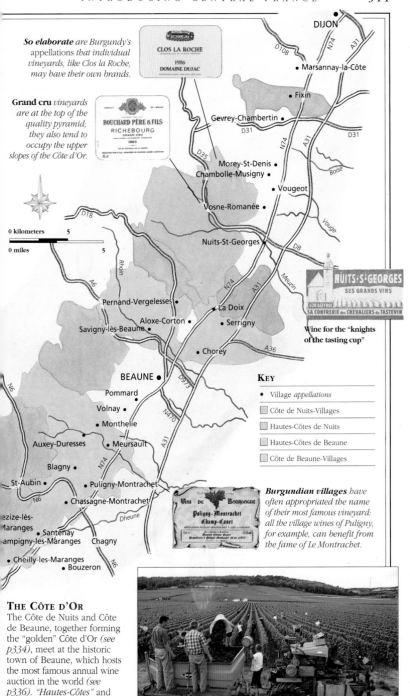

So elaborate are Burgundy's appellations *that individual vineyards, like Clos la Roche, may have their own brands.*

CLOS LA ROCHE
1986
DOMAINE DUJAC

Grand cru *vineyards are at the top of the quality pyramid; they also tend to occupy the upper slopes of the Côte d'Or.*

BOUCHARD PÈRE & FILS
RICHEBOURG
GRAND CRU
1985

DIJON

D108
N74
A31

Marsannay-la-Côte

Fixin

Gevrey-Chambertin
D31
N74
A31
D31

Boise

Morey-St-Denis
Chambolle-Musigny

Vougeot

Vosne-Romanée

Vouge

Nuits-St-Georges
D8

Meuzin

N74
A31

NUITS·S·GEORGES
SES GRANDS VINS
SON BEFFROI
SA CONFRERIE des CHEVALIERS du TASTEVIN

Wine for the "knights of the tasting cup"

0 kilometers 5
0 miles 5

Rhoin

A6

Pernand-Vergelesses
La Doix
Aloxe-Corton
Serrigny
Savigny-lès-Beaune

Chorey

A36

BEAUNE
D973

Pommard

Volnay

Monthélie

Auxey-Duresses
Meursault

Blagny

St-Aubin

Puligny-Montrachet

Chassagne-Montrachet

N6

N74

A31

N470

Dheune

ezize-lès-
Maranges
Santenay
ampigny-lès-Maranges   Chagny

Cheilly-lès-Maranges
Bouzeron

N6

KEY

• Village *appellations*

☐ Côte de Nuits-Villages

☐ Hautes-Côtes de Nuits

☐ Hautes-Côtes de Beaune

☐ Côte de Beaune-Villages

Vins de Bourgogne
Puligny-Montrachet
Champ-Canet

Burgundian villages have often appropriated the name of their most famous vineyard: all the village wines of Puligny, for example, can benefit from the fame of Le Montrachet.

THE CÔTE D'OR
The Côte de Nuits and Côte de Beaune, together forming the "golden" Côte d'Or *(see p334),* meet at the historic town of Beaune, which hosts the most famous annual wine auction in the world *(see p336).* "Hautes-Côtes" and "Villages" wines are made by those not fortunate enough to possess land in the starry individual *appellations.*

Teams of grape-pickers at the vineyards of Nuits-St-Georges

The French Alps

IN ANY SEASON, the Alps are one of the most spectacular regions of France – a majestic mountain range stretching south from Lake Geneva almost to the Mediterranean, and climaxing in Europe's loftiest peak, the 4,800-m (15,770-ft) Mont Blanc. The area encompasses the old regions of Dauphiné and Savoie, once remote and independent (Savoie only became part of France in 1860). They have prospered since alpine holidays and skiing became popular during the last century, but are still very conscious of their distinct identity.

Children in traditional Savoie costumes

The Alpine landscape in winter: chalets and skiers on the slopes at Courchevel

WINTER

THE SKI SEASON usually starts just before Christmas, and finishes at the end of April. Most resorts offer both cross-country and downhill skiing,

A cable car at Courchevel, part of Les Trois Vallées complex

with many pistes (ski trails) linking two or more ski stations. The less energetic can enjoy the landscape from some of the highest cable cars (*téléphériques*) in the world.

Of the 100 or more French Alpine resorts, the most popular include **Chamonix-Mont Blanc**, the historic capital of Alpine skiing and site of the first Winter Olympics in 1924; **Megève**, which boasts one of the best ski schools in Europe; **Morzine**, a year-round resort on the Swiss border, adjacent to the modern, car-free resort of **Avoriaz**; modern **Albertville**, site of the 1992 Winter Olympics; **Les Trois Vallées**, which include glamorous

A downhill skier at Val d'Isère

Courchevel and **Méribel**, and the lesser-known **Val Thorens/Les Ménuires**; **Tignes**, a year-round resort; **Les Arcs** and **La Plagne**, both custom built; and **Val d'Isère**, a favorite among the rich and famous.

ALPINE FLOWERS

In spring and early summer the pastures of the French Alps are ablaze with flowers. These include blue and yellow gentians, bellflowers, lilies, saxifrages and a variety of orchids. Steep mountain meadows cannot be farmed intensively, and the absence of fertilizers and weed killers enables wild flowers to flourish.

Spring gentian (*Gentiana verna*)

Martagon lily (*Lilium martagon*)

The French Alps in spring: flower-filled meadows bordered by dramatic white peaks

SPRING AND SUMMER

THE ALPINE summer season starts in late June, extending to early September – most resorts close in October and November

Belled dairy cows in an Alpine pasture

between the hiking and skiing seasons. After the spring thaw, flower-filled pastures, snow-fed mountain lakes and a huge number of marked trails make this area a hiker's paradise. In the Chamonix area alone there are over 310 km (195 miles) of hiking trails. The best known long-distance route is the **Tour du Mont Blanc**, a 10-day hike via France, Italy and Switzerland. The **GR5** traverses the entire Alps, passing through the **Parc National de la Vanoise** and **Parc Régional du Queyras** (*see p377*) to the south. *Téléphériques* give access to the higher trails, where the views are even more awesome. Be sure to bring plenty of warm, waterproof clothing: the weather can change very quickly.

Many resorts are now concentrating on broadening their summer appeal – golf, tennis, mountain biking, horse riding, paragliding, canoeing, white water rafting, glacier skiing and mountain climbing are all widely available.

Mountain climbers scaling the heights around Mont Blanc

Geology of the Massif Central

THE MASSIF CENTRAL covers almost one-fifth of France and is over 250 million years old. Most of its peaks have been eroded to form a vast plateau split into deep valleys. The heart of the Massif consists of hard, igneous rocks like granite, with softer rocks such as limestone at its margins. Different rock types are reflected in the landscape and buildings; in the eroded Gorges du Tarn, the houses are built of russet-colored limestone. Massive granite farmhouses are a feature of Limousin, and Le Puy-en-Velay is known for its giant basalt pillars.

LOCATOR MAP

☐ *Extent of the Massif Central*

Basalt *is a dark, fine-grained rock formed by volcanic lava. A common building stone in the Auvergne, it is often cut into blocks and bonded with lighter-colored mortar. In the medieval town of Salers (see p353), basalt was used for most of the buildings, including this one in the Grande Place.*

This granite portal *is found in the Romanesque church at Moutier d'Ahun (see p346). Granite underlies much of the Massif Central.*

Montluçon •

Moutier d'Ahun •

Limoges •

Clermon Ferran

Dordogne

• Salers

Schist tiling *is featured on these roofs at Argentat. Schist is a crystalline rock that splits readily into layers. It is particularly common on the edge of the Massif, and provides an effective roofing material.*

• Argentat

Cère

Lot

Limestone walls *can be seen on houses in Espalion (see p356). Of all the rocks in the Massif Central, it is among the most easily worked. It splits readily and is soft enough to be cut into blocks with a handsaw. As with granite, its color and consistency vary from area to area.*

Mi

Tarn

0 kilometers   50

0 miles   50

Crystalized lava, *like this dramatic curtain of columns at Prades, formed when liquid basalt seeped through the surrounding rock and solidified to form giant crystals.*

KEY

- Sedimentary rock
- Surface volcanic rock
- Granite
- Metamorphic rock

ievers

Loire

Saône

Lyon •

•
St-Etienne

• Le-Puy-en-Velay

Rhône

Limestone plateaus (causses) *are typical of this region. Gorges, where rivers have cut through layers of this slightly soluble rock, run deep into the Massif Central.*

This mature landscape *at Mont Aigoual is the highest point in the Cévennes (see p357), dividing rivers flowing into the Atlantic and the Mediterranean. Its granite and schist rocks show erosion.*

RECOGNIZING ROCKS

Geologists divide rocks into three groups. Igneous rocks, like granite, are formed by volcanic activity and either extrude onto the surface or intrude into other rocks below ground. Sedimentary rocks are produced by sediment buildup. Metamorphic rocks have been transformed by heat or pressure.

SEDIMENTARY ROCK

Oolitic limestone *often contains fossils and small amounts of quartz.*

SURFACE VOLCANIC ROCK

Basalt, *which can form very thick sheets, is the most common lava rock.*

GRANITE

Pink granite, *a coarse-grained rock, is formed deep in the earth's crust.*

METAMORPHIC ROCK

Muscovite schist *is a medium-grained mud or clay-based rock.*

BURGUNDY
AND FRANCHE-COMTÉ

YONNE · NIÈVRE · CÔTE D'OR · SAÔNE-ET-LOIRE
HAUTE-SAÔNE · DOUBS · JURA

BURGUNDY CONSIDERS *itself the heart of France, a prosperous region with world-renowned wine, earthy but excellent cuisine and magnificent architecture. Franche-Comté to the east combines gentle farmland with lofty Alpine forests.*

Under the dukes of Valois, Burgundy was France's most powerful rival, with territory extending well beyond its present boundaries. By the 16th century, however, the duchy was ruled by governors appointed by the French king, but it still managed to keep its privileges and traditions. Once a part of Burgundy, Franche-Comté – the Free County – struggled to remain independent of the French crown, and was a province of the Holy Roman Empire until annexed by Louis XIV in 1674.

Burgundy is a wealthy region, a center of medieval religious faith that produced Romanesque masterpieces at Vézelay, Fontenay, and Cluny. Dijon is a splendid city, filled with the palaces of the old Burgundian nobility and a collection of great paintings and sculptures in the Musée des Beaux Arts. The vineyards of the Côte d'Or, the Côte de Beaune and Chablis yield some of the world's most venerated wines. Other richly varied landscapes – from the wild forests of the Morvan to the lush farmland of the Brionnais – produce snails, Bresse chickens and Charolais beef.

Franche-Comté has none of this opulence, though its capital, Besançon, is an elegant 17th-century city with a tradition of clockmaking. Topographically the Franche-Comté is divided in two, with gently rolling farmland in the Saône Valley and high Alpine scenery to the east. This forest country of Alpine torrents filled with trout is also the home of great cheeses, notably Vacherin and Comté, and of the well-known yellow wine of Arbois.

The prehistoric site of the Roche de Solutré near Mâcon

◁ Vineyards at Santenay in the world-renowned Côte de Beaune district

Exploring Burgundy and Franche-Comté

BURGUNDY IS FRANCE'S RICHEST province – historically, culturally, gastronomically and economically. This lush kernel of a once-great power possesses a concentration of unique Romanesque architecture in Fontenay and Vézelay, along with some of the world's most venerated wines. Dijon is a must for lovers of art, architecture and food. Franche-Comté is better suited for outdoor vacations, such as hiking and canoeing in wild scenery and crystal-clear rivers.

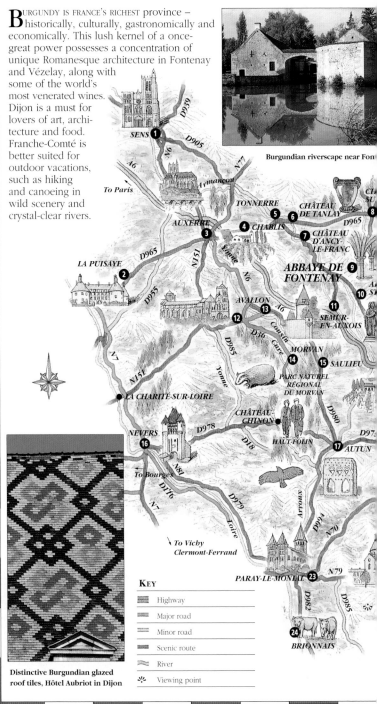

Burgundian riverscape near Fon

SENS 1
D939
D905
N6
A6
To Paris
N77
Armançon
TONNERRE 5
6 CHÂTEAU DE TANLAY
8
D965
AUXERRE 3
4 CHABLIS
7 CHÂTEAU D'ANCY-LE-FRANC
Yonne
N151
D965
LA PUISAYE 2
ABBAYE DE FONTENAY 9
N6
10
D955
AVALLON 13
12
A6
11 SEMUR-EN-AUXOIS
Cousin
D36
Cure
D985
MORVAN
14
15 SAULIEU
N7
Yonne
N151
PARC NATUREL RÉGIONAL DU MORVAN
LA CHARITÉ-SUR-LOIRE
CHÂTEAU-CHINON
D980
NEVERS 16
D978
D18
HAUT-FOLIN
17 AUTUN
To Bourges
N81
D976
N7
D979
Arroux
Loire
D994
N70
To Vichy
Clermont-Ferrand
PARAY-LE-MONIAL 23
N79
D982
D985
24
BRIONNAIS
KEY
Highway
Major road
Minor road
Scenic route
River
Viewing point

Distinctive Burgundian glazed roof tiles, Hôtel Aubriot in Dijon

SIGHTS AT A GLANCE

Wine harvest in Nuits-St-Georges, Côte d'Or

GETTING AROUND

Burgundy is well-served by the A6 autoroute from Paris to Lyon and Marseille, which is joined by the A31 from Nancy and Dijon (and the Channel ports via the A26), and the A36 from Besançon. An alternative route through the region from Dijon to Lyon is the A39. If you have time and a taste for quiet country roads, those in Burgundy and Franche-Comté are some of the most rewarding in France. The TGV links Dijon and Mâcon with Paris, Geneva and Marseille. Dijon is a major rail hub, and connects other towns in the region; and its international airport serves most European destinations.

0 kilometers   25

0 miles   25

La Sainte Châsse, 11th-century
reliquary in the Treasury in Sens

Sens ❶

Yonne. 🏛 *29,000.* 🚉 🚌
ℹ *place Jean-Jaurès (03 86 65 19 49).* 🐓 *Mon & Fri.*

T HE LITTLE TOWN of Sens, at the confluence of the rivers Yonne and Vanne, was important well before Caesar came to Gaul. Indeed, it was the Senones whose attempt to sack the Roman Capitol in 390 BC was so famously thwarted by a flock of geese.

The **Cathédrale St-Etienne** is Sens' outstanding glory. Begun before 1140, it is the oldest of the great Gothic cathedrals and its noble simplicity influenced many other churches. Louis IX *(see p47)* did the town the honor of getting married here in 1234.

The exquisite stained-glass windows from the 12th–16th centuries show biblical scenes, including the Tree of Jesse, and a tribute to Thomas à Becket who was exiled here. His liturgical robes are in the Treasury (part of the **Musée de Sens**), which has one of the finest collections in France, including a beautiful Byzantine reliquary.

🏛 **Les Musées de Sens**
Pl de la Cathédrale. 📞 *03 86 64 46 22.* 🕐 *Jun–Sep: daily; Oct–May: Wed–Mon (except Mon, Thu & Fri ams).* 🎫 ♿

La Puisaye ❷

Yonne, Nièvre. 🚉 *Auxerre, Clamecy, Bonny-sur-Loire, Cosne-Cours-sur-Loire.* 🚌 *St-Fargeau, St-Sauveur-en-Puisaye.* ℹ *Charny (03 86 63 65 51).*

T HE STRANGE, secret forest country of the Puisaye was immortalized by Colette (1873–1954), who was born at **St-Sauveur** in "a house that smiled only on its garden side . . .". The town's 17th-century château now houses the **Musée Colette**.

The best way to explore the region is on foot or by bike around its watery woodlands, orchards and meadows, so unlike the rest of Burgundy. Alternatively, take a ride on the *Transpoyaudin*, a 27 km (17 mile) train ride from St-Saveur to Villiers St-Benoit.

An unusual hands-on visit can be made to **Château de Guédelon**, a 25-year project exactly recreating a medieval castle, using only original building methods and materials, found locally. Nearby is the genuine 13th-century **Château de Ratilly**, with a pottery workshop and art exhibitions. More of this can be seen in **St-Amand**, the center of Puisaye stoneware production, much of which was traditionally fired in the still operational vast 18th-century horizontal kiln at Moutiers. Both the pottery and local frescoes (see the

Colette in the 1880s at St-Sauveur

churches at **Moutiers** and **La Ferté-Loupière**) made use of locally-mined ocher, a major export in the 19th century. The pink-brick **Château de St-Fargeau** housed the exiled Grande Mademoiselle *(p53)*.

🏛 **Musée Collete**
Château St-Sauveur-en-Puisaye. 📞 *03 86 45 61 95.* 🕐 *Apr–Oct: Wed– Mon; Nov–Mar: w/e & sch. vacs pms.* 🎫

Auxerre ❸

Yonne. 🏛 *40,000.* 🚉 ℹ *1–2 quai de la République (03 86 52 06 19).* 🐓 *Tue & Fri.*

B EAUTIFULLY SITUATED overlooking the Yonne River, Auxerre justly prides itself on a fine collection of churches, along with a charming pedestrianized main square, the place Charles-Surugue.

The Gothic **Cathédrale St-Etienne** took over three centuries to build and was completed in about 1560. It is famous for its intricate 13th-century stained glass. The choir, with its slender columns and colonettes, is the epitome of Gothic weightlessness and elegance, while the western portals are decorated with beautiful Flamboyant sculpture that has been sadly mutilated by war and weather. The Romanesque crypt is adorned with unique 11th–13th-century frescoes, including one depicting Christ on a white horse. The badly pillaged treasury is less impressive, but still has an interesting collection of beautifully illuminated manuscripts.

Château de St-Fargeau in the Puisaye region

St. Germanus, mentor of St. Patrick and bishop of Auxerre in the 5th century, was buried at the former abbey church of **St-Germain**. The abbey was founded by Queen Clothilde, wife of Clovis *(see pp44–5)*, the first Christian king of France, and is an important shrine. The crypt is partly Carolingian, with tombs and 11th–13th century frescoes. The former abbey houses the **Musée St-Germain** with local Gallo-Roman finds.

🏛 Musée St-Germain
2 place St-Germain. 📞 *03 86 18 05 50.* ⬤ *Wed–Mon.* ⬤ *some public hols.* 📷

The intriguing spring of Fosse Dionne in Tonnerre

Medieval fresco in Cathédrale St-Etienne at Auxerre

Chablis ❹

Yonne. 🏠 *2,600.* 🚍 🛈 *quai du Biez (03 86 42 80 80).* ⬤ *Sun.*

T HERE CAN BE no question that Chablis tastes best in Chablis. Although this is one of the most famous wine villages on earth, its narrow stone streets still have an air of sleepy prosperity. February, processions in nearby Fyé, attended by the wine brotherhood of Piliers Chablisiens, honor Saint Vincent, the patron saint of wine-growers.

Tonnerre ❺

Yonne. 🏠 *6,357.* 🚍 🚍 🛈 *rue F-Mitteraud (03 86 55 14 48).* ⬤ *Sat.*

T HE MYSTICAL, cloudy green spring of **Fosse Dionne** is a good reason to visit the small town of Tonnerre. An astonishing volume of water bursts up from the ground into an 18th-century washing site. Due to its depth and strong currents it has never been thoroughly explored, and local legend has it that a serpent lives on undisturbed at the bottom.

The **Hôtel-Dieu** is 150 years older than the Hôtel-Dieu in Beaune *(see p336–7)*. It was founded by Margaret of Burgundy in 1293 to care for the poor. It lost its tiling during the Revolution, but the barrel-vaulted oak ceiling survived.

⛪ Hôtel-Dieu & Musée
Rue du Prieuré. 📞 *03 86 55 33 00.* ⬤ *Apr–May: w/e & publ hols pms only; Jun–Sep: Wed–Mon.* 📷 ♿ 📷

Château de Tanlay ❻

Tanlay. 📞 *03 86 75 70 61.* ⬤ *Apr–mid-Nov: Wed–Mon.* 📷 📷 *oblig.* ♿

T HE MOATED Château de Tanlay is a beautiful example of French Renaissance, built in the mid-16th century. There is a *trompe l'oeil* in the Grande Galerie and, in the corner tower, an intriguing School of Fontainebleau painted ceiling. Its antique divinities represent famous Protestants and Catholics in the 16th century, such as Diane de Poitiers as Venus.

The Renaissance façade and *cour d'honneur* of Château de Tanlay

Abbaye de Fontenay **9**

THE TRANQUIL ABBEY of Fontenay is the oldest surviving Cistercian foundation in France and offers a rare insight into the Cistercian way of life. It represents the spirit of the order in the sublime gravity of its Romanesque church and its plain but elegant chapter house, in early Gothic style. The abbey was founded in 1118 by St. Bernard. Situated deep in the forest, it offered the peace and seclusion the Cistercians sought. Supported by the local aristocracy, the abbey began to thrive and remained in use until the Revolution when it was sold and converted into a paper mill. In 1906 the abbey came under new ownership and was restored to its original appearance.

Dovecote
A magnificent circular dovecote, built in the 13th century, is situated next to the kennel where the precious hunting dogs of the dukes of Burgundy were guarded by servants.

The 17th-century abbot's lodgings were built when the abbots were appointed by royal favor.

The bakehouse is no longer intact, but the 13th-century oven and chimney have survived.

The visitors' hostel is where weary wanderers and pilgrims were offered board and lodging by the monks.

★ Cloisters
For a 12th-century monk, a walk through the cloisters was an opportunity for meditation and provided shelter from the weather.

Warming Room

In the forge monks produced their own tools and hardware.

Fontenay "Prison"
It may be that this 15th-century building was actually used to lock up not local miscreants but important abbey archives, in order to protect them against damage by rats.

Scriptorium
Manuscripts were copied here. The adjacent warming room was used to warm chilled hands.

★ **Abbey Church**
Rich decoration has no place in this church from the 1140s. But the severe architectural forms, the warm color of the stone and the diffused light convey a grandeur of their own.

VISITORS' CHECKLIST

Marmagne. ☎ *03 80 92 15 00.*
🚌 Montbard. ○ *10am–5pm daily (Nov 11–Mar: 10am–noon, 2–5pm daily).* 🅿 ♿ ✉
Ⓦ *www.abbayedefontenay.com*

Dormitory
Monks slept in long rows on straw mattresses in this large, unheated room. The timberwork roof is from the late 15th century.

The herb garden was skillfully cultivated by the monks in order to grow healing herbs for medicines and potions.

STAR FEATURES

★ **Abbey Church**

★ **Cloisters**

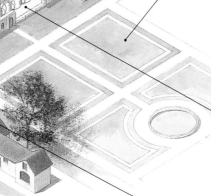

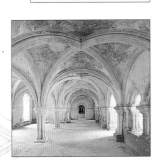

Chapter house
Once a day, monks and abbot assembled in this room to discuss matters concerning the community. It derives much of its charm from the elegant 12th-century piers and ribbed vaults.

Infirmary

ST. BERNARD AND THE CISTERCIANS

In 1112 Bernard, a young Burgundian nobleman, joined the Cistercians. At the time the order was still obscure, founded 14 years earlier by a group of monks who wanted to turn their back on the elaborate lifestyle of Cluny *(see pp44–5)*, renounce the world and espouse poverty and simplicity of life. During Bernard's lifetime the Cistercians became one of the largest and most famous orders of its time. Part of this success was clearly due to Bernard's powerful personality and his skills as a writer, theologian and statesman. He reinforced the poverty rule, rejecting all forms of embellishment. In 1174, only 21 years after his death, he was canonized.

The Virgin Protecting the Cistercian Order, by Jean Bellegambe

Château d'Ancy-le-Franc ❼

Ancy-le-Franc. ☎ 03 86 75 14 63. ☐ Apr–mid-Nov: Tue–Sun. ✔ obligatory. ▨

THE CLASSICAL Renaissance façade of Château d'Ancy-le-Franc gives an austere impression. Its inner courtyard, however, has a rich ornamentation. The château was built in the 1540s by the Italian Sebastiano Serlio, for the Duke of Clermont-Tonnerre. Most of the interior decorations were carried out by Primaticcio and other members of the Fontainebleau School (see pp170–71). Diane de Poitiers, the duke's sister-in-law and mistress of Henry II, is portrayed in the *Chambre de Judith e Holophernes*.

In the outbuildings a vintage car and carriage museum displays over 80 vehicles.

The staid façade of Château d'Ancy-le-Franc

The vase of Vix in the Musée du Châtillonnais, Châtillon-sur-Seine

Châtillon-sur-Seine ❽

Côte d'Or. ▨ 6,850. ▨ ▨ ▮ place Marmont (03 80 91 13 19). ▨ Sat.

WORLD WAR II left Châtillon a smoking ruin, hence the town's resolutely modern aspect. But the past is still present in the **Musée du Châtillonnais**, where the magnificent Vix treasure is displayed. In 1953, the tomb of a Gaulish princess, dating from the 6th century BC, was discovered near Vix at Mont Lassois. The trove of jewelry and artifacts of Greek origin includes a stunning bronze vase, 164 cm (66 in) high and weighing 208 kg (459 lb).

Another point of interest is the Romanesque **Eglise St-Vorles** containing an *Entombment* with Christ and mourners splendidly sculpted (1527).

At the nearby source of the Douix River, which runs into the Seine, is a beautiful grotto.

🏛 **Musée du Châtillonnais**
7 rue du Bourg. ☎ 03 80 91 24 67. ☐ Jul–Aug: daily; Sep–Jun: Wed–Mon ● Jan 1, May 1, Dec 25. ▨

Abbaye de Fontenay ❾

See pp322–3.

Alise-Ste-Reine ❿

Côte d'Or. ▨ 670. ▮ Venarey-les-Laumes, 3 km (2 miles) (03 80 96 89 13).

MONT AUXOIS, above the little village of Alise-Ste-Reine, was the site of Caesar's final victory over the heroic Gaulish chieftain Vercingetorix in 52 BC after a six-week siege (see p42). The first excavations here were undertaken in the mid-19th century, and they uncovered the vestiges of a thriving Gallo-Roman town, with theater, forum and well laid-out street plan. The **Musée Alésia** has a collection of artifacts, jewelry and bronze figures from the site.

Alise is dominated by Aimé Millet's gigantic moustachioed statue of Vercingetorix, which was placed here in 1865 to commemorate the first excavations. Cynics feel that it bears a more than passing resemblance to Napoleon III, who sponsored the dig.

🏛 **Musée Alésia**
Rue de l'Hôpital. ☎ 03 80 96 10 95. ☐ Mar–mid-Nov: daily. ▨

Environs
In the vicinity lies **Château de Bussy-Rabutin**. The spiteful 17th-century soldier and wit Roger de Bussy-Rabutin created its highly individualistic

Excavations at the Roman site near Alise-Ste-Reine

decor while exiled from Louis XIV's court. One room is dedicated to portraits of his many mistresses, as well as to some imaginary ones.

♣ **Château de Bussy-Rabutin**
Bussy-le-Grand. **C** 03 80 96 00 03.
○ Apr–Sep: Tue–Sun; Oct–Mar: Thu–Mon. ● Jan 1, Nov 1 & 11, Dec 25. &

Semur-en-Auxois ⓫

Côte d'Or. 🏠 4,500. 🚐
🛈 2 place Gaveau (03 80 97 05 96).
🗓 Sun.

Semur-en-Auxois by the Armançon River

APPROACHED from the west, Semur-en-Auxois comes as a surprise on an otherwise uneventful road. Its massive round bastions built in the 14th century (one of them with an unnerving gash in it) suddenly appear, towering over the Pont Joly and the peaceful Armançon River.

The **Eglise Notre-Dame** dates from the 13th and 14th centuries, and was modeled on the cathedral of Auxerre. The fragile high walls had to be restored in the 15th and 19th centuries. The church houses significant artworks, from the tympanum showing the legend of Doubting Thomas on the north doorway, to the 15th-century *Entombment* by Antoine le Moiturier. The stained glass presents the legend of Sainte Barbara, and the work of different guilds, such as butchers and drapers.

Environs
The village of Epoisses is the site of the moated **Château d'Epoisses**, its 11th–18th-century construction blending medieval towers with fine Renaissance details, and a huge 15th-century dovecote. Epoisses is also the home of one of Burgundy's most re-

Stained-glass window in Eglise Notre-Dame at Semur-en-Auxois

vered cheeses, to be sampled at the local café or *fromagerie*.

♣ **Château d'Epoisses**
Epoisses. **C** 03 80 96 40 56.
○ Jul–Aug: Wed–Mon (grounds: all year). & 🎫 👟 ground floor only.

Vézelay ⓬

See pp326–7.

Avallon ⓭

Yonne. 🏠 8,600. 🚐 🚂
🛈 6 rue Bocquillot (03 86 34 14 19).
🗓 Sat.

A FINE OLD fortified town, Avallon is situated on a granite spur between two ravines by the Cousin River.

Avallon suffered much in the wars of Saracens, Normans, English and French, which accounts for its coldly defensive aspect. Today the town is quiet and quite beautiful, full of charming details. The principal monument is the 12th-century Romanesque **Eglise St-Lazare**, with two magnificent carved doorways. The larger illustrates the signs of the zodiac, the labors of the month and the musicians of the Apocalypse.

The nave is decorated with sophisticated acanthus capitals and polychrome statuary.

The **Musée de l'Avallonnais** has a wide-ranging collection, featuring an intricate Venus mosaic from the 2nd century AD, and Georges Rouault's (1871–1958) series of Expressionist etchings, the *Miserere*.

🏛 **Musée de l'Avallonnais**
Place de la Collégiale. **C** 03 86 34 03 19. ○ May–Oct: Wed–Mon pms. &

Environs
To the southwest of Avallon is the 12th-century Château de Bazoches, given to Maréchal de Vauban by Louis XIV in 1675, and transformed by him into a military garrison.

***Miserere* by Georges Rouault in the Musée d'Avallonnais, Avallon**

Vézelay ⑫

Decorated capital

T HE GOLDEN GLOW of the Basilique Ste-Madeleine crowning Vézelay's hill is visible from afar. Tourists follow in the footsteps of medieval pilgrims, ascending the narrow street up to the former abbey church. In the 12th century, at the height of its glory, the abbey claimed to house relics of Mary Magdalene, and was also an important meeting point for pilgrims en route to Santiago de Compostela in Spain *(see pp390–91)*. Today its attraction lies in the Romanesque church with its magnificent sculpture and Gothic choir.

View of Vézelay
The abbey dominates Vézelay's surroundings as it once dominated the religious and worldly affairs of the area.

Tour St-Michel was built in 1230–40. It derives its name from the statue of the archangel in the tower's southwest corner.

Nave of Ste-Madeleine

Nave of Ste-Madeleine
The nave was rebuilt between 1120–35, using alternate dark and light stone in the transverse arches.

The façade dates from 1150 and has a large 13th-century window. It was about to collapse when Viollet-le-Duc was commissioned to restore it according to old plans in 1840.

The narthex used to be a gathering point for medieval processions.

★ **Tympanum**
This masterpiece of sculpture (1120–35) shows Christ on His throne, stretching out His hands from which rays of light descend onto the apostles.

STAR FEATURES
★ Tympanum
★ Capitals

Tour St-Antoine was built at the same time as the choir, in the late 12th century. Its counterpart on the north side was never finished.

VISITORS' CHECKLIST

Basilique Ste-Madeleine, Vézelay.
(03 86 33 39 50. **▯** Sermizelles,
◯ 6am–8pm daily (7am–6pm winter). **✝** 6:30pm Mon–Sat; 11am Sun. Daily office (sung in 4-part harmony): 7am, 12:30pm, 6pm Tue–Fri (8am w/e). **◉**

The chapter house and cloister are the only parts remaining from the 12th-century monastic buildings. Viollet-le-Duc rebuilt the cloister and restored the rib-vaulted chapter house, once a graceful background for the monks' daily assemblies.

Crypt of Ste-Madeleine
The Romanseque crypt houses relics once thought to be Mary Magdalene's. The vault was rebuilt in 1165.

★ Capitals
The capitals in the nave and narthex are exquisitely carved, and provide a vivid rendering of the stories of Classical antiquity and the Bible. The master who created them remains unknown.

Choir of Ste-Madeleine
The choir was rebuilt in the last quarter of the 12th century in the then-modern Gothic style of the Ile de France.

Morvan, a region of rivers and forests, well-suited to fishing and other outdoor pursuits

Morvan

Yonne, Côte d'Or, Nièvre, Saône et Loire. *Dijon.* *Autun, Corbigny.* *Château-Chinon, Saulieu, Avallon.* *Château-Chinon (03 86 85 06 58); Maison du Parc, St-Brisson (03 86 78 79 00).*

MORVAN is a Celtic word meaning Black Mountain, which is a good description of this area seen from afar. The immense, sparsely inhabited plateau of granite and woodland appears suddenly in the center of the rich Burgundy hills and farmland. Stretching roughly north to south, it gains altitude as it proceeds southward, reaching a culminating point of 901 m (2,928 ft) at **Haut-Folin**.

The Morvan's two sources of natural wealth are abundant water and dense forests of oak, beech and conifer. In the old days lumber used to be floated out of the area to Paris via a network of lakes and rivers. Today it travels by truck, and the Yonne, Cousin and Cure rivers are instead used for recreation and the production of electricity.

The population continues to shrink, for the Morvan has always been a poor, remote area. Each of its largest towns, Château-Chinon in the center and Saulieu on the outskirts, has barely 3,000 inhabitants.

During World War II, the Morvan was a bastion of the French Resistance. Today a Regional Nature Park, its attraction is its wildness. Information on a wide variety of outdoor activities, including bicycling, canoeing, skiing, and horseback riding, is available at the Maison du Parc at St-Brisson, where there is also a **Musée de la Resistance**. There are plenty of short walking trails, in addition to two well-marked long distance paths: the GR13 (Vézelay to Autun) and the Tour du Morvan par les Grands Lacs.

🏛 Musée de la Résistance
Maison du Parc, St-Brisson. *03 86 78 72 99.* *Easter–mid-Nov: daily.*

Saulieu

Côte d'Or. *3,000.* *24 rue d'Argentine (03 80 64 00 21).* *Thu & Sat.*

ON THE EDGE of the Morvan, Saulieu has been a shrine of Burgundian cooking since the 17th century. The town was then a stop on the Paris to Lyon coach road. To-day the tradition is maintained by world-famous chef Bernard Loiseau at the **Côte d'Or** restaurant (*see p598*). Yet there is more to Saulieu than *ris de veau de lait braisé* or *poularde truffée à la vapeur.* The Romanesque **Basilique St-Andoche**, built in the early 12th century, has decorated capitals with representations of the Flight into Egypt and a comical version of the story of Balaam and his donkey waylaid by the Angel.

Nevers faïence vase

Nevers

Nièvre. *44,000.* *Palais Ducal, rue Sabatier (03 86 68 46 00).* *Sat.*

LIKE ALL Burgundian towns fronting the Loire, Nevers should be approached from the west side of the river for a full appreciation of its noble site. Though lacking historical importance, the town is interesting. Considered to be the earliest of the Loire châteaux, the **Palais Ducal** has a long Renaissance façade framed by polygonal towers and a broad esplanade. The Romanesque 11th-century **Eglise St-Etienne** has monolithic columns and a wreath of radiating chapels. In the crypt of the Gothic **Cathédrale St-Cyr** is a 16th-century sculpted *Entombment*, and the foundations of a 6th-century baptistry, discovered in 1944 after heavy bombing. The contemporary stained-glass windows are also noteworthy. The overlordship of Nevers passed to the Gonzaga family in the 16th century. They brought with them an Italian school of artists skilled in faïence making and glassblowing.

The industry has remained, and the modern pottery is still traditionally decorated in white, blue, yellow and green with its curious trademark, the little green arabesque knot, or *noeud vert*. The best place to view it is at the **Musée Municipal**, and the best place to buy it is the 17th-century **Faïencerie Montagnon**.

🏛 Musée Municipal Frédéric Blandin
Promenade des Remparts. ☎ 03 86 71 67 90. ◯ Wed–Mon (Oct–Apr: pms only). ● May 1, Dec 25–Jan 2.

Environs
Just south of Nevers, the 19th-century **Pont du Guetin** carries the Loire Canal majestically across the Allier River. The church at **St-Parize-le-Châtel** has a jolly Burgundian menagerie sculpted on the capitals of the crypt.

The *Temptation of Eve* in Autun

Autun 🟡

Saône-et-Loire. 🚶 17,900. 🚃 🚌 ℹ️ 2 av Charles de Gaulle (03 85 86 80 38). 🛒 Wed & Fri.

AUGUSTODUNUM, the town of Augustus, was founded in the late 1st century BC. It was a great center of learning,

The imposing Porte St-André in Autun, once part of the Roman wall

with a population four times what it is today. Its theater, built in the 1st century AD, could seat 20,000 people.

Today Autun is still a delight, deserving gastronomic as well as cultural investigation.

The magical **Cathédrale St-Lazare** was built in the 12th century. It is special because of the genius of its sculptures, most of them by the mysterious 12th-century artist Gislebertus. He sculpted both the capitals inside and the glorious Last Judgment tympanum over the main portal. This masterpiece, called a "Romanesque Cézanne" by writer André Malraux, escaped notice and was saved from destruction during the Revolution because it had been plastered over in the 18th century. Inside, some of the capitals can be seen close up in a room in the tower. Look also for the sculpture of Pierre Jeannin

and his wife. Jeannin was the president of the Dijon parliament who prevented the Massacre of St. Bartholomew *(see pp50–51)* spreading to Burgundy with the immortal remark, "the commands of very angry monarchs should be obeyed very slowly."

The fine collection of medieval art at the **Musée Rolin** includes the lovely bas relief *Temptation of Eve*, by Gislebertus. There is also the painted stone Virgin of Autun (15th century), and the *Nativity of Cardinal Rolin* by the Master of Moulins, from about 1480.

The monumental **Porte St-André** and **Porte d'Arroux** and the ruins of the **Théâtre Romain** and the **Temple de Janus**, are reminders of Autun's glorious Roman past.

🏛 Musée Rolin
5 rue des Bancs. ☎ 03 85 52 09 76. ◯ Wed–Mon. ● public hols & end-Dec–mid-Jan.

Remains of the Roman theater at Autun, dating from the 1st century AD

Street by Street: Dijon ⑱

THE CENTER of Dijon is noted for its architectural splendor – a legacy from the Dukes of Burgundy *(see p333)*. Wealthy parliament members also had elegant *hôtels particuliers* built in the 17th–18th centuries. The capital of Burgundy, Dijon today has a rich cultural life and a renowned university. The city's great art treasures are housed in the Palais des Ducs. Dijon is also famous for its mustard *(see p308)* and *pain d'épice* (gingerbread), a reminder of the town's position on the spice route. It became a major rail hub during the 19th century and now has a TGV link to Paris.

Hôtel de Vogüé
This elegant 17th-century mansion is decorated with Burgundian cabbages and fruit garlands by Hugues Sambin.

★ Notre-Dame
This magnificent 13th-century Gothic church has a façade with gargoyles, columns and the popular Jacquemart clock. The chouette (owl) is reputed to bring good luck when touched.

Musée des Beaux Arts
The collection of Flemish masters here includes this 14th-century triptych by Jacques de Baerze and Melchior Broederlam.

Place de la Libération was created by Mansart in the 17th century.

★ Palais des Ducs
The Dukes of Burgundy held court here, but the building seen today was mainly built in the 17th century for the parliament. It now houses the Musée des Beaux Arts.

Rue Verrerie
This cobbled street in the old merchants' quarter is lined with medieval half-timbered houses. Some have fine wood carvings, such as Nos. 8, 10 and 12.

VISITORS' CHECKLIST

Côte d'Or. 151,000. 5 km (3 miles) SSE Dijon. Cours de la Gare. rue des Forges (03 80 44 11 44). Tue, Thu–Sat. Florissimo (3 yearly: 2005 next); Festival de Musique (Jun); Fêtes de la Vigne (Sep). **Hôtel de Vogüé** only inner courtyard open to the public. **Musée Magnin** (03 80 67 11 10) Tue–Sun. Jan 1, Dec 25. first floor. W www.ot-dijon.fr

★ St-Michel
Begun in the 15th century and completed in the 17th century, St-Michel's façade combines Flamboyant Gothic with Renaissance details. On the richly carved porch, angels and biblical motifs mingle with mythological themes.

Musée Magnin
A collection of French and foreign 16th–19th-century paintings are displayed among period furniture in this 17th-century mansion.

Eglise St-Etienne dates back to the 11th century but has been rebuilt many times. Its characteristic lantern was added in 1686.

STAR SIGHTS

★ Palais des Ducs

★ Notre-Dame

★ St-Michel

KEY

– – – Suggested route

0 meters   100

0 yards   100

Well of Moses by Claus Sluter, in the Chartreuse de Champmol

Exploring Dijon

The center of Dijon is a warren of little streets well worth exploring. The rue des Forges, behind the Palais de Ducs, was the main street until the 18th century and is named after the jewelers and goldsmiths who had workshops there. The tourist office, housed in Hôtel Chambellan at No. 34, is Flamboyant Gothic with a stone spiral staircase and wooden galleries. At No. 38 the Maison Maillard, built in 1560, has a stone façade decorated by Hugues Sambin.

Rue Chaudronnerie has a number of houses of note, especially the Maison des Cariatides at No. 28, with ten fine stone- carved caryatids framing the windows. Place Darcy is lined with hotels and restaurants; the Jardin Darcy is delightful.

🏛 Musée des Beaux Arts
Place de la Ste-Chapelle. ☎ 03 80 74 52 70. ☐ Wed–Mon. ● Jan 1, May 1, May 8, Jul 14, Nov 1 & 11, Dec 25. 📷 ♿ limited.

Dijon's prestigious art collection is housed in the former Palais des Ducs *(see p330).* The Salle des Gardes on the first floor is dominated by the giant mausoleums of the dukes, with tombs sculpted by Claus Sluter (c.1345–1405). Other exhibits include two gilded Flemish retables and a portrait of Philip the Good by Rogier van der Weyden.

The art collection has many Dutch and Flemish masters and sculpture by Sluter and François Rude. There is also a large collection of Swiss and German primitives, 16th–18th century French paintings, and the Donation Granville of 19th- and 20th-century French art. Also note the vast ducal kitchens with six giant fireplaces, and the Tour Philippe le Bon, 46 m (150 ft) tall with a fine view of Burgundian tiled rooftops.

⛪ Cathédrale St-Benigne
Little remains of the 11th-century Benedictine abbey first founded in honor of St. Benigne, but beneath the Gothic church is a magnificent Romanesque crypt with a fine rotunda ringed by three circles of columns.

🏛 Musée Archéologique
5 rue du Docteur Maret. ☎ 03 80 30 88 54. ☐ Wed–Mon. ● most public hols. 📷

The museum is housed in the old dormitory of the Benedictine abbey of St-Benigne. The 11th-century chapterhouse, its stocky columns supporting a barrel-vaulted roof, houses a fine collection of Gallo-Roman sculpture. The ground floor, with its lovely fan vaulting, houses the famous head of Christ by Claus Sluter, originally from the *Well of Moses.*

⚰ Chartreuse de Champmol
1 bd Chanoine Kir. ● for renovation.

This was originally the site of a family necropolis built by Philip the Bold, destroyed during the Revolution. All that remains is a chapel doorway and the famous *Well of Moses* by Claus Sluter. It is now in the grounds of a psychiatric hospital east of Dijon train station, not very easy to find but definitely worth the effort. Despite its name, it is not a well, but a monument, its lower part probably originally surrounded by water. Sluter is renowned for his deeply cut carving, and this work, depicting six prophets, is exquisitely lifelike.

The tomb of Philip the Bold by Claus Sluter, now in the Salle des Gardes of the Musée des Beaux Arts

The Golden Age of Burgundy

WHILE THE FRENCH Capetian Dynasty fought in the Hundred Years' War *(see pp48–9)*, the dukes of Burgundy built up one of the most powerful states in Europe, which included Flanders and parts of Holland. From the time of Philip the Bold (1342–1404), the ducal court became a cultural force, supporting many of Europe's finest artists, such as painters Rogier Van der Weyden and the Van Eyck brothers and sculptor Claus Sluter. The duchy's dominions were, however, broken up after the death of Duke Charles the Bold in 1477.

The tomb of Philip the Bold in Dijon was made by the Flemish sculptor Claus Sluter, who was among the most brilliant artists of the Burgundian golden age. The dramatic realism of the mourners is one of the most striking features of this spectacular tomb, begun while the duke was still alive.

BURGUNDY IN 1477

▨ *Extent of the duchy at its peak*

THE MARRIAGE OF PHILIP THE GOOD

Philip the Good, duke from 1419–67, married Isabella of Portugal in 1430. This 17th-century copy of a painting by Van Eyck shows the sumptuous wedding feast, when Philip also inaugurated the chivalric Order of the Golden Fleece.

The dukes surrounded themselves with luxury, including fine gold and silverware.

Isabella of Portugal

The Duchess of Bedford, Philip's sister

Greyhounds were popular hunting animals at the Burgundian court.

Philip the Good is dressed in white ceremonial finery.

***Burgundian art**, such as this Franco-Flemish Book of Hours, reflected the Flemish origins of many of the dukes' favorite artists.*

***Dijon's Palais des Ducs** was rebuilt in 1450 by Philip the Good to reflect the glory of the Burgundian court, a center of art, chivalry and glorious feasts. Empty after Charles the Bold's death, it was reconstructed in the 17th century.*

Wine harvest in the vineyards of Nuits-St-Georges, part of the Côte d'Or district

Côte d'Or ⑲

Côte d'Or. ✈ Dijon. 🚃 🚌 Dijon,
Nuits-St-Georges, Beaune, Santenay.
🛈 Santenay (03 80 20 63 15: summer
only); Beaune (03 80 26 21 30).

Iₙ WINEMAKING TERMS, the Côte
d'Or includes the Côte de
Beaune and the Côte de Nuits
in a nearly unbroken line of
vines from Dijon to Santenay.
Squeezed in between the flat
plain of the Saône to the
southeast and a plateau of
rough woodland to the northwest, this narrow escarpment
is about 50 km (30 miles)
long. The grapes of the great
Burgundy vineyards grow in
the golden-reddish soil of the
slope (hence the name).
    The classification of the
characteristics of the land is
extremely technical and elaborate, but for the layman a
rough rule of thumb might be
that 95 percent of the best

**Narrow street in Beaune's historic
center**

vines are on the uphill side of
the N74 thoroughfare *(see
pp310–11)*. The names on the
signs haunt the dreams of
wine lovers the world over:
Gevrey-Chambertin, Vougeot,
Chambolle-Musigny, Vosne-
Romanée, Nuits-St-Georges,
Aloxe-Corton, Meursault and
Chassagne Montrachet.

**Typical grape basket in the Musée
du Vin de Bourgogne at Beaune**

Beaune ⑳

Côte d'Or. 🏠 22,000. 🚃 🚌 🛈 rue
de l'Hôtel Dieu (03 80 26 21 30).
🗓 Sat & Wed. 🎵 Baroque Music (Jul).

Tₕᴇ OLD CENTER of Beaune,
snug within its ramparts
and encircling boulevards, is
easy to explore on foot. Its
indisputable treasure is the
Hôtel-Dieu *(see pp336–7)*. The
Hôtel des Ducs de Bourgogne,
built in the 14th–16th
centuries, houses the **Musée
du Vin de Bourgogne**. The
building, with its flamboyant
façade, is as interesting as its
display of traditional wine-
making equipment.
    Farther to the north lies
the **Collégiale Notre-Dame**,
begun in the early 12th
century. Inside this mainly
Romanesque church hang five
very fine 15th-century woollen
and silk tapestries. With hints

of early Renaissance style they
delicately illustrate the life of
the Virgin Mary in 19 scenes.

🏛 Musée du Vin de
Bourgogne
Rue d'Enfer. 📞 03 80 22 08 19.
⏲ Apr–Nov: daily; Dec–Mar:
Wed–Mon. ⊘

Tournus ㉑

Saône-et-Loire. 🏠 6,000. 🚃 🚌 🛈
place Carnot (03 85 27 00 20). 🗓 Sat.

Tₕᴇ ABBAYE DE St-Philibert is
one of Burgundy's oldest
and greatest Romanesque
buildings. It was founded by
a group of monks from Noirmoutier who had been driven
from their island by invading
Normans in the 9th century.
They brought with them relics
of their patron saint, Philibert
(still in the choir). Rebuilt in
the 10th–12th centuries, the
well-fortified abbey church is
made from lovely pale-pink

**Dovecote in Cormatin château
gardens, Mâconnais**

Nave of St-Philibert in Tournus

stone with black and white vaulting inside.

The 17th-century Hotel-Dieu has its original rooms intact with the furniture, equipment and pharmacy on display. It also houses the **Musée Greuze** dedicated to Tournus' most famous son, the artist Jean-Baptiste Greuze (1725–1805).

Environs
Southwest of Tournus lies the Mâconnais landscape of hills, vineyards, orchards, red-tiled farmhouses and Romanesque churches. **Brancion** is a pretty hill village; **Chapaize** has an 11th-century church; and there is a sumptuous Renaissance château at **Cormatin**. The village of **Taizé** is the center of a world-famous ecumenical community. To the north, **Chalon-sur-Saône** features old quarters and the Musée Niepce dedicated to the inventor of photography.

Cluny ㉒

Saône-et-Loire. 4,800. 6 rue Mercière (03 85 59 05 34). Sat.

THE LITTLE TOWN of Cluny is overshadowed by the ruins of its great abbey. The **Ancienne Abbaye de Cluny** was once the most powerful monastic foundation in Europe (see pp44–5).

The abbey was founded by William the Pious, Duke of Aquitaine in 910. Within 200 years, Cluny had become the head of a major reforming order with monasteries all over Europe. Its abbots were consid-

ered as powerful as monarchs or popes, and four of them are venerated as saints. By the 14th century, however, the system was in decline. The abbey was closed in 1790 and the church was later dismantled for building materials.

The guided tour presents the abbey remains, notably the Clocher de l'Eau Bénite (Holy Water Bell Tower), **Musée d'Art**, housed in the former abbot's palace, and its figured capitals displayed in the 13th-century flour storage. In town, don't miss the 12th-century **Eglise St-Marcel**.

Southwest of town, the chapel in **Berzé-la-Ville** is decorated with superb 12th-century frescoes, similar to those once seen at Cluny.

🏠 **Ancienne Abbaye de Cluny**
☎ 03 85 59 12 79. ⬜ daily.
🏛 **Musée d'Art**
Palais Jean de Bourbon. ☎ 03 85 59 12 79. ⬜ daily. ● Jan 1, May 1, Nov 1 & 11, Dec 25. ◨ &

Paray-le-Monial ㉓

Saône-et-Loire. 10,500. 25 av Jean-Paul II (03 85 81 10 92). Fri.

DEDICATED to the cult of the Sacred Heart of Jesus, the **Basilique du Sacré-Coeur** has made Paray-le-Monial one of the most important sites of pilgrimage in modern France. Marguerite-Marie Alacoque who was born here in 1647, had rather gory visions from which the cult later developed, sweeping across France in the 19th century. The church is a small version of the now lost abbey church of Cluny, with particularly harmonious and pure Romanesque architecture.

A visit to the **Musée de Paul Charnoz** provides an interesting insight into industrial artistic tile production from the 19th-century to the present.

Situated on place Guignaud is the ornate **Maison Jayet**, dating from the 16th century, which houses the town hall.

Basilique du Sacré-Coeur at Paray-le-Monial

Hôtel-Dieu

Christ-de-Pitié

AFTER THE HUNDRED Years' War, many of Beaune's inhabitants suffered the effects of poverty and famine. To remedy this, the chancellor, Nicolas Rolin, and his wife founded a hospice here in 1443, which was inspired by the architecture of Northern French hospitals. The Rolins provided an annual grant, and vines and saltworks for income. Today the hospice is considered a medieval jewel, with its superb geometric multi-colored Burgundian roof tiles. It houses two religious masterpieces: the *Christ-de-Pitié* statue, carved from wood, and Rogier van der Weyden's polyptych.

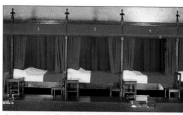

★ Great Hall of the Poor
The hall, with its carved, painted roof, has 28 four-poster beds, each one often used by several patients at a time. Meals were served from central tables.

Tribute to Rolin's Wife
A recurring motif features the entwined letters N and G, birds and stars, and the word "Seulle" referring to Rolin's wife Guigone, his "one and only."

Saint Hugues' Room contains a painting of the saint curing two children. Frescoes by Isaac Moillon show the miracles of Christ.

Entrance

Saint Anne's Room has a tableau of nuns working in what was once the linen room, and a colorful feast-day tapestry.

ANNUAL CHARITY WINE AUCTION

On the third Sunday in November, Beaune's annual charity auction is the centerpiece of three days of festivities known as *Les Trois Glorieuses*. The banquet of the Con- frérie des Chevaliers du Tastevin is held on Saturday at the Château Clos de Vougeot. On Sunday the auction of wine from 151 acres of vineyards owned by nearby hospitals takes place. Its prices are the benchmark for the entire vintage. On Monday at La Paulée de Meursault there is a party where growers bring along bottles of their best vintages to enjoy.

Hospices de Beaune
1986
BEAUNE
Appellation Beaune Contrôlée
Cuvée Nicolas-Rolin

75 cl

Wine sold at the famous auction

STAR FEATURES

- **★ Great Hall**

- **★ Last Judgment Polyptych by Rogier van der Weyden**

Kitchen
The centerpiece of the kitchen is a Gothic fireplace with a dual hearth and a mechanical spit, made in 1698, which is turned by a wooden "robot."

Cour d'Honneur
The buildings of Hôtel-Dieu are arranged around a splendid central courtyard. This is flanked by a wooden gallery, above which rise high dormer windows topped by weather-vanes. The courtyard well is a fine example of Gothic wrought-iron work.

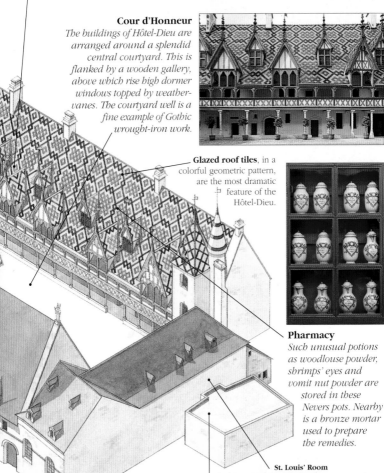

Glazed roof tiles, in a colorful geometric pattern, are the most dramatic feature of the Hôtel-Dieu.

Pharmacy
Such unusual potions as woodlouse powder, shrimps' eyes and vomit nut powder are stored in these Nevers pots. Nearby is a bronze mortar used to prepare the remedies.

St. Louis' Room

★ Last Judgment Polyptych
The naked figures shown in Rogier van der Weyden's 15th-century polyptych were briefly given clothing in the 19th century. At the same time, the altarpiece was cut in half so that the outer and inner panels could be seen together.

Château de Pierreclos in the Mâconnais region

Brionnais

Saône-et-Loire. 🚉 Mâcon.
🚌 Paray-le-Monial, La Clayette.
🚏 Paray-le-Monial, Anzy-le-Duc.
🛈 Marcigny (03 85 25 39 06).

THE BRIONNAIS is a small and peaceful rural district, squeezed between the Loire River and the Beaujolais foothills in the far south of Burgundy.

Its agricultural staple is the white Charolais cow, which can be seen grazing everywhere. For a closer look at this regional symbol, visit the lively cattle market in **St-Christophe** early on Thursday mornings.

The area has an abundance of Romanesque churches, most of which are built of the local ocher-colored stone. The 11th-century church of **Anzy-le-Duc** has a majestic

Capital in St-Julien-de-Jonzy

three-tiered polygonal tower and exquisitely carved capitals. **Semur-en-Brionnais** was the birthplace of Cluny's famous abbot, St. Hugues. Its church is inspired by his great monastery. The church at **St-Julien-de-Jonzy** has a very finely carved tympanum.

A small town by the Genette River, **La Clayette** is graced by a château set in a lake. It is not open to the public, but has a vintage car museum and a *son et lumière* show in summer.

Southeast of La Clayette the lonely **Montagne de Dun** rises just over 700 m (2,300 ft) and offers a panorama over the gentle, green Brionnais hills. This is some of the best picnic country in Burgundy, full of sleepy corners and quiet byways.

Mâcon ㉕

Saône-et-Loire. 👥 36,000. ✈ 🚉
🚌 🛈 1 pl Saint Pierre (03 85 21 07 07). 🛒 Sat.

AT THE FRONTIER between Burgundy and the south, Mâcon is an industrial town and wine center on the Saône.

The lack of churches is due to fervent anti-clericalism during the Revolution, when 14 were destroyed. A 17th-century convent has been turned into the **Musée des Ursulines**. Its collections include French and Flemish painting and an exhibition on the prehistoric site of Solutré. On the charming place aux Herbes, where the market is held, the **Maison de Bois** is a 15th-century wooden house covered with bizarre carvings.

🏛 **Musée des Ursulines**
Allée de Matisco. 📞 03 85 39 90 38. 🕐 Tue–Sat, Sun pm.
⬤ some public hols. 🎫

Environs
The great **Roche de Solutré** rises dramatically above the Pouilly-Fuissé vineyards in the Mâconnais district (see p335). Below the rock, bones and flints from the Stone Ages have established it as an important archaeological site.

Mâconnais is also the land of the Romantic poet Lamartine (1790–1869). Born in Mâcon, he spent his childhood at Milly Lamartine and later lived at Château de St-Point. **Château de Pierreclos** is associated with his epic poem *Jocelyn*.

Charolais cattle grazing on the gentle hills of the Brionnais

Franche-Comté

A REGION OF WOODS and water, the Franche-Comté offers exceptional natural beauty combined with opportunities for canoeing, hiking and skiing. In addition to its interesting towns, this is a region to explore in the wild. Glorious scenery with grottoes and waterfalls are found all along the Vallée du Doubs. Farther south are the spectacular sources of the Lison and Loue rivers. The Reculées is an area of extraordinary formations of ridges and waterfalls such as Baume-les-Messieurs. In Région des Lacs, the silent, peaceful lakes are surrounded by mountain peaks and virgin forests.

Cascades du Hérisson

Pays-des-Lacs. ℹ *Clairvaux-les-Lacs (03 84 25 27 47).*

Nature at its purest at Source du Lison in the Franche-Comté

THE VILLAGE of Doucier, at the foot of the Pic de l'Aigle, is the start of the Hérisson River valley, one of the finest natural settings in the Jura. Park the car by the Moulin Jacquand windmill and walk up the trail through the woods to a spectacular waterfall, the 65-m (213-ft) Cascade de L'Eventail, and beyond to the equally impressive Cascade du Grand Saut. The walk, which takes about two hours there and back, is steep at times, and can be slippery so proper shoes are essential.

Arbois ㉗

Jura. ⚐ 4,000. 🚆 🚌 ℹ *10 rue de l'Hôtel de Ville (03 84 66 55 50).* 🛒 *Fri.*

THE WINE TOWN of Arbois lies on the vine-covered banks of the Cuisance River. It is famous for its wines, especially the sherrylike *vin jaune* (yellow wine) of the district. On the north side of the town is **Maison de Pasteur**, the preserved house and laboratory of the great practical scientist Louis Pasteur (1822–95), the first to test vaccines on humans.

Environs

Southeast of Dole is the 18th-century **Château d'Arlay**, with immaculately kept gardens

Dole ㉘

Jura. ⚐ 27,000. 🚆 🚌 ℹ *6 pl Grevy (03 84 72 11 22).* 🛒 *Tue, Thu & Sat.*

THE BUSY TOWN of Dole lies where the Doubs meets the Rhine-Rhône Canal. The former capital of the Comté was always a symbol of the region's resistance to the French. The region had become used to relative independence under the Counts of Burgundy and then as part of the Holy Roman Empire. Though always French-speaking, its people did not appreciate the idea of the French absolute monarchy and in 1636 endured a very long siege. The town finally submitted to Louis XIV first in 1668 and again in 1674.

There is a charming historic quarter in the center of town, full of winding alleys, houses dating back to the 15th century, and quiet inner courtyards. Place aux Fleurs offers an excellent view of this part of town and the mossy-roofed, 16th-century **Eglise Notre-Dame** with its high bell tower.

Virgin and Child on the north portal of Eglise Notre-Dame, Dole

The Saline Royale at Arc-et-Senans

Arc-et-Senans ㉙

Doubs. 🏘 *1,300.* 🚇 ℹ️ *Ancienne Saline Royale (03 81 57 43 21).*

DESIGNATED a world heritage site since 1982, the Saline Royale (royal salt works) at Arc-et-Senans were designed by the great French architect Claude-Nicolas Ledoux (1736–1806). He envisaged a development built in concentric circles around the main buildings. However, the only ones to be completed (in 1775) were the buildings used for salt production. Nevertheless, these show the staggering scale of Ledoux's idea: saltwater was to be piped from Salins-les-Bains nearby, and fuel to reduce it was to come from the Chaux Forest. The enterprise, which was never a financial success, was closed down in 1895, but the terrific buildings remain.

The **Musée Ledoux Lieu du Sel** displays intriguing models of the grand projects imagined by the visionary architect.

🏛 **Musée Ledoux Lieu du Sel**
Ancienne Saline Royale.
📞 *03 81 54 45 45.* ⭕ *daily.* ⬤ *Jan 1, Dec 25.* 🎦 ✅ ♿ *ground floor.*

Champlitte ㉚

Haute Saône. 🏘 *1,900.* 🚇 ℹ️ *La Mairie (03 84 67 64 10).*

THE **Musée des Arts et Traditions Populaires** in the small town of Champlitte was created by a local shepherd who collected objects and artifacts connected with disappearing local customs. One of the most poignant displays housed in this Renaissance château, recalls the emigration of 400 inhabitants to Mexico in mid-19th century.

🏛 **Musée des Arts et Traditions Populaires**
Place de l'Eglise. 📞 *03 84 67 82 00.* ⭕ *Jun–Aug: daily; Sep–May: Wed–Mon.* ⬤ *Sun am, Jan 1, Nov 1, Dec 25.* 🎦 ✅

Besançon ㉛

Doubs. 🏘 *120,000.* 🚇 🚌 ℹ️ *2 pl de la Première Armée Française (03 81 80 92 55).* 🛒 *Tue, Fri & Sun.* 🌐 *www.besancon.com*

BESANÇON supplanted Dole as the capital of the Franche-Comté in the 17th century. It began as an ecclesiastical center and is now an industrial one, specializing in precision engineering. The stately architecture of the old town, often enriched with elegant wrought-iron work, is a 17th-century legacy.

Behind the fine Renaissance façade of the Palais Granvelle, in the Grande Rue, lies the new **Musée du Temps**, a staggering collection of millions of "time-pieces" of all ages, sizes and shapes – a timely tribute to Besançon's renown as a clock- and watch-making center. An interactive exhibition on the fourth floor invites reflection on the relativity of the notion of time. Farther along the same street are the birthplaces of novelist Victor Hugo (1802–85) at No. 140 and the Lumière brothers *(see p59)* at place Victor Hugo. Behind **Porte Noire**, a Roman arch, is the 12th-century Cathédrale St-Jean. In its bell tower is the extraordinary **Horloge Astronomique** – try to be there on the hour, when the automats pop out.

The stunning **Musée des Beaux Arts et d'Archéologie** occupies the old corn market. Its collection includes works by Bellini, Cranach, Rubens, Fragonard, Boucher, Ingres, Goya, Matisse and Picasso.

Vauban's citadel, built on a strategic site overlooking the Doubs River, offers magnificent views and houses the intriguing **Musée Comtoise**, with a collection of local artifacts.

🏛 **Musée du Temps**
Palais Granvelle, 96 Grande Rue.
📞 *03 81 87 81 50* ⭕ *Wed–Sun pms only.* ⬤ *Jan 1, May 1, Nov 1, Dec 25.* 🎦 ♿

🕐 **Horloge Astronomique**
Rue de la Convention. 📞 *03 81 81 12 76.* ⭕ *Apr–Sep: Wed–Mon; (Thu–Mon winter).* ⬤ *Jan.* 🎦

🏛 **Musée des Beaux Arts et d'Archéologie**
1 pl de la Révolution. 📞 *03 81 87 80 49.* ⭕ *Wed–Mon.* 🎦 *Sat pm.* ♿

🏛 **Musée Comtoise**
La Citadelle, rue des Fusillés de la Résistance. 📞 *03 81 87 83 16.* ⭕ *daily.* ⬤ *Tue in winter, Jan 1, Dec 25.* 🎦

The fantastic astronomical clock in Besançon, made in 1857–60

Ornans ㉜

Doubs. 🏘 *4,300.* 🚇 ℹ️ *7 rue Pierre Vernier (03 81 62 21 50).*

THE GREAT Realist painter Gustave Courbet was born in Ornans in 1819. He painted the town in every possible light. His *Enterrement à Ornans* proved to be one of the most influential paintings

The striking Chapelle Notre-Dame-du-Haut by Le Corbusier at Ronchamp

of the 19th century. A stream of Courbet enthusiasts makes the pilgrimage to this delightful riverside town to see his grave and the paintings in his childhood home, now turned into the **Musée Courbet**.

🏛 Musée Courbet
Place Robert Fernier. 📞 03 81 62 23 30. ⬜ Apr–Oct: daily; Nov–Mar: Wed–Mon. ⬤ Jan 1, May 1, Nov 1, Dec 25. 📷

Environs
A canoeist's paradise, the **Vallée de la Loue** is the loveliest in the Jura. The D67 follows the river from Ornans eastward to Ouhans; from there it is only a 15-minute walk to its magnificent source. Various belvederes offer splendid views over the area.

Southwest of Ornans, the spectacular **Source du Lison** *(see p339)* is a 20-minute walk from Nans-sous-Ste-Anne.

Belfort ㉝

Territoire de Belfort. 👥 60,000. 🚂 🚌 ℹ 2 bis rue Clemenceau (03 84 55 90 90). ⬤ Wed, Fri–Sat.

THE SYMBOL of Belfort is an enormous pink sandstone lion. It was built (rather than carved) by Frédéric Bartholdi

(1834–1904), whose other major undertaking was the Statue of Liberty.

Belfort's immensely strong **citadel**, designed by Vauban under Louis XIV, withstood three sieges, in 1814, 1815 and 1870. Today this remarkable array of fortifications provides an interesting walk and extensive views. The **Musée d'Art et d'Histoire**, housed in some of the billets, displays models of the original fortifications as well as regional art and artifacts and contemporary exhibitions (closed Tuesdays).

Ronchamp ㉞

Haute Saône. 👥 3,100. 🚌 ℹ place du 14 juillet 03 84 63 50 82). ⬤ Sat.

LE COURBUSIER'S remarkable **Chapelle Notre-Dame-du-Haut** dominates this former miners' town. A sculpture rather than a building, its swelling concrete form was finalized in 1955. Light, shape and space form a successful unity in the interior.

There is also the **Musée de la Mine,** evoking the industry and the life of local miners.

Le Miroir d'Ornans in the Musée Courbet, Ornans

THE MASSIF CENTRAL

ALLIER · AVEYRON · CANTAL · CORRÈZE · CREUSE · HAUTE-LOIRE
HAUTE-VIENNE · LOZÈRE · PUY DE DÔME

THE MASSIF CENTRAL *is a region of strange, wild beauty – one of France's best-kept secrets. It is surprisingly little known beyond its sprinkling of spas and the major cities of Clermont-Ferrand, Vichy and Limoges. However, the new autoroutes through the heart of its uplands have started to open up this previously remote region.*

The huge central plateau of ancient granite and crystalline rock that makes up the Massif Central embraces the dramatic landscapes of the Auvergne, Limousin, Aveyron and Lozère. Once a testing crossroads for pilgrims, and strung with giant volcanoes, it is a region of unsuspected richness, from the spectacular town of Le Puy-en-Velay, to the unique treasures of Conques.

With its crater lakes and hot springs, the Auvergne is the Massif Central's lush volcanic core, an outdoor paradise offering activities from hiking in summer to skiing in winter. It also has some of France's most beautiful Romanesque churches, medieval castles and Renaissance palaces. To the east are the mountain ranges of Forez, Livardois and Velay; to the west are the giant chains of extinct volcanoes – the Monts Dômes, Monts Dore and the Monts du Cantal. The Limousin, on the northwestern edge of the Massif Central, is gentler country, with green pastures and blissfully empty roads.

The Aveyron spreads into the southwest from the Aubrac Mountains, carrying with it the Lot, Aveyron and Tarn rivers through gorges and valleys with their cliff-hanging villages. To the east in the Lozère are the Grands Causses, the vast, isolated uplands of the Cévennes. These barren plateaus give farmers a poor living, but have been a favorite place for adventurous travelers throughout the centuries.

La Bourboule, a spa town in the Monts Dore

◁ The summit of Puy Mary, 1,787 m (5,863 ft), offering a superb view to walkers who attempt the ascent

Exploring the Massif Central

NATURE IS AT ITS MOST MAGNIFICENT in the volcanic mountain ranges and wild river gorges of the Massif Central. This is a vast and unspoiled territory that offers spectacular sightseeing and every imaginable outdoor activity, with rafting, paragliding, canoeing and hiking among the many choices. There are hundreds of churches, châteaux and museums to nourish lovers of history, architecture and art; and good, hearty regional cooking and wonderful local wines for lovers of good living.

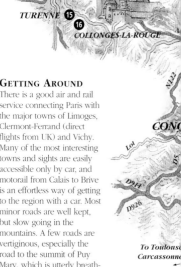

KEY

▰▰	Highway
▰▰	Major road
▰▰	Minor road
▰▰	Scenic route
～	River
✲	Viewing point

0 kilometers   25

0 miles   25

Limestone cliffs of the Gorges du Tarn

GETTING AROUND

There is a good air and rail service connecting Paris with the major towns of Limoges, Clermont-Ferrand (direct flights from UK) and Vichy. Many of the most interesting towns and sights are easily accessible only by car, and motorail from Calais to Brive is an effortless way of getting to the region with a car. Most minor roads are well kept, but slow going in the mountains. A few roads are vertiginous, especially the road to the summit of Puy Mary, which is utterly breath-taking. The A71/A75 through the Auvergne is a magni-ficent road (and toll-free).

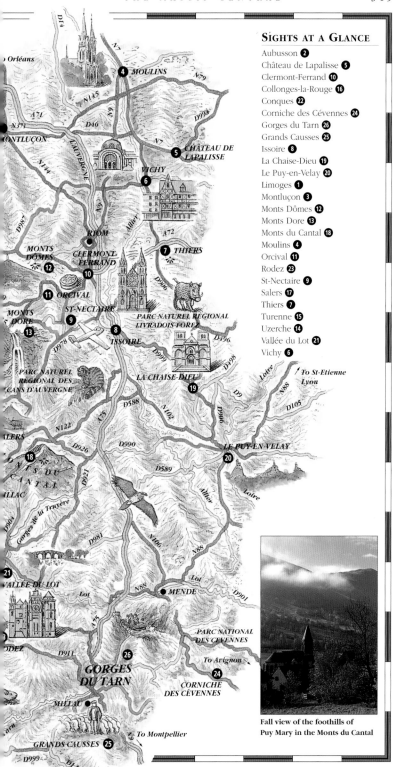

Fall view of the foothills of Puy Mary in the Monts du Cantal

IE NY SCAY QVEL REMEDDE METT
RE AVX OVELLES PVSSAYGE
COVRIR TOVES NE LES PVIS SE
COVRIS MIEVX MEVLT VALVT
DEVX ME DEMETRE
1577

A Limoges enamel plaque, *The Bad Shepherd*

Limoges ❶

Haute-Vienne. 🏠 140,000. ✈ 🚉
🚌 🛈 *12 bvd de Fleurus (05 55 34 46 87)*. 🚌 daily.

THE CAPITAL of the Limousin has two hearts: the old Cité, which grew up around the cathedral on a plateau overlooking the Vienne River, and the rival château on an adjacent rise, now the commercial center of the modern city. The Cité was ravaged by the Black Prince in 1370 during the Hundred Years' War and never recovered; today, it is a quiet place to wander among half-timbered houses and narrow streets.

The area was famous for enamelwork in the Middle Ages and Renaissance period, but it was not until the 1770s, when kaolin deposits were discovered nearby, that Limoges became synonymous with porcelain. The legendary local ware is on display at the superb **Musée National Adrien-Dubouché**. More than 10,000 exhibits, including early Greek and Chinese pieces, trace the history of ceramics to the present day. The **Musée Municipal de l'Evêché** houses some 500 Limousin enamels.

🏛 **Musée National Adrien-Dubouché**
Place Winston Churchill.
📞 *05 55 33 08 50*. **Open** Wed–Mon.
Closed Jan 1, May 1, Dec 25. 📷
🏛 **Musée Municipal de l'Evêché, Musée de l'Email**
Place de la Cathédrale. 📞 *05 55 35 98 10*. ◯ Jul, Aug: daily; Oct–Jun: Wed–Mon. ● some public hols.

Environs

Intense Resistance activity in the Limousin during World War II led to severe reprisals by the occupying army. On June 10, 1944, at the village of Oradour-sur-Glane, 25 km (16 miles) NW of Limoges, SS troops burned alive the entire population. The ruins have been kept as a shrine, and a new village built nearby, with an information and research center in between. The lively town of St-Junien nearby has been a glove-making center since the Middle Ages, and it still supplies today's designers with luxury leather items; keep a sharp eye out for bargains!

Aubusson ❷

Creuse. 🏠 5,000. 🚌 🛈 *rue Vieille (05 55 66 32 12)*. 🚌 Sat.

AUBUSSON OWES its renown to the exceptionally pure waters of the Creuse, perfect for making the delicately colored dyes used for tapestries and rugs. Tapestry production was at its zenith in the 16th and 17th centuries, but by the end of the 18th century, the Revolution and patterned wallpaper had swept away the clientele.

In the 1940s, Aubusson was revived, largely due to the artist Jean Lurçat, who persuaded other modern artists to design for tapestry. The **Musée Départemental de la Tapisserie**, across the river from the Old Town, displays a permanent collection of these modern works. All 30 workshops welcome visitors – at the **Manufacture St. Jean**, you can watch tapestries and custom-made carpets being made by hand and restored.

🏛 **Musée Départemental de la Tapisserie**
Avenue des Lissiers. 📞 *05 55 66 33 06.*
◯ Wed–Mon (Tue pm Jul–Aug). 📷 ♿
🏛 **Manufacture St. Jean**
3 rue St. Jean. 📞 *05 55 66 10 08.*
◯ Mar–Oct: daily; Nov–Feb: Mon–Fri. ● Dec 23–Jan 1. 📷

Environs

A single street of 15th-century houses and a Roman bridge comprise **Moûtier-d'Ahun**,

Tapestry restoration at the Manufacture St. Jean in Aubusson

Romanesque church at Moûtier-d'Ahun near Aubusson

tucked into the lush Creuse Valley. Vestiges of a Benedictine abbey still remain in the half-Romanesque, half-Gothic church with its elaborate stone portal. The choir has wooden stalls, for which it is worth paying a visit to the church. They are masterpieces of late 17th-century carving with intricately worked motifs of flora and fauna representing the different facets of Good and Evil in figurative form. There is a garden where the nave once was.

Montluçon ❸

Allier. 🏘 42,500. 🚃 🚍 🚹
5 Pl Piquand (04 70 05 11 44). 🍲
Tue–Sun.

Montlucon is the economic center of the region, a small town with a medieval core. At its heart there is a Bourbon château, now the **Musée des Musiques Populaires**, housing a collection of *vielles* (hurdy-gurdies). Upstairs is a display of traditional instruments – bagpipes, oboes – and some regional faïence. The 12th-century **Eglise de St-Pierre** is a surprise, with giant stone columns and a huge barrel-vaulted ceiling.

🏛 **Musée des Musiques Populaires**
Château des Ducs de Bourbon.
📞 04 70 02 56 57. 🕐 Wed–Mon pms. 🌑 some public hols. 🈚

Moulins ❹

Allier. 🏘 22,000. 🚃 🚍 🚹 *rue François Péron (04 70 44 14 14).* 🍲 *Tue & Fri.*

CAPITAL of the Bourbonnais and seat of the Bourbon Dukes since the 10th century, Moulins flourished during the early Renaissance and is now an appealing backwater.

Moulins' most celebrated sight is the Flamboyant Gothic **Cathédrale Notre-Dame**, where members of the Bourbon court appear amid the saints in the 15th- and 16th-century stained-glass windows.

The treasury contains a luminous 15th-century Virgin and Child triptych by the "Master of Moulins." Benefactors Pierre II, Duke of Bourbon, and his wife, Anne de Beaujeu, bedecked in embroidery and jewels, are shown being introduced to a less richly dressed Madonna in the central panel.

The tower keep and the single remaining wing of the Bourbon **Vieux Château** house a superb collection of sculpture, paintings and decorative art from the 12th to the 16th centuries.

🔒 **Cathédrale Notre-Dame**
Rue Louis Mantin. **Treasury** 🕐 *daily.*
🌑 *Tue & Sun am.* 🈔

Stained-glass windows at the Cathédrale Notre-Dame in Moulins

Château de Lapalisse **⑤**

Allier. 📞 *04 70 55 01 12.*
🕐 *Apr–Oct: daily.* 🏛️

In the early 16th century, the Marshal of France, Jacques II de Chabannes, hired Florentine architects to reconstruct the feudal château-fort in Lapalisse, creating a refined Renaissance castle, inhabited ever since by his descendants. The *salon doré* (gilded room) has a beamed ceiling paneled in gold, and two huge 15th-century Flemish tapestries showing the Crusader Knight Godefroy de Bouillon and Greek hero Hector, two of the nine classic braves of chivalric legend.

Environs
From Lapalisse, the D480 leads up through the beautiful Besbre Valley past a handful of other small, well-preserved châteaux. Only **Château de Thoury**, with ancient hunting memorabilia and *objets d'art* on display, is open to the public.

⚓ Château de Thoury
Dompierre. 📞 *04 70 42 00 41.* 🕐
Easter–Oct: daily. 🏛️ 🚹 *restr.* 🚗 *oblig.*

Gilded ceiling, Château de Lapalisse

Vichy **⑥**

Allier. 🚶 *27,000.* 🚉 🚌 ℹ️ *19 rue du Parc (04 70 98 71 94).* 🛒 *Wed.*

This small city on the Allier River has been known since the Roman era for its hot and cold springs, and reputed cures for rheumatism, arthritis and digestive complaints. The celebrated letter-writer Madame de Sévigné and the daughters of Louis XV came here in the late 17th and 18th centuries – the former compared the showers to "a rehearsal for Purgatory." The

Interior of the original Thermal Establishment building in Vichy

visits of Napoleon III in the 1860s put Vichy on the map and made taking the waters fashionable. The small town was spruced up and became a favorite among the French nobility and the world's wealthy middle classes. These days, the grand old Thermal Establishment, built in 1900, has been turned into a shopping center The modern baths are state-of-the-art and

Vichy poster (about 1930–50) by Badia-Vilato

strictly for medical purposes. A doctor's prescription and a reservation 30 days in advance are required for all aquatic treatments.

Vichy's fortunes changed for the better once again in the 1960s with the damming of the Allier, creating a huge lake in the town center. Vichy soon became a thriving center for watersports and international events. For a small fee, you can have a taste of sports from aikido to water-skiing or learn canoeing on the 3-km-long (2-mile) artificial river.

The focal point of life in Vichy is the **Parc des Sources** in the center of town, with its turn-of-the-century bandstand (afternoon concerts in season), Belle Epoque glass-roofed shopping centers, and the Grand Casino and Opera House. Here there is gambling every afternoon and musical performances in the evenings, and an atmosphere of gaiety pervades. Also open to the public are the beautiful bronze taps of the **Source**

Célestin, in a riverside park containing vestiges of a convent bearing the same name. Only by making an effort to imagine the city in grainy black-and-white newsreel style is there the slightest reminder of the wartime Vichy government which was based in the town from 1940–44 *(see p61)*.

🔹 **Source Célestin**
Boulevard Kennedy.
◯ *daily.* ◑ *Dec–Jan* ♿

Thiers ❼

Puy de Dôme. 🚶 *13,000.* 🚉 🚌
🛈 *rue Conchette (04 73 80 65 65).*
🛒 *Thu & Sat.*

A CCORDING TO the writer La Bruyère, Thiers "seems painted on the slope of the hill," hanging dramatically as it does on a ravine over a sharp bend in the Durolle River. The city has been renowned for cutlery since the Middle Ages, when legend has it that Crusaders brought back techniques of metalwork from the Middle East. With grindstones powered by dozens of waterfalls on the opposite bank of the river, Thiers produced everything from table knives to guillotine blades, and cutlery remains its major industry today, much of it on display in the Cutlery Museum, the **Musée de la Coutellerie**.

The Old Town is filled with mysterious quarters like "the Corner of Chance" and "Hell's Hollow," honeycombed with tortuous streets and well-restored 14th–17th-century houses. Many have elaborately-carved wooden façades, like the Maison du Pirou in place

Pirou. The view west from the rampart terrace, toward Monts Dômes and Monts Dore, is splendid at sunset.

🏛 **Musée de la Coutellerie**
Maison des Coutelliers, 21–23 & 58 rue de la Coutellerie. 📞 *04 73 80 58 86.*
◯ *Jun–Sep: daily; Oct–May: Tue–Sun.*
● *May 1, Nov 1, Dec 25 & Jan (except in school hols).* 📷

Issoire ❽

Puy de Dôme. 🚶 *15,000.* 🚉 🚌
🛈 *place Charles de Gaulle (04 73 89 15 90).* 🛒 *Sat.*

M OST OF OLD ISSOIRE was destroyed in the 16th-century Wars of Religion. The present-day town has been an important industrial center since the end of World War II.

PILGRIMAGES AND OSTENSIONS

Parishes in the Auvergne and the Limousin are renowned for honoring their saints in outdoor processions. Ascension Day sees the Virgin of Orcival carried above the village by night, accompanied by gypsies and their children for baptism. Every seven years a score of villages in the Limousin hold *Ostensions*, when the saints' relics are paraded through the streets into the surrounding woods. The *Ostension* season begins the Sunday after Easter and runs until June. The next event in the seven-year cycle will be held in 2009.

The Virgin of Orcival, carried in procession above the village (1903)

Not only does Issoire have a thriving aeronautical tradition, it is also a mecca for glider pilots, who come from miles around to take advantage of the strong local air currents.

Issoire's colorful 12th-century abbey church of **St-Austremoine** is one of the great Romanesque churches of the region. The capitals depict scenes from the *Life of Christ* (one of the Apostles at the Last Supper has fallen asleep at table), and imaginary demons and beasts. The 15th-century fresco of the *Last Judgment* shows Bosch-like figures of sinners being cast into the mouth of a dragon, with one damsel being carted off to hell in a handbasket. The nearby Tour de l'Horloge has scenes of Renaissance history.

Thiers from the south, spreading over the slopes above the Durolle River

St-Nectaire ❾

Puy de Dôme. 🏃 *750.* 🚾 🛈 *Les Grands Thermes (04 73 88 50 86).*

THE AUVERGNE is noted for Romanesque churches. The **Eglise St-Nectaire** in the upper village of St-Nectaire-le-Haut, with its soaring, elegant proportions, is one of the most beautiful. The 103 stone capitals, 22 of them polychrome, are vividly carved, and the treasury includes a gold bust of St. Baudime and a wooden Notre-Dame-du-Mont-Cornadore, both marvels of 12th-century workmanship. The lower village, St-Nectaire-le-Bas, is a spa with more than 40 hot and cold springs, used in the treatment of kidney and metabolic problems.

Environs
The 12th-century citadel of **Château de Murol**, partially in ruins, offers costumed guides demonstrating medieval life and knightly pursuits. It is wonderful for children.

🏛 **Château de Murol**
Murol. 🕿 *04 73 88 67 11.*
🕒 *Apr–Oct: daily; Nov–Mar: Sat, Sun & public & school hols.* 🚫

Fontaine d'Amboise (1515) in Clermont-Ferrand

Clermont-Ferrand ❿

Puy de Dôme. 🏃 *140,000.* ✈ 🚂 🚾 🛈 *place de la Victoire (04 73 98 65 00).* 🛒 *Mon–Sat.*

CLERMONT-FERRAND began as two distinct – and rival – cities, united only in 1630. Clermont is a lively commercial center and student town, with thriving cafés and restaurants. It was a Celtic settlement before the Roman era, had a cathedral as early as the 5th century, and by 1095 was significant enough for the pope to announce the First Crusade there. The Counts of Auvergne, challenging the episcopal power of Clermont, made their base in what is now old Montferrand, a short drive from Clermont city center. Built on a bastide pattern, it is a time warp of quiet streets and Renaissance houses.

Clermont's more ancient origins are well-illustrated at the **Musée Bargoin** with its remarkable collections of locally-found Roman domestic artefacts (closed Mondays).

Place St-Pierre is Clermont's principal marketplace, with a daily food market – especially good on Saturdays. Nearby, the pedestrianized Rue du Port, lined with small shops, leads steeply downhill from the **Fontaine d'Amboise** (1515), to the **Basilique Notre-Dame-du-Port**. This is one of the most important Romanesque churches in the region. The stone interior is beautifully proportioned, with a magnificent raised choir and vivid carved capitals – look for Largesse battling Avarice, in the form of two knights with chain mail and pikes.

The contrast with the black lava **Cathédrale de Notre-Dame-de-l'Assomption** is startling, from austere 12th-century Romanesque to high-flying 13th-century Gothic.

Raised choir in the Basilique Notre-Dame-du-Port

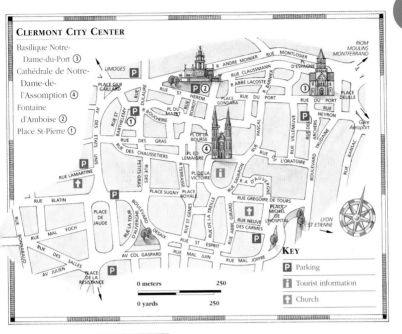

CLERMONT CITY CENTER

Basilique Notre-
Dame-du-Port ③
Cathédrale de Notre-
Dame-de-
l'Assomption ④
Fontaine
d'Amboise ②
Place St-Pierre ①

KEY

P Parking

i Tourist information

Church

0 meters 250

0 yards 250

The graceful lines of the interior are due to the strong local stone used for construction, allowing pillars to be thinner and the whole structure lighter. The dark volcanic rock provides a foil for the jewel-like 12th–15th-century stained-glass windows, believed to be from the same workshop as Sainte-Chapelle's in Paris *(see pp80–81)*.

The old section of Mont-ferrand thrived from the 13th to the 17th centuries, and many fine houses – known as *hôtels particuliers* – built by prosperous merchants have survived. Some of the best of

Michelin Man, c.1910

these, with Italianate loggias, mullioned windows and intriguing courtyards, line ancient **rue Kléber**. Between Clermont and old Montferrand lies a third mini-city, the headquarters and factories of the Michelin rubber and tire company, founded here in 1830, which dominates the town.

Environs

Once the rival of Clermont-Ferrand for supremacy in Auvergne, **Riom** is a somber provincial town of black stone houses and lava fountains. The 14th-century château of Duke Jean de Berry was razed in the 19th century to build the Palais de Justice; all that remains is the delicate Sainte-Chapelle, with its lovely 15th-century stained-glass windows.

Riom's greatest treasure is a graceful Madonna holding an infant with a small bird in his hand. The statue is housed in the Eglise de Notre-Dame-du-Marthuret, originally built in the 14th century, but much changed since then.

**Choir inside the Cathédrale de
Notre-Dame-de-l'Assomption**

Orcival ⓫

Puy de Dôme. 🏠 300.
🚌 04 73 65 82 55.

CRAMMED WITH HOTELS and crowded in summer, Orcival is nevertheless well worth visiting for its Romanesque church, the **Basilique d'Orcival**, which many would say is the best in the region. Completed at the beginning of the 12th century, and typically Auvergne Romanesque in style, the apse is multi-tiered and the side walls are supported by powerful buttresses and strong arches. Inside, the ornate silver and vermilion *Virgin and Child* (in the formal, forward-facing position known as "in majesty") is enigmatic in its rigid, square chair. With an interior lit by 14 windows, and a spacious crypt, the proportions of the building itself are the most graceful aspect.

*Virgin and
Child* in the
**Basilique
d'Orcival**

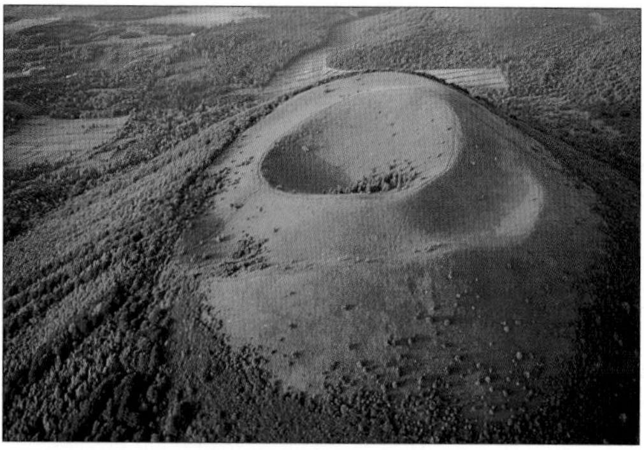

Aerial view of Puy de Dôme in the Monts Dômes range

Monts Dômes ⓬

Puy de Dôme. Clermont-Ferrand. Puy de Dôme summit (04 73 62 21 45: Apr–mid-Nov). Montlosier (04 73 65 64 00).

THE YOUNGEST RANGE of the Auvergne volcanoes at 4,000 years old, the Monts Dômes, or Chaîne des Puys, encompasses 112 extinct volcanoes aligned over a 30-km (19-mile) stretch just west of Clermont-Ferrand. At the center, the **Puy de Dôme** towers above a high plateau. A concentric road off the N922 spirals up the peak at a steady 12 percent gradient, while the steeper, original switchback Roman path is still used by hikers.

At the summit, a half-hour farther, are the vestiges of the Roman temple of Mercury and a meteorological/telecommunications tower. On a rare clear day, the view across the volcano will take away whatever breath you have left.

The controversial new **Parc Européen du Volcanisme, Vulcania**, uses the latest technology to simulate volcanic activity in its 2-ha (5-acre) underground circuit.

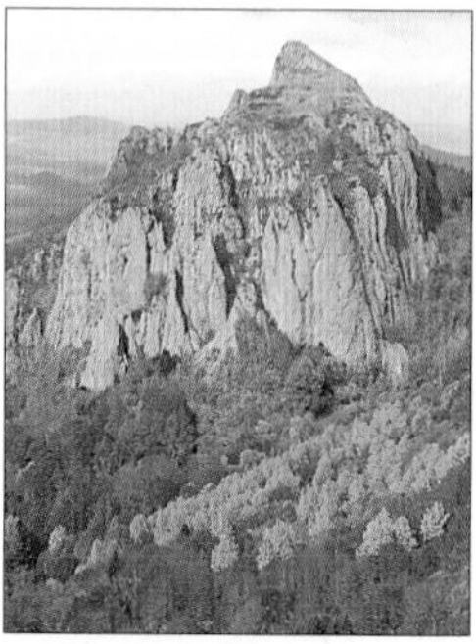

The volcanic Roche Tuilière below Col de Guéry in the Monts Dore

In the southwest corner of the Monts Dômes region is the **Château de Cordès**, a small, privately-owned 15th-century manor house with formal gardens designed by Le Nôtre *(see p169)*.

Vulcania
D941B, Saint-Ours-les-Roches. *04 73 31 02 05. Feb–Nov: Wed–Sun; Jun–Aug & sch. hols: daily.*
Documentation center

Château de Cordès
Orcival. *04 73 65 81 34.*
Easter–Oct: daily (call for appointments out of season).

Monts Dore ⓭

Puy de Dôme. Clermont-Ferrand. Le Mont-Dore. Montlosier (04 73 65 64 00).

THREE GIANT VOLCANOES – the Puy de Sancy, the Banne d'Ordanche and the Puy de l'Aiguiller – and their secondary cones make up the Monts Dore: dark green, heavily wooded mountains laced with rivers and lakes and dotted with summer and winter resorts for skiing, hiking, paragliding, canoeing and sailing.

The 1,886-m (6,185-ft) **Puy de Sancy** is the highest point in Central France. It can be reached by taking a shuttle from the town of Le Mont-Dore to the cable car which goes up to the peak, followed by a long hike across open terrain. From Le Mont-Dore, there is an exhilarating scenic drive on the D36 which leads to the **Couze-Chambon Valley**, a beautiful stretch of high moorland threaded with waterfalls.

The area has two popular spa towns: **La Bourboule**, for children's ailments, with its casino, and Le Mont-Dore, with its grandiose turn-of-the-century **Etablis-sement Thermal**.

Below the Col de Guéry on the D983, the eroded volcanic **Roche Sanadoire** and **Roche Tuilière** stand up like two gigantic gateposts. From their peaks are far-reaching views over the wooded Cirque de Chausse and beyond.

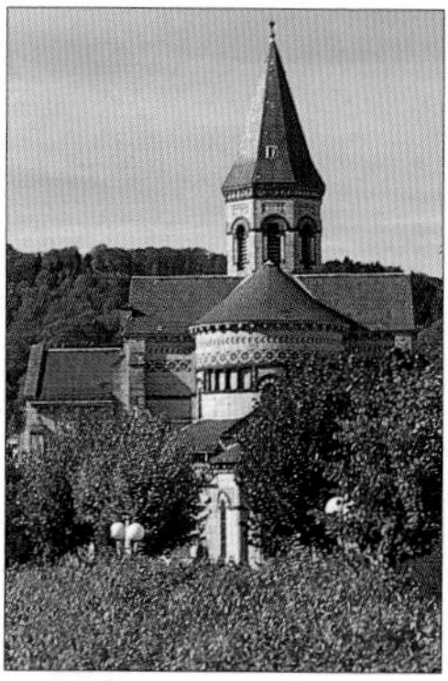

Church at La Bourboule in the Monts Dore

Uzerche ⓮

Corrèze. 3,000. place de la Libération (05 55 73 15 71).

UZERCHE is an impressive sight: gray slate roofs, turrets and bell towers rising from a hill above the Vézère River. This prosperous town never capitulated during the conflicts of the Middle Ages, and earlier withstood a seven-year siege by Moorish forces in 732. On the point of surrender, the townspeople sent a feast out to their enemy – in fact, the last of their supplies. The Moors, thinking such lavish offerings meant the city had stores to spare, gave up.

The Romanesque **Église St-Pierre** crests the hill above the town. Beyond Uzerche, the Vézère cuts through the green gorges of the Saillant.

CANTAL CHEESE

Transhumance is still practiced in the Auvergne, with the local Salers cattle kept in barns in the valleys during winter and led up to mountain pastures for the summer. The robust grasses and flowers – gentian, myrtle, anemone – on which the cows graze produce a flavorful milk that is the basis for the region's great cheese, Cantal. Curds were once pressed through cheesecloth by hand, but now modern methods prevail. Cantal is the key ingredient in *aligot* – the potato-and-cheese purée flavored with garlic that is one of the region's most famous dishes.

Salers cattle enjoying rich pastures

Turenne ⓯

Corrèze. 👥 *750.* 🚗 🚌
ℹ️ *Ancienne Mairie (summer: 05 55 85 94 38; winter: 05 55 85 91 15).*

TURENNE IS one of the most appealing medieval towns in the Corrèze. Crescent-shaped and clustered on the cliffside, the town was the last independent feudal fiefdom in France, under the absolute rule of the La Tour d'Auvergne family until 1738. Henri de la Tour d'Auvergne, their most illustrious member, was a marshal of France under Louis XIV, and one of the greatest soldiers of modern times.

Now the sole remains of the **Château de Turenne** are the 13th-century Clock Tower and 11th-century Tower of Caesar, from which there is an amazing 360-degree view of the Cantal Mountains across to the Dordogne Valley. Not far away is the 16th-century collegiate chuch and the **Chapelle des Capucins** dating from the 18th century.

⚜ **Château de Turenne**
📞 *05 55 85 90 66.* ⏰ *Apr–Oct: daily; Nov–Mar: Sun pm.* 📷

Collonges-la-Rouge ⓰

Corrèze. 👥 *400.* 🚗
ℹ️ *Mairie (05 55 25 41 09).*

THERE'S SOMETHING a little unsettling about Collonges' unique carmine sandstone architecture, quite beautiful in individual houses, though the overall effect takes some getting used to, for it is both austere and fairytale like.

Founded in the 8th century, Collonges came under the rule of Turenne, whose burghers built the sturdy turreted houses in the surrounding vineyards. Be sure to see the communal bread oven in the marketplace, and the 11th-century church, later fortified with a tower keep. The church's unusual carved white limestone tympanum shows a man driving a bear, and other lively figures.

Salers ⓱

Cantal. 👥 *450.* 🚌 *summer only.*
ℹ️ *place Tyssandier d'Escous (04 71 40 70 68).* 🛒 *Wed.*

A SOLID, HANDSOME TOWN of gray lava houses and 15th-century ramparts, Salers sits atop a steep escarpment at the edge of the Cantal Mountains. It is one of few virtually intact Renaissance villages in the region. The church has an admirable polychrome *mise au tombeau* (entombment), dated 1495, and five elaborate 17th-century Aubusson tapestries.

From the fountain, streets lead up to the cliff edge, and allow views of the surrounding valleys, with the ever-present sound of cowbells in the distance. The town is very crowded in the summer, but it makes a good starting point for excursions to the Puy Mary (*see p354*), the huge barrage in Bort-les-Orgues, the nearby Château de Val and the Cère Valley to the south.

Medieval Château de Val in Bort-les-Orgues near Salers

Puy Mary Peak in the volcanic Monts du Cantal

Monts du Cantal ⑱

Cantal. ✈ *Aurillac.* ▤ ▤ *Lioran.*
ℹ *Aurillac (04 71 48 46 58).*

THE CANTAL MOUNTAINS were originally one enormous volcano – the oldest and the largest in Europe, dating from the Tertiary period. The highest peaks, the **Plomb du Cantal** at 1,855 m (6,086 ft) and the **Puy Mary** at 1,787 m (5,863 ft), are surrounded by ranges of smaller crests and deep river valleys. Driving the narrow, precipitous roads is a giddy experience, compounded by the grand vistas at every hairpin turn. Between peaks and gorges, rich mountain pastures provide summer grazing for red-gold Salers cows *(see p353)*. From the **Pas de Peyrol**, the highest road pass in the country at 1,589 m (5,191 ft), it's about a 25-minute journey on foot to the summit of the Puy Mary.

Environs
One of the finest of the Auvergne châteaux, **Château d'Anjony** was built by Louis II d'Anjony, a supporter of Joan of Arc *(see pp290–91)*. Highlights are the 16th-century frescoes: in the chapel, scenes from the Life and Passion of Christ, and upstairs in the *Salle des Preux* (Room of the Knights), a dazzling series of the nine heroes of chivalry. To the south lies the small market town of **Aurillac**, a good base from which to explore the Cantal region.

♣ **Château d'Anjony**
Tournemire. 📞 04 71 47 61 67.
◯ *mid-Feb–mid-Nov: daily pms.* ▨

La Chaise-Dieu ⑲

Haute-Loire. ♨ 800. ▤ ℹ *place de la Mairie (04 71 00 01 16).* 🚌 *Thu.*

SOMBER AND MASSIVE, midway between Romanesque and Gothic, the abbey church of **St-Robert** is the prime reason to visit the small village of La Chaise-Dieu. The building dates from the 14th century and is an amalgam of styles and tastes. The choir, however, is sensational: 144 oak stalls carved with figures of Vice and Virtue. Above them, entirely covering the walls, are some of the loveliest tapestries in France. Made in Brussels and Arras in the early 16th century and depicting scenes from the Old and New Testaments, they are rich in color and detail.

On the outer walls of the choir, the 15th-century wall painting of the *Danse Macabre* shows Death in the form of skeletons leading rich and poor alike to their inevitable end. Beyond the cloister is the Echo room, in which two people whispering in opposite corners can hear one another perfectly – this was a clever medieval solution for hearing the confessions of lepers and monks.

Le Puy-en-Velay ⑳

Haute-Loire. ♨ 23,000. ✈ ▤ ▤
ℹ *place du Breuil (04 71 09 38 41).*
🚌 *Sat.* 🎪 *Sep.*

Statue of Notre-Dame-de-France at Le Puy

LOCATED IN THE BOWL of a volcanic cone, the extraordinary town of Le Puy teeters on a stunning series of rock outcrops and giant basalt pillars. The town appears to have three peaks, each topped with a landmark church or statue. Seen from afar, the ensemble is one of the most dramatic sights in France.

Now a commercial and tourist-oriented town, Le Puy's star attraction is its medieval **Holy City**. This became a pilgrimage center after the Bishop of Le Puy, Gotescalk, made one of the first pilgrimages to Santiago de Compostela in 962, and built the **Chapelle St-Michel d'Aiguilhe** upon his return.

Detail of *Danse Macabre* at St-Robert, in La Chaise-Dieu

THE AUVERGNE'S BLACK MADONNAS

The cult of the Virgin Mary has always been strong in the Auvergne and this is reflected in the concentration of her statues in the region. Carved in dark walnut or cedar, now blackened with age, the Madonnas are believed to originate from the Byzantine influence of the Crusaders. Perhaps the most famous Madonna is the one in Le-Puy-en-Velay, a 17th-century copy of one which belonged to Louis IX in the Middle Ages.

Louis IX's Black Virgin

Pilgrims from eastern France and Germany assembled at the **Cathédrale de Notre-Dame**, with its famous Black Madonna and "fever stone" – a Druid ceremonial stone with healing powers embedded in one of its walls – before setting off for Compostela.

Built on an early pagan site, the Cathédrale de Notre-Dame is a huge Romanesque structure. Multiform arches, carved palm and leaf designs and a checkerboard façade show the influences of Moorish Spain, and indicate the considerable cultural exchange that took place with southern France in the 11th and 12th centuries. In the transept are Romanesque frescoes, notably an 11th–12th-century St. Michael; in the sacristy, the treasury includes the Bible of Theodolphus, a handwritten document from the era of Charlemagne. The cathedral is the center of the Holy City complex that dominates the upper town, encompassing a baptistry, cloister, Prior's house and Penitents' chapel.

The colossal red statue of **Notre-Dame-de-France**, on the pinnacle of the Rocher Corneille, was erected in 1860, cast from 213 cannons captured at Sebastopol during the Crimean War. The statue is reached by a steep pathway, and can be climbed by an iron ladder on the inside.

The Chapelle St-Michel, like the cathedral, shows Moorish influences in the trefoil decoration and colored mosaics on the rounded arch over the main entrance. It seems to grow out of a giant finger of lava rock and is reached by a steep climb. The church is thought to be located on the site of a Roman temple to Mercury, and its center dates from the 10th century, although most of the building was constructed a century later. The floor has been constructed to follow the contours of the rock in places, and the interior is ornamented with faded 10th-century murals and 20th-century stained-glass.

In the lower city, narrow streets of 15th- and 16th-century houses lead to the Vinay Garden and the **Musée Crozatier**, which has a collection of handmade lace from the 16th century to the present – a craft that is now enjoying a revival. The museum also has a surprisingly good collection of medieval *objets d'art* and 15th-century paintings, with works attributed to de Heem and Salomon Ruysdael.

In mid-September, Le Puy transforms itself into a masked and costumed Renaissance carnival for the Bird King Festival, an ancient tradition celebrating the skill of the city's best archers *(see p.34)*.

Chapelle St-Michel d'Aiguilhe
Aiguilhe. 04 71 09 50 03.
Feb–mid-Nov: daily; Xmas hols: pms only. Jan 1, Dec 25.

Notre-Dame-de-France
Rocher Corneille. 04 71 04 11 33.
Feb–Nov: daily; Xmas hols: pms only.
Dec–Jan.

Musée Crozatier
Jardin Henri Vinay. 04 71 09 38 90.
Wed–Mon (summer: daily). Oct–Apr: Sun am; Jan 1, Nov 1, Dec 25.

Chapelle St-Michel d'Aiguilhe, standing on a finger of lava rock

Ruins of the Castle of Calmont d'Olt in Espalion in the Lot Valley

Vallée du Lot ㉑

Aveyron. ✈ *Aurillac, Rodez.* 🚊 *Rodez, Séverac-le-Château.* 🚌 *St-Géniez, Conques.* 🛈 *Espalion (05 65 44 10 63).*

FROM MENDE and the old river port of La Canourgue all the way to Conques, the Lot River (or Olt in old usage) courses through its fertile valley past orchards, vineyards and pine forests. **St. Côme d'Olt**, near the Aubrac mountains, is an unspoiled, fortified village whose 15th-century church is surrounded by Medieval and Renaissance houses. At **Espalion**, the pastel stone houses and a turreted 16th-century castle are reflected in the river, which runs beneath a 13th-century arched stone bridge. The town has one of the best markets in the region on Friday mornings. Just outside town is the 11th-century Perse Church, whose carved capitals portray battling knights and imaginary birds sipping from a chalice.

Estaing was once the fiefdom of one of the greatest families of the Rouergue, dating back to the 13th century. The village nestles beneath its massive château (now a convent) on the river bank. The road passes through the Lot Gorge on the way to **Entraygues** ("between waters"), where the old quarter and 13th-century Gothic bridge are worth a visit. Beyond Entraygues, the river widens to join the Garonne.

Conques ㉒

See pp358–9.

Rodez ㉓

Aveyron. 🏠 *26,000.* ✈ 🚊 🚌 🛈 *place Foch (05 65 68 02 27).* 📅 *Wed, Fri (eve) & Sat.*

LIKE MANY medieval French cities, Rodez was politically divided: the shop-lined **place du Bourg** on one side of town and **place de la Cité**, near the cathedral, on the other, reflect conflicting secular and ecclesiastical interests. Rodez's commercial center, the largest in the region, is probably the main attraction now, though the 13th-century huge pink stone **Cathédrale Notre-Dame** is worth a look, with its fortress-like west façade, and its magnificent, ornate belltower. The 15th-century choir stalls show a superb panoply of creatures, including a winged lion, some fair demoiselles and a naughty fellow exposing his derrière.

Entombment in Rodez Cathedral

Environs

Just 45km (28 miles) southeast lies the small village of Saint Léons, birthplace of Jean-Henri Fabre, the famous entymologist. Here is **Micropolis**, part interactive museum, part theme park, dedicated to the glory of insects (open daily). Go to see the breathtaking film of the same name, if nothing else.

ROBERT LOUIS STEVENSON

Robert Louis Stevenson (1850–94), best known for his novels *Treasure Island, Kidnapped* and *Dr. Jekyll and Mr. Hyde*, was also an accomplished travel writer. In 1878, he set off across the remote Cévennes mountain range with only a small donkey, Modestine, for company. His classic account of this eventful journey, *Travels with a Donkey in the Cévennes*, was published in the following year.

Robert Louis Stevenson

Dramatic scenery in Corniche des Cévennes national park

Corniche des Cévennes ㉔

Lozère, Gard. ✈ *Rodez-Marcillac.*
🚌 *Alès.* 🚌 *St-Jean-du-Gard.*
ℹ *St-Jean-du-Gard (04 66 85 32 11).*

THE DRAMATIC corniche road from Florac on the Tarn to St-Jean-du-Gard was cut in the early 18th century by the army of Louis XIV in pursuit of the Camisards, Protestant rebels who had no uniforms but fought in their ordinary shirts (*camiso* in the *langue d'oc*). The route of the D983 makes a spectacular drive. Fascination with the history of the Camisards was one of the reasons that the famous Scots writer Robert Louis Stevenson undertook his fabled trek in the Cévennes with Modestine, recounted in his *Travels with a Donkey*.

In St-Laurent-de-Trèves, where fossil remains suggest dinosaurs once roamed the lagoon, there is a sweeping view of the Grands Causses and the peaks of Lozère and Aigoual. The Corniche finishes in St-Jean-du-Gard, where the **Musée des Vallées Cévenoles**, depicting typical peasant life, is located in a former 17th-century inn.

🏛 Musée des Vallées Cévenoles

95 Grand' rue, St-Jean-du-Gard.
📞 *04 66 85 10 48.* 🕐 *Jul–Aug: daily; Apr–Jun, Sep–Oct: 10am–noon, 2–7pm daily; Nov–Mar: Tue, Thu, Sun pm.* ● *Jan 1, Dec 25.* 📷 ♿ *gr. fl.*

Grands Causses ㉕

Aveyron. ✈ *Rodez-Marcillac.* 🚌
🚌 *Millau.* ℹ *Millau (05 65 60 02 42).*

THE CAUSSES are vast, arid limestone plateaus, alternating with surprisingly green, fertile canyon valleys. The only sign of life at times is a bird of prey wheeling in the sky, or an isolated stone farm or shepherd's hut. The whole area makes for some desolate hiking for those who like solitude.

The four Grands Causses – Sauveterre, Méjean, Noir and Larzac – stretch out east of the city of Millau, from Mende in the north to the valley of the Vis River in the south.

Among the sights in the Causses are the *chaos* – bizarre rock formations reputed to resemble ruined cities, and named accordingly: there's the *chaos* of **Montpellier-le-Vieux**, **Nîmes-le-Vieux** and **Roquesaltes**. **Aven Armand** and the **Dargilan Grotto** are vast and deep natural underground grottoes with equally astonishing formations.

A good place to head in the windy reaches of the Larzac Causse is the strange, rough-hewn stone village of **La Couvertoirade**, a fully enclosed citadel of the Knights Templar in the 12th century. The unpaved streets and medieval houses are an austere reminder of the dark side of the Middle Ages. Entrance to the village is free, with a fee for the tour of the ramparts.

The Causse du Larzac's best-known village is probably **Roquefort-sur-Soulzon**, a small gray town terraced on the side of a crumbled limestone outcrop. It has one main street and one major product, Roquefort cheese. This is made from unpasteurized sheep's milk, seeded with a distinctive blue mold grown on loaves of bread, and aged in the warren of damp caves above the town.

View over Méjean, one of the four plateaus of the Grands Causses

Conques ❷

12th-century reliquary

THE VILLAGE of Conques clusters around the splendid Abbaye de Ste-Foy, hemmed into a rugged site against the hillside. Sainte Foy was a young girl who became an early Christian martyr; her relics were first kept at a rival monastery in Agen. In the 9th century a monk from Conques stole the relics, thereby attracting pilgrims to this remote spot and firmly establishing Conques as a stop on the route to Santiago de Compostela *(see pp390–91)*.

The treasury holds the most important collection of medieval and Renaissance gold work in western Europe. Some of it was made in the abbey's own workshops as early as the 9th century. The Romanesque abbey church has beautiful stained-glass windows by Pierre Soulages (1994) and its tympanum is a triumph of medieval sculpture.

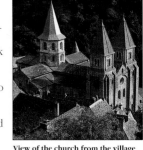

View of the church from the village

The broad transepts were able to accommodate crowds of pilgrims.

Nave Interior
Pure and elegantly austere, the Romanesque interior dates from 1050–1135. The short nave soars to a height of 22 m (72 ft), with three tiers of arches topped by 250 decorative carved capitals.

Tympanum
This sculpture of 1135 depicts the Last Judgment, *with the Devil in Hell (shown here) in the lower part of the sculpture and Christ in Heaven in the tympanum's central position.*

CONQUES' TREASURES

The treasures date from the 9th to the 16th century, and are prized for both their beauty and their rarity. The gold-plated wood and silver reliquary of Ste. Foy is studded with gems, rock crystal and even an *intaglio* of Roman Emperor Caracalla. The body is 9th century, but the face may be older, possibly 5th century. Other magnificent pieces include an "A"-shaped reliquary said to be a gift from Charlemagne; the small but exquisite Pépin's shrine from AD 1000; and a late 15th-century processional cross.

The precious reliquary of Ste-Foy

VISITORS' CHECKLIST

Abbaye de Sainte-Foy, Conques.
📞 05 65 72 85 00. 🚌 🚌 from Rodez. **Treasuries** ☐ daily: Jul–Aug: 9 am–12:30 pm, 1:30–7 pm; Sep–Jun: 9 am–noon, 2–6 pm (Oct–Mar: 10 am). 🕭 🕭 8:15 am (Sep–Jun), 11:30 am Mon–Sat (Jul–Aug), 7:45 am, 11 am Sun. 📷
♿ restr. 🅿 W www.conques.fr

Romanesque Chapels
The east end is three-tiered, topped by the blind arcades of the choir and a central bell tower. Three chapels surround the eastern apse, built to accommodate extra altars for the celebration of mass.

Treasury I
The precious contents of the treasury were hidden by the townspeople to prevent their destruction during the French Revolution. Perhaps surprisingly, all were returned.

Entrance to Treasury I

The Cloister consists of a reconstructed square: only two sections of the original early 12th-century arcades remain. However, 30 of the original carved capitals are displayed in the refectory and in the Treasury II above the tourist office.

Gorges du Tarn ㉖

NEAR THE BEGINNING of its journey to meet the Garonne River, the Tarn flows through some of Europe's most spectacular gorges. For millions of years, the Tarn and its tributary, the Jonte, have eaten their way down through the limestone plateaus of the Cévennes, creating a sinuous forked canyon some 25 km (15 miles) long and nearly 400 m (1,300 ft) deep. The gorges are flanked by rocky bluffs and scaled by roads with dizzying bends and panoramic views, which are incredibly popular in the high season. The surrounding plateaus, or *causses*, are eerily different, forming an open, austere landscape, dry in summer and snow-clad in winter, where wandering sheep and isolated farms are sometimes the only signs of life.

Point Sublime
From 800 m (2,600 ft) up, there are stunning views of a major bend in the Tarn Gorge, with the Causse Méjean visible in the distance.

Outdoor Activities
The Tarn and Jonte gorges are popular for canoeing and rafting. Although relatively placid in summer, melting snow can make the rivers hazardous in spring.

Pas de Souci
Just upriver from Les Vignes, Pas de Souci flanks a narrow point in the gorge as the Tarn makes its way northward.

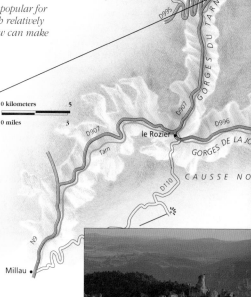

Chaos de Montpellier-le-Vieux
Situated on the flank of the Causse Noir off the D110 is a remarkable geological site – bizarre rock formations created by limestone erosion.

La Malène
*An old crossing-point between the Causse de Sauveterre
and the Causse Méjean, this village, with its 16th-century
fortified manor, is a good starting point for boat trips.*

VISITORS' CHECKLIST

Lozère. ✈ Rodez-Marcillac. ▭
Mende, Banassac, Séverac-le-
Château. ▭ Florac, Le Rozier. ❚
Le Rozier (summer: 05 65 62 60
89). St-Enimie (04 66 48 53 44).

AUSSE DE SAUVETERRE

Ste-Enimie   D907   Ispagnac

Tarn

la Malène

CAUSSE MEJEAN

D996

Aven
mand

otte de
argilan   D39   Jonte   D996

Meyrueis

Aven Armand Caves
*On the Causse Méjean, many
stalactites in the caves are
tinted by minerals that
are deposited by the
slowly trickling water.*

Causse Méjean
The high plateaus or causses *are a botanist's
paradise in spring and summer, with over
900 species of wildflowers, including orchids.*

THE WILD CÉVENNES

One of the least populated parts
of France, this area is well known
for its wildflowers and birds of
prey, and griffon
vultures were once
common here. These
giant but harmless
scavengers nearly died
out earlier this century
through being hunted, but now
a reintroduction program has led
to growing numbers breeding in
the Gorges de la Jonte.

Yellow wort

Kidney
vetch

Green-
winged
orchid

*Wildflowers found in this
thinly populated area include
unusual alpine plants.*

*The griffon vulture, which
now breeds in the region, has a
wingspan of over 2.5 m (8 ft).*

THE RHÔNE VALLEY AND FRENCH ALPS

···

LOIRE · RHÔNE · AIN · ISÈRE · DRÔME
ARDÈCHE · HAUTE-SAVOIE · SAVOIE · HAUTES-ALPES

*I*TS TWO MOST IMPORTANT *geographical features, the Alps and the Rhône River, give this region both its name and its dramatic character. The east is dominated by majestic snowcapped peaks, while the Rhône provides a vital conduit between north and south.*

The Romans recognized this strategic route when they founded Lyon over 2,000 years ago. Today Lyon, with its great museums and fine Renaissance buildings, is the second city of France. It is one of the country's most vital commercial and cultural centers as well as the undisputed capital of French gastronomy. To the north lie the flat marshlands of the Dombes and the rich agricultural Bresse plain. Here, too, are the famous Beaujolais vineyards which, along with the Côtes du Rhône, make the region such an important wine producer.

The French Alps have some of the world's most popular year-round resort areas: internationally renowned ski resorts such as Chamonix, Mégève and Courchevel, and historic cities like Chambéry, capital of Savoy before it joined France. Elegant spa towns line the shores of Lac Léman (Lake Geneva). Grenoble, a bustling university city and high-tech center, is flanked by two of the most spectacular nature reserves in France, the Chartreuse and the Vercors.

To the south, orchards and fields of sunflowers give way to brilliant rows of lavender interspersed with vineyards and olive groves. Châteaux and ancient towns dot the landscape. Mountains and pretty, old-fashioned spa towns characterize the rugged Ardèche, and the deeply scoured gorges along the Ardèche River offer some of the wildest scenery in France.

The restored Ferme de la Forêt at St-Trivier-de-Courtes, north of Bourg-en-Bresse

◁ **Annecy's medieval quarter**

Exploring the Rhône Valley and French Alps

LYON is the region's largest city, famed for its historic buildings and gastronomic tradition. Wine lovers can choose between the vineyards of the Beaujolais, Rhône Valley and Drôme region to the south. To the west, the Ardèche offers rugged wilderness, canoeing and climbing. Spa devotees from around the world flock to Évian-les-Bains and Aix-les-Bains, while the Alps are a favorite destination for sports enthusiasts *(see pp312–13)*.

SIGHTS AT A GLANCE

Aix-les-Bains ㉒
Annecy ㉓
The Ardèche ⑪
Bourg-en-Bresse ①
Briançon ⑯
Chambéry ㉑
The Chartreuse ⑳
The Dombes ②
Grenoble ⑱
Grignan ⑭
Lac Léman ㉔
Le Bourg d'Oisans ⑰
Lyon ④
Montélimar ⑬
Nyons ⑮
Palais Idéal du
  Facteur Cheval ⑧
Pérouges ③
St-Étienne ⑦
St-Romain-en-Gal ⑥
Tournon-sur-Rhône ⑨
Valence ⑩
Vals-les-Bains ⑫
The Vercors ⑲
Vienne ⑤

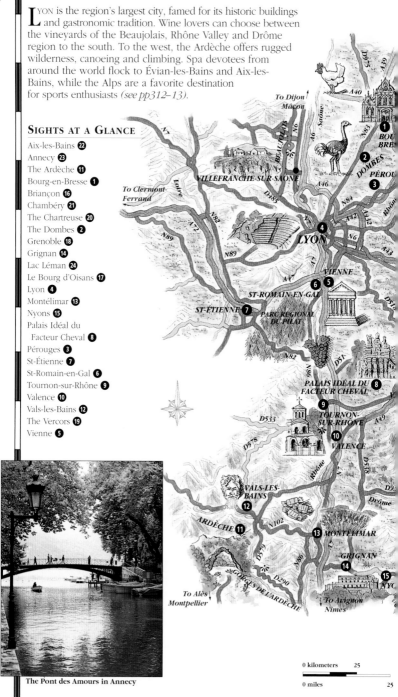

To Dijon
Mâcon

To Clermont-
Ferrand

To Alès
Montpellier

The Pont des Amours in Annecy

0 kilometers   25

0 miles   25

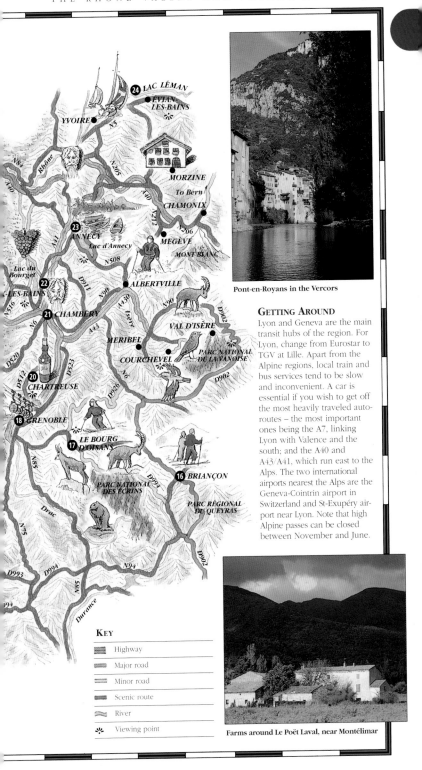

24 LAC LÉMAN

EVIAN-LES-BAINS

YVOIRE

N5

Rhône

N84

A40

A41

N205

MORZINE

A40

To Bern

CHAMONIX

N212

N206

23 ANNECY

Lac d'Annecy

MEGÈVE

MONT BLANC

N508

Lac du Bourget

22 LES-BAINS

N516

N6

D911

ALBERTVILLE

A430

21 CHAMBERY

A43

Isère

N90

VAL D'ISÈRE

D902

MERIBEL

N6

COURCHEVEL

PARC NATIONAL DE LA VANOISE

D520

D523

D902

20 CHARTREUSE

D512

D926

18 GRENOBLE

N85

17 LE BOURG D'OISANS

D991

16 BRIANÇON

PARC NATIONAL DES ECRINS

Drac

PARC RÉGIONAL DU QUEYRAS

N75

D902

D993

D994

N94

N85

994

Durance

Pont-en-Royans in the Vercors

GETTING AROUND

Lyon and Geneva are the main transit hubs of the region. For Lyon, change from Eurostar to TGV at Lille. Apart from the Alpine regions, local train and bus services tend to be slow and inconvenient. A car is essential if you wish to get off the most heavily traveled auto-routes – the most important ones being the A7, linking Lyon with Valence and the south; and the A40 and A43/A41, which run east to the Alps. The two international airports nearest the Alps are the Geneva-Cointrin airport in Switzerland and St-Exupéry air-port near Lyon. Note that high Alpine passes can be closed between November and June.

KEY

�	Highway
▬▬▬	Major road
══	Minor road
▬▬	Scenic route
～	River
✴	Viewing point

Farms around Le Poët Laval, near Montélimar

Bourg-en-Bresse ❶

Ain. ☒ *43,000.* ▣ ▣ ▊ *Centre Culturel Albert Camus, 6 av Alsace-Lorraine (04 74 22 49 40).* ▣ *Wed, Sat–Sun.* ▣ *www.bourg-en-bresse.org*

BOURG-EN-BRESSE is a busy market town, with some beautifully restored half-timbered buildings. It is best known for its tasty *poulet de Bresse* (chickens raised in the flat agricultural region of Bresse and designated *appellation contrôlée, see p309);* and its abbey church of **Brou** on the southeast edge of town.

The latter (no longer a place of worship) has become one of the most visited sites in France. Flamboyant Gothic in style, it was built between 1505 and 1536 by Margaret of Austria after the death of her husband Philibert, Duke of Savoy, in 1504.

The couple's finely sculpted Carrara marble tombs can be seen in the choir, along with the tomb of Margaret of Bourbon, Philibert's mother, who died in 1483. Notice also the beautifully carved choir stalls, stained-glass windows, and rood screen with its elegant basket-handle arching.

The adjacent cloisters house a small museum with a good collection of 16th- and 17th-century Dutch and Flemish masters, as well as contemporary works by local artists.

Environs
About 24 km (15 miles) north of Bourg-en-Bresse at St-Trivier-de-Courtes, the restored **Ferme-Musée de la Forêt** offers a look at farm life in the region during the 17th century. The ancient house has what is known locally as a Saracen chimney, with a brick hood in the center of the room, similar to constructions in Sicily and Portugal, and a collection of antique farm implements.

Tomb of Margaret of Austria in the abbey church of Brou at Bourg-en-Bresse

🏛 **Ferme-Musée de la Forêt**
▐ *04 74 30 71 89.* ▢ *Jul–Sep: daily; Apr–Jun & Oct: w/e & public hols.* ▨ ▧

The Dombes ❷

Ain. ▲ *Lyon.* ▣ *Lyon, Villars les Dombes, Bourg-en-Bresse.* ▣ *Villars-les-Dombes (from Bourg-en-Bresse).* ▊ *3 pl de Hôtel de Ville, Villars-les-Dombes (04 74 98 06 29).*

THIS FLAT, glacier-gouged plateau south of Bourg-en-Bresse is dotted with small hills, ponds and marshes, making it popular with anglers and bird-watchers.
In the middle of the area at
▶**Villars-les-Dombes** is
an ornithological
park, the **Parc des
Oiseaux**. Over 400
species of native
and exotic birds live
here, including tufted herons, vultures, pink flamingos, emus, and ostriches.

Bresse chickens

✗ **Parc des Oiseaux**
Route Nationale 83, Villars-les-Dombes. ▐ *04 74 98 05 54.* ▢ *daily.* ▨ ▧

Pérouges ❸

Ain. ☒ *900.* ▣ *Meximieux-Pérouges.* ▣ ▊ *04 74 61 01 14.*

ORIGINALLY the home of a colony of immigrants from Perugia, Pérouges is a fortified hilltop village of medieval houses and cobblestone streets. In its heyday in the 13th century it was a thriving center of linen weaving, but with the mechanization of the industry in the 19th century, the local population dwindled from 1,500 to 90.

Restoration of its historic buildings and a new influx of craftsmen have breathed new life into Pérouges. Not surprisingly, the village has often been used as the setting for historical dramas such as *The Three Musketeers* and *Monsieur Vincent.* The village's main square, place de la Halle, is shaded by a huge lime tree planted in 1792 to honor the Revolution.

A Tour of Beaujolais

BEAUJOLAIS is an ideal area for wine tasting, offering delicious, affordable wine and glorious countryside. The south of the region produces most of the Beaujolais Nouveau, released fresh from the cellars on the third Thursday of November each year. In the north are the ten superior quality *cru* wines – St-Amour, Juliénas, Moulin-à-Vent, Chénas, Fleurie, Chiroubles, Morgon, Brouilly, Côte de Brouilly and Regnié – most of which can be visited in a day's drive. The distinctive *maisons du pays* have living quarters built over the wine cellar. Almost every village has its *cave* (wine cellar), offering tastings and a glimpse of the wine culture that dominates local life.

Côte de Brouilly

Moulin-à-Vent ②
This 17th-century windmill has lovely views of the Saône Valley. Tastings of the oldest *cru* in the region are held in the *caves* next door.

Juliénas ①
Famous for *coq au vin*, this village stores and sells wine in its church, and château, and in the Maison de la Dime, a 16th-century tithe house.

MACON →

D26

Chénas

D32

D68

D266

Romanèche-Thorins

Vineyard of Gamay grapes

Chiroubles ⑦
A bust in the village square honors Victor Pulliat, who saved the vines from the phylloxera blight in the 1880s by using American vine stocks.

D18

D26

Fleurie ③
The chapel of the Madonna (1875) stands guard over the vineyards, and village restaurants serve local *andouillettes au Fleurie*.

Villié-Morgon ④
Wine tasting is in the cellars of the 18th-century château in the village center. The Château de Corcelles has a Renaissance courtyard.

D68

D9

D68

KEY

▬	Tour route
═	Other roads
⁂	Viewing point

0 kilometers 2

0 miles 1

Régnié-Durette

Beaujeu ⑥
Once the ancient capital of the region, Beaujeu offers tastings in this Renaissance wooden house, and in the 17th-century Hospices de Beaujeu.

D37

Cercié

Brouilly ⑤
The hill, with its tiny 19th-century chapel of Notre-Dame du Raisin, offers fine views and an annual Beaujolais wine festival.

VILLEFRANCHE-SUR-SAONE

Street-by-Street: Lyon ➍

ON THE WEST BANK of the Saône River, the restored old quarter of Vieux Lyon is an atmospheric warren of cobbled streets, *traboules* (covered passageways), Renaissance palaces, first-class restaurants, lively *bouchons* (bistros) and chic designer shops. It is also the site of the Roman city of Lugdunum, the commercial and military capital of Gaul founded by Julius Caesar in 44 BC. Vestiges of this prosperous city can be seen in the superb Gallo-Roman museum at the top of Fourvière Hill. Two excavated Roman theaters still stage performances from opera to rock concerts. At the foot of the hill is the finest collection of Renaissance mansions in France – a testimony to the enormous wealth brought to the city by banking, printing and the silk trade.

★ Théâtres Romains
There are two Roman amphitheaters here: the Grand Théâtre, the oldest theater in France, built in 15 BC to seat 30,000 spectators and still used for modern performances; and the smaller Odéon, with its geometric tiled flooring.

★ Musée de la Civilisation Gallo-Romaine
This underground museum contains a rich collection of statues, mosaics, coins and inscriptions evoking Lyon's Roman past.

Entrance to funicular

Cathédrale St-Jean
Begun in the late 12th century, cathedral has a 14th-century as nomical clock that shows religi feast days till the year 2019.

STAR SIGHTS

- ★ Théâtres Romains

- ★ Musée de la Civilisation Gallo-Romaine

- ★ Basilique Notre-Dame de Fourvière

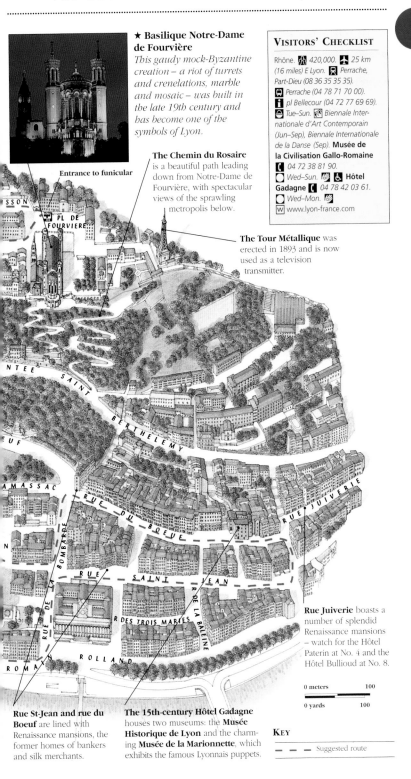

★ Basilique Notre-Dame de Fourvière

This gaudy mock-Byzantine creation – a riot of turrets and crenelations, marble and mosaic – was built in the late 19th century and has become one of the symbols of Lyon.

Entrance to funicular

The Chemin du Rosaire is a beautiful path leading down from Notre-Dame de Fourvière, with spectacular views of the sprawling metropolis below.

The Tour Métallique was erected in 1893 and is now used as a television transmitter.

VISITORS' CHECKLIST

Rhône. 420,000. ✈ 25 km (16 miles) E Lyon. 🚆 Perrache, Part-Dieu (08 36 35 35 35). 🚏 Perrache (04 78 71 70 00). 🛈 pl Bellecour (04 72 77 69 69). 🎭 Tue–Sun. 🎭 Biennale Internationale d'Art Contemporain (Jun–Sep), Biennale Internationale de la Danse (Sep). **Musée de la Civilisation Gallo-Romaine** 📞 04 72 38 81 90. 🕐 Wed–Sun. 🎟 ⚿ **Hôtel Gadagne** 📞 04 78 42 03 61. 🕐 Wed–Mon. 🎟 🌐 www.lyon-france.com

Rue Juiverie boasts a number of splendid Renaissance mansions – watch for the Hôtel Paterin at No. 4 and the Hôtel Bullioud at No. 8.

0 meters 100
0 yards 100

Rue St-Jean and rue du Boeuf are lined with Renaissance mansions, the former homes of bankers and silk merchants.

The 15th-century Hôtel Gadagne houses two museums: the **Musée Historique de Lyon** and the charming **Musée de la Marionnette**, which exhibits the famous Lyonnais puppets.

KEY

– – – Suggested route

Exploring Lyon

FRANCE'S SECOND CITY, dramatically sited on the banks of the Rhône and Saône rivers, has been a vital gateway between north and south since ancient times. Upon arriving you immediately feel a *brin du sud*, or touch of the south. The crowds are not as quick-stepping as they are in Paris, and the sun is often shining here when it's rainy and cold in the north. Despite its importance as a banking, textile and pharmaceutical center, most of the French immediately associate Lyon with their palates. The city is packed with restaurants, ranging from simple *bouchons* (bistros) to some of the most opulent tables in France.

The rue St-Jean in Vieux Lyon

The Presqu'île

The heart of Lyon is the Presqu'île, the narrow peninsula of land between the Saône and Rhône rivers, just north of their confluence. A pedestrianized shopping street, the rue de la République, links the twin poles of civic life: the vast **place Bellecour**, with its equestrian statue of Louis XIV in the middle, and the **place des Terreaux**. The latter is overlooked by Lyon's ornate 17th-century Hôtel de Ville (town hall) and the Palais St-Pierre, a former Benedictine convent and now the home of the **Musée des Beaux Arts**. In the middle of the square is a monumental 19th-century fountain by Bartholdi, sculptor of the Statue of Liberty.

Behind the town hall, architect Jean Nouvel's futuristic **Opéra de Lyon** – a black barrel vault of steel and glass encased in a Neo-Classical shell – reopened its doors in 1993 to a storm of public criticism.

A few blocks to the south, the **Musée de l'Imprimerie** illustrates Lyon's contribution to the early days of printing in the late 15th century.

Two other museums worth visiting in the Presqu'île are the **Musée des Tissus**, which houses an extraordinary collection of silks and tapestries dating from early Christian times to the present day, and the **Musée des Arts Décoratifs**, which displays a range of tapestries, furniture, porcelain and *objets d'art*.

Nearby, the **Abbaye St-Martin d'Ainay** is an impressively restored Carolingian church dating from 1107.

LYON CITY CENTER

Abbaye St-Martin d'Ainay ⑬
Amphithéâtre des Trois Gaulles ①
Basilique Notre-Dame
   de Fourvière ⑨
Cathédrale St-Jean ⑫
Eglise St-Polycarpe ②
Hôtel Gadagne ⑦
Hôtel de Ville ④
Musée de la Civilisation
   Gallo-Romaine ⑩
Musée de l'Imprimerie
   et de la Banque ⑥
Musée des Arts Décoratifs ⑭
Musée des Beaux Arts ⑤
Musée Historique des Tissus ⑮
Opéra de Lyon ③
Théâtres Romains ⑪
Tour Métallique ⑧

KEY

▨	See pp368–9
Ⓜ	Metro station
Ⓟ	Parking
ⓘ	Tourist information
✝	Church

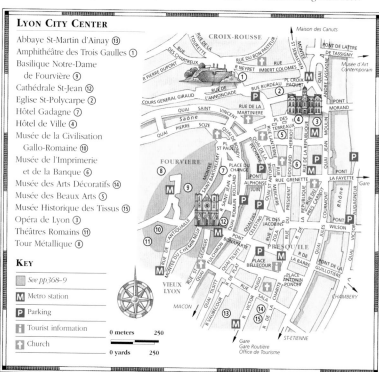

0 meters 250

0 yards 250

Musée des Beaux Arts

LYON'S RECENTLY RENOVATED musee des beaux arts showcases the country's largest and most important collection of art after the Louvre. The museum is housed in the 17th-century Palais St-Pierre, a former Benedictine convent for the daughters of the nobility. The Musée d'Art Contemporain, formerly located in the Palais St-Pierre, is now at 81 quai Charles de Gaulle, north of the Jardin Tête d'Or. Housed in a building designed by Renzo Piano, it specializes in works dating from after the mid-1900s.

Food market on quai St-Antoine

La Croix-Rousse

This industrial area north of the Presqu'île became the center of the city's silk-weaving industry in the 15th century. It still has covered passages known as *traboules*, used by the weavers to transport their finished fabrics. To get a sense of them, enter at No. 6 place des Terreaux and continue along till you reach the **Eglise St-Polycarpe**. From here, it is a short walk to the ruins of the **Amphithéâtre des Trois Gaulles**, built in AD 19, and the **Maison des Canuts**, where you can see a traditional silk loom in operation.

La Part-Dieu

This modern business area on the east bank of the Rhône has one of the TGV stations, a huge shopping complex, a public library and the **Auditorium Maurice-Ravel** for important cultural events.

🏛 Musée de l'Imprimerie
13 rue de la Poulaillerie.
📞 04 78 37 65 98. ○
Wed–Sun. ● *public hols.*
🏛 Musée des Tissus
34 rue de la Charité.
📞 04 78 38 42 00.
○ *Wed–Sun.* ● *public hols.* 📷
🏛 Musée des Arts Décoratifs
30 rue de la Charité. 📞 04 78 38 42 00. ○ *Tue–Sun.* ● *public hols.* 📷
🏛 Maison des Canuts
10–12 rue d'Ivry. 📞 04 78 28 62 04. ○ *Mon–Sat.* ● *public hols.* 📷 ♿

Environs

Southeast of Lyon, Bourgoin-Jallieu prints silk for fashion houses, and has an excellent renovated **Musée du Textile**.

ANTIQUITIES

INCLUDED in this wide-ranging collection are Egyptian archaeological finds, Etruscan statuettes and 4,000-year-old Cypriot ceramics. The antiquities department occupies the ground floor of the museum, the rest of which is devoted to temporary exhibits.

SCULPTURE AND OBJETS D'ART

OCCUPYING the old chapel on the ground floor, the sculpture department includes works from the French Romanesque period and Italian Renaissance, as well as late 19th- and early 20th-century pieces. Represented are Rodin and Bourdelle (whose statues also appear in the courtyard), Maillol, Despiau and Pompon among others. The huge *objets d'art* collection on the first floor, comprises medieval ivories, bronzes and ceramics, coins, medals, weapons, jewelry, furniture and tapestries.

Odalisque (1841) by James Pradier

PAINTINGS AND DRAWINGS

THE MUSEUM'S superb collection of paintings occupies the first and second floors. It covers all periods and includes works by Spanish and Dutch masters; the French schools of the 17th, 18th and 19th centuries; Impressionist

Fleurs des Champs (1845) by Louis Janmot of the Lyon School

and modern paintings; and works by the Lyon School, whose exquisite flower paintings were used as sources of inspiration by the designers of silk fabrics through the ages. On the first floor, the Cabinet d'Arts Graphiques has over 4,000 drawings and etchings by such artists as Delacroix, Poussin, Géricault, Degas and Rodin (by appointment only).

🏛 Musée des Beaux Arts
Palais St-Pierre, 20 place des Terreaux.
📞 04 72 10 17 40. ○ *Wed–Mon.*
● *public hols.* 📷 ♿

La Méduse (1923) by Alexeï von Jawlensky

Châtiment de Lycurgue in the Musée Archéologique, St-Romain-en-Gal

Vienne **⑤**

Isère. **🏃** *29,000.* 🚄 🚌 **ℹ** *cours Brillier (04 74 53 80 30).* 🛒 *Sat.*
W *www.vienne-tourisme.fr*

No OTHER CITY in the Rhône Valley offers such a concentration of architectural history as Vienne. Located in a natural basin of land between the river and the hills, this site was recognized for both its strategic and aesthetic advantages by the Romans, who vastly expanded an existing village when they invaded the area in the 1st century BC.

The center of the Roman town was the **Temple d'Auguste et Livie** (10 BC) on place du Palais, a handsome structure supported by Corinthian columns. Not far

Vienne's Temple d'Auguste et Livie (1st century BC)

away off place de Miremont are the remains of the **Théâtre de Cybèle**, a temple dedicated to the goddess Cybele, whose worship involved orgiastic rites.

The **Théâtre Romain**, at the foot of Mont Pipet off rue du Cirque, was one of the largest amphitheaters in Roman France, capable of seating over 13,000 spectators. It was restored in 1938, and is now used for a variety of events, including an international jazz festival in the first two weeks of July each year. From the very top seats the view of the town and river is spectacular.

Other interesting Roman vestiges include a fragment of Roman road in the public gardens and, on the southern edge of town, the **Pyramide du Cirque**, a curious structure about 20 m (65 feet) high that was once the centerpiece of the chariot racetrack. The **Musée des Beaux Arts et d'Archéologie** also has a good collection of Gallo-Roman artifacts, as well as 18th-century French faïence and 17th-century paintings by lesser-known artists from the region.

The **Cathédrale de St-Maurice** is the city's most important medieval monument. It was built between the 12th and 16th centuries and represents an unusual hybrid of Romanesque and Gothic styles. The interior has three aisles but no transept, and contains many fine

Romanesque sculptures. Two of Vienne's earliest Christian churches are the 12th-century **Eglise St-André-le-Bas**, with richly carved capitals in its nave and cloister, and the **Eglise St-Pierre**, parts of which date from the 5th and 6th centuries. The latter houses the **Musée Lapidaire**, a museum of stone carving with a collection of bas-reliefs and statues of Gallo-Roman buildings.

🏛 Musée des Beaux Arts et d'Archéologie
Place de Miremont **📞** *04 74 85 50 42.* ⏰ *Apr–Oct: Tue–Sun; Nov–Mar: Tue–Sat, Sun pm.* ● *Jan 1, May 1, Nov 1 & 11, Dec 25.* 📷

🏛 Musée Lapidaire
Place St-Pierre. **📞** *04 74 85 20 35.* ⏰ *Tue–Sun.* ● *Nov–Mar: Sun am, Jan 1, May 1, Nov 1 & 11, Dec 25.* 📷 ♿

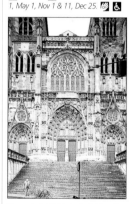

Vienne's Cathédrale de St-Maurice

St-Romain-en-Gal **⑥**

Rhône. **🏃** *1,300.* 🚄 *Vienne.*
ℹ *Vienne (04 74 53 80 30).*

IN 1967, BUILDING WORK in this commercial town directly across the Rhône from Vienne revealed extensive remains of a significant Roman community dating from 100 BC to AD 300. It comprises the remnants of villas, public baths, shops and warehouses. Of particular interest is the House of the Ocean Gods, with a magnificent mosaic floor depicting the bearded Neptune and other ocean images.

Much of what has been unearthed during the ongoing excavations is housed in the

Musée Archéologique
adjoining the ruins. The
impressive collection includes
household objects, murals
and mosaics. The star exhibit
is the *Châtiment de Lycurgue*,
a mosaic discovered in 1907.

🏛 **Musée Archéologique**
📞 *04 74 53 74 01.* ⏰ *Tue–Sun.* ⬤
some publ hols. ▨ ♿ *restr.* ❚ ❚

St-Étienne **❼**

Loire. 🏙 *200,000.* ✈ ▯ ▯
ℹ *av de la Libération (04 77 49 39 00).*
⬤ *Tue–Sun.* [W] *www.tourisme-st-
etienne.com*

T HE DOUR industrial renown
brought to this city by
coal-mining and armaments is
slowly being shaken off, with
urban redevelopment well
underway and a brand new
tramway. The downtown area
around place des Peuple is
lively. Nearby, Jean Michel
Wilmotte has overhauled the
Musée d'Art et d'Industrie,
which covers St-Étienne's industrial background, including
the development of the revolutionary jacquard loom, and
world-class collections of,
among other things, cycles
and ribbon-making machines.
   To the north of the city, the
Musée d'Art Moderne has a
collection of 20th-century art,
including works by Andy
Warhol and Frank Stella.

🏛 **Musée d'Art et
d'Industrie**
Place Louis Comte. 📞 *04 77 49 73
00.* ⏰ *Wed–Mon.* ⬤ *some public
hols.* ▨ ♿ ▭ ❚
🏛 **Musée d'Art Moderne**
La Terrasse. 📞 *04 77 79 52 52.*
⏰ *Wed–Mon.* ⬤ *some public hols.*
▨ ♿

Detail of the bizarre Palais Idéal du Facteur Cheval at Hauterives

Palais Idéal du Facteur Cheval **❽**

Hauterives, Drôme. ▯ *Romans-sur-
Isère.* 📞 *04 75 68 81 19.* ⏰ *daily.*
⬤ *Jan 1–15, Dec 25.* ▨ ♿

A T HAUTERIVES, 25 km (15
miles) north of Roman-
sur-Isère on the D538, is
one of the greatest follies of
France, an eccentric "palace"
constructed entirely of stones
and evoking Egyptian, Roman,
Aztec and Siamese styles of
architecture. It was built
single-handedly by a local
postman, Ferdinand Cheval,
who collected the stones
during his daily rounds on
horseback. His neighbors
thought he was crazy, but the
project attracted the admiring
attention of surrealist André
Breton and other artists.
   The interior of the palace is
inscribed with numerous mottos
and exortations by Cheval,
the most poignant of which
refers to his assiduous efforts
to realize his lifelong fantasy:
"1879–1912: 10,000 days,
93,000 hours, 33 years of toil."

THE RHÔNE'S BRIDGES

The Rhône has played a crucial role in French history,
transporting armies and commercial traffic between the
north and south. It has always been dangerous, a
challenge to boatmen and builders for centuries. In 1825
the brilliant engineer Marc Seguin built the first suspension
bridge using steel wire cables. This was followed by
another 20 along the length of the Rhône, forever transforming communications between east and west.

Suspension bridge over the Rhône at Tournon-sur-Rhône

The town of Tournon-sur-Rhône

Tournon-sur-Rhône **9**

Ardèche. 🏠 10,000. 🚆 🚌 🛈 Hôtel de la Tourette (04 75 08 10 23). 🔄 Wed & Sat.

SITUATED AT THE FOOT of impressive granite hills, Tournon is a lovely town with gracious tree-lined promenades and an imposing 11th-16th-century **château**. The latter houses a museum of local history, and has fine views of the town and river from its terraces.

The adjacent **Collégiale St-Julien**, with its square bell tower and elaborate façade, is an interesting example of the Italian influence on architecture in the region during the 14th century. Inside is the powerful *Resurrection*, painted in 1576 by Capassin, a pupil of Raphael.

On quai Charles de Gaulle, the **Lycée Gabriel-Faure** is the oldest secondary school in France, dating from 1536.

Directly across the Rhône from Tournon, the village of **Tain l'Hermitage** is famous for its steep-climbing vineyards that produce both red and white Hermitage, the finest (and most some of the most expensive) of all Côtes du Rhône wines.

Environs

From Tournon's main square, the place Jean Jaurès, a narrow, twisting road marked the **Route Panoramique** leads via the villages of Plats and St-Romain-de-Lerps to St-Péray. This route offers breathtaking views at every turn, and, at St-Romain, you are rewarded with a superb panorama extending over 13 *départements*.

Valence **10**

Drôme. 🏠 65,000. 🚆 🚌 🛈 parvis de la Gare (04 75 44 90 40). 🔄 Wed & Sat. 🌐 www.tourisme-valence.com

VALENCE is a large, thriving market town set on the east bank of the Rhône and looking across to the cliffs of the Ardèche. Its principal sight is the Romanesque **Cathédrale St-Apollinaire** on place des Clercs, founded in 1095 and rebuilt in the 17th century.

Alongside the cathedral in the former bishop's palace, the small **Musée des Beaux Arts** contains a collection of late 18th-century chalk drawings of Rome by Hubert Robert.

A short walk from here are two Renaissance mansions. The **Maison des Têtes** at No. 57 Grande Rue was built in 1532 and is embellished

with the sculpted heads of various ancient Greeks including Aristotle, Homer and Hippocrates. On rue Pérollerie, the **Maison Dupré-Latour** has a finely sculptured porch and staircase.

The **Parc Jouvet**, south of avenue Gambetta, offers 14 acres (6 hectares) of pools and gardens, with fine views across the river to the ruined **Château de Crussol**.

🏛 **Musée des Beaux Arts**
4 place des Ormeaux. 📞 04 75 79 20 80. ◻ Tue–Sun pms only. ⬤ public hols. 📷

The limestone Pont d'Arc

The Ardèche **11**

Ardèche. ✈ Avignon. 🚆 Montélimar, Pont St-Esprit. 🚌 Montélimar, Vallon Pont d'Arc. 🛈 Vallon Pont d'Arc (04 75 88 04 01).

OVER THE COURSE OF thousands of years, wind and water have endowed this south-central region of France

---

CÔTES DU RHÔNE

Rising in the Swiss Alps and traveling south to the Mediterranean, the mighty Rhône is the common thread that links the many vineyards of the Rhône Valley. A hierarchy of *appellations* is divided into three levels of quality: at the base, the regional Côtes du Rhône provides the bulk of the Rhône's wines; next, Côtes du Rhône-Villages comprises a plethora of picturesque villages; and, at the top, there are 13 individual *appellations*. The most famous are the steep slopes of Hermitage and Côte Rôtie in the northern Rhône, and historic Châteauneuf-du-Pape (*see p493*) in the south. The lion's share of production is of red wine based on the syrah grape, which is often spicy, full-bodied and robust.

Harvest in a Côtes du Rhône vineyard

with such a wild and rugged landscape that it is often more reminiscent of the American Southwest than the verdure commonly associated with the French countryside. This visible drama is repeated underground as well, since the Ardèche is honeycombed with enormous stalagmite- and stalactite-ornamented caves. The most impressive are the **Aven d'Orgnac** (*aven* meaning pothole) to the south of Vallon-Pont-d'Arc, and the **Grotte de la Madeleine**, reached via a marked path from the D290.

For those who prefer to stay above ground, the most arresting natural scenery in the region is the **Gorges de l'Ardèche**, best seen from the D290, a two-lane road with frequent viewing points that parallels the recessed river for 32 km (20 miles). Nearly at the head of the gorge, heading west, is the **Pont d'Arc**, a natural limestone "bridge" spanning the river, created by erosion and the elements.

Canoeing and white-water rafting are the two most popular sports here. All the equipment necessary can be rented locally; operators at Vallon-Pont-d'Arc (among many other places) rent out two-person canoes and arrange return transportation from St-Martin d'Ardèche, 32 km (20 miles) downstream. Note that the Ardèche River is one of France's fastest flowing rivers – it is safest in May and June; by fall its waters can be

The village of Vogüé on the banks of the Ardèche River

unpredictable and dangerous, especially for beginners.

The softer side of the region is found in its ancient and picturesque villages, gracious spa towns, vineyards and plantations of Spanish chestnuts (from which the delectable *marron glacé* is produced).

Some 13 km (8 miles) south of Aubenas, the 12th-century village of **Balazuc** is typical of the region, its stone houses built on a clifftop overlooking a secluded gorge of the Ardèche River. There are fine views as you approach and leave the village on the D294.

Neighboring **Vogüé** is nestled between the Ardèche River and a limestone cliff. A tiny but atmospheric village, its most commanding sight is the 12th-century **Château de Vogüé**, once the seat of the barons of Languedoc. Rebuilt in the 17th century, the building houses a museum featuring exhibitions about the region.

⌂ **Château de Vogüé**
[04 75 37 01 95. **]** *Easter–Jun: Thu–Sun pms; Jul–mid-Sep: daily; mid-Sep–mid-Nov: w/e pms.* 🖼 🗹

Vals-les-Bains ⑫

Ardèche. 🏠 3,700. ⎅ Montelimar
ℹ️ Gare Routière (04 75 37 49 27).
🗓 Thu & Sun (& Wed in summer).

THIS SMALL SPA TOWN retains a hint of its past elegance. It is situated in the valley of the Volane, where there are at least 150 springs, of which all but two are cold. The water, which contains bicarbonate of soda and other minerals, is said to help with digestive problems, rheumatism and diabetes.

Discovered around 1600, Vals-les-Bains is one of the few spas in southern France to have been overlooked by the Romans. The town reached the height of its popularity in the late 19th century, and most of its parks and architecture retain something of the *Belle Epoque*. Vals is a convenient first stop for an exploration of the Ardèche, with plenty of hotels and restaurants.

Environs
About 8 km (5 miles) east of Vals is the superb Romanesque church of **St-Julien du Serre**.

The Gorges de l'Ardèche, between
Vallon-Pont-d'Arc and Pont St-Esprit

A farm near Le Poët Laval, east of Montélimar

Montélimar ®

Drôme. 🏠 32,000. 🚊 🚌
🛈 Allées Provençales (04 75 01 00
20). 🖪 Wed–Sat.

WHETHER you choose to make a detour to Montélimar will largely depend on how sweet a tooth you might have. The main curiosity of this market town is its medieval center, chock-full of shops selling almond-studded nougat. This splendid confection has been made here since the start of the 17th century, when the almond tree was first introduced into France from Asia.

The 12th–16th century **Château des Adhémar** overlooks the town from a tall hill to the east and houses a contemporary art center.

♣ Château des Adhémar
📞 04 75 00 62 30. ◯ Apr–Oct:
daily; Nov–Mar: Wed–Mon. ⬤ Jan 1,
Nov 1, Dec 25. 🌠

Environs
The countryside east of Montélimar is full of picturesque medieval villages and scenic routes. **La Bégude-de-Mazenc** is a thriving little vacation center, with its fortified Old Town perched on a hilltop. Farther east is **Le Poët Laval**, a tiny medieval village of honey-colored stone buildings set in the Alpine foothills. **Dieulefit**, the main town of this beautiful region, has several small hotels and restaurants, as well as facilities for tennis, swimming and fishing. To the south, the fortified village of **Taulignan** is known for its cuisine based on truffles, the local delicacy.

Grignan ®

Drôme. 🏠 1,300. 🚊 🛈 Grande
Rue (04 75 46 56 75). 🖪 Tue.

ATTRACTIVELY SITUATED on a rocky hill surrounded by fields of lavender, this charming little village owes its fame to Madame de Sévigné, who wrote many of her celebrated letters while staying with her daughter at the **Château de Grignan**. Built during the 15th and 16th centuries, it is one of the finest Renaissance structures in this part of France. Its interior contains a good collection of Louis XII furniture and Aubusson tapestries.

From the château's terrace, a panoramic view extends as far as the Vivarais Mountains in the Ardèche. Directly below the terrace, the **Eglise de St-Saveur** was built in the 1530s, and contains the tomb of Madame de Sévigné, who died in the château in 1696 at the age of 69.

♣ Château de Grignan
📞 04 75 46 51 56. ◯ Apr–Oct:
daily; Nov–Mar: Wed–Mon.
⬤ Jan 1, Dec 25. 🌠 📷 oblig.

Nyons ®

Drôme. 🏠 7,000. 🚊 🛈 place de la
Libération (04 75 26 10 35). 🖪 Thu.

NYONS is synonymous with olives in France, since the region is a major center of olive production. A variety of olive products can be bought here at the colorful Thursday morning market, from soap to *tapenade*, the olive paste so popular in the south.

The **quartier des Forts** is Nyons' oldest quarter, a warren of narrow streets and stepped alleyways, the most rewarding of which is the covered rue des Grands Forts. Spanning the Aygues River is a graceful 13th-century bridge; on its town side are several old mills turned into shops where you can see the enormous presses once used to extract olive oil. The **Musée de l'Olivier** further explains the cultivation of the olive tree and the myriad local uses found for its fruit.

There is a fine view of the area from the belvedere overlooking the town. Sheltered as it is by mountains, Nyons enjoys an almost exotic climate, with all the trees and plants of the Riviera to be found here.

🏛 Musée de l'Olivier
Ave des Tilleuls. 📞 04 75 26 12 12.
◯ Mar–Oct: Mon–Sat pms; Nov–Feb:
Tue–Sat pms. 🌠 ♿

Environs
From Nyons, the D94 leads west to **Suze-la-Rousse**, a pleasant wine-producing village that, during the Middle Ages, was the most important town in the area. Today, it is best known for its "university of wine," a highly respected center of enology. It is housed

The hilltop town of Grignan and its Renaissance château

Olive groves just outside Nyons

in the 14th-century **Château de Suze-la-Rousse**, the hunting lodge of the princes of Orange. The interior courtyard is a Renaissance masterpiece and some rooms preserve original paint and stuccowork.

♣ **Château de Suze-la-Rousse**
📞 04 75 04 81 44. ☐ Apr–Oct: daily; Nov–Mar: Wed–Mon. ● Jan 1, Dec 25. 🖼 🖫 🖬

Playing *boules* in Nyons

Briançon ❶

Hautes Alpes. 🏠 12,000. 🚂 🚌
🅸 place du Temple (04 92 21 08 50).
🅰 Wed.

BRIANÇON – the highest town in Europe at 1,326 m (4,330 feet) – has been an important stronghold since pre-Roman times, guarding as it does the road to the Col de Montgenèvre, one of the oldest and most important passes into Italy. At the beginning of the 18th century, the town was fortified with ramparts and gates – still splendidly intact – by Louis XIV's military architect, Vauban. If driving, park at the Champs de Mars, and enter the pedestrianized Old Town via the **Porte de Pignerol**.

This leads to the **Grande Rue**, a steep, narrow street with a stream running down the middle, bordered by lovely period houses. The nearby **Eglise de Notre-Dame** dates from 1718, and was also built by Vauban with an eye to defense. To visit Vauban's **citadel**, stop by the tourist office, which organizes guided tours.

Today, Briançon is a major sports center, offering skiing in winter, and rafting, cycling and *parapente* in summer.

Environs
Just west of Briançon, the **Parc National des Ecrins** is the largest of the French national parks, offering lofty peaks and glaciers, and a magnificent variety of Alpine flowers.

The **Parc Régional du Queyras** is reached from Briançon over the rugged Col de l'Izoard. A wall of 3,000-m (9,850-ft) peaks separates this wild and beautiful national park from neighboring Italy.

Le Bourg d'Oisans ❶

Isère. 🏠 2,900. 🅸 quai Girard (04 76 80 03 25). 🅰 Sat.

LE BOURG D'OISANS is an ideal base from which to explore the Romanche Valley and other adjoining valleys. The area provides numerous opportunities for outdoor sports including cycling, rock-climbing, and skiing, in the nearby resort of **L'Alpe d'Huez**.

Silver and other minerals have been mined here since the Middle Ages, and today the town has a scientific reputation as a center for geology and mineralogy. Its **Musée des Mineraux et de la Faune des Alpes** is renowned for its collection of crystals and precious stones.

🏛 **Musée des Minéraux et de la Faune des Alpes**
📞 04 76 80 27 54. ☐ 2–6 pm daily (Jul–Aug:11 am–7 pm) ● mid-Nov–mid-Dec; Dec 25, Jan 1. 🖼 ♿

LIFE ON HIGH

The Alpine ibex is one of the rarest inhabitants of the French Alps, living high above the tree line in all but the coldest part of the year. Until the creation of the Parc National de la Vanoise, this sure-footed climber had become almost extinct in France, but as a result of rigorous conservation there are now over 500. Both males and females have horns; in the oldest males they can be almost 1 m (3 ft) long.

An ibex in the Parc National de la Vanoise

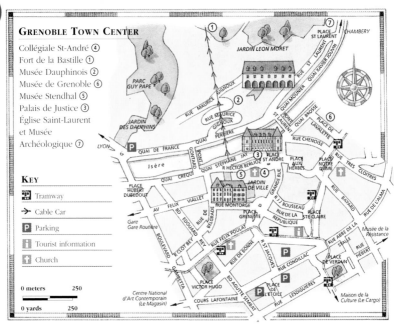

GRENOBLE TOWN CENTER

Collégiale St-André ④
Fort de la Bastille ①
Musée Dauphinois ②
Musée de Grenoble ⑥
Musée Stendhal ⑤
Palais de Justice ③
Église Saint-Laurent
et Musée
Archéologique ⑦

KEY

🚋 Tramway

✈ Cable Car

🅿 Parking

ℹ Tourist information

✝ Church

0 meters   250
0 yards   250

Grenoble's former town hall, now the Musée Stendhal

Grenoble ⑱

Isère. 🏠 165,000. ✈ 🚉 🚌
ℹ 14 rue de la République
(04 76 42 41 41). 🗓 Tue–Sun.

ANCIENT CAPITAL of the
Dauphiné region and site
of the 1968 Winter Olympics,
Grenoble is a thriving city,
home to the science-oriented
University of Grenoble, and a
center of chemical and electronics industries and nuclear
research. It is attractively situated at the confluence of the
Drac and Isère rivers, with the
Vercors and Chartreuse mountains to the west and north.

A cable car starting at quai
Stéphane-Jay whisks you up
to the 19th-century **Fort de
la Bastille**, where you are
rewarded with superb views of
the city and surrounding mountains. From here, paths lead
down through the Parc Guy
Pape and Jardin des Dauphins
to the **Musée Dauphinois**, a
regional museum in a 17th-
century convent devoted to
local history, arts and crafts.

On the left bank of the Isère,
the focus of life is the pedestrian area around the lively
place Grenette, lined with
sidewalk cafés. Nearby, the
place St-André is the heart of
the medieval city, overlooked
by Grenoble's oldest buildings
including the 13th-century
Collégiale St-André and
16th-century **Palais de Justice**.
In the former town hall, the
Musée Stendhal houses an exhibition on the life of the 19th-
century novelist from Grenoble.
The **Musée de Grenoble**, on
the place de Lavalette, exhibits
art from every period, including
a superb modern collection
with works by Chagall, Picasso
and Matisse, among others. The
Musée de l'Ancien Evêché
nearby recounts the history of
Isère, and includes a visit to the
4th-century baptistery. On rue
Hébert, the **Musée de la
Résistance** contains a collection of documents relating to
the French Resistance.

Temporary displays of
modern art can be seen at
Le Magasin (Centre National
d'Art Contemporain), a renovated warehouse on the Cours
Berriat. In the quartier Mal-
herbe, **Le Cargo** (Maison de
la Culture) hosts everything
from film festivals to concerts.

🏛 **Musée Dauphinois**
30 rue Maurice Gignoux. 📞 04 76
85 19 01. 🗓 Wed–Mon. 🔴 Jan 1,
May 1, Dec 25. 🔲 ♿
🏛 **Musée Stendhal**
1 rue Hector Berlioz. 📞 04 76 54 44
14. 🗓 Tue–Sun pms only (mid-Jul–
mid-Sep: daily). 🔴 public hols. ♿

Grenoble's gondola cable car

🏛 **Musée de Grenoble**
5 place de Lavalette. 📞 04 76 63 44
44. 🕐 Wed–Mon. ● Jan 1, May 1,
Dec 25. 🎦 & 🎥 🔲 🔲

🏛 **Musée de l'Ancien Evêché**
3 rue Très Cloîtres. 📞 04 76 03 15
25. 🕐 Wed–Mon. 🎥

🏛 **Musée de la Résistance**
14 rue Hébert. 📞 04 76 42 38 53.
🕐 Wed–Mon. ● Jan 1, May 1,
Dec 25. 🎥 &

🏛 **Le Magasin** (CNAC)
155 Cours Berriat. 📞 04 76 21 95 84.
🕐 Tue–Sun pms only (during
exhibitions). ● mid-Sep–Oct. 🎥 &

🏛 **Le Cargo**
4 rue Paul Claudel. 📞 04 38 49 95 95.
● for renovation until 2004. 🎥 &

The Vercors ⑲

Isère & Drôme. ✈ Grenoble. 🚉
Romans-sur-Isère, St-Marcellin,
Grenoble. 🚌 Pont-en-Royans,
Romans-sur-Isère. 🛈 Pont-en-Royans
(04 76 36 09 10).

To the south and west of
Grenoble, the Vercors is
one of the most magnificent
regional parks in France – a
wilderness of pine forests,
mountains, waterfalls, caves
and deep, narrow gorges.
The D531 out of Grenoble
passes through **Villard-de-
Lans** – a good base for
excursions in the area – and
continues west to the dark
Gorges de la Bournes. About
8 km (5 miles) farther west,
the hamlet of **Pont-en-Royans**
is situated on a very narrow
limestone gorge, its stone
houses built into the rocks
overlooking the Bourne River.
South of Pont-en-Royans
along the D76, the **Route de
Combe-Laval** snakes along a
sheer cliff above the roaring
river. The **Grands Goulets**,
6.5 km (4 miles) to the east,
is a spectacularly deep,
narrow gorge overlooked by
sheer cliffs that virtually shut
out the sky above. The best-
known mountain in the park
is the **Mont Aiguille**, a soaring
outcrop rising 2,086 m (6,844 ft).
The Vercors was a key base
for the French Resistance
during World War II. In July
1944 the Germans launched
an aerial attack on the region,
flattening several of its villages.
There are Resistance museums
at Vassieux and Grenoble.

Cows grazing in the Chartreuse

The Chartreuse ⑳

Isère & Savoie. ✈ Grenoble,
Chambéry. 🚉 Grenoble, Voiron.
🚌 St-Pierre-de-Chartreuse. 🛈 St-
Pierre-de-Chartreuse (04 76 88 62 08).

From Grenoble, the D512
leads north toward
Chambéry into the Chartreuse,
a majestic region of mountains
and forests where hydroelec-
tricity was invented in the late
19th century. The **Monastère
de la Grande Chartreuse** is
the main local landmark, situated just west of St-Pierre-de-
Chartreuse off the D520-B.
Founded by St. Bruno in
1084, the monastery owes its
fame to the sticky green and
yellow Chartreuse liqueurs first
produced by the monks in
1605. The recipe, based on
a secret herbal elixir of 130
ingredients, is now produced
in the nearby town of Voiron.
The monastery itself is
inhabited by about 40 monks
who live in silence and seclusion. It is not open to visitors,
but there is a museum at the
entrance, the **Musée de la
Correrie**, which faithfully
depicts the daily routine of
the Carthusian monks.

🏛 **Musée de la Correrie**
St-Pierre-de-Chartreuse. 📞 04 76 88
60 45. 🕐 Apr–Oct: daily. 🎥

A farm in the pine-clad mountains of the Chartreuse

Chambéry ㉑

Savoie. 🏠 *56,000.* ✈ 🚆 🚌
ℹ️ *24 boulevard de la Colonne
(04 79 33 42 47).* 🛒 *Tue, Sat.*

ONCE THE CAPITAL of Savoy, this dignified city has aristocratic airs and a distinctly Italianate feel. Its best-loved monument is the splendidly extravagant **Fontaine des Eléphants** on rue de Boigne. It was erected in 1838 to honor the Comte de Boigne, a native son who left to his hometown some of the fortune he amassed in India.

The **Château des Ducs de Savoie**, at the opposite end of rue de Boigne, was built in the 14th century and is now mostly occupied by the Préfecture (police). Only parts of the building can be visited, such as the late Gothic Ste-Chapelle.

On the southeast edge of town is the 17th-century country house, **Les Charmettes**, where the Romantic philosopher Rousseau lived with his mistress Madame de Warens from 1732–42. It is wortisit for its vine-covered gardens and small museum of Rousseau memorabilia.

♣ **Les Charmettes**
892 chemin des Charmettes.
📞 *04 79 33 39 44.*
⬜ *Wed–Mon.* ⚫ *public hols.* 📷 🎦

Roman statue in the Temple of Diana

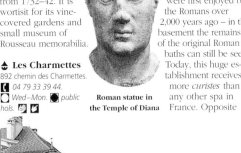
The Lac du Bourget at Aix-les-Bains

Aix-les-Bains ㉒

Savoie. 🏠 *30,000.* ✈ 🚆
ℹ️ *place Maurice Mollard (04 79 88 68 00).* 🛒 *Wed & Sat.*

THE GREAT Romantic poet Lamartine rhapsodized over the beauty of Lac du Bourget, site of the gracious spa town of Aix-les-Bains. The heart of the town is the 19th-century **Thermes Nationaux**, thermal baths which were first enjoyed by the Romans over 2,000 years ago – in the basement the remains of the original Roman baths can still be seen. Today, this huge establishment receives more *curistes* than any other spa in France. Opposite the baths, the 2nd-century AD **Temple of Diana** contains a collection of Gallo-Roman artifacts. The nearby **Musée Faure** is an art-lover's paradise, with its collection of Impressionist paintings, including Degas and Sisley, Rodin sculptures and Lamartine memorabilia.

🚿 **Thermes Nationaux**
Pl Maurice Mollard. 📞 *04 79 35 38 50.*
⬜ *Mar –Oct: Mon–Sat; Nov–Feb: Wed–Sat.* 🎦 *obligatory.* ⚫ *mid-Dec–Jan, May 1, Jul 14, Aug 15.* 📷

🏛 **Musée Faure**
Villa des Chimères, 10 bd des Côtes.
📞 *04 79 61 06 57.* ⬜ *Wed–Mon.*
⚫ *Dec 18–Jan 2, public hols.*
📷 ♿

Environs
Boats leave from Aix's Grand Port and sail across Lac du Bourget to the **Abbaye d'Hautecombe**, a Benedictine abbey containing the mausoleum of the Savoyard dynasty.

The small town of **Le Revard**, just east of Aix on the D913, has spectacular views of the lake on one side and Mont Blanc on the other.

Annecy ㉓

Haute Savoie. 🏠 *50,000.* ✈ 🚆 🚌
ℹ️ *1 rue Jean Jaurès (04 50 45 00 33).* 🛒 *Tue, Fri–Sun.*

ANNECY IS ONE of the most charming and attractive towns in the Alps, set at the

Annecy's 12th-century Palais de l'Isle, with the Thiou Canal in the foreground

Cycling along the shores of Lac Léman (Lake Geneva)

northern tip of Lac d'Annecy and surrounded by snow-capped mountains. Its small medieval quarter is laced with canals, flower-covered bridges and arcaded streets. Strolling around is the main attraction, particularly on market day, though there are also specific sights well worth a visit: the formidable **Palais de l'Isle**, a 12th-century prison in the middle of the Thiou Canal; and the turreted **Château d'Annecy**, set high on a hill above the town, with fine views of Vieil Annecy and the crystal-clear lake beyond.

The best spot for swimming and water sports is at the eastern end of the avenue d'Albigny near the Imperial Palace hotel, while boat trips leave from the quai Thiou.

Environs
One of the best ways to enjoy the area's spectacular scenery is to take a boat from Annecy to **Talloires**, a tiny lakeside village celebrated for its prestigious hotels and restaurants. Facing Talloires across the narrowest part of the lake is the 15th-century **Château de Duingt** (not open to visitors).

On the west bank of the lake, Semnoz Mountain and its summit, the **Crêt de Châtillon**, offer superb views of Mont Blanc and the Alps.

Lac Léman ㉔

Haute Savoie & Switzerland. 🚠 Geneva. 🚇 🚌 Geneva, Thonon-les-Bains, Évian-les-Bains. 🛈 Thonon-les-Bains (04 50 71 55 55).

THE STIRRING SCENERY and gentle climate of the French shore of Lake Geneva (Lac Léman to the French) has made it a popular and fashionable resort area since the first spa buildings were erected at Évian-les-Bains in 1839.

Yvoire is a fine place to begin a visit to the area. This medieval walled fishing port is guarded by a massive 14th-century castle, and its tightly-packed houses are bedecked with colorful flower boxes.

Farther east along Lac Léman is **Thonon-les-Bains**, a prosperous, well-manicured little spa town perched on a cliff overlooking the lake. A funicular takes you down to Rives, the small harbor at the foot of the cliffs, where you can rent a sailboat or take an excursion boat to the Swiss cities of Geneva and Lausanne. Just outside the town is the 15th-century **Château de Ripaille**, made famous by its onetime resident, Duke Amadeus VIII, who later became antipope (Felix V).

Though it has been modernized and acquired an international reputation for its eponymous spring water, **Évian-les-Bains** still exudes a polite *vie en rose* charm. The tree-lined lakefront promenade teems with leisurely strollers, while more energetic types can avail themselves of all kinds of sports activities including tennis, golf, riding, sailing and skiing in the winter. State-of-the-art spa treatments are available, and the exotic domed casino is busy at night, offering blackjack, roulette and baccarat as well as other games.

From Évian there are daily ferries across Lake Geneva to Lausanne in Switzerland, as well as bus excursions into the surrounding mountains.

Évian-les-Bains' Hôtel Royal
(see p563)

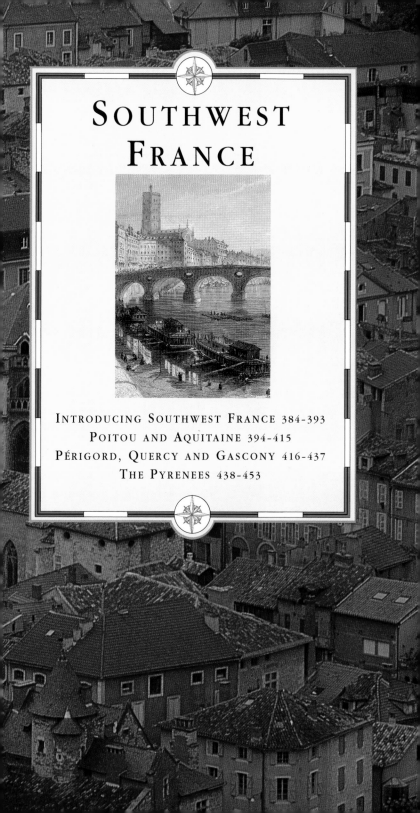

SOUTHWEST
FRANCE

Introducing Southwest France

THE SOUTHWEST IS FARMING FRANCE, a green and peaceful land
nurturing crops from sunflowers to *foie gras*. Other key country
products include Landes forest timber, Bordeaux wines and Cognac.
Major modern industries, including aerospace, are focused on the
two chief cities, Bordeaux and Toulouse. Visitors are mainly drawn to
the wide Atlantic beaches, the ski slopes of the Pyrenees and
the rural calm of the Dordogne. The major sights of this
popular region are shown here and include some of
France's most celebrated Romanesque buildings.

La Rochelle

Roman Ruins, Saintes

La Rochelle's harbor *is today a haven for pleasure
yachts as well as an important commercial port* (see p406).
*Tour de la Chaîne and Tour St-Nicolas protect the
entrance of the old port. The town's historic center is filled
with cobbled streets lined by merchants' houses.*

Grand Théâtre, E

POITOU AND AQUITAIN
(See pp394–415)

THE PYRENEES
(See pp438–53)

Bordeaux *is a town of grand buildings
and monuments, including its theater.
The Monument aux Girondins, with its
magnificent bronze statues and fountains, stands at the 18th-century Esplanade des Quinconces* (see pp410–12).

| 0 kilometers | 50 |
| 0 miles | 50 |

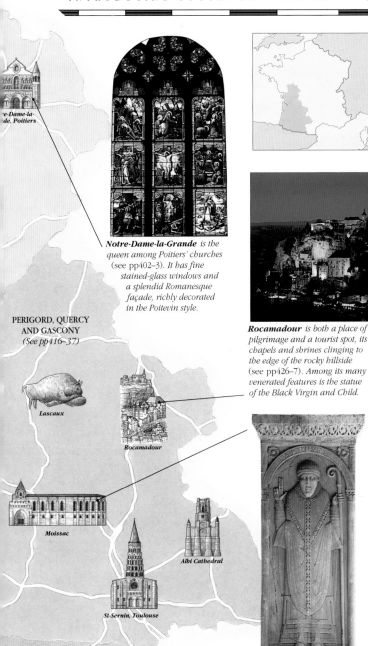

Notre-Dame-la-Grande *is the queen among Poitiers' churches (see pp402–3). It has fine stained-glass windows and a splendid Romanesque façade, richly decorated in the Poitevin style.*

PERIGORD, QUERCY AND GASCONY
(See pp416–37)

Lascaux

Rocamadour

Moissac

Albi Cathedral

St-Sernin, Toulouse

Cirque de Gavarnie

Rocamadour *is both a place of pilgrimage and a tourist spot, its chapels and shrines clinging to the edge of the rocky hillside (see pp426–7). Among its many venerated features is the statue of the Black Virgin and Child.*

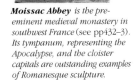

Moissac Abbey *is the pre-eminent medieval monastery in southwest France (see pp432–3). Its tympanum, representing the Apocalypse, and the cloister capitals are outstanding examples of Romanesque sculpture.*

Regional Food: Southwest France

THE RENAISSANCE KING HENRI IV's declaration, "Great cooking and great wines make a paradise on earth," sums up the wonderful and varied cuisine of southwest France. Oysters and mussels proliferate along the Arcachon and Marennes coastline, and in the countryside around Bordeaux, the vine dominates to such an extent that wines are used in the cooking of practically every regional dish – *à la bordelaise* generally translates as "with a wine sauce."

Garlic

In Périgord, Quercy and Gascony, geese, ducks and goats are raised for *foie gras*, *confit* and cheese. Truffles found in the forests are highly prized and costly and are used sparingly in soups, sauces, *pâté* and stuffings. Goose fat is used for cooking dishes such as *cassoulet* and *daube de boeuf*.

In Basque country, the local chili pepper, the *piment d'Espelette*, spices everything from Bayonne's famous ham and *piperade*, to fish and stews.

Piperade *is a popular Basque country dish of a fluffy omelette or scrambled eggs mixed with garlic, peppers and ham.*

Pain de campagne, *the traditional round, rustic country loaf, is quite hard to find today, but a few dedicated bakers still make it. The sour dough is baked in a traditional wood-fired oven, with the smoke from the fire helping to flavor the bread.*

Foie gras *is the enlarged liver of a goose or duck that has been force-fed on maize. It may be cooked in port or brandy.*

Toulouse sausage

Duck

Homard persillé *is a lobster terrine cooked in a flavored stock with parsley and herbs.*

Haricot beans

Garlic sausage

Cassoulet *is a dish that arouses fierce competition among the dedicated cooks of the southwest. It is a thick stew of white haricot beans, cooked with a variety of sausages and cuts of meat. There are several versions of cassoulet, which can include duck, fresh or salt pork, or mutton.*

Chèvre tiède sur un lit de salade *is grilled goat's cheese, served on a bed of green salad, usually with croûtons.*

Duck with cèpes *is made from confit of duck (meat cooked and preserved in its own fat) with wild mushrooms and garlic.*

Fresh truffles *are often cooked in an omelette to bring out their earthy flavor. Périgord truffles are considered the best.*

Rabbit *with prunes is a classic casserole combination, using the celebrated local Agen prunes for a sweet-sour flavor.*

Saucisson sec

Saucisson au poivre

Saucissons *are fresh or dried (sec) sausages available all over France. They can include a variety of meat, herbs and spices.*

Goat's cheese *is often preserved in olive oil, with bay leaves, black peppercorns and thyme added for flavor.*

Marzipan loaf, *a Basque specialty known as touron, is made of almond paste with pistachios, hazelnuts and fruit.*

WILD MUSHROOMS

Mushroom hunting is a favorite pastime for the French. Varieties include the big and fleshy *cèpes (Boletus edulis)*, the egg-yolk colored *chanterelles (Cantharellus cibarius)*, and the brown *morilles* (morels). Fresh wild mushrooms make a less expensive but equally delicious substitute for truffles.

Chanterelles

Morille

Cèpe

Walnut oil *is a popular dressing for salads in the southwest. Walnut trees grow in the valleys here, thriving even in the thin soil of the uplands. The Dordogne produces more walnuts than any other French region.*

FOLLE DE NOIX

HUILE DE NOIX

DRINKS

Besides fine wines, the region's most famous drink is brandy, a spirit made from white grapes. Brandies are distilled in both Cognac and Armagnac, and are best drunk following a meal. In Quercy, there is an aperitif called Quercy Noix, which is made from walnuts.

Armagnac   Cognac   Quercy Noix

France's Wine Regions: Bordeaux

Barrel-making

Bordeaux is the world's largest fine wine region, and, for red wines, certainly the most familiar outside France. Following Henry II's marriage to Eleanor of Aquitaine, three centuries of courtly commerce with England ensured that claret was served at the finest foreign tables. In the 19th century, canny merchants capitalized on this fame and brought fantastic financial prosperity to the region, and with it, the famous 1855 Classification of the Médoc, a rating system for châteaux that is still used today.

LOCATOR MAP

Bordeaux wine region

Cos d'Estournel, like all the châteaux included in the 1855 league of crus classés *("classed growths"), proudly proclaims the fact on its label.*

Picking red Merlot grapes at Château Palmer

WINE REGIONS

The great wine-producing areas of Bordeaux straddle two great rivers; the land between the rivers ("Entre-Deux-Mers") produces lesser, mainly white wines. The rivers, and the river port of Bordeaux itself, have been crucial to the trade in Bordeaux wines; some of the prettiest châteaux line the river banks, enabling easy transportation.

Lac d

KEY FACTS ABOUT BORDEAUX WINES

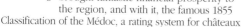

Location and Climate
Climatic conditions may vary not only from one year to another, but also within the region itself. The soils tend to be gravelly in the Médoc and Graves, and clayey on the right bank.

Grape Varieties
The five main red grape varieties are **Cabernet Franc, Cabernet Sauvignon, Merlot, Petit Verdot** and **Malbec**. Cabernet Sauvignon is the dominant grape on the west side of the Gironde, Merlot to the east. Most Bordeaux reds are, however, a blend of grapes. **Sauvignon Blanc** and **Sémillon** are grown and often blended for both dry and sweet whites.

Good Producers
(reds) Latour, Margaux, Haut-Brion, Cos d'Estournel, Léoville Las Cases, Léoville Barton, Lascombes, Pichon Longueville, Pichon Lalande, Lynch-Bages, Palmer, Rausan-Ségla, Duhart Milon, d'Angludet, Léoville Poyferré, Branaire Ducru, Ducru Beaucaillou, Malescot St.-Exupéry, Cantemerle, Phélan-Segur, Chasse-Spleen, Poujeaux, Domaine de Chevalier, Pape Clément, Cheval Blanc, Canon, Pavie, l'Angelus, Troplong Mondot, La Conseillante, Lafleur, Trotanoy.

Good Vintages
(reds) 1996, 1995, 1990, 1989, 1988.

Haut-Brion, in the top division of Bordeaux's Classification, was and still is the single Graves château in this league of Médoc properties.

Arcacho

Cap
Ferret

Lac de C
et de San

The famous legend that guarantees château-bottling originated in Bordeaux, as a check to unscrupulous merchants.

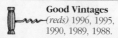

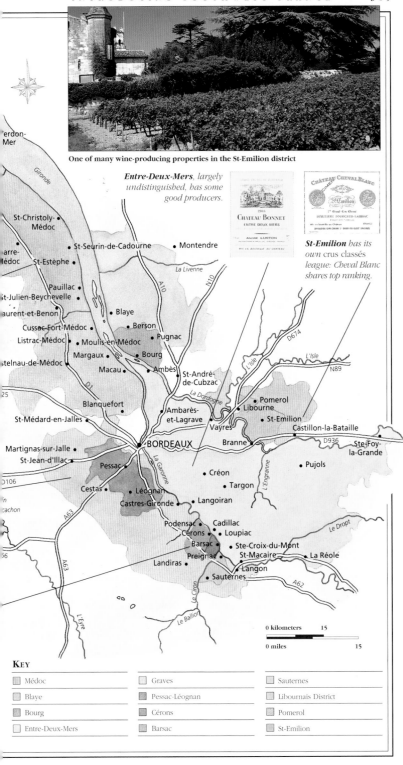

One of many wine-producing properties in the St-Emilion district

Entre-Deux-Mers, largely undistinguished, has some good producers.

CHÂTEAU BONNET
ENTRE DEUX MERS

André LURTON

CHÂTEAU CHEVAL BLANC

St-Emilion

St-Emilion has its own crus classés league: Cheval Blanc shares top ranking.

'erdon-Mer

Gironde

St-Christoly-Médoc

arre-Médoc   St-Estèphe   St-Seurin-de-Cadourne   Montendre

La Livenne   A10   N10

Pauillac

t-Julien-Beychevelle   Blaye

aurent-et-Benon   Berson   D674

Cussac-Fort-Médoc   Pugnac   L'Isle   L'Isle   N89

Listrac-Médoc   Moulis-en-Médoc

Margaux   Bourg

stelnau-de-Médoc   Macau   Ambès   St-André-de-Cubzac

25   D1   La Dordogne   Pomerol

Blanquefort   Libourne

St-Médard-en-Jalles   Ambarès-et-Lagrave   St-Emilion

Vayres   Castillon-la-Bataille

Martignas-sur-Jalle   **BORDEAUX**   Branne   D936   Ste-Foy-la-Grande

St-Jean-d'Illac   La Garonne   Pujols

0106   Pessac   Créon   L'Engranne

n   Targon

cachon   Cestas   Léognan

Castres-Gironde   Langoiran

66   A63   Podensac   Cadillac   Le Dropt

Cérons   Loupiac

Barsac   Ste-Croix-du-Mont

Preignac   St-Macaire   La Réole

Landiras   Langon

Sauternes   A62

A63   Le Ciron

L'Eyre   Le Ballion

0 kilometers   15

0 miles   15

KEY

Médoc	Graves	Sauternes
Blaye	Pessac-Léognan	Libournais District
Bourg	Cérons	Pomerol
Entre-Deux-Mers	Barsac	St-Emilion

The Road to Compostela

Scallop symbol

Throughout the Middle Ages millions of Christians visited Santiago de Compostela in Spain to pay homage at the shrine of St. James (Santiago). They traveled across France staying in monasteries or simple shelters and would return with a scallop shell, the symbol of St. James, as a souvenir. Most pilgrims went in hope of redemption and were often on the road for years. In 1140, a monk named Picaud wrote one of the world's first travel guides about the pilgrimage. Today, travelers can follow the same routes, passing through ancient towns and villages with their magnificent shrines and churches.

Foreign pilgrims joined at ports such as St-Malo.

The original cathedral of Santiago de Compostela was built in 813 by Alfonso II over the tomb of St. James. In 1075 construction started on the grandiose Romanesque church seen today, which has, among other later additions, a resplendent 17th–18th-century Baroque façade.

The routes converged on Santiago de Compostela.

Most pilgrims crossed the Pyrenees at Roncesvalles.

James the Greater, an apostle, came to Spain to spread the Gospel, according to legend. On his return to Judea, he was martyred by Herod. His remains were taken to Spain by boat and lay hidden for 800 years.

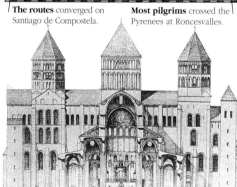

The powerful Cluny Monastery in Burgundy (see pp44–5), and its affiliated monasteries, played an important role in promoting the pilgrimage. They built shelters and set up churches and shrines housing precious relics, to encourage the pilgrims on their way.

THE PILGRIMS' WAY

Paris, Vézelay *(see pp326–7)*, Le Puy *(see p354)* and Arles are the rallying points for the four "official" routes across France. They cross the Pyrenees at Roncesvalles and Somport, and merge at Puente la Reina to form one route, culminating at the shrine on the Galician coast.

WHAT TO SEE TODAY

Huge Romanesque churches, including Ste-Madeleine at Vézelay *(see p326)*, Ste-Foy at Conques *(pp358–9)* and St-Sernin at Toulouse *(p437)*, along with many small chapels, were built to accommodate large numbers of pilgrims.

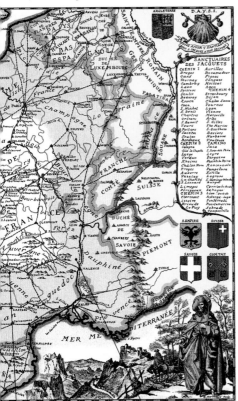

Basilique Ste-Madeleine, Vézelay

Conques purloined relics to boost its prestige.

Le Puy was a main rallying point for pilgrims.

The first recorded pilgrim was the bishop of Le Puy in 951. But pilgrims have probably been coming to Santiago since 814, soon after the saint's tomb was found.

The reliquary of Ste-Foy, at Conques, is in one of many elaborate shrines on the way that drew crowds of pilgrims. A saint's relics were thought to have miraculous powers.

The name Santiago de Compostela is believed to originate from the Latin Campus stellae (field of stars). Legend has it that strange stars were seen hovering over a field in 814, and on July 25, now the feast of Santiago, the saint's remains were found. Subsequent evidence showed that St. James' remains were never in Compostela after all.

Caves of the Southwest

SOUTHWEST FRANCE is well known for its spectacular rock formations, created by the slow accumulation of dissolved mineral deposits. Caves and rock shelters exist throughout limestone country in France. But in the foothills of the Pyrenees and the Dordogne they also have something else to offer the visitor: a collection of extraordinary rock paintings, some dating back to the last Ice Age. These art forms were created when prehistoric peoples evolved and began engraving, painting and carving. This unique artistic tradition lasted for more than 25,000 years, reaching its zenith around 17,000 years ago. Some very fine examples of cave painting are still visible today.

Ancient cave paintings at Lascaux

CAVES OF THE DORDOGNE

There are many different cave systems to visit in or near the Dordogne Valley. The entire Périgord region contains one of the densest concentrations of prehistoric sites anywhere in the world. In an uncertain climate, its rivers flanked by caves and rock shelters proved very attractive to prehistoric man.

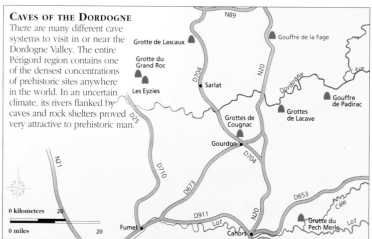

CAVE FORMATION

Limestone is laid down in layers containing fissures that allow water to penetrate beneath the surface. Over thousands of years, the water slowly dissolves the rock, first forming potholes and then larger caverns. Stalactites develop where water drips from the cave roof; stalagmites grow upward from the floor.

Grotte du Grand Roc in the Vézère Valley, Périgord

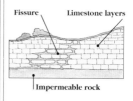

Fissure   Limestone layers

Impermeable rock

1 *Water percolates through fissures, slowly dissolving the surrounding rock.*

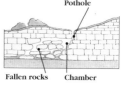

Pothole

Fallen rocks   Chamber

2 *The water produces potholes and loosens surrounding rocks, which gradually fall away.*

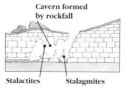

Cavern formed by rockfall

Stalactites   Stalagmites

3 *Dripping water containing dissolved limestone forms stalactites and stalagmites.*

GOUFFRE DE PADIRAC

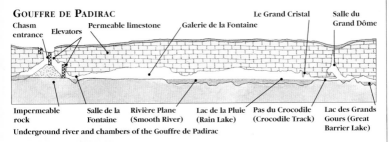

Chasm entrance · Elevators · Permeable limestone · Galerie de la Fontaine · Le Grand Cristal · Salle du Grand Dôme

Impermeable rock · Salle de la Fontaine · Rivière Plane (Smooth River) · Lac de la Pluie (Rain Lake) · Pas du Crocodile (Crocodile Track) · Lac des Grands Gours (Great Barrier Lake)

Underground river and chambers of the Gouffre de Padirac

Prehistoric caves at Les Eyzies

VISITING THE CAVES

Cougnac contains chasms ("gouffres") and galleries and its prehistoric paintings include human figures. Around **Les Eyzies** (see pp424–5) are the major caves of **La Mouthe**, **Les Combarelles**, and **Font de Gaume** which have some beautiful prehistoric paintings, drawings and engravings, as does **Rouffignac** in its extensive network of caves. **Grand Roc** has chambers containing a profusion of stalactites and stalagmites. For more unusual rock formations, the chasm at **La Fage**, northeast of Les Eyzies, leads to chambers and galleries with some magnificent examples.

On the south bank of the Dordogne, an underground river and lake with extraordinary rock formations can be seen at **Lacave**. The gigantic chasm and caverns at **Padirac** (p428) are even more spectacular. The caves at **Lascaux** with the finest prehistoric paintings have been closed, but the exceptional replica at **Lascaux II** (p424) is well worth seeing. Farther south, **Pech-Merle's** caverns (p428) have impressive rock formations.

THE STORY OF CAVE ART

The first prehistoric cave paintings in Europe were discovered in northwest Spain in 1879. Since then, over 200 decorated caves and rock shelters have been found in Spain and France, mainly in the Dordogne region. A wide range of clues, from stone lamps to miraculously preserved footprints, has helped prehistorians work out the techniques the cave artists used. But their motives remain mysterious. Nearly all the paintings are of animals, with few humans, and many of them are in inaccessible underground chambers. The paintings undoubtedly had a symbolic or magical significance; a new theory suggests they were the work of shamans.

The techniques used by Ice Age artists, who worked by lamplight, included cutting outlines into soft rock, using natural contours as part of the design. Black lines and shading were produced by charcoal, while color washes were applied with mineral pigments such as kaolin and hematite. Hand silhouettes were made by sucking up diluted pigment and blowing it through a plant stem to form a fine spray. When the hand was removed from the rock, its eerie shape was left behind.

Decorated stone lamp discovered in Lascaux cave

Kaolin

Charcoal

Hematite

The Great Bull from the Hall of Bulls frieze at Lascaux

POITOU AND AQUITAINE

DEUX-SÈVRES · VIENNE · CHARENTE-MARITIME
CHARENTE · GIRONDE · LANDES

THIS VAST AREA *of southwest France spans a quarter of the country's windswept Atlantic coastline, a great expanse of fine sandy beaches. The region stretches from the marshes of the Marais Poitevin to the great pine forests of the Landes. Central to it is the celebrated wine region of Bordeaux and its great châteaux.*

The turbulent history of Poitou and Aquitaine, fought over for centuries, has left a rich architectural and cultural heritage. The great arch and amphitheater at Saintes bear witness to Roman influence in the area. In the Middle Ages, the pilgrimage route to Santiago de Compostela *(see pp390–91)* created an impressive legacy of Romanesque churches, such as those at Poitiers and Parthenay, as well as tiny chapels and glowing frescoes. The Hundred Years' War *(see pp48–9)* caused great upheaval but also resulted in the construction of mighty defense keeps by the English Plantagenet kings. As a result of the Wars of Religion *(see pp50–51)*, many towns, churches and châteaux were destroyed and had to be rebuilt.

Present-day Poitiers is a big, thriving commercial center. To the west are the historic ports of La Rochelle and Rochefort. Farther south, the wine-producing district of Bordeaux combines with Cognac, famous for its brandy, to supply an important part of the region's income. The city of Bordeaux is as prosperous today as in Roman times, combining a lively cultural scene with elegant 18th-century architecture. Its wines complement the region's cuisine: eels, mussels and oysters from the coast; and salty lamb and goat's cheeses from the inland pastures.

Shuttered houses in St-Martin-de-Ré, on Ile de Ré, off the coast of La Rochelle

◁ **The seaside resort of Arcachon by the sandy dunes of the Bassin d'Arcachon**

Exploring Poitou and Aquitaine

BLESSED WITH a seemingly endless Atlantic coastline, abundant navigable waterways, excellent ports and the finest wine and brandy in the world, the region is ideal for a relaxing vacation. Today most summer visitors head straight for the beaches with their thundering waves, but there is also lush countryside inland with a lot to offer. Fine medieval architecture can be seen along the pilgrim's route to Santiago de Compostela *(see pp390–91)*, and châteaux of all shapes and sizes characterize the wine districts around Bordeaux. The only modern city of major importance in the region, Bordeaux is worth a visit for its elegant 18th-century architecture as well as for its rich cultural life. The vast man-made forest of Les Landes also adds to this greatly undervalued corner of France.

Beachlife in Bassin d'Arcachon on the Côte d'Argent

GETTING AROUND

The region's main highway is the A10 connecting Paris and Poitiers with Bordeaux and points east, such as Toulouse, west to Rochefort and south to Bayonne and Spain. This road carries most of the area's heavy traffic, relieving the excellent smaller roads. Bordeaux can be reached by TGV direct from Lille (Eurostar interchange), and the Paris-Poitiers-Angoulême-Bordeaux TGV line has halved rail travel times (Paris–Bordeaux 3 1/4 hr). Bordeaux has an international airport (direct flights to UK), and has coach services to most European capitals. Poitiers has buses to nearby towns, including Parthenay, Chauvigny and St-Savin.

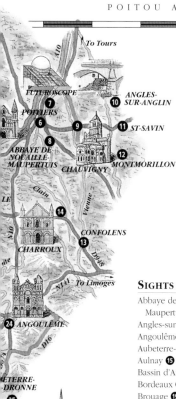

One of the Ile de Ré's picturesque harbors

SIGHTS AT A GLANCE

Boats moored at Coulon in the Marais Poitevin

KEY

▬ Highway

▬ Major road

▬ Minor road

▬ Scenic route

〰 River

☆ Viewing point

0 kilometers   25

0 miles   25

Rose window of St-Médard, Thouars

Thouars ❶

Deux-Sèvres. 🏠 12,000. 🚗 🚌 🛈
3 bis Bd Pierre Curie (05 49 66 17 65).
🗓 Tue & Fri.

Thouars, on a rocky outcrop surrounded by the Thouet River, is on the border between Anjou and Poitou. There are as many roofs of northern slate as of southern red tiles.

In the center lies **Eglise St-Médard**. Its Romanesque façade is a perfect example of the Poitevin style that is typical of the region *(see p402)*, although a splendid Gothic rose window has been added. Lined with half-timbered medieval houses, the rue du Château leads up to the 17th-century château that dominates the town. It now houses a lycée and is open to the public during the summer.

East of Thouars lies the moated **Château d'Oiron**, which now hosts contemporary art exhibitions. A masterpiece of Renaissance architecture, it was largely built in 1518–49.

🏰 Château d'Oiron
79100 Oiron. 📞 05 49 96 51 25.
⬜ daily. ⬤ some public hols. 🈯

Parthenay ❷

Deux-Sèvres. 🏠 10,400. 🚗 🚌
🛈 8 rue de la Vau-St-Jacques (05 49
64 24 24). 🗓 Wed.

Parthenay is a classic, sleepy provincial town, typical of western France – except on Wednesday mornings, when France's second biggest livestock market is held here. In the Middle Ages, the town was an important stop on the route to Santiago de Compostela *(see pp390–91)*, and it is easy to imagine the processions of pilgrims in the medieval quarter. Steep and cobbled, rue de la Vau-St-Jacques winds up to the 13th-century ramparts, leading on from the fortified Porte St-Jacques, which guards a 13th-century bridge over the Thouet River.

West of Parthenay, the 12th-century church of **St-Pierre de Parthenay-le-Vieux** has a splendid Poitevin façade, featuring Samson and the Lion and a cavalier with a falcon.

Marais Poitevin ❸

Charente-Maritime, Deux-Sèvres,
Vendée. ✈ La Rochelle. 🚌 Niort,
🚌 Coulon, Arçais, Marans.
🛈 Coulon (05 49 35 99 29).

The poitevin marshes, which have been slowly drained with canals, dikes and sluices for a thousand years, cover about 80,000 hectares (197,000 acres) between Niort and the sea. The area is now a regional park, divided into two parts. To the north and south of the Sèvre estuary is the Marais Désséché (dry marsh), where cereal and other crops are grown. The huge swath of the Marais Mouillé (wet marsh) is upstream toward Niort.

The wet marshes, known as Venise Verte (Green Venice), are the most interesting. They are crisscrossed by a labyrinth of weed-choked canals, adorned with waterlilies and irises, shaded by poplars and beeches, and support a rich variety of birds and other wildlife. The *maraîchins* who live here stoutly maintain that much of the huge, waterlogged forest is unexplored. The picturesque whitewashed villages hereabouts are all built on higher ground, and the customary means of transportation is a flat-bottomed boat, known as a *platte*.

Coulon, St-Hilaire-la-Palud, La Garette, and Arçais, as well as Damvix and Maillezais in the Vendée, are all convenient starting points for boat trips around the marshes (allow at least two hours). Boats can

Medieval houses lining the cobbled rue de la Vau-St-Jacques in Parthenay

Flat-bottomed boats moored at Coulon in the Marais Poitevin

be rented with or without a guide. Make sure you bring plenty of insect repellent.

Coulon is the largest and best equipped village, and a popular base for visiting the area. In the aquarium there lurks the ugliest freshwater fish in captivity in France, the *silure*, or sheat-fish. From here there are also river cruises departing along the main channel of the Sèvre.

The Plantagenet donjon in Niort, now housing a local museum

Niort **4**

Deux-Sèvres. 🏠 58,000. 🚊 🚌
🛈 16 rue du Petit St-Jean (05 49 24 18 79). 🛍 Thu & Sat.

ONCE A MEDIEVAL PORT by the green waters of the Sèvre, Niort is now a prosperous industrial town specializing in machine tools, electronics, chemicals and insurance.

Its closeness to the marshes is evident in local specialties – eels, snails and angelica. This herb has been cultivated in the wetlands for centuries and is used for anything from liqueur to ice cream.

The town's immediate attraction is the huge 12th-century donjon overlooking the Vieux Pont. Built by Henry II and Richard the Lion-Heart, it played an important role during the Hundred Years' War and was later used as a prison. One prisoner was the father of Madame de Maintenon *(see p52)*, who was born in Niort and spent her childhood there. The donjon is now a museum concentrating on local arts and crafts, and archaeology.

Environs
Halfway to Poitiers is the small town of **St-Maixent-L'Ecole**. A marvel of light and space, its abbey church is a Flamboyant Gothic reconstruction by François Le Duc (1670) of a building destroyed during the Wars of Religion. Farther west, the **Tumulus de Bougon** consists of five tumuli (burial mounds), the oldest dating from 4500 BC.

Melle **5**

Deux-Sèvres. 🏠 4,000. 🚌 🛈 rue E Travers (05 49 29 15 10). 🛍 Fri.

A ROMAN SILVER MINE was the origin of Melle, which in the 9th century had the only mint in Aquitaine. Later, its fame derived from the *baudet du Poitou,* an especially sturdy mule bred in the area. Now Melle is better known for its churches, of which the finest is **St-Hilaire**. Built in a delightful riverside setting, it has a 12th-century Poitevin façade with an equestrian statue, thought to be of the Emperor Constantine, above the north door. The capitals in the nave have elaborate motifs ranging from angels to bizarre beasts.

Environs
To the northwest, the abbey in **Celles-sur-Belle** has a great Moorish doorway that contrasts strongly with the rest of the church, a 17th-century restoration in Gothic style.

Equestrian statue of Constantine on the façade of St-Hilaire, Melle

Canal in the Venise Verte region of the Marais Poitevin ▷

Poitiers ❻

THREE OF THE GREATEST BATTLES in French history were
fought around Poitiers, the most famous in 732
when Charles Martel halted the Arab invasion. After
two periods of English rule *(see p47)*, the town thrived
during the reign of Jean de Berry (1369–1416), the great
sponsor of the arts. Its university, founded in 1431,
made Poitiers a major intellectual center and boasted
Rabelais among its students. The Wars of Religion left
Poitiers in chaos, and not until the late 19th century did
any major development take place. Today, however,
the town is a modern and dynamic regional capital,
with a rich architectural heritage in its historic center.

Fresco in Eglise
St-Hilaire-le-Grand

🏛 Notre-Dame-la-Grande
Despite its name, Notre-Dame-
la-Grande is not a large church.
One of Poitiers' great pilgrim
churches, it is most celebrated
as a masterpiece of lively 12th-
century Poitevin sculpture,
notably its polychrome facade.
In the choir is a Romanesque
fresco of Christ and the Virgin.
Most of the chapels were
added during the Renaissance.

🏛 Palais de Justice
Pl Alphonse Lepetit. **[** 05 49 50 22
00. **◻** Mon–Fri; Jul & Aug:daily.
Behind the bland Renaissance
façade is the 12th-century
great hall of the palace of the
Angevin kings, Henry II and
Richard the Lion-Heart. This
is thought to be the scene of
Joan of Arc's examination by a
council of theologians in 1429.

🏛 Cathédrale St-Pierre
The 13th-century carved choir
stalls in St-Pierre are by far
the oldest in France. Note the
huge 12th-century east window
showing the Crucifixion. The

Pillars with colorful geometrical patterns in Notre-Dame-la-Grande

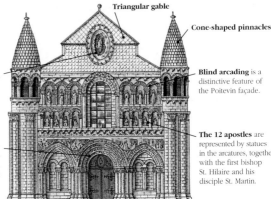

NOTRE-DAME-LA-GRANDE

Triangular gable

Cone-shaped pinnacles

Christ in Majesty is
shown in the center of
the gable, surrounded
by symbols of the
evangelists.

Blind arcading is a
distinctive feature of
the Poitevin façade.

The portals on the
Poitevin façade are deep
and richly sculpted, often
showing a pronounced
Moorish influence.

The 12 apostles are
represented by statues
in the arcatures, together
with the first bishop
St. Hilaire and his
disciple St. Martin.

tiny figures of the cathedral's patrons (Henry II and Eleanor of Aquitaine) are crouched at the foot of the window. Its organ (1787–1791), made by François-Henri Cliquot, is one of the most prestigious and beautiful in Europe.

🏛 Eglise Ste-Radegonde

Housed in this church is the 6th-century tomb of Radegonde, who founded the Abbaye de Ste-Croix – the first nunnery in France – on this site. In the choir are 13th-century windows recounting the life of the saint.

🏛 Eglise St-Hilaire-le-Grand

Fires and reconstructions have made St-Hilaire a mosaic of different styles. With its origins in the 6th century, the church still displays an 11th-century bell tower and a 12th-century nave.

🏛 Baptistère St-Jean

Rue Jean Jaurès. ◯ *Jul–Aug: daily; Sep–Jun: Wed–Mon.* 🈺
The polygonal 4th-century Baptistère St-Jean is one of the oldest Christian buildings in France. Many of the earliest converts were baptized here. Now a museum, it contains Romanesque frescoes of Christ

and Emperor Constantine, and some Merovingian sarcophagi.

🏛 Musée Sainte-Croix

3 bis rue Jean Jaurès. 📞 *05 49 41 07 53.* ◯ *Jun–Sep: Mon pm–Sun; Oct–May: Tue–Fri all day, Sat–Mon pms only.* ● *some public hols.* 🈺
Musée Sainte-Croix exhibits prehistoric, Gallo-Roman and medieval archaeology, and a wide range of paintings and 19th-century sculpture. Five bronzes by Camille Claudel are on show, including *La Valse.* There is also a large collection of contemporary art.

🏛 Médiathèque François Mitterrand

4 rue de l'Université. 📞 *05 49 52 31 51.* ◯ *Tue–Sat.* ● *public hols.*
This modern building, in the historic quarter, is renowned for its communications technology. Inside, the **Maison du Moyen Age** displays medieval manuscripts and engravings.

VISITORS' CHECKLIST

Vienne. 🏠 *84,000.* ✈ *5 km (3 miles) W Poitiers.* 🚉 🚌
🛈 *45 pl Charles de Gaulle (05 49 41 21 24).* 🍴 *Tue–Sun.*
🎵 *Colla-Voce (end Aug–Sep).*
🌐 *www.interpc.fr/ot-poitiers*

One of Futuroscope's most popular attractions: the vast movie theater

Futuroscope 🕖

Jaunay-Clan. 🚉 📞 *05 49 49 30 00.* ◯ *daily.* ● *Nov 3–Feb 6.* 🈺 🍴 🎁

FUTUROSCOPE is a fantastic theme park 7 km (4.5 miles) north of Poitiers, exploring state-of-the-art visual technology in a futuristic architectural environment. Attractions evolve yearly and include simulators, 3D and 360° screens and the "magic carpet" cinema, with one of its two screens placed on the floor, creating the sensation of "flying" over land. The crystal-like movie theater has the biggest screen in Europe.

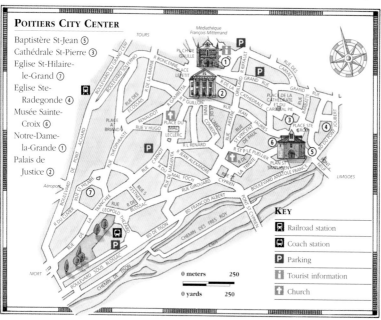

POITIERS CITY CENTER

Baptistère St-Jean ⑤
Cathédrale St-Pierre ③
Eglise St-Hilaire-le-Grand ⑦
Eglise Ste-Radegonde ④
Musée Sainte-Croix ⑥
Notre-Dame-la-Grande ①
Palais de Justice ②

KEY

🚉 Railroad station

🚌 Coach station

🅿 Parking

🛈 Tourist information

✝ Church

0 meters   250

0 yards   250

The castle ruins of Angles-sur-Anglin with the old watermill in the foreground

Abbaye de Nouaillé-Maupertuis **8**

Nouaillé-Maupertuis. **☎** 05 49 55 35 69. **Church** ☐ 9am–6pm. **&** restricted.

ON THE BANKS of the Miosson River lies the Abbaye de Nouaillé-Maupertuis. First mentioned in 780, the abbey became independent in 808 and followed the Benedictine rule. Apart from the beauty of the site, it is also worth visiting the church, built in the 11th–12th centuries and reconstructed several times. Behind the altar is the 10th-century sarcophagus of St. Junien, with three great heraldic carved eagles on the front.

More interesting is the nearby battlefield, scene of the great English victory at Poitiers by the Black Prince in 1356. The view has changed little in 600 years. Drive down the small road to La Cardinerie (to the right off the D142), which leads to the river crossing at Gué de L'Omme, the epicenter of the battle. There is a monument halfway up the hill where the heaviest fighting took place, and where the French king Jean le Bon was isolated and captured. He had put up a heroic single-handed resistance with nothing but his battle-ax and his small son Philippe to tell him where the next English knight was coming from.

Chauvigny **9**

Vienne. **🚶** 7,000. **🚌** **ℹ** 5 rue St-Pierre (05 49 46 39 01). **🛒** Sat.

CHAUVIGNY, on its steep promontory overlooking the broad Vienne River, has the distinction of being able to display the ruins of no fewer than four fortified medieval castles. Stone from the local quarry was so plentiful that nobody ever bothered to demolish earlier castles for building material.

Nevertheless, the best thing in this town is the 11th–12th-century **Eglise St-Pierre**, whose decorated capitals are a real treasure – particularly those in the choir. The carvings represent biblical scenes, along with monsters,

Monster capitals in Eglise St-Pierre in Chauvigny

sphinxes and sirens. Look for the one that says *Gofridus me fecit* (Gofridus made me), with wonderfully natural scenes of the Epiphany.

Environs
Nearby is the lovely **Château de Touffou**, a Renaissance dream on the banks of the Vienne, with terraces and hanging flowers. Just north of it is the sleepy village of **Bonneuil-Matours**, with fine choir stalls in its Romanesque church.

🏰 Château de Touffou
Bonnes. **☎** 05 49 56 08 48. ☐ May–mid-Jun: Thu–Sun pms; mid-Jun–mid-Sep: Wed–Mon; mid–end Sep & Apr: w/e & publ hols pms. **●** Oct–Mar.

Angles-sur-Anglin **10**

Vienne. **🚶** 360. **ℹ** 14 La Place (05 49 48 86 87). **🛒** Sun.

THE VILLAGE OF ANGLES lies in an extremely beautiful riverside setting, dominated by its castle ruins. Adding to the charm is an old watermill by the slow-running Anglin River, graced by waterlilies and swaying reeds. Try to avoid visiting in summer, as the narrow streets become too close for comfort.

Angles is also famous for its tradition of fine needlework, the *jours d'Angles*, which is determinedly maintained by the local women today (their workshops can be visited).

St-Savin ⓫

Vienne. 🏠 1,100. 🚉
🏛 20 pl de la Libération (05 49 48
11 00). 🛒 Fri.

THE GLORY of St-Savin is its
11th-century abbey church
with its slender Gothic spire
and huge nave.

The abbey had enormous
influence until the Hundred
Years' War, when it was burned
down. It was later pillaged
several times during the Wars
of Religion. Despite restoration work by monks in the
17th century and again in the
19th century, the church
seems quite untouched.

Its interior contains the most
magnificent series of 12th-
century Romanesque frescoes
in Europe. These wallpaintings
were among the very first in
France to be classified as a
Monument Historique in 1836.
Some of the frescoes were
restored in 1967–74 and since
1983 they have been protected by UNESCO. A full-scale
replica of the St-Savin murals
can be seen at the Palais de
Chaillot in Paris *(see pp106–7)*.
The abbey-museum explains
the techniques and historical
context of these murals.

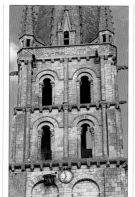

Bell tower of St-Savin

Montmorillon ⓬

Vienne. 🏠 7,000. 🚉 🏛 2 pl du
Maréchal Leclerc (05 49 91 11 96).
🛒 Wed & Sat.

MONTMORILLON, built on
both banks of the calm
Gartempe River, has its
origins in the 11th century.
Like most towns in the region,
it had a difficult time during
the Hundred Years' War and
the Wars of Religion. Some
buildings survived, such as
Eglise Notre-Dame, which

has beautiful frescoes in its
12th-century crypt. They
include scenes from the life
of St. Catherine of Alexandria.

Environs
Half an hour's walk from the
Pont de Chez Ragon, south of
Montmorillon, is the **Portes
d'Enfer**, a dramatically shaped
rock above the sudden rapids
of the Gartempe.

Confolens ⓭

Charente. 🏠 3,150. 🚉 🏛 place
des Marronniers (05 45 84 22 22).
🛒 Wed & Sat.

ON THE BORDER with Limou-
sin, Confolens was once
an important frontier town
with several churches, but
now suffers from rural exodus.
Efforts to prevent the town's
isolation include the annual
international folklore festival.
Every August, the town is
transformed into a tumultuous
mix of music, costumes and
crafts from all over the world.

Of historical interest is the
medieval bridge across the
Vienne, heavily restored in
the early 18th century.

Charroux ⓮

Vienne. 🏠 1,400. 🏛 2 route de
Chatain (05 49 87 60 12). 🛒 Thu.

THE 8TH-CENTURY **Abbaye St-
Sauveur** in Charroux was
once one of the richest
abbeys in the region. Today,
it has become no more than a
ruin open to the sky.

Its chief contribution to
history was made in the 10th
century, when the Council of
Charroux declared the "Truce
of God," the earliest-known
attempt to regulate war in the
manner of the Geneva
convention. Rules included:
"Christian soldiers may not
plunder churches, strike
priests or steal peasants' livestock while campaigning."

The huge tower marking
the center of the church, and
some superb sculpture from
the original abbey portal in
the small museum here, give
an idea of what Charroux must
have been like in its heyday.

ST-SAVIN WALL PAINTINGS

The frescoes of St-Savin represent Old Testament history
from the Creation to the Ten Commandments. The sequence
starts to the left of the entrance with the Creation of the
stars and of Eve. It continues with scenes from Noah's Ark
to the Tower of Babel, the story of Joseph and the parting
of the Red Sea. It is believed that all the frescoes were
created by the same group of artists, due to the similarity
in style. Their harmonious colors – red and yellow ocher,
green, black and white – have been softened by time.

Noah's Ark, from a 12th-century wall painting in St-Savin

Aulnay ⓖ

Charente-Maritime. 👥 *1,400.*
🛈 *290 avenue de l'Eglise (05 46 33 14 44).* 🛒 *Thu & Sun.*

PERHAPS the most unusual fact about the lovely 12th-century **Eglise St-Pierre** in Aulnay is that it was all built at once; there is no ill-fitting apse or transept added to an original nave. Surrounded by nothing but cypresses, it has remained the same since the time of the great pilgrimages.

The church is covered in glorious sculpture, particularly the outside of the south transept. It is a rare example of a complete Romanesque façade, with rank on rank of raucous monsters and graceful human figures. Look for the donkey with a harp. Inside the church there is a pillar decorated with elephants, inscribed "Here be Elephants."

Façade of Eglise St-Pierre at Aulnay

La Rochelle ⓗ

Charente-Maritime. 👥 *78,000.* ✈
🚉 🚌 🛈 *place de la Petite Sirène, Le Gabut (05 46 41 14 68).* 🛒 *daily.*

LA ROCHELLE, a commercial center and busy port since the 11th century, has suffered much from a distressing tendency to back the wrong side – the English and the Calvinists, for example. This led to a ruthless siege of the city by Cardinal Richelieu in 1628, during which 23,000 people starved to death. The walls were destroyed and the city's

Tour St-Nicolas in La Rochelle

privileges withdrawn. The glory of La Rochelle is the old harbor surrounded by stately buildings. The harbor is now the biggest yachting center on France's Atlantic coast. On either side of its entrance are **Tour de la Chaîne** and **Tour St-Nicolas**. A huge chain used to be strung between them to ward off attack from the sea.

La Rochelle is easy to explore on foot, though its cobbled streets and many arcades can be impossibly congested in high summer. To get an overview, climb the 15th-century **Tour de la Lanterne**. Its inner walls were covered in graffiti by prisoners, mostly foreign mariners, in the 17th–19th centuries. Ships are the most common motif.

The study of the 18th-century scientist Clément Lafaille is preserved in the **Muséum d'Histoire Naturelle**, complete with shell collection and display cabinets. There are also stuffed animals and African masks. The town's relation to the New World is treated in the **Musée du Nouveau Monde**. Emigration as well as commerce and the slave trade are explained through old maps, paintings and artifacts.

The richly decorated 16th-century courtyard façade of the **Hôtel de Ville** is worth a visit, as is the delightful collection of perfume bottles in the **Musée du Flacon à Parfum** in the parfumerie at No. 33 rue du Temple.

Next to the Vieux Port is the huge **Aquarium**. Transparent tunnels lead through tanks with different marine biotopes, including sharks and turtles.

🏰 **Tour de la Lanterne**
Le Port. 📞 *05 46 41 56 04.* 🕐 *mid-May–mid-Sep: daily; mid-Sep–mid-May: Tue–Sun.* ⬤ *Jan 1, May 1, Nov 1 & 11, Dec 25.* 🎟

🏛 **Muséum d'Histoire Naturelle**
28 rue Albert Premier. 📞 *05 46 41 18 25* ⬤ *for renovation (gdn open)* 🎟 ♿

🏛 **Musée du Nouveau Monde**
10 rue Fleuriau. 📞 *05 46 41 46 50.* 🕐 *Wed–Mon.* ⬤ *Sun am, Jan 1, May 1, Jul 14, Nov 1 & 11, Dec 25.* 🎟

🐟 **Aquarium**
Bassin des Grands Yachts. 📞 *05 46 34 00 00.* 🕐 *daily.* 🎟 ♿ 🅿 📷 🎧

Environs

Ile de Ré, also known as the white island, is a long stretch of chalky cliffs and dunes, with a rich birdlife. Since 1988 it has been connected to the mainland by a 3-km-long (2-mile) bridge. Head for **Ars-en-Ré**, in the middle, or **St-Martin-de-Ré**, the island's main town. Apart from its 17th-century ramparts, there are plenty of seafood restaurants serving locally-grown oysters. Salt pans also cover the island.

Arcade in rue du Palais, La Rochelle

Rochefort ⓘ

Charente-Maritime. 👥 *28,000.* 🚉
🚌 🛈 *av Sadi-Carnot (05 46 99 08 60).* 🛒 *Tue, Thu & Sat.*

THE HISTORIC RIVAL of La Rochelle, Rochefort was built by Colbert *(see pp52–3)* in the 17th century to be the

Phare des Baleines on the eastern point of Ile de Ré, opposite La Rochelle

greatest shipyard in France, producing over 300 sailing vessels per year.

Today, this maritime heritage can be traced in the **Corderie Royale** (royal ropeworks) from 1670. Beautifully restored, the building now houses an exhibition on ropemaking. The **Musée de la Marine** displays splendid models of all the ships built in the arsenal. The reconstruction of the frigate *Hermione* can be seen nearby.

Rochefort is also famous as the birthplace of the flamboyant writer Pierre Loti (1850–1923). The author's extravagant **Maison de Pierre Loti** is filled with lush souvenirs in an oriental decor.

The **Musée d'Art et d'Histoire** has an interesting ethnographic collection and a relief map of the old shipyard.

🚇 **La Corderie Royale**
Centre International de la Mer, rue Audebert. 🔲 05 46 87 01 90.
🔵 daily. ⚫ Jan 1, Dec 25. 🔳 ♿ 🔲
🏛 **Musée de la Marine**
Place de la Galissonnière. 🔲 05 46 99 86 57. 🔵 Tue–Sun. ⚫ May 1, mid-Dec–Jan. 🔳 🔲
🏛 **Maison de Pierre Loti**
141 rue Pierre Loti. 🔲 05 46 99 16 88.
🔵 Apr–Sep: daily; Oct–March: Wed–Mon. ⚫ Jan, Nov 1 & 11, Dec 25.
🏛 **Musée d'Art et d'Histoire**
63 avenue Charles de Gaulle.
🔲 05 46 99 83 99. ⚫ for renovation until 2004. 🔳 only.

Environs
Ile d'Aix is served by a ferry from Fouras on the mainland. Napoleon was briefly kept here before being exiled to St.

Helena. There are Napoleonic mementos in the **Musée Napoléonien**. The camel he rode in the Egyptian campaign is in the **Musée Africain**.

🏛 **Musée Napoléonien**
30 rue Napoléon. 🔲 05 46 84 66 40.
🔵 Wed–Mon. ⚫ May 1. 🔳
🏛 **Musée Africain**
Rue Napoléon. 🔲 05 46 84 66 40.
🔵 Thu–Tue. ⚫ May 1. 🔳 ♿

Napoleon, who was detained on Ile d'Aix in 1814

Île d'Oléron ⓲

Charente-Maritime. ✈ La Rochelle.
🚆 Rochefort, La Rochelle, Saintes then bus. ⛴ from La Rochelle (in summer).
🅸 Bourcefranc (05 46 85 65 23).

Oléron is the second largest French island after Corsica, and a very popular holiday resort. Its south coast, the **Côte Sauvage**, is all dunes and pine forest, with excellent beaches at Vert Bois and Grande Plage, near the fishing

port of La Cotinière. The north is more prosaic, largely given over to farming and fishing.

The train from **St-Trojan** makes an interesting excursion through dunes and woodlands to the Pointe de Maumusson (Easter–Oct).

Brouage ⓳

Charente-Maritime. 🏘 130.
🅸 2 rue de Québec, Hiers-Brouage (05 46 85 19 16).

Cardinal Richelieu's fortress in Brouage, his base during the Siege of La Rochelle (1627–8), once overlooked a thriving harbor, but its wealth and population declined in the 18th century as the ocean receded. In 1659, Marie Mancini was sent into exile here by her uncle, Cardinal Mazarin, who did not approve of her liaison with Louis XIV. The king never forgot the beautiful Marie. Even on his way back from his wedding, he stayed alone at Brouage in the room once occupied by his first great love. Today, the **ramparts** form a peaceful backdrop for the villagers working in the mussel beds below.

Environs
There are two reasons to go to **Marennes**, southwest of Brouage: the famous green-tinged oysters and the view from the steeple of Eglise St-Pierre-de-Sales. Nearby is the 18th-century **Château de la Gataudière,** with an exhibition of horsedrawn vehicles.

One of Royan's five popular beaches

Royan ⑳

Charente-Maritime. 🏃 *17,500.* 🚌 🚗 ⛴ *to Verdon only.* 🚶 *Rond-Point de la Poste (05 46 05 04 71).* 🍴 *Tue–Sun.*

Badly damaged by Allied carpet-bombing at the end of World War II, Royan is now thoroughly modern and completely different in tone from the rest of the towns on this weather-beaten coast. With five beaches of fine sand, here called *conches*, it becomes a heavily populated resort in the summer months.

Built between 1955 and 1958, **Eglise Notre-Dame** is a remarkable early example of reinforced concrete architecture. Its interior is flooded with color and light through the stained-glass windows.

A change from all the modern architecture is offered by the outstanding Renaissance **Phare de Cordouan**. Various lighthouses have been erected on the site since the 11th century. The present one was finished in 1611, with a chapel inside. The construction was later reinforced and 30 m (130 ft) added to its height. Since 1789, the only thing that has changed is the lighting method. Boat trips that include Phare de Cordouan leave from Royan harbor.

Talmont-sur-Gironde ㉑

Charente-Maritime. 🏃 *83.* 🚶 *rue de L'Église (05 46 90 16 25).*

The tiny Romanesque **Eglise Ste-Radegonde** is perched on a spit of land overlooking the Gironde. Built in 1094, the church's apse was designed to resemble the bow of a ship – which is apt, since the nave has already fallen into the sea. A 15th-century façade closes off what's left. Inside are richly decorated capitals, including a tableau of St. George and the Dragon.

Talmont is a jewel of a village, packed full of little white houses, decorated with colorful hollyhocks in summer.

Saintes ㉒

Charente-Maritime. 🏃 *27,000.* 🚌 🚗 🚶 ℹ *Villa Musso, 62 cours National (05 46 74 23 82).* 🍴 *Tue–Sun.*

Saintes, capital of the Saintonge region, has an extraordinarily rich architectural heritage. For centuries, it possessed the only bridge on the lower Charente, well used by pilgrims heading for Santiago de Compostela. The Roman bridge no longer exists, but you can still admire the magnificent **Arch of Germanicus** (AD 19) that used to mark its entrance.

On the same side of the river is the simple and beautiful **Abbaye aux Dames**. Consecrated in 1047, the church was modernized in the 12th century. During the 17th–18th centuries, many young noble ladies were educated here. Look for the decorated portal and the vigorous 12th-century head of Christ in the apse.

On the left bank is the 1st-century Roman **amphitheater**. Farther away lies the more unknown gem, **Eglise St-Eutrope**. In the 15th century, this church had the misfortune to effect a miraculous cure of the dropsy on Louis XI. In a paroxysm of gratitude, he did his best to wreck it with unsightly Gothic additions. Luckily, its rare Romanesque capitals have survived.

Arch of Germanicus in Saintes

Cognac ㉓

Charente. 🏃 *20,000.* 🚌 🚗 🚶 ℹ *16 rue du 14 Juillet (05 45 82 10 71).* 🍴 *Tue–Sat.*

Wherever you spot the telltale black lichen stains from alcohol evaporation on the exterior of the buildings

Necropolis in the monolithic Eglise St-Jean in Aubeterre-sur-Dronne

here, you may be sure that you are looking at yet another storehouse of cognac.

All the great cognac houses do tours – a good one is chez **Cognac Otard**, situated in the 15th–16th-century château where François I was born. The distillery was established in 1795 by a Scot named Otard, who ruthlessly demolished an old chapel in the process. Luckily, much of the Renaissance architecture was saved and can be seen during the tour, which includes a cognac-tasting.

Cognac in traditional snifter

The basic material for cognac is local white wine low in alcohol, which is then distilled. The resultant pale spirit is aged in oak barrels for 4–40 years before being bottled. The skill lies in the blending – therefore, the only guide to quality is the name and the duration of aging.

🍷 Cognac Otard
Château de Cognac, 127 bd Denfert-Rochereau. ▐ 05 45 36 88 86.
◖ Apr–Oct: daily; Nov–Dec: Mon–Fri.
● May 1 & public hols in winter. ▨

Angoulême ②④

Charente. ▨ 46,000. ▣ ▣
▐ 7 bis, rue du Chat (05 45 95 16 84). ▣ Wed & Sat.

THE CELEBRATED 12th-century **Cathédrale St-Pierre**, which dominates this thriving industrial center, is the fourth

to be built on the site. One of its most interesting features is the Romanesque frieze on the façade, wonderfully rich in detail. Some exaggerated restoration work was carried out by the 19th-century architect Abadie. In his eagerness to wipe out all details added after the 12th century, he even managed to destroy a 6th-century crypt. Unfortunately, he was also let loose on the old château, transforming it into a Neo-Gothic **Hôtel de Ville** (town hall). However, the 15th-century tower where Marguerite d'Angoulême was born in 1492 still stands. A statue of her can be seen in the garden. Sister of François I, she spoke six languages, had an important role in foreign politics and wrote the very popular novel *Heptameon*.

The ramparts offer a long bracing walk with views over the Charente Valley. A vintage car race takes place along the ramparts in mid-September.

The **Centre National de la Bande Dessinée et de l'Image** has a reference collection of French print and film cartoons dating back to 1946.

🏛 Centre National de la Bande Dessinée et de l'Image
121 rue de Bordeaux. ▐ 05 45 38 65 65. ◖ Tue–Sun (w/e pms only). ● Jan, public hols. ▨ ♿ ▯ ▯ Cinema

Environs
Angoulême used to be famous for its papermills. The **Moulin du Verger** at Puymoyen has a museum and still produces rag paper in the traditional 18th-century manner.

🌾 Moulin du Verger
▐ 05 45 61 10 38. ◖ daily.

Aubeterre-sur-Dronne ②⑤

Charente. ▨ 390. ▣ ▐ place du Château (05 45 98 57 18). ▣ Thu, Sun.

THE CHIEF ORNAMENT of this pretty white village is the staggering monolithic **Eglise St-Jean**. Dug out of the white chalky cliff that gave the village its name (Alba Terra – White Earth), some parts of it date back to the 6th century. Between the Revolution and 1860, it served as the village's cemetery. It contains an early Christian baptismal font and an octagonal reliquary.

The Romanesque Eglise St-Jacques at the top of the village has a fine sculpted façade.

Detail from the Romanesque façade of Cathédrale St-Pierre in Angoulême

Street-by-Street: Bordeaux ㉖

UILT ON A CURVE of the Garonne River,
Bordeaux has been a major port since
pre-Roman times and for centuries a focus
and crossroads of European trade. Today
Bordeaux shows little visible evidence of
the Romans, Franks and English or the Wars
of Religion that have marked its past. This
forward-looking town, the fifth-largest in
France, is an industrial and maritime sprawl
surrounding a noble 18th-century center.

Along the waterfront of this wealthy wine
metropolis is a long sweep of elegant
Classical façades, first built to mask the
medieval slums behind. Adding to the
magnificence is the Esplanade des
Quinconces, the Grand Théâtre
and the Place de la Bourse.

Eglise Notre-Dame, built 1684–1707

The Maison du Vin gives information on wine tours.

RUE CONDILLAC

COURS DE L'INTENDANCE

RUE MAUTREC

ALLÉES DE TO

PL DE LA COMEDIE

RUE STE CATHERINE

COURS DU 30

RUE ST REMI

COURS DU CHAPEAU ROUGE

RUE ESPRIT DES LOIS

ALLÉES D'ORLÉA

★ **Grand Théâtre**
*Built in 1773–80, the theater
is a masterpiece of the
Classical style, crowned by
12 statues of the muses.*

STAR SIGHTS

★ **Grand Théâtre**

★ **Esplanade des Quinconces**

★ **Place de la Bourse**

KEY

— — — Suggested route

0 meters   100

0 yards   100

PL DE LA BOURSE

The quais, lined with graceful
façades, make a beautiful
walk along the Garonne.

LA GARONNE

★ **Place de la Bourse**
*This elegant and harmonious
square is flanked by two
majestic 18th-century
buildings, Palais de la Bourse
and Hôtel des Douanes.*

★ Esplanade des Quinconces
Replacing the 15th-century Château de Trompette, this vast space of tree-lined esplanades with statues and fountains was created in 1827–58.

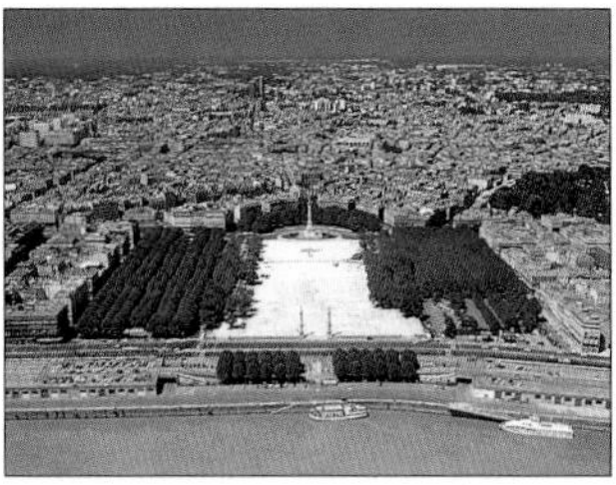

Visitors' Checklist

Gironde. 215,000. 10 km (6 miles) W Bordeaux. Gare St-Jean, rue Charles Domerq. Allée de Chartres. 12 cours du 30 Juillet (05 56 00 66 00). daily. L'Eté Girondin (jazz: Jul–Aug); Fête du Vin Nouveau (Oct). www.bordeaux-tourisme.com

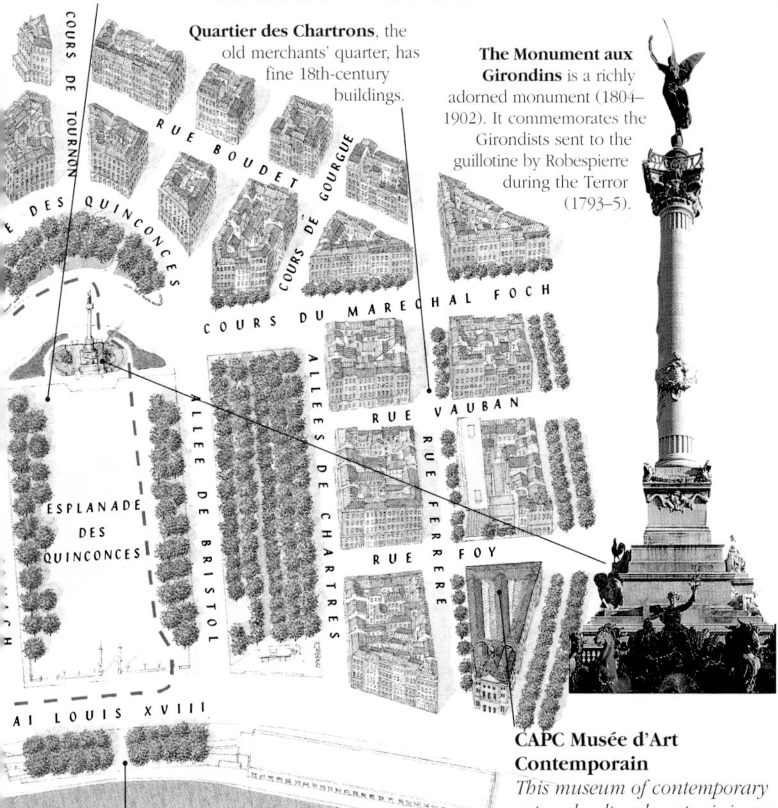

Quartier des Chartrons, the old merchants' quarter, has fine 18th-century buildings.

The Monument aux Girondins is a richly adorned monument (1804–1902). It commemorates the Girondists sent to the guillotine by Robespierre during the Terror (1793–5).

CAPC Musée d'Art Contemporain
This museum of contemporary art and cultural center is in an early 19th-century warehouse.

Terraces provide good views over the river.

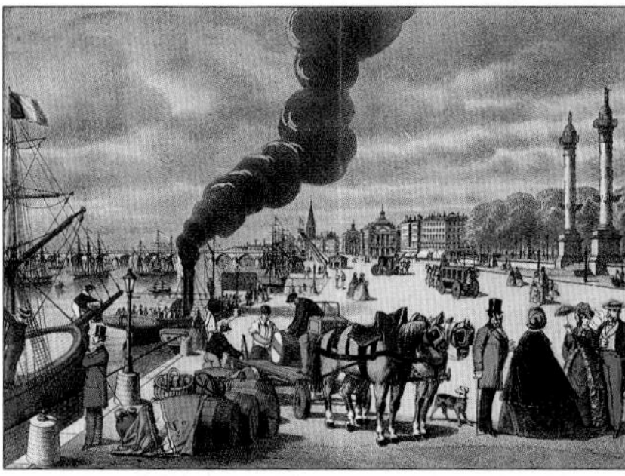

Loading wine barrels in 19th-century Bordeaux

The Bordeaux Wine Trade

After Marseille, Bordeaux is the oldest trading port in France. From Roman times the export of wine was the basis for a modest prosperity, but under English rule (1154–1453, *see pp46–9*), the merchants began making immense fortunes from their monopoly of wine sales to England. After the discovery of the New World, Bordeaux took advantage of its Atlantic position to diversify and extend its wine market. Today the Bordeaux region produces over 44 million cases of wine per year.

GRAND THÉÂTRE DE BORDEAUX

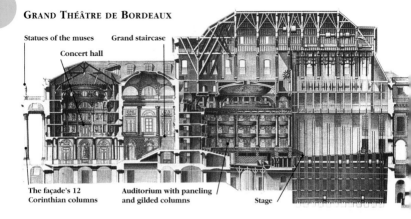

Statues of the muses   Grand staircase

Concert hall

The façade's 12
Corinthian columns

Auditorium with paneling
and gilded columns

Stage

Exploring Bordeaux

Much of central Bordeaux is grand streets and 18th-century mansions. A triangle made by Cours Clemenceau, Cours de l'Intendance and Allées de Tourny has chic boutiques and cafés. Cathédrale St-André is another focal point, with good museums nearby. Both the *quais* and the Chartrons district around the Jardin Public are being renovated and are well worth exploring.

⛲ Grand Théâtre

Place de la Comédie. **(** 05 56 00 85 20.
Built by the architect Victor Louis, the 18th-century Grand Théâtre is one of the finest Classical constructions of its type in France. The auditorium is renowned for its extraordinary acoustics. The spectacular main staircase was later imitated by Garnier for the Paris Opéra *(see p93)*.

⛪ Eglise St-Seurin

This church is somewhat chaotic, with a patchwork of styles ranging from the 11th to the 18th century. Most interesting are the 6th-century Gallo-Roman sarcophagi in the crypt, and a fine 14th century bishop's throne.

⛪ Basilique St-Michel

It took 200 years to build the huge Basilique St-Michel, begun in 1350. Recently restored, this triple-naved edifice has a remarkable statue of St. Ursula with her flock of penitents. Its freestanding belfry, built in 1472–92, is the tallest in southern France at 114 m (375 ft).

⛫ Musée des Beaux-Arts

20 cours d'Albret. **(** 05 56 10 20 56.
◯ *Wed–Mon.* ◉ *public hols.* 🏷 🚻
Housed in two wings of the Hôtel de Ville, the excellent collection of paintings here, ranges from the Renaissance to our time. Masterpieces include works by Titian, Rubens, Veronese, Delacroix, Corot, Renoir, Matisse and Boudin.

⛫ Musée des Arts Décoratifs

39 rue Bouffard. **(** 05 56 00 72 50.
◯ *Wed–Mon.* ◉ *public hols.* 🏷 🚻
If you're interested in elegant furnishings and fine porcelain, stop off at this exceptional collection, housed in the suitably refined 18th-century Hôtel de Lalande.

⛫ Musée d'Aquitaine

20 cours Pasteur. **(** 05 56 01 51 00.
◯ *Tue–Sun.* ◉ *public hols.* 🏷 🚻 🛗
This important museum traces life in the region from prehistoric times to the present, through artifacts, furniture and viticulture tools. Among its

Calm street in Bordeaux by the Porte de la Grosse Cloche

more spectacular exhibits are the Tayac treasure from the 2nd century BC, and the Garonne treasure, a hoard of over 4,000 Roman coins.

⛪ Cathédrale St-André

The nave of this gigantic church was begun in the 11th century and modified 200 years later. The Gothic choir and transepts were added in the 14th and 15th centuries. The excellent medieval sculptures on the Porte Royale include scenes from the Last Judgment.

⛫ CAPC Musée d'Art Contemporain

Entrepôt Lainé, 7 rue Ferrère. **(** 05 56 00 81 50. ◯ *Tue–Sun.* ◉ *public hols.* 🏷 🚻 🛗 🛗
This superbly converted 19th-century warehouse merits a visit, whatever you make of its high profile temporary exhibitions and permanent collection of contemporary art.

St-Émilion ❷⃞

Gironde. 🏠 *2,800.* 🚌 🚉 🛈 *pl des Créneaux (05 57 55 28 28).* 🛒 *Sun.*

THIS CHARMING village in the middle of the prestigious red wine district to which it gives its name, dates back to an 8th-century hermit, Émilion, who dug out a cave for himself in the rock. A monastery followed, and by the Middle Ages St-Émilion had become a small town. Today medieval houses still line the narrow streets, and parts of the 12th-century ramparts remain. The magical interior of the monolithic church dug out of the chalky cliff by followers of Saint Émilion after his death is sadly somewhat ruined at present by concrete columns put up to prevent its collapse.

Famous châteaux in the district include the elegant **Figeac**, **Cheval Blanc** and **Ausone**, all of them St-Émilion Premier Grands Crus Classés.

Vineyard close to Margaux in the Médoc region west of Bordeaux

Pauillac ㉘

Gironde. 🏠 *5,700.* 🚃 🚌
ℹ️ *La Verrerie (05 56 59 03 08).*
📅 *Tue & Sat.*

ONE OF THE MOST famous areas in the Médoc wine region *(see pp388–9)* is the commune of Pauillac. Three of its châteaux are Médoc Premier Grands Crus Classés.

The **Château Mouton-Rothschild** uses leading artists to create its wine labels and has a small museum of paintings on wine themes from all over the world. The **Château Lafite-Rothschild** is of medieval origin and the **Château Latour** is recognizable by its distinctive stone turret. They can be visited by appointment

(contact the tourist office). The town of Pauillac is on the west bank of the Gironde. In the 19th century it was the bustling arrival point for transatlantic steamships, but now the sleepy port is mostly used by pleasure boats. There are picturesque river views from the quais and plenty of cafés serving the local wine.

BORDEAUX WINE CHÂTEAUX

The château is at the heart of the quality system in Bordeaux, the world's largest fine wine region. A château includes a vineyard and a building, which can range from the most basic to the grandest, from historic to modern. But the château is also the symbol of a tradition and of the philosophy that a wine's quality and character spring from the soil. Some châteaux welcome visitors for wine tasting as well as buying. The Maison du Vin and the tourist office in Bordeaux *(see p411)* offer information and tours.

Latour *in Pauillac is famous for its powerful wines and the medieval stone turret which appears on its label.*

Cheval Blanc, *a great château in the St-Émilion area, boasts a rich, spicy Premier Grand Cru.*

Margaux, *built in 1802, produces a classic Margaux Premier Cru of the same elegant proportions as its Palladian façade.*

Palmer, *dating from 1856, is Neo-Renaissance in style and produces a very fine Margaux Troisième Cru.*

Gruaud-Larose *is a cream-colored château with a Classical façade, distinguished by its full-bodied St-Julien Deuxième Cru Classé.*

Vieux Château Certan *is Belgian-owned and one of the great historic properties of Pomerol. Its wines are consistently in the first rank in the district, challenged only by Pétrus.*

The immense Dune du Pilat, stretching almost 3 km (2 miles) south of the inlet to Bassin d'Arcachon

La Côte d'Argent **㉙**

Gironde, Landes. ⊠ *Bordeaux, Biarritz.*
⊠ *Soulac-sur-Mer, Arcachon, Labenne,*
Dax. ⊠ *Lacanau, Arcachon, Mimizan.*
ℹ️ *Lacanau (05 56 03 21 01),*
Mimizan-Plage (05 58 09 11 20),
Capbreton (05 58 72 12 11).

THE LONG STRETCH of coast
between Pointe de Grave
on the Gironde estuary and
Bayonne *(see p442)* is called
La Côte d'Argent – the "Silver
Coast." It is virtually one vast
beach of shifting sand dunes.
Treeplanting has now slowed
down their progress.

The coast is dotted with seaside resorts like **Soulac-sur-**
Mer in the north, followed by
the big **Lacanau-Océan** and
Mimizan-Plage. Down in the
south is **Hossegor** with its
salty lake, and **Capbreton**.
Modern vacation resorts have
been integrated with the old.

Inland is a string of lakes
popular for fishing and boating. They are connected to
each other and the ocean by
courants, lively water currents,
such as the **Courant d'Huchet**
from Etang de Léon. Boat trips
are available.

Bassin
d'Arcachon **㉚**

Gironde. 👥 *11,500.* 🚢 *to Cap Ferret.*
🚌 🚲 ℹ️ *esp Georges Pompidou*
(05 57 52 97 97). 🏪 *Wed, Sat & Sun.*

IN THE MIDDLE of the Côte
d'Argent the straight coastline suddenly forms a lagoon.
Famous for its natural beauty,
fine beaches and oysters, the
Bassin d'Arcachon is a
protected area, perfect for
vacationers, sailing enthusiasts and seafood lovers.

The basin is dotted with
smaller amorphous resorts,
beaches and fishing/oyster
villages, all worth exploring.

Cap Ferret, the northern
headland that protects the
basin from stiff Atlantic
winds, is a preserve of the
wealthy, whose luxurious
villas stand among the pines.
Look for the small road under
the trees from Lège, which
leads to the wild, magnificent
beach of Grand-Crohot.

Between Cap Ferret and
Arcachon, near Gujan-
Mestras, the **Parc Ornitho-**
logique du Teich provides
care and shelter for damaged
birds and endangered species.
For the bird-watcher, there
are two fascinating walks,
each carefully marked: an
introductory one, and another
of greater length. Both

provide concealed observation
points from which people can
watch the wildfowl without
disturbing them.

Arcachon was created as
a seaside resort in 1845. Its
popularity grew, and in the
late 19th and early 20th
centuries, the elegant villas in
the calm Ville d'Hiver were
built. The livelier Ville d'Eté,
facing the lagoon, has a
casino and sports facilities.

The immense **Dune du**
Pilat is the largest sand dune
in Europe. It is nearly 3 km
(2 miles) long, 104 m (340 ft)
high and 500 m (1,625 ft)
wide. Aside from its panoramic view, the dune is a
magnificent vantage point in
autumn for viewing flocks of
migratory birds as they pass
overhead on their way to the
sanctuary at Le Teich.

🦆 **Parc Ornithologique**
du Teich

Le Teich. 📞 *05 56 22 80 93.*
⊙ *daily.* 🈺 🚻 💻 📷

Parc Ornithologique du Teich, a bird sanctuary in Bassin d'Arcachon

LANDES FOREST

The vast, totally artificial 19th-century forest of Les Landes was an ambitious project to make use of an area of sand and marshes. Pines and grasses were planted to anchor the coastal dunes, and inland dunes were stabilized with a mixture of pines, reeds and broom. In 1855 the land was drained, and is now covered with pine groves and undergrowth, preserving a delicate ecological balance.

Pine trees in the Landes forest

Les Landes ③

Gironde, Landes. ✈ *Bordeaux, Biarritz.* 🚆 *Morcenx, Dax, Mont-de-Marsan.* 🚌 *Mont-de-Marsan.* 🛈 *Mont-de-Marsan (05 58 05 87 37).*

Almost entirely covered by an immense pine forest, the Landes area extends over the two *départements* of Gironde and Landes. The soil here is uniformly sandy. Until a century ago, the whole region became a swamp in winter, because of a layer of tufa (porous rock) just under the surface that retained water from the brackish lakes. Any settlement or agriculture close to the sea was impossible due to the constantly shifting dunes. Furthermore, the mouth of the Adour River kept moving from Capbreton to Vieux-Boucau and back, a distance of 32 km (20 miles).

The Adour was stabilized near Bayonne by a canal in the 16th century. This was the start of the slow conquest of the Landes. The planting of pine trees ultimately wiped out the migrant shepherds and their flocks. Today, the inner Landes is still very underpopulated, but wealthy from its pinewood and pine derivatives. The coastal strip has a large influx of vacationers.

In 1970, part of the forest was made into a nature park. Here, a small steam train takes visitors to **Marqueze**, where a typical 19th-century *airial* (clearing) has been restored. It commemorates the vanished world of Les Landes before the draining of the marshes, when shepherds still used stilts to get about. There are traditional *auberges landaises*, wooden houses with sloping roofs, as well as henhouses built on stilts because of the foxes. In **Luxey**, a museum recalls old techniques of tapping and distilling of resin.

Lévignacq, near the coast, is a perfect Landais village with a remarkable 14th-century fortified church full of charming naive frescoes.

Mont-de-Marsan ㉜

Landes. ♟ *32,000.* 🚆 🚌
🛈 *6 place du Général Leclerc (05 58 05 87 37).* 🛒 *Tue & Sat.*

A bullfighting mecca, Mont-de-Marsan attracts all the great bullfighters of France and Spain during the summer season. A less bloodthirsty local variant of the sport, very popular here, is the *course landaise*, in which the object is to vault over the horns and back of a charging cow.

The administrative capital of the Landes is also known for its hippodrome and the production of poultry and *foie gras*.

Sculpture from the first half of the 20th century can be seen at **Musée Despiau-Wlérick**.

Dax ㉝

Landes. ♟ *20,000.* 🚆 🚌 🛈 *place Thiers (05 58 56 86 86).* 🛒 *Sat, Sun am.*

The thermal spa of Dax is second only to Aix-les-Bains (*see p380*) in importance. Its hot springs, with a constant temperature of 64° C (147° F) and tonic mud from the Adour, have been soothing aches and pains and promoting tranquillity since the time of Emperor Augustus.

Apart from the 13th-century doorway of the otherwise 17th-century **Cathédrale Notre-Dame**, there isn't much of architectural interest in this warm, peaceful town. But the promenade along the Adour River is charming, and the bullring is world-renowned.

La Force (1937) by Raoul Lamourdieu, in the bullfighting capital of Mont-de-Marsan

PÉRIGORD, QUERCY AND GASCONY

DORDOGNE · LOT · TARN · HAUTE GARONNE · LOT-ET-GARONNE
TARN-ET-GARONNE · GERS · CORRÈZE

SOUTHWEST FRANCE IS AN ARCHAEOLOGISTS' *heaven, for the region has been continuously inhabited by mankind for tens of thousands of years, longer than any other area in Europe. The landscape of these historic regions seems to have an ancient familiarity, derived from centuries of people living in harmony with the land.*

The great cave sites around Les Eyzies and Lascaux harbor the earliest evidence known of primitive art. The castles, bastides *(see p435)* and churches that grace the countryside from Périgueux to the Pyrenees, and from the Bay of Biscay to Toulouse and to the Mediterranean, belong to a far more recent past. From the coming of Christianity until the late 18th century, this region was the battlefield for a string of conflicts. The English fought and lost the Hundred Years' War for Aquitaine (1345–1453); this was followed by intermittent Wars of Religion, in which Catholics fought Huguenots (French Protestants) in a series of massacres and guerilla wars *(see pp48–49)*.

Today nothing is left of these old struggles but crumbling ramparts, keeps and bastides, which are part of the region's cultural and artistic heritage, attracting thousands of visitors every year. Yet it is as well to remember that all the great sights here, from the impressive abbey church at Moissac, whose 12th-century portal is a masterpiece of Romanesque art, to the awesome clifftop site of Rocamadour; these, too, have suffered badly at one time or another from the attacks of marauding soldiers.

This region may seem incomparably rich in all the ingredients for a good vacation – uncluttered landscapes, empty roads, clean rivers and good regional cuisine – but the economy is rather fragile. Over the last century, the southwest has suffered from a decline in the old peasant way of life, resulting in a population migration away from the countryside to the surrounding towns.

Périgord geese, raised for the area's celebrated *foie gras*

◁ La Roque-Gageac in the Dordogne Valley

Exploring Périgord, Quercy and Gascony

THE MARKET TOWNS of Périgueux, Cahors and Albi make good bases for exploring the region, and are quieter alternatives to Toulouse – the only major urban center. Elsewhere, the green hills and sleepy villages of Gascony and Périgord (also known as the Dordogne) are mainly for those who appreciate the slow pace of life in the countryside. But if you want more than peace and good food, this region offers some of France's finest medieval architecture, and Europe's most important prehistoric caves, notably Lascaux.

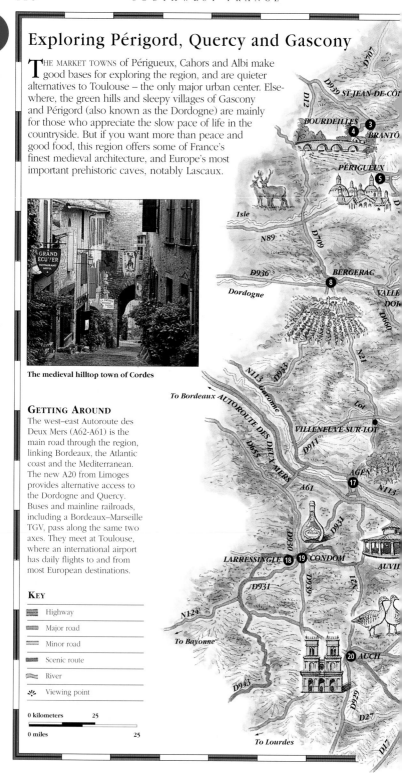

The medieval hilltop town of Cordes

GETTING AROUND

The west–east Autoroute des Deux Mers (A62-A61) is the main road through the region, linking Bordeaux, the Atlantic coast and the Mediterranean. The new A20 from Limoges provides alternative access to the Dordogne and Quercy. Buses and mainline railroads, including a Bordeaux–Marseille TGV, pass along the same two axes. They meet at Toulouse, where an international airport has daily flights to and from most European destinations.

KEY

▨▨	Highway
▨▨	Major road
▨▨	Minor road
▨▨	Scenic route
〰	River
⋇	Viewing point

0 kilometers 25

0 miles 25

Limoges
itiers

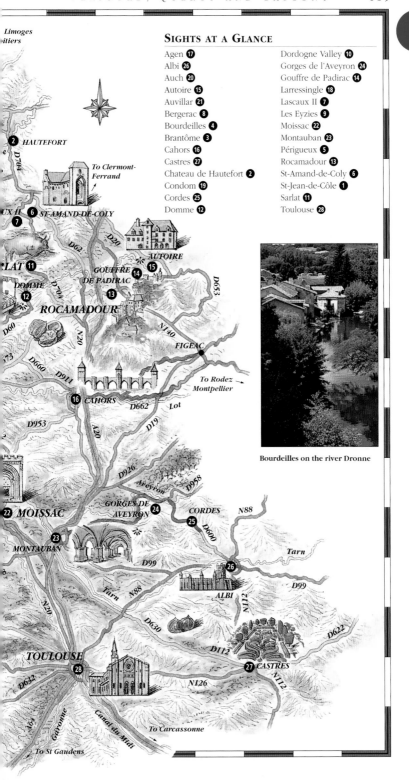

SIGHTS AT A GLANCE

HAUTEFORT

To Clermont-
Ferrand

UX II **6** ST-AMAND-DE-COLY
7

AUTOIRE

LAT **11**

DOMME
12

GOUFFRE
DE PADIRAC **14** **15**

13

ROCAMADOUR

FIGEAC

To Rodez
Montpellier

16 CAHORS   Lot

Bourdeilles on the river Dronne

22 MOISSAC

GORGES DE
AVEYRON **24**

CORDES   N88

25

23

MONTAUBAN

Tarn

ALBI   **26**

TOULOUSE
28

27 CASTRES

To Carcassonne

To St Gaudens

St-Jean-de-Côle ❶

Dordogne. 🚶 350. 🚹 *place du Château (05 53 62 14 15).*

ST-JEAN-DE-CÔLE's medieval, humpbacked bridge gives the best view of this lovely Dordogne village set in hilly countryside. Stone and half-timbered houses, roofed with the distinctive red-brown tiles of the region, cram the narrow streets around the main square. Here stand a covered marketplace, château, and 12th-century church.

The cupola of the church used to be the largest in the region, bigger even than those of the cathedrals. Too large, it seems, for it fell down twice in the 18th and 19th centuries. The second time it happened the builders gave up, and there has been a plank ceiling ever since.

Main square in the lovely village of St-Jean-de-Côle

Hautefort ❷

📞 *05 53 50 51 23.* **Château** 🕐 *Apr–Sep: daily (Feb–Mar & Oct: pms only); Nov: Sun pms & publ hols.* ⬤ *Dec–Jan* 🈲 ▣ *oblig.* ♿ *gr. floor & gdn only.*

HAUTEFORT clings to the sides of a steep hill topped by a massive 17th-century château, one of the finest in southwest France. Partially fortified, built as a pleasure palace in honor of King Louis XIII's secret love, the Marquis de Hautefort's beautiful sister Marie, the castle is surrounded by French gardens on terraces with superb views of the rolling green country of northeast Perigord. In the village, the hospice, of a similar date, has a fascinating museum of early medical and dental implements.

Brantôme Abbey, with belfry

Brantôme ❸

Dordogne. 🚶 2,100. 🚊 🚹 *Pavillon Renaissance (05 53 05 80 52).* 🏪 *Fri.*

SURROUNDED on all sides by the river Dronne, Brantôme is sometimes called the Venice of the Périgord Vert. Its medieval abbey and 11th-century belfry (reputedly the oldest still standing in France), together with the verdant rockface behind, provide a dramatic backdrop for this picturesque town.

Pierre de Bourdeille, the poet (1540–1614), was appointed abbot here in his youth. His lovers allegedly included Mary, Queen of Scots. After a crippling fall, Bourdeille retired here in 1569 to write his racy memoirs. It is possible to wander the stone staircases and cloisters, and through the main courtyard to the intriguing troglodyte dwellings in the cliff behind. In one is a huge crucifixion scene cut into the stone during the 16th century.

Across the river is the **Musée Rêve et Miniatures**, a private collection of doll houses in a variety of period styles. Each one is authentically furnished, down to the smallest detail.

12 km (7 miles) northeast, near Villars, lies the Renaissance **Château de Puyguilhem**, as well as Boschaud Abbey and the **Grotte de Villars**.

🏛 **Musée Rêve et Miniatures**
8 rue Puyjoli. 📞 *05 53 35 29 00.* 🕐 *Easter–Nov 11: Sat–Thur pms. (Jul–Aug: daily all day).* 🈲 ♿
♣ **Château de Puyguilhem**
Villars. 📞 *05 53 54 82 18.* 🕐 *Apr–Oct: daily; Nov–Mar: Tue–Sun.* ⬤ *Jan 1, Dec 25.* 🈲 ♿

Bourdeilles ❹

Dordogne. 🚶 800. 🚹 *Le Mairie (05 53 03 42 96).*

THIS SMALL TOWN has everything – a narrow Gothic bridge with cutwater piers spanning the Dronne, a mill upstream and a medieval **château**. The 16th-century additions to the castle were designed in a hurry by the châtelaine Jacquette de Montbron, when expecting Queen Catherine de' Medici to visit. When the royal visit was called off, so were the building works. The highlight of the château is the gilded first floor salon, decorated in the 1560s by Ambroise le Noble, of the Fontainebleau School.

♣ **Château de Bourdeilles**
📞 *05 53 03 73 36.* 🕐 *Apr–Nov: Wed–Mon (Feb–Mar & Dec: Mon, Wed–Thu & Sun; Jul–Aug: daily).* ⬤ *Jan.* 🈲 ▣

The impressive Château de Bourdeilles towering above the town

Cathédrale St-Front in Périgueux, restored in the 19th century

Périgueux ❺

Dordogne. 32,000. *26 place Francheville (05 53 53 10 63).* *daily.*

THE ANCIENT and truly gastronomic city of Périgueux, like its neighbors Bergerac and Riberac, should be visited on market day, when stalls in the lively squares in the medieval part of town offer the pick of local specialties, including truffles, *charcuterie* (prepared meats) and the succulent pies called *pâtés de Périgueux*.

Périgueux, now the busy regional capital, has long been the crossroads of Périgord. The earliest part remaining today is the quarter known as **La Cité**, once the important Gallo-Roman settlement of Vesunna. La Domus de Vesonne, a Gallo-Roman museum, has just opened on site. From Roman times to the Middle Ages, this was the focus of Périgueux. Most of the fabric of Vesunna was torn down in the 3rd century, but some vestiges of a temple, a huge arena and a sumptuous villa remain. The **Eglise St-Etienne**, nearby dates back to the 12th century.

Walking up the hill from La Cité to the city's dazzling white cathedral, you pass through bustling streets and squares, each with its market activity. This is the medieval quarter of **Le Puy St-Front**, which began to flourish as pilgrims on their way to Santiago de Compostela *(see pp390–91)* visited the cathedral. They brought wealth and prestige to the quarter and it gradually eclipsed La Cité in political importance.

At the top stands the imposing **Cathédrale St-Front**, the largest in southwestern France. The Romanesque construction was heavily restored (some say to death) in the 19th century, when architect Paul Abadie added the fanciful domes and cones. He later used St-Front as inspiration for the Sacré-Coeur in Paris *(see p130)*.

19th-century stained glass in Cathédrale St-Front

Other gems of medieval and Renaissance architecture in this recently restored area include **Maison Estignard**, at No. 3 rue Limogeanne, with its unusual corkscrew staircase, and houses along rue Aubergerie and rue de la Constitution.

Also in the cathedral quarter is the **Musée du Périgord**, one of the most comprehensive prehistory museums in France, with remnants of burials dating back 70,000 years. Beautiful Roman mosaics, glass, earthenware and other artifacts from Vesunna are in the Gallo-Roman museum.

Musée du Périgord
22 cours Tourny. *05 53 06 40 70.* *Wed–Mon.* *public hols.*

St-Amand-de-Coly ❻

Dordogne. *La Mairie (05 53 51 67 50.* *daily.*

THIS abbey church is an outstanding example of fortress architecture, built in the 12th–13th century by Augustinian monks to protect their monastery. There are two lines of defense: a high stone rampart and, behind it, the arched tower of the church itself. The tower looks more like a castle keep, and slits show where it was once pierced by a score of arrows.

Inside, the church is beautifully simple, with pure lines, a flat ribbed vault, a 12th-century cupola, a soaring nave, and a stone floor sloping upward to the altar. Yet even this interior was arranged for defense, with a gallery from which enemies within the building could be attacked.

St-Amand was heavily damaged during the Hundred Years' War. In 1575, it survived a siege by 2,000 Huguenot cavalry-men and a six-day bombardment by cannon. Religious life here came to an end after the Revolution.

Sarlat

Sculptures of geese in Sarlat

SARLAT-LA-CANEDA features the highest concentration of medieval, Renaissance and 17th-century façades of any town in France. Its prosperity was a reflection of the privileged status it was granted in return for loyalty to the French crown during the Hundred Years' War. Behind the nondescript rue de la République are narrow lanes and archways, and ancient, ocher-colored stone town houses rich in ornamental detail. Protected by law since 1962, Sarlat's buildings now form an outdoor museum. The town is also famous for one of the best markets in France.

Place de la Liberté
The Renaissance heart of Sarlat is now lined with luxury shops and cafés.

Rue des Consuls contains 15th-, 16th- and 17th-century mansions, built for the town's middle-class merchants, magistrates and church officials.

Rue Jean-Jacques Rousseau was the main street until rue de la République (known as "La Traverse") was built in the 19th century.

Walnuts, a key Périgord crop

SARLAT MARKET

Every Wednesday, the great Sarlat food market is held in place de la Liberté, and every Saturday there is a full-scale fair that attracts locals from all around. Sarlat lies at the heart of the nation's *foie gras* and walnut trades. These typical Périgord products absorb much of the town's attention and supply a good proportion of its revenue, as they did during Sarlat's heyday in the 13th and 14th centuries. Other local specialties are black truffles dug up in the woods in January, and wild mushrooms. Seek out, too, the cheeses of every shape, age and hue, and the huge range of pork delicacies available – choose from canned, fresh, smoked, dried, salted, fried, baked or boiled.

Bulbs of pink garlic

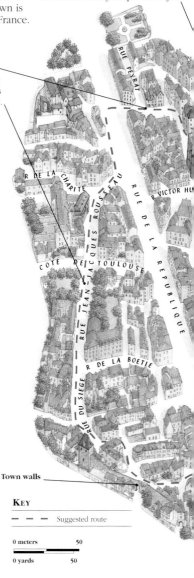

Town walls

KEY

– – – Suggested route

0 meters   50
0 yards   50

Rue de la Salamandre

This lane was named after the salamander emblem of King François I, seen on many of the town's 16th-century houses.

VISITORS' CHECKLIST

Dordogne. 🏠 10,500. 🚉 ave de la Gare (05 53 59 00 21). 🚌 15 ave Aristide Briand (05 53 59 01 48). 🛈 rue Tourny (05 53 31 45 45). 🛒 Wed & Sat. 🎭 Theater (Jul–Aug); Film (Nov).

Lanterne des Morts (Lantern of the Dead)

The conical tower in the cemetery was built to commemorate St. Bernard's sermons in Sarlat in August 1147.

Cathédrale St-Sacerdos

Built largely in the 16th and 17th centuries, the cathedral is remarkable for its magnificent 18th-century organ.

The Chapelle des Pénitents Bleus, built in pure Romanesque style, is the last vestige of the 12th-century abbey.

The former Bishop's Palace, with remains of a 16th-century loggia and a Renaissance interior, is now the municipal theater.

Cour des Fontaines

A pure spring here attracted the monks who founded Sarlat's first abbey in the 9th century.

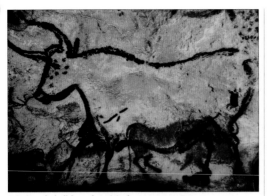

Painting of a bull from the original cave at Lascaux

Lascaux II ❼

Montignac. **☎** *05 53 51 95 03.*
◻ *Apr–Oct: daily; Nov–Dec & Feb–Mar: Tue–Sun.* **●** *Jan, Dec 25.* 🖼️ 🎟️

L ASCAUX is the most famous of the prehistoric sites clustered around the junction of the Vézère and Beune rivers *(see pp392–3).* Four young boys and their dog, Robot, came across the caves and their astonishing palaeolithic paintings in 1940, and the importance of their discovery was swiftly recognized.

Lascaux has been closed to the public since 1963 because of deterioration, but an exact copy, known as Lascaux II, has been created a few minutes' walk down the hillside, using the same materials. The replica is beautiful and is well worth seeing: high-antlered elk, bison, bulls and plump horses cover the walls, moving in herds or files, surrounded by arrows and geometric symbols thought to have had ritual significance.

Bergerac ❽

Dordogne. **🏚️** *28,000.* **✈** **🚆** **🚌** **ℹ️** *rue Neuve d'Argenson (05 53 57 03 11).* **🗓️** *Wed & Sat.*

T HIS SMALL PORT, a tobacco farming and commercial center, spreads itself over both sides of the Dordogne. Chief attractions are its extraordinary **Musée du Tabac** (tobacco museum), and its food and wine, which are invariably excellent. Bergerac's most celebrated wine is Monbazillac, a sweet white wine, often drunk on ceremonial occasions. On display in the small, lively museum are some American Indian pipes and ivory tobacco graters.

🏛️ Musée du Tabac
Maison Peyrarède, place du Feu.
☎ *05 53 63 04 13.* **◻** *Tue–Sun.* **●** *public hols.* 🖼️ 🎟️

Les Eyzies ❾

Dordogne. **🏚️** *900.* **🚆** **ℹ️** *19 ave de la Préhistoire (05 53 06 97 05).* **🗓️** *Mon (Apr–Oct).*

F OUR MAJOR prehistoric sites and a group of smaller caves cluster around the unassuming village of Les Eyzies. Head first for the **Musée National de Préhistoire**, in a 16th-century castle overlooking the village. The timelines and other exhibits are useful for putting the vast area of prehistoric painting and sculpture into context.

The **Grotte de Font de Gaume**, a good 20-minute walk from the road, is the logical first stop after the museum in Les Eyzies. This cave, discovered in 1901, contains the finest ensemble of prehistoric paintings still open to the public in France. Close by is the **Grotte des Combarelles**, with engravings of bison, reindeer, magic symbols and human figures.

Les Eyzies, a center for the area's concentration of prehistoric caves

Farther on, you reach the rock shelter of **Abri du Cap Blanc**, discovered in 1909, with a rare, life-size frieze of horses and bison sculpted in the rock.

On the other side of Les Eyzies is the cave system in **Rouffignac**, a favorite place for excursions since the 15th century. There are 8 km (5 miles) of caves here, 2.5 km (1.5 miles) of which are served by electric train. The paintings include drawings of mammoths, and a frieze of two bison challenging each other to combat.

Tickets for all the caves sell out fast, especially in summer, so arrive early. Some must be booked a fortnight ahead!

Musée National de Préhistoire

🏛 **Musée National de Préhistoire**
🔹 05 53 06 45 45. ⬛ Wed–Mon.
⬤ Dec 25, Jan 1. 🎟 ♿ 🚻 🔊
🔹 **Grotte de Font de Gaume**
🔹 05 53 06 86 00. ⬛ Thu–Tue by appt (book fortnight ahead). ⬤ some public hols. 🎟
🔹 **Grotte des Combarelles**
🔹 05 53 06 86 00. ⬛ Thu–Tue by appt (book fortnight ahead). ⬤ some public hols. 🎟
🔹 **Abri du Cap Blanc**
Marquay, Les Eyzies. 🔹 05 53 59 21 74.
⬛ Apr–Oct: daily. 🎟 ♿
🔹 **Grotte de Rouffignac**
🔹 05 53 05 41 71. ⬛ Apr–Oct: daily. 🎟 ♿

Dordogne Valley ⑩

Dordogne. ✈ Bergerac. 🚍 Bergerac, Le Buisson de Cadouin. 🚍 Beynac, 🛈 Le Buisson de Cadouin (05 53 22 06 09).

Probably no river in France crosses so varied a landscape and such different geological formations as the

View of Domme from the medieval gateway of Porte de la Combe

Dordogne. Starting in deep granite gorges in the Massif Central, it continues through fertile lowlands, then enters the limestone Causse country around Souillac. By the time the Dordogne has wound down to the Garonne, it is almost 3 km (2 miles) wide.

Don't be put off by the touristy image of this famous valley. Despite being a popular vacation spot, it is a beautiful area for wandering. Several villages make good stopping-off points, including Limeuil, Beynac, and La Roque-Gageac from where flat-bottomed *gabarres* (river-boats) ferry visitors (Easter–Oct).

Perched high above the river, southwest of Sarlat, is the 17th-century **Château de Marqueyssac**. Its topiary park offers panoramic views from Domme to Beynac, and of the Château de Castelnaud on the opposite river bank.

Sarlat ⑪

See pp422–3.

Domme ⑫

Dordogne. 🏠 1,000. 🛈 place de la Halle (05 53 31 71 00). 🗓 Thu.

Henry Miller wrote: "Just to glimpse the black, mysterious river at Domme from the beautiful bluff . . . is something to be grateful for all one's life." Domme itself is a neat bastide (see p435) of golden stone, with medieval gateways still standing. People come here to admire the view, which takes in the Dordogne Valley from Beynac in the west to Montfort in the east, and wander the maze of old streets inside the walls. There is also a large cavern under the 17th-century covered market (return by elevator; from February to mid-November) where the inhabitants hid at tense moments during the Hundred Years' War and the 16th-century Wars of Religion. Despite a seemingly impregnable position, 30 Huguenots captured Domme by scaling the cliffs at night and opening the gates.

A cingle (loop) of the Dordogne River, seen from the town of Domme

Rocamadour ⑬

ROCAMADOUR BECAME one of the most famous centers of pilgrimage following the discovery in 1166 of an ancient grave and sepulcher containing an undecayed body, said to be that of the early Christian hermit St. Amadour. The discovery unleashed a spate of miracles heralded, it is claimed, by the bell above the Black Virgin and Child in the Chapel of Notre-Dame. Although the town suffered with the decline of pilgrimages in the 17th and 18th centuries, it was heavily restored in the 19th century. Still a holy shrine, as well as a popular tourist destination, Rocamadour's site on a rocky plateau above the Alzou Valley is phenomenal. The best views are to be had from the hamlet of L'Hospitalet.

Black Virgin and Child

The château stands on the site of a fort which protected the sanctuary from the west.

St. Michael's Chapel contains well-preserved 12th-century frescoes.

General View

Rocamadour is at its most breathtaking in the sunlight of early morning: the cluster of medieval houses, towers and battlements seems to sprout from the base of the cliff.

The Tomb of St. Amadour once held the body of the hermit called *roc amator* (lover of rock), from whom the town took its name.

Museum of Sacred Art

Grand Stairway

Pilgrims would climb this broad flight of steps on their knees as they said their rosaries. The stairway leads to a square on the next level, around which the main pilgrim chapels are grouped.

The Chapel of St. John the Baptist faces the fine Gothic portal of the Basilica of St-Sauveur.

The Basilica of St-Sauveur, a late 12th-century sanctuary, backs onto the bare rock face.

St. Anne's Chapel dates from the 13th century, and contains a 17th-century gilded altar screen.

Ramparts

Cross of Jerusalem

Stations of the Cross
Pilgrims encounter the Cross of Jerusalem and 14 stations marking Jesus's journey to the Cross on their way up the hill-side to the château.

Chapel of St. Blaise (13th-century)

Rocamadour Town
Now a pedestrian precinct, its main street is lined with souvenir shops to tempt the throngs of pilgrims.

Chapel of Notre-Dame (Miracles)
St Amadour's body was found in the cliff, near the Black Virgin Chapel. A statue of the Black Virgin, the supreme object of veneration, stands on the altar.

Gouffre de Padirac 🄯

Lot. 🄲 *05 65 33 64 56.* 🄾 *Apr–mid-Oct: daily.* 🄰 🄱

FORMED BY THE COLLAPSE of a cave, this huge crater measures 35 m (115 ft) wide and 103 m (337 ft) deep. The underground river and stunning succession of galleries at the bottom (*see p393*) have been great tourist attractions since their discovery in 1889. The immense chamber known as the Salle du Grand Dôme dwarfs the tallest of cathedrals.

Autoire 🄯

Lot. 🄰 *250.*

THIS IS ONE of the loveliest places in Quercy, the fertile area east of Périgord. There are no grand monuments or dramatic history, just a beautifully unspoiled site at the mouth of the Autoire gorge. The **Château de Limarque** on the main square, and the **Château de Busqueille** overlooking it, are both built in characteristic Quercy style, with turrets and small towers. Elsewhere, elaborate, raised dovecotes typical of the region stand in the middle of fields or are attached to houses.

Outside Autoire, past a 30-m (100-ft) waterfall, a path leads to a rock amphitheater giving panoramic views of the region.

The picturesque village of Autoire, seen from across the gorge

Cahors 🄯

Lot. 🄰 *20,000.* 🄿 🄿 🄸 *place François Mitterrand (05 65 53 20 65).* 🄰 *Wed & Sat.*

THE CHIEF TOWN of rural Quercy, 2,000-year-old Cahors, is encircled by the natural defenses of the Lot River. This small commercial center is famous for truffles, a Saturday morning market, and the dark, heady Cahors wine that was produced as far back as Roman times. Cahors' main street is boulevard Gambetta, a typical southern thoroughfare lined with plane trees, cafés, and shops. This street, like many others in France, was named after the dashing radical Léon Gambetta (1838–82), who was born in Cahors and led France to recovery after the war with Prussia in 1870.

Cathédrale de St-Etienne, entrenched behind the narrow streets of Cahors' Old Town,

A Tour of Two Rivers

FLANKED BY SPECTACULAR LIMESTONE CLIFFS, the beautiful Lot and Célé valleys feature ancient medieval villages and castles, narrow gorges, and rushing waterfalls along lazy stretches of river. An unhurried tour of both valleys, around 160 km (100 miles), is best spread over two days, to savor the gastronomic delights as well as the superb views. A relaxing way to enjoy the beautiful scenery of the Lot valley is by train (all-day or half-day trips with Quercyrail) from Cahor to Cajarc. The slow, winding road from Cahors, well-known for the 14th-century Pont Valentré, meanders beside the wide river Lot. This is the home of truffles, *confit* (conserve) of duck and goose, delicious goat's cheese, and the almost black Cahors wine.

Grotte de Pech-Merle ①
This 25,000-year-old prehistoric site outside Cabrerets has huge chambers painted with mammoths, horses, bison, and human figures.

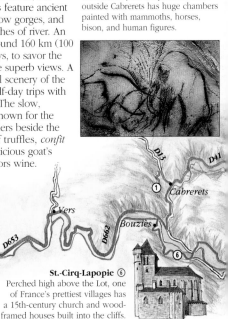

St.-Cirq-Lapopie ⑥
Perched high above the Lot, one of France's prettiest villages has a 15th-century church and wood-framed houses built into the cliffs.

dates back to 1119. It has
some fine medieval details:
don't miss the lively figures of
the Romanesque north door
and tympanum, depicting the
Ascension, or the huge cupola
above the nave (said to be
the largest in France). They
are covered in 14th-century
frescoes depicting
the stoning of St. Stephen
(St. Étienne). The Renaissance
cloisters are decorated with
some intricate, though
damaged, carvings.

Also worth seeking out in
the cathedral quarter is the
ornate 16th-century **Maison
de Roaldès**, its north facade
decorated with the tree, sun,
and rose of Quercy motifs. It
was here that Henri of
Navarre (who later became
King Henri IV) stayed for one
night in 1580 after surrounding
and capturing Cahors.

The town's landmark
monument is the **Pont
Valentré**, a fortified bridge
with seven pointed arches and

The fortified Pont Valentré spanning the Lot River at Cahors

three towers that spans the
river. It was built between
1308 and 1360 and has withstood many attacks since
then. A breathtaking sight, it
is claimed that the bridge is
one of the most photographed
monuments in all of France.

An alternative way to
enjoy the scenery is to take
a leisurely 90-minute boat

trip through the lock from
a wharf near the bridge
(Apr–Oct).

Environs
Situated about 60 km (37
miles) to the west of Cahors
is the **Château de Bonaguil**,
a superb example of military
architecture dating from the
Middle Ages.

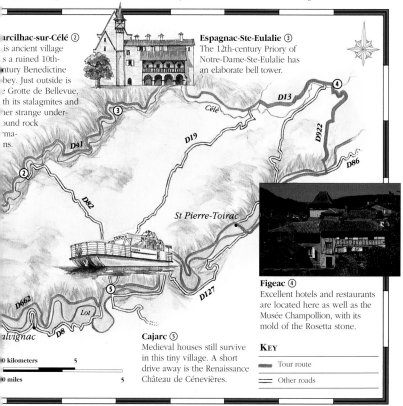

arcilhac-sur-Célé ②
is ancient village
s a ruined 10th-
ntury Benedictine
bey. Just outside is
e Grotte de Bellevue,
th its stalagmites and
her strange under-
ound rock
rma-
ns.

Espagnac-Ste-Eulalie ③
The 12th-century Priory of
Notre-Dame-Ste-Eulalie has
an elaborate bell tower.

Figeac ④
Excellent hotels and restaurants
are located here as well as the
Musée Champollion, with its
mold of the Rosetta stone.

Cajarc ⑤
Medieval houses still survive
in this tiny village. A short
drive away is the Renaissance
Château de Cénevières.

KEY

Tour route

Other roads

0 kilometers 5

0 miles 5

Orchards and vineyards outside Agen

Agen **17**

Lot-et-Garonne. <N /> 32,180. <N /> <N />
<N /> <N /> 107 boulevard Carnot
(05 53 47 36 09). <N /> Wed, Sat & Sun.

IN A RECENT nationwide poll, the inhabitants of Agen – an attractive, unhurried provincial capital on the Garonne – were shown to be easily the most contented people in France. The town is the mecca of French rugby (its team has won three championship titles in recent years), and the prune production center of France.

But the town has other treasures in addition to happy citizens and succulent plums. The **Musée Municipal des Beaux-Arts** contains fine paintings by Goya, including his *Ascent in a Hot-Air Balloon;* Sisley's *September Morning;* Corot's landscape *L'étang de Ville d'Avray* and works by Picabia and Caillebotte. Undisputed jewel of the collection is the *Vénus du Mas*, a beautifully proportioned marble statue dating from the 1st century BC, discovered nearby in 1876.

Around the town, vast orchards of regimented plum trees are a prominent feature of the landscape. Crusaders returning from the Middle East brought the fruit to France in the 11th century, and monks in the nearby Lot Valley were the first to dry plums for prunes in commercial quantities. Agen's factories now produce approximately 35,500 tons of prunes each year.

<N /> Musée Municipal des Beaux-Arts

Place du Docteur Esquirol. <N /> 05 53 69 47 23. <N /> Wed–Mon. <N /> Jan 1, May 1, Nov 1, Dec 25. <N />

Environs

The fortified village of Moirax has a 12th-century Romanesque church of great beauty and symmetry, formerly part of a Cluniac priory. Two of the appealingly sculpted capitals depict biblical accounts of Daniel in the lions' den, and Original Sin.

Larressingle **18**

Gers. <N /> 150. <N /> to Condom. <N /> Condom (05 62 28 00 80).

WITH ITS RAMPARTS, ruined donjon (defense tower) and fortress gate, Larressingle is a tiny fortified village in the middle of the Gascon countryside. It dates from the 13th century, and is one of the last remaining Gascon villages with its walls still intact. The state of preservation is unique, and gives an idea of what life must have been like for the small, embattled local communities, who had to live for decades under conditions of perpetual warfare.

Condom **19**

Gers. <N /> 8,000. <N /> <N /> place Bossuet (05 62 28 00 80). <N /> Wed.

LONG A CENTER for the Armagnac trade, Condom is a market town built around the late-Gothic **Cathédrale St-Pierre**. In 1569 during the Wars of Religion, the Huguenot (French Protestant) army threatened to demolish the cathedral, but Condom's citizens averted this by paying a huge ransom.

The Baïse River skirts the town center. Notable among Condom's fine 17th–18th-century mansions is the **Hôtel de Cugnac** on Rue Jean-Jaurès, with its ancient *chai* (wine and spirit storehouse) and distillery. On the other side of the town center, the **Musée de l'Armagnac** is the place to find out, finally, what the difference between the brandy of Armagnac and Cognac really is.

<N /> Musée de l'Armagnac

2 rue Jules Ferry. <N /> 05 62 28 47 17. <N /> Apr–Oct: Wed–Mon; Nov–Mar: Wed–Sun pms. <N /> Jan, public hols. <N /> <N /> gr.fl.

ARMAGNAC

Armagnac is one of the world's most expensive brandies. It is also one of the leading products of southwest France: approximately 6 million bottles are produced annually, 45 per cent of which are exported to 132 countries. The vineyards of Armagnac roughly straddle the border between the Gers and the Lot-et-Garonne regions and the Landes. Similar in style to Cognac, its more famous neighbor, Armagnac's single distillation leaves more individual flavors in the spirit. The majority of small, independent producers offer direct sale to the public: watch for the battered, often half-hidden farm signs advertising *Vente Directe.*

A Tenarèze Armagnac

D'ARTAGNAN

Gascons call their domain the "Pays d'Artagnan" after Alexandre Dumas' rollicking hero from *The Three Musketeers* (1844). The character of d'Artagnan was based on Charles de Batz, a typical Gascon whose chivalry, passion and impetuousness made him ideal as a musketeer, or royal body-guard. De Batz's life was as fast and furious as that of the fictional hero, and he performed a feat of courtliness by arresting Louis XIV's most formidable minister without causing the slightest offense. The French have other opinions of the Gascon nature too: a *promesse de Gascon,* for example, means an empty promise.

Statue of Dumas' musketeer d'Artagnan in Auch

The windows show a mix of prophets, patriarchs and apostles, with 360 individually characterized figures and exceptional colors. Three depict the key biblical events of the Creation, the Crucifixion and the Resurrection.

Auch went through an urbanization program in the 18th century, when the Allées d'Etigny, flanked by the grand Hôtel de Ville and Palais de Justice, were built. Some fine houses from this period line the pedestrianized rue Dessoles. Auch's restaurants are known for their hearty dishes, including *foie gras de canard* (fattened duck liver).

Auch ㉠

Gers. 🔼 25,000. 🚇 🚌 ℹ 1 rue Dessoles (05 62 05 22 89). 🛒 Thu & Sat.

THE ANCIENT capital of the Gers department, Auch (pronounced "Ohsh") has long been a sleepy place that comes alive on market days. The new town by the station is not a place that encourages you to linger. Head instead for the Old Town on the out-

Medallion from Cathédrale Ste-Marie

crop overlooking the Gers River. If you climb the 234 stone steps from the river, you arrive directly in front of the late-Gothic **Cathédrale Ste-Marie**, begun in 1489 (under restoration). The furnishings of the cathedral are remarkable; highlights are the carved wooden choir stalls depicting more than 1,500 biblical, historical and mythological characters, and the equally magnificent 15th-century stained-glass, attributed to Arnaud de Moles.

Auvillar ㉡

Tarn-et-Garonne. 🔼 1,000. ℹ place de la Halle (05 63 39 89 82).

A PERFECT complement to the high emotion of Moissac (*see pp432–3*), Auvillar is one of the loveliest hilltop villages in France. It has a triangular marketplace lined with half-timbered arcades at its center, and extensive views from the promenade overlooking the Garonne River. There are picnic spots along this panoramic path plus an orientation map. This includes all but the chimneys visible in the distance, belonging to the nuclear plant at Golfech.

Sunflowers, a popular crop in southwest France, grown for their seeds and oil

Moissac ⓐ

Abbot Durand

THE VILLAGE OF MOISSAC nestles among vineyards of sweet Chasselas grapes, with the abbey of St-Pierre its undisputed highlight. Founded in the 7th century by a Benedictine monk, the abbey was subsequently ransacked by Arabs, Normans and Hungarians. In 1047, the Moissac Abbey was united with the rich foundation at Cluny and prospered under the direction of Abbot Durand de Bredon. By the 12th century it had become the preeminent monastery in southwest France. The south portal created during this period is a masterpiece of Romanesque sculpture.

Abbey of St-Pierre
The church's exterior belongs to two periods: one part, in stone, is Romanesque, the other, in brick, is Gothic.

Tympanum
The lower register of the balanced, compact tympanum shows the expressive "24 Elders with crowns of gold" from St. John's vision.

Christ in Majesty
The figure of Christ sits in judgment at the center of the scene. He holds the Book of Life in His left hand and raises His right in benediction.

★ South Portal
The carved south portal (1100–1130) is a masterful translation into stone of St. John's dramatic vision of the Apocalypse (Book of Revelation, Chapters 4 and 5). The Evangelists Matthew, Mark, Luke and John appear as "four beasts full of eyes." Moorish details on the door jambs reflect the contemporary cultural exchange between France and Spain.

★ Cloister
*The late 11th-century
cloister is lined with
alternate double and single
columns in white, pink,
green and gray marble. In
all, there are 76 richly
decorated arches.*

FLOORPLAN: CHURCH AND CLOISTER

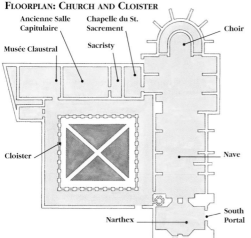

Ancienne Salle
Capitulaire

Chapelle du St.
Sacrement

Musée Claustral

Sacristy

Choir

Cloister

Nave

Narthex

South
Portal

Cloister Capitals
*Flowers, beasts and scenes
from both the Old and New
Testaments are featured in
these superbly sculptured
11th-century Romanesque
capitals.*

STAR FEATURES

★ South Portal

★ Cloister

Montauban ㉓

Tarn-et-Garonne. 🏘️ 55,000. 🚉 🚌
ℹ️ place Prax-Paris (05 63 63 60 60).
🛒 Sat.

MONTAUBAN deserves more
attention than it usually
gets, as Toulouse's little pink-
brick sister and the capital of
the 17th-century "Protestant
Republic" of southern France.
The painter Ingres was born
in Montauban in 1780, and
the town's great treasure is the
Musée Ingres, an exceptional
bequest of several paintings
and 4,000 drawings. Part of
the museum's collection
includes works by sculptor
Emile Bourdelle, an associate
of Rodin, also from the town.

Above all, Montauban is a
civilized shopping center,
with a double-arcaded main
square (place Nationale) built
in the 17th and 18th centuries.
A few streets away lies the
stark white **Cathédrale Notre-
Dame**, built on the orders of
Louis XIV in 1692, in the back-
lash against Protestant heresy.

🏛️ **Musée Ingres**
Palais Episcopal. 📞 05 63 22 12 91.
⏰ Tue–Sun (Jul–Aug: daily). ⛔ Jan
1, Jul 14, Nov 1, Nov 11, Dec 25. 🎫

Gorges
de l'Aveyron ㉔

Tarn-et-Garonne. ✈️ Toulouse. 🚉
Montauban, Lexos. 🚌 Montauban.
ℹ️ Montauban (05 63 63 31 40).

AT THE Gorges de l'Aveyron,
the sweltering plains of
Montauban change abruptly
to cool, chestnut-wooded hills.
Unlike the other villages
of Périgord and Quercy, these
precariously perched villages
were obsessed with defense.

The château in Bruniquel,
founded in the 6th century, is
built over the lip of a preci-
pice, reached by a steep walk
through the village. Farther
along the D115, the village of
Penne's position on the tip of
a giant rock fang is even more
extreme. The gorge narrows
and darkens; from St-Antonin-
Noble-Val, fixed firmly to its
rock face, the valley turns
toward Cordes.

Cordes ㉕

Tarn. **1,050. Maison Fonpeyrouse (05 63 56 00 52). Sat.**

SOMETIMES KNOWN as Cordes-sur-Ciel, this is a fitting description as the town seems suspended against the sky-line. During the 13th-century Cathar wars the entire town was excommunicated. Devastating epidemics of plague later sent it into decline, and the town was in an advanced state of decay at the beginning of this century.

Restoration work under the care of the artist Yves Brayer began in the 1940s. The ramparts and many of the gates built in 1222 by the town's founder, Albigensian Count Raymond VII of Toulouse, have been well-preserved. Also intact are Gothic houses such as the 14th-century **Maison du Grand Fauconnier**, with falcons carved on its façade, and the **Maison du Grand Veneur** (Great Huntsman's House), which line the unbelievably steep cobbled streets.

Today, lovely as it is from a distance, Cordes on its hilltop still exudes a sense of loss. The town of which Albert Camus once wrote, "Everything is beautiful there, even regret," is now dependent on tourism. "Medieval" crafts for visitors abound, but nothing remains of the weaving, *pastel* (blue pigment) and leather industries that paid for so many of Cordes' ancient buildings. The **Jardin du Paradis** offers a corner of beauty and hope.

Cathédrale Ste-Cécile perched above the town of Albi

Albi ㉖

Tarn. **50,000. Palais de la Berbie, place Ste-Cécile (05 63 49 48 80). Sat.**

LIKE MANY other large towns in this part of the world, Albi is not only red, but also red-hot, and definitely not for brief afternoon visits. You need to get up in the cool early morning to walk the streets around the market and the cathedral.

Then head for the **Musée Henri de Toulouse-Lautrec** in the Palais de la Berbie, ahead of the crowds. The museum contains the most complete permanent collection of the artist's work in existence, including paintings, drawings, and his famous posters for the Moulin-Rouge. There are also canvases by Matisse, Dufy, and Yves Brayer.

After a stroll around the beautiful terraced gardens of the Palais de la Berbie overlooking the river Tarn, head for the vast red-brick **Cathédrale Ste-Cécile**, built in the aftermath of the Albigensian crusade in 1265. It was intended as a reminder to potential heretics that the Church meant business. From a distance, its semicircular towers and narrow windows give it the appearance more of a fortress than a place of worship. Every feature, from the huge bell tower to the apocalyptic fresco of the *Last Judgement*, is on a giant scale built deliberately to dwarf the average human being. The effect is absolutely breathtaking.

🏛 Musée Toulouse-Lautrec
Palais de la Berbie. **📞** 05 63 49 48 70. **◻** Apr–Sep: daily; Oct–Mar: Wed–Mon. **●** Jan 1, May 1, Nov 1, Dec 25. 🈲 🅰 🚹 🔄

Castres ㉗

Tarn. **45,500. ✕ 3 rue Milhau-Ducommun (05 63 62 63 62). Tue–Sat.**

CASTRES HAS BEEN a center for the fabric industry since the 14th century. Today it is also the headquarters of one of France's biggest pharmaceutical companies and a busy, relaxed, southern town. In the large collection of Spanish art in the **Musée Goya**, the artist himself is well represented by a large, misty council scene and by a series of powerful prints, *Los Caprichos*. Outside, the formal gardens between the town hall and the Agout River were designed in the 17th century by Le Nôtre (*see p169*), the landscape architect of Vaux-le-Vicomte and Versailles.

🏛 Musée Goya
Hôtel de Ville. **📞** 05 63 71 59 30 or 05 63 71 59 27. **◻** Jul–Aug: daily; Sep–Jun: Tue–Sun. **●** Jan 1, May 1, Nov 1, Dec 25. 🈲

TOULOUSE-LAUTREC

Comte Henri de Toulouse-Lautrec was born in Albi in 1864. Crippled at 15 as a result of two falls, he moved to Paris in 1882, recording the life of the city's cabarets, brothels, racecourses and circuses. A dedicated craftsman, his bold, vivid posters did much to establish lithography as a major art form. Alcoholism and syphilis led to his early death at the age of 36.

Lautrec's *La Modiste* (1900)

Bastide Towns

BASTIDE TOWNS were hurriedly built in the 13th century by both the English and the French, to encourage settlement of empty areas before the Hundred Years' War. They are the medieval equivalent of "new towns," with their planned grid of streets and fortified perimeters. Over 300 bastide towns and villages still survive between Périgord and the Pyrenees.

A broad arcaded marketplace is the central feature of most bastides. Montauban's arcades still shelter a variety of shops.

Lauzerte, founded in 1241 by the Count of Toulouse, is a typical bastide town of gray stone houses. The town, long an English outpost, is perched for security on the brow of a hill.

The church could be used as a keep when the bastide's outer fortifications had been breached.

The central square is surrounded by a grid of interconnecting streets and alleys. This differs markedly from the usual jumble of medieval houses and lanes.

Stone houses protected the perimeter.

MONFLANQUIN

This military bastide town was built by the French in 1256 on a strategic north–south route. It changed hands several times during the Hundred Years' War.

Today, the bastides form a convenient network of market towns, known as the route des bastides. The best time to visit them is on market day, when the central squares are crammed with stalls.

Porte de la Jane in Cordes is a typical bastide feature. These narrow gateways were easily barred by portcullises.

Toulouse ㉘

TOULOUSE, THE MOST IMPORTANT TOWN in southwest France, is the country's fourth largest metropolis, and a major industrial and university city. The area is also famous for its aerospace industry (Concorde, Airbus, the Ariane space rocket all originated here), as shown by the new Cité de l'Espace just outside the city.

Best seen on foot, Toulouse has fine regional cuisine, two striking cathedrals, lively street life and a rose-brick Old Town which, as the French say, is "Pink at dawn, red at noon and mauve at dusk."

The river Garonne, crossed by the Pont Neuf, and bordered by tree-lined quays

Houseboats at their moorings on the Canal du Midi

Exploring Toulouse

This warm southern city has steadily expanded, crescentlike, from its original Roman site on the Garonne. First it was a flourishing Visigoth city, then a Renaissance town of towered brick palaces built with the wealth generated by the *pastel* (blue pigment) and grain trades. The grandest of these palaces still survive in the Old Town, centered around place du Capitole and the huge 18th-century **Hôtel de Ville**. Here, and in place St-Georges and rue Alsace-Lorraine, is the main concentration of shops, bars and cafés. The city's large student population keeps prices down in the numerous cafés, oyster bars and bookstores, and in the fleamarket, held on Sundays in place St-Sernin.

A ring of 18th- and 19th-century boulevards encircles the city, surrounded in turn by a tangle of autoroutes. The left bank of the Garonne is under development (St-Cyprien) and is linked by Toulouse's new driverless metro. The former abattoir has been superbly converted into a center for modern and contemporary art, **Les Abattoirs** (Tue–Sun), the highlight of which is Picasso's theater backdrop *Minotaur disguised as Harlequin.*

🔒 Les Jacobins

This church was begun in 1229 and completed over the next two centuries. It was the first Dominican convent, founded to combat dissent in the region. The Jacobins' convent became the founding institution of Toulouse University. Its church, a Gothic masterpiece, features a soaring, 22-branched palm tree vault in the apse. The delicate Gothic Chapelle St-Antonin (1337) contains frescoes of the Apocalypse dating from 1341.

🏛 Musée des Augustins

21 rue de Metz. 📞 05 61 22 21 82. ⭘ Wed–Mon. ⬤ Jan 1, May 1, Dec 25. 🈺 ♿ 📷
Toulouse became a center of Romanesque art due to its pos-

Palm vaulting in the apse of Les Jacobins

ition on the route to Santiago de Compostela *(see p390).* The museum has sculpture from the period and 12th-century Romanesque capitals, as well as cloisters from a 14th-century Augustinian priory. There are also 16th–19th-century French, Italian and Flemish paintings here.

Façade of Musée des Augustins

♣ Fondation Bemberg

Hôtel d'Assézat, Place d'Assézat. **☎** 05 61 12 06 89. ◯ *Tue–Sun.* ⬤ *1 Jan, 25 Dec.* 🎫 ♿ 🛒

This 16th-century palace houses the collection of local art lover Georges Bemberg, and covers Renais-

sance paintings, *objets d'art* and bronzes, as well as 19th–20th-century French paintings.

⛪ Basilique de St-Sernin

This is the largest Romanesque basilica in Europe, built in the 11th–12th centuries to accommodate pilgrims on their way to Santiago de Compostela. Highlights are the octagonal brick belfry, with rows of decorative brick arches topped by pepper pot turrets and a spire. Beautiful 11th-century marble bas-reliefs of Christ and the symbols of the Evangelists by Bernard Gilduin are in the ambulatory.

🏛 Cité de l'Espace

Avenue Jean Gonord. **☎** 05 62 71 64 80. ◯ Apr–Sep: daily; Oct–Mar: Tue–Sun. 🎫 ♿ 🛈 🍴 🛒 Southeast of Toulouse, this vast "space park" includes a planetarium, interactive exhibits related to the exploration of space, the Terradome "film experience" on the history of the earth, and a lifesize replica of the Ariane 5 rocket, where visitors can learn how to launch rockets and satellites.

KEY

🅿 Parking
🛈 Tourist information
🕆 Church
Ⓜ Metro

0 meters 250
0 yards 250

SIGHTS AT A GLANCE

Basilique de Notre-Dame-de-la Daurade ④
Basilique de St-Sernin ①
Hôtel d'Assézat ⑤
Hôtel de Ville ②
Les Jacobins ③
Musée des Augustins ⑥

The tiered, 12th-century tower of Basilique de St-Sernin

THE PYRENEES

PYRÉNÉES-ATLANTIQUES · HAUTES-PYRÉNÉES · ARIÈGE
HAUTE-GARONNE

THE MOUNTAINS *dominate life in the French Pyrenees. A region in many ways more Spanish than French, for centuries its remote terrain and tenacious people have given heretics a hiding place and refugees an escape route. Today it is the last remaining wilderness in southern Europe and a habitat for rare animal species.*

Heading east from the Atlantic coast, the hills are wonderfully lush after the plains of Aquitaine. The deeper the Pyrenees are penetrated, the steeper the valley sides and the more gigantic the snow-clad peaks become. This is magnificent, empty, dangerous country, to be approached with caution and respect. In summer the region offers over 1,600 km (1,000 miles) of walking trails, as well as camping, fishing and climbing. In winter there is both cross-country and downhill skiing at the busy resorts along the border, which are much livelier than their Spanish counterparts.

Historically, the Pyrenees are known as the birthplace of Henri IV, who put an end to the Wars of Religion in 1593 and united France, though the region has been characterized more often by independent fiefdoms. The region's oldest inhabitants, the Basque people *(see p445)* have maintained their own language and culture, and their resorts of Bayonne, Biarritz and St-Jean-de-Luz reflect this, looking to the sea and to summer visitors for their livelihood.

Inland, Pau, Tarbes and Foix rely on tourism and medium-scale industry, while Lourdes receives four million pilgrims every year. For the rest, life has been regulated by agriculture, though economic constraints today are causing an exodus from the land.

Countryside around St-Lizier, in the heart of the Pyrenean countryside

◁ **Barèges, a ski resort and spa town in the Hautes-Pyrénées**

Exploring the Pyrenees

THE TOWERING PYRENEES cut across southwest
France from the Mediterranean to the Atlantic
coast, encompassing the craggy citadel of
Montségur, the pilgrimage center of Lourdes, Pau
in the hilly Béarn country, and the Basque port of
Bayonne. This formidable range, an unspoiled
paradise for hikers, anglers and skiers, is as lush
on its French side as it is arid in Spain, and
contains the wild and beautiful Parc National des
Pyrénées. Throughout the region, visitors can
expect cool temperatures and grandiose scenery.
Lovers of art and architecture will be richly
rewarded by St-Bertrand-de-Comminges and St-
Jean-de-Luz, among the region's important sights.

**Marzipan sweets, a specialty of
southwest France** *(see p387)*

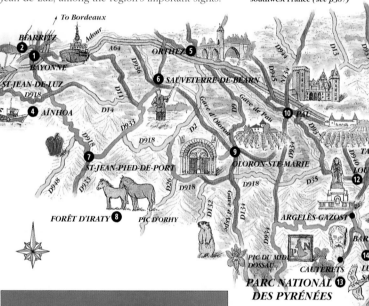

The galleried church in the Basque village of Espelette

GETTING AROUND

Access to the Basque coast in the
western Pyrenees is via the A63
from Bordeaux. The length of the
Pyrenees, including the mountain
valleys, is served by the A64 which
now runs all the way from Bayonne
to Toulouse, via Orthez, Pau, Tarbes
and St-Gaudens. Once you are high
up, expect narrow, twisting roads
and slow driving. The scenic but
demanding D918/118 corniche road
crosses 18 high passes between the
Atlantic and the Mediterranean.

There are airports at Biarritz, Pau
and Lourdes. These three towns,
together with Orthez and Tarbes, are
on the rail route which loops south
between Bordeaux and Toulouse.

Sights at a Glance

Wild pottock ponies on moorland in the Forêt d'Iraty

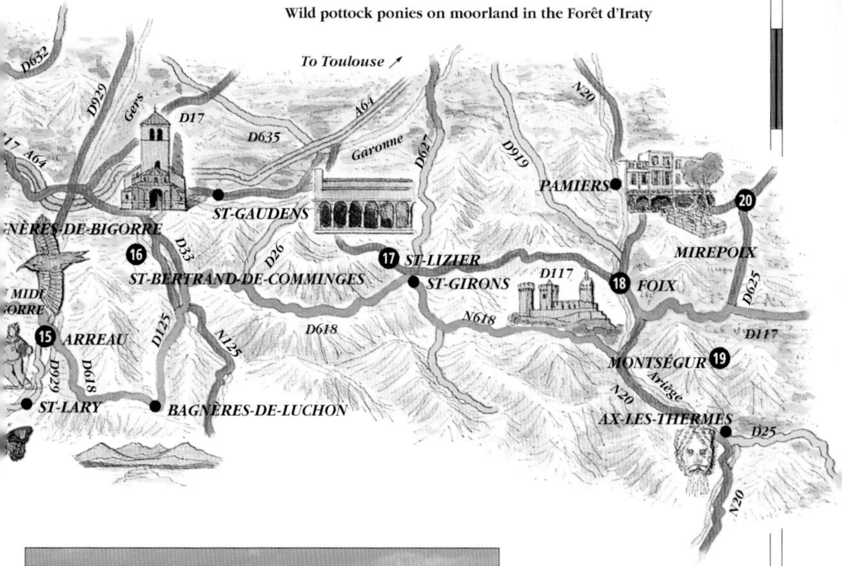

St-Jean-de-Luz seen from Ciboure, across the Nivelle estuary

Key

- Highway
- Major road
- Minor road
- Scenic route
- River
- Viewing point

0 kilometers 25

0 miles 25

Bayonne ❶

Pyrénées-Atlantiques. 🏛 *40,000.* 🚉
🚌 ℹ *place des Basques (05 59 46 01 46).* 🛒 *Mon–Sat (am only).*

BAYONNE, capital of the French Basque country, lies between two rivers – the turbulent Nive, which arrives straight from the mountains, and the wide, languid Adour. An important town since Roman times because of its command of one of the few easily passable roads to Spain, Bayonne prospered as a free port under English rule from 1154 to 1451. Since then, it has successfully withstood 14 sieges, including a particularly bloody one directed by Wellington in 1813.

Grand Bayonne, the district around the cathedral, can be easily explored on foot. The 13th-century **Cathédrale Ste-Marie** was begun under English rule and is northern Gothic in style rather than Pyrenean Romanesque. Look for the handsome cloister and the 15th-century knocker on the north door – if a fugitive could put a hand to this, he was entitled to sanctuary. The surrounding pedestrian streets form a lively shopping area, especially the arcaded rue du Port Neuf, with cafés serving hot chocolate, a Bayonne specialty. (Quality chocolate-making was introduced by Jews who fled Spain at the end of the 15th century, and it has remained a specialty of the

Lighthouse at Biarritz

town ever since.) Bayonne is also known worldwide for its ham.

Petit Bayonne lies on the opposite side of the quay-lined Nive River. The **Musée Basque** gives an excellent introduction to the customs and traditions of the Basque nation, with reconstructed home interiors and exhibits on seafaring. Nearby, the **Musée Bonnat** has a superb art gallery. The first floor here is a must for art lovers, with sketches by Leonardo, Van Dyck, Rembrandt and Rubens, and paintings by Goya, Corot, Ingres and Constable.

🏛 Musée Basque
37 quai des Corsaires. ☎ *05 59 46 61 90.* 🕐 *Tue–Sun.* ⬤ *public hols.*
📷 ♿ 🚻

🏛 Musée Bonnat
5 rue Jacques Lafitte. ☎ *05 59 59 08 52.* 🕐 *Wed–Mon.* ⬤ *public hols.*
📷 ♿

Biarritz ❷

Pyrénées-Atlantiques. 🏛 *29,000.* ✈
🚉 🚌 ℹ *Javalquinto, square d'Ixelles (05 59 22 37 10).* 🛒 *daily.*

BIARRITZ, WEST of Bayonne, has a grandiose center, but has been developed along the coast by residential suburbs. The resort began as a whaling port but was transformed into a playground for the European rich in the 19th century. Its popularity was assured when Empress Eugénie discovered its mild winter climate during the reign of her husband, Napoleon III.

The town has three good beaches, with the best surfing in Europe, two casinos, and one of the last great luxury hotels in France, the Palais *(see p569),* formerly the residence of Eugénie.

In the port des Pêcheurs, the **Musée de la Mer** aquarium is home to specimens of marine life found in the Bay of Biscay. Below it, a narrow causeway leads across to the Rocher de la Vierge, offering views along the whole of the Basque coast. The Musée du Chocolat is fine compensation for a rainy day.

🏛 Musée de la Mer
Esplanade du Rocher-de-la-Vierge, 14 plateau de l'Atalaye. ☎ *05 59 22 75 40.* 🕐 *Apr–Oct: daily; Nov–Mar: Tue–Sun.* ⬤ *2nd–3rd wk Jan, Jan 1, Dec 25.* 📷 ♿ 🚻 🖥

Altar in Eglise St-Jean-Baptiste

St-Jean-de-Luz ❸

Pyrénées-Atlantiques. 🏛 *13,000.*
✈ *Biarritz* 🚉 🚌 ℹ *pl Maréchal Foch (05 59 26 03 16).* 🛒 *Tue & Fri.*

ST-JEAN is a sleepy fishing village out of season and a scorching tourist town in August, with shops to rival the chic rue du Faubourg St-Honoré in Paris. In the 11th century, whale carcasses were towed into St-Jean to be divided up by the whole village. The natural harbor protects the shoreline, making it one of the few beaches safe for swimming along this stretch of coast.

One of the most important historical events in St-Jean was the wedding of Louis XIV and the Infanta Maria Teresa

Grand Bayonne, clustered around the twin-spired cathedral

St-Jean-de-Luz, a fishing village that explodes into life in summer

of Spain in 1660, a union that had the effect of sealing the long-awaited alliance between France and Spain, only to embroil the two countries ultimately in the War of the Spanish Succession. This wedding took place at the **Eglise St-Jean-Baptiste**, still the biggest and best of the great Basque churches, a triple-galleried marvel with a glittering 17th-century altar-piece and an atmosphere of gaiety and fervor. The gate through which the Sun King led his bride was immediately walled up by masons: a plaque now marks the place. The **Maison Louis XIV**, with its contemporary furnishings, is where the king stayed in 1660, and is worth a look.

The port is busy in the summer, while the restaurants behind the covered markets serve sizzling bowls full of *chipirons* – squid cooked in their own ink – a local specialty. Place St.-Louis is a delightful place to sit and watch the world go by.

🏛 **Maison Louis XIV**
Place Louis XIV. 📞 05 59 26 01 56.
⏰ *Jun–Sep.* 🎦

Environs
On the other side of the Nivelle River, **Ciboure** was the birthplace of composer Maurice Ravel. It is character-ized by 18th-century mer-chants' houses, steep narrow streets and seafood restau-rants. A two-hour coastal walk leads to the neighboring village of **Socoa**, where the lighthouse on the clifftop offers a fine view of the coast all the way to Biarritz.

Basque men in traditional berets

Ainhoa ❹

Pyrénées-Atlantiques. 🏠 *600.* 🚌
🛈 *La Mairie (05 59 29 92 60).*

A TINY TOWNSHIP on the road to the Spanish border, Ainhoa was founded in the 12th century as a waystation on the road to Santiago de Compostela *(see pp390–91).* The main street of 17th-century whitewashed Basque houses and a galleried church from the same period survive.

Environs
There is a similar church in the village of **Espelette** nearby. Typically Basque in style, the galleries boosted the seating capacity and had the added effect of separating the men from the women and children in the main part of the church. Espelette is the trading center for *pottocks*, an ancient local breed of pony, auctioned here at the end of January. It is also the shrine of the local crop, the red pimento pepper, especially in October when a pepper festival is held here.

At the foot of the St-Ignace Pass lies the pretty mountain village of **Sare**. From here you can reach the summit of la Rhune by cog railroad. This provides the best vantage point in the entire Pays Basque. The descent on foot is worthwhile.

Basque farmhouse near Espelette

Sauveterre-de-Béarn and the remains of the fortified bridge over the Gave d'Oloron, the Pont de la Légende

Orthez **5**

Pyrénées-Atlantiques. 🏠 10,700. 🚉
🚌 **i** *Maison Jeanne d'Albret, rue
Bourg Vieux (05 59 69 02 75, 05
59 69 37 50).* 🌢 *Tue.*

ORTHEZ is an important
Béarn market town, its
13th–14th-century bridge a
vital river-crossing point over
the Gave de Pau in the Middle
Ages. It has a Tuesday
morning market held from
November to February, selling
foie gras, smoked and air-
cured Bayonne hams, and all
kinds of poultry and fresh
produce. Fine buildings line
the rue Bourg Vieux,
especially the house of Jeanne
d'Albret, mother of Henry IV,
on the corner of rue Roarie.
Jeanne's enthusiasm for the
Protestant faith alienated both
her own subjects and Charles
X, and ultimately caused the
Béarn region to be drawn into
the Wars of Religion (1562–93).

Sauveterre-de-Béarn **6**

Pyrénées-Atlantiques. 🏠 1,300.
🚌 **i** *Parc de la Mairie, (05 59 38
58 65).* 🌢 *Sat.*

AN ATTRACTIVE market town,
Sauveterre is worth an
overnight stay. It has breathtaking views southward over
the Gave d'Oloron, the single

arch of the river's fortified
bridge, and the 16th-century
Château de Nays. Fishermen
gather here for the annual
world salmon-fishing cham-
pionships, held in the Oloron
between April and July.
　Be sure, also, to visit the
Château de Laàs, located
9 km (5.5 miles) along the
D27 from Sauveterre, which
has an excellent collection of
18th-century decorative art
and furniture – notably the
bed that Napoleon slept in (if
the bitter taste of failure
allowed him to enjoy any
repose) on the night after his
defeat at Waterloo.

♠ Château de Laàs
(*05 59 38 91 53.* ⏱ *May–Oct: Wed–
Mon (Apr: pm only; Jul–Aug: daily).* 🖼

**The Château de Nays at Sauveterre
in the Béarn region**

St-Jean-Pied-de-Port **7**

Pyrénées-Atlantiques. 🏠 1,500.
🚌 **i** *14 place Charles de Gaulle
(05 59 37 03 57).* 🌢 *Mon.*

ST-JEAN-PIED-DE-PORT is the
old capital of Basse-
Navarre and lies at the foot of
the Roncesvalles Pass. Here
the Basques crushed the rear-
guard of Charlemagne's army
in 778 and killed its commander, Roland, later glorified
in the *Chanson de Roland.*
　Throughout the Middle Ages
this red sandstone fortress
town was famous as the last
rallying point before entering
Spain on the pilgrim road to
Santiago de Compostela *(see
pp390–91).* As soon as a
group of pilgrims was
spotted, the townsfolk would
ring the church bells to show
them the way, and the pilgrims
would sing in response.
　Visitors and pilgrims in all
seasons still provide St-Jean
with its income. They enter
the narrow streets of the upper
town on foot from the Porte
d'Espagne, and pass cafés,
hotels and restaurants on the
way up. The ramparts are
worth the steep climb, as is the
citadel with panoramic view.
　On Mondays the town hosts
a livestock market, Basque
pelote matches and, in summer, shows with bulls.

Forêt d'Iraty ❽

Pyrénées-Aquitaine. 🚉 *St-Jean-Pied-de-Port*. 🚌 ℹ️ *St-Jean-Pied-de-Port (05 59 37 03 57), Larrau (05 59 28 51 29).*

A WILD PLATEAU of beech woods and moorland, the Forêt d'Iraty is famous for its cross-country skiing and walking. Here the ancient breed of Basque ponies, the *pottocks*, run half-wild. These creatures have not changed at all since the prehistoric inhabitants of the region traced their silhouettes on the walls of local caves.

The tourist office at St-Jean-Pied-de-Port publishes maps of local walks. The best begins at the Chalet Pedro parking lot, south of the lake on the Iraty Plateau, and follows the GR10 to 3,000-year-old standing stones on the western side of the Sommet d'Occabé.

Oloron-Ste-Marie ❾

Pyrénées-Atlantiques. 👥 *11,000.* 🚉 🚌 ℹ️ *Villa Bourdeu, place Pompidou (05 59 39 98 00).* 🛒 *Fri.*

O LORON, A SMALL TOWN at the junction of the Aspe and Ossau valleys, has grown from a Celtiberian settlement. There are huge agricultural fairs here in May and September, and the town is famed for producing the famous classic French berets.

BASQUE CULTURE

Most of Basque country is in Spain, but around 10 percent lies within France. The Basque people have their own complex language, isolated from other European tongues, and their music, games and folklore are equally distinct. French Basques are less fiercely separatist than their Spanish counterparts, but both are still deeply attached to their unique way of life.

Pelota, the traditional Basque game

Cathédrale Ste-Marie

The town's great glory is the doorway of the Romanesque **Cathédrale Ste-Marie**, with its biblical and Pyrenean scenes. Spain lies just on the other side of the Somport Pass, at the head of the mountainous Aspe Valley, and the influence of Spanish stonemasons is evident in Oloron's **Eglise Sainte-Croix** with its Moorish-style vaulting. These two churches are Oloron's only sights, leaving time to head up the Aspe Valley to try one of the area's famous ewe's cheeses, or mixed cow and goat's cheeses.

A side road leads to Lescun, huddled around its church, beyond which is a spectacular range of saw-toothed peaks topped by the **Pic d'Anie** at 2,504 m (8,215 ft), one of the most beautiful spots in the Pyrenees. Sadly, at nearby Somport, a controversial highway and tunnel project was permitted, despite it posing a threat to the traditional mountain agricultural economy, and the last habitat of the Pyrenean brown bear.

High moorland above the Forêt d'Iraty, long stripped of timber for use by the French and Spanish navies

Gobelin tapestry in the Château de Pau

Pau ❿

Pyrénées-Atlantiques. 🏠 *87,000.* ✈
🚃 🚌 ℹ *place Royale (05 59 27 27 08).* 🛒 *Mon–Sat.*

A LIVELY university town, with elegant Belle Epoque architecture and shady parks, Pau is the capital of the Béarn region, and the most interesting big town in the central Pyrenees. The weather in fall and winter is mild, so this has been a favorite resort of affluent foreigners, especially the English, since the early 19th century.

Pau is chiefly famous as the birthplace of King Henry IV. His mother, Jeanne d'Albret, traveled for 19 days by carriage from Picardy, in the eighth month of her pregnancy, just to have her baby here. She sang during her labor, convinced that if she did so, Henry would grow up as tough and resilient as she was. As soon as the infant was born, his lips were smeared with garlic and local Jurançon wine, in keeping with the traditional custom.

The town's principal sight is the **Château de Pau**, first remodeled in the 14th century for the ruler of Béarn, Gaston Phoebus *(see p453).* It was heavily restored 400 years later. Marguerite d'Angoulême, sister of the King of France, resided here in the late 16th century, and transformed the town into a center for the arts and free thinking.

The château's 16th-century Gobelin tapestries, made by Flemish weavers working in Paris, are fabulous. (The Maison Carré in Nay – 18 km (11 miles) toward Lourdes – exhibits the former Musée Béarnais' important collection of artifacts retracing the history, traditions and culture of the Béarn.)

Outside, the boulevard des Pyrénées affords both glorious views of the gardens below and a glimpse of the highest Pyrenean peaks, which are often snow-capped all year round. Continue from here to the eclectic **Musée des Beaux-Arts**, where there is a splendid Degas, the *Cotton Exchange, New Orleans*; Rubens' *Last Judgment*; and a work by El Greco.

♣ Château de Pau
Rue du Château. 📞 *05 59 82 38 00.* 🕐 *daily.* ⬤ *Jan 1, May 1, Dec 25.* 📷 ♿ 🅿

🏛 Musée des Beaux-Arts
Rue Mathieu Lalanne. 📞 *05 59 27 33 02.* 🕐 *Wed–Mon.* ⬤ *some public hols.* 📷 ♿ *restricted.*

Tarbes ⓫

Hautes-Pyrénées. 🏠 *48,000.* 🚶
🚃 🚌 ℹ *3 cours Gambetta (05 62 51 30 31).* 🛒 *Thu.*

T ARBES is the most prosperous town in the Bigorre region, a center for chemical and engineering industries with good shops and a major agricultural market. The **Jardin Massey** in the middle of town was designed at the turn of the 19th century and is one of the loveliest parks in the southwest. It has many rare plants, including the North American sassafras. Its museum has a collection of 16th–20th-century European art.

The **Maison du Cheval** and the Haras National (National Stud) in the town center, with its thoroughbred stallions, should not be missed.

🏛 La Maison du Cheval
Chemin du Mauhourat. 📞 *05 62 56 30 80.* 🕐 *Mon–Fri.* ⬤ *public hols.* 📷

Lourdes ⓬

Hautes-Pyrénées. 🏠 *15,000.* 🚶 🚃
🚌 *Easter–mid-Oct.* ℹ *pl Peyramale (05 62 42 77 40).* 🛒 *alternate Thu.*

L OURDES, one of the great modern shrines of Europe, owes its celebrity to visions of the Virgin experienced by a 14-year-old girl, Bernadette Soubirous, in 1858.

Château de Pau, birthplace of Henry IV in 1553

◁ **Foothills of the Pyrenees**

Four million people annually visit the **Grotte Massabielle**, the cave where the visions occurred, and the one room on rue des Petits-Fossés where Bernadette's family lived, in search of a miracle cure for disability or disease.

If one is not led there by faith, Lourdes is best avoided, or left to those who really need it. Visit the **Grottes de Bétharram** for underground rides by boat and train through its vast caverns, or the **Musée Pyrénéen**, with fascinating exhibits on the pioneers who opened up these ranges.

Grottes de Bétharram
St-Pé-de-Bigorre. 05 62 41 80 04. Feb–Mar 25: Mon–Fri pms; Mar 26–Oct 25: daily.

Spectacular limestone formations at the Grottes de Bétharram

Pilgrims participating in open-air mass at Lourdes

Musée Pyrénéen
Château Fort, rue du Fort. 05 62 42 37 37. Apr–Oct: daily; Nov–Mar: Wed–Mon. public hols (winter only).

Parc National des Pyrénées ⑬

See pp450–51.

Luz-St-Sauveur ⑭

Hautes-Pyrénées. 1,200. Lourdes. place du 8 mai (05 62 92 81 60). Mon.

LUZ-ST-SAUVEUR is an attractive spa town, with an unusual church built in the 14th century by the Hospitaliers de Saint Jean de Jérusalem (later the Knights of Malta), an order established to protect pilgrims. The church is fortified with gun slits that look out over the town and valley. These provided protection for pilgrims on the way to Santiago de Compostela.

Environs
The elegant spa town of **Cauterets** makes a good base for climbing, skiing and walking in the rugged mountains of the Bigorre region.

Gavarnie is a former way-station on the Santiago de Compostela pilgrim route. A good track, accessible on foot or by donkey, leads from the village to the spectacular natural rock amphitheater known as the **Cirque de Gavarnie**. Here the longest waterfall in Europe, at 240 m (787 ft), cascades off the mountain into space, encircled by eleven 3,000-m (9,800-ft) peaks.

Tourists can now share much of the **Observatoire Pic du Midi de Bigorre** with scientists. Access is by cable-car from La Mongie to Le Taoulet and then up to the summit. Alternatively there are a number of walks up to the Pic (4 hours minimum).

The French are justly proud of the Observatory, which has supplied the clearest images of Venus and other planets in the solar system so far obtained from the Earth's surface. The vast 1-m (3.2-ft) telescope mapped out the moon for NASA's Apollo missions.

Observatoire Pic du Midi de Bigorre
05 62 56 71 02. daily (unless weather forbids). Nov.

THE MIRACLE OF LOURDES

In 1858 a young girl named Bernadette Soubirous experienced 18 visions of the Virgin at the Grotte Massabielle near the town. Despite being told to keep away from the cave by her mother – and the local magistrate – she was guided to a spring with miraculous healing powers. The church endorsed the miracles in the 1860s, and since then, many people claim to have been cured by the holy water. A huge Religious City of shrines, churches and hospices has since grown up around the spring, with a dynamic tourist industry to match.

Bernadette's vision

Parc National des Pyrénées ⑬

Pyrenean ibex

THE PYRENEES National Park, designated in 1967, extends 100 km (62 miles) along the French and Spanish frontier. It boasts some of the most spectacular scenery in Europe, ranging from meadows glimmering with butterflies to high peaks, snowcapped even in summer. Variations in altitude and climate make the park rich in flora and fauna. One of the most enjoyable ways to see it is on foot: within the park are 350 km (217 miles) of well-marked footpaths.

Vallée d'Aspe
Jagged peaks tower above the Vallée d'Aspe and the Cirque de Lescun. This area is now threatened by a new highway (see p445).

Pic d'Anie
The limestone-flanked 2,504-m (8,215-ft) Pic d'Anie overlooks rich upland pastures watered by melting snow. In spring, the ground is ablaze with Pyrenean varieties of gentian and columbine, found nowhere else.

Col du Somport, the Somport pass (1,632 m/5,354 ft), is a rugged route into Spain, snow-bound December–April.

PIC D'ANIE
2,504 m
(8,215 ft)

PAU
Laruns
VALLÉE D'OSSAU
D934
PIC DE LA SAGETTE
2,301 m
(7,550 ft)
VALLÉE D'ASPE
N134
PIC DU MIDI D'OSSAU
2,884 m
(9,462 ft)

Pic du Midi d'Ossau
A tough trail leads from the Bious-Artigues Lake at the base of the Pic du Midi d'Ossau and encircles the formidable, tooth-shaped summit (2,884 m/9,462 ft).

PYRENEAN WILDLIFE

The Pyrenees are home to a rich variety of wild creatures, many of them unique to the range. The ibex, a member of the antelope family, is still numerous in the valleys of Ossau and Cauterets. Birds of prey include the Egyptian, griffon and bearded vultures. Ground predators range from the rare Pyrenean lynx to civet, pine marten and stoat. The desman, a tiny aquatic mammal related to the mole, is found in many of the mountain streams.

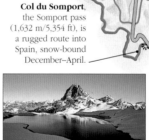

Pyrenean fritillary *flowers through late spring and early summer in mountain pastures.*

The Turk's Cap Lily *flowers June–August on rocky slopes at t to 2,200 m (7,218 ft).*

Brèche de Roland
The famous breach in the sheer crest of the Cirque de Gavarnie forms a gateway between France and Spain.

TIPS FOR WALKERS

The park is crossed by a network of numbered trails. Each is well marked and shows the length of time needed. En route are mountain huts offering a meal and a bed for the night. For maps and information visit the Park Office at Cauterets (05 62 92 52 56) or at Luz-St-Sauveur (05 62 92 38 38), both open year-round.

Walking the trail in high summer

The GR10 long-distance trail is one of the great walks of France, linking the Atlantic with the Mediterranean.

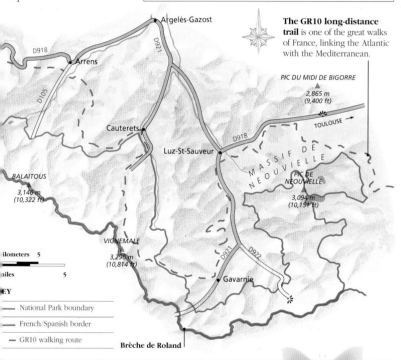

Argelès-Gazost

D918

Arrens

D105

D921

Cauterets

Luz-St-Sauveur

D918

PIC DU MIDI DE BIGORRE
2,865 m
(9,400 ft)

TOULOUSE

BALAITOUS
3,146 m
(10,322 ft)

MASSIF DE NEOUVIELLE

PIC DE NEOUVIELLE
3,094 m
(10,151 ft)

VIGNEMALE
3,296 m
(10,814 ft)

D921

D922

Gavarnie

Kilometers 5

Miles 5

KEY

― National Park boundary

― French/Spanish border

― GR10 walking route

Brèche de Roland

*The **Egyptian vulture** is seen over the Pyrenees, especially over rocky cliff faces.*

Pyrenean bears *are close to extinction but a few still live in the Ossau and Aspe valleys.*

Cleopatra

Scarce Swallowtail

These butterflies *are among several colorful species found at high altitudes.*

Arreau

Hautes-Pyrénées. ⚐ *860.* ⌷
ℹ *Château des Nestes (05 62 98 63 15).* 🛒 *Thu.*

ARREAU STANDS at the junction of the Aure and Louron rivers. A small, bustling half-timbered town with good shops and restaurants, this is the place to buy the basics (maps, walking boots, spiked walking sticks) for hiking or fishing in the mountains.

Environs
St-Lary Soulan is a ski resort up the valley, a base for exploring the entire Massif du Néouvielle in summer; the roads leading from the town will get you up to very high altitudes by car, and then you need to walk. Head for the village of Fabian and the smattering of lakes above it, where the GR10 *(see p451)* and other well-marked trails crisscross the peaks. Here you may see golden eagles or an enormous lammergeier (vulture) soaring overhead.

St-Bertrand-de-Comminges

Haute-Garonne. ⚐ *220.* ⌷
Montrejeau, then taxi. ℹ *Les Olivetains, parvis de la Cathédrale (05 61 95 44 44).*

THE PRETTY hilltop town of St-Bertrand is the most remarkable artistic and historic site in the Central Pyrenees and the site of an acclaimed summer music festival *(see p33)*. Some of

Cloisters in the Cathédrale Ste-Marie, St-Bertrand-de-Comminges

the best sculpture in the region adorns the portal of the **Cathédrale Ste-Marie**. The adjoining Romanesque and Gothic cloisters contain sarcophagi, carved capitals and statues of the four Evangelists.

St-Bertrand's origins lie on the plain below, in the city founded by the great Roman statesman Pompey in 72 BC. At that time it consisted of two thermal baths, a theater, a temple, a market and a Christian basilica. All were destroyed by Gontran, the grandson of Clovis *(see p202)*, in 585, and six centuries were to pass before the Bishop of Comminges, Bertrand de l'Isle, saw the site as a potential location for a new cathedral and monastery. The town, which was relatively unimportant in political terms, became reestablished as a major religious center.

Inside the cathedral, look out for the 66 magnificently carved choirstalls and the 16th-century organ case. The tomb of Bertrand de l'Isle is situated at the far end of the choir, with

an altar beside it; the beautiful marble tomb in the Virgin's chapel just off the nave is that of Hugues de Châtillon, a bishop who provided funds for the completion of the cathedral in the 14th century.

⛪ Cathédrale Ste-Marie
☎ *05 61 89 04 91.* ⏰ *daily.*
● *Sun am.* 📷 🎥

Fresco in the Cathédrale St-Lizier

St-Lizier

Ariège. ⚐ *1,800.* ⌷ ℹ *place de l'Eglise (05 61 96 77 77).*

ST-LIZIER is located in the Ariège, a region famous for its steep-sided valleys and wild mountain scenery. The village dates back to Roman times, and by the Middle Ages was an important religious center, only to be superseded in the 12th century by St-Girons nearby. St-Lizier has the distinction of possessing two cathedrals; the finest is the 12th–14th-century **Cathédrale St-Lizier** in the lower town. It boasts Romanesque frescoes and a cloister with carved columns,

The imposing 12th-century Cathédrale Ste-Marie above St-Bertrand

St-Lizier, with snow-capped mountains in the distance

but the **Cathédrale de la Sède** in the upper town, reached on foot through narrow streets, has the better view.

Foix ⑱

Ariège. 👥 9,700. 🚉 🚌 ℹ️ *29 rue Delcassé (05 61 65 12 12).* 🛒 *1st, 3rd & 5th Mon of each month & Fri.*

WITH ITS BATTLEMENTS and towers, Foix stands directly at the junction of the Arget and Ariège rivers. In the Middle Ages, Foix's dynasty of counts ruled the whole of the Béarn area. Count Gaston Phoebus (1331–91) was the most flamboyant, a poet who surrounded himself with troubadours and wrote a famous treatise on hunting. He was a ruthless politician, who also had his own brother and his only son put to death.

Some of the pleasures of the medieval court are recreated in the local summer fair, the largest in the southwest. At any time, the 15th-century keep of the **Château de Foix** is worth climbing just for the view. The small and much-restored 14th-century **Eglise de St-Volusien**, on the banks of the river Ariège, is delightful in its simplicity and grace.

♦ Château de Foix
📞 *05 61 65 56 05.* 🕐 *daily.* ● *Nov–Apr: Mon–Tue; Jan 1, Dec 25.* 🏷️

Montségur ⑲

Ariège. 👥 *100.* ℹ️ *05 61 03 03 03.* 🏛️ 🅿️ *for the château.*

THE TOWN of Montségur is famous as the last strong-hold of the Cathars *(see p481)*. From the parking area at the foot of the mount, a path leads up to the castle above, occupied in the 13th century by *faidits* (dispossessed aristo-crats) and a Cathar community. The Cathars lived outside the fortress, in houses clinging to the rock. Staunchly opposed to Catholic authority, the Cathar troops unwisely marched on Avignonnet in 1243 and massacred members of the Inquisitional tribunal. In retaliation, an army of 10,000 laid siege to Montségur for ten months. When captured, 205 Cathars refused to convert and were burned alive.

Mirepoix ⑳

Ariège. 👥 *3,300.* 🚌 ℹ️ *place du Maréchal Leclerc (05 61 68 83 76).* 🛒 *Mon & Thu.*

MIREPOIX IS A TRADITIONAL bastide town *(see p435)* with a huge main square – one of the loveliest in the south-west – surrounded by beamed 13th–15th-century arcades and half-timbered houses.

The **cathedral**, begun in 1317 with the last additions made in 1867, boasts the widest Gothic nave (22 m/72 ft) in France.

The best times to visit the town are on market days, when the square is covered with vendors selling a mass of local produce.

The arcaded main square at Mirepoix

THE SOUTH OF FRANCE

Introducing the South of France

THE SOUTH is France's most popular vacation region, drawing millions of visitors each year to the Riviera resorts and modern beach cities to the west. Agriculture is a mainstay of the economy, producing early fruits and an abundance of affordable wine. The new high-tech industries of Nice and Montpellier reflect the region's key role in the developing south coast sunbelt, while Corsica still preserves much of its natural beauty. The map shows the major sights of this sun-blessed region.

Pont du Gard, *a 2,000-year-old bridge* (see p485), *is a major feat of Roman engineering. It was a key link in the 17-km (10.5-mile) aqueduct, parts of which were underground, carrying fresh water from a spring at Uzes to Nîmes.*

St-Guilhem-le-Désert

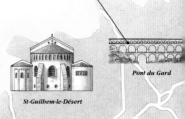

Pont du Gard

LANGUEDOC-ROUSSILLON
(See pp466–87)

Carcassonne

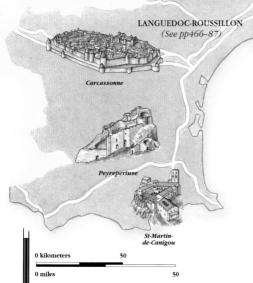

Peyrepertuse

St-Martin-de-Canigou

| 0 kilometers | 50 |
| 0 miles | 50 |

The Camargue *lies at the mouth of the Rhône delta, where marshland and inland seas support a rich selection of wildlife. Three visitors' centers give a good introduction to this fragile area with its population of pink flamingos and white horses (see pp500–1).*

INTRODUCING THE SOUTH OF FRANCE

***Avignon**, enclosed by massive ramparts, became papal territory when popes decamped from Rome (see p493) in the 14th century, taking up residence in the Palais des Papes that towers over the town. In summer the town is the scene of the popular Avignon Festival.*

lais des Papes, Avignon

PROVENCE AND THE COTE D'AZUR
(See pp488–521)

Musée Matisse, Nice

*Giacometti statue,
St-Paul-de-Vence*

margue

CORSICA
(See pp522–33)

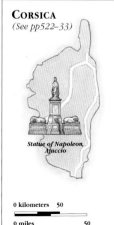

*Statue of Napoleon,
Ajaccio*

0 kilometers   50

0 miles   50

***The Côte d'Azur** has attracted sun worshipers and celebrities since the 1920s (see pp464–5). The coast also offers some prize collections of 20th-century art (pp462–3) and such famous yearly events as the Cannes Film Festival and Antibes Jazz Festival.*

Regional Food: the South

IT'S A HEADY EXPERIENCE just to stand, look and sniff in a Provençal market. Tables sag under piles of braided pink garlic, fresh and colorful peppers, tomatoes, eggplant, zucchini and asparagus. The Cavaillon melons are so ripe they've split, leaking sweet perfume. In the fall and winter an earthy, fragrant scent fills the air; wild mushrooms, Swiss chards, cardoons, walnuts, quinces, pumpkins, fennel and wrinkled black olives all crowd the stalls. Coastal Provence is famous for fish soups, including *bouillabaisse* and *bourride*, a garlic fish stew. Lamb is the most common meat in Provence, the best coming from the margins of the Camargue and the Crau where lambs graze on herbs and salt-marsh grass.

Rosemary

Roussillon's Pyrenean villages provide delectable sausages, hams and *charcuterie*. Roussillon supplies France with the first of the season's peaches, cherries and apricots. Its coastal waters provide a bountiful sea harvest of plump mussels, oysters and *tellines* (tiny clams). Farther south, the island of Corsica has a robust cuisine with strong Italian influences.

Salade Niçoise *comes in many versions but always includes lettuce, green beans, tomatoes, black olives, eggs and anchovies.*

Pistou soup *is a rich vegetable and bean soup flavored with* pistou, *a sauce of basil, garlic and olive oil.*

Fish broth

Croutons

Red snapper

Rouille (meaning "rust"), a mayonnaise of chilies and garlic

Conger eel

Monkfish

Red mullet

Bouillabaisse, *a fish soup originating in Marseille, is a luxury today. It consists of an assortment of local seafood including monkfish, mullet, snapper, scorpion fish and conger eel, flavored with tomatoes, saffron and olive oil. Traditionally, the fish broth is served first with croutons spread with* rouille, *a spicy mayonnaise. The fish is eaten afterward.*

Ratatouille *is a stew of onions, eggplant, zucchini, tomatoes and peppers, cooked in olive oil and garlic.*

Pissaladière *is similar to pizza, garnished with onions, olives and anchovies. Every* boulangerie *in Provence sells it.*

Aïoli *is a sauce made of egg yolks, garlic and olive oil. It is served with salt cod, boiled eggs, snails or raw vegetables.*

Boeuf en daube *is a beef stew with red wine, cooked slowly in a pot-bellied casserole called a "daubière."*

Brandade de morue, *a specialty of Nîmes, is a purée of salt cod with cream, olive oil, garlic and potatoes.*

Tarte au citron *is a sweet-pastry pie filled with a creamy lemon mixture. Menton is well known for its lemon crop.*

Fougasse *is a flattish, lattice-like bread variously studded with black olives, anchovies, onions and spices. The sweet version is flavored with almonds.*

OLIVES AND OLIVE OIL

Most of the olive crop is crushed for oil. Ripe olives are black and the unripe ones are green; both can be preserved in brine or oil. At the end of the olive harvest it is customary to eat bread with *tapenade,* a paste of black olives, capers, anchovies and olive oil.

Tapenade

Honey *comes in many flavors, depending on the diet of the bees, which can include a wide variety of flowers and herbs such as lavender, orange blossom, rosemary or thyme.*

Black olives

Olive oil

Pitted olives

Lemon verbena   Camomile   Lime flower

TISANES

In the south of France, tisanes (flower and herb infusions or teas) are popular drinks, especially after meals. Lime flower *(tilleul)* is the most popular, considered good for the digestion and for sleep. Camomile tea stimulates the kidneys, and lemon verbena *(verveine)* soothes the liver.

France's Wine Regions: the South

AMASSIVE ARC stretching from Banyuls, in the extreme southern corner of France, to Nice, close to the Italian border, encompasses the Mediterranean vineyards of Languedoc-Roussillon and Provence. This was for a century an area of mass-produced wine, and much is still of *vin de table* quality. Today, however, the more dynamic producers are applying new technology to traditional and classic grape varieties to revive southern France's nobler heritage of generous, warm, aromatic wines, evocative of sun-baked stone, the scent of wild herbs, and the shimmering waters of the Mediterranean.

Cellar sign, Banyuls

LOCATOR MAP
▨ *Languedoc-Roussillon & Provence*

Coteaux du Languedoc is a large and varied appellation stretching from Narbonne toward Nîmes.

This full, red Fitou bears a name that reflects the importance of the *terroir*, or native soil, to many southern French winemakers.

Stop here to try the wines of Rivesaltes – idiosyncratic yet distinctive, exotic sweet white Muscats and rich, portlike reds.

Rugged valley slopes in Corbières

KEY

- Collioure & Banyuls
- Côtes de Roussillon
- Côtes de Roussillon Villages
- Fitou
- Corbières
- Minervois
- Coteaux du Languedoc
- Costières du Gard
- Coteaux d'Aix en Provence
- Côtes de Provence
- Cassis
- Bandol & Côtes de Provence
- Coteaux Varois
- Bellet

Hand-picking grapes for Côtes de Provence red wine

WINE REGIONS

Both in the Provence wine region, east of Aix and Marseille, and in the larger Languedoc-Roussillon area to the west, new, quality wine *appellations*, such as Cabardès (north of Carcassonne), are joining the more familiar names.

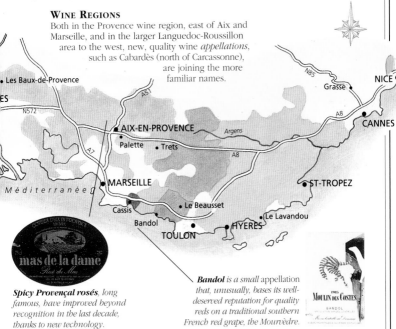

Spicy Provençal rosés, long famous, have improved beyond recognition in the last decade, thanks to new technology.

Bandol is a small appellation *that, unusually, bases its well-deserved reputation for quality reds on a traditional southern French red grape, the Mourvèdre.*

KEY FACTS ABOUT WINES OF THE SOUTH

 Location and Climate
A warm and sunny climate helps to create generously alcoholic wines. The flat coastal plains support acres of vines, but generally the best sites are on the schist and limestone hillsides.

Grape Varieties
Mass-produced grapes such as **Carignan** and **Aramon** are giving way to quality varieties such as **Syrah, Mourvèdre** and **Grenache**. **Cabernet Sauvignon**, **Merlot** and **Syrah**, and the whites **Chardonnay**, **Sauvignon Blanc** and **Viognier**, are increasingly used for *vins de pays*. Rich, sweet whites are made from the aromatic, honeyed **Muscat** grape.

Good Producers
Corbières & Minervois: La Voulte Gasparets, Saint Auriol, Lastours, Villerambert-Julien.
Faugères: Château des Estanilles, Château de la Liquière. *Faugères*: Château Cazal-Viel, Domaine Navarre, Cave de Roquebrun.
St. Chinian: Château Cazal-Viel, Domaine Navarre, Cave de Roquebrun.
Coteaux du Languedoc and vins de pays: Mas Jullien, Château de Capitoul, Prieuré de St. Jean de Bébian, Mas de Daumas Gassac, Pech-Celeyran. *Roussillon*: Domaine Gauby, Domaine Sarda Malet. *Provence*: Domaine Tempier, Château Pibarnon, Domaine de Trévallon, Mas de la Dame, Domaine Richeaume, La Courtade, Château Simone, Château Pradeaux, Château de Bellet.

Artists and Writers in the South of France

Monet's palette

ARTISTS AND WRITERS have helped create our image of the South of France – the poet Stephen Liégeard even gave the Côte d'Azur its name in 1887. Many writers, French and foreign, found a haven in the warmth of the south. From Cézanne to Van Gogh, Monet to Picasso, artists have been inspired by the special light and brilliant colors of this seductive region. Today it is rich in art museums, some devoted to single artists like Matisse, Picasso and Chagall, others with varied collections such as those in Céret, Nîmes, Montpellier, St-Tropez, St-Paul-de-Vence and Nice *(see pp472–517)*.

Picasso and Françoise Gilot on the Golfe Juan, 1948

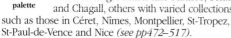

Paul Cézanne's studio in Aix-en-Provence *(see p501)*

THE WILD BEASTS

THE FAUVES, DUBBED "Wild Beasts" for their unnaturally bright and wild colors, led one of the first 20th-century avant-garde movements, founded by Matisse in Collioure in 1905 *(see p25)*. Other Fauves included Derain, Vlaminck, Marquet, Van Dongen and Dufy. Matisse visited Corsica in 1898, and then St-Tropez, and was inspired by the lushness of Provence to paint the celebrated *Luxe, Calme et Volupté.* Eventually he settled in Nice, where he painted his great series of Odalisques. He wrote, "What made me stay are the great colored reflections of January, the luminosity of daylight." The exquisite blue-and-white chapel he designed in Vence is one of the most moving of his later works *(see p513)*.

FESTIVE LIGHT

THE IMPRESSIONISTS were fascinated by the effects of light, and Monet was entranced by "the glaring festive light" of the south that made colors so intense he said no one would believe they were real if painted accurately. In 1883 Renoir came with him to the south, returning often to paint his voluptuous nudes in the filtered golden light. Bonnard, too, settled here, painting endless views of the red tiled roofs and palm trees.

Post-Impressionists Van Gogh and Gauguin arrived in 1888, attracted by the region's rich colors. Cézanne, who was born in Aix in 1839, analyzed and painted the structure of nature, above all the landscape of Provence and his beloved Mont-Ste-Victoire. Pointillist Paul Signac came to St-Tropez to paint sea and sky in a rainbow palette of dots.

Vincent Van Gogh's *Sunflowers* (1888)

PICASSO COUNTRY

THE SOUTH of France is, without question, Picasso country. His nymphs and sea urchins, his monumental women running on the beach, his shapes and colors, ceramics and sculpture are all derived from the hard shadows and bright colors of the south.

Pablo Picasso was born in Malaga in Spain in 1881 but spent much of his life on the French Mediterranean, developing Cubism with Braque in Céret in 1911, and arriving in Juan-les-Pins in 1920. He was in Antibes when war broke out in 1939, where he painted *Night Fishing at Antibes*, a luminous nocturnal seascape. He returned in 1946 and was given the Grimaldi Palace to use as a studio. It is now a Picasso Museum *(see p511)*. He also worked in Vallauris, producing ceramics and sculptures *(see p512)*.

Deux Femmes Courant sur la Plage (1933) by Pablo Picasso

LOST CAVIAR DAYS

JUST AS F. Scott Fitzgerald wrote the Jazz Age into existence, so he captured the glittering life on the Riviera with *Tender is the Night*. He and Zelda arrived in 1924 attracted, like many expatriate writers, by the warm climate and the cheap, easy living. "One could get away with more on

Scott and Zelda Fitzgerald with daughter Scottie

the summer Riviera, and whatever happened seemed to have something to do with art," he wrote. They passed their villa on to another American, Ernest Hemingway. Many other writers flocked there including Katherine Mansfield, D.H. Lawrence, Aldous Huxley, Friedrich Nietzsche, Lawrence Durrell and Graham Greene. Some, like Somerset Maugham, led a glamorous lifestyle surrounded by exotic guests. Colette was an early visitor to St-Tropez, and in 1954, Françoise Sagan captured the youthful hedonism of the time in her novel, *Bonjour Tristesse*.

NEW REALISM

IN THE 1950s Nice produced its own school of artists, the *Nouveaux Réalistes*, including Yves Klein, Arman, Martial Raysse, Tinguely, César, Niki de Saint Phalle and Daniel Spoerri *(see pp516–17)*. They explored the possibilities of everyday objects – Arman sliced violins, packaged and displayed trash; Tinguely exploded TV sets and cars. They had a light-hearted approach: "We live in a land of vacations, which gives us the spirit of nonsense," said Klein. He painted solid blue canvases of his personal color, International Klein Blue, taking the inspiration of the Mediterranean to its limit.

PROVENÇAL WRITERS

The regions of Provence and Languedoc have always had a distinct literary identity, ever since the troubadours in the 12th–13th centuries composed their love poetry in the *langue d'oc* Provençal, a Latin-based language. In the last century, many regional writers have been inspired by the landscape and local traditions. They were influenced by the 19th-century Felibrige movement to revive the language, led by Nobel prize-winning poet Frédéric Mistral. Some, like Daudet and filmmaker-turned-writer Marcel Pagnol, celebrate the Provençal character. Others, such as Jean Giono, explore the connection between nature and humanity.

Frédéric Mistral in the *Petit Journal*

Beaches in the South of France

The Carlton Hotel logo

THE GLAMOROUS Mediterranean coast is France's foremost vacation playground. To the east lie the Riviera's big, traditional resorts such as Menton, Nice, Cannes and Monte-Carlo. To the west are smaller resorts in coves and bays like St-Tropez and Cassis. Farther on is the Camargue reserve at the mouth of the Rhone. West of the Rhone, making a majestic curve reaching almost to the Spanish border, is the long, sandy shore of Languedoc-Roussillon, where a string of purpose-built resorts range from modern beach cities to replicas of fishing villages.

The beaches are sandy west of Antibes; eastward, they are naturally rocky, so any sand is imported. Antipollution drives mean that most beaches are now clean, except in a few spots west of Marseille and around Nice. Beaches around towns often charge fees but are usually well-equipped.

A train poster by Domergue advertising the Côte d'Azur

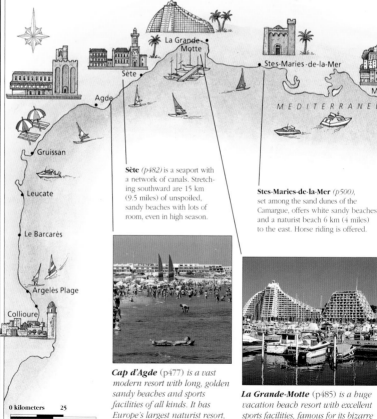

Sète (p482) is a seaport with a network of canals. Stretching southward are 15 km (9.5 miles) of unspoiled, sandy beaches with lots of room, even in high season.

Stes-Maries-de-la-Mer (p500), set among the sand dunes of the Camargue, offers white sandy beaches and a naturist beach 6 km (4 miles) to the east. Horse riding is offered.

Cap d'Agde (p477) is a vast modern resort with long, golden sandy beaches and sports facilities of all kinds. It has Europe's largest naturist resort, accommodating 20,000 visitors.

La Grande-Motte (p485) is a huge vacation beach resort with excellent sports facilities, famous for its bizarre ziggurat architecture.

0 kilometers   25

0 miles   25

In Victorian times *the Côte d'Azur, or Riviera, was the fashionable vacation spot for Europe's royalty and rich. They came to gamble and escape northern winters. Summer bathing did not come into vogue until the 1920s. Today the Riviera is busy all year-round, with the glamorous beaches and nightlife still a major attraction.*

Menton *(p519)* has a warm climate in winter, and year-round beach weather. Its sheltered, rocky beaches are backed by beautiful villas.

Cannes *(p510)* takes great pride in its golden beaches, keeping them scrupulously clean: most are private with entrance fees.

Cassis *(p503)* is a charming fishing village with a popular casino, white cliffs and some lovely hidden creeks nearby.

St-Tropez (p506) *is flanked by golden beaches mostly occupied by stylish "clubs," offering amenities at a price.*

Nice (p516), *Although the town's waterfront is visually dramatic, with a wide, handsome prom-enade, the beach is stony and has a busy highway alongside.*

Cap Ferrat (p518) *is a wooded peninsula that has a 10-km (6-mile) craggy cliff walk offering glimpses of grand villas and private beaches.*

LANGUEDOC-ROUSSILLON

AUDE · GARD · HÉRAULT · PYRÉNÉES-ORIENTALES

T HE TWO DISTINCT PROVINCES *of Languedoc and Roussillon stretch from the foothills of the Pyrenees on the Spanish border to the mouth of the Rhône. The flat beaches and lagoons of the coast form a perfect sunbelt accommodating millions of vacationers every year. In between is a dry, sunburned land producing half of France's table wine and the season's first peaches and cherries.*

Beyond such sensuous pleasures are many layers of history, including the unification of the two provinces. The formerly independent Languedoc once spoke Occitan, the tongue of the troubadours, and still cherishes its separate identity. Roussillon was a Spanish possession until the treaty of the Pyrenees in 1659. Its Catalan heritage is displayed everywhere from the road signs to the Sardana dance, and the flavor of Spain is evident in the popularity of bullfights, paella and gaudily painted façades.

This stretch of coastline was the first place in Gaul to be settled by the Romans, their enduring legacy evident in the great amphitheater at Nîmes and the magnificent engineering of the Pont du Gard. The abbeys of St-Martin-du-Canigou, St-Michel-de-Cuxa and St-Guilhem-le-Désert are superb examples of early Romanesque architecture, unaffected by Northern Gothic. The great craggy Cathar castles and the perfectly restored medieval Cité of Carcassonne bear witness to the bloody battles of the Middle Ages.

In parts, the region remains wild and untamed: from the high plateaus of the Cerdagne, to the wild hills of the Corbières or the remote uplands of Haut Languedoc. But it also has the most youthful and progressive cities in France: Montpellier, the ancient university city and capital of the region, and Nîmes, with its exuberant *feria* and bullfights. The whole area is typified by an insouciant mixture of ancient and modern, from Roman temples and postmodern architecture in its cities to solar power and ancient abbeys in the mountains.

A sunny stretch of coastline at Cap d'Agde

◁ **The abbey of Saint-Martin-du-Canigou perched on Mount Canigou**

Exploring Languedoc-Roussillon

Languedoc-Roussillon combines miles of gentle
coastline with a rugged hinterland. Its clean,
sandy beaches are perfect for family vacations, with
resorts ranging from traditional fishing villages to
new purpose-built resorts. Inland is quieter, with
acres of vineyards in the Corbières and Minervois
and mountain walks in the Haut Languedoc and
Cerdagne. A rich architectural heritage ranges from
Roman to Romanesque, contrasting with the
modern, vibrant atmosphere of the main cities.

**Jousting on the canal, a regular
summer event in Sète**

Sights at a Glance

To Orange
Montélimar

To Avignon

To Arles
Marseille

RC NATIONAL
DES
CÉVENNES

Rodez

GROTTE DES
DEMOISELLES

ST-GUILHEM-
LE-DÉSERT

DEVE

MONTPELLIER

PÉZENAS

SÈTE

GOLFE DU LION

PONT
DU GARD

NÎMES

AIGUES-
MORTES

LA
GRANDE
MOTTE

GETTING AROUND

Montpellier's international airport serves the region; smaller
airports at Carcassonne, Perpignan
and Nîmes have direct flights to
the UK. The TGV runs beyond
Montpellier to Béziers, and a
good rail network connects the
region's main towns. The A61
highway provides access from
the west and the A9 follows the
coast. The A75 now enters from
the north. Smaller roads, even in
the mountains, are well-maintain-
ed. Barges along the Canal du
Midi are a leisurely alternative.

KEY

	Highway
	Major road
	Minor road
	Scenic route
	River
⥾	Viewing point

0 kilometers　　　　25

0 miles　　　　25

The ruined Barbarossa tower at Gruissan on the Golfe du Lion

Cerdagne **❶**

Pyrénées-Orientales. 🚉 *Perpignan.*
🚌 🚏 *Mont Louis, Bourg Madame.*
ℹ️ *Mont Louis (04 68 04 21 97 or 04 68 04 21 18).*

Tᴀᴇ ʀᴇᴍᴏᴛᴇ ᴄᴇʀᴅᴀɢɴᴇ, an independent state in the Middle Ages, is today divided between Spain and France. Its high plateaus offer skiing and walking along clear mountain lakes in pine and chestnut forests. The Little Yellow Train is an excellent way to sample the area in a day. Stops include **Mont Louis**, a town fortified by Vauban, Louis XIV's military architect, which still accommodates French troops; the ski resort of **Font-Romeu**; and **Latour-de-Carol**, along with the tiny village of **Yravals** below it. Nearby **Odeillo** is the site of a huge solar furnace, 45 m (150 ft) tall and 50 m (165 ft) wide. Established in 1969, its giant curved mirrors are a remarkable sight in the valley.

Villefranche-de-Conflent **❷**

Pyrénées-Orientales. 🚶 *225.* 🚌 🚏
ℹ️ *34 bis rue St-Jacques (04 68 96 22 96).*

Iɴ ᴍᴇᴅɪᴇᴠᴀʟ ᴛɪᴍᴇs Villefranche's position at the narrowest point of the Têt Valley made it an eminently defensible fortress against Moorish invasion. Today, fragments of 11th-century walls remain, along with massive ramparts, gates and Fort Liberia, high

Abbey cloisters of St-Michel-de-Cuxa

above the gorge, all built by Vauban in the 17th century. The 12th-century **Eglise de St-Jacques** has fine carved capitals from the workshops of St-Michel-de-Cuxa, and Catalan painted wooden statues, including a 14th-century *Virgin and Child*. The 13th-century oak door is embellished with intricate wrought ironwork, a craft still apparent on many of the shop signs in town. From

Statue in St-Jacques, Villefranche

the streets of locally quarried pink marble you can make the climb up to the **Grottes des Canalettes**, a superb underground setting for concerts. Or, climb aboard the Little Yellow Train up to the magnificent mountain plain of the Cerdagne (04 68 96 56 62).

St-Michel-de-Cuxa **❸**

Prades, Pyrénées-Orientales.
☎ *04 68 96 15 35.* ◐ *daily.* ● *Sun am, religious hols.* 📷

Pʀᴀᴅᴇs, a small, pink marble town in the Têt Valley, is typical of the local style. The **Eglise St-Pierre** has a southern Gothic wrought-iron belfry and a Baroque Catalan interior. But the town is distinguished by the beautiful pre-Romanesque abbey of St-Michel-de-Cuxa, which lies 3 km (2 miles) farther up the valley, and by the legacy of the Spanish cellist Pablo Casals. Casals spent many years here in exile from Franco's Spain; every August the abbey provides the setting for the Prades music festival held in his memory.

An early example of monastic architecture, St-Michel-de-Cuxa Abbey was founded by Benedictine monks in 878 and rapidly became renowned throughout France and Spain. Distinctive keyhole arches showing Moorish influence pierce the massive walls of the abbey church, which was consecrated in 974. The mottled pink marble cloisters, with their superbly carved capitals, were added later, in the 12th century.

After the Revolution the building was abandoned, and

Tʜᴇ Lɪᴛᴛʟᴇ Yᴇʟʟᴏᴡ Tʀᴀɪɴ

Arrive early for the best seats in the carriages of *Le Petit Train Jaune*, which winds its way on narrow-gauge tracks through gorges and across towering viaducts up into the Cerdagne, stopping at small mountain stations along the way. Built in 1910 to improve access to the mountains, it now operates mainly for tourists, beginning at Villefranche-de-Conflent and terminating at Latour-de-Carol.

The Little Yellow Train, with open carriages for summer visitors

its famous carvings looted. From 1913, George Grey Bernard, a visiting American artist, began to discover some of the capitals incorporated in local buildings. He sold the carvings to the Metropolitan Museum of Art in New York in 1925, where they formed the basis of the Cloisters Museum – a faithful re-creation of a Romanesque abbey in the unlikely setting of Manhattan.

St-Martin-du-Canigou ❹

Casteil. ☎ 04 68 05 50 03.
⬜ (guided tours only: tour lasts one hour, times vary with seasons) Easter–Sep: daily; Oct–Easter: Wed–Mon. ▨

SAINT-MARTIN-DU-CANIGOU is situated in a spectacularly remote site a third of the way up Pic du Canigou, on a jagged spur of rock approached only by jeep or a 40-minute climb on foot from Casteil or by hiring a jeep from Vernet-les-Bains. The abbey was built between 1001 and 1026, and financed by Guifred, Count of Cerdagne, who abandoned his family and entered the monastery in 1035. He was buried there 14 years later in a tomb he carved from the rock himself, and which can still be seen. The church is early

Nun at St-Martin

Romanesque, based on a simple basilican plan. Two churches are built, quite literally, one on top of the other, making the lower church the crypt for the upper building.

The abbey complex is best viewed from above by continuing up the path. From there, its irregular design clinging to the rock is framed by the dramatic mountain setting – the ensemble a tribute to the ingenuity and vitality of its early builders.

Serrabone Priory's chapel tribune, with columns of local marble

Prieuré de Serrabone ❺

Boule d'Amont. ☎ 04 68 84 09 30.
⬜ daily. ● Jan 1, May 1, Nov 1, Dec 25. ▨

PERCHED HIGH UP on the northern flanks of Pic du Canigou, the sacred mountain of the Catalans, is the priory of Serrabone. A final lap of hairpin turns on the approach road (the D618) reveals the simple square tower and round apse of this remote Romanesque abbey, surrounded by a botanical garden of local herbs and woodland plants clinging to the mountain side.

Inside the cool, austere 12th-century building is a surprisingly elaborate chapel tribune, its columns and arches glowing from the local red-veined marble, carved by the anonymous Master of Cuxa, whose work appears throughout the region. Note the strange beasts and verdant flora featured in the capital carvings, especially the rose of Roussillon.

The 11th-century cloister of St-Martin-du-Canigou

Céret ❻

Pyrénées-Orientales. 🏠 *8,000.* ▣
🛈 *av Clémenceau (04 68 87 00 53).*
📅 *Sat.* 🎉 *Fête des Cerises (May/Jun).*

CÉRET IS A CHERRY TREE TOWN,
surrounded by a glorious
cloud of pink blossoms in the
early spring, and producing
the very first fruits of the year.
The tiled and painted façades
and loggias of the buildings
have a Spanish feel, and
the town was popular with
Picasso, Braque and Matisse.
Today, as a result, Céret is
distinguished by the recently
extended **Musée d'Art
Moderne**, its sophisticated
modern architecture housing
a remarkable collection that
includes Catalan artists Tapiès
and Capdeville, a series of
bowls by Picasso painted
with bullfighting scenes, and
works by Matisse, Chagall,
Juan Gris and Salvador Dalí.
    The town's Catalan heritage
is evident in regular bullfights
held in the arena, and in its
Sardana dance festival held
towards the end of July.

🏛 **Musée d'Art Moderne**
Bd Maréchal Joffre. 📞 *04 68 87 27 76.*
⬜ *May–Sep: daily; Oct–Apr:
Wed–Mon.* ⬤ *Jan 1, May 1,
Nov 1, Dec 25.* 🎫 ♿

Environs
From Céret the D115 follows
the Tech Valley to the spa

Statue by Aristide Maillol, Banyuls

town of **Amélie-les-Bains**,
where fragments of Roman
baths have been discovered.
Beyond, in **Arles-sur-Tech**,
the Eglise de Ste-Marie contains 12th-century frescoes,
and a sarcophagus
beside the church
door which, ac-
cording to local
legend, produces
drops of unac-
countably pure
water every year.

Catalan flag

Côte Vermeille ❼

Pyrénées-Orientales. ✈ *Perpignan.*
▣ *Collioure, Cerbère.* ▣ *Collioure,
Banyuls-sur-Mer.* 🛈 *Collioure (04 68
82 15 47), Cerbère (04 68 88 42 36).*

HERE THE PYRENEES meet the
Mediterranean, the coast
road twisting and turning
around secluded pebbly coves
and rocky outcrops. The

vermeille (vermilion-tinted)
rock of the headlands gives
this stretch of coast, the loveliest to be found in Languedoc-
Roussillon, its name.
    The Côte Vermeille extends
all the way to the Costa Brava
in northern Spain. With its
Catalan character, it is as redo-
lent of Spain as of France.
Argelès-Plage has three
sandy beaches and a palm-
fringed promenade, and is
the largest camping center in
Europe. The small resort of
Cerbère is the last French
town before the border, flying
the red and gold Catalan flag
to signal its true allegiance.
All along the coast, terraced
vineyards cling to the rocky
hillsides, producing
strong, sweet wines
like Banyuls and
Muscat. The difficult
terrain makes harvest-
ing a laborious process.
Vines were first
planted here by Greek
settlers in the 7th century BC,
and Banyuls itself has wine
cellars dating back to the
Middle Ages.
    Banyuls is also famous as
the birthplace of Aristide
Maillol, the 19th-century
sculptor, whose work can be
seen all over the region. **Port
Vendres**, with fortifications
built by the indefatigable
Vauban (architect to Louis XIV),
is a fishing port renowned for
its anchovies and sardines.

The spectacular Côte Vermeille, seen from the coast road south of Banyuls

Collioure Harbor, with one of its beaches and the Eglise Notre-Dame-des-Anges

Collioure ❽

Pyrénées-Orientales. 🏠 2,900. 🚊
🚌 🛈 *place du 18 juin (04 68 82 15 47).* 🛥 *Wed & Sun.*

T HE COLORS of Collioure first
attracted Matisse here in
1905: brightly stuccoed houses
sheltered by cypresses and
gaily painted fishing boats, all
bathed in the famous luminous
light, and washed by a gentle
sea. Other artists including
André Derain worked here
under Matisse's influence and
were dubbed *fauves* (wild
beasts) for their wild experiments with color. Art galleries
and souvenir shops now fill
the cobbled streets, but this
small fishing port has changed
surprisingly little since then,
with anchovies still its main
business. Three salting houses
are evidence of this tradition.

Three sheltered beaches,
both pebble and sand, nestle
around the harbor, dominated
by the bulk of the **Château
Royal**, which forms part of the
harbor wall. It was first built
by the Knights Templar in
the 13th century, and
Collioure became the main
port of entry for Perpignan,
remaining under the rule of
Spanish Aragon until France
took over in 1659. The outer
fortifications were reinforced
ten years later by Vauban,
who demolished much of the
original town in the process.
Today the château can be

toured, or visited for its
exhibitions of modern art.

The **Eglise Notre-Dame-
des-Anges** on Collioure's
quayside was rebuilt in the
17th century to replace the
church that was destroyed by
Vauban. A former lighthouse
was incorporated into the
fabric of the new church as a
bell tower. Inside the church
are no fewer than five
Baroque altarpieces by
Joseph Sunyer and other
Catalan masters of the genre.

Be warned that Collioure
is extremely popular in July
and August, with visitors cram-
ming the tiny streets. Long
lines of traffic are possible,
too, though the building of
another route, the D86, has
helped to ease congestion.

⚓ **Château Royal**
🅲 *04 68 82 06 43.* 🔵 *daily.* ⬤ *Jan 1,
May 1, Dec 25.* 📷

Elne ❾

Pyrénées-Orientales. 🏠 6,500.
🚊 🚌 🛈 *place Sant-Jordi (04 68 22
05 07).* 🛥 *Mon, Wed & Fri.*

T HE ANCIENT TOWN of Elne
accommodated Hannibal
and his elephants in 218 BC
on his epic journey to Rome,
and was one of the most important towns in Roussillon
until the 16th century. Today
it is famed for the 11th-century
**Cathédrale de Ste-Eulalie et
Ste-Julie**, with its superb
cloister. Milky blue-veined
marble has been carved into
exquisite capitals, embellished
with a riot of flowers, figures
and arabesques. The side nearest the cathedral dates from
the 1100s; the remaining three are
13th- to 14th-century. From the
front of the cathedral are views
of the vines and orchards of
the surrounding plain.

Carved capital at Elne, showing "The Dream of the Magi"

A wide, sandy beach near Perpignan, ideally suited to family vacations

Perpignan ⑩

Pyrénées-Orientales. 🏠 108,000.
★ 🚍 ⊟ 🛈 Palais des Congrès (04
68 66 30 30). 🅐 daily.

CATALAN PERPIGNAN has a
distinctly southern feel,
with palm trees lining the Têt
River promenade, house and
shop façades painted vibrant
turquoise and pink, and the
streets of the Arab quarter
selling aromatic spices, couscous and paella.

Today Perpignan is the
vibrant capital of Roussillon,
and has an important position
on the developing Mediterranean sunbelt. But it reached
its zenith in the 13th and 14th
centuries under the kings of
Majorca and the kings of
Aragon, who controlled great
swathes of northern Spain and
southern France. Their vast
Palais des Rois de Majorque
still straddles a substantial
area in the southern part of

the city. Perpignan's strong
Catalan identity is evident
during the twice-weekly
summer celebrations when
the Sardana is danced in
the place de la Loge. It is a
key Catalan
symbol, danced
proudly by
young and old.
Arms raised,
concentric circles of
dancers keep step to the
heady accompaniment of
a Catalan woodwind band.

One of Perpignan's finest
buildings, the **Loge de
Mer**, lies at the head of
the square. Built in 1397 to
house the Maritime
Exchange, only the eastern
section retains the original
Gothic design. The rest of
the building was
rebuilt in Renaissance
style in 1540 with
sumptuous carved
wooden ceilings and sculpted
window frames. While visitors

**Devout Christ
in St-Jean**

are sometimes offended by
the sight of a fast-food restaurant inside, the result is that
the Loge de Mer has avoided
becoming a hushed mu-
seum piece. Instead, it
remains the
center of
Perpignan life
– elegant cafés
cluster around it,
producing a constant
buzz of activity.

Next door is the **Hôtel
de Ville** with its stone
façade and wrought-iron
gates. Inside, parts of the
arcaded courtyard date
back to 1315; at the center
is Aristide Maillol's allegorical sculpture, *The
Mediterranean* (1950).

To the east is the laby-
rinthine cathedral
quarter of St-Jean,
made up of small
streets and squares
containing some fine 14th-
and 15th-century buildings.

🏠 Cathédrale St-Jean
Place de Gambetta.
Topped by a wrought-iron
belfry, this cathedral was
begun in 1324 and was finally
completed in 1509. It is
constructed almost entirely
from river pebbles layered
with red brick, a style
common throughout the
region due to the scarcity of
other building materials.

Inside the gloomy interior,
the nave is flanked by gilded
altarpieces and painted wood-
en statues, with a massive pre-
Romanesque marble font. A
cloistered cemetery adjoins
the Church and the Chapel of

THE ANNUAL PROCESSION DE LA SANCH

There is a very Catalan
atmosphere in Perpignan
during the annual Good
Friday procession of the
Confraternity of La Sanch
(Brotherhood of the Holy
Blood). Originally dedicated
to the comfort of condemned
prisoners in the 15th century,
members of the brotherhood
still wear macabre red or
black robes as they carry
sacred relics and the crucifix
from the Chapel of the
Devout Christ to the
cathedral.

the Devout Christ with its precious, poignantly realistic medieval wooden Crucifixion. The cathedral replaced the 11th-century church of St-Jean-le-Vieux, whose superb Romanesque doorway can be glimpsed through the gates to the left of the main entrance.

🏛 Palais des Rois de Majorque

2 rue des Archers. 📞 04 68 34 48 29. 🕐 daily. 🔴 Jan 1, May 1, Nov 1, Dec 25. 🈹

Access to the vast 13th-century fortified palace of the Kings of Majorca is as circuitous today as it was intended to be for invading soldiers. Flights of steps zigzag within the sheer red-brick ramparts, begun in the 15th century and added to successively over the next two centuries. Eventually, the elegant gardens and substantial castle within are revealed, entered by way of the Tour de l'Hommage, from the top of which is a panoramic view of the city, mountains and sea.

The palace itself is built around a central arcaded courtyard, flanked on one side by the Salle de Majorque, a great hall with a triple fireplace and giant Gothic arched windows. Adjacent, two royal chapels built one above the other show southern Gothic style at its best: pointed arches, patterned frescoes and elaborate tilework demonstrating a distinct Moorish influence. The fine rose marble doorway of the upper King's Chapel is a typical example of the Roussillon Romanesque style,

Courtyard in the Hôtel de Ville

although the sculpted capitals are Gothic. Today the great courtyard is sometimes used for concerts.

🏛 Musée Catalan

Le Castillet. 📞 04 68 35 42 05. 🕐 Wed–Mon. 🔴 Jan 1, May 1, Nov 1. 🈹

The red-brick tower and pink belfry of the Castillet, built as the town gate in 1368, was at one time a prison and is all that remains of the town walls. It now houses a collection of Catalan craft objects, including agricultural implements, kitchen furniture, looms, and glazed terra-cotta pots used for storing water and oil.

🏛 Musée Hyacinthe-Rigaud

16 rue de l'Ange. 📞 04 68 35 81 23. 🕐 Wed–Mon. 🔴 public hols. 🈹

This magnificent 17th-century mansion has an eclectic art collection dominated by the work of Hyacinthe Rigaud (1659–1743), who was born in Perpignan and was court painter to both Louis XIV and Louis XV.

The first floor has a room of portraits, including work by David, Greuze, and Ingres; the Dufy, Picasso and Maillol room; and the Primitifs Catalan, 14th–16th-century Catalan and Spanish paintings, among them the *Retable de la Trinité* (1489) by the Master of Canapost.

The museum also represents the 20th century: Alechinsky, Appel and others from the late 1940s European Cobra movement; the Catalan artist Pierre Daura; and modern Roussillon painters like Brune, Terrus and Violet.

Fort tower and ramparts, Salses

Salses ⑪

Pyrénées-Orientales. 🚉 2,500. 🚉
🚌 ℹ Place de la République (04 68 38 66 13). 🛒 Wed.

LOOKING LIKE a giant sand-castle against the ocher earth of the Corbières vineyards, the **Fort de Salses** stands at the old frontier of Spain and France. It guards the narrow passage between the mountains and the Mediterranean lagoons, and was built by King Ferdinand of Aragon between 1497 and 1506 to defend Spain's possession of Roussillon. Its massive walls and rounded towers are a classic example of Spanish military architecture, designed to deflect the new threat posed by gunpowder.

Inside were underground stabling for 300 horses and a subterranean passageway around the inner courtyard.

There is a wonderful view from the keep over the lagoons and surrounding coastline.

The pebble and red-brick Cathédrale de St-Jean in Perpignan

Vineyards covering the hilly terrain of the Corbières

Corbières ⑫

Aude. ✈ Perpignan. 🚆 Narbonne, Carcassonne, Lézignan-Corbières. 🚌 Narbonne, Carcassonne, Lézignan-Corbières. ℹ Lézignan-Corbières (04 68 27 05 42).

STILL ONE of the wildest parts of France, with few roads, let alone villages, the Corbières is best known for its wine and the great craggy hulks of the Cathar castles *(see p481)*. Much of the land is untamed *garrigue* (scrubland), fragrant with honeysuckle and broom; promising south-facing slopes have been cleared and are planted with vines.

To the south are the spectacular medieval castles of **Peyrepertuse** and **Quéribus**, the latter one of the last Cathar strongholds. **Villerouge-Termenes** celebrates its turbulent past with an annual medieval banquet. To the west is the barren, uninhabited Razès area in the upper Aude Valley. Its best-kept secret is the village of **Alet-les-Bains**, with beautifully preserved half-timbered houses and the remains of a Benedictine abbey, battle-scarred from the Wars of Religion.

Narbonne ⑬

Aude. 🚶 48,000. 🚆 🚌 ℹ Place Roger Salengro (04 68 65 15 60). 🛳 Thu & Sun.

NARBONNE is a medium-sized, cheerful town profiting from the booming wine region that surrounds it. The town is bisected by the tree-shaded Canal de la Robine; to the north is the restored medieval quarter with many elegant shops and good restaurants. Located here is one of Narbonne's most intriguing tourist attractions, the **Horreum**. These underground granaries and grain chutes date from the 1st century BC, when Narbonne was a major port and capital of the largest Roman province in Gaul.

The town prospered through the Middle Ages until the 15th century, when the harbor silted up and the course of the Aude River changed, taking Narbonne's fortunes with it. By then, an important bishopric had been established and an ambitious cathedral project, modeled on the great Gothic cathedrals of the North, was underway. However, the full

grandiose design was abandoned and just the chancel, begun in 1272, became the **Cathédrale St-Just et St-Pasteur** we see today.

It is still enormous, enhanced by 14th-century sculptures, fine stained-glass windows and an 18th-century carved organ. Aubusson and Gobelin tapestries adorn the walls, and the Chapel of the Anonciade houses a treasury of manuscripts, jeweled reliquaries and tapestries.

The unfinished transept now forms a courtyard, and between the cathedral and the adjacent **Palais des Archevêques** (Archbishops' Palace) lie cloisters with four magnificent galleries of 14th-century vaulting.

This huge palace and cathedral complex dominates the center of Narbonne. Between the Palais des Archevêques' massive 14th-century towers is the town hall, with a 19th-century Neo-Gothic façade by Viollet le Duc *(see p190)*, the architect who so determinedly

The vaulted chancel of Cathédrale St-Just et St-Pasteur in Narbonne

CANAL DU MIDI

From Sète to Toulouse the 240-km (149-mile) Canal du Midi winds its way between plane trees, vineyards and sleepy villages. The complex system of locks, aqueducts and bridges is a remarkable feat of engineering, built by the Béziers salt-tax baron Paul Riquet. Completed in 1681, it encouraged Languedoc trade and was a vital link, via the Garonne River, between the Atlantic and the Mediterranean. Today it is used by tourist barges (04 67 22 81 00).

Tranquil waterway of the Canal du Midi

The Cistercian Abbaye de Fontfroide (1093), southwest of Narbonne

🏛 **Musée Lapidaire**
Eglise Notre-Dame de Lamourguié.
📞 04 68 65 53 58. ⏲ Jul–Aug:
daily. ● for restoration until 2004.
🖼 ♿

Environs

Southwest (13 km/8 miles), the Cistercian **Abbaye de Fontfroide** has an elegant cloister. The abbey is tucked away in a quiet valley, surrounded by cypress trees.

Golfe du Lion ⓮

Aude, Hérault. 🚶 🚆 🚌 Montpellier.
🚢 Sète. ℹ La Grande Motte (04 67 56 42 00).

LANGUEDOC-Roussillon's shore line (100 km/65 miles long) forms an almost unbroken sweep of sandy beach. Only at its southern limits does it break into the rocky inlets of the Cote Vermeille. Purpose-built resorts created since the 1960s emphasize eco-friendly, low-rise family accommodation, some in local styles, others with imaginative architecture (some now look rather dated).

La Grand Motte marina has distinctive ziggurat-style buildings (see p485). **Cap d'Agde** has Europe's largest naturist quarter. Inland **Agde**, founded by ancient Greek traders, is built of black basalt and has a fortified cathedral. **Port Leucate** and **Port Bacarès** are ideal for watersports. An older town is **Sète** (see p482). A feature of the flat Languedoc coast is its étanges – large, shallow lagoons. Those nearest the Camargue are the haunt of thousands of wading birds.

restored medieval France. The palace itself is divided into the Palais Vieux (Old Palace) and the Palais Neuf (New Palace). Narbonne's most important museums are in the Palais Neuf, on the left as you enter through the low medieval arches of the passage de l'Ancre. The **Musée d'Archéologie et de Pré-histoire** collection includes fragments of Narbonne's Roman heritage, from milestones and parts of the original walls to an assemblage of domestic objects, coins, tools and glassware. The **Chapelle de la Madeleine** is decorated with a 14th-century wall painting and houses a collection of Greek vases, sarcophagi and mosaics.

In the archbishops' former apartments is the **Musée d'Art et d'Histoire**, which is as interesting for its luxurious furnishings and richly decorated ceilings as for its art collection. This includes some fine paintings by Canaletto, Brueghel, Boucher and Veronese as well as a large selection of local earthenware.

South of the Canal de la Robine are a number of fine mansions, including the Renaissance **Maison des Trois Nourrices** on the corner of rue des Trois-Nourrices and rue Edgard-Quinet. Nearby is the **Musée Lapidaire**, with architectural fragments from Gallo-Roman Narbonne, and the 13th-century Gothic **Basilique St-Paul-Serge**. The present building retains the crypt and some sarcophagi of an earlier church on this site.

🏛 Horreum

Rue Rouget-de-l'Isle. 📞 04 68 32 45 30. ⏲ Apr–Sep: daily; Oct–Mar: Tue–Sun. ● Jan 1, May 1, Nov 1 & 11, Dec 25. 🖼

🏛 **Musée d'Archéologie et de Préhistoire/Musée d'Art et d'Histoire**
Palais des Archevêques. 📞 04 68 90 30 54. ⏲ Apr–Sep: daily; Oct–Mar: Tue–Sun. ● Jan 1, May 1, Nov 1 & 11, Dec 25. 🖼

A wide, sandy beach on the Cap d'Agde

Carcassonne ⓯

THE CITADEL OF CARCASSONNE is a perfectly restored medieval town. It crowns a steep bank above the Aude River, a fairy-tale sight of turrets and ramparts overlooking the Basse Ville below. The strategic position of the citadel, between the Atlantic and the Mediterranean and on the corridor between the Iberian Peninsula and the rest of Europe, led to its original settlement, consolidated by the Romans in the 2nd century BC. It became a key element in medieval military conflicts. At its zenith in the 12th century, it was ruled by the Trencavels, who built the château and cathedral. Military advances and the Treaty of the Pyrenees in 1659, which relocated the French-Spanish border, left its superb fortifications obsolete, and it fell into decline. The attentions of architectural historian Viollet-le-Duc *(see p190)* led to its restoration in the 19th century.

The Restored Citadel
Restoration of La Cité has always been controversial. Critics complain it looks too new, favoring a more romantic ruin.

★ **Château Comtal**
A fortress within a fortress, the château has a moat, five towers and defensive wooden galleries on the walls.

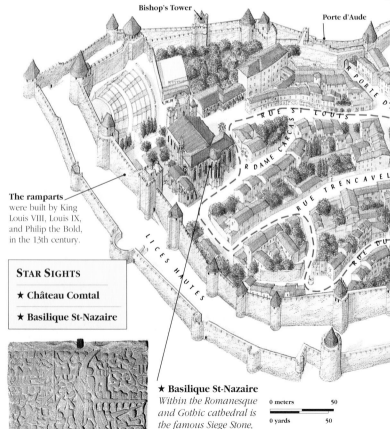

Bishop's Tower

Porte d'Aude

RUE ST LOUIS

R DAME CARCAS

RUE TRENCAVEL

R PORTE D'A

RUE DU

LICES HAUTES

The ramparts
were built by King Louis VIII, Louis IX, and Philip the Bold, in the 13th century.

STAR SIGHTS

★ **Château Comtal**

★ **Basilique St-Nazaire**

★ **Basilique St-Nazaire**
Within the Romanesque and Gothic cathedral is the famous Siege Stone, said to depict the 1209 Siege of Carcassonne by crusaders.

| 0 meters | 50 |
| 0 yards | 50 |

KEY

– – – Suggested route

RELIGIOUS PERSECUTION

Carcassonne's strategic position meant it was often at the center of religious conflict. The Cathars *(see p481)* were given sanctuary here in 1209 by Raymond-Roger Trencavel when besieged by Simon de Montfort in his crusade against heresy. In the 14th century the Inquisition continued to root out the Cathars. This painting depicts intended victims.

Les Emmurés de Carcassonne,
J.P. Laurens

VISITORS' CHECKLIST

Aude. 🏠 45,000. ✈ 4 km
(2 miles) W Carcassonne. 🚢
Port du Canal du Midi (04 68 71
74 55). 🚌 bd de Varsovie. ℹ
Tour Narbonnaise, La Cité (04 68
10 24 36/30). 🛒 Tue, Thu & Sat.
🎭 Festival de la Cité (Jul);
l'Embrasement de la Cité (Jul);
Les Spectacles Médiévaux (two
weeks, mid-Aug). **Château
Comtal** ⏰ daily. ● Jan 1,
May 1, Nov 1 & 11, Dec 25. 🎟
W www.tourisme.fr/carcassonne

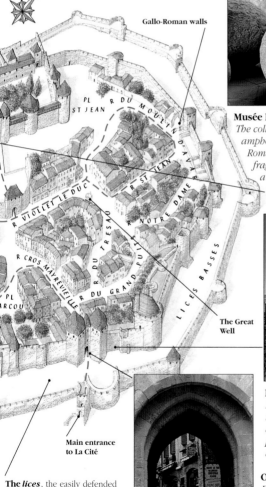

Gallo-Roman walls

PL ST JEAN
R DU MOULIN D'AVAR
R ST JEAN
R VIOLLET LE DUC
R NOTRE DAME
R CROS MAYREVIEILLE
R DU TRESAU
R DU GRAND PUITS
LICES BASSES
PL ARCOU

The Great Well

Main entrance to La Cité

The *lices*, the easily defended spaces between the inner and outer ramparts, were also used for jousting, crossbow practice and for storage of timber and other materials.

Musée Lapidaire
The collection includes Roman amphorae and terra-cotta, Romanesque murals and fragments from the cathedral, a set of Gothic windows and these medieval stone missiles.

Porte Narbonnaise
Flanked by two sandstone towers, built in 1280, the defenses included two portcullises, two iron doors, a moat and a drawbridge.

Old City Entrance
Entering La Cité is still a step back in time, although it is one of France's top tourist destinations, filled with souvenir shops.

Béziers with its medieval cathedral, seen from Pont Vieux in the southwest

Minerve

Hérault. 🏘 100. 🛈 place du Monument (04 68 91 81 43).

IN THE PARCHED, arid hills of the Minervois, surrounded by grapevines and not much else, Minerve appears defiant on its rocky outcropping at the confluence of the Cesse and Briant rivers. It is defended by what the Minervois call the "Candela" (Candle), an octagonal tower, which is all that remains of the medieval château. In 1210, the small town resisted the vengeful Simon de Montfort, scourge of the Cathars, in a siege lasting seven weeks. This culminated in the execution of 140 Cathars, who were burned at the stake after refusing to renounce their faith.

Today visitors enter Minerve by a high bridge spanning the gorge. Turn right and follow the route of the Cathars past the Romanesque arch of the Porte des Templiers to the 12th-century **Eglise St-Etienne**. Outside the church is a crudely carved dove, symbol of the Cathars, and within is a 5th-century white marble altar table, one of the oldest artifacts in the region.

A rocky path follows the riverbed below the town, where the water has cut out caves and two bridges – the Grand Pont and the Petit Pont – from the soft limestone.

Béziers **⑰**

Hérault. 🏘 71,000. ✈ 🚉 🚌 🛈 Palais des Congrès, 29 av Saint Saëns (04 67 76 47 00). 🗓 Fri.

FAMOUS FOR its bullfights and rugby, and the wine of the surrounding region, Béziers has several other points of interest. It seems turned in on itself, its roads leading up to the massive 14th-century **Cathédrale St-Nazaire**, with its fine sculpture, stained glass and frescoes. In 1209, several thousand citizens were massacred in the crusade against the Cathars. The papal legate's troops were ordered not to discriminate between Catholics and Cathars, but to "Kill them all. God will recognize his own!"

Statue of the engineer Paul Riquet in the allées Paul Riquet, Béziers

The **Musée du Biterrois** holds exhibitions on local history, wine and the Canal du Midi, engineered in the late 17th century by Paul Riquet, Béziers' most famous son (see p476). His statue presides over the allées Paul Riquet, the broad esplanade at the foot of the hill. This is lined by two double rows of plane trees and large canopied restaurants, a civilized focus to this otherwise businesslike town.

🏛 **Musée du Biterrois**
Caserne St-Jacques. 📞 04 67 36 71 01. ⏰ Tue–Sun. ⚫ Jan 1, May 1, Dec 25. 🎟 ♿

Environs
Overlooking the Béziers plain and the mountains to the north is Oppidum d'Ensérune, a superb Roman site with substantial foundations. The **Musée de l'Oppidum d'Ensérune** has a good archaeological collection, from Celtic, Greek and Roman vases to jewelry, funeral fragments and weapons.

The **Château de Raissac** (between Béziers and Lignan) houses an unusual 19th-century faïence museum and modern workshop in its stables (Tue–Sat).

🏛 **Musée de l'Oppidum d'Ensérune**
Nissan lez Ensérune. 📞 04 67 37 01 23. ⏰ daily (mid-Sep–mid-May: Tue–Sun). ⚫ public hols. 🎟 ♿ limited.

The Cathars

THE CATHARS (from Greek *katharos*, meaning pure) were a 13th-century Christian sect critical of corruption in the established church. Cathar dissent flourished in independent Languedoc as an expression of separatism, but the rebellion was rapidly exploited for political purposes. Peter II of Aragon was eager to annex Languedoc, and Philippe II of France joined forces with the pope to crush the Cathar heretics in a crusade led by Simon de Montfort in 1209. This heralded the start of over a century of ruthless killing and torture.

CATHAR CASTLES
The Cathars took refuge in the defensive castles of the Corbières and Ariège. Peyrepertuse is one of the most remote, difficult to get to even today: a long, narrow stone citadel hacked from a high, craggy peak over 609 m (2,000 ft) high.

Cathars (also known as Albigensians) believed in the duality of good and evil. They considered the material world entirely evil. To be truly pure they had to renounce the world and be nonviolent, vegetarian and sexually abstinent.

The crusade against the Cathars was vicious. Heretics' land was promised to the crusaders by the pope, who assured forgiveness in advance of their crimes. In 1209, 20,000 citizens were massacred in Béziers and, the following year, 140 were burned to death in Minerve. In 1244, 225 Cathars died defending one of their last fortresses at Montségur.

CATHAR COUNTRY
Castles and towns with a Cathar association, some of them spectacular sites, are concentrated in Languedoc-Roussillon, the center of Catharism in the Middle Ages.

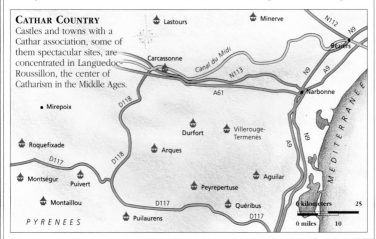

Lastours · Minerve · N112 · N9 · Béziers · Carcassonne · Canal du Midi · N113 · N9 · A9 · A61 · Narbonne · Mirepoix · D118 · Durfort · Villerouge-Termenès · Roquefixade · D117 · D118 · Arques · Aguilar · Montségur · Puivert · Peyrepertuse · MEDITERRANEAN · Montaillou · D117 · Quéribus · 0 kilometers 25 · PYRENEES · Puilaurens · D117 · 0 miles 10

The impressive Grand Hotel *(see p571)* on quai de la Résistance, Sète

Sète ⑱

Hérault. 🏙 *40,000.* 🚉 🚌 ⛴
🛈 *60 Grand' Rue Mario Roustan
(04 67 74 71 71).* 🛒 *Mon, Wed–Fri.*

SÈTE IS A MAJOR FISHING and
industrial port. It has a
gutsier, more raffish air than
much of the leisure-oriented
Mediterranean, with its shops
selling ships' lamps and

**Cimetière Marin in Sète, burial
place of the poet Paul Valéry**

propellers, and its quayside
restaurants full of hungry
sailors demolishing vast
platters of mussels, oysters
and sea snails straight off the
boat. Most of Sète's restaurants can be found in a stroll
along the Grand Canal, with
its Italianate houses painted
in pastel colors and with
wrought-iron balconies overlooking Sète's network of
canals and bridges. Boisterous
water-jousting tournaments,
which date back to 1666, form
part of the patron saint's
festival in August *(see p33).*
   The new **Musée
International des Arts
Modestes** displays everyday
objects (including some by
well-known contemporary
designers) in amusing new
contexts, within a renovated
canalside warehouse.
   Above the town is the
Cimetière Marin, where
Sète's most famous son, poet
Paul Valéry (1871-1945), is
buried. There is a small museum and breathtaking views
of the coast and the mountains.

🏛 **Musée International des
Arts Modestes**
23 quai du Maréchal de Lattre de
Tassigny. 🕻 *04 67 18 64 00.*
🕙 *Jul–Aug: daily; Sep–Jun:
Wed–Mon.* ● *public hols.* 🅿 ♿

Pézenas ⑲

Hérault. 🏙 *8,000.* 🚉 🛈 *place
Gambetta (04 67 98 36 40).* 🛒 *Sat.*

PÉZENAS IS A COMPACT and
charming little town easily
appreciated in a gentle stroll of
its main sights and abounding
in small details, fragmentary
evidence of Pézenas' past
glory as the seat of local
government in the 16th–17th
centuries. Then the town also
played artistic host to glittering troupes of musicians and
actors, including Molière.
   Best of all are the glimpses
of fine houses through courtyard doorways, such as the
Hôtel des Barons de Lacoste,
at 8 rue François-Oustrin,
with its beautiful stone
staircase, and the **Maison des
Pauvres** at 12 rue Alfred
Sabatier, with its three
galleries and staircase.
   Look for the medieval shop
window on rue Triperie-Vieille,
and within the 14th-century
Porte Faugères (Faugères
Gate) the narrow streets of
the Jewish ghetto, which has
a chilling feeling of enclosure.
Shops selling antiques, secondhand goods and books abound.
Around the town, vines cover
the prosperous plain as far as
the eye can see.

**The stone foyer of the Hôtel des
Barons de Lacoste in Pézenas**

Parc Régional du Haut Languedoc ⓴

Hérault, Tarn. ✕ *Béziers.*
▣ *Béziers, Bédarieux.* ▣ *St-Pons-de-Thomières, Mazamet, Lamalou-les-Bains.* ⓱ *St-Pons-de-Thomières (04 67 97 06 65).*
ⓦ *www.vivrehautlanguedoc.com*

THE HIGH LIMESTONE plateaus and wooded slopes of upper Languedoc are a world away from the coast. From the Montagne Noire, a mountainous region between Béziers and Castres, up into the Cévennes is a landscape of remote sheep farms, eroded rock formations and deep river gorges. Much of this area has been designated the Parc Régional du Haut Languedoc, the second largest of the French national parks after Ecrins.

St-Pons-de-Thomières is the entrance, with access to forest and mountain trails for walking and riding, plus a wildlife research center, where one can glimpse the mouflons (wild mountain sheep), eagles and wild boar, which were once a common sight in the region.

If you take the D908 from St-Pons through the park you pass the village of **Olargues** with its 12th-century bridge over the Jaur River. **Lamalou-les-Bains**, on the park's eastern edge, is a small spa town with a restored Belle Epoque spa building and a theater and a soporifically slow pace.

Outside the park boundaries to the northeast there are spectacular natural phenomena. At the **Cirque de Navacelles**, the Vis River has joined up with itself, cutting out an entire island. On it sits the peaceful village of Navacelles, visible from the road higher up. The **Grotte des Demoiselles** is one of the most magnificent in an area full of caves, where you walk through a calcified world. A funicular train takes visitors from the foot of the mountain to the top.

The **Grotte de Clamouse** is also an extraordinary experience, the reflections from underground rivers and pools flickering on the cavern roofs, with stalagmites resembling dripping candles and stalactites soaring Gothic columns.

▨ Grotte des Demoiselles
St-Bauzille-de-Putois. ▮ *04 67 73 70 02.* ◯ *daily.* ⬤ *Jan 1, Dec 25.* ▨
▨ Grotte de Clamouse
Rte de St-Guilhem-le-Désert, St-Jean-de-Fos. ▮ *04 67 57 71 05.* ◯ *Feb–Oct: daily; Nov–Jan: Sun–Fri.* ▨

Apse of St-Guilhem-le-Désert

St-Guilhem-le-Désert ⓴

Hérault. ▨ *250.* ▣ ⓱ *Maison Communale (04 67 57 44 33).*

TUCKED AWAY in the Celette Mountains, St-Guilhem-le-Désert is no longer as remote as when Guillaume of Aquitaine retired here as a hermit in the 9th century. After a lifetime as a soldier, Guillaume received a fragment of the True Cross from Emperor Charlemagne and established a monastery in this ravine above the Hérault River.

Vestiges of the first 10th-century church have been discovered but most of the building is a superb example of 11th–12th-century Romanesque architecture. Its lovely apsidal chapels dominate the heights of the village, behind which the carved doorway opens onto a central square.

Within the church is a somber barrel-vaulted central aisle leading to the sunlit central apse. Only two galleries of the cloisters remain: the rest are in New York's Cloisters Museum, along with carvings from St-Michel-de-Cuxa (*see p471*).

Extraordinary limestone formations at the Grotte de Clamouse

MONTPELLIER CITY CENTER

Cathédrale de St-Pierre ⑤
Château d'Eau ①
CORUM ⑫
Hôtel de Manse ⑧
Hôtel de Mirman ⑨
Hôtel des Trésoriers
  de la Bourse ⑥
Jardin des Plantes ③
Musée Fabre ⑩
Musée
  Languedocien ⑦
Notre-Dame
  des Tables ⑪
Place de
  la Comédie ⑬
Promenade de Peyrou ②
Tour de la Babote ⑭
Tours des Pins ④

KEY

🅿 Parking

⛪ Church

0 meters 250
0 yards 250

Open-air café in the place de la Comédie, Montpellier

Montpellier ㉒

Hérault. 👥 250,000. 🚆 🚌 ✈
ℹ 30 allée Jean de Lattré de Tassigny
(04 67 60 60 60). 🕐 daily. 🎭 Festival
International Montpellier Danse
(Jun–Jul). 🌐 www.ot-montpellier.fr

MONTPELLIER is one of the liveliest and most progressive cities in the south, with a quarter of its population under 25. On a summer evening when its university is in session, it may seem more like a rock festival than the capital of Languedoc-Roussillon. The center of the action is the egg-shaped **Place de la Comédie**, known as "l'Oeuf," ("the egg") with its 19th-century opera house fronted by the Fontaine des Trois Graces and surrounded by buzzing cafés. An esplanade of plane trees and fountains leads to the **CORUM**, an opera and conference center typical of the city's brave new architectural projects. The best of these is Ricardo Bofill's Postmodern housing complex known as Antigone, which is modeled on St. Peter's in Rome.

Montpellier was founded relatively late for this region of ancient Roman towns, developing in the 10th century as a result of the spice trade with the Middle East. The city's medical school was founded in 1220, partly as a result of this cross-fertilization of knowledge between the two cultures, and remains one of the most respected in France.

Most of Montpellier was ravaged by the Wars of Religion in the 16th century. Only the **Tour de la Babote** and the **Tours des Pins** remain of the 12th-century fortifications. There are few fine churches, with the exception of the **Cathédrale de St-Pierre** and the 18th-century **Notre-Dame des Tables.**

Reconstruction in the 17th century included the building of mansions with elegant court-yards, stone staircases and balconies. Examples open to the public include **Hôtel de Manse** on rue Embouque-d'Or, **Hôtel de Mirman** near place des Martyrs de la Resistance and **Hôtel des Trésoriers de la Bourse**. The Hôtel des Lunaret houses the **Musée Languedocien** which exhibits Romanesque and prehistoric artifacts.

Another 17th-century building houses the **Musée Fabre,** with its collection of mainly

PONT DU GARD ← To Uzès

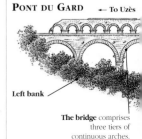

Left bank

The bridge comprises three tiers of continuous arches.

French paintings. Highlights include Courbet's famous *Bonjour M. Courbet*, Berthe Morisot's *L'Eté*, Robert Delaunay's *Nature Morte Portugaise*, and some evocative paintings of the region by Raoul Dufy and François Desnoyer.

A good place to view the city's position between mountains and sea is from the **Promenade de Peyrou**, a grand 18th-century square dominated by the **Château d'Eau** and the aqueduct that used to serve the city. Just to the north is the **Jardin des Plantes**, France's oldest botanical gardens (1593).

🏛 **Musée Languedocien**
7 rue Jacques Coeur. **[** *04 67 52 93 03.* **○** *Mon–Sat.* **●** *public hols.* **▓**

🏛 **Musée Fabre**
39 bd Bonne Nouvelle. **[** *04 67 14 83 00.* **○** *Tue–Sun (some temp. closures).*
● *Jan 1, May 1, Jul 14, Nov 1, Dec 25.*
▓ **&** **w** *www.ville-montpellier.fr*

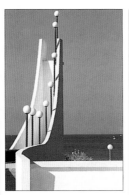

Château d'Eau, Montpellier

La Grande-Motte ㉓

Hérault. **🏃** *6,500.* **🚂** **🚌** *av Jean-Bene (04 67 56 42 00).* **🛒** *Sun (& Thu: mid-Jun–mid-Sep).*

Tʜᴇ ʙɪᴢᴀʀʀᴇ white towers of this modern marina exemplify the development of the Languedoc-Roussillon coast. One of a number of

La Grande-Motte

new cities on the lakes south of Montpellier, there are marinas and facilities for every kind of sport from tennis and golf to water sports, all flanked by golden beaches and pine forests. To the east are Le Grau-du-Roi, once a tiny fishing village, and Port-Camargue, with its big marina.

Aigues-Mortes ㉔

Gard. **🏃** *6,000.* **🚂** **🚌** **🛈** *Porte de la Gardette (04 66 53 73 00).*
🛒 *Wed & Sun.*

Tʜᴇ ʙᴇsᴛ ᴀᴘᴘʀᴏᴀᴄʜ to this perfectly preserved walled town is across the salt marshes of the Petite Camargue. Now marooned 5 km (3 miles) from the sea, the defenses of this once-important port have become a tourist experience, worth visiting more for the effect of the ensemble than for the tacky shops within. Aigues-Mortes ("Place of Dead Waters") was established by Louis XI in the 13th century to consolidate his power, and built according to a strict grid pattern. By climbing up the

Tour de Constance you can walk out onto the rectangular walls, that afford a superb view over the Camargue.

Environs
Across the salt lagoons to the northeast is **St-Gilles-du-Gard**, also once an important medieval port. Today it is worth a detour to see the superbly sculpted 12th-century façade of its abbey church. This was originally established by the monks of Cluny Abbey as a shrine to St. Gilles, and a resting place on the famous pilgrimage route to Santiago de Compostela *(see pp390–91)*.

Pont du Gard ㉕

Gard. **[** *04 66 37 51 10.* **🚌** *from Nîmes.*

Nᴏ ᴀᴍᴏᴜɴᴛ ᴏꜰ ꜰᴀᴍᴇ can diminish the first sight of the 2,000-year-old Pont du Gard. The Romans themselves considered it the best testimony to the greatness of the Roman Empire, and at 49 m (160 ft) it was the highest bridge they ever built. It is made from enormous blocks of stone, hauled into place with an ingenious system of pulleys and a vast phalanx of slave labor. The huge build-up of calcium in the water channels suggests that the aqueduct was in continuous use for 400–500 years.

The aqueduct, which originally carried water to Nîmes along a 50-km (31-mile) route from the springs at **Uzès**. This charming town has an arcaded marketplace and several fine medieval towers including the lovely 12th-century Tour Fenestrelle.

A museum recently opened on site (08 20 90 33 30).

Water channel ———

To Nîmes →

Right bank

Roman inscriptions
include a damaged phallus carving as a good luck symbol.

Some stones weighed up to six tonnes.

Nîmes ㉖

Listed number one on the tourist map of Nîmes is the bus stop designed by Philippe Starck, who is also credited with reworking the city's pedestrian zone. Such innovations are part of the city's current design renaissance. Architectural projects range from imaginative housing to a glittering new arts complex, under the guidance of a dynamic mayor. An important crossroads in the ancient world, Nîmes is equally well-known for its Roman antiquities such as the amphitheater, the best preserved of its kind. The city is also famous for its festivals and bullfights. These are good times to see the rest of Nîmes with its museums, archaeological collections and Old Town of narrow streets and intimate squares.

Arches of the Roman amphitheater

Historic Nîmes

Nîmes has always had a turbulent history, and suffered particularly during the 16th-century Wars of Religion when the Romanesque **Cathédrale Notre-Dame et St-Castor** was badly damaged. During the 17th and 18th centuries the town prospered from textile manufacturing, one of the most enduring products being denim, or "de Nîmes." Many of the fine houses of this period have been restored, and elegant examples can be seen on rue de l'Aspic, rue des Marchands and rue de Chapitre in the Old Town. Just outside the town center is the futuristic apartment building, **Nemausus I**.

The Roman gate, the **Porte Auguste**, built 20 years before the temple of **Maison Carrée**, was once part of one

Jug from Musée Archéologique

of the longest city walls in Gaul. Of the original arches still standing, two (large) were for carts and chariots and two (smaller) ones for pedestrians. The other major Roman remnant is the **Castellum**, where water used to arrive from the Pont du Gard (see p485). From the Castellum it was distributed around the city through thick pipes.

🌸 Jardin de la Fontaine

Quai de la Fontaine. ⬭ daily. ♿
When the Romans arrived in Nîmes, they found a town established by the Gauls, centered on source of a spring. They named the town Nemausus, after their river god. In the 18th century, formal gardens were constructed,

Jardin de la Fontaine, with a view over the city

Sights at a Glance

and a network of limpid pools and cool stone terraces remains. High above the garden on Mont Cavalier is the octagonal Tour Magne, once a key part of the Roman walls.

Arms of the city in a sculpture by Martial Raysse

♁ Les Arènes

Bd des Arènes. **📞** *04 66 76 72 77.* ◯ *daily.* ● *Jan 1, May 1, Dec 25 & on performance days.* 🎫 ♿

All roads lead to the amphitheater, Les Arènes. Built at the end of the 1st century AD, the design of the oval arena and tiers of stone seats accommodated huge crowds of up to 25,000 spectators. Today it is in use again, a perfect spot for concerts, sporting events and bullfights.

🏛 Maison Carrée

Pl de la Maison Carrée. **📞** *04 66 36 26 76.* ◯ *daily.* ● *publ hols.* Square House is a very prosaic name for this elegant Roman temple, the pride of Nîmes. Built between 2-3 AD, it is one of the best preserved in the world, with fluted Corinthian columns and a sculpted frieze.

🏛 Musée des Beaux Arts

Rue Cité Foulc. **📞** *04 66 67 38 21.* ◯ *Tue–Sun.* ● *Jan 1, May 1, Nov 11, Dec 25.* ♿

This fine arts museum houses an eclectic collection of Dutch, French, Italian and Flemish works, notably Jacopo Bassano's *Susanna and the Elders*, and the *Mystic Marriage of St. Catherine* by Michele Giambono. The Gallo-Roman mosaic of *The Marriage of Admetus*, discovered in 1882, is displayed on the main floor.

🏛 Musée Archéologique

Musée d'Histoire Naturelle, 13 bis bd Amiral Courbet. **📞** *04 66 76 74 80.* ◯ *Tue–Sun.* ● *Jan 1, May 1, Nov 11, Dec 25.* 🎫

The museum's collection of Roman statues, ceramics, glass, coins and mosaics is housed in Nîmes' natural history museum. The exhibits include important Iron Age menhir statues.

VISITORS' CHECKLIST

Gard. ⚑ *137,000.* ✈ *12 km (7.5 miles) SSE Nîmes.* 🚉 *bd Talabot (08 36 35 35 35).* 🚌 *rue St Félicité (04 66 29 52 00).* 🛈 *6 rue Auguste (04 66 58 38 00).* ⛪ *Mon, Fri, Sun.* 🎭 *Ferias d'Hiver (Feb), de Pentecôte (Pentecost), des Vendanges (Sep).* 🌐 *www.ot-nimes.fr*

The Maison Carrée, now a museum

🏛 Carré d'Art

Place de la Maison Carrée. **📞** *04 66 76 35 35.* ◯ *Tue–Sun.* ● *Jan 1, May 1, Nov 1, Dec 25.* 🎫 ♿

Nîmes' controversial arts complex, by the British architect Sir Norman Foster, opened in 1993. Five floors of this glass and steel temple, that was built in tribute to the Maison Carrée opposite, lie underground. The complex incorporates a library, a roof-terrace restaurant around a huge glass atrium, and the Musée d'Art Contemporain. The museum's 300 works cover the main European art movements from the 1960s on, and include works by Raysse, Boltanski and Lavier for France.

KEY

🅿 Parking

🛈 Tourist information

✝ Church

0 meters	250
0 yards	250

Bullfight at Les Arènes in Nîmes

PROVENCE AND THE CÔTE D'AZUR

BOUCHES-DU-RHÔNE · VAUCLUSE · VAR
ALPES-DE-HAUTE-PROVENCE · ALPES-MARITIMES

FROM ITS HERB-SCENTED HILLS *to its yacht-filled harbors, no other region of France fires the imagination as strongly as Provence. The vivid landscape and luminous light have inspired artists and writers from Van Gogh to Picasso, F. Scott Fitzgerald to Pagnol.*

The borders of Provence are defined by nature: to the west, the Rhône; south, the Mediterranean; and north, where the olive trees end. To the east are the Alps and a border which has shifted over the centuries between France and Italy. Within is a contrasting terrain of plummeting gorges, Camargue saltflats, lavender fields and sun-drenched beaches.

Past visitors have left their mark. In Orange and Arles, the buildings of Roman *Provincia* are still in use. Fortified villages like Èze were built to withstand the Saracen pirates who plagued the coast in the 6th century.

In the 19th century, rich Europeans sought winter warmth on the Riviera; by the 1920s, high society was in residence all year, and their elegant villas remain. The warm sunlight nurtures intense flavors and colors. Peppers, garlic and olives transform a netful of Mediterranean fish into that vibrant epitome of Provençal cuisine, *bouillabaisse*.

The image of Provence bathed in sunshine is marred only when the bitter Mistral wind scours the land. It has shaped a people as hardy as the olive tree, yet quick to embrace life to the full the moment the sun returns.

Cap Martin, seen from the village of Roquebrune

◁ **Lavender fields near the Gorges du Verdon**

Exploring Provence

THIS SUN-DRENCHED southeastern region is France's most popular vacation destination. Sunworshippers cram the beaches in the summer months, and entertainment includes opera, dance and jazz festivals, bull fights, casinos and *boules* games. Inland is a paradise for walkers and nature lovers, with remote mountain plateaux, perched villages and dramatic river gorges.

Promenade des Anglais, Nice

To Valence
St-Étienne

Rhône

VAISON-
LA-ROMAINE ❷

ORANGE ❸

Aigues

MONT VENTOUX ❶

SISTERO

D5

D938

D974

D950

D12

❹

❻ CARPENTRAS

D51

CHÂTEAUNEUF-
DU-PAPE

FONTAINE-
DE-VAUCLUSE ❼

To Nîmes

❺ AVIGNON

❽

N100

GORDES

D57

D973

❾ LUBERON

TARASCON ⓬

❿

ST-RÉMY-
DE-PROVENCE

Durance

Canal de Provence

LES-BAUX-DE-PROVENCE ⓫

ARLES ⓭

N113

SALON-
DE-PROVENCE

D5

To Montpellier

D570

D35

D5

A54

A7

Rhône

⓮

CAMARGUE

⓯ AIX-EN-
PROVENCE

D80

A55

MARSEILLE

⓰

D559

A50

⓱

CASSIS

To Briançon

D900

BARCELONNETTE

D64

D2205

MERCANTOUR

DIGNE-LES-BAINS

N85

Bléone

Verdon

Var

N204

N85

ALPES-MARITIMES **41**

23

D907

N85

D2565

N202

MENTON **42**

GORGES DU LOUP

GORGES DU VERDON

D2211

ÉZE

ROQUEBRUNE-CAP-MARTIN **40**

N85

33

VENCE

ST-PAUL-DE-VENCE

MONACO

39 **43**

34

D21

35

36 **37**

VILLEFRANCHE-SUR-MER

D30

D557

GRASSE **26**

BIOT

VALLAURIS

32

38 NICE

CAP FERRAT

31

CAGNES-SUR-MER

DRAGUIGNAN

30

29 ANTIBES

A84

27

28 CAP D'ANTIBES

Argens

CANNES

PROVENÇALE

FRÉJUS **24**

N7

25

ST-RAPHAËL

MASSIF DES MAURES

ST-MAXIME

N97

21

22 ST-TROPEZ

D14

HYÈRES

LE LAVANDOU

19

ÎLES D'HYÈRES

20

GETTING AROUND

The largest airport in the region, and second busiest in France, is Nice. Fly-drive packages are popular, although mainly recommended for touring inland. Traffic jams on coastal roads in high season can usually be avoided by using the autoroutes. Main coastal towns have good bus and rail links, and bikes can be hired at most rail stations. The Chemin de Fer de Provence railroad runs from Nice to Digne-les-Bains through spectacular mountain scenery. Mountain roads, though tortuous, are good.

KEY

▨	Highway
▨	Major road
▨	Minor road
▨	Scenic route
〰	River
☀	Viewing point

0 kilometers 25

0 miles 25

Spectacular scenery near the quiet market town of Forcalquier

Mont Ventoux ❶

Vaucluse. ✈ *Avignon.* ▤ *Orange.*
▤ *Bedoin.* ℹ *Bedoin (04 90 65 63 95).*

THE NAME means "Windy
Mountain" in Provençal,
and deservedly so. A variety
of flora and fauna may be
found on the lower slopes, but
moss is the only plant life to
survive at the peak, where the
winter temperature can drop
to −27° C (−17° F). The bare
white scree at the summit
makes it look snowcapped
even during summer.

In 1336, the poet Petrarch
made the first recorded ascent
of the 1,912-m (6,242-ft) peak.
Today, a road leads to the
radio beacon pinnacle, but the
trip should not be attempted in
bad weather. At other times,
spectacular views from the top
make the effort worthwhile.

**Roman mosaic from the Villa du
Paon in Vaison-la-Romaine**

Vaison-la-Romaine ❷

Vaucluse. ♟ *5,600.* ▤ ℹ *place du
Chanoine Sautel (04 90 36 02 11).*
🛒 *Tue.*

THIS SITE on the banks of the
Ouvèze has been settled
since the Bronze Age, but its
name stems from five centuries
as a prosperous Roman town.
Although the upper town,
dominated by the ruins of a
12th-century castle, has some
charming narrow streets, stone
houses and fountains, Vaison's
main attractions lie on the
opposite side of the river.

The **Roman City** is split into
two districts: Puymin and La
Villasse. At Puymin, an opulent
mansion, the Villa du Paon,
and a Roman theater have
been uncovered.

In 1992, the Ouvèze River
burst its banks, taking many

lives in Vaison and the nearby
area. Damage to some ruins,
such as the Roman bridge, has
since been repaired. Also at
Vaison is the fine, Romanesque
**Cathédrale Notre-Dame-de-
Nazareth** with medieval
cloisters.

🏛 Roman City
Fouilles de Puymin & Musée Théo
Desplans, pl du Chanoine Sautel.
📞 *04 90 36 02 11.* 🕐 *daily.*
⬤ *Jan 1, Dec 25.* 🈵 ✔ 👍 ℹ

Orange ❸

Vaucluse. ♟ *29,000.* ▤ ▤ ℹ *cours
Aristide Briand (04 90 34 70 88).* 🛒 *Thu.*

ORANGE IS A thriving regional
center. The fields and
orchards and, in particular, the
great vineyards of the Côtes du
Rhône, make it an important
marketplace for produce such
as grapes, honey and
truffles. In contrast, visitors
should explore the area around
the 17th-century Hôtel de Ville,
where attractive streets open
onto quiet, shady squares.
Orange has two of the greatest
Roman monuments in Europe.

🏛 Roman Theater
Place de Frères-Mounet. 📞 *04 90 51
17 60.* 🕐 *daily.* 🈵 ✔ *entrance also
valid for Musée Municipal.* 👍 ℹ 🖥
Dating from the 1st-century
AD reign of Augustus, the
well-preserved theater has
perfect acoustics. It is still
used for theater performances
and concerts. The back wall
("the finest wall in my
kingdom," said Louis XIV)
rises to a height of 36 m (120
ft) and is 103 m (338 ft) wide.

🏛 Triumphal Arch
Avenue de l'Arc de Triomphe.
The triple-arched monument

**Statue of Augustus Caesar in the
Roman Theater at Orange**

was built about AD 20. It is
elaborately decorated: battle
scenes and military trophies
are mingled with flowers and
fruits. Inscriptions to the glory
of Tiberius were added later.

🏛 Musée Municipal
Rue Madeleine-Roch. 📞 *04 90 51
18 24.* 🕐 *daily.* 🈵
Relics here reflect the history
of Orange, including 400
marble fragments which
proved to be plans of the
area based on three surveys.
The earliest dates to the reign
of the Emperor Vespasian in
the 1st century BC.

Châteauneuf-du-Pape ❹

Vaucluse. ♟ *2,100.* ▤ *Sorgues,
then taxi.* ℹ *place du Portail
(04 90 83 71 08).* 🛒 *Fri.*

HERE, IN THE 14TH CENTURY,
the popes of Avignon
chose to build a new castle
(*château neuf*) and plant the
vineyards from which one of

View across the vineyards of Châteauneuf-du-Pape

the finest wines of the Côtes du Rhône is produced. Now, almost every doorway in this attractive little town seems to open into a *vigneron's* cellar.

After the Wars of Religion *(see pp50–51)*, all that remained of the papal fortress were a few fragments of walls and tower, but the ruins look spectacular and offer magnificent views across to Avignon and the Vaucluse uplands beyond.

Wine festivals punctuate the year, including the Fête de la Véraison in August *(see p34)*, when the grapes start to ripen, and the Ban des Vendages in September, when the grapes are ready to be harvested.

Avignon ❺

Vaucluse. 🏠 *100,000.* ✈ 🚉 🚌
🛈 *41 cours Jean Jaurès (04 32 74 32 74).* 🛒 *Tue–Sun.*

Massive ramparts enclose one of the most fascinating towns in southern France. The huge **Palais des Papes** *(see pp494–5)* is the dominant feature, but the town contains other riches. To the north of the Palais is the 13th-century **Petit Palais**, once the Archbishop of Avignon's residence. It has received such notorious guests as Cesare Borgia and Louis XIV. Now a museum, it displays Romanesque and Gothic sculpture and medieval paintings of the Avignon and Italian Schools, with works by Botticelli and Carpaccio.

The rue Joseph-Vernet and rue du Roi-René are lined with many splendid 17th- and 18th-century houses. There are also some notable churches, such as the **Cathédrale de Notre-Dame-des-Doms**, with its Romanesque cupola, and the 14th-century **Eglise St-Didier**. The **Musée Lapidaire** contains statues, mosaics and carvings from pre-Roman Provence. The **Musée Calvet** features a superb array of exhibits, such as wrought-iron works and Roman finds. It also gives an overview of French art during the past 500 years, with works by Rodin, Utrillo and Dufy.

Two major modern and contemporary art collections, the **Musée Angladon** and the

Pont St-Bénézet and the Palais des Papes in Avignon

Collection Lambert, have recently been added to the city's cultural repertoire.

The place de l'Horloge is the center of Avignon's social life, with sidewalk cafés and a merry-go-round from 1900. One of the prettiest streets is the rue des Teinturiers. Until the 19th century, brightly patterned calico called *indiennes* was printed here – inspiration for today's Provençal patterns.

Outdoor performance at the Avignon Festival

Avignon's renowned 12-century bridge, the **Pont St-Bénézet**, was largely destroyed by floods in 1668. One of the remaining arches bears the tiny Chapelle St-Nicolas. People danced on an island below the bridge but over the years, as the famous song testifies, *sous* has become *sur*.

Avignon hosts France's largest festival (mid-Jul–mid-Aug), which includes ballet, drama and classical concerts *(see p33)*. The "Off" festival has street theater and music from folk to jazz.

🏛 **Petit Palais**
Place du Palais. 🕻 *04 90 86 44 58.* 🔲 *Wed–Mon.* ⬤ *Jan 1, May 1, Jul 14, Nov 1, Dec 25.* 🔲 🔲

🏛 **Musée Lapidaire**
27 rue de la République. 🕻 *04 90 85 75 38.* 🔲 *Wed–Mon.* ⬤ *Jan 1, May 1, Dec 25.* 🔲 *restricted.*

🏛 **Musée Calvet**
65 rue Joseph Vernet. 🕻 *04 90 86 33 84.* 🔲 *Wed–Mon.* ⬤ *Jan 1, May 1, Dec 25.* 🔲 *restricted.* 🔲 🔲

Palais des Papes

CONFRONTED WITH FACTIONAL STRIFE in Rome and encouraged by the scheming of Philippe IV of France, Pope Clement V moved the papal court to Avignon in 1309. Here it remained until 1377, during which time his successors transformed the modest episcopal building into the present magnificent palace. Its heavy fortification was vital to defend against rogue bands of mercenaries. Today it is empty of the luxurious trappings of 14th-century court life – virtually all the furnishings and works of art were destroyed or looted in the course of the centuries.

Pope Clement VI (1342–52)

Benedict XII's cloister incorporates the guest and staff wings, and the Benedictine chapel.

Trouillas tower

Bell tower

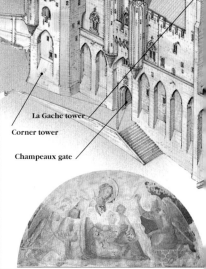

La Gache tower

Corner tower

Champeaux gate

Military Architecture
The palace and its ten towers were designed as an impregnable fortress. It eventually covered an area of 15,000 sq m (148,000 sq ft).

THE AVIGNON POPES

Seven "official" popes reigned in Avignon until 1376. They were followed by two "anti-popes," the last of whom, Benedict XIII, fled in 1403. Popes or anti-popes, few were known for their sanctity. Clement V died eating powdered emeralds, prescribed as an indigestion cure; Clement VI (1342–52) thought that the best way to honor God was through luxury. Petrarch was shocked by "the filth of the universe" at court. In 1367, Urban V tried to return the Curia (papal court) to Rome, a move that became permanent in 1377.

Benedict XII (1334–42)

Consistory Hall
Simone Martini's frescoes (1340) were taken from the cathedral to replace works destroyed by fire in the papal reception hall in 1413.

Papal Power
More like a war-lord's citadel than a papal palace, the building's heavy fortification reflects the insecure climate of 14th-century religious life.

VISITORS' CHECKLIST

Place du Palais, Avignon.
04 90 27 50 73.
Nov–Mar: 9:30am–5:45pm;
Apr–Oct: 9am–7pm (Jul–mid-Sep:
9am–8pm). Last adm: 1 hr before
closing.
www.palais-des-papes.com

★ Grand Tinel
A series of fine 17th- and 19th century Gobelin tapestries now hang in the vast banquet hall, where cardinals gathered to elect a new pope.

★ Stag Room
Fourteenth-century hunting frescoes and ceramic tiles make Clement VI's study the palace's most lovely room.

Angels' tower

Pope's chamber

Great courtyard

BUILDING THE PALACE

The palace comprises Pope Benedict XII's simple Palais Vieux (1334–42) and Clement VI's flamboyant Palais Neuf (1342–52). Ten towers, some of which are more than 50 m (164 ft) high, are set in the walls to protect its four wings.

The Great Chapel is 20 m (66 ft) high and covers an area of 780 sq m (8,400 sq ft).

The Great Audience Hall is divided into two naves by five columns with bestiary sculpture on their capitals.

STAR FEATURES

★ Grand Tinel

★ Stag Room

KEY

☐ By Benedict XII (1334–42)

☐ By Clement VI (1342–52)

Carpentras ❻

Vaucluse. 🏛 *25,500.* 🚉 ℹ *Hôtel-Dieu, pl A Briand (04 90 63 57 88).* 🔄 *Fri.*

I N 1320, CARPENTRAS became capital of the papal county of Venaissin, and remained so until 1791. Modern boulevards trace the former ramparts, with only one original gate, the Porte d'Orange, surviving.

In the Middle Ages, the town had a large Jewish community; today, that community is small. The 1367 **Synagogue** is the oldest in France. The Sanctuary has been restored but the baths and bakery are unchanged.

While not openly persecuted under papal rule, many Jews changed faith, entering **Cathédrale St-Siffrein** by the Porte Juive (Jews' Door).

The Law Courts were built in 1640 as the episcopal palace. Its Criminal Court has 17th-century carved tablets of the local towns. In the pharmacy of the Hôtel-Dieu, the 18th-century cupboards are painted with quaint figures of monkey "doctors." More regional art and history is on display at the **Musée Sobirats**.

⬛ Synagogue
Place Maurice Charretier. 📞 *04 90 63 39 97.* 🕐 *Mon–Fri.* ⬤ *Jewish feast days.*

🏛 Musée Sobirats
Rue du Collège. 📞 *04 90 63 04 92.* 🕐 *Wed–Mon.* ⬤ *public hols.* 📷

Riverfront and watermill at Fontaine-de-Vaucluse

Fontaine-de-Vaucluse ❼

Vaucluse. 🏛 *500.* 🚉 ℹ *chemin de la Fontaine (04 90 20 32 22).*

T HE MAIN ATTRACTION here is the source of the Sorgue River. It is the most powerful spring in France, gushing at up to 90,000 liters (19,800 gallons) per second from an underground river at the foot of a cliff. It powers the Moulin à Papier Vallis Clausa (paper mill), which produces handmade paper using the same methods as in the 15th century, and now sells maps, prints and lampshades. There are also several museums. One is devoted to the poet Petrarch, who lived and wrote here, and another to the French Resistance of World War II.

Gordes ❽

Vaucluse. 🏛 *2,000.* ℹ *Le Château (04 90 72 02 75).* 🔄 *Tue.*

P ERCHED VILLAGES abound in Provence, but Gordes is said to attract the most visitors, and it is easy to understand why. Dominated by a 16th-century château, the town forms such a harmonious whole that it might have been designed by an architect. The arcaded medieval lanes add to the attractive hilltop position.

Just south lies the **Village des Bories**, a bizarre, primitive habitat. Bories are tiny beehive-shaped huts built of overlapping dry stones. The construction techniques are thought to date back to Neolithic times. This group was inhabited from the 16th to the early 20th centuries.

The **Abbaye de Sénanque**, north of Gordes, is one of the finest Romanesque Cistercian monastries in France.

♔ Château de Gordes
📞 *04 90 72 02 75.* 🕐 *daily.* ⬤ *Jan 1, Dec 25.* 📷

⛺ Village des Bories
rte de Cavaillon. 📞 *04 90 72 03 48.* 🕐 *daily.* ⬤ *Jan 1, Dec 25.* 📷

Luberon ❾

Vaucluse. ✈ *Avignon.* 🚉 *Cavaillon, Avignon.* 🚌 *Apt.* ℹ *Apt (04 90 74 03 18).*

A HUGE LIMESTONE range, the Montagne du Luberon is one of the most appealing areas of Provence. Rising to 1,125 m (3,690 ft), it combines

Perched village of Gordes

wild areas with picturesque villages. Almost the entire area is designated a regional nature park. Within it are more than 1,000 plant species and cedar and oak forests. The wildlife is varied, with eagles, vultures, snakes, beavers, wild boar and the largest European lizards. The park headquarters are in **Apt**, the capital of the Luberon.

Once notorious as the haunt of highwaymen, the Luberon hills now hide sumptuous vacation homes. The major village is **Bonnieux**, with its 12th-century church and 13th-century walls. Also popular are **Roussillon**, with red ocher buildings; **Lacoste**, the site of the ruins of the Marquis de Sade's castle; and **Ansouis**, with its 14th-century Eglise St-Martin and 17th-century castle. **Ménerbes**, drew to it the writer Peter Mayle, whose tales of life here brought this quiet region a worldwide audience.

Herb stall at St-Rémy-de-Provence

St-Rémy-de-Provence ⑩

Bouches-du-Rhône. 🅜 9,500. 🚌
🛈 place Jean Jaurès (04 90 92 05 22). 🔴 Wed.

FOR CENTURIES St-Rémy, with its tree-lined boulevards, fountains and narrow streets, had two claims to fame. One was that Vincent Van Gogh spent a year here, in 1889–90, at the St-Paul-de-Mausole hospital. *Wheat Field with Cypress* and *Ravine* are among the 150 works he produced here. St-Rémy-de-Provence was also the birthplace in 1503 of

Nostradamus, known for his cryptic prophecies. But, in 1921, St-Rémy found new fame when archaeologists unearthed the fascinating Roman ruins at **Glanum**. Little remains of the ancient city, sacked in AD 480 by the Goths, but the site is very impressive. Around the ruins of an arch from the first century BC are the foundations of buildings, fragments of walls and a vast mausoleum, decorated with such scenes as the death of Adonis.

🏛 **Glanum**
🅒 04 90 92 23 79. 🔘 daily. 🔴 Jan 1, May 1, Nov 1 & 11, Dec 25. 🔖 ♿ 🏠

Les Baux-de-Provence ⑪

Bouches-du-Rhône. 🅜 460. 🚌 Arles.
🛈 La Maison du Roy (04 90 54 34 39).

ONE OF THE STRANGEST places in Provence, the deserted citadel of Les Baux stands like a natural extension of a huge rocky plateau. The ruined castle and old houses overlook the Val d'Enfer (Infernal Valley), with its weird rocks, once the haunt of witches and goblins according to legend.

In the Middle Ages, Les Baux was home to powerful feudal lords, who claimed descent from the Magus Balthazar. It was the most famous of the Provençal Cours d'Amour, at which troubadours sang the praises of high-born ladies. The ideal of everlasting but unrequited courtly love contrasts with the war-like nature of the citadel's lords.

The glory of Les Baux ended in 1632. It had become a Protestant stronghold and Louis XIII ordered its destruction. The living village below has

Deserted medieval citadel of Les Baux-de-Provence

a pleasant little square, the 12th-century **Eglise St-Vincent** and the **Chapelle des Pénitents Blancs** next door, decorated by local artist Yves Brayer, whose work can be seen in the **Musée Yves Brayer**.

In 1821, bauxite was discovered (and named) here, and the closed quarries now form the backdrop for spectacular audio-visual theme programs, known as the **Cathédrale d'Images**.

To the southwest are the ruins of the **Abbaye de Montmajour**. It has a 12th-century Romanesque church, noted for its circular crypt.

Parading the Tarasque, 1850

Tarascon ⑫

Bouches-du-Rhône. 🅜 11,300. 🚉
🚌 🛈 59 rue des Halles (04 90 91 03 52). 🔴 Tue & Fri.

ACCORDING TO LEGEND, the town takes its name from the Tarasque, a monster, half-animal and half-fish, which terrorized the countryside. It was tamed by Sainte Marthe, who is buried in the church here. An effigy of the Tarasque is still paraded through the streets each June *(see p33)*.

The striking, perfectly preserved 15th-century **château** on the banks of the Rhône is one of the finest examples of Gothic military architecture in Provence. Its somber exterior gives no hint of the beauties within: the Flemish-Gothic courtyard; the spiral staircase; and the painted ceilings of the banqueting hall.

On the opposite bank is Beaucaire, with its own ruined castle surrounded by gardens.

🏰 **Château**
Bd du Roi René. 🅒 04 90 91 01 93.
🔘 May–Aug: daily; Sep–Apr: Tue–Sun.
🔴 some public hols 🔖 🏠

Arles ⑬

EW OTHER TOWNS IN PROVENCE combine all the region's charms as well as Arles. Its position on the Rhône makes it a natural, historic gateway to the Camargue *(see pp500–1)*. Its Roman remains, such as the arena and Constantine's baths, are complemented by the ocher walls and Roman-tiled roofs of later buildings. A bastion of Provençal tradition and culture, its museums are among the best in the region. Van Gogh spent time here in 1888–9, but Arles is no longer the industrial town he painted. Visitors are now its main business, and entertainment ranges from the Arles Festival to bullfights.

Emperor Constantine

Palais Constantine was once a grand imperial palace. Now only its vast Roman baths remain, dating from the 4th century AD. They are remarkably well preserved and give an idea of the luxury that bathers enjoyed.

Musée Réattu
This museum, in the old Commandery of the Knights of Malta, houses witty Picasso sketches, paintings by the local artist Jacques Réattu (1760–1833) and sculptures by Ossip Zadkine, including La Grande Odalisque *(1932), above.*

Museon Arlaten
In 1904 the poet Frédéric Mistral used his Nobel Prize money to establish this museum devoted to his beloved native Provence. Parts of the collection are arranged in room settings, and even the museum attendants wear traditional Arles costume.

Espace Van Gogh, in a former hospital where the artist was treated in 1889, is a cultural center devoted to his life and work.

★ Eglise St-Trophime
This church combines a noble 12th-century Romanesque exterior with superb Romanesque and Gothic cloisters. The ornate main portal is carved with saints and apostles.

Tourist information

0 meters		100
0 yards		100

LES ALYSCAMPS

A tree-lined avenue of broken medieval tombs is the focal point of these "Elysian Fields" to the southeast of Arles. It became Christian in the 4th century and was a prestigious burial ground until the 12th century. Some sarcophagi were sold and are in museums; others have been neglected. Mentioned in Dante's *Inferno*, painted by Van Gogh and Gauguin, it is a place for thought and inspiration.

Les Alyscamps by Paul Gauguin

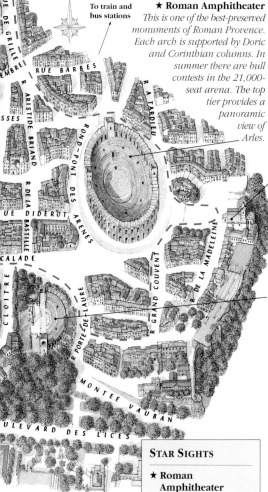

To train and bus stations

★ Roman Amphitheater

This is one of the best-preserved monuments of Roman Provence. Each arch is supported by Doric and Corinthian columns. In summer there are bull contests in the 21,000-seat arena. The top tier provides a panoramic view of Arles.

Notre-Dame-de-la-Major is the church in which the *gardians* (cowboys) of the Camargue celebrate the feast day of their patron saint, St. George. Although the building dates from the 12th to 17th centuries, a Roman temple existed on this spot hundreds of years earlier.

STAR SIGHTS

- ★ Roman Amphitheater
- ★ Roman Theater
- ★ Eglise St-Trophime

KEY

– – – Suggested route

★ Roman Theater

Once a fortress, its stones were later used for other buildings. Today, the theater stages the Arles Festival. Its remaining columns are called the "two widows."

The Camargue

T HE RHÔNE DELTA was responsible for the formation of the 140,000 ha (346,000 acres) of wetlands, pastures, dunes and salt flats that make up the Camargue, but human efforts are needed to preserve it. The region now maintains a fragile ecological balance, in which a unique collection of flora flourishes, including tamarisk and narcissi, and fauna such as egrets and ibises. The pastures provide grazing for sheep, cattle and small white Arabian-type horses, ridden by the *gardians* or cowboys, a hardy community who traditionally lived in thatched huts *(cabanes)* and still play their part in keeping Camargue traditions alive.

Camargue gardian

Sunset over the Camargue

Black Bulls
In a Provençal bull contest (known as a course), the animals are not killed. Instead, red rosettes are plucked from between their horns with a small hook.

Mas du Pont de R...

Méjanes

PLAINE DE LA CAMARGUE

Etang de Vacc...

PARC REGIONAL DE CAM...

PETITE CAMARGUE

Centre de Ginès

Stes-Maries-de-la-Mer

MEDITERRANEE

0 kilometers 5
0 miles 5

Les Stes-Maries-de-la-Mer
The May gypsy pilgrimage to this fortified church marks the legendary arrival by boat in AD 18 of Mary Magdalene, St. Martha and the sister of the Virgin Mary. Statues in the church depict the event.

Flamingoes
These striking birds are always associated with the Camargue, but the region supports many other breeds, including herons, kingfishers, owls and birds of prey. The area around Ginès is the best place to see them.

KEY

—— Nature preserve boundary

– – Walking routes

– – Walking and cycling routes

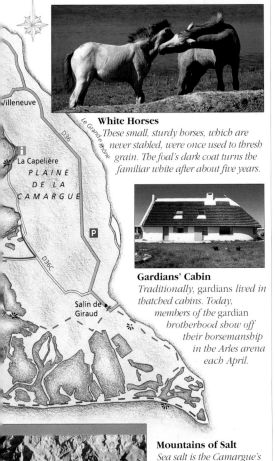

White Horses
These small, sturdy horses, which are never stabled, were once used to thresh grain. The foal's dark coat turns the familiar white after about five years.

Gardians' Cabin
Traditionally, gardians *lived in thatched cabins. Today, members of the* gardian *brotherhood show off their horsemanship in the Arles arena each April.*

Mountains of Salt
Sea salt is the Camargue's main "harvest." Throughout the summer, sea water evaporates from huge brine pans and the crystals are heaped into camelles *up to 8 m (26 ft) high.*

Aix-en-Provence ⓯

Bouches du Rhône. 👥 126,000. 🚉 🚌 🛈 2 place du Général de Gaulle (04 42 16 11 61). 🛒 daily.

FOUNDED BY the Romans in 103 BC, Aix was frequently attacked, first by the Visigoths in AD 477, later by Lombards, Franks and Saracens. Despite this, the city prospered. By the end of the 12th century it was capital of Provence. A center of art and learning, it reached its peak in the 15th century during the reign of "Good King" René. He is shown in Nicolas Froment's *Triptych of the Burning Bush* in the 13th-century Gothic **Cathédrale de St-Sauveur**, also noted for its 16th-century walnut doors, Merovingian baptistry and Romanesque cloisters.

Aix is still a center of art and learning, and its many museums include the **Musée Granet** of fine arts and archaeology, and the **Musée des Tapisseries** (tapestries), in the Palais de l'Archevêché.

Aix has been called "the city of a thousand fountains." Three of the best are situated along cours Mirabeau. On one side of this tree-lined avenue are 17th- and 18th-century buildings with wrought-iron balconies. On the other are the cafés that are so much a part of the city's social life.

The Old Town is centered on place de l'Hôtel de Ville, with its colorful flower market. In the northwest of the town is the **Pavillon de Vendôme**, housing furniture and works of art by Van Loo.

Aix's most famous son is Paul Cézanne. The **Atelier de Cézanne** is kept as it was when he died in 1906. Montagne Ste-Victoire, which inspired many of his paintings, lies 15 km (9 miles) east of Aix.

🏛 **Musée Granet**
13 rue Cardinale. 📞 04 42 38 14 70. ⏰ closed for renovation until 2006.
🏛 **Musée des Tapisseries**
28 pl des Martyrs de la Résistance. 📞 04 42 23 09 91. ⏰ Wed–Mon. ⏰ some public hols. ♿
🏠 **Atelier de Cézanne**
9 av Paul Cézanne. 📞 04 42 21 06 53. ⏰ daily. ⏰ some public hols. ♿ 🏠

Old harbor of Marseille, looking toward the quai de Rive Neuve

Marseille **⑯**

Bouches-du-Rhône. 🚶 *800,500.*
✈ 🚃 🚌 ⛴ 🚏 *4 La Canebière*
(04 91 13 89 00). ☀ *daily.*

A GREEK SETTLEMENT founded in the 7th century BC, then called Massilia, Marseille was seized by the Romans in 49 BC. It became the "Gateway to the West" for most Oriental trade. France's largest port and second-largest city has close links with the Middle East and North Africa. It is exotic, cosmopolitan and lively, with an outdated reputation for corruption and drug trafficking.

In Marseille, narrow, stepped streets, quiet squares and fine 18th-century façades contrast with the bustle of boulevard Canebière and the Cité Radieuse, Le Corbusier's post-war radical housing complex.

The old harbor now only handles small boats, but its daily fish market is renowned.

Marseille has many excellent museums. Those in the old harbor area include the **Musée des Docks Romains**, the **Musée d'Histoire de Marseille**, the **Musée du Vieux Marseille** and the upbeat **Musée de la Mode**.

In the shopping area to the south is the **Musée Cantini**, housing the 20th-century art collection of sculptor Jules Cantini. It includes Surrealist, Cubist and Fauve paintings.

Right the other side of the city, in one of the finest houses in Marseille, is the **Musée Grobet-Labadié**, with its fine furniture, tapestries, 17th–19th century paintings and rare musical instruments.

🏛 Musée des Beaux-Arts

Palais Longchamp, place Henri Dunan.
📞 *04 91 14 59 30.* ☀ *Tue–Sun.*
⬤ *public hols.* 📷 ♿
This museum is housed in the handsome 19th-century Palais Longchamp. Works include Michel Serre's graphic views of Marseille's plague of 1721, Pierre Puget's town plans for the city, and murals depicting it in Greek and Roman times.

⚓ Château d'If

📞 *04 91 59 02 30.* ☀ *May–Aug: daily; Sep–Apr: Tue–Sun.* 📷 🏛

The Château d'If (Castle of Yew) stands on a tiny island 2 km (1 mile) southwest of the port. A formidable fortress, it was built in 1529 to house artillery, but was never put to military use and later became a prison. Alexandre Dumas' fictional "Count of Monte Cristo" was supposed to have been imprisoned here, and visitors can see a special cell, complete with escape hole. Most real-life inmates were either common criminals or political prisoners.

🔒 Notre-Dame-de-la-Garde

Built between 1853 and 1864, this Neo-Byzantine basilica dominates the city. Its belfry, 46 m (151 ft) high, is capped by a huge gilded statue of the Virgin. The lavishly decorated interior has colored marble and mosaic facings.

🔒 Abbaye de St-Victor

Similar to a fortress in appearance, the abbey was rebuilt in the 11th century after destruction by the Saracens. In the French Revolution, the rebels used it as a barracks and prison.

There is an intriguing crypt in the abbey's church, with an original catacomb chapel and a number of pagan and Christian sarcophagi.

On February 2 each year, St-Victor becomes a place of pilgrimage. Boat-shaped cakes are sold to commemorate the legendary arrival of St. Mary Magdalene, Lazarus and St. Martha nearly 2,000 years ago.

🔒 Cathédrale de la Major

Built in Neo-Byzantine style, this is the largest 19th-century church in France, 70 m (230 ft) high and 141 m (463 ft) long. In the crypt are the tombs of the bishops of Marseille. By it

Le Corbusier's innovative Cité Radieuse in Marseille

Fish market at Marseille

is the small and beautiful Ancienne Cathédrale de la Major.

♿ Vieille Charité

Rue de la Charité. 📞 04 91 14 58 80. ☐ Tue–Sun. ◑ public hols. ✦ ♿
In 1640, the construction of a shelter "for the poor and beggars" of Marseille was begun by royal decree. Pierre Puget's hospital and domed church were opened one hundred years later. Now, the restored building houses the Musée d'Archéologie Egyptienne, with its fine collection of Egyptian artifacts; the Musée des Arts Africains is on the second floor.

Cassis ⓱

Bouches-du-Rhône. 🏠 8,000. 🚊
🚌 ℹ Le Port (04 42 01 71 17).
☐ Wed & Fri.

MANY OF THE VILLAGES along this coast have been built up to the point where they have all but lost their original charm, but Cassis is still much the same little fishing port that attracted such artists as Dufy, Signac and Derain. This is a place in which to relax at a waterside café, watching the fishermen or street performers, while enjoying a plate of seafood and a bottle of the local dry white wine for which Cassis is famous.

From Marseille to Cassis, the coastline forms narrow inlets, called **Calanques**, their jagged white cliffs (some as much as 400 m/1,312 ft high) reflected in dazzling turquoise water. Wildlife abounds here, with countless seabirds, foxes, stone martens, bats, large snakes and lizards. The flora is no less impressive, with more than 900 plant species, of which 50 are classified as rare. The En-Vau and Sormiou Calanques are especially lovely.

Toulon ⓲

Var. 🏠 170,000. ✈ 🚊 🚌 ⛴ ℹ
Place Raimu (04 94 18 53 00).
☐ Tue–Sun.

THIS NAVAL BASE has a long maritime history. In 1793 it was captured by an Anglo-Spanish fleet, but was boldly retaken by the then-unknown young commander Napoleon Bonaparte. Nearly 150 years later, Nazi troops took Toulon. The French fleet, trapped in the harbor, sank its own ships to keep them from the enemy.

The **Musée de la Marine** is a focus for this history, with such artifacts as finely crafted figureheads and model ships.

The tower of the former town hall is virtually all that remains of the prewar quai Cronstadt. Rebuilt and renamed quai Stalingrad, its many cafés and shops make it a favorite meeting place for Toulonnais. The war-damaged Old Town has a few original buildings, and the market is well worth a visit.

🏛 Musée de la Marine

Place Monsenergue. 📞 04 94 02 10 61. ☐ Apr–Sep: daily; Oct–Mar: Wed–Mon. ◑ mid-Dec–Jan. ✦ ♿ 🚻

Paul Signac's *Cap Canaille*, painted at Cassis in 1889

Tour of the Gorges du Verdon

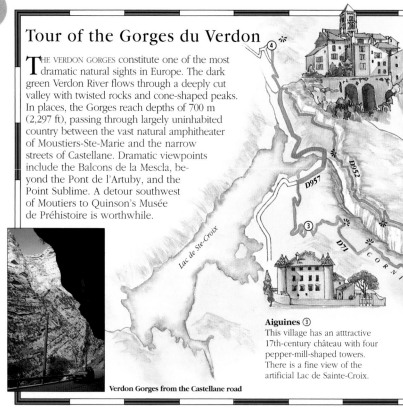

THE VERDON GORGES constitute one of the most dramatic natural sights in Europe. The dark green Verdon River flows through a deeply cut valley with twisted rocks and cone-shaped peaks. In places, the Gorges reach depths of 700 m (2,297 ft), passing through largely uninhabited country between the vast natural amphitheater of Moustiers-Ste-Marie and the narrow streets of Castellane. Dramatic viewpoints include the Balcons de la Mescla, beyond the Pont de l'Artuby, and the Point Sublime. A detour southwest of Moutiers to Quinson's Musée de Préhistoire is worthwhile.

Lac de Ste-Croix

Aiguines ③
This village has an atttractive 17th-century château with four pepper-mill-shaped towers. There is a fine view of the artificial Lac de Sainte-Croix.

Verdon Gorges from the Castellane road

Hyères ⑲

Var. 🏛 52,000. ✈ 🚌 🚗 ⛴
ℹ av Ambroise Thomas (04 94 01 84 50). 🗓 Tue, Sat & 3rd Thu of month.

TOWARD THE END of the 18th century, Hyères became one of the first health resorts of the Côte d'Azur. Among its many distinguished visitors during the next century were Queen Victoria, Robert Louis Stevenson and Edith Wharton.

The main sights are found in the medieval streets of the Vieille Ville that lead past the spacious, flagstoned place Massillon (scene of a colorful daily market) to a ruined castle and panoramic views over the coast.

Modern Hyères is imbued with a lingering Belle Epoque charm that has become popular with experimental filmmakers. It continues to attract a health-conscious crowd and is a major center for aquatic sports.

Fishing off Porquerolles, the largest of the Iles d'Hyères

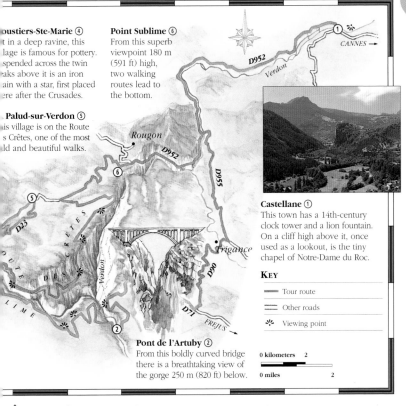

oustiers-Ste-Marie ④
t in a deep ravine, this
lage is famous for pottery.
spended across the twin
aks above it is an iron
ain with a star, first placed
re after the Crusades.

Palud-sur-Verdon ⑤
is village is on the Route
s Crêtes, one of the most
ld and beautiful walks.

Point Sublime ⑥
From this superb
viewpoint 180 m
(591 ft) high,
two walking
routes lead to
the bottom.

CANNES →

Rougon

Trigance

Castellane ①
This town has a 14th-century
clock tower and a lion fountain.
On a cliff high above it, once
used as a lookout, is the tiny
chapel of Notre-Dame du Roc.

KEY

▬▬▬	Tour route
═══	Other roads
☀	Viewing point

Pont de l'Artuby ②
From this boldly curved bridge
there is a breathtaking view of
the gorge 250 m (820 ft) below.

0 kilometers 2

0 miles 2

Îles d'Hyères ⑳

Var. ✈ Toulon-Hyères. 🚌 🚌 ⛴
Hyères. 🛈 Hyères (04 94 01 84 50).

L OCALLY KNOWN as the Iles
d'Or, after the gold color
of their cliffs, this glamorous
trio of islands can be reached
by boat from Hyères, Le
Lavandou and, in summer,
Cavalaire and Port-de-Miramar.

Porquerolles, the largest
of the three, measures 7 km
(4.5 miles) by 3 km (2 miles).
It is covered in rich vegetation,
much of which, for instance
the Mexican bellombra tree,
was introduced from a variety
of exotic foreign climes.

The island's main town, also
known as Porquerolles, looks
more like a North African
colonial settlement than any
Provençal village. It was
established in 1820 as a
retirement town for Napoleon's
most honored troops.

All the island's beaches lie
along the northern coastline.

The long, sandy Plage Notre-
Dame, one of the finest
beaches in Provence, sits in a
sheltered bay about an hour's
walk from Porquerolles.

A stroll around lush, hilly
Port-Cros, covering just 2.5
sq km (1 sq mile), takes the
best part of a day. It rises to
195 m (640 ft), the highest
point on any of the islands.

Port-Cros has been a national park since 1963. A unique
reserve of Mediterranean flora
and fauna, its surrounding
waters are also protected.
There is even a 300 m (984 ft)
scenic swimming route. You
can buy a waterproof guide to
the underwater life, which
includes rare rock fish.

The wild, virtually treeless
Île du Levant is reached by
boat from Port-Cros. Its main
draw is the oldest naturist
resort in France, Héliopolis,
founded in 1931. The eastern
half of the island, controlled
by the French navy, is permanently closed to the public.

Massif des Maures ㉑

Var. ✈ Toulon-Hyères. 🚌 Fréjus,
Hyères, or Toulon. 🚌 Bormes-les-
Mimosas. ⛴ Toulon. 🛈 Bormes-
les-Mimosas (04 94 01 38 38).

T HE DENSE WILDERNESS of
pine, oak and sweet
chestnut covering the Maures
mountain range probably gave
rise to its name, meaning dark
or gloomy. It extends nearly
65 km (40 miles) between
Hyères and Fréjus.

The D558 north of Cogolin
offers a route to the heart of
the Maures. Along the way is
La Garde-Freinet, well known
for its bottle cork industry.

Northwest of Cannet-des-
Maures, in splendid isolation,
lies the Romanesque Abbaye
de Thoronet. With the abbeys
at Sénanque, in Vaucluse, and
Silvacane, in the Bouches-du-
Rhône, it is known as one of
the "Three Sisters" of Provence.

Harborside at St-Tropez

St-Tropez ❷

Var. 🏘 6,000. 🚉 🛈 quai Jean
Jaurès (04 94 97 45 21). 🛒 Tue & Sat.

THE GEOGRAPHY of St-Tropez
kept it untouched by the
earliest development of the
Côte d'Azur. Tucked away at
the tip of a peninsula, it is the
only north-facing town on the
coast and so did not appeal
to those seeking a warm and
sheltered winter resort. In
1892, the painter Paul Signac
was among the first outsiders
to respond to its unspoiled
charm, encouraging friends,
such as the painters Van
Dongen, Matisse and Bonnard,
to join him. In the 1920s, the
chic Parisian writer Colette
also made her home here. St-
Tropez also began to attract
star-spotters, hoping for a
glimpse of celebrities such
as the Prince of Wales.

During World War II, the
beaches around St-Tropez were
the scene of Allied landings,
and the town was heavily
bombed. Then, in the 1950s,
young Parisians began to
arrive, and the Bardot-Vadim
film helped to create the
reputation of modern St-Tropez
as a playground for gilded
youth. The wild public
behavior and turbulent love
affairs of Roger Vadim, Brigitte
Bardot, Sacha Distel and others
left fiction far behind. Mass
tourism followed, with visitors
once again more interested in
spotting a celebrity than in
visiting the **Musée de la
Citadelle** in the 16th-century
citadel above the town, or the
Musée de l'Annonciade with
its outstanding collection of
works by Signac, Derain,
Rouault, Bonnard and others.
Bardot had a villa at La
Madrague, but tourists invaded
her privacy, so she left.

Today, there are far more
luxury yachts than fishing
boats moored in St-Tropez
harbor. Its cafés make ideal
bases for people- and yacht-
watching. Another center of
the action is place des Lices,
both for the Harley-Davidson
set and the morning market.

St-Tropez has its own small
beaches but the best are to be
found just outside the town,
including the golden curve of
Pampelonne, jammed with
beach clubs and fashionable
restaurants. This is the beach
on which to see and be seen.
St-Tropez has no train station,
so driving and parking can be
a nightmare in summer.

It is said that St-Tropez
takes its name from a Roman
soldier martyred as a Christian
by the Emperor Nero. Each
year in May, a *bravade* in his
honor takes place, when an
effigy of the saint is carried
through the town to the accompaniment of musket fire.

Nearby are two small towns
of differing character but equal
charm. **Port-Grimaud** was
only built in 1966 but the sensitive use of traditional architecture makes it seem older.
Most of its "streets" are canals
and many homes have their
own mooring. Up in the hills,
the winding streets of **Rama-
tuelle** have been restored to
bijou perfection by the largely
celebrity population.

🏛 **Musée de la Citadelle**
Montée de la Citadelle. 📞 04 94 97
59 43. 🕐 daily. 🚫 Jan 1, May 1,
Ascension, May 17, Dec 25. 🈸
🏛 **Musée de l'Annonciade**
Place Grammont. 📞 04 94 97 04 01.
🕐 Dec–Oct: Wed–Mon. 🚫 Jan 1,
Ascension, May 1, Nov, Dec 25.
🈸 🅿 🚫 🅰 ground floor only.

**Stylish solution to the traffic
problems in St-Tropez**

BRIGITTE BARDOT

In 1956, Brigitte Bardot's film,
And God Created Woman,
was shot in St-Tropez by her
new husband, Roger Vadim.
By settling in St-Tropez, "BB"
the sex goddess changed the
fortunes of the sleepy little
fishing village and ultimately
the Côte d'Azur, making it
the center of her hedonistic
lifestyle. In 1974, on her 40th
birthday, she celebrated her
retirement from films at Club
55 on Pampelonne Beach, and
now devotes her time to her
animal sanctuary.

Brigitte Bardot in 1956

Digne-les-Bains ㉓

Alpes-de-Haute-Provence. 17,000. place du Tampinet (04 92 36 62 62). Wed & Sat.

THIS CHARMING town in the foothills of the Alps appears in Victor Hugo's *Les Misérables*: the hero stole a bishop's candlesticks. A trip on the *Train des Pignes* from Nice offers superb views. Digne's attractions include a spa, the lavender festival *(see p34)* and the **Fondation Alexandra David-Néel**, a Tibetan center.

Fondation Alexandra David-Néel,
27 av du Maréchal Juin. 04 92 31 32 38. daily.

Fréjus ㉔

Var. 52,000. 325 rue Jean Jaurès (04 94 51 83 83). Wed & Sat.

THE MODERN TOWN of Fréjus is dwarfed in importance by two impressive historic sites. The remains of the Roman port of **Amphithéâtre** (founded by Julius Caesar in 49 BC) may not be as complete as those at Orange or Arles, but they are of exceptional variety. A great amphitheater, fragments of an aqueduct, a theater and part of a rampart gateway remain. The sea has receded over the centuries and there are few traces of the original harbor.

The cathedral on place Formigé marks the entrance to the **Cité Episcopale**. The fortified enclave includes the 5th-century baptistry, one of the oldest in France, and the cathedral cloister, its coffered medieval roof decorated with scenes from the Apocalypse.

In 1959, Fréjus was hit by a wall of water as the Malpasset Barrage burst. To the north, the ruined dam can still be seen.

Amphithéâtre
Rue Henri Vadon. 04 94 51 83 83. Wed – Mon. Jan 1, May 1, Dec 25.

Cité Episcopale
58 rue de Fleury. 04 94 51 26 30. Apr–Aug: daily; Sep–Mar: Tue–Sun. Jan 1, May 1, Nov 1 & 11, Dec 25. cloisters.

THE CREATION OF A PERFUME

The best perfumes begin as a formula of essential oils extracted from natural sources. The blend of aromas is created by a perfumer called a "nose" because of his or her exceptional sense of smell. A perfume may use as many as 300 essences, all painstakingly extracted from plants by various methods: steam distillation, extraction by volatile solvents, and *enfleurage à froid* (for costly or potent essences). With this process, pungent blossoms are placed onto layers of fats

Lavender for several days until the fats are saturated. The

water oils are then "washed" out with alcohol, and when this evaporates, it leaves the pure perfume essence behind.

Grasse flowers

St-Raphaël ㉕

Var. 28,000. Rue Waldeck Rousseau (04 94 19 52 52). daily.

DELIGHTFULLY SITUATED, St-Raphaël is a charming, old-style Côte d'Azur resort with Art Nouveau architecture and a palm-fronded promenade. Aside from its beaches, it offers a marina, a casino, Roman ruins, a 12th-century church and a museum that displays treasures salvaged from a Roman wreck.

It was here that Napoleon Bonaparte landed in 1799 upon his return from Egypt.

Grasse ㉖

Alpes-Maritimes. 44,000. Palais des Congrès. (04 93 36 03 56). Tue–Sun.

CRADLED BY HILLS, with views out to sea, Grasse is surrounded by fields of flowers: lavender, mimosa, jasmine and roses. Grasse has been the center of the world's perfume industry since the 16th century, when Catherine de' Médici set the fashion for scented leather gloves. At that time, Grasse was also known as the center for leather tanning. The tanneries

have gone, but the perfume houses founded in the 18th and 19th centuries are still in business; however today Grasse perfumes are mostly made from imported flowers or chemical essences. Fragonard and Molinard have their own museums, but the best place to learn more is at the **Musée Internationale de la Parfumerie**, which has a garden of fragrant plants.

Grasse was the birthplace of Jean-Honoré Fragonard, the artist. The **Villa-Musée Fragonard** is decorated with murals by his son. Fragonard's only known religious work is in the **Cathédrale de Nôtre-Dame-du-Puy** in the Old Town, with two paintings by Rubens. The place aux Aires and the place du Cours typify the unspoiled charm of Grasse, surrounded by narrow arcaded streets with Renaissance staircases and balconies.

Musée International de la Parfumerie
8 place du Cours. 04 93 36 80 20. Jun–Sep: daily; Oct, Dec–May: Wed–Mon. public hols.

Villa-Musée Fragonard
23 bd Fragonard. 04 93 36 01 61. Jun–Sep: daily; Oct, Dec–May: Wed–Mon. public hols.

Statue honoring Jean-Honoré Fragonard in Grasse

Lavender fields near Puimoisson, Alpes-de-Haute-Provence ▷

High summer on the beach at Cannes, overlooked by the Carlton Hotel

Cannes ㉗

Alpes-Maritimes. 🏛 *70,000.* 🚉 🚌
🚢 ⓘ *Palais des Festivals, 1 La
Croisette (04 93 39 24 53).* 📅 *daily.*

JUST AS GRASSE is synonymous
with the perfume industry,
the first thing that most people
associate with Cannes is its
many festivals, especially the
International Film Festival
held each May. There is,
however, much more to the
city than these glittering events.
It was Lord Brougham, the
British Lord Chancellor, who
put Cannes on the map,
although Prosper Mérimée,
Inspector of Historic Monuments, allegedly visited Cannes
two months before him. Lord
Brougham stopped here in
1834, unable to reach Nice
due to a cholera outbreak
there. Struck by the beauty
and mild climate of what was
then just a small fishing port,

he built a villa here. Other
foreigners followed, and
Cannes became established as
a top Mediterranean resort.

The Old Town that Lord
Brougham knew is centered
in the Le Suquet district, on
the slopes of Mont Chevalier.
Part of the old city wall can
still be seen on place de la
Castre, which is dominated
by the **Notre-Dame de
l'Espérance**, built in the 16th
and 17th centuries in the
Provençal Gothic style. An
11th-century watchtower is
another attraction, and the
castle keep houses the **Musée
de la Castre**, the eclectic
finds of a 19th-century Dutch
explorer, Baron Lycklama.

The famed **boulevard de
la Croisette** is lined with
gardens and palm trees. One
side is occupied by luxury
boutiques and hotels such as
the Carlton, built in Belle
Epoque style, whose twin
cupolas were modeled on the
breasts of La Belle Otero, a
famous member of the 19th-
century *demi-monde*. Opposite
are some of the finest sandy
beaches on this coast. Once
one of the world's grandest
thoroughfares, the faded
glamour of the Croisette
revives at festival time.

🏝 Iles de Lérins
🚢 depart from: Gare Maritime, Vieux
Port. ⓘ *Esterel Chanteclair (04 93 39
11 82), Compagnie Maritime Cannoise
(04 93 38 66 33 for Ste M), Planaria
(04 92 98 71 38 for Ile St-H).*
Just off the coast from Cannes
are the Iles de Lérins. The fort
on **Ile Sainte-Marguerite** is
where the mysterious Man in
the Iron Mask was imprisoned

CANNES FILM FESTIVAL

The first Cannes Film Festival took place in 1946 and,
for almost 20 years, it remained a small and exclusive
affair, attended by the artists and celebrities who lived
or were staying on the coast. The arrival of the "starlet,"
especially Brigitte Bardot, in the mid-1950s marked the
change from artistic event to media circus, but Cannes
remains the international marketplace for filmmakers
and distributors, with the *Palme d'Or* award conferring
high status on its winner. The annual film festival is
held in the huge Palais des Festivals, opened in 1982.
It has three auditoriums, two exhibition halls, conference rooms, a casino, a nightclub and a restaurant.

Gérard Depardieu and family arriving at the festival

in the late 17th century. A popular theory is that his face had to be hidden because he resembled some one very important indeed – possibly even Louis XIV. Visitors can see the tiny cell that held him for over ten years. **Ile Saint-Honorat** has an 11th-century tower in which the resident monks took refuge during raids by Saracens. There are also five ancient chapels. Both islands offer peaceful woodland walks, fine views and quiet coves for swimming.

Beside the boulevard de la Croisette

Cap d'Antibes ②

Alpes-Maritimes. ✈ *Nice.* 🚉 🚌
Antibes. 🚢 *Nice.* ℹ️ *Antibes (04 92 90 53 00).*

W ITH ITS SUMPTUOUS villas in their lush grounds, this rocky, wooded peninsula, known as "the Cap" to its regular visitors, has been a symbol of luxury life on the Riviera since it was frequented by F. Scott Fitzgerald and the rich American set in the 1920s. One of the wealthiest of all, magnate Frank Jay Gould, invested in the resort of Juan-les-Pins, and it became the focus of high life on the Cap. Today, memories of the Jazz Age live on at the Jazz Festival, when international stars perform under the pines (*see p33*).

At the highest point of the peninsula, the sailors' chapel of **La Garoupe** has a collection of votive offerings and a 14th-century Russian icon. Nearby is the **Jardin Thuret,** created in 1856 to acclimatize

tropical plants. Much of the exotic flora of the region began its naturalization here.

🌿 **Jardin Thuret**
62 blvd du Cap. ☎ 04 93 67 88 00.
◯ *Mon – Fri.* ● *public hols.*

Antibes ②

Alpes-Maritimes. 👥 *70,000.* 🚉 🚌
🚢 ℹ️ *11 place du Gal de Gaulle
(04 92 90 53 00).* 🕐 *Tue–Sun.*

T HE LIVELY TOWN of Antibes was founded by the Greeks as Antipolis and settled by the Romans. In the 14th century, Savoy's possession of the town was contended by France until it fell to them in 1481, after which **Fort Carré** was built and the port, now a center of Mediterranean yachting, was remodelled by Vauban.

The Château Grimaldi, formerly a residence of Monaco's ruling family, was built in the 12th century and retains its Romanesque tower. It now houses the **Musée Picasso.** In 1946, the artist used part of the castle as a studio and, in gratitude, donated all 150 works completed during his

***The Goat** (1946) by Pablo Picasso*

stay, including *The Goat.* Most are inspired by his love of the sea, including *La Joie de Vivre.*

The pottery in the **Musée d'Archéologie** includes objects salvaged from shipwrecks from the Middle Ages to the 18th century.

🏛 **Musée Picasso**
Château Grimaldi. ☎ 04 92 90 54 20. ◯ *Tue–Sun.* ● *public hols.* 📷
⛔ 🚻
🏛 **Musée d'Archéologie**
1 av Mézière. ☎ 04 92 90 54 35.
◯ *Tue–Sun.* ● *public hols.*
📷 ⛔ 🚻

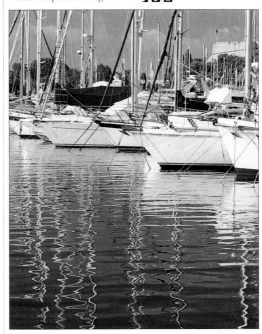
Sailboats in the harbor at Antibes

Vallauris ❸⓪

Alpes-Maritimes. 🏠 24,000. ☐ ☐
🛈 square 8 mai 1945 (04 93 63 82 58).
☐ Tue–Sun.

VALLAURIS OWES its fame to the influence of Pablo Picasso, who rescued the town's dying pottery industry and stimulated a revival of the craft. In 1951, the village commissioned Picasso to paint a mural in the decon-secrated chapel next to the castle, and his *War and Peace* (1952) is the chief ex-hibit of the **Musée National Picasso**. In the main square is a bronze statue, *Man with a Sheep*, donated by Picasso.

🏛 **Musée National Picasso**
Place de la Libération. ☎ 04 93 64
98 05. ☐ Wed–Mon. ● Jan 1, Dec
25. 📷 ♿ ground floor only. ☐

Biot ❸①

Alpes-Maritimes. 🏠 8,000. ☐ ☐
🛈 46 rue St-Sebastien (04 93 65 78
00). ☐ Tue & Fri.

A TYPICAL LITTLE hill village, Biot has retained its charm and has always attracted artists and artisans. The best known is Fernand Léger, who made his first ceramics here in 1949. Examples of these, and other works by him are shown in the **Musée Fernand Léger** outside town. Its external wall boasts a huge mosaic by the artist.
  The town is also famous for its bubble-flecked glassware. The craft of the glassblowers can be seen (and purchased) at the **Verrerie de Biot**.

🏛 **Musée Fernand Léger**
Chemin du Val-de-Pome. ☎ 04 92 91
50 30. ☐ Wed–Mon. ● Jan 1, May
1, Dec 25. 📷 ♿ ☐ ☐
☐ **La Verrerie de Biot**
Chemin des Combes. ☎ 04 93 65 03
00. ☐ daily. ● Dec 25. ♿

Renoir's studio at the Maison Les Collettes in Cagnes-sur-Mer

Cagnes-sur-Mer ❸②

Alpes-Maritimes. 🏠 43,000. ☐ ☐
🛈 6 bd Maréchal Juin (04 93 20
61 64). ☐ Tue–Sun.

C AGNES-SUR-MER is divided into three districts. The oldest and most interesting is Haut-de-Cagnes, with its steep streets, covered passageways and ancient buildings, includ-ing a number of Renaissance arcaded houses. The other districts are Cagnes-Ville, the modern town where hotels and shops are concentrated, and Cros-de-Cagnes, a sea-side fishing resort and yachting

harbor. The **Château Grimaldi** in Haut-de-Cagnes was built in the 14th century and reworked in the 17th by Henri Grimaldi. Behind the fortress walls is a shady court-yard with a 200-year-old pepper tree. The surrounding marble columns conceal a museum devoted to the olive tree, and a small collection of modern Mediterranean art. There is also a group of paint-ings bequeathed by *chanteuse* Suzy Solidor. The 40 works, all portraits of her, are by such artists as Marie Laurencin and Cocteau. On the ceiling of the banquet hall is a vast illusionistic fresco of the *Fall of Phaeton* attributed to Carlone in the 1620s.
  The last 12 years of Pierre Auguste Renoir's life were spent in Cagnes, at the **Maison Les Collettes**, where the warm, dry climate eased his arthritis. The house has been kept almost exactly as it was

Exterior of the Musée Fernand Léger in Biot, with a mural by the artist when he died in 1919 and contains ten of his paintings. It is set in a magnificent olive grove, in which can be seen his great bronze *Venus Victrix*.

⚓ Château Grimaldi
[04 92 02 47 30. **○** Dec–mid-Nov: Wed–Mon. **●** Jan 1, May 1, mid-Nov–Dec 2, Dec 25. **▨**
🏛 Maison Les Collettes
[04 93 20 61 07. **○** Wed–Mon. **●** Nov 1–22. **▨**

La Ferme des Colettes (1915) by Renoir, in Cagnes-sur-Mer

Gorges du Loup 🔢

Alpes-Maritimes. **✈** Nice.
🚃 Cagnes-sur-Mer. **🚃** Grasse.
🚌 Nice. **🛈** Grasse (04 93 36 66 66).

THE LOUP RIVER rises in the Pre-Alps behind Grasse and cuts a deep path down to the Mediterranean. Along its route are dramatic cascades and spectacular views. The superb countryside is crowned by the perched villages for which the region is famous.

Gourdon owes much of its appeal to its ancient houses, grouped around a 12th-century **Château** built on the site of a Saracen stronghold and perched dizzyingly on the cliffside. Its terraced gardens were laid out by Le Nôtre *(see p169)*, who landscaped the gardens of Versailles. The museum houses a collection of naive art, including a work by Henri Rousseau.

Tourrette-sur-Loup is a fortified village in which the ramparts are formed by the outer houses. It is surrounded by fields of violets, for which it is famous, grown for use in perfume and candied sweets.

⚓ Château de Gourdon
[04 93 09 68 02. **○** Jun–Sep: daily; Oct–May: Wed–Mon pm. **▨**

Vence 🔢

Alpes-Maritimes. **🚗** 15,000. **🚃** **🛈** place du Grand Jardin (04 93 58 06 38). **☐** Tue & Fri.

VENCE'S GENTLE CLIMATE has always been its main attraction; today it is surrounded by vacation villas. It was an important religious center in the Middle Ages. The **Cathédrale**, built on the site of a temple of Mars, was restored by Vence's most famous bishop, Antoine Godeau. A 5th-century Roman sarcophagus serves as its altar. Also noteworthy are the Carolingian wall carvings, the 15th-century carved choir stalls and Godeau's tomb.

Just within the ramparts of the Old Town, which retains its 13th–14th-century town gates, is place du Peyra, once a Roman forum. Its urn-shaped fountain, built in 1822, still provides fresh water. On the edge of town, the **Chapelle du Rosaire** was built from 1947–51 and decorated by Henri Matisse,

Domed roof in Vence

in gratitude to the nuns who nursed him during an illness. On its white walls, biblical scenes are reduced to simple black lines tinted by splashes of light from the blue and yellow stained-glass windows.

🔒 Chapelle du Rosaire
Av Henri Matisse. **[** 04 93 58 03 26. **○** Mon, Wed & Sat pm only; Tue & Thu am only. **●** mid-Nov–mid-Dec, and public hols. **▨ ♿**

Market day in the Old Town of Vence

Street-by-Street: St-Paul-de-Vence ⑤

Restaurant sign,
St-Paul-de-Vence

ONE OF THE MOST famous and visited hill villages of the Nice hinterland, St-Paul-de-Vence was once a French frontier post facing Savoy. Its 16th-century ramparts offer views over a landscape of cypress trees, and red-roofed villas with palm trees and swimming pools. The village has been heavily restored but its winding streets and medieval buildings are authentic. It has proved a magnet for artists, both established and aspiring, throughout the 20th century. Today galleries and studios dominate the village.

View of St-Paul-de-Vence
The local landscape is a favorite subject for artists. Neo-Impressionist Paul Signac (1863–1935) painted this view of St. Paul.

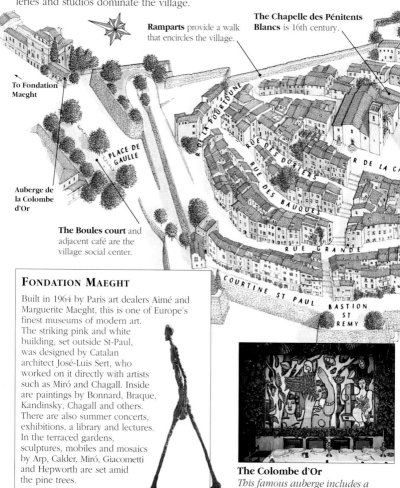

The Chapelle des Pénitents Blancs is 16th century.

Ramparts provide a walk that encircles the village.

To Fondation Maeght

PLACE DE GAULLE

R DE LA FOURTOUNE

RUE DES DORIERS

R DE LA CAS

RUE DES BAUQUES

RUE GRANDE

COURTINE ST PAUL

BASTION ST REMY

Auberge de la Colombe d'Or

The Boules court and adjacent café are the village social center.

FONDATION MAEGHT

Built in 1964 by Paris art dealers Aimé and Marguerite Maeght, this is one of Europe's finest museums of modern art. The striking pink and white building, set outside St-Paul, was designed by Catalan architect José-Luis Sert, who worked on it directly with artists such as Miró and Chagall. Inside are paintings by Bonnard, Braque, Kandinsky, Chagall and others. There are also summer concerts, exhibitions, a library and lectures. In the terraced gardens, sculptures, mobiles and mosaics by Arp, Calder, Miró, Giacometti and Hepworth are set amid the pine trees.

L'Homme qui Marche
by Giacometti

The Colombe d'Or
This famous auberge includes a Léger mural (above) on the terrace; a Braque dove by the pool; a Picasso and a Matisse in the dining room.

The Musée d'Histoire de Saint-Paul, has local waxwork scenes from the town's past.

Le Donjon, a grim medieval building, was used as a prison until the 19th century.

Eglise Collégiale
Begun in the 12th century, the church's treasures include a painting of St. Catherine, attributed to Tintoretto.

Grand Fountain
This charming cobble-stoned place has a pretty urn-shaped fountain.

VISITORS' CHECKLIST

Alpes-Maritimes. 🚶 *2,900.*
🚃 *12 place du Grand Jardin, Vence (04 93 58 37 60).*
ℹ️ *2 rue Grande (04 93 32 86 95).*
Fondation Maeght ⭘ *daily.* ♿
Library, lectures, concerts.

Rue Grande
The doors of the 16th- and 17th-century houses bear coats-of-arms.

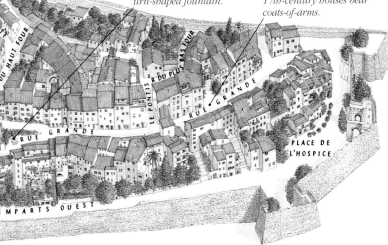

SEITE
R DU HAUT FOUR
R DU PLUS BAS FOUR
LE PONTIS
RUE GRANDE
RUE GRANDE
PLACE DE L'HOSPICE
REMPARTS OUEST

CELEBRITY VILLAGE

The Colombe d'Or (Golden Dove) auberge *(see p574)* was popular with many of the artists and writers who flocked to the Riviera in the 1920s. Early patrons included Picasso, Soutine, Modigliani, Signac, Colette and Cocteau. They often paid for their rooms and meals with paintings, resulting in the priceless collection that can be seen by diners today. The rich and famous have continued to come to St-Paul: Zelda and F. Scott Fitzgerald had a dramatic fight over Isadora Duncan at dinner here one night, and Yves Montand married Simone Signoret on the terrace. A photo display of celebrity visitors in the St-Paul museum features Sartre and de Beauvoir, Greta Garbo, Sophia Loren, Burt Lancaster and Catherine Deneuve.

Artist Marc Chagall (1887–1985), who moved to St-Paul-de-Vence in 1950

Nice 36

THE LARGEST RESORT on the Mediterranean coast and the fifth biggest city in France, with its second busiest airport, Nice was founded by the Greeks and colonized by the Romans. Its temperate winter climate and verdant subtropical vegetation have long attracted visitors. Until World War II, it was popular with aristocrats, including Tsar Nicholas I's widow who visited in 1856, and Queen Victoria who stayed in 1895. This glittering past has contributed to Nice becoming capital of the Côte d'Azur, and today it is also a center for business conferences and package vacations. Nice has good museums, good beaches and an atmospheric street life. Best of all is Carnival: 18 days of celebrations finishing on Shrove Tuesday in a fireworks display and the Battle of the Flowers *(see p35)*.

Yachts at anchor in Nice harbour

Exploring Nice

The promenade des Anglais, running right along the seafront, was built in the 1830s with funds raised by the English colony. Today it is an 8-lane, 5-km (3-mile) highway, with galleries, shops and grand hotels like the **Negresco**, reflecting Nice's prosperity.

Nice also has a dark side, recorded in 1982 by English author, Graham Greene. He wrote a controversial attack on Jacques Médecin, the city's right-wing mayor, who fled to South America to avoid standing trial in France.

Nice was Italian until 1860, and the pastel façades and balconies of the Old Town have a distinctly Italianate feel. It lies at the foot of a hill still known as the Château for the castle which once stood there. The district is largely restored and its tall, narrow buildings house artists and galleries, boutiques and restaurants. The daily flower market in the cours Saleya should not be missed.

The **Cimiez** district, on the hills overlooking the town, is the fashionable quarter of Nice. The old monastery of Notre-Dame-de-Cimiez is well worth a visit. Lower down the Cimiez hillside are Les Arènes, remains of an extensive Roman settlement with vestiges of the great baths and an amphitheatre. Artifacts from the excavations are on show at the archaeological museum, next to the Musée Matisse. At the foot of the Cimiez hill is the **Musée Chagall**.

Musée Matisse

164 av des Arènes de Cimiez. *04 93 81 08 08.* *Wed–Mon.* *some public hols.*

Inspired by the Mediterranean light, Matisse spent many years in Nice. The museum, housed in and below the 17th-century Arena Villa, displays drawings, paintings, bronzes, fabrics and artifacts. Highlights include *Still Life With Pomegranates* and his last completed work, *Flowers and Fruits*.

Nice's Old Quarter

Palais Lascaris

15 rue Droite. *04 93 62 05 54.* *Tue–Sun.* *some public hols & 2 wks Nov.*

This 17th-century stucco palace is decorated with ornate woodwork, Flemish tapestries and illusionistic ceilings thought to be by Carlone. Its small but delightful collection includes a reconstruction of an 18th-century apothecary's shop.

Musée d'Art Contemporain

Promenade des Arts. *04 93 62 61 62.* *Wed–Mon.* *Jan 1, Easter, May 1, Dec 25.*

The museum occupies a strikingly original complex of four marble-faced towers linked by glass passageways. The collection is particularly strong in Neo-Realism and Pop Art, with works by Andy Warhol, Jean Tinguely and Niki de Saint-Phalle. Also well represented are such Ecole de Nice artists as César, Arman and Yves Klein.

***Blue Nude IV* (1952) by Henri Matisse**

An azure view – relaxing on the promenade des Anglais

VISITORS' CHECKLIST

Alpes-Maritimes. 345,000.
7 km (4.5 miles) SW. av Thiers
(08 36 35 35 35). 5 blvd Jean
Jaurès (04 93 85 61 81). quai
du Commerce (04 93 13 66 66).
5 prom des Anglais (04 92 14 48
00). Tue–Sun. Carnival (Feb).

Cathédrale Ste-Réparate
This 17th-century Baroque
building is surmounted by a
handsome tiled dome. Its
interior is lavishly decorated
with plasterwork, marble and
original paneling.

Musée Chagall
36 Avenue du Docteur Ménard.
04 93 53 87 20. Wed–Mon.
Jan 1, May 1, Dec 25.
This is the largest collection of
works by Marc Chagall, with
paintings, drawings, sculpture,
stained glass and mosaics. Best
of all are the 17 canvases of
the artist's *Biblical Message*.

Musée des Beaux-Arts
33 avenue des Baumettes. 04 92
15 28 28. Tue–Sun. Jan 1,
Easter, May 1, Dec 25.
The 19th-century home of a
Ukrainian princess displays
works sent to Nice by Napoleon III after Italy ceded the
city to France in 1860, as well
as paintings by Impressionists
and Post-Impressionists, such
as Renoir, Monet and Dufy.

Palais Masséna
65 rue de France. 04 93 88 11
34. until 2004.
This 19th-century Italianate
villa exhibits religious works,

paintings by Niçois primitives,
white-glazed faïence and
Josephine's gold cloak.

Cathédrale Orthodoxe Russe St-Nicolas
Completed in 1912, the
cathedral was built in memory
of a young Tsarevitch who
died of consumption here
in 1865. The exterior is of
pink brick and gray marble,
with elaborate mosaics. The
interior is resplendent with
icons and fine woodwork.

Musée des Arts Asiatiques
405 prom des Anglais. 04 92 29
37 00. Wed–Sun. Jan 1,
May 1, Dec 25.
Exhibits of ancient and contemporary art from across Asia,
in Kenzo Tange's uncluttered
white marble and glass setting.

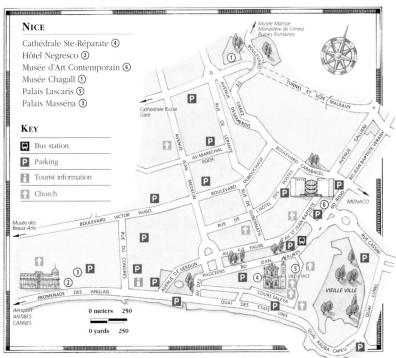

NICE

KEY

🚌 Bus station

P Parking

ℹ Tourist information

⛪ Church

Chapelle St-Pierre, Villefranche

Villefranche-sur-Mer ③⑦

Alpes-Maritimes. 👥 8,000. 🚊 🚌
ℹ️ Jardin François Binon (04 93 01 73 68). 🛥️ Sat.

O NE OF THE MOST perfectly situated towns on the coast, Villefranche lies at the foot of hills forming a sheltered amphitheater. The town overlooks a beautiful natural harbor that is deep enough to be a naval port of call.

The bright and animated waterfront is lined by Italianate façades with cafés and bars from which to watch the fishermen. Here, too, is the medieval **Chapelle St-Pierre**, which, after years of service storing fishing nets, was restored in 1957 and decorated by Jean Cocteau. His frescoes depict non-religious images as well as the life of St. Peter.

Also worth a visit is the 16th-century **Citadelle St-Elme**, incorporating the town hall and two art galleries.

Behind the harbor, the streets are narrow, winding, and often stepped or enclosed by overhanging buildings. Walking through them, you get the odd glimpse of the harbor. The vaulted 13th-century rue Obscure has always provided shelter from bombardment, right up to World War II.

🏛️ **Chapelle St-Pierre**
Quai Amiral Courbet. 📞 04 93 76 90 70. 🕐 mid-Dec–mid-Nov: Tue–Sun. 🔴 Dec 25. 🈸

Cap Ferrat ③⑧

Alpes-Maritimes. ✈️ Nice. 🚊 Nice.
🚌 Beaulieu-sur-Mer. 🚌 ℹ️ St-Jean-Cap-Ferrat (04 93 76 08 90).

T HE PENINSULA of Cap Ferrat boasts some of the most sumptuous villas found on the Riviera. From 1926 until the author's death, the best-known was Somerset Maugham's Villa Mauresque, where Maugham received celebrities from Noël Coward and Winston Churchill to the Duke of Windsor.

High walls guard most of the exclusive villas, but possibly the finest of all is open to the public. The **Musée Ephrussi de Rothschild** is a terra-cotta and marble mansion set in themed gardens on the crest of the cape. It belonged to the Baroness Ephrussi de Rothschild, who bequeathed it to the Institut de France in 1934. It is furnished as she left it, with her collections of priceless porcelain, items that belonged to Marie Antoinette, tapestries and paintings, and a unique collection of working drawings by Fragonard.

The town of **Beaulieu** lies where the cape joins the mainland, overlooking the Baie des Fourmis. A pleasant marina with an exceptionally mild climate and very fine hotels, it is the site of another unique house, the extraordinary **Villa Kerylos**. Built between 1902 and 1908 for archaeologist Theodore Reinach in imitation of an ancient Greek residence, it contains lovingly reproduced mosaics, frescoes and furniture.

🏛️ **Musée Ephrussi de Rothschild**
Cap Ferrat. 📞 04 93 01 33 09. 🕐 Feb–Oct: daily; Nov–Jan: Mon–Fri pms, w/e & school & publ hols: daily. 🈸 ♿ 🅿️ 🛍️

🏛️ **Villa Kerylos**
Imp Gustave Eiffel, Beaulieu. 📞 04 93 01 01 44. 🕐 as above. 🈸 ♿ 🛍️

Greek-style Villa Kerylos at Beaulieu on Cap Ferrat

Louis XV salon at the Fondation Ephrussi de Rothschild, Cap Ferrat

Èze ❸❾

Alpes-Maritimes. 🏠 2,600. 🚂 🚌
🛈 place de Gaulle (04 93 41 26 00).

FOR MANY, EZE is the ultimate perched village, balancing on a rocky pinnacle high above the Mediterranean. Every summer, thousands of visitors stream through the 14th-century fortified gate and throng the narrow streets. The carefully restored, flower-decked buildings mainly house shops, galleries and craft workshops. At the top of the village, the ruined château is surrounded by the lush tropical plants of the **Jardin Exotique**. The view from here is superb.

Farther along the Upper Corniche is the Roman Alpine Trophy of **La Turbie** *(see pp42–3)*. This vast 6 BC structure dominates the surrounding village, with magnificent views toward Monaco and Italy.

🌿 **Jardin Exotique**
Rue du Château. 🚻 04 93 41 10 30.
⬜ daily. 🌑 Jan 1, Dec 25. 📷
♫ **La Turbie**
⬜ Apr–mid-Sep: daily; mid-Sep–Mar: Tue–Sun. 🌑 public hols. 📷 📷 📷

Roquebrune-Cap-Martin ❹⓪

Alpes-Maritimes. 🚉 Nice. 🚂 🚌
🛈 218 av Aristide Briand (04 93 35 62 87). 🚌 Wed.

THE MEDIEVAL VILLAGE of Roquebrune overlooks the wooded cape where the villas of the rich and famous still abound. Visitors here have included Coco Chanel and

Greta Garbo. The cape has not always been kind to its guests. Poet W.B. Yeats died here in 1939, and the architect Le Corbusier was drowned off the coast in 1965.

In 1467, Roquebrune believed that by acting scenes from the Passion it escaped the plague, and every August it continues this tradition.

View from Roquebrune

Alpes-Maritimes ❹❶

Alpes-Maritimes. 🚉 Nice. 🚂 Nice.
🚌 Peille. 🚌 Nice. 🛈 La Mairie,
Peille (04 93 79 71 71).

IN THE HINTERLAND of the Côte d'Azur, it is still possible to find quiet, unspoiled villages off the tourist track. The tiny twin villages of **Peille** and **Peillon** are typical. Both have changed little since the Middle Ages, perched on outcrops over the Paillon River, their streets a mass of steps and arches. Peille, the more remote, even has its own dialect. The Alpes-Maritimes countryside is also unspoiled, its

craggy gorges, tumbling rivers and wind-swept plateaus just a few hours from the coast. Of note are the ancient rock carvings of the **Vallée des Merveilles** and rare wildlife in the **Parc National du Mercantour**.

Menton ❹❷

Alpes-Maritimes. 🏠 30,000. 🚂 🚌
🛈 Palais de l'Europe, 8 avenue Boyer
(04 92 41 76 50). 🚌 daily.

MENTON'S BEACHES, with the Alps and the golden buildings and Belle Epoque villas of the Old Town as a backdrop, would be enough to lure most visitors. In the 19th century, Queen Victoria and famous writers and poets often vacationed here. Tropical gardens and citrus fruits thrive in its perfect climate, mild even in February for the famous lemon festival *(see p35)*.

The **Basilica St-Michel** is a superb example of Baroque architecture in yellow and pink stone. The square before it is paved with a mosaic of the Grimaldi coat of arms. The **Salle des Mariages** in the Hôtel de Ville was decorated in 1957 by Jean Cocteau. Drawings, paintings, ceramics and stage designs by the renowned artist are displayed in the **Musée Cocteau**, housed in a 17th-century fort. Inside the Palais Carnolès, the **Musée des Beaux-Arts** features works from the Middle ages to the 20th century.

🏛 **Salle des Mariages**
Hôtel de Ville. 🚻 04 92 10 50 00.
⬜ Mon–Fri. 🌑 public hols. 📷
🏛 **Musée Cocteau**
Quai de Monléon. 🚻 04 93 57 72 30. ⬜ Wed–Mon. 🌑 public hols. 📷
🏛 **Musée des Beaux-Arts**
3 av de la Madone. 🚻 04 93 35 49 71. ⬜ Wed–Mon. 🌑 public hols.

Mosaic at the Musée Cocteau in Menton

Monaco

Aerial view of Monaco

Travelers to Monaco by car would do well to take the Moyenne Corniche, one of the most beautiful highways in the world, with incomparable views of the Mediterranean coastline. Arriving among the skyscrapers of Monaco today, it is hard to imagine the turbulence of its history. At first a Greek settlement, later taken by the Romans, it was bought from the Genoese in 1297 by the Grimaldis who, in spite of bitter family feuds and at least one political assassination, still rule as the world's oldest monarchy. Monaco covers 1.9 sq km (0.74 sq miles) and, although its size has increased by one-third in the form of landfills, it still occupies an area smaller than that of New York City's Central Park.

Grand Casino

Exploring Monaco

Monaco owes its renown principally to its Grand Casino. Source of countless legends, it was instituted in 1856 by Charles III to save himself from bankruptcy. The first casino was opened in 1865 on a barren promontory (later named Monte-Carlo in his honor) across the harbor from ancient Monaco-Ville. So successful was Charles's money-making venture that, by 1870, he was able to abolish taxation for his people. Today, Monaco is a tax haven for thousands, and its residents have the highest per capita income in the world.

Visitors come from all over the world for the Grand Prix de Monaco in May and the Monte Carlo Rally in January *(see p35)*. Many of the greatest singers perform in the opera season. There is a fireworks festival (July–August), and an international circus festival at the end of January as well as world-class ballet and concerts. Facilities exist for every sort of leisure activity, and there is plenty else to enjoy without going broke, including **Fort Antoine** and the Neo-Romanesque **Cathédrale**.

♛ Grand Casino

Place du Casino. 📞 *00 377 92 16 23 00*. 🕐 *daily, from noon.* ♿
Designed in 1878 by Charles Garnier, architect of the Paris Opéra *(see p93)*, and set in formal gardens, the Casino gives a splendid view over Monaco. The lavish interior is still decorated in Belle Epoque style, recalling an era when this was the rendezvous of Russian Grand Dukes, English lords and other adventurers. Anyone can play the odds on the one-armed bandits of the Salle Blanche or the roulette wheels of the Salle Europe. Even the most exclusive of the gaming rooms can be visited at a price, but their tables are for the big spenders only.

♟ Palais Princier

Place du Palais. 📞 *00 377 93 25 18 31*. 🕐 *Jun–Oct: daily.* 📷
Monaco-Ville, the seat of government, is the site of the 13th-century Palais Princier. The interior, with its priceless furniture and carpets and its

Skyscrapers and apartment blocks of modern Monte-Carlo

MONACO'S ROYAL FAMILY

Since 1949, Monaco has been in the charge of its most effective ruler ever. Businesslike Prince Rainier III is descended from a Grimaldi who entered the Monaco fortress in 1297 disguised as a monk. Rainier's wife, former film star Grace Kelly, died tragically in 1982. Their son, Albert, is heir to the throne but his sisters, Caroline and Stephanie, are the main focus of media attention.

Prince Rainier III, Princess Grace and Princess Caroline

VISITORS' CHECKLIST

Monaco. 🏙 30,000. ✈ 7 km (4.5 miles) SW Nice. 🚉 av Prince Pierre (00 377 93 10 60 15). ℹ 2a bd des Moulins (00 377 92 16 61 16). 🛒 daily. 🎪 Festival du Cirque (Jan–Feb); International Fireworks Festival (Jul–Aug); Fête Nationale Monégasque (19 Nov).

Cousteau established his research center here.

♣ Jardin Exotique

62 bd du Jardin Exotique. ☎ 00 377 93 30 33 65. 🕐 daily. 🚫 Nov 19, Dec 25. 🎫 ♿ to part of garden only. 🅿 These gardens are considered to be the finest in Europe, with a huge range of tropical and subtropical plants. In the park, a museum of anthropology offers evidence that bears, mammoths and hippopotami once lived on the coast here.

magnificent frescoes, is only open to the public in the summer. The changing of the guard is at 11:55 am.

🏛 Musée des Souvenirs Napoléoniens

Place du Palais. ☎ 00 377 93 25 18 31. 🕐 Jun–mid-Nov: daily; mid-Dec–May: Tue–Sun. 🚫 Jan 1, May 1, Grand Prix, Dec 25. 🎫 ♿ A genealogical tree on the wall traces the family links between the Grimaldis and Bonapartes. Also on display are Napoleon's

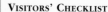

Guard outside the Palais Princier

personal effects and clothing, and numerous portraits.

⚓ Musée Océano-graphique

Av Saint-Martin. ☎ 00 377 93 15 36 00. 🕐 daily. 🎫 ♿ 🍴 🅿 This museum was founded in 1910 by Prince Albert I, using his casino profits. Its aquarium, fed with sea water, holds rare species of marine plants and animals. The museum houses an important scientific collection, diving equipment and model ships. Marine explorer Jacques

🏛 Musée des Automates et Poupées d'Autrefois

17 av Princesse Grace. ☎ 00 377 93 30 91 26. 🕐 daily. 🚫 Jan 1, May 1, Grand Prix, Nov 19, Dec 25. 🎫 🅿 This museum houses over 400 dolls from the 18th and 19th centuries. The delightful automata are set in motion several times each day.

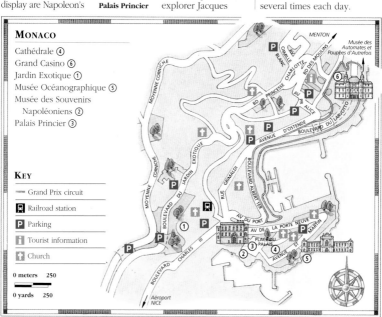

MONACO

Cathédrale ④
Grand Casino ⑥
Jardin Exotique ①
Musée Océanographique ⑤
Musée des Souvenirs Napoléoniens ②
Palais Princier ③

KEY

═══ Grand Prix circuit
🚉 Railroad station
🅿 Parking
ℹ Tourist information
✝ Church

0 meters 250
0 yards 250

CORSICA

HAUTE-CORSE · CORSE-DU-SUD

*C*ORSICA, *where the people speak their own Italian dialect, has all the attributes of a mini-continent. There are tropical palm trees, vineyards, olive and orange groves, forests of chestnut and indigenous pine, alpine lakes and cool mountain torrents filled with trout. Most distinctive of all is the parched maquis (scrub), heavy with the scent of myrtle, which Napoleon swore he could smell from the sea.*

The fourth-largest island in the Mediterranean after Sicily and Sardinia, Corsica has been a problem and a bafflement to mainland France ever since 1769, when it was "sold" to Louis XV by the Genoese for 40 million francs. Before that, following years of struggle, the Corsican people had enjoyed 14 years of independence under the revered leadership of Pasquale Paoli. They understandably felt cheated by the deal with the French, and have resented them ever since. To vacationers visiting the island – in July and August tourists outnumber the inhabitants six to one – the Corsican-French relationship may not appear to be an adverse one. However, there is a strong (and sometimes violent) separatist movement, which does deter some tourists. As a result, Corsica's wild beauty has been preserved to an extent not seen in the rest of the Mediterranean.

From the 11th to the 13th century, Corsica was a colony of the old Tuscan republic of Pisa, whose builders founded beautifully proportioned Romanesque churches. These buildings are, along with the megalithic stone warriors in Filitosa, the noblest monuments to be seen here. Otherwise, this birthplace of Napoleon remains a place of wild seacoasts and mountain peaks, one of the last unspoiled corners of the Mediterranean: poor, depopulated, beautiful, old-fashioned and doggedly aloof.

The village of Oletta in the Nebbio region around St-Florent

◁ **A fisherman with feline friends in Bastia**

Exploring Corsica

CORSICA'S MAIN APPEAL is its scenery: a wildly beautiful landscape of mountains, forests, myrtle-scented maquis and countless miles of sandy beaches. Late spring (when the wild flowers are in bloom) and early fall are the best times to visit – the temperature is moderate and there aren't too many visitors. The island is renowned for its superb hiking trails, some of which become cross-country skiing trails during the winter. Downhill skiing is also possible in February and March.

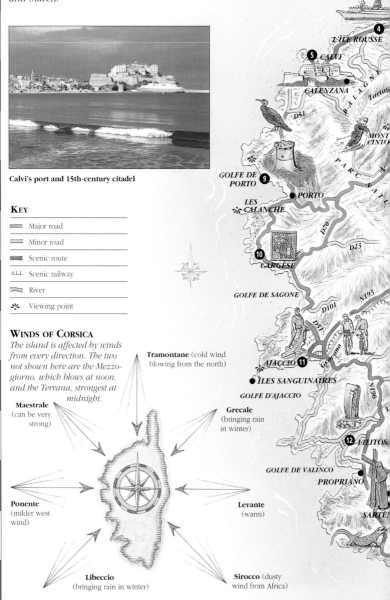

Calvi's port and 15th-century citadel

KEY

▭▭▭	Major road
▭▭▭	Minor road
▭▭▭	Scenic route
⊥⊥⊥	Scenic railway
〜〜	River
☼	Viewing point

WINDS OF CORSICA

The island is affected by winds from every direction. The two not shown here are the Mezzogiorno, which blows at noon, and the Terrana, strongest at midnight.

Tramontane (cold wind blowing from the north)

Maestrale (can be very strong)

Grecale (bringing rain in winter)

Ponente (milder west wind)

Levante (warm)

Libeccio (bringing rain in winter)

Sirocco (dusty wind from Africa)

Map labels

L'ÎLE ROUSSE ④

⑤ CALVI

CALENZANA

BALAGNE

D51 · Tartag

MONT CINTO

PARC N

GOLFE DE PORTO ⑨

● PORTO

LES CALANCHE

D70 · D23

⑩ CARGESE

GOLFE DE SAGONE

D101 · N193

D51 · Gravona

AJACCIO ⑪

● ÎLES SANGUINAIRES

GOLFE D'AJACCIO

⑫ FILITOS

N196

GOLFE DE VALINCO

PROPRIANO

SARTÈ

SIGHTS AT A GLANCE

Ajaccio **11** Côte Orientale **15**
Bastia **2** Filitosa **12**
Bonifacio **14** Golfe de Porto **9**
Calvi **5** L'Île Rousse **4**
Cap Corse **1** The Niolo **6**
Cargèse **10** St-Florent **3**
The Castagniccia **8** Sartène **13**
Corte **7**

The Calanche cliffs in the Golfe de Porto

GETTING AROUND

Car ferries (which should be booked well in advance)
depart from Marseille, Nice and Toulon, arriving at
Bastia, L'Île Rousse, Calvi, Ajaccio and Propriano.
There are also ferries from Sardinia and the Italian
ports of Genoa, Livorno and La Spezia. Small airports
are based at Ajaccio, Bastia, Calvi and Figari (near
Bonifacio). Corsica's roads are narrow, twisting and
often tortuously slow, though breathtaking views
reward the effort. A car is almost a must for exploring
the island, as public transportation is limited. Carry
spare petrol – gas stations are few and far between.

0 kilometers   20
0 miles   10

Corte's Old Town, with its citadel high up on a rocky outcrop

Cap Corse ❶

Haute-Corse. 🚊 Bastia. 🚌 Bastia,
Macinaggio, Rogliano. 🚢 Bastia.
ℹ️ Bastia (04 95 54 20 40).

The village of Erbalunga on the east coast of Cap Corse

Cᴀᴘ ᴄᴏʀsᴇ is the northern tip of Corsica, 40 km (25 miles) in length but seldom more than 12 km (7.5 miles) wide, pointing like an accusatory finger toward Genoa.

There are two roads out of Bastia to the cape: the D81 leading west across the mountains and joining up with the D80 after the wine village of Patrimonio; and the D80 traveling north along the eastern shore to **Erbalunga** and **Macinaggio**. Either way the road is narrow and twisting, a foretaste of what awaits you nearly everywhere in Corsica.

From the coastal village of **Lavasina**, the D54 leads left off the D80 to Pozzo; from here it is a 5-hour round-trip on foot to the 1,307-m (4,300-ft) summit of **Monte Stello**, the highest peak on the cape. The 360-degree view from the top takes in St-Florent to the west, the massif of central Corsica to the south and the Italian island of Elba to the east.

Farther up the coast, the restored **Tour de Losse** is one of many 16th-century Genoese towers along the coast – part of an elaborate system which enabled all Corsican towns to be warned within two hours of impending barbarian raids.

The charming 18th-century fishing port of **Centuri**, near the tip of the peninsula on the west coast, is an ideal spot for a delicious seafood feast. **Pino**, a pretty little village straggling down the green mountainside farther to the south, has no hotel, only a lovely little church dedicated to the Virgin, full of model ships placed there by mariners grateful for her protection.

On the way south along the vertiginous lower corniche, be sure to turn left up the hill to **Canari**. One of the larger villages in this area, Canari has a jewel of a 12th-century Pisan church, Santa Maria Assunta, a magnificent view across the sea, and a thoroughly convivial hotel-restaurant. All the by-roads in this thickly wooded area seem to lead somewhere interesting. There are literally dozens of picturesque hamlets in the vicinity, and it should be borne in mind that from this point onward the landscape becomes steadily less attractive as the road winds on past the old asbestos works and beaches of black sand below **Nonza**.

Bastia ❷

Haute-Corse. 🏛 39,000. ✈ 🚊 🚌
🚢 ℹ️ pl St-Nicolas (04 95 54 20 40).
🏛 Tue–Sun. 🌐 www.ville-bastia.fr

A ᴛʜʀɪᴠɪɴɢ ᴘᴏʀᴛ and the administrative capital of Upper Corsica, Bastia is utterly different in style from its sedate west coast rival, Ajaccio. The Genoese citadel and colorful 19th-century Italianate buildings around the old port are for many people their first taste of the authentic Mediterranean – as it was half a century ago, and as it stubbornly remains in our imagination.

The center of Bastiais life is the **place St-Nicolas**, facing the wharf where ferries from the mainland and Italy arrive. Heading south along the waterfront you come to the **place de l'Hôtel de Ville**, site of a bustling outdoor food market each morning. Bordering the square are the early 17th-century **Chapelle de l'Immaculée Conception**, with its ornate 18th-century interior, and the mid-17th-century **Eglise de St-Jean-Baptiste**, whose façade dominates the Vieux Port.

From here it is a short walk up to the 16th-century **citadel**, where there are two more churches worth seeing: the Baroque **Chapelle Sainte-Croix**, with its striking *Black Christ*, fished out of the sea by Bastiais fishermen in 1428; and the 15th-century **Sainte-Marie**, which has a *Virgin* made of a ton of solid silver.

Bastia's Vieux Port seen from the Jetée du Dragon

St-Florent ❸

Haute-Corse. 🏛 *1,500.* 🅿 ℹ
Bâtiment Administratif (04 95 37 06 04).
✉ *1st Wed of month.*

S T-FLORENT IS almost a
Corsican St-Tropez – chic,
affluent and packed with
yachts from all over the
Mediterranean. Its citadel
(closed to visitors) dates from
1439, and is a fine example of
Genoese military architecture.
The town itself is pleasant to
wander through; its main
attraction, the 12th-century
Pisan **Cathédrale de Santa
Maria Assunta**, lies just inland
on the road to Poggio-d'Oletta.

Environs
A leisurely 4-hour tour by car
of the **Nebbio** region, which
extends in an amphitheater
around St-Florent, might take
in the following: **Santo Pietro
di Tenda**; **Murato**, famous for
its magnificent **Eglise de San
Michele de Murato**, a 12th-
century Pisan Romanesque
construction built of white and
green stone; the **San Stefano**
pass, with the sea on either
side; **Oletta**, which produces a
special blue cheese made from
ewes' milk; the **Teghime** pass;
and finally, the wine village of
Patrimonio, where there is
a strange, big-eared menhir
dating from 900–800 BC.

Along the coast to the west
of St-Florent lies the barren, uninhabited **Désert des Agriates**.
If you can face the 10-km
(6-mile) trip to the sea – on
foot, by bike or by motorcycle
– the Saleccia beach here is
by far the most beautiful and
solitary beach on the island.

San Michele de Murato

L'Île Rousse ❹

Haute-Corse. 🏛 *2,850.* 🅿 🅿 ⛴
ℹ *place Paoli (04 95 60 04 35).*
✉ *daily.* 🅦 www.ot-ile-rousse.fr

F OUNDED IN 1758 by
Pasquale Paoli, leader of
independent Corsica, L'Île
Rousse is today a major
vacation resort and
ferry terminal. The
center of town is the
plane-shaded place
Paoli, dominated by
a marble statue of
Corsica's national hero.
On the north side of the
square is the covered
market, with the Old
Town just beyond.

In the summer, L'Île
Rousse becomes hid-
eously crowded, its
beaches a mass of
bodies. It is worth
traveling 10 km (6 miles) up
the coast to **Lozari**, which
offers a magnificent, virtually
unspoiled stretch of sand.

**French foreign
legionnaire**

Environs
One very pleasant way to
discover the **Balagne** region
is to take the tram-train from
L'Île Rousse to Calvi and
back. This odd little service
runs all year (more frequent
in summer), roughly along
to the coastline and stopping
at Algajola, Lumio and various
villages along the way.

Calvi ❺

Haute-Corse. 🏛 *5,200.* 🅿 🅿 ⛴
ℹ *Port de Plaisance (04 95 65 16 67).*
✉ *daily.* 🅦 www.calvitravel.com

C ALVI, where Nelson lost his
eye in an "explosion of
stones" in 1794, is today half
military town, half cheap vacation resort. Its 15th-century
citadel is garrisoned by a
crack French regiment of the
foreign legion; while beyond
the ferry port is a seedy,
apparently endless camp-
site and trailer park.
The town makes a
halfhearted case for
being the birthplace of
Christopher Columbus,
but there is no real evi-
dence to support this.
A much better claim to
fame is the food, which is
very good and reasonably
priced by Corsican stan-
dards. There is also a very
respectable jazz festival
at Calvi towards the
end of June.

Outside of town, the
19th-century **Chapelle
de Notre-Dame de la Serra**
is gloriously situated on a hilltop commanding extensive
views in all directions.

The Chapelle de Notre-Dame de la Serra, 6 km (3.5 miles) southwest of Calvi

Corte's 15th-century citadel at dawn

The Niolo ❻

Haute-Corse. ☐ *Corte.* ℹ *Calacuccia (04 95 48 05 22).* ☒ *www.niolo.st.fr*

THE NIOLO, west of Corte, extends westward to the Vergio pass and the upper Golo basin, and to the east as far as the Scala di Santa Regina. It includes Corsica's highest mountain, the 2,700-m (8,859-ft) **Monte Cinto**, and its biggest river, the **Golo**, which meets the sea south of Bastia.

Unique among the regions of Corsica, the Niolo persists in the cultivation of livestock as its economic mainstay.

The main town, **Calacuccia**, is convenient for excursions to Monte Cinto. The nearby ski resort of **Haut Asco** is best reached by the D147 from **Asco**, but enthusiasts can walk from Calacuccia (8–9 hours). To the south is the huge forest of **Valdu Niello**.

Corte ❼

Haute-Corse. 🏔 *6,000.* ☐ ☐ ℹ *La Citadelle (04 95 46 26 70).* 🗓 *Fri.* ☒ *www.corte-tourisme.com*

IN THE geographical center of Corsica, Corte was the chosen capital of the independence leader Pasquale Paoli from 1755–69, and today is the seat of the island's university. In the Old Town is the 15th-century citadel, housing the **Musée de la Corse**. Its exhibits relate to traditional Corsican life and anthropology.

Corte is the best base for exploring nearby mountain areas, because it stands exactly halfway along the GR20, the legendary 220-km (137-mile) trail from Calenzana to Conca.

🏛 Musée de la Corse

La Citadelle. 🕻 *04 95 45 25 45.* ◯ *Apr–mid-Jun & Oct–Nov: Tue–Sun; mid-Jun–Sep: daily; Dec–Mar: Tue–Sat* ⬤ *public hols.* 🌐 🚻 💳 🎧

Environs
Don't miss the wildly beautiful **Gorges de la Restonica**, about 12 km (7.5 miles) out of town via the D623. Above these gorges adventurous walkers may wish to make the well-marked climb to the snow-fed **Lac de Melo** (allow 60–90 minutes); or the **Lac de Capitello**, 30 minutes farther on, where the snow stays as late as early June. The path – in winter a cross-country ski trail – follows the river.

South of Corte, the **Forêt de Vizzavona** features beech and pine woodland crisscrossed by trout-filled streams and walking trails (notably the GR20). It is a perfect refuge from the summer heat and is also an excuse to take the small train up from Ajaccio or Bastia, which stops at Vizzavona.

The Castagniccia ❽

Haute-Corse. 🚉 *Bastia.* ☐ *Corte, Ponte Leccia.* ☐ *Piedicroce, La Porta, Valle-d'Alesani.* ℹ *Piedicroce (04 95 35 82 54).*

EAST OF CORTE is the hilly, chestnut-covered region of Castagniccia (literally "small chestnut grove"), which most Corsicans agree is the very heart and kernel of the island. It was here that independence leader Pasquale Paoli was born in 1725, and that the revolts against Genoa and later France began in earnest in 1729. Alas, many of the villages in this beautiful, remote area are nearly empty, their inhabitants having joined the 800,000 or so Corsicans (almost three times the present population) who live and work in mainland France or Italy. It seems hard to believe that in the 17th century, when the great chestnut forests introduced here by the Genoese were at the height of their production, this was the most prosperous and populated region in Corsica.

The D71 from Ponte Leccia (north of Corte) to the east coast winds through the center of the Castagniccia region, and to see it at a leisurely pace will take the best part of a day. Arm yourself with a picnic before you start, because there are few supplies available to buy en route.

◁ **Limestone cliffs of Bonifacio** *(see p533)*

Golfe de Porto ❾

Corse-du-Sud. 🚶 🚌 ⛴ *Ajaccio.*
🚌 *Porto.* ℹ *Porto (04 95 26 10 55).*
ⓦ www.porto-tourisme.com

PORTO IS SITED at the head of the Golfe de Porto, one of the most beautiful bays in the Mediterranean, which for the sake of its fauna and flora has been included in UNESCO's list of the world's common cultural heritage sites. The town has a magnificent Genoese watchtower – the perfect spot for admiring the sunset – and regular boat excursions (Apr–Oct) to the Calanche, Scandola and Girolata.

The **Calanche** begin 2 km (1.2 miles) out of Porto, on the road to Piana. These 300-m (1,000-ft) red granite cliffs plunge truly to the sea, and are breathtaking. They are accessible only by boat or on foot: well-defined trails start from the Tête du Chien and the Pont de Mezanu, while boat tickets are available at Porto's Hôtel Le Cyrnée.

East of Porto are the Gorges de la Spelunca, accessed by a mule route punctuated by Genoese bridges.

Just south of Porto along a spectacular corniche drive passing under granite archways, lies the pretty village of **Piana**, a good base for visiting this whole area, with information on recommended walks. One particularly worthwhile destination is the cove at **Ficajola** just below Piana – a truly delightful beach.

Porto's marina and Genoese watchtower

Environs
The road over the mountains from Porto to Calvi offers no more than a taste of this grandiose corner of Corsica – you have to take to the sea to view it properly (ferries from Porto and Galéria). **Girolata**, a tiny hamlet north of Porto, can be reached only by sea or by walking a mule path (4 hours round-trip) from a clearly marked point 23 km (14 miles) north of Porto on the D81.

At the mouth of the Golfe de Girolata, the **Réserve Naturelle de Scandola**, instituted in 1975, is the first land-and-sea reserve in France, covering over 1,000 hectares (2,500 acres) of sea, and a similar area of cliffs, caves and maquis (shrubbery). Marine life is abundant in these protected waters; there are ospreys, puffins and falcons.

CORSICAN FLOWERS

For lovers of wildflowers, Corsica is a Mediterranean jewel. Much of the island is covered with maquis, a tangle of aromatic shrubs and low trees that flowers from late winter onward. Among its dense variety are the showy rock-

Rock-rose

roses, which shower the ground with short-lived pink or white petals, and brilliant yellow broom. Grassy and rocky slopes are good places to spot the widespread tassel hyacinth and the Illyrian sea lily, which grows only in Corsica and Sardinia.

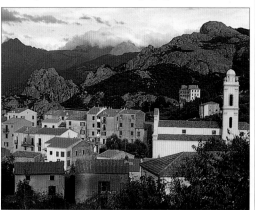

The town of Piana with the Calanche in the background

Spanish broom

Illyrian sea lily

Tassel hyacinth

Cargèse's Greek rite church

Cargèse ⓾

Corse-du-Sud. 🚶 *1,000.* 🚌 🛈 *rue du Docteur Dragacci (04 95 26 41 31).*

CARGÈSE overlooks the sea from a promontory between the bays of Sagone and Pero. It is a small town with an odd history: many of the people who live here are the descendants of 17th-century Greek refugees from Turkish rule, given asylum in Corsica.

A few Cargèsiens still speak Greek, and their icon-filled Eastern (Greek) rite church still faces its Catholic counterpart in an attitude that must once have seemed deliberately confrontational. Nowadays the old rivalries have long since vanished, and the Orthodox priest and Catholic *curé* often stand in for one another.

There are many splendid beaches in the vicinity, notably at **Pero** and **Chiuni** just to the north, and at **Ménasina** and **Stagnoli** to the south.

Ajaccio ⓫

Corse-du-Sud. 🚶 *60,000.* ✈ 🚢
🚌 🚆 🛈 *3 bd du Roi Jérôme (04 95 51 53 03).* 🛍 *Tue–Sun.*

AJACCIO, a noisy, busy town by Corsican standards, was the birthplace of Napoleon Bonaparte in 1769. Napoleon never returned to Corsica after crowning himself emperor of the French in 1804, but the town – the modern capital of nationalist Corsica – celebrates his birthday every August 15.

The 16th-century **Cathédrale Notre-Dame de la Miséricorde**, where Napoleon was baptized in 1771, houses Delacroix's famous painting *Vierge du Sacré-Coeur*.

A few streets away, the **Maison Bonaparte**, where Napoleon was born and spent his childhood, contains family portraits, period furniture and assorted memorabilia.

More interesting is the superb collection of artworks assembled on the coattails of Napoleon by his uncle, Cardinal Fesch, who looted numerous churches, palaces and museums during the Italian campaign and brought the priceless swag home to Ajaccio. Housed in the 19th-century Palais Fesch, the **Musée Fesch** contains the finest collection of Italian primitive art in France after the Louvre. Among its masterpieces are works by Bellini, Botticelli, Bernini, Poussin, Titian and Veronese. Next to the Palais Fesch stands the **Chapelle Impériale**, built in 1855 by Napoleon III to accommodate the tombs of the Bonapartes.

From here, walk back along the quay to the Jetée de la Citadelle, which offers superb views of the town, the marina and the Golfe d'Ajaccio. The adjacent 16th-century **citadel** is occupied by the army.

🏛 **Maison Bonaparte**
Rue St-Charles. 📞 *04 95 21 43 89.*
🕐 *Mon pm–Sun.*

🏛 **Musée Fesch**
50 rue Fesch. 📞 *04 95 21 48 17.*
🕐 *Apr–Sep: Mon pm–Sun; Oct–Mar: Mon–Fri.* ● *public hols.* 🎟 🚻
🌐 *www.musee-fesch.com*

Environs
From the quai de la Citadelle there are daily excursions to the **Îles Sanguinaires** at the mouth of the Golfe d'Ajaccio.

At Vero, 21 km (13 miles) northeast on the N193, is an unusual park, **A Cupulatta**, with over 150 species of tortoises and turtles (Apr–Oct).

A statue-menhir at Filitosa

Filitosa ⓬

Centre Préhistorique de Filitosa, Corse-du-Sud. 📞 *04 95 74 00 91.*
🕐 *Apr–Oct: daily.* 🎟 🚻 *mus. only.*

THE 4,000-YEAR-OLD, life-size stone warriors of Filitosa are the most spectacular relics of megalithic man in Corsica. Discovered in 1946, these phallic granite menhirs represent an interesting progression from mere silhouettes to more detailed sculpture, etched with human features and even weapons.

The five most recent and most sophisticated figures (about 1500 BC) stand around a thousand-year-old olive

Statue of Napoleon by Laboureur in place Maréchal Foch, Ajaccio

The fortified Old Town of Bonifacio, with the harbor in the foreground

tree, in the field below a tumulus. Other finds, which include a heavily armed warrior with shield, helmet and sword, can be seen in the site's archaeological museum.

Sartène ⓭

Corse-du-Sud. 🏠 3,400. 🚌 🛈 6 rue Borgo (04 95 77 15 40). 🛒 summer: daily; winter: Sat.

Sartène is a medieval fortified town of narrow cobbled streets and gray granite houses rising above the Rizzanese Valley. Founded by the Genoese in the early 16th century, it has survived attacks by Barbary pirates and centuries of bloody feuding among the town's leading families.

Despite all this, Sartène has a reputation for deep piety, reinforced each year by the oldest and most intense Christian ceremony in Corsica, the Good Friday *Catenacciu* – literally, the "chained one." A red-hooded penitent, barefoot and in chains, drags a wooden cross through the Old Town in a reenactment of Christ's ascent to Golgotha.

Environs
Just outside of town in Sartène's former prison, the **Musée de Préhistoire Corse** contains fascinating artifacts from the Neolithic period, the Bronze Age and Iron Age.

🏛 Musée de Préhistoire Corse
Rue Croce. 📞 04 95 77 01 09. 🔓 (due to reopen Oct 2002) mid-Jun–mid-Sep: Mon–Sat; mid-Sep–mid-Jun: Mon–Fri. ⬤ public hols. 🈶

Bonifacio ⓮

Corse-du-Sud. 🏠 3,000. 🚌 ⛴ 🛈 rue Fred Scamaroni (04 95 73 11 88). 🛒 Wed. 🌐 www.bonifacio.com

Bonifacio is the southernmost town in Corsica, dramatically sited on a limestone cliff peninsula with some of the most stunning views in the Mediterranean (*see pp528–9*). Its handsome harbor at the foot of the cliffs is the focus of life: cafés, restaurants and boutiques abound and boats depart regularly for neighboring Sardinia and the uninhabited islands of Lavezzi and Cavallo.

From the harbor, steps lead up to Bonifacio's fortified Old Town. The citadel, built by the conquering Genoese at the end of the 12th century, has long been the town's main defensive post, and from 1963–83 was the headquarters of the French foreign legion. From here, wander down to the tip of the promontory to see the two old windmills and the ruins of a Franciscan monastery.

Côte Orientale ⓯

Haute-Corse & Corse-du-Sud. 🚌 Bastia. 🚉 Aléria, Salenzara, Porto-Vecchio. ⛴ Bastia, Porto-Vecchio. 🛈 Aléria (04 95 57 01 51), Porto-Vecchio (04 95 70 09 58).

The FLAT and dreary alluvial plain stretching from Bastia to Solenzara has been rich farmland since 1945, the year it was finally drained and rid of malaria. More recently, vacation resorts and even high-rise hotels have mushroomed along the coast, cashing in on its long, sandy beaches.

The best sight in **Mariana**, which is otherwise uncomfortably close to the Bastia-Poretta airport, is the early 12th-century cathedral of Mariana known as **La Canonica**. A short distance away is the slightly older **Eglise de San Perteo**, surrounded by meadows.

About halfway down the coast, the port of **Aléria**, originally a Greek colony and the base for Rome's conquest of Corsica in 259 BC, is interesting for its rich archaeological heritage. Just outside town, a museum housed in the 16th-century Fort de Matra chronicles daily life in Roman Aléria.

Toward the southern tip of the island, the fortified town of **Porto-Vecchio**, built by Corsica's Genoese conquerors, is now an extremely popular seaside resort. The setting is perfect for the conventional seaside vacation, with umbrella pines, cork oak forests and glorious white sandy beaches within easy reach of the town, especially at **Palombaggia** and **Pinarello**.

The Golfe de Porto-Vecchio

TRAVELERS'
NEEDS

WHERE TO STAY

MANY OF FRANCE'S 22,000 registered hotels are charming, unique and well priced. These four pages describe the types of hotels we have reviewed and provide tips on what to expect from French hotels. The hotel listings pages *(see pp540–75)* describe some of the best hotels around the country in every price category and style, from slick, modern chain hotels to small, classic, family-run establishments. Also included are *chambres d'hôte* (a sort of French bed-and-breakfast), which range from simple farms to grand châteaux, as well as the best hostels. France is full of furnished vacation apartments and houses, and information is given on renting a rural home, or *gîte*, and on how to get the most out of a camping vacation.

The Hôtel Euzkadi at Espelette in the Pyrenees *(see p569)*

THE CLASSIC FAMILY HOTEL

IF YOU'RE TOURING on a budget, the small, family-run, family-oriented hotel lurking in virtually every village and town is for you. It's likely to be the focal point of the village, with the bar and dining room (if the food is fairly good) full of locals. The atmosphere is entirely informal, with children, cats and dogs happily at home. In the hotel's dozen or so bedrooms, old-fashioned charm will make up for a lack of up-to-date decor and for the mere trickle of hot water in the shower.

The annual *Logis de France* guide details over 4,000 of these family-run, mainly one- and two-star hotel-restaurants. They tend to be located in small towns or rural locations; there are none in Paris. Most are no more than roadside inns, but off the beaten track you will discover many converted farmhouses and inexpensive seaside hotels. The *Logis* is a useful reference, but the quality of places listed can be uneven.

THE CHÂTEAU HOTEL

MANY OF FRANCE'S châteaux and mansions have been converted into luxury hotels. They include everything from Renaissance buildings with sweeping lawns to medieval castles with battlements and keeps. Grand hotels are found all over France, with rich pickings in the Loire, the Savoie, the Haute-Savoie and the Rhône Delta. Properties included in the **Relais et Châteaux** brochure are recommended.

Typically, rooms are beautifully designed and the food is *haute cuisine*. Bedrooms range from grand suites to more simple abodes, often in converted farm buildings, making it possible, if you're willing to forgo four-poster beds and antiques, to live in luxury without going broke.

THE CITY HOTEL

EVERY BIG CITY has a group of hotels close to the train station or port. They range from cheap accommodations to a grand hotel or two. The most famous city hotels are the palace hotels in Paris and the Riviera resorts such as Nice and Cannes. Note that many city hotels do not have a restaurant. It is always worth checking the quality of the bedroom before you officially check in.

THE MODERN CHAIN HOTEL

BRANCHES OF MODERN hotel chains are useful for inexpensive pitstops if you're traveling through France. Many are situated on the outskirts of towns, near highways or main roads. The cheapest are the one-star, no-frills **Formula 1** motels, offering bedrooms with a double and single bed and no private bathroom.

Two-star chains include **Ibis/Arcade**, **Campanile**, **Climat de France** and **Primevère**. Three-star chains include **Novotel** and **Mercure**; both offer private bathrooms and allow one child to stay at no charge, provided the whole

Le Négresco in Nice on the Côte d'Azur *(see p573)*

The Meurice Hotel in the Tuileries Quarter of Paris *(see p541)*

family sleeps in one room (Novotel has free accommodations for two under-16s).

THE RESTAURANT-WITH-ROOMS

THROUGHOUT FRANCE, many of the better restaurants offer accommodations. Usually, the bedrooms match the restaurant's quality and are priced accordingly. Sometimes, though, gourmet restaurants have simple bedrooms hidden away upstairs – great finds for those who like to splurge on food while saving on lodging. Refer to the restaurant listings on pages 580–613.

MEALS AND FACILITIES

IN HIGH SEASON, many resort hotels insist on half board, or *demi-pension* (a per-person rate for the room, dinner and breakfast). There is also full board, or *pension*, which covers lunch too. While it is cheaper to opt for inclusive rates, meals come from set or limited-choice menus, which often omit the more interesting dishes.

Many smaller family-run hotels do not provide meals on Sunday evenings and often stop serving dinner as early as 9pm on other days.

Rooms usually have double beds; twin or single beds must be requested when booking. All mid-range hotels have a choice of bathroom facilities. A walk down the corridor to a separate bathroom can reduce the room rate considerably. A bathroom with a bath *(un bain)* usually costs more than one with a shower *(une douche); un cabinet de toilette* has a sink and bidet, without a bath, shower or toilet. If you do not have *pension* or *demi-pension* accommodations, breakfast is often an added charge. Go instead to the local café, which may be cheaper and more filling.

Hôtel de l'Abbaye at Talloires in the French Alps *(see p564)*

GRADINGS

FRENCH HOTELS ARE GRADED from zero stars to four stars (plus "four star luxury"). Stars indicate the hotel's facilities. Hotels with two or more stars must have an elevator where appropriate and a phone in every bedroom and at least 40 percent of their rooms must have bathrooms. Three-star hotels must provide room service breakfast and have 80 percent of rooms with baths. Only four-star hotels must have a restaurant and all of their rooms with baths.

PRICES

RATES, inclusive of tax and service, are quoted per room (apart from *pension* and *demi-pension* arrangements). There is usually a small supplement for a third person in a room for two, and little reduction for single travelers.

As a rule, the higher the star rating, the more you pay. Rates for a double room start from about 25€ per night for a one-star hotel and go up to 80€ or more for a four-star hotel. Costs also vary geographically, with remote rural areas like Brittany being the cheapest. In fashionable areas like the Dordogne and Provence, expect to pay 20 percent more, and another 20 percent again for Paris and the Côte d'Azur. Prices vary seasonally too, with coastal and alpine areas raising rates by up to 50 percent in peak periods.

BOOKING

ALWAYS BOOK well in advance for Paris, and for hotels in popular tourist areas in July and August.

In resort areas, most hotels close from October to March, so it is wise to phone ahead when traveling out of season to make sure the place is open.

Reservations can normally be held with a credit card at all but the humblest hotels. If you want to make a booking while you are in France, there are tourist offices in all main cities that provide a hotel reservation service up to eight days in advance.

The dining room of the Grand Hôtel, Sète *(see p571)*

BED-AND-BREAKFASTS

FRENCH bed-and-breakfasts, called *chambres d'hôte*, come in all shapes and sizes, from tiny cottages to elaborate châteaux full of family portraits and antiques, plus some *ferme-auberges (see p577)*. In all cases you will stay in a private home, and should not expect hotel services or amenities. Many offer dinner – *table d'hôte* – on request, where you usually dine *en famille*. Over 25,000 rural *chambres d'hôte* are registered and inspected by **Gîtes de France**. Watch for the yellow and green *chambres d'hôte* signs on the roadside.

Roadside signs also lead to many B&Bs that are not registered. Information on these is available from local tourist offices.

HOUSE RENTALS

THE FABLED *gîte* is a rural vaca- tion home often converted from a farmhouse or its outbuildings. A *gîte* vacation is a popular and relatively cheap way to see France, particularly out of season, but you must book many months in advance for the best *gîtes*.

Gîtes de France registers some 42,000 *gîtes*, all inspected and graded to indicate the level of facilities. You can choose from a selection of 2,500 in the company's main brochure (available from the French Government Tourist Office), or book direct. Each of its 95 regional offices produces a booklet with all the *gîtes* in its *département*, which comes with a booking form. These are also available through the head office in Paris, **Maison des Gîtes de France**, which itself publishes a series of listings catering for those with more specialised requirements. These include *gîtes* for skiing, *gîtes* with horses, rural *gîtes*, and serious luxury *gîtes*.

France has many other kinds of furnished home rentals: expensive south-coast villas; ski resort chalets; city and coastal apartments. The *Allo Vacances* brochure, from the **French Government Tourist Office**, lists real estate agents offering vacation rentals.

The Gîtes de France logo

CAMPING

ELEVEN THOUSAND official sites are spread around France's diverse countryside. The **Fédération Française de Camping et de Caravaning** publishes a comprehensive list, updated every year. Gîtes de France's *Camping à la Ferme* guide covers some simpler sites on farm land.

Campsites are graded from one to four stars. Three- and four-star sites are usually impressively spacious with many amenities and electricity connections for most tents and campers. One- and two-star sites always have toilets, a public phone and running water (though one-star sites sometimes have only cold water). What they lack in facilities they often make up for in peacefulness and rural charm.

Note that some sites accept only visitors with a **camping carnet** (pass). *Carnets* are available from the organizations listed opposite.

HOSTELS

HOSTELS are a money-saving option for single travelers, though for those traveling with a partner, cheap hotels are often no more expensive.

The IYHF's hosteling guide details the **FUAJ**'s (Fédération Unie des Auberges de Jeunesse) 220 hostels around France, open to all ages and offering dormitory accommodations. If you are not a member of the **YHA** (Youth Hostel Association) in your home

A Bordeaux campsite in high season

country, you have to pay a small surcharge each time you stay in a French youth hostel.

UCRIF (Union des Centres de Rencontres Internationales de France) has 50 centers with a cultural bias throughout France. All have single, shared and dormitory accommodations and a restaurant.

In the summer, it is possible to stay in university rooms. Contact **CROUS** (Centre Régional des Oeuvres Universitaires et Scolaires) for details.

Gîtes d'étapes are usually large farmhouses with dormitories close to walking, bicycling and horse riding trails. Gîtes de France's *Gîtes d'Etape et de Séjour* guide lists 1,600 sites throughout the country.

DISABLED TRAVELERS

A NUMBER OF associations publish information on accommodations with wheelchair access throughout France: the **Association des Paralysés de France (APF)**, the **Groupement pour l'Insertion des Personnes Handicapées**

The Carlton Intercontinental in Cannes *(see p572)*

Physiques (GIHP), and Gîtes de France's guide *Accessibles*. APF have their own travel company, APF Evasion, as do **Voyages Asa**, who have a team of specially adapted vehicles. **Les Compagnons du Voyage** (part of SNCF/RATP) can organize transportation, escorted or not, on all public transportation networks throughout France (see Directory below for details).

FURTHER INFORMATION

T HE INVALUABLE *Traveler in France Reference Guide*, listing hotel chains, reservation agencies and companies for every type of package vacation, is published by the French Government Tourist Office. It also distributes *Logis de France* guides, and all the booklets for château-hotels and château-B&Bs. However, it only distributes the *Relais et Châteaux* guide over the counter.

The first port of call for all non-hotel accommodations in the French countryside should be Gîtes de France, including for B&B (brochures available from their Paris shop).

When in France, local tourist offices are the best source of information for B&Bs and furnished rentals.

Loisirs Accueil are special booking agencies that offer information on hotels, campsites, *gîtes* and B&Bs in their areas. A list of all 53 offices in France is available from the French Tourist Office.

DIRECTORY

CHAIN HOTELS

Campanile
📞 *01 64 62 46 46 France.*
🌐 *www.campanile.fr*

Climat de France
📞 *01 64 62 46 62 France.*
🌐 *www.climatdefrance.fr*

Formula 1
📞 *0836 685 685 France.*
🌐 *www.hotelformule1. com*

Ibis, Novotel, Sofitel, Mercure
📞 *020 8283 4500 in UK.*
📞 *01 60 87 90 00 France.*
🌐 *www.accorhotel.com*

Primevère
📞 *0800 12 12 12 (free)*
🌐 *www.choicehotels.com*

Relais et Châteaux
📞 *0870 242 0052 in UK.*
📞 *0825 32 32 32 France*
🌐 *www.relaischateaux. com*

HOUSE RENTALS & B&B

Gîtes de France
59 St-Lazare, 75009 Paris.
📞 *01 49 70 75 75.*
🌐 *www.gites-de-france.fr*
Brochures can be obtained from French Goverment Tourist Office.

CAMPING

Fédération Française de Camping et de Caravaning
78 rue de Rivoli, 75004 Paris. 📞 *01 42 72 84 08.*

CAMPING ASSOCS IN US AND UK

American Automobile Association
📞 *(407) 444 7000.*

American Automobile Touring Alliance
📞 *(617) 237 2600.*

Camping and Caravaning Club
📞 *(02476) 422 024 (UK).*

HOSTELS

CROUS
39 av G-Bernanos, 75231 Paris Cedex 05.
📞 *01 40 51 36 00.*

FUAJ (Fédération Unie des Auberges de Jeunesse)
9 rue Brantome, 75003 Paris. 📞 *01 48 04 70 40.*
🌐 *www.fuaj.fr*

UCRIF
27 rue de Turbigo, 75002 Paris. 📞 *01 40 26 57 64.*

American Youth Hostel Association
1108 K Street NW, Washington, DC 20005.
📞 *(202) 783 0717.*

DISABLED TRAVELERS

APF
17 bd August Blanqui 75013 Paris.
📞 *01 40 78 69 00.*
📠 *01 45 89 40 57.*
🌐 *www.apf-asso.com*

GIHP

10 rue Georges de Porto-Riche, 75014 Paris.
📞 *01 43 95 66 36.*
📠 *01 45 40 40 26.*
🌐 *www.crava-cicat.com*

Les Compagnons du Voyage
17 quai d'Austerlitz 75013 Paris
📞 *01 45 83 67 77.*
🌐 *www.compagnons.com*

Voyages Asa
21 rue Richard Lenoir, 75011 Paris.
📞 *01 40 09 09 65.*
📠 *01 40 09 27 80.*

ADDITIONAL INFORMATION

French Government Tourist Office
444 Madison Avenue, New York, NY 10022.
📞 *(212) 838 7800.*
🌐 *www.franceguide.com*
🌐 *www.en-france.com*
(for Tourist Offices in France).

Choosing a Hotel

THE HOTELS in this guide have been selected across a wide price range for their excellent facilities and location. Many also have a highly recommended restaurant. The chart lists the hotels by region, starting with Paris; color-coded thumb tabs indicate the regions covered on each page. For more details on restaurants, see pp580–613.

	CREDIT CARDS	CHILDREN'S FACILITIES	PARKING FACILITIES	SWIMMING POOL	GARDEN
PARIS					
ILE ST-LOUIS: *Hôtel des Deux Iles.* **Map 9 C4.** €€€€ 59 rue St-Louis-en-l'Ile, 75004. **℃** *01 43 26 13 35.* **FAX** *01 43 29 60 25.* **Rooms:** *17.* It's a privilege to stay on the Ile St-Louis. The prices here are reasonable, although the bedrooms are quite small. 🛏 📺	AE MC V				
ILE ST-LOUIS: *Hôtel du Jeu de Paume.* **Map 9 C4.** €€€€€ 54 rue St-Louis-en-l'Ile, 75005. **℃** *01 43 26 14 18.* **FAX** *01 40 46 02 76.* **Rooms:** *31* A welcoming, exemplary family hotel. Features include a glass-walled elevator, old terra-cotta paving and a sauna. 🛏 📺 ⓦ www.jeudepaumehotel.com	AE DC MC V				▦
MARAIS: *Hôtel de la Place des Vosges.* **Map 10 D4.** €€€ 12 rue de Birague, 75004. **℃** *01 42 72 60 46.* **FAX** *01 42 72 02 64.* **Rooms:** *16.* A charming old building close to one of the prettiest squares in Paris. The large top floor rooms have good views. 🛏 📺 ⓐ hotel.place.des.vosges@gofornet.com	AE DC MC V				
MARAIS: *Hôtel de la Bretonnerie.* **Map 9 C3.** €€€€ 22 rue Ste-Croix de la Bretonnerie, 75004. **℃** *01 48 87 77 63.* **FAX** *01 42 77 26 78.* **ⓦ** www.delabretonnerie.com **Rooms:** *29.* Situated on a charming street, this is one of the most comfortable hotels in the Marais. Spacious bedrooms with antique furniture. 🛏 📺	MC V				
MARAIS: *St-Paul-le-Marais.* **Map 10 D3.** €€€€ 8 rue de Sévigné, 75004. **℃** *01 48 04 97 27.* **FAX** *01 48 87 37 04.* **Rooms:** *27* Old timber and stone create a rustic environment. The rooms facing the courtyard are quieter. 🛏 📺 ⓦ www.hotel-paris-marais.com	AE DC MC V	●			▦
MARAIS: *Pavillon de la Reine.* **Map10 D3.** €€€€€ 28 place des Vosges, 75003. **℃** *01 40 29 19 19.* **FAX** *01 40 29 19 20.* **Rooms:** *55.* This is the luxury hotel of the Marais. The bedrooms are sumptuous and the courtyard is a haven of peace. 🛏 ▤ 📺 ⓦ www.pavillon-de-la-reine.com	AE DC MC V	●	▦		▦
BEAUBOURG: *Hôtel Beaubourg.* **Map 9 B2.** ⓦ www.hotelbeaubourg.com €€€€ 11 rue Simon Lefranc, 75004. **℃** *01 42 74 34 24.* **FAX** *01 42 78 68 11.* **Rooms:** *28.* An extremely comfortable and well-equipped hotel, tastefully restored and decorated, with a pretty courtyard garden. 🛏 📺	AE DC MC V				▦
LES HALLES: *Hôtel Agora.* **Map 9 A2.** ⓦ www.123france.com €€€€ 7 rue de la Cossonerie, 75001. **℃** *01 43 33 46 02.* **FAX** *01 42 33 80 99.* **Rooms:** *29* A quirkily renovated hotel in a relatively quiet street. The cozy rooms are decorated with canopied chests and old paintings. 🛏 📺	AE MC V				
LES HALLES: *Hôtel St-Merry.* **Map 9 B3.** €€€€ 78 rue de la Verrerie, 75004. **℃** *01 42 78 14 15.* **FAX** *01 40 29 06 82.* **Rooms:** *12* The building incorporates the austere St-Merry church and is decorated in 17th-century style with canopied beds and period rugs. 🛏	AE MC V				
TUILERIES: *Hôtel Brighton.* **Map 8 D1.** ⓦ www.esprit-de-france.com €€€€ 218 rue de Rivoli, 75001. **℃** *01 47 03 61 61.* **FAX** *01 42 60 41 78.* **Rooms:** *65.* The bedrooms have high molded ceilings and large windows looking either on to the courtyard or the Jardin des Tuileries. Courtyard rooms are quieter but less attractive. 🛏 📺	AE DC MC V	●			
TUILERIES: *Clarion St-James et Albany.* **Map 8 D1.** €€€€€ 202 rue de Rivoli, 75001. **℃** *01 44 58 43 21.* **FAX** *01 44 58 43 11.* **Rooms:** *208.* Part of the hotel is in the elegant-facaded Hôtel Noailles. Although perfectly situated, it can be a bit noisy. 🛏 📺 ▯ ⓦ clarionstjames.com	AE DC MC V	●			▦
TUILERIES: *Hôtel de Crillon.* **Map 7 C1.** ⓦ www.crillon-paris.com €€€€€ 10 pl de la Concorde, 75008. **℃** *01 44 71 15 00.* **FAX** *01 44 71 15 02.* **Rooms:** *197.* Occupying an unrivaled position in the heart of the city, this hotel offers luxurious yet restrained elegance. Magnificent terrace. 🛏 ▤ 📺 ▯	AE DC MC V	●			▦

			CREDIT CARDS	CHILDREN'S FACILITIES	PARKING FACILITIES	SWIMMING POOL	GARDEN

Price categories for a standard double room (not per person) for one night, including tax and service charges, but not including breakfast.
€ under 30€
€€ 30€–60€
€€€ 61€–90€
€€€€ 91€–150€
€€€€€ over 150€

CHILDREN'S FACILITIES
Cribs and baby-sitting available. Some hotels provide children's portions and high chairs in the restaurant.

PARKING FACILITIES
Parking provided by the hotel in either a private lot or a private garage very close by.

SWIMMING POOL
Hotel pools are often quite small and are outdoors unless otherwise stated.

GARDEN
Hotel with garden, courtyard or terrace, often providing tables for eating outside.

	CREDIT CARDS	CHILDREN'S FACILITIES	PARKING FACILITIES	SWIMMING POOL	GARDEN
TUILERIES: *Hôtel du Louvre.* **Map** 8 E1. W www.hoteldulouvre.com €€€€€ Place André Malraux, 75001. 01 44 58 38 38. FAX 01 44 58 38 01. **Rooms:** 200. If you stay in this hotel, book the Pissaro suite where the artist painted *Place du Théâtre Français.* Very good brasserie. ⌨ ▤ TV ⅼⅼ	AE DC MC V	●			
TUILERIES: *Intercontinental.* **Map** 8 D1. W www.paris.interconti.com €€€€€ 3 rue de Castiglione, 75001. 01 44 77 11 11. FAX 01 44 77 14 60. **Rooms:** 445. This elegant late 19th-century hotel was designed by Charles Garnier, architect of the Paris Opéra, and is used for fashion shows. ⌨ ▤ TV ⅼⅼ	AE DC MC V	●			
TUILERIES: *Meurice.* **Map** 8 D1. W www.meuricehotel.com €€€€€ 228 rue de Rivoli, 75001. 01 44 58 10 10. FAX 01 44 58 10 15. **Rooms:** 160. A perfect example of successful restoration, with excellent replicas of the original plasterwork and furnishings. ⌨ ▤ TV ⅼⅼ	AE DC MC V				
TUILERIES: *Ritz.* **Map** 4 D5. W www.ritzparis.com. €€€€€ 15 place Vendôme, 75001. 01 43 16 30 30. FAX 01 43 16 36 88. **Rooms:** 170. After a century, this hotel still lives up to its discreet, high reputation. Original Louis XVI furniture, fireplaces, and chandeliers. ⌨ ▤ TV ⅼⅼ	AE DC MC V	●	■	●	■
OPÉRA: *Ambassador.* **Map** 4 E4. W www.hotelambassador-paris.com €€€€€ 16 bd Haussmann, 75009. 01 44 83 40 40. FAX 01 53 24 66 96. **Rooms:** 300. One of the best examples of Paris's Art Deco hotels, restored to its former glory with deep carpeting and antique furniture. The ground floor has crystal chandeliers and the food is outstanding. ⌨ ▤ TV ⅼⅼ	AE DC MC V	●			
OPÉRA: *Grand Hôtel Intercontinental.* **Map** 4 D5. €€€€€ 2 rue Scribe, 75009. 01 40 07 32 32. FAX 01 42 66 12 51. **Rooms:** 514. Millions have been invested in this hotel – bedrooms are equipped with every comfort and there is a health club. ⌨ ▤ TV ⅼⅼ W www.paris.interconti.com	AE DC MC V	●			
OPÉRA: *Westminster.* **Map** 4 D5. W www.warwickhotels.com €€€€€ 13 rue de la Paix, 75002. 01 42 61 57 46. FAX 01 42 60 30 66. **Rooms:** 101. The bedrooms are pleasantly furnished, some in period style with marble mantelpieces, chandeliers, and 18th-century clocks. ⌨ ▤ TV ⅼⅼ	AE DC MC V	●	■		
INVALIDES: *Pavillon.* **Map** 7 A2. @ patrickpavillon@aol.com €€€ 54 rue Saint Dominique, 75007. 01 45 51 42 87. FAX 01 45 51 32 79. **Rooms:** 18. A small, family-run hotel that guarantees peace and quiet. Although the rooms are small, they are pleasantly decorated. Breakfast is served in the courtyard in summer. ⌨ TV	AE DC MC V				■
INVALIDES: *Hôtel de Suède St-Germain.* **Map** 7 B4. €€€€ 31 rue Vaneau, 75007. 01 47 05 00 08. FAX 01 47 05 69 27. **Rooms:** 39. This elegant, late 18th-century style hotel overlooks the park of the Hôtel Matignon, home of the prime minister. ⌨ ▤ TV W www.hoteldesuede.com	AE DC MC V	●			■
INVALIDES: *Hôtel de Varenne.* **Map** 7 B2. W www.hoteldevarenne.com €€€€ 44 rue de Bourgogne, 75007. 01 45 51 45 55. FAX 01 45 51 86 63. **Rooms:** 24. A severe façade conceals a narrow courtyard where guests breakfast in the summer. Sound proofing in the bedrooms minimizes street noise. Rooms overlooking the courtyard are quiet and cheerful. ⌨ ▤ TV	AE MC V				■
INVALIDES: *Hôtel Bourgogne & Montana.* **Map** 7 B2. €€€€€ 3 rue de Bourgogne, 75007. 01 45 51 20 22. FAX 01 45 56 11 98. **Rooms:** 32. This is a relaxing, intimate hotel with an air of sobriety. Features include a mahogany bar, old elevator, and circular hall with pink marble columns. ⌨ ▤ TV W www.bourgogne-montana.com	AE DC MC V				
EIFFEL TOWER: *Grand Hôtel Lévêque.* **Map** 6 F3. €€€ 29 rue Cler, 75007. 01 47 05 49 15. FAX 01 45 50 49 36. **Rooms:** 50. Very reasonable hotel with a superb location and friendly owners. Rooms vary in price and size but are all bright and airy. ▤ TV W www.hotel-leveque.com	AE MC V	●			

For key to symbols see back flap

Price categories for a standard double room (not per person) for one night, including tax and service charges, but not including breakfast.
€ under 30€
€€ 30€–60€
€€€ 61€–90€
€€€€ 91€–150€
€€€€€ over 150€

CHILDREN'S FACILITIES
Cribs and baby-sitting available. Some hotels provide children's portions and high chairs in the restaurant.

PARKING FACILITIES
Parking provided by the hotel in either a private lot or a private garage very close by.

SWIMMING POOL
Hotel pools are often quite small and are outdoors unless otherwise stated.

GARDEN
Hotel with garden, courtyard or terrace, often providing tables for eating outside.

	CREDIT CARDS	CHILDREN'S FACILITIES	PARKING FACILITIES	SWIMMING POOL	GARDEN
CHAILLOT: *Melia-Alexander*. **Map** 1 B5. W www.solmelia.com €€€€€ 102 av Victor Hugo, 75016. 01 54 90 62 00. FAX 01 56 90 61 01. *Rooms:* 62. This comfortable, traditional hotel reflects the bourgeois self-confidence of avenue Victor Hugo. The small, quiet public rooms convey a sense of warmth and intimacy.	AE DC MC V				■
CHAILLOT: *Hôtel Square*. **Map** 5 A4. W www.hotelsquare.com €€€€€ 3 rue de Boulainvilliers, 75016. 01 44 14 91 90. FAX 01 44 14 91 99. *Rooms:* 22. The rooms are furnished with sumptuous fabrics and exotic woods, each with marble bathroom. Great views over the river to the Eiffel Tower.	AE DC MC V		■		
CHAILLOT: *Raphaël*. **Map** 2 D4. W www.raphael-hotel.com €€€€€ 17 avenue Kléber, 75016. 01 53 64 32 00. FAX 01 53 64 32 01. *Rooms:* 90. Many movies are shot in the Neo-Gothic bar of this timeless hotel where stars shelter from the paparazzi. A Turner hangs in the hall.	AE DC MC V	●			
CHAILLOT: *Villa Maillot*. **Map** 1 C4. W www.lavillamaillot.fr €€€€€ 143 avenue de Malakoff, 75016. 01 53 64 52 52. FAX 01 45 00 60 61. *Rooms:* 42. A modern hotel with furnishings inspired by Art Deco. The rooms have large beds, jewelry safes, and marble bathrooms.	AE DC MC V	●	■		■
CHAILLOT: *Concorde La Fayette*. **Map** 1 C2. €€€€€ 3 pl du Général Koenig, 75017. 01 40 68 50 68. FAX 01 40 68 50 43. *Rooms:* 950. A high-tech tower bristling with facilities including a fitness club and an amazing bar on the 33rd floor. W www.concorde-lafayette.com	AE DC MC V	●			
CHAMPS-ELYSÉES: *Résidence Lord Byron*. **Map** 2 E4. €€€€ 5 rue Chateaubriand, 75008. 01 43 59 89 98. FAX 01 42 89 46 04. *Rooms:* 31. This small, discreet hotel has a courtyard garden for summer breakfasts. The bedrooms are relatively quiet but not large. W www.escapade-paris.com	AE DC MC V				■
CHAMPS-ELYSÉES: *Atala*. **Map** 2 E4. W www.hotelatala.com €€€€€ 10 rue Chateaubriand, 75008. 01 45 62 01 62. FAX 01 42 25 66 38. *Rooms:* 48. Situated in a quiet street close to the busy Champs-Elysées, the Atala's rooms overlook a tranquil garden with tall trees. The eighth-floor bedrooms have spectacular views of the Eiffel Tower.	AE DC MC V	●	■		■
CHAMPS-ELYSÉES: *Bristol*. **Map** 3 A4. €€€€€ 112 rue du Faubourg St-Honoré, 75008. 01 53 43 43 00. FAX 01 53 43 43 01. W www.hotel-bristol.com *Rooms:* 175. One of the city's finest hotels. The large rooms are sumptuously decorated with antiques and have magnificent bathrooms.	AE DC MC V	●	■	●	■
CHAMPS-ELYSÉES: *Four Seasons Georges V*. **Map** 2 E5. €€€€€ 31 avenue George V, 75008. 01 49 52 70 00. FAX 01 49 52 70 20. *Rooms:* 245. A legendary hotel dotted with secret salons, old furniture, and paintings, with an excellent restaurant. W www.fourseasons.com	AE DC MC V	●	■		■
CHAMPS-ELYSÉES: *Plaza Athénée*. **Map** 6 F1. €€€€€ 25 avenue Montaigne, 75008. 01 53 67 66 65. FAX 01 53 67 66 76. *Rooms:* 188. A hotel for honeymooners and old aristocracy which conforms to the highest contemporary standards of luxury. W www.plaza-athenee-paris.com	AE DC MC V	●			■
CHAMPS-ELYSÉES: *Royal Monceau*. **Map** 2 F3. €€€€€ 37 avenue Hoche, 75008. 01 42 99 88 00. FAX 01 42 99 89 90. *Rooms:* 200. This elegant hotel has one of Paris's most luxurious health clubs and one of the city's best Italian restaurants. W www.royalmonceau.com	AE DC MC V	●	■	●	
ST-GERMAIN-DES-PRÉS: *Hôtel d'Orsay*. **Map** 7 C2. €€€€ 93 rue de Lille, 75007. 01 47 05 85 54. FAX 01 45 55 51 16. *Rooms:* 41. Under new management, the entire hotel has been renovated. It has a splendid rooftop view. W www.hotel-esprit-de-france.com	AE DC MC V				

ST-GERMAIN-DES-PRÉS: *Buci Latin.* **Map 8E4.** €€€€€ AE DC MC V
34 rue du Buci, 75006. [01 43 29 07 20. FAX 01 43 29 67 44. ***Rooms:*** 27.
A trendy hotel with minimalist decor which attracts a young crowd. Several suites have balconies and big whirlpool baths. www.bucilatin.com

ST-GERMAIN-DES-PRÉS: *Hôtel St-Germain-des-Prés.* **Map 8 E4.** €€€€€ AE MC V
36 rue Bonaparte, 75006. [01 43 26 00 19. FAX 01 40 46 83 63. ***Rooms:*** 30.
Although this charming and unusual hotel is on a busy street, the noise rarely intrudes. Bedroom size varies. www.hotel-staint-germain.com

ST-GERMAIN-DES-PRÉS: *Hôtel de l'Université.* **Map 8 D3.** €€€€€ AE MC V
22 rue de l'Université, 75007. [01 42 61 09 39. FAX 01 42 60 40 84. ***Rooms:*** 27.
A converted 17th-century town house with antiques and tapestries in its public rooms. The cellar is a 14th-century crypt. www.hoteluniversite.com

ST-GERMAIN-DES-PRÉS: *Hôtel de Fleurie.* **Map 8 F4.** €€€€€ AE DC MC V
32 rue Grégoire de Tours, 75006. [01 53 73 70 00. FAX 01 53 73 70 20. ***Rooms:*** 29.
A welcoming, family-run hotel with a delightful facade, light interiors, and comfort throughout. www.hotel-de-fleurie.fr

LATIN QUARTER: *Esmeralda.* **Map 9 A4.** €€ AE V
4 rue St-Julien-le Pauvre, 75005. [01 43 54 19 20. FAX 01 40 51 00 68. ***Rooms:*** 19.
The decor reflects contrasting ages and styles behind old stone walls and under beamed ceilings. The best rooms overlook Notre-Dame.

LATIN QUARTER: *Hôtel des Grandes Ecoles.* **Map 9 B5.** €€€€ MC V
75 rue Cardinal Lemoine, 75005. [01 43 26 79 23. FAX 01 43 25 28 15. ***Rooms:*** 51.
A cluster of three small houses with a garden. Two of the buildings have retained their old-fashioned charm. www.hotel-grandes-ecoles.com

LATIN QUARTER: *Hôtel des Grands Hommes.* **Map 13 A1.** €€€€€ AE DC MC V
17 place du Panthéon, 75005. [01 46 34 19 60. FAX 01 43 26 67 32. ***Rooms:*** 31.
Sorbonne teachers frequent this quiet family hotel near the Jardin du Luxembourg. Attic rooms have views of the Panthéon. www.hoteldesgrandshommes.com

LATIN QUARTER: *Hôtel de Notre-Dame.* **Map 9 B5.** €€€€ AE DC MC V
19 rue Maître Albert, 75005. [01 43 26 79 00. FAX 01 46 33 50 11. ***Rooms:*** 34.
Situated in a quiet street with Notre-Dame just across the river, this small hotel makes an ideal base for exploring old Paris. www.france-hotel-guide.com

LATIN QUARTER: *Hôtel du Panthéon.* **Map 13 A1.** €€€€€ AE DC MC V
19 place du Panthéon, 75005. [01 43 54 32 95. FAX 01 43 26 64 65. ***Rooms:*** 36.
This hotel is managed by the same family as the Hôtel des Grands Hommes and the welcome is equally warm. www.hoteldupanthenon.com

LATIN QUARTER: *Hôtel les Degrés de Notre-Dame.* **Map 9 B4.** €€€€ MC V
10 rue des Grands-Degrés, 75005. [01 55 42 88 88. FAX 01 40 46 95 34. ***Rooms:*** 11.
Choose between a quiet bedroom or one with a wonderful view of Notre-Dame from the window. Conveniently located.

LUXEMBOURG QUARTER: *Perreyve.* **Map 8 E5.** €€€ AE DC MC V
63 rue Madame, 75006. [01 45 48 35 01. FAX 01 42 84 03 30. ***Rooms:*** 30.
The bedrooms here are simple and clean. The corner ones and those in the attic on the sixth floor are the best. @ perreyvehotel@gofornet.com

LUXEMBOURG QUARTER: *Récamier.* **Map 8 E4.** €€€€ MC V
3 bis place St-Sulpice, 75006. [01 43 26 04 89. FAX 01 46 33 27 73. ***Rooms:*** 30.
A family hotel with no television sets nor restaurant. Try to get a room which looks onto both the courtyard and the square.

LUXEMBOURG QUARTER: *Hôtel de l'Abbaye.* **Map 8 D5.** €€€€€ AE MC V
10 rue Cassette, 75006. [01 45 44 38 11. FAX 01 45 48 07 86. ***Rooms:*** 44.
Once an abbey, this elegant hotel still basks in a tranquil atmosphere. There is a pretty courtyard. www.hotel-abbaye.com

JARDIN DES PLANTES: *Le Jardin des Plantes.* **Map 13 B1.** €€€€ AE DC MC V
5 rue Linné, 75005. [01 47 07 06 20. FAX 01 47 07 62 74. ***Rooms:*** 33.
This cheerfully decorated hotel in a residential area near the gardens has a rooftop terrace and a sauna in the vaulted cellar. www.timhotel.com

MONTPARNASSE: *Ferrandi.* **Map 11 C1.** www.123france.com €€€€€ AE DC MC V
92 rue du Cherche-Midi, 75006. [01 42 22 97 40. FAX 01 45 44 89 97. ***Rooms:*** 42.
A quiet hotel with a fireplace in the lounge and comfortable bedrooms, many with four-poster or canopied beds.

Price categories for a standard double room (not per person) for one night, including tax and service charges, but not including breakfast.
€ under 30€
€€ 30€–60€
€€€ 61€–90€
€€€€ 91€–150€
€€€€€ over 150€

CHILDREN'S FACILITIES
Cribs and baby-sitting available. Some hotels provide children's portions and high chairs in the restaurant.

PARKING FACILITIES
Parking provided by the hotel in either a private lot or a private garage very close by.

SWIMMING POOL
Hotel pools are often quite small and are outdoors unless otherwise stated.

GARDEN
Hotel with garden, courtyard or terrace, often providing tables for eating outside.

	CREDIT CARDS	CHILDREN'S FACILITIES	PARKING FACILITIES	SWIMMING POOL	GARDEN
MONTPARNASSE: *Hôtel la Ste-Beuve*. Map 12 D1. €€€€€ 9 rue Ste Beuve, 75006. ℂ 01 45 48 20 07. FAX 01 45 48 67 52. **Rooms:** 22. A warm and cozy atmosphere in this carefully restored hotel. Breakfast is served at bridge tables or at sofas in the salon. www.paris-hotel-charme.com	AE DC MC V	●			
MONTPARNASSE: *Lenox Montparnasse*. Map 12 D2. €€€€ 15 rue Delambre, 75014. ℂ 01 43 35 34 50. FAX 01 43 20 46 64. **Rooms:** 52. The overall atmosphere is one of restrained elegance. Each of the six large suites on the upper floor has a fireplace. www.hotellennox.com	AE MC V	●			
MONTPARNASSE: *Villa des Artistes*. Map 12 D2. €€€€ 9 rue de la Grande Chaumière, 75006. ℂ 01 43 26 60 86. FAX 01 43 54 73 70. www.villa-artistes.com **Rooms:** 59. The main charm of this hotel, which aims to evoke the Belle Epoque, is the large patio garden where you can breakfast in peace.	AE DC MC V	●			▦
MONTMARTRE: *Timhôtel*. Map 4 E1. www.timhotel.com €€€€ 11 rue Ravignan, 75018. ℂ 01 42 55 74 79. FAX 01 42 55 71 01. **Rooms:** 60. This is one of Montmartre's most delightful hotels. It borders a quiet, charming square and there are good views from the top floors.	AE DC MC V	●			
MONTMARTRE: *Terrass'Hôtel*. Map 4 E1. www.terrass-hotel.com €€€€€ 12 rue Joseph-de-Maistre, 75018. ℂ 01 46 06 72 85. FAX 01 42 52 29 11. **Rooms:** 101. There are panoramic views over the rooftops of Paris from the upper floors. A few bedrooms retain original Art Deco woodwork.	AE DC MC V	●	▦		

ILE DE FRANCE

	CREDIT CARDS	CHILDREN'S FACILITIES	PARKING FACILITIES	SWIMMING POOL	GARDEN
BARBIZON: *Hostellerie la Dague*. @ ladague@wanadoo.fr €€€ 5 Grand rue, 77630. ℂ 01 60 66 40 49. FAX 01 60 69 24 59. **Rooms:** 25. This rustic yet smart ivy-hung hotel is popular with Parisians, so book well in advance. The traditional French restaurant is charming.	MC V		▦		▦
ENGHIEN-LES-BAINS: *Grand Hôtel* www.lucienbarriere.com €€€€€ 85 rue Général de Gaulle, 95880. ℂ 01 39 34 10 00. FAX 01 39 34 10 01. **Rooms:** 47. Situated in the heart of this bustling spa town, the *Grand Hôtel* lives up to its name, with its own casino to complete the image.	AE DC MC V		▦		▦
FONTAINEBLEAU: *Grand Hôtel de l'Aigle Noir* €€€€€ 27 pl Napoléon Bonaparte, 77300. ℂ 01 60 74 60 00. FAX 01 60 74 60 01. **Rooms:** 56. This prestigious mansion overlooks Fontainebleau château and its vast park. Gourmet cuisine and impeccable service. www.hotelaiglenoir.com	AE DC MC V	●	▦	▦	▦
HERBEVILLE: *Le Mont au Vent* €€€ 2 rue de Maule, 78580. ℂ 01 30 90 65 22. FAX 01 34 75 12 54. **Rooms:** 6. Set in appealing countryside, this small village hotel makes a good base for visiting Versailles. Price includes breakfast. Cash only.			▦	●	
ROISSY-CHARLES-DE-GAULLE: *Novotel Roissy Charles-de-Gaulle* €€€€ Charles de Gaulle Airport, 95705. ℂ 01 49 19 27 27. FAX 01 49 19 27 99. **Rooms:** 200. This standard chain hotel is one of the best emergency or en route stop-overs. @ h1014@accor-hotels.com	AE DC MC V	●	▦		
ST-SYMPHORIEN LE CHATEAU: *Château d'Esclimont* €€€€€ 28700 ℂ 02 37 31 15 15. FAX 02 37 31 57 91. **Rooms:** 53. A fairytale castle with its own private forest, near Paris. The rooms are extremely comfortable and the cuisine is truly gastronomic.	AE DC MC V	●	▦	●	▦
ST-GERMAIN-EN-LAYE: *La Forestière* www.cazaudehore.fr €€€€€ 1 av du Président Kennedy, 78100. ℂ 01 39 10 38 38. FAX 01 39 73 73 88. **Rooms:** 30. Exuding an air of rural sophistication, this secluded hotel is set in woodland. Enjoy the gastronomic delights in the restaurant.	AE DC MC V	●	▦		▦

St-Germain-en-Laye: *Pavillon Henri IV* Ⓦ www.pavillonhenri4.fr €€€€€ — AE DC MC V
19–21 rue Thiers, 78100. **℡** *01 39 10 15 15.* **FAX** *01 39 73 93 73.* **Rooms:** *42.*
This sumptuous hotel occupies an elegant lodge built by
Henri IV where Louis XIV was born and Alexandre Dumas wrote
The Three Musketeers. Panoramic views over the Seine Valley. 🚗 TV

Versailles: *Hôtel de Clagny* €€ — MC V
6 impasse de Clagny, 78000. **℡** *01 39 50 18 09.* **FAX** *01 39 50 85 17.* **Rooms:** *21.*
Conveniently close to the station and in a quiet location. The rooms are
simply furnished and unremarkable but the welcome is genuine. 🚗 TV

Versailles: *Trianon Palace* Ⓦ www.westin.com €€€€€ — AE DC MC V
1 bd de la Reine, 78000. **℡** *01 30 84 50 00.* **FAX** *01 30 84 50 01.* **Rooms:** *192.*
Undoubtedly the most spendid hotel in the region, deserving the
accolade "palace," blending in with the Classical lines of the Versailles
park. The gourmet restaurant is the jewel in the crown. 🚗 🍴 TV 🍴

Le Nord and Picardy

Amiens: *Hôtel de Normandie* Ⓦ www.hotelnormandie-80.com €€ — AE MC V
1 bis rue Lamartine, 80000. **℡** *03 22 91 74 99.* **FAX** *03 22 92 06 56.* **Rooms:** *28.*
Five minutes' walk from the station and near the cathedral, this turn-of-
the-century hotel represents quiet and simplicity in a busy city. 🚗 TV

Amiens: *Le Prieuré* €€ — MC V
17 rue Porion, 80000. **℡** *03 22 92 27 67.* **FAX** *03 22 92 46 16.* **Rooms:** *21.*
An exceptionally comfortable hotel with tastefully decorated rooms
and antique furniture. Only a few steps from the cathedral. 🚗 TV 🍴

Armbouts-Cappel: *Hôtel du Lac* Ⓦ www.hoteldulacdk.com €€€ — AE DC MC V
2 bordure du lac, 59380. **℡** *03 28 60 70 60.* **FAX** *03 28 61 06 39.* **Rooms:** *66.*
South of Dunkerque, set beside a lake known for its abundant bird
life, this is an extremely comfortable, modern hotel. 🚗 TV 🍴

Berck-sur-Mer: *Hôtel Neptune* Ⓦ www.hotel-cote-opale.com €€ — AE DC MC V
Esplanade Parmentier, 62600. **℡** *03 21 09 21 21.* **FAX** *03 21 09 29 29.* **Rooms:** *63.*
An airy and elegant hotel on the seafront. Rooms are simple but stylish
with white and blue decor. The restaurant has great sea views. 🚗 TV 🍴

Boulogne-sur-Mer: *Hôtel Métropole* Ⓦ www.hotel-metropole-boulogne.com €€€ — AE DC MC V
51 rue Thiers, 62200. **℡** *03 21 31 54 30.* **FAX** *03 21 30 45 72.* **Rooms:** *25.*
Boulogne is notoriously short of hotels with character, but this one is
both comfortable and convenient for shopping. 🚗 🍴 TV

Calais: *Kyriad* Ⓦ www.hotel-plage-calais.com €€ — AE MC V
Digue G Berthe, 62100. **℡** *03 21 34 64 64.* **FAX** *03 21 34 35 39.* **Rooms:** *44.*
Overlooking the beach is this comfortable and convenient hotel, a
welcoming establishment with an inexpensive restaurant. 🚗 TV 🍴

Cambrai: *Le Mouton Blanc* @ hotelmoutonblanc@wanadoo.com €€€ — MC V
33 rue Alsace Lorraine, 59400. **℡** *03 27 81 30 16.* **FAX** *03 27 81 83 54.* **Rooms:** *32.*
Situated between the beautiful old church of St-Géry and the center
of the historic town, this hotel offers convenience and comfort. 🚗 TV 🍴

Cambrai: *Château de la Motte Fénelon* Ⓦ www.hroy.com €€€ — AE DC MC V
59403. **℡** *03 27 83 61 38.* **FAX** *03 27 83 71 61.* **Rooms:** *40.*
Set in a large park, this is a peaceful place to stay, with refined cuisine.
Half of the rooms are in the elegant 19th-century château and orangery, designed
by Parisian architect Hittorf, and half in modern annexes in the park. 🚗 TV

Dunkerque: *Trianon Hôtel* €€ — V MC
20 rue de la Colline, 59240. **℡** *03 28 63 39 15.* **FAX** *03 28 63 34 57.* **Rooms:** *12.*
Peacefully situated, this charming hotel offers good value for your money. 🚗 TV

Gosnay: *La Chartreuse du Val St-Esprit* Ⓦ www.lachartreuse.com €€€€ — AE DC MC V
1 rue de Fouquières, 62199. **℡** *03 21 62 80 00.* **FAX** *03 21 62 42 50.* **Rooms:** *67.*
A sumptuous, peaceful château with much of its original furniture.
Its *restaurant gastronomique* specializes in fresh seafood, and the
dining room is a setting in which to enjoy dining in style. 🚗 🍴 TV 🍴

Laon: *Hôtel de la Bannière de France* @ banniere.de.france@wanadoo.fr €€ — AE DC MC V
11 rue Franklin Roosevelt, 02000. **℡** *03 23 23 21 44.* **FAX** *03 23 23 31 56.* **Rooms:** *18.*
Charming coaching inn within the ancient walled town of Laon. Good
views and a convenient stop to and from the Channel ports. 🚗 TV 🍴

For key to symbols see back flap

<table>
<tr><td colspan="2">

Price categories for a standard double room (not per person) for one night, including tax and service charges, but not including breakfast.
€ under 30€
€€ 30€–60€
€€€ 61€–90€
€€€€ 91€–150€
€€€€€ over 150€

</td><td colspan="5">

CHILDREN'S FACILITIES
Cribs and baby-sitting available. Some hotels provide children's portions and high chairs in the restaurant.
PARKING FACILITIES
Parking provided by the hotel in either a private lot or a private garage very close by.
SWIMMING POOL
Hotel pools are often quite small and are outdoors unless otherwise stated.
GARDEN
Hotel with garden, courtyard or terrace, often providing tables for eating outside.

</td></tr>
</table>

	CREDIT CARDS	CHILDREN'S FACILITIES	PARKING FACILITIES	SWIMMING POOL	GARDEN
LAON: *Hostellerie St-Vincent* @ hotel.st.vincent@wanadoo.fr €€ 111 avenue Charles de Gaulle, 02000. **(** *03 23 23 42 43.* **FAX** *03 23 79 22 55.* **Rooms:** *47.* A comfortable and modern establishment, easy to find on the east side of this ancient town. Both hotel and restaurant are good value. 🚗 TV 🍴	AE DC MC V		▨		▨
LE TOUQUET: *Hôtel Blue Cottage* @ blue.cottage@wanadoo.fr €€€ 41 re Jean-Monnet, 62520. **(** *03 21 05 15 33.* **FAX** *03 21 05 41 60.* **Rooms:** *26.* Not far from the market place, this is an accessible hotel where, like many provincial establishments, half board is preferred in July and August. 🚗 TV 🍴	AE DC MC V	●			▨
LE TOUQUET: *Novotel-Thalamer* @ ho449@accorhotels.com €€€€€ Front de Mer, 62520. **(** *03 21 09 85 00.* **FAX** *03 21 09 85 10.* **Rooms:** *149.* Large hotel on the seafront offering bright, functional rooms with superb views. Relax in the saltwater spa and sauna. 🚗 TV 🍴	AE DC MC V	●	▨	●	▨
LILLE: *Alliance* @ alliance@alliance-hospitality.com €€€€€ 17 quai du Wault, 59800. **(** *03 20 30 62 62.* **FAX** *03 20 42 94 25.* **Rooms:** *83.* This converted 17th-century convent is remarkably quiet for a city hotel. Suspended gardens overhang the glass-covered cloister and bar area. 🚗 TV 🍴	AE DC MC V		▨		
LONGPONT: *Hôtel de l'Abbaye* €€ 8 rue des Tourelles, 02600. **(** *03 23 96 02 44.* **FAX** *03 23 96 02 44.* **Rooms:** *11.* The name is taken from a 12th-century ruined abbey nearby and the hotel is almost as old. Good restaurant serving local cuisine. 🚗 🍴	MC V	●	▨		
MAUBEUGE: *Hôtel Shakespeare* W www.grandhotelmaubeuge.fr €€ 3 rue du Commerce, 59600. **(** *03 27 65 14 14.* **FAX** *03 27 64 04 66.* **Rooms:** *35.* Modern, functional and efficiently run hotel with a friendly atmosphere. There is a restaurant and a comfortable bar. 🚗 TV 🍴	AE DC MC V	●	▨		
MONTREUIL: *Le Darnetal* €€ Place Darnetal, 62170. **(** *03 21 06 04 87.* **FAX** *03 21 86 64 67.* **Rooms:** *4.* Booking is essential at this hotel-restaurant in the old fortified town of Montreuil. Old-style rooms all with en-suite bathrooms. The dinner menu is excellent value, especially the oyster dishes. 🚗 🍴	AE DC MC V				
PÉRONNE: *Hostellerie des Remparts* W www.logisdefrance.fr €€ 21 rue Beaubois, 80200. **(** *03 22 84 01 22.* **FAX** *03 22 84 31 96.* **Rooms:** *39.* Some rooms overlook the old fortifications of the town and their ornamental gardens. Substantial refurbishment has lessened its old-fashioned character. 🚗 TV 🍴	AE DC MC V	●			
REUILLY-SAUVIGNY: *L'Auberge le Relais* @ auberge.relais.de.reuilly@wanadoo.fr €€€ 2 rue de Paris, 02850. **(** *03 23 70 35 36.* **FAX** *03 23 70 27 76.* **Rooms:** *7.* An old *ferme-auberge* with some modern additions in this tiny village. It has a glass conservatory overlooking a lovely garden. 🚗 ▤ TV 🍴	AE DC MC V				▨
ST-OMER: *Hôtel St-Louis* W www.hotel-stlouis.com €€ 25 rue d'Arras, 62500. **(** *03 21 38 35 21.* **FAX** *03 21 38 57 26.* **Rooms:** *30.* Situated right in the center of a historic cathedral town is this 18th-century coaching inn. The bedrooms have been modernized, but the restaurant retains the flavor of the old days. 🚗 TV 🍴	AE MC V	●	▨		
ST-QUENTIN: *Grand Hôtel* €€€ 6–8 rue Dachery, 02100. **(** *03 23 62 69 77.* **FAX** *03 23 62 53 52.* **Rooms:** *24.* Well-designed and tastefully decorated rooms. The restaurant, *Le Président*, is a must for dinner and breakfast as well. 🚗 TV 🍴	AE DC MC V		▨		
SARS-POTERIES: *Hôtel du Marquais* €€ 65 rue du Général de Gaulle, 59216. **(** *03 27 61 62 72.* **FAX** *03 27 57 47 35.* **Rooms:** *11.* Simple but charming accommodation with an excellent restaurant next door. 🚗	MC V		▨		▨

VERVINS: *La Tour de Roy* @ latourduroy@wanadoo.fr €€€€€ AE DC MC V
45 rue du Général Leclerc, 02140. **(** *03 23 98 00 10.* **FAX** *03 23 98 00 72.* **Rooms:** *22.*
An exceptionally comfortable and quiet hotel, with hand-painted
bathrooms. There is a splendid garden and outdoor tables. 🛏 ▤ TV 🍴

WIMEREUX: *Hôtel du Centre* w www.hotelducentre-wimereux.com €€ AE MC V
78 rue Carnot, 62930. **(** *03 21 32 41 08.* **FAX** *03 21 33 82 48.* **Rooms:** *25.*
This small, comfortable hotel is centrally located with the
beach nearby. 🛏 TV 🍴

CHAMPAGNE

ANDELOT: *Le Cantarel* w www.hotel-cantarel.com €€ MC V
Place Cantarel, 52700. **(** *03 25 01 31 13.* **FAX** *03 25 03 15 41.* **Rooms:** *8.*
Andelot lies northeast of Chaumont on the road to Neufchâteau. This
hotel in the village square has a good restaurant. 🛏 TV 🍴

BOURBONNE-LES-BAINS: *Hôtel Jeanne d'Arc* w www.hotel-jda.fr €€ AE DC MC V
Rue Amiral-Pierre, 52400. **(** *03 25 90 46 00.* **FAX** *03 25 88 78 71.* **Rooms:** *29.*
The town is a thermal spa and this well-equipped hotel is right beside
the pump room. The surrounding countryside is magnificent. 🛏 TV 🍴

CHÂLONS-EN-CHAMPAGNE: *Hôtel du Pot d'Etain* w www.hotel-lepotdetain.com €€ AE MC V
18 place de la République, 51000. **(** *03 26 68 09 09.* **FAX** *03 26 68 58 18.* **Rooms:** *27*
This 15th-century private hotel in the center of town is run by a family
of bakers and there are fresh-baked croissants for breakfast. 🛏 TV

CHAMPILLON: *Royal Champagne* @ royalchampagne@wanadoo.fr €€€€€ AE DC MC V
Bellevue, 51160. **(** *03 26 52 87 11.* **FAX** *03 26 52 89 69.* **Rooms:** *25.*
Situated on the summit of the wooded Montagne de Reims, this
16th-century staging-post houses a welcoming hotel-restaurant. 🛏 TV 🍴

CHARLEVILLE-MÉZIÈRES: *Le Relais du Square* €€ AE DC MC V
3 place de la Gare, 08000. **(** *03 24 33 38 76.* **FAX** *03 24 33 56 66.* **Rooms:** *49.*
Despite the address, the hotel is out of earshot of the trains. There is a
cozy bar and the hotel is connected to a decent restaurant. 🛏 TV

CHAUMONT: *Le Grand Val* w www.hotel-legrandval.fr €€ AE DC MC V
Route de Langres, 52000. **(** *03 25 03 90 35.* **FAX** *03 25 32 11 80.* **Rooms:** *52.*
On the road to Langres and Dijon stands this simple stone-built hotel
with wood-paneling and fine views over the Marne Valley. 🛏 TV 🍴

EPERNAY: *Hôtel de la Cloche* €€ AE DC MC V
3 place Mendès-France, 51200. **(** *03 26 55 15 15.* **FAX** *03 26 55 64 88.* **Rooms:** *19.*
The best hotel-restaurant in its category in Epernay, *La Cloche*
offers modest but sunny rooms and a good restaurant serving
a choice of regional specialties. 🛏 TV 🍴

EPERNAY: *Micheline & Jean-Marie Tarlant* w www.tarlant.com €€ MC V
Oeuilly, RN3, 51480. **(** *03 26 58 30 60.* **FAX** *03 26 58 37 31.* **Rooms:** *4.*
Grapepickers' cottages have been converted into guest rooms on
this family-run wine estate. Breakfast is in a charming conservatory
and can be followed by a visit to the champagne cellars below. 🛏

ETOGES: *Château d'Etoges* w www.etoges.com €€€€ AE DC MC V
4 rue Richebourg, 51270. **(** *03 26 59 30 08.* **FAX** *03 26 59 35 57.* **Rooms:** *20.*
This impressive 17th-century château, with moat and decorative towers,
is still inhabited and presented very much as a grand private home. 🛏 TV 🍴

FAGNON: *Abbaye de Sept Fontaines* w www.abbayedeseptfontaines.fr €€€€ AE DC MC V
08090 Fagnon. **(** *03 24 37 38 24.* **FAX** *03 24 37 58 75.* **Rooms:** *23.*
Located 6 miles from Charleville-Mézières, this 18th-century château is built on
a 12th-century abbey, set in a large park with a 9-hole golf course. 🛏 TV 🍴

HAYBES-SUR-MEUSE: *L'Ermitage Moulin Labotte* €€ MC V
08170 Haybes-sur-Meuse. **(** *03 24 41 13 44.* **FAX** *03 24 40 46 72.* **Rooms:** *10.*
A remote 18th-century converted mill set in woodland. There is
an atmospheric dining room with a mill-wheel. 🛏 TV 🍴
w www.perso.wanadoo-moulin-labotte.fr

LANGRES: *Grand Hôtel de l'Europe* €€ MC V
23–25 rue Diderot, 52200. **(** *03 25 87 10 88.* **FAX** *03 25 87 60 65.* **Rooms:** *26.*
The hotel is a listed 17th-century building, with a beautifully preserved
dining room of the period, but with modernized bedrooms. 🛏 TV 🍴

<table>
<tr><td>
Price categories for a standard double room (not per person) for one night, including tax and service charges, but not including breakfast.
€ under 30€
€€ 30€–60€
€€€ 61€–90€
€€€€ 91€–150€
€€€€€ over 150€
</td></tr>
</table>

CHILDREN'S FACILITIES
Cribs and baby-sitting available. Some hotels provide children's portions and high chairs in the restaurant.

PARKING FACILITIES
Parking provided by the hotel in either a private lot or a private garage very close by.

SWIMMING POOL
Hotel pools are often quite small and are outdoors unless otherwise stated.

GARDEN
Hotel with garden, courtyard or terrace, often providing tables for eating outside.

	CREDIT CARDS	CHILDREN'S FACILITIES	PARKING FACILITIES	SWIMMING POOL	GARDEN
MAGNANT: *Le Val Moret* €€ 10110 Magnant. ☎ 03 25 29 85 12. FAX 03 25 29 70 81. **Rooms:** 42. A single-story modern motel on the A5 from Troyes to Dijon. Comfortable with a good and reasonably priced restaurant. 🛏 TV 🍴	AE DC MC V	●	▨		▨
MESNIL-ST-PÉRE: *L'Auberge du Lac* W www.auberge-du-lac.fr €€€€ 10140 Mesnil-St-Pére. ☎ 03 25 41 27 16. FAX 03 25 41 57 59. **Rooms:** 21. This old-fashioned inn takes its name from the nearby lake in the Forêt d'Orient, where fishing, bathing and tennis are all available. 🛏 ▤ TV 🍴	MC V		▨		▨
MONTHERMÉ: *Le Franco-Belge* €€ 2 rue Pasteur, 08800. ☎ 03 24 53 01 20. FAX 03 24 53 54 49. **Rooms:** 15. A family-run hotel overlooking the village square. The cuisine is home prepared using fresh garden produce. 🛏 TV 🍴	MC V	●	▨		▨
REIMS: *Hôtel Crystal* W www.hotel-crystal.fr €€ 86 place Drouet d'Erlon, 51100. ☎ 03 26 88 44 44. FAX 03 26 47 49 28. **Rooms:** 31. This old-fashioned hotel borders the liveliest square in Reims yet is surprisingly quiet. In summer breakfast is served on the terrace. 🛏 TV	AE MC V				▨
REIMS: *Boyer les Crayères* W www.gerardboyer.com €€€€€ 64 bd Henri Vasnier, 51100. ☎ 03 26 82 80 80. FAX 03 26 82 65 52. **Rooms:** 19. This is a famous hotel on the gastronomic and champagne-tasting trail. Discreetly sumptuous, it occupies a Belle Epoque mansion, set in attractive grounds on the outskirts of Reims. 🛏 ▤ TV 🍴	AE DC MC V	●	▨		▨
RETHEL: *Le Moderne* €€ Place de la Gare, 08300. ☎ 03 24 38 44 54. FAX 03 24 38 37 84. **Rooms:** 22. A thoroughly modernized establishment that guarantees peace and comfort. Excellent local cuisine is served in the restaurant. 🛏 TV 🍴	AE MC V	●	▨		▨
ST-DIZIER: *Hôtel Gambetta* W www.citotel.com €€ 62 rue Gambetta, 52100. ☎ 03 25 56 52 10. FAX 03 25 56 39 47. **Rooms:** 63. A modern establishment with conference facilities and an inexpensive restaurant. Many tourists come to St-Dizier to see the bird-life at the famous Lac du Der-Chantecoq nearby. 🛏 TV 🍴	AE DC MC V	●	▨		
SEDAN: *L'Auberge du Port* W www.auberge-du-port.com €€ Bazeilles, 08140. ☎ 03 24 27 13 89. FAX 03 24 29 35 58. **Rooms:** 20. Exceptionally comfortable hotel on the banks of the river Meuse, ideal for visitors in search of peace and quiet. Meals on the terrace. 🛏 TV 🍴	AE DC MC V	●	▨		▨
SEPT-SAULX: *Le Cheval Blanc* W www.chevalblanc-sept-saulx.com €€€ Rue du Moulin, 51400. ☎ 03 26 03 90 27. FAX 03 26 03 97 09. **Rooms:** 25. Set among Champagne vineyards, this hotel-restaurant makes a convenient stop-over for visitors to Alsace and Burgundy. The gourmet restaurant is worth visiting in its own right. 🛏 TV 🍴	AE DC MC V	●	▨		▨
TROYES: *Grand Hôtel* W www.grandhotel-troyes.com €€€ 4 av Maréchal-Joffre, 10000. ☎ 03 25 79 90 90. FAX 03 25 78 48 93. **Rooms:** 80. A large, modern establishment incorporating no less than four restaurants, including a brasserie, pizzeria, and *gastronomique*. 🛏 TV 🍴	AE MC V	●	▨	●	▨
TROYES: *Hôtel des Comtes de Champagne* W www.comtesdechampagne.com €€ 54–56 rue de la Monnaie, 10000. ☎ 03 25 73 11 70. FAX 03 25 73 06 02. **Rooms:** 30. This solid private mansion, located on a quiet street, was once the medieval bank of the Counts of Champagne. Individualistic rooms with period furniture. Perfect for exploring the city center. 🛏 TV	MC V		▨		
VIGNORY: *Le Relais Verdoyant* @ le-relais-verdoyant@wanadoo.fr €€ Quartier de la Gare, 52320. ☎ 03 25 02 44 49. FAX 03 25 01 96 89. **Rooms:** 7. An old converted country farm in a peaceful hamlet. Halfway between Chaumont and Joinville. Friendly and totally relaxing. 🛏 TV 🍴	MC V	●	▨		▨

ALSACE AND LORRAINE

COLMAR: *Hôtel Beauséjour* W www.beausejour.fr €€ AE DC MC V
25 rue du Ladhof, 68000. (03 89 41 37 16. FAX 03 89 41 43 07. **Rooms:** 44.
A family hotel – reasonably priced family rooms, some with kitchenette.
Facilities include children's play area, sauna and fitness room. 🚐 TV 🍴

COLMAR: *Hôtel le Maréchal* @ marechal@calixo.net €€€€ AE MC V
4–6 place des Six-Montagnes-Noires, 68000. (03 89 41 60 32.
FAX 03 89 24 59 40. **Rooms:** 30.
A 16th-century timber-framed house, Colmar's premier city-center hotel
is on the waterfront in the atmospheric Petite Venise quarter. 🚐 ☰ TV

EGUISHEIM: *Hostellerie du Pape* @ info@hostellerie-pape.com €€€ AE DC MC V
10 Grand rue, 68420. (03 89 41 41 21. FAX 03 89 41 41 31. **Rooms:** 33.
An appealing hotel-restaurant set in the most perfectly preserved small
town, bordering the oldest quarter and well-placed for shops. 🚐 TV 🍴

EPINAL: *Hôtel Azur* W www.azurhotelepinal.com €€ AE DC MC V
54 quai des Bons Enfants, 88000. (03 29 64 05 25. FAX 03 29 64 00 40. **Rooms:** 20.
A simple but welcoming hotel in the center of town.
Some rooms overlook the canal. 🚐 TV

GÉRARDMER: *Manoir au Lac* W www.manoir-au-lac.com €€€€€ AE DC MC V
Route d'Epinal, 88400. (03 29 27 10 20. FAX 03 29 27 10 27. **Rooms:** 14.
Barely half a mile from the town center, this manor house is set in
its own grounds, with an exceptional view of the lake. 🚐 TV

LUNÉVILLE: *Château d'Adoménil* W www.relaischateaux.fr €€€€€ AE DC MC V
Route d'Epinal, 88400. (03 29 27 10 20. FAX 03 29 27 10 27. **Rooms:** 14.
Swans and mallards glide around the moat of the elegant 17th-century château,
where refined cuisine is served on the pretty, local Lunéville faïence. 🚐 ☰ TV 🍴

METZ: *Grand Hôtel de Metz* @ grandhoteldemetz@wanadoo.fr €€ AE DC MC V
3 rue des Clercs, 57000. (03 87 36 16 33. FAX 03 87 74 17 04. **Rooms:** 62.
Close to the cathedral, market and restaurants, this established hotel
combines a Neo-Baroque lobby with countrified rooms. 🚐 TV

MOLSHEIM: *Hôtel Bugatti* @ hotel-le-bugatti@wanadoo.fr €€ AE MC V
Rue de la Commanderie, 67120. (03 88 49 89 00. FAX 03 88 38 36 00. **Rooms:** 45.
Molsheim is where the great motor manufacturer Bugatti lived, and the
factory still stands across from the hotel. Guests can use the pool at the
Hôtel Diana and there are riding stables nearby. 🚐 TV

NANCY: *Hôtel Albert Ier et Astoria* €€ AE DC MC V
3 rue Armée-Patton, 54000. (03 83 40 31 24. FAX 03 83 28 47 78. **Rooms:** 85.
This welcoming hotel is just a few minutes' walk from place Stanislas. The
decor is modern and the rooms well-equipped, comfortable, and quiet. 🚐 TV

NANCY: *Grand Hôtel de la Reine* W www.concorde-hotels.com €€€€€ AE DC MC V
2 place Stanislas, 54000. (03 83 35 03 01. FAX 03 83 32 86 04. **Rooms:** 42.
As well as the elegant luxury of this 18th-century palace in the town's main
square, the Stanislas restaurant is excellent. 🚐 ☰ TV 🍴

OBERNAI: *Hôtel Restaurant des Vosges* €€ AE MC V
5 place de la Gare, 67210. (03 88 95 53 78. FAX 03 88 49 92 65. **Rooms:** 20.
There is nothing pretentious about this functional, modern hotel.
Standards are high and the restaurant is excellent value. 🚐 TV 🍴

REMIREMONT: *Hôtel du Cheval de Bronze* €€ AE MC V
59 rue Charles de Gaulle, 88200. (03 29 62 52 24. FAX 03 29 62 34 90. **Rooms:** 35.
An old-fashioned hotel that is a useful stop-over for travelers crossing
Alsace or Lorraine and a good base for exploring the Vosges. No restaurant but
the owner is happy to recommend. 🚐 TV @ hotel-du-cheval-de-bronze@wanadoo.fr

RIBEAUVILLE: *Hôtel de Mouton* €€ MC V
5 place de la Sinne, 68150. (03 89 73 60 11. FAX 03 89 73 74 62. **Rooms:** 14
A delightful 14th-century wine-grower's house in the old quarter.
The rooms are spacious and charming. 🚐 TV 🍴

SAUSHEIM: *Novotel Mulhouse–Sausheim* @ ho452@accor-hotels.com €€€€ AE DC MC V
Rue de L'Ile-Napoléon, 68390. (03 89 61 84 84. FAX 03 89 61 77 99. **Rooms:** 77.
The Novotel chain offers great family bargains and caters well for
children – there is a toddlers' play area and restaurant. 🚐 ☰ TV 🍴

For key to symbols see back flap

Price categories for a standard double room (not per person) for one night, including tax and service charges, but not including breakfast.
€ under 30€
€€ 30€–60€
€€€ 61€–90€
€€€€ 91€–150€
€€€€€ over 150€

CHILDREN'S FACILITIES
Cribs and baby-sitting available. Some hotels provide children's portions and high chairs in the restaurant.

PARKING FACILITIES
Parking provided by the hotel in either a private lot or a private garage very close by.

SWIMMING POOL
Hotel pools are often quite small and are outdoors unless otherwise stated.

GARDEN
Hotel with garden, courtyard or terrace, often providing tables for eating outside.

Hotel		Credit Cards	Children's Facilities	Parking Facilities	Swimming Pool	Garden
SAVERNE: *Chez Jean* ⓦ www.chez-jean.com €€€ 3 rue de la Gare, 67700. ☎ 03 88 91 10 19. FAX 03 88 91 27 45. *Rooms: 25.* A four-storied traditional Alsatian house with views of the hills behind the town. There is a sauna and a delightful wine bar downstairs.		AE DC MC V	●			
SELESTAT: *Auberge des Alliés* @ auberge.allies@libertysurf.fr €€ 39 rue des Chevaliers, 67600. ☎ 03 88 92 09 34. FAX 03 88 92 12 88. *Rooms: 19.* The decor of this charming *logis de France* is one of exposed beams, polished wood and decorative knick-knacks.		MC V				■
STRASBOURG: *Au Cerf d'Or* €€€ 6 place de l'Hôpital, 67000. ☎ 03 88 36 20 05. FAX 03 88 36 68 67. *Rooms: 37.* The main hotel has more charming rooms, but the annex offers a small pool and sauna. Nearby are several waterfront restaurants.		MC V		■	●	
STRASBOURG: *Relais Mercure* @ h1813@accord-hotels.com €€€ 3 rue du Maire Kuss, 67000. ☎ 03 88 32 80 80. FAX 03 88 23 05 39. *Rooms: 52.* Although part of the vast Mercure chain, this is an old-fashioned red-brick hotel with very helpful management.		AE DC MC V				■
STRASBOURG: *Régent Petite France* ⓦ www.regent-hotels.com €€€€€ 5 rue des Moulins, 67000. ☎ 03 88 76 43 43. FAX 03 88 76 43 76. *Rooms: 72.* The city's most prestigious and ideally located deluxe hotel. Set in a converted watermill, it overlooks the Petite France district.		AE DC MC V		■		■
VERDUN: *Hostellerie du Coq Hardi* ⓦ www.coq-hardi.com €€€ 8 avenue de la Victoire, 55100. ☎ 03 29 86 36 36. FAX 03 29 86 09 21. *Rooms: 35.* This handsome Lorraine hotel offers traditional comfort and a friendly reception. Delicious traditional cooking.		AE DC MC V	●	■		
WANTZENAU: *Le Moulin de la Wantzenau* @ moulin-wantzenau@wanadoo.fr €€ 3 impasse du Moulin, 67610. ☎ 03 88 59 22 22. FAX 03 88 59 22 00. *Rooms: 20.* An imposing converted mill that makes a pleasant place to stop en route to Lorraine and Germany. Peaceful atmosphere.		AE MC V		■		■

NORMANDY

Hotel		Credit Cards	Children's Facilities	Parking Facilities	Swimming Pool	Garden
L'AIGLE: *Hôtel du Dauphin* @ regis.ligot@free.fr €€€ Place de la Halle, 61300. ☎ 02 33 84 18 00. FAX 02 33 34 09 28. *Rooms: 30.* A fine stone-built inn close to the biggest market in Normandy. High-class, traditional hospitality and business facilities.		AE DC MC V	●	■		
ALENÇON: *Hôtel le Chapeau Rouge* €€ 3 boulevard Duchamp, 61000. ☎ 02 33 26 20 23. FAX 02 33 26 54 05. *Rooms: 14.* A modern, serviceable hotel ten minutes' walk from the town center.		MC V		■		
BAGNOLES DE L'ORNE: *Hôtel Le Normandie* @ hotel-le-normandie@wanadoo.fr €€ 2 av du Dr Paul Lemuet, 61140. ☎ 02 33 30 71 30. FAX 02 33 30 71 31. *Rooms: 22.* A handsome old stone-built inn with a highly recommended restaurant. In summer, meals are served in the attractive garden. There is a fine view from the front across wooded countryside and park. Reasonably priced.		AE MC V	●	■		■
BALINES: *Auberge du Moulin de Bâlines* ⓦ www.moulin-de-balines.fr €€€ RN12, 27130. ☎ 02 32 32 03 48. FAX 02 32 60 11 22. *Rooms: 12.* Set in its own vast park, this delightful country hotel is good value. The conversion of the ancient mill has been tastefully done.		DC MC V	●	■		■
BÉNOUVILLE: *Le Manoir d'Hastings* €€€ 18 avenue de la Côte-de-Nacre, 14970. ☎ 02 31 44 62 43 FAX 02 31 44 76 18. *Rooms: 16.* A modern hotel built on to a 17th-century building which is now the restaurant. Each bedroom has its own sitting-room. Helpful staff.		AE DC MC V	●	■		■

BRIONNE: *Auberge du Vieux Donjon*   €€   AE MC V
19 rue de la Soie, 27800. **[** 02 32 44 80 62. **FAX** 02 32 45 83 23. **Rooms:** 8.
A perfect old-fashioned country inn on the edge of the market square.
For centuries farmers have come here to enjoy a hearty meal. 🛏 📺 ▮

CABOURG: *Grand Hôtel* **W** www.grandhotelcabourg.com   €€€€   AE DC MC V
Promenade Marcel-Proust, 14390. **[** 02 31 91 01 79. **FAX** 02 31 24 03 20. **Rooms:** 70.
A huge, white Belle Epoque hotel standing on the seafront with vast
rooms and balconies. Marcel Proust often stayed here. 🛏 📺 ▮

CAEN: *Le Dauphin* **@** dauphin.caen@wanadoo.fr   €€€€   AE DC MC V
29 rue Gemare, 14000. **[** 02 31 86 22 26. **FAX** 02 31 86 35 14. **Rooms:** 22.
In a quiet but central location, this old priory has been well renovated, with
comfortable rooms. Its restaurant serves excellent Norman cuisine. 🛏 📺 ▮

CAEN: *Hôtel Mercure* **@** h0869@accord-hotels.com   €€€€   AE DC MC V
1 rue Courtonne, 14000. **[** 02 31 47 24 24. **FAX** 02 31 47 43 88. **Rooms:** 114.
Despite its central location, an atmosphere of quiet elegance pervades,
with every attention paid to the comfort of the guests. 🛏 ▤ 📺 ▮

CEAUX: *Le Relais du Mont* **W** www.hotel-mont-st-michel.com   €€   AE DC MC V
La Buvette, 50220. (Route N175.) **[** 02 33 70 92 55. **FAX** 02 33 70 94 57. **Rooms:** 30.
Facing west with splendid sunsets over Mont-St-Michel, this modern
hotel has family rooms available and an excellent restaurant. 🛏 📺 ▮

DEAUVILLE: *Hôtel Normandy* **@** normandy@lucienbarriere.com   €€€€€   AE DC MC V
38 rue J-Mermoz, 14800. **[** 02 31 98 66 22. **FAX** 02 31 98 66 23. **Rooms:** 291.
Despite its modernization, this friendly hotel has retained its original
charm. Meals are served in the courtyard under the apple trees. 🛏 📺 ▮

EVREUX: *Le Paris*   €
32 rue de la Harpe, 27000. **[** 02 32 39 12 97. **Rooms:** 6.
Quietly situated close to the cathedral and the town center. Clean,
simple rooms are sensibly priced, and the welcome is warm.

FALAISE: *Hôtel de la Poste* **@** hoteldelaposte@wanadoo.fr   €€   AE MC V
38 rue Georges-Clemenceau,14700. **[** 02 31 90 13 14. **FAX** 02 31 90 01 81. **Rooms:** 17.
The hotel accommodation is comfortable and the restaurant is very
good value. The busy street quietens down at night. 🛏 📺 ▮

FÉCAMP: *Vent d'Ouest* **W** www.hotelventdouest.tm.fr   €€   AE MC V
3 ave Gambetta, 76400. **[** 02 35 28 04 04. **FAX** 02 35 27 75 96. **Rooms:** 15.
A friendly welcome awaits guests in this centrally-located hotel The decor
has a maritime theme in keeping with Fécamp's busy fishing port. 🛏 ▤ ▮

FONTENAI-SUR-ORNE: *Le Faisan Doré* **@** lefaisandore@wanadoo.fr   €€   MC V
D924, 61200. **[** 02 33 67 18 11. **FAX** 02 33 35 82 15. **Rooms:** 14.
A large, moderately priced hotel, with freshly renovated rooms. There
is a beautiful garden with a terrace for dining out in summer. 🛏 📺 ▮

GRANDCAMP-MAISY: *Hôtel Duguésclin*   €€   AE MC V
4 quai Henri Crampon, 14450. **[** 02 31 22 64 22. **FAX** 02 31 22 34 79. **Rooms:** 25.
Friendly and efficiently run modern hotel on the seafront in this small
fishing port. Boasts an excellent restaurant. 🛏 📺 ▮

GRANVILLE: *Hôtel Michelet*   €€   MC V
5 rue Jules Michelet, 50400. **[** 02 33 50 06 55 **FAX** 02 33 50 12 25. **Rooms:** 20.
The hotel is close to shops, restaurants, and the casino in this charming
town. Plain rooms and friendly owners. 🛏

HONFLEUR: *La Ferme St-Siméon* **W** www.st-simeon.com   €€€€€   AE MC V
Rue A-Marais, 14600. **[** 02 31 81 78 00. **FAX** 02 31 89 48 48. **Rooms:** 34.
Ancient farmhouse on the Seine estuary, beautifully converted in to guest
rooms. Renoir, Cézanne, and other Impressionists used to meet here. 🛏 📺 ▮

ISIGNY-SUR-MER: *Hôtel de France*   €€   AE MC V
17 rue Emile-Demagny, 14230. **[** 02 31 22 00 33. **FAX** 02 31 22 79 19. **Rooms:** 19.
A friendly and comfortable small hotel in this picturesque fishing port.
Local ingredients are favored in the excellent restaurant. 🛏 📺 ▮

LISIEUX: *Grand Hôtel de l'Espérance* **W** www.lisieux-hotel.com   €€€   AE DC MC V
16 boulevard Ste-Anne, 14100. **[** 02 31 62 17 53. **FAX** 02 31 62 34 00. **Rooms:** 100.
This traditional half-timbered Norman building is on a busy street but
sound proofing ensures peace and quiet. 🛏 📺 ▮

<table>
<tr><td colspan="2">

Price categories for a standard double room (not per person) for one night, including tax and service charges, but not including breakfast.
€ under 30€
€€ 30€–60€
€€€ 61€–90€
€€€€ 91€–150€
€€€€€ over 150€

</td><td colspan="2">

CHILDREN'S FACILITIES
Cribs and baby-sitting available. Some hotels provide children's portions and high chairs in the restaurant.
PARKING FACILITIES
Parking provided by the hotel in either a private lot or a private garage very close by.
SWIMMING POOL
Hotel pools are often quite small and are outdoors unless otherwise stated.
GARDEN
Hotel with garden, courtyard or terrace, often providing tables for eating outside.

</td></tr>
</table>

	Price	Credit Cards	Children's Facilities	Parking Facilities	Swimming Pool	Garden
MACE: *Ile de Sees* ⓦ www.ile-sees.fr Vandel, 61500. ☎ 02 33 27 98 65. FAX 02 33 28 41 22. *Rooms:* 16. This traditional half-timbered former dairy is now a friendly hotel, set in wooded parkland, at the heart of chateaux and studfarm country. 🚗 TV ⑪	€€	MC V	●	●		
MESNIL-VAL: *Hostellerie de la Vieille Ferme* 23 rue de la Mer, 76910. ☎ 02 35 86 72 18. FAX 02 35 86 12 67. *Rooms:* 31. Set in its own park, this 18th-century farmhouse has several attractively converted outbuildings that make up the hotel complex. 🚗 TV ⑪	€€€	AE DC MC V	●			●
MORTAGNE-AU-PERCHE: *Hostellerie Genty-Home* ⓦ www.genty-home.com 4 rue Notre-Dame, 61400. ☎ 02 33 25 11 53. FAX 02 33 25 41 38. *Rooms:* 8. A traditional stone-built inn in the center of this unspoiled market town. Inside the decor varies from functional in the hotel to ornate in the reproduction Louis XV gastronomic restaurant. 🚗 TV ⑪	€€	AE MC V	●	●		
MORTAIN: *Hôtel de la Poste* ⓦ www.hoteldelaposte.fr Place des Arcades, 50140. ☎ 02 33 59 00 05. FAX 02 33 69 53 89. *Rooms:* 28. Situated on the spectacular Cherbourg peninsula, Mortain has a lovely river overlooked by this family-run hotel. 🚗 TV ⑪	€€	AE MC V	●	●		
PONT-AUDEMER: *Belle-Isle-sur-Risle* ⓦ www.bellisle.com 112 Route de Rouen, 27500. ☎ 02 32 56 96 22. FAX 02 32 42 88 96. *Rooms:* 20. Set on an island in its own large garden of ancient trees and roses, the hotel has a fitness center, sauna, and two pools (outdoor and indoor), as well as exceptionally comfortable bedrooms and superb cuisine, served in the 19th-century rotunda overlooking the river. 🚗 TV ⑪	€€€€	AE DC MC V	●	●	●	●
PONT DE L'ARCHE: *Hôtel de la Tour* @ hotel-de-la-tour@wanadoo.fr 41 quai Foch, 27340. ☎ 02 35 23 00 99. FAX 02 35 23 46 22. *Rooms:* 18. A pretty 18th-century Norman house with comfortably renovated rooms, overlooking either the patio garden, the ramparts or the river. 🚗 TV	€€	AE DC MC V		●		●
ROUEN: *Hôtel de Bordeaux* ⓦ www.perso.wanadoo.fr/interhotel.rouen 9 place de la République, 76000. ☎ 02 35 71 93 58. FAX 02 35 71 92 15. *Rooms:* 48. A functional, friendly and well-run hotel overlooking the Seine on one side and the cathedral towers on the other. English spoken. 🚗 TV	€€	AE DC MC V				
ROUEN: *Hôtel Notre-Dame* ⓦ www.hotelnotredame.com 4 rue de la Savonnerie, 76000. ☎ 02 35 71 87 73. FAX 02 35 89 31 52. *Rooms:* 30. The staff are friendly and helpful, the rooms are spacious, some of them with views of the river and cathedral. 🚗 TV	€€	AE DC MC				
SAINT-LÔ: *Hôtel des Voyageurs* 5–7 avenue de Briovère, 50000. ☎ 02 33 05 08 63. FAX 02 33 05 14 34. *Rooms:* 31. A professional establishment where the rooms are comfortable and quiet. The restaurant specializes in fish. 🚗 TV ⑪	€€€	DC MC V	●	●		●
ST-PATERNE: *Château de St-Paterne* ⓦ www.chateau-saintpaterne.com 72610 St-Paterne. ☎ 02 33 27 54 71. FAX 02 33 29 16 71. *Rooms:* 8. This is not so much a hotel as a family château, where a fixed-menu is served *en famille*. The De Valbrays still live in this beautiful château, set in its own park just on the outskirts of Alençon. 🚗	€€€€€	MC V	●	●	●	●
SÉES: *Hôtel du Cheval Blanc* 1 place St-Pierre, 61500. ☎ 02 33 27 80 48. FAX 02 33 28 58 05. *Rooms:* 9. A discreet and comfortable hotel on the route south from the Channel ports. It represents the best of French provincial hospitality. 🚗 TV ⑪	€€	MC V	●	●		●
VERNON: *Hôtel d'Evreux* @ hotel.devreux@libertysurf.fr 11 place d'Evreux, 27200. ☎ 02 32 21 16 12. FAX 02 32 21 32 73. *Rooms:* 12. An 18th-century coaching inn with a romantic courtyard where, on warm summer evenings, guests can enjoy fine cuisine outside. 🚗 TV ⑪	€€	AE DC MC V	●	●		●

BRITTANY

AUDIERNE: *Le Goyen* Ⓦ www.chateauxhotels.com/goyen €€€€ AE MC V
Place Jean-Simon, 29770. ☎ 02 98 70 08 88. FAX 02 98 70 18 77. **Rooms:** 27.
Most of the bedrooms in this restored old building overlook the fishing
port which supplies the hotel's superb restaurant.

BREST: *Hôtel de la Corniche* Ⓦ www.lacorniche.brest.com €€€ AE MC V
1 rue Amiral-Nicol, 29200. ☎ 02 98 45 12 42. FAX 02 98 49 01 53. **Rooms:** 16.
This modern hotel, built of local stone in the Breton style, is on the west
side of the city near the naval base. It is convenient as a base for walks
along the scenic coastline.

CARNAC: *Lann Roz* @ hotel.lan-roz@club-internet.fr €€€ MC V
36 avenue de la Poste, 56340. ☎ 02 97 52 10 48. FAX 02 97 52 24 36. **Rooms:** 13.
A friendly hotel with a pretty garden ten minutes' walk from the beach.
The restaurant has a fine wine list.

CESSON-SÉVIGNÉ: *Hôtel Germinal* €€€ AE MC V
9 cours de la Vilaine, 35510. ☎ 02 99 83 11 01. FAX 02 99 83 45 16. **Rooms:** 20.
A river runs on both sides of this converted mill. The decor is rustic
with traditional wooden furniture.

DINAN: *Moulin de la Fontaine des Eaux* @ denisnoel@aol.com €€€ AE MC
22100. ☎ & FAX 02 96 87 92 09. **Rooms:** 5.
Set in a wooded valley 5 mins from the port of Dinan, this converted 18th-century
watermill overlooks its own lake and grounds. Chambre d'hôte only.

DINARD: *Hôtel Printania* @ printania.dinard@wanadoo.fr €€€ AE MC V
5 ave Georges V, 35800. ☎ 02 99 46 13 07. FAX 02 99 46 26 32. **Rooms:** 60.
A friendly family run hotel with typical Breton decor: ornate box beds, Quimper
faïence, carved wooden furniture. Near the beach with fine sea views.

FOUGÈRES: *Balzac Hôtel* €€ AE DC MC V
15 rue Nationale, 35300. ☎ 02 99 99 42 46. FAX 02 99 99 65 43. **Rooms:** 20.
In one of the prettiest towns in western France, this quiet, recently renovated
hotel furnished in 18th-century style offers a warm welcome.

GROIX (ÎLE DE): *Hôtel de la Marine* Ⓦ www.hoteldelamarine.com €€ MC V
7 rue Général-de-Gaulle, 56590. ☎ 02 97 86 80 05. FAX 02 97 86 56 37. **Rooms:** 22.
An old stone house filled with traditional furniture standing in the
middle of the island of Groix. A relaxing hideaway.

LA FORÊT-FOUESNANT: *Le Manoir du Stang* €€€€
29940 La Forêt-Fouesnant. ☎ & FAX 02 98 56 97 37. **Rooms:** 24.
A fabulous Renaissance manor house set in a large park with
woodland and a lake. The interior features ancient paneling and
antique furniture which has been in the family for generations.

LAMBALLE: *La Tour d'Argent* @ latourdargent@wanadoo.fr €€ AE DC MC V
2 rue du Docteur Lavergne, 22400. ☎ 02 96 31 01 37. FAX 02 96 31 37 59. **Rooms:** 31.
Unrelated to the famous Paris restaurant of the same name,
this private home is full of charm and makes a pleasant stay.

MORLAIX: *Hôtel de l'Europe* Ⓦ www.hotel-europe-com.fr €€ AE DC MC V
1 rue d' Aiguillon, 29600. ☎ 02 98 62 11 99. FAX 02 98 88 83 38. **Rooms:** 60.
This Second Empire hotel is filled with furniture from earlier periods.
The brasserie is excellent value. Centrally located.

PÉNESTIN: *Hôtel Loscolo* Ⓦ www.hotelloscolo.com €€€€ MC V
La Pointe de Loscolo, 56760. ☎ 02 99 90 31 90. FAX 02 99 90 32 14. **Rooms:** 15.
A modern building on a cape with magnificent ocean views to both sides
and good walking nearby. The restaurant serves rich cuisine.

PLÉVEN: *Le Manoir de Vaumadeuc* Ⓦ www.vaumadeuc.com €€€€ AE DC MC V
22130 Pléven. ☎ 02 96 84 46 17. FAX 02 96 84 40 16. **Rooms:** 14.
This old manor house, with its graceful bay windows and fine
staircase, dates back to the 15th century. The park around it
includes a beautiful rose garden. (in summer only).

PLOUGASTEL-DAOULAS: *Hôtel Kastel Roc'h* @ kastel-roch@wanadoo.fr €€ AE MC V
91 ave du Général de Gaulle, 29470. ☎ 02 98 40 32 00. FAX 02 98 04 25 40. **Rooms:** 45.
Near Océanopolis and the marina, this hotel has some family rooms
which makes it a good base for a vacation with children.

For key to symbols see back flap

Price categories for a standard double room (not per person) for one night, including tax and service charges, but not including breakfast.

€ under 30€
€€ 30€–60€
€€€ 61€–90€
€€€€ 91€–150€
€€€€€ over 150€

CHILDREN'S FACILITIES
Cribs and baby-sitting available. Some hotels provide children's portions and high chairs in the restaurant.

PARKING FACILITIES
Parking provided by the hotel in either a private lot or a private garage very close by.

SWIMMING POOL
Hotel pools are often quite small and are outdoors unless otherwise stated.

GARDEN
Hotel with garden, courtyard or terrace, often providing tables for eating outside.

	CREDIT CARDS	CHILDREN'S FACILITIES	PARKING FACILITIES	SWIMMING POOL	GARDEN
QUIBERON: *Hôtel Bellevue* €€€ Rue Tiviec, 56170. **C** 02 97 50 16 28. **FAX** 02 97 30 44 34. *Rooms:* 39. Forming an L-shape around its swimming pool, the Bellevue is near the seafront and casino. It has a comfortable lounge and bar. ☷ TV ⊺	AE MC V	●	■	●	■
QUIMPER: *Hotel Gradlon* W www.hotel-gradlon.com €€€€ 30 rue Brest, 29000. **C** 02 98 95 04 39. **FAX** 02 98 95 61 25. *Rooms:* 22. Most of the rooms in the quiet, traditionally decorated hotel overlook the enclosed garden, just a few minutes' walk from the historic center. ☷ TV	AE MC V	●	■		■
ROSCOFF: *Hôtel Bellevue* €€ Rue Jeanne-d'Arc, 29680. **C** 02 98 61 23 38. **FAX** 02 98 61 11 80. *Rooms:* 18. An old Breton house enjoying fine views of the sea and the old port. To the rear is a pleasant garden with deckchairs where drinks are served. ☷ TV	MC V	●			
ST-MALO: *Hôtel Elizabeth* W www.st-malo-elizabeth.com €€€€ 2 rue des Cordiers, 35400. **C** 02 99 56 24 98. **FAX** 02 99 56 39 24. *Rooms:* 17. Situated within the ramparts of the old town, the building has a 16th-century façade. English satellite TV is available. ☷ TV	AE DC MC V		■		
ST-MÉLOIR DES ONDES: *Hôtel Richeux* W www.maisons-de-bricourt.com €€€€€ Le Point du Jour, 35350. **C** 02 99 89 64 76. **FAX** 02 99 89 88 47. *Rooms:* 13. A charming Art-Deco villa with views of the bay of Mont-St-Michel. The rooms are furnished with antiques. ☷ TV ⊺	AE DC MC V	●	■		■
VANNES: *La Marébaudière* W www.marebaudiere.com €€€ 4 rue Aristide-Briand, 56000. **C** 02 97 47 34 29. **FAX** 02 97 54 14 11. *Rooms:* 41. A peaceful hotel decorated with flair. The beautifully preserved old walled town is a short walk away. ☷ TV	AE DC MC V	●	■		

THE LOIRE VALLEY

	CREDIT CARDS	CHILDREN'S FACILITIES	PARKING FACILITIES	SWIMMING POOL	GARDEN
AMBOISE: *Le Choiseul* W www.le-choiseul.com €€€€€ 36 quai Charles-Guinot, 37400. **C** 02 47 30 45 45. **FAX** 02 47 30 46 10. *Rooms:* 32. An ivy-covered manor set in elegant grounds. The famous cellars can be visited. A sophisticated restaurant and musical evenings. ☷ ☰ TV ⊺	AE DC MC V	●	■	●	■
AZAY-LE-RIDEAU: *Le Clos Philippa* €€€ 10 rue Pineau, 37190. **C** 02 47 45 26 49. **FAX** 02 47 45 31 46. *Rooms:* 5. Guests at this 18th-century house have the use of the owner's drawing room, sitting room, library, and grounds. Meals can be served on the terrace. ☷	DC MC V	●	■		■
AZAY-LE-RIDEAU: *Manoir de la Rémonière* W www.chateaux-france.com €€€€ La Chapelle St-Blaise, 37190. **C** 02 47 45 24 88. **FAX** 02 47 45 45 69. *Rooms:* 9. A 15th-century manor house standing in romantic grounds that are perfect for children to play in. ☷		●	■		■
BEAUGENCY: *Hotel de la Sologne* W www.hoteldelasologne.com €€ 6 place St-Firmin, 45190. **C** 02 38 44 50 27. **FAX** 02 38 44 90 19. *Rooms:* 16. This recently refurbished hotel on the main square overlooks the ruined castle keep. Breakfast is served in an attractive conservatory. ☷ TV	MC V	●			
BEAUGENCY: *Hotel de l'Abbaye* €€€€ 2 quai de l'Abbaye, 45190. **C** 02 38 44 67 35. **FAX** 02 38 44 87 92. *Rooms:* 17. Ask for a room in one of the former monastic cells of this restored abbey beside the river. The restaurant is good but overpriced. ☷ TV ⊺	AE DC MC V	●	■		
BRÉHÉMONT: *Le Castel de Bray et Monts* W www.castelhotel-bray.com €€€ Le Bourg, 37130. **C** 02 47 96 70 47. **FAX** 02 47 96 57 36. *Rooms:* 9. An attractive 18th-century mansion in the heart of the village, set in ample grounds along the Loire river. The rooms are charming and breakfast is excellent. Cooking classes possible. ☷ TV ⊺	MC V	●	■		■

CHAMBORD: *Hôtel Saint-Michel* €€ | MC V
41250 Chambord. 02 54 20 31 31. FAX 02 54 20 36 40. **Rooms:** 38.
Reserve early at this old-fashioned hotel and ask for a room with a view of the château. The restaurant is stuffy but the cuisine good.

CHAMPIGNÉ: *Château des Briottières* www.briottieres.com €€€€€ | MC V
49330 Champigné. 02 41 42 00 02. FAX 02 41 42 01 55. **Rooms:** 15.
Family-run château set in 50 hectare-grounds. Romantic dinners are on offer as well as wine-tasting trips and cooking classes.

CHARTRES: *Grand Monarque* www.bw-grand-monarque.com €€€€ | AE DC MC V
22 place des Epars, 28005. 02 37 21 00 72. FAX 02 37 36 34 18. **Rooms:** 55.
This converted 16th-century staging post, with massively thick walls, is part of the Best Western network, and has a recommended gourmet restaurant.

CHÊNEHUTTE-LES-TUFFEAUX: *Hostellerie du Prieuré* www.prieure.com €€€€ | AE DC MC V
49350. 02 41 67 90 14. FAX 02 02 41 67 92 24. **Rooms:** 36.
18 rooms are in the luxurious 10th–16th-century former priory, with magnificent views over the Loire. A gourmet restaurant adds to the appeal.

CHENONCEAUX: *Hostel du Roy* www.hostelduroy.com €€ | AE DC MC V
9 rue du Dr Bretonneau, 37150. 02 47 23 90 17. FAX 02 47 23 89 81. **Rooms:** 32.
A sprawling hotel-restaurant with simple but appealing bedrooms and a dining room hung with hunting trophies. Local wines served.

CHINON: *Hôtel Diderot* www.hoteldiderot.com €€ | AE MC V
4 rue Buffon, 37500. 02 47 93 18 87. FAX 02 47 93 37 10. **Rooms:** 28.
An elegant, ivy-clad 18th-century house on a quiet street. The bedrooms are simple but some have good views.

CHINON: *Hôtel de France* www.bestwestern.com €€€€ | AE DC MC V
47 place de Gen-de-Gaulle, 37500. 02 47 93 33 91. FAX 02 47 98 37 03. **Rooms:** 31.
This underrated hotel, comfortable and friendly but without frills, is situated in the Old Quarter a short way from the scenic main street.

CHINON: *Hostellerie Gargantua* €€€ | MC V
73 rue Voltaire, 37500. 02 47 93 04 71. FAX 02 47 93 08 02. **Rooms:** 8.
With its pointed roof and turret, this old building overlooking the river is a local landmark. Its cuisine blends the traditional and modern.

CHOUZÉ-SUR-LOIRE: *Château des Réaux* www.chateaus-france.com €€€€ | AE MC V
Le Port-Boulet, 37140. 02 47 95 14 40. FAX 02 47 95 18 34. **Rooms:** 17.
A lovingly restored brick and stone Renaissance château in a wine-growing area. The owners enjoy showing is to visitors.

FONTEVRAUD-L'ABBAYE: *Hôtellerie Prieuré St-Lazare* €€€ | AE MC V
49590 Fontevraud-L'Abbaye. 02 41 51 73 16. FAX 02 41 51 75 50. **Rooms:** 52.
This atmospheric hotel is housed in the former St-Lazare priory, within the famous abbey complex, and has a gourmet restaurant. www.hotelfp-fontevraud.com

GENNES: *Les Naulets* €€ | AE MC
18 rue Croix de la Mission, 49350. 02 41 51 81 88. FAX 02 41 38 00 78. **Rooms:** 19.
The warm welcome, good value food and quiet location on the edge of this village more than compensate for the lack of architectural interest.

GIEN: *Hôtel La Poularde* lapoularde@wanadoo.fr €€ | AE DC MC V
13 quai de Nice, 45500. 02 38 67 36 05. FAX 02 38 38 18 78. **Rooms:** 9.
Located on the banks of the Loire, this 19th-century bourgeois house has pleasant rooms with Louis-Philippe furniture. Try the excellent restaurant.

LA CHARTRE-SUR-LE-LOIR: *Hôtel de France* €€ | MC V
20 place de la République, 72340. 02 43 44 40 16. FAX 02 43 79 62 20. **Rooms:** 24.
This hotel in the town center has a garden beside the river. Its restaurant serves generous portions and has won awards.

LE MANS: *Ibis Centre* €€ | AE DC MC V
Quai Ledru-Rolin, 72000. 02 43 23 18 23. FAX 02 43 24 00 72. **Rooms:** 85.
Overlooking the river and the Old Quarter, this is the best hotel in Le Mans for budget travelers. It serves a good buffet breakfast.

LOCHES: *Hôtel de France* €€ | DC MC V
6 rue Picois, 37600. 02 47 59 00 32. FAX 02 47 59 28 66. **Rooms:** 17.
This elegant hotel is situated near the medieval gate. The restaurant is excellent, and smokes its own salmon.

For key to symbols see back flap

Price categories for a standard double room (not per person) for one night, including tax and service charges, but not including breakfast.
€ under 30€
€€ 30€–60€
€€€ 61€–90€
€€€€ 91€–150€
€€€€€ over 150€

CHILDREN'S FACILITIES
Cribs and baby-sitting available. Some hotels provide children's portions and high chairs in the restaurant.

PARKING FACILITIES
Parking provided by the hotel in either a private lot or a private garage very close by.

SWIMMING POOL
Hotel pools are often quite small and are outdoors unless otherwise stated.

GARDEN
Hotel with garden, courtyard or terrace, often providing tables for eating outside.

	CREDIT CARDS	CHILDREN'S FACILITIES	PARKING FACILITIES	SWIMMING POOL	GARDEN
LUYNES: *Domaine de Beauvois* W www.beauvois.com €€€€€ Route de Cleré-les-Pins, 37230. ☎ 02 47 55 50 11. FAX 02 47 55 59 62. **Rooms:** 36. Built around a 15th-century tower and overlooking its own lake, the Domaine has large rooms, a Michelin-rated restaurant and jazz evenings. 🚗 TV ¶	AE DC MC V	●	▨	●	▨
MARÇAY: *Château de Marçay* W www.chateaudemarcay.com €€€€ 37500 Marçay. ☎ 02 47 93 03 47. FAX 02 47 93 45 33. **Rooms:** 34. Service and cuisine in this elegant château-hotel is impeccable. There are good views over the surrounding parkland and vineyards. 🚗 TV ♿ ¶	AE DC MC V	●	▨	●	▨
MONTBAZON: *Château d'Artigny* W www.artigny.com €€€€€ Route de Monts, 37250. ☎ 02 47 34 30 30. FAX 02 47 34 30 39. **Rooms:** 65. The grandiose classical exterior is matched by a formal Empire-style interior. A gourmet restaurant serves regional specialties. 🚗 TV ¶	AE DC MC V	●	▨	●	▨
MONTLOUIS-SUR-LOIRE: *Château de la Bourdaisière* €€€€ 25 rue de la Bourdaisière, 37270. ☎ 02 47 45 16 31. FAX 02 47 45 09 11. **Rooms:** 20. A magnificent château refurbished as luxury accommodations. Gabrielle d'Estrées, Henri IV's mistress, was born here in 1565. The famous kitchen gardens are open to the public. 🚗 ¶ (for min 6). W www.chateaulabourdaisiere.com	AE MC V	●	▨	●	▨
MONTREUIL-BELLAY: *Demeure des Petits Augustins* €€ 321 rue Nationale, 49260. ☎ 02 41 52 33 88. FAX 02 41 52 33 88. **Rooms:** 3. Guests are made welcome in this 17th-century town mansion. The spacious, individually styled bedrooms look over a charming courtyard. The "white" suite is especially recommended. 🚗 ♿ @ moniquguezenec@minitel.net	MC V	●			▨
MONTREUIL-BELLAY: *Relais du Bellay* W www.splendid-hotel.fr €€ 96 rue Nationale, 49260. ☎ 02 41 53 10 10. FAX 02 41 38 70 61. **Rooms:** 42. Rooms are in the 17th-century main building and the stylishly-furnished annex, with heated pool, sauna, Turkish bath, jacuzzi and gym. All are quiet. 🚗 TV ♿	MC V	●	▨	●	▨
MUIDES-SUR-LOIRE: *Château de Colliers* W www.chateauxandcountry.com €€€€ 41500 Muides-sur-Loire. ☎ 02 54 87 50 75. FAX 02 54 87 03 64. **Rooms:** 5. This château, set among woods a short drive east of Blois, combines grandeur with rusticity. In the 18th century it belonged to an aristocratic governor of Louisiana. 🚗 ♿	MC V	●	▨	●	▨
NANTES: *Jules Verne* W www.hoteljulesverne.fr €€€ 3 rue du Couëdic, 44000. ☎ 02 40 35 74 50. FAX 02 40 20 09 35. **Rooms:** 65. A modern hotel on a pedestrianized square, offering friendly service and comfortable rooms. Free tended parking in the nearby place du Commerce. 🚗 ▤ TV ♿	AE DC MC V	●	▨		
NANTES: *Hôtel la Perouse* W www.hotel-laperouse.fr €€€ 3 allée Duquesne, 44000. ☎ 02 40 89 75 00. **Rooms:** 47 This smart hotel which opened in 1993 offers crisp, contemporary design and efficient service. It is reasonably quiet for a city hotel. 🚗 ▤ TV	AE DC MC V	●	▨		
NOIZAY: *Château de Noizay* W www.chateaudenoizay.com €€€€€ 37210 Noizay. ☎ 02 47 52 11 01. FAX 02 47 52 04 64. **Rooms:** 19. A compact Renaissance château set in Classical gardens on the right bank of the Loire. The rooms are discreetly and elegantly furnished. In good weather breakfast is served on the terrace. 🚗 TV ¶	AE DC MC V	●	▨	●	▨
ONZAIN: *Domaine des Hauts de Loire* W www.domainehautsloire.com €€€€ Route d'Herbault, 41150. ☎ 02 54 20 72 57. FAX 02 54 20 77 32. **Rooms:** 35. A count's former hunting lodge with large grounds and a lake, this is an unashamedly expensive place to relax and enjoy good food. 🚗 TV ♿ ¶	AE DC MC V	●	▨	●	▨
ROCHECORBON: *Domaine des Hautes Roches* €€€€€ 86 quai de la Loire, 37210. ☎ 02 47 52 88 88. FAX 02 47 52 81 30. **Rooms:** 15. The underground rooms hewn into the chalk in this "troglodyte" hotel are particulary spacious and atmospheric. 🚗 TV ♿ ¶ W www.leshautesroches.com	AE DC MC V	●	▨	●	▨

ROMORANTIN-LANTHENAY: *Grand Hôtel du Lion d'Or* €€€€€ | AE DC MC V
69 rue G.Clémenceau, 41200. **(** 02 54 94 15 15. **FAX** 02 54 88 24 87. **Rooms:** 16.
This former 16th-century staging post is now a gastronomic halt in a
historic but untouristy town. 🔒 🍽 TV 🍴 W www.hotel-liondor.fr

ST-JULIEN-LE-PAUVRE: *Château de la Renaudière* €€€
72240 St-Julien-le-Pauvre. **(** 02 43 20 71 09. **FAX** 02 43 20 75 56. **Rooms:** 3.
A gracious château, owned by the Marquis de Mascureau, set among rolling
meadows between Le Mans and Laval. The family enjoys introducing visitors
to the lesser-known châteaux of the region. 🔒 @ pdemascureau@wanadoo.fr

ST-LAMBERT-DES-LEVÉES: *La Croix de la Voulte* €€
Route de Boumois, 49400. **(** **FAX** 02 41 38 46 66. **Rooms:** 4.
The rooms in this old manor outside Saumur are all different and the
furnishings stylish. The welcome is very friendly. 🔒

SAUMUR: *Hôtel Anne d'Anjou* W www.hotel-anneanjou.com €€€€€ | AE DC MC V
32–34 quai Mayaud, 49400. **(** 02 41 67 30 30. **FAX** 02 41 67 51 00. **Rooms:** 45.
The decor in this elegant mansion beside the river Loire is sophisticated and
romantic: the painted ceiling ove the grand staircase is very impressive. 🔒 TV ♿

TOURS: *Hôtel Moderne* W www.touraine-hotel.org €€ | MC V
1–3, rue Victor Laloux, 37000. **(** 02 47 05 32 81. **FAX** 02 47 05 71 50. **Rooms:** 23.
Conveniently located in a quiet side street in the center of Tours, the rooms
are gradually being refurbished by the new owners. 🔒 TV 🍴

TOURS: *Hôtel de l'Univers* W www.hotel-univers-loirevalley.com €€€€€ | AE DC MC V
5 boulevard Heurteloup, 37000. **(** 02 47 05 37 12. **FAX** 02 47 61 51 80. **Rooms:** 85.
Statesmen, including Winston Churchill, and royals have stayed at this
luxurious Belle Epoque hotel. Some rooms have antique furniture. 🔒 🍽 TV ♿ 🍴

VANNES-SUR-COSSON: *Le Ludion* €€
Les Hauts de Tuileries, 45510. **(** 02 38 58 12 87. **Rooms:** 2.
Down a dirt track, surrounded by forest, this friendly *chambre d'hôte* provides
an excellent dinner and homemade jelly and *pâtisseries* for breakfast. 🔒 TV 🍴

VARADES: *Le Grand Patis* €€
44370 Varades. **(** 02 40 83 42 28. **Rooms:** 5.
Rooms in this restored château are simple, clean and spacious and two have
stone balconies overlooking the peaceful, leafy grounds. 🔒 🍴

VITRY-AUX-LOGES: *Château de Plessis-Beauregard* €€€
Vitry-aux-Lodges, 45530. **(** 02 38 59 47 24. **FAX** 02 38 59 47 48. **Rooms:** 3.
Beside the Forêt d'Orléans, this turreted, brick château has light, airy rooms and
a swimming pool. A set dinner is available if ordered well in advance. 🔒

VOUVRAY: *Château de Jallanges* W www.jallanges.com €€€€ | MC V
37210 Vouvray. **(** 02 47 52 06 66. **FAX** 02 47 52 11 18. **Rooms:** 7
An imposing Renaissance brick château, now a family home, with
stylish and comfortable rooms. Guests are taken on a guided tour
from chapel to turrets. A good base for exploring Touraine. 🔒 ♿ 🍴

YZEURES-SUR-CREUSE: *Hôtel de la Promenade* €€ | MC V
1 pl du 11 Novembre, 37290. **(** 02 47 91 49 00. **FAX** 02 47 94 46 12. **Rooms:** 15.
This former coaching inn in Touraine is near the archeological sites of Le
Grand-Pressigny and Preuilly-sur-Claise, and La Brenne nature preserve. 🔒 TV 🍴

BURGUNDY AND FRANCHE-COMTÉ

ARBOIS: *Jean-Paul Jeunet* @ jeunet@receptionfrance.com €€€€€ | AE DC MC V
9 rue de l'Hôtel de Ville, 39600. **(** 03 84 66 05 67. **FAX** 03 84 66 24 20. **Rooms:** 18.
In the center of this picturesque town, Jeunet offers modern amenities
and comfort. Good selection of Jura wines in the restaurant. 🔒 TV 🍴

ARNAY-LE-DUC: *Chez Camille* W www.chezcamille.fr €€€ | AE DC MC V
1 place Edouard-Herriot, 21230. **(** 03 80 90 01 38. **FAX** 03 80 90 04 64. **Rooms:** 11.
An attractive and tastefully decorated hotel with spacious bedrooms
and antique furniture. The hotel offers warmth and peace with its huge
open fire in the salon and sound proofing. Traditional cuisine. 🔒 🍽 TV 🍴

AUTUN: *Les Granges* €€
Monthélon, 71400. **(** 03 85 52 22 99. **Rooms:** 3.
This working farm is a good base to explore the Burgundian countryside and
Autun. Homemade butter and marmalade make breakfast a true pleasure. 🔒

<table>
<tr><td colspan="6">

Price categories for a standard double room (not per person) for one night, including tax and service charges, but not including breakfast.
€ under 30€
€€ 30€–60€
€€€ 61€–90€
€€€€ 91€–150€
€€€€€ over 150€

</td></tr>
</table>

CHILDREN'S FACILITIES
Cribs and baby-sitting available. Some hotels provide children's portions and high chairs in the restaurant.

PARKING FACILITIES
Parking provided by the hotel in either a private lot or a private garage very close by.

SWIMMING POOL
Hotel pools are often quite small and are outdoors unless otherwise stated.

GARDEN
Hotel with garden, courtyard or terrace, often providing tables for eating outside.

	CREDIT CARDS	CHILDREN'S FACILITIES	PARKING FACILITIES	SWIMMING POOL	GARDEN
AUTUN: *Hôtel St-Louis et de la Poste* W www.amadeusprop.com €€€ 6 rue de l'Arbalète, 71400. [03 85 52 01 01. FAX 03 85 86 32 54. **Rooms:** 39. This quiet hotel was once a staging post. Rooms vary in price, the most expensive being Napoleon's former bedchamber. ▭ TV ⌗	AE DC MC V		▪		▪
BEAUNE: *Le Home* €€ 138 route Dijon, 21200. [03 80 22 16 43. FAX 03 80 24 90 74. **Rooms:** 23. Set back from the main road in a charming courtyard is this simple, homely hotel just outside the town. Clean and comfortable. ▭	MC V		▪		▪
BEAUNE: *Hôtel du Cep* W www.hotel-cep-beaune.com €€€€€ 27 rue Maufoux, 21200. [03 80 22 35 48. FAX 03 80 22 76 80. **Rooms:** 57. In the heart of the Old Town is this subdued and elegant hotel, tastefully renovated in a Renaissance style. Each bedroom is named after a wine of the Côte d'Or vineyards. ▭ ▤ TV ⌗	AE DC MC V		▪		▪
BESANÇON: *Hôtel Mercure Parc Micaud* @ h1220@accor-hotels.com €€€€€ 3 avenue E Droz, 25000. [03 81 40 34 34. FAX 03 81 40 34 39. **Rooms:** 91. A luxury modern hotel on the waterfront offering comfort, good breakfasts. ▭ ▤ TV ⌗	AE DC MC V	●	▪		
BOUILLAND: *Le Vieux Moulin* W www.chateauxhotels.com/levieuxmoulin €€€€ 21420 Bouilland. [03 80 21 51 16. FAX 03 80 21 59 90. **Rooms:** 20. A recently renovated mill located in one of the most spectacular villages in Burgundy. The chef is famous for his creativity. ▭ TV ⌗	MC V	●	▪	●	▪
CHABLIS: *Hostellerie des Clos* W www.hostellerie-des-clos.fr €€ Rue Jules-Rathier, 89800. [03 86 42 10 63. FAX 03 86 42 17 11. **Rooms:** 26. The owner has renovated a medieval convent in the middle of this famed village. The rooms are modern and comfortable, the garden is delightful and the restaurant is one of the best in the region. ▭ TV ⌗	AE MC V		▪		▪
CHAILLY-SUR-ARMANÇON: *Château de Chailly* W www.chailly.com €€€€€ 21320 Chailly-sur-Armançon. [03 80 90 30 30. FAX 03 80 90 30 00. **Rooms:** 45. Recently restored, this magnificent Renaissance château is extremely luxurious, and has its own golf course, tennis courts, outdoor swimming pool and two restaurants. ▭ TV ⌗	AE DC MC V	●	▪	●	▪
CHÂTEAU CHINON: *Hôtel du Vieux Morvan* €€ 8 place Gudin, 58120. [03 86 85 05 01. FAX 03 86 85 02 78. **Rooms:** 24. François Mitterrand learned he had become President here – for years he visited this hotel and always stayed in room 15. The manageress has since retired but the hotel retains its rustic, old-world style. ▭ TV ⌗	MC V	●	▪		
CLUNY: *Hostellerie de Bourgogne* W www.hotel-cluny.com €€ Place de l'Abbaye, 71250. [03 85 59 00 58. FAX 03 85 59 03 73. **Rooms:** 16. This old-fashioned auberge is located next door to the magnificent Cluny abbey. Excellent restaurant serving refined cuisine. ▭ TV ⌗	AE MC V	●	▪		
DIJON: *Hostellerie le Sauvage* €€ 64 rue Monge, 21000. [03 80 41 31 21. FAX 03 80 42 06 07. **Rooms:** 21. This city hotel is conveniently located for the main sights and the historic center. ▭ TV	AE MC V		▪		
FLAVIGNY-SUR-OZERAIN: *Mme Marc Brigand* € 21150 Flavigny-sur-Ozerain. [03 80 96 20 91. **Rooms:** 3. Simple accommodation in an old-fashioned house brought to life by its breezy owners. Meals available and cash only.					▪
FONTETTE: *Hôtel Crispol* €€€ St-Père-sous-Vezelay, 89450. [03 86 33 26 25. FAX 03 86 33 33 10. **Rooms:** 12. Well-planned and smart decor in this very luxurious and modern hotel. Generous and imaginative local cooking. ▭ TV ⌗	MC V	●	▪		

GEVREY-CHAMBERTIN: *Mme Geneviève Sylvain* €€
14 rue de l'Eglise, 21220. **[** FAX *03 80 51 86 39*. **Rooms:** 3.
Welcoming owners run this spacious *chambres d'hôte*. Ideal location
for exploring the village restaurants and local wine-tastings.

GEVREY-CHAMBERTIN: *Hôtel des Grands Crus* €€€ MC V
Route des Grands Crus, 21220. **[** *03 80 34 34 15*. FAX *03 80 51 89 07*. **Rooms:** 24.
A light and airy, old-style hotel with wonderful views over the vineyards. No
restaurant but several good ones in the village. W www.hoteldesgrandscrus.com

JOIGNY: *La Côte St-Jacques* W www.relaischateaux.com/lorrain €€€€ AE DC MC V
14 Faubourg de Paris, 89300. **[** *03 86 62 09 70*. FAX *03 86 91 49 70*. **Rooms:** 32.
Known as a mini Versailles, this glamorous and glossy hotel
sits beside the river Yonne. The restaurant is outstanding.

LEVERNOIS: *Le Parc* @ hotel.le.parc@wanadoo.fr €€€ AE V
21200 Levernois. **[** *03 80 22 22 51*. FAX *03 80 24 21 19*. **Rooms:** 25.
Set in the heart of beautiful park land, this hotel offers a relaxing retreat.
Hot-air ballooning is possible in the area.

LIGNY-LE-CHÂTEL: *Relais Saint-Vincent* @ relais.saint.vincent@libertysurf.fr €€ AE DC MC V
14 Grande-Rue, 89144. **[** *03 86 47 53 38*. FAX *03 86 47 54 16*. **Rooms:** 15.
An ancient half-timbered house, well equipped with modern comforts.
The restaurant serves regional specialities.

MAILLY LE CHATEAU: *Le Castel* @ lecastelmailly@aol.com €€ MC V
89660 Mailly le Chateau. **[** *03 86 81 43 06*. FAX *03 86 81 49 26*. **Rooms:** 12.
In this charming village, Le Castel offers simple rooms in a haven
of peace. Its *table d'hôte* also has good-value Burgundy cuisine.

OYE-ET-PALLET: *Hôtel Parnet* W www.pagesjaunes.fr/hotelparnet €€ AE MC V
11 rue de la Fauconnière, 25160. **[** *03 81 89 42 03*. FAX *03 81 89 41 47*. **Rooms:** 16.
In the Jura mountains, this is a great place to take a cross-country
skiing vacation. Clean, comfortable and calm. Good food.

POLIGNY: *Hostellerie des Monts de Vaux* W www.hostellerie.com €€€€€ AE DC MC V
39800 Poligny. **[** *03 84 37 12 50*. FAX *03 84 37 09 07*. **Rooms:** 10
An elegant old coaching inn on the outskirts of Poligny. Friendly
owners, good Jura cuisine and wine, and tennis courts.

PULIGNY-MONTRACHET: *Le Montrachet* W www.le-montrachet.com €€€€ AE DC MC V
Place des Marroniers, 21190. **[** *03 80 21 30 06*. FAX *03 80 21 39 06*. **Rooms:** 32.
A quiet resting spot in the heart of Burgundy wine country. The
restaurant serves good food and has an excellent wine list.

ST-GERVAIS-EN-VALLIÈRE: *Moulin d'Hauterive* W www.chateauxhotels.com €€€€ AE DC MC V
Chaublanc, 71350. **[** *03 85 91 55 56*. FAX *03 85 91 89 65*. **Rooms:** 21.
A converted watermill in a secluded setting with a tennis court and
sauna. The owner serves inventive home-cooking.

ST-PÈRE-SOUS-VÉZELAY: *Mme Demeule* €€
Le Petit Cléret, Fontette, 89450. **[** *03 86 33 25 87*. **Rooms:** 2.
This charming period house is run as a *chambres d'hôte* by two
animal lovers. Choose the upstairs room under the eaves.

SAULIEU: *La Côte d'Or* W www.bernard-loiseau.com €€€€€ AE DC MC V
2 rue Argentine, 21210. **[** *03 80 90 53 53*. FAX *03 80 64 08 92*. **Rooms:** 32.
Regarded as one of the best and most innovative restaurants in France.

TONNERRE: *L'Abbaye St-Michel* @ abbayestmichel@wannado.fr €€€€€ AE DC MC V
Montée de St-Michel, 89700. **[** *03 86 55 05 99*. FAX *03 86 55 00 10*. **Rooms:** 12.
A renovated abbey which now houses a celebrated Burgundy
restaurant. The hotel blends old and modern styles.

TOURNUS: *Château de Beaufer* @ beaufer@aol.com €€€€ MC V
71700 Tournus. **[** *03 85 51 18 24*. FAX *03 85 51 25 04*. **Rooms:** 6.
Choose between a room in the ivy-clad 16th-century château or one in the
annex. Meals are now served in the château, and riding is also available.

VÉZELAY: *Cabalus* @ contact@cabalus.com €€ AE MC V
Rue St Pierre, 89450. **[** *03 86 33 20 66*. FAX *03 86 33 38 03*. **Rooms:** 4.
This 12th-century building, the abbey's former hostelry, is in the middle
of the old town. Evening meals are available.

For key to symbols see back flap

Price categories for a standard double room (not per person) for one night, including tax and service charges, but not including breakfast. € under 30€ €€ 30€–60€ €€€ 61€–90€ €€€€ 91€–150€ €€€€€ over 150€	CHILDREN'S FACILITIES Cribs and baby-sitting available. Some hotels provide children's portions and high chairs in the restaurant. PARKING FACILITIES Parking provided by the hotel in either a private lot or a private garage very close by. SWIMMING POOL Hotel pools are often quite small and are outdoors unless otherwise stated. GARDEN Hotel with garden, courtyard or terrace, often providing tables for eating outside.	CREDIT CARDS	CHILDREN'S FACILITIES	PARKING FACILITIES	SWIMMING POOL	GARDEN
VÉZELAY: *L'Espérance* @ marc.meneau@wanadoo.fr €€€€€ St-Père-sous-Vézelay, 89450. **[** 03 86 33 39 10. FAX 03 86 33 26 15. ***Rooms:*** 30. Some of the rooms overlook the garden; others are in a renovated mill. Above all, guests come for the famous restaurant. ▣ TV ❚❚		AE DC MC V		■	●	■
VONNAS: *Georges Blanc* W www.georgesblanc.com €€€€€ 01540 Vonnas. **[** 04 74 50 90 90. FAX 04 74 50 08 80. ***Rooms:*** 48. A sumptuous hotel-restaurant with luxurious rooms built and furnished in a modern country style using stone, tiles, and tapestries. ▣ ▤ TV ❚❚		AE DC MC V	●	■	●	■

THE MASSIF CENTRAL

	CREDIT CARDS	CHILDREN'S FACILITIES	PARKING FACILITIES	SWIMMING POOL	GARDEN
AUBUSSON-D'AUVERGNE: *Au Bon Coin* €€ 63120 Aubusson-d'Auvergne. **[** 04 73 53 55 78. FAX 04 73 53 56 29. ***Rooms:*** 6. The friendly owner of this rustic inn is also the mayor of the town and the tasty cuisine reflects his pride in local culinary traditions. ▣ ❚❚	MC V	●			
BEAULIEU-SUR-DORDOGNE: *Château d'Arnac* €€€ Nonards, 19120. **[** 05 55 91 54 13. FAX 05 55 91 52 62. ***Rooms:*** 4. The hospitable English owners have restored this château, keeping some original details. The grounds include a small lake. ▣ W www.chateau.mcmail.com			●	■		■
BELCASTEL: *Le Vieux Pont* W www.hotelbelcastel.com €€€ 12390 Belcastel. **[** 05 65 64 52 29. FAX 05 65 64 44 32. ***Rooms:*** 7. An annex to the Fagegaltier sisters' imaginative but affordable restaurant which overlooks the medieval village and its castle. ▣ ▤ TV ❚❚	AE DC MC V	●	■		■
CALVINET: *Hôtel Beauséjour* W www.cantal-restaurant-puech.com €€ Route de Maurs, 15340. **[** 04 71 49 91 68. FAX 04 71 49 98 63. ***Rooms:*** 12. A recently renovated hotel filled with light which has a highly distinctive cuisine. The town is famous for its schist roofs. ▣ TV ❚❚	AE DC MC V	●	■		
CHAMALIÈRES: *Hôtel Radio* W www.hotel-radio.fr €€€ 43 avenue Pierre et Marie Curie, 63400. **[** 04 73 30 87 83. FAX 04 73 36 42 44. ***Rooms:*** 26. Quiet Art Deco building perched on a hill overlooking Clermont-Ferrand and dotted with early radio sets. First-class cuisine. ▣ TV ❚❚	AE DC MC V	●	■		
COUPIAC: *L'Hostellerie du Château* W www.hostellerie-coupiac.fr €€ Ave Raymond Bel, 12550. **[** 05 65 98 12 60. FAX 05 65 98 12 61. ***Rooms:*** 9. This no frills Logis de France hotel is an excellent base for exploring the region. Its restaurant plays strongly on the local gastronomy. ▣ TV ❚❚	DC MC V	●	■		
FLORAC: *Grand Hôtel du Parc* W www.grandhotelduparc.fr €€ 47 avenue Jean-Monestier, 48400. **[** 04 66 45 03 05. FAX 04 66 45 11 81. ***Rooms:*** 60. There is an old-fashioned atmosphere to this cavernous hotel set in attractive grounds. The prices are not those of a grand hotel. ▣ TV ❚❚	AE DC MC V	●	■	●	■
LAGUIOLE: *Michel Bras* W www.michel-bras.fr €€€€€ Route de l'Aubrac, 12210. **[** 05 65 51 18 20. FAX 05 65 48 47 02. ***Rooms:*** 15. The Auvergne's most prestigious chef, whose cuisine is famous for its use of wild plants, offers superb, ultra-modern rooms overlooking the Aubrac plateau. The atmosphere is surprisingly unstuffy. ▣ TV ❚❚	AE DC MC V	●	■		
LAQUEUILLE: *Les Clarines* €€ Laqueuille-Gare, 63820. **[** 04 73 22 00 43. FAX 04 73 22 06 10. ***Rooms:*** 12. Simple rooms and dependable food are available at this converted farmhouse high up in the midst of rolling countryside. ▣ TV ❚❚	AE DC MC V	●	■		■
MILLAU: *Château de Creissels* W www.chateau-de-creissels.com €€ Route de Ste-Afrique, 12100. **[** 05 65 60 16 59. FAX 05 65 61 24 63. ***Rooms:*** 30. A converted 11th-century *bastide* with a vaulted dining room and modern bedrooms. Straightforward regional food is on the menu. There are stunning views over the Tarn valley. ▣ TV ❚❚	AE DC MC V	●	■		

MOULINS: *Hôtel de Paris* W www.chateauxhotels.com/paris €€ AE DC MC V
21 rue de Paris, 03000. 04 70 44 00 58. FAX 04 70 34 05 39. **Rooms:** 27.
A stylish stopover, near the cathedral at the gateway to the Massif
Central. The restaurant has a garden.

MUR-DE-BARREZ: *Auberge de Barrez* W www.aubergedebarrez.com €€ AE DC MC V
Avenue du Carladez, 12600. 05 65 66 00 76. FAX 05 65 66 07 98. **Rooms:** 18.
A welcoming and comfortable modern hotel in the heart of hiking
country. Christian Gaudel's excellent cooking is a bonus.

NAJAC: *Oustal del Barry* W www.oustal.del.barry.com €€ AE DC MC V
Place du Bourg, 12270. 05 65 29 74 32. FAX 05 65 29 75 32. **Rooms:** 20.
This rustic inn overlooks the square of one of France's most
picturesque villages. The cuisine is highly distinctive.

NEUVÈGLISE: *Auberge du Pont de Lanau* W www.aubergedupontdelanau.fr €€ MC V
15260 Neuvèglise. 04 71 23 57 76. FAX 04 71 23 53 84. **Rooms:** 8.
This inn in the Gorges de la Truyère has small but well-proportioned
rooms, some with a view of the mountains.

PONTAUMUR: *Hôtel de la Poste* @ hotel-poste2@wanadoo.fr €€ MC V
Avenue du Marronnier, 63380. 04 73 79 90 15. FAX 04 73 79 73 17. **Rooms:** 15.
A pleasantly decorated modern hotel in a small country town. The
owner-chef believes in promoting the finest local ingredients.

PONTEMPEYRAT: *Moulin de Mistou* W www.mistou.fr €€€ AE MC V
Craponne-sur-Arzon, 43500. 04 77 50 62 46. FAX 04 77 50 66 70. **Rooms:** 14.
A delightfully quiet and secluded hotel in a converted old mill. Fun-
loving Bernard Roux offers consistently inventive cooking.

ROANNE: *Troisgros* W www.troisgros.fr €€€€€€ AE DC MC V
Place Jean-Troisgros, 42300. 04 77 71 66 97. FAX 04 77 70 39 77. **Rooms:** 18.
What was once a humble station hotel has become a luxurious
place to stay and a world-famous culinary attraction.

ST-BONNET-LE-FROID: *Auberge des Cimes* W www.regismarcon.fr €€€€ AE MC V
43290 St-Bonnet-le-Froid. 04 71 59 93 72. FAX 04 71 59 93 40. **Rooms:** 12.
Gourmet pilgrims compete for rooms at this exceptional village
inn run by an inspired chef whose reputation is growing.

ST-FLOUR: *Le Bout du Monde* W www.saint-flour.com/leboutdumonde €€ MC V
St-Georges, 15100. 04 71 60 15 84. FAX 04 71 60 72 90. **Rooms:** 14.
You'll get an old-fashioned welcome at this hotel in a quiet river valley.
The restaurant serves local dishes at unbeatable prices.

ST-HILAIRE-LE-CHÂTEAU: *Hôtel du Thaurion* €€ AE DC MC V
23250 St-Hilaire-le-Château. 05 55 64 50 12. FAX 05 55 64 90 92. **Rooms:** 8.
This renovated staging post has been in the owner's family for 200
years. His cuisine is based on old local recipes.

ST-JEAN-DU-BRUEL: *Hôtel du Midi Papillon* €€ MC V
12230 St-Jean-du-Bruel. 05 65 62 26 04. FAX 05 65 62 12 97. **Rooms:** 18.
A quiet, friendly hotel overlooking a flower garden and a river. The
food is good and breakfast especially recommended.

ST-PRIVAT-D'ALLIER: *La Vieille Auberge* W www.francehotelreservation.com €€
Route de Saugues, 43580. 04 71 57 20 56. FAX 04 71 57 22 50. **Rooms:** 19.
A recently renovated, pleasantly rustic village inn. The rooms and
the food (hearty and straightforward) are excellent value.

SALERS: *Hostellerie de la Maronne* W www.cfi15.fr/hotelmaronne €€€€ AE DC MC V
Le Theil, St Martin Valmeroux 15140. 04 71 69 20 33. FAX 04 71 69 28 22. **Rooms:** 21.
Built as a 19th-century mansion, this stylish hotel, located 4 miles from Salers,
is a haven of peace. Its restaurant is a treat for gourmets.

VICHY: *Le Pavillon d'Enghien* @ catherine.belabed@wanadoo.fr €€€ AE DC MC V
32 rue Callou, 03200. 04 70 98 33 30. FAX 04 70 31 67 82. **Rooms:** 22.
There's something of Vichy's pre-war spa atmosphere to this small
hotel opposite the Callou Baths.

VILLEFORT: *Hôtel Balme* W www.villefort.free.fr €€ AE DC MC V
Place du Portalet, 48800. 04 66 46 80 14. FAX 04 66 46 85 26. **Rooms:** 16.
An unusual hotel which has a mini-museum devoted to the chestnut.
The cuisine is influenced by the chef's travels in the Orient.

For key to symbols see back flap

<table>
<tr><td colspan="2">

Price categories for a standard double room (not per person) for one night, including tax and service charges, but not including breakfast.
€ under 30€
€€ 30€–60€
€€€ 61€–90€
€€€€ 91€–150€
€€€€€ over 150€

CHILDREN'S FACILITIES
Cribs and baby-sitting available. Some hotels provide children's portions and high chairs in the restaurant.

PARKING FACILITIES
Parking provided by the hotel in either a private lot or a private garage very close by.

SWIMMING POOL
Hotel pools are often quite small and are outdoors unless otherwise stated.

GARDEN
Hotel with garden, courtyard or terrace, often providing tables for eating outside.

</td></tr>
</table>

	CREDIT CARDS	CHILDREN'S FACILITIES	PARKING FACILITIES	SWIMMING POOL	GARDEN
VITRAC: *Auberge de la Tomette* W www.auberge-la-tomette.com €€ 15220 Vitrac. 📞 04 71 64 70 94. FAX 04 71 64 77 11. **Rooms:** 15. The main hotel stands in a flowery park, and has sports facilities and a sauna. Its handsome diningroom has attractive panelling. 🛏 TV 🍴	AE DC MC V	●	■		
YDES: *Château de Trancis* W www.trancis.com €€€€ 15210 Ydes. 📞 04 71 40 60 40. FAX 04 71 40 62 13. **Rooms:** 7. On the fringes of the Auvergne regional park, this stylish château offers well-equipped rooms and an ornate Louis XIV salon. 🛏 TV 🍴	AE DC MC V	●	■	●	■

THE RHÔNE VALLEY AND FRENCH ALPS

	CREDIT CARDS	CHILDREN'S FACILITIES	PARKING FACILITIES	SWIMMING POOL	GARDEN
AIX-LES-BAINS: *Hôtel Le Manoir* W www.hotel-lemanoir.com €€€€ 37 rue Georges-1er, 73105. 📞 04 79 61 44 00. FAX 04 79 35 67 67. **Rooms:** 73. A charming old hotel in the Parc du Splendide-Royal, within walking distance of the thermal baths. 🛏 TV 🍴	AE DC MC V	●	■		
ALBERTVILLE: *Hôtel Million* W www.hotelmillion.com €€€€ 8 place de la Liberté, 73200. 📞 04 79 32 25 15. FAX 04 79 32 25 36. **Rooms:** 26. Established in 1770, with traditionally furnished, comfortable rooms, the hotel is known for its restaurant which serves good gastronomic cuisine. 🛏 TV 🍴	AE DC MC V	●	■		
ANNECY: *Hôtel de l'Abbaye* W www.hotelabbaye-annecy.com €€€€ 15 chemin de l'Abbaye, 74940. 📞 04 50 23 61 08. FAX 04 50 23 61 71. **Rooms:** 18. A charming hotel-restaurant occupying a former 15th-century Dominican convent surrounded by gardens. 🛏 TV 🍴	AE DC MC V		■		■
BAGNOLS: *Château de Bagnols* W www.bagnols.com €€€€€€ 69620 Bagnols. 📞 04 74 71 40 00. FAX 04 74 71 40 49. **Rooms:** 20. This exquisite 13th-century château north of Lyon is set on a hilltop surrounded by Beaujolais vineyards. 🛏 ▤ TV 🍴	AE DC MC V	●	■		■
BOURG-EN-BRESSE: *Hôtel du Prieuré* @ hotel-du-prieure@wanadoo.fr €€€ 51 boulevard de Brou, 01000. 📞 04 74 22 44 60. FAX 04 74 22 71 07. **Rooms:** 14. A charming hotel surrounded by gardens and 16th-century stone walls, only a minute's walk from the famous Eglise de Brou. The large bedrooms are furnished in French country style. 🛏 TV	AE DC MC V		■		■
CHAMBÉRY: *Hôtel des Princes* @ hoteldesprinces@wanadoo.fr €€€€ 4 rue de Boigne, 73000. 📞 04 79 33 45 36. FAX 04 79 70 31 47. **Rooms:** 45. Set in the grandest section of the Old Town, this is a pleasantly old-fashioned hotel with comfortable rooms. 🛏 TV	AE DC MC V				
CHAMONIX-MONT-BLANC: *Le Hameau Albert 1er* €€€€€€ 119 impasse du Montenvers, 74402. 📞 04 50 53 05 09. FAX 04 50 55 95 48. **Rooms:** 42. This large, welcoming chalet-style hotel has stupendous views of Mont Blanc and a good restaurant. 🛏 TV 🍴 W www.hameaualbert.fr	AE DC MC	●	■	●	■
CHONAS L'AMBALLAN: *Domaine de Clairefontaine* €€€ 38121. 📞 04 74 58 81 52. FAX 04 74 58 80 93. **Rooms:** 26 & 2 suites. Set in a magnificent park just south of Vienne, among 300-hundred year old trees, it combines impeccably designed and furnished rooms with the exquisite cuisine of Philippe Girardon. 🛏 TV 🍴 W www.domaine-de-clairefontaine.fr	AE MC V	●	■		■
COMBLOUX: *Aux Ducs de Savoie* W www.ducs-de-savoie.com €€€€ 253 route du Bouchet, 74920. 📞 04 50 58 61 43. FAX 04 50 58 67 43. **Rooms:** 50. The rooms in this modern hotel are well-equipped, some with views of Mont Blanc, and it has a restaurant *panoramique*. 🛏 TV 🍴	AE DC MC V		■	●	■
CORDON: *Le Cordonant* €€ 74700 Cordon. 📞 04 50 58 34 56. FAX 04 50 47 95 57. **Rooms:** 16. A friendly family-run hotel west of Chamonix offering comfortable rooms with views of Mont Blanc. 🛏 TV 🍴	MC V		■		■

COURCHEVEL: *La Sivolière* Ⓦ www.hotel-la-sivoliere.com   €€€€€ DC MC V
Rue des Chenus, 73120. █ 04 79 08 08 33. FAX 04 79 08 15 73. **Rooms:** *33.*
Attracting such distinguished guests as the Spanish royal family,
this tastefully decorated hotel lies at the foot of the pistes. 🛏 TV 🍴

EVIAN-LES-BAINS: *Hôtel de la Verniaz et ses Chalets*   €€€€ AE DC MC V
Avenue d' Abondance, 74500. █ 04 50 75 04 90. FAX 04 50 70 78 92. **Rooms:** *30.*
Set on a hill above Evian, this glamorous establishment consists of a central villa
and five chalets, each with its own garden. 🛏 TV 🍴 Ⓦ www.relaischateaux.com/verniaz

EVIAN-LES-BAINS: *Hôtel Royal* Ⓦ www.royalparcevian.com   €€€€€ AE DC MC V
Rive Sud du Lac-de-Genève, 74500. █ 04 50 26 85 00. FAX 04 50 75 61 00. **Rooms:** *154.*
An imposing turn-of-the-century hotel offering four restaurants, jogging trails,
and a children's club. 🛏 TV 🍴

GRENOBLE: *Park Hôtel* Ⓦ www.park-hotel-grenoble.fr   €€€€€ AE DC MC V
10 place Paul-Mistral, 38027. █ 04 76 85 81 23. FAX 04 76 46 49 88. **Rooms:** *52.*
Grenoble's leading modern hotel offers comfortably furnished rooms
with many amenities. Staff are friendly and helpful. 🛏 ▤ TV 🍴

LA CHAPELLE-EN-VERCORS: *Hôtel Bellier*   €€ AE DC MC V
26420 La Chapelle-en-Vercors. █ 04 75 48 20 03. FAX 04 75 48 25 31. **Rooms:** *12.*
Set in the Vercors massif southwest of Grenoble, this family-run chalet-style
hotel is friendly and unassuming, and offers meals in the high season 🛏 TV

LAMASTRE: *Château d'Urbillac*   €€€ AE DC MC V
Route de Vernoux, 07270. █ 04 75 06 42 11. FAX 04 75 06 52 75. **Rooms:** *12.*
A 16th-century château restored with rooms in 19th-century style and
set in a vast area of parkland in the beautiful Ardèche region. 🛏 🍴

LE POËT LAVAL: *Les Hospitaliers* Ⓦ www.hotel-les-hospitaliers.com   €€€ AE DC MC V
26160 Le Poët Laval. █ 04 75 46 22 32. FAX 04 75 46 49 99. **Rooms:** *22.*
A beautifully restored hotel in the center of a tiny medieval hilltop
village east of Montélimar. First-class service and cuisine. 🛏 TV 🍴

LYON: *Hôtel des Artistes* @ artiste@club-internet.fr   €€€ AE DC MC V
8 rue Gaspard-André, 69002. █ 04 78 42 04 88. FAX 04 78 42 93 76. **Rooms:** *45.*
Close to place Bellecour and next door to the Théâtre des Célestins, this
delightful hotel is a favorite haunt of actors and revue artists. 🛏 ▤ TV

LYON: *Hôtel Carlton* @ h2950@accor-hotels.com   €€€€€ AE DC MC V
4 rue Jussieu, 69002. █ 04 78 42 56 51. FAX 04 78 42 10 71. **Rooms:** *83.*
In the heart of the Presqu'île near the Rhône, this recently renovated
hotel still retains traces of its elegant Belle Epoque days. 🛏 ▤ TV

LYON: *Cour des Loges* Ⓦ www.courdesloges.com   €€€€€ AE DC MC V
6 rue du Boeuf, 69005. █ 04 72 77 44 44. FAX 04 72 40 93 61. **Rooms:** *62.*
A luxury hotel occupying four renovated Renaissance mansions in
the heart of Vieux Lyon. 🛏 ▤ TV 🍴

MALATAVERNE: *Domaine du Colombier* Ⓦ www.domaine-colombier.com   €€€ AE DC MC V
Route de Donzère, 26780. █ 04 75 90 86 86. FAX 04 75 90 79 40. **Rooms:** *25.*
Occupying a 14th-century abbey south of Montélimar, this welcoming
hotel has stylish rooms and a big garden with swimming pool. 🛏 TV 🍴

MANIGOD: *Chalets-hôtel de la Croix-Fry* Ⓦ www.hotelchaletcroixfry.com   €€€€ AE MC V
Route du Col de la Croix-Fry, 74230. █ 04 50 44 90 16. FAX 04 50 44 94 87. **Rooms:** *12.*
High on a mountain pass east of Annecy, this chalet-style
hotel combines Alpine rustic with comfort and facilities. 🛏 TV 🍴

MEGÈVE: *Le Fer à Cheval* Ⓦ www.feracheval-megeve.com   €€€€€ AE MC V
36 route du Crêt-d'Arbois, 74120. █ 04 50 21 30 39. FAX 04 50 93 07 60. **Rooms:** *47.*
A charming hotel with an authentic Savoy atmosphere. Guests are
served dinner around a stone fireplace in winter. 🛏 TV 🍴

MORZINE: *Hôtel Les Prodains* @ hotellesprodains@aol.com   €€ MC V
Village des Prodains, 74110. █ 04 50 79 25 26. FAX 04 50 75 76 17. **Rooms:** *15.*
Situated at the foot of the slopes in the village, facilities at Les Prodains
include an outdoor swimming pool and a sauna. 🛏 TV 🍴

PÉROUGES: *Hostellerie du Vieux Pérouges* Ⓦ www.ostellerie.com   €€€€€ AE MC V
Place du Tilleul, 01800. █ 04 74 61 00 88. FAX 04 74 34 77 90. **Rooms:** *28.*
This historic Bresson inn is a movie maker's dream, converted from
13th-century buildings and set in a medieval hilltop village. 🛏 TV 🍴

Price categories for a standard double room (not per person) for one night, including tax and service charges, but not including breakfast.
€ under 30€
€€ 30€–60€
€€€ 61€–90€
€€€€ 91€–150€
€€€€€ over 150€

CHILDREN'S FACILITIES
Cribs and baby-sitting available. Some hotels provide children's portions and high chairs in the restaurant.

PARKING FACILITIES
Parking provided by the hotel in either a private lot or a private garage very close by.

SWIMMING POOL
Hotel pools are often quite small and are outdoors unless otherwise stated.

GARDEN
Hotel with garden, courtyard or terrace, often providing tables for eating outside.

	CREDIT CARDS	CHILDREN'S FACILITIES	PARKING FACILITIES	SWIMMING POOL	GARDEN
ST-NAZAIRE-EN-ROYANS: *Hôtel Rome* €€ 26190. ☎ 04 75 48 40 69. FAX 04 75 48 31 17. **Rooms:** 13. Spectacularly sited on the edge of Lake de la Bourne, with the Vercors as a backdrop, this renovated hotel provides good basic comfort. � TV 🍴	AE DC MC V	●	▓		▓
TALLOIRES: *Hôtel Beau-Site* W www.hotel-beausite-fr.com €€€€€ 74290 Talloires. ☎ 04 50 60 71 04. FAX 04 50 60 79 22. **Rooms:** 29. This elegant hotel is especially noted for its warm and friendly atmosphere. Boating and watersports on the nearby lake. 🚗 TV 🍴	AE DC MC V	●	▓		▓
TALLOIRES: *Abbaye de Talloires* W www.abbaye-talloires.com €€€€€ Chemin des Moines, 74290. ☎ 04 50 60 77 33. FAX 04 50 60 78 81. **Rooms:** 32. An elegant hotel occupying a former 17th-century Benedictine abbey, beautifully situated on the shores of Lac d'Annecy. 🚗 TV 🍴	AE DC MC V	●	▓		▓

POITOU AND AQUITAINE

	CREDIT CARDS	CHILDREN'S FACILITIES	PARKING FACILITIES	SWIMMING POOL	GARDEN
ARCACHON: *Arc-Hôtel-sur-Mer* W www.arc-hotel-sur-mer.com €€€€ 89 boulevard de la Plage, 33120. ☎ 05 56 83 06 85. FAX 05 56 83 53 72. **Rooms:** 30. An outdoor pool, sandy beach nearby, sea views and pleasant location enhance the appeal of this comfortable resort hotel. 🚗 ▤ TV	AE DC MC V	●	▓	●	▓
BEQUEY-CADILLAC: *Hôtel du Château de la Tour* €€€€ Route départementale 10, 33410. ☎ 05 56 76 92 00. FAX 05 56 62 11 59. **Rooms:** 32. An appealing hotel with good facilities in a historic village. A good base to explore surrounding wine country. 🚗 ▤ TV 🍴 W www.francehotelreservation.com	AE MC V	●	▓	●	▓
BORDEAUX: *Grand Hôtel Français* W www.grand-hotel-francais.com €€€ 12 rue du Temple, 33000. ☎ 05 56 48 10 35. FAX 05 56 81 76 18. **Rooms:** 35. A good value hotel in the center of town with attractively decorated, comfortable and quiet rooms. 🚗 ▤ TV	AE DC MC V	●			
CHASSENEUIL-DU-POITOU: *Château Clos de la Ribaudière* €€€ 86360 Chasseneuil-du-Poitou. ☎ 05 49 52 86 66. FAX 05 49 52 86 32. **Rooms:** 41. A restored 19th-century house in a riverside park 6 miles from Poitiers, this is a haven of peace and comfort. 🚗 TV 🍴 W www.ribaudiere.com	AE DC MC V	●	▓	●	▓
CIERZAC: *Moulin de Cierzac* W www.moulindecierzac.com €€ 17520 Cierzac. ☎ 05 45 83 01 32. FAX 05 45 83 03 59. **Rooms:** 10. South of Cognac is this small hotel-restaurant in a 17th-century country house with a vast collection of Cognac, "the water of life." 🚗 TV 🍴	AE MC V	●	▓		▓
COGNAC: *Les Pigeons Blancs* @ pigeonsblancs@wanadoo.fr €€€ 110 rue Jules Brisson, 16100. ☎ 05 45 82 16 36. FAX 05 45 82 29 29. **Rooms:** 7. A small, excellent value hotel-restaurant which has been in the same family since the 18th-century. 🚗 🍴	AE V	●	▓		▓
CONFOLENS: *Hôtel Emeraude* €€ 20 rue Emile Roux, 16500. ☎ 05 45 84 12 77. FAX 05 45 84 15 55. **Rooms:** 19. A basic but good value hotel with a perfect setting beside the river Vienne, with a lovely flowered terrace used for meals. Traditional decor and food. Ask for a room with a view. 🚗 🍴	MC V	●			
COULON: *Hôtel au Marais* W www.hotel-aumarais.com €€ 46-48 quai Louis Tardy, 79510. ☎ 05 49 35 90 43. FAX 05 49 35 81 98. **Rooms:** 18. Situated in the mysterious fens of the Marais Poitevin is this lovely little hotel. Boat hire is available in the town. 🚗 TV	MC V				▓
EUGÉNIE-LES-BAINS: *Les Prés d'Eugénie* @ guerard@relaischateaux.fr €€€€€ 40320 Eugénie-les-Bains. ☎ 05 58 05 06 07. FAX 05 58 51 10 10. **Rooms:** 40. The illustrious chef Michel Guérard draws worshipers to his delightful hotel, cuisine, and thermal spa. Less costly accommodation is available in the same grounds. Truly a treat to stay here. 🚗 TV 🍴	AE DC MC V	●	▓	●	▓

GRADIGNAN: *Le Chalet Lyrique* w www.chalet-lyrique.fr €€€ — AE MC V
169 cours du Général-de-Gaulle, 33170. ℂ 05 56 89 11 59. FAX 05 56 89 53 37. *Rooms: 44.*
Not too far away from the Bordeaux-Mérignac airport, this is a
pleasant stop-over with a magnificent patio.

GRENADE-SUR-L'ADOUR: *Pain Adour et Fantasie* €€€ — AE DC MC V
14–16 place des Tilleuls, 40270. ℂ 05 58 45 18 80. FAX 05 58 45 16 57. *Rooms: 11.*
Timber and stone adorn this graceful 18th-century hotel set beside the river
Adour, with an acclaimed restaurant. @ pain.adour.fantasie@wanadoo.fr

HIERSAC: *Hostellerie du Maine Brun* @ hostellerie-du-maine-brun@wanadoo.fr €€€€ — AE DC MC V
La Vigerie, 16290. ℂ 05 45 90 83 00. FAX 05 45 96 91 14. *Rooms: 20.*
A mill on the pretty banks of the Nouère has become a supremely
relaxing hotel with much to enjoy – cuisine, wines and Cognac.

HOSSEGOR: *Barbary Lane* w www.barbary-lane.com €€ — MC V
156 ave Côte d'Argent, 40150. ℂ 05 58 43 52 19. FAX 05 58 43 95 19. *Rooms: 18.*
Located in a quiet pine forest just 500 meters from the sea, this
charming hotel is a haven of peace.

LA ROCHELLE: *Les Brises* €€€ — AE MC V
Ch. de la Digue de Richelieu, 17000. ℂ 05 46 43 89 37. FAX 05 46 43 27 97. *Rooms: 50.*
A comfortable and well-liked hotel to the west of this handsome and
bustling city. Wonderful views out to sea and the offshore islands.

MAGESCQ: *Relais de la Poste* w www.coussau.fr €€€€ — AE DC MC V
24 ave de Maremne, 40140. ℂ 05 58 47 70 25. FAX 05 58 47 76 17. *Rooms: 13.*
A small hotel with gardens and pools perfectly combining comfort,
celebrated cuisine, fine wines, and family tradition.

MARGAUX: *Relais de Margaux* w www.relais-margaux.fr €€€€€ — AE DC MC V
Chemin de l'Ile Vincent, 33460. ℂ 05 57 88 38 30. FAX 05 57 88 31 73. *Rooms: 64.*
The high price at this luxurious hotel is money well spent. Peaceful
setting, handsome grounds, pool, tennis, and exquisite food.

MIMIZAN: *Au Bon Coin du Lac* w www.jp-caule.com €€€ — AE DC MC V
34 avenue du Lac, 40200 . ℂ 05 58 09 01 55. FAX 05 58 09 40 84. *Rooms: 8.*
The cuisine at this small hotel is a prime draw, not to mention its very
agreeable setting among pine trees and beside a lake.

MONTBRON: *Hostellerie Château Sainte Catherine* €€€ — AE DC MC V
Rte de Marthon, 16380. ℂ 05 45 23 60 03. FAX 05 45 70 72 00. *Rooms: 10.*
Napoleon's wife, Josephine de Beauharnais, lived in this elegant
18th-century house and park. It offers excellent local cuisine.

NIEUIL: *Château de Nieuil* w www.relaischateaux.com/nieuil €€€€ — AE DC MC V
16270 Nieuil. ℂ 05 45 71 36 38. FAX 05 45 71 46 45. *Rooms: 14.*
King François I hunted in the extensive park embracing this spectacular
Renaissance château, transformed in the 1930s into a hotel.

RETJONS: *L'Hostellerie Landaise* €€ — MC V
40120 Retjons. ℂ FAX 05 58 93 36 33. *Rooms: 8.*
Architecturally a true *auberge landaise*, set in its own park with duck-
dimpled lake. A delightful overnight stop.

ROYAN: *Family Golf Hôtel* €€€ — MC V
28 boulevard Garnier, 17200. ℂ 05 46 05 14 66. FAX 05 46 06 52 56. *Rooms: 33.*
An unpretentious hotel on the seafront in a large and lively resort just
north of the Gironde.

SABRES: *Auberge des Pins* w www.auberge-des-pins.com €€ — AE MC V
Route de la Piscine, 40630. ℂ 05 58 08 30 00. FAX 05 58 07 56 74. *Rooms: 25.*
Deep in the forests of the Landes Regional Park, this comfortable
auberge has been called the very model of a family hotel.

ST-EMILION: *Château Meylet* €€
"La Gomerie", 33330. ℂ 05 57 24 68 85. FAX 05 57 24 77 35. *Rooms: 4.*
A renovated, homey farmhouse surrounded by its own vineyards –
perfect for exploring the area. Price includes a lovely breakfast.

ST-EMILION: *Hostellerie Plaisance* w www.hostellerie.plaisance.com €€€€ — AE DC MC V
5 place du Clocher, 33330. ℂ 05 57 55 07 55. FAX 05 57 74 41 11. *Rooms: 16.*
An excellent small hotel in a striking building in the upper part of this
town, famous for its wine.

	Credit Cards	Children's Facilities	Parking Facilities	Swimming Pool	Garden
Price categories for a standard double room (not per person) for one night, including tax and service charges, but not including breakfast. € under 30€ €€ 30€–60€ €€€ 61€–90€ €€€€ 91€–150€ €€€€€ over 150€ **Children's Facilities** Cribs and baby-sitting available. Some hotels provide children's portions and high chairs in the restaurant. **Parking Facilities** Parking provided by the hotel in either a private lot or a private garage very close by. **Swimming Pool** Hotel pools are often quite small and are outdoors unless otherwise stated. **Garden** Hotel with garden, courtyard or terrace, often providing tables for eating outside.					
ST-EMILION: *Château Grand Barrail* W www.grand-barrail.com €€€€€ Route de Libourne, 33330. (05 57 55 37 00. FAX 05 57 55 37 49. **Rooms:** 28. Set in beautiful grounds, this luxurious château-hotel pampers to one's every need, and has a good restaurant. 🛗 ▤ TV ‖	AE DC MC V	●	▪	●	▪
VELLUIRE: *Auberge de la Rivière* €€€ Rue de la Fouarne, 85770. (02 51 52 32 15. FAX 02 51 52 37 42. **Rooms:** 11. A secluded, ivy-covered inn on the banks of the river Vendée. Rooms are comfortable with river views. Worth staying for the superb food. 🛗 TV ‖	MC V	●			▪

PÉRIGORD, QUERCY AND GASCONY

	Credit Cards	Children's Facilities	Parking Facilities	Swimming Pool	Garden
ALBI: *Hostellerie du Vigan* W www.hostellerieduvigan.com €€ 16 place du Vigan, 81000. (05 63 43 31 31. FAX 05 63 47 05 42. **Rooms:** 40. A very good value hotel in the center of town which is unpretentious, comfortable and inexpensive. 🛗 ▤ TV ‖	AE DC MC V	●	▪		
ALBI: *Hôtel St-Clair* W www.andrieu.michele.free.fr €€ 8 rue St-Clair, 81000. (05 63 54 25 66. FAX 05 63 47 27 58. **Rooms:** 11. An old-fashioned hotel in a converted 18th-century building, exotically furnished by the owner with finds from her travels though Indonesia and Turkey. 🛗 TV	MC V		▪		
BEYNAC: *Hôtel Bonnet* @ hbonnet@free.fr €€ 24220 Beynac. (05 53 29 50 01. FAX 05 53 29 83 74. **Rooms:** 20. This small village hotel is named after the family who have owned it for years. Simple, airy, and traditional in style. 🛗 ‖	AE DC MC V		▪		▪
BRANTÔME: *Le Chatenet* @ chatenet.hotel@wanadoo.fr €€€€ 24310 Brantôme. (05 53 05 81 08. FAX 05 53 05 85 52. **Rooms:** 9. Off the busy riverside road lies this beautifully restored 17th-century manor house. Facilities include tennis courts and a clubhouse. 🛗 TV		●	▪	●	▪
BRANTÔME: *Le Moulin de l'Abbaye* W www.relaischateaux.com €€€€€ 1 route de Bourdeilles, 24310. (05 53 05 80 22. FAX 05 53 05 75 27. **Rooms:** 19. A handsome, old creeper-covered mill standing next to the river Dronne. The dining room extends to a terrace over the river. 🛗 TV	AE DC MC V	●	▪		▪
CAHORS: *Terminus* @ terminus.balandre@wanadoo.fr €€€ 5 avenue Charles-de-Freycinet, 46000. (05 65 53 32 00. FAX 05 65 53 32 26. **Rooms:** 22 A good find in the heart of truffle country, only two minutes from the station. Elegant 1920s-style decor and stained-glass windows. 🛗 ▤ TV ‖	AE DC MC V		▪		
CARSAC-AILLAC: *Le Relais du Touron* W www.relaisdutouron.free.fr €€ 24200 Carsac-Aillac. (05 53 28 16 70. FAX 05 53 28 52 51. **Rooms:** 12. Set in wooded countryside just east of Sarlat is this serene, 19th-century small mansion. 🛗 TV ‖	MC V		▪	●	▪
CASTILLONNÈS: *Hôtel Restaurant Les Remparts* W www.logisderance47.com €€ 26–28 rue de la Paix, 47330. (05 53 49 55 85. FAX 05 53 49 55 89. **Rooms:** 9. This attractive hotel in the middle of Castillonnès, a medieval bastide, has a lovely garden and courtyard. The restaurant is excellent. 🛗 TV ‖	AE DC MC V	●	▪		▪
CHAMPAGNAC-DE-BELAIR: *Hôtel Moulin du Roc* W www.moulinduroc.com €€€€ 24530 Champagnac-de-Belair. (05 53 02 86 00. FAX 05 53 54 21 31. **Rooms:** 13. In a beautiful setting by a quiet stream just outside Brantôme is this converted walnut mill. Indoor pool and wonderful food. 🛗 ▤ TV ‖	AE DC MC V	●	▪	●	▪
COLY: *Manoir d'Hautegente* W www.manoir-hautegente.com €€€€ 24120 Coly. (05 53 51 68 03. FAX 05 53 50 38 52. **Rooms:** 15. Just north of Sarlat is this picturesque mansion, once the mill and forge of an abbey. Family-run, friendly hotel with log fires, private fishing, swimming pool, and library. 🛗 TV ‖	AE DC MC V	●	▪	●	▪

CONDOM: *Hôtel Les Trois Lys* W www.les-trois-lys.com €€€€ MC V
38 rue Gambetta, 32100. 05 62 28 33 33. FAX 05 62 28 41 85. **Rooms:** 10.
In the heart of Armagnac country is this well-run 17th-century hotel.
Breakfast is served on the patio.

DOMME: *Hôtel de l'Esplanade* @ esplanade.domme@wanadoo.fr €€€ AE DC MC V
24250 Domme. 05 53 28 31 41. FAX 05 53 28 49 92. **Rooms:** 25.
Perched on the cliff-top is this hotel with a panoramic dining terrace.
Rooms are tastefully decorated, some with fantastic views.

DURAS: *Hostellerie des Ducs* W www.hostellerieducs-duras.com €€ AE DC MC V
47120 Duras. 05 53 83 74 58. FAX 05 53 83 75 03. **Rooms:** 15.
Situated between the Dordogne and Garonne rivers is this simple,
family-run hostelry overlooking a 14th-century fortress.

FLORIMONT-GAUMIERS: *La Daille* €€€€
24250 Dordogne. 05 53 28 40 71. **Rooms:** 3.
A short drive from Gaumiers, this stone-built farmhouse
has marvelous views (minimum stay: 3 nights in season).

LACAVE: *Le Pont de l'Ouysse* W www.lepontdelouysse.fr €€€€ AE DC MC V
46200 Lacave. 05 65 37 87 04. FAX 05 65 32 77 41. **Rooms:** 14.
A smart restaurant-with-rooms not far from Rocamadour. Inventive
variations on local dishes are on offer.

LA COQUILLE: *Hôtel des Voyageurs* W www.hotels-restau-dordogne.org €€ MC V
Rue de la République, 24450. 05 53 52 80 13. FAX 05 53 60 18 29. **Rooms:** 10.
This small village hotel is friendly and comfortable.
Enjoy delicious regional food.

LES EYZIES-DE-TAYAC: *Le Moulin de la Beune* @ souliebeune@perigord.com €€ MC V
24620 Les Eyzies-de-Tayac. 05 53 06 94 33. FAX 05 53 62 98 06. **Rooms:** 20
Huge, comfortable rooms in this converted mill. Reasonably priced
and efficiently run.

LES EYZIES-DE-TAYAC: *Le Centenaire* W www.hotelducentenaire.fr €€€€ AE DC MC V
24620 Les Eyzies-de-Tayac. 05 53 06 68 68. FAX 05 53 06 92 41. **Rooms:** 20.
A luxurious, modern hotel just outside the town. Spacious bedrooms
with balconies overlooking the lawn and swimming pool.

MARQUAY: *Hôtel des Bories* W www.membreslycos.fr €€ MC V
24620 Marquay. 05 53 29 67 02. FAX 05 53 29 64 15. **Rooms:** 30.
An unassuming hotel offering outstanding value. Family-run with basic
rooms and beamed ceilings. Lake with watersports nearby.

MERCUÈS: *Château de Mercuès* @ mercues@relaischateaux.fr €€€€€ AE DC MC V
46090 Mercuès. 05 65 20 00 01. FAX 05 65 20 05 72. **Rooms:** 30.
Situated beside the Lot river is this 12th-century turreted château, luxuriously
modernized, with tennis court and helicopter pad! Generous breakfasts.

MEYRONNE: *La Terrasse* W www.hotel-la-terrasse.com €€€ AE DC MC V
46200 Meyronne. 05 65 32 21 60. FAX 05 65 32 26 93. **Rooms:** 17.
This converted monastery has some of its bedrooms in the adjacent
14th-century château. Meals are eaten in the large dining room.

MONBAHUS: *Tresfonds Ouest* @ bridricherrington@wannado.fr €€
47290 Cancon. 05 53 01 06 33. **Rooms:** 2.
This lovely stone farmhouse, full of antiques, provides a comfortable and
relaxed base for exploring the bastide towns.

NONTRON: *Le Grand Hôtel Pelisson* @ grand-hotel-pelisson@wanadoo.fr €€ MC V
3 place A-Agard, 24300. 05 53 56 11 22. FAX 05 53 56 59 94. **Rooms:** 23.
Very reasonably priced and well-run hotel in the center of this market
town. Swimming pool, pretty garden, and good, honest food.

PÉRIGUEUX: *Hôtel du Midi et Terminus* W www.hotel-du-midi.fr €€ MC V
18 rue Denis Papin, 24000. 05 53 53 41 06. FAX 05 53 08 19 32. **Rooms:** 23.
Just in front of the train station in this delightful town – the "capital"
of the Dordogne – the hotel has simple but comfortable rooms.

RIBÉRAC: *Pauliac* @ pauliac@infonie.fr €€ MC V
Celles, 24600. 05 53 91 97 45. FAX 05 53 90 43 46. **Rooms:** 5.
A basic, well-restored farmhouse set in a tiny hamlet. There is a
terraced garden and tables outside. Good, wholesome food.

Price categories for a standard double room (not per person) for one night, including tax and service charges, but not including breakfast.

€ under 30€
€€ 30€–60€
€€€ 61€–90€
€€€€ 91€–150€
€€€€€ over 150€

CHILDREN'S FACILITIES
Cribs and baby-sitting available. Some hotels provide children's portions and high chairs in the restaurant.

PARKING FACILITIES
Parking provided by the hotel in either a private lot or a private garage very close by.

SWIMMING POOL
Hotel pools are often quite small and are outdoors unless otherwise stated.

GARDEN
Hotel with garden, courtyard or terrace, often providing tables for eating outside.

	CREDIT CARDS	CHILDREN'S FACILITIES	PARKING FACILITIES	SWIMMING POOL	GARDEN
ROCAMADOUR: *Domaine de la Rhue* W www.domainedelarhue.com €€€ 46500 Rocamadour. ☎ 05 65 33 71 50. FAX 05 65 33 72 48. **Rooms:** 14. Only a few minutes' drive from Rocamadour is this peaceful hotel – a 19th-century stone building, imaginatively converted. Spacious rooms. 🛏 🗏	DC MC V	●	▦	●	▦
ST-CIRC-LAPOPIE: *Hôtel de la Pélissaria* €€€ 46330 St-Cirq-Lapopie. ☎ 05 65 31 25 14. FAX 05 65 30 25 52. **Rooms:** 10. A tiny hotel in a cliff-top village above the Lot river. The rooms have tiled floors, white walls, exposed beams and pine doors. 🛏 TV	MC V		▦		
SARLAT-LA-CANÉDA: *Hostellerie de Meysset* €€ 62 rte d'Argentouleau, 24200. ☎ 05 53 59 08 29. FAX 05 53 28 47 61. **Rooms:** 26. Built in local style and set in its own park is this pleasant rural hotel. French windows open on to the lawn. Excellent food. 🛏 TV 🍴	AE DC MC V	●	▦		
TAMNIÈS: *Hôtel Laborderie* @ hotel.laborderie@worldonline.fr €€ 24620 Tamniès. ☎ 05 53 29 68 59. FAX 05 53 29 65 31. **Rooms:** 44. Between Sarlat and Les Eyzies lies this family-run, modern hotel. Log fires in winter and swimming and outdoor meals in summer. 🛏 TV 🍴	MC V				
TOULOUSE: *Hôtel Albert 1er* W www.hotel-albert1.com €€ 8 rue Rivals, 31000. ☎ 05 61 21 17 91. FAX 05 61 21 09 64. **Rooms:** 50. A good value hotel, centrally situated with cheerful rooms and modern bathrooms. Small lounge and breakfast room. 🛏 🗏 TV	AE DC MC V	●			
TOULOUSE: *Hôtel Jean-Mermoz* W www.hotel-mermoz.com €€€ 50 rue Matabiau, 31000. ☎ 05 61 63 04 04. FAX 05 61 63 15 64. **Rooms:** 52. Modern hotel in the center of town which is comfortable, friendly and surprisingly quiet. Pleasant garden. 🛏 🗏 TV	AE DC MC V		▦		▦
VIEUX MAREUIL: *Auberge de l'Etang Blue* W www.perigord-hotel.com €€€ 24340. ☎ 05 53 60 92 63. FAX 05 53 56 33 20. **Rooms:** 11. Set in 10 hectares of peaceful woodland with 5 fishing and swimming lakes, this hotel is simple yet full of character and charm, with friendly service. 🛏 TV 🍴	MC V	●	▦		▦

THE PYRENEES

	CREDIT CARDS	CHILDREN'S FACILITIES	PARKING FACILITIES	SWIMMING POOL	GARDEN
AÏNHOA: *Hôtel-Restaurant Ithurria* W www.ithurria.com €€€€ 64250 Aïnhoa. ☎ 05 59 29 92 11. FAX 05 59 29 81 28. **Rooms:** 26. With its cozy rooms, beamed dining room and gourmet cooking, this old coaching inn in one of the prettiest Basque villages is a satisfying place to stay. 🛏 🗏 TV 🍴	AE MC V		▦		
ANGLET: *Château de Brindos* @ brindos@thalassoblanco.com €€€€€ Allée du Château, 64600. ☎ 05 59 23 17 68. FAX 05 59 23 48 47. **Rooms:** 30. Life is calm and gracious here beside the peaceful lake. The beach is only a short drive away and there is also a golf course nearby. 🛏 🗏 TV 🍴	AE MC DC V	●	▦	●	▦
ARGELÈS-GAZOST: *Hôtel le Miramont* W www.hotelmizamont.com €€€€ 44 avenue des Pyrénées, 65400. ☎ 05 62 97 01 26. FAX 05 62 97 56 67. **Rooms:** 27. A stylish, comfortable hotel with a garden in a small spa town. The attractive restaurant serves delicious food. 🛏 TV 🍴	AE DC MC V	●	▦		▦
ARREAU: *Hôtel d'Angleterre* €€ Route de Luchon, 65240. ☎ 05 62 98 63 30. FAX 05 62 98 69 66. **Rooms:** 24. Four rivers flow through little Arreau, past slate-roofed houses. This 17th-century inn serving savoury mountain food is good value. It makes a suitable base for exploring the stunning countryside. 🛏 TV 🍴	MC V	●	▦		▦
BARBAZAN: *Hostellerie de L'Aristou* €€ Route de Sauveterre, 31510. ☎ 05 61 88 30 67. FAX 05 61 95 55 66. **Rooms:** 7. This pleasant country house has a fine restaurant and is ideal for exploring the nearby Roman ruins. 🛏 TV 🍴	AE MC V	●	▦		▦

BIARRITZ: *Château du Clair de Lune* ⓦ www.chateauduclairdelune.com €€€€ — DC MC V
48 avenue Alan-Seeger, 64200. ☎ 05 59 41 53 20. FAX 05 59 41 53 29. **Rooms:** 17.
This Belle-Époque mansion converted into a relaxing hotel is
set back from the crowded coast amid scented gardens.

BIARRITZ: *Hôtel Windsor* @ hotelwindsor-biarritz@wanadoo.fr €€€ — AE DC MC V
Grande Plage, 64200. ☎ 05 59 24 08 52. FAX 05 59 24 98 90. **Rooms:** 48.
Standing above the famous Grande Plage, and with recently decorated
family rooms, this is a great spot for a lively vacation.

BIARRITZ: *Hôtel du Palais* ⓦ www.hotel-du-palais.com €€€€€ — AE DC MC V
1 avenue de l'Impératrice, 64200. ☎ 05 59 41 64 00. FAX 05 59 41 67 99. **Rooms:** 156.
A magnificent hotel of enduring grandeur and elegance. The service
and food are impeccable; the mood refreshingly unstuffy.

ESPELETTE: *Hôtel Euzkadi* ⓦ www.hotel-restaurant-euzkadi.com €€ — MC V
64250 Espelette. ☎ 05 59 93 91 88. FAX 05 59 93 90 19. **Rooms:** 32.
The generous, savory Basque cooking has made this characterful
hotel enormously popular.

FOIX: *Hôtel Lons* @ hotel-lons-foix@wanadoo.fr €€ — AE DC MC V
6 place G-Dutilh, 09000. ☎ 05 61 65 52 44. FAX 05 61 02 68 18. **Rooms:** 39.
The big, period bedrooms and glass-enclosed dining room of this half-
timbered house in the Old Town are right above the river.

GAVARNIE: *Hôtel Vignemale* ⓦ www.hotel-vignemale.com €€€€ — AE DC MC V
65120 Gavarnie. ☎ 05 62 92 40 00. FAX 05 62 92 40 08. **Rooms:** 25.
This recently modernized hotel makes a comfortable base to walk the
mountain trails or merely to enjoy the Cirque de Gavarnie.

NUZENAC: *L'Oustal* €€
Unac, 09250. ☎ 05 61 64 48 44. **Rooms:** 2.
High in the wild Ariège, not far from Ax-les-Thermes, is this appealing rural
hostelry with marvelous views and excellent cuisine. *Chambre d'hôte* only

OLORON-STE-MARIE: *L'Alysson* ⓦ www.alysson-hotel.fr €€€€ — AE DC MC V
Boulevard des Pyrénées, 64400. ☎ 05 59 39 70 70. FAX 05 59 39 24 47. **Rooms:** 32.
The most comfortable hotel in a picturesque riverside town, with
good food served in a modern dining room.

PAU: *Grand Hôtel du Commerce* @ hotel.commerce.pau@wanadoo.fr €€ — AE DC MC V
9 rue Maréchal-Joffre, 64000. ☎ 05 59 27 24 40. FAX 05 59 83 81 74. **Rooms:** 51.
Conveniently located near the royal château, this popular, traditional
hotel has comfortable rooms and a reasonable restaurant.

ST-ETIENNE-DE-BAÏGORRY: *Hôtel Arcé* ⓦ www.hotel-arce.com €€€€ — DC MC V
64430 St-Etienne-de-Baïgorry. ☎ 05 59 37 40 14. FAX 05 59 37 40 27. **Rooms:** 22.
Deep in the Basque Country is this welcoming family hotel in a
wonderful setting beside the fast-flowing Nive des Aldudes.

ST-GIRONS: *Hôtel Eychenne* ⓦ www.ariege.com/hotel-eychenne €€€ — AE DC MC V
8 avenue Paul-Laffont, 09200. ☎ 05 61 04 04 50. FAX 05 61 96 07 20. **Rooms:** 41.
The antique furnishings, garden, swimming pool and excellent
restaurant combine to give this hotel true distinction.

ST-JEAN-DE-LUZ: *La Devinière* €€€€ — MC V
5 rue Loquin, 64500. ☎ 05 59 26 05 51. FAX 05 59 51 26 38. **Rooms:** 11.
Quiet and tiny, with snug rooms elegantly furnished and an intimate
garden, this gem of a hotel is in the heart of the old city.

ST-JEAN-DE-LUZ: *Le Parc Victoria* ⓦ www.relaischateaux.com €€€€€ — AE MC V
5 rue Cépé, 64500. ☎ 05 59 26 78 78. FAX 05 59 26 78 08. **Rooms:** 18.
A glorious garden and swimming pool set off this Victorian mansion,
furnished in the style of the 1930s, near the beach.

ST-JEAN-PIED-DE-PORT: *Hôtel les Pyrénées* @ hotel.pyrenees@wanadoo.fr €€€€ — AE DC MC V
19 pl du Gén-de-Gaulle, 64220. ☎ 05 59 37 01 01. FAX 05 59 37 18 97. **Rooms:** 21.
Relaxing, if pricy, this hotel with its famous Basque-based cuisine
provides a refuge from the summer crowds.

ST-JEAN-PIED-DE-PORT: *Hôtel Larramendy Andreinia* €€ — MC V
Esterençuby, 64220. ☎ 05 59 37 09 70. FAX 05 59 37 36 05. **Rooms:** 28.
Set in a tiny village on the rippling river Nive, this Basque hotel
is an ideal base for ramblers. ⓦ www.hotel-restaurant-larramendy.fr

<table>
<tr><td>

Price categories for a standard double room (not per person) for one night, including tax and service charges, but not including breakfast.
€ under 30€
€€ 30€–60€
€€€ 61€–90€
€€€€ 91€–150€
€€€€€ over 150€

</td><td>

CHILDREN'S FACILITIES
Cribs and baby-sitting available. Some hotels provide children's portions and high chairs in the restaurant.
PARKING FACILITIES
Parking provided by the hotel in either a private lot or a private garage very close by.
SWIMMING POOL
Hotel pools are often quite small and are outdoors unless otherwise stated.
GARDEN
Hotel with garden, courtyard or terrace, often providing tables for eating outside.

</td></tr>
</table>

	CREDIT CARDS	CHILDREN'S FACILITIES	PARKING FACILITIES	SWIMMING POOL	GARDEN
SARE: *Hôtel Arraya* W www.arraya.com €€€ Place du village, 64310. (05 59 54 20 46. FAX 05 59 54 27 04. **Rooms:** 20. This centrally located, modern hotel guarantees peace and comfort. Every bedroom has an en-suite bathroom. 🛏 TV ❚❚	AE MC V	●			▪
TARBES: *Hôtel de l'Avenue* € 80 av Bertrand-Barère, 65000. (FAX 05 62 93 06 36. **Rooms:** 26. A small family-run hotel only a two-minute walk from the station. The quietest rooms overlook an interior courtyard. 🛏 TV	MC V	●			

LANGUEDOC-ROUSSILLON

	CREDIT CARDS	CHILDREN'S FACILITIES	PARKING FACILITIES	SWIMMING POOL	GARDEN
AIGUES-MORTES: *Hôtel des Croisades* €€ 2 rue du Port, 30220. (04 66 53 67 85. FAX 04 66 53 72 95. **Rooms:** 14. With friendly staff and a delightful garden, this hotel is excellent value for money. 🛏 ▤ TV	MC V				▪
AIGUES-MORTES: *Hôtel Saint-Louis* @ hotel.saint-louis@wanadoo.fr €€€€ 10 rue de l'Amiral-Courbet, 30220. (04 66 53 72 68. FAX 04 66 53 75 92. **Rooms:** 22. This charming hotel is tucked within the stout stone walls of a lively city built by the saint-king Louis IX. The Camargue is nearby. 🛏 TV ❚❚	AE MC V	●			▪
BARJAC: *Hôtel le Mas du Terme* €€€€ Route de Bagnols-sur-Cèze, 30430. (04 66 24 56 31. FAX 04 66 24 58 54. **Rooms:** 23. Situated in beautiful country near the Ardèche gorges is this distinctive old hotel. The restaurant serves home-produced wine. 🛏 TV ❚❚	MC V	●	▪	●	▪
BÉZIERS: *Le Champ-de-Mars* €€ 17 rue de Metz, 34500. (04 67 28 35 53. FAX 04 67 28 61 42. **Rooms:** 10. Newly renovated, the rooms here overlook the garden and offer excellent value for money. 🛏 TV	AE DC MC V		▪		▪
BOUZIGUES: *La Côte Bleue* W www.epicuria.fr/cotebleue €€€ Avenue Louis-Tudesq, 34140. (04 67 78 31 42. FAX 04 67 78 35 49. **Rooms:** 32. With its comfortable rooms, swimming pool and famous terraced restaurant on the seashore, this hotel is justifiably popular. 🛏 TV ❚❚	AE MC V	●	▪	●	▪
CARCASSONNE: *Hôtel Le Donjon des Remparts* €€€ 2 rue du Comte-Roger, 11000. (04 68 11 23 00. FAX 04 68 25 06 60. **Rooms:** 62. In the heart of the medieval city, this superb 14th-century building has every modern comfort. 🛏 ▤ TV ❚❚ W www.bestwestern-donjon.com	AE DC MC V	●	▪		▪
CARCASSONNE: *Hôtel Mercure Porte de la Cité* @ h1622@accor.hotels.com €€€€ 18 rue C Saint-Saens, 11000. (04 68 11 92 82. FAX 04 68 71 11 45. **Rooms:** 61. At the eastern entry to the medieval city, this is a comfortable place for a stopover away from the summer crowds. 🛏 ▤ TV ❚❚	AE DC MC V	●	▪	●	▪
CASTILLON-DU-GARD: *Le Vieux Castillon* €€€€€ Rue Turion Sabatier, 30210. (04 66 37 61 61. FAX 04 66 37 28 17. **Rooms:** 35. Restored buildings in a medieval village have been made into a stylish and discreet hotel. Even the pool is artfully set beside a ruined wall. 🛏 ▤ TV ❚❚ @ vieux.castillon@wanadoo.fr	AE DC MC V	●	▪	●	▪
CÉRET: *La Terrasse au Soleil* W www.la-terrasse-au-soleil.fr €€€€€ Route de Fontfrède, 66400. (04 68 87 01 94. FAX 04 68 87 39 24. **Rooms:** 21. A peaceful and comfortable hotel set between the mountains and the sea giving splendid views. There is a good restaurant. 🛏 ▤ TV ❚❚	AE DC MC V	●	▪	●	▪
COLLIOURE: *Relais des Trois Mas* €€€€€ Route de Port-Vendres, 66190. (04 68 82 05 07. FAX 04 68 82 38 08. **Rooms:** 23. The hotel consists of several tastefully restored buildings amid pine-shaded gardens. Every room has a sea or harbor view and some have terraces. The restaurant, La Balette, is famous. 🛏 ▤ TV ❚❚	MC V		▪	●	▪

FUILLA: *Rozinante* @ mrozinante@aol.com €€
7 Cami Ribere Enclose, 66820. (04 68 96 34 50. FAX 04 68 96 34 50. **Rooms:** 3.
Nestling under Mount Canigou, this delightful guesthouse
boasts its own pool and luxurious lawns. No animals.

MINERVE: *Relais Chantovent* €€
34210 Minerve. (04 68 91 14 18. FAX 04 68 91 81 99. **Rooms:** 10.
The hotel buildings are spread out in the narrow streets. The rooms
in the annex, a converted village house, have great character. 🛏 🍽
MC V

MONTPELLIER: *Hôtel Guilhem* @ hotel-le-guilhem@mnet.fr €€€
18 rue JJ-Rousseau, 34000. (04 67 52 90 90. FAX 04 67 60 67 67. **Rooms:** 33.
An appealing bed-and-breakfast hotel, run by friendly owners, which
provides peace and seclusion in a busy city. 🛏 TV
AE DC MC V

NARBONNE: *Grand Hôtel du Languedoc* w www.hoteldulanguedoc.com €€€
22 boulevard Gambetta, 11100. (04 68 65 14 74. FAX 04 68 65 81 48. **Rooms:** 40.
A cheerful city hotel only a short walk from the cathedral, shops
and museums. Its Belle Epoque-style restaurant is popular. 🛏 TV 🍽
AE DC MC V

NÎMES: *Kyriad Hôtel* @ kyriad.nimcentre@le-plazza.fr €€€
10 rue Roussy, 30000. (04 66 76 16 20. FAX 04 66 67 65 99. **Rooms:** 28.
A peaceful location and well-equipped bathrooms and bedrooms
make this modernized hotel good value. 🛏 ▤ TV
AE DC MC V

NÎMES: *Imperator Concorde* w www.hotel-imperator.com €€€€
Quai de la Fontaine, 30900. (04 66 21 90 30. FAX 04 66 67 70 25. **Rooms:** 62.
Nîmes' grandest hotel stands close to 17th-century gardens and
fountains, and some remarkable Roman architecture. 🛏 ▤ TV 🍽
AE DC MC V

PERPIGNAN: *Hôtel de la Loge* w www.hoteldelaloge.fr €€
1 rue des Fabriques-Nabot, 66000. (04 68 34 41 02. FAX 04 68 34 25 13. **Rooms:** 22.
In the heart of the city, close to the sights, is this calm, 16th-century
Catalan mansion with a mosaic forecourt and fountain. 🛏 ▤ TV
AE DC MC V

PEYRIAC-MINERVOIS: *Château de Violet* w www.chateau-de-violet.com €€€€
Route de Pépieux, 11160. (04 68 78 10 42. FAX 04 68 78 30 01. **Rooms:** 17.
Timbered ceilings and huge fireplaces add atmosphere to this château
which presides over its own domain of parks and vineyards. 🛏 TV 🍽
AE DC MC V

PONT DE MONTVERT: *Hôtel des Cévennes* €€
48220 Pont de Montvert. (04 66 45 80 01. **Rooms:** 10.
This traditional granite auberge (closed in winter), overlooks the rushing Tarn.
Rooms 1–3 have a river view; the dining room has a village panorama. 🛏 🍽

PRADES: *Grand Hôtel Thermal* €€€
Molitg-les-Bains, 66500. (04 68 05 00 50. FAX 04 68 05 02 91. **Rooms:** 62.
A spa hotel in the mountains, surrounded by palm trees and
adjacent to a lake. Spacious, peaceful, and very good value. 🛏 TV 🍽
AE V

QUILLAN: *Hôtel Cartier* @ hot.cart@wanadoo.fr €€
31 bd Charles de Gaulle, 11500. (04 68 20 05 14. FAX 04 68 20 22 57. **Rooms:** 28.
A comfortable, modest hotel-restaurant in the center of town. 🛏 TV 🍽
AE MC V

ST-CYPRIEN-PLAGE: *Le Mas d'Huston* w www.opengolfclub.com €€€€
66750 St-Cyprien-Plage. (04 68 37 63 63. FAX 04 68 37 64 64. **Rooms:** 50.
A relaxing hotel by the beach with all the pleasures of a bustling
resort to hand. The restaurant overlooks a golf course. 🛏 ▤ TV 🍽
AE DC MC V

SÈTE: *Grand Hôtel* w www.sete-hotel.com €€€
17 quai du Mar de Lattre de Tassigny, 34200. (04 67 74 71 77.
FAX 04 67 74 29 27. **Rooms:** 43.
Built in Belle Epoque style, this hotel overlooking Sète's Grand Canal
has a splendid palm-filled atrium and rooms with balconies. 🛏 ▤ TV
AE DC MC V

SOMMIÈRES: *Auberge du Pont-Romain* €€€
2 rue Emile-Jamais, 30250. (04 66 80 00 58. FAX 04 66 80 31 52. **Rooms:** 18.
Behind a forbidding façade, this wonderful garden leads down to the river.
Some large bedrooms overlook it. 🛏 TV 🍽 @ aubergedupontromain@wanadoo.com
AE MC V

UZÈS: *Le Mas d'Oléandre* w www.provence-sud.com/oleandre €€€
Saint-Médiers, 30700. (04 66 22 63 43. FAX 04 66 03 14 06. **Rooms:** 6.
A carefully restored farmhouse set in a secluded village surrounded by
vineyards. A good base for exploring and close to local restaurants. 🛏
MC V

Price categories for a standard double room (not per person) for one night, including tax and service charges, but not including breakfast.
€ under 30€
€€ 30€–60€
€€€ 61€–90€
€€€€ 91€–150€
€€€€€ over 150€

CHILDREN'S FACILITIES
Cribs and baby-sitting available. Some hotels provide children's portions and high chairs in the restaurant.
PARKING FACILITIES
Parking provided by the hotel in either a private lot or a private garage very close by.
SWIMMING POOL
Hotel pools are often quite small and are outdoors unless otherwise stated.
GARDEN
Hotel with garden, courtyard or terrace, often providing tables for eating outside.

	CREDIT CARDS	CHILDREN'S FACILITIES	PARKING FACILITIES	SWIMMING POOL	GARDEN
UZÈS: *Château d'Arpaillargues* W www.lcm.fr/savry €€€€ 30700 Uzès. (04 66 22 14 48. FAX 04 66 22 56 10. *Rooms: 29.* An 18th-century château with tastefully decorated bedrooms, varying in size. Enjoy the exquisite cuisine by the pool or on the terrace.	AE MC V	●	■	●	■
VILLENEUVE-LES-BÉZIERS: *Maison Viner* €€ 7 rue de la Fontaine, 34420. (04 67 39 87 15. FAX 04 67 32 00 95. *Rooms: 4.* Beautifully restored period bed-and-breakfast just 5 km (3 miles) from the Mediterranean. Evening meals and picnic lunches available.	MC V	●	■		

PROVENCE AND THE CÔTE D'AZUR

	CREDIT CARDS	CHILDREN'S FACILITIES	PARKING FACILITIES	SWIMMING POOL	GARDEN
AIX-EN-PROVENCE: *Hôtel des Augustins* €€€€ 3 rue de la Masse, 13100. (04 42 27 28 59. FAX 04 42 26 74 87. *Rooms: 29.* A converted 12th-century convent with large and commodious rooms in traditional Provençal style. A haven of peace in the heart of Aix.	AE DC MC V	●			
AIX-EN-PROVENCE: *Mas d'Entremont* W www.masdentremont.com €€€€ Montée d'Avignon, Célony, 13090. (04 42 17 42 42. FAX 04 42 21 15 83. *Rooms: 17.* This old Provençal farmhouse is now a luxurious hotel set in terraced tennis grounds just outside Aix. Spacious and tastefully decorated.	MC V	●	■	●	■
ANTIBES: *Mas Djoliba* W www.hotel-djoliba.com €€€ 29 av de Provence, 06600. (04 93 34 02 48. FAX 04 93 34 05 81. *Rooms: 13.* A traditional Provençal hotel just a short walk from the center and beach. Set in a pretty garden it offers comfortable rooms in a rustic style.	AE DC MC V		■	●	■
ARLES: *Hôtel d'Arlatan* W www.hotel-arlatan.com €€€€ 26 rue du Sauvage, 13631. (04 90 93 56 66. FAX 04 90 49 68 45. *Rooms: 54.* Situated in the heart of Arles, this hotel dates from the 16th-century. Stone walls and a cavernous fireplace decorate the salon.	AE DC MC V	●	■		
AVIGNON: *Hôtel de la Mirande* W www.la-mirande.fr €€€€€ 4 place de la Mirande, 84000. (04 90 85 93 93. FAX 04 90 86 26 85. *Rooms: 20.* An exquisite establishment with richly decorated rooms in Provençal style and fine antiques. There is a relaxing inner courtyard.	AE DC MC V	●	■		■
AVIGNON: *Hôtel d'Europe* W www.hotel-d-europe.fr €€€€ 12 place Crillon, 84000. (04 90 14 76 76. FAX 04 90 14 76 71. *Rooms: 45.* This has been Avignon's most refined hotel since Napoleon's day. Bedrooms are vast and elegant; the salon is splendidly bedecked with tapestries above marble floors. Superb restaurant.	AE DC MC V	●	■		
BEAULIEU-SUR-MER: *Le Métropole* W www.le-metropole.com €€€€€ 15 bd du Marechal Leclerc, 06310. (04 93 01 00 08. FAX 04 93 01 18 51. *Rooms: 40.* An Italianate palace complete with Mediterranean terrace, offering luxurious rooms and views across to St-Jean-Cap-Ferrat.	AE DC MC V	●	■	●	■
BEAURECUEIL: *Relais Sainte-Victoire* W www.relais-sainte-victoire.com €€€ 13100 Beaurecueil. (04 42 66 94 98. FAX 04 42 66 85 96. *Rooms: 12.* A small hotel set in a beautiful pastoral scene next to open fields under Mont-Ste-Victoire.	AE MC V	●	■	●	■
BORMES-LES-MIMOSAS: *Le Bellevue* W www.bellevuebormes.fr.st €€ 14 place Gambetta, 83230. (04 94 71 15 15. FAX 04 94 05 96 04. *Rooms: 12.* Small, simple family-run hotel with spacious bedrooms and balconies, overlooking a nest of terra-cotta roofs to the sea.	MC V	·	■		■
CANNES: *Carlton Intercontinental* W www.cannes.interconti.com €€€€€ 58 bd de la Croissette, 06400. (04 93 06 40 06. FAX 04 93 06 40 25. *Rooms: 338.* Home to stars during the movie festival and business people the rest of the year, the Carlton rivals Le Négresco as the Riviera's glittering jewel. A private beach allows you to book in direct from your yacht.	AE DC MC V	●	■		■

DIGNE-LES-BAINS: *Hôtel du Grand-Paris* w www.chateauxhotels.com €€€
19 bd Thiers, 04000. ☎ 04 92 31 11 15. FAX 04 92 32 32 82. **Rooms:** 23.
Once a convent, this atmospheric hotel offers comfortable rooms and
medieval surroundings in the heart of the town. 🚗 TV ⅋ — AE DC MC V

FONTVIEILLE: *La Régalido* w www.laregalido.com €€€€€
Rue Mistral, 13990. ☎ 04 90 54 60 22. FAX 04 90 54 64 29. **Rooms:** 15.
This peaceful converted olive mill is one of the most welcoming and
luxurious hotels in the area – covered in ivy, with a flowery garden.
Rooms are tastefully decorated, some with terraces. 🚗 ⅋ TV ⅋ — AE DC MC V

FOX AMPHOUX: *L'Auberge du Vieux Fox* €€€
Place de l'Eglise, 83670. ☎ 04 94 80 71 69. FAX 04 94 80 78 38. **Rooms:** 8.
Parts of this hotel date back to the 11th century, when it was a staging
post. Rooms are small but the sweeping views are splendid. 🚗 TV ⅋ — AE MC V

JUAN-LES-PINS: *La Jabotte* w www.jabotte.com €€€
13 av M-Mauray, Cap d'Antibes, 06160. ☎ 04 93 61 45 89. FAX 04 93 61 07 04. **Rooms:** 10.
Five minutes' walk from the centers of Juan-les-Pins and Antibes,
this friendly hotel has a lot to offer for its price. It is also possible
to stay in one of the bungalows on the terrace. 🚗 — AE MC V

LA CADIÈRE D'AZUR: *Hostellerie Bérard* w www.hotelberard.com €€€€
Rue Gabriel Peri, 83740. ☎ 04 94 90 11 43. FAX 04 94 90 01 94. **Rooms:** 40.
A friendly hotel and restaurant on the high street of this village. Four
converted buildings with individually styled bedrooms. 🚗 ⅋ TV ⅋ — AE DC MC V

LES ARCS-SUR-ARGENS: *Logis du Guetteur* w www.logisduguetteur.com €€€€
Place du Château, 83460. ☎ 04 94 99 51 10. FAX 04 94 99 51 29. **Rooms:** 13.
This 11th-century château sits on top of a hill overlooking the village.
Atmospheric vaulted dining room and spacious bedrooms. 🚗 ⅋ TV — AE DC MC V

LES BAUX-DE-PROVENCE: *Le Mas d'Aigret* w www.masdaigret.com €€€€
13520 Les Baux-de-Provence. ☎ 04 90 54 20 00. FAX 04 90 54 44 00. **Rooms:** 16.
A smart, personal hotel only a short walk from the medieval citadel.
The dining room and some of the bedrooms of this intriguing old
farmhouse have been cut out of rock. 🚗 ⅋ TV ⅋ — AE MC V

NICE: *Hôtel Windsor* w www.hotelwindsornice.com €€€
11 rue Dalpozzo, 06000. ☎ 04 93 88 59 35. FAX 04 93 88 94 57. **Rooms:** 57.
A friendly, family-run hotel with a palmed garden. Simple bedrooms
with modern murals, some with French windows and balconies. 🚗 ⅋ TV ⅋ — AE DC MC V

NICE: *Le Négresco* w www.hotel-negresco-nice.com €€€€€
37 prom des Anglais, 06000. ☎ 04 93 16 64 00. FAX 04 93 88 35 68. **Rooms:** 140.
The most famous hotel on the Riviera, recently renovated to even
more lofty heights of Belle Epoque grandeur. 🚗 ⅋ TV ⅋ — AE DC MC V

PEILLON: *Auberge de la Madone* w www.chateauxhotels.com/madone €€€€
06440 Peillon. ☎ 04 93 79 91 17. FAX 04 93 79 99 36. **Rooms:** 20.
A family-run modern inn in the remarkable perched village of Peillon.
Imaginative regional menus and comfortable bedrooms. 🚗 ⅋ — MC V

REILLANNE: *Auberge de Reillanne* €€€
Le Pigeonnier, 04110. ☎ FAX 04 92 76 45 95. **Rooms:** 6.
A beautiful old country house in the east Luberon, secluded and off
the tourist track. The hotel is simple yet alluring – books line the
ancient shelves and the 20th century seems to have barely begun. 🚗 ⅋ — MC V

ROUSSILLON: *Le Mas de Garrigon* @ mas.de.garrigon@wanadoo.fr €€€€
Route de St-Saturnin d'Apt, 84220. ☎ 04 90 05 63 22. FAX 04 90 05 70 01. **Rooms:** 9.
Set in pines in a secluded corner of Haute Provence, this traditional
country house is a perfect retreat. Classical music plays in the comfortable salons and each room has a private terrace. 🚗 TV ⅋ — AE DC MC V

SAIGNON: *Auberge du Presbytère* w www.provence-luberon.com €€€
Place de la Fontaine, 84400. ☎ 04 90 74 11 50. FAX 04 90 04 68 51. **Rooms:** 12.
A small auberge in the square of this unspoiled hilltop village. Simple,
atmospheric bedrooms, local cuisine and the village bar. 🚗 ⅋ — MC V

ST-JEAN-CAP-FERRAT: *Clair Logis* w www.hotel-clair-logis.fr €€€
12 av Centrale, 06230. ☎ 04 93 76 51 81. FAX 04 93 76 51 82. **Rooms:** 18.
This seductively old-fashioned villa with its large, mature garden is
very good value. The larger rooms are in the main building. 🚗 TV — AE MC V

Price categories for a standard double room (not per person) for one night, including tax and service charges, but not including breakfast.

€ under 30€
€€ 30€–60€
€€€ 61€–90€
€€€€ 91€–150€
€€€€€ over 150€

CHILDREN'S FACILITIES
Cribs and baby-sitting available. Some hotels provide children's portions and high chairs in the restaurant.

PARKING FACILITIES
Parking provided by the hotel in either a private lot or a private garage very close by.

SWIMMING POOL
Hotel pools are often quite small and are outdoors unless otherwise stated.

GARDEN
Hotel with garden, courtyard or terrace, often providing tables for eating outside.

	CREDIT CARDS	CHILDREN'S FACILITIES	PARKING FACILITIES	SWIMMING POOL	GARDEN
LES SAINTES-MARIES-DE-LA-MER: *Hostellerie de Cacharel* €€€€ Route de Cacharel, 13460. **[** 04 90 97 95 44. **FAX** 04 90 97 87 97. **Rooms:** 16. *Gardians* or Provençal cowboys used to inhabit this ancient ranch in the heart of the marshes. The hotel is surprisingly comfortable with large rooms and relaxing salons. Riding. 🔲 W www.hotel-cacharel.com	MC V		▪	●	▪
ST-PAUL-DE-VENCE: *La Colombe d'Or* W www.la-colombe-dor.com €€€€€ Place De-Gaulle, 06570. **[** 04 93 32 80 02. **FAX** 04 93 32 77 78. **Rooms:** 26. An old farmhouse once populated by Impressionist painters is now home to movie stars and models. The rooms are luxurious but the real stars are originals by Picasso and Matisse (*see p514*). 🔲 ▤ TV ❚❚	AE DC MC V	●	▪	●	▪
ST-RÉMY-DE-PROVENCE: *Le Mas des Carassins* €€€ 1 chemin Gaulois, 13210. **[** 04 90 92 15 48. **FAX** 04 90 92 63 47. **Rooms:** 14. A 19th-century farmhouse on the outskirts of town, decorated in a country-style. A friendly atmosphere and helpful staff. 🔲 ▤ TV ❚❚ W www.hoteldescarassins.com	MC V			●	▪
ST-TROPEZ: *Lou Cagnard* €€ Avenue P Roussel, 83990. **[** 04 94 97 04 24. **FAX** 04 94 97 09 44. **Rooms:** 19. A very popular, good value hotel in the newest part of town, a short walk to the port. Cheerful bedrooms and pleasant courtyard. 🔲 TV	MC V		▪		▪
SALON-DE-PROVENCE: *L'Abbaye de Sainte-Croix* €€€€€ Route du Val-de-Cuech, 13300. **[** 04 90 56 24 55. **FAX** 04 90 56 31 12. **Rooms:** 25. This converted 12th-century abbey retains its medieval charm. The bedrooms, originally monks' cells, vary in size. 🔲 ▤ TV ❚❚ W www.hotel-provence.com	AE DC MC V		▪	●	▪
SEILLANS: *Hôtel des Deux Rocs* €€€ Place Font d'Amont, 83440. **[** 04 94 76 87 32. **FAX** 04 94 76 88 68. **Rooms:** 14. A captivating 18th-century mansion hotel in the peaceful village square. Strong family atmosphere and mediterranean cuisine. 🔲 ❚❚	MC V	●			▪
TARASCON: *Les Mazets des Roches* @ mazets-roches@wanadoo.fr €€€ Route de Fontvieille, 13150. **[** 04 90 91 34 89. **FAX** 04 90 43 53 29. **Rooms:** 37. Set in densely wooded grounds, 12 km from St-Rémy, this typically Provençal hotel offers cycling, tennis, and *boules*. 🔲 ▤ TV ❚❚	AE DC MC V	●	▪	●	▪
TOURTOUR: *La Petite Auberge* W www.look.net/auberge €€€€ 83690 Tourtour. **[** 04 98 10 26 16. **FAX** 04 98 10 26 50. **Rooms:** 15. For peace and quiet, beautiful views and a rustic setting, head to Tourtour and this small auberge. 🔲 TV ❚❚	AE DC MC V	●	▪	●	▪
TRIGANCE: *Château de Trigance* W www.chateau-de-trigance.fr €€€€ 83840 Trigance. **[** 04 94 76 91 18. **FAX** 04 94 85 68 99. **Rooms:** 10. A unique and romantic hideaway in the mountain valleys. Four-poster beds, tapestries, and vaulted ceilings adorn this 11th-century château, carefully restored by the owner. Access by private road. 🔲 TV ❚❚	AE DC MC V		▪		▪
VAISON-LA-ROMAINE: *Le Beffroi* W www.le-beffroi.com €€€€ Rue de L'Evêché, Haute Ville, 84110. **[** 04 90 36 04 71. **FAX** 04 90 36 24 78. **Rooms:** 22. This 16th-century hotel seduces its guests with antiques, fireplaces, tiled floors, and paintings. Each room is individually furnished. 🔲 TV ❚❚	AE DC MC V	●	▪	●	▪
VENCE: *Auberge des Seigneurs* €€€ Place du Frêne, 06140. **[** 04 93 58 04 24. **FAX** 04 93 24 08 01. **Rooms:** 6. This restaurant-with-rooms is a medieval time capsule. Bedrooms are spartan but cheap. Good choice of Provençal specialities. 🔲	DC MC V		▪		
VILLEFRANCHE-SUR-MER: *Hôtel Welcome* W www.welcomehotel.com €€€€ 1 quai Courbet, 06230. **[** 04 93 76 27 62. **FAX** 04 93 76 27 66. **Rooms:** 37. This tall, narrow building stands over a fish restaurant near the old port. Most of the small but comfortable bedrooms have seaside balconies. The same family has run this hotel for half a century. 🔲 ▤ TV	AE DC MC V		▪		

CORSICA

AJACCIO: *Hôtel Napoléon* [W] www.hotelnapoleonajaccio.com €€€ | AE DC MC V
4 rue Lorenzo Véro, 20000. [C] 04 95 51 54 00. FAX 04 95 21 80 40. *Rooms: 62.*
In a quiet street just off the Cours Napoléon, in the center of town,
this is a modern, friendly, family-run hotel. 🛏 ▤ TV

BARCAGGIO: *La Giraglia* €€€
Ersa, 20275. [C] 04 95 35 60 54. FAX 04 95 35 65 92. *Rooms: 14.*
Off the tourist track, this modest seaside hotel with rustic rooms is ideal
for a peaceful stay. There are good seafood restaurants next door. 🛏

BASTIA: *Hôtel de la Corniche* [W] www.hotel-lacorniche.com €€€ | AE MC V
San-Martino-di-Lota, 20200. [C] 04 95 31 40 98. FAX 04 95 32 37 69. *Rooms: 19.*
A simple but good value hotel on a winding road 10 minutes' drive
from Bastia. Breathtaking views from the terrace. 🛏 TV 🍴

BONIFACIO: *Résidence du Centre Nautique* [W] www.centre-nautique.com €€€€ | AE MC V
Quai Nord, 20169. [C] 04 95 73 02 11. FAX 04 95 73 17 47. *Rooms: 10.*
A perfect stop by the harbor for sailing enthusiasts. The rooms have
been converted into small duplexes. 🛏 ▤ TV 🍴

BONIFACIO: *Hôtel Genovese* [W] www.hotel-genovese.com €€€€€ | AE DC MC V
Quartier de la Citadelle, 20169. [C] 04 95 73 12 34. FAX 04 95 73 09 03. *Rooms: 15.*
A luxury hotel in the Old Town that was once the legionnaires' barracks.
Refined, modern decor with grand rooms and suites. 🛏 ▤ TV

CALVI: *Hôtel Balanéa* [W] www.hotel-balanea.com €€€ | AE DC MC V
6 rue Clémenceau, 20260. [C] 04 95 65 94 94. FAX 04 95 65 29 71. *Rooms: 38.*
This renovated hotel in the center of town, beside the harbor,
has spacious and well-decorated rooms with large bathrooms. 🛏 ▤ TV

CALVI: *Auberge de la Signoria* [W] www.hotel-la-signoria.com €€€€€ | AE MC V
Rte de la Forêt de Bonifato, 20260. [C] 04 95 65 93 00. FAX 04 95 65 38 77. *Rooms: 18.*
The owners have renovated their large house, retaining its
original character. A haven of seclusion and peace – candlelit dinners
served on the terrace under the palm trees. 🛏 ▤ TV 🍴

FELICETO: *Hôtel Mare e Monti* €€€ | MC V
20225 Feliceto. [C] 04 95 63 02 00. FAX 04 95 63 02 01. *Rooms: 18.*
Set at the foot of rocky cliffs overlooking the ocean, the house has been
in the same family since 1870. Expect a warm welcome.
🛏 TV

L'ILE ROUSSE: *A Pastorella* [W] www.oda.fr/aa/hotel-a-pastorella €€€ | AE MC V
Monticello, 20220. [C] 04 95 60 05 65. FAX 04 95 60 21 78. *Rooms: 12.*
Just inland, this traditional hotel sits in the village square. Originally a
bar and restaurant, rooms of various sizes have been added. 🛏 TV 🍴

L'ILE ROUSSE: *Santa Maria* [W] www.hotelsantamaria.com €€€€ | AE DC MC V
Route du Port, 20220. [C] 04 95 63 05 05. FAX 04 95 60 32 48. *Rooms: 56.*
A modern hotel situated between two beaches with small but light and
comfortable rooms with balconies. 🛏 ▤ TV

PIANA: *Les Roches Rouges* €€€ | AE DC MC V
20115 Piana. [C] 04 95 27 81 81. FAX 04 95 27 81 76. *Rooms: 30.*
An old Corsican house that has been refurbished – the rooms are plain
but there is a lovely restaurant with terrace and superb views. 🛏 🍴

PORTICCIO: *Le Maquis* [W] www.lemaquis.com €€€€€ | AE DC MC V
20166 Porticcio. [C] 04 95 25 05 55. FAX 04 95 25 11 70. *Rooms: 25.*
A stylish hotel consisting of white-shuttered buildings centered on a
terrace and freshwater pool. Tennis court. Excellent cuisine. 🛏 ▤ TV 🍴

SARTÈNE: *Villa Piana* [@] hotel-la-villa-piana@wanadoo.fr €€€ | AE DC MC V
Route de Propriano, 20100. [C] 04 95 77 07 04. FAX 04 95 73 45 65. *Rooms: 32.*
A large, friendly Provençal-style villa with a splendid view across the
town to the mountains. The rooms are bright and airy, decorated in a
rustic style. Floodlit tennis courts. 🛏

SPELONCATO: *A Spelunca* €€ | MC V
20226 Speloncato. [C] 04 95 61 50 38. FAX 04 95 61 53 14. *Rooms: 18.*
A magnificent hotel in the former palace of a local cardinal. Huge grand
rooms and excellent value. 🛏

For key to symbols see back flap

WHERE TO EAT

THE FRENCH consider eating well an essential part of their national birthright. There are few other places where people are as passionately knowledgeable about their cuisine and their wine. Restaurant reviews, as well as cooking and food shows on television, are avidly followed, and the general quality of both fresh food and restaurant meals is vastly better in France than it is in most other European countries.

This section begins with an overview of the different types of restaurants in France, with tips on eating out, reading the menu, ordering and service. Following this is a list of restaurants we have sampled, arranged by region and town *(see pp580–613)*. At the front of the book *(see pp20–3)*, there is a guide to a typical menu and an introduction to French wine. And, at the start of each of the five regional sections can be found the food and wine features of that particular area.

FRENCH EATING HABITS

THE TRADITIONAL large meal at noon survives mainly in rural regions. In cities, lunch is increasingly likely to consist of a sandwich, a salad or a steak in a café, while dinner is the main meal of the day. Usually, lunch is from noon to 2pm and dinner is from 8 to 10pm, with last orders taken 30 minutes before closing time.

Some family-owned places are closed on weekends, so it may be difficult to find a meal anywhere outside your hotel on Sundays, except in large cities. Outside major cities and in resort towns, restaurants and hotels are often closed out of season, so it is advisable to phone ahead.

Over the past few decades, French eating habits have changed dramatically. The growing popularity of the cuisine of former French colonies means that North African and Vietnamese places are now easy to find, as are Chinese restaurants. Burger and Tex-Mex joints are also popular with young people. As city-dwellers and suburbanites in France have become almost as health-conscious as other Europeans, there has been an explosion of "light" foods; and the rise of the *hypermarchés* (hypermarkets) has resulted in less fresh produce on the menu, as more frozen and prepared food is eaten.

REGIONAL COOKING

ONE OF the great pleasures of traveling in France is sampling the country's regional

Typical elegant terrace restaurant in Provence

cuisine. In every *département* of France, menus will nearly always include local specialties, which reflect predominant local products and agriculture. A good way to divide France gastronomically is the butter/olive oil divide. In the north, butter is generally used in cooking; in the south, olive oil; and in the southwest, goose and duck fat predominate.

Each region takes great pride in its own cuisine. Nationally, the best known dishes come from four regions: Alsace, a province with close German ties; the southwest, where cassoulet, a rich stew of white beans, tomatoes, sausage and duck is a well-loved dish; the Alps, which gave fondue to the nation; and Provence, famed for bouillabaisse, a rich fish soup from Marseille.

The gastronomic capital of France is, however, considered to be Lyon, which boasts a significant proportion of France's best restaurants and many superb no-nonsense bistros known as *bouchons*.

La Cigale, a Belle Epoque brasserie in Nantes *(see p595)*

RESTAURANTS

ENCOMPASSING the whole alphabet of French cuisine, restaurants in France range from tiny white-washed places with rush-bottomed chairs to stately, wood-paneled château dining rooms and the top kitchens of famous chefs. Many hotels have fine restaurants open to non-residents, a selection of which can be found in the hotel listings *(see pp540–75)*.

Prices for restaurants of the same rating are more or less consistent throughout France except in large cities, where they can be more expensive. The quality of the food and service, though, is the most significant price factor, and a meal can easily cost up to 150€ a person at one of the leading restaurants.

There are several different kinds of French cuisine that you may come across. *Haute cuisine* is the traditional cooking method, where the flavor of the food is enhanced with rich sauces. *Nouvelle cuisine* challenged this method, especially for the diet-conscious, in using light rather than creamy sauces, which bring out the texture and color of the ingredients. *Cuisine bourgeoise* is French home cooking. *Cuisine des Provinces* uses high-quality ingredients to prepare traditional rural dishes. Many top chefs favor *cuisine moderne,* which releases the natural flavor of the food. There has also been a revival of traditional methods.

The restaurant L'Excelsior at Nancy in Lorraine *(see p589)*

Camembert

BISTROS

WHEN THE FRENCH go out to eat, they are most likely to visit the broadest class of restaurant, the bistro. Bistros vary enormously – some urban bistros are formally decorated, while those in smaller cities and in the country tend to be more casual. They offer a good, moderately priced meal from a traditional menu of an *entrée* or *hors d'oeuvre* (appetizer), *plats mijotés* (simmered dishes) and *grillades* (grilled fish and meats), followed by cheese and dessert.

BRASSERIES

BRASSERIES have their origin in Alsace and were originally attached to breweries; the name brasserie actually means brewery. Usually found in larger cities, they are big, bustling places, many with fresh shellfish stands outside. They serve beer on tap, as well as a *vin de la maison* (house wine) and a variety of regional wines. Menus include simple fish and grilled meat dishes along with Alsatian specialties like *choucroute garnie* (sauerkraut with sausage and pork). Prices are very much on a par with those you would pay at bistros. Like cafés, brasseries are usually open from morning until night and serve food all day long.

FERME-AUBERGES

IN THE COUNTRY you may eat at a simple "farm inn," where good, inexpensive meals, often made with fresh farm produce, are taken with your host's family as part of your room and board. For more details on *ferme-auberges*, see Bed-and-Breakfasts on page 538.

CAFÉS

CAFÉS REPRESENT the soul of France. Every place but the tiniest hamlet can be counted on to have a café, open as a rule from early in the morning until 10pm or so. They serve drinks, coffee, tea, simple meals, and snacks such as salads, omelettes and sandwiches throughout the day, and usually provide a cheaper breakfast than most hotels.

In addition to serving refreshments, cafés are a good source of information and offer the traveler opportunities to observe the French at their most relaxed.

In villages, almost the entire population might drift in and out of the single café during the course of a day, while large cities have cafés that cater to a specific clientele, such as workers or students. Paris's most famous cafés were traditional meeting places for intellectuals and artists to exchange ideas *(see p142)*.

Auberge du XII Siécle at Saché in the Loire Valley *(see p595)*

Tables outside a café in the Old Town of Nice on the Côte d'Azur

BISTRO ANNEXES

OVER THE PAST few years, "baby" bistros, or bistro annexes, have appeared in large cities, especially Paris and Lyon, as a new category of restaurant. They are lower-priced sister eateries of the famous – and more expensive – restaurants run by well-known chefs. Many of them offer *prix-fixe* (fixed-price) menus and the chance to sample the cooking of a celebrated kitchen in relaxed surroundings.

FAST FOOD

IF YOU WANT to avoid the American fast-food chains, wine bars and *salons du thé* are also affordable for light meals. Cafeterias, found in some shopping centers, serve tasty food at reasonable prices.

RESERVATIONS

IN CITIES and larger towns it is always best to make a reservation, especially from May to September. This rarely applies to cafés or in the country, where you can walk into most places without a reservation. However, if you are traveling in remote rural and resort areas off season, it is worth finding out first if the restaurant is open year-round.

If you have a reservation and your plans change, then you should call and cancel. Smaller restaurants, in particular, must fill all their tables to make a profit, and no-shows threaten their livelihood.

READING THE MENU AND ORDERING

WHEN THE MENU is presented, you'll usually be asked if you'd like an aperitif. Since many French people do not drink spirits before a meal, this could be Kir (white wine mixed with a dash of black-currant liqueur), vermouth, light port (drunk in France as a cocktail) or a soft drink.

Opening the menu, *les entrées* or *hors d'oeuvre* are appetizers. *Les plats* are the main courses, and most restaurants will offer a *plat du jour*, or daily special; these are often seasonal or local dishes of particular interest. A selection of dishes from a classic French menu is given on pages 20–21.

Cheese is served as a separate course between the main course and dessert. Coffee is always served black, unless you specify *"crème."* Alternatively, you can ask for a *tisane*, or herbal tea.

WINE

RESTAURANTS mark wine up considerably, so it can be expensive to drink fine wine with your meal. Local wine, however, is often served in carafes and is good value. Ordering a *demi* (50 cl) or *quart* (25 cl) carafe is a cheap and enjoyable way to try out a region's wines.

French law divides the country's wines into the following four classes, in ascending order of quality: Vin de Table, Vin de Pays, Vin Délimité de Qualité Supérieure (VDQS)

and Appellation d'Origine Contrôlée (AOC). The Vin de Table wines are rarely found in restaurants, but to choose a regional wine (Vins de Pays upward), refer to the wine features in the regional sections of this book. For an introduction to French wine, see pages 22–3.

When in doubt, order the house wine. These are usually good and also affordable.

WATER

TAP WATER is supplied upon request free of charge and is perfectly safe to drink. The French also pride themselves on their wide range of mineral waters. Favorite mealtime brands include Evian and the slightly carbonated Badoit.

Le Moulin de Mougins *(see p612)*

HOW TO PAY

VISA/CARTE BLEUE (V) is the most widely accepted credit card in France. Master-card/Access (MC), American Express (AE) and Diners Club (DC) are also commonly used. The abbreviations shown in brackets are used in the restaurant listings to indicate which card(s) each restaurant accepts.

La Tour d'Argent in the Latin Quarter of Paris *(see p583)*

Always carry plenty of cash, especially when touring the countryside, because many smaller restaurants still do not take credit cards. If in doubt, ask when you book a table.

SERVICE AND TIPPING

THE PACE of a French meal is generally leisurely. People think nothing of spending four hours at the table, so if you are pressed for time, go to a café or brasserie. A service charge of 12.5 to 15 percent is almost always included in the price of your meal, but most French people leave a few euro cents behind in a café, and an additional 5 percent or so of the total bill in other restaurants. In the grander restaurants, which pride themselves on their service, an additional tip of 5 to 10 percent is correct.

Thirty euro cents is sufficient for toilet attendants, and fifty or seventy euro cents an item is appropriate for the cloakroom attendant.

DRESS CODE

EVEN WHEN DRESSED casually, the French are generally well turned out; visitors should aim for the same level of presentable comfort. Running shoes, shorts, and athletic wear or beachwear are unacceptable everywhere except cafés or beachside places.

The restaurant listings indicate which restaurants require men to wear a jacket and tie (see pp580-613).

CHILDREN

FRENCH CHILDREN are introduced early to restaurants and are well received almost everywhere in France. However, few restaurants provide special facilities like high chairs or baby seats, because children are expected to behave sensibly and also because there is often not much extra room at the table.

PETS

DOGS are usually accepted at all but the most elegant restaurants. The French are

The Eychenne hotel-restaurant at St-Girons in the Pyrenees (see p607)

great dog lovers, so do not be surprised to see your neighbor's lapdog sitting at the adjacent *banquette*.

SMOKING

IN SPITE OF recent strict legislation requiring restaurants to provide their clientele with smoking and nonsmoking sections, a laissez-faire attitude prevails in most places. The owner of one Paris bistro now carries a portable no-smoking sign that he hangs on the wall over the table of anyone who requests a nonsmoking table. If you are sensitive to smoke, ask for a window table.

The Hôtel Royal at Evian-les-Bains in the French Alps (see p563)

WHEELCHAIR ACCESS

THOUGH THE RESTAURANTS of newer hotels usually provide wheelchair access, it is often limited elsewhere. A word when you are booking your table should ensure that you are given a conveniently located table and assistance, if needed, when you arrive.

The listings show restaurants with wheelchair access.

Refer also to page 539 of this book, which gives the names and addresses of organizations that provide advice to disabled travelers in France.

VEGETARIAN FOOD

FRANCE REMAINS difficult for vegetarians, although some progress has been made in recent years. In most nonvegetarian restaurants the main courses are firmly oriented toward meat and fish. However, you can often do well by ordering from the *entrées* and should never be timid about asking for a dish to be served without its meat content. If you make an advance request, most of the better restaurants will prepare a special vegetarian dish.

Only larger cities and university towns are likely to have completely vegetarian restaurants. Otherwise cafés, pizzerias, crêperies and oriental restaurants are good places to find vegetarian meals.

PICNICS

PICNICKING is the best way to enjoy the wonderful fresh produce, local bread, cheeses and *charcuterie* from the markets and enticing shops to be found all over France. For more details see pages 622–3.

Picnics are also a good way to eat cheaply and enjoy the French countryside. Picnicking areas along major roads are well marked and have tables and chairs, but country lanes are better still.

Choosing a Restaurant

T HE RESTAURANTS in this guide have been selected across a wide range of price categories for their good value, exceptional food and interesting location. This chart lists the restaurants by region, starting with Paris. Use the color-coded thumb tabs, which indicate the regions covered on each page, to guide you to the relevant section of the chart. *Bon Appétit!*

		CREDIT CARDS	CHILDREN'S FACILITIES	FIXED-PRICE MENU	GOOD WINE LIST	OUTDOOR TABLES
PARIS						
ILE DE LA CITÉ: *Le Vieux Bistrot.* **Map 9 B4.** 14 rue du Cloître-Notre-Dame, 75004. **(** 01 43 54 18 95. An authentic, honest bistro, frequented by many Parisian restaurateurs and entertainment stars. The food here is unpretentious and very good. ● *Dec 24–25.*	€€€€	MC V			●	▨
THE MARAIS: *Baracane.* **Map 10 E4.** 38 rue des Tournelles, 75004. **(** 01 42 71 43 33. In spite of its touristy location this tiny restaurant serving ethnic cuisine has very good quality food at reasonable prices. ● *Sat L; Sun.*	€€	MC V		▨		
THE MARAIS: *Aux Vins des Pyrénées.* **Map 10 D4.** 25 rue Beautreillis, 75004. **(** 01 42 72 64 94. A very old bistro whose friendly and typically Parisian atmosphere make it eternally popular. Unusually good selection of wines by the glass. ● *Sat L; mid–end Aug.*	€€€	MC V		▨		
THE MARAIS: *La Guirlande de Julie.* **Map 10 D3.** 25 place des Vosges, 75003. **(** 01 48 87 97 07. The food is impeccable and the setting unbeatable. In good weather meals are served under the stone vaults around the 17th-century *place.* ● *Mon.*	€€€	MC V				▨
THE MARAIS: *Le Passage des Carmagnoles.* **Map 10 F4.** 18 passage de la Bonne-Graine, 75011. **(** 01 47 00 73 30. A bistro in a 300-year-old house serving traditional family cooking made only with fresh produce. ● *Sat L, Sun.*	€€	AE MC V			●	
THE MARAIS: *Le Bar à Huîtres.* **Map 10 E3.** 33 bd Beaumarchais, 75003. **(** 01 48 87 98 92. Oysters and other shellfish predominate here. Compose your own appetizer platter, then follow with a choice of fish or meat dishes.	€€€	AE MC V	●	▨		▨
THE MARAIS: *L'Ambroisie.* **Map 10 D3.** 9 pl des Vosges, 75004. **(** 01 42 78 51 45. This discreet, romantic spot is one of only seven Michelin three-star restaurants in Paris. Reservations accepted one month ahead. ⑁ ● *Sun–Mon; 1 wk Feb, Aug.*	€€€€€	AE MC V			●	
BEAUBOURG: *Le 404.* **Map 9 C1.** 69 rue Gravilliers, 75003. **(** 01 42 74 57 81. Magnificently located in a 1737 hôtel particulier, the food is rooted in Morocco, and the interior resembles a bedouin tent.	€€	AE MC V				
LES HALLES: *Chez Elle.* **Map 9 A2.** 7 rue des Prouvaires, 75001. **(** 01 45 08 04 10. The menu is classic bistro, changing with the seasons and always based on fresh, local produce. Desserts are traditional and delicious, including the crème caramel. ● *Sat–Sun.*	€€	AE MC V				
LES HALLES: *Aux Tonneaux des Halles.* **Map 9 A1.** 28 rue Montorgueil, 75001. **(** 01 42 33 36 19. One of the last of its kind, with real zinc bar and one of the tiniest kitchens in Paris, this bistro serves excellent food, with good value wines. ⑁ ● *Sun.*	€€€	V			●	▨
LES HALLES: *Le Grizzli.* **Map 9 B3.** 7 rue St-Martin, 75004. **(** 01 48 87 77 56. This restaurant provides hearty, traditional Italian and southwestern French food.	€€	AE MC V				▨
LES HALLES: *Au Pied de Cochon.* **Map 8 F1.** 6 rue Coquillière, 75001. **(** 01 40 13 77 00. This famous institution in the heart of Les Halles is open every day, all day and all night, serving copious amounts of grilled pigs' trotters and shellfish. Hearty cuisine and atmosphere but be prepared for lines after 10pm.	€€€	AE DC MC V				▨

Average prices for a three-course meal for one, including a half-bottle of house wine, tax and service: € under 25€ €€ 25€–35€ €€€ 36€–50€ €€€€ 51€–75€ €€€€€ over 75€	**CHILDREN'S FACILITIES** Where high chairs and smaller portions are available. **FIXED-PRICE MENU** A good-value fixed-price menu on offer at lunch, dinner or both, often with three or more courses. **GOOD WINE LIST** Denotes a wide range of good wines, or otherwise a more specialised selection of local wines. **OUTDOOR TABLES** Facilities for eating outdoors, often with a good view. **WEEKLY & ANNUAL CLOSURE** Double check as may change (L = lunch; D = dinner).	CREDIT CARDS	CHILDREN'S FACILITIES	FIXED-PRICE MENU	GOOD WINE LIST	OUTDOOR TABLES
TUILERIES QUARTER: *Le Grand Louvre.* **Map 8 F2.** €€ Le Louvre, 75001. (01 40 20 53 41. It is rare to find such a good restaurant in a museum. New chef Yves Pinard is putting his own mark on the southwestern menu. ● *Tue.*		AE DC MC V	●	■		
TUILERIES QUARTER: *Goumard.* **Map 3 C5.** €€€€€ 9 rue Duphot, 75001. (01 42 60 36 07. No expense has been spared with the fabulous Lalique lights and sculptures in this restored 19th-century restaurant. Excellent fish and desserts. ▯ ● *2wks Aug.*		AE DC MC V		■	●	
TUILERIES QUARTER: *L'Espadon.* **Map 4 D5.** €€€€€ 15 pl Vendôme, 75001. (01 43 16 30 80. Part of the Ritz, this is one of the Parisian restaurants most highly rated by Michelin. Modern classic cuisine from chef Michel Roth. & ▯		AE DC MC V	●	■	●	■
TUILERIES QUARTER: *Le Grand Véfour.* **Map 8 F1.** €€€€€ 17 rue de Beaujolais, 75001. (01 42 96 56 27. An 18th-century 3-star Michelin restaurant, considered by many to be the most attractive in the city. This is the place for special occasions. & ▯ ● *Fri D–Sun; Aug. V*		AE DC MC		■	●	
OPÉRA QUARTER: *Chartier.* **Map 4 F4.** € 7 rue du Faubourg Montmartre, 75009. (01 47 70 86 29. This cavernous restaurant packs in the crowds with its quick service and basic French food at budget prices. Popular with students, travelers and local *habitués*, the place bustles with an infectious bonhomie.		MC V				
OPERA QUARTER: *A G Le Poète.* **Map 3 C4.** €€ 27 rue Pasquier, 75008. (01 47 42 00 64. Soft lighting and red velvet decor provide a romantic setting for inspired cooking, with dishes such as red mullet and baby scallops on creamed wild nettles. ● *Sat–Sun; 1 wk Aug.*		AE MC V		■		
OPÉRA QUARTER: *Café Runtz.* **Map 4 F5.** €€€ 16 rue Favart, 75002. (01 42 96 69 86. This pleasant brasserie is one of the few genuine Alsatian places in Paris where copious amounts of regional specialties are served. ● *Sat D–Sun, publ hols; Aug.*		AE DC MC V		■		
OPÉRA QUARTER: *Le Vaudeville.* **Map 4 F5.** €€€ 29 rue Vivienne, 75002. (01 40 20 04 62. The attractive Art Deco interior provides an appealing backdrop to the food: good shellfish, the chef's famous smoked salmon, and classic standbys like pigs' trotters and *andouillette* (tripe sausage).		AE DC MC V	●	■		■
OPÉRA QUARTER: *Lucas Carton.* **Map 3 C5.** €€€€€ 9 pl de la Madeleine, 75008. (01 42 65 22 90. Awarded 3 Michelin stars, the cuisine here is imaginative and exotic. The decor is stunning, the service crisp and the crowd very dressy. ▯ ● *Sat L, Sun L, Mon L; Aug.*		AE DC MC V		■	●	
INVALIDES QUARTER: *Thoumieux.* **Map 7 A2.** €€€ 79 rue St-Dominique, 75007. (01 47 05 49 75. Ingredients are fresh, and virtually everything is made on the premises of this well-run restaurant, including *foie gras* and *rillettes* (similar to pâté). The *cassoulet* (stew of white beans and meat) is a specialty here.		AE MC V	●	■		
INVALIDES QUARTER: *L'Arpège.* **Map 7 B3.** €€€€€ 84 rue de Varenne, 75007. (01 45 51 47 33. Chef owner Alain Passard's 3-star Michelin restaurant is near the Musée Rodin. His lobster and turnip vinaigrette, and the duck Louise Passard are classics. ● *Sat–Sun.V*		AE DC MC		■	●	
EIFFEL TOWER QUARTER: *La Serre.* **Map 6 F3.** €€ 29 rue de l'Exposition, 75007. (01 45 55 20 96. A small, cozy neighborhood restaurant of a type that is becoming increasingly rare. Rustic specialties include *pot au feu* and *cassoulet.* ● *Sun L–Mon; 2 wks Aug.*		MC V	●	■		

For key to symbols see back flap

		CREDIT CARDS	CHILDREN'S FACILITIES	FIXED-PRICE MENU	GOOD WINE LIST	OUTDOOR TABLES

Average prices for a three-course meal for one, including a half-bottle of house wine, tax and service:
€ under 25€
€€ 25€–35€
€€€ 36€–50€
€€€€ 51€–75€
€€€€€ over 75€

CHILDREN'S FACILITIES
Where high chairs and smaller portions are available.
FIXED-PRICE MENU
A good-value fixed-price menu on offer at lunch, dinner or both, often with three or more courses.
GOOD WINE LIST
Denotes a wide range of good wines, or otherwise a more specialised selection of local wines.
OUTDOOR TABLES
Facilities for eating outdoors, often with a good view.
WEEKLY & ANNUAL CLOSURE
Double check as may change (L = lunch; D = dinner).

	CREDIT CARDS	CHILDREN'S FACILITIES	FIXED-PRICE MENU	GOOD WINE LIST	OUTDOOR TABLES
CHAILLOT QUARTER: *La Butte Chaillot*. **Map** 2 D5. €€€ 110 bis, av Kleber, 75116. **(** *01 47 27 88 88.* This is one of chef Guy Savoy's most recent restaurants. The sophisticated cuisine and the modern decor attract a very stylish crowd. **& ●** *Sat L; Aug.*	AE DC MC V		■		
CHAILLOT QUARTER: *L'Astrance*. **Map** 5 C3. €€€€€ 4 rue Beethoven, 75016. **(** *01 40 50 84 40.* The skillfully inventive dishes have made this place so popular you have to book a month ahead. Try the *Menu Surprise*. **●** *Mon–Tue L; 1 wk Feb, Aug.*	AE MC V		■		■
CHAILLOT QUARTER: *Amphyclès*. **Map** 1 C2. €€€€€ 78 avenue des Ternes, 75017. **(** *01 40 68 01 01.* Philippe Groult's creative dishes include steamed *foie gras* with beans, fillet of sea bass with sesame, and pigeon in a seaweed crust. **●** *Sat L, Sun; Jul.*	AE DC MC V		■	●	
CHAILLOT QUARTER: *Alain Ducasse*. **Map** 6 F1. €€€€€ 25 avenue Montaigne, 75008. **(** *01 53 67 65 00.* In a dining room decorated with *trompe l'oeil* and sculptures, Alain Ducasse creates the great classic dishes from meticulously chosen ingredients, worthy of the restaurant's 3 Michelin stars. **¶ ●** *Sat–Mon L, Tue L, Wed L; mid-Jul–mid-Aug.*	AE DC MC V	●	■	●	
CHAMPS-ELYSÉES: *Le Cercle Ledoyen*. **Map** 7 B1. €€ 1 av Dutuit, 75008. **(** *01 53 05 10 02.* Walls and ceiling of the handsome dining room are decorated with Parisian scenes. Food is simple yet refined: grilled brill with wild mushrooms, pheasant with quince and a wonderful range of chocolate desserts. **●** *Sat–Mon L; Aug.*	AE MC V				■
CHAMPS-ELYSÉES: *La Fermette Marbeuf 1900*. **Map** 2 F5. €€€ 5 rue Marbeuf, 75008. **(** *01 53 23 08 00.* Come here to dine amid the stunning Belle Epoque decor. La Fermette serves good brasserie-style food, including a commendable set menu with many wines of *appellations contrôlées* status.	AE DC MC V		■	●	■
CHAMPS-ELYSÉES: *Lasserre*. **Map** 7 A1. €€€€€ 17 av Franklin D Roosevelt, 75008. **(** *01 43 59 53 43.* For over 50 years, charismatic owner René Lasserre has labored to maintain one of Paris' finest menus. Main courses are classics, desserts sublime. **¶ ●** *Sun–Mon; Aug.*	AE DC MC V		■	●	
CHAMPS-ELYSÉES: *Au Petit Colombier*. **Map** 2 D3. €€€€ 42 rue des Acacias, 75017. **(** *01 43 80 28 54.* The slightly rustic ambience of this comfortable restaurant complements the traditional provincial cuisine. Excellent for a relaxing evening. **& ●** *mid-Jul–mid-Aug*	AE MC V		■		
CHAMPS-ELYSÉES: *Taillevent*. **Map** 2 F4. €€€€€ 15 rue Lamennais, 75008. **(** *01 44 95 15 01.* Taillevent is the most elegant of Paris's three-star restaurants. The service, wine list and cuisine of Michel del Burgo make it memorable. **& ¶ ●** *Sat–Sun; late Jul–late Aug.*	AE DC MC V			●	
CHAMPS-ELYSÉES: *Guy Savoy*. **Map** 2 D3. €€€€€ 44–46 rue de Naples, 75008. **(** *01 40 75 01 56.* A large, handsome dining room, professional service, and the remarkable cuisine of Guy Savoy himself, which looks as good as it tastes, including cold oysters in aspic and mussels with mushrooms. **¶ ●** *Sat L, Sun–Mon; 3 wks Aug.*	AE DC MC V			●	
ST-GERMAIN-DES-PRÉS: *Le Petit St-Benoît*. **Map** 8 E3. €€ 4 rue St-Benoît, 75006. **(** *01 42 60 27 92.* This is the place for anyone who's on a budget or who wants to mix with the locals. The food is simple and tasty, and good value. **& ●** *Sun; 1 wk Feb, Aug.*					■
ST-GERMAIN-DES-PRÉS: *Rôtisserie d'en Face*. **Map** 8 F4. €€€ 2 rue Christine, 75006. **(** *01 43 26 40 98.* Even the wealthy appreciate a bargain – they come here for Jacques Cagna's reasonable menu including farm chicken with mashed potatoes. **●** *Sat L, Sun.*	AE MC V		■		

St-Germain-des-Prés: *Alcazar*. Map8 F4. €€€
62 rue Mazarine, 75006. 01 53 10 19 99.
Sir Terence Conran created this huge, elegant and thoroughly modern
establishment which serves simple but well-made cuisine. Sat D, Sun, Mon D.

AE DC MC V

St-Germain-des-Prés: *Le Procope*. Map 8 F4. €€€
13 rue de l'Ancienne Comédie, 75006. 01 40 46 79 00.
Paris' longest-surviving restaurant, it has long been the chosen place
for writers, artists, politicians, and philosophers.

AE MC V

St-Germain-des-Prés: *Brasserie Lipp*. Map 8 E4. €€€€
151 blvd St-Germain, 75006. 01 45 48 53 91.
This is the brasserie that everyone loves to hate. But they keep on returning.
Ask to be seated downstairs – the first floor is referred to as Siberia.

AE DC MC V

St-Germain-des-Prés: *Restaurant Jacques Cagna*. Map 8 F4. €€€€€
14 rue des Grands Augustins, 75006. 01 43 26 49 39.
This elegant 17th century town house is a showcase for the excellent classic-cum-
contemporary cuisine of the chef/owner Jacques Cagna. Sat, Mon L; Aug

AE DC MC V

Latin Quarter: *Loubnane*. Map 9 A4. €€
29 rue Galande, 75005. 01 43 26 70 60.
This Lebanese restaurant serves generous mezzes under the watchful eye of a
patron whose main aim in life is the happiness of his customers. Mon–Tue L.

AE DC MC V

Latin Quarter: *La Rôtisserie du Beaujolais*. Map 9 B5. €€€
19 quai de la Tournelle, 75005. 01 43 54 17 47.
Facing the Seine and owned by Claude Terrail of the Tour d'Argent next door,
much of the meat comes from the best suppliers in Lyon. Mon–Tue L.

MC V

Latin Quarter: *La Tour d'Argent*. Map 9 B5. €€€€€€
15–17 quai de la Tournelle, 75005. 01 43 54 23 31.
Established in 1582, La Tour d'Argent consistently maintains top-class
status. The wine cellar must be one of the best in the world. Mon–Tue L.

AE DC MC V

Luxembourg Quarter: *Perraudin*. Map 12 F1. €€
157 rue St-Jacques, 75005. 01 46 33 15 75.
Generations of students have come here to tuck into the home-spun meals
at this authentic bistro. The set menu is a bargain. Sun; Aug.

Luxembourg Quarter: *Au Petit Marguéry*. Map 13 B3. €€€
9 bd de Port-Royal, 75013. 01 43 31 58 59.
Cold lobster *consommé* with caviar, mushroom salad with *foie gras* and
cod with spices are some of the unusual dishes served here. Sun, Mon.

AE MC V

Montparnasse: *La Maison du Cantal*. Map 11 A3. €€
1 place Falguière, 75015. 01 47 34 12 24.
Come on a chilly evening for the hearty country dishes of the Auvergne,
such as tender rump steak with *bleu d'Auvergne* cheese sauce. Sun, Mon; 1 wk Aug.

MC V

Montparnasse: *La Coupole*. Map 12 D2. €€€
102 bd du Montparnasse, 75014. 01 43 20 14 20.
This is a lively and boisterous place all through the day and night. It has
been popular with artists and thinkers since 1927. Serves vegetarian dishes.

AE DC MC V

Montparnasse: *La Cagouille*. Map 11 C3. €€€
10–12 pl Constantin Brancusi, 75014. 01 43 22 09 01.
This is considered one of the best fish restaurants in Paris. The shellfish
platter is recommended. Also look out for the seasonal items on the menu.

AE MC V

Montmartre: *Le Clos des Morillons*. Metro Convention. €€€
50 rue des Morillons, 75015. 01 48 28 04 37.
The experience of chef Vincent Beneteau is evident in the
constantly evolving menu of this discreet family-run restaurant. Sat L, Sun–Mon L.

AE MC V

Montmartre: *La Table d'Anvers*. Metro Anvers. €€€€
2 place d'Anvers, 75009. 01 48 78 35 21.
Near the Butte Montmartre, the menu at this family establishment has powerful
hints of Italy and Provence. The pastries and desserts are excellent. Sat L, Sun.

AE MC V

Montmartre: *Beauvilliers*. €€€€€
52 rue Lamarck, 75018. 01 42 54 54 42.
Stepping into this restaurant, you are imbued with a sense of *joie de vivre*.
Chef Edouard Carlier's cuisine is always exciting.

AE MC V

Average prices for a three-course meal for one, including a half-bottle of house wine, tax and service:
€ under 25€
€€ 25€–35€
€€€ 36€–50€
€€€€ 51€–75€
€€€€€ over 75€

CHILDREN'S FACILITIES
Where high chairs and smaller portions are available.
FIXED-PRICE MENU
A good-value fixed-price menu on offer at lunch, dinner or both, often with three or more courses.
GOOD WINE LIST
Denotes a wide range of good wines, or otherwise a more specialised selection of local wines.
OUTDOOR TABLES
Facilities for eating outdoors, often with a good view.
WEEKLY & ANNUAL CLOSURE
Double check as may change (L = lunch; D = dinner).

	CREDIT CARDS	CHILDREN'S FACILITIES	FIXED-PRICE MENU	GOOD WINE LIST	OUTDOOR TABLES
NATION: *Les Allobroges.* **Metro** Avron. €€ 71 rue des Grands Champs, 75020. ☎ 01 43 73 40 00. Olivier Pateyron's fresh and innovative cooking makes the hike worthwhile, but the decor and ambience might not impress a hot date. ● Sun–Mon; Aug.	AE MC V		■		
REPUBLIQUE/MARAIS: *Astier.* **Map** 10 E1. €€ 44 rue Jean Pierre Timbaud, 75011. ☎ 01 43 57 16 35. The food is excellent and at unbeatable prices, so the dining rooms are always full. The cheeses and wines are also good. ● Sat–Sun; Christmas & Spring hols.	MC V		■		
OBERKAMPF/MARAIS: *Le Villaret* **Map** 10 E1. €€€ 13 rue Ternaux, 75011. ☎ 01 43 57 89 76. Venture to the northern fringes of the fast-developing Oberkampf district for this excellent "cuisine du marché." Packed on weekends. ● Sat L, Sun; Aug.	MC V		■	●	
OBERKAMPF/MARAIS: *Le Repaire de Cartouche* **Map** 10 D2. €€€ 8 bvd Filles du Calvaire, 75011. ☎ 01 47 00 25 86. Like its 'sister' establishment, Le Villaret, this restaurant is run by former employees of Astier, to the same standards. ♿ ● Sun–Mon; 1st wk May, Aug.	DC MC V			●	
BASTILLE/NATION: *Les Amognes.* **Metro** Faidherbe Chaligny. €€€ 243 rue du Faubourg St-Antoine, 75011. ☎ 01 43 72 73 05. Thierry Coue's small restaurant is not pretty, but the food is good and original. Try sardine tart or sea bream with chilli-oil. ● Sat L, Sun–Mon L; 1st 3 wks Aug.	MC V		■		
BASTILLE: *Le Train Bleu.* **Map** 14 E1. €€€ 20 bvd Diderot, 75012. ☎ 01 43 43 09 06. Named for the fast train that once carried the élite down to the Riviera, Le Train Bleu in the Gare de Lyon, with its fabulous Belle Epoque decor and upscale brasserie cuisine, is a pleasant exception to most station restaurants. ♿	AE DC MC V	●	■		

ILE DE FRANCE

	CREDIT CARDS	CHILDREN'S FACILITIES	FIXED-PRICE MENU	GOOD WINE LIST	OUTDOOR TABLES
BARBIZON: *La Clé d'Or* €€€ 73 rue Grande. ☎ 01 60 66 40 96. This recently restored inn retains its old-world charm. Its specialties are shellfish, seafood, and game in season. ● Nov–Mar: Sun D.	AE DC MC V	●	■	●	■
BARBIZON: *Hostellerie les Pléiades* €€€ 21 rue Grande. ☎ 01 60 66 40 25. Once the artist Daubigny's studio, this restaurant offers traditional cuisine such as veal with morel mushrooms. ● Sun D, Mon; Nov–Mar.	AE MC DC V	●	■		
DAMPIERRE: *Auberge Saint-Pierre* €€€ 1 rue de Chevreuse. ☎ 01 30 52 53 53. This half-timbered inn faces the grand Château de Dampierre. The menu offers classics such as *foie gras* and *joue de boeuf* (ox cheek). ● Sun D–Mon; Aug.	MC V		■	●	
DAMPIERRE: *Les Ecuries du Château* €€€ Château de Dampierre. ☎ 01 30 52 52 99. Situated within the château, Les Ecuries offers a classic menu of fish and meat dishes in a sophisticated setting. ● Tue–Wed; 2 wks Feb, 1st 3 wks Aug.	AE DC MC V		■		
FONTAINEBLEAU: *Le Caveau des Ducs* €€€ 24 rue de Ferrare. ☎ 01 64 22 05 05. Offers standard classic French cuisine in intimate rustic surroundings near to the fabulous Château de Fontainebleau. ● 1st 2 wks Aug.	AE DC MC V	●	■	●	■
MAISONS-LAFFITTE: *Le Tastevin* €€€€ 9 avenue Eglé. ☎ 01 39 62 11 67. Great cooking and carefully selected wines served in delightful surroundings make Michel Blanchet's restaurant one of the best in the suburbs. Specialties include fish, seafood, and poultry. ● Mon–Tue; 2 wks Feb, 1st 3 wks Aug.	AE DC MC V		■	●	■

RAMBOUILLET: *Le Cheval Rouge* €€ — AE MC V
78 rue du Général de Gaulle. (*01 30 88 80 61.*
The specialties in this small restaurant near the château include
stuffed quail *à la champenoise* (*foie gras* and champagne). & ● *Tue D, Wed.*

RUEIL-MALMAISON: *Relais de St-Cucufa* €€€ — AE MC V
114 rue Général-de-Miribel. (*01 47 49 79 05.*
Whether lunching in the garden or dining by the fire, guests can enjoy
specialties such as the crayfish ravioli or grilled shellfish. ● *Sun L, Mon; Aug.*

VERSAILLES: *Restaurant Chez Lazare* €€ — MC V
18 rue de Satory. (*01 39 50 41 45.*
This fun South-American restaurant makes a change from French
classic cuisine. Seated below tiers of copper pots, diners tuck into
grilled fish and steaks. ● *Sun–Mon.*

VERSAILLES: *Les Petites Marches* €€€ — AE DC MC V
1 bd de la Reine. (*01 39 50 13 21.*
This little place, an annex of the famous Les Trois Marches
next door, serves good daily specials at affordable prices. ● *Sun–Mon; Aug.*

VERSAILLES: *Les Trois Marches (Trianon Palace)* €€€€€ — AE DC MC V
1 bd de la Reine. (*01 39 50 13 21.*
The restaurant is part of the sumptuous palace overlooking the formal
gardens. The *haute cuisine* matches the splendor of the place. ● *Sun–Mon; Aug.*

LE NORD AND PICARDY

ABBEVILLE: *Au Châteaubriant* €€ — AE MC V
1 place de l'Hôtel de Ville. (*03 22 24 08 23.*
Quiche Picarde (with sweet onions, ham and sour cream) and steak in mushroom
and Calvados sauce are praised. ● *Sun D, Mon; 2 wks Mar, last wk Jul–1st wk Aug.*

AMIENS: *La Couronne* €€ — AE V
64 rue Saint-Leu. (*03 22 91 88 57.*
To start, try a portion of homemade spicy duck pâté, followed
by a local specialty of salt marsh lamb from the Somme Abbey
nearby, accompanied by a Chinon wine. ● *Sat–Sun D; 1st wk Jan, mid–end Jul.*

ARRAS: *La Rapière* €€ — AE MC V
44 Grand'Place. (*03 21 55 09 92.*
There are several menus, but the *menu régional* offers good value and
a varied selection of dishes. The chicken cooked in beer is delicious. & ● *Sun D.*

ARRAS: *La Faisanderie* €€€€ — AE DC MC V
45 Grand'Place. (*03 21 48 20 76.*
This is a classified historic building with a splendid brick-vaulted dining
room. The menu is seasonal. ● *Sun D–Tue L; 1st wk Jan, 1st wk Feb, 1st–3rd wk Aug.*

AVESNES-SUR-HELPE: *La Crémaillière* €€€ — AE MC V
26 place Général Leclerc. (*03 27 61 02 30.*
A great place, with a menu featuring stuffed quails and other local dishes
such as *flamiche* and *maroilles tart*. ● *Sun D, Mon, Tue D; 1st wk Jan, 2 wks Aug.*

CALAIS: *Le Channel* €€ — AE DC MC V
3 bd de la Résistance, 62100. (*03 21 34 42 30.*
Watch the ships come and go as you enjoy a menu based on fresh
ingredients from the North Sea. ● *Sun D, Tue; Dec 23–Jan 15, last wk Jul–mid-Aug.*

CAMBRAI: *L'Escargot* €€ — MC V
10 rue Général de Gaulle. (*03 27 81 24 54.*
Local ingredients feature highly in this innovative cuisine: try the snails
with melted *Tome de Cambrai*, or *andouillette de Cambrai* with mustard sauce.
● *Wed, Fri D; last wk Dec, 1st wk Feb, last wk Jul–1st wk Aug.*

DOUAI: *La Terrasse* €€€ — AE MC V
36 terrasse St-Pierre. (*03 27 88 70 04.*
Breast of duck with fresh figs, and fillet of *sandre* (pike-perch) on a bed
of sweet onions give some idea of the splendid cuisine available here.

DUNKERQUE: *Estaminet Flamand* € — MC V
6 rue des Fusillers-Marins. (*03 28 66 98 35*
Delicious and authentic Flemish cuisine including *maroilles* (cheese) or
beer tart and sugar tart. ● *Sat L, Sun–Mon.*

<table>
<tr><td colspan="2">

Average prices for a three-course meal for one, including a half-bottle of house wine, tax and service:

€ under 25€
€€ 25€–35€
€€€ 36€–50€
€€€€ 51€–75€
€€€€€ over 75€

</td></tr>
</table>

CHILDREN'S FACILITIES
Where high chairs and smaller portions are available.
FIXED-PRICE MENU
A good-value fixed-price menu on offer at lunch, dinner or both, often with three or more courses.
GOOD WINE LIST
Denotes a wide range of good wines, or otherwise a more specialised selection of local wines.
OUTDOOR TABLES
Facilities for eating outdoors, often with a good view.
WEEKLY & ANNUAL CLOSURE
Double check as may change (L = lunch; D = dinner).

	CREDIT CARDS	CHILDREN'S FACILITIES	FIXED-PRICE MENU	GOOD WINE LIST	OUTDOOR TABLES
DURY-LES-AMIENS: *L'Aubergade* €€€ 78 Route Nationale. 03 22 89 51 41. High standard, traditional French cuisine – try the *terrine de foie gras.* & ● *Sun D, Mon.*	AE MC V		■	●	
HALLINES: *L'Hostellerie St-Hubert* €€€ 1 rue du Moulin. 03 21 39 77 77. Situated in its own park at the edge of the river Aa. Offers a classic French menu with an impressive selection of cheeses. ● *Sun D, Mon & Tue L.*	MC V		■	●	
LILLE: *La Pâte Brisée* € 65 rue de la Monnaie. 03 20 74 29 00. Set in the Old Town, this rustic bistro specializes in bountiful servings of quiches, tarts, gratins, and mixed salads. It's always packed at lunchtime, so arrive early.	MC V		■		▨
LILLE: *Restaurant aux Moules* €€ 34 rue de Béthune. 03 20 57 12 46. As its name suggests, mussels are the order of the day here, served in many guises. Local dishes such as *carbonnade flamande* are also good. Wash down your choice with local beer and enjoy the bustling, 1930s brasserie atmosphere. &	MC V		▨		▨
LONGUEAU: *La Potinière* €€ 2 av Henri Barbusse. 03 22 46 22 83. Popular with the locals, this cozy restaurant offers a daily menu based on freshly bought produce. Dishes are richer in winter. ● *Sun D, Mon; Aug.*	MC V	●	■		
MONTREUIL-SUR-MER: *Auberge de la Grenouillère* €€€ Rue de la Grenouillère, La Madeleine-sous-Montreuil. 03 21 06 07 22. This is an excellent restaurant, only 3 km (2 miles) west of Montreuil, for sampling French provincial cooking: braised quails with langoustines and frogs' legs are just two of the specialties. ● *Sep–Jun: Tue & Wed; Jan.*	AE DC MC V		■	●	▨
POIX-DE-PICARDIE: *L'Auberge de la Forge* €€ Route Nationale 29, Caulières. 03 22 38 00 91. A traditional Picardy inn that serves good, old-fashioned, hearty fare: try the salt-marsh lamb or trout with *foie gras.*	MC V	●	■		▨
ROYE: *La Flamiche* €€€ 20 place de l'Hôtel de Ville. 03 22 87 00 56. Eel terrine and local wild duck with forest mushrooms are two favorites with diners here. Start with a *flamiche* (covered tart) of leeks or pan-fried scallops. & ● *Sun D, Mon, Tue L; Dec 22–Jan 15, 1 wk Aug.*	AE DC MC V	●	■	●	
ST-QUENTIN: *Le Pot d'Etain* €€€ Route Nationale 29, Holnon. 03 23 09 34 35. Located 5 km from St-Quentin, this hotel-restaurant offers practicality and good service. The food is unpretentiously wholesome. &	AE DC MC V	●	■		
SANGATTE: *Les Dunes* €€ Route Nationale 48, Blériot-Plage. 03 21 34 54 30. Near the Channel Tunnel, this beachside restaurant serves great seafood: try the cassoulet of mussels or cockles flambéed in whisky. & ● *Sep–Jun: Sun D, Mon.*	AE DC MC V	●	■		▨
SARS-POTERIES: *L'Auberge Fleurie* €€€ 67 rue Général de Gaulle. 03 27 61 62 48. Set in pretty countryside, L'Auberge is an ancient, rather grand converted farmhouse. Game, venison, wild boar, and partridge are in abundance in winter. A variety of shellfish also appears on the menu. & ● *Mon; last 2 wks Jan, 2 wks Aug.*	AE DC MC V		■	●	
WIMEREUX: *La Liégeoise* €€€ Digue de Mer. 03 21 32 41 01. At this fish restaurant, a salad of red mullet with balsamic vinegar makes a good start to the meal, followed by turbot with asparagus. & ● *Sun D, Mon L, Feb.*	AE DC MC V	●	■	●	

CHAMPAGNE

AMBONNAY: *Auberge Saint-Vincent* €€ — AE DC MC V
1 rue St Vincent. (03 26 57 01 98.
This elegant restaurant with Louis XIII ceilings is a pleasure to dine in.
The menu is seasonal. & ● *Sun D, Mon; 2 wks Feb, last wk Aug.*

AUBRIVES: *Debette* €€ — AE MC V
2 place Louis Debette. (03 24 41 64 72.
Ardennes specialties here include smoked ham, trout, and game *terrines*. Desserts
are made with fruit from the owner's garden. & ● *Sun D, Mon L; 20 Dec–5 Jan.*

BAR-SUR-AUBE: *Le Cellier aux Moines* € — MC V
Rue du General Vouillemont. (03 25 27 08 01.
The 12th-century vaulted dining room, with roaring fire, adds to the pleasure
of such dishes as *andouillette* gratin with *chaource*. ● *D on Sun–Thu.*

CHALONS-EN-CHAMPAGNE: *Les Ardennes* €€€ — AE V
34 place de la République. (03 26 68 21 42.
The *patron*, M Bouffonais, worked at the Savoy in London in the 1950s. His
restaurant is a fine 17th-century house in this picturesque town. The menu is
exceptionally wide with an extravagant selection of desserts. ● *Sun D, Mon D.*

CHALONS-EN-CHAMPAGNE: *Au Carillon Gourmand* €€€ — MC V
15bis place Monseigneur Tissier. (03 26 64 45 07.
Located in the town center, in the Notre-Dame-en-Vaux district, this friendly place
serves good daily specials. ● *Sun D, Mon, Wed D; 1 wk Feb, 1 wk Apr, 1st 3 wks Aug.*

CHAUMONT: *Bleu Comme Orange* € — AE MC V
11 rue Saint-Louis. (03 25 01 26 87.
Situated in the Old Quarter of Chaumont, this lively restaurant is always
packed with locals at midday. It is essentially a *crêperie*, providing
imaginative combinations of fillings. ● *Sun, Mon D; 3 wks Aug.*

EPERNAY: *L'Auberge Champenoise* € — AE DC MC V
Moussy. (03 26 54 03 48.
After visiting some of the vast champagne cellars in Epernay, this friendly inn
is an excellent place for an inexpensive meal. & ● *1st 2 wks Jan.*

L'EPINE: *Aux Armes de Champagne* €€€€ — AE DC MC V
31 avenue du Luxembourg. (03 26 69 30 30.
This gourmet restaurant situated in a pretty village just north of Châlons-en-
Champagne serves delicious regional specialties. ● *Nov–Mar: Sun D & Mon; Jan.*

JOINVILLE: *Le Soleil d'Or* €€€ — AE DC MC V
9 rue des Capucins. (03 25 94 15 66.
Its monastic interior belies the elegant service and eclectic menu: scallop tart with
sweet basil or chestnut butter. & ● *D on Mon–Sat; last 2 wks Feb, 1 wk Aug, 1 wk Nov.*

LANGRES: *Le Lion d'Or* €€€ — MC V
Rue des Auges. (03 25 87 03 30.
This charming restaurant not only offers good regional food but also a
panoramic view of Lake Liez. ● *Sun D; Jan 15–Feb 9.*

LE MESNIL-SUR-OGER: *Le Mesnil* €€ — MC V
2 rue Pasteur. (03 26 57 95 57.
Just south of Epernay, this gourmet restaurant is situated in one of the
prettiest villages in Champagne, amid vineyards. The *patron* is happy to show
diners around his cellars. & ● *Wed L; Jan 21–Feb 5, Aug 15–Sep 5.*

NOGENT-SUR-SEINE: *Au Beau Rivage* €€ — MC V
20 rue Villiers-aux-Choux. (03 25 39 84 22.
Situated at the water's edge, this restaurant has a terrace overlooking the river.
The menu features fish cooked with fresh herbs. ● *Sun D, Mon; 2 wks Feb.*

REIMS: *Le Vigneron* €€ — MC V
Place Paul Jamot. (03 26 79 86 86.
This popular restaurant is particularly recommended for those who wish to sample
dishes with a strong local flavor. A reservation is essential. ● *Sat L, Sun; 2 wks Aug.*

REIMS: *Les Crayères* €€€€€ — AE DC MC V
64 boulevard Vasnier. (03 26 82 80 80.
Specialties in this celebrated restaurant include smoked salmon and cream
of caviar. Tours are also given of its wine cellar. & ● *Mon, Tue L; Dec 26 –Jan 15.*

For key to symbols see back flap

<table>
<tr><td colspan="2">

Average prices for a three-course meal for one, including a half-bottle of house wine, tax and service:

€ under 25€
€€ 25€–35€
€€€ 36€–50€
€€€€ 51€–75€
€€€€€ over 75€

</td><td colspan="2">

CHILDREN'S FACILITIES
Where high chairs and smaller portions are available.
FIXED-PRICE MENU
A good-value fixed-price menu on offer at lunch, dinner or both, often with three or more courses.
GOOD WINE LIST
Denotes a wide range of good wines, or otherwise a more specialised selection of local wines.
OUTDOOR TABLES
Facilities for eating outdoors, often with a good view.
WEEKLY & ANNUAL CLOSURE
Double check as may change (L = lunch; D = dinner).

</td></tr>
</table>

		CREDIT CARDS	CHILDREN'S FACILITIES	FIXED-PRICE MENU	GOOD WINE LIST	OUTDOOR TABLES
REVIGNY-SUR-ORNAIN: *Agape et Maison Forte* €€ Place Henriot du Coudray. 📞 03 29 70 56 00. Traditional ingredients and game are given an innovative twist here: try the *pot au feu de foie gras* with balsamic vinegar. You can also stay here. ♿ ● Sun D.		AE MC V	●	▨		▨
ST-DIZIER: *La Gentilhommière* €€€ 29 rue Jean Jaurès. 📞 03 25 56 32 97. Fillet of lamb wrapped in hazelnut pastry, and *foie gras* in Sauterne, are two favorites here. ♿ ● Sat L, Sun D, Mon; 1st 3 wks Aug.		MC V		▨		
ST-DIZIER: *Hôtellerie du Moulin* €€ Eclaron (9 km from St-Dizier). 📞 03 25 04 17 76. Estimable food cooked with a light touch across a wide range of dishes in this wood-frame logis. ♿ ● Mon L, Sat L, Sun D; 3 wks Jan, mid–end Sep.		MC V	●	▨	●	▨
ST-IMOGES: *La Maison du Vigneron* €€€ Route Nationale 51. 📞 03 26 52 88 00. Both a champagne house and a chic restaurant. Regional dishes are served and diners can accompany their meals with the owner's champagne. ♿ ● Wed.		AE DC MC V	●	▨	●	▨
STE-MÉNEHOULD: *Le Cheval Rouge* € 1 rue Chanzy. 📞 03 26 60 81 04. Overlooking Ste-Ménehould's main square, many interesting dishes are served here, including the local specialty, *pied de cochon*. ♿ ● Sun D, Mon D; mid-Nov–mid-Dec.		AE DC MC V	●	▨		
TROYES: *Le Jardin Gourmand* € 31 rue Paillot de Montabert. 📞 03 25 73 36 13. Set in the heart of the historic quarter, the restaurant occupies a romantic courtyard. This is the place to try the town's specialty – *andouillettes*. ● Sun–Mon L.		MC V	●			▨
TROYES: *Le Bourgogne* €€€ 40 rue Général de Gaulle. 📞 03 25 73 02 67. Le Bourgogne is considered Troyes' finest restaurant. Try the *mousseline* of pike or the iced soufflé with Armagnac. ● Sun D, Mon (& mid-Jun–mid-Oct: Sun L).		MC V		▨	●	

ALSACE AND LORRAINE

		CREDIT CARDS	CHILDREN'S FACILITIES	FIXED-PRICE MENU	GOOD WINE LIST	OUTDOOR TABLES
COLMAR: *Le Caveau Saint-Pierre* € 24 rue de la Herse. 📞 03 89 41 99 33. Reached by a boardwalk running alongside a canal in Colmar's pretty "Little Venice." On weekends in winter, the specialty to choose is the classic *baeckoff* (stew). ● Sun D, Mon, Fri L; Jan.		MC V	●	▨		▨
COLMAR: *La Maison des Têtes* €€€ 19 rue des Têtes. 📞 03 89 24 43 43. The façade of this 17th-century brasserie is a classified historic monument. Serves traditional Alsace fare such as *choucroute*. ♿ ● Sun D, Mon, Feb.		AE DC MC V	●	▨	●	▨
DOLE: *Les Templiers* €€€ 35 Grande Rue. 📞 03 84 82 78 78. Adventurous dishes served in a truly sumptuous Gothic setting, and all at reasonable prices. ● Sat L, Sun D, Mon.		AE DC MC V	●	▨		
HAGUENAU: *Restaurant Barberousse* €€€ 8 place Barberousse. 📞 03 88 73 31 09. Astonishingly good value, the lunchtime menu particularly. The dishes are unpretentious local fare: homemade *foie gras* and *terrines*, *choucroute* with meat or fish and good hot desserts. ♿ ● Sun D, Mon, Tue D; Jul 20–Aug 15.		MC V	●	▨		▨
MARLENHEIM: *Le Cerf* €€€€€ 30 rue du Général de Gaulle. 📞 03 88 87 73 73. This fine restaurant likes customers to arrive hungry, for its rich Alsatian cuisine – the portions are immense. Vegetarians are welcomed. ♿ ● Tue–Wed.		AE DC MC V	●	▨	●	▨

METZ: *Le Bistrot des Sommeliers* €€ | MC V
10 rue Pasteur. (03 87 63 40 20.
The day's menu is dreamed up according to what the market has to offer. The wine list is impressive and is available by the glass. 🔆 ● *Sat L, Sun.*

METZ: *Restaurant des Roches* €€ | AE DC MC V
29 rue des Roches. (03 87 74 06 51.
Predominantly a fish restaurant, but there are plenty of meat–dishes. The *soufflé glacé* is recommended. ● *Sun D, Mon D.*

MULHOUSE: *Restaurant de la Poste* · €€€ | AE MC V
7 rue Général de Gaulle, Riedisheim. (03 89 44 07 71.
Six generations of chefs have worked to establish the reputation of this fine restaurant. The menu is imaginative. ● *Sun D, Mon, Tue L; 2 wks Feb, 1st 3 wks Aug.*

NANCY: *L'Excelsior* €€€ | AE DC MC V
50 rue Henri Poincaré. (03 83 35 24 57.
Take a step back in time and enjoy a delightful meal in this magnificent listed historic monument. The cuisine, like everything else about this brasserie, is classic French.

RIQUEWIHR: *Au Péché Mignon* €€ | MC V
5 rue de Dinzheim. (03 89 49 04 17.
This rustic restaurant offers robust Alsatian specialties, the food is described as *cuisine grand-mère* – homey, copious, and old-fashioned. ● *Thu.*

SAVERNE: *Taverne Katz* €€ | AE MC V
80 Grand-Rue. (03 88 71 16 56.
The cozy, polished-wood interior provides a perfect setting for traditional food such as *spaetzle* (Alsatian noodles) and *jambonneau braisé* (knuckle of ham).

SÉLESTAT: *Restaurant Jean-Frédèric Edel* €€€€ | AE DC MC V
7 rue des Serruriers. (03 88 92 86 55.
Homemade *foie gras*, and breast of veal in beer with an excellent *choucroute* are two of the specialties here. ● *Sun D, Tue L, Wed; Dec 25 –Jan 2, end Jul–mid-Aug.*

STRASBOURG: *Zum Strissel* €€ | AE DC MC V
5 place de la Grande Boucherie. (03 88 32 14 73.
An old-fashioned wine cellar in a 14th-century building, serving mixed-meat stew, onion tart, and pitchers of Alsatian wines. 🔆 ● *Sun–Mon; 10 days Feb, Jul.*

STRASBOURG: *Au Crocodile* €€€€€ | AE DC MC V
10 rue de l'Outre. (03 88 32 13 02.
This is probably Strasbourg's most exclusive restaurant. Visitors dine in opulent surroundings with every whim attended to. Recommended dishes include pike-perch and innovative fish dishes. ● *Sun–Mon; 3 wks Jul, Dec 25–Jan 2.*

TURCKHEIM: *Auberge du Brand* €€ | AE DC MC V
8 Grand Rue. (03 89 27 06 10.
The cuisine has a regional flavor but it is not as resolutely Alsatian as in the neighboring *winstubs* (winebars). The service is prompt and discreet. 🔆 ● *L on Mon–Sat; 1st 2 wks Jul.*

VERDUN: *Le Coq Hardi* €€€€ | AE DC MC V
8 avenue de la Victoire. (03 29 86 36 36.
This gourmet restaurant is the best in Verdun, a city with few good quality, moderately priced restaurants. ● *Fri.*

NORMANDY

ARGENTAN: *Restaurant d'Argentan* € | MC V
22 rue Beigle. (02 33 36 19 38.
Traditional peasant dishes, including Camembert salad and salmon with cider sauce, are served up here in this friendly restaurant. ● *Tue D–Wed.*

AUDRIEU: *Château d'Audrieu* €€€€ | AE MC V
Audrieu. (02 31 80 21 52.
This 18th-century château was transformed into a luxurious hotel and restaurant in 1976. ● *L on Mon–Fri, Mon D exc hotel guests; Dec–mid-Feb.*

BAYEUX: *Le Lion d'Or* €€€ | AE DC MC V
71 rue St-Jean. (02 31 92 06 90.
This 17th-century inn serves delicious food: unusual duck *foie gras* with honey, or Vire *andouille* (tripe sausage) tart with apple and camembert. ● *Dec 20–Jan 20.*

For key to symbols see back flap

		CREDIT CARDS	CHILDREN'S FACILITIES	FIXED-PRICE MENU	GOOD WINE LIST	OUTDOOR TABLES

Average prices for a three-course meal for one, including a half-bottle of house wine, tax and service:

€ under 25€
€€ 25€–35€
€€€ 36€–50€
€€€€ 51€–75€
€€€€€ over 75€

CHILDREN'S FACILITIES
Where high chairs and smaller portions are available.

FIXED-PRICE MENU
A good-value fixed-price menu on offer at lunch, dinner or both, often with three or more courses.

GOOD WINE LIST
Denotes a wide range of good wines, or otherwise a more specialised selection of local wines.

OUTDOOR TABLES
Facilities for eating outdoors, often with a good view.

WEEKLY & ANNUAL CLOSURE
Double check as may change (L = lunch; D = dinner).

	CC	CF	FP	GW	OT
LE BEC-HELLOUIN: *Restaurant de la Tour* € Place Guillaume-le-Conquérant. (02 32 44 86 15. It's best to reserve in advance to sample the traditional Norman cuisine here. Duck – including *foie gras* – is the house specialty. ● *Wed D, Thu; last 2 wks Nov.*	MC V	●	■		
CHAMPEAUX: *Au Marquis de Tombelaine* € Route de Carolles. (02 33 61 85 94. Dishes to go for are homemade *foie gras*, oysters and lobster Thermidor, served with a bottle of Burgundy and ending with cheese. ● *Tue D–Wed; Jan, last wk Nov.*	MC V	●	■	●	
CHERBOURG: *La Cendrée* € 18–20 passage Digard. (02 33 93 67 04. This simple but friendly restaurant offers probably the best value in town. It is popular with the locals and reservation is advisable. ● *Sun–Mon.*	MC V		■		
COSQUEVILLE: *Au Bouquet de Cosqueville* €€ Hameau Remond. (02 33 54 32 81. The specialties include lobster cooked in cider, local fish and shellfish. For dessert try a fresh *crêpe* or *crème brûlée.* & ● *Tue–Wed except in Jul–Aug; Jan.*	AE MC V	●	■	●	●
CRESSERONS: *La Valise Gourmande* €€ 7 route de Lion-sur-Mer. (02 31 37 39 10. Traditional Normandy food in a setting of old beams and oak furniture. Try the cod with *andouille* and cider butter. & ● *Sun D, Mon; 1st 2 wks Mar, last 2 wks Sep.*	MC V	●	■	●	●
DEAUVILLE: *Le Dauphin* €€€€ Le Breuil-en-Auge, Pont l'Evêque. (02 31 65 08 11. A reservation is essential for this much sought-after restaurant, 20 kms from Deauville. The owners spare no effort in making your visit a memorable one, and they take great pride in their cooking. ● *Sun D, Mon; mid-Nov–Dec 7.*	AE MC V		■	●	
DEAUVILLE: *Le Spinnaker* €€€ 52 rue Mirabeau. (02 31 88 24 40. This is one of Normandy's finest fish restaurants. The baked lobster in cider vinegar or turbot with shallots must be sampled. & ● *Mon (& Oct–Mar: Tue); Jan, last 2 wks Nov.*	AE DC MC V		■	●	
DIEPPE: *A la Marmite Dieppoise* €€ 8 rue St Jean. (02 35 84 24 26. Try the *Marmite Dieppoise* here – a tasty combination of fish and shellfish in a cream sauce. ● *Sun D, Mon (& Sep–Jun: Thu D); last wk Nov, 2 wks Dec, 1 wk Jun.*	MC V	●			
DOZULÉ: *Le Pavé d'Auge* €€€ Beuvron-en-Auge. (02 31 79 26 71. The highly talented chef at Le Pavé d'Auge likes to serve food made from local ingredients. The menu is strong on fish, with a assortment of meat and poultry dishes. The cheese platter has a good selection. ● *Mon (& Sep–Jun: Tue); Dec.*	MC V	●	■		
GISORS: *Le Cappeville* €€ 17 rue Cappeville. (02 32 55 11 08. Traditional cooking with local specialties including *camembert millefeuille* or monkfish with *andouille* and cider cream. ● *Wed D, Thu; 1st 2 wks Jan, Sep 1–10.*	AE MC V	●	■	●	
HONFLEUR: *Le Champlain* € 6 place Hamelin. (02 31 89 14 91. Seasonal favorites at this family-run business are scallops in puff pastry with orange butter, and *tombe* (tub gurnard – a Channel fish) with onion fondu and cider. ● *Wed D, Thu; Jan–Feb 10.*	AE MC V		■		
HONFLEUR: *La Ferme St-Siméon* €€€€€ Rue A-Marais. (02 31 81 78 00. It is a delight to enjoy a light lunch here on the terrace. The food is exquisitely prepared, featuring local seafood, poultry, and cheese. ● *Mon, Tue L.*	AE MC V		■	●	■

LA FERTÉ MACÉ: *Auberge de Clouet* €€ AE MC V
Chemin le Clouet. 02 33 37 18 22.
An hour or two spent exploring the delightful, historic market town should end with a meal of local specialties on this floral terrrace. ● *Sun D.*

LOUVIERS: *Le Clos Normand* € DC MC V
16 rue de la Gare. 02 32 40 03 56.
M. Grenot, the owner, loves to prepare food in his attractive 1890's town house. Vegetarian dishes served on request. ● *Sun D, Mon; last 2 wks Aug.*

LYONS-LA-FORÊT: *La Licorne* €€€ AE DC MC V
Place Benserade. 02 32 49 62 02.
The high quality belies the price in this 17th-century inn, where diners eat in front of a massive fireplace. & ● *Mon, Tue L (& Oct–Mar: Sun D); Dec–Jan.*

MONT-ST-MICHEL: *Hôtel Saint-Pierre* € AE DC MC V
Grande-Rue. 02 33 60 14 03.
Lamb grazed on the salt marshes, known as *agneau pré-salé*, features on the menu. Crab and salmon are other favorites in this 15th-century building.

MONT-ST-MICHEL: *La Mère Poulard* €€€€ AE DC MC V
Grande-Rue. 02 33 89 68 68.
Visitors from all over Europe come here to sample the famous *omelette Mère Poulard* cooked in a long-handled pan over a wood fire.

PUTANGES-PONT-ECREPIN: *Hôtel du Lion Verd* €€ MC V
Place de l'Hôtel-de-Ville. 02 33 35 01 86.
The owner is rightly proud of her beef with Camembert cream. Lunch menu is good value. Vegetarian dishes available. ● *Nov–Apr: Sun D & Mon; mid- Dec–Jan.*

ROUEN: *La Marmite* €€ AE MC V
3 rue Florence 02 35 71 75 55.
This attractive restaurant, housed in an 18th-century building, stays open late so guests can enjoy the romantic candle-lit ambience. ● *Sun D, Mon; 1st 2 wks Aug.*

ROUEN: *Restaurant Gill* €€€€ AE DC MC V
9 quai de la Bourse. 02 35 71 16 14.
House specialties include the crayfish salad with chutney, and *Pigeon à la rouennaise*. & ● *Sun D, Mon (& Oct–Apr: Sun L & Tue L); 1st wk Jan & Apr, 1st 3 wks Aug.*

STE-CECILE ACHERIE: *Le Manoir de l'Acherie* € AE MC V
St-Cécile Acherie. 02 33 51 13 87.
Calvados is the flavor here – ham and lamb are cooked in it and the apple tart is flambéed with it. & ● *Sun D (Oct 15–Apr 10), Mon (Sep–Jun); 2wks Feb, 3 wks Nov.*

ST-GERMAIN DE TALLEVENDE: *Auberge Saint-Germain* €€ MC V
Place de l'Eglise. 02 31 68 24 13.
This is an ideal restaurant for families, with a menu of good home-cooking that caters to all tastes, including vegetarian. ● *Sun D, Mon; 2 wks Feb.*

SEES: *Le Gourmand Candide* €€ MC V
14 place du Général de Gaulle. 02 33 27 91 28.
This friendly establishment serves fine Normandy cuisine, including *andouille* with apple and *pommeau*. ● *Mon, Tue D (& Sep–Jun: Sun D); 1st 3 wks Jan.*

THIBERVILLE: *La Levrette* € MC V
10 rue de Lieurey. 02 32 46 80 22.
Plain home cooking at competitive prices is the attractive feature of this friendly place. Try the specialty, scallops Marco Polo. ● *Thu, Sun D; 3 wks Feb, last 2 wks Aug.*

TROUVILLE-SUR-MER: *Brasserie les Vapeurs* €€ AE MC V
160 boulevard Fernand-Moureaux. 02 31 88 15 24.
Situated opposite the fish market, the seafood served here is truly fresh and full of flavor. You will be tempted to come back for more. &

VEULES-LES-ROSES: *Les Galets* €€€ AE MC V V
3 rue Victor Hugo. 02 35 97 61 33.
If you wish to have a meal by the sea, Les Galets is just the place, but you must book. Vegetarian dishes to order. & ● *Tue D, Wed (& Sep–Jun: Tue L); mid-Dec–mid-Jan.*

VILLERS-BOCAGE: *Les Trois Rois* €€ AE DC MC V
2 place Jeanne d'Arc. 02 31 77 00 32.
The dishes are created by the owner from the catch of the day, fresh every morning. ● *Sun D, Mon (& Sep–Jun: Tue L); Jan, last wk Jun.*

For key to symbols see back flap

<table>
<tr><td>

Average prices for a three-course meal for one, including a half-bottle of house wine, tax and service:

€ under 25€
€€ 25€–35€
€€€ 36€–50€
€€€€ 51€–75€
€€€€€ over 75€

</td><td>

CHILDREN'S FACILITIES
Where high chairs and smaller portions are available.
FIXED-PRICE MENU
A good-value fixed-price menu on offer at lunch, dinner or both, often with three or more courses.
GOOD WINE LIST
Denotes a wide range of good wines, or otherwise a more specialised selection of local wines.
OUTDOOR TABLES
Facilities for eating outdoors, often with a good view.
WEEKLY & ANNUAL CLOSURE
Double check as may change (L = lunch; D = dinner).

</td></tr>
</table>

		CREDIT CARDS	CHILDREN'S FACILITIES	FIXED-PRICE MENU	GOOD WINE LIST	OUTDOOR TABLES

BRITTANY

AURAY: *L'Églantine* €€
17 place Saint-Sauveur, Saint-Goustan. ☎ 02 97 56 46 55.
Right on the port of Saint-Goustan, wonderfully fresh fish are presented to clients before being simply prepared and cooked.
Cards: MC V · Children ● · Fixed-price ▨ · Outdoor ▨

AURAY: *La Closerie de Kerdrain* €€€€
20 rue Louis Billet. ☎ 02 97 56 61 27.
First Empire tapestries adorn the dining room of this manor house, where specialties include sea bass, lobster, and scallops. ● Mon, Wed L (all day in winter); 1st 3 wks Mar.
Cards: AE DC MC V · Children ● · Fixed-price ▨ · Good Wine ● · Outdoor ▨

BELLE-ISLE-EN-TERRE: *Le Relais de l'Argoat* €€
9 rue de Guic. ☎ 02 96 43 00 34.
This coaching inn on the edge of a pretty village has two dining rooms with a friendly atmosphere. Excellent cheese. & ● Sep–Jun: Sun D & Mon; Jan.
Cards: MC V · Children ● · Fixed-price ▨

CARANTEC: *Restaurant Patrick Jeffroy* €€€€
20 rue Kelenn. ☎ 02 98 67 00 47.
A magnificent view over Kelenn beach. Specialties include warm lobster salad and grilled oysters in cider sauce. ● Oct–Jun: Sun D–Tue L; 2 wks Jan.
Cards: AE MC V · Children ● · Fixed-price ▨ · Good Wine ●

CONCARNEAU: *La Coquille* €€
1 quai de Moros. ☎ 02 98 97 08 52.
Feast yourself on the very freshest of seafood whilst watching the fishing boats come into port. ● Sun D, Mon; last 2 wks Jan, 2 wks end May/beg Jun.
Cards: AE DC MC V · Children ● · Fixed-price ▨ · Good Wine ●

DINAN: *Chez la Mère Pourcel* €€€
3 place des Merciers. ☎ 02 96 39 03 80.
This restaurant is in a stunning old Gothic building. The menu is seasonal and consistently good, with excellent Loire wines. ● Sun D–Mon (& Tue:Oct–Feb).
Cards: AE DC MC V · Fixed-price ▨ · Good Wine ● · Outdoor ▨

HÉDÉ: *L'Hostellerie du Vieux Moulin* €€
Ancienne route de St-Malo. ☎ 02 99 45 45 70.
Part of a complex built in the 19th century to supply water power, it has views of the ruins of Hédé Castle. Particularly good lunches of scallops, grilled langoustines, and duck. ● Mon L (& Sep–Jun: Mon D, Thu L, Sun); Jan, 1st 2 wks Oct.
Cards: AE MC V · Children ● · Fixed-price ▨ · Outdoor ▨

LE CONQUET: *Le Relais du Vieux Port* €
1 quai Drellach. ☎ 02 98 89 15 91.
You can almost dip your feet in the water while enjoying a crêpe filled with fresh scallops, followed by the *Bonne Maman*, with caramelized apples and cream. &
Cards: MC V · Children ● · Fixed-price ▨ · Outdoor ▨

LORIENT: *Le Neptune* €
15 ave de la Perrière. ☎ 02 97 37 04 56.
Try for a table in the rear dining room with conservatory. The wide choice includes lobster flambé and fricassée of monkfish. ● Sun; 1 wk May, 2 wks Sep.
Cards: AE DC MC V · Children ● · Fixed-price ▨

MORLAIX: *La Marée Bleue* €€
3 rampe St-Melaine. ☎ 02 98 63 24 21.
Standing in the shadow of the viaduct is a first-class restaurant. Customers return often for the flawless fish dishes. ● Sep–Jun: Sun D & Mon; Oct.
Cards: MC V · Children ● · Fixed-price ▨ · Good Wine ●

PAIMPOL: *La Vieille Tour* €€
13 rue de l'Eglise. ☎ 02 96 20 83 18.
This is a friendly, old-fashioned restaurant. Some rare delicacies are served, including ravioli stuffed with crayfish tails or cherry-filled chocolate mousse in raspberry sauce. ● Sep–Jun: Wed, Sun D.
Cards: MC V · Children ● · Fixed-price ▨

PLÉLAN-LE-GRAND: *L'Auberge du Presbytère* €€
Treffendel. ☎ 02 99 61 00 76.
In an old priest's house that has altered little over the centuries, the chef serves poultry and pigeon in several traditional ways. & ● Sun D–Mon (& Tue: Oct–Apr).
Cards: MC V · Children ● · Fixed-price ▨ · Outdoor ▨

PLOMEUR: *Le Relais Bigouden* — €
Rue Pen Allée. (02 98 82 04 79. — MC V
A cheerful and friendly restaurant full of fresh flowers; specialties include lobster in a ragoût (pre-order) and fresh seafood. ● *Nov–Mar: Fri & Sun D.*

PLOUBALAY: *Restaurant de la Gare* — €€€
4 rue Ormelets. (02 96 27 25 16. — AE V
This unassuming restaurant uses the freshest local produce: St-Jacut oysters, marinaded scallops, turbot, John Dory. Leave room for the excellent desserts.
& ● *Mon D, Tue D–Wed (Jul–Aug: Mon L, Tue L, Wed); 2 wks Jan, last wk Jun, 2 wks Oct.*

PONT L'ABBÉ: *Le Relais de Ty-Boutic* — €
Route de Plomeur. (02 98 87 03 90. — MC V
A serious "foodie," the chef has won several prizes. His specialty: langoustines with leeks. Vegetarian dishes to order. ● *Sun D, Mon; mid-Feb–mid-Mar.*

QUIBERON: *Le Relax* — €€
27 boulevard Castéro. (02 97 50 12 84. — AE DC MC V
With lovely ocean views and a pretty garden, you'll find a wide selection of superbly cooked fish here, changing seasonally. & ● *Mon (ex Aug); Jan–mid-Feb.*

QUIMPER: *L'Ambroisie* — €€
49 rue Elie Fréron. (02 98 95 00 02. — AE MC V
A short walk from the cathedral, the interior has Francis Bacon prints on the walls. Fish and desserts are excellent. ● *Sun D, Mon; last wk Jun.*

RENNES: *Le Corsaire* — €€
52 rue d'Antrain. (02 99 36 33 69. — AE DC MC V
With a deservedly good reputation locally, specialties here include braised oxtail and *abalones* (shellfish). ● *Sep–Jun: Sun D & Wed; Jul–Aug: Sun–Mon.*

RENNES: *Le Piano Blanc* — €€
Route de Sainte-Foix. (02 99 31 20 21. — AE MC V
Just outside the town, fish dishes are served under the lime trees in summer, and in front of a roaring fire in winter. & ● *Sat–Sun; 1 wk Aug, 25 Dec–2 Jan.*

ST-BRIEUC: *Amadeus* — €€€
22 rue de Gouët. (02 96 33 92 44. — MC V
In one of this historic town's oldest buildings, it is fish which predominates here – fillet of sole with duck liver is outstanding – and there is a wide range of desserts.
● *Sat L, Sun, Mon L; 2 wks Feb, last 2 wks Aug.*

ST-MALO: *Le Franklin* — €€
4 chaussée du Sillon. (02 99 40 50 93. — MC V
A restaurant overlooking the sea. Specialties include fish cooked with spice. The service is efficient and friendly.

VITRÉ: *La Taverne de l'Ecu* — €€
12 rue Baudrairie. (02 99 75 11 09. — AE MC V
A half-timbered Renaissance house. The fish is excellent, and the bread is homemade. ● *Sep–Jun: Tue D & Wed (& Oct– May: Sun D); 2 wks Feb & 1 wk Nov.*

THE LOIRE VALLEY

AMBOISE: *Le Choiseul* — €€€€
36 quai C.Guinot. (02 47 30 45 45. — AE DC MC V
For asparagus fans, the themed spring menu runs to ice cream with crystallized green asparagus tips. *A la carte* has equally avant-garde dishes. ● *mid-Dec–Jan.*

ANGERS: *La Ferme* — €
2 place Freppel. (02 41 87 09 90. — AE DC V
A hectic restaurant which spills outdoors in summer. Rustic dishes like *poule au pot*, and a friendly *patronne*. & ● *Sun D, Wed; Jul 20–Aug 12, Dec 23–Jan 10.*

ANGERS: *La Salamandre* — €€€
1 boulevard du Maréchal-Foch. (02 41 88 99 55. — AE DC MC
The slightly kitsch interior belies the strength of the food. Sample squid stuffed with courgette or *foie gras* stew with Banyuls. ● *Sun.*

BEAUGENCY: *Le P'tit Bateau* — €€
54 rue du Pont. (02 38 44 56 38. — AE V
Near the château, Le P'tit Bateau is the most appealing restaurant in town. It is popular with the locals and offers fresh fish, game, and wild mushrooms, and regional wines. & ● *Sun D–Tue L; 1 wk Apr, mid-end Aug, 1 wk Nov.*

Average prices for a three-course meal for one, including a half-bottle of house wine, tax and service: € under 25€ €€ 25€–35€ €€€ 36€–50€ €€€€ 51€–75€ €€€€€ over 75€	**CHILDREN'S FACILITIES** Where high chairs and smaller portions are available. **FIXED-PRICE MENU** A good-value fixed-price menu on offer at lunch, dinner or both, often with three or more courses. **GOOD WINE LIST** Denotes a wide range of good wines, or otherwise a more specialised selection of local wines. **OUTDOOR TABLES** Facilities for eating outdoors, often with a good view. **WEEKLY & ANNUAL CLOSURE** Double check as may change (L = lunch; D = dinner).				

	CREDIT CARDS	CHILDREN'S FACILITIES	FIXED-PRICE MENU	GOOD WINE LIST	OUTDOOR TABLES
BLOIS: *L'Orangerie du Château* €€€ 1 avenue Jean Laigret. **(** 02 54 78 05 36. Housed in the castle's former winter garden (a 15th-century conservatory), the fine setting is matched by the food and wine. & ● *Sun D, Wed; mid-Feb–mid-Mar.*	MC V	●	▥	●	▥
BLOIS: *Le Duc de Guise* € 15 place Louis XII. **(** 02 54 78 22 39. A boisterous family-orientated Italian restaurant by the château. Pizzas are cooked in traditional fashion, in wood-fired ovens. ● *Mon (& Oct–May: Tue L).*	DC MC V	●	▥		▥
BOUCHEMAINE: *La Terrasse* €€ La Pointe de Bouchemaine. **(** 02 41 77 14 46. Located in a hamlet on the confluence of the rivers Loire and Maine, this panoramic restaurant offers freshly caught eels, pike-perch, salmon and other freshwater fish. & ● *Oct–Easter: Sun D; Nov 15–30.*	AE MC V	●	▥		
BOURGES: *La Courcillière* € Rue de Babylone. **(** 02 48 24 41 91. By the marshes with a view over the river Yèvre, it's worth the 20-minute walk from town for freshwater fish and local cooking. & ● *Tue D–Wed (& Sun D in winter).*	AE MC V	●	▥		▥
BOURGES: *Le Jardin Gourmand* €€ 15 bis, boulevard Ernest-Renan. **(** 02 48 21 35 91. A gourmet restaurant in an old town house decorated with style. Specialties include homemade sorbets. & ● *Sun D, Mon, Tue L; 2 wks Jul, mid-Dec–mid-Jan.*	AE MC V		▥	●	▥
BOURGUEIL: *L'Auberge la Lande* € 24 rue la Lande. **(** 02 47 97 92 41. This auberge, in an old town house, uses only local produce for its simple but delicious dishes. Good choice of local Loire Valley wines. & ● *Sun D–Mon.*	MC V	●	▥		▥
CHARTRES: *Le Buisson Ardent* €€ 10 rue au Lait. **(** 02 37 34 04 66. Close to the cathedral, in the oldest part of Chartres, the fish specialties and warm *foie gras* served in this restaurant are all extremely tasty. ● *Sun D, Wed.*	MC V	●	▥		
CHARTRES: *Le Grand Monarque* €€€€ 22 place des Epars. **(** 02 37 21 00 72. Within this large 17th-century farmhouse, refurbished in 1987, are both a gourmet restaurant (where the food is variable but can be excellent, with a first-rate wine cellar), and a brasserie with more traditional food. ● *Sun D–Mon.*	AE DC MC V	●	▥	●	▥
CHINON: *Les Années 30* €€ 78 rue Voltaire. **(** 02 47 93 37 18. An elegant little eatery on the way up to the château. Pike-perch in butter and *coq au vin* are served in an airy dining room, or out on the terrace. & ● *Tue L, Wed, Thu L; 2 wks Mar, 1 wk Jun, 2 wks Oct.*	DC MC V	●	▥		▥
CONTRES: *La Botte d'Asperges* €€€ 52 rue Pierre-Henri Mauger. **(** 02 54 79 50 49. Once the asparagus capital of France, asparagus specialties still feature prominently in season, together with homemade smoked *foie gras.* ● *Mon (& Sun D in winter).*	MC V	●	▥		
FAY-AUX-LOGES: *La Fortune du Pot* €€€ 2 chemin du Halage. **(** 02 38 59 56 54. Traditional gourmet cuisine in a former wine depot: *foie gras* specialties followed by honey-caramelized pears in pastry. ● *Sun D, Mon D–Wed; 2 wks Feb, 3 wks summer.*	MC V	●	▥		
FONTEVRAUD-L'ABBAYE: *La Licorne* €€€ Allée Sainte-Catérine. **(** 02 41 51 72 49. The elegant setting and pretty courtyard, plus the seafood ravioli and unusual rhubarb desserts, make this a popular place to dine. ● *Sun D–Mon (& Sep–Apr: Wed D); mid-Dec–mid-Jan.*	AE DC MC V	●	▥		▥

GENNES: *Auberge du Moulin de Sarré* €
Route de Louerre. **(** *02 41 51 81 32.*
The menu in this working watermill includes freshly-caught trout, and *fouées* (warm bread puffs filled with goat's cheese, *rillettes* or beans). & ● *Christmas–mid-Jan.*

	●	■			■

GIEN: *Restaurant La Poularde* €€ AE DC MC V
13 quai de Nice. **(** *02 38 67 36 05.*
Game, such as venison, and old-fashioned vegetables like Jerusalem artichokes are served here, overlooking the Loire River. & ● *Sun D–Mon L; Jan 1–14.*

| AE DC MC V | ● | ■ | | | ■ |

LA BOHALLE: *Auberge de la Gare* € MC V
3 impasse de la Gare. **(** *02 41 80 41 20.*
After a dinner of snails, eel or steak and good local cheeses take a stroll down to the riverbank behind this welcoming inn. &

| MC V | ● | ■ | | | ■ |

LAMOTTE-BEUVRON: *Hôtel Tatin* €€ AE MC V
5 avenue de Vierzon. **(** *02 54 88 00 03.*
The menu of game, pike-perch and local red wine is overshadowed by the famous *tarte Tatin*. ● *Sun D–Mon; 1 wk Jan, 2 wks Feb, 1 wk summer.*

| AE MC V | ● | ■ | ● | | ■ |

LE MANS: *La Cité d'Aleth* € MC V
7 & 9 rue de la Vieille Porte. **(** *02 43 28 73 81.*
A family-run crêperie in Le Vieux Mans, which offers *crêpes* and *galettes* of all descriptions, complemented by salads and fruity desserts. & ● *Tue–Wed L, Sun L.*

| MC V | | ■ | | | |

LE MANS: *Le Grenier à Sel* €€ AE DC MC V
26 place de L'Eperon. **(** *02 43 23 26 30.*
Well-situated for exploring the Old Town, this restaurant specializes in fish served with light sauces. & ● *Sun D, Fri.*

| AE DC MC V | ● | ■ | | | |

LE MANS: *Restaurant La Chamade* € MC V
9 rue Dorée. **(** *02 43 28 22 96.*
The cuisine comes from the southwest, Brittany, Eastern France and Provence. The lunch menu is very good value. ● *Tue D–Wed; 10 days Apr, 2 wks Oct.*

| MC V | ● | ■ | | | ■ |

MONTBAZON: *La Chancelière* €€ MC V
1 place des Marronniers. **(** *02 47 26 00 67.*
A firm favorite with the locals, dishes include rabbit stuffed with *foie gras* or oyster ravioli in champagne. & ● *Sun–Mon; 3 wks Feb, last wk Aug.*

| MC V | ● | ■ | ● | | |

NANTES: *La Taverne de Maitre Kanter* € AE MC V
1 place Royale. **(** *02 40 48 55 28.*
Part of a reliable chain, this Alsatian tavern excels with its offerings of *choucroute* (sauerkraut) and cold meats. Try the beers, too. &

| AE MC V | ● | ■ | | | ■ |

NANTES: *La Cigale* €€ MC V
4 place Graslin. **(** *02 51 84 94 94.*
The interior of this Belle Epoque brasserie is decorated with tiles and gilding; the quality and choice of cuisine are also exceptional.

| MC V | ● | ■ | ● | | ■ |

NANTES: *L'Atlantic* € AE DC MC V
26 bd Stalingrad. **(** *02 40 74 00 72.*
Good home cooking is on offer at this simple restaurant not far from the railway station. ● *Sat.*

| AE DC MC V | ● | ■ | | | |

ORLÉANS: *La Petite Marmite* €€ AE MC V
178 rue de Bourgogne. **(** *02 38 54 23 83.*
This small restaurant serves good traditional cuisine. Try the rabbit *orléannaise*, with a honey sauce, or the goat's cheese *feuilleté*. ● *Mon–Sat L.*

| AE MC V | | ■ | | | |

ORLÉANS: *La Chancellerie* €€ AE MC V
27 place du Martroi. **(** *02 38 53 57 54.*
This lively brasserie is on the town's main square and is always busy. Staple brasserie fare is enlivened by the wines. There is a separate restaurant. & ● *Sun.*

| AE MC V | ● | ■ | ● | | ■ |

ORLÉANS: *Les Antiquaires* €€€ AE MC V
2 rue au Lin. **(** *02 38 53 52 35.*
A popular place with locals for its inventive cuisine. In season, Sologne game is served, including the house specialty: young partridge casserole. ● *Sun D–Mon.*

| AE MC V | ● | ■ | | | |

SACHÉ: *Auberge du XII Siécle* €€€ MC V
1 rue Principal. **(** *02 47 26 88 77.*
In a listed building in the center of town, regional specialties and *escargots* are on the menu. & ● *Sun D–Tue L; last 3 wks Jan, 1st wk May & Jun.*

| MC V | ● | ■ | ● | | ■ |

		CHILDREN'S FACILITIES	FIXED-PRICE MENU	GOOD WINE LIST	OUTDOOR TABLES

Average prices for a three-course meal for one, including a half-bottle of house wine, tax and service:
€ under 25€
€€ 25€–35€
€€€ 36€–50€
€€€€ 51€–75€
€€€€€ over 75€

CHILDREN'S FACILITIES
Where high chairs and smaller portions are available.
FIXED-PRICE MENU
A good-value fixed-price menu on offer at lunch, dinner or both, often with three or more courses.
GOOD WINE LIST
Denotes a wide range of good wines, or otherwise a more specialised selection of local wines.
OUTDOOR TABLES
Facilities for eating outdoors, often with a good view.
WEEKLY & ANNUAL CLOSURE
Double check as may change (L = lunch; D = dinner).

	CREDIT CARDS	CHILDREN'S FACILITIES	FIXED-PRICE MENU	GOOD WINE LIST	OUTDOOR TABLES
SAUMUR: *Auberge St-Pierre* € 6 place St-Pierre. 02 41 51 26 25. On a square near the château, its regional specialties include *sandre au Saumur Champigny*. ● Mon (& Sep–Jun: Sun).	AE MC V	●	▨		▨
TOURS: *L'Atelier Gourmand* € 37 rue Etienne-Marcel. 02 47 38 59 87. The specialties at this welcoming restaurant include goat cheese and sweet pepper flan, and spare rib of pork with spices. & ● mid-Dec–Jan 5.	AE MC V		▨	●	▨
TOURS: *Chez Jean-Michel/Le Charolais* €€ 123 rue Colbert. 02 47 20 80 20. A short menu of traditional dishes complements the excellent range of wine, by the glass, in this lively wine bar. & ● Sat–Sun; 1 wk Christmas, 3 wks Aug.	MC V		▨	●	
TOURS: *L'Arche de Meslay* €€ Milletière Zone Industrielle. 02 47 29 00 07. Well worth a detour despite the unpromising address. Try the *bouillabaisse tourangelle* and the almond cookie with fruit. & ● Sun–Mon; 3 wks Aug.	AE MC V	●	▨	●	
TOURS: *La Roche Le Roy* €€€€ 55 route de St-Avertin. 02 47 27 22 00. A rather formal Michelin-starred establishment in a romantic manor house. The emphasis is on seasonal fish and game. ● Sun–Mon; 1st 3 wks Aug.	AE DC MC V	●	▨	●	▨
TOURS: *Jean Bardet* €€€€€ 57 rue Groison. 02 47 41 41 11. The gastronomic temple of the Loire. With two Michelin stars and a dazzling wine list, diners revel in lobster, scallops and salmon. Prices are better not taken into consideration!	AE DC MC V	●	▨	●	▨
VENDOME: *Le Petit Bilboquet* €€ Ancienne route de Tours. 02 54 77 16 60. Most of the dishes are traditional here, such as duck with a honey sauce – but just wait for the fantastic array of desserts. ● Sun D–Mon, Thu; 3 wks Aug.	AE MC V	●	▨		▨
VILLANDRY: *Domaine de la Giraudière* € Route de Druye. 02 47 50 08 60. A working farm for a countrified lunch. The food is all home-produced: pâtés, quiches, omelettes with truffle or goat cheese ice cream. & ● Nov 11–Mar 15.	MC V	●	▨		▨
VOUVRAY: *La Cave Martin* € 66 vallée Coquette. 02 47 52 62 18. Carved into the rock, this restaurant has a rustic menu of *andouillettes* (tripe sausages), duck and salads. ● Sun D–Mon; Dec.	MC V	●	▨		▨

BURGUNDY AND FRANCHE-COMTÉ

	CREDIT CARDS	CHILDREN'S FACILITIES	FIXED-PRICE MENU	GOOD WINE LIST	OUTDOOR TABLES
BEAUNE: *La Bouzerotte* €€ Bouze les Beaune. 03 80 26 01 37. In winter, a roaring fire makes this the cosiest place in Burgundy. In summer, enjoy dining on the terrace. The hearty regional dishes are all cooked to order. ● Mon–Tue; Feb 10–Mar 1, 1 wk Sep; Dec 24–Jan 1.	MC V	●	▨		▨
BEAUNE: *La Ciboulette* €€ 69 rue Lorraine. 03 80 24 70 72. The basic decor is in contrast with the standard of bistro cooking, which is the best value in Beaune. Solid, simple dishes. ● Mon–Tue; 3 wks Feb, 2 wks Aug.	MC V		▨		
BEAUNE: *Le Gourmandin* €€€ 8 place Carnot. 03 80 24 07 88. A stainless steel modern interior is warmed by the buzzing crowds. The chef provides good, satisfying bistro cooking like *boeuf bourguignon*.	MC V	●	▨		▨

BEAUNE: *Les Coquines*   €€€   AE DC MC V
Ladoix Serrigny. 03 80 26 43 58.
Feast on solid Burgundy cooking, with the emphasis on quantity.
Located in a vineyard, the wines are exceptional here. ● Wed–Thu; Dec 25–Jan 2.

BEAUNE: *Jean Crotet*   €€€€€   AE DC MC V
Route de Combertault, Levernois. 03 80 24 73 58.
"Serious" cuisine is served up in a beautiful old mansion. The Bresse
chicken and Bourgogne snails are carefully cooked. ● Tue–Wed L.

CHAGNY: *Château de Bellecroix*   €€€€   AE DC MC V
Route Nationale 6. 03 85 87 13 86.
This charming mansion was once the property of the Order of the Knights of
Malta and boasts a Neo-Gothic dining room. Local dishes are a specialty
and the desserts are mouth-watering. ● Wed; Dec 20–Feb 15.

CHAGNY: *Lameloise*   €€€€€   AE DC MC V
36 place d'Armes. 03 85 87 65 65.
The cheapest Michelin three-star restaurant in France, this family-run place
is not in the slightest pretentious. It exudes warmth and offers classic Burgundy cooking, done to perfection. ● Tue L, Wed, Thu L; Dec 20–Jan 15.

CHATEAUNEUF: *La Fontaine*   €€   AE MC V
Chateauneuf. 03 85 26 26 87.
An extravagant pink and pistachio mosaic interior sets the scene for inventive
interpretations of traditional dishes. ● Tue D, Wed (& Oct–Mar: Sun D); Jan.

CHATEAUNEUF: *Hostellerie du Château*   €€€   AE DC MC V
Chateauneuf. 03 80 49 22 00.
Set in a picturesque medieval village, this modestly priced inn is simple
and welcoming, as is its food. ● Mon–Tue; Dec–Jan.

DIJON: *Le Bistrot des Halles*   €   MC V
10 rue Bannelier. 03 80 49 94 15.
At lunchtime, this bistro is roaring. Next to the market, it attracts all
sorts of food merchants and local business people, who come here
to enjoy meat pie, *jambon persillé* and *boeuf bourgignon*. ● Sun–Mon.

DIJON: *Le Chabrot*   €€€   AE V
36 rue Monge. 03 80 30 69 61.
The cosy interior and chatty owner make this restaurant as popular as
the good fixed-price menu. Burgundy wine is served by the glass. ● Sun.

DIJON: *La Chouette*   €€   MC V
1 rue de la Chouette. 03 80 30 18 10.
An exponent of "old school" cuisine, the chef has injected new life
into classics such as snails and salmon. Huge cellar
of Burgundy wines.

DIJON: *Jean-Pierre Billoux*   €€€€   AE DC MC V
13 place de la Libération. 03 80 38 05 05.
Run by the most famous chef in Dijon, its cooking effectively combines
rustic traditional ingredients with novel flavours. ● Sun D, Mon; 1 wk Aug.

FONTANGY: *Ferme Auberge de la Morvandelle*   €   AE MC V
Précy-sous-Thil. 03 80 84 33 32.
This is a working farm, open to guests only at the weekend. Reserve ahead
to experience chicken, guinea fowl and homemade desserts. ● Dec–Mar.

GEVREY-CHAMBERTIN: *Le Bon Bistrot*   €€€   MC V
Rue de Chambertin. 03 80 34 33 20.
Mouthwatering Burgundy delicacies are served at very reasonable prices for
this region. On fine days, dine on the terrace. ● Sun D, Mon; 2 wks Feb, Aug 1–15.

GEVREY-CHAMBERTIN: *Chez Guy*   €€   MC V
3 place de la Mairie. 03 80 58 51 51.
Local cuisine such as *joue de boeuf*, cooked for five hours in red wine. A
pleasant terrace for the summer. ● Wed (& Oct–Apr: Tue); 2 wks Feb.

GEVREY-CHAMBERTIN: *Les Millésimes*   €€€€€   AE MC V
25 rue de l'Eglise. 03 80 51 84 24.
This family concern, in a wine-making cellar, offers friendly service, excellent
cuisine and wonderful wines. Veal, lobster, truffles and a superb cheeseboard
make it a firm favorite with all who visit. ● Sun L, Tue–Wed L; Dec 10–Jan 25.

Average prices for a three-course meal for one, including a half-bottle of house wine, tax and service:
€ under 25€
€€ 25€–35€
€€€ 36€–50€
€€€€ 51€–75€
€€€€€ over 75€

CHILDREN'S FACILITIES
Where high chairs and smaller portions are available.
FIXED-PRICE MENU
A good-value fixed-price menu on offer at lunch, dinner or both, often with three or more courses.
GOOD WINE LIST
Denotes a wide range of good wines, or otherwise a more specialised selection of local wines.
OUTDOOR TABLES
Facilities for eating outdoors, often with a good view.
WEEKLY & ANNUAL CLOSURE
Double check as may change (L = lunch; D = dinner).

	CREDIT CARDS	CHILDREN'S FACILITIES	FIXED-PRICE MENU	GOOD WINE LIST	OUTDOOR TABLES
LA CROIX-BLANCHE: *Le Relais Mâconnais* €€€ Berze la Ville. 03 85 36 60 72. Burgundy beef with red Mâcon wine, and sliced duck liver in strawberry vinegar are typical of this acclaimed restaurant. Mon L (& Oct–Jun: Mon D & Sun); Jan.	AE DC MC V	●	▥		▥
MEURSAULT: *Relais de la Diligence* €€ 23 rue de la Gare. 03 80 21 21 32. In a drab location by an old station, the Relais bulges with locals on Sunday lunchtimes. The quantity and quality of dishes such as *tourte* and *boeuf bourguignon* is superb. Nov–mid-Jun: Tue D, Wed; Dec 12–Jan 20.	AE DC MC V	●	▥	●	▥
NITRY: *La Beursaudière* €€€ Chemin de Ronde. 03 86 33 69 69. The staff wear peasant costume. A full four-course meal – plainly presented but very appetizing – is served at a reasonable price. Oct–Easter: Mon D.	AE DC MC V	●	▥		▥
PIERRE PERTHUIS: *Les Deux Ponts* €€€ Pierre Perthuis. 03 86 32 31 31. This freshly renovated old inn on the Compostela pilgrimage route serves a varied menu with the freshest produce in season. Mon (& Oct–mid-Apr: Tue).	MC V	●	▥		▥
QUARRÉ-LES-TOMBES: *Auberge de l'Atre* €€€€ Les Lavaults. 03 86 32 20 79. The decorative interior of this restaurant in the Morvan region contrasts with the rustic simplicity of the building. It is known locally to offer the best value in its price range. Tue D, Wed; Feb, Jun 25–Jul 6.	AE DC MC V	●	▥		▥
RABOLIOT: *Le Raboliot* € Place Marché. 02 38 97 44 52. In a village just off the A6, the style here is an eclectic mixture of Corsican and French cooking, with hefty portions of game in season. Lunchtime only.	MC V	●	▥		
SAINTE-MAGNANCE: *Auberge des Cordoix* €€ Sainte Magnance. 03 86 33 11 79. In this old staging post, good simple local cuisine: *oeufs en meurette* or beef with a morel (mushroom) sauce. Tue–Wed; 3wks Jan, 1st wk Jun, 1st wk Nov.	MC V	●	▥		▥
ST-LAURENT-SUR-SAÔNE: *Le St-Laurent* €€ 1 quai Bouchacourt. 03 85 39 29 19. 1900s kitsch fills George Blanc's city bistro, which serves adventurous versions of local specialties. The white Mâcon wine is good value.	AE DC MC V	●	▥		▥
ST-PÈRE-SOUS-VÉZELAY: *L'Espérance* €€€€€ St-Père-sous-Vézelay. 03 86 33 39 10. Perhaps the greatest eating in Burgundy. The dining room opens onto a terrace with superb views. Marc Meneau, one of France's finest chefs, turns traditional dishes into modern classics. Tue L (& mid-Oct–mid-Jun: Tue D, Wed L); Feb.	AE DC MC V		▥	●	▥
SAULIEU: *La Poste* €€ 1 rue Grillot. 03 80 64 05 67. This is a former coaching inn with well-preserved charm. Sample *boeuf Charolais*, along with good local wines.	AE DC MC V	●	▥	●	▥
SAULIEU: *La Côte d'Or* €€€€€ 2 rue d'Argentine. 03 80 90 53 53. Old-fashioned decor misleads here. The chef serves up imaginative interpretations of traditional dishes such as pike-perch with a shallot fondu and wine. Very sumptuous with an extensive wine list.	AE DC MC V	●	▥		
SEMUR-EN-AUXOIS: *Les Minimes* €€€ 39 rue de Vaux. 03 80 97 26 86. Simple, traditional, regional cuisine in a no-frills, bistro-style interior, combine with a friendly welcome here. Sun D, Mon.	MC V	●	▥		

SENS: *Hôtel de Paris et de la Poste* €€€
97 rue de la République. 📞 03 86 65 17 43.
Run by the same family for three generations, diners watch as roasts are carved, and desserts are flambéed at the table. ● *Sun D–Mon L; 2 wks Jan, 2 wks Aug.*

	AE			
DC	●	▦		▦
MC				
V				

TOURNUS: *Restaurant Greuze* €€€€€
1 rue A Thibaudet. 📞 03 85 51 09 11.
Here's the place to enjoy some of the best classic cooking in France, and the restaurant itself is a monument to a bygone age, but it is not without its surprises, including several exquisite dishes featuring raw fish. 🖔 ● *mid–end Dec*

AE	●	▦	●	
DC				
MC				
V				

VILLARS-FONTAINE: *Auberge du Coteau* €€
Villars-Fontaine, D35 W of Nuits St-Georges. 📞 03 80 61 10 50.
Set among the vineyards of the Haute-Côtes de Nuits, this cozy inn serves hearty Burgundy fare at great prices. ● *Tue D, Wed; last 2 wks Feb, Aug 15–Sep 7.*

| MC | ● | ▦ | | ▦ |
| V | | | | |

VILLENEUVE-SUR-YONNE: *Auberge la Lucarne aux Chouettes* €€€
Quai Bretoche. 📞 03 86 87 18 26.
Renovated by actress Leslie Caron, this restaurant has a lovely setting by the river Yonne. The staff try very hard to please. 🖔 ● *Sun D, Mon; mid-Nov–mid-Dec.*

| MC | ● | ▦ | | ▦ |
| V | | | | |

VONNAS: *L'Ancienne Auberge* €€€
Place du Marché. 📞 04 74 50 90 50.
The clientele is often wealthy Parisians rather than locals. Fancier and more expensive than most bistros, it is still well worth a visit. 🖔 ● *Jan.*

AE	●	▦		▦
DC				
MC				
V				

VONNAS: *Georges Blanc* €€€€€
Vonnas. 📞 04 74 50 90 90.
A popular shrine of cooking (three Michelin stars), with smooth service in a dining room crammed with antiques. The inventive menu includes fish and game. 🖔 ● *Mon–Tue, Wed L; Jan.*

AE	●	▦	●	
DC				
MC				
V				

THE MASSIF CENTRAL

AUMONT-AUBRAC: *Restaurant Prouhèze* €€€
2 route du Languedoc. 📞 04 66 42 80 07.
The award-winning chef uses only the freshest ingredients to create elegant and unusual flavors. 🖔 ● *Sun D, Mon, Tue L (Jul–Aug: Mon L only); Nov–Mar.*

AE	●	▦		
MC				
V				

AURILLAC: *La Reine Margot* €€
19 rue Guy-de-Veyre. 📞 04 71 48 26 46.
The place to sample the rustic dishes of the Auvergne, with high-quality hams, pork and beef. ● *Sun D, Mon; 1st wk Jan, last wk Jun–1st wk Jul, last wk Aug.*

| MC | ● | ▦ | | |
| V | | | | |

BESSE-EN-CHANDESSE: *Hostellery du Beffroy* €€€
26 rue de l'Abbé Blot. 📞 04 73 79 50 08.
In this former guardsroom, chef Thierry Legros performs his magic. Try the *mille feuille de Panis* or the sea bream with a root vegetable sauce. ● *Mon–Tue; Nov–Dec.*

AE		▦	●	
DC				
MC				
V				

BOUSSAC: *Le Relais Creusois* €€
Route de la Châtre. 📞 05 55 65 02 20.
Luxurious cuisine, though not surroundings. Desserts are exquisite, as are the Bordeaux wines. Book for dinner. ● *Sep–Jun: Tue D–Wed; Jan–Feb, 1 wk Jun.*

| MC | ● | ▦ | | ▦ |
| V | | | | |

CLERMONT-FERRAND: *Le Chardonnay* €
1 place Philippe-Marcombes. 📞 04 73 90 18 28.
As well as enjoying hearty Auvergne cuisine, wine-lovers can choose from the wide range of superb wines, direct from the producers, many of which can be sampled by the glass. ● *Sat L, Sun, public hols.*

| V | ● | ▦ | ● | ▦ |

CLERMONT-FERRAND: *Clos Maréchal* €
51 rue Bonnabaud. 📞 04 73 93 59 69.
The new chef is gaining confidence and making tasty salads, duck and a range of delicious desserts. 🖔 ● *Sat–Sun.*

AE	●	▦		▦
MC				
V				

ESPALION: *Le Méjane* €€
8 rue Méjane. 📞 05 65 48 22 37.
Exceptionally good value menu with dishes like *fouace* stuffed with *foie gras* or pig's trotter terrine. 🖔 ● *Sun D (& Sep–Jun: Mon L, Wed, Jul–Aug: Mon); Feb–Mar.*

AE	●	▦		
DC				
MC				
V				

LAGUIOLE: *Michel Bras* €€€€€
Route de l'Aubrac. 📞 05 65 51 18 20.
A wall of glass overlooks the Aubrac countryside from this 3-star hilltop restaurant. The early-vegetable stew is excellent. 🖔 ● *Nov–early Apr: Mon–Wed L.*

AE	●	▦	●	
DC				
MC				
V				

Average prices for a three-course meal for one, including a half-bottle of house wine, tax and service:
€ under 25€
€€ 25€–35€
€€€ 36€–50€
€€€€ 51€–75€
€€€€€ over 75€

CHILDREN'S FACILITIES
Where high chairs and smaller portions are available.
FIXED-PRICE MENU
A good-value fixed-price menu on offer at lunch, dinner or both, often with three or more courses.
GOOD WINE LIST
Denotes a wide range of good wines, or otherwise a more specialised selection of local wines.
OUTDOOR TABLES
Facilities for eating outdoors, often with a good view.
WEEKLY & ANNUAL CLOSURE
Double check as may change (L = lunch; D = dinner).

	CREDIT CARDS	CHILDREN'S FACILITIES	FIXED-PRICE MENU	GOOD WINE LIST	OUTDOOR TABLES
LIMOGES: *Philippe Redon* €€ 3 rue d'Aguesseau. 05 55 34 66 22. First-class local ingredients are used in conventional but well-cooked dishes. The wines are good value. ● *Sat L–Mon L.*	AE MC V	●	■	●	
MONTSALVY: *Auberge Fleurie* € Place du Barry. 04 71 49 20 02. A friendly village inn with a chef who prepares wonderfully imaginative dishes made with the best local produce. & ● *mid-Jan–mid-Feb.*	MC V	●	■	●	■
MURAT: *Le Jarrousset* €€ Route Nationale 122. 04 71 20 10 69. This is a discreet, unfussy restaurant. The chef uses local ingredients like green lentils and "free-range" veal, cooked to perfection. & ● *Mon, Wed; Jan.*	MC V	●	■	●	■
RODEZ: *Le St-Amans* €€ 12 rue de la Madeleine. 05 65 68 03 18. Traditional cooking with sophistication – pigeon flavored with cocoa, *aligot* (mashed potato and *tomme*) with roquefort sauce. & ● *Sun D, Mon; Mar.*	MC V	●	■		
ROYAT: *La Belle Meunière* €€ 25 avenue de la Vallée. 04 73 35 80 17. The chef, Jean-Claude Bon, won a Gault Millau award for his repertoire of regional dishes. The menu is regularly updated, but the classics include duck *foie gras* with lentils and red wine. & ● *Sat L, Sun D, Mon; last 2 wks Feb, Nov 1–21.*	AE DC V	●	■		■
ST-ENIMIE: *Château de la Caze* €€€ D907 bis, route des Gorges du Tarn. 04 66 48 51 01. This 15th-century castle set in extensive grounds near the river Tarn is an idyllic gastronomic stopover. & ● *Thu L (& Wed out of season); Nov 11–Easter.*	AE DC MC V	●	■		■
ST-ETIENNE: *Nouvelle* €€€ 30 rue St-Jean. 04 77 32 32 60. Elegant setting and attentive staff as well as the culinary treats make this a very popular restaurant. Reserving ahead is advised to ensure a chance to sample the inventive cuisine. ● *Sun D–Mon; 1st 2 wks Jan, 1st 3 wks Aug.*	AE MC V	●	■		
ST-JEAN-EN-VAL: *La Bergerie* €€ Sarpoil. 04 73 71 02 54. This restaurant is a local favorite, so reserving is essential in the evening. Choose from an ever-changing, inventive menu. & ● *Sun D, Mon; 1st 3 wks Jan.*	AE MC V	●	■		
ST-JULIEN-CHAPTEUIL: *Vidal* €€ Place du Marché. 04 71 08 70 50. Top quality local produce is served here, and the menus change according to the season. & ● *Mon D (& Sep–Jun: Sun D & Tue); mid-Jan–Feb.*	AE MC V	●	■	●	
VICHY: *La Veranda* €€ 3 place Joseph-Aletti. 04 70 31 78 77. Part of the Aletti Palace Hotel, La Veranda serves traditional cooking and regional cheeses in modern surroundings. &	AE DC MC V	●	■		■

THE RHÔNE VALLEY AND FRENCH ALPS

	CREDIT CARDS	CHILDREN'S FACILITIES	FIXED-PRICE MENU	GOOD WINE LIST	OUTDOOR TABLES
AIX-LES-BAINS: *Le Salon d'Elvire* €€€ 20 blvd Bertholiet. 04 79 88 04 38. Dine in full view of the spectacular Dent du Chat mountain. Specialties include a *vivier de homards* (lobster extravaganza). ● *Mon.*	MC V	●	■		■
BOURG-EN-BRESSE: *Chez Blanc* €€ 19 place Bernard. 04 74 45 29 11. The local specialty, *Bresse* chicken, is perfection, as are the frogs' legs and the grilled sea bream. &	AE DC MC V	●	■	●	■

CHAMBÉRY: *La Chaumière* €€ | AE MC V

14 rue Denfert-Rochereau. **(** 04 79 33 16 26.
A cozy dining room that serves good quality traditional dishes. The
fish, duck, and *foie gras* are particular bargains. 🔆 ● *Sun.*

CHAMBÉRY: *L'Essentiel* €€€€ | AE DC MC V

183 place de la Gare. **(** 04 79 96 97 27.
Talented young chef Jean-Michel Bouvier creates generous specialties such
as *canette de Bresse* cooked in honey. ● *Sat L, Sun.*

CHAMONIX: *Le Hameau Albert 1er* €€€€€ | AE DC MC V

119 impasse Montenvers. **(** 04 50 53 05 09.
The superb cooking of chef Pierre Carrier at this two-Michelin-star
restaurant is matched by the wonderful views over Mont Blanc.
The *foie gras* is especially recommended. 🔆 ● *Wed, Thu L; 2 wks May, Nov.*

CHAMONIX: *L'Impossible* €€€ | MC V

9 chemin du Cry. **(** 04 50 53 20 36.
Originally a farmhouse, the rustic dining room is warmed by a huge fire. There
is an emphasis on cheese dishes like traditional *raclette* and fondue. Entrecôte
and tournedos steaks are grilled in the fireplace. ● *May–Oct: Tue; Nov–1st wk Dec.*

COLLONGES-AU-MONT-D'OR: *Paul Bocuse* €€€€€ | AE DC MC V

40 rue de la Plage. **(** 04 72 42 90 90.
Try specialties like black truffle soup with pastry and Bresse poultry with
cream and morels. The wines are also of a high standard. 🔆

COURCHEVEL: *La Bergerie* €€€€€ | AE MC V

Route du Nogentil. **(** 04 79 08 24 70.
Popular with the rich and famous, this two-tiered restaurant has dancing on the
ground floor, lunches and drinks served upstairs. ● *Sun D, Mon D.*

COURCHEVEL: *Le Chabichou* €€€€€ | AE DC MC V

Quartier des Chenus. **(** 04 79 08 00 55.
Reserve seats by the huge windows to enjoy views of the mountains.
The cuisine is creative and exotic at one of the most popular (but
expensive) restaurants in this extensive resort. ● *May–Jun, Sep–Oct.*

EVIAN-LES-BAINS: *Savoy* €€ | AE MC V

17 quai Charles Besson. **(** 04 50 83 15 00.
The restaurant offers views of the lake and across into Switzerland. The
Savoyard specialties include *fondue* and *gratin dauphinois.* ● *Nov–Mar.*

GRENOBLE: *Amerindia* €€ | MC V

4 place des Gordes. **(** 04 76 51 58 39.
A bright and cheerful restaurant on a South American theme, with an enjoyable
choice of vegetarian options on the menu. ● *Sun (& Oct–Apr: Mon); last wk Dec.*

GRENOBLE: *Le Berlioz* €€ | AE DC MC V

4 rue de Strasbourg. **(** 04 76 56 22 39.
Housed in an 18th-century mansion, this restaurant features a different
seasonal menu with regional specialties each month. 🔆 ● *Sun; Aug.*

LYON: *Le Bouchon aux Vins* €€ | AE MC V

62 rue Mercière. **(** 04 78 38 47 40.
A very popular restaurant serving regional cuisine. Try the
charcuterie and *l'assiette du bouchon* or selection of specialties. 🔆

LYON: *Le Mercière* €€ | AE MC V

56 rue Mercière. **(** 04 78 37 67 35.
A busy, top-value restaurant where booking is essential. The fixed-
price menu provides very substantial dishes, and the *à la carte* is a
rare treat. 🔆

LYON: *Léon de Lyon* €€€€€ | AE MC V

1 rue Pléney. **(** 04 72 10 11 12.
The expert chef and owner serves local food with a modern twist in a
two-story building set on the Presqu'Île in the heart of the city. The menu
changes ten times a year. 🔆 ● *Sun, Mon (& Apr–Sep: Sat L); 1st 3 wks Aug.*

LYON: *La Tour Rose* €€€€€ | AE DC MC V

22 rue du Boeuf. **(** 04 78 37 25 90.
In a Renaissance convent, the chef concentrates on flavorsome fish
and vegetables, also providing a huge cheeseboard and good wines. ● *Sun.*

Average prices for a three-course meal for one, including a half-bottle of house wine, tax and service:
€ under 25€
€€ 25€–35€
€€€ 36€–50€
€€€€ 51€–75€
€€€€€ over 75€

CHILDREN'S FACILITIES Where high chairs and smaller portions are available.
FIXED-PRICE MENU A good-value fixed-price menu on offer at lunch, dinner or both, often with three or more courses.
GOOD WINE LIST Denotes a wide range of good wines, or otherwise a more specialised selection of local wines.
OUTDOOR TABLES Facilities for eating outdoors, often with a good view.
WEEKLY & ANNUAL CLOSURE Double check as may change (L = lunch; D = dinner).

	Price	CREDIT CARDS	CHILDREN'S FACILITIES	FIXED-PRICE MENU	GOOD WINE LIST	OUTDOOR TABLES
MEGÈVE: *Le Chamoix* Place de l'Eglise. 04 50 21 25 01. A popular restaurant in the center of town, serving regional specialties like *fondue savoyarde.* ● Wed–Thu L; May–Jun, Nov 11–Dec11.	€€	MC V				▪
MEGÈVE: *Les Enfants Terribles* Place de l'Eglise. 04 50 58 76 69. A refined menu on which expensive ingredients like morels and scallops are used to brighten up locally inspired dishes. & ● Tue; May.	€€€	AE DC MC V	●	▪		▪
MORZINE: *La Chamade* Morzine. 04 50 79 13 91. Traditional ingredients, like pig's trotters and *omble chevalier* (char), cooked in an open fire. Tasty mountain piglet. & ● May, mid-Nov–mid-Dec.	€€€	DC MC V	●	▪	●	▪
PÉROUGES: *Hostellerie du Vieux Pérouges* Place du Tilleul. 04 74 61 00 88. In a 13th-century timbered building, this restaurant is exceptionally good. Try *Ypocras*, a liqueur made to a recipe from medieval times.	€€€€	AE MC V	●	▪		
ROANNE: *La Maison Troisgros* Place de la Gare. 04 77 71 66 97. One of the most prestigious restaurants in France, with elegant contemporary decor. Dishes include salmon with sorrel. & ● Tue–Wed, 2 wks Feb, Aug 1–15.	€€€€€	AE DC MC V	●	▪	●	
TALLOIRES: *Villa des Fleurs* Route du Port. 04 50 60 71 14. The lake in the grounds here is picturesque, and it also provides the restaurant's main attraction – a succulent fish called *féra.* ● Sun D, Mon, Tue L; Nov 12–Dec 12.	€€€	AE MC V	●	▪		▪
TALLOIRES: *Le Père Bise* Route du Port. 04 50 60 72 01. A mix of locals and wealthy tourists worship at one of France's gastronomic shrines. Faultless food and panoramic views go some way towards offsetting the prices. & ● Feb 10–mid-Apr: Tue–Wed, mid-Apr–Nov: Tue L, Fri L; Dec–Jan.	€€€€€	AE DC MC V	●	▪	●	▪
THONON-LES-BAINS: *Le Comte Rouge* 10 bvd du Canal, Place des Arts. 04 50 71 06 04. Fish dishes are the specialty in this somewhat rustic hotel-restaurant: *gratin de queues d'écrevisses* or *filets de féra* (a lake fish). ● Sep–Jun: Sun D & Wed.	€€	MC V		▪		
VALENCE: *Restaurant Pic* 285 avenue Victor-Hugo. 04 75 44 15 32. Fillet of sea bass in caviar, *charolais* beef and intricate desserts have all enhanced the reputation of this establishment. & ● Sun D–Mon & Nov–Mar: Tue); 1st 2 wks Jan.	€€€€€	AE DC MC V	●	▪	●	
VIENNE: *La Cloître* 2 rue des Cloîtres. 04 74 31 93 57. Situated next to the cathedral, this establishment serves classic French cuisine, and local specialties such as *ravioles de homard au fenouil.* & ● Sun.	€€€€	MC V	●	▪		▪

POITOU AND AQUITAINE

	Price	CREDIT CARDS	CHILDREN'S FACILITIES	FIXED-PRICE MENU	GOOD WINE LIST	OUTDOOR TABLES
ANGOULÊME: *Auberge du Pont de la Meure* Nersac. 05 45 90 60 48. Beside the Charente river, the Oysters *à la charentaise* (with sausage), stewed eel and goat in garlic are worth a special trip. ● Fri D, Sat; last 2 wks Aug.	€€	AE DC MC V	●	▪	●	
BORDEAUX: *La Mamounia* 51 rue Lafourie-Monbadon. 05 56 81 21 84. A draped ceiling lends a tent-like atmosphere to this smart Moroccan restaurant, which is a haven for vegetarians. Couscous is the main item on the menu. Sweet mint tea is served with your meal. &	€	AE DC MC V			●	

BORDEAUX: *Chez Philippe* €€€
1 place du Parlement. ☎ 05 56 81 83 15.
A casual, lively spot with the deserved reputation of being the best fish restaurant in Bordeaux. ● Sun, Mon; 1st 3 wks Aug.
AE DC MC V

BORDEAUX: *La Tupina* €€€€
6 rue Porte de la Monnaie. ☎ 05 56 91 56 37.
Dishes are cooked over an open fire in a friendly atmosphere – the grilled poultry is a must.
AE DC MC V

BORDEAUX: *L'Olivier du Clavel* €€
44 rue Charles-Domercq. ☎ 05 57 95 09 50.
This modern bistro is one of the few places where Bordeaux wine can be sampled by the glass. The cuisine is Mediterranean. 🔗 ● Sat L, Sun–Mon; Aug.
DC V

BORDEAUX: *Le Chapon Fin* €€€€
5 rue de Montesquieu. ☎ 05 56 79 10 10.
Crayfish ravioli, young pigeon and local oysters are some of the treats in store here. 🔗 ● Sun–Mon.
AE DC MC V

BOULIAC: *Le Bistroy* €€€
3 place Camille-Hostein. ☎ 05 57 97 06 06.
This buzzing place gets its food from the neighbouring top restaurant St-James, meaning the same sensational cuisine at lower price. 🔗 ● Sun; 1 mth in winter
AE DC MC V

COGNAC: *Les Pigeons Blancs* €€€
110 rue Jules Brisson. ☎ 05 45 82 16 36.
Owned by the same family since the 17th century, this old post house has excellent service, wine and food. 🔗 ● Sun D–Mon L; 1st 2 wks Jan.
AE DC MC V

CROUTELLE: *La Chenaie* €€
La Berlanderie. ☎ 05 49 57 11 52.
Deep in the Poitevin hills, this cheery farmhouse offers *foie gras* cooked in various ways and rich local goat's cheese. 🔗 ● Sun D, Mon; last wk Jan.
AE MC V

ILE DE RÉ: *Café du Phare* €
St-Clément-des-Baleines. ☎ 05 46 29 46 66.
An Art Deco café beneath the lighthouse serves the local specialty, *poutargue* (cod's roe, shallots, and sour cream). 🔗 ● Jan–Mar: Tue; mid-Nov–Dec 20, 3 wks Jan.
MC V

JARNAC: *Restaurant du Château* €€
15 place du Château. ☎ 05 45 81 07 17.
Immensely popular with the locals, with a delicious *potée à la charentaise* (duck *magret, confit* and beans). ● Sun D, Mon; Wed D; last 2 wks Jan, 3 wks Aug.
AE MC V

LANGON: *Claude Darroze* €€€€
95 cours du Général Leclerc. ☎ 05 56 63 00 48.
Gaudy *trompe l'oeil* decor does not detract from the generosity and quality of the food, or the local claret. 🔗 ● Oct–mid-May: Sun L & Mon L; 2 wks Jan, 3 wks Oct.
AE MC V

LA ROCHELLE: *A Côté de Chez Fred* €€
30 rue Saint Nicholas. ☎ 05 46 41 65 76.
Fred, the owner-chef, is a former fishmonger, and his seafood dishes vary according to the previous evening's catch. ● Sun, Mon; last wk Oct–mid-Nov.
MC V

LA ROCHELLE: *Richard Coutanceau* €€€€
Plage de la Concurrence. ☎ 05 46 41 48 19.
Overlooking the beach, this is a big, bright restaurant run by a rising young chef. Simple, authentic seafood dishes such as lobster sautéd in olive oil. 🔗 ● Sun.
AE DC MC V

MARGAUX: *Le Savoie* €€
Rue de la Poste. ☎ 05 57 88 31 76.
This little town house offers good-value menus of simple yet original dishes. 🔗 ● Sun D.
AE DC MC V

MIMIZAN: *Au Bon Coin du Lac* €€€
34 avenue du Lac. ☎ 05 58 09 01 55.
Plushness and luxury abound at this lakeside eatery. There are views of the lake from both the dining room and pretty terrace. 🔗 ● Sun D, Mon; Feb.
AE DC MC V

NIORT: *Les Mangeux du Lumas* €€
La Garette. ☎ 05 49 35 82 89.
Sample a favorite local treat, *lumas* – tiny snails – bathed in butter, cream or a regional aperitif, *pineau des Charentes*. 🔗 ● Mon D–Tue (& Sep–Jun: Wed D).
AE MC V

Average prices for a three-course meal for one, including a half-bottle of house wine, tax and service:
€ under 25€
€€ 25€–35€
€€€ 36€–50€
€€€€ 51€–75€
€€€€€ over 75€

CHILDREN'S FACILITIES
Where high chairs and smaller portions are available.
FIXED-PRICE MENU
A good-value fixed-price menu on offer at lunch, dinner or both, often with three or more courses.
GOOD WINE LIST
Denotes a wide range of good wines, or otherwise a more specialised selection of local wines.
OUTDOOR TABLES
Facilities for eating outdoors, often with a good view.
WEEKLY & ANNUAL CLOSURE
Double check as may change (L = lunch; D = dinner).

	CREDIT CARDS	CHILDREN'S FACILITIES	FIXED-PRICE MENU	GOOD WINE LIST	OUTDOOR TABLES
PAUILLAC: *Château Cordeillan-Bages* €€€€ Route des Châteaux. (05 56 59 24 24. The award-winning wine waiter at this establishment, right in the heart of Bordeaux country, will guide you through the extensive wine list to find the perfect accompaniment to a splendid meal. & ● *Mon, Tue L, Sat L; mid-Dec–Jan.*	AE DC MC V	●	■	●	
POITIERS: *Maxime* €€ 4 rue St-Nicolas. (05 49 41 09 55. A chic restaurant for sophisticated palates. Dishes include game, tender duck and ravioli of hot oysters. ● *Sat L, Sun (& Nov–Feb: Sat D); Jul 14–Aug 21.*	AE DC MC V	●	■		
ROYAN: *La Jabotière* €€€ Pontaillac. (05 46 39 91 29. Modern cuisine is offered in a renovated beachfront restaurant. Sample sea bream with tomatoes and curry or cannelloni. & ● *Sun D, Mon; Christmas, Jan.*	AE MC V	●	■		■
ST-EMILION: *Hostellerie de Plaisance* €€€€ Place du Clocher. (05 57 55 07 55. Enjoy the view over the roofs of the medieval town and sample good regional cuisine along with superb wines from across the country. & ● *Jan.*	AE DC MC V	●	■	●	■
SAINTES: *Taverne de Maître Kanter* €€ 116 avenue Gambetta. (05 46 74 16 85. Classic crowded brasserie serving wonderful seafood – the *fruits de mer* are a must – and *choucroute.* Very good value.	MC V	●	■		

PÉRIGORD, QUERCY AND GASCONY

	CREDIT CARDS	CHILDREN'S FACILITIES	FIXED-PRICE MENU	GOOD WINE LIST	OUTDOOR TABLES
AGEN: *L'Atelier* €€ 14 rue Jeu de Paume. (05 53 87 89 22. Formerly a carpenter's workshop, the selection here includes duck dishes and good grilled fish *à la plancha.* & ● *Mon L, Sat L, sun; 2 wks end Jul–early Aug.*	AE MC V	●	■		
ALBI: *Hostellerie du Vigan* € 16 place du Vigan. (05 63 43 31 31. An unpretentious and inexpensive, rather business-like place to eat, which produces good local dishes at remarkable value. & ● *Sun L.*	AE DC MC V	●	■		
ALBI: *Le Moulin de la Mothe* €€ Rue de la Mothe. (05 63 60 38 15. Set in pretty grounds by the river, opposite the cathedral, the typical Tarn dishes here include duck and *foie gras.* & ● *Wed (& Sep–Jun: Sun D); 1 wk Nov, 2 wks Feb.*	AE DC MC V	●	■	●	■
AUCH: *Restaurant Roland Garreau* €€€ 2 place de la Libération. (05 62 61 71 71. Gascon cuisine with *assiette de trois foie gras aux quatre saveurs* and *magret de canard* served with sweet wines. ● *Sun D.*	AE DC MC V	●	■	●	
BARBOTAN-LES-THERMES: *La Bastide Gasconne* €€€ Barbotan-les-Thermes. (05 62 08 31 00. The reputation of this restaurant is going up with the locals, always a good sign. Flawless dishes such as braised knuckle of veal or crêpe with praline and Armagnac are served impeccably. & ● *Nov–Mar.*	AE MC V	●	■		■
BERGERAC: *L'Enfance de Lard* €€ Place Pélissière. (05 53 57 52 88. Excellent southwest cooking including meat grilled over vine cuttings on the open fire. Reserving is advisable. ● *L (& mid-Sep–mid-Jun: Tue); last 2 wks Sep.*	MC V		■	●	
BRANTÔME: *Les Frères Charbonnel* €€€ 57 rue Gambetta. (05 53 05 70 15. Bargain-priced wines, hearty salad, pike-perch with truffles and *foie gras* can be enjoyed overlooking the Dronne. & ● *Oct–Jun: Sun D, Mon; mid-Nov–mid-Dec, Feb.*	AE DC MC V	●	■	●	■

605

BRANTÔME: *Moulin de L'Abbaye* €€€€ | AE DC MC V | ● | ▦ | ● | ▦
1 route de Bourdeilles. (05 53 05 80 22.
Dine in luxury on traditional Perigord cooking complemented by dishes such as pike-perch filet or sole *paupiette*. & T ● every L (Jul–Aug: Mon L only); Nov–Mar.

CAHORS: *La Paix* € | AE MC V | | ▦ | | ▦
30 place St-Maurice. (05 65 35 03 40.
This is a locals' restaurant right beside the market. The food is traditional and good – with a very cheap fixed-price menu. ● Sat D–Sun; 1st wk Oct; Dec 22–Jan 8.

CAHORS: *Claude Marco* €€ | AE DC MC V | ● | ▦ | | ▦
Lamagdelaine. (05 65 35 30 64.
A rustic restaurant, 7 km east of Cahors, with a cozy dining room and a delightful terrace. Abundant regional specialties. ● Mon L (& mid-Sep–mid-Jun: Sun D & Tue L).

CAHORS: *Le Balandre* €€€ | AE DC MC V | ● | ▦ | ●
5 avenue Charles-de-Freycinet. (05 65 53 32 00.
An immaculate dining room where generous southwestern cuisine is served, with a good selection of Cahors wines. & ● Sep–Jun: Sun–Mon; last 2 wks Nov.

CASTELJALOUX: *La Vieille Auberge* €€ | MC V | ● | ▦
11 rue Posterne. (05 53 93 01 36.
Delicious Gasconne specialties can be enjoyed at very reasonable prices.
& ● Sun D, Wed L (& mid-Sep–mid-Jun: Tue D & Wed D); 1 wk Feb, 2 wks Jun, 2 wks Nov.

CHAMPAGNAC DE BELAIR: *Le Moulin du Roc* €€€€ | AE DC MC V | ● | ▦ | ● | ▦
Champagnac-de-Belair. (05 53 02 86 00.
A converted oil mill in a romantic spot by the river Dronne. The cooking is inconsistent but the fish is recommended. ● Tue (& mid-Sep–Jun: Mon–Wed); Jan–beg Feb.

DOMME: *L'Esplanade* €€€ | AE DC MC V | ● | ▦ | ● | ▦
Rue Pontcaret. (05 53 28 31 41.
The views are panoramic but the prices are high so stick to trout, salmon or rack of lamb. & ● Mon, Wed L; Nov 11–Feb.

LES-EYZIES-DE-TAYAC: *Le Moulin de la Beune* €€ | MC V | ● | ▦ | | ▦
2 rue des Moulins bas. (05 53 06 94 33.
Local produce is served in one of the two mills or on the riverside terrace. Try the *jarret de porc* or *foie gras millefeuille*. & ● Tue L, Wed L, Sat L; Nov–Mar.

LARTIGUE: *L'Auberge de Lartigue* € | | ● | ▦ | | ▦
Lartigue. (05 62 65 41 22.
Don't be put off by appearances – this is wonderful, off-the-beaten track Gascony. The *foie gras* comes in a variety of forms, all superb. & ● Thu; Oct.

MARMANDE: *Auberge du Moulin d'Ané* €€ | AE DC MC V | ● | ▦ | | ▦
Virazeil, route de Gontaud. (05 53 20 18 25.
The cuisine is seasonal and consistently excellent in this beautifully-restored 18th-century mill. & ● Tue–Wed in winter; 1 wk each in Feb, Jun & Nov.

MONTAUBAN: *Le Ventadour* €€ | MC V | | ▦
23 quai Villebourbon. (05 63 63 34 58.
A popular place with the local townspeople, who appreciate the plain cooking and reasonable prices at this central restaurant. ● Sat L, Sun–Mon; 2–3 wks Aug.

MONTRÉAL-DU-GERS: *Chez Simone* € | AE MC V | ● | ▦ | | ▦
Montréal-du-Gers. (05 62 29 44 40.
Another restaurant very much admired by people in the know, due to the generous helpings of excellent locally produced *foie gras*. ● Sun D–Mon (& Sep–Jun: Tue); 1 wk Jan.

PERIGUEUX: *Au Petit Chef* € | AE DC MC V | ● | ▦ | | ▦
5 place du Coderc. (05 53 53 16 03.
The cheapest lunch menu comprises soup, a buffet of hors d'oeuvres, main course and pâtisserie – all homemade. ● Sep–Jun: Sat D–Sun; 1 wk in Feb, Jun & Sep each.

PÉRIGUEUX: *Hercule Poirot* €€ | AE DC MC V | ● | ▦ | ●
2 rue de la Nation. (05 53 08 90 76.
In this magnificent Renaissance vaulted dining room, three types of cuisine are available: traditional or Perigourdine cuisine, or fish dishes. &

PUYMIROL: *Les Loges de l'Aubergade* €€€€ | AE DC MC V | ● | ▦ | ● | ▦
52 rue Royale. (05 53 95 31 46.
This is one of the southwest's great restaurants, set in a beautiful medieval building on a hilltop. & ● Mon L (& Nov–Mar: Sun D–Tue L); Feb school hols.

For key to symbols see back flap

Average prices for a three-course meal for one, including a half-bottle of house wine, tax and service:
€ under 25€
€€ 25€–35€
€€€ 36€–50€
€€€€ 51€–75€
€€€€€ over 75€

CHILDREN'S FACILITIES
Where high chairs and smaller portions are available.
FIXED-PRICE MENU
A good-value fixed-price menu on offer at lunch, dinner or both, often with three or more courses.
GOOD WINE LIST
Denotes a wide range of good wines, or otherwise a more specialised selection of local wines.
OUTDOOR TABLES
Facilities for eating outdoors, often with a good view.
WEEKLY & ANNUAL CLOSURE
Double check as may change (L = lunch; D = dinner).

	CREDIT CARDS	CHILDREN'S FACILITIES	FIXED-PRICE MENU	GOOD WINE LIST	OUTDOOR TABLES
ROCAMADOUR: *Jehan de Valon* €€ Cité Médiévale. 05 65 33 63 08. There are great views from this restaurant in the pedestrianized medieval town center. Lamb and *foie gras* are specialties. ● mid-Nov–mid-Feb.	AE DC MC V	●	■	●	
TOULOUSE: *A la Truffe de Quercy* € 17 rue Croix-Baragnon. 05 61 53 34 24. Traditional recipes have been handed down from father to son for over 150 years in this rustic family restaurant. Try the *cassoulet*. & ● Sun; public hols, Aug.	V		■		
TOULOUSE: *La Côte de Bœuf* €€ 12 rue des Gestes. 05 61 21 19 61. Small, efficient and supremely friendly restaurant offering huge steaks and known for its generous portions. & ● every L, Sun; 3 wks Aug.	MC V		■		■
TOULOUSE: *Brasserie des Beaux-Arts* €€€ 1 quai de la Daurade. 05 61 21 12 12. An authentic brasserie serving local dishes. There is always a line. Try the oysters with house Riesling wine.	AE DC MC V	●	■	●	■
TOULOUSE: *Les Jardins de l'Opéra (D. Toulousy)* €€€€€ 1 place du Capitole. 05 61 23 07 76. In a pretty courtyard in the middle of town, this is unquestionably one of the best places to eat, and has great local cuisine. ● Sun–Mon; 1 wk Jan, Aug.	AE MC V	●	■	●	■
VILLEFRANCHE-DE-LAURAGAIS: *Hôtel de France* € 106 rue de la République. 05 61 81 62 17. You are in *cassoulet* country here, and this 19th-century auberge prides itself on making one of the best and most authentic in the region. ● Nov–Apr: Sun D.	MC V	●	■		

THE PYRENEES					
AINHOA: *Ithurria* €€€ Ainhoa. 05 59 29 92 11. In the prettiest village of the Basque region, this eatery serves delicious local fare such as peppers stuffed with cod. ● mid-Sep–Jun: Wed–Thu L; Nov–Apr.	AE MC V		■	●	
ARCANGUES: *Moulin d'Alotz* €€€ Arcangues. 05 59 43 04 54. A well-converted mill where the chef offers light country cooking such as langoustine or sole roasted with ceps. ● Tue–Wed; 2 wks each in Jan & Nov.	DC MC V	●	■		■
ARGELÈS-GAZOST: *Le Casaou* €€ 44 ave des Pyrénées. 05 62 97 01 26. A traditional establishment with local cuisine such as fried pigeon with Madiran sauce or baked pike-perch with mussels and cockles. ● Sun D, Wed; Nov 5–Dec 20.	AE MC V	●	■	●	
AUDRESSEIN: *l'Auberge d'Audressein* €€ Route de Luchon. 05 61 96 11 80. This family-run logis is housed in a converted 19th-century forge and serves some of the best local cuisine around, with game and *foie gras* strongly featured. & ● Oct–Easter: Sun D–Mon (ex public hols); Jan, 1 wk Dec.	DC MC V	●	■	●	■
BAYONNE: *Le Cheval Blanc* €€€ 68 rue Bourgneuf. 05 59 59 01 33. You will find creative traditional cooking here. Taste the baked hake with onions and sweet peppers, and the chocolate Amandine with wild cherries for dessert. ● Sun D, Mon; Feb school hols.	AE MC V	●	■	●	
BIARRITZ: *Les Platanes* €€€€ 32 avenue Beausoleil. 05 59 23 13 68. Top-flight cooking, using only fresh products, in a friendly setting. The dining room only seats 25 so it is advisable to reserve. & ● Mon–Tue.	AE DC MC V		■		

BIARRITZ: *Plaisir des Mets* €€€ | MC V
5 rue Centre. (05 59 24 34 66.
Enjoy the fish dishes and shellfish in this gastronomic
restaurant. & ● Sep–Jun: Tue D, Wed; last 2 wks Jun, last 2 wks Nov.

CIBOURE: *Arrantzaleak* €€ | AE DC MC V
Avenue Jean-Poulou. (05 59 47 10 75.
An unassuming seafront building hides a dream. Wonderfully fresh fish is grilled
on the simple dining room's open fire. ● Mon (& Sep–Jun: Sun D); mid-Dec–Jan 20.

ESPELETTE: *Euzkadi* € | MC V
Espelette. (05 59 93 91 88.
The locals gather here on Sundays for their favorite seasonal game, peppers,
omelette, *boudins* and substantial Rioja wines. ● Sep–Jun: Mon–Tue; Nov–mid-Dec.

EUGÉNIE-LES-BAINS: *Les Prés d'Eugénie-Michel Guérard* €€€€€ | AE DC MC V
Eugénie-les-Bains. (05 58 05 06 07.
Run by the creator of *cuisine minceur*, there is a low-calorie menu or a truly
gourmet one. All desserts are made to order. & ● Sep–Jun: Mon–Tue; Dec–Feb.

GUÉTHARY-BIDART: *Les Frères Ibarboure* €€€€ | AE DC MC V
Chemin de Talienia. (05 59 54 81 64.
In an 18th-century manor amid woods, this is a rare treat – the regional
fare is full-flavored and faultless. & ● Sun D (& Sep–Jun:Wed); 2 wks Nov, 2 wks Jan.

JURANÇON: *Ruffet* €€€€ | DC MC V
3 avenue Charles-Touzet. (05 59 06 25 13.
Good, traditional cuisine with a different menu every day. The warm
welcome and amiable service entice diners to return. & ● Sun D, Mon.

PAU: *La Gousse d'Ail* €€ | MC V
12 rue du Hédas. (05 59 27 31 55.
A pleasant, brick and stucco restaurant with beams and a big fireplace. Its
excellent value makes it stand out in an area full of bistros. & ● Tue–Wed L, Sat L.

PAU: *Chez Pierre* €€ | AE DC MC V
16 rue Louis-Barthou. (05 59 27 76 86.
A fine chef, an elegant town house setting and a series of creative dishes ensure
the reputation of this restaurant. ● Sat L, Sun, Mon L; 2 wks each in Jan & Aug.

ST-GIRONS: *Eychenne* €€ | AE DC MC V
8 avenue Paul Laffont. (05 61 04 04 50.
A pretty restaurant in an old seminary with two gardens where diners can
enjoy pigeon, duck and fish specialties. & ● Nov–Mar: Sun D, Mon; Dec–Jan.

ST-JEAN-DE-LUZ: *Auberge Kaïku* €€ | AE MC V
17 rue de la République. (05 59 26 13 20.
Regional Basque dishes such as *parilladas* (mixed fried and grilled fish), served
in the oldest house in town. & ● Mon L (& mid-Sep–mid-Jun: Wed); Nov 12–Dec 20.

ST-JEAN-DE-LUZ: *Petit Grill Basque* € | AE DC MC V
2 rue St Jacques. (05 59 26 80 76.
Simple, good Basque home-cooking – fish soup, squid, turkey croquettes,
piquillos (peppers) stuffed with cod. & ● Wed (& mid-Sep–Jun: Thu); Dec 20–Jan 20.

ST-JEAN-PIED-DE-PORT: *Chalet Pedro* € |
Forêt d'Iraty. (05 59 28 55 98.
A mountain chalet that caters for skiers and locals alike. Slow service does not
spoil fresh trout or *cèpes* omelette. & ● every D, Tue (except Jul–Aug & Oct); Nov 11–Easter.

ST-JEAN-PIED-DE-PORT: *Pyrénées* €€€€ | AE MC V
19 place Charles de Gaulle. (05 59 37 01 01.
A famous restaurant serving the best local produce: suckling lamb, salmon and,
in season, wild morels. ● Sep 20–Jun: Tue (& Nov–Mar: Mon D); Nov 20–Dec 20, Jan 5–28.

ST-SAVIN: *Le Viscos* €€ | AE DC MC V
St-Savin. (05 62 97 02 28.
In summer, eat outside on the flower-filled terrace overlooking the Lavedan
valley. Specialties are *cèpes*, duck and *foie gras*. & ● Sep–Jun: Sun D–Mon; 2 wks Jan.

URT: *Auberge de la Galupe* €€€€ | AE DC MC V
Place du Port. (05 59 56 21 84.
A fishermans' inn with fine local produce – Jabugo ham, salmon and
eels, and sweet Jurançon wine. & ● Sep–Jun: Sun D, Mon–Tue; 2 wks Jan.

<table>
<tr><td colspan="2">

Average prices for a three-course meal for one, including a half-bottle of house wine, tax and service:

€ under 25€
€€ 25€–35€
€€€ 36€–50€
€€€€ 51€–75€
€€€€€ over 75€

</td><td colspan="2">

CHILDREN'S FACILITIES
Where high chairs and smaller portions are available.
FIXED-PRICE MENU
A good-value fixed-price menu on offer at lunch, dinner or both, often with three or more courses.
GOOD WINE LIST
Denotes a wide range of good wines, or otherwise a more specialised selection of local wines.
OUTDOOR TABLES
Facilities for eating outdoors, often with a good view.
WEEKLY & ANNUAL CLOSURE
Double check as may change (L = lunch; D = dinner).

</td></tr>
</table>

	CREDIT CARDS	CHILDREN'S FACILITIES	FIXED-PRICE MENU	GOOD WINE LIST	OUTDOOR TABLES
LANGUEDOC-ROUSSILLON					
AIGUES-MORTES: *Café de Bouzigues* € 7 rue Pasteur. ☎ 04 66 53 93 95. Staff are friendly and specialties include lamb and aubergine *tian*, and peach salad. ☷ ◗ *mid-Jan–mid-Mar.*	AE MC V		▩		▩
AIGUES-MORTES: *Restaurant les Enganettes* € 12 rue Morceau. ☎ 04 66 53 69 11. Excellent regional specialties in a rustic setting. Portions are very generous and all the food is freshly prepared. ◗ *Tue D, Wed; Nov.*	MC V	●	▩		
ANDUZE: *Auberge des Trois Barbus* €€€ Générargues. ☎ 04 66 61 72 12. Imaginative cooking with *foie gras* and truffles in a rustic auberge. Lunch by the pool with views across the valley. ◗ *Oct–May: Sun D, Mon; Jan–Mar.*	AE MC V	●	▩		
ANDUZE: *Les Demeures du Ranquet* €€€ Le Ranquet, route de Saint-Hippolyte-du-Fort. ☎ 04 66 77 51 63. Located 6 km (4 miles) from Anduze, the owners of this lovingly restored building set in a forest of oak trees offer well-cooked traditional dishes. ☷ ◗ *Jun–Aug: Tue, mid-Sep–May: Tue D–Wed; Nov–Dec.*	DC MC V	●	▩	●	▩
ARLES-SUR-TECH: *Hôtel les Glycines* €€€ Rue du Jeu-de-Paume. ☎ 04 68 39 10 09. Tasty food based on local produce, and many regional wines. There is a pretty garden which is ideal for summer dining. ☷ ◗ *mid-Nov–mid-Feb.*	AE DC MC V	●	▩	●	▩
BÉZIERS: *Le Framboisier* €€€ 12 rue Boeildieu. ☎ 04 67 49 90 00. This is an elegant establishment with a classic menu and long list of fine Languedoc-Roussillon wines. ◗ *Sun–Mon; 2 wks Feb, last 2 wks Aug.*	AE DC MC V	●	▩	●	
BOUZIGUES: *La Côte Bleue* €€€ Avenue Louis Tudesq. ☎ 04 67 78 30 87. Overlooking the saltwater lagoon of the Bassin de Thau, this airy restaurant offers fresh seafood and fish. ☷ ◗ *Sep–Jun: Tue D–Wed (& Oct–Mar: Sun); mid-Jan–mid-Feb.*	AE MC V	●	▩		
CARCASSONNE: *Le Languedoc* €€ 32 allée d'Iéna. ☎ 04 68 25 22 17. This pleasant restaurant is below the walled city. *Cassoulet*, the filling bean stew that is the regional specialty, is a must, and there is a range of salads, savory dishes, and desserts. ◗ *Mon (& Sep–Jun: Sun D); mid-Dec–mid-Jan.*	AE DC MC V	●	▩		
CARCASSONNE: *Brasserie Le Donjon* € 4 rue Porte d'Aude. ☎ 04 68 25 95 72. An elegant, refreshingly modern brasserie in an otherwise completely medieval town. Regional specialties of *foie gras* and cassoulet. ◗ *Nov–Mar: Sun D.*	AE DC MC V	●	▩		▩
CASTELNAUDARY: *Grand Hôtel Fourcade* € 14 rue des Carmes. ☎ 04 68 23 02 08. In the Old Town bordering the Canal du Midi, this old-fashioned place has *cassoulet* as the highlight of an interesting menu. ◗ *Sun D, Mon; last 3 wks Jan.*	AE DC MC V	●	▩		
CASTELNOU: *L'Hostal* € Carrer de la Patore. ☎ 04 68 53 45 42. In an artists' village, this restaurant fills up on the weekend, when locals flock in for *cargolade*, the Catalan feast of grilled meat and snails. ◗ *Sun D, Mon, Wed D; Jan.*	AE DC MC V	●	▩		▩
COLLIOURE: *La Frégate* €€ Quai de l'Amirauté. ☎ 04 68 82 06 05. Wonderful fish soups, local anchovies, and *bouillinades* (fish platters) are among the favorites in this jolly, quayside restaurant.	MC V	●	▩		▩

COLLIOURE: *La Balette* €€€ | MC V
Route de Port-Vendres. 📞 04 68 82 05 07.
Beautifully set above the bay, this is very popular in summer – booking is essential. Seafood stars in a wide range of Catalan dishes. ● *Nov 12–Dec 20.*

CUCUGNAN: *Auberge du Vigneron* €€ | MC V
2 rue Achille-Mir. 📞 04 68 45 03 00.
Atmospheric restaurant in the former wine cellar of a charming inn, serving dishes of duck and fruit in tasty combinations. ● *Sun D, Mon; Dec–mid-Feb.*

MINERVE: *Relais Chantovent* €€ | MC V
Minerve. 📞 04 68 91 14 18.
The pretty medieval town, with its deep ravine, shouldn't be missed, nor should the regional cooking and wines. ♿ ● *Sun D–Mon (& Oct–Jun: Sun); mid-Dec–mid-Mar.*

MONTPELLIER: *Chandelier* €€€€€ | AE DC MC V
39 place Zeus. 📞 04 67 15 34 38.
Inventive fish dishes such as *St-Pierre* (John Dory) in an olive pastry or lobster stew with herbs and lasagna are the stock-in-trade here. ● *Sun, Mon L.*

MONTPELLIER: *La Réserve Rimbaud* €€€ | AE DC MC V
820 avenue de St-Maur. 📞 04 67 72 52 53.
Sophisticated food at affordable prices in a relaxed riverside setting. Grilled clams, and monkfish with herbs, olives and aïoli. ♿ ● *Sun D–Mon, Wed L; Jan–mid-Mar.*

MOSSET: *Mas Lluganas "Ferme Auberge"* €€€ | MC V
2 place de l'Oratori. 📞 04 68 05 00 36.
All the meat is produced on the farm. Local producers provide the cheese and vegetables. Le Canigou and the Pyrenees provide the backdrop. ♿ ● *early Oct–Apr.*

NARBONNE: *L'Auberge des Vignes* €€ | MC V
Domaine de l'Hospitalet, route de Narbonne Plage. 📞 04 68 45 28 50.
In a vineyard this restaurant serves Mediterranean cuisine, such as fish of the day with *tapenade* and saffron juice. ♿ ● *Sep–Dec & Mar–Jun: Sun D–Mon; Jan–Feb.*

NARBONNE: *La Table St-Créscent* €€€ | AE DC MC V
Domaine St-Crésent le Viel. 📞 04 68 41 37 37.
In an 8th-century oratory, this delightful restaurant serves elegant food including shrimp casserole with purple artichokes. ♿ ● *Sat L, Sun D, Mon.*

NÎMES: *Nicolas* € | MC V
1 rue Poise. 📞 04 66 67 50 47.
Regional fare at good-value prices in a packed but friendly and unpretentious atmosphere. ● *Sat L, Mon; 1st 2 wks Jul.*

OLARGUES: *Domaine de Rieumégé* €€€€ | AE DC MC V
Route de Saint-Pons. 📞 04 67 97 73 99.
Traditional local cuisine is served in this restored 17th-century *mas*, including lamb curry with garlic, rosemary and spicy oil. ● *mid-Nov–Mar.*

PERPIGNAN: *Casa Sansa* €€€ | AE MC V
3 rue Fabriques-Couvertes. 📞 04 68 34 21 84.
A 14th-century wine cellar decorated with Catalan artifacts provides the setting for true Catalan food: spicy meatballs, shrimp, and anchovies. ● *Sun–Mon.*

PERPIGNAN: *Le Chapon Fin* €€€ | AE DC MC V
18 boulevard Jean-Bourrat. 📞 04 68 35 14 14.
The restaurant serves fine Mediterranean food such as lobster stew with Banyuls, as well as seafood and truffles. ♿ ● *Sun; 1st 2 wks Jan, last 2 wks Aug.*

PERPIGNAN: *Le Mas Vermeil* €€€ | AE MC V
Traverse de Cabestany. 📞 04 68 66 95 96.
The menu is unpretentious and simple, leaning towards the rich Catalan style. Dine in the garden restaurant, complete with fountains. ♿ ● *Jan.*

PÉZENAS: *Après le Déluge* €€ | AE MC V
5 rue du Maréchal Plantavit. 📞 04 67 98 10 77.
This former smithy in the ramparts is now a restaurant, run by a family of artists. Traditional Languedoc cuisine with a twist. ● *L: Mon–Sat; last wk Jun, 1st 2 wks Dec.*

PORT-VENDRES: *La Côte Vermeille* €€€€ | AE MC V
Quai du Fanal. 📞 04 68 82 05 71.
At this quayside restaurant, the food concentrates on delicate seafood and fish, but other dishes can be ordered. ♿ ● *Mon (& Sep–Jun: Sun); Jan.*

Average prices for a three-course meal for one, including a half-bottle of house wine, tax and service:
€ under 25€
€€ 25€–35€
€€€ 36€–50€
€€€€ 51€–75€
€€€€€ over 75€

CHILDREN'S FACILITIES
Where high chairs and smaller portions are available.
FIXED-PRICE MENU
A good-value fixed-price menu on offer at lunch, dinner or both, often with three or more courses.
GOOD WINE LIST
Denotes a wide range of good wines, or otherwise a more specialised selection of local wines.
OUTDOOR TABLES
Facilities for eating outdoors, often with a good view.
WEEKLY & ANNUAL CLOSURE
Double check as may change (L = lunch; D = dinner).

	CREDIT CARDS	CHILDREN'S FACILITIES	FIXED-PRICE MENU	GOOD WINE LIST	OUTDOOR TABLES

SAILLAGOUSE: *L'Atalaya* €€€
Saillagouse. ☎ 04 68 04 70 04.
A pretty auberge perched above the village. The cuisine includes roast pigeon and *foie gras.* ● *Apr–mid-Jun & mid-Sep–Nov: L Mon–Thu; mid-Jan–Mar, Nov–mid-Dec.*
MC V · · · — | ■ | ● | ■

ST-MARTIN-DE-LONDRES: *Les Muscardins* €€€€
19 route des Cévennes. ☎ 04 67 55 75 90.
A bright, cheerful restaurant with a notable list of local wines. Gourmets often return to savor the adventurous cooking of the Rousset family, who base their menu on regional produce – fish, lamb and pigeon. 🅱 ● *Mon–Tue; Feb.*
AE DC MC V — ● | ■ | ●

ST-PONS-DE-THOMIÈRES: *Auberge de Cabarétou* €€€
St-Pons-de-Thomières. ☎ 04 67 97 02 31.
Set in a forest with views across Haut Languedoc, this auberge combines classic and modern local cuisine. 🅱 ● *Sun D–Tue (& mid-Jan–mid-Feb: Mon–Fri).*
AE DC MC V — ● | ■ | ● | ■

SÈTE: *Palangrotte* €€
1 rampe Paul-Valéry. ☎ 04 67 74 80 35.
A good place to go to sample a plate of oysters, for which this area is justifiably famous. ● *Sun D–Mon.*
AE MC V — ● | ■ | ●

VILLEFRANCHE-DE-CONFLENT: *Auberge St-Paul* €€€
7 Place de l'Eglise. ☎ 04 68 96 30 95.
Originally a 13th-century chapel, this inn offers good local produce, cooked with a personal touch. ● *Sun–Mon (& Oct–Easter: Tue); 3 wks Jan, 1 wk Jun, 1 wk end Nov.*
AE DC — | ■ | ● | ■

PROVENCE AND THE CÔTE D'AZUR

AIX-EN-PROVENCE: *Mas d'Entremont* €€€
315 Route Nationale 7, Célony. ☎ 04 42 17 42 42.
Glass walls open onto the surrounding park, and the menu is wonderful, but with few local dishes. A good Provençal wine list. 🅱 ● *Sun D–Mon L; Nov–mid-Mar.*
MC V — ● | ■ | ● | ■

AIX-EN-PROVENCE: *Le Bistro Latin* €€
18 rue de la Couronne. ☎ 04 42 38 22 88.
An intimate restaurant on two floors, serving excellent meals at good prices, and imaginative local specialties baked sole with fennel sauce. ● *Sun–Mon L.*
MC V — | ■ | ●

AIX-EN-PROVENCE: *L'Aix Quis.* €€€
22 rue Leydet. ☎ 04 42 27 76 16.
Stylish fish and meat dishes in a restaurant that is fast becoming the culinary headquarters of Aix. Try the delicious six-course menu. ● *Sun–Mon.*
AE MC V — ● | ■

ARLES: *L'Escaladou* €€
23 rue de la Porte de Laure. ☎ 04 90 96 70 43.
This pretty Provençal restaurant is close to the bull ring in the center of town. Choose the good local fish with piles of fresh vegetables.
● | ■ | | ■

ARLES: *L'Olivier* €€€
1 bis rue Reattu. ☎ 04 90 49 64 88.
Fine Provençal food. The freshest ingredients are used for dishes like honey-coated roast pigeon and bull with a caper and anchovy sauce. There is a charming interior courtyard. ● *Sun–Mon L (& Oct–May: Mon D); Nov, 2 wks Jan.*
MC V — | ■ | | ■

AVIGNON: *Hiély-Lucullus* €€€
5 rue de la République. ☎ 04 90 86 17 07.
Avignon gastronomes have been flocking here for 60 years. Try specialties like *foie gras* and *meringue glacée.* ● *Tue–Wed; last 2 wks Jan, last 2 wks Jun.*
AE MC V — ● | ■ | ●

AVIGNON: *La Fourchette* €€
17 rue Racine. ☎ 04 90 85 20 93.
A relaxed alternative to Avignon's smarter restaurants. Prices are reasonable and the desserts are mouthwatering. ● *Sat–Sun; 2 wks Feb, 2 wks mid-Aug, 1 wk Sep.*
MC V — | ■

BIOT: *Auberge du Jarrier* €€€ | AE MC V
30 passage de la Bourgade. 04 93 65 11 68.
An unpretentious restaurant with an array of seafood, delicate fish and local goat's cheeses. Reserve a week in advance in season. Mon–Wed L, Sep–Jun: Mon–Tue.

CAGNES-SUR-MER: *Le Cagnard* €€€€ | AE DC MC V
Rue Sous-barri. 04 93 20 73 21.
Housed in a medieval inn in the ramparts of the village, this superb restaurant has a classic menu with delicacies such as roast pigeon. Mon L, Tue L, Thu L; Nov–mid-Dec.

CANNES: *Royal Gray* €€€€ | AE DC MC V
38 rue des Serbes. 04 92 99 79 60.
It is difficult to eat more lavishly than at the Royal Gray, long the doyen of Cannes' restaurants. Sun–Mon (& mid-Jul–Aug: Sat–Sun L).

CAVAILLON: *Restaurant Prévot* €€€ | AE MC V
353 avenue de Verdun. 04 90 71 32 43.
A gastronomic treat in the heart of a pretty market town. The food is elegant and delicious; try the melon and scallops. Sun D, Mon; 2 wks Aug.

CHÂTEAUNEUF-DU-PAPE: *La Mère Germaine* €€€ | MC V
Place de la Fontaine. 04 90 83 54 37.
This restaurant serves delicious dishes and has an outstanding local wine list. Superb views of the vineyards and pleasant service. Tue D–Wed; Feb.

CHÂTEAUX-ARNOUX: *La Bonne Etape* €€€€ | AE DC MC V
Chemin du Lac. 04 92 64 00 09.
Set among lavender fields and olive groves, the flavor is Provençal, with dishes such as *courgettes farcies* and lamb. end Nov–mid-Mar: Mon–Tue; Jan–mid-Feb.

COL D'EZE: *La Bergerie* €€€ | AE MC V
Grande Corniche. 04 93 41 03 67.
Winter by the fire, summer on the terrace – the hearty, warming food includes lamb in herbs; local wines. L (& Dec–Mar: Mon–Thu & Sun D); mid-Jan–mid-Feb.

CUERS: *Le Lingoustou* €€€ | AE DC MC V
Route de Pierrefeu. 04 94 28 69 10.
Traditional Provençal specialties served in refined style, although the setting remains suitably rustic, amid rolling vineyards. Sun D–Mon; Jan.

GIGONDAS: *Les Florets* €€ | AE DC MC V
Route des Dentelles. 04 90 65 85 01.
Locals pack the dining room for the good regional food. The terrace overlooks the Dentelles de Montmirail. Wed (& Nov–Dec & Mar: Mon D, Tue); Jan–mid-Mar.

LA GARDE FREINET: *Auberge Sarrazine* €€
Route Nationale 98. 04 94 43 65 98.
A rural dining room where a fire roars in winter and flowers adorn the tables in summer. Try rabbit with polenta and honey. Sep–Jun: Sun D–Mon.

LES BAUX-DE-PROVENCE: *L'Oustaù de Baumanière* €€€€€ | AE DC MC V
Val d'Enfer. 04 90 54 33 07.
Two Michelin stars, views over the medieval village and a menu blending ancient local dishes and *nouvelle cuisine*. Nov–Apr: Wed, Thu L; Jan 7–Mar 7.

LOURMARIN: *Le Moulin de Lourmarin* €€€€€ | AE DC MC V
Rue du Temple. 04 90 68 06 69.
This luxurious converted olive mill serves delicious food, especially the fish and Luberon game. Tue, Thu L; mid-Jan–Feb, mid-Nov–mid-Dec.

MARSEILLE: *Dar Djerba* €€ | MC V
15 cours Julien. 04 91 48 55 36.
A North African restaurant serving delicious couscous dishes in an intimate atmosphere. Mon L; 2 wks Aug.

MARSEILLE: *Miramar* €€€€ | AE DC MC V
12 quai du Port. 04 91 91 10 40.
The *bouillabaisse* is one of the most authentic in Marseille – but at a price. There is also a huge selection of seafood. Sun–Mon; 3 wks Aug, 2 wks Dec.

MONACO: *Le Périgourdin* €€€ | AE MC V
5 rue des Oliviers. 00377 93 30 06 02.
Two minutes walk from the casino, this friendly restaurant offers all the riches of Périgord cuisine at bargain prices. Sat L, Sun; last 2 wks Aug.

Average prices for a three-course meal for one, including a half-bottle of house wine, tax and service:
€ under 25€
€€ 25€–35€
€€€ 36€–50€
€€€€ 51€–75€
€€€€€ over 75€

CHILDREN'S FACILITIES
Where high chairs and smaller portions are available.
FIXED-PRICE MENU
A good-value fixed-price menu on offer at lunch, dinner or both, often with three or more courses.
GOOD WINE LIST
Denotes a wide range of good wines, or otherwise a more specialised selection of local wines.
OUTDOOR TABLES
Facilities for eating outdoors, often with a good view.
WEEKLY & ANNUAL CLOSURE
Double check as may change (L = lunch; D = dinner).

	CREDIT CARDS	CHILDREN'S FACILITIES	FIXED-PRICE MENU	GOOD WINE LIST	OUTDOOR TABLES
MONTE-CARLO: *Café de Paris* €€€ Place du Casino. ☎ 00377 92 16 20 20. A recreation of a Belle Epoque brasserie. Among the specialties are *pavé de saumon* and Charolais beef with morels. ♿	AE DC MC V				■
MOUGINS: *Le Moulin de Mougins* €€€€€ Notre Dame-de-Vie. ☎ 04 93 75 78 24. With two Michelin stars, this restaurant still manages to stay ahead of competition, as well as being *the* place for those other stars during the Cannes Film Festival. ♿	AE DC MC V	●	■		■
NICE: *Nissa Socca* € 5 rue Sainte-Réparate. ☎ 04 93 80 18 35. Features vast plates of *socca* (chick-pea bread) with pasta and carafes of red wine. Crowded, often taking over the street in summer. ◑ *Sun, Mon L; 2 wks Jun*			■		■
NICE: *Le Chantecler (Negresco)* €€€€€ 37 promenade des Anglais. ☎ 04 93 16 64 00. Long the bastion of gastronomy in Nice, the restaurant retains immaculate standards established when Russian princes came to dine in the last century. Seafood and fish feature strongly. ♿ ◑ *mid-Nov–mid-Dec.*	AE DC MC V	●	■		
ORANGE: *La Roselière* € 4 rue du Renoyer. ☎ 04 90 34 50 42. Chalkboards propped against stone walls display the daily-changing menu, with every dish lovingly prepared from local produce. ◑ *Sun–Mon; 2 wks Aug.*			■		
ST-AGNES: *Le Logis Sarrasin* € 40 rue des Sarrasins. ☎ 04 93 35 86 89. A plain, family-run restaurant in the Alpine foothills, offering six huge courses of local game and Italian specialties. ◑ *Mon (& Sep–Jun: every D); Oct 20–Nov 20.*	MC V		■		■
ST-JEAN-CAP-FERRAT: *Le St-Jean* € Place Clemenceau. ☎ 04 93 76 04 75. In the busy town square, this restaurant serves up simple but excellent food, such as pizzas, pastas and fish. The first floor terrace is perfect for balmy summer evenings. ♿ ◑ *Tue D–Wed; Dec 15–25, mid-Jan–mid-Feb.*	AE MC V				■
ST-JEAN-CAP-FERRAT: *Le Sloop* €€€ Nouveau port de St-Jean. ☎ 04 93 01 48 63. Amid the smart yachts of St-Jean's picturesque port, Le Sloop specializes in light and delicious seafood. ♿ ◑ *mid Sep–Jun: Wed, Jul–mid-Sep: Tue L, Wed L; mid-Nov–Dec 20.*	MC V		■	●	■
ST-RÉMY-DE-PROVENCE: *Le Jardin de Fréderic* €€ 8 bd Gambetta. ☎ 04 90 92 27 76. This small, family-run restaurant housed in a villa serves local dishes such as rack of lamb with garlic cream. ◑ *Wed, Thu L; Feb.*	MC V	●	■		■
ST-VALLIER-DE-THIEY: *Le Relais Impérial* €€ Route Napoléon, Route Nationale 85. ☎ 04 93 60 36 36. In an agreeable atmosphere, and with friendly service, this is one of the few places to offer an authentic *pissaladière* – onions, olives, and anchovies cooked in dough – with superb Provençal white wines. ♿	AE DC MC V	●	■	●	■
SÉGURET: *La Table du Comtat* €€€ Séguret. ☎ 04 90 46 91 49. Truffles, pigeon and wild boar grace a menu of local produce. A memorable view forms the backdrop and the cellar stuffed with Côtes du Rhône provides a fitting accompaniment. ♿ ◑ *Oct–Jun: Tue D–Wed (& Oct–Mar: Sun D); Feb.*	AE DC MC V	●	■	●	■
TOUËT-SUR-VAR: *Auberge des Chasseurs* € Touët. ☎ 04 93 05 71 11. Local game makes for appetizing and filling dishes at this country auberge, and the stockfish *à la niçoise* is excellent. ♿ ◑ *Tue (& Oct–Jun: Sun–Thu); Nov.*	AE DC MC V	●	■		■

VENCE: *Auberge des Seigneurs* €€ Place du Frêne. **[** 04 93 58 04 24. Come with an appetite to this medieval *auberge*, complete with roaring fire and five succulent courses, including chicken and rack of lamb curry. ● *Mon L, Sat L.* ● *Mon, Tue L, Wed L; Nov–mid-Mar.*	DC MC V	■			
VENCE: *Le Vieux Couvent* €€€ 68 av Général Leclerc. **[** 04 93 58 78 58. Housed in a former 17th-century convent, this restaurant is popular for Provençal fare with an inventive touch. ● *Wed, Thu L; Jan 10–mid-Mar.*	MC V	■	●	
VILLEFRANCHE-SUR-MER: *Mère Germaine* €€€ Quai Courbet. **[** 04 93 01 71 39. Bouillabaisse and *sole tante marie* (poached sole with mushrooms) are served in this friendly restaurant overlooking the beach. **&** ● *Nov 12–Dec 21.*	AE MC V	■		■

CORSICA

AJACCIO: *Le 20123* €€ 2 rue du Roi-de-Rome. **[** 04 95 21 50 05. At the heart of the old town, M Albani has recreated his native mountain village, Pina Canale, within his restaurant. Top quality regional products are used, and the wine is a local organic red. ● *Mon; mid-Jan–mid-Feb.*		●	■	
BASTIA: *A Casarella* €€ Route Ste-Croix. **[** 04 95 32 02 32. Within the Citadelle, overlooking the port, Corsican specialties like *stozzapreti* (grated cheese with tomato/herb sauce) are served here. ● *Sat L, Sun; Nov.*	MC V	■	●	■
BONIFACIO: *L'Archivolto* €€ Rue de l'Archivolto. **[** 04 95 73 17 58. Part of the flea market, the chef at l'Archivolto makes the most of fresh seasonal produce. The terrace makes outdoor dining a pleasure. ● *Sun L; Oct–Mar.*	MC V	■		
BONIFACIO: *Stella d'Oro* € 7 rue Doria. **[** 04 95 73 03 63. A family institution, with a hearty local atmosphere. Fish and fowl feature heavily on the menu. ● *Oct–Easter.*	AE DC MC V	■		
CALVI: *L'Ile de Beauté* €€ Quai Landry. **[** 04 95 65 00 46. This restaurant is on the quayside and concentrates on perfect fish creations such as terrines or red mullet salad. The seafood selection varies according to what the market has to offer. ● *Oct–Mar 25.*	AE DC MC V	■		
CORTE: *Auberge de la Restonica* €€ Vallée de la Restonica. **[** 04 95 46 09 58. Run by an ex-international soccer player, this is a rural hillside inn with a dining room opening on to views of the forest. Simple, good food. **&** ● *Nov–Feb.*	MC V	●	■	
L'ILE ROUSSE: *La Bergerie* €€€€ Route de Monticello. **[** 04 95 60 01 28. Dine in the shady garden of this pretty converted farmhouse. Try a sea-urchin omelette with some local wine. **&** ● *Apr–mid-Jun & mid-Sep–Oct: Mon; Nov–Mar.*	MC V			■
PORTO: *Le Soleil Couchant* € Porto Marine. **[** 04 95 26 10 12. On the terrace, there are wonderful views over the marina. The local fare is very good value; the *charcuterie* and sheeps' cheeses excel. **&** ● *Nov–Mar.*	MC V	■		
PORTO-VECCHIO: *Auberge du Maquis* €€€ Ferruccio. **[** 04 95 70 20 39. In this peaceful country retreat, a short drive from Porto-Vecchio, the cuisine is local and simple – baked trout with olive oil or stuffed eggplant. ● *Apr–Jun: Wed; Oct–Dec.*		●	■	■
ST-FLORENT: *La Gaffe* €€ Port de St-Florent. **[** 04 95 37 00 12. Savor fresh, appetizing mussels and crayfish in lemon and mint, while sitting on the shady terrace watching the boats sail by. **&** ● *Mon L, Tue L; mid-Nov–Jan.*	AE DC MC V	●	■	●	■
SARTÈNE: *La Chaumière* €€ 39 rue du Capitaine-Benedetti. **[** 04 95 77 07 13. Carved out of the granite hillside, this Corsican inn serves traditional island cooking: *charcuterie*, tripe, and wild boar, with local wines. ● *mid-Jan–mid-Mar.*	AE DC MC V	●	■		■

For key to symbols see back flap

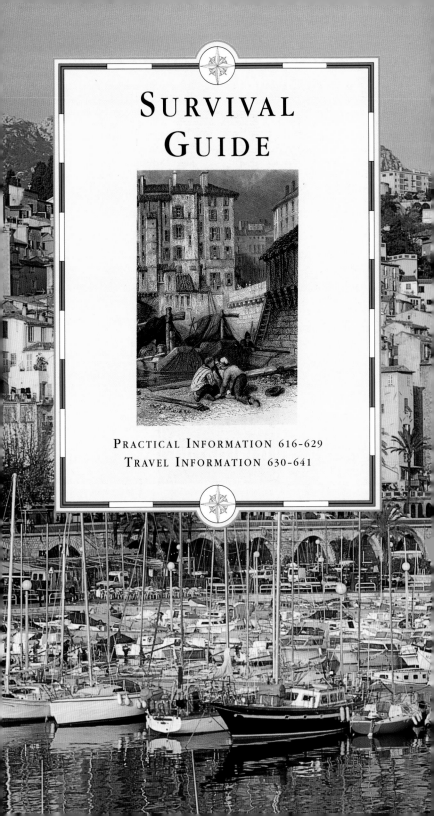

SURVIVAL
GUIDE

PRACTICAL INFORMATION

FRANCE is justifiably proud of its many attractions, for which it has excellent tourist information facilities. Both in France and abroad, French Government Tourist Offices are an invaluable source of reference for practical aspects of your stay. Most towns and large villages in France have a tourist information office; the relevant

Tourist information logo

address and telephone number is provided for each town and area listed in this guide. Domestic tourism in France creates peak vacation migration periods, especially between July 14 and August 31. Consequently, the hotel and restaurant trades are seasonal. A little advance planning will allow you to avoid the disappointment of seasonal closings.

MANNERS

THE FRENCH have rituals of politeness that are easy to pick up. In shops be ready to say *Bonjour Monsieur/Madame* before asking for what you want, then *merci* when you receive your change, and *merci, au revoir Monsieur/ Madame* when you get your purchases and leave.

Shake hands when introduced to someone, or at any time when you see a hand offered. In small communities, locals may greet you with a *Bonjour Monsieur/Madame* in the street even if they have never seen you before. For other useful expressions, refer to the phrase book *(pp671–2)*.

VISAS

CURRENTLY THERE are no visa requirements for EU nationals or visitors from the United States, Canada, Australia, or New Zealand who plan to stay in France for under three months. For trips over three months, visas should be obtained prior to departure from your local French consulate. Visitors from most other countries require a tourist visa. Anyone planning to study or work in France should apply to their local French consulate several months in advance about visa requirements.

TAX-FREE GOODS AND CUSTOMS INFORMATION

VISITORS RESIDING outside the EU can reclaim the sales tax TVA or VAT on French goods if more than 175 is spent in one shop in one day. Get a *détaxe* receipt and take

the goods (untouched) out of the country within 3 months. The form should be presented to customs when leaving the country. The reimbursement will be sent to you.

Exceptions for *détaxe* rebate are food and alcohol, medicines, tobacco, cars and motorcycles. Tax can be reimbursed for bicycles. More information and advice is available from the **Centre des Renseignements des Douanes**.

Sign for tourist office in smaller towns and villages

TOURIST INFORMATION

ALL MAJOR CITIES and large towns have *offices de tourisme*. Small towns and even villages have *syndicats d'initiative*. Both can provide town maps, advice on accommodations, and information on regional recreational and cultural activities.

You can also get information before you leave for France from **French Government Tourist Offices (FGTO)** (or Maisons de la France as they are officially known), or by

phoning or writing to local tourist offices (see headings for each town in this guide) or to the appropriate Regional Tourist Board *(Comité Régional de Tourisme)* – ask the FGTO for the address.

ADMISSION CHARGES

MOST MUSEUMS and monuments in France charge an entrance fee, usually from 2 to 7.5 . This may be reduced or waived on Sundays. Discounts are usually available to under 7s, under 18s, students under 26 (carrying valid student identification) and over 60s.

OPENING HOURS

THIS GUIDE lists which days of the week sights are open. Generally, hours are from 10am–5:40pm with one late evening per week. Most sights close on major public holidays. National museums and sights are normally closed on Tuesdays, with a few exceptions which close on Mondays. Municipal museums normally close on Mondays. Churches open every day but close at lunchtime. Check the opening hours for private museums because they do not always have standard opening times.

See page 622 for details on opening hours for shops; page 620 for banks; and pages 576–7 for restaurants.

Colonne de la Grande Armée

Sign to monument of cultural importance

Visitors taking the weight off weary feet

FACILITIES FOR THE DISABLED

WHEN PARKING, the international orange card scheme applies. In general, however, France is not yet very wheelchair friendly. While most larger museums and major sites, as well as restaurants, now provide at least partial wheelchair access, the very nature of many chateaux and fortified monuments implies inaccessibility. Various organizations (with websites) have more or less complete information: the **GIHP** (Groupement pour l'Insertion des Personnes Handicapées Physiques), and the **Association des Paralysés de France**, whose travel branch, APF Evasion, runs specialist holidays, as do Voyages Asa (*see p539*). The **CIDJ** (Centre d'Information et de Documentation Jeunesse) has information for young disabled travelers.

FRENCH TIME

FRANCE IS ONE HOUR ahead of Greenwich Mean Time (GMT) in winter, and 2 hours in summer. The French use the 24-hour clock, eg 7pm = 19:00.

Lining up for the Eiffel Tower

STUDENT INFORMATION

STUDENTS WITH valid identity cards (the ISIC International Student Identity Card) benefit from many discounts. **CIDJ** offices provide a comprehensive service for students.

ELECTRICAL ADAPTORS

THE VOLTAGE in France is 220 volts. Plugs have two round pins, or three round pins for applications which need to be earthed. Some hotels offer built-in adaptors for shavers only.

Standard French two-pin plug for electrical appliances

CONVERSION CHART

Imperial to metric
1 inch = 2.54 centimeters
1 foot = 30 centimeters
1 mile = 1.6 kilometers
1 ounce = 28 grams
1 pound = 454 grams
1 US pint = 0.47 liter
1 US gallon = 3.8 liters

Metric to imperial
1 millimeter = 0.04 inch
1 centimeter = 0.4 inch
1 meter = 3 feet 3 inches
1 kilometer = 0.6 mile
1 gram = 0.04 ounce
1 kilogram = 2.2 pounds
1 liter = 2.1 US pints

DIRECTORY

EMBASSIES

United States
2 av Gabriel, 75008 Paris.
Map 3 A5. 01 43 12 22 22.
Consulate: 2 rue St. Florentin, 75001 Paris. **Map** 11 C1.
01 43 12 23 47.
Consular offices: Nice, Marseilles, Strasbourg.

United Kingdom
35 rue du Faubourg St-Honoré
Paris 75008. **Map** 3 C5.

FRENCH GOVERNMENT TOURIST OFFICES

United States
French Government Tourist Office, 444 Madison Avenue, New York, NY 10022.
(212) 838 7800.

UK
French Government Tourist Office (Maison de la France), 178 Piccadilly, London W1V 0AL.
0906 8244 123 within UK only.
FAX 020 7493 6594.
W www.franceguide.com

USEFUL ADDRESSES

Centre des Renseignements des Douanes
84 rue d'Hauteville, 75010 Paris.
Map 14 F3. 01 53 24 68 24.
FAX 01 53 24 68 30.
9am–5pm Mon–Fri.
W www.douane.minese.gouv.fr

CIDJ
101 quai Branly, 75015 Paris.
Map 6 E2. 01 44 49 12 00.
9:30am–6pm Mon–Fri (5pm Tue & Fri, 1pm Sat).
W www.cidj.com

GIHP
10 rue de Georges de Porto-Riche, 75014 Paris. 01 43 95 66 36.
W www.crava-cicat.com

Paris Convention and Visitors Bureau Headquarters
127 av des Champs-Elysées, 75008 Paris. **Map** 2 E4. 08 36 68 31 12 (in English). 9am–8pm daily, (11am–6pm Sun in winter). May 1
W www.paris-touristoffice.com

Personal Security and Health

On the whole, France is a safe place for visitors: take normal precautions, such as sensible care of your possessions at all times, and avoid unfamiliar or unfrequented residential urban areas after dark. If you become ill during your stay, pharmacies are an excellent source of advice. Consulates and consular departments at your embassy are a good source of help and advice in an emergency *(see p617)*. For serious medical problems, this section gives the numbers of the most important emergency services.

French pharmacy sign

PERSONAL SECURITY

Violent crime is not a major problem in France. Take the usual precautions you would at home. Avoid risky city neighborhoods. If you are involved in an argument or car accident, avoid confrontation. In potentially difficult situations you should above all stay calm and speak French if you can; this may defuse the situation.

LEGAL ASSISTANCE

Nearly all travel insurance policies cover legal costs up to a certain level, as do comprehensive motor policies, in the event of any legal action or advice being needed, for example after an accident. If you do not have this coverage, phone your nearest consulate or, as a last resort, phone the local *Ordre des Avocats* (lawyers' association) for the name of a good local lawyer.

INTERPRETERS

Translation and interpretation is offered by professional translators. Contact the **Société Française des Traducteurs** *(see below)*.

PERSONAL PROPERTY

Make sure you insure your possessions before arrival. Beware of pickpockets, especially on the Paris metro during the rush hour. Keep all valuables securely concealed, and if carrying a purse or briefcase, never let it out of your sight. Also, only take as much cash as you think you will need. Traveler's checks are the safest method of carrying large sums of money.

Phone or visit the area police to report crimes, missing persons or stolen property, muggings or assault. The *commissariat de police* is the headquarters. In small towns and villages, go to the *mairie* (town hall), which will only be open during office hours. If your passport is lost or stolen, call your consulate *(see p617)*.

The white-gloved motorcyclists who patrol the highways are the *CRS (Compagnie Républicaine de Sécurité)*.

If you are involved in a traffic accident outside a town you may be asked to accompany the other driver to the nearest *gendarmerie*. The *gendarmerie nationale* is a military organization that deals with all crimes outside urban areas. Making a statement (a *PV* or *procès-verbal*) can be a lengthy process. Take your

identity papers (and your vehicle papers, if relevant) with you when you go to make a statement.

MEDICAL TREATMENT

All travelers should consider purchasing travel insurance. Non-EU nationals are obliged to carry medical insurance, taken out before they arrive.

Discuss your medical coverage with your insurer before leaving the US. If you know that you will need to obtain prescriptions while you are abroad, find out in advance exactly how to do this. Your local consulate may be able to help.

In the case of a medical emergency call **SAMU** *(Service d'Aide Médicale Urgence)*. However, it is often faster to call **Sapeurs Pompiers** (the fire service), who offer a first-aid and ambulance service. This is particularly true in rural areas of France where the local fire department is likely to be much closer than

---

Gendarme

Fireman

DIRECTORY

EMERGENCY NUMBERS

Ambulance (SAMU)
📞 15 or 18 *(Sapeurs Pompiers)*.

Fire (Sapeurs Pompiers)
📞 18.

Police and Gendarmerie
📞 17.

INTERPRETERS

Société Française des Traducteurs
📞 01 48 78 43 32.
🌐 www.sft.fr

the ambulance service based in town. The paramedics are called *secouristes*.

Emergency rooms *(service des urgences)* in public hospitals can deal with most medical problems. Your consulate should be able to recommend an English-speaking doctor in the area.

PHARMACIES

IN FRANCE, pharmacists can diagnose health problems and suggest appropriate treatments. They are also trained to identify mushrooms, and you can take any you are unsure about to them to eliminate the danger of poisoning.

Pharmacies have a green cross outside. A card in the window will give details of the nearest *pharmacie de garde* for night openings.

Police car

Fire engine

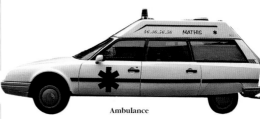

Ambulance

Fire hazard poster

OUTDOOR EMERGENCIES

FOREST FIRES are a major risk in many parts of France. High winds can make fires spread rapidly in winter as well as summer. Keep well away from an area where there is a fire, as its direction can change quickly. Make sure you do not start a fire with campfires or a cigarette butt.

When walking in the mountains or sailing, notify the relevant authority of your route and observe local regulations posted in the area.

During the hunting season (Sep–Feb and especially Sundays) dress in bright colors when out walking. Avoid areas where hunters may be concealed in blinds or stalking game in the woods *(see p629)*.

PUBLIC TOILETS IN FRANCE

Modern pay toilets are now found in many towns. Do not let children under ten use the toilets on their own as the automatic cleaning function can be dangerous. The best policy is to use toilets in cafés or restaurants where you are a customer, or go to a department store. Traditional *pissoirs* and keyhole toilets, still found in some towns, are often not very clean. Toilet facilities are provided on the *autoroute* at drive-in rest areas every 20 km (12 miles), as well as at the major service areas.

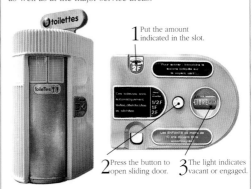

1 Put the amount indicated in the slot.

2 Press the button to open sliding door.

3 The light indicates vacant or engaged.

Banking and Local Currency

YOU MAY BRING any amount of currency into France, but anything over 7,500€ (cash and checks) must be declared on arrival. The same applies when you leave. Traveler's checks are the safest way to carry money abroad, but credit cards, which can be used to withdraw local currency, are by far the most convenient. Bureaux de change are located at airports, main train stations, and in some hotels and shops, but banks usually offer the best rates of exchange.

Credit card cash dispenser

USING BANKS

MOST FRENCH BANKS have a bureau de change, but rates can vary. Most banks also now have ATMs (automatic teller machines) outside (or an indoor area open 24 hr/day), which accept credit cards in the **Visa/Carte Bleue** or **Mastercard** groups and debit cards (Switch, Maestro, Cirrus), enabling you to withdraw money in local currency directly from your own bank account. Bear in mind that ATMs may run out of bills before the end of the weekend.

If there is no ATM, you can withdraw up to 300€ per day on Visa at the foreign counter of a bank showing the Visa sign. The Bank may need to obtain telephone authorization for such withdrawals first.

BANKING HOURS

AS A GENERAL RULE, banks in northern France are open Mon–Fri approximately 9am–4:30 or 5:15pm. However, some are open only till noon, and many will close at noon on the working day before a holiday. In southern France, banks are normally open Tue–Sat, approximately 8am–12 noon and from 1:30–4:30pm. Around a public holiday, they are usually closed from Friday noon to Tuesday morning.

BUREAUX DE CHANGE

OUTSIDE PARIS, independent bureaux de change are rare except in main train stations and areas with a high density of tourists. Privately owned bureaux de change can have variable rates: check commission and minimum charges first.

CARDS AND CHECKS

TRAVELERS' CHECKS can be obtained from **American Express**, **Thomas Cook** or your bank. If you know that you will spend most of them, it is best to have them issued in Euros. American Express checks are widely accepted in France. If checks are exchanged at an Amex office no commission is charged. In the case of theft, checks are replaced at once.

Because of the high commissions charged, many French businesses do not accept the American Express credit card. The most commonly used credit card is Carte Bleue/Visa. Eurocard/Mastercard is also widely accepted.

Credit cards issued in France are now "smart cards," which means they have a *puce* (a microchip capable of storing data instead of a magnetic strip on the back). Many retailers have machines designed to read both smart cards and magnetic strips. Conventional non-French cards cannot be read in the smart card slot. Persuade the cashier to swipe the card through the magnetic reader *(bande magnétique)*. You may also be asked to tap in your PIN code *(code confidentiel)* and press the green key *(validez)* on a small keypad by the cash desk.

Machine to read credit cards

CONVERSION CHART

THE FOLLOWING chart is a rough guide to equivalent currency values, rounded up or down for ease of use.

EUROS	FRANCS
1	6.5
5	33
10	65
20	130
25	165
50	330
75	495
100	650
150	980

THE EURO

The euro (€), the single European currency, is now operational in 12 of the 15 member states of the EU. Austria, Belgium, Finland, France, Germany, Greece, Ireland, Italy, Luxembourg, Netherlands, Portugal, and Spain all chose to join the new currency; Denmark, the UK, and Sweden chose to stay out, with an option to review their decision. France's Overseas Departments (Réunion etc) also all now use the euro.

Euro notes are identical throughout all 12 countries, bearing architectural drawings of fictitious monuments. The coins, however, have one side identical (the value side), and one side unique to each country. Both notes and coins are valid and interchangeable within each of the 12 countries.

Bank Notes

Euro bills have seven denominations. The 5€ note (gray in color) is the smallest, followed by the 10€ note (pink), 20€ bill (blue), 50€ bill (orange), 100€ bill (green), 200€ bill (yellow), and 500€ bill (purple). All notes show the stars of the European Union.

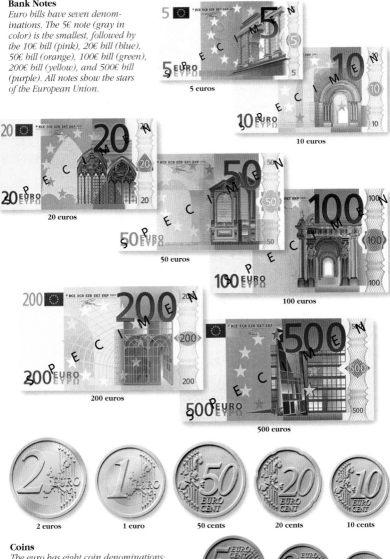

5 euros

10 euros

20 euros

50 euros

100 euros

200 euros

500 euros

Coins

The euro has eight coin denominations: 1 euro and 2 euros; 50 cents, 20 cents, 10 cents, 5 cents, 2 cents, and 1 cent. The 2- and 1-euro coins are both silver and gold in color. The 50-, 20- and 10-cent coins are gold. The 5-, 2- and 1-cent coins are bronze.

2 euros

1 euro

50 cents

20 cents

10 cents

5 cents

2 cents

1 cent

Shopping

Sᴴᴏᴘᴘɪɴɢ ɪɴ ꜰʀᴀɴᴄᴇ is a delight. Whether you go to the hypermarkets and department stores, or seek out the small specialist stores and markets, you will be tempted by stylish French presentation and the quality of goods for sale. Renowned for its food and wine, France also offers world-famous fashion, pottery, porcelain and crystal.

This section gives guidelines on opening hours, and the range of goods stocked by the different types of stores and markets. There are also tips on how to buy wine straight from the vineyards and wine cooperatives, and a size conversion chart to make clothes shopping easier.

Olive oil from Baux

Fresh nectarines and melons for sale at a market stall

Opening Hours

Fᴏᴏᴅ ꜱʜᴏᴘꜱ open anytime between 7 and 8am and close around noon for lunch. In the North, this is generally for 2 hours; in the South, it is usually for 3–4 hours (except in resorts). After lunch most are open until 7pm or later. Bakeries often stay open until 1pm or later, to catch the late baguette buyers, as well as serving snacks at lunchtime.

Shops that do not close at lunchtime include some supermarkets, department stores and most hypermarkets.

General opening hours for nonfood shops are around 9am–6pm Mon–Sat, often with a break for lunch. Many of these shops are closed Monday mornings.

Most food shops (and newsagents) are open on Sunday mornings. Virtually every shop in France is closed on Sunday afternoon. Smaller shops may be closed one day of the week, usually Monday. However, those in tourist regions are often open every day in the high season.

Larger Shops

Hʏᴘᴇʀᴍᴀʀᴋᴇᴛꜱ (*hypermarchés* or *grandes surfaces*) can be found on the outskirts of every sizable town: look for signs indicating *centre commercial*. Among the biggest are Carrefour, Casino, Auchan, Leclerc and Continent. They sell discount gas.

Department stores (*grands magasins*), such as the cheap and cheerful Monoprix and Prisunic, are often found in town centers. Others, like the more upscale Printemps and Galeries Lafayette, can be found both in town and out-of-town centers.

A local bakery, which will often sell pâtisseries as well as bread

Specialist Shops

Oɴᴇ ᴏꜰ ᴛʜᴇ ᴘʟᴇᴀꜱᴜʀᴇꜱ of shopping in France is that specialist food shops still flourish despite the new large supermarkets. The *boulangerie*, for bread, is frequently combined with a *pâtisserie* selling cakes and pastries. The *traiteur* sells prepared foods. Cheese shops (*fromagerie*) and other shops specializing in dairy products (*laiterie*) may also be combined, while the *boucherie* (butcher's) and *charcuterie* (pork butcher's/delicatessen) are often separate shops. For general groceries go to an *épicerie* or *alimentation*; an *épicerie fine* is a delicatessen.

Cleaning and household products are available from a *droguerie*, but hardware is bought from a *quincaillerie*. The term *Papeterie* (stationer's) covers both the expensive, specialist retailers and their hypermarket equivalent.

Markets

Tʜɪꜱ ɢᴜɪᴅᴇ ʟɪꜱᴛꜱ the market days for every town featured. To find out where the market is, ask a passerby for *le marché*. Markets usually close promptly at noon and don't re-open in the afternoon.

Look for local producers, including those with only one or two special items to sell, because their goods are often cheaper and of better quality.

By law, price tags include the origin of all produce: *pays* means local. Chickens from Bresse are marketed wearing a red, white and blue badge giving the name of the producer as proof of authenticity. If you are visiting markets over several weeks, look for items just coming into season, such as fresh walnuts, the first wild asparagus, early artichokes or wild strawberries.

At the market, you can also buy spices, shoes and clothes, and some unusual items such as decorative cabbages.

There is a full calendar of important seasonal regional markets in France, specializing in such things as truffles, hams, garlic, *foie gras* and livestock. *Foires artisanales* may be held at the same time as the seasonal fairs, selling local produce and crafts.

REGIONAL PRODUCE

F RENCH REGIONAL specialties can be bought outside their area of origin. It is, however, interesting to buy them locally because their creation and flavor reflect the region's traditions, tastes and climate.

Provence, in the south, prides itself on the quality of its olive oil, the best of which is made from the first cold pressing and lovingly decanted every day for a week. In the temperate north, Camembert is the product of fresh Norman milk that has been cured for at least three weeks. Popular drinks are also associated with particular regions. Pastis, made from aniseed, is popular in the south, while calvados, made from apples, is from the north (see p245).

Location also determines quality. For example, the culinary tradition of Lyon, France's premier gastronomic city, comes from the proximity of Charolais cattle, Bresse chickens and pork, game from La Dombes, and the finest Rhône Valley wines.

Sausages and cheeses, regional specialties for sale in a Lyon market

WINE

I N WINE-producing areas, follow the *dégustation* (tasting) signs to vineyards (*domaines*) where you can taste the wine. While not usually compulsory, you will be expected to buy at least one bottle, except in those regions (eg. Beaujolais) where a small fee is normally charged for a wine-tasting. Wine cooperatives make and sell the wine of small produc-

ers. Here you can buy wine in 5- and 10-liter containers (*en vrac*), as well as in bottles. As wine sold *en vrac* is duty-free, customers get a permit (*laissez-passer*) indicating their destination. Bottled wine sold by coops is duty-paid.

HOUSEHOLD AND KITCHEN GOODS

W HEN BUYING goods for the home, try the best department stores such as Alinéa, Cèdre Rouge and Habitat, whose stock is geared to the Gallic market. Despalles is good for garden furniture, and Le Roy Merlin is the home-improvement hypermarket.

It is surprisingly rare to see the whole range of kitchen

Pastis 51, drunk in the south

goods available in a specialist shop. Try the kitchen section of department stores. General hardware stores stock cast-iron cooking equipment. White china is sold in specialist shops.

A good variety of pottery is available throughout France at reasonable prices, especially near centers of production, such as Aubagne near Marseille and Vallauris near Grasse.

Other fine examples of French craftmanship come from Limoges, a world-famous center for porcelain since the 18th century (see p346), and Baccarat in Lorraine, renowned for fine crystal since 1764.

CLOTHING

E LEGANT AND CASUAL clothes can be found even in quite small towns. Paris, however, remains the center for fashion; refer to pages 136–7 for details on men's and women's fashion.

Provençal dried herbs for culinary use and making teas

SIZE CHART

For Australian sizes follow the British and American conversions.

Women's dresses, coats and skirts

French	36	38	40	42	44	46	48
British	8	10	12	14	16	18	20
American	6	8	10	12	14	16	18

Women's shoes

French	36	37	38	39	40	41
British	3	4	5	6	7	8
American	5	6	7	8	9	10

Men's suits

French	44	46	48	50	52	54	56	58
British	34	36	38	40	42	44	46	48
American	34	36	38	40	42	44	46	48

Men's shirts

French	36	38	39	41	42	43	44	45
British	14	15	$15^{1}/_{2}$	16	$16^{1}/_{2}$	17	$17^{1}/_{2}$	18
American	14	15	$15^{1}/_{2}$	16	$16^{1}/_{2}$	17	$17^{1}/_{2}$	18

Men's shoes

French	39	40	41	42	43	44	45	46
British	6	7	$7^{1}/_{2}$	8	9	10	11	12
American	7	$7^{1}/_{2}$	8	$8^{1}/_{2}$	$9^{1}/_{2}$	$10^{1}/_{2}$	11	$11^{1}/_{2}$

Communications

FRENCH TELECOMMUNICATIONS are sophisticated and efficient. They are run by France Télécom; the postal service is *La Poste*. Public telephones are located in most public places. To use them, you usually need a phonecard (*télécarte*).

Post offices (*bureaux des postes*) are identified by the blue-on-yellow La Poste sign. La Poste used to be called the PTT, so road signs often still indicate PTT.

Foreign language newspapers are available in most large towns. Some TV channels and radio stations broadcast foreign-language programs.

Sign for public telephone

TELEPHONING IN FRANCE

TO USE A PAYPHONE (*cabine*), you generally need a phone card (*télécarte*). Sold in tabacs, post offices and some newsagents, these are available in 50 or 120 telephone units, and are simple to use. Remember to buy a new card *before* the old one runs out! For local calls, a unit lasts up to six minutes. Many phones now also accept credit cards (with a PIN number).

Few payphones take coins. Cheap rates, giving 50% lower call charges, operate from 7pm to 8am Monday to Friday, from midnight to 8am and noon to midnight on Saturday, and all day Sunday. In cafés, payphones are token-operated and are reserved for the use of patrons. Post offices have telephone booths (*cabines*) where you can telephone first and pay after the call. This is cheaper than making long-distance calls from hotels, which often add hefty surcharges.

The Minitel electronic directory can also be used free in post offices.

Home Direct calling service, or *pays directe*, lets you book the call through an operator in your country, and pay by credit card or by reversing the charges. Sometimes you can also call a third country.

All French telephone numbers have ten digits. The first two digits indicate the region: 01 indicates Paris and the Ile de France; 02, the northwest; 03, the northeast; 04, the southeast (including Corsica); and 05, the southwest. Do not dial the initial zero when phoning from abroad.

USING A PHONECARD TELEPHONE

1 Lift receiver and wait for a dial tone.

2 Insert the *télécarte,* arrow side up, in the direction that the arrow is pointing.

3 The display will show how many units are stored on the card and then tell you to dial.

4 Key in the number and wait to be connected.

5 If you want to make another call, do not replace the receiver; simply press the green follow-on call button.

6 When you have finished the call, replace the receiver. The card will emerge from the slot. Remove it.

7 If card runs out in mid-call, it will re-emerge; remove it and insert another.

French phonecard

HOW TO KEY INTO MINITEL

Minitel provides a variety of services through a screen and keyboard connected to the telephone line. To use Minitel, press the telephone symbol and enter the Minitel number and code. For directory information, press the telephone symbol and key in 3611. When beeping starts, press Connexion/Fin. Specify the service or name of supplier required. Enter town or area. Press Envoi to search. To disconnect, press Veille or Connexion/Fin. Charges vary and are displayed on the screen.

TV AND RADIO

ALL TV CHANNELS in France show commercials. The major nationwide TV channels are *TF1* and *France 2*, both offering a lightweight mass-audience mix of soaps, game shows, discussion and movies. *France 3*, with wildlife, documentaries, debate, arts programs and classic films, is regional television, locally made and presented in every part of France, though national and international issues are also covered. *5ᵉ (La Cinquième)* and the Franco-German high-culture *ARTE*, specialising in arts, classical music and films, share a channel (and show relatively few commercials). *M6* shows magazine programs on topical issues, money, etc, as well as devoting a lot of time to pop music. *Canal Plus* (or *Canal +*) is the popular "extra channel" available to subscribers only, though a few programs are shown uncoded. Most hotels subscribe, allowing guests to enjoy the channel's diverse mix of music, sport exclusives, family programs screened early in the day, and adult movies (including porn) in the late evening.

Other popular subscription cable and satellite channels in France (collectively known as *TPS*, or *télévision par satellite*) include English-language *MTV*, *CNN*, *Sky* and *BBC World*, as well as several in French and other languages. English-language films on French television are generally subtitled at first (look out for the letters "*VO*" – *Version Originale*); dubbed versions appear later ("*VF*" – *Version Française*).

UK radio stations can be picked up in France, including *Radio 4* during the day (648 AM or 198 Long Wave). On the same wavelength, *BBC World Service* broadcasts through the night, with news in English every hour. *Voice of America* can be found at 90.5, 98.8 and 102.4 FM. *Radio France International* (738 AM) gives daily news in English from 3-4pm. French radio stations favour phone-ins and French pop music, or, on more highbrow stations, lengthy intellectual discussions – for fluent French speakers.

CELL PHONES

MOST NEW CELL phones brought from another European or Mediterranean country can be used in France exactly as at home. However, US-based cell phones need to be "triple band" to be used in France. Cell phones are also readily available for hire in France if required. Remember that making and receiving international mobile calls can be very expensive.

INTERNET ACCESS

AFTER A SLOW start, the number of French language sites grew rapidly and the internet is now widely accessible everywhere in France, including in many hotels and in internet cafes. The French modem socket is incompatible with US and UK plugs. Although adaptors are available, it is cheaper to buy a French modem lead.

Foreign newspapers sold in France

NEWSPAPERS AND MAGAZINES

BUY YOUR NEWSPAPERS and magazines at a newsagent (*maison de la presse*) or a news-stand (*kiosque*). Every region of France is served by major local newspapers, which are much more popular than Paris-based national ones. The main national dailies are – from right to left on the political spectrum – weighty, intelligent *Le Figaro*, tabloid *France Soir*, quirky *Le Monde* (comes out in the afternoon), *Libération* on the intellectual left and the Communist paper *L'Humanité*.

In resorts and large cities, many British newspapers are available on the day of publication. Some are European editions, like *Financial Times Europe* and *The Guardian Europe*. Other papers may arrive a day or two late, as do Sunday newspapers. English-language international papers and magazines include *The Weekly Telegraph*, *Guardian International*, *USA Today*, *The Economist*, *Newsweek*, and *The International Herald Tribune*.

USEFUL FRENCH DIALLING CODES

- **Directory enquiries** dial 12.
- **International directory enquiries**, for all countries, dial 32 12.
- **International telegrams** dial 0800 33 44 11.
- **Home Direct** (collect call), dial 0800 99, then the country code (preceded by 00).
- To ring **France** dial: from the UK and US: 00 33; from Australia: 00 11 33. Omit the first 0 of the French area code.
- To make direct international calls, dial 00, wait for the tone, then dial the country

code, area code (omit the intital zero) and the number.
- The middle pages of the telephone directory give the cost of calls per minute for each country and list their country codes, Home direct codes etc.
- The country codes for the following are: **Australia**: 61; **Canada and USA**: 1; **Eire**: 353; **New Zealand**: 64; **UK**: 44.
- **Low-rate period** (for most places): 7pm–8am Mon–Fri, all day Sun and public hols.
In the case of emergencies, dial 17.

Road sign giving directions to the post office

USING LA POSTE

LA POSTE (the Post Office) used to be called the P.T.T. *(postes, télégraphes, téléphones)* and although the signs have been changed on post office buildings, some road signs still give directions to the P.T.T.

The postal service in France is fast and reliable. However, it is not cheap, especially when sending a parcel abroad, as all sea-mail services have been discontinued.

At La Poste, postage stamps *(timbres)* are sold singly or in *carnets* of seven or ten. Common postage stamps are also sold at *tabacs*. You can also consult the electronic telephone directory on Minitel for free, buy phonecards *(télécartes)*, cash or send international money orders *(mandats)*, and call abroad.

Post offices also provide, for a small collection fee, a mail holding service so you can receive mail care of post offices in France. As an address, the sender should write the recipient's surname in block capitals before the first name, followed by "Poste Restante," then the postcode and name of the town it is to be sent to. Unless specified otherwise, mail will go to that town's main post office *(recette principale)*. When sending a letter poste restante it is wise to underline the

surname, as French officials may otherwise assume the first name is the family name.

Post offices usually open from 9am–5pm Mon–Fri, often with a break for lunch, and 9am–noon on Saturdays.

SENDING A LETTER

LETTERS ARE MAILED in yellow mailboxes that often have separate slots for the town you are in, the *département* and other destinations *(autres destinations)*.

There are eight different price zones for international mail. EU countries are the cheapest, Australasia the most expensive. You can also buy aerograms, which cost the same for all countries.

A mailman *(un facteur)*

POSTCODES

ALL FRENCH ADDRESSES have five-digit postcodes. The first two digits represent the *département (see opposite)*. If they are followed by 000, this indicates the main town in that *département*, so, for example, Bordeaux is 33000. France's largest cities, Paris, Lyon and Marseille, are divided into *arrondissements*, which are shown in the last two digits of the postcode.

The town hall in Compiègne

LOCAL GOVERNMENT IN FRANCE

A COMPLEX JIGSAW, France's local government operates in a three-tier system – *région, département* and *commune*. The country used to comprise separate semi-autonomous provinces or duchies, like Provence and the smaller Anjou. During the Revolution, these were replaced by a standard-sized network of 96 *départements*. These are administrative units mostly named after rivers, for example Haute-Loire, each ruled by a *préfet* appointed in Paris.

The system had its strengths, but was too state-controlled for a modern democracy. Now some of the prefect's power has gone to the *département's* elected council. For some functions the *départements* have been grouped into 22 *régions*, each with an elected assembly. Several, like Brittany and Alsace, roughly correspond to the old provinces; others are hybrids, like Centre and Rhône-Alpes.

At a lower level, France remains split up into around 35,000 *communes* (parishes or boroughs), ranging from big cities like Paris or Lyon to tiny villages. Each *commune* has its elected mayor, a figure of great local influence, ruling from the *mairie* (town hall). This system is cumbersome, yet village communes refuse to merge, so great is the pull of local pride.

A distinctive yellow French mailbox

***Carnet* of ten stamps**

Regions of France
In 1972, France was officially divided into 22 regions. This map shows the 15 regional divisions used in this guide and all France's 96 départements.

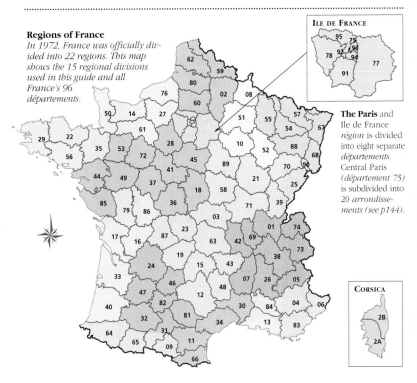

ILE DE FRANCE

The Paris and Ile de France *région* is divided into eight separate *départements.* Central Paris *(département 75)* is subdivided into 20 *arrondissements (see p144).*

CORSICA

THE DÉPARTEMENTS OF FRANCE

PARIS AND ILE DE FRANCE
75 Paris
77 Seine-et-Marne
78 Yvelines
91 Essonne
92 Hauts-de-Seine
93 Seine-St-Denis
94 Val-de-Marne
95 Val-d'Oise

NORTHEAST FRANCE
Le Nord and Picardy
02 Aisne
59 Nord
60 Oise
62 Pas-de-Calais
80 Somme

Champagne
08 Ardennes
10 Aube
51 Marne
52 Haute-Marne

Alsace and Lorraine
54 Meurthe-et-Moselle
55 Meuse
57 Moselle
67 Bas-Rhin
68 Haut-Rhin
88 Vosges

WESTERN FRANCE
Normandy
14 Calvados
27 Eure
50 Manche
61 Orne
76 Seine-Maritime

Brittany
22 Côtes-du-Nord
29 Finistère

35 Ille-et-Vilaine
56 Morbihan

The Loire Valley
18 Cher
28 Eure-et-Loir
36 Indre
37 Indre-et-Loire
41 Loir-et-Cher
44 Loire-Atlantique
45 Loiret
49 Maine-et-Loire
53 Mayenne
72 Sarthe
85 Vendee

CENTRAL FRANCE
Burgundy and Franche-Comté
21 Côte d'Or
25 Doubs
39 Jura
58 Nièvre
70 Haute-Saône
71 Saône-et-Loire
89 Yonne
90 Territoire de Belfort

The Massif Central
03 Allier
12 Aveyron
15 Cantal
19 Corrèze
23 Creuse
43 Haute-Loire
48 Lozère
63 Puy-de-Dôme
87 Haute-Vienne

Rhône Valley and French Alps
01 Ain
05 Hautes Alpes
07 Ardèche
26 Drôme
38 Isère
42 Loire

69 Rhône
73 Savoie
74 Haute-Savoie

SOUTHWEST FRANCE
Poitou and Aquitaine
16 Charente
17 Charente-Maritime
33 Gironde
40 Landes
79 Deux-Sèvres
86 Vienne

Périgord, Quercy and Gascony
24 Dordogne
32 Gers
46 Lot
47 Lot-et-Garonne
81 Tarn
82 Tarn-et-Garonne

The Pyrenees
09 Ariège
31 Haute-Garonne
64 Pyrénées-Atlantiques
65 Hautes-Pyrénées

THE SOUTH OF FRANCE
Languedoc-Roussillon
11 Aude
30 Gard
34 Hérault
66 Pyrénées-Orientales

Provence and the Côte d'Azur
04 Alpes-de-Haut-Provence
06 Alpes-Maritimes
13 Bouches-du-Rhône
83 Var
84 Vaucluse

Corsica
2A Corse-du-Sud
2B Haute-Corse

Special Vacations and Outdoor Activities

A COUNTRY AS RICHLY DIVERSE in culture and geography as France offers an amazing variety of sports and leisure activities. For the best in entertainment and spectator sports, festivals and annual events, see *France through the Year* on pages 32–5. Information on current leisure and sporting activities in a particular region is available from the tourist offices listed for each town in this guide. The suggestions below cover some of the most popular as well as some more unusual pursuits.

Hiking along the Gorges du Verdon in Provence *(see pp504–5)*

SPECIAL VACATIONS

FRENCH GOVERNMENT TOURIST Offices *(see p617)* have extensive information on travel companies offering special-interest vacations. Send for *The Traveler in France Reference Guide*.

Educational courses include language learning, often combined with other activities. Ask for *Cours de français pour étudiants étrangers* from the **French Institute** – write or fax the librarian.

Young people can enjoy a French-speaking vacation by working part-time on the restoration of historic sites with **Union REMPART** *(Union pour la Réhabilitation et Entretien des Monuments et du Patrimoine Artistique)*.

There is a wide choice of gastronomic courses available, offering classical cuisine or regional cooking. Wine appreciation courses for various levels of expertise are also available. There are numerous art and

crafts courses throughout France. for all levels and varying lengths of time.

Nature lovers can enjoy the *parcs nationaux* and can join organized bird-watching and botanical trips in many areas, including the Camargue, the Cévennes and Corsica. *Le Guide des Jardins de France* published by Hachette is a useful reference guide when visiting France's many beautiful gardens.

GOLF AND TENNIS

THERE ARE golf courses all over France, especially along the north and south coasts and in Aquitaine. French players have to reach a minimum standard and obtain a license in order to play, so take your handicap certificate with you. Most top courses offer weekend or longer tutored breaks geared to any level of player. *Le Guide des Golfs de France* published by Editions Sand et Menges gives details.

Tennis is very popular in France and courts for hourly rental can be found in almost every town. Take your own equipment with you as rental facilities may not be available.

Mountain bikes, wonderful for exploring

Escaping into the forest at Fontainebleau *(see pp170–71)*

WALKING, BICYCLING AND HORSE RIDING

MORE THAN 30,000 km (19,000 miles) of *Grandes Randonnées* (long-distance tracks) and the shorter *Petites Randonnées* are clearly marked. The routes vary in difficulty and include long pilgrim routes, alpine crossings and tracks through national parks. *Topo Guides*, published by **Fédération Française de la Randonnée Pédestre**, describe the *GR* tracks in French with details of transportation connections, overnight stops and food shopping. They also publish a general walking guide, *Guide du Randonneur*.

Some *Grandes and Petites Randonnées* are open to mountain bikes and horses. For detailed advice on bicycling in France, contact the **CTC** (Cyclists' Touring Club) or **Fédération Française de Cyclotourisme**. Local tourist offices in France provide details about area riding facilities. *Gîtes d'étapes* *(see p539)* offer dormitory accommodations close to well-known tracks.

MOUNTAIN SPORTS

APART FROM downhill skiing and *ski de fond* (cross-country skiing), catered for by numerous travel operators, the mountains, especially the Alps and Pyrenees, are enjoyed in the

Canoes at St-Chély, near the Gorges du Tarn *(see pp360–61)*

summer by rock-climbers and mountaineers. Contact the **Féderation Française de la Montagne et de l'Escalade** for more information.

AERONAUTICAL SPORTS

Learning to fly in France can be much cheaper than in the US. Information on schools can be obtained from the **Fédération Nationale Aéronautique**. There are also plenty of opportunities to learn the exhilarating skills of gliding, paragliding and hang gliding. For more information, contact the **Fédération Française de Vol Libre**.

Paragliding or *parapente* off the cliffs of Chamonix *(see pp312–13)*

WATER SPORTS

White-water rafting, kayaking and canoeing take place on many French rivers, especially in the Massif Central. More information can be obtained from The **Fédération Française de Canoë-Kayak**. The Atlantic coast around Biarritz offers some of the best surfing and windsurfing in Europe. Sailing and water-skiing are also popular all over France. Training schools and equipment rentals are found at the coast and near lakes.

Swimming facilities are generally good, although beaches in the South of France can be very crowded *(see pp464–5)*.

FIELD SPORTS

Although hunting is a popular sport in France, a *permis de chasse* is essential. This involves passing an exam in French, which makes it difficult for visitors to take part. There are regional variations of season depending on the activity. Details are displayed in local town halls.

All kinds of fishing, for both fresh and seawater fish, are available, depending on the area. Local fishing shops sell the *carte de pêche*, which gives details of regulations.

NATURISM

There are nearly 90 centers in France for naturism, mostly in the south, south-west and Corsica. Information is available in English from French Government Tourist Offices or from the **Fédération Française de Naturisme**.

PUBLIC EVENTS

To join the French enjoying their spare time, look for football (soccer) and rugby matches, or bicycling races. Seasonal markets and local *fêtes* often combine antiques fairs and *boules* tournaments with rock and pop concerts.

TRAVEL INFORMATION

FRANCE has advanced transportation systems, with Paris at the hub. Paris's two main airports, Roissy-Charles-de-Gaulle and Orly, have direct flights to North America, Africa, Japan, and the rest of Europe. The city's six major train stations connect it to some 6,000 destinations in France and provide links to all of Europe. France is also well connected by sea, with frequent ferry crossings in the English Channel and the Mediterranean.

ARRIVING BY AIR

FRANCE IS SERVED by nearly all international airlines. Some airports near the border, such as Geneva, Basle, and Luxembourg, can also be used for destinations in France.

The main British airlines with regular flights to France are **British Airways**, **British Midland**, **Ryanair**, **buzz**, **EasyJet** and **Air France**. From the United States there are regular flights through **American Airlines** and **Delta**. **Air Canada** runs flights from Canada, and **Qantas** provides connecting flights from Australia and New Zealand.

AIR FARES

AIRLINE FARES are at their highest during the peak summer season in France, usually from July to September. Different airlines, however, may have slightly different high summer season periods, so check with the airlines or an

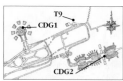

CDG Airport *Terminals CDG1, CDG2, and T9 are linked by shuttle buses and mini-subway trains. Departures are on the lower level and arrivals on the upper.*

CDG1 is used for international flights, except those of Air France.

Taxis
(Door 20)

Roissybus &
Disneyland Paris
bus (Door 30)

Car-rental
agencies
(Doors 10,
18 & 20)

Air France buses
(Door 34)

Shuttle buses
(Shopping Level)

PARIS ROISSY-CHARLES-DE-GAULLE (CDG)

THERE ARE TWO main terminals: CDG1 and CDG2. T9 is for charter flights. Taxis to central Paris cost 23€–30€.

Air France buses go to Porte Maillot and Charles de Gaulle-Etoile. The journey takes about 40 minutes. Air France buses also go to Montparnasse TGV train station. The journey takes around 50 minutes. RATP buses (Roissybus) leave every 15 minutes for L'Opéra.

The journey takes about 45 minutes, depending on traffic conditions, and costs 7€.

All the major car rental companies can be found at the airport. A limousine service is also available, but this must be reserved in advance, and costs 105€–140€ to Paris.

A fast, reliable and cheap way to the center is by train. With a station in CDG2, and linked to CDG1 by a free shuttle bus, the RER reaches Châtelet-les-Halles, in the heart of Paris, in less than 30 minutes and the Gare de Nord in 35 minutes.

CDG2 also has its own TGV station, with direct lines to Lille (1hr), Bordeaux (4hrs), and Lyon (2hrs), and connections to much of the TGV network.

CDG2E is the airport's latest extension, opposite CDG2F, due to open in 2003.

Airport Information
01 48 62 22 80.

CDG2 is used for all Air France flights and for short-hop international flights by other carriers.

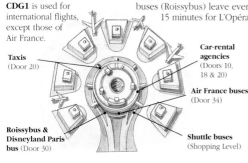

Roissybus (Door 11)

TGV and RER stations

Air France & shuttle
buses (Doors 2 & 6)

Taxis
(Door 7)

CDG2D

CDG2F

CDG2B

Disneyland
Paris bus
(Door 11)

Air France bus
to Etoile &
shuttle buses
(Doors 5 & 8)

CDG2A

Roissybus
(Door 9)

CDG2C

Taxis
(Door 6)

Air France buses to Montparnasse &
Orly; & shuttle buses (Doors 2, 5 & 8)

Air France bus to Etoile
& shuttle buses (Door 6)

CDG2E
(due to
open in
2003)

agent to find out which fares will apply when you travel.

APEX (Advance Purchase Excursion) fares are booked in advance. They cannot be changed or canceled without penalty, and there are also minimum and maximum stay requirements. Note that children often travel more cheaply than adults.

Fierce competition among airlines means there are some very attractive discounts available. Look for the best deals; reputable travel agents provide some very good ones. The addresses of a selection of recommended discount travel agents are listed on page 633. These agents offer both charter and regular scheduled flights at competitive prices. Many of them have representatives in other countries.

Getting to or from France on the national carrier, Air France

FLIGHT TIMES

FLIGHT TIMES to Paris from various cities are: London: 1 hour; Dublin: 90 minutes; Montreal: 7½ hours; New York: 8 hours; Los Angeles: 12 hours; Sydney: 23 hours.

INTERNATIONAL AIRPORTS

MAIN AIRPORTS in France serving international and domestic flights are on pages 632-3, with transportation details. Details of Paris's two main airports are listed below.

Orly Airport
The two terminals, Orly Sud and Orly Ouest, are linked by a mini-subway, but they are within walking distance of one another.

Orly Ouest is largely used for domestic flights.

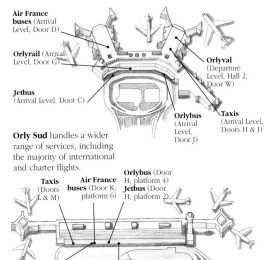

Air France buses (Arrival Level, Door D)

Orlyrail (Arrival Level, Door G)

Jetbus (Arrival Level, Door C)

Orlyval (Departure Level, Hall 2, Door W)

Orlybus (Arrival Level, Door J)

Taxis (Arrival Level, Doors H & I)

Orly Sud handles a wider range of services, including the majority of international and charter flights.

Taxis (Doors L & M)
Air France buses (Door K, platform 6)
Orlybus (Door H, platform 4)
Jetbus (Door H, platform 2)
Orlyval (Door K)
Orlyrail (Door G, platform 1)

ORLY AIRPORT (ORY)

THERE ARE two terminals: Orly Sud and Orly Ouest. Taxis take 25–45 minutes to the city center, depending on the traffic, and cost about 25€.

Air France buses leave the airport every 12 minutes and take around 30 minutes to central Paris (stops at Les Invalides and Montparnasse).

The RATP Orlybus leaves every 13 minutes and takes about 25 minutes to reach the Denfert-Rochereau metro.

The Jetbus service connects Orly to Villejuif-Louis Aragon metro, and departs from the airport every 15 minutes.

Shuttle buses (confusingly called Orlyrail) link the airport with RER line C at Pont de Rungis, from where trains leave every 15 minutes for Gare d'Austerlitz (25 minute journey). An automatic train, Orlyval, links the airport with RER line B at Antony, from where trains depart every 4–8 minutes for Châtelet in central Paris (35 minute journey).

Car rental companies at the airport include Avis, Budget, Europcar, Hertz and National Citer. A chauffeur-driven limousine to central Paris costs around 70€.

Airport Information
📋 01 49 75 15 15.

FRANCE BY AIR

THE MAIN domestic airline is Air Lib. **Air Littoral** and **Air France** also have a number of routes, and there are smaller local airlines. **Buzz** also now flies several domestic routes, forcing down prices.

Unless you are eligible for discounts (usually based on various combinations of age and frequency of travel), it may be cheaper and faster, for some routes, to travel on the high-speed trains *(see p635)*.

CHANNEL FERRIES

IN ADDITION TO the Eurotunnel vehicle-carrying rail shuttles through the Channel Tunnel *(see p634)*, there are several ship or catamaran crossings between the UK and Continental ports.

P&O Stena runs between Dover and Calais, with frequent crossings (1½ hours). **P&O Portsmouth** runs between Portsmouth and Le Havre (5½ hrs) or Cherbourg (5 hrs). The Channel Island specialists, **Condor**, have a fast ferry from Poole to St Malo (4½ hours). **Brittany Ferries** runs a 9-hour service from Portsmouth to St-Malo, a 6-hour service from Portsmouth to Caen, and a 6-hour service from Plymouth to Roscoff. From Poole to Cherbourg, Brittany have a conventional ship (4¼ hours), and a fast ferry, the Condor Vitesse (2¼ hours). They also have a service to Santander in Spain

and to Biarritz, near the French border, and sail from Cork in Eire to Roscoff.

Freight carrier **Norfolkline** also takes cars on its 2-hour Dover to Dunkerque crossing, while **P&O North Sea Ferries** sail from Hull to Zeebrugge in Belgium, with good road links to northeast France.

Hoverspeed, who no longer operate hovercraft, use Super Seacat high-speed craft from Dover to Calais (45 minutes) and catamarans from Newhaven to Dieppe (2hrs). **Transmanche Ferries** (oper-ated by Corsica Ferries) also goes from Newhaven to Dieppe (3¾ hrs).

THE CHANNEL TUNNEL

THE CHANNEL TUNNEL is a 52km (31 miles) rail tunnel which runs beneath the English Channel – 39 km (23 miles) of it under the water, in the earth beneath the bottom of the sea. Its English terminal is at Folkestone in Kent, and the French terminal at Sangatte, 3km (2 miles) from Calais. The terminal leads directly onto highway – the M20 in England, the A16 in France.

Eurotunnel logo

There are two ways to use the Channel Tunnel. For vehicles and their passengers, **Eurotunnel** rail shuttles carry vehicles (passengers remain with their cars) on specially constructed trains between Folkestone and Calais (35 minutes). Eurotunnel trains depart every 15-60 minutes according to demand.

Alternatively, rail passengers without vehicles can board

AIRPORT
Bâle-Mulhouse
Bastia-Poretta
Bordeaux-Mérignac
Lille-Lesquin
Lyon-St-Exupéry
Marseille-Provence
Montpellier-Méditerranée
Nantes Atlantique
Nice-Côte d'Azur
Strasbourg
Toulouse-Blagnac

Eurostar trains at London or Ashford and disembark at Calais-Fréthun, Lille or Paris. On the French side of the Channel, Eurostar cruises at 300 km/hr (186mph). The journey from London to Paris takes 3 hours, or to Lille 2 hours. There are up to 24 departures daily from London to Paris. There are also weekly Eurostar services direct to Disneyland Paris (daily during school vacations), and in winter there are two trains weekly from London direct to the ski resorts of the French Alps. Pre-booking is advised, and often entails much lower advance-purchase fares.

OTHER CROSSINGS

CAR FERRIES sail to Corsica from Marseille, Nice and Toulon all year round. The ferries are run by **SNCM Ferryterranée**, **CTN** and **Corsica Ferries**. In the high season, SNCM sail weekly to Sardinia from Toulon and Marseille. SNCM and CTN also go to Tunis and Algiers from Marseille.

Corsica Ferries, **Corsica Marittima**, **Moby Lines** and **CMN** connect Corsica to Italy, with crossings from Bastia, Calvi, Ajaccio, L'Ile Rousse, Porto-Vecchio and Propriano to Genoa, Livorno, Elba and Sardinia (mainly in summer). **Compagnie Marocaine de Navigation** (Comanov) has a luxury two-night car ferry service between Sète and Tangier.

Plying the Mediterranean with SNCM Ferryterranée

Information	Distance from City	Taxi to City	Bus Details
03 89 90 31 11	25 km (16 miles)	40€–45€	Mulhouse centre 30 mins
04 95 54 54 54	20 km (13 miles)	32€–42€	City centre 25 mins
05 56 34 50 50	12 km (8 miles)	23€–30€	Gare St-Jean 30–45 mins
03 20 49 68 68	10 km (5 miles)	18€–23€	Lille SNCF 30 mins
04 72 22 72 21	25 km (16 miles)	38€–45€	Perrache SNCF 40 mins.
04 42 14 14 14	25 km (16 miles)	35€–45€	St-Charles SNCF 25 mins
04 67 20 85 00	7 km (4 miles)	15€–18€	City centre 20 mins
02 40 84 80 00	12 km (8 miles)	18€–23€	City centre 20 mins
0820 423 333	6 km (4 miles)	23€–30€	Gare Routière 20 mins
03 88 64 67 67	15 km (9 miles)	23€–30€	City centre 30 mins
05 61 42 44 00	9 km (5 miles)	23€–30€	Gare Routière Marengo 30 mins

DIRECTORY

AIRLINES

Air France
0820 820 820.
w www.airfrance.com

Air Lib
0825 805 805.
w www.air-lib.fr

Air Littoral
0803 834 834.
w www.airlittoral.com

American Airlines
0810 872 872.

British Airways
0825 825 400.
0845 779 9977 in UK.
w www.britishairways.com

British Midland
01 48 91 87 04.
0870 609 0555 in UK.
w www.flybmi.com

buzz
01 55 17 42 42.
w www.buzzaway.com

Delta Airlines
0800 354 080.

Easyjet
0870 6000 000 in UK.
08 25 08 25 08.
w www.easyjet.com

Qantas
0820 820 500.
020-8846 0466 in UK
w www.qantas.com

Ryanair
08 25 07 16 26.
w www.ryanair.com

FERRY SERVICES

Brittany Ferries
02 33 88 44 88.
08705 360 360 (UK).
w www.brittanyferries.com

Compagnie Marocaine de Navigation
01 45 22 27 52.

Corsica Ferries,
04 95 32 95 95.
w www.corsicaferries.com

Hoverspeed
08 20 00 35 55.
01304 865 000 in UK.
w www.hoverspeed.co.uk

Moby Lines
04 95 34 84 94.

Norfolkline
03 28 59 01 01.

North Sea Ferries
01482 377 177 in UK.

P&O Stena
03 21 46 10 10.
w www.posl.com

P&O Portsmouth
0825 013 013. w www.poportsmouth.com

SNCM Ferryterranée, Corsica Marittima CTN & CMN
08 91 70 18 01 (24-hrs for all ports).
w www.sncm.fr

Transmanche Ferries
0800 650 100.

TRAVEL AGENCIES

Aix-en-Provence
Usit Connections,
7 cours Sextius,
13100 Aix-en-Provence.
04 42 93 48 48.

Bordeaux
Usit Connections,
284 rue St-Cathérine,
33000 Bordeaux.
05 56 33 89 90.

Lyon
Forum Voyages, 10 rue
President Carnot, 69002
Lyon. 04 78 92 86 00.

Nice
Havas,
12 ave Felix Faure, 06000
Nice. 04 93 62 76 30.

Paris
Directours,
90 ave des Champs-
Elysées, 75008 Paris.
01 45 62 62 62.

Nouvelles Frontières,
66 bd St-Michel, 75006
Paris. 01 46 34 55 30.
w www.nouvelles-frontieres.fr

O. T. U.
119 rue St-Martin, 75004
Paris. 0820 817 817.

Usit Connections,
14 rue Vivienne, 75002
Paris. 01 44 55 32 60.
w www.usitconnection.fr

Usit Connections,
6 rue de Vaugirard,
75006 Paris.
01 42 34 56 90.

Toulouse
Usit Connections,
5 rue des Lois,
31000 Toulouse.
05 61 11 52 42.

London
Usit Campus,
52 Grosvenor Gardens,
London SW1W 0AG,
08702 401 010.
w www.usitcampus.co.uk

Usit Campus,
YHA Adventure Shop,
152–160 Wardour St,
London W1F 8YA.
020-7437 7767.

Trailfinders,
215 Kensington High St,
London W8 6BD.
020-7937 5400.
w www.trailfinders.com

Travel Cuts,
295 Regent Street,
London W1R 7YA.
020-7255 1944.
w www.travelcuts.co.uk

CHANNEL TUNNEL

Eurostar
08705 186 186 in UK.
w www.eurostar.com

Eurotunnel
03 21 00 61 00..
08705 35 35 35 in UK.

Traveling by Train

SNCF logo

THE FRENCH state railroad, Société Nationale des Chemins de Fer (**SNCF**), runs Europe's most comprehensive national rail network. Its services include high-speed long-distance TGVs and mainline expresses, overnight sleepers, Motorail, and rural lines that reach every corner of the country. Lines closed for economic reasons are replaced by SNCF's modern buses, free to rail pass holders. Travel off the main lines can be slow, though – some cross-country journeys are quicker via Paris.

ARRIVING IN FRANCE

FOR TRAVELERS arriving from Britain, **Eurostar** gives access to the whole French rail network. At Lille, two hours from London, passen-gers can change to onward TGVs by-passing Paris and continuing southeast to Lyon, the Rhone valley and the Mediterranean, or southwest to Brittany, the Loire Valley, and SW France. Three hours from London Waterloo, Eurostar reaches Paris Gare du Nord, as do high-speed **Thalys** trains serving Brussels, Amsterdam, and Cologne.

Rail traveler with luggage trolley

From the capital's six train stations, trains fan out to about 6,000 destinations throughout France. Non-TGV trains depart from Gare de l'Est (east), Gare St-Lazare (north), and Gare d'Austerlitz (southeast). The main TGV stations are Gare du Nord, Gare Montparnasse, which serves Brittany, and soutwest France, and Gare de Lyon, for Burgundy, Lyon and the Rhône, Marseille and the Mediterranean.

TRAVELING AROUND FRANCE BY TRAIN

FRANCE HAS ALWAYS been known for the punctuality of its trains, and also for a positive attitude to investment in the state-owned rail system. It is easy and enjoyable to travel in France by train. TGVs running on new High Speed Lines are the pride of the SNCF (the national railroad company), with journey times such as Lille-Lyon or Paris-Marseille in just 3 hrs. Note that in some towns, the new TGV station is separate from the main station, and can be out of the town center. Apart from TGVs, frequent, fast and comfortable main-line express trains provide a compre-hensive city-to-city service, while the rural lines provide connections to smaller towns and villages, sometimes on rather older, slower rolling stock. Some of these train journeys, for example in mountain regions, are a worthwhile experience in their own right. SNCF is also the largest bus operator in France, filling in the gaps where railroad lines have been closed. There are also very good local and sub-urban train services in the largest cities, and the excellent RER (*Reseau Express Régionale*) train network in the Paris area. When purchasing a rail ticket – whether in France or

Symbol for Paris suburban trains

abroad – it is also possible to pre-book a car (*Train + Auto*), bike (*Train + Velo*) or hotel (*Train + Hôtel*) to await you at your destination.

Sleeper trains are a convenient way to travel long distances at night with accom-modation in first or second class *couchette* (bunk bed) compartments. Motorists can travel overnight with their cars on **Motorail**, in France called TAC (*Train-Auto-Couchette*) or TAA (*Train-Auto-Accompagné*) from Paris Bercy. Motorail trains run (May–September only) direct from Calais to the Dordogne, Toulouse, Narbonne, Avignon or Nice. As well as enjoying a less stressful journey, Motorail customers may also book Channel crossings at lower fares. An alternative way to avoid a long drive is to send your car by **AutoTrain** from Paris while driver/passengers travel separately by train.

Not all trains have restaurant cars or bars, even on long journeys. TGV trains have bars with light meals, but reservations must be made in advance for the at-seat meal service available in first class.

Information on these services is available from **Rail Europe** in London and New York, or the SNCF in France as well as from their respective websites *(see p637)*. Leaflets are available at most French stations.

FARES AND PASSES

THERE IS A basic fare for each rail journey, but numerous discounts are available on French trains. These reduced fares and travel passes are for certain categories of passengers. Substantial fare discounts of 25–50% are offered to over 60s (*Découverte Senior*), under 26s (*Découverte 12–25*), up to four adults traveling with a child under 12 (*Découverte Enfant Plus*), or anyone booking more than 30 days or more than 8 days in advance (*Découverte J30 or J8*).

Traveling by train and car through France with Motorail

Rail **passes** give even larger fare reductions. Strictly for non-residents, the **France Railpass** can only be bought outside France. It gives unlimited travel for 3 to 7 days. If you are planning to travel in other countries too, choose **Eurodomino** passes for individual countries, allowing travel between 3 and 8 days, or **InterRail**, which gives 12-, 22-, or 30 days travel for under 26s (or, for a higher price, over 26s) in different zones of Europe.

Discounts and passes are not valid on certain dates and times. The SNCF *Calendrier Voyageurs* (Travelers' Calendar), available at all stations, shows blue and white periods. Almost all fare reductions are valid only in blue periods. The white period is normally only Monday 5–10am, and Friday and Sunday 3–8pm.

The TGV, with its distinctive-looking "nose"

TGV RAIL SERVICE

Trains à Grande Vitesse, or high-speed trains, travel at speeds up to 300 km/h (186 mph). There are three routes. TGV Nord from Paris Gare du Nord, TGV Atlantique from Paris Gare Montparnasse and TGV Sud-Est from Paris Gare de Lyon.

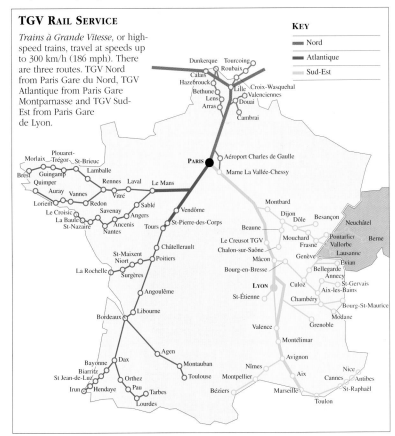

PRIVATE RAILROADS

PRIVATELY RUN RAILROADS are numerous but mostly serve as tourist attractions rather than as transportation. However, **Chemins de Fer de Provence** runs the Train des Pignes over the 150-km (90-mile) spectacular route from Nice to Digne. In Corsica, **Chemins de Fer de Corse** operates two routes, Bastia-Calvi and Calvi-Ajaccio.

BOOKING WITHIN FRANCE

AUTOMATIC TICKET and reservation machines *(billetterie automatique)* are found at main stations. They take credit cards or coins. You can also check train times and fares and

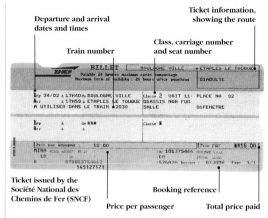

Departure and arrival dates and times

Train number

Ticket information, showing the route

Class, carriage number and seat number

Ticket issued by the Société National des Chemins de Fer (SNCF)

Price per passenger

Booking reference

Total price paid

An automatic ticket machine

make reservations by phoning **SNCF** or by using the Minitel system *(see p624)*, or via their website *(see p637)*. Tickets may be purchased by credit card, then picked up at the station.

Reservations are compulsory for travel by TGV, for all trains on public holidays, and for a *couchette* or *siège inclinable* (reclinable seat) and must be made at least five minutes before departure. Both reservations and tickets must be validated in a *composteur* machine before boarding the train *(see right)* – failure to do so can incur an on-the-spot fine.

BOOKING OUTSIDE FRANCE

TICKETS AND PASSES for rail travel (including Motorail) in France can be booked and paid for in advance direct from **SNCF**. Book on-line on their website (allow 7 days for ticket delivery), or by phone on 08 36 35 35 39, a special SNCF bookings line for English speakers (7am to 10pm daily). You can pay for your tickets by credit card. On-line booking is also possible on the **Eurostar** website.

Rail Europe, and other foreign rail travel agents, can take bookings by post, by phone, on-line, or in person at their London shop. Rail Europe bookings must be made between 14 and 60 days in advance, and a small charge is made for credit card

bookings. Note that reservations made in another country may be difficult or impossible to change in France; any alterations to your booking should be made by the original issuing company.

TIMETABLES

FRENCH RAILWAY timetables change twice a year, in May and September.

Stations sell the SNCF's *Ville-à-Ville* timetable which details all mainline routes nationwide. SNCF also sell regional timetables.

Free leaflets give information on traveling with children, reduced fares, train travel for the disabled, and the TGV network *(see pp634–5)*. Some regions, such as Provence-Alpes-Côte d'Azur, have a

Composteur Machine
Orange composteur *machines are located in station halls and at the head of each platform. Insert tickets and reservations separately, printed side up, in the machine. The* composteur *will punch your ticket and print the time and date on the back. A penalty may be imposed by the inspector on the train if you fail to do this.*

regional TER *(Transports Express Régionaux)* timetable that includes bus travel.

Bear in mind that trains in France are punctual. Your train will almost certainly leave on time!

ARRIVING BY BUS

THE MODERN BUSES operated by **Eurolines** travel to 270 destinations in Europe, including many in France.

There are three departures daily (five in summer) to Paris from Victoria Coach Station in London, with stops in Bagnolet in eastern Paris. The trip takes about nine hours – tickets may be purchased from the booking office at Victoria. Eurolines have one-way tickets, returns and round trips throughout Europe.

TRAVELING AROUND FRANCE BY BUS

LONG-DISTANCE buses generally only operate where trains don't offer a good service (eg. Geneva to Nice). SNCF (the state railroad) operates buses and issues regional TER *(Transports Express Régionaux)* combined bus and train timetables and tickets.

Eurolines offers a wider range of destinations than most. It also offers excursions and arranges accommodations.

Local buses run from a town's *Gare Routière* (which is often at the Gare SNCF). Timetables are geared to carry students and people going to work, so the morning departure time from a village may be very early.

TAXIS

IN THE PROVINCES prices vary from one region to another. All taxis must carry meters *(compteurs)*. The pickup charge should be about 2€ plus 0.5€ or more per km. You may be able to agree on a price for a long journey. Look for a *station de taxi* outside airports or train stations or in the center of town. Because hailing a taxi is only common practice in France's large cities, you have to book a taxi by telephone in rural areas.

BICYCLE TRAVEL

ALTHOUGH CYCLING is popular in France, few long-distance trains carry bicycles. TER (ie. regional) trains generally do carry bikes. They are indicated on the timetable by a bicycle symbol. In most instances, however, a bicycle has to be sent as a separate package. The drawback is that you may have to wait up to four days for delivery.

Alternatively, you can rent a bicycle. Through the SNCF, you can reserve a rental bike at a number of stations when you buy your ticket *(see Train + Vélo p634)*. Bicycle shops in many towns have touring bikes or mountain bikes for rent, and may also rent mopeds and light motorcycles.

Rural France is ideal for cycling due to its large network of uncrowded roads. There are, however, few bike lanes in towns. For more details on marked bicycle routes, see page 628.

HITCH-HIKING

IT IS NOT EASY to get around France by hitch-hiking. You must look clean and "normal" to have any chance of a lift, especially since it is car, rather than truck drivers who will be your best bet. The safest and easiest way to hitch-hike long-distance is through **Allo-stop** who have branches in many major towns and will arrange rides for a reasonable rate.

DIRECTORY

INFORMATION AND RESERVATIONS

SNCF France
08 36 35 35 35.
08 36 35 35 39 *(English)*.
Minitel 36 15 SNCF.
W www.sncf.fr

Eurostar
London Waterloo
International
08705 186 186.
W www.eurostar.com

Rail Europe
179 Piccadilly
London W1V 0BA.
08705 848 848.
020-7647 4900.
W www.raileurope.co.uk

W www.britcities.com
(non UK European travel)

Rail Europe Group
Westchester One, 44 South
Broadway, White Plains,
New York, NY 10601.
888 4387 245 *(freephone)*
W www.raileurope.com

PRIVATE RAILWAYS

Chemins de Fer de Provence
04 97 03 80 80.

Chemins de Fer de Corse:
Ajaccio
04 95 23 11 03.

Bastia
04 95 32 80 61.

Calvi
04 95 65 00 61.

EUROLINES

London
52 Grosvenor Gardens

Victoria, London SW1.
08705 143 219.
W www.eurolines.co.uk

Victoria Coach Station
164 Buckingham Palace
Road, London SW1 9TP.
020 7730 3499.

Paris
28 av du Général de
Gaulle, 93170 Bagnolet.
08 36 69 52 52.

BUS STATIONS IN FRANCE

Paris (Eurolines)
Porte de Bagnolet.
08 36 69 52 52.

Bordeaux
Place des Quinconces.
05 56 43 68 43.

Lyon
Gare de Perrache.
04 72 61 72 61.

Marseille
Place Victor Hugo.
04 91 50 57 55.

Nice
5 boulevard Jean Jaurès.
04 93 85 61 81.

Strasbourg
Place des Halles.
03 88 77 70 09.

Toulouse
68–70 Blvd Pierre Semard.
05 61 61 67 67.

HITCH-HIKING

Allo-stop
8 rue Rochambeau,
Paris 75009.
01 53 20 42 42.
W www.ecritel.fr

On the Road

The classic Citroën 2 CV

Fᴿᴀɴᴄᴇ ʜᴀꜱ one of the densest road networks in Europe, with modern highways that allow quick and easy access to all parts of the country. However, you can save money on tolls and explore France in a more leisurely way by using some of the other high quality roads that dissect the country. This section gives instructions on how to use the highway tollbooths and French parking meters (*horodateurs*), as well as explaining some of the rules governing driving in France. There are also various travel tips, such as where to buy gas, how to get weather and traffic forecasts, where to rent a car and where to find the best road maps.

Highway and main road signs

Gᴇᴛᴛɪɴɢ ᴛᴏ Fʀᴀɴᴄᴇ ʙʏ Cᴀʀ

Tʜᴇʀᴇ ɪꜱ ᴀ ɢᴏᴏᴅ choice of car-ferry operators from the UK (*see p632*). You can profit from discount fares for short trips, a flat rate for a car with up to five passengers, or by buying tickets for the crossing in conjunction with Motorail (*see pp634 and 637*).

You can also take the car on the **Eurotunnel** shuttle (*see p632*) via the Channel Tunnel.

Wʜᴀᴛ ᴛᴏ Tᴀᴋᴇ

Cʜᴇᴄᴋ with your car insurance agent (and any automotive club you belong to, such as AAA) before leaving for France to determine the extent of your coverage abroad. An international driver's license is recommended but not mandatory.

If you drive your own car, you must have the original registration insurance certificate and a valid driver's license. You should also carry a passport or National ID card. A sticker showing the country

of registration must be displayed close to the rear number plate. The headlights of right-hand drive cars must be adjusted for left-hand driving. You must also carry a red warning triangle, spare headlight bulbs, a first-aid kit and a fire extinguisher. If you are caught without these you are liable to be fined. When driving around ski resorts in winter, snow chains (*chaînes*) are essential.

Bᴜʏɪɴɢ Gᴀꜱ ɪɴ Fʀᴀɴᴄᴇ

Dɪᴇꜱᴇʟ ꜰᴜᴇʟ (*gazole* or *gasoil*) is comparatively cheap and is sold everywhere. Leaded gas (*super*) and unleaded gas (*sans plomb*) are more expensive, and leaded is sometimes hard to find. Large supermarkets and hypermarkets sell gas at a discount. Gas coupons are not accepted.

A map (*la carte de l'essence moins chère*), available from French Government Tourist Offices (*see p617*), shows the location of stores that are close to highway exits. Rural stations may close on Sundays. Filling up the tank is known as *faire le plein*.

Some of the most widely available car rental firms in France

Rᴜʟᴇꜱ ᴏꜰ ᴛʜᴇ Rᴏᴀᴅ

Uɴʟᴇꜱꜱ ʀᴏᴀᴅ signs indicate otherwise, *priorité à droite* means that you must give way to any vehicle joining the road from the right, except on roundabouts or from private property. Most major roads outside built-up areas have the right of way indicated by *passage protegé* signs.

Contrary to convention in the US and UK, flashing headlights in France mean the driver is claiming the right of way.

Other French driving rules include the compulsory wearing of seat belts, the use of booster seats for all children under 10, and the obligation to carry a valid driving license or identification papers at all times. For farther details consult the RAC website (*see p641*).

40 km/h (25 mph) speed limit

Sᴘᴇᴇᴅ Lɪᴍɪᴛꜱ ᴀɴᴅ Fɪɴᴇꜱ

Sᴘᴇᴇᴅ ʟɪᴍɪᴛꜱ in France are as follows:
• On autoroutes: 130 km/h (80 mph); 110 km/h (70 mph) when it rains.
• On divided highways: 110 km/h (70 mph); 90–100 km/h (55–60 mph) when it rains.
• On other roads: 90 km/h (55 mph), 80 km/h (50 mph) when it rains.
• In towns: 50 km/h (30 mph). This applies anywhere in a village, hamlet or city, unless marked otherwise. In some places it may be lower. Normal limits may not be shown.

On-the-spot fines of around $125 are summarily levied for not stopping at a Stop sign, for overtaking where forbidden, or other diving offenses. Drunk-driving can lead to confiscation of the vehicle or even imprisonment.

Sign indicating one-way system

No entry for any vehicles

Passage protegé ends, priorité à droite starts

HIGHWAYS

Most highways in France have a toll system (*autoroutes à péage*), and vary considerably in price. City bypasses are usually free. Some longer sections of highway may also be free, eg. on the A26 and A75. Tolls can be paid with either credit cards or cash. Where only small sums are involved, you throw coins into a large receptacle and change is given automatically.

Much of the *autoroute* network has been built in the last 20 years. It includes good rest areas and picnic spots 10–20 km (6–12 miles) apart, gas stations at every 40 km (25 miles), and emergency telephones every 2 km (1¼ miles). Service areas include shops, takeout food and restaurants, fax and telephone facilities.

OTHER ROADS

In France the RN (*route nationale*) and D (*départementale*) roads are a good alternative to highways. *Bis/Bison futée* signs are posted for alternative routes away from heavy traffic.

Sunday is usually a good day to travel since there are very few trucks on the road. Try to avoid traveling at the French vacation rush periods known as *grands départs*. The worst times are weekends in mid-July, and the beginning and end of August when vacations begin and end.

If you are bypassing rather than driving into Paris, it is more advisable to take the highways on either side of the city, avoiding the busy *boulevard péripherique* that encircles Paris.

ROAD CONDITIONS AND WEATHER FORECASTS

Local radio stations report on road conditions – look for highway signs listing their frequencies. **CRICR** (Centre Régional d'Information et de Coordination Routière) lines give general information on regional road conditions. The **CNIR** (Centre National d'Information Routière) line covers the whole of France.

The **RAC** sells a tailormade route-planning information service, giving scenic options and road conditions.

To get weather forecasts in English for the English Channel and throughout France call **The Met Office** or **Holiday Weatherline**.

Sign for Channel Tunnel terminal

USING THE AUTOROUTE TOLL

When you enter an autoroute, take a ticket from the machine. This identifies your starting point on the autoroute. You do not pay until you reach an exit toll. You are charged according to the distance traveled and the type of vehicle driven.

Highway Sign
These signs indicate the name and distance to the next toll booth. They are usually blue and white; some show the tariff rates for cars, motorcycles, trucks and caravans.

Tollbooth with Attendant
When you hand in your ticket at a staffed tollbooth, the attendant will tell you the cost of your journey on the autoroute, and the charge will be displayed. You can pay with coins, notes, credit cards or with a Eurocheque in French francs. A receipt is issued on request.

Automatic Machine
On reaching the exit toll, insert your ticket into the machine and the price of your journey will be displayed in French francs. You can pay either with coins or by credit card. The machine will give change and can issue a receipt.

USING AN HORODATEUR MACHINE

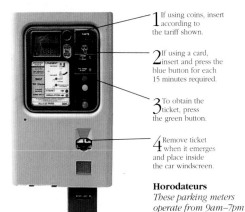

1 If using coins, insert according to the tariff shown.

2 If using a card, insert and press the blue button for each 15 minutes required.

3 To obtain the ticket, press the green button.

4 Remove ticket when it emerges and place inside the car windscreen.

Horodateurs
These parking meters operate from 9am–7pm Mon–Fri. Unless otherwise indicated, parking is free Sat–Sun, public holidays and in August.

PARKING

PARKING REGULATIONS vary from town to town. Most operate pay-and-display systems *(horodateurs)*. Some machines accept a parking payment card, which can be bought at tobacconists. Provincial towns offer free parking from noon to 1:30pm. Parking is normally limited to two hours. In small towns, parking is confined to one side of the street only, alternating at different times of the month. Signs show where parking is allowed.

In larger cities, especially Paris, finding a parking space can be hard. Because space is so limited, cars frequently "bump" one another to squeeze into a space.

If you are in an area where parking permits are in use, the local tourist office will supply you with one.

CAR RENTAL

ALL THE MAIN international car-rental companies operate in France. It is worth making arrangements before you leave for France because discount rentals can often be booked and prepaid in the UK or USA. In France, two smaller companies offer very competitive rates.

F.P.Lock operates outside airport terminal buildings, usually from a hotel lobby in the immediate vicinity and will pick you up when you arrive. The other option is **Autos Abroad**, brokers who use cars owned by other car-rental companies, like **Budget** and **Citer**. Renting from either of these companies may be half the price of the standard rental.

For car hire booked in combination with flights, your travel agent can usually organize a good deal. SNCF (the French state railroad) offers combined train and car-rental fares called *(see p634)*

with pick-up points at 200 stations in France. Phone **Rail Europe** for information *(see directory opposite).*

For non-EU residents planning to drive in France for a minimum of three weeks, the best option is the short-term tax-free purchase-and-buy-back service (sometimes called TT leasing) offered by **Citroën**, **Peugeot** and **Renault**.

Information on chauffeur-driven car rentals can be obtained from the **Automobile Club de l'Ile de France**.

MAPS

IN THIS GUIDE, each chapter begins with a map of the region showing all the sights and giving useful tips on getting around. If you wish to avoid using highways the *Bison Futé* map of France recommends alternative routes. It is available from French Government Tourist Offices *(see p617).*

For driving shorter distances and for cycling, it is very pleasant to use the smaller D *(département)* roads marked in yellow or white on **Michelin** maps, and often quite empty of traffic. The red Michelin maps of France (scale 1:1,000,000) are useful for planning a trip. The excellent Michelin atlas of France has generously overlapping maps at a scale of 1:200,000, and is by far the most comprehensive and legible atlas for driving currently available. At the same scale, a series of

Mountain cyclists in the Alps

regional maps with yellow covers is sold in different sheet sizes. Maps showing the whole country are also available (red covers). Larger scale maps (green covers) are currently only available for the south of France and the area surrounding Paris. A series called *Alentours de,* also at 1:100,000 scale, focus on the areas round Bordeaux, Nancy, Nantes, Poitiers, Rouen and Strasbourg.

IGN (Institut Géographique National) is the equivalent of the British Ordnance Survey mapping organization. The whole of France is available in sheets at 1:250,000, 1:100,000, 1:50,000 and 1:25,000. **Espace IGN**, just off the Champs-Elysées in Paris, is a haven for map

lovers. The **Roger Lascelles Touring Map**, at 1:1,000,000, is recommended, as are their Red Cover Maps at 1:250,000. Refer to page 628 for walking and cycling maps.

In France, all newsagents and gas stations stock the more commonly used maps. In the US **Rand McNally** have a good selection. For more specialized requests try **Roger Lascelles** or **France Magasin**, a specialist French bookstore (*see below*).

The town maps included in this guide locate all the important sights. You can usually get town plans free from tourist offices, although

A selection of French road maps

for large towns you might need the more detailed maps published by Michelin or Blay (available from Roger Lascelles in the UK).

DIRECTORY

CAR HIRE

ADA
☎ 01 42 93 65 13 (Paris).

Autos Abroad
☎ 0870 066 7788 (UK).

Avis
☎ (1) (800) 331 1212 (US).
☎ 01 49 75 44 91 (Paris).

Budget
☎ (1) (800) 527 0700 (US).
☎ 0825 003 564.

Europcar
☎ (1) (800) 227 3876 (US).
☎ 0803 861 861.

F.P.Lock
☎ 01 34 29 80 08 (Paris).
☎ 04 92 27 05 10 (Nice).

Hertz
☎ (1) (800) 654 3131 (US).
☎ 0803 861 861.

Hire for Lower
☎ 020 7491 1111 (UK).

National Citer
☎ 01 44 38 61 61 (Paris).

Rent a Car
☎ 0836 694 695 (Paris)

Sixt-Eurorent
☎ 01 44 38 55 55 (Paris).

Rail Europe
☎ 08705 848 848 (UK).
W www.raileurope.co.uk

TT LEASING

Citroën
25 rue de Constantinople
75008 Paris.
Map 3 B2.
☎ 01 53 04 34 80.
FAX 01 55 30 05 49.

Peugeot Sodexa
115 av de l'Arche,
92400 Courbevoie.
☎ 01 49 04 81 81 (Paris).
FAX 01 47 89 49 40.

Renault Eurodrive
Renault Ventes Spéciales
Exportation, 186 av Jean-
Jaurès, 75019 Paris.
☎ 01 40 40 32 32 (Paris).
FAX 01 40 40 34 20 (Paris).

CHAUFFEUR CAR HIRE

Automobile Club de l'Ile de France
14 av de la Grande
Armeé, 75017 Paris.
Map 2 D4.
☎ 01 40 55 43 00.

WEATHER FORECASTS

Holiday Weatherline
☎ 0870 600 4242 (from UK only) France forecasts.

The Met Office
☎ 0845 300 0300 (within UK). ☎ 1344 855 680 (from abroad).
W www.met-office.gov.uk

ROAD CONDITIONS

RAC
Great Park Road, Bradley
Stoke, Bristol BS32 4QN.
☎ 09064 701 740.
W www.rac.co.uk

CNIR
☎ 01 48 12 44 44 (Paris).

Autoroute
☎ 01 47 05 90 01.

CRICR Bordeaux
☎ 05 56 96 33 33.

Lille
☎ 03 20 47 33 33.

Lyon
☎ 04 72 81 57 33.

Marseille
☎ 04 91 78 78 78.

Metz
☎ 03 87 63 33 33.
Paris Region
☎ 01 48 99 33 33.

Rennes
☎ 02 99 32 33 33.

MAPS

AA
30–31 Haymarket
London SW1X 4EU.
☎ 08706 000 371.
W www.theaa.co.uk

Espace IGN
107 rue la Boétie
75008 Paris.
Map 2 F5.
☎ 01 43 98 80 00.
FAX 01 43 98 85 89.

Michelin
Espace Opéra
32 av de l'Opéra
75002 Paris. **Map** 4 F5.
☎ 01 42 68 05 20.
☎ (803) 458 6470 (US).
W www.viamichelin.fr

Rand McNally
150 East 52nd Street,
New York, NY 10022.
☎ (212) 758 7488.

Roger Lascelles
47 York Road,
Brentford,
Mddx TW8 0QP.
☎ 020-8847 0935.
FAX 020-8568 3886.

General Index

Acknowledgments

Dorling Kindersley would like to thank the following people whose contributions and assistance have made the preparation of this book possible.

Main Contributors
John Ardagh, Rosemary Bailey, Judith Fayard, Lisa Gerard-Sharp, Alister Kershaw, Alec Lobrano, Anthony Roberts, Alan Tillier, Nigel Tisdall.

Contributors and Consultants
John Ardagh is a writer and broadcaster, and author of many books on France, among them *France Today* and *Writers' France*.

Rosemary Bailey has written and edited several guides to regional France, including *Burgundy*, the *Loire Valley* and the *Côte d'Azur*.

Alexandra Boyle is a writer and editor who has worked in publishing in England and France for 20 years.

Elsie Burch Donald, editor and writer, is the author of *The French Farmhouse*.

David Burnie B.Sc. has written over 30 books on natural sciences, including *How Nature Works*.

Judith Fayard, an American based in Paris, was Paris bureau chief for *Life* magazine for 10 years, and is now European editor of *Town & Country*. She contributes to various publications, including the *Wall Street Journal*.

Lisa Gerard-Sharp is a writer and broadcaster and author of several regional guides to France and Italy.

Colin Jones is Professor of History at Exeter University. His books include *The Longman Companion to the French Revolution* and *The Cambridge Illustrated History of France*.

Alister Kershaw is an Australian writer and broadcaster who has lived in the Loire Valley for 30 years.

Alec Lobrano is an American writer, based in Paris. He is the European editor of *Departures* magazine and contributes to *International Herald Tribune*, *Los Angeles Times* and *The Independent*.

Anthony Roberts is a writer and translator who has lived in Gascony for 15 years, contributing to various publications including *The Times*, *World of Interiors* and *Architectural Digest*.

Anthony Rose is the wine correspondent of *The Independent* and co-author of *The Grapevine*.

Jane Sigal is the author of two books on French food, *Normandy Gastronomique* and *Backroom Bistros, Farmhouse Fare*.

Alan Tillier is the main contributor to the *Eyewitness Guide to Paris*. He has lived in Paris for more than 20 years as correspondent for various journals, including the *International Herald Tribune, Newsweek* and *The Times*.

Nigel Tisdall is a travel writer and author of guides to Brittany and Normandy.

Patricia Wells is food critic of the *International Herald Tribune* and author of the *Food Lovers' Guide to Paris* and the *Food Lovers' Guide to France*.

Additional Contributors
Nathalie Boyer, Caroline Bugler, Ann Cremin, Bill Echikson, Adrian Gilbert, Peter Graham, Marion Kaplan, Jim Keeble, Alexandra Kennedy, Fred Mawer, Andrew Sanger, Clive Unger-Hamilton.

Additional Photography
Jo Craig, Michael Crockett, Mike Dunning, Philip Enticknap, Steve Gorton, Alison Harris, John Heseltine, Roger Hilton, Eric Meacher, Neil Mersh, Roger Moss, Robert O'Dea, Alan Williams, Peter Wilson.

Additional Illustrations
Dinwiddie Maclaren, John Fox, Nick Gibbard, Paul Guest, Stephen Gyapay, Kevin Jones Associates, Chris Orr, Robbie Polley, Sue Sharples.

Additional Cartography
Colourmap Scanning Limited; Contour Publishing; Cosmographics; European Map Graphics; Meteo-France. Street Finder maps: ERA Maptec Ltd (Dublin), adapted with permission from original survey and mapping by Shobunsha (Japan).

Cartographic Research
Jennifer Skelley, Rachel Hawtin (Lovell Johns); James Mills-Hicks, Peter Winfield, Claudine Zarte (Dorling Kindersley Cartography).

Design and Editorial Assistance
Peter Adams, Laetitia Benloulou, Steve Bere, Arwen Burnett, Janet Clayton, Cate Craker, Maggie Crowley, Fay Franklin, Tom Fraser, Emily Green, Elaine Harries, Paul Hines, Nicholas Inman, Nancy Jones, Siri Lowe, Francesca Machiavelli, Lesley McCave, Ella Milroy, Malcolm Parchment, Lyn Parry, Shirin Patel, Alice Peebles, Alice Pennington-Mellor, Marianne Petrou, Salim Qurashi, Marisa Renzullo, Philippa Richmond, Andrew Szudek, Fiona Wild, Nicholas Wood, Irina Zarb.

Special Assistance
Mme Jassinger, French Embassy Press Department; Peter Mills and Christine Lagardère, French Railways Ltd.

Photographic Reference
Altitude, Paris; Sea and See, Paris; Editions Combier, Mâcon; Thomas d'Hoste, Paris.

PHOTOGRAPHY PERMISSIONS

DORLING KINDERSLEY would like to thank the following for their assistance and kind permission to photograph at their establishments: The Caisse Nationale des Monuments Historiques et des Sites; M. A. Leonetti, the Abbey of Mont St-Michel; Chartres Cathedral; M. Voisin, Château de Chenonceau; M. P Mistral, Cité de Carcassonne, M. D. Vingtain, Palais des Papes, Avignon; Château de Fontainebleau; Amiens Cathedral; Conques Abbey; Fontenay Abbey; Moissac Abbey; Vézelay Abbey, Reims Cathedral and all the other churches, museums, hotels, restaurants, shops, galleries and sights too numerous to thank individually.

PICTURE CREDITS

t = top; tl = top left; tc = top center; tr = top right; cla = center left above; ca = center above; cra = center right above; cl = center left; c = center; cr = center right; clb = center left below; cb = center below; crb = center right below; bl = bottom left; b = bottom; bc = bottom center; br = bottom right; (d) = detail.

Works of art have been reproduced with the permission of the following copyright holders; ©ADAGP, Paris and DACS, London 1994: 25tl, 59tl, 61tl (detail), 88c, 89ca, 95t, 109b, 514bl; ©DACS, London 1994: 24c, 24cb, 25c, 25cb, 26bl, 60–61, 84cl, 86t, 86b, 89t, 203t, 341t, 371br, 412t, 463t, 472t, 498ca, 503b, 511t, 512b, 514tr, 514br, 519b; © J Fabris: 25c; © Succession H. Matisse/DACS 1994; 25b, 88b, 516b.

Photos achieved with the assistance of the EPPV and the CSI: 132–3; Photo of Euro Disneyland ® Park and the Euro Disneyland Paris ® 168cr; The characters, architectural works and trademarks are the property of The Walt Disney Company. All rights reserved; Courtesy of the Maison Victor Hugo, Ville de Paris: 87t; Musée National des Châteaux de Malmaison et Bois-Preau: 163b; Musée de Montmartre, Paris: 129t; Musée National de la Legion d'Honneur: 56t; © Sundancer: 138bl.

The publisher would like to thank the following individuals, companies and picture libraries for permission to reproduce their photographs: AIR FRANCE/D TOULORGE: 631t; ALPINE GARDEN SOCIETY/CHRISTOPHER GREY-WILSON: 450bl, 450br; AGENCE PHOTO AQUITAINE: D. Lelann 411tl; ANCIENT ART AND ARCHITECTURE COLLECTION: 43 crb, 46c, 46cb, 48br, 53bl, 242–3b, 325bl, 372t, 424t, 428b; PHOTO AKG, BERLIN: 41cra, 42bl, 50bc, 51crb, 392t, 393b; ARCHIVES PHOTOGRAPHIQUES, PARIS/DACS: 412t; ATELIER BRANCUSI/CENTRE GEORGES POMPIDOU, Paris: Bernard Prerost 89br; ATELIER DU REGARD/A ALLEMAND: 432cl, 432cr, 432b.

BIBLIOTHÈQUE NATIONALE, DIJON: 45cb; F. BLACKBURN: 451bl; GERARD BOULLAY/PHOTOLA: 83bl, 83cra; BRIDGEMAN ART LIBRARY: Albright Knox Art Gallery, Buffalo, New York 265br; Anthony Crane

Collection 201br; Bibliothèque Nationale, Paris 46cr–47cl, 48t, 49cr, 65bl; British Library, London 48bl, 64br, 282c, 283br, 283tl; Bonhams, London 55tc, 58tl; Château de Versailles, France 65tr; Christies, London 25c, 503b; Giraudon 24tr, 24tl, 52cr–53cl, 53tl, 55tl, 65bc, 171b, 324c, 333c, 355tl; Guildhall Library, Corporation of London 407b; Hermitage, St. Petersburg 25bl; Index 462b; Kress Collection, Washington DC 283bl; Lauros-Giraudon 42t, 65br; Musée des Beaux Arts, Quimper 233c; Musée Condé, Chantilly 46tl, 53tr, 64bl, 65tc, 65tcl, 65cb, 194t, 283c; Musée d'Orsay, Paris 24cb; Paul Bremen Collection 245t; Sotheby's New York 51tl; V&A Museum, London 328b; Walters Art Gallery, Baltimore, Maryland 346t; JOHN BRUNTON: 504b; MICHAEL BUSSELLE: 172–3.

CAMPAGNE, CAMPAGNE: 340t; C. Guy 315t; Lara 181cr; B. Lichtstein 207b, 314cl; Pyszel 180bl; CNMHS, PARIS/DACS: Longchamps Delehaye 203tl; CASTELET/GROTTE DE CLAMOUSE: 483b; COLLECTION CDT GARD: 315bl; CDT LOT: 429b; CEPHAS: Stuart Boreham 250–1; Hervé Champollion 312tr, 324t, 340b; Mick Rock 34c, 388tl, 388tl, 461t, 508–9; JEAN LOUP CHARMET: 43b, 46br, 48clb, 54t, 58cl, 58clb, 59tl, 59tc, 59tc, 60bl, 60br, 61crb, 204b, 233b, 255br, 259b, 264t, 271b, 290br, 333br, 348b, 349t, 351c, 391cr, 391br, 411b, 465t, 497t.

CITÉ DES SCIENCES ET L'INDUSTRIE: Michel Lamoureux 133c; Pascal Prieur 132tr, 132ca; Michel Viard 132cb; BRUCE COLEMAN: Udo Hirsch 361br; Flip de Nooyer 377br; Hans Reinhard 313tl, 313tr; PHOTOS EDITIONS COMBIER, MÂCON: 193t; JOE CORNISH: 112, 224–5, 360br, 438.

DANSMUSEET, STOCKHOLM/PETER STENWALL: 60cr–61cl; DOHERTY: 235tc; E. DONARD: 31tr, 31c, 31cl, 31bc; EDITIONS D'ART DANIEL DERVEAUX: 390cr–391cl; PHOTO DASPET, AVIGNON: 494bl.

ET ARCHIVE: 290bl; Cathedral Treasury, Aachen 4t; 44cl; Musée Carnavalet, Paris 57tl; Museum of Fine Arts, Lausanne 51br; Musée d'Orsay, Paris 57cra; Musée de Versailles 52b; 289bl; National Gallery, Scotland 54br; Victoria and Albert Museum, London 49tl; 333bl; EUROPEAN COMMISSION: 621; MARY EVANS PICTURE LIBRARY: 9c, 42br, 46bl, 47c, 49b, 50tl, 52cla, 54c, 58b, 59cr, 59br, 61br, 108c, 109cl, 167b, 173c, 181t, 187b, 225c, 269t, 281b, 283tr, 291bl, 305c, 356b, 383c, 445t, 455c, 463b, 498tl, 535c, 615c; Explorer 27b, 50clb.

PHOTO FLANDRE, AMIENS: 193b; FRANCE TÉLÉCOM: 624cr; M Reynard 624b; FRENCH RAILWAYS/SNCF: 634bl, 635t.

GIRAUDON, PARIS: 8–9, 15t, 25cra, 52br, 42ca, 44tl, 44clb, 45tl, 46cl, 48cr–49cl, 52tl, 52clb, 54cl, 56cl, 56cr–57cl, 323br, 337br, 359b, 481cb MS Nero EII pt.2 fol. 20V0; Lauros-Giraudon 40tl, 40bc, 41t, 41crb, 41cb, 41br, 43tc, 45tr, 47crb, 51cr, 56clb, 56br, 341b, 481cl; Musée d'Art Moderne, Paris

25tr; Musée de Beaux Arts, Quimper 24cl; Telarci 45cr; RONALD GRANT ARCHIVE: 17b, 62clb.
SONIA HALLIDAY PHOTOGRAPHS: Laura Lushington 299tr; ROBERT HARDING PICTURE LIBRARY: 26bl, 33tr, 35tr, 35cl, 39b, 108tr, 230tl, 233tr, 312bl, 312br, 313br, 339t, 390cla, 427cr, 451tr, 479b, C. Bowman 442t; Explorer, Paris 35cr, 63br, 97br, 169b, 352t, 361tr, 450cb, 451tl, 474b, 487br, 617b, 628b, 640b; R.Francis 82clb, 626c; D.Hughes 382–3; W.Rawlings 45br, 63tl, 227tl, 246b; A.Wolfitt 22tr, 160, 538bl; JOHN HESELTINE: 135c; HONFLEUR, MUSÉE BOUDIN: 252b; DAVID HUGHES: 2–3, 357t, 357b; THE HULTON DEUTSCH COLLECTION: 181br, 291br, 463c, 506b; FJ Mortimer 180tl.

THE IMAGE BANK: Peter Miller 362; IMAGES: 313c, 450cl, 450tr; JACANA: F Gohier 450tl; JM Labat 451bc; TREVOR JONES: 194b.

MAGNUM PHOTOS LTD: Bruno Barbey 16b, 27tr, 32bl; R Capa 462tr; P Halsman 515b; THE MANSELL COLLECTION: 27tl, 272t, 285b, 449b, 494tl; MILEPOST 91$^1/_2$: Bob Walkley 635t; JOHN MILLER: 214b, 326tr, 397b; MUSÉE DE L'ANNONCIADE, ST-TROPEZ: 514tr; MUSÉE D'ART MODERNE ET CONTEMPORAIN DE STRASBOURG: Edith Rodeghiero 221t; MUSÉE DES BEAUX ARTS, CARCASSONNE: 479tl; MUSÉE DES BEAUX ARTS, DIJON: 333tl; MUSÉE DES BEAUX ARTS DE LYON: 371tr, 371bl, 371br; MUSÉE DE LA CIVILISATION GALLO-ROMAINE, LYON: 43cr, 368cl; MUSÉE DEPARTMENTAL BRETON, QUIMPER: 264bl; MUSÉE FLAUBERT, ROUEN: 255bl; MUSEUM NATIONAL D'HISTOIRE NATURELLE, PARIS: 134c; COURTESY OF THE MUSÉE MATISSE, NICE: 516b; MUSÉE NATIONAL D'ART MODERNE, PARIS: 88clb, 89t, 89cr, 89cb, 325br; Succession Henri Matisse 88bl; MUSÉE RÉATTU, ARLES: M Lacanaud 498ca; CLICHÉ MUSÉE DE SENS/J.P. ELIE: 320tl; MUSÉE TOULOUSE-LAUTREC, ALBI: 434b.

SERVICE NATIONAL DES TIMBRES POSTE ET DE LA PHILATÉLIE: designed by Eve Luquet 626bl; NETWORK PHOTOGRAPHERS: Barry Lewis 328t; Rapho/Mark Buscail 628tl; Rapho/De Sazo 628tr; Rapho/Michael Serraillier 629b; PICTURES COLOUR LIBRARY: 392b, 416, 534, 614–5; MICHEL LE POER TRENCH: 26br; CENTRE GEORGES POMPIDOU: Bernard Prerost 89b; POPPERFOTO: 241c; PYRENEES MAGAZINE/DR: 390bl. REDFERNS: William Gottlieb: 60clb; RETROGRAPH ARCHIVE: M. Breese 464tl, 464tr; RÉUNION DES MUSÉES NATIONAUX: Musée des Antiquités Nationales 393c; Musée Guimet 107t; Musée du Louvre 53ca, 97bl, 98t, 98bl, 98br, 99tl, 99c, 99b; Musée Picasso 84cl, 86b, 463t; Musée de Versailles 169t; RF REYNOLDS: 235bc.

REX FEATURES: Sipa 18t; ROCAMADOUR: 427t; ROGER-VIOLLET: 109tc; FOUNDATION ROYAUMONT: J Johnson 162t; RÉUNION DES MUSÉES NATIONAUX: *Le Duo* (1937) by Georges Braque, Collections du Centre Pompidou, Musée Nationaux d'Art Moderne, © ADAGP, Paris and DACS, London 2001 89ra.

SIPA PRESS: 128bl; PHOTO SNCM/SOUTHERN FERRIES: 632b; SPECTRUM COLOUR LIBRARY: P Thompson 239b; FRANK SPOONER PICTURES: Bolcina 33b; Uzan 62br; Simon 63ca; Gamma Press 35b, 63crb; JEAN MARIE STEINLEN: 394; TONY STONE IMAGES: 312c, 316; SYGMA: 521t; C de Bare 32t; Walter Carone 140t; P Forestier 304–5; Frederic de la Fosse 510b; D Goldberg 17c; L'Illustration 104tl; T Prat 426c; L de Raemy 63bl.

EDITIONS TALLANDIER: 38, 40cb, 43tl, 44br, 44br–45bl, 47t, 47b, 48cl, 49tr, 50br, 54clb, 54bl, 54cr–55cl, 55crb, 55bl, 57tr, 57crb, 57br, 59bl, 59bc, 60cla, 60crb, 61tc, 61tr; TOURIST OFFICE SEMUR-EN-AUXOIS: 325t; © TMR/A.D.A.G.P. PARIS and DACS, LONDON 1994 – COLLECTION L. TREILLARD: 61tl detail.

JEAN VERTUT: 40br–41bl; VISUAL ARTS LIBRARY: 24b; VIEW PICTURES: Paul Rafferty 131b.

WORLD PICTURES: 313bl.

ZEFA: 168c, 341t; O. ZIMMERMAN/MUSÉE D'UNTERLINDEN 6800 COLMAR: 217t.

Front Endpaper: All special photography except JOE CORNISH lbl; THE IMAGE BANK rcb; PICTURES COLOUR LIBRARY lcr; JEAN MARIE STEINLEIN lcl; TONY STONE IMAGES rca.

JACKET
Front - DK PICTURE LIBRARY: John Parker cl; Kim Sayer b; GETTY IMAGES: Suzanne & Nick Geary main image. Back - DK PICTURE LIBRARY: Kim Sayer b, t. Spine - GETTY IMAGES: Suzanne & Nick Geary.

All other images © Dorling Kindersley. For more information see www.DKimages.com

Phrase Book

IN EMERGENCY

Help!	Au secours!	oh se**koor**
Stop!	Arrêtez!	aret-**ay**
Call a	Appelez un	apuh-**lay** uñ
doctor!	médecin!	med**sañ**
Call an	Appelez une	apuh-**lay** oon
ambulance!	ambulance!	oñboo-**loñs**
Call the	Appelez la	apuh-**lay** lah
police!	police!	poh-**lees**
Call the fire	Appelez les	apuh-lay leh
department!	pompiers!	poñ-**peeyay**
Where is the	Où est le téléphone	oo ay luh tehleh**fon**
nearest telephone?	le plus proche?	luh ploo **prosh**
Where is the	Où est l'hôpital	oo ay l'**opee**tal luh
nearest hospital?	le plus proche?	ploo **prosh**

COMMUNICATION ESSENTIALS

Yes	Oui	wee
No	Non	noñ
Please	S'il vous plaît	seel voo **play**
Thank you	Merci	mer-**see**
Excuse me	Excusez-moi	exkoo-**zay** mwah
Hello	Bonjour	boñ**zhoor**
Goodbye	Au revoir	oh ruh-**vwar**
Good night	Bonsoir	boñ-**swar**
Morning	Le matin	ma**tañ**
Afternoon	L'après-midi	l'apreh-**meedee**
Evening	Le soir	swar
Yesterday	Hier	ee**yehr**
Today	Aujourd'hui	oh-zhoor-**dwee**
Tomorrow	Demain	duh**mañ**
Here	Ici	ee-**see**
There	Là	lah
What?	Quel, quelle?	kel, kel
When?	Quand?	koñ
Why?	Pourquoi?	poor-**kwah**
Where?	Où?	oo

USEFUL PHRASES

How are you?	Comment allez-vous?	kom-moñ tal**ay** voo
Very well,	Très bien,	treh byañ,
thank you.	merci.	mer-**see**
Pleased to	Enchanté de faire	oñshoñ-**tay** duh fehr
meet you.	votre connaissance.	votr kon-ay-**sans**
See you soon.	A bientôt.	byañ-**toh**
That's fine	Voilà qui est parfait	vwalah kee ay par**fay**
Where is/are...?	Où est/sont...?	oo ay/soñ
How far	Combien de	kom-**byañ** duh keelo-
is it to...?	kilomètres d'ici à...?	metr d'ee-**see** ah
Which	Quelle est la	kel ay lah **deer**-
way to...?	direction pour...?	ek-**syoñ** poor
Do you speak	Parlez-vous	par-lay voo
English?	anglais?	oñg-**lay**
I don't	Je ne	zhuh nuh kom-
understand.	comprends pas.	**proñ** pah
Could you	Pouvez-vous parler	poo-**vay** voo par-lay
speak slowly	moins vite s'il	mwañ veet seel
please?	vous plaît?	voo play
I'm sorry.	Excusez-moi.	exkoo-**zay** mwah

USEFUL WORDS

big	grand	groñ
small	petit	puh-**tee**
hot	chaud	show
cold	froid	frwah
good	bon	boñ
bad	mauvais	moh-**veh**
enough	assez	as**say**
well	bien	byañ
open	ouvert	oo-**ver**
closed	fermé	fer-**meh**
left	gauche	gohsh
right	droit	drwah
straight ahead	tout droit	too drwah
near	près	preh
far	loin	lwañ
up	en haut	oñ **oh**
down	en bas	oñ **bah**
early	de bonne heure	duh bon **urr**
late	en retard	oñ ruh-**tar**
entrance	l'entrée	l'on-**tray**
exit	la sortie	sor-**tee**
toilet	les toilettes, les WC	twah-let, vay-**see**
free, unoccupied	libre	leebr
free, no charge	gratuit	grah-**twee**

MAKING A TELEPHONE CALL

I'd like to place a	Je voudrais faire	zhuh voo-dreh fehr
long-distance call.	un interurbain.	uñ añter-oorbañ
I'd like to make	Je voudrais faire une	zhuh voo**dreh** fehr
a collect call.	communication	oon komoonikah-
	PCV.	**syoñ** peh-seh-veh
I'll try again	Je rappelerai	zhuh rapel-
later.	plus tard.	**eray** ploo tar
Can I leave a	Est-ce que je peux	es-**keh** zhuh puh
message?	laisser un message?	leh-**say** uñ mehs**azh**
Hold on.	Ne quittez pas,	nuh kee-**tay** pah
	s'il vous plaît.	seel voo play
Could you speak	Pouvez-vous parler	poo-**vay** voo par-
up a little please?	un peu plus fort?	**lay** uñ puh foor
local call	la communication	komoonikah-
	locale	**syoñ** low-**kal**

SHOPPING

How much	C'est combien	say kom-**byañ**
does this cost?	s'il vous plaît?	seel voo play
I would like ...	je voudrais...	zhuh voo-**dray**
Do you have?	Est-ce que vous avez?	es-**kuh** voo zav**ay**
I'm just	Je regarde	zhuh ruh**gar**
looking.	seulement.	suhl**moñ**
Do you take	Est-ce que vous	es-**kuh** voo
credit cards?	acceptez les cartes	zaksept-**ay** leh kart
	de crédit?	duh kreh-**dee**
Do you take	Est-ce que vous	es-**kuh** voo
traveler's	acceptez les	zaksept-**ay** leh
checks?	chèques de voyage?	shek duh vwa**yazh**
What time	A quelle heure	ah kel urr
do you open?	vous êtes ouvert?	voo zet oo-**ver**
What time	A quelle heure	ah kel urr
do you close?	vous êtes fermé?	voo zet fer-**may**
This one.	Celui-ci.	suhl-wee-**see**
That one.	Celui-là.	suhl-wee-**lah**
expensive	cher	shehr
cheap	pas cher,	pah shehr,
	bon marché	boñ mar-**shay**
size, clothes	la taille	tye
size, shoes	la pointure	pwañ-**tur**
white	blanc	bloñ
black	noir	nwahr
red	rouge	roozh
yellow	jaune	zhohwn
green	vert	vehr
blue	bleu	bluh

TYPES OF SHOPS

antiques	le magasin	maga-**zañ**
shop	d'antiquités	d'oñteekee-**tay**
bakery	la boulangerie	booloñ-**zhuree**
bank	la banque	boñk
book store	la librairie	lee-**brehree**
butcher	la boucherie	boo-**shehree**
cake shop	la pâtisserie	patee-**sree**
cheese shop	la fromagerie	fromazh-**ree**
dairy	la crémerie	krem-**ree**
department store	le grand magasin	groñ maga-**zañ**
delicatessen	la charcuterie	sharkoot-**ree**
drugstore	la pharmacie	farmah-**see**
fish seller	la poissonnerie	pwasson-**ree**
gift shop	le magasin de	maga-**zañ** duh
	cadeaux	ka**doh**
greengrocer	le marchand	mar-**shoñ** duh
	de légumes	lay-**goom**
grocery	l'alimentation	alee-moñta-**syoñ**
hairdresser	le coiffeur	kwa**fuhr**
market	le marché	marsh-**ay**
newsstand	le magasin de	maga-**zañ** duh
	journaux	zhoor-**no**
post office	la poste,	pohst,
	le bureau de poste,	boo**roh** duh pohst,
	le PTT	peh-teh-teh
shoe store	le magasin	maga-**zañ**
	de chaussures	duh show-**soor**
supermarket	le supermarché	soo pehr-**marshay**
tobacconist	le tabac	tabah
travel agent	l'agence	l'azhoñs
	de voyages	duh vwayazh

SIGHTSEEING

abbey	l'abbaye	l'abay-**ee**
art gallery	la galerie d'art	galer-**ree** dart
bus station	la gare routière	gahr roo-tee-**yehr**

cathedral	la cathédrale	katay-**dral**
church	l'église	l'ay**gleez**
garden	le jardin	zhar-**dañ**
library	la bibliothèque	beeb**leeo**-tek
museum	le musée	moo-**zay**
tourist information office	les renseignements touristiques, le syndicat d'initiative	roñsayn-**moñ** too-rees-**teek**, sandee-ka d'eenee-syat**eev**
town hall	l'hôtel de ville	l'ohtel duh veel
train station	la gare (SNCF)	gahr (es-en-say-ef)
private mansion	l'hôtel particulier	l'ohtel partikoo-**lyay**
closed for	fermeture	fehrmeh-**tur**
public holiday	jour férié	zhoor fehree-**ay**

STAYING IN A HOTEL

Do you have a vacant room?	Est-ce que vous avez une chambre?	es-kuh voo-**zavay** oon shambr
double room, with double bed	la chambre à deux personnes, avec un grand lit	shambr ah duh pehr-son avek un gronñ lee
twin room	la chambre à deux lits	shambr ah duh lee
single room	la chambre à une personne	shambr ah oon pehr-**son**
room with a bath, shower	la chambre avec salle de bains, une douche	shambr avek sal duh bañ, oon doosh
porter	le garçon	gar-**soñ**
key	la clef	klay
I have a reservation.	J'ai fait une réservation.	zhay fay oon rayzehrva-**syoñ**

EATING OUT

Have you got a table?	Avez-vous une table libre?	avay-**voo** oon tahbl leebr
I want to reserve a table.	Je voudrais réserver une table.	zhuh voo-**dray** rayzehr-**vay** oon tahbl
The check please.	L'addition s'il vous plaît.	l'adee-**syoñ** seel voo **play**
I am a vegetarian.	Je suis végétarien.	zhuh swee vezhay-**tehryañ**
Waitress/ waiter	Madame, Mademoiselle/ Monsieur	mah-**dam**, mah-demwah**zel**/ muh-**syuh**
menu	le menu, la carte	men-**oo**, kart
fixed-price menu	le menu à prix fixe	men-**oo** ah pree feeks
cover charge	le couvert	koo-**vehr**
wine list	la carte des vins	**kart**-deh vañ
glass	le verre	vehr
bottle	la bouteille	boo-**tay**
knife	le couteau	koo-**toh**
fork	la fourchette	for-**shet**
spoon	la cuillère	kwee-**yehr**
breakfast	le petit déjeuner	puh-**tee** deh-**zhuh-nay**
lunch	le déjeuner	deh-**zhuh-nay**
dinner	le dîner	dee-**nay**
main course	le plat principal	plah prañsee-**pal**
appetizer, first course	l'entrée, le hors d'oeuvre	l'oñ-**tray**, or-duhvr
dish of the day	le plat du jour	plah doo zhoor
wine bar	le bar à vin	bar ah vañ
café	le café	ka-**fay**
rare	saignant	say-noñ
medium	à point	ah **pwañ**
well-done	bien cuit	byañ **kwee**

MENU DECODER

l'agneau	l'anyoh	lamb
l'ail	l'eye	garlic
la banane	banan	banana
le beurre	burr	butter
la bière, bière à la pression	bee-**yehr**, bee-**yehr** ah lah pres-**syoñ**	beer, draft beer
le bifteck, le steak	beef-**tek**, stek	steak
le boeuf	buhf	beef
bouilli	boo-**yee**	boiled
le café	kah-**fay**	coffee
le canard	kanar	duck
le chocolat	shoko-lah	chocolate
le citron	see-**troñ**	lemon
le citron pressé	see-**troñ** press-**eh**	fresh lemon juice
les crevettes	kruh-**vet**	prawns
les crustacés	kroos-ta-**say**	shellfish
cuit au four	kweet oh foor	baked
le dessert	deh-**ser**	dessert
l'eau minérale	l'oh **meeney**-ral	mineral water
les escargots	leh zes-kar-**goh**	snails
les frites	freet	chips
le fromage	from-**azh**	cheese
le fruit frais	frwee freh	fresh fruit
les fruits de mer	frwee duh mer	seafood
le gâteau	gah-**toh**	cake
la glace	glas	ice, ice cream
grillé	gree-**yay**	grilled
le homard	omahr	lobster
l'huile	l'weel	oil
le jambon	zhoñ-**boñ**	ham
le lait	leh	milk
les légumes	lay-**goom**	vegetables
la moutarde	moo-**tard**	mustard
l'oeuf	l'uf	egg
les oignons	leh zonyoñ	onions
les olives	leh zoleev	olives
l'orange	l'oroñzh	orange
l'orange pressée	l'oroñzh press-**eh**	fresh orange juice
le pain	pan	bread
le petit pain	puh-**tee** pañ	roll
poché	posh-**ay**	poached
le poisson	pwah-**ssoñ**	fish
le poivre	pwavr	pepper
la pomme	pom	apple
les pommes de terre	pom-duh **tehr**	potatoes
le porc	por	pork
le potage	poh-**tazh**	soup
le poulet	poo-**lay**	chicken
le riz	ree	rice
rôti	row-**tee**	roast
la sauce	sohs	sauce
la saucisse	soh**sees**	sausage, fresh
sec	sek	dry
le sel	sel	salt
la soupe	soop	soup
le sucre	sookr	sugar
le thé	tay	tea
le toast	toast	toast
la viande	vee-**yand**	meat
le vin blanc	vañ bloñ	white wine
le vin rouge	vañ roozh	red wine
le vinaigre	veenaygr	vinegar

NUMBERS

0	zéro	zeh-**roh**
1	un, une	uñ, oon
2	deux	duh
3	trois	trwah
4	quatre	katr
5	cinq	sañk
6	six	sees
7	sept	set
8	huit	weet
9	neuf	nerf
10	dix	dees
11	onze	oñz
12	douze	dooz
13	treize	trehz
14	quatorze	ka**torz**
15	quinze	kañz
16	seize	sehz
17	dix-sept	dees-**set**
18	dix-huit	dees-**weet**
19	dix-neuf	dees-**nerf**
20	vingt	vañ
30	trente	tront
40	quarante	karoñt
50	cinquante	sañk**oñt**
60	soixante	swas**oñt**
70	soixante-dix	swasoñt-**dees**
80	quatre-vingts	katr-**vañ**
90	quatre-vingt-dix	katr-vañ-**dees**
100	cent	soñ
1,000	mille	meel

TIME

one minute	une minute	oon mee-**noot**
one hour	une heure	oon urr
half an hour	une demi-heure	oon **duh-mee** urr
Monday	lundi	luñ-**dee**
Tuesday	mardi	mar-**dee**
Wednesday	mercredi	mehrkruh-**dee**
Thursday	jeudi	zhuh-**dee**
Friday	vendredi	voñdruh-**dee**
Saturday	samedi	sam-**dee**
Sunday	dimanche	dee-**moñsh**

Central Paris

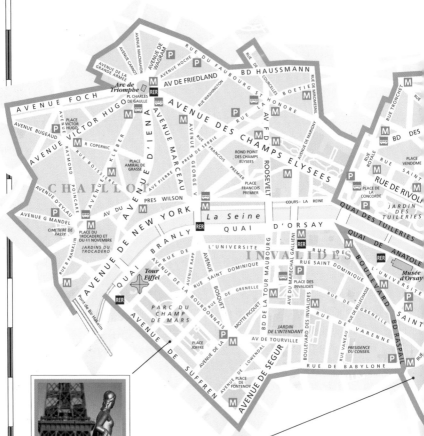

La Seine

ARC DE TRIOMPHE
PL CHARLES DE GAULLE

AVENUE FOCH

AVENUE DE LA GRANDE ARMEE

AVENUE CARNOT

AVENUE MACMAHON

AVENUE DE WAGRAM

AVENUE HOCHE

RUE DU FAUBOURG ST HONORE

RUE DE COURCELLES

BD HAUSSMANN

AV DE FRIEDLAND

RUE DE MONCEAU

RUE LA BOETIE

RUE TRONCHET

RUE

M

BD DES

AVENUE DES CHAMPS ELYSEES

RUE WASHINGTON

RUE LA BOETIE

AV F D ROOSEVELT

AVENUE DE MARIGNY

RUE ROYALE

RUE

PLACE VENDOME

RUE SAINT

RUE DE RIVOLI

AVENUE BUGEAUD

PLACE VICTOR HUGO

AVENUE VICTOR HUGO

R COPERNIC

RUE BOISSIERE

RAYMOND POINCARE

AVENUE KLEBER

AVENUE D'IENA

AVENUE MARCEAU

RUE PIERRE

AVE PIERRE

PREM GEORGE V

RUE DE SERBIE

RUE FRANCOIS PREMIER

ROND POINT DES CHAMPS ELYSEES

PLACE FRANCOIS PREMIER

COURS LA REINE

PLACE DE LA CONCORDE

JARDIN DES TUILERIES

CHAILLOT

PLACE AMIRAL DE GRASSE

AVENUE D'EYLAU

AV DU PRES WILSON

AVENUE DE NEW YORK

AVENUE G MANDEL

CIMETIERE DE PASSY

PLACE DU TROCADERO ET DU 11 NOVEMBRE

JARDINS DU TROCADERO

RUE B FRANKLIN

QUAI BRANLY

AVENUE DE LA BOURDONNAIS

Tour Eiffel

PARC DU CHAMP DE MARS

AVENUE DE SUFFREN

PLACE JOFFRE

RUE DE L'UNIVERSITE

RUE DE RUE RAPP

AVENUE BOSQUET

RUE SAINT DOMINIQUE

RUE DE GRENELLE

RUE MOTTE PICQUET

BD DE LA TOUR MAUBOURG

AVE DU MARECHAL GALLIENI

QUAI D'ORSAY

QUAI

L'UNIVERSITE

RUE SAINT DOMINIQUE

PLACE DES INVALIDES

INVALIDES

QUAI DE ANATOLE

BOULEVARD SAINT

Musée d'Orsay

RER

RUE DE

RUE DE BELLECHASSE

RUE DE VARENNE

RUE VANEAU

BD RASPAIL

RUE

JARDIN DE L'INTENDANT

AVENUE DE LA MOTTE PICQUET

AV DE TOURVILLE

AVENUE DE LOWENDAL

AVENUE DE SEGUR

PLACE DE FONTENOY

BOULEVARD DES INVALIDES

PRESIDENCE DU CONSEIL

RUE DE BABYLONE

Pont de Bir-Hakeim

CHAMPS-ELYSÉES AND INVALIDES
Pages 100–111
Street Finder maps 1–3, 6, 7

THE LEFT BANK
Pages 112–123
Street Finder maps 7–9, 12, 13

KEY

	Major sight
M	Metro station
RER	RER station
	Main bus stop
P	Main parking area
✚	Hospital with emergency unit

0 meters   500
0 yards   500